SIXTH EDITION

Organizational Behavior

Science, the Real World, and You

Debra L. Nelson
Oklahoma State University

James Campbell Quick
University of Texas at Arlington

Australia • Brazil • Japan • Korea • Mexico • Singapore • Spain • United Kingdom • United States

Organizational Behavior: Science, the Real World, and You, Sixth Edition
Debra L. Nelson, James Campbell Quick

Vice President of Editorial, Business: Jack W. Calhoun

Editor-in-Chief: Melissa Acuña

Sr. Acquisitions Editor: Michele Rhoades

Developmental Editor: Erin Berger

Editorial Assistant: Ruth Belanger

Marketing Manager: Clint Kernen

Sr. Marketing Coordinator: Sarah Rose

Sr. Marketing Communications Manager: Jim Overly

Sr. Content Project Manager: Martha Conway

Managing Media Editor: Pam Wallace

Media Editor: Kristen Meere

Manufacturing Coordinator: Doug Wilke

Production Service: Macmillan Publishing Solutions

Copyeditor: Gary Morris

Sr. Art Director: Tippy McIntosh

Cover and Internal Designer: Red Hangar Design, Joe DeVine

Cover Image: © iStock

Text Permissions: Roberta Broyer

Photography Manager: John Hill

Photo Researcher: Sam Marshall

Library of Congress Control Number: 2008920399

Student Edition ISBN 13: 978-0-324-57873-7
Student Edition ISBN 10: 0-324-57873-3
Instructor's Edition ISBN 13: 978-0-324-58096-9
Instructor's Edition ISBN 10: 0-324-58096-7

South-Western Cengage Learning
5191 Natorp Boulevard
Mason, OH 45040
USA

Cengage Learning products are represented in Canada by
Nelson Education, Ltd.

For your course and learning solutions, visit **academic.cengage.com**
Purchase any of our products at your local college store or at our preferred online store **www.ichapters.com**

Printed in Canada
1 2 3 4 5 6 7 12 11 10 09 08

Brief Contents

Contents

Part 2 Individual Processes and Behavior 79

Chapter 17 Career Management 576

Preface

Much has changed in the world since the fifth edition of ***Organizational Behavior: Foundations, Realities & Challenges*** appeared three years ago, and considerable new knowledge has been discovered about organizational behavior to add to the last 100 years of research. Our knowledge base has been refined and advanced in the context of a professional world hungry for authentic leaders and a more positive approach to understanding and leading people in organizations. The sixth edition represents the opportunities and optimism that form the heart of organizational behavior. Opportunity is "a favorable time" or "a chance for progress and advancement." More than responding to change, we encourage students of organizational behavior and leaders in organizations to be the instigators of positive change. Using the knowledge and insights offered in the study of organizational behavior, we can take responsible actions to create the kinds of organizations in which we thrive, grow strong, and experience fulfillment in the spirit of the happy/productive worker. These are favorable times in which to advance the science and practice the art of organizational behavior in a manner that it is beneficial to all concerned. This includes workers and leaders, men and women, those of all ethnic groups and occupations, and all those of diverse faith traditions.

The distinctiveness of ***Organizational Behavior*** has always been reflected in its subtitle: ***Foundations, Realities & Challenges***. We chose this subtitle for our first five editions because it represents the solid scholarly foundations on which the science of organizational behavior was built, the realities of contemporary life in organizations, and the challenges that constantly arise. As we move into this sixth edition, we wanted to retain these values but contemporize their communication; hence our new subtitle ***Science, the Real World, and You***. "Science" refers to the broad and deep research roots of our discipline. Our book is anchored in research tradition and contains not only classic research but also leading-edge scholarship in the field. This research and theory form the foundations of our knowledge base. "The Real World" reflects what is going on in organizations of all types: public and private, large and small, product and service oriented. In our text, these realities take shape as examples from all types of organizations. Some of the examples show success, while others show failure, in cases where managers apply organizational behavior knowledge in the real world. "You" features are the opportunities we have to grow and develop both as individuals and organizations. In the book, they take the form of individual and group activities for proactive learning.

Organizational behavior is the study of individual behavior and group dynamics in organizational settings. It focuses on timeless topics like motivation, leadership, teamwork, and communication. Such issues have captured our attention for decades. Organizational behavior also encompasses contemporary issues in organizations. How do we encourage employees to act ethically, to engage in organizational citizenship behaviors, to go above and beyond the call of duty to exhibit exceptional performance? How do we restructure organizations in the face of increasing competition? What is the new psychological contract between employees and organizations? How have careers changed, and what can we expect in the future? How do you manage employee behavior in virtual organizations or teams? What happens when organizations with strong cultures and a need for constancy face the pressure to become current, competitive, and agile? ***Organizational Behavior*** thus engages both classic and emerging issues.

Our overarching theme of change continues to drive the book, along with the subthemes: globalization, diversity, ethics, and technology. These subthemes continue to reflect the challenges that managers face. The sequence in which we address these subthemes and the ways in which we elaborate upon them *has* changed, however, as it should. The global marketplace continues to bring with it a world with no boundaries, with no constraints on time and distance. Diversity can be a tremendous asset, with its wealth of skills and knowledge, if managers can build organizational cultures that view differences as assets. Managing ethical behavior means doing the right thing in an age of increased white-collar crime and public scrutiny of organizations. While new technologies have vastly improved the efficiency of work, managers must balance high tech with high touch.

Organizations expect all employees to learn continually. Our book rests on the assumption that learning involves not only acquiring knowledge but also developing skills. The rich theory and research in organizational behavior must be translated into application. Thus, the text presents the opportunity to know concepts, ideas, and theories, and to practice skills, abilities, and behaviors to enhance the management of human behavior at work. Both knowledge and skills are essential for our future managers. We hope the knowledge and skills presented here empower them to succeed in the changing world of work.

SPECIAL FEATURES

Several special features of the book extend the subtitle ***Science, the Real World, and You*** to specific applications. These features are designed to enhance the application of theory and research in practice, to stimulate student interest and discussion, and to facilitate cognitive as well as skill-based learning. The sixth edition reflects a change in how we refer to some of our special features. You learn in Chapter 1, Figure 1.4, that basic knowledge is concerned with Science, that skill application is concerned with the Real World, and that knowledge and skill development concerns You directly. The pedagogical features included in each chapter are titled Science (Foundations), The Real World (Realities), and You (Challenges).

SCIENCE

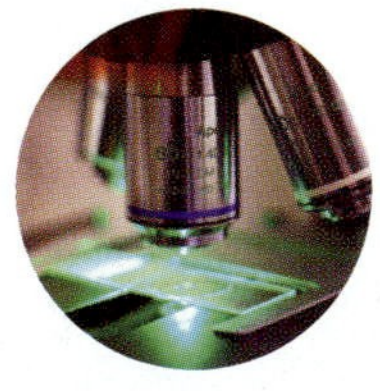

Each chapter includes a Science feature that summarizes a leading-edge research study related to the chapter's topic. This feature exposes students to the way knowledge is advanced in organizational behavior and the scientific nature of the discipline. For example, the Science feature in Chapter 18 shows how mergers and acquisitions often fail because employees feel that the organization has violated its psychological contract with them.

EXTENSIVE TEXT REFERENCES

The book is based on extensive classic and contemporary research literature. At the end of the book is a lengthy chapter-by-chapter reference list that students can refer to for in-depth treatments of the chapter topics. In this edition, over 200 new research studies, theory articles, and scholarly books have been reviewed and cited. In addition to this freshening of the content base for the text, chapters have new content and key words that reflect positive changes. For example, Chapter 4 now has extensive coverage of emotions at work; so much so that the chapter is now titled "Attitudes, Emotions, and Ethics." Other research on emotions is integrated throughout the sixth edition. Chapter 7 brings attention to the continuing work/life balance issue of workaholism while the importance of heartfelt communication as an antidote to social isolation is emphasized in Chapter 8. Chapter 12 reflects enhanced coverage of the inspirational leadership theories (transformational, charismatic, authentic) along with emotional intelligence.

THINKING AHEAD AND LOOKING BACK

The opening and closing features for the sixth edition, as in previous editions, frame the chapter with a vignette from one of six focus organizations. The organizations in the sixth edition are all new: American Express, Caribou Coffee, Genentech, Google, Timberland, and Toyota. As in the past, these companies represent manufacturing and service, profit and nonprofit, and large and small organizations. By featuring these six key organizations throughout the book, students can familiarize themselves with the companies in greater depth than a single appearance would allow. The Looking Back feature is a continuation of the Thinking Ahead feature on that particular organization and brings closure to the example.

THE REAL WORLD

The purpose of including two new The Real World features in each chapter is to spotlight contemporary organizational life. The realities reflect the themes of globalization, diversity, technology, and ethics. They include not only examples of successes but also examples of failures, which are opportunities for learning. In Chapter 4, a Real World feature highlights PepsiCo's challenges in India related to cultural differences in views of ethical behavior. The Real World 12.1 reflects Anne Mulcahy's leadership journey at Xerox.

YOU

These self-assessment exercises provide the student with feedback on an important aspect of the topic. Examples are the Frazzle Factor (You 7.1) in Chapter 7, in which students discover how much stress and anger they have, and You 11.1 that helps students assess their political skills. Each You is designed to enhance self-knowledge or to promote skill development in the subject matter. The student is able to use the results of the You feature for self-discovery and behavioral change.

DIVERSITY DIALOGUES

These are real-life stories drawn from news headlines that are presented in a way designed to stimulate frank dialogue and discussion. The aim is to present content that can be used to create a psychologically safe environment in which to discuss these often emotionally loaded and sensitive issues. There are Diversity Dialogues designed into the body of nine chapters in the book. Two examples are "When Domestic Violence 'Goes to Work'" in Chapter 7 and "White Males: Diversity Programs' Newest Leaders?" in Chapter 12.

DISCUSSION AND COMMUNICATION QUESTIONS

All students need help in developing their oral and written communication skills. Discussion and communication questions are included at the end of each chapter to give students practice in applying chapter material using some form of communication. The questions challenge students to write memos and brief reports, prepare oral presentations for class, interview experts in the field, and conduct research to gather information on important management topics for discussion in class.

ETHICAL DILEMMAS

Learning to develop moral reasoning and the capacity to resolve ethical dilemmas is hard work. Simple answers to complex questions just do not exist. Therefore, an Ethical Dilemma has been crafted for each chapter that offers students an opportunity to engage in ethical debate and moral reasoning concerning tough decisions and situations. Each chapter's feature poses a scenario and then a series of questions for use in probing the ethical dilemma.

EXPERIENTIAL EXERCISES

Two group-oriented experiential exercises are included at the end of each chapter. They are designed for students to work in teams to learn more about an important aspect of the chapter's topic. The exercises give students opportunities to develop interpersonal skills and to process their thinking within a teamwork setting. In Experiential Exercise 4.2, for example, students are presented with twelve ethical issues faced in organizations, and they meet in groups to discuss all sides of the issue and a proposed resolution. Experiential Exercise 10.1 places students in the role of a manager who must make a layoff decision. Students are given summaries of their "employees'" résumés and asked to propose a decision in terms of who should be laid off.

CASES (NEW AND REVISED)

A case is included at the end of each chapter. Half of these chapter cases are completely new, and the other half have been updated. Each case is based on a real-world situation that has been modified slightly for learning purposes. Students have an opportunity to discuss and reflect on the content of the case, drawing on and then applying the content material of the chapter within the framework of the case. All of the Cohesion Cases that appear at the end of the four parts of the book are new and feature an ongoing scenario of the global energy company, BP. The Workplace Video Cases are all new, as well.

SOME DISTINCTIVE FEATURES STUDENTS LIKE

Organizational Behavior offers a number of distinctive, time-tested, and interesting features for students, as well as new and innovative features. Each chapter begins with a clear statement of learning objectives to provide students with expectations about what is to come. The chapter summaries are designed to bring closure to these learning objectives. Graphics and tables enhance students' ease in grasping the topical material and involve them actively in the learning process. Photos throughout each chapter reinforce, and in many cases supplement, the text.

Engaging and relevant end-of-chapter features such as the list of key terms, review questions, discussion questions, and cases reflect practical and applied aspects of organizational behavior.

Examples from diverse organizations (multinational, regional, nonprofit, public) and industries (manufacturing, service, defense) are included. These examples are integrated throughout the text. A unique feature of the book is its focus on the six organizations mentioned earlier. These represent many different types of organizations—large and small, profit and nonprofit, product and service oriented. The purpose of this approach is to provide a sense of continuity and depth not achieved in single examples.

STUDY AIDS

To help you learn, understand, and apply the material in ***Organizational Behavior,*** the sixth edition provides many unique and comprehensive study tools.

Web Site A rich Web site at academic.cengage.com/management/nelson-quick complements the text, providing extras for students. Resources include chapter glossaries and interactive quizzes.

CengageNOW This powerful and fully integrated online teaching and learning system provides you with flexibility and control, saves valuable time, and improves outcomes. Students benefit by having choices in the way they learn through their unique personalized learning paths. All this is made possible by CengageNOW!

- Homework, assignable and automatically graded
- Integrated eBook
- Personalized Learning Paths
- Interactive Course Assignments
- Assessment Options, including **AACSB learning standards achievement reporting**
- Test Delivery
- Course Management Tools, including Grade Book
- WebCT and Blackboard Integration

Speak with your South-Western Cengage Learning sales representative about integrating CengageNOW into your courses.

SOME DISTINCTIVE FEATURES INSTRUCTORS LIKE

Professors have demanding jobs. They should expect textbook authors and publishers to provide them with the support they need to do an excellent job for students. Among their expectations should be a well-integrated, complete ancillary package. ***Organizational Behavior*** has this package.

ANCILLARY PACKAGE

A comprehensive set of ancillaries supports the basic text: an Instructor's Manual with Video Guide, a Test Bank, ExamView (computerized testing software), PowerPoint® presentation files, a product support Web site, and a video program. The videos include clips about real companies with which your students may already be familiar as well as a variety of short vignettes from real Hollywood films. Using video in the classroom will enhance the text presentation and reinforce its themes, adding continuity and integration to the overall understanding of organizational behavior.

Instructor's Manual with Video Guide The Instructor's Manual with Video Guide for ***Organizational Behavior*** was prepared by David A. Foote (Middle Tennessee State University), Joseph E. Champoux (University of New Mexico), and B. J. Parker. For this edition, the Instructor's Manual is available only on the Instructor's Resource CD-ROM and on the product support Web site, academic.cengage .com/management/nelson-quick. Each chapter contains the following information:

- Chapter scan—a brief overview of the chapter.
- Learning objectives that are presented in the textbook.
- Key terms—a list of key terms from the chapter.
- The chapter summarized—an extended outline with narratives under each major point to flesh out the discussion and offer alternative examples and issues to bring forward. The extended outlines are several pages long and incorporate many teaching suggestions.
- Answer guidelines for end-of-chapter materials—detailed responses to the review questions, discussion and communication questions, and ethical dilemmas, with suggestions for keeping discussion on track in the classroom.
- Suggested answers for the You features.
- Experiential exercises—a brief description of each exercise as well as a detailed summary of anticipated results. Also included are alternative experiential exercises not found in the text. Discussion questions are provided with selected experiential exercises. Finally, a list of sources for still more exercises may be found under "Extra Experiential Exercises."
- Cases—suggested answers for case discussion questions are provided in a detailed form.
- Integration of Myers-Briggs Type Indicator material (optional)—including full descriptions and exercises in communication, leadership, motivation, decision making, conflict resolution, power, stress and time management, and managing change. For instructors unfamiliar with Myers-Briggs, a general introduction to this instrument is provided at the end of Chapter 3 of the Instructor's Manual. The introduction includes several good references for additional information about testing.
- Video cases—suggested answers to the Biz Flix and Workplace video cases are included for all chapters.

Test Bank The Test Bank, prepared by Jon G. Kalinowski (Minnesota State University, Mankato), has been thoroughly revised for this edition. The Test Bank contains more than 1,200 multiple-choice, true/false, matching, and essay questions. Each question has been coded according to Bloom's taxonomy, a widely known testing and measurement device used to classify questions according to level (easy, medium, or hard) and type (application, recall, or comprehension). Each question has also been associated to AACSB learning standards. For this edition, the Test Bank is available only on the Instructor's Resource CD-ROM.

ExamView This supplement contains all of the questions in the Test Bank. The program is easy-to-use test creation software compatible with Microsoft Windows and Macintosh. Instructors can add or edit questions, instructions, and answers, and select questions (randomly or numerically) by previewing them on the screen. Instructors can also create and administer quizzes online, whether over the Internet, a local area network (LAN), or a wide area network (WAN). ExamView is available on the Instructor's Resource CD-ROM.

PowerPoint Presentation Files Marilyn Bergmann and Donna Raleigh (University of Wisconsin, Eau Claire) have developed more than 300 PowerPoint slides for this text. These slides feature figures from the text, lecture outlines, and innovative adaptations to enhance classroom presentation. PowerPoint presentation files are available on the Instructor's Resource CD-ROM and on the product support Web site, academic.cengage.com/management/nelson-quick.

Instructor's Resource CD-ROM (ISBN: 0-324-58090-8) Key instructor ancillaries (Instructor's Manual with Video Guide, Test Bank, ExamView, and PowerPoint slides) are provided on CD-ROM, giving instructors the ultimate tool for customizing lectures and presentations.

Web Site ***Organizational Behavior*** has its own product support Web site at academic.cengage.com/management/nelson-quick. The full PowerPoint presentation is available for you to download as lecture support. The Instructor's Manual is also available for download.

WebTutor™ Advantage on WEBCT™ and on Blackboard® WebTutor Advantage complements ***Organizational Behavior*** by providing interactive reinforcement. WebTutor Advantage's online teaching and learning environment brings together content management, assessment, communication, and collaboration capabilities for enhancing in-class instruction or for delivering distance learning. For more information, including a demo, visit academic.cengage.com/webtutor.

"Take 2" Video Program (ISBN: 0-324-58094-0) Available in DVD format, an updated video program has been developed for use with ***Organizational Behavior.*** Video segments have been selected to support the themes of the book and to deepen students' understanding of the organizational behavior concepts presented throughout the text. Biz Flix video cases, developed by Joseph E. Champoux of the University of New Mexico, incorporate clips from popular films such as *8 Mile, Meet the Parents,* and *Reality Bites* into the classroom. Companies profiled in the Workplace video series include Honda, McDonald's, Yahoo, and Cold Stone Creamery, among others. Information on using the videos can be found in the Instructor's Manual.

Organizational Behavior: Experiences and Cases (ISBN: 0-324-04850-5) Written by Dorothy Marcic, Joseph Seltzer, and Peter Vaill, ***Organizational Behavior: Experiences and Cases*** contains experiential exercises and cases that emphasize management skill development and practical application of theory integral to the study of organizational behavior.

OUR REVIEWERS ARE APPRECIATED

We would like to thank our professional peers and colleagues who reviewed the text to evaluate scholarly accuracy, writing style, and pedagogy. The many changes we made are based on their suggestions. We gratefully acknowledge the help of the following individuals:

Robert F. Abbey, Jr., *Troy State University*
Stephen R. Ball, *Cleary University*
Deborah Bashaw, *Harding University*
Talya Bauer, *Portland State University*
Angela D. Boston, *University of Texas, Arlington*
Mark C. Butler, *San Diego State University*
Ceasar Douglas, *Florida State University*
Tracey Rockett Hanft, *University of Texas, Dallas*
Theodore T. Herbert, *Rollins College*
Jacqueline A. Gilbert, *Middle Tennessee State University*
Don Jung, *San Diego State University*
Bryan Kennedy, *Athens State University*
Jalane M. Meloun, *Barry University*
Floyd S. Ormsbee, *Clarkson University*
Linda Beats Putchinski, *University of Central Florida*
Elizabeth C. Ravlin, *University of South Carolina*
Harriet L. Rojas, *Indiana Wesleyan University*
Chris John Sablynski, *California State University, Sacramento*
Marian C. Schultz, *University of West Florida*
M. Shane Spiller, *Morehead State University*
William H. Turnley, *Kansas State University*

ACKNOWLEDGMENTS

The sixth edition of ***Organizational Behavior*, like its predecessors,** is the product of great teamwork, and we are indebted to all of our team members who made the revision process a pleasure. Our editor Michele Rhoades was a great creative resource and sounding board, contributing terrific energy to the project. Erin Berger, our developmental editor, was a constant source of positive feedback and ideas, and kept us going strong throughout the process. Martha Conway, our production editor, took us through the final stages with ease, and Gary Morris had an eagle eye for the details in the copyediting phase.

Faye Cocchiara, a veteran colleague and collaborator, has worked with us since the fifth edition. Her voice can easily be detected throughout the book. Her voice and her research are most evident in the emphasis on diversity. Faye conceptualized, designed, authored, and executed the nine Diversity Dialogues featured in nine of the chapters in the book, first in Chapter 2 and last in Chapter 17.

Janaki Gooty's energetic presence can also be seen throughout the book. Her expertise in emotions at work and leadership particularly shine through. The many organizational examples throughout the sixth edition reflect Janaki's ingenuity and eye for the application of organizational behavior.

Joanne H. Gavin's presence continues to be felt in her passion for moral and ethical action, which is a positive presence in the Ethical Dilemmas that she conceptualized and executed first in the fifth edition. Her character continues to be with us. So too it is with Marilyn Macik-Frey, whose expertise in communication added new content to how we think about communication and about healthy, heartfelt relationships.

Joseph Champoux of the University of New Mexico was kind enough to lend us materials from his *At the Movies* series of texts for our new Biz Flix video cases, and B. J. Parker wrote our all-new Workplace video cases.

Michael McCuddy of Valparaiso University did his customary outstanding job on the cases that appear at the end of each chapter and the cohesion cases that appear at the end of each part. He has a way of making organizational problems fascinating to students. Jeff McGee was most helpful with small business and entrepreneurship advice and contacts as well as his support as chairman of the Department of Management. Additionally, Carol Byrne and Ruthie Brock, business librarians at the University of Texas at Arlington, provided much support in the preparation of this textbook.

Preparation of the ancillary materials to enhance classroom efforts required a host of people. David A. Foote, Middle Tennessee State University, Joseph E. Champoux, the University of New Mexico, and B. J. Parker created a superb Instructor's Manual and Video Guide. Jon Kalinowski of Minnesota State University, Mankato, was great in preparing the Test Bank that accompanies the textbook. Many thanks go to Marilyn Bergmann and Donna Raleigh of University of Wisconsin, Eau Claire, for developing the PowerPoint presentation files. We are also grateful to Floyd Ormsbee, Clarkson University; Amit Shah, Frostburg State University; and Susan Carson, who created materials that appear in the CengageNOW product.

We are fortunate to have several colleagues who have made helpful contributions and supported our development through all six editions of the textbook: Mike Hitt of Texas A&M University; Lisa Kennedy of Baylor College of Medicine; Robert Dooley, Mark Gavin, and Laura Little, all of Oklahoma State University; Jo Anne Wilson of AT&T; Tammy Manning of Galligan & Manning; David Mack, David Gray, Myrtle Bell, Ken Price, Jim Lavelle, and Steve Colburn, all of the University of Texas at Arlington; Juliana Lilly of Sam Houston State University; and J. Lee Whittington of University of Dallas.

Our families and friends have encouraged us throughout the development of the book. They have provided us with emotional support and examples for the book and have graciously allowed us the time to do the book justice. We are truly grateful for their support.

This book has been a labor of love for both of us. It has made us better teachers and also better learners. And that is our wish for you!

Debra L. Nelson
James Campbell Quick

About the Authors

Debra L. Nelson

Dr. Debra L. Nelson is The Spears School of Business Associates' Professor of Business Administration and Professor of Management at Oklahoma State University. She received her Ph.D. from the University of Texas at Arlington, where she was the recipient of the R. D. Irwin Dissertation Fellowship Award. Dr. Nelson is the author of over 90 journal articles focusing on organizational stress management, gender at work, and leadership. Her research has been published in the *Academy of Management Executive, Academy of Management Journal, Academy of Management Review, MIS Quarterly, Organizational Dynamics, Journal of Organizational Behavior*, and other journals. In addition, she is coauthor/coeditor of several books, including *Organizational Behavior: Science, the Real World, and You* (6th ed., South-Western, Cengage Learning, 2008); *Positive Organizational Behavior* (Sage, 2007); *Organizational Leadership* (South-Western, Cengage Learning, 2004); *Gender, Work Stress, and Health* (American Psychological Association, 2002); *Advancing Women in Management* (Blackwell, 2002); and *Preventive Stress Management in Organizations* (American Psychological Association, 1997). Dr. Nelson has also served as a consultant to several organizations including AT&T, American Fidelity Assurance, Sonic, State Farm Insurance Companies, and Southwestern Bell. She has presented leadership and preventive stress management seminars for a host of organizations, including Blue Cross/Blue Shield, Conoco/Phillips, Oklahoma Gas and Electric, Oklahoma Natural Gas, and the Federal Aviation Administration. She has been honored with the Greiner Graduate Teaching Award, the Chandler-Frates and Reitz Graduate Teaching Award, the Regents' Distinguished Teaching Award, the Regents' Distinguished Research Award, and the Burlington Northern Faculty Achievement Award at OSU. Dr. Nelson also serves on the editorial review boards of the *Journal of Organizational Behavior, Journal of Leadership and Organizational Studies*, and *Leadership*.

James Campbell Quick

Dr. James Campbell (Jim) Quick is John and Judy Goolsby Distinguished Professor and Professor of Organizational Behavior in the College of Business Administration at the University of Texas at Arlington. He is Visiting Professor, Lancaster University Management School, UK. He earned an A.B. with Honors from Colgate University, where he was a George Cobb Fellow and Harvard Business School Association intern. He earned an M.B.A. and a Ph.D. at the University of Houston. He completed postgraduate courses in behavioral medicine (Harvard Medical School) and combat stress (University of Texas Health Science Center at San Antonio).

Dr. Quick is a Fellow of the Society for Industrial and Organizational Psychology, the American Psychological Association, the American Psychological Society, and the American Institute of Stress. He was awarded the 2002 Harry and Miriam Levinson Award by the American Psychological Foundation.

With his brother (Jonathan D. Quick, M.D., M.P.H.), Dr. Quick framed the area of preventive stress management, a term now listed in the *APA Dictionary of Psychology* (2007). He has received over $300,000 in funded support for research, scholarship, and intellectual contributions from the Society for Human Resource Management, Hospital Corporation of America, the State of Texas, and the American Psychological Association. His articles have been published in leading journals such as the *Academy of Management's Journal* and *Review*, *Journal of Organizational Behavior*, *Air University Review*, *Journal of Bone & Joint Surgery*, and the *Journal of Medical Education*. He received the 1990 Distinguished Professional Publication Award for *Corporate Warfare: Preventing Combat Stress and Battle Fatigue,* coauthored with Debra L. Nelson and Jonathan D. Quick for the American Management Association's *Organizational Dynamics* and used in the curriculum of the United States Air Force Academy and the U.S. Army War College.

Dr. Quick is coauthor of *Managing Executive Health* (Cambridge University Press, 2008), published in seven languages; *Preventive Stress Management in Organizations* (American Psychological Association, 1997), originally published in 1984 and released as *Unternehmen ohne Stress* in German; and *Stress and Challenge at the Top: The Paradox of the Successful Executive* (John Wiley & Sons, 1990). He is coeditor of the *Handbook of Occupational Health Psychology* (APA, 2002); *The New Organizational Reality: Downsizing, Restructuring, and Revitalization* (APA, 1998); *Stress and Well-Being at Work* (APA, 1992); and *Work Stress: Health Care Systems in the Workplace* (Praeger Scientific, 1987), for which he received the 1987 Distinguished Service Award from the UTA College of Business. He is a member of Beta Gamma Sigma and Phi Beta Delta honor societies and the Great Southwest Rotary Club, where he is a past president and a Paul Harris Fellow.

Dr. Quick was the American Psychological Association's stress expert to the National Academy of Sciences on National Health Objectives for the Year 2000. He was also a scientific exchange delegate to the People's Republic of China.

Dr. Quick was recognized with the Texas Volunteer Recognition Award (American Heart Association, 1985); a listing in *Who's Who in the World*, 7th Edition (1984–85); The Maroon Citation (Colgate University Alumni Corporation, 1993); two Minnie Stevens Piper Professorship Award nominations (1995, 2001); and a Presidential Citation from the American Psychological Association (2001).

Dr. Quick, U.S. Air Force Colonel (Retired), was the Senior Individual Mobilization Augmentee at the San Antonio Air Logistics Center (AFMC), Kelly AFB, Texas, in his last assignment. He was Distinguished Visiting Professor of Psychology, 59th Medical Wing (1999). His awards and decorations include the Legion of Merit, Meritorious Service Medal, and National Defense Service Medal with Bronze Star.

Dr. Quick is married to the former Sheri Grimes Schember; both are members of the Presidents' Club of Colgate University and the Chancellor's Council of the University of Texas System.

Dedication

To our students, who challenge us to be better than we are, who keep us in touch with reality, and who are the foundations of our careers.

© DIGITAL VISION

PART 1

Introduction

CHAPTER 1

Organizational Behavior and Opportunity

LEARNING OBJECTIVES

After reading this chapter, you should be able to do the following:

1 Define *organizational behavior*.

2 Identify four action steps for responding positively in times of change.

3 Identify the important system components of an organization.

4 Describe the formal and informal elements of an organization.

5 Understand the diversity of organizations in the economy, as exemplified by the six focus organizations.

6 Recognize the opportunities that change creates for organizational behavior.

7 Demonstrate the value of objective knowledge and skill development in the study of organizational behavior.

THINKING AHEAD: CARIBOU COFFEE

Competing on Experience . . . for the Hearts of Customers

Caribou Coffee's chief competitor is Starbucks. Every organization has a chief competitor or set of competitors operating within its business environment, just as Starbucks is Caribou Coffee's chief competitor. Competitive markets increase the need for change and innovation within the firm as well as across the industry. When well managed and legally operated, they benefit the customer by delivering better products and services at lower rates. In addition, they benefit the competitors by challenging them to engage in innovations and serve their customers better without gouging, abusing, or shortchanging them. The rules of the competition need to be clear, the competitors well matched, and regulators engaged appropriately to insure competition that is fair to all concerned, including the public and society at large.[1]

Competition can be head-to-head or asymmetrical. Head-to-head competition occurs when two companies are competing for the same customers and on the same basis, such as price or size. Caribou Coffee's Michael Coles aims to compete with Starbucks asymmetrically, not head-to-head. That is, he is not trying to compete with Starbucks on the basis of size, and to keep up with his chief competitor on that basis. Size is only one dimension along which competition may occur. Competition may occur along other dimensions too, such as market share, quality of product or service, or a specialized, niche-customer strategy. Using asymmetrical competition, a company surrenders certain advantages or territory to the competition while capitalizing on their own distinctive strengths and advantages. Asymmetrical competition changes the rules of the game.

In the case of Caribou Coffee, Michael Coles has set the goal of being number one in "experience." Thus, Caribou has defined the competition in terms of a quality rather than a number, be that number of stores, number of customers, number of dollars earned in revenue, or number of profit dollars earned. This goes to the heart of the marketplace and to the heart of customer satisfaction. Customers, one at a time, are the ones who define experience for Caribou Coffee, Starbucks, and any other coffee chain. That is how Southwest Airlines succeeded and grew in the airline industry, by focusing on customer satisfaction and the traveler's experience, not on the size of their airline. When organizations like Caribou Coffee define the rules of the competition and state clearly what their goal is, they are engaging in asymmetrical competition and changing the game to how they want to play it. Can they win that way?

HUMAN BEHAVIOR IN ORGANIZATIONS

1 Define *organizational behavior*.

Human behavior in organizations is complex and often difficult to understand. Organizations have been described as clockworks in which human behavior is logical and rational, but they often seem like snake pits to those who work in them.[2] The clockwork metaphor reflects an orderly, idealized view of organizational behavior devoid of conflict or dilemma because all the working parts (the people) mesh smoothly. The snake pit metaphor conveys the daily conflict, stress, and struggle in organizations. Each metaphor reflects reality from a different perspective—the organization's versus the individual's point of view. These metaphors reflect the complexity of human behavior, the dark side of which is seen in cases of air rage and workplace violence. On the positive side, the Gallup Organization's Marcus Buckingham suggests that people's psychological makeup is at the heart of the emotional economy.[3]

This chapter is an introduction to organizational behavior. The first section provides an overview of human behavior in organizations, its interdisciplinary origins, and behavior in times of change. The second section presents an organizational context within which behavior occurs and briefly introduces the six focus companies used selectively in the book. The third section highlights the *opportunities* that exist in times of *change* and *challenge* for people at work.[4] The fourth section addresses the ways people learn about organizational behavior and explains how the text's pedagogical features relate to the various ways of learning. The final section of the chapter presents the plan for the book.

Organizational behavior is individual behavior and group dynamics in organizations. The study of organizational behavior is primarily concerned with the psychosocial, interpersonal, and behavioral dynamics in organizations. However, organizational variables that affect human behavior at work are also relevant to

opportunities
Favorable times or chances for progress and advancement.

change
The transformation or modification of an organization and/or its stakeholders.

challenge
The call to competition, contest, or battle.

organizational behavior
The study of individual behavior and group dynamics in organizations.

the study of organizational behavior. These organizational variables include jobs, the design of work, communication, performance appraisal, organizational design, and organizational structure. Therefore, although individual behavior and group dynamics are the primary concerns in the study of organizational behavior, organizational variables are also important.

This section briefly contrasts two perspectives for understanding human behavior, the external and the internal perspectives. The section then discusses six scientific disciplines from which the study of organizational behavior has emerged and concludes with a discussion of behavior in times of change.

Understanding Human Behavior

The vast majority of theories and models of human behavior fall into one of two basic categories. One category has an internal perspective, and the other has an external perspective. The internal perspective considers factors inside the person to understand behavior. This view is psychodynamically oriented. People who subscribe to this view understand human behavior in terms of the thoughts, feelings, past experiences, and needs of the individual. The internal perspective explains people's actions and behavior in terms of their history and personal value systems. The internal processes of thinking, feeling, perceiving, and judging lead people to act in specific ways. The internal perspective has given rise to a wide range of motivational and leadership theories. This perspective implies that people are best understood from the inside and that their behavior is best interpreted after understanding their thoughts and feelings.

The other category of theories and models of human behavior takes an external perspective. This perspective focuses on factors outside the person to understand behavior. People who subscribe to this view understand human behavior in terms of external events, consequences of behavior, and the environmental forces to which a person is subject. From the external perspective, a person's history, feelings, thoughts, and personal value systems are not very important in interpreting actions and behavior. This perspective has given rise to an alternative set of motivational and leadership theories, which are covered in Chapters 5 and 12 of the text. The external perspective implies that a person's behavior is best understood by examining the surrounding external events and environmental forces.

The internal and external perspectives offer alternative explanations for human behavior. For example, the internal perspective might say Mary is an outstanding employee because she has a high need for achievement, whereas the external perspective might say Mary is an outstanding employee because she is paid extremely well for her work. Kurt Lewin captured both perspectives in saying that behavior is a function of both the person and the environment.[5]

Interdisciplinary Influences

Organizational behavior is a blended discipline that has grown out of contributions from numerous earlier fields of study, only one of which is the psychological discipline from which Kurt Lewin came. These interdisciplinary influences are the roots for what is increasingly recognized as the independent discipline of organizational behavior. The sciences of psychology, sociology, engineering, anthropology, management, and medicine have each contributed to our understanding of human behavior in organizations.

Psychology is the science of human behavior and dates back to the closing decades of the nineteenth century. Psychology traces its own origins to philosophy and the science of physiology. One of the most prominent early psychologists,

psychology
The science of human behavior.

William James, actually held a degree in medicine (M.D.). Since its origin, psychology has itself become differentiated into a number of specialized fields, such as clinical, experimental, military, organizational, and social psychology. Organizational psychology includes the study of many topics, such as work motivation, which are also covered by organizational behavior.[6] Early psychological research for the American military during World War I had later implications for sophisticated personnel selection methods used by corporations such as Johnson & Johnson, Valero Energy, and Texas Instruments.[7]

Sociology, the science of society, has made important contributions to knowledge about group and intergroup dynamics in the study of organizational behavior. Because sociology takes society rather than the individual as its point of departure, the sociologist is concerned with the variety of roles within a society or culture, the norms and standards of behavior in groups, and the consequences of compliant and deviant behavior. For example, the concept of *role set,* a key contribution to role theory in 1957 by Robert Merton, was used by a team of Harvard educators to study the school superintendent role in Massachusetts.[8] More recently, the role set concept has been used to study the effects of codes of ethics in organizations.[9]

Engineering is the applied science of energy and matter. Engineering has made important contributions to our understanding of the design of work. By taking basic engineering ideas and applying them to human behavior at work, Frederick Taylor had a profound influence on the early years of the study of organizational behavior.[10] Taylor's engineering background led him to place special emphasis on human productivity and efficiency in work behavior. His notions of performance standards and differential piece-rate systems have had lasting impact. Taylor's original ideas are embedded in organizational goal-setting programs, such as those at Black & Decker, IBM, and Weyerhaeuser.[11]

Anthropology, the science of human learned behavior, is especially important to understanding organizational culture. Cultural anthropology focuses on the origins of culture and the patterns of behavior as culture is communicated symbolically. Research in this tradition has examined the effects of efficient cultures on organization performance[12] and how pathological personalities may lead to dysfunctional organizational cultures.[13] Schwartz used a psychodynamic, anthropological mode of inquiry in exploring corporate decay at General Motors and NASA.[14]

Management, originally called administrative science, is a discipline concerned with the study of overseeing activities and supervising people in organizations. It emphasizes the design, implementation, and management of various administrative and organizational systems. March and Simon take the human organization as their point of departure and concern themselves with the administrative practices that will enhance the effectiveness of the system.[15] Management is the first discipline to take the modern corporation as the unit of analysis, and this viewpoint distinguishes the discipline's contribution to the study of organizational behavior.

Medicine is the applied science of healing or treatment of diseases to enhance an individual's health and well-being. Medicine has long-standing concern for both physical and psychological health, as well as for industrial mental health.[16] More recently, as the war against acute diseases is being won, medical attention has shifted to more chronic diseases, such as hypertension, and to occupational health and well-being.[17] Individual behavior and lifestyle patterns play important roles in treating chronic diseases.[18] These trends have contributed to the growth of corporate wellness programs, such as Johnson & Johnson's "Live for Life Program." The surge in health care costs over the past two decades has contributed to increased organizational concern with medicine and health care in the workplace.[19]

sociology
The science of society.

engineering
The applied science of energy and matter.

anthropology
The science of the learned behavior of human beings.

management
The study of overseeing activities and supervising people in organizations.

medicine
The applied science of healing or treatment of diseases to enhance an individual's health and well-being.

Behavior in Times of Change

② Identify four action steps for responding positively in times of change.

Early research with individuals, groups, and organizations in the midst of environmental change found that change is often experienced as a threat that leads to a reliance on well-learned and dominant forms of behavior.[20] That is, in the midst of change, people often become rigid and reactive, rather than open and responsive. This may be useful if the change is neither dramatic nor rapid because we are often effective at coping with incremental change. However, if significant change occurs, then rigid and well-learned behavior may be counterproductive. The practice of outsourcing is a significant change in American industry that has been facilitated by dramatic advances in the Internet and networking technology.[21] Big changes disrupt people's habitual behavior and require learning if they are to be managed successfully. Eric Brown, ProLine International's VP of Global Business Development, offers some sage words of advice to see the opportunity in change.[22] He recommends adapting to change by seeing it as positive and seeing challenge as good rather than bad. His action steps for doing this are to (1) have a positive attitude, (2) ask questions, (3) listen to the answers, and (4) be committed to success.

However, success is never guaranteed, and change sometimes results in failure. If this happens, do not despair. Some of the world's greatest leaders, such as Winston Churchill, experienced dramatic failure before achieving lasting success. The key to their eventual success was their capacity to learn from the failure and to respond positively to the opportunities presented to them. One venture capitalist with whom the authors have worked likes to ask those seeking to build a business to tell him about their greatest failure. What the venture capitalist is looking for in the answer is how the executive responded to the failure and what he or she learned from the experience. While change carries with it the risk of failure as well as the opportunity for success, it is often how we behave in the midst of change that determines which outcome results. Success can come through the accumulation of small wins and through the use of microprocesses, as has been found with middle managers engaged in institutional change.[23]

THE ORGANIZATIONAL CONTEXT

③ Identify the important system components of an organization.

A complete understanding of organizational behavior requires an understanding of both human behavior and the organizational context where behavior is enacted. This section discusses the organizational context. First, organizations are presented as systems. Second, the formal and informal organizations are discussed. Finally, six focus companies are presented as contemporary examples and drawn on throughout the text.

Organizations as Open Systems

As with human behavior, two different perspectives offer complementary explanations of organizations. Organizations are open systems of interacting components, which are people, tasks, technology, and structure. These internal components also interact with components in the organization's task environment. Organizations as open systems have people, technology, structure, and purpose, which interact with elements in the organization's environment.

What, exactly, is an organization? Today, the corporation is the dominant organizational form for much of the Western world, but other organizational forms have dominated other times and societies. Some societies have been dominated by religious organizations, such as the temple corporations of ancient Mesopotamia and the churches in colonial America.[24] Other societies have been dominated by military organizations, such as the clans of the Scottish Highlands and the regional armies of the People's Republic of China.[25, 26] All of these societies are woven together by family organizations, which themselves may vary from nuclear and extended families to small, collective communities.[27, 28] The purpose and structure of the religious, military, and family organizational forms may vary, but people's behavior in these organizations may be very similar. In fact, early discoveries about power and leadership in work organizations were remarkably similar to findings about power and leadership within families.[29]

Organizations may manufacture products, such as aircraft components or steel, or deliver services, such as managing money or providing insurance protection. To understand how organizations do these things requires an understanding of the open system components of the organization and the components of its task environment.

task
An organization's mission, purpose, or goal for existing.

people
The human resources of the organization.

technology
The tools, knowledge, and/or techniques used to transform inputs into outputs.

structure
The systems of communication, authority and roles, and workflow.

Katz, Kahn, and Leavitt set out open system frameworks for understanding organizations.[30] The four major internal components—task, people, technology, and structure—along with the organization's inputs, outputs, and key elements in the task environment, are depicted in Figure 1.1. The *task* of the organization is its mission, purpose, or goal for existing. The *people* are the human resources of the organization. The *technology* is the wide range of tools, knowledge, and/or techniques used to transform the inputs into outputs. The *structure* is the systems of communication, the systems of authority, and the systems of workflow.

In addition to these major internal components, the organization as a system also has an external task environment. The task environment is composed of different constituents, such as suppliers, customers, and federal regulators. Thompson describes the task environment as that element of the environment related to the

FIGURE 1.1 An Open Systems View of Organization

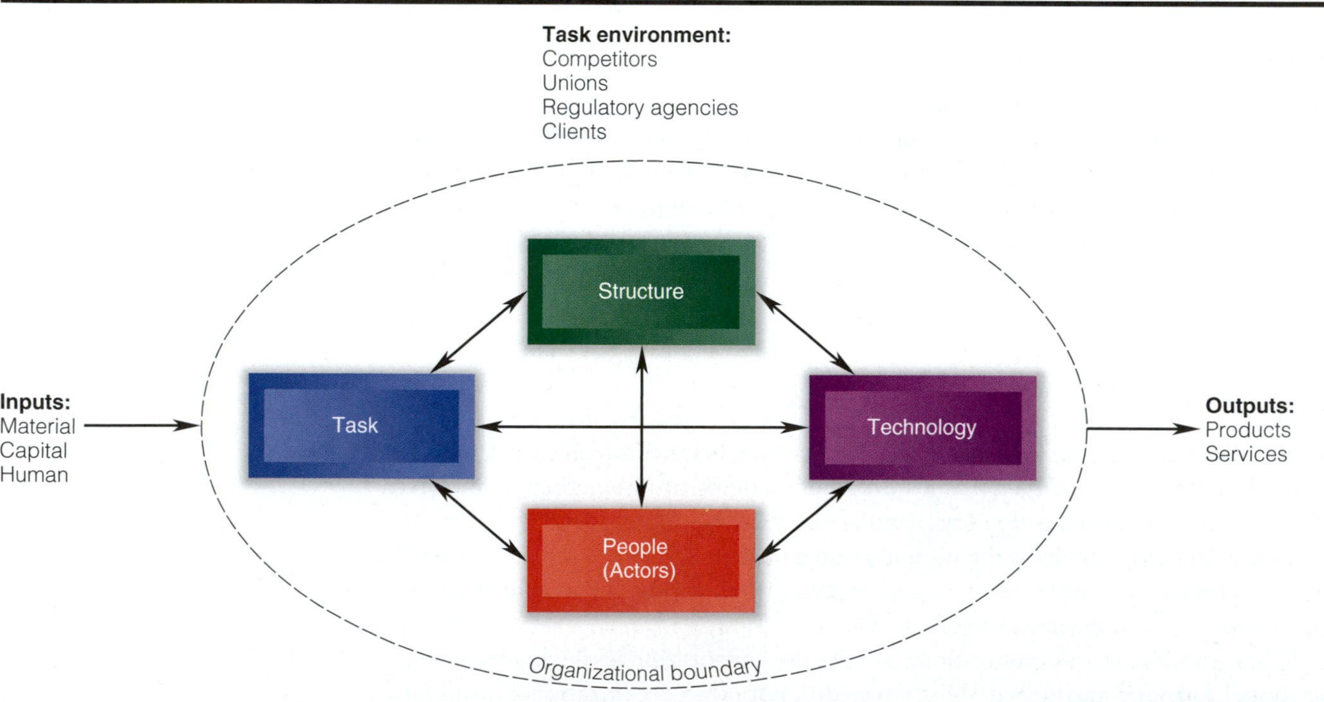

SOURCE: Based on Harold Leavitt, "Applied Organizational Change in Industry: Structural, Technological, and Humanistic Approaches," in J. G. March, ed., *Handbook of Organizations* (Chicago: Rand McNally, 1965), 1145. Reprinted by permission of James G. March.

organization's degree of goal attainment; that is, it is composed of those elements of the environment related to the organization's basic task.[31] For example, competitors are part of any organization's task environment, as we saw in Thinking Ahead with Caribou Coffee. Starbucks is the chief competitor for Caribou and thus a key element in Caribou's task environment. Therefore, Caribou has to develop a business strategy and approach to succeed that considers the actions and activities of Starbucks.

The organization system works by taking inputs, converting them into throughputs, and delivering outputs to its task environment. Inputs consist of the human, informational, material, and financial resources used by the organization. Throughputs are the materials and resources as they are transformed by the organization's technology component. Once the transformation is complete, they become outputs for customers, consumers, and clients. The actions of suppliers, customers, regulators, and other elements of the task environment affect the organization and the behavior of people at work. For example, Onsite Engineering and Management experienced a threat to its survival in the mid-1980s by being totally dependent on one large utility for its outputs. By broadening its client base and improving the quality of its services (that is, its outputs) over the next several years, Onsite became a healthier, more successful small company. Transforming inputs into high-quality outputs is critical to an organization's success.

The Formal and Informal Organization

(4) Describe the formal and informal elements of an organization.

The open systems view of organization may lead one to see the design of an organization as a clockwork with a neat, precise, interrelated functioning. The *formal organization* is the official, legitimate, and most visible part that enables people to think of organizations in logical and rational ways. The snake pit organizational metaphor mentioned earlier has its roots in the study and examination of the *informal organization*, which is unofficial and less visible. The informal elements were first fully appreciated as a result of the *Hawthorne studies*, conducted during the 1920s and 1930s. It was during the interview study, the third of the four Hawthorne studies, that the researchers began to develop a deeper understanding of the informal elements of the Hawthorne Works as an organization.[32] The formal and informal elements of the organization are depicted in Figure 1.2.

Potential conflict between the formal and informal organization makes an understanding of both important. Conflicts between these two elements erupted in many organizations during the early years of the twentieth century and were embodied in the union–management strife of that era. The conflicts escalated into violence in a number of cases. For example, during the 1920s, supervisors at the Homestead Works of U.S. Steel were issued pistols and boxes of ammunition "just in case" it became necessary to shoot unruly, dangerous steelworkers. Such potential formal–informal, management–labor conflict does not characterize all organizations. During the same era, Eastman Kodak was very progressive. The company helped with financial backing for employees' neighborhood communities, such as Meadowbrook in Rochester, New York. Kodak's concern for employees and attention to informal issues made unions unnecessary within the company.

formal organization
The official, legitimate, and most visible part of the system.

informal organization
The unofficial and less visible part of the system.

Hawthorne studies
Studies conducted during the 1920s and 1930s that discovered the existence of the informal organization.

The informal elements of the organization are frequent points of diagnostic and intervention activities in organization development, though the formal elements must always be considered as well because they provide the context for the informal.[33] These informal elements are important because people's feelings, thoughts, and attitudes about their work do make a difference in their behavior and performance. Individual behavior plays out in the context of the formal and informal elements of the system, becoming organizational behavior. The uncovering

FIGURE 1.2 Formal and Informal Organization

Formal organization (overt)
Goals and objectives
Policies and procedures
Job descriptions
Financial resources
Authority structure
Communication channels
Products and services

Social surface

Informal organization (covert)
Beliefs and assumptions
Perceptions and attitudes
Values
Feelings, such as fear, joy, anger, trust, and hope
Group norms
Informal leaders

of the informal elements in an organization was one of the major discoveries of the Hawthorne studies. The importance of employees' moods, emotions, and dispositional affect is being re-recognized as a key influence on critical organizational outcomes, such as job performance, decision making, creativity, turnover, teamwork, negotiation, and leadership.[34]

Six Focus Organizations

(5) Understand the diversity of organizations in the economy, as exemplified by the six focus organizations.

Organizational behavior always occurs in the context of a specific organizational setting. Most attempts at explaining or predicting organizational behavior rely heavily on factors within the organization and give less weight to external environmental considerations.[35] Students can benefit from being sensitive to the industrial context of organizations and from developing an appreciation for each organization as a whole.[36] In this vein, six organizations each appear three times for a total of eighteen Thinking Ahead and Looking Back features. Caribou Coffee is illustrated in this chapter. We challenge you in each chapter to anticipate what is in the Looking Back feature once you read Thinking Ahead.

The U.S. economy is the largest in the world, with a gross domestic product of more than \$13.2 trillion in 2006. Figure 1.3 shows the major sectors of the economy. The largest sectors are service (41 percent) and product manufacture of nondurable goods (20 percent) and durable goods (8 percent). Taken together, the manufacture of products and the delivery of services account for 69 percent of

FIGURE 1.3 U.S. Gross Domestic Product (Approximately $13.2 Trillion for 2006)

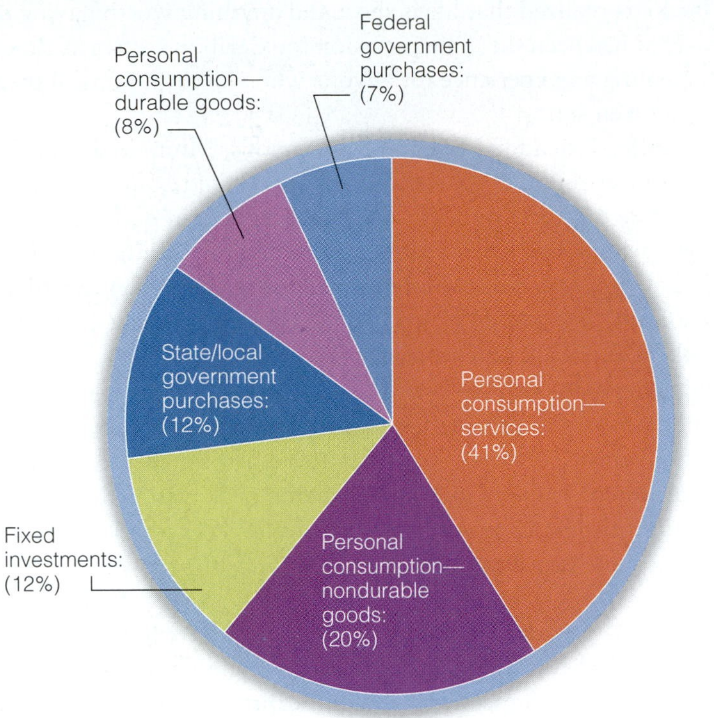

the U.S. economy. Government and fixed investments account for the remaining 31 percent. Large and small organizations operate in each sector of the economy shown in Figure 1.3.

The private sectors are an important part of the economy. The manufacturing sector includes the production of basic materials, such as steel, and the production of finished products, such as automobiles and electronic equipment. The service sector includes transportation, financial services, insurance, and retail sales. The government sectors, which provide essential infrastructure, and nonprofit organizations are also important to our collective well-being because they meet needs not addressed in these economic sectors. We have chosen organizations that reflect the manufacturing service, retail, and nonprofit sections of business: Caribou Coffee, Genentech, Inc., Google, The Timberland Company, American Express, and Toyota Motor Corporation.

Each of these six organizations makes an important and unique contribution to the manufacturing or service sectors of the national economy and/or to our national well-being. These organizations are not alone, however. Hundreds of other small, medium, and large organizations are making valuable and significant contributions to the economic health and human welfare of the United States. Brief examples from many organizations are used throughout the book. We hope that by better understanding these organizations, you may have a greater appreciation for your own organization and others within the diverse world of private business enterprises and nonprofit organizations.

Caribou Coffee. Caribou Coffee is the second largest retailer of specialty and gourmet coffee in the United States. It was born out of an entrepreneurial dream of newlyweds John and Kim Puckett on a trip through Alaska. They went through an arduous climb to the top of Sable Mountain and took in the breathtaking view of the beautiful countryside and a herd of caribou passing through the valley. In that moment, the Pucketts realized that life is short and anything worth having takes a lot of hard work. That has been the defining vision for Caribou Coffee as they pride themselves with creating an experience for anyone who walks into one of their thousands of stores in eighteen states.

Caribou Coffee is headquartered in Minneapolis, Minnesota. The company currently employs over 5,000 employees across the United States. Caribou also offers its specialty coffee products through several grocery chain outlets, college campuses, airlines, sports venues, and other vendors. Recently, the Rainforest Alliance awarded the prestigious Corporate Green Globe Award to Caribou. This award highlights the company's socially responsible practices, focusing on growing coffee in a way that balances ecological, social, and economic considerations.

Caribou's corporate culture is relaxed and informal. Employees are seen as a real asset and encouraged to hone their entrepreneurial spirit. New ideas are always encouraged and most of the company's offices are set in scenic mountain lodge locations. Caribou offers very attractive benefits packages to attract and retain the best talent. They also place a huge emphasis on diversity and recently appointed a woman to their Chief Operating Officer (COO) position.[37]

Genentech, Inc. Led by its chairman and CEO, Arthur D. Levinson, Ph.D., Genentech was founded in 1976 by two venture capitalists to develop, manufacture, and commercialize biotherapeutics for "significant unmet medical needs." And meet unmet medical needs the company has done. Through their basic and applied research, Genentech's more than 800 scientists have amassed a pipeline of over 50 projects in the areas of oncology, immunology, and tissue growth and repair. While Genentech is known for its new product development, it has also had great success in identifying multiple uses for existing drugs to fight not just a particular disease but evolving forms of it.

Genentech is headquartered in San Francisco, California, and has research facilities in Vacaville and Oceanside, California. With over 10,600 full-time employees, Genentech has been recognized as a top employer by *Fortune, Working Mother*, and *Science* magazines. Genentech was named one of *Fortune's* "100 Best Companies to Work For" in the United States for the ninth consecutive year in 2007. The company is also known for its commitment to making sure that the patients who need their products can afford them, donating nearly $205 million in free drugs to uninsured patients in 2006 and capping the price of per patient costs of certain drugs in 2007.

Genentech is publicly traded on the NYSE and reported total operating revenues of $2.84 million for the first quarter of 2007. The company's total cash and investments portfolio totaled nearly $4.9 billion as of March 31, 2007.[38]

Google. Founded in September 1998 by two Stanford University doctoral students, Larry Page and Sergey Brin, Google is currently home to one of the most popular search engines in the country, Google .com. Referred to by *FastCompany* in 2003 as having been "founded by geeks and run by geeks," Google has developed

At the Google headquarters in Mountain View, California, the lobby is complete with lava lamps, a piano, and live projections of Google.com queries from around the world.

© AP PHOTO/PAUL SAKUMA

a product that has changed the lives of more than 380 million Internet users a month by providing information that is fast, accurate, and easy to use.

Google employs more than 7,900 full-time employees ("Googlers" as they call themselves) worldwide. The company's corporate culture is relatively intimate and uniquely "geek." Its Mountain View, California, headquarters lobby is complete with lava lamps, a piano, and live projections of Google.com queries from around the world. Rather than expensive Porsches, most of the cars in the parking lot are beat-up Volvos and Subarus. Googlers seem to be driven by an impossible quest for perfection—in speed, relevant content, and user trust.

While online search continues to be the heart of Google, the company has developed a number of other Internet-related products including Google Maps, Google Earth, Google Book Search, and Google Video. In 2006, the company acquired YouTube, the enormously popular repository of commercial and user-generated video content. Google reported over $10.6 billion in total revenue and a net income of over $3 billion for the year ending December 31, 2006.[39]

The Timberland Company. The birth of Timberland can be traced back to when Nathan Schwartz bought a part of the Abington Shoe Company in 1952. It was in 1978 that the official Timberland company name took shape after the introduction of their first Timberland boot. Since then, the company has never looked back. Today it exports to several foreign locations.

In 1998, Jeffrey Schwartz, grandson of founder Nathan Schwartz, took over as the President and CEO of Timberland. He has been instrumental in creating the company's distinct corporate image. For example, in 2001, they introduced the Path of Service program for employees. This allows employees to take a sabbatical and engage in long-term service projects. Timberland ranked 78 in the *Fortune* "100 Best Companies to Work For" list in 2007. It employs just over 2,000 employees and is headquartered in Stratham, New Hampshire. Timberland encourages employees to give back to the communities they live in. It gives employees 40 hours of paid time per year to volunteer.

Today, the race to engage in socially responsible business practices seems to be more heated than ever for people at Timberland. The company recruited 9,000 volunteers across the globe to celebrate Earth Day. These service hours totaling about 53,000 hours were invested in activities such as planting tress and restoration of native species. Jeff Schwartz claims that such activities help achieve Timberland's larger corporate goal of being carbon neutral by 2010.[40]

American Express (AMEX). Founded in 1850 in New York, American Express started out as a business delivery service for large financial corporations. They specialized in delivering small bank parcels such as money orders, checks, and financial certificates. It was only much later in the late 1800s and early 1900s that they began to focus on financial services. Soon American Express evolved into a banking and financial services conglomerate with locations all over the world. In 1958, the company issued its first charge card and since then has been known for its credit card products and services.

American Express ranked 74 on *Fortune*'s "100 Best Companies to Work For" in America in 2007. With over 29,000 employees in the United States and over 35,000 outside the United States, the company has a strong corporate culture founded and built on values such as trust, integrity, and teamwork. During the 9/11 attacks, employees of the company, headquartered directly across from Ground Zero, demonstrated undeniable courage and commitment by continuing to work from temporary locations to help customers and colleagues get through the difficult time.

Fully realizing that investors care as much about company image as they do about bottom-line numbers, AMEX has transformed itself into a model corporate citizen. It heavily invests in three major themes related to corporate social responsibility: preservation and enrichment of cultural heritage; development of leadership; and encouragement of community service in the communities where it operates.[41]

Toyota Motor Corporation. The Toyota Motor Corporation was born when Kiichiro Toyoda completed his A1 prototype passenger car in 1935. More than seven decades later, Toyota has become a force in the automobile industry and is the fourth largest automaker in North America, having sold over 7.4 million passenger cars, trucks, and buses in 2005.

Since its founding, Toyota's aim has been to "enrich society through car making." To that end, the company has made good on its commitment to develop vehicles that are safe, environmentally advanced, and fun to drive. To date, Toyota has sold over 500,000 hybrid vehicles worldwide including the Lexus RX and GS, Highlander, Prius, and Camry models. Under the leadership of its chairman, Fujio Cho, and its president, Katsuaki Watanabe, Toyota deploys *monozukuri*—the manufacturing of value-added products—to help achieve its goals of creating a more prosperous society and innovating into the future.

Along with its subsidiaries, Toyota manufactures in 27 countries and sells vehicles in more than 170 countries. In addition to its worldwide presence, Toyota's economic impact in North America continues to grow. Nearly two-thirds of all its vehicles sold in the United States are built in the United States. The North American operations group expects that by 2008, it will have the capacity to build over 1.8 million cars and trucks. Toyota employs approximately 300,000 people worldwide; it has net sales of 23.95 billion yen ($194.08 million) and a net income of 1.64 billion yen ($13.32 million) for the fiscal year ending March 31, 2007.[42]

CHANGE CREATES OPPORTUNITIES

(6) Recognize the opportunities that change creates for organizational behavior.

Change creates opportunities and risks, as mentioned earlier in the chapter. Global competition is a leading force driving change at work. Competition in the United States and world economies has increased significantly during the past couple of decades, especially in industries such as banking, finance, and air transportation. Corporate competition creates performance and cost pressures, which have a ripple effect on people and their behavior at work. While one risk for employees is the marginalization of part-time professionals, good management practice can ensure the integration of these part-time professionals.[43] The competition may lead to downsizing and restructuring, yet it provides the opportunity for revitalization as well.[44] Further, small companies are not necessarily the losers in this competitive environment. Scientech, a small power and energy company, found it had to enhance its managerial talent and service quality to meet the challenges of growth and big-company competitors. Product and service quality is one tool that can help companies become winners in a competitive environment. Problem-solving skills are another tool used by IBM, Control Data Services, Inc., Northwest Airlines, and Southwest Airlines to help achieve high-quality products and services.

Too much change leads to chaos; too little change leads to stagnation. Change in the coffee industry is a key stimulus for both Caribou Coffee and for Starbucks as they innovate and improve as organizations. Winning in a competitive industry can be a transient victory however; continuous change is required to stay ahead of the

THE REAL WORLD 1.1

Nintendo "Gets It" and Is Back in the Game

By the 1980s, Nintendo, which had ushered in the modern age of videogames, was the most successful company in the gaming world. However, over the next twenty years they watched Sony and Microsoft cut their market share of U.S. hardware sales in half by the introduction of newer, more powerful systems. This occurred within the context of a booming industry that grew to $30 billion globally. Nintendo began its dramatic turnaround in the early 2000s when its top two strategists, CEO Satoru Iwata and legendary game designer Shigeru Miyamoto, identified two troubling trends. First, as young consumers started careers and families, they cut back on game time. Second, as consoles became more powerful, the games became more expensive. Nintendo needed a paradigm shift and an entirely new way of engaging in the competition with Sony and Microsoft. Iwata and Miyamoto decided they needed to do something about the game controller, whose basic design had remained unchanged for decades. They made the risky decision to build the Wii around a chip similar to one of Nintendo's early entries in gaming, which meant success would not be on the strength of breathtaking graphics. Then they designed a sleek, small, white exterior console that would sit right next to the TV. Finally, they went for a motion-sensitive wireless controller. While risky, the new controller paradigm paid off and demand well outstripped supply of Wiis during 2006. The Wii is reversing twenty years of declining Nintendo console sales.

© REUTERS/TORU HANAI/LANDOV

Nintendo's Wii game console was released abroad as well as in the United States. Here is a Wii display at a game shop in Tokyo's Akihabara electronic district.

SOURCE: J. Gaudiosi, "Why Wii Won," *Business 2.0* 8 (May 2007): 35–37.

competition. For example, in 2006 it looked like the game was over for Nintendo's storied console business. Then again, maybe not, as we see in The Real World 1.1. The gaming world is full of changes. What are your perceptions of change? Complete You 1.1 and see how you perceive change.

Four Challenges for Managers Related to Change

Chapter 2 develops four challenges for managers related to change in contemporary organizations: globalization, workforce diversity, ethics and character, and technological innovation. These are four driving forces creating and shaping changes at work. Further, success in global competition requires organizations to be more responsive to ethnic, religious, and gender diversity as well as personal integrity in the workforce, in addition to responding positively to the competition in the international marketplace. Workforce demographic change and diversity are critical challenges in themselves for the study and management of organizational behavior.[45] The theories of motivation, leadership, and group behavior based on research in a workforce of one composition may not be applicable in a workforce of a very different composition.[46] This may be especially problematic if ethnic, gender, and/or religious differences lead to conflict between leaders and followers in organizations. For example, the Russian military establishment has found ethnic and religious conflicts between the officers and enlisted corps a serious impediment to unit cohesion and performance at times.

YOU 1.1

Analyze Your Perceptions of a Change

Everyone perceives change differently. Think of a change situation you are currently experiencing. It can be any business, school-related, or personal experience that requires a significant change in your attitude or behavior. Rate your feelings about this change using the following scales. For instance, if you feel the change is more of a threat than an opportunity, you would circle 0, 2, or 4 on the first scale.

1. Threat	0	2	4	6	8	10	Opportunity
2. Holding on to the past	0	2	4	6	8	10	Reaching for the future
3. Immobilized	0	2	4	6	8	10	Activated
4. Rigid	0	2	4	6	8	10	Versatile
5. A loss	0	2	4	6	8	10	A gain
6. Victim of change	0	2	4	6	8	10	Agent of change
7. Reactive	0	2	4	6	8	10	Proactive
8. Focused on the past	0	2	4	6	8	10	Focused on the future
9. Separate from change	0	2	4	6	8	10	Involved with change
10. Confused	0	2	4	6	8	10	Clear

How positive are your perceptions of this change?

SOURCE: H. Woodward and S. Buchholz, *Aftershock: Helping People through Corporate Change*, 15. Copyright © 1987 John Wiley & Sons, Inc. Reprinted by permission of John Wiley & Sons, Inc.

Global Competition in Business

Managers and executives in the United States face radical change in response to increased global competition. According to noted economist Lester Thurow, this competition is characterized by intense rivalry between the United States, Japan, and Europe in core industries.[47] Economic competition places pressure on all categories of employees to be productive and to add value to the firm. The uncertainty of unemployment resulting from corporate warfare and competition is an ongoing feature of organizational life for people in companies or industries that pursue cost-cutting strategies to achieve economic success. The global competition in the automotive industry among the Japanese, U.S., and European car companies embodies the intensity that can be expected in other industries in the future.

Some people feel that the future must be the focus in coming to grips with this international competition; others believe we can deal with the future only by studying the past.[48] Global, economic, and organizational changes have dramatic effects on the study and management of organizational behavior. How positive were your perceptions of the change you analyzed in You 1.1? Are you an optimist who sees opportunity, or a pessimist who sees threat?

Customer Focused for High Quality

Global competition has challenged organizations to become more customer focused, to meet changing product and service demands, and to exceed customers' expectations of high quality. Quality has the potential for giving organizations in viable industries a competitive edge in meeting international competition. By striving to be number one in experience, Caribou Coffee aims to compete with a customer-focused, high-quality approach.

SCIENCE

Is TQM a Fleeting Fashion?

This research studied the provision of TQM consulting services between 1992 and 2001, a period during which TQM consulting went from the limelight to the background of the management stage. TQM consulting was a fleeting fashion with a boom and a bust during this period, and yet it has staying power. This study helps us to understand the boom-to-bust cycle that occurred. As TQM consulting boomed, the demand for qualified consultants outstripped the supply and led more generalists into the arena of offering TQM consulting services. However, these generalists had weak links to the technical foundations of this type of consulting and, as a result, were often uncommitted, unprepared, and superficial providers of services. These "fashion surfers" damaged the credibility of the consulting services offered by all, tarnishing the industry. As a result, they contributed to the downturn and eventual bust in TQM consulting services. TQM was a legitimate managerial innovation and the question became: how could it survive the collapse of a boom? The answer lay in the commitment of consulting specialists with strong links to quality control expertise. The emergence of a hard core of knowledgeable TQM providers of management consulting services helped this innovation to survive and will improve the average TQM program success, refine industry best practice, and increase the legitimacy of an innovation that went through a real bust. Yes, TQM was a fleeting fashion but one that is still here because of a solid technical foundation.

SOURCE: R. J. David and D. Strang, "When Fashion Is Fleeting: Transitory Collective Beliefs and the Dynamics of TQM Consulting," *Academy of Management Journal* 49 (2006): 215–233.

Quality became a rubric for products and services of high status. Total quality is defined in many ways.[49] Total quality management (TQM) is the complete dedication to continuous improvement and to customers so that their needs are met and their expectations exceeded. Quality is a customer-oriented philosophy of management with important implications for virtually all aspects of organizational behavior. Quality cannot be optimized, because customer needs and expectations are always changing. It is a cultural value embedded in highly successful organizations. Ford Motor Company's dramatic metamorphosis as an automotive leader is attributable to the decision to "make quality Job One" in all aspects of the design and manufacture of cars. As we see in the Science feature, while TQM management consulting went through a boom-to-bust cycle, it is here to stay.

Quality improvement enhances the probability of organizational success in increasingly competitive industries. One study of 193 general medical hospitals examined seven TQM practices and found them positively related to the financial performance of the hospitals.[50] Quality improvement is an enduring feature of an organization's culture and of the economic competition we face today. It leads to competitive advantage through customer responsiveness, results acceleration, and resource effectiveness.[51] The three key questions in evaluating quality-improvement ideas for people at work are these: (1) Does the idea improve customer response? (2) Does the idea accelerate results? (3) Does the idea increase the effectiveness of resources? A "yes" answer means the idea should be implemented to improve quality.

Six Sigma is a philosophy for company-wide quality improvement developed by Motorola and popularized by General Electric. The Six Sigma program is characterized by its customer-driven approach, its emphasis on decision making based on quantitative data, and its priority on saving money.[52] It has evolved into a high-performance system to execute business strategy. Part of its quality program is a 12-step problem-solving method specifically designed to lead a Six Sigma "Black Belt" to significant improvement within a defined process. It tackles problems in

Six Sigma
A high-performance system to execute business strategy that is customer driven, emphasizes quantitative decision making, and places a priority on saving money.

TABLE 1.1 Contrasting Six Sigma and Total Quality Management

Six Sigma	Total Quality Management
Executive ownership	Self-directed work teams
Business strategy execution system	Quality initiative
Truly cross-functional	Largely within a single function
Focused training with verifiable	No mass training in statistics and quality
return on investment	Return on investment
Business results oriented	Quality oriented

SOURCE: M. Barney, "Motorola's Second Generation," *Six Sigma Forum Magazine* (May 2002): 13.

four phases: (1) measure, (2) analyze, (3) improve, and (4) control. In addition, it demands that executives be aligned to the right objective and targets, quality improvement teams be mobilized for action, results be accelerated, and sustained improvement be monitored. Six Sigma is set up in a way that it can be applied to a range of problems and areas, from manufacturing settings to service work environments. Table 1.1 contrasts Six Sigma and TQM. One study compared Six Sigma to two other methods for quality improvement (specifically, Taguchi's methods and the Shainin system) and found it to be the most complete strategy of the three, with a strong emphasis on exploiting statistical modeling techniques.[53]

Behavior and Quality at Work

Whereas total quality may draw on reliability engineering or just-in-time management, total quality improvement can be successful only when employees have the skills and authority to respond to customer needs.[54] Total quality has direct and important effects on the behavior of employees at all levels in the organization, not just on employees working directly with customers. Chief executives can advance total quality by engaging in participative management, being willing to change everything, focusing quality efforts on customer service (not cost cutting), including quality as a criterion in reward systems, improving the flow of information regarding quality-improvement successes or failures, and being actively and personally involved in quality efforts. While serving as chairman of Motorola, George Fisher emphasized the behavioral attributes of leadership, cooperation, communication, and participation as important elements in the company's Six Sigma program.

Quality improvement continues to be important to our competitiveness. The U.S. Department of Commerce's sponsorship of an annual award in the name of Malcolm Baldrige, former secretary of commerce in the Reagan administration, recognizes companies excelling in quality improvement and management. The Malcolm Baldrige National Quality Award examination evaluates an organization in seven categories: leadership, information and analysis, strategic quality planning, human resource utilization, quality assurance of products and services, quality results, and customer satisfaction.

According to former President George H. W. Bush, quality management is not just a strategy. It must be a new style of working, even a new style of thinking. A dedication to quality and excellence is more than good business. It is a way of life, giving something back to society, offering your best to others.

Quality is one watchword for competitive success. Organizations that do not respond to customer needs find their customers choosing alternative product and service suppliers who are willing to exceed their expectations. With this said, you should not conclude that total quality is a panacea for all organizations or that it guarantees unqualified success.

Managing Organizational Behavior in Changing Times

Over and above the challenge of quality improvement to meet international competition, managing organizational behavior during changing times is challenging for at least four reasons: (1) the increasing globalization of organizations' operating territory, (2) the increasing diversity of organizational workforces, (3) the continuing demand for higher levels of moral and ethical behavior at work, and (4) continuing technological innovation with its companion need for skill enhancement. These are the important issues to address in managing people at work.

Each of these four issues is explored in detail in Chapter 2 and highlighted throughout the text because they are intertwined in the contemporary practice of organizational behavior. For example, the issue of women in the workplace concerns workforce diversity and at the same time overlaps the globalization issue. Gender roles are often defined differently in various cultures, and sexual harassment is a frequent ethical problem for organizations in the United States, Europe, Israel, and South Africa. For another example, process and technology innovations require attention to behavioral issues if they are to be successful. One study of innovation in 47 German companies found that organizational support and psychological safety were positively related to return on assets and goal achievement, suggesting that attention to behavioral factors along with technical factors in implementing successful process innovations is important.[55] Therefore, students of organizational behavior must appreciate and understand these important issues.

LEARNING ABOUT ORGANIZATIONAL BEHAVIOR

7 Demonstrate the value of objective knowledge and skill development in the study of organizational behavior.

Organizational behavior is based on scientific knowledge and applied practice. It involves the study of abstract ideas, such as valence and expectancy in motivation, as well as the study of concrete matters, such as observable behaviors and medical symptoms of distress at work. Therefore, learning about organizational behavior includes at least three activities, as shown in Figure 1.4. First, the science of organizational behavior requires the mastery of a certain body of *objective knowledge*. Objective knowledge results from research and scientific activities, as reflected in the Science feature in each chapter. Second, the practice of organizational behavior requires *skill development* based on knowledge and an understanding of yourself in order to master the abilities essential to success. The You features in each chapter challenge you to know yourself and apply what you are learning. Third, both objective knowledge and skill development must be applied in real-world settings. The Real World features in each chapter open windows into organizational realities where science and skills are applied.

Learning is challenging and fun because we are all different. The Real World 1.2 feature shows that while diversity is very important, it does have its limits. Within learning environments, student diversity is best addressed in the learning process through more options for students and greater responsibility on the part of students as coproducers in the effort and fun of learning.[56] For those who are blind or have vision impairments, learning can be a special challenge. The alignment of teaching styles with learning styles is important for the best fit, and teaching is no longer just verbal and visual but also virtual with a new generation of students.[57] To gain a better understanding of yourself as a learner, thereby maximizing your potential and developing strategies in specific learning environments, you need to evaluate the way you prefer to learn and process information. You 1.2 offers a quick way

objective knowledge
Knowledge that results from research and scientific activities.

skill development
The mastery of abilities essential to successful functioning in organizations.

THE REAL WORLD 1.2

The Limits of Diversity

Diversity is critically important in the real world just as it is in learning environments. Appreciating, understanding, and working effectively with those who are different from us have huge value in achieving great results by working together. However, one Florida city manager learned that even diversity tolerance has its limits. Largo, Florida, is a city whose motto is "The City of Progress." According to Susan Sinz, the city's human resources director, Largo created a diversity program in 2004 to respond to the small number of employees who were terminated for making racial slurs or using derogatory remarks. The program focused primarily on the appreciation of diversity in knowledge, skills, and abilities without taking on a specific demographic diversity dimension, such as race or gender. The result was substantive tolerance for diversity among the employees of the city of Largo. However, when city manager Steven Stanton began undergoing hormone therapy in preparation for a sex-change operation, a very active group of churches became involved and worked to set limits on how much diversity the city should tolerate. The city found that transgender issues are still on the periphery of most diversity initiatives. As a result, while it still preaches and practices tolerance, Largo fired Stanton after the story created a firestorm locally and broke nationwide. Tolerance and appreciation of diversity do have limits.

SOURCE: J. Marquez, "Limits of Diversity Program Revealed," *Workforce Management* 86 (2007): 1–4.

of assessing your learning style. If you are a visual learner, then use charts, maps, PowerPoint slides, videos, the Internet, notes, or flash cards, and write things out for visual review. If you are an auditory learner, then listen, take notes during lectures, and consider taping them so you can fill in gaps later; review your notes frequently; and recite key concepts out loud. If you are a tactile learner, trace words as you are saying them, write down facts several times, and make study sheets.

FIGURE  **1.4** Learning about Organizational Behavior

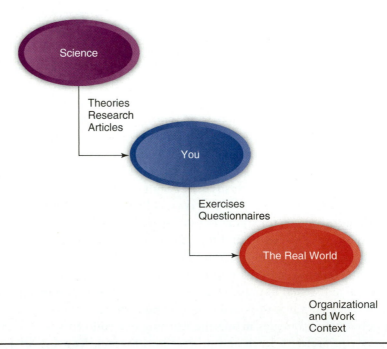

Learning Style Inventory

Directions: This 24-item survey is not timed. Answer each question as honestly as you can. Place a check on the appropriate line after each statement.

	OFTEN	SOMETIMES	SELDOM
1. Can remember more about a subject through the lecture method with information, explanations, and discussion.			
2. Prefer information to be written on the chalkboard, with the use of visual aids and assigned readings.			
3. Like to write things down or to take notes for visual review.			
4. Prefer to use posters, models, or actual practice and some activities in class.			
5. Require explanations of diagrams, graphs, or visual directions.			
6. Enjoy working with my hands or making things.			
7. Am skillful with and enjoy developing and making graphs and charts.			
8. Can tell if sounds match when presented with pairs of sounds.			
9. Remember best by writing things down several times.			
10. Can understand and follow directions on maps.			
11. Do better at academic subjects by listening to lectures and tapes.			
12. Play with coins or keys in pockets.			
13. Learn to spell better by repeating the word out loud than by writing the word on paper.			
14. Can better understand a news development by reading about it in the paper than by listening to the radio.			
15. Chew gum, smoke, or snack during studies.			
16. Feel the best way to remember is to picture it in your head.			
17. Learn spelling by "finger spelling" words.			
18. Would rather listen to a good lecture or speech than read about the same material in a textbook.			
19. Am good at working and solving jigsaw puzzles and mazes.			
20. Grip objects in hands during learning period.			
21. Prefer listening to the news on the radio rather than reading about it in the newspaper.			
22. Obtain information on an interesting subject by reading relevant materials.			
23. Feel very comfortable touching others, hugging, hand-shaking, etc.			
24. Follow oral directions better than written ones.			

Scoring Procedures

Score 5 points for each OFTEN, 3 points for each SOMETIMES, and 1 point for each SELDOM.

Visual Preference Score 5 Points for questions 2 + 3 + 7 + 10 + 14 + 16 + 19 + 22 = ____

Auditory Preference Score 5 Points for questions 1 + 5 + 8 + 11 + 13 + 18 + 21 + 24 = ____

Tactile Preference Score 5 Points for questions 4 + 6 + 9 + 12 + 15 + 17 + 20 + 23 = ____

SOURCE: Adapted from J. N. Gardner and A. J. Jewler, *Your College Experience: Strategies for Success, Third Concise Edition* (Belmont, Calif.: Wadsworth/ITP, 1998), pp. 62–63; E. Jensen, *Student Success Secrets*, 4th ed. (Hauppauge, N.Y.: Barron's, 1996), 33–36.

Objective Knowledge

Objective knowledge, in any field of study, is developed through basic and applied research. Research in organizational behavior has continued since early research on scientific management. Acquiring objective knowledge requires the cognitive mastery of theories, conceptual models, and research findings. In this book, the objective knowledge in each chapter is reflected in the notes that support the text and in the Science feature included in each chapter. Mastering the concepts and ideas that come from these notes enables you to intelligently discuss topics such as motivation, performance, leadership,[58] and executive stress.[59]

We encourage instructors and students of organizational behavior to think critically about the objective knowledge in organizational behavior. Only by engaging in critical thinking can one question or challenge the results of specific research and responsibly consider how to apply research results in a particular work setting. Rote memorization does not enable the student to appreciate the complexity of specific theories or the interrelationships among concepts, ideas, and topics. Good critical thinking, in contrast, enables the student to identify inconsistencies and limitations in the current body of objective knowledge.

Critical thinking, based on knowledge and understanding of basic ideas, leads to inquisitive exploration and is a key to accepting the responsibility of coproducer in the learning process. A questioning, probing attitude is at the core of critical thinking. The student of organizational behavior should evolve into a critical consumer of knowledge related to organizational behavior—one who is able to intelligently question the latest research results and distinguish plausible, sound new approaches from fads that lack substance or adequate foundation. Ideally, the student of organizational behavior develops into a scientific professional manager who is knowledgeable in the art and science of organizational behavior.

Skill Development

Learning about organizational behavior requires doing as well as knowing. The development of skills and abilities requires that students be challenged by the instructor and by themselves. Skill development is a very active component of the learning process. The You features in each chapter give you a chance to learn about yourself, challenge yourself, and developmentally apply what you are learning.

The U.S. Department of Labor wants people to achieve the necessary skills to be successful in the workplace.[60] The essential skills identified by the Department of Labor are (1) resource management skills, such as time management; (2) information management skills, such as data interpretation; (3) personal interaction skills, such as teamwork; (4) systems behavior and performance skills, such as cause–effect relationships; and (5) technology utilization skills, such as troubleshooting. Many of these skills, such as decision making and information management, are directly related to the study of organizational behavior.[61]

Developing skills is different from acquiring objective knowledge in that it requires structured practice and feedback. A key function of experiential learning is to engage the student in individual or group activities that are systematically reviewed, leading to new skills and understandings. Objective knowledge acquisition and skill development are interrelated. The process for learning from structured or experiential activities is depicted in Figure 1.5. The student engages in an individual or group-structured activity and systematically reviews that activity, which leads to new or modified knowledge and skills.

FIGURE 1.5 Learning from Structured Activity

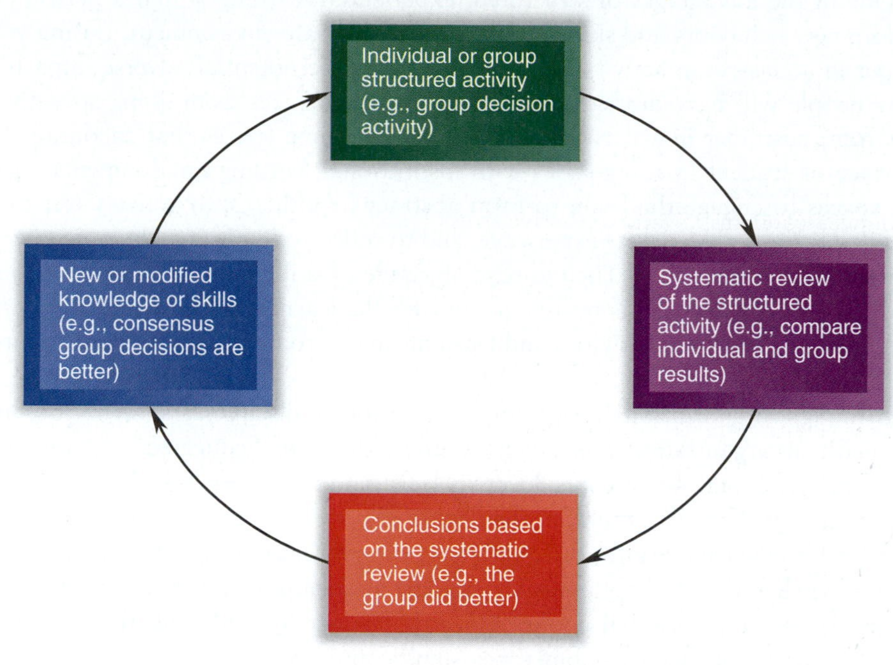

If skill development and structured learning occur in this way, there should be an inherently self-correcting element to learning because of the modification of the student's knowledge and skills over time.[62] To ensure that skill development does occur and that the learning is self-correcting as it occurs, three basic assumptions that underlie the previous model must be followed.

First, each student must accept responsibility for his or her own behavior, actions, and learning. This is a key to the coproducer role in the learning process. A group cannot learn for its members. Each member must accept responsibility for what he or she does and learns. Denial of responsibility helps no one, least of all the learner.

Second, each student must actively participate in the individual or group-structured learning activity. Structured learning is an active process. In group activities, everyone suffers if just one person adopts a passive attitude. Hence, all must actively participate.

Third, each student must be open to new information, new skills, new ideas, and experimentation. This does not mean that students should be indiscriminate. It does mean that they should have a nondefensive, open attitude so that change is possible through the learning process.

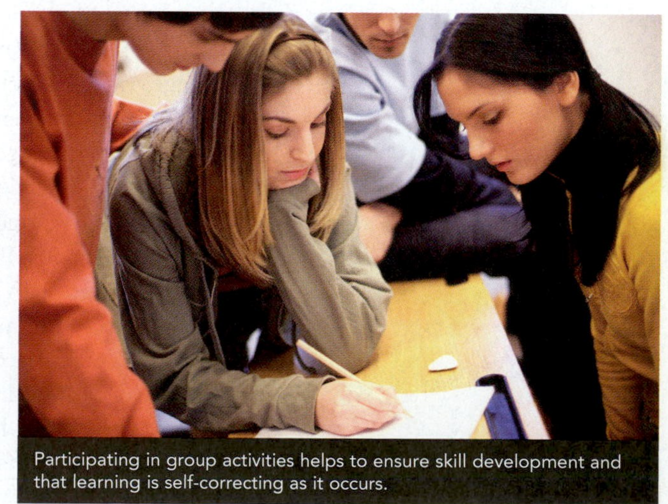

Participating in group activities helps to ensure skill development and that learning is self-correcting as it occurs.

Application of Knowledge and Skills

The Real World features in each chapter give you a window into organizational realities and help you assess your own knowledge of the real world at work. Understanding the real world is one essential aspect of appreciating organizational behavior, the other two being understanding scientific knowledge and understanding yourself.

One of the advantages of structured, experiential learning is that a person can explore new behaviors and skills in a comparatively safe environment. Losing your temper in a classroom activity and learning about the potential adverse impact on other people will have dramatically different consequences from doing so with an important customer in a tense work situation. Learning spaces that encourage the interface of student learning styles with institutional learning environments create safe spaces to engage the brain to form abstract hypotheses, to actively test these hypotheses through concrete experience, and to reflectively observe the outcomes in behavior and experience.[63] The ultimate objective of skill application and experiential learning is that students be able to transfer the learning process they employed in structured classroom activities and learning spaces to unstructured opportunities in the workplace.

Although organizational behavior is an applied discipline, students are not "trained" in organizational behavior. Rather, they are "educated" in organizational behavior and are a coproducer in learning. The distinction between these two modes of learning is found in the degree of direct and immediate applicability of either knowledge or skills. As an activity, training more nearly ties direct objective knowledge or skill development to specific applications. By contrast, education enhances a person's residual pool of objective knowledge and skills that may then be selectively applied later—sometimes significantly later—when the opportunity presents itself. Hence, education is highly consistent with the concept of lifelong learning. Especially in a growing area of knowledge such as organizational behavior, the student can think of the first course as the outset of lifelong learning about the topics and subject.

PLAN FOR THE BOOK

Challenge and opportunity are watchwords in organizations during these changing times. Managers and employees alike are challenged to meet change in positive and optimistic ways: change in how work gets done, change in psychological and legal contracts between individuals and organizations, change in who is working in the organization, and change in the basis for organization. Four challenges for managers are the global environment, workplace diversity, ethical issues at work, and technological innovation. These four challenges, which are discussed in detail in Chapter 2, are shaping the changes occurring in organizations throughout the world. For example, the increasing globalization of business has led to intense international competition in core industries, and the changing demographics of the workplace have led to gender, age, racial, and ethnic diversity among working populations.

The first two chapters compose Part 1 of the book, the introduction. Against the backdrop of the challenges discussed here, we develop and explore the specific subjects in organizational behavior. In addition to the introduction, the text has three major parts. Part 2 addresses individual processes and behavior. Part 3 addresses interpersonal processes and behavior. Part 4 addresses organizational processes and structure.

The five chapters in Part 2 are designed to help the reader understand specific aspects of human behavior. Chapter 3 discusses personality, perception, and attribution. Chapter 4 examines attitudes, values, and ethics. What was your attitude toward change in You 1.1? Chapters 5 and 6 address the broad range of motivational theories, learning, and performance management in organizations. Finally, Chapter 7 considers stress and well-being, including healthy aspects of life, at work.

Part 3 is composed of six chapters designed to help the reader better understand interpersonal and group dynamics in organizations. Chapter 8 addresses communication in organizations. Chapter 9 focuses on teamwork and groups as an increasingly prominent feature of the workplace. Chapter 10 examines how individuals and groups make decisions. Chapter 11 is about power and politics, one very dynamic aspect of organizational life. Chapter 12 addresses the companion topics of leadership and followership. Finally, Chapter 13 examines conflict at work, not all of which we consider bad.

The five chapters in Part 4 are designed to help the reader better understand organizational processes and the organizational context of behavior at work. Chapter 14 examines traditional and contemporary approaches to job design. Chapter 15 develops the topics of organizational design and structure, giving special attention to contemporary forces reshaping organizations and to emerging forms of organization. Chapter 16 addresses the culture of the organization. Chapter 17 focuses on the important issue of career management. Finally, Chapter 18 brings closure to the text and the main theme of change by addressing the topic of managing change.

MANAGERIAL IMPLICATIONS: FOUNDATIONS FOR THE FUTURE

Managers must consider personal and environmental factors to understand fully how people behave in organizations and to help them reach their maximum potential. Human behavior is complex and at times confusing. Characteristics of the organizational system and formal–informal dynamics at work are important environmental factors that influence people's behavior. Managers should look for similarities and differences in manufacturing, service-oriented, nonprofit, and governmental organizations.

Change may be seen as a threat or as an opportunity by contemporary managers. For example, hospital managers face not only clinical challenges but also organizational learning and the implementation of effective high involvement management practices with a professional workforce.[64] Changing customer demands for high-quality outputs in other industries challenges companies to beat the global competition. Globalization, workforce diversity, ethics, and technology are four challenges for managers that are developed in Chapter 2. Another aspect of meeting the competition is learning. Managers must continually upgrade their knowledge about all aspects of their businesses, to include especially the human side of the enterprise. They must hone both their technical and interpersonal skills, engaging in a lifelong educational process. This is a fun and somewhat unpredictable process that can at times be frustrating, while always challenging and exciting.

Several business trends and ongoing changes are affecting managers across the globe. These include continuing industrial restructuring, a dramatic increase in the amount and availability of information, a need to attract and retain the best employees, a need to understand a wide range of human and cultural differences, and a rapid shortening of response times in all aspects of business activities. Further, the old company towns are largely relics of the past, and managers are being called on to reintegrate their businesses with communities, cultures, and societies at a much broader level than has ever been required before. Trust, predictability, and a sense of security become important issues in this context. Reweaving the fabric of human relationships within, across, and outside the organization is a challenge for managers today.

Knowledge becomes power in tracking these trends and addressing these issues. Facts and information are two elements of knowledge in this context. Theories are a third element of a manager's knowledge base. Good theories are tools that help managers understand human and organizational behavior, help them make good business decisions, and inform them about actions to take or to refrain from taking. Managers always use theories, if not those generated from systematic research, then those evolved from the manager's implicit observation. Theories tell us how organizations, business, and people work—or do not work. Therefore, the student is challenged to master the theories in each topic area, and then apply and test the theory in the real world of organizational life. The challenge for the student and the manager is to see what works and what does not work in their specific work context.

LOOKING BACK: CARIBOU COFFEE

Winning the Experience Game

Consumer Reports rated Caribou Coffee's brew higher than their chief competitor's coffee in 2004, giving Caribou an argument that they offer better coffee. That is not their main claim to fame in the competition. Caribou believes that they offer a more inviting atmosphere and a broader lineup of coffee than does Starbucks. Caribou CEO Coles is clear that his company is not aiming to compete for location. They do not intend to have as many locations as Starbucks. However, this does not mean that Caribou does not plan to grow. It plans to open franchises in the United States as well as other countries. By 2014 Caribou expects to double the size of their chain and have 1,000 locations. This is still less than 10 percent of their chief competitor's base.

There are four dimensions of experience in which Caribou takes direct aim at its chief competitor to win the hearts of its customers.[65] These are the Internet, square tables, customer names, and coffee selection. Free wireless Internet service is a positive draw for the company, enabling every customer who wants to stay connected during a coffee break to do so. A stop at Caribou Coffee may be more than a coffee break, too. The company plans to stay with square tables and not go to the round ones of its chief competitor. This makes it possible to shuffle a couple or more together and have a meeting of the minds at Caribou, not just a coffee break on the Internet. The average Caribou customer visits one of its locations between three and five times per week. Hence, Caribou employees are expected to learn either a customer's name or drink by the second or third visit.

Winning in very competitive industries is challenging, hard, risky work to do. Setbacks occur too, and Caribou is still not a highly profitable business. In fact, the company continues to operate at a loss. However, they are in a booming industry of coffeehouses nationally, which is cause for optimism for the long term. Initially, the company underestimated how many new products would have to be launched to move ahead in the game, so for 2007 they plan to double the number of new product rollouts. Having large, strong, strategic partners helps, too. Caribou is partnering with Atlanta-based Coke to roll out a new iced coffee drink. Thus, being number one in experience does not mean ignoring size altogether.

Chapter Summary

1. Organizational behavior is individual behavior and group dynamics in organizations.
2. Change is an opportunity when one has a positive attitude, asks questions, listens, and is committed to succeed.
3. Organizations are open systems composed of people, structure, and technology committed to a task.
4. Organizations have formal and informal elements within them.
5. Manufacturing organizations, service organizations, privately owned companies, and nonprofit organizations all contribute to our national well-being.
6. The changes and challenges facing managers are driven by international competition and customer demands.
7. Learning about organizational behavior requires a mastery of objective knowledge, specific skill development, and thoughtful application.

Key Terms

anthropology (p. 6)
challenge (p. 4)
change (p. 4)
engineering (p. 6)
formal organization (p. 9)
Hawthorne studies (p. 9)
informal organization (p. 9)
management (p. 6)
medicine (p. 6)
objective knowledge (p. 19)
opportunities (p. 4)
organizational behavior (p. 4)
people (p. 8)
psychology (p. 5)
Six Sigma (p. 17)
skill development (p. 19)
sociology (p. 6)
structure (p. 8)
task (p. 8)
technology (p. 8)

Review Questions

1. Define *organizational behavior*. What is its focus?
2. Identify the four action steps for responding positively to change.
3. What is an organization? What are its four system components? Give an example of each.
4. Briefly describe the elements of the formal and the informal organization. Give examples of each.
5. Discuss the six focus organizations used in the book.
6. Describe how competition and total quality are affecting organizational behavior. Why is managing organizational behavior in changing times challenging?

Discussion and Communication Questions

1. How do the formal aspects of your work environment affect you? What informal aspects of your work environment are important?
2. What is the biggest competitive challenge or change facing the businesses in your industry today? Will that be different in the next five years?
3. Describe the next chief executive of your company and what she or he must do to succeed.
4. Discuss two ways people learn about organizational behavior.
5. Which of the focus companies is your own company most like? Do you work for one of these focus companies? Which company would you most like to work for?
6. *(communication question)* Prepare a memo about an organizational change occurring where you work or in your college or university. Write a 100-word description of the change and, using Figure 1.1, identify how it is affecting the people, structure, task, and/or technology of the organization.
7. *(communication question)* Develop an oral presentation about the changes and challenges facing your college or university based on an interview with a faculty member or administrator. Be prepared to describe the changes and challenges. Are these good or bad changes? Why?
8. *(communication question)* Prepare a brief description of a service or manufacturing company, entrepreneurial venture, or nonprofit organization of your choice. Go to the library and read about the organization from several sources; then use these multiple sources to write your description.

Ethical Dilemma

The afternoon was as gloomy as Brian's mood. It had not been a very productive day. All Brian could think about was the decision before him. He found the current situation interesting in that he had never before struggled with decisions. In the past, he had always been able to make quick and good decisions. His gut gave him the answer and he trusted his instincts. This time he felt nothing, and he was unsure how to proceed without that guiding force.

Brian Cowell was 62 years old and the CEO of Data Solutions, a company he had run for the last 20 years. Brian had been very successful at the helm. Data Solutions had grown from a small data processing business to one of the largest employers in the area. Brian's good instincts had guided them through the challenging times of the '80s and '90s, and the company was in just the right place to meet the challenges ahead. Or was it? This was the question that plagued Brian.

Changes in technology were providing some interesting possibilities for the future. A part of Brian said that he needed to step up and lead Data Solutions into the global environment. He could do that and continue the growth he had begun so many years ago. That was a big step and would take Brian down a very challenging road. The other option was to continue on the company's current path. Not a bad one; the company had its most profitable year last year and everyone was very happy. Deep inside, Brian knew the answer: move the company forward to the next logical step, globalization. But he was tired and really wanted to spend his last years at Data Solutions reaping the benefits of his hard work, not gearing up for the biggest challenge of his career. Didn't he deserve the right to enjoy his final years at the company he built?

Questions

1. Does Brian have an obligation to lead the company to globalization?
2. What is Brian's responsibility to himself and his family?
3. Consider Brian's decision in light of consequential, rule-based, and character theories.

Experiential Exercises

1.1 What's Changing at Work?

This exercise provides an opportunity to discuss changes occurring in your workplace and university. These changes may be for the better or the worse. However, rather than evaluating whether they are good or bad changes, begin by simply identifying the changes that are occurring. Later, you can evaluate whether they are good or bad.

Step 1. The class forms into groups of approximately six members each. Each group elects a spokesperson and answers the following questions. The group should spend at least five minutes on each question. Make sure that each member of the group makes a contribution to each question. The spokesperson for each group should be ready to share the group's collective responses.

a. *What are the changes occurring in your workplace and university?* Members should focus both on internal changes, such as reorganizations, and on external changes, such as new customers or competitors. Develop a list of the changes discussed in your group.

b. *What are the forces that are driving the changes?* To answer this question, look for the causes of the changes members of the group are observing. For example, a reorganization may be caused by new business opportunities, by new technologies, or by a combination of factors.

c. *What signs of resistance to change do you see occurring?* Change is not always easy for people or organizations. Do you see signs of resistance, such as frustration, anger, increased absences, or other forms of discomfort with the changes you observe?

Step 2. Once you have answered the three questions in Step 1, your group needs to spend some time evaluating whether these changes are good or bad. Decide whether each change on the list developed in Step 1a is good or bad. In addition, answer the question "Why?" That is, why is this change good? Why is that change bad?

Step 3. Each group shares the results of its answers to the questions in Step 1 and its evaluation of the changes completed in Step 2. Cross-team questions and discussion follow.

Step 4. Your instructor may allow a few minutes at the end of the class period to comment on his or her perceptions of changes occurring within the university, or businesses with which he or she is familiar.

1.2 My Absolute Worst Job

Purpose: To become acquainted with fellow classmates.
Group size: Any number of groups of two.
Exercise schedule:

1. Write answers to the following questions:
   a. What was the worst job you ever had? Describe the following:
      (1) The type of work you did
      (2) Your boss
      (3) Your coworkers
      (4) The organization and its policies
      (5) What made the job so bad
   b. What is your dream job?
2. Find someone you do not know, and share your responses.
3. Get together with another dyad (pair), preferably new people. Partner "a" of one dyad introduces partner "b" to the other dyad; then "b" introduces "a." The same process is followed by the other dyad. The introduction should follow this format: "This is Mary Cullen. Her very worst job was putting appliqués on bibs at a clothing factory, and she disliked it for the following reason. What she would rather do is be a financial analyst for a big corporation."
4. Each group of four meets with another quartet and is introduced, as before.
5. Your instructor asks for a show of hands on the number of people whose worst jobs fit into the following categories:
   a. Factory
   b. Restaurant
   c. Manual labor
   d. Driving or delivery
   e. Professional
   f. Health care
   g. Phone sales or communication
   h. Other
6. Your instructor gathers data on worst jobs from each group and asks the groups to answer these questions:
   a. What are the common characteristics of the worst jobs in your group?
   b. How did your coworkers feel about their jobs?
   c. What happens to morale and productivity when a worker hates the job?
   d. What was the difference between your own morale and productivity in your worst job and in a job you really enjoyed?
   e. Why do organizations continue to allow unpleasant working conditions to exist?
7. Your instructor leads a group discussion on Parts (a) through (e) of Question 6.

SOURCE: D. Marcic, "My Absolute Worst Job: An Icebreaker," *Organizational Behavior: Experiences and Cases* (St. Paul, Minn.: West, 1989), 5–6.

TAKE 2

Biz Flix | 8 Mile

Jimmy "B-Rabbit" Smith, Jr., (Eminem) wants to succeed as a rapper and to prove that a white man can create moving sounds. His job at the North Detroit Stamping (NDS) plant fills his days while he pursues his music at night—and sometimes on the plant's grounds. The film's title refers to Detroit's northern city boundary, well known to local people. *8 Mile* is a gritty look at Detroit's hip-hop culture in 1995 and Jimmy's desire for acceptance by it. Eminem's original songs, "Lose Yourself" and "8 Mile," received several award nominations. "Lose Yourself" won the 2003 Academy Award for best original song.

The scene has two parts. It is an edited composite of two brief NDS plant sequences that appear in different places in the film. Part I of the scene appears early in the film in the sequence "The Franchise." Part II appears in the last twenty-five minutes of the film in the "Papa Doc Payback" sequence. Jimmy arrives late for work in the first part of the scene, after riding the city bus because his car did not start. The second part occurs after his beating by Papa Doc (Anthony Mackie) and Papa Doc's gang. The film continues to its end with Jimmy's last battle (a rapper competition).

What to Watch for and Ask Yourself:

- What is your perception of the quality of Jimmy's job and his work environment?
- What is the quality of Jimmy's relationship with Manny (Paul Bates), his foreman? Does it change? If it does, why?
- How would you react to this type of work experience?

Workplace Video | Managerial and Quality Control at Honda

When Honda announced in 1982 that it was building its first auto assembly plant in North America, many analysts felt that American labor could not produce the same quality automobiles as the Japanese. Quality had been a strategic focus of Japanese manufacturers since World War II, and automakers like Honda and Toyota were undisputed leaders of Japan's quality movement. Confident that American workers could produce award-winning Civics and Accords, Honda moved ahead with its plans and became the first Japanese company to establish manufacturing operations in the United States.

Relocating to North America was nearly inevitable for Honda's manufacturing division. Turbulent changes in the global economic environment had put a financial squeeze on the automaker, and moving overseas was the only way it could reduce transportation costs and counter unfavorable exchange rates, which had raised the price of materials in Japan.

Change proved favorable. Despite the cultural challenges involved in transplanting Japanese manufacturing methods to the United States, Honda's North American facilities have attained remarkable efficiency. Sam Kennedy, associate chief inspecting engineer at Honda, uses quality circles, statistical process control, and weekly managers' meetings to establish a culture of continuous improvement at Honda's Marysville, Ohio, plant. For

TAKE 2

Kennedy, quality management means taking a proactive approach to problem solving. "If you simply wait and react to a problem," the inspection chief remarks, "you're going to be dealing with nothing but problems."

Honda's preventative approach to quality is apparent throughout the assembly process. The paint department, for example, places white protective film over vehicle frames to prevent assembly-line workers from chipping and scratching paint while installing parts and components. Likewise, Honda's welding zone, a bustling area formerly occupied by human workers, is now filled with speedy high-precision robots that make millions of welds but few errors. According to Kennedy, Honda's high-tech welding zone is emblematic of Honda's commitment to quality: "We have improved the accuracy of our product and the consistency of the product, which is really what quality is all about."

Discussion Questions

1. What opportunities and challenges would you expect Honda to encounter as a result of establishing manufacturing facilities in the United States?
2. What are some managerial techniques that help Honda's workers achieve higher quality and efficiency in their production tasks?
3. How might changes associated with Honda's move to the United States affect the behavior of plant workers and managers?

Johnson & Johnson: Using a Credo for Business Guidance

Johnson & Johnson, founded by Robert Wood Johnson and his brothers James and Mead in 1886, has grown into the world's most comprehensive manufacturer of health care products and related services for the consumer, pharmaceutical, and medical devices and diagnostics markets. Today, Johnson & Johnson consists of more than 250 operating companies, employing approximately 121,000 employees, with more than 50,000 of those in the United States. The company has operations in 57 nations and sells products all around the world.[1] Product categories include, but are not limited to: allergy, colds, and flu; baby care; cardiology; dental care; diabetes care; first aid; medical devices and diagnostics; oncology; prescription drugs; skin and hair care; and vision care.[2] The company's sales have increased every year for since 1946, and in 2006, global sales were $53.9 billion and net earnings were $11.1 billion.[3] Moreover, Johnson & Johnson was ranked ninth on *Fortune's* 2006 "America's Most Admired Companies" list and fourth on the magazine's 2006 "Global Most Admired Companies."[4]

The worldwide success of Johnson & Johnson is widely attributed to an unwavering commitment to a business philosophy that puts customers first and stockholders last. Robert Wood Johnson II first articulated this philosophy in 1943; it was called the *Johnson & Johnson Credo*.[5] Like his father before him, Robert Wood Johnson II could be dogmatic, autocratic, and prone to micromanagement. Yet he was not inflexible; in fact, he encouraged innovation in every part of the company. There was, however, one thing about him that was inflexible—adherence to the Johnson & Johnson Credo. Even after the company went from being family owned to having public ownership and trading of its stock in the early 1960s, the Johnson & Johnson Credo has provided fundamental managerial and operational guidance to which the company has unwaveringly adhered.[6]

The key points of the Johnson & Johnson Credo address the company's four responsibilities. In descending order of emphasis, these responsibilities may be summarized as follows:

- The company's first responsibility is to meet the needs of everyone—doctors, nurses, patients, mothers, fathers, and others—who use its products. Johnson & Johnson does this by providing quality products that are reasonably priced, and by ensuring that suppliers and distributors have the opportunity to make a fair profit.
- The company's second responsibility is to its employees throughout the world, treating them fairly and with dignity, seeking to involve them, and providing them with competent and ethical management.
- The company's third responsibility is to the various communities where it operates, seeking to improve those communities and sharing in the burden of such improvements.
- The company's last responsibility is to the stockholders, seeking to make a sound profit in order to provide a fair return to the owners and to enable the company to innovate and grow so that fair returns are maintained in the future.[7]

The full credo was in a format that people could understand, and Robert Wood Johnson II demanded that people follow it. Very importantly, the company created appropriate organizational mechanisms to bring the credo to life, and to support and reinforce it. The credo "may sound a bit corny—and so may J&J's devotion to it: It's posted in every J&J facility around the world and carved in an eight-foot chunk of limestone at company headquarters in New Brunswick, N.J. But Johnson made sure everyone bought into it."[8]

The credo has served the company well during normal operating conditions and in times of crisis, such as in 1982 and 1986 when the Tylenol® acetaminophen product was adulterated with cyanide and used as a murder weapon. During the

Tylenol crises, Johnson & Johnson's "managers and employees made countless decisions that were inspired by the philosophy embedded in the credo."[9] Tylenol was immediately cleared from store shelves, and the company was very proactive and open in addressing each crisis. As a result, J&J's good reputation was maintained and the Tylenol business was reinvigorated.

The Johnson & Johnson Credo continues to guide the company's decisions and actions regarding its responsibilities to customers, employees, the community, and stockholders. The credo guides the company's operations in Africa, Asia and the Pacific Rim, Eastern and Western Europe, Latin America, the Middle East, and North America.[10] Ralph Larsen, a former chief executive officer of Johnson & Johnson, maintains that the credo provides a constant source of guidance for the company and that it is the foundation for everything the company does.[11] Although the credo has been revised and updated at different points throughout its existence, the essential responsibilities endure.[12] To help ensure the credo's continuing viability, Johnson & Johnson employees periodically participate in a survey to evaluate how the company performs its responsibilities.[13]

Discussion Questions

1. From your perspective, what role(s) should business play in the contemporary world?
2. What implications does the credo have for Johnson & Johnson's view of the role(s) it should play in the contemporary world?
3. What implications does the credo have for the attitudes and job behavior of the company's employees?
4. Would you like to work for a company like Johnson & Johnson? Why or why not?

SOURCE: This case was written by Michael K. McCuddy, The Louis S. and Mary L. Morgal Chair of Christian Business Ethics and Professor of Management, College of Business Administration, Valparaiso University.

CHAPTER 2

Challenges for Managers

LEARNING OBJECTIVES

After reading this chapter, you should be able to do the following:

1 Describe the dimensions of cultural differences in societies that affect work-related attitudes.

2 Explain the social and demographic changes that are producing diversity in organizations.

3 Describe actions managers can take to help their employees value diversity.

4 Discuss the assumptions of consequential, rule-based, and character theories of ethics.

5 Explain six issues that pose ethical dilemmas for managers.

6 Understand the alternative work arrangements produced by technological advances.

7 Explain the ways managers can help employees adjust to technological change.

THINKING AHEAD: GENENTECH, INC.

Do Business and Science Mix?

Genentech, Inc. is the world's foremost biotechnology company and a leader in nurturing a culture of creativity. This combination has put the company in the top 25 most innovative companies along with Intel Corp. and GE. According to Chairman and Chief Executive Arthur Levinson, you can make it really complicated or really simple. Genentech does it simply; it hires innovative people, listens to them, and then does what they suggest. The company uses a unique approach to attracting and cultivating the best scientists to attain success in the world of business.[1]

First and foremost, Genentech is committed to doing great science. If a drug cannot be first in class or best in class, they do not pursue it. They do not work to achieve incremental advances or extend patents unless it is going to really matter to patients. Their most talented scientists are thus encouraged to do important basic and translational research.

Second, the company decided in the early 1990s that they would be committed to oncology, which at the time was new for them. By 2007 they were the leading producer of anticancer drugs in the United States. They did take a lot of risks, many of which paid off. That is a central tenet in business; knowing the right risks to take and then working extremely hard and wisely to make the risk pay off. The company has now broadened into immunology, where the role of management is to set broad direction, and then hire the best scientists, and to tell them: "Do your stuff." But there are always trade-offs in the short term between the cancer patient who needs treatment now and the immunology patient who needs long-term defense.

Third, Genentech places a huge emphasis on making the company a great place to work. In the late 1990s, it did not appear in the many lists of the best places to work. This led the company to begin employee surveys that asked some key questions: What do you like about the company? More importantly, what don't you like? What bothers you? By listening to employees and then taking action, Genentech management led the company to *Fortune*'s Top 20 list four years in a row. The firm was number one in 2006 and number two in 2007, just behind Google Inc. Genentech operates in the new industrial technology arena of biotechnology and has successfully mixed business with science. The company cannot do everything for everyone, so how do they address the ethical trade-offs?

MANAGEMENT CHALLENGES IN A NEW TIME

Most U.S. executives continue to believe that U.S. firms are encountering unprecedented global competition.[2] Globalization is being driven on the one hand by the spread of economic logics centered on freeing, opening, deregulating, and privatizing economies to make them more attractive for investment and, on the other hand, by the digitization of technologies that is revolutionizing communication.[3] The challenges for managers in this context are manifest in both opportunities and threats, as briefly touched upon in Chapter 1. The long, robust economic expansion in the United States during the 1990s led to a bubble that burst and several years of economic difficulty. Managers are challenged to lead people in the good times and the bad times, as Anne Mulcahy did in addressing Xerox's financial difficulties, because business cycles ultimately produce both. Over time, managers face both opportunities and threats.

What major challenges must managers overcome in order to remain competitive? Chief executive officers of U.S. corporations cite four issues that are paramount: (1) globalizing the firm's operations to compete in the global village; (2) leading a diverse workforce; (3) encouraging positive ethics, character, and personal integrity; and (4) advancing and implementing technological innovation in the workplace.[4,5]

Successful organizations and managers respond to these four challenges as opportunities rather than as threats. Our six focus companies—Caribou Coffee, Genentech, American Express, Toyota Motor Corporation, Timberland, and Google—and their managers have wrestled with one or more of these four challenges as they pursue success and achievement. We see in the Looking Back feature that some of the trade-offs that companies like Genentech face are not simple ethical dilemmas with simple solutions. While Caribou Coffee, as we detailed in Chapter 1, wanted to be number one in experience, Genentech's industry offers a different challenge. In this chapter, we focus on these four challenges that, when well managed, lead to success and healthy organizational outcomes.

Globalization has led to the emergence of the global village in the world economy. The Internet, along with rapid political and social changes, has broken down old national barriers to competition. What has emerged is a world characterized by an ongoing process of integration and interconnection of states, markets, technologies, and firms. This world as a global macroeconomic village is a boundaryless market in which all firms, large and small, must compete.[6]

Managing a diverse workforce is something organizations like Alcon Laboratories and Coors Brewing Company do extremely well. Both companies reap success from their efforts. The workforce of today is more diverse than ever before. Managers are challenged to bring together employees of different backgrounds in work teams. This requires going beyond the surface to deep-level diversity.[7]

Good character, ethical behavior, and *personal integrity* are hallmarks of managers in organizations like Johnson & Johnson. The company's credo guides employee behavior and has helped employees do the right thing in tough situations. Ethical behavior in business has been at the forefront of public consciousness for some time now. Insider trading scandals, influence peddling, and contract frauds are in the news daily. It need not be that way. Many executives lead with a spirit of personal integrity.[8]

Technological innovation is one of the keys to strategic competitiveness. Imagine yourself as a small business owner of a package delivery firm. You'll be competing with FedEx, which owns the most technologically advanced package tracking and delivery system in the world. Would you be able to compete? Technological change can be complex and risky. It may also create ethical dilemmas, as in the case of Genentech's biotechnology advances.

Organizations and managers who see opportunity in these four challenges will remain competitive, rather than just survive, in today's turbulent environment. Throughout the book, you'll see how organizational behavior can contribute to successfully managing the challenges.

THE GLOBAL VILLAGE

Only a few years ago, business conducted across national borders was referred to as "international" activity. The word *international* carries with it a connotation that the individual's or the organization's nationality is held strongly in consciousness.[9] *Globalization,* in contrast, implies that the world is free from national boundaries and that it is really a borderless world.[10] U.S. workers are now competing with workers in other countries. Foreign-based organizations are locating subsidiaries in the United States, such as the U.S. manufacturing locations of Honda, Toyota, Mazda, and Mercedes. The reverse is true as well, as we see in The Real World 2.1, which shows how Volkswagen's German workers had to come to grips with globalization.

Similarly, what were once referred to as multinational organizations (those doing business in several countries) are now called transnational companies. In *transnational organizations,* the global viewpoint supersedes national issues.[11] Transnational organizations operate over large global distances and are multicultural in terms of the people they employ. 3M, Dow Chemical, Coca-Cola, and other transnational organizations operate worldwide with diverse employee populations.

Changes in the Global Marketplace

Social and political upheavals have led organizations to change the way they conduct business and to encourage their members to think globally. Toyota is one Japanese company thinking big, thinking globally, and thinking differently by learning to speak to the 60-million-strong Generation Y, or millennials.[12] The collapse of Eastern Europe was followed quickly by the demise of the Berlin Wall. East and West

transnational organization
An organization in which the global viewpoint supersedes national issues.

Globalization Comes to Wolfsburg, Germany

Wolfsburg, Germany, is the home of Volkswagen (VW), Europe's largest automaker, and has a population of 125,000. Actually, VW has prospered greatly from globalization throughout its history, which began in 1938 when the town was formed with the mission to manufacture an affordable "people's car." After World War II, the company churned out millions of Beetles and exported them to every continent except Antarctica. The postwar years were a globalization boom for the company. By the early 2000s, it was saddled with some of the highest labor costs in the world, with factory employees generally working four-day weeks and earning as much as $50 per hour. The company was forced to slash 20,000 jobs and faced the prospect of being taken over by an international hedge fund or merge with an Asian competitor. Waves of panic swept through Wolfsburg. By 2007, however, the mood was good according to Hartmut Meine, a district manager for IG Metal, the metalworkers' union that represents 97 percent of VW's German employees. Negotiations have led to a pact that includes no more job cuts before 2011 in exchange for wage freezes and longer workweeks. The company is ramping up production on its all-time best-selling car, the Golf, and expecting a pretax profit of more than $6 billion for 2007. Thus, VW is doing well in the global automotive shakeout that has devastated the U.S. auto industry.

SOURCE: C. Whitlock, "VW's Home Town Finds Ways to Cope with Globalization," *The Washington Post* (June 5, 2007): A10.

Germany were united into a single country. In the Soviet Union, perestroika led to liberation and brought about many opportunities for U.S. businesses, as witnessed by the press releases showing extremely long waiting lines at Moscow's first McDonald's restaurant.

guanxi
The Chinese practice of building networks for social exchange.

Business ventures in China have become increasingly attractive to U.S. companies. Coca-Cola has led the way. One challenge U.S. managers have faced is understanding the Chinese way of doing business. Chinese managers' business practices have been shaped by the Communist Party, socialism, feudalistic values, and *guanxi* (building networks for social exchange). Once *guanxi* is established, individuals can ask favors of each other with the expectation that the favor will be returned. For example, it is common in China to use *guanxi* to conduct business or to obtain jobs. *Guanxi* is sometimes a sensitive word, because Communist Party policies oppose the use of such practices to gain influence. In China, the family is regarded as being responsible for a worker's productivity, and in turn, the company is responsible for the worker's family. Because of socialism, Chinese managers have very little experience with rewards and punishments and are reluctant to use them in the workplace. The concept of *guanxi* is not unique to China. There are similar concepts in many other countries, including Russia and Haiti. It is a broad term that can mean anything from strongly loyal relationships to ceremonial gift-giving, sometimes seen as bribery. *Guanxi* is more common in societies with underdeveloped legal support for private businesses.[13]

One challenge that U.S. managers pursuing business ventures in China face is understanding the Chinese way of doing business.

To work with Chinese managers, Americans can learn to build their own *guanxi;* understand the Chinese chain of command; and negotiate slow, general agreements in order to interact effectively. Using the foreign government as the local franchisee may be effective in China. For example, KFC Corporation's operation in China is a joint venture between KFC (60 percent) and two Chinese government bodies (40 percent).[14]

In 1993, the European Union integrated fifteen nations into a single market by removing trade barriers. At that time, the member nations of the European Union were Belgium, Denmark, France, Germany, Greece, Ireland, Italy, Luxembourg, the Netherlands, Portugal, Spain, Austria, Finland, Sweden, and the United Kingdom. As of 2004, Estonia, Hungary, Latvia, Lithuania, Malta, Poland, Slovakia, and Slovenia were also members. The integration of Europe provides many opportunities for U.S. organizations, including 350 million potential customers. Companies like Ford Motor Company and IBM, which entered the market early with wholly owned subsidiaries, will have a head start on these opportunities.[15] Competition within the European Union will increase, however, as will competition from Japan and the former Soviet nations.

The United States, Canada, and Mexico have dramatically reduced trade barriers in accordance with the North American Free Trade Agreement (NAFTA), which took effect in 1994. Organizations have found promising new markets for their products, and many companies have located plants in Mexico to take advantage of low labor costs. DaimlerChrysler, for example, has a massive assembly plant in Saltillo. Prior to NAFTA, Mexico placed heavy tariffs on U.S. exports. The agreement immediately eliminated many of these tariffs and provided that the remaining tariffs be phased out over time.

All of these changes have brought about the need to think globally. Managers can benefit from global thinking by taking a long-term view. Entry into global markets requires long-term strategies.

Understanding Cultural Differences

1 Describe the dimensions of cultural differences in societies that affect work-related attitudes.

One of the keys for any company competing in the global marketplace is to understand diverse cultures. Whether managing culturally diverse individuals within a single location or managing individuals at remote locations around the globe, an appreciation of the differences among cultures is crucial. Edgar Schein suggests that to understand an organization's culture, or more broadly any culture, it is important to dig below the surface of visible artifacts and uncover the basic underlying assumptions at the core of the culture.[16] His definition of organizational culture is the pattern of basic assumptions that a given group has invented, discovered, or developed in learning to cope with its problems of external adaptation and internal integration, and that have worked well enough to be considered valid. These basic assumptions are then taught to new members as the correct way to perceive, think, and feel in relation to those problems. We develop Schein's culture model of basic assumptions, values, visible artifacts, and creations more fully in Chapter 16.

Microcultural differences (i.e., differences within cultures) can play an important role in understanding the global work environment.[17] Knowing cultural differences in symbols is extremely important. Computer icons may not translate well in other cultures. The thumbs-up sign, for example, means approval in the United States. In Australia, however, it is an obscene gesture. And manila file folders, like the icons used in Windows applications, aren't used in many European countries and therefore aren't recognized.[18]

Do cultural differences translate into differences in work-related attitudes? The pioneering Dutch researcher Geert Hofstede focused on this question.[19] He and his colleagues surveyed 160,000 managers and employees of IBM who were working in 60 different countries.[20] In this way, the researchers were able to study individuals from the same company in the same jobs, but working in different countries. Hofstede's work is important because his studies showed that national culture explains more differences in work-related attitudes than do age, gender, profession, or position within the organization. Thus, cultural differences do affect individuals' work-related attitudes. Hofstede found five dimensions of cultural differences that

FIGURE 2.1 Hofstede's Dimensions of Cultural Differences

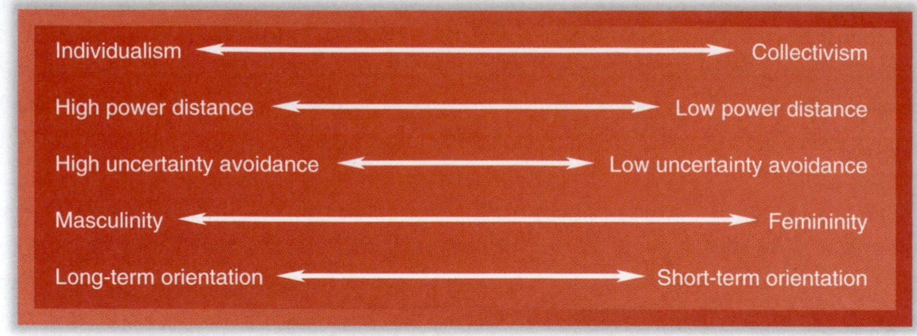

SOURCE: Reprinted with permission of Academy of Management, PO Box 3020, Briar Cliff, NY 10510-8020. *Cultural Constraints in Management Theories* (Figure). G. Hofstede, *Academy of Management Executive 7* (1993). Reproduced by permission of the publisher via Copyright Clearance Center, Inc.

formed the basis for work-related attitudes. These dimensions are shown in Figure 2.1 and are described next.

Individualism versus Collectivism In cultures where *individualism* predominates, people belong to loose social frameworks, but their primary concern is for themselves and their families. People are responsible for taking care of their own interests. They believe that individuals should make decisions. Cultures characterized by *collectivism* are tightly knit social frameworks in which individual members depend strongly on extended families or clans. Group decisions are valued and accepted.

The North American culture is individualistic in orientation. It is a "can-do" culture that values individual freedom and responsibility. In contrast, collectivist cultures emphasize group welfare and harmony. Israeli kibbutzim and Japanese culture are examples of societies in which group loyalty and unity are paramount. Organization charts show these orientations. In Canada and the United States, which are individualistic cultures, organization charts show individual positions. In Malaysia, which is a collectivist culture, organization charts show only sections or departments.

This dimension of cultural differences has other workplace implications. Individualistic managers, as found in Great Britain and the Netherlands, emphasize and encourage individual achievement. In contrast, collectivistic managers, such as in Japan and Colombia, seek to fit harmoniously within the group. They also encourage these behaviors among their employees. Further, there are cultural differences within regions of the world. Arabs are more collectivist than Americans. Within the Arab culture, however, Egyptians are more individualistic than Arabs from the Gulf States (Saudi Arabia, Oman, Bahrain, Kuwait, Qatar, United Arab Emirates). This may be due to the fact that Egyptian businesspeople tend to have longer and more intensive exposures to Western culture.[21]

individualism
A cultural orientation in which people belong to loose social frameworks, and their primary concern is for themselves and their families.

collectivism
A cultural orientation in which individuals belong to tightly knit social frameworks, and they depend strongly on large extended families or clans.

power distance
The degree to which a culture accepts unequal distribution of power.

Power Distance The second dimension of cultural differences examines the acceptance of unequal distribution of power. In countries with a high *power distance,* bosses are afforded more power simply because they are the bosses. Titles are used, formality is the rule, and authority is seldom bypassed. Power holders are entitled to their privileges, and managers and employees see one another as fundamentally

different kinds of people. India is a country with a high power distance, as are Venezuela and Mexico.

In countries with a low power distance, people believe that inequality in society should be minimized. People at various power levels are less threatened by, and more willing to trust, one another. Managers and employees see one another as similar. Managers are given power only if they have expertise. Employees frequently bypass the boss in order to get work done in countries with a low power distance, such as Denmark and Australia.

Uncertainty Avoidance Some cultures are quite comfortable with ambiguity and uncertainty, whereas others do not tolerate these conditions well. Cultures with high *uncertainty avoidance* are concerned with security and tend to avoid conflict. People have a need for consensus. The inherent uncertainty in life is a threat against which people in such cultures constantly struggle.

Cultures with low uncertainty avoidance are more tolerant of ambiguity. People are more willing to take risks and are more tolerant of individual differences. Conflict is seen as constructive, and people accept dissenting viewpoints. Norway and Australia are characterized by low uncertainty avoidance, and this trait is seen in the value placed on job mobility. Japan and Italy are characterized by high uncertainty avoidance, so career stability is emphasized.

Masculinity versus Femininity In cultures that are characterized by *masculinity,* assertiveness and materialism are valued. Men are expected to be assertive, tough, and decisive, and women to be nurturing, modest, and tender.[22] Money and possessions are important, and performance is what counts. Achievement is admired. Cultures that are characterized by *femininity* emphasize relationships and concern for others. Men and women are expected to assume both assertive and nurturing roles. Quality of life is important, and people and the environment are emphasized.

Masculine societies, such as in Austria and Venezuela, define gender roles strictly. Feminine societies, in contrast, tend to blur gender roles. Women may be the providers, and men may stay home with the children. The Scandinavian countries of Norway, Sweden, and Denmark exemplify the feminine orientation.

Time Orientation Cultures also differ in *time orientation;* that is, whether the culture's values are oriented toward the future (long-term orientation) or toward the past and present (short-term orientation).[23] In China, a culture with a long-term orientation, values such as thrift and persistence, which focus on the future, are emphasized. In Russia, the orientation is short-term. Values such as respect for tradition (past) and meeting social obligations (present) are emphasized.

U.S. Culture The position of the United States on these five dimensions is interesting. Hofstede found the United States to be the most individualistic country of any studied. On the power distance dimension, it ranked among the countries with weak power distance. Its rank on uncertainty avoidance indicated a tolerance of uncertainty. The United States also ranked as a masculine culture with a short-term orientation. These values have shaped U.S. management theory, so Hofstede's work casts doubt on the universal applicability of U.S. management theories. Because cultures differ so widely on these dimensions, management practices should be adjusted to account for cultural differences. Managers in transnational organizations must learn as much as they can about other cultures in order to lead their culturally diverse organizations effectively.

uncertainty avoidance
The degree to which a culture tolerates ambiguity and uncertainty.

masculinity
The cultural orientation in which assertiveness and materialism are valued.

femininity
The cultural orientation in which relationships and concern for others are valued.

time orientation
Whether a culture's values are oriented toward the future (long-term orientation) or toward the past and present (short-term orientation).

Planning for a Global Career

Think of a country you would like to work in, do business in, or visit. Find out about its culture, using Hofstede's dimensions as guidelines. You can use a variety of sources to accomplish this, particularly your school library, government offices, faculty members, or others who have global experience. You will want to answer the following questions:

1. Is the culture individualistic or collectivist?
2. Is the power distance high or low?
3. Is uncertainty avoidance high or low?
4. Is the country masculine or feminine in its orientation?
5. Is the time orientation short-term or long-term?
6. How did you arrive at your answers to the first five questions?
7. How will these characteristics affect business practices in the country you chose to investigate?

Careers in management have taken on a global dimension. Working in transnational organizations may well give managers the opportunity to work in other countries. *Expatriate managers,* those who work outside their home country, benefit from having as much knowledge as possible about cultural differences. Because managers are increasingly exposed to global work experiences, it is never too early to begin planning for this aspect of your career. You 2.1 asks you to begin gathering information about a country in which you would like to work, including information on its culture.

International executives are executives whose jobs have international scope, whether in an expatriate assignment or in a job dealing with international issues. What kind of competencies should an individual develop in order to prepare for an international career? There seem to be several attributes, all of them centering on core competencies and the ability to learn from experience. Some of the key competencies are integrity, insightfulness, risk taking, courage to take a stand, and ability to bring out the best in people. Learning-oriented attributes of international executives include cultural adventurousness, flexibility, openness to criticism, desire to seek learning opportunities, and sensitivity to cultural differences.[24] Further, strong human capital has a generally positive effect on internationalization.[25]

Understanding cultural differences becomes especially important for companies that are considering opening foreign offices, because workplace customs can vary widely from one country to another. Carefully searching out this information in advance can help companies successfully manage foreign operations. Consulate offices and companies operating within the foreign country are excellent sources of information about national customs and legal requirements. Table 2.1 presents a business guide to cultural differences in three countries: Japan, Mexico, and Saudi Arabia.

Another reality that can affect global business practices is the cost of layoffs in other countries. The practice of downsizing is not unique to the United States. Dismissing a forty-five-year-old middle manager with twenty years of service and a $50,000 annual salary can vary in cost from a low of $13,000 in Ireland to a high of $130,000 in Italy.[26] The cost of laying off this manager in the United States would be approximately $19,000. The wide variability in costs stems from the various legal protections that certain countries give workers. In Italy, laid-off employees must receive a "notice period" payment (one year's pay if they have nine years or

expatriate manager

A manager who works in a country other than his or her home country.

TABLE 2.1 Business Guide to Cultural Differences

Country	Appointments	Dress	Gifts	Negotiations
Japan	Punctuality is necessary when doing business here. It is considered rude to be late.	Conservative for men and women in large to medium companies, though pastel shirts are common. May be expected to remove shoes in temples and homes, as well as in some *ryokan* (inn) style restaurants. In that case, slip-on shoes should be worn.	Important part of Japanese business protocol. Gifts are typically exchanged among colleagues on July 15 and January 1 to commemorate midyear and the year's end, respectively.	Business cards (*meishi*) are an important part of doing business in Japan and key for establishing credentials. One side of your card should be in English and the reverse in Japanese. It is an asset to include information such as membership in professional associations.
Mexico	Punctuality is not always as much of a priority in Mexican business culture. Nonetheless, Mexicans are accustomed to North Americans arriving on time, and most Mexicans in business, if not government, will try to return the favor.	Dark, conservative suits and ties are the norm for most men. Standard office attire for women includes dresses, skirted suits, or skirts and blouses. Femininity is strongly encouraged in women's dress. Women business travelers will want to bring hosiery and high heels.	Not usually a requirement in business dealings though presenting a small gift will generally be appreciated as a gesture of goodwill. If giving a gift, be aware that inquiring about what the receiver would like to receive can be offensive.	Mexicans avoid directly saying "no." A "no" is often disguised in responses such as "maybe" or "We'll see." You should also use this indirect approach in your dealings. Otherwise, your Mexican counterparts may perceive you as being rude and pushy.
Saudi Arabia	Customary to make appointments for times of day rather than precise hours. The importance Saudis attach to courtesy and hospitality can cause delays that prevent keeping to a strict schedule.	The only absolute requirement of dress code in Saudi Arabia is modesty. For men, this means covering everything from navel to knee. Females are required to cover everything except the face, hands, and feet in public; they can wear literally anything they want providing they cover it with an *abaya* (standard black cloak) and headscarf when they go out.	Should only be given to the most intimate of friends. For a Saudi to receive a present from a lesser acquaintance is so embarrassing that it is considered offensive.	Business cards are common but not essential. If used, the common practice is to have both English and Arabic printed, one on each side so that neither language is perceived as less important by being on the reverse of the same card.

SOURCE: Adapted from information obtained from business culture guides accessed online at http://www.executiveplanet.com.

more of service) plus a severance payment (based on pay and years of service). U.S. companies operating overseas often adopt the European tradition of training and retraining workers to avoid overstaffing and potential layoffs. An appreciation of the customs and rules for doing business in another country is essential if a company wants to go global.

Developing Cross-Cultural Sensitivity

As organizations compete in the global marketplace, employees must learn to deal with individuals from diverse cultural backgrounds. Stereotypes may pervade employees' perceptions of other cultures. In addition, employees may be unaware of others' perceptions of the employees' national culture. A potentially valuable exercise is to ask members of various cultures to describe one another's cultures. This provides a lesson on the misinterpretation of culture.

Intel wants interns and employees to understand the company's culture, but more importantly, it wants to understand the employees' cultures. In an effort to increase diversity, Intel's proportion of ethnic minorities in managerial positions increased from 13 percent in 1993 to 20 percent in 2003, and is still climbing.[27] Many individuals feel their cultural heritage is important and may walk into uncomfortable situations at work. To prevent this, Intel's new workers are paired carefully with mentors, and mentors and protégés learn about each others' cultures.

Cultural sensitivity training is a popular method for helping employees recognize and appreciate cultural differences. Another way of developing sensitivity is to use cross-cultural task forces or teams. The Milwaukee-based GE Medical Systems Group (GEMS) has 19,000 employees working worldwide. GEMS has developed a vehicle for bringing managers from each of its three regions (the Americas, Europe, and Asia) together to work on a variety of business projects. Under the Global Leadership Program, several work groups made up of managers from various regions of the world are formed. The teams work on important projects, such as worldwide employee integration to increase the employees' sense of belonging throughout the GEMS international organization.[28]

The globalization of business affects all parts of the organization, and human resource management is affected in particular. Companies have employees around the world, and human resource managers face the daunting task of effectively supporting a culturally diverse workforce. Human resource managers must adopt a global view of all functions, including human resource planning, recruitment and selection, compensation, and training and development. They must have a working knowledge of the legal systems in various countries, as well as of global economics, culture, and customs. Human resource managers must not only prepare U.S. workers to live outside their native country but also help foreign employees interact with U.S. culture. Global human resource management is a complex endeavor, but it is critical to the success of organizations in the global marketplace.

Globalization is one challenge managers must meet in order to remain competitive in the changing world. Related to globalization is the challenge of managing an increasingly diverse workforce. Cultural differences contribute a great deal to the diversity of the workforce, but there are other forms of diversity as well.

THE DIVERSE WORKFORCE

Workforce diversity is an important issue for organizations. The United States, as a melting pot nation, has always had a mix of individuals in its workforce. We once sought to be all alike, as in the melting pot, but we now recognize and appreciate individual differences. *Diversity* encompasses all forms of differences among individuals, including culture, gender, age, ability, religion, personality, social status, and sexual orientation. Catalyst's Sheila Wellington believed 2003 was the year in which business made the case for diversity and inclusion, and then matched it with action.

Attention to diversity has increased in recent years. This is largely because of the changing demographics of the working population. Managers feel that dealing with diversity successfully is a paramount concern for two reasons. First, managers need to know how to motivate diverse work groups. Second, managers need to know how to communicate effectively with employees who have different values and language skills.

Several demographic trends are affecting organizations. By the year 2020, the workforce will be more culturally diverse, more female, and older than ever. In addition, legislation and new technologies have brought more workers with disabilities into the workforce. Hence, learning to work together is an increasingly important skill, just as it is important to work with an open mind.[29] Alcon Laboratories, the Swiss-owned and Fort Worth–based international company whose mission is to improve and preserve eyesight and hearing, creates an opportunity for learning to work together through diversity training.[30] Valuing diversity in organizations is an important issue.[31]

Cultural Diversity

2 Explain the social and demographic changes that are producing diversity in organizations.

Cultural diversity in the workplace is growing because of the globalization of business, as we discussed earlier. People of diverse national origins—Koreans, Bolivians, Pakistanis, Vietnamese, Swedes, Australians, and others—find themselves cooperating in teams to perform the work of the organization. In addition, changing demographics within the United States significantly affect the cultural diversity in organizations. By 2020, minorities will constitute more than one-half of the new entrants to the U.S. workforce. The participation rates of African Americans and Hispanic Americans in the labor force increased dramatically in recent years. By 2020, white non-Hispanics will constitute 68 percent of the labor force (down from 83 percent in 2002); 14 percent of the workforce will be Hispanic (up from 12 percent); African Americans' share will remain at 11 percent; and 5 percent will be Asian.[32]

These trends have important implications for organizations. African Americans and Hispanic Americans are overrepresented in declining occupations, thus limiting their opportunities. Further, both groups tend to live in a small number of large cities that are facing severe economic difficulties and high crime rates. Because of these factors, minority workers are likely to be at a disadvantage within organizations. It does not have to be this way. For example, by monitoring its human resource systems, Coco-Cola has made substantial progress on diversity.[33]

The jobs available in the future will require more skill than has been the case in the past. Often, minority workers have not had opportunities to develop leading-edge skills. Minority skill deficits are large, and the proportions of African Americans and Hispanic Americans who are qualified for higher-level jobs are often much lower than the proportions of qualified whites and Asian Americans.[34] Minority workers are less likely to be prepared because they are less likely to have had satisfactory schooling and on-the-job training. Educational systems within the workplace are needed to supply minority workers the skills necessary for success. Companies such as Motorola are already recognizing and meeting this need by focusing on basic skills training.

The globalization of business and changing demographic trends present organizations with a tremendously culturally diverse workforce. This represents both a

diversity
All forms of individual differences, including culture, gender, age, ability, religion, personality, social status, and sexual orientation.

challenge and a risk. The challenge is to harness the wealth of differences that cultural diversity provides. The risk is that prejudices and stereotypes may prevent managers and employees from developing synergies that can benefit the organization.

Gender Diversity

The feminization of the workforce has increased substantially. The number of women in the labor force increased from 31.5 million in 1970 to 64 million in 2003. This increase accounts for almost 60 percent of the overall expansion of the entire labor force in the United States for this time period. In 2004, women made up over 60 percent of the labor force, and it is predicted that by the year 2010, 70 percent of new entrants into the workforce will be women and/or people of color. Women are better prepared to contribute in organizations than ever before. Women now earn 32 percent of all doctorates, 52 percent of master's degrees, and 50 percent of all undergraduate degrees. Thus, women are better educated, and more are electing to work. In 2004, almost 58 percent of U.S. women were employed.[35] However, women comprised only 14.7 percent of corporate board members in 2005.[36]

Women's participation in the workforce is increasing, but their share of the rewards of participation is not increasing commensurately. Women hold only 16.4 percent of corporate officer positions in the *Fortune* 500 companies.[37] In 2005, only eight *Fortune* 500 companies had women CEOs.[38] Xerox CEO Anne Mulcahy is a very positive example yet still the exception, not the rule. Median weekly earnings for women persist at a level of 81 percent of their male counterparts' earnings.[39] Furthermore, because benefits are tied to compensation, women also receive lower levels of benefits.

In addition to lower earnings, women face other obstacles at work. The *glass ceiling* is an intangible barrier that keeps women (and minorities) from rising above a certain level in organizations. In the United States, it is rare to find women in positions above middle management in corporations.[40] The ultimate glass ceiling may well be the corporate board room and the professional partnership. One study found no substantive increase in female corporate board members between 1996 and 2002.[41] While women account for 40 percent of the legal professionals, they are not 40 percent of the partners.

There is reason to believe that, on a global basis, the leadership picture for women is improving and will continue to improve. For example, the number of female political leaders around the world increased dramatically in recent decades. In the 1970s, there were only five such leaders. In the 1990s, twenty-one female leaders came into power. Countries such as Ireland, Sri Lanka, Iceland, and Norway all had female political leaders in the 1990s. Women around the world are leading major global companies, albeit not in the United States. These global female business leaders do not come predominantly from the West. In addition, a large number of women have founded entrepreneurial businesses. Women now own nearly 10.4 million of all American businesses, and these women-owned businesses employ more than 12.8 million people and generate $1.9 trillion in sales.[42]

Removing the glass ceiling and other obstacles to women's success represents a major challenge to organizations. Policies that promote equity in pay and benefits, encourage benefit programs of special interest to women, and provide equal starting salaries for jobs of equal value are needed in organizations. Corporations that shatter the glass ceiling have several practices in common. Upper managers clearly demonstrate support for the advancement of women, often with a statement of commitment issued by the CEO. Leaders incorporate practices into their diversity management programs to ensure that women perceive the organization as attractive.[43] Women are represented on standing committees that address strategic

glass ceiling
An intangible barrier that keeps women and minorities from rising above a certain level in organizations.

business issues of importance to the company. Women are targeted for participation in executive education programs, and systems are in place for identifying women with high potential for advancement.[44] Three of the best companies in terms of their advancement and development of women are Motorola, Deloitte & Touche, and the Bank of Montreal.[45]

Although women in our society have adopted the provider role, men have not been as quick to share domestic responsibilities. Managing the home and arranging for child care are still seen as the woman's domain. In addition, working women often find themselves having to care for their elderly parents. Because of their multiple roles, women are more likely than men to experience conflicts between work and home. Organizations can offer incentives such as flexible work schedules, child care, elder care, and work site health promotion programs to assist working women in managing the stress of their lives.[46]

More women in the workforce means that organizations must help them achieve their potential. To do less would be to underutilize the talents of half of the U.S. workforce.

The glass ceiling is not the only gender barrier in organizations. Males may suffer from discrimination when they are employed in traditionally female jobs such as nursing, elementary school teaching, and social work. Males may be overlooked as candidates for managerial positions in traditionally female occupations.[47]

Age Diversity

The graying of the U.S. workforce is another source of diversity in organizations. Aging baby boomers (those individuals born from 1946 through 1964) contributed to the rise of the median age in the United States to thirty-six in the year 2000—six years older than at any earlier time in history. This also means that the number of middle-aged Americans is rising dramatically. In the workforce, the number of younger workers is declining, as is the number of older workers (over age sixty-five). The net result will be a gain in workers aged thirty-five to fifty-four. By 2030, there will be 70 million older persons, more than twice their number in 1996. People over age sixty-five will comprise 13 percent of the population in 2010, and 20 percent of the population by 2030.[48]

This change in worker profile has profound implications for organizations. The job crunch among middle-aged workers will become more intense as companies seek flatter organizations and the elimination of middle-management jobs. Older workers are often higher paid, and companies that employ large numbers of aging baby boomers may find these pay scales a handicap to competitiveness.[49] However, a more experienced, stable, reliable, and healthy workforce can pay dividends to companies. The baby boomers are well trained and educated, and their knowledge can be a definite asset to organizations.

Another effect of the aging workforce is greater intergenerational contact in the workplace.[50] As organizations grow flatter, workers who were traditionally segregated by old corporate hierarchies (with older workers at the top and younger workers at the bottom) are working together. Four generations are cooperating: the silent generation (people born from 1930 through 1945), a small group that includes most organizations' top managers; the baby boomers, whose substantial numbers give them a strong influence; the baby bust generation, popularly known as Generation X (those born from 1965 through 1976); and the subsequent generation, tentatively called Generation Y, millennials, or the baby boomlet.[51] The millennials bring new challenges to the workplace because of their access to technology since a young age and a perpetual connection to parents.[52] While there is diversity among these various generations, there is diversity within each as well.

The differences in attitudes and values among these four generations can be substantial, and managers face the challenge of integrating these individuals into a cohesive group. Currently, as already noted, most positions of leadership are held by members of the silent generation. Baby boomers regard the silent generation as complacent and as having done little to reduce social inequities. Baby boomers strive for moral rights in the workplace and take a more activist position regarding employee rights. The baby busters, newer to the workplace, are impatient, want short-term gratification, and believe that family should come before work. They scorn the achievement orientation and materialism of the baby boomers. The millennials generate much controversy in both the definition of who they are and what constitute their distinguishing characteristics. Managing such diverse, conflicting perspectives is a challenge that must be addressed.

One company that is succeeding in accommodating the baby busters is Patagonia, a manufacturer of products for outdoor enthusiasts. Although the company does not actively recruit twenty-year-olds, approximately 20 percent of Patagonia's workers are in this age group because they are attracted to its products. To retain baby busters, the company offers several options, one of which is flextime. Employees can arrive at work as early as 6 a.m., and work as late as 6 p.m., as long as they work the core hours between 9 a.m. and 3 p.m. Workers also have the option of working at the office for five hours a day and at home for three hours.

Personal leaves of absence are also offered, generally unpaid, for as much as four months per year. This allows employees to take an extended summer break and prevents job burnout. Patagonia has taken into consideration the baby busters' desire for more time for personal concerns and has incorporated that desire into the company.[53]

Younger workers may have false impressions of older workers, viewing them as resistant to change, unable to learn new work methods, less physically capable, and less creative than younger employees. Research indicates, however, that older employees are more satisfied with their jobs, are more committed to the organization, and possess more internal work motivation than their younger cohorts.[54] Research also shows that direct experience with older workers reduces younger workers' negative beliefs.[55] Motivating aging workers and helping them maintain high levels of contribution to the organization is a key task for managers.

Ability Diversity

The workforce is full of individuals with different abilities, presenting another form of diversity. Individuals with disabilities are an underutilized human resource. An estimated 50 million individuals with disabilities live in the United States, and their unemployment rate is estimated to exceed 50 percent.[56] Nevertheless, the representation of individuals with disabilities in the workforce has increased because of the Americans with Disabilities Act, which went into effect in the summer of 1992. Under this law, employers are required to make reasonable accommodations to permit workers with disabilities to perform jobs. The act defines a person with a disability as "anyone possessing a physical or mental impairment that substantially limits one or more major life activities."[57] The law protects individuals with temporary, as well as permanent, disabilities. Its protection encompasses a broad range of illnesses that produce disabilities. Among these are acquired immune deficiency syndrome (AIDS), cancer, hypertension, anxiety disorders, dyslexia, blindness, and cerebral palsy, to name only a few. The Real World 2.2 examines an ability/disability debate in the case of a successful amputee sprinter.

Some companies recognized the value of employing workers with disabilities long before the legislation. Pizza Hut employs 3,000 workers with disabilities and

An Equalizer or an Edge?

Oscar Pistorius of South Africa is facing resistance from the track and field's world governing body to his desire to be the first amputee runner to compete in the Olympics. He wants to compete in the 2008 Beijing Games. Pistorius calls himself the fastest man on no legs; he sprints on a pair of j-shaped blades made of carbon fiber and known as Cheetahs. Born with a birth defect, he had both legs amputated below the knee when he was 11 months old. During 2007, Pistorius delivered startling record performances for disabled athletes at 100 meters (10.91 seconds), 200 meters (21.58 seconds), and 400 meters (46.34 seconds). He did win second place in the 2007 South African national championships against able-bodied runners with a 46.56 second finish in the 400. Do his prosthetic legs simply level the playing field for him by compensating for his disability, or do they give him an unfair edge via what some call techno-doping? Track and field's world governing body prohibited the use of technological aids like springs and wheels starting in 2007. Since 2004, transgender athletes have been allowed to compete in the Olympics. One scientist argues that Pistorius has no advantage, only that he competes at a disadvantage, because a prosthetic leg returns only about 80 percent of the energy absorbed in each stride compared to 240 percent for a natural leg. Overall, Pisotrius' success presents more questions than answers.

SOURCE: J. Longman, "Debate on Amputee Sprinter: Is He Disabled or Too-Abled?" *The New York Times* (May 15, 2007): 1.

plans to hire more. The turnover rate for Pizza Hut workers with disabilities is only one-fifth of the normal turnover rate.[58]

McDonald's created McJOBS, a program that has trained and hired more than 9,000 mentally and physically challenged individuals since 1981.[59] McJOBS is a corporate plan to recruit, train, and retain individuals with disabilities. Its participants include workers with visual, hearing, or orthopedic impairments; learning disabilities; and mental retardation. Through classroom and on-site training, the McJOBS program prepares individuals with disabilities for the work environment. Before McJOBS workers go on-site, sensitivity training sessions are held with store managers and crew members. These sessions help workers without disabilities understand what it means to be a worker with a disabling condition. Most McJOBS workers start part-time and advance according to their abilities and the opportunities available. Some McJOBS workers with visual impairments prefer to work on the back line, whereas others who use wheelchairs can work the drive-thru window.

Companies like Pizza Hut and McDonald's have led the way in hiring individuals with disabilities. One key to their success is helping able-bodied employees understand how workers with disabilities can contribute to the organization. In this way, ability diversity becomes an asset and helps organizations meet the challenge of unleashing the talents of workers with disabilities.

Differences Are Assets

Diversity involves much more than culture, gender, age, ability, or personality. It also encompasses religion, social status, and sexual orientation. The scope of diversity is broad and inclusive. All these types of diversity lend heterogeneity to the workforce. Some programs aimed at enhancing appreciation and understanding diversity are required while some are voluntary. As we see in the accompanying Science feature, not everyone participates equally in voluntary diversity training.

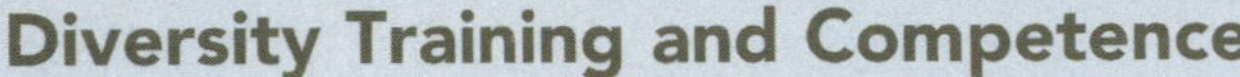

Diversity Training and Competence

Diversity training is an umbrella term that encompasses a wide array of specific programs designed to train and direct employees in behaviors aimed at displaying openness and receptiveness to diversity. Early on, diversity training focused specifically on race and gender. Because of its concern with human resource recruiting, hiring, and promotion practices that might limit opportunities for women and minorities, it was often described as equal opportunity training. More recently there has been an expansion to diversity dimensions such as disability status and culture. In a two-part study by Kulik and colleagues, interest and actual participation in voluntary diversity training were examined. The results found that demographic characteristics played no significant role in either a person's interest or participation in voluntary diversity training. That is, characteristics such as age, sex, and race made no difference. However, what did make a difference was the pretraining competence of the person. Specifically, persons with more competence in the diversity domain displayed significantly more interest in additional diversity training and were more likely to attend a voluntary training session. The researchers concluded that trainees with low competence in the diversity domain are unaware of their low competence levels and therefore are not motivated to participate in training designed to increase diversity competence. Hence, the competent become more competent and those low in competence miss the opportunity to increase their knowledge and awareness.

SOURCE: C. T. Kulik, M. B. Pepper, L. Robertson, and S. K. Parker, "The Rich Get Richer: Predicting Participation in Voluntary Diversity Training," *Journal of Organizational Behavior*. In press.

The issue of sexual orientation as a form of diversity has received increasing attention from organizations. Approximately 1.5 million households in the United States are identified as homosexual domestic partnerships.[60] Sexual orientation is an emotionally charged issue. Often, heterosexual resistance to accepting gay, lesbian, or bisexual workers is caused by moral beliefs. Although organizations must respect these beliefs, they must also send a message that all people are valued. The threat of job discrimination leads many gay men and lesbians to keep their sexual orientation secret at work. This secrecy has a cost, however. Closeted gay workers report lower job satisfaction and organizational commitment and more role conflict and conflict between work and home life issues than do openly gay workers or heterosexual workers.[61] To counteract these problems, companies like NCR are actively seeking gay job applicants. Other companies like IBM, Ford Motor Company, JPMorgan Chase, and American Airlines are offering benefits, training, support groups, and marketing strategies in support of gay rights. These initiatives help gay employees become more integrated and productive organizational members. Education and training can be supplemented by everyday practices like using inclusive language—for example, using the term "partner" instead of "spouse" in verbal and written communication.

Combating prejudice and discrimination is a challenge in managing diversity. Whereas prejudice is an attitude, discrimination is behavior. Both are detrimental to organizations that depend on productivity from every single worker. Often, in studies of ratings of promotion potential, minorities are rated lower than whites, and females are rated lower than males.[62] The disparity between the pay of women and minority-group members relative to white men increases with age.[63] It is to organizations' benefit to make sure that good workers are promoted and compensated fairly, but as the workforce becomes increasingly diverse, the potential for unfair treatment also increases.

Diversity is advantageous to the organization in a multitude of ways. Some organizations have recognized the potential benefits of aggressively working to increase the diversity of their workforces. Yum! Brands' Kentucky Fried Chicken (KFC) has a goal of attracting and retaining female and minority-group executives. A president of KFC's U.S. operations said, "We want to bring in the best people. If there are two equally qualified people, we'd clearly like to have diversity."[64]

(3) Describe actions managers can take to help their employees value diversity.

In an effort to understand and encourage diversity, Alcon Laboratories developed a diversity training class called Working Together. The course takes advantage of two key ideas. First, people work best when they are valued and when diversity is taken into account. Second, when people feel valued, they build relationships and work together as a team.[65] Even majority group managers may be more supportive of diversity training if they appreciate their own ethnic identity. One evaluation of diversity training found that participants were more favorable if the training was framed with a traditional title and had a broad focus.[66] Further, women react more positively to diversity training than men. Companies can get positive payoffs from diversity training and should, therefore, measure the effect of training.

Managing diversity is one way a company can become more competitive. It is more than simply being a good corporate citizen or complying with affirmative action.[67] It is also more than assimilating women and minorities into a dominant male culture. Managing diversity includes a painful examination of hidden assumptions that employees hold. Biases and prejudices about people's differences must be uncovered and dealt with so that differences can be celebrated and exploited to their full advantage.

Diversity's Benefits and Problems

Diversity can enhance organizational performance. Table 2.2 summarizes the main benefits, as well as problems, with diversity at work. Organizations can reap five main benefits from diversity. First, diversity management can help firms attract and retain the best available talent. The companies that appear at the top of "Best Places to Work" lists are usually excellent at managing diversity. Second, diversity can enhance marketing efforts. Just as workforces are becoming more diverse, so are markets. Having a diverse workforce can help the company improve its marketing plans by drawing on insights of employees from various cultural backgrounds. Third, diversity promotes creativity and innovation. The most innovative companies, such as HP, deliberately put together diverse teams to foster creativity. Fourth, diversity results in better problem solving. Diverse groups bring more expertise and experience to bear on problems and decisions. They also encourage higher levels of critical thinking. Fifth, diversity enhances organizational flexibility. Inflexible organizations are characterized by narrow thinking, rigidity, and standard definitions of "good" work styles. In contrast, diversity makes an organization challenge old assumptions

TABLE 2.2 Diversity's Benefits and Problems

Benefits	Problems
• Attracts and retains the best human talent	• Resistance to change
• Improves marketing efforts	• Lack of cohesiveness
• Promotes creativity and innovation	• Communication problems
• Results in better problem solving	• Interpersonal conflicts
• Enhances organizational flexibility	• Slowed decision making

and become more adaptable. These five benefits can add up to competitive advantage for a company that manages diversity well.

Lest we paint an overly rosy picture of diversity, we must recognize its potential problems. Five problems are particularly important: resistance to change, lack of cohesiveness, communication problems, conflicts, and decision making. People are more highly attracted to, and feel more comfortable with, others like themselves. It stands to reason that diversity efforts may be met with considerable resistance when individuals are forced to interact with others unlike themselves. Managers should be prepared for this resistance rather than naively assuming that everybody supports diversity. (Managing resistance to change is presented at length in Chapter 18.) Another potential problem with diversity is the issue of cohesiveness, that invisible "glue" that holds a group together. Cohesive, or tightly knit, groups are preferred by most people. It takes longer for a diverse group of individuals to become cohesive. In addition, cohesive groups have higher morale and better communication. We can reason that it may take longer for diverse groups to develop high morale.

Another obstacle to performance in diverse groups is communication. Culturally diverse groups may encounter special challenges in terms of communication barriers. Misunderstandings can occur that can lower work group effectiveness. Conflicts can also arise, and decision making may take more time.[68]

In summary, diversity has several advantages that can lead to improved productivity and competitive advantage. In diverse groups, however, certain aspects of group functioning can become problematic. The key is to maximize the benefits of diversity and prevent or resolve the potential problems.

Pillsbury is one company that lays out the performance case for managing and valuing differences. Pillsbury's managers argue that the same business rationale for cross-functional teams is relevant to all kinds of diversity. Managing differences includes bringing race and gender, as well as marketing expertise, into a team. The company lacked the language expertise and cultural access to the Hispanic community. To open up a very profitable baked-goods market in a tough-to-crack niche, Pillsbury hired a group of Spanish-speaking Americans of Hispanic descent. Pillsbury's vice president of human resources conducted his own study of the food industry, asking an independent group to rate the diversity performance of ten companies and correlating it with financial performance over a ten-year period. Along with many other studies, the Pillsbury research suggests that diversity is a strong contributor to financial performance.[69]

Whereas the struggle for equal employment opportunity is a battle against racism and prejudice, managing diversity is a battle to value the differences that individuals bring to the workplace. Organizations that manage diversity effectively can reap the rewards of increased productivity and improved organizational health. Another aspect of a healthy organization is employees of good character, ethical behavior, and personal integrity.

ETHICS, CHARACTER, AND PERSONAL INTEGRITY

(4) Discuss the assumptions of consequential, rule-based, and character theories of ethics.

In addition to the challenges of globalization and workforce diversity, managers frequently face ethical dilemmas and trade-offs. Some organizations display good character and their executives are known for personal integrity. Johnson & Johnson employees operate with an organizational credo, presented later in this section. Merck & Company is another organization that manages ethical issues well; its emphasis on ethical behavior has earned it recognition as one of America's most admired companies in *Fortune*'s polls of CEOs. We saw that Genentech is a biotechnology company facing ethical dilemmas and trade-offs in its decision making between cancer patients and immunology patients.

Despite the positive way some organizations handle ethical issues, however, unethical conduct can still occur. A few of the ethical problems that managers report as toughest to resolve include employee theft, environmental issues, comparable worth of employees, conflicts of interest, and sexual harassment.[70]

How can people in organizations rationally think through ethical decisions so that they make the "right" choices? Ethical theories help us understand, evaluate, and classify moral arguments; make decisions; and then defend conclusions about what is right and wrong. Ethical theories can be classified as consequential, rule based, or character based.

Consequential theories of ethics emphasize the consequences or results of behavior. John Stuart Mill's utilitarianism, a well-known consequential theory, suggests that right and wrong are determined by the consequences of the action.[71] "Good" is the ultimate moral value, and we should maximize the most good for the greatest number of people. But do good ethics make for good business?[72] Right actions do not always produce good consequences, and good consequences do not always follow from right actions. And how do we determine the greatest good—in short-term or long-term consequences? Using the "greatest number" criterion can imply that minorities (less than 50 percent) might be excluded in evaluating the morality of actions. An issue that may be important for a minority but unimportant for the majority might be ignored. These are but a few of the dilemmas raised by utilitarianism.

© AP PHOTO/DAVID J. PHILLIP

Despite the positive way some organizations handle ethical issues, unethical conduct does occur. Andrew S. Fastow, former chief financial officer of Enron Corp., was convicted on charges related to his role in the company's collapse.

In contrast, *rule-based theories* of ethics emphasize the character of the act itself, not its effects, in arriving at universal moral rights and wrongs.[73] Moral rights, the basis for legal rights, are associated with such theories. In a theological context, the Bible, the Talmud, and the Koran are rule-based guides to ethical behavior. Immanuel Kant worked toward the ultimate moral principle in formulating his categorical imperative, a universal standard of behavior.[74] Kant argued that individuals should be treated with respect and dignity and that they should not be used as a means to an end. He argued that we should put ourselves in the other person's position and ask if we would make the same decision if we were in his or her situation.

Corporations and business enterprises are more prone to subscribe to consequential ethics than rule-based ethics, in part due to the persuasive arguments of the Scottish political economist and moral philosopher Adam Smith.[75] He believed that the self-interest of human beings is God's providence, not the government's. Smith set forth a doctrine of natural liberty, presenting the classical argument for open market competition and free trade. Within this framework, people should be allowed to pursue what is in their economic self-interest, and the natural efficiency of the marketplace would serve the well-being of society. However, an alternative to those theories is offered through virtue-ethics.

Character theories of ethics emphasize the character of the individual and the intent of the actor, in contrast to either the character of the act itself or its consequences. These theories emphasize virtue-ethics and are based on an Aristotelian approach to character. Robert Solomon is the best-known advocate of this approach.[76] He supports a business ethics theory that centers on the individual within the corporation, thus emphasizing both corporate roles and personal virtues. The center of Aristotle's vision was on the inner character and virtuousness of the individual, not on her or his behavior or actions. Thus, the "good" person who acted out of virtuous and "right" intentions was one with integrity and ultimately good ethical standards. For Solomon, the six dimensions of virtue-ethics are community,

consequential theory
An ethical theory that emphasizes the consequences or results of behavior.

rule-based theory
An ethical theory that emphasizes the character of the act itself rather than its effects.

character theory
An ethical theory that emphasizes the character, personal virtues, and integrity of the individual.

excellence, role identity, integrity, judgment (*phronesis*), and holism. Further, "the virtues" are a shorthand way of summarizing the ideals that define good character. These include honesty, loyalty, sincerity, courage, reliability, trustworthiness, benevolence, sensitivity, helpfulness, cooperativeness, civility, decency, modesty, openness, and gracefulness, to name a few.

Cultural relativism contends that there are no universal ethical principles and that people should not impose their own ethical standards on others. Local standards should be the guides for ethical behavior. Cultural relativism encourages individuals to operate under the old adage "When in Rome, do as the Romans do." Unfortunately, strict adherence to cultural relativism can lead individuals to deny accountability for their decisions and to avoid difficult ethical dilemmas.

(5) Explain six issues that pose ethical dilemmas for managers.

People need ethical theories to help them think through confusing, complex, difficult moral choices and ethical decisions. In contemporary organizations, people face ethical and moral dilemmas in many diverse areas. The key areas we address are employee rights, sexual harassment, romantic involvements, organizational justice, whistle-blowing, and social responsibility. We conclude with a discussion of professionalism and codes of ethics.

Employee Rights

Managing the rights of employees at work creates many ethical dilemmas in organizations. Some of these dilemmas are privacy issues related to technology. Computerized monitoring, discussed later in the chapter, constitutes an invasion of privacy in the minds of some individuals. The use of employee data from computerized information systems presents many ethical concerns. Safeguarding the employee's right to privacy and at the same time preserving access to the data for those who need it requires that the manager balance competing interests.

Drug testing, free speech, downsizing and layoffs, and due process are but a few of the issues involving employee rights that managers face. Perhaps no issue generates as much need for managers to balance the interests of employees and the interests of the organization as AIDS in the workplace. New drugs have shown the promise of extended lives for people with human immunodeficiency virus (HIV), and this means that HIV-infected individuals can remain in the workforce and stay productive. Managers may be caught in the middle of a conflict between the rights of HIV-infected workers and the rights of their coworkers who feel threatened.

Employers are not required to make concessions to coworkers but do have obligations to educate, reassure, and provide emotional support to them. Confidentiality may also be a difficult issue. Some employees with HIV or AIDS do not wish to waive confidentiality and do not want to reveal their condition to their coworkers because of fears of stigmatization or even reprisals. In any case, management should discuss with the affected employee the ramifications of trying to maintain confidentiality and should assure the employee that every effort will be made to prevent negative consequences for him or her in the workplace.[77]

Laws exist that protect HIV-infected workers. As mentioned earlier, the Americans with Disabilities Act requires employees to treat HIV-infected workers as disabled individuals and to make reasonable accommodations for them. The ethical dilemmas involved with this situation, however, go far beyond the legal issues. How does a manager protect the dignity of the person with AIDS and preserve the morale and productivity of the work group when so much prejudice and ignorance surround this disease? Many organizations, such as Wells Fargo, believe the answer is education.[78] Wells Fargo has a written AIDS policy because of the special issues associated with the disease—such as confidentiality, employee socialization, coworker education, and counseling—that must be addressed. The Body Shop's employee

How Much Do You Know about Sexual Harassment?

Indicate whether you believe each statement below is true (T) or false (F).

_____ 1. Sexual harassment is unprofessional behavior.
_____ 2. Sexual harassment is against the law in all fifty states.
_____ 3. Sexual advances are a form of sexual harassment.
_____ 4. A request for sexual activity is a form of sexual harassment.
_____ 5. Verbal or physical conduct of a sexual nature may be sexual harassment.
_____ 6. Sexual harassment occurs when submission to sex acts is a condition of employment.
_____ 7. Sexual harassment occurs when submission to or rejection of sexual acts is a basis for performance evaluation.
_____ 8. Sexual harassment occurs when such behavior interferes with an employee's performance or creates an intimidating, hostile, and offensive environment.
_____ 9. Sexual harassment includes physical contact of a sexual nature, such as touching.
_____ 10. Sexual harassment requires that a person have the intent to harass, harm, or intimidate.

All of the items are true except item 10, which is false. While somewhat ambiguous, sexual harassment is defined in the eyes of the beholder. Give yourself 1 point for each correct answer. This score reflects how much you know about sexual harassment. Scores can range from 0 (poorly informed) to 10 (well informed). If your score was less than 5, you need to learn more about sexual harassment.

SOURCE: See W. O'Donohue, ed., *Sexual Harassment* (Boston: Allyn and Bacon, 1997) for theory, research, and treatment. See http://www.eeoc.gov/stats/harass.html for the latest statistics.

education program consists of factual seminars combined with interactive theater workshops. The workshops depict a scenario in which an HIV-positive worker must make decisions, and the audience decides what the worker should do. This helps participants explore the emotional and social issues surrounding HIV.[79] Many fears arise because of a lack of knowledge about AIDS.

Sexual Harassment

According to the Equal Employment Opportunity Commission, sexual harassment is unwelcome sexual attention, whether verbal or physical, that affects an employee's job conditions or creates a hostile working environment.[80] Court rulings, too, have broadened the definition of sexual harassment beyond job-related abuse to include acts that create a hostile work environment. In addition, Supreme Court rulings presume companies are to blame when managers create a sexually hostile working environment. Some organizations are more tolerant of sexual harassment. Complaints are not taken seriously, it is risky to complain, and perpetrators are unlikely to be punished. In such organizations, sexual harassment is more likely to occur. It is also more likely to occur in male-dominated workplaces.[81] Managers can defend themselves by demonstrating that they took action to eliminate workplace harassment and that the complaining employee did not take advantage of company procedures to deal with it. Even the best sexual harassment policy, however, will not absolve a company when harassment leads to firing, demotions, or undesirable working assignments.[82] How much do you know about sexual harassment? Complete You 2.2 to get an idea.

There are three types of sexual harassment. *Gender harassment* includes crude comments or sexual jokes and behaviors that disparage someone's gender or convey hostility toward a particular gender. *Unwanted sexual attention* involves unwanted touching or repeated unwanted pressures for dates. *Sexual coercion* consists of implicit or explicit demands for sexual favors by threatening negative job-related consequences or promising job-related rewards.[83] Recent theory has focused attention on the aggressive behavior of sexual harassers.[84]

Sexual harassment costs the typical *Fortune* 500 company $6.7 million per year in absenteeism, turnover, and loss of productivity. Valeant Pharmaceuticals International has paid out millions to settle four sexual harassment complaints against former CEO Milan Panic. One U.S. airline reached a $2.6 million settlement with the EEOC in 2001 after the agency found widespread sexual harassment of female employees at the airline's New York JFK International Airport facility. Plaintiffs may now sue not only for back pay but also for compensatory and punitive damages. And these costs do not take into account the negative publicity that firms may encounter from sexual harassment cases, which can cost untold millions. Sexual harassment can have strong negative effects on victims. Victims are less satisfied with their work, supervisors, and coworkers and may psychologically withdraw at work. They may suffer poorer mental health and even exhibit symptoms of post-traumatic stress disorder in conjunction with the harassment experience. Some victims report alcohol abuse, depression, headaches, and nausea.[85]

Several companies have created comprehensive sexual harassment programs that seem to work. Atlantic Richfield (ARCO), owned by British Petroleum and a player in the male-dominated energy industry, has a handbook on preventing sexual harassment that includes phone numbers of state agencies where employees can file complaints. In essence, it gives employees a road map to the courthouse, and the openness seems to work. Lawsuits rarely happen at ARCO. When sexual harassment complaints come in, the company assumes the allegations are true and investigates thoroughly. The process has resulted in the firing of highly placed managers, including the captain of an oil tanker. Other companies believe in the power of training programs. Some of the best training programs use role-playing, videotapes, and group discussions of real cases to help supervisors recognize unlawful sexual harassment and investigate complaints properly.

Romantic Involvements

Hugging, sexual innuendos, and repeated requests for dates may constitute sexual harassment for some but a prelude to romance for others. This situation carries with it a different set of ethical dilemmas for organizations.

A recent fax poll indicated that three-fourths of the respondents felt it was okay to date a coworker, while three-fourths disapproved of dating a superior or subordinate. In *Meritor vs. Vinson*, the Supreme Court ruled that the agency principle applies to supervisor–subordinate relationships. Employers are liable for acts of their agents (supervisors) and can thus be held liable for sexual harassment. Other employees might claim that the subordinate who is romantically involved with the supervisor gets preferential treatment. Dating between coworkers poses less liability for the company because the agency principle does not apply. Policing coworker dating can also backfire: Wal-Mart lost a lawsuit when it tried to forbid coworkers from dating.

Workplace romances may result, for the participants, in experiences that can be positive or negative, temporary or permanent, exploitative to nonexploitative. The effects of office romances can similarly be positive or negative, or they can simply be mild diversions. Romances can be damaging to organizational effectiveness, or they can occasionally enhance effectiveness through their positive effects on participants. Two particular kinds of romances are hazardous in the workplace. Hierarchical romances, in which one person directly reports to another, can create tremendous conflicts of interest. Utilitarian romances, in which one person satisfies the needs of another in exchange for task-related or career-related favors, are potentially damaging in the workplace. Although most managers realize that workplace romance cannot be eliminated through rules and policies, they believe that intervention is a must when romance constitutes a serious threat to productivity or workplace morale.[86]

Organizational Justice

Another area in which moral and ethical dilemmas may arise for people at work concerns organizational justice, both distributive and procedural. *Distributive justice* concerns the fairness of outcomes individuals receive. For example, the salaries and bonuses of U.S. corporate executives became a central issue with Japanese executives when former President George H. W. Bush and American CEOs in key industries visited Japan in 1992. The Japanese CEOs questioned the distributive justice in keeping the American CEOs' salaries at high levels at a time when so many companies were having financial difficulty and laying off workers.

Procedural justice concerns the fairness of the process by which outcomes are allocated. The ethical questions here do not concern the just or unjust distribution of organizational resources but rather, the process. Has the organization used the correct procedures in allocating resources? Have the right considerations, such as competence and skill, been brought to bear in the decision process? And have the wrong considerations, such as race and gender, been excluded from the decision process? One study in a work-scheduling context found voluntary turnover negatively related to advance notice and consistency, two dimensions of procedural justice.[87] Some research found cultural differences in the effects of distributive and procedural justice, such as between Hong Kong and the United States.[88]

Whistle-Blowing

Whistle-blowers are employees who inform authorities of wrongdoings by their company or coworkers. Whistle-blowers can be perceived as either heroes or villains depending on the circumstances. For a whistle-blower to be considered a public hero, the situation the whistle-blower reports to authorities must be so serious as to be perceived as abhorrent by others.[89] In contrast, the whistle-blower is considered a villain if others see the act of whistle-blowing as more offensive than the situation being reported.

Whistle-blowing is important in the United States because workers sometimes engage in unethical behavior in an intense desire to succeed. Many examples of whistle-blowing can be found in corporate America. For example, one former Coca-Cola employee made a number of allegations against the company and issued an ultimatum: Coca-Cola must pay him nearly $45 million or he would go to the media.[90] While a Georgia state court dismissed most of the allegations, Coca-Cola still had to defend itself against claims related to wrongful termination. One of the former employee's allegations relating to a falsified marketing test did force Coca-Cola to make a public apology and offer to pay Burger King $21 million.

Organizations can manage whistle-blowing by communicating the conditions that are appropriate for the disclosure of wrongdoing. Clearly delineating wrongful behavior and the appropriate ways to respond are important organizational actions.

distributive justice
The fairness of the outcomes that individuals receive in an organization.

procedural justice
The fairness of the process by which outcomes are allocated in an organization.

whistle-blower
An employee who informs authorities of the wrongdoings of his or her company or coworkers.

Social Responsibility

Corporate *social responsibility* is the obligation of an organization to behave in ethical ways in the social environment in which it operates. Ethical conduct at the individual level can translate into social responsibility at the organizational level. When Malden Mills, the maker of Polartec, burned down in 1995, the company's president, Aaron Feuerstein, paid workers during the months it took to rebuild the company. Although doing so cost the company a lot of money and was not required by law, Feuerstein said his own values caused him to do the socially responsible thing. Malden Mills recovered financially and continues its success with Polartec.

Socially responsible actions are expected of organizations. Current concerns include protecting the environment, promoting worker safety, supporting social issues, and investing in the community, among others. Some organizations, like IBM, loan executives to inner-city schools to teach science and math. Other organizations, like Patagonia, demonstrate social responsibility through environmentalism. Firms that are seen as socially responsible have a competitive advantage in attracting applicants.[91]

Codes of Ethics

One of the characteristics of mature professions is the existence of a code of ethics to which the practitioners adhere in their actions and behavior. An example is the Hippocratic oath in medicine. Although some of the individual differences we address in Chapter 4 produce ethical or unethical orientations in specific people, a profession's code of ethics becomes a standard against which members can measure themselves in the absence of internalized standards.

No universal code of ethics or oath exists for business as it does for medicine. However, Paul Harris and four business colleagues, who founded Rotary International in 1905, made an effort to address ethical and moral behavior right from the beginning. They developed the four-way test, shown in Figure 2.2, which is now used in more than 166 nations throughout the world by the 1.2 million Rotarians in more than 30,000 Rotary clubs. Figure 2.2 focuses the questioner on key ethical and moral questions.

Beyond the individual and professional level, corporate culture is another excellent starting point for addressing ethics and morality. In Chapter 16 we examine how corporate culture and leader behavior trickle down the company, setting a standard for all below. In some cases, the corporate ethics may be captured in

FIGURE 2.2 The Four-Way Test

The Four-Way Test
OF WHAT WE THINK, SAY, OR DO

1. Is it the TRUTH?
2. Is it FAIR to all concerned?
3. Will it build GOODWILL and better friendships?
4. Will it be BENEFICIAL to all concerned?

social responsibility
The obligation of an organization to behave in ethical ways.

a regulation. For example, the Joint Ethics Regulation (DOD 5500.7-R, August 1993) specifies the ethical standards to which all U.S. military personnel are to adhere. In other cases, the corporate ethics may be in the form of a credo. Johnson & Johnson's credo, shown in Figure 2.3, helped hundreds of employees ethically address the criminal tampering with Tylenol products. In its 1986 centennial annual report, J & J attributed its success in this crisis, as well as its long-term business growth (a compound sales rate of 11.6 percent for 100 years), to "our unique form of decentralized management, our adherence to the ethical principles embodied in our credo, and our emphasis on managing the business for the long term."

Individual codes of ethics, professional oaths, and organizational credos all must be anchored in a moral, ethical framework. They are always open to question and continuous improvement using ethical theories as a tool for reexamining the soundness of the current standard. Although a universal right and wrong may exist, it would be hard to argue that there is only one code of ethics to which all individuals, professions, and organizations can subscribe.

FIGURE 2.3 The Johnson & Johnson Credo

We believe our first responsibility is to the doctors, nurses, and patients,
to mothers and all others who use our products and services.
In meeting their needs everything we do must be of high quality.
We must constantly strive to reduce our costs
in order to maintain reasonable prices.
Customers' orders must be serviced promptly and accurately.
Our suppliers and distributors must have an opportunity
to make a fair profit.

We are responsible to our employees,
the men and women who work with us throughout the world.
Everyone must be considered as an individual.
We must respect their dignity and recognize their merit.
They must have a sense of security in their jobs.
Compensation must be fair and adequate,
and working conditions clean, orderly, and safe.
Employees must feel free to make suggestions and complaints.
There must be equal opportunity for employment, development
and advancement for those qualified.
We must provide competent management,
and their actions must be just and ethical.

We are responsible to the communities in which we live and work
and to the world community as well.
We must be good citizens—support good works and charities
and bear our fair share of taxes.
We must encourage civic improvements and better health and education.
We must maintain in good order
the property we are privileged to use,
protecting the environment and natural resources.

Our final responsibility is to our stockholders.
Business must make a sound profit.
We must experiment with new ideas.
Research must be carried on, innovative programs developed
and mistakes paid for.
New equipment must be purchased, new facilities provided,
and new products launched.
Reserves must be created to provide for adverse times.
When we operate according to these principles,
the stockholders should realize a fair return.

TECHNOLOGICAL INNOVATION

A fourth challenge that managers face is effectively managing technological innovation. *Technology* consists of the intellectual and mechanical processes used by an organization to transform inputs into products or services that meet organizational goals. Managers face the challenge of rapidly changing technology and of putting the technology to optimum use in organizations. The inability of managers to incorporate new technologies successfully into their organizations is a major factor that has limited economic growth in the United States.[92] Although the United States still leads the way in developing new technologies, it lags behind in making productive use of these new technologies in workplace settings.[93] Good-to-great organizations avoid technology fads and bandwagons, yet become pioneers in the application of carefully selected technologies.[94]

© YOSHIKAZU TSUNG/AFP/GETTY IMAGES

Managers face the challenge of effectively managing technological innovation, such as Hitachi's electronic paper display.

The Internet has radically changed the way organizations communicate and perform work. By integrating computer, cable, and telecommunications technologies, businesses have learned new ways to compete. For example, Kmart takes advantage of the Internet through BlueLight.com for online retailing. In networked organizations, time, distance, and space become irrelevant. A networked organization can do business anytime and anywhere, which is essential in the global marketplace. This allows retailers to drastically cut their investments in inventories. The World Wide Web has created a virtual commercial district. Customers can book air travel, buy compact discs, and "surf the Net" to conduct business around the globe.[95]

The Internet and electronic innovation have made surveillance of employees more widespread. However, companies need to balance the use of spyware, monitoring of employee e-mails and Web sites, and video monitoring systems with respect for employee rights to privacy. Managers with excellent interpersonal skills go a long way in ensuring high productivity, commitment, and appropriate behavior on the part of employees versus the use of intense employee performance monitoring systems using electronic surveillance. Companies with clearly written policies that spell out their approach to monitoring employees may succeed better in walking the fine line between respecting employees' privacy and protecting the interests of the organization.

technology
The intellectual and mechanical processes used by an organization to transform inputs into products or services that meet organizational goals.

expert system
A computer-based application that uses a representation of human expertise in a specialized field of knowledge to solve problems.

robotics
The use of robots in organizations.

One fascinating technological change is the development of *expert systems*, computer-based applications that use a representation of human expertise in a specialized field of knowledge to solve problems. Expert systems can be used in many ways, including providing advice to nonexperts, offering assistance to experts, replacing experts, and serving as a training and development tool in organizations.[96] They are used in medical decision making, diagnosis, and medical informatics.[97] Anheuser-Busch has used an expert system to assist managers in ensuring that personnel decisions comply with antidiscrimination laws.[98]

Robots, another technological innovation, were invented in the United States, and advanced research on *robotics* is still conducted here. However, Japan leads the world in the use of robotics in organizations. Organizations in the United States have fewer total robots than were added in 1989 alone in Japan.[99] Robots in Japan are treated like part of the family. They are even named after favorite celebrities, singers, and movie stars. Whereas Japanese workers are happy to let robots take over repetitive or dangerous work, Americans are more suspicious of labor-saving robots because employers often use them to cut jobs.[100] The main reason for the reluctance of U.S. organizations to use robots is their slow payout. Robotics represents a big investment that does not pay off in the short term. Japanese managers are more willing to use a long-term horizon to evaluate the effectiveness of robotics technology. Labor unions may also resist robotics because of the fear that robots will replace employees.

Some U.S. companies that experimented with robotics had bad experiences. Deere & Company originally used robots to paint its tractors, but the company scrapped them because programming the robots for the multitude of types of paint used took too long. Now Deere uses robots to torque cap screws on tractors, a repetitive job that once had a high degree of human error.

It is tempting to view technology from only the positive side; however, a reality check is in order. Some firms that have been disappointed with costly technologies are electing to *de*-engineer. And computer innovations often fail; 42 percent of information technology projects are abandoned before completion, and half of all technology projects fail to meet managers' expectations. Pacific Gas and Electric (part of PG&E Corporation) spent tens of millions of dollars on a new IBM-based system. Deregulation then hit the utility industry, and customers were permitted to choose among utility companies. Keeping up with multiple suppliers and fast-changing prices was too much, and the massive new system couldn't handle the additional burden quickly enough. It was scrapped in favor of a new project using the old first-generation computer system, which is being updated and gradually replaced. Because some innovations fail to live up to expectations, and some simply fail, it is important to effectively manage both revolutionary and evolutionary approaches to technological transitions.[101]

Alternative Work Arrangements

(6) Understand the alternative work arrangements produced by technological advances.

Technological advances have been responsible, to a large degree, for the advent of alternative work arrangements, the nontraditional work practices, settings, and locations that are now supplementing traditional workplaces. One alternative work arrangement is *telecommuting*, transmitting work from a home computer to the office using a modem. IBM, for example, was one of the first companies to experiment with the notion of installing computer terminals in employees' homes. By telecommuting, employees gain flexibility, save the commute to work, and enjoy the comforts of being at home. Telecommuting also has disadvantages, however, including distractions, lack of opportunities to socialize with other workers, lack of interaction with supervisors, and decreased identification with the organization. Despite these disadvantages, telecommuters still feel "plugged in" to the communication system at the office. Studies show that telecommuters often report higher satisfaction with office communication than do workers in traditional office environments.[102]

Estimates are that about 28 million Americans are telecommuting. Why do companies encourage telecommuting? Cost reductions are an obvious motivator. Since 1991, AT&T has gained $550 million in cash flow from eliminating office space and reducing overhead costs. Another reason is to increase productivity. At IBM, a survey of telecommuters indicated that 87 percent believed they were more

telecommuting
Transmitting work from a home computer to the office using a modem.

productive in the alternative work arrangement. Telecommuting also allows companies access to workers with key skills regardless of their location. Alternative workplaces also give companies an advantage in hiring and keeping talented employees who find the flexibility of working at home very attractive.

There is a spectrum of other alternative work arrangements. *Hoteling* is a shared-office arrangement wherein employees have mobile file cabinets and lockers for personal storage, and "hotel" work spaces are furnished for them. These spaces must be reserved instead of being permanently assigned. The computer system routes phone calls and e-mail as necessary. Individuals' personal photos and memorabilia are stored electronically and "placed" on occupants' computer desktops upon arrival.

Satellite offices comprise another alternative work arrangement. In such offices, large facilities are broken into a network of smaller workplaces close to employees' homes. Satellites are often located in comparatively inexpensive cities and suburban areas. They usually have simpler and less costly furnishings and fixtures than the more centrally located offices. Satellites can save a company as much as 50 percent in real estate costs and can be quite appealing to employees who do not want to work in a large urban area. This can broaden the pool of potential employees, who can communicate with the home office via various technologies.[103]

All of these alternative work arrangements signal a trend toward *virtual offices*, in which people work anytime, anywhere, and with anyone. The concept involves work being where people are, rather than people moving to where the work is. Information technologies make connectivity, collaboration, and communication easy. Critical voice mails and messages can be delivered to and from the central office, a client's office, the airport, the car, or home. Wireless Internet access and online meeting software such as WebEx make it possible for employees to participate in meetings anywhere at any time.

Emerging Managerial Realities

Technological innovation affects the very nature of the management job. Managers who once had to coax workers back to their desks from coffee breaks now find that they need to encourage workers mesmerized by new technology to take more frequent breaks.[104] Working with a computer can be stressful, both physically and psychologically. Eyestrain, neck and back strain, and headaches can result from sitting at a computer terminal too long. In addition, workers can become accustomed to the fast response time of the computer and expect the same from their coworkers. When coworkers do not respond with the speed and accuracy of the computer, they may receive a harsh retort. New technology combined with globalization and intensified business pressures has led to the rise of extreme workers, pushing up the ranks of workaholics.[105] These extreme workers pay a price in relationships; other dimensions of a full, rich life; and levels of stress.

Computerized monitoring provides managers with a wealth of information about employee performance, and it holds great potential for misuse as mentioned earlier in this section. The telecommunications, airline, and mail-order merchandise industries make wide use of systems that secretly monitor employees' interactions with customers. Employers praise such systems because they improve customer service. Workers, however, are not so positive; they react with higher levels of depression, anxiety, and exhaustion from working under such secret scrutiny. At Bell Canada, operators were evaluated on a system that tabulated average working time with customers. Operators found the practice highly stressful, and they sabotaged the system by giving callers wrong directory assistance numbers rather than taking the time to look up the correct ones. As a result, Bell

Canada now uses average working time scores for entire offices rather than for individuals.[106]

New technologies and rapid innovation place a premium on a manager's technical skills. Early management theories rated technical skills as less important than human and conceptual skill. This is past reality. Managers today must develop technical competence in order to gain workers' respect. Computer-integrated manufacturing systems, for example, have been shown to require managers to use participative management styles, open communication, and greater technical expertise to be effective.[107] In a world of rapid technological innovation, managers must focus more carefully on helping workers manage the stress of their work. They must take advantage of the wealth of information at their disposal to motivate, coach, and counsel workers rather than try to control them more stringently or police them. The management of intellectual property, however, cannot be left to technology managers or corporate lawyers.[108] Roughly 75 percent of *Fortune* 100's total market capitalization is in intangible assets, such as patents, copyrights, and trademarks. Managers and companies with well-conceived strategies and policies for their intellectual property can use it for competitive advantage in the global marketplace.

Technological change occurs so rapidly that turbulence characterizes most organizations. Workers must constantly learn and adapt to changing technology so that organizations can remain competitive. Managers must grapple with the challenge of helping workers adapt and make effective use of new technologies.

Helping Employees Adjust to Technological Change

Most workers are well aware of the benefits of modern technologies. The availability of skilled jobs and improved working conditions have been by-products of innovation in many organizations. Technology is also bringing disadvantaged individuals into the workforce. Microchips have dramatically increased opportunities for workers with visual impairments. Information can be decoded into speech using a speech synthesizer, into braille using a hard-copy printer, or into enlarged print visible on a computer monitor. Workers with visual impairments are no longer dependent on sighted persons to translate printed information for them, and this has opened new doors of opportunity.[109] Engineers at Carnegie Mellon University have developed PizzaBot, a robot that individuals with disabilities can operate using a voice-recognition system. Despite these and other benefits of new technology in the workplace, however, employees may still resist change.

Technological innovations bring about changes in employees' work environments, and change has been described as the ultimate stressor. Many workers react negatively to change that they perceive as threatening to their work situation. Many of their fears center around loss—of freedom, of control, of the things they like about their jobs.[110] Employees may fear deterioration of their quality of work life and increased pressure at work. Further, they may fear being replaced by technology or being displaced into jobs of lower skill levels.

(7) Explain the ways managers can help employees adjust to technological change.

Managers can take several actions to help employees adjust to changing technology. The workers' participation in early phases of the decision-making process regarding technological changes is important. This helps them gain important information about the potential changes in their jobs, making them less resistant to the change. Workers are the users of the new technology. Their input in early stages can lead to a smoother transition into the new ways of performing work.

Managers should also keep in mind the effects that new technology has on the skill requirements of workers. Many employees support changes that increase the skill requirements of their jobs. Increased skill requirements often lead to increases in job autonomy, more responsibility, and potential pay increases, all of which are received positively by employees. Whenever possible, managers should select technology that increases workers' skill requirements.

Providing effective training about ways to use the new technology also is essential. Training helps employees feel that they control the technology rather than being controlled by it. The training should be designed to match workers' needs, and it should increase the workers' sense of mastery of the new technology.

Support groups within the organization are another way of helping employees adjust to technological change. Such change is stressful, and support groups are important emotional outlets for workers. Support groups can also function as information exchanges so that workers can share advice on using the technology. Workers feel less alone with the problem when they know that other workers share their frustration.

A related challenge is to encourage workers to invent new uses for technology already in place. *Reinvention* is the term for creatively applying new technology.[111] Innovators should be rewarded for their efforts. Individuals who explore the boundaries of a new technology can personalize the technology and adapt it to their own job needs, as well as share this information with others in the work group. In one large public utility, service representatives, without their supervisor's knowledge, developed a personal note-passing system that later became the basis of a formal communication system that improved the efficiency of their work group.

Managers face a substantial challenge in leading organizations to adopt new technologies more humanely and effectively. Technological changes are essential for earnings growth and for expanded employment opportunities. The adoption of new technologies is a critical determinant of U.S. competitiveness in the global marketplace.

MANAGERIAL IMPLICATIONS: BEATING THE CHALLENGES

Organizational success depends on managers' ability to address the four challenges of globalization, workforce diversity, ethics, and technological innovation. Failure to address the challenges can be costly. Think about Pepsi's losses to Coke in the global cola wars. Coke is winning the battle and capitalizing on the huge opportunities and profits from global markets. A racial discrimination lawsuit against Texaco cost the company millions in a settlement and damaged its reputation. Managers' behavioral integrity (i.e., word-deed alignment) is judged by all employees, most especially African American employees.[112] Mitsubishi suffered a similar fate in a sexual harassment scandal. Failure to address these challenges can mean costly losses, damage to reputations, and ultimately an organization's demise.

These four challenges are important because the way managers handle them shapes employee behavior. Developing global mindsets among employees expands their worldview and puts competition on a larger scale. Knowing that diversity is valued and differences are assets causes employees to think twice about engaging in discriminatory behaviors. Valuing technological change leads employees to experiment with new technologies and develop innovative ways to perform their jobs. Sending a message that unethical behavior is not tolerated lets employees know that doing the right thing pays off.

These four challenges are recurring themes that you will see throughout our book. You will learn how companies are tackling these challenges and how organizational behavior can be used to create opportunity in organizations, which is a must if they are to remain competitive.

reinvention

The creative application of new technology.

"You're Hired!" . . . Not . . . if You're Over 40

Donald Trump's hugely popular reality series, *The Apprentice*, was mired in controversy at the beginning of its sixth and final season. R. Joseph Hewett, a 51-year-old technology manager, alleged in an age-discrimination lawsuit that he never got a chance to hear the words, "You're fired!" because the show's organizers and producers felt he was too old to compete.

Hewett maintained that he was unjustifiably turned down for the reality show given his "many years of experience managing large commercial properties." Among his qualifications, Hewett graduated magna cum laude from college and worked as a technology manager at a commercial real estate company. He was also 49 years old at the time he applied for the show in 2005. In his lawsuit, Hewett asserted that only two of the finalists in the first six seasons of show had been over 40 years of age, a claim that a Trump spokesman did not deny. According to the Trump organization, while they actively sought participants from "all age groups," few applicants were over the age of 40.

Hewett reached a settlement with the Trump organization that in his words was "satisfactory to all." He stated that the lawsuit was never about a disgruntled applicant trying to get back at Trump's organization but rather an opportunity to advocate on behalf of an entire class of people he believed had been victimized.

1. Was Hewett justified in bringing age-discrimination litigation against *The Apprentice*? Why or why not?
2. What could the Trump organization have done to encourage more people over 40 to apply for the show?

SOURCE: M. Pratt. "Apprentice Reject Who Claimed Age Discrimination Settles Suit," *The Associated Press* (May 22, 2007).

LOOKING BACK: GENENTECH, INC.

You Can't Do Everything for Everybody

Science and business have their limitations. No company, no government, no agency can meet the needs of everyone; those are the constraints of reality. However, no one knows what the actual limits are until they push them. For example, in 2006, Genentech spent $1.8 billion in research and development. That is a significant budget for one company, but Genentech still had to do some serious prioritizing to decide where to spend those precious resources. The budget was large; it was not unlimited. Imagination is great, and reality provides a set of constraint limitations. As a result, trade-offs must be made both in the short term and the long term, giving rise to ethical dilemmas.

At the same time it wrestles with priorities of resource allocation, Genentech has nurtured a culture that fosters innovation, creativity, and new ideas. The company is committed to the proper treatment of employees and scientists in creative cultures, which takes more than training and lip service. Innovation and creativity need to be underscored at every turn. Within Genentech, the implication of this commitment has been, from the beginning, to allow its researchers to publish their findings in academic journals. Publication in leading scientific journals is an important career status marker for scientists.[113] The company's position is very different from most pharmaceutical companies that tightly guard their research secrets.

The good news for Genentech is that their "publish your research" policy allows them to compete with Harvard, Stanford, Lancaster, Cambridge, and other leading research universities of the world when recruiting top scientists. This is because these scientists know that they can continue to build their academic reputations while also doing important research and earning corporate salaries. They have helped lead Genentech to scientific and financial successes, for example with a drug like Lucetis, which treats the leading cause of blindness. Approved in mid-2006, Lucetis had sales of $380 million for the year, making it one of Genentech's most successful launches ever. Science and business can mix!

Chapter Summary

1. To ensure that their organizations meet the competition, managers must tackle four important challenges: globalization, workforce diversity, ethical behavior, and technological change at work.
2. The five cultural differences that affect work-related attitudes are individualism versus collectivism, power distance, uncertainty avoidance, masculinity versus femininity, and time orientation.
3. Diversity encompasses gender, culture, personality, sexual orientation, religion, ability, social status, and a host of other differences.
4. Managers must take a proactive approach to managing diversity so that differences are valued and capitalized upon.
5. Three types of ethical theories include consequential theories, rule-based theories, and character theories.
6. Ethical dilemmas emerge for people at work in the areas of employee rights, sexual harassment, romantic involvements, organizational justice, whistle-blowing, and social responsibility.
7. Alternative work arrangements, facilitated by technology, are changing the way work is performed.
8. Through supportive relationships and training, managers can help employees adjust to technological change.

Key Terms

character theory (p. 53)
collectivism (p. 40)
consequential theory (p. 53)
distributive justice (p. 57)
diversity (p. 45)
expatriate manager (p. 42)
expert system (p. 60)
femininity (p. 41)
glass ceiling (p. 46)
guanxi (p. 38)
individualism (p. 40)
masculinity (p. 41)
power distance (p. 40)
procedural justice (p. 57)
reinvention (p. 64)
robotics (p. 60)
rule-based theory (p. 53)
social responsibility (p. 58)
technology (p. 60)
telecommuting (p. 61)
time orientation (p. 41)
transnational organization (p. 37)
uncertainty avoidance (p. 41)
whistle-blower (p. 57)

Review Questions

1. What are Hofstede's five dimensions of cultural differences that affect work attitudes? Using these dimensions, describe the United States.
2. What are the primary sources of diversity in the U.S. workforce?
3. What are the potential benefits and problems of diversity?
4. What is the reality of the glass ceiling? What would it take to change this reality?
5. What are some of the ethical challenges encountered in organizations?
6. Describe the difference between distributive and procedural justice.
7. Why do employees fear technological innovations, and how can managers help employees adjust?

Discussion and Communication Questions

1. How can managers be encouraged to develop global thinking? How can managers dispel stereotypes about other cultures?
2. Some people have argued that in designing expert systems, human judgment is made obsolete. What do you think?
3. Why do some companies encourage alternative work arrangements?
4. What effects will the globalization of business have on a company's culture? How can an organization with a strong "made in America" identity compete in the global marketplace?
5. Why is diversity such an important issue? Is the workforce more diverse today than in the past?
6. How does a manager strike a balance between encouraging employees to celebrate their own cultures and forming a single unified culture within the organization?
7. Do you agree with Hofstede's findings about U.S. culture? Other cultures? On what do you base your agreement or disagreement?
8. (*communication question*) Select one of the four challenges (globalization, diversity, ethics, technology) and write a brief position paper arguing for its importance to managers.
9. (*communication question*) Find someone whose culture is different from your own. This could be a classmate or an international student at your university. Interview the person about his or her culture, using Hofstede's dimensions. Also ask what you might need to know about doing business in that person's culture (e.g., customs, etiquette). Be prepared to share this information in class.

Ethical Dilemma

Jill Warner, President of Ace Toys, sat looking at the monthly profit and loss statement. For the fifth month in a row, the company had lost money. Labor costs were killing them. Jill had done everything she could think of to reduce costs and still produce a quality product. She was beginning to face the fact that soon she would no longer be able to avoid the idea of outsourcing. It was a concept that Jill had done everything to avoid, but it was beginning to look inevitable.

Jill felt strongly about making a quality American product using American workers in an American factory. But if things continued the way they were, she was going to have to do something. She owed it to her stockholders and board of directors to keep the company financially healthy. They had entrusted her with the future of the company, and she could not let them down. It was not her money or company to do with as she pleased. Her job was to make sure that Ace Toys flourished.

However, if she chose to outsource the production segment of the company, only management and the sales force would keep their jobs. How could she face the 500 people who would lose their jobs? How would the small community that depended on those 500 jobs survive? She also worried about the customers who had come to depend on Ace Toys to produce a safe product that they could give to their children with confidence. Would that quality suffer if she sent production halfway around the world? How could she ensure that the company she hired to produce their toys would live up to Ace's standards? Would the other company pay a fair wage and not employ children? The questions seemed endless, but Jill needed to decide how to save the company.

Questions

1. Is sending jobs out of the country unethical?
2. Using consequential, rule-based, and character theories, evaluate Jill's options.

Experiential Exercises

2.1 International Orientations

1. Preparation (preclass)

Read the background on the International Orientation Scale and the case study "Office Supplies International—Marketing Associate," complete the ratings and questions, and fill out the self-assessment inventory.

2. Group Discussions

Groups of four to six people discuss their answers to the case study questions and their own responses to the self-assessment.

3. Class Discussion

Instructor leads a discussion on the International Orientation Scale and the difficulties and challenges of adjusting to a new culture. Why do some people adjust more easily than others? What can you do to adjust to a new culture? What can you regularly do that will help you adjust in the future to almost any new culture?

Office Supplies International—Marketing Associate*

Jonathan Fraser is a marketing associate for a large multinational corporation, Office Supplies International (OSI), in Buffalo, New York. He is being considered for a transfer to the international division of OSI. This position will require that he spend between one and three years working abroad in one of OSI's three foreign subsidiaries: OSI-France, OSI-Japan, or OSI-Australia. This transfer is considered a fast-track career move at OSI, and Jonathan feels honored to be in the running for the position.

Jonathan has been working at OSI since he graduated with his bachelor's degree in marketing ten years ago. He is married and has lived and worked in Buffalo all his life. Jonathan's parents are first-generation German Americans. His grandparents, although deceased, spoke only German at home and upheld many of their ethnic traditions. His parents, although quite "Americanized," have retained some of their German traditions. To communicate better with his grandparents, Jonathan took German in high school but never used it because his grandparents had passed away.

In college, Jonathan joined the German Club and was a club officer for two years. His other collegiate extracurricular activity was playing for the varsity baseball team. Jonathan still enjoys playing in a summer softball league with his college friends. Given his athletic interests, he volunteered to be the athletic programming coordinator at OSI, where he organizes the company's softball and volleyball teams. Jonathan has been making steady progress at OSI. Last year, he was named marketing associate of the year.

His wife, Sue, is also a Buffalo native. She teaches English literature at the high school in one of the middle-class suburbs of Buffalo. Sue took five years off after she had a baby but returned to teaching this year when Janine, their five-year-old daughter, started kindergarten. She is happy to be resuming her career. One or two nights a week, Sue volunteers at the city mission where she works as a career counselor and a basic skills trainer. For fun, she takes pottery and ethnic cooking classes.

Both Sue and Jonathan are excited about the potential transfer and accompanying pay raise. They are, however, also feeling apprehensive and cautious. Neither Sue nor Jonathan has ever lived away from their families in Buffalo, and Sue is concerned about giving up her newly reestablished career. Their daughter Janine has just started school, and Jonathan and Sue are uncertain whether living abroad is the best thing for her at her age.

Using the following three-point scale, try to rate Jonathan and Sue as potential expatriates. Write a sentence or two on why you gave the ratings you did.

Rating Scale

1. Based on this dimension, this person would adjust well to living abroad.
2. Based on this dimension, this person may or may not adjust well to living abroad.
3. Based on this dimension, this person would not adjust well to living abroad.

Jonathan's International Orientation

rating dimension	rating and reason for rating
International attitudes	
Foreign experiences	
Comfort with differences	
Participation in cultural events	

Sue's International Orientation

rating dimension	rating and reason for rating
International attitudes	
Foreign experiences	
Comfort with differences	
Participation in cultural events	

Discussion Questions: Office Supplies International

1. Imagine that you are the international human resource manager for OSI. Your job is to interview both Jonathan and Sue to determine whether they should be sent abroad. What are some of the questions you would ask? What critical information do you feel is missing? It might be helpful to role-play the three parts and evaluate your classmates' responses as Jonathan and Sue.
2. Suppose France is the country where they would be sent. To what extent would your ratings change? What else would you change about the way you are assessing the couple?
3. Now answer the same questions, except this time they are being sent to Japan. Repeat the exercise for Australia.
4. For those dimensions that you rated Sue and Jonathan either 2 or 3 (indicating that they might have a potential adjustment problem), what would you suggest for training and development? What might be included in a training program?
5. Reflect on your own life for a moment and give yourself a rating on each of the following dimensions. Try to justify why you rated yourself as you did. Do you feel that you would adjust well to living abroad? What might be difficult for you?

rating dimension	rating and reason for rating France, Japan, Australia (or other)
International attitudes	
Foreign experiences	
Comfort with differences	
Participation in cultural events	

6. Generally, what are some of the potential problems a dual-career couple might face? What are some of the solutions to those problems?
7. How would the ages of children affect the expatriate's assignment? At what age should the children's international orientations be assessed along with their parents?

International Orientation Scale

The following sample items are taken from the International Orientation Scale. Answer each question and give yourself a score for each dimension. The highest possible score for any dimension is 20 points.

Dimension 1: International Attitudes

Use the following scale to answer questions Q1 through Q4.

1 *Strongly agree*
2 *Agree somewhat*
3 *Maybe or unsure*
4 *Disagree somewhat*
5 *Strongly disagree*

Q1. Foreign language skills should be taught as early as elementary school. _____

Q2. Traveling the world is a priority in my life. _____

Q3. A yearlong overseas assignment (from my company) would be a fantastic opportunity for my family and me. _____

Q4. Other countries fascinate me. _____

Total Dimension 1 _____

Dimension 2: Foreign Experiences

Q1. I have studied a foreign language.

1 Never
2 For less than a year
3 For a year
4 For a few years
5 For several years

Q2. I am fluent in another language.

1 I don't know another language.
2 I am limited to very short and simple phrases.
3 I know basic grammatical structure and speak with a limited vocabulary.
4 I understand conversation on most topics.
5 I am very fluent in another language.

Q3. I have spent time overseas (traveling, studying abroad, etc.).

1 Never
2 About a week
3 A few weeks
4 A few months
5 Several months or years

Q4. I was overseas before the age of 18.

1 Never
2 About a week
3 A few weeks
4 A few months
5 Several months or years

Total Dimension 2 _____

Dimension 3: Comfort with Differences

Use the following scale for questions Q1 through Q4.

1	*Quite similar*
2	*Mostly similar*
3	*Somewhat different*
4	*Quite different*
5	*Extremely different*

Q1. My friends' career goals, interests, and education are . . . _____

Q2. My friends' ethnic backgrounds are . . . _____

Q3. My friends' religious affiliations are . . . _____

Q4. My friends' first languages are . . . _____

Total Dimension 3 _____

Dimension 4: Participation in Cultural Events

Use the following scale to answer questions Q1 through Q4.

1	*Never*
2	*Seldom*
3	*Sometimes*
4	*Frequently*
5	*As often as possible*

Q1. I eat at a variety of ethnic restaurants (e.g., Greek, Polynesian, Thai, German). _____

Q2. I watch the major networks' world news programs. _____

Q3. I attend ethnic festivals. _____

Q4. I visit art galleries and museums. _____

Total Dimension 4 _____

Self-Assessment Discussion Questions:

Do any of these scores suprise you?

Would you like to improve your international orientation?

If so, what could you do to change various aspects of your life?

*"Office Supplies International—Marketing Associate" by Paula Caligiuri. Copyright © 1994 by Paula Caligiuri, Ph.D. Information for the International Orientation Scale can be obtained by contacting Paula Caligiuri, Ph.D. at 732-445-5228 or e-mail: paula@caligiuri.com. Reprinted by permission of the author.

Dorothy Marcic and Sheila M. Puffer, *Management International: Cases, Exercises, and Readings* (Eagan, MN: West Publishing, 1994). *All rights reserved. May not be reproduced without written permission of the publisher.*

2.2 Ethical Dilemmas

Divide the class into five groups. Each group should choose one of the following scenarios and agree on a course of action.

1. Sam works for you. He is technically capable and a good worker, but he does not get along well with others in the work group. When Sam has an opportunity to transfer, you encourage him to take it. What would you say to Sam's potential supervisor when he asks about Sam?
2. Your boss has told you that you must reduce your work group by 30 percent. Which of the following criteria would you use to lay off workers?
   a. Lay off older, higher-paid employees.
   b. Lay off younger, lower-paid employees.
   c. Lay off workers based on seniority only.
   d. Lay off workers based on performance only.
3. You are an engineer, but you are not working on your company's Department of Transportation (DOT) project. One day you overhear a conversation in the cafeteria between the program manager and the project engineer that makes you reasonably sure a large contract will soon be given to the ABC Company to develop and manufacture a key DOT subsystem. ABC is a small firm, and its stock is traded over the counter. You feel sure that the stock will rise from its present $2.25 per share as soon as news of the DOT contract gets out. Would you go out and buy ABC's stock?
4. You are the project engineer working on the development of a small liquid rocket engine. You know that if you could achieve a throttling ratio greater than 8 to 1, your system would be considered a success and continue to receive funding support. To date, the best you have achieved is a 4-to-1 ratio. You have an unproven idea that you feel has a 50 percent chance of being successful. Your project is currently being reviewed to determine if it should be continued. You would like to continue it. How optimistically should you present the test results?
5. Imagine that you are the president of a company in a highly competitive industry. You learn that a competitor has made an important scientific discovery that is not patentable and will give that company an advantage that will substantially reduce the profits of your company for about a year. There is some hope of hiring one of the competitor's employees

who knows the details of the discovery. Would you try to hire this person?

Each group should present its scenario and chosen course of action to the class. The class should then evaluate the ethics of the course of action, using the following questions to guide discussion:

1. Are you following rules that are understood and accepted?
2. Are you comfortable discussing and defending your action?
3. Would you want someone to do this to you?
4. What if everyone acted this way?
5. Are there alternatives that rest on firmer ethical ground?

Scenarios adapted from R. A. DiBattista, "Providing a Rationale for Ethical Conduct from Alternatives Taken in Ethical Dilemmas," *Journal of General Psychology* 116 (1989): 207–214; discussion questions adapted with the permission of The Free Press, a Division of Simon & Schuster, Inc. from *The Manager as Negotiator: Bargaining for Cooperation and Competitive Gain* by David A. Lax and James K. Sebenius 0-02-918770-2. Copyright © 1986 by David A. Lax and James K. Sebenius.

TAKE 2

Biz Flix | Mr. Baseball

The New York Yankees trade aging baseball player Jack Elliot (Tom Selleck) to the Chunichi Dragons, a Japanese team. This lighthearted comedy traces Jack's bungling entry into Japanese culture and exposes his cultural misconceptions, which almost cost him everything—including his new girlfriend Hiroko Uchiyama (Aya Takanashi). Unknown to Jack, Hiroko's father is "The Chief" (Ken Takakura), the Chunichi Dragons' manager. After Jack slowly begins to understand Japanese culture and Japanese baseball, his teammates finally accept him. This film shows many examples of Japanese culture, especially its love for baseball.

The *Mr. Baseball* scene takes place after "The Chief" has removed Jack from a baseball game. It shows Jack dining with Hiroko and her grandmother (Mineko Yorozuya), grandfather (Jun Hamamura), and father. The film continues with a dispute between Jack and Hiroko. Jack also learns from "The Chief" what he must do to succeed on the team.

What to Watch for and Ask Yourself:

- Does Jack Elliot behave as if he had cross-cultural training before arriving in Japan?
- Is he culturally sensitive or insensitive?
- What do you propose that Jack Elliot do for the rest of his time in Japan?

Workplace Video | Meeting the Challenge of Diversity at Whirlpool

In today's global marketplace, managers must routinely interact with people of different cultures, languages, beliefs, and values. Recognizing diversity and the unique way people of different backgrounds communicate is essential to success in the international arena.

Whirlpool Corporation, the number-one name in home appliances, has a long history of managing diversity. Established in 1911, Whirlpool has become a global corporation with manufacturing locations on every major continent. Approximately 60 percent of Whirlpool's 68,000 employees work outside of North America, and those within North America represent a diverse mix of people.

Building a cohesive team of diverse individuals is one of the great challenges of management. Whirlpool's leaders are committed to cultivating a broad workforce, and that means eliminating glass ceilings and biases that discourage certain groups from participating fully in the company. Attaining these objectives is the job of Whirlpool's award-winning diversity program. To enter the program, workers join the particular employee-network group with which they self-identify. Once joined to a network, workers have access to career resources and training opportunities.

Although the diversity program is designed for employees, it also helps Whirlpool achieve specific business objectives, such as understanding the needs and desires of its global customer base. "Whirlpool has recognized that having diverse people making decisions and giving input to the factors that we consider on a daily basis is extremely important to the business," says Kathy Nelson, VP of Consumer & Appliance Care at Whirlpool. "It's important because we need to make sure that the people who are making business decisions are reflective of who our consumers are."

Mark McLane, director of Global Diversity and Inclusion, sees diversity as a vehicle through which Whirlpool can find innovative solutions to problems. "The greatest strength of our employee base today is its diversity—the diversity of thought and what that brings to our innovation processes," McLane remarks. "We've embedded innovation throughout the entire organization; we've really leveraged the strengths of each individual Whirlpool employee."

Discussion Questions

1. What are the three main objectives of Whirlpool's diversity networks?
2. What challenges do managers at Whirlpool face in establishing a diverse workplace? How might they respond to these challenges?
3. Do you think Whirlpool's encouragement of employee networks always leads to a culture of diversity and the formation of effective multicultural teams? Why or why not?

CASE

The Timberland Company: Challenges and Opportunities

The Timberland Company, headquartered in Stratham, New Hampshire, makes and markets footwear, apparel, and accessories. Its footwear includes hiking boots, boat shoes, sandals, outdoor casual footwear, and dress shoes. The apparel line includes socks, shirts, pants, and outerwear, whereas accessories involve such products as watches, sunglasses, and belts. Timberland sells its products around the world through department stores and athletic stores and operates over 220 company-owned and franchised outlets in the United States, Canada, Latin America, Europe, the Middle East, and Asia.[1]

Timberland has a strong international operation with a growing market in China; however, it has experienced increased labor costs and tariffs in Europe. In 2006 the tariff issue became very important due to the sourcing of approximately 30 percent of Timberland's total volume from factories in China and Vietnam. The company's international strength has been offset somewhat by its declining market fortunes in the United States. Timberland also faces increased competition globally, particularly from Nike and Adidas. From 2001 to 2005, Timberland had an average annual revenue growth of 7.5 percent, compared to the industry average of 9 percent during the same period. Moreover, revenue growth has been decelerating.[2] In 2006, Timberland had $1.6 billion in revenues that reflected growth in the business segments serving casual, outdoor, and industrial consumers. However, the boot business declined due to significant fashion changes that diminished demand for those products.[3]

Although Timberland experienced some market difficulty in 2006, it was still recognized as a great place to work. The company was honored by *Working Mother* magazine as "One of the Best Places to Work" and by *Fortune* magazine as "One of the 100 Best Companies to Work For."[4]

Timberland develops and uses technology to further its business interests and to benefit its customers and distributors. For example, Timberland uses innovative technology that enables customers to customize their footwear online. The company's configuration software allows shoppers to "specify so many product details—including colors, hardware, laces and typefaces for monogramming—that more than one million combinations are possible for any one base [footwear] style."[5] The results are visualized instantaneously on the customer's own computer. A company spokesperson observed, ". . . no one else out there has this technology. It was really important to us to include that because the challenge in the online environment is trying to replicate that tactile-visual experience of an offline environment."[6]

Another application of innovative technology occurred in the summer of 2005 with Timberland's test of its PreciseFit System in 54 stores in Europe, Asia, and the United States. The PreciseFit System, tested in the men's casual footwear category, enables Timberland to exactly fit footwear for the 60 percent of men who can't get an optimal fit otherwise and for those men—about 35 percent of the market—who have a half-size or greater difference between their left foot and right foot. Each pair of shoes comes with inserts that fit full and half-sizes in narrow, medium, and wide widths, thereby enabling retailers to more easily service hard-to-fit customers, maintain a smaller inventory, and have fewer lost sales.[7]

In addition to its efforts to run the business more effectively and efficiently, to provide customers with continually improving service, and to meaningfully support suppliers and distributors, Timberland is also committed to social and environmental causes. Part of its mission is to use "the resources, energy, and profits of a publicly traded footwear-and-apparel company to combat social ills, help the environment, and improve conditions for laborers around the globe."[8] Jeffrey Swartz, Timberland's CEO, believes that the best way to pursue social objectives is through a publicly traded company rather than through a privately owned company or a nonprofit organization because it forces commerce and justice—business interests and social/

environmental interests—to be enacted in a public and transparent manner.[9]

Timberland's social and environmental commitments and efforts are evident in its products and operations as well as in its relationships with suppliers and customers. In terms of its products and operations, Timberland practices full-disclosure labeling on its footwear. Every footwear box has a label describing the ecological impact with respect to the amount of energy used in the manufacture and distribution of each product. Timberland's goal is to decrease its ecological footprint by increasing the use of wind or solar power in the manufacture and distribution of its products. Future plans for full-disclosure packaging include labeling that details the environmental impact of the chemicals and organic materials contained in Timberland's products.[10]

In dealing with suppliers around the world, Timberland promotes fair labor practices and human rights. According to the company's Global Human Rights Standards, "[W]e're equally committed to improving the quality of life for our business partners' employees. Through our Code of Conduct program, Timberland works to ensure that our products are made in workplaces that are fair, safe and nondiscriminatory. Beyond training factory management, educating factory workers, and auditing for compliance with our Code of Conduct, we also partner with nongovernmental organizations and international agencies such as Verité, CARE, and Social Accountability International to help us develop programs focused on continuous improvement and sustainable change."[11] How does Timberland operationalize these standards? One way is by constructively engaging suppliers who commit labor infractions. Rather than immediately discharging such suppliers, Timberland works at getting them to change their policies so as to keep the workers employed.[12]

Timberland engages in similar influence attempts with its customers. For instance, in making a sales presentation to executives from McDonald's Corporation regarding the possibility of Timberland becoming the contract supplier of new uniforms for the fast food giant, CEO Swartz used a novel approach. To the surprise of the McDonald's executives, he did not provide product prototypes or pitch the company's creativity or craftsmanship. Instead, he talked enthusiastically about Timberland's corporate culture and what the company was doing in terms of social, environmental, and labor commitments. Swartz's message was that he expected Timberland's culture would rub off on McDonald's, thereby helping McDonald's to build a unified, purposeful, motivated workforce.[13]

Can commerce and justice—business interests and social/environmental interests—peacefully coexist and mutually reinforce each other for Timberland and its stakeholders over the long term?

Discussion Questions

1. Jeffrey Swartz's approach to running Timberland is based on the belief that business success is compatible with a corporate social and environmental responsibility. Do you share this belief? Why or why not?
2. How does Timberland's commitment to social and environmental responsibility influence the ways in which it deals with the diversity, technology, and globalization challenges that it faces?
3. Consider the ethical, diversity, technology, and globalization challenges that have confronted Timberland. How has the company converted these challenges into opportunities?
4. What are some advantages and disadvantages of Timberland's attempts to influence suppliers and customers regarding corporate social and environmental responsibility? How can these influence efforts help Timberland as it seeks to deal with its own ethical, diversity, technology, and globalization challenges?

SOURCE: This case was written by Michael K. McCuddy, The Louis S. and Mary L. Morgal Chair of Christian Business Ethics and Professor of Management, College of Business Administration, Valparaiso University.

BP: Facing Multiple Challenges (A)

During its 100-year history, BP PLC has grown from a local oil company into a global energy group that employs over 96,000 people and, on a daily basis, serves approximately 13 million customers in over 100 nations.[1] In the early 1900s, struggling against the elements and a variety of disappointments, George Reynolds and a group of explorers searched for seven years before discovering oil in Persia. To capitalize on their discovery, the Anglo-Persian Oil Company was formed. This company would eventually become BP. In the years leading up to World War I, the British government sought to secure a reliable source of Oil for its navy, consequently becoming a major investor in the Anglo-Persian Oil Company. Although British Petroleum was created by a German firm to market products in Britain, Britain seized those assets during World War I and sold them to the Anglo-Persian oil Company. Thus, British Petroleum became a company largely owned by the British government.[2]

Over the ensuing decades, British Petroleum continued to grow. Then in the 1970s, political changes in the Middle East had profound effects on world oil supplies. Nearly every oil-rich nation in the Middle East announced the immediate or impending nationalization of their petroleum resources. These moves profoundly influenced BP's subsequent corporate strategy, which to that point had been entirely focused on the supply of Middle Eastern oil. About the same time, the company discovered and began developing a major oil field in Prudhoe Bay, Alaska, and an oil field off the coast of Scotland. Development of the Prudhoe Bay oil field and building the Trans-Alaska Pipeline System taught BP "the value of dealing with potentially contentious environmental considerations at the very start of major projects."[3]

With no refineries or distribution outlets in the United States, BP acquired a stake in Standard Oil of Ohio (Sohio) in order to bring Alaskan products to market. In 1987, two major events occurred for BP. First, the company acquired complete ownership and control of Sohio and incorporated it into BP America. Second, the British government completed privatization of the company, selling the last of the BP shares it owned.[4] As a government-owned entity, BP was a rigid, hierarchical company. However, this dramatically changed when the company was split into 150 business units with managers' pay being linked to their unit's profitability. In this milieu, an aggressive and entrepreneurial corporate culture was born.[5]

Enter John Browne

In 1995, John P. Browne became CEO of BP and began pursuing a strategy of vigorous growth through mergers and acquisitions. During the next several years, BP acquired Amoco, ARCO, and Burmah Castrol while also negotiating oil deals in Russia. In the process, BP was transformed into a global force in the oil industry, becoming the second largest major oil company in the world, behind ExxonMobil.[6] Browne was the first leader in the oil industry to acknowledge the problem of climate change and the need for the oil industry as a whole to recognize this problem and deal with it appropriately and effectively.[7] BP also became engaged in significant efforts to develop alternative energy sources, including biofuels, solar energy, and hydrogen fuels.[8] By 2003, under Browne's guidance and with the help of advertising company Ogilvy & Mather, BP rebranded itself—BP was to stand for *Beyond Petroleum.*[9] With this orientation, BP reinforced its commitment to the environment and the development of alternative energy sources.

Current Challenges and Opportunities

In the past few years, however, BP has encountered several challenges that have threatened its expressed commitments to the environment and the development of alternative energy sources. Some of these challenges are in the United States; others are elsewhere in the global community. Most prominent among the American challenges are safety issues, charges of market manipulation, and environmental pollution.

In March 2005, an explosion at BP's Texas City, Texas, refinery—the company's largest in the United States—claimed 15 lives and injured 180 people. An investigation by the United States Chemical Safety Board attributed the explosion to BP management's "check-book mentality" with its emphasis on cutting costs, and to the failure of management to acknowledge warnings of safety problems and provide effective safety oversight.[10] Another investigation, headed by James Baker, the noted American elder statesman and problem solver, concluded that the safety budget was inadequate and safety staff was overstretched.[11] BP was faulted for not learning the lessons of poor safety management following refinery accidents in Grangemouth, Scotland, in 2000.[12] To the company's credit, it has offered to settle all lawsuits arising from the Texas City disaster and initially set aside $1.6 billion for victim compensation. This is in contrast to ExxonMobil, which is still engaged in a legal battle over liability for the 1989 Alaskan oil spill from the *Exxon Valdez*.[13]

In March 2006, a significant oil spill occurred on BP's Prudhoe Bay pipeline due to its corrosion. Standard operating procedure in the industry is for pipelines to be inspected every five years with "a smart-pig"—a high-tech device used for testing the internal wear and tear of the pipeline.[14] Although BP had conducted external inspections, the company admitted that it had not conducted a smart-pig inspection of the Alaska pipeline since 1992, a test that would have enabled the company to monitor the pipeline's health over time.[15] Jon Birger, writing in *Fortune* magazine, observes that "BP's current pipeline woes are receiving disproportionate attention because of when and where they occurred—at a time of high prices and in a place where every accident is an argument against further Alaska drilling."[16]

In June 2006, the Commodity Futures Trading Commission (CFTC), which oversees energy trading in the United States, charged BP's North American subsidiary and traders with manipulating the propane market in February 2004. Although it denied any wrongdoing, BP nonetheless fired some of the traders who were involved in the alleged scandal.[17]

BP's refinery in Whiting, Indiana has been the scene of several major controversies in 2006 and 2007. In November 2006, U.S. health and safety regulators imposed a $384,000 fine on BP for deficient lights and wiring, wrongly set heat alarms, and untested fire hydrants.[18] In April 2007, a fire at the Whiting refinery cut daily production in half. The fire was caused by a compressor unit that was inspected shortly before the outbreak of the fire. Employees at the refinery had previously "complained of a 'run until it breaks' approach at the plant."[19]

The Whiting refinery, BP's second largest in the United States, is located along the shores of Lake Michigan in northwest Indiana, just a few miles east of the Indiana/Illinois border. In late spring of 2007, BP sought and received a permit from Indiana regulators to increase the amount of pollutants that the Whiting refinery discharges into Lake Michigan. The permit allows BP to discharge an average of 1,584 pounds of ammonia and 4,925 pounds of suspended solids into Lake Michigan on a daily basis, both significant increases over current discharge levels. The additional pollutants are viewed as a threat to human health as well as fish and wildlife. Chicago and numerous other communities take their drinking water from Lake Michigan. The Whiting refinery is already one of the largest sources of industrial pollution discharged into Lake Michigan. An Illinois Congressman commented that BP apparently stands for "Back to Pollution."[20]

In addition to its American challenges, BP faces significant energy supply challenges on a global basis. Perhaps the most notable are with respect to deals in Russia and Venezuela. Under Browne, BP partnered with TNK to develop energy resources in Eastern Siberia. Investors now worry that BP may be pressured by the Russian government into giving up some of its interests in the Kovykta gas fields.[21] Officials of the Russian government charge that TNK-BP has not fulfilled the terms of its license due to underproduction in the Kovykta fields. BP counters that since TNK-BP is barred from exporting gas from Russia, there is no market for the volume of production required by the license.[22] BP's energy exploration and oil supplies may also be significantly disrupted in Venezuela, as President Hugo Chavez implements his strategy of nationalizing that country's oil production. Although in late June 2007, ExxonMobil and Conoco Phillips decided to pull out of Venezuela, BP, along with three other international oil companies, decided to "stick it out [in Venezuela] despite the unilateral abrogation of their contracts."[23]

BP's handling of these challenges will determine whether they become opportunities for growth or threats to future success. The company's approach will be influenced, perhaps even complicated, by the mantle of executive leadership changing on May 1, 2007, with John Browne's resignation and Tony Hayward's assumption of the CEO position. As J. Robinson West, head of a Washington-based energy consulting firm, observed, "BP is the most challenged of the super majors at this time."[24]

Discussion Questions

1. What lessons about leading people and managing organizations does BP provide?
2. Which of the four management challenges—globalization; leading a diverse workforce; ethics, character, and personal integrity; or technological innovation—have had the greatest impact on BP in the past few years? Explain your answer.
3. Which of the management challenges are likely to have the greatest impact on BP's future operations? Explain your answer.
4. What advice would you give Tony Hayward as he takes over the helm of BP? Why would you give this advice?
5. What can BP do to transform its challenges into opportunities?

SOURCE: This case was written by Michael K. McCuddy, The Louis S. and Mary L. Morgal Chair of Christian Business Ethics and Professor of Management, College of Business Administration, Valparaiso University.

© DIGITAL VISION

Individual Processes and Behavior

CHAPTER 3

Personality, Perception, and Attribution

LEARNING OBJECTIVES

After reading this chapter, you should be able to do the following:

1 Describe individual differences and their importance in understanding behavior.

2 Define *personality*.

3 Identify several personality characteristics and their influences on behavior in organizations.

4 Give examples of each personality characteristic from your own work experience and how you would apply your knowledge in managing personality differences.

5 Discuss Carl Jung's contribution to our understanding of individual differences, and explain how his theory is used in the Myers-Briggs Type Indicator.

6 Evaluate the importance of the MBTI to managers.

7 Define *social perception* and explain how characteristics of the perceiver, the target, and the situation affect it.

8 Identify five common barriers to social perception.

9 Explain the attribution process and how attributions affect managerial behavior.

10 Evaluate the accuracy of managerial attributions from the standpoint of attribution biases and errors.

THINKING AHEAD: SERGEY BRIN: A REBELLIOUS CHILD BECOMES ONE OF THE MOST IMPORTANT PERSONS ON THE WEB

Sergey Brin cofounded Google while he and Larry Page were students at Stanford. In 2006, *Forbes* magazine named Brin the twelfth richest person in the United States with a net worth of $14.1 billion. So what is the story behind the young entrepreneur's rise to the top?

Brin's parents emigrated from the Soviet Union in 1979. His father is a mathematics professor at University of Maryland, and his mother is a research scientist at NASA's Goddard Space Flight Center. Such educated parents undoubtedly passed on some of their appreciation for science and mathematics to their son. Brin himself contends that his Russian heritage and skepticism toward authority drove his rebellious side. This aspect of his personality may have led him and Page to create a company that invented a new way of finding information on the Internet.

Brin also defies the stereotypical image of a successful CEO. He and Page have consistently highlighted the relaxed corporate culture at Google. He rarely wears business suits to work, and his behavior is full of boyish enthusiasm and restless energy. He shares an office space with Larry Page that looks like a playroom full of gadgets and monitors instead of a sleek corporate office.

In the Looking Back feature, you'll see how Sergey Brin's personality affects the culture and tremendous success of Google.[1]

INDIVIDUAL DIFFERENCES AND ORGANIZATIONAL BEHAVIOR

(1) Describe individual differences and their importance in understanding behavior.

In this chapter and continuing in Chapter 4, we explore the concept of *individual differences*. Individuals are unique in terms of their skills, abilities, personalities, perceptions, attitudes, emotions, and ethics. These are just a few of the ways people may be similar to or different from one another. Individual differences represent the essence of the challenge of management, because no two people are completely alike. Managers face the challenge of working with people who possess a multitude of individual characteristics, so the more managers understand those differences, the better they can work with others. Figure 3.1 illustrates how individual differences affect human behavior.

The basis for understanding individual differences stems from Lewin's early contention that behavior is a function of the person and the environment.[2] Lewin

individual differences The way in which factors such as skills, abilities, personalities, perceptions, attitudes, values, and ethics differ from one individual to another.

FIGURE 3.1 Variables Influencing Individual Behavior

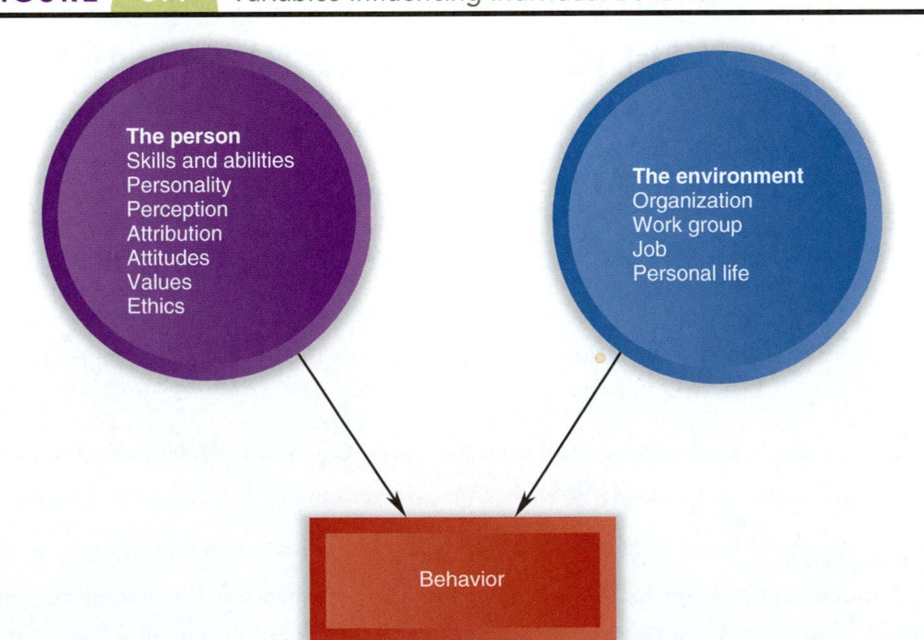

expressed this idea in an equation: $B = f(P, E)$, where B = behavior, P = person, and E = environment. This idea has been developed by the *interactional psychology* approach.[3] Basically, it says that in order to understand human behavior, we must know something about the person and the situation. There are four basic propositions of interactional psychology:

1. Behavior is a function of a continuous, multidirectional interaction between the person and the situation.
2. The person is active in this process and both changes, and is changed by, situations.
3. People vary in many characteristics, including cognitive, affective, motivational, and ability factors.
4. Two interpretations of situations are important: the objective situation and the person's subjective view of the situation.[4]

The interactional psychology approach points out the need to study both persons and situations. We will focus on personal and situational factors throughout the text. The person consists of individual differences such as those we emphasize in this chapter and Chapter 4: personality, perception, attribution, attitudes, emotions, and ethics. The situation consists of the environment the person operates in, and it can include things like the organization, work group, personal life situation, job characteristics, and many other environmental influences. One important and fascinating individual difference is personality.

SKILLS AND ABILITIES

There are many skills and abilities that relate to work outcomes. *General mental ability* (*GMA*) was introduced by Spearman (1904)[5] almost a hundred years ago. It is defined as an individual's innate cognitive intelligence. It was the single best predictor of work performance across many occupations studied both here in the United States[6] and across different cultures.[7]

PERSONALITY

(2) Define *personality.*

What makes an individual behave in consistent ways in a variety of situations? Personality is an individual difference that lends consistency to a person's behavior. *Personality* is defined as a relatively stable set of characteristics that influence an individual's behavior. Although there is debate about the determinants of personality, there appear to be several origins. One determinant is heredity, and some interesting studies have supported this position. Identical twins who are separated at birth and raised apart in very different situations have been found to share personality traits and job preferences. For example, about half of the variation in traits like extraversion, impulsiveness, and flexibility was found to be genetically determined; that is, identical twins who grew up in different environments shared these traits.[8] For example, the opening discussion of Sergey Brin highlights his parents' penchant for the hard sciences that seems to have fed his own interest in computer sciences. In addition, the twins held similar jobs.[9] Thus, there does appear to be a genetic influence on personality.

Another determinant of personality is the environment a person is exposed to. Family, culture, education, and other environmental forces shape personality. Personality is therefore shaped by both heredity and environment.

interactional psychology
The psychological approach that says in order to understand human behavior, we must know something about the person and about the situation.

personality
A relatively stable set of characteristics that influence an individual's behavior.

Personality Theories

Two major theories of personality are the trait theory and the integrative approach. Each theory has influenced the study of personality in organizations.

Trait Theory Some early personality researchers believed that to understand individuals, we must break down behavior patterns into a series of observable traits. According to *trait theory*, combining these traits into a group forms an individual's personality. Gordon Allport, a leading trait theorist, saw traits as broad, general guides that lend consistency to behavior.[10] Thousands of traits have been identified over the years. Raymond Cattell, another prominent trait theorist, identified sixteen traits that formed the basis for differences in individual behavior. He described traits in bipolar adjective combinations such as self-assured/apprehensive, reserved/outgoing, and submissive/dominant.[11]

Big Five Personality Model

Personality theorists have long argued that in order to understand individual behavior, people's behavioral patterns can be broken down into a series of observable traits. One popular personality classification is the "Big Five." The Big Five traits include extraversion, agreeableness, conscientiousness, emotional stability, and openness to experience.[12] These are broad, global traits that are associated with behaviors at work. Descriptions of the Big Five appear in Table 3.1.

From preliminary research, we know that introverted and conscientious employees are less likely to be absent from work.[13] In making peer evaluations, individuals with high agreeableness tend to rate others more leniently, while individuals with high conscientiousness tend to be tougher as raters.[14] Extraverts tend to have higher salaries, receive more promotions, and are more satisfied with their careers.[15] Across many occupations, people who are conscientious are more motivated and are high performers.[16] Viewing more specific occupations, however, shows that different patterns of the Big Five factors are related to high performance. For customer service jobs, individuals high in emotional stability, agreeableness, and openness to experience perform best. For managers, emotional stability and extraversion are traits of

TABLE 3.1 The Big Five Personality Traits

Trait	Description
Extraversion	The person is gregarious, assertive, and sociable (as opposed to reserved, timid, and quiet).
Agreeableness	The person is cooperative, warm, and agreeable (rather than cold, disagreeable, and antagonistic).
Conscientiousness	The person is hardworking, organized, and dependable (as opposed to lazy, disorganized, and unreliable).
Emotional stability	The person is calm, self-confident, and cool (as opposed to insecure, anxious, and depressed).
Openness to experience	The person is creative, curious, and cultured (rather than practical with narrow interests).

SOURCES: P. T. Costa and R. R. McCrae, *The NEO-PI Personality Inventory* (Odessa, Fla.: Psychological Assessment Resources, 1992); J. F. Salgado, "The Five Factor Model of Personality and Job Performance in the European Community," *Journal of Applied Psychology* 82 (1997): 30–43.

trait theory
The personality theory that states that in order to understand individuals, we must break down behavior patterns into a series of observable traits.

SCIENCE

Does Your Personality Affect Life Outcomes?

This question has long perplexed personality researchers. As noted earlier, some personality characteristics like conscientiousness and self efficacy have been shown to affect job performance. Are there more far-reaching impacts of an individuals' personality?

The answer seems to be a resounding yes. In a recent comprehensive review of research on the Big Five personality model, researchers predicted that personality characteristics could affect important individual outcomes (e.g., happiness, spirituality and virtues, depression, longevity, risky behavior), interpersonal outcomes (e.g., dating variety, attractiveness, status, family satisfaction) and social and institutional outcomes (e.g., occupational choice and performance, volunteerism, leadership, antisocial and criminal behavior).

They found that extraverts, for example, are happier, more satisfied with romantic relationships, and less likely to be depressed. Agreeable individuals are less likely to have heart disease, and more likely to have a positive leadership style. Conscientious people are healthier and enjoy greater occupational success, and they are less likely to engage in criminal or antisocial behaviors. Emotionally stable individuals experience greater job satisfaction, commitment, and occupational success. Those who are open to new experiences tend to choose occupations that involve creative and artistic skills, but they are also more likely to engage in substance abuse.

So it appears that the impact of the Big Five goes beyond the workplace and affects many facets of life.

SOURCE: D. J. Ozer and V. Benet-Martínez, "Personality and the Prediction of Consequential Outcomes," *Annual Review of Psychology* 57 (2006): 401–421.

top performers.[17] Recent research indicates that in work teams, the minimum level of agreeableness in a team as well as the mean levels of conscientiousness and openness to experience had a strong effect on overall team performance.[18]

Read about how the Big Five personality traits affect a broad range of personal and work outcomes in the Science feature above. The Big Five framework has also been applied across cultures. It has held up well among Spanish and Mexican populations.[19] It remains to be seen whether or not the Big Five traits will emerge in studies of cultures that are extremely different from Western cultures.[20]

The trait approach has been the subject of considerable criticism. Some theorists argue that simply identifying traits is not enough; instead, personality is dynamic and not completely stable. Further, early trait theorists tended to ignore the influence of situations.[21] Also, the trait theory tends to ignore process—that is, how we get from a trait to a particular outcome.

Integrative Approach Recently, researchers have taken a broader, more *integrative approach* to the study of personality.[22] To capture its influence on behavior, personality is described as a composite of the individual's psychological processes. Personality dispositions include emotions, cognitions, attitudes, expectancies, and fantasies.[23] *Dispositions,* in this approach, simply mean the tendencies of individuals to respond to situations in consistent ways. Influenced by both genetics and experiences, dispositions can be modified. The integrative approach focuses on both person (dispositions) and situational variables as combined predictors of behavior.

integrative approach
The broad theory that describes personality as a composite of an individual's psychological processes.

Personality Characteristics in Organizations

3 Identify several personality characteristics and their influences on behavior in organizations.

Managers should learn as much as possible about personality in order to understand their employees. Hundreds of personality characteristics have been identified. We have selected three characteristics because of their particular influences on individual behavior in organizations: core self-evaluations (CSE), self-monitoring, and

YOU 3.1

What's Your Locus of Control?

Below is a short scale that can give you an idea of your locus of control. For each of the four items, circle either choice a or choice b.

1. a. Becoming a success is a matter of hard work; luck has little or nothing to do with it.
   b. Getting a good job depends mainly on being in the right place at the right time.
2. a. The average citizen can have an influence in government decisions.
   b. This world is run by the few people in power, and there is not much the little guy can do about it.
3. a. As far as world affairs are concerned, most of us are the victims of forces we can neither understand nor control.
   b. By taking an active part in political and social affairs, people can control world events.
4. a. With enough effort we can wipe out political corruption.
   b. It is difficult for people to have much control over the things politicians do in office.

Scoring Key:

The internal locus of control answers are:
1a, 2a, 3b, 4a
The external locus of control answers are:
1b, 2b, 3a, 4b

Determine which category you circled most frequently using the key to the left. This gives you an approximation of your locus of control.

SOURCES: T. Adeyemi-Bello, "Validating Rotter's Locus of Control Scale with a Sample of Not-for-Profit Leaders," *Management Research News* 24 (2001): 25–35; J. B. Rotter, "Generalized Expectancies for Internal vs. External Locus of Control of Reinforcement," *Psychological Monographs* 80, whole No. 609 (1966).

4 Give examples of each personality characteristic from your own work experience and how you would apply your knowledge in managing personality differences.

positive/negative affect. Because these characteristics affect performance at work, managers need to have a working knowledge of them.

Core Self-Evaluation (CSE) Core self-evaluation (CSE) is a broad set of personality traits that refers to self-concept.[24] It is comprised of locus of control, self-esteem, generalized self-efficacy, and emotional stability. CSE has been found to predict both goal-directed behavior and performance,[25] even in non-U.S. cultures (e.g., Japan).[26] Each characteristic comprising CSE with the exception of emotional stability (as we discussed in the Big Five approach) is addressed next.

Locus of Control An individual's generalized belief about internal (self) versus external (situation or others) control is called *locus of control*. People who believe they control what happens to them are said to have an internal locus of control, whereas people who believe that circumstances or other people control their fate have an external locus of control.[27] Research on locus of control has strong implications for organizations. Internals (those with an internal locus of control) have been found to have higher job satisfaction and performance, to be more likely to assume managerial positions, and to prefer participative management styles.[28] For example, Sergey Brin's parents emigrated from Russia because they believed they would have greater control over their destinies in the United Sates. This action reflects internal locus of control. They believed they could have more control of their destiny here in the United States. You can assess your locus of control in You 3.1.

locus of control
An individual's generalized belief about internal control (self-control) versus external control (control by the situation or by others).

Internals and externals have similar positive reactions to being promoted, which include high job satisfaction, job involvement, and organizational commitment. The difference between the two is that internals continue to be happy long after the promotion, whereas externals' joy over the promotion is short-lived. This might occur because externals do not believe their own performance led to the promotion.[29]

Knowing about locus of control can prove valuable to managers. Because internals believe they control what happens to them, they will want to exercise control in their work environment. Allowing internals considerable voice in how work is performed is important. Internals will not react well to being closely supervised. Externals, in contrast, may prefer a more structured work setting, and they may be more reluctant to participate in decision making.

Self-Efficacy *General self-efficacy* is a person's overall view of himself/herself as being able to perform effectively in a wide variety of situations.[30] Employees with high general self-efficacy have more confidence in their job-related abilities and other personal resources (i.e., energy, influence over others, etc.) that help them function effectively on the job. People with low general self-efficacy often feel ineffective at work and may express doubts about performing a new task well. Previous success or performance is one of the most important determinants of self-efficacy. People who have positive beliefs about their efficacy for performance are more likely to attempt difficult tasks, to persist in overcoming obstacles, and to experience less anxiety when faced with adversity.[31] People with high self-efficacy also value the ability to provide input, or "voice," at work. Because they are confident in this capability, they value the opportunity to participate.[32] High self-efficacy has also been recently related to higher job satisfaction and performance.

COURTESY OF PENGUIN GROUPS (USA) INC.

Employees with high general self-efficacy have more confidence in their job-related abilities and personal resources. This "I think I can" attitude helps them function effectively on the job.

There is another form of self-efficacy, called task-specific self-efficacy, which we will cover in Chapter 6. *Task-specific self-efficacy* is a person's belief that he or she can perform a specific task ("I believe I can do this sales presentation today"). In contrast, general self-efficacy is broader ("I believe I can perform well in just about any part of the job").

Self-Esteem *Self-esteem* is an individual's general feeling of self-worth. Individuals with high self-esteem have positive feelings about themselves, perceive themselves to have strengths as well as weaknesses, and believe their strengths are more important than their weaknesses.[33] Individuals with low self-esteem view themselves negatively. They are more strongly affected by what other people think of them, and they compliment individuals who give them positive feedback while cutting down people who give them negative feedback.[34]

Evaluations from other people affect our self-esteem. For example, you might be liked for who you are or for your achievements. Being liked for who you are is more stable, and people who have this type of self-esteem are less defensive and more honest with themselves. Being liked for your achievement is more unstable; it waxes and wanes depending on how high your achievements are.[35]

A person's self-esteem affects a host of other attitudes and has important implications for behavior in organizations. People with high self-esteem perform better and are more satisfied with their jobs.[36] For example, a recent study of 288 R&D engineers from four organizations found that self-esteem predicted supervisor ratings of job performance. This research indicates that self-esteem might be important to performance in knowledge-based occupations.[37] When they are involved in a job search, those with high self-esteem seek out higher-status jobs.[38] A work team made up of such individuals is more likely to be successful than a team with low or average self-esteem.[39]

general self-efficacy
An individual's general belief that he or she is capable of meeting job demands in a wide variety of situations.

self-esteem
An individual's general feeling of self-worth.

Very high self-esteem may be too much of a good thing. When people with high self-esteem find themselves in stressful situations, they may brag inappropriately.[40] This may be viewed negatively by others, who see spontaneous boasting as egotistical. Very high self-esteem may also lead to overconfidence and to relationship conflicts with others who may not evaluate this behavior favorably.[41] Individuals with high self-esteem may shift their social identities to protect themselves when they do not live up to some standard. Take two students, Denise and Teresa, for example. If Denise outperforms Teresa on a statistics exam, Teresa may convince herself that Denise is not really a good person to compare against because Denise is an engineering major and Teresa is a physical education major. Teresa's high self-esteem is protecting her from this unfavorable comparison.[42]

Self-esteem may be strongly affected by situations. Success tends to raise self-esteem, whereas failure tends to lower it. Given that high self-esteem is generally a positive characteristic, managers should encourage employees to raise their self-esteem by giving them appropriate challenges and opportunities for success. These three characteristics, along with the effects of emotional stability as discussed in the section on the Big Five, then, constitute an important personality trait known as core self-evaluations. CSE is a strong predictor of both job satisfaction and job performance next only to GMA.[43]

Self-Monitoring A characteristic with great potential for affecting behavior in organizations is *self-monitoring*—the extent to which people base their behavior on cues from other people and situations.[44] High self-monitors pay attention to what is appropriate in particular situations and to the behavior of other people, and they behave accordingly. Low self-monitors, in contrast, are not as vigilant to situational cues and act from internal states rather than paying attention to the situation. As a result, the behavior of low self-monitors is consistent across situations. High self-monitors, because their behavior varies with the situation, appear to be more unpredictable and less consistent. One study amongst managers of a recruitment firm found that high self-monitors were more likely to offer emotional help to others in dealing with work related anxiety. Low self-monitors, on the hand, even when tasked with managerial responsibilities were less likely to offer such emotional support and help.[44a] You can use You 3.2 to assess your own self-monitoring tendencies.

Research is currently focusing on the effects of self-monitoring in organizations. In one study, the authors tracked the careers of 139 MBAs for five years to see whether high self-monitors were more likely to be promoted, change employers, or make a job-related geographic move. The results were "yes" to each question. High self-monitors get promoted because they accomplish tasks through meeting the expectations of others and because they seek out central positions in social networks.[45] They are also more likely to use self-promotion to make others aware of their skills and accomplishments.[46] However, the high self-monitor's flexibility may not be suited for every job, and the tendency to move may not fit every organization.[47] Because high self-monitors base their behavior on cues from others and from the situation, they demonstrate higher levels of managerial self-awareness. This means that, as managers, they assess their own workplace behavior accurately.[48] Managers who are high self-monitors are also good at reading their employees' needs and changing the way they interact with employees depending on those needs.[49]

self-monitoring
The extent to which people base their behavior on cues from other people and situations.

Although research on self-monitoring in organizations is in its early stages, we can speculate that high self-monitors respond more readily to work group norms, organizational culture, and supervisory feedback than do low self-monitors, who

YOU 3.2

Are You a High or Low Self-Monitor?

For the following items, circle T (true) if the statement is characteristic of your behavior. Circle F (false) if the statement does not reflect your behavior.

1. I find it hard to imitate the behavior of other people. T F
2. At parties and social gatherings, I do not attempt to do or say things that others will like. T F
3. I can only argue for ideas that I already believe. T F
4. I can make impromptu speeches even on topics about which I have almost no information. T F
5. I guess I put on a show to impress or entertain others. T F
6. I would probably make a good actor. T F
7. In a group of people, I am rarely the center of attention. T F
8. In different situations and with different people, I often act like very different persons. T F
9. I am not particularly good at making other people like me. T F
10. I am not always the person I appear to be. T F
11. I would not change my opinions (or the way I do things) in order to please others or win their favor. T F
12. I have considered being an entertainer. T F
13. I have never been good at games like charades or at improvisational acting. T F
14. I have trouble changing my behavior to suit different people and different situations. T F
15. At a party, I let others keep the jokes and stories going. T F
16. I feel a bit awkward in company and do not show up quite as well as I should. T F
17. I can look anyone in the eye and tell a lie with a straight face (if it is for a good cause). T F
18. I may deceive people by being friendly when I really dislike them. T F

Scoring:

To score this questionnaire, give yourself 1 point for each of the following items that you answered T (true): 4, 5, 6, 8, 10, 12, 17, and 18. Now give yourself 1 point for each of the following items that you answered F (false): 1, 2, 3, 7, 9, 11, 13, 14, 15, and 16. Add both subtotals to find your overall score. If you scored 11 or above, you are probably a *high self-monitor.* If you scored 10 or under, you are probably a *low self-monitor.*

SOURCE: From *Public Appearances, Private Realities: The Psychology of Self-Monitoring* by M. Snyder. Copyright © 1987 by W. H. Freeman and Company. Used with permission.

adhere more to internal guidelines for behavior ("I am who I am"). In addition, high self-monitors may be enthusiastic participants in the trend toward work teams because of their ability to assume flexible roles.

Positive/Negative Affect Recently, researchers have explored the effects of persistent mood dispositions at work. Individuals who focus on the positive aspects of themselves, other people, and the world in general are said to have *positive affect*.[50] In contrast, those who accentuate the negative in themselves, others, and the world are said to possess *negative affect* (also referred to as negative affectivity).[51] Positive affect is linked with job satisfaction, which we discuss at length in Chapter 4. Individuals with positive affect are more satisfied with their jobs.[52] In addition, those with positive affect are more likely to help others at work and also engage in more organizational citizenship behaviors (OCBs).[53] Employees with positive affect are also absent from work less often.[54] Positive affect has also been linked to more life satisfaction and better performance across a variety of life and work domains.[55]

positive affect
An individual's tendency to accentuate the positive aspects of himself or herself, other people, and the world in general.

negative affect
An individual's tendency to accentuate the negative aspects of himself or herself, other people, and the world in general.

Individuals with negative affect report more work stress.[56] Individual affect also influences the work group. Positive individual affect produces positive team affect, which leads to more cooperation and less conflict within the team.[57] Leader affectivity can have an impact on subordinate outcomes. For example, a recent study of leaders and subordinates found that leader negative affectivity had a negative effect on subordinate attitudinal outcomes such as organizational commitment, job satisfaction, and anxiety.[58]

Positive affect is a definite asset in work settings. Managers can do several things to promote this trait, including allowing participative decision making and providing pleasant working conditions. We need to know more about inducing positive affect in the workplace.

The characteristics previously described are but a few of the personality characteristics that affect behavior and performance in organizations. Negative affect, for example, affects work stress, as you'll see in Chapter 7. Another personality characteristic related to stress is Type A behavior, also presented in Chapter 7. Other personality characteristics are woven in throughout the book. Can managers predict the behavior of their employees by knowing their personalities? Not completely. You may recall that the interactional psychology model (Figure 3.1) requires both person and situation variables to predict behavior. Another idea to remember in predicting behavior is the strength of situational influences. Some situations are *strong situations* in that they overwhelm the effects of individual personalities. These situations are interpreted in the same way by different individuals, evoke agreement on the appropriate behavior in the situation, and provide cues to appropriate behavior. A performance appraisal session is an example of a strong situation. Employees know to listen to their boss and to contribute when asked to do so.

A weak situation, in contrast, is one that is open to many interpretations. It provides few cues to appropriate behavior and no obvious rewards for one behavior over another. Thus, individual personalities have a stronger influence in weak situations than in strong situations. An informal meeting without an agenda can be seen as a weak situation.

Organizations present combinations of strong and weak situations; therefore, personality has a stronger effect on behavior in some situations than in others.[59]

Measuring Personality

Several methods can be used to assess personality. These include projective tests, behavioral measures, and self-report questionnaires.

The *projective test* is one method used to measure personality. In these tests, individuals are shown a picture, abstract image, or photo and are asked to describe what they see or tell a story about it. The rationale behind projective tests is that each individual responds to the stimulus in a way that reflects his or her unique personality. The Rorschach inkblot test is a projective test commonly used to assess personality.[60] Like other projective tests, however, it has low reliability. The individual being assessed may look at the same picture and see different things at different times. Also, the assessor may apply his or her own biases in interpreting the information about the individual's personality.

There are *behavioral measures* of personality as well. Measuring an individual's behavior involves observing it in a controlled situation. We might assess a person's sociability, for example, by counting the number of times he or she approaches strangers at a party. The behavior is scored in some manner to produce an index of personality. Some potential problems with behavioral measures include the observer's ability

strong situation
A situation that overwhelms the effects of individual personalities by providing strong cues for appropriate behavior.

projective test
A personality test that elicits an individual's response to abstract stimuli.

behavioral measures
Personality assessments that involve observing an individual's behavior in a controlled situation.

to stay focused and the way the observer interprets the behavior. In addition, some people behave differently when they know they are being observed.

The most common method of assessing personality is the *self-report questionnaire*. Individuals respond to a series of questions, usually in an agree/disagree or true/false format. One of the more widely recognized questionnaires is the Minnesota Multiphasic Personality Inventory (MMPI). The MMPI is comprehensive and assesses a variety of traits, as well as various neurotic or psychotic disorders. Used extensively in psychological counseling to identify disorders, the MMPI is a long questionnaire. The Big Five traits we discussed earlier are measured by another self-report questionnaire, the NEO Personality Inventory. Self-report questionnaires also suffer from potential biases. It is difficult to be objective about your own personality. People often answer the questionnaires in terms of how they want to be seen, rather than as they really are.

Another approach to applying personality theory in organizations is the Jungian approach and its measurement tool, the MBTI® instrument. The Myers-Briggs Type Indicator® instrument has been developed to measure Jung's ideas about individual differences. Many organizations use the MBTI instrument, and we will focus on it as an example of how some organizations use personality concepts to help employees appreciate diversity.

APPLICATION OF PERSONALITY THEORY IN ORGANIZATIONS: THE MYERS-BRIGGS TYPE INDICATOR INSTRUMENT

One approach to applying personality theory in organizations is the Jungian approach and its measurement tool, the MBTI instrument.

5 Discuss Carl Jung's contribution to our understanding of individual differences, and explain how his theory is used in the Myers-Briggs Type Indicator instrument.

6 Evaluate the importance of the MBTI to managers.

Swiss psychiatrist Carl Jung built his work on the notion that people are fundamentally different, but also fundamentally alike. His classic treatise *Psychological Types* proposed that the population was made up of two basic types—Extraverted types and Introverted types.[61] He went on to identify two types of Perceiving (Sensing and Intuition) and two types of Judgment (Thinking and Feeling). Perceiving (how we gather information) and Judging (how we make decisions) represent the basic mental functions that everyone uses.

Jung suggested that human similarities and differences could be understood by combining preferences. We prefer and choose one way of doing things over another. We are not exclusively one way or another; rather, we have a preference for Extraversion or Introversion, just as we have a preference for right-handedness or left-handedness. We may use each hand equally well, but when a ball is thrown at us by surprise, we will reach to catch it with our preferred hand. Jung's type theory argues that no preferences are better than others. Differences are to be understood, celebrated, and appreciated.

During the 1940s, a mother–daughter team became fascinated with individual differences among people and with the work of Carl Jung. Katharine Briggs and her daughter, Isabel Briggs Myers, developed the *Myers-Briggs Type Indicator instrument* to put Jung's type theory into practical use. The MBTI instrument is used extensively in organizations as a basis for understanding individual differences. More than 3 million people complete the instrument per year in the United States.[62] The MBTI instrument has been used in career counseling, team building, conflict management, and understanding management styles.[63] In Experiential Exercise 3.1 at the end of this chapter, you can assess your own MBTI type. You might find it helpful to do this before reading on.

self-report questionnaire
A common personality assessment that involves an individual's responses to a series of questions.

Myers-Briggs Type Indicator (MBTI) instrument
An instrument developed to measure Carl Jung's theory of individual differences.

The Preferences

There are four scale dichotomies in type theory with two possible choices for each scale. Table 3.2 shows these preferences. The combination of these preferences makes up an individual's psychological type.

Extraversion
A preference indicating that an individual is energized by interaction with other people.

Introversion
A preference indicating that an individual is energized by time alone.

Sensing
Gathering information through the five senses.

Intuition
Gathering information through "sixth sense" and focusing on what could be rather than what actually exists.

Extraversion/Introversion The *Extraversion/Introversion* preference represents where you get your energy. The Extraverted type (E) is energized by interaction with other people. The Introverted type (I) is energized by time alone. Extraverted types typically have a wide social network, whereas Introverted types have a more narrow range of relationships. As articulated by Jung, this preference has nothing to do with social skills. Many Introverted types have excellent social skills but prefer the internal world of ideas, thoughts, and concepts. Extraverted types represent approximately 70 percent of the U.S. population.[64] Our culture rewards Extraverted types and nurtures them. Jung contended that the Extraversion/Introversion preference reflects the most important distinction between individuals.

In work settings, Extraverted types prefer variety, and they do not mind the interruptions of the phone or visits from coworkers. They communicate freely but may say things that they regret later. Read the Real World 3.1 in which Doug Parker (CEO of US Airways) is known for extraversion, yet sometimes has to be reined in by his staff.

Introverted types prefer quiet for concentration, and they like to think things through in private. They do not mind working on a project for a long time and are careful with details. Introverted types dislike telephone interruptions, and they may have trouble recalling names and faces.

Sensing/Intuition The *Sensing/Intuition* preference represents perception, or how we prefer to gather information. In essence, it reflects what we pay attention to. The Sensing type (S) pays attention to information gathered through the five senses and

TABLE 3.2 Type Theory Preferences and Descriptions

Extraversion	**Introversion**	**Thinking**	**Feeling**
Outgoing	Quiet	Analytical	Subjective
Publicly expressive	Reserved	Clarity	Harmony
Interacting	Concentrating	Head	Heart
Speaks, then thinks	Thinks, then speaks	Justice	Mercy
Gregarious	Reflective	Rules	Circumstances
Sensing	**Intuition**	**Judging**	**Perceiving**
Practical	General	Structured	Flexible
Specific	Abstract	Time oriented	Open ended
Feet on the ground	Head in the clouds	Decisive	Exploring
Details	Possibilities	Makes lists/uses them	Makes lists/loses them
Concrete	Theoretical	Organized	Spontaneous

Doug Parker: Extraversion in Business

Doug Parker is one of the most interesting yet contradictory top executives in American business today. He is credited with taking over the ailing America West Airlines just days before the 9/11 attacks. He also drew a lot of flak for merging America West with another fiscally unhealthy airline (US Airways). Industry analysts speculated that this would be the worst merger in airline history.

Parker proved the skeptics wrong. US Airways made more money than any other airline in 2006 except Southwest. Parker is described as an extroverted, gregarious guy with the tendency to talk a lot, and is also known for a sharp, analytical mind. For example, on one occasion when he was on a US Airways flight, he kept saying that the Washington airport where they were supposed to land was shut down due to weather. He speculated that they would have to land in Boston. His immediate staff had to rein him in and remind him that he should not be making such comments to passengers. Instead, any news of change in landing plans should come from the cockpit. His drinking habits are also well documented, and he was arrested for a DUI.

Yet Parker seems to be able to channel his extraverted personality into profitable business. He surrounds himself with talented executives at all times, whether for business or leisure activities. This helps him learn aspects of the business that he is not necessarily well versed in.

SOURCE: B. Gimbel, "Onboard the Wild Ride of Doug Parker." *Fortune* (April 30, 2007): 137–141.

to what actually exists. The Intuitive type (N) pays attention to a "sixth sense" and to what could be rather than what is.[65] Approximately 70 percent of people in the United States are Sensing types.[66]

At work, Sensing types prefer specific answers to questions and can become frustrated with vague instructions. They like jobs that yield tangible results, and they enjoy using established skills more than learning new ones. Intuitive types like solving new problems and are impatient with routine details. They enjoy learning new skills more than actually using them. Intuitive types tend to think about several things at once, and they may be seen by others as absentminded. They like figuring out how things work just for the fun of it.

Thinking/Feeling The *Thinking/Feeling* preference represents the way we prefer to make decisions. The Thinking type (T) makes decisions in a logical, objective fashion, whereas the Feeling type (F) makes decisions in a personal, value-oriented way. The general U.S. population is divided 50/50 on the Thinking/Feeling type preference, but it is interesting that two-thirds of all males are Thinking types, whereas two-thirds of all females are Feeling types. It is the one preference in type theory that has a strong gender difference. Thinking types tend to analyze decisions, whereas Feeling types sympathize. Thinking types try to be impersonal, while Feeling types base their decisions on how the outcome will affect the people involved.

In work settings, Thinking types tend to show less emotion, and they may become uncomfortable with more emotional people. They are likely to respond more readily to other people's thoughts. They tend to be firm minded and like putting things into a logical framework. Feeling types, in contrast, tend to be more comfortable with emotion in the workplace. They enjoy pleasing people as well as frequent praise and encouragement.

Thinking
Making decisions in a logical, objective fashion.

Feeling
Making decisions in a personal, value-oriented way.

TABLE 3.3 Characteristics Frequently Associated with Each Type

Sensing Types		Intuitive Types	
ISTJ Quiet, serious, earn success by thoroughness and dependability. Practical, matter-of-fact, realistic, and responsible. Decide logically what should be done and work toward it steadily, regardless of distractions. Take pleasure in making everything orderly and organized—their work, their home, their life. Value traditions and loyalty.	**ISFJ** Quiet, friendly, responsible, and conscientious. Committed and steady in meeting their obligations. Thorough, painstaking, and accurate. Loyal, considerate, notice and remember specifics about people who are important to them, concerned with how others feel. Strive to create an orderly and harmonious environment at work and at home.	**INFJ** Seek meaning and connection in ideas, relationships, and material possessions. Want to understand what motivates people and are insightful about others. Conscientious and committed to their firm values. Develop a clear vision about how best to serve the common good. Organized and decisive in implementing their vision.	**INTJ** Have original minds and great drive for implementing their ideas and achieving their goals. Quickly see patterns in external events and develop long-range explanatory perspectives. When committed, organize a job and carry it through. Skeptical and independent, have high standards of competence and performance for themselves and others.
ISTP Tolerant and flexible, quiet observers until a problem appears, then act quickly to find workable solutions. Analyze what makes things work and readily get through large amounts of data to isolate the core of practical problems. Interested in cause and effect, organize facts using logical principles, value efficiency.	**ISFP** Quiet, friendly, sensitive, and kind. Enjoy the present moment, what's going on around them. Like to have their own space and to work within their own time frame. Loyal and committed to their values and to people who are important to them. Dislike disagreements and conflicts, do not force their opinions or values on others.	**INFP** Idealistic, loyal to their values and to people who are important to them. Want an external life that is congruent with their values. Curious, quick to see possibilities, can be catalysts for implementing ideas. Seek to understand people and to help them fulfill their potential. Adaptable, flexible, and accepting unless a value is threatened.	**INTP** Seek to develop logical explanations for everything that interests them. Theoretical and abstract, interested more in ideas than in social interaction. Quiet, contained, flexible, and adaptable. Have unusual ability to focus in depth to solve problems in their area of interest. Skeptical, sometimes critical, always analytical.

(*Continues*)

Judging Preference
Preferring closure and completion in making decisions.

Perceiving Preference
Preferring to explore many alternatives and flexibility.

Judging/Perceiving The *Judging-Perceiving* dichotomy reflects one's orientation to the outer world. The Judging type (J) loves closure. Judging types prefer to lead a planned, organized life and like making decisions. A Perceiving type (P), in contrast, prefers a more flexible and spontaneous life and wants to keep options open. Imagine two people, one with a preference for Judging and the other for Perceiving, going out for dinner. The J asks the P to choose a restaurant, and the P suggests ten alternatives. The J just wants to decide and get on with it, whereas the P wants to explore all the options.

In all arenas of life, and especially at work, Judging types love getting things accomplished and delight in marking off the completed items on their calendars. Perceiving types tend to adopt a wait-and-see attitude and to collect new information rather than draw conclusions. Perceiving types are curious and welcome new information. They may start too many projects and not finish them.

TABLE 3.3 Continued

Sensing Types		Intuitive Types	
ESTP Flexible and tolerant, they take a pragmatic approach focused on immediate results. Theories and conceptual explanations bore them—they want to act energetically to solve the problem. Focus on the here-and-now, spontaneous, enjoy each moment that they can be active with others. Enjoy material comforts and style. Learn best through doing.	**ESFP** Outgoing, friendly, and accepting. Exuberant lovers of life, people, and material comforts. Enjoy working with others to make things happen. Bring common sense and a realistic approach to their work and make work fun. Flexible and spontaneous, adapt readily to new people and environments. Learn best by trying a new skill with other people.	**ENFP** Warmly enthusiastic and imaginative. See life as full of possibilities. Make connections between events and information very quickly, and confidently proceed based on the patterns they see. Want a lot of affirmation from others, and readily give appreciation and support. Spontaneous and flexible, often rely on their ability to improvise and their verbal fluency.	**ENTP** Quick, ingenious, stimulating, alert, and outspoken. Resourceful in solving new and challenging problems. Adept at generating conceptual possibilities and then analyzing them strategically. Good at reading other people. Bored by routine, will seldom do the same thing the same way, apt to turn to one new interest after another.
ESTJ Practical, realistic, matter-of-fact. Decisive, quickly move to implement decisions. Organize projects and people to get things done, focus on getting results in the most efficient way possible. Take care of routine details. Have a clear set of logical standards, systematically follow them and want others to also. Forceful in implementing their plans.	**ESFJ** Warmhearted, conscientious, and cooperative. Want harmony in their environment, work with determination to establish it. Like to work with others to complete tasks accurately and on time. Loyal, follow through even in small matters. Notice what others need in their day-by-day lives and try to provide it. Want to be appreciated for who they are and for what they contribute.	**ENFJ** Warm, empathetic, responsive, and responsible. Highly attuned to the emotions, needs, and motivations of others. Find potential in everyone, want to help others fulfill their potential. May act as catalysts for individual and group growth. Loyal, responsive to praise and criticism. Sociable, facilitate others in a group, and provide inspiring leadership.	**ENTJ** Frank, decisive, assume leadership readily. Quickly see logical and inefficient procedures and policies, develop and implement comprehensive systems to solve organizational problems. Enjoy long-term planning and goal setting. Usually well informed, well read, enjoy expanding their knowledge and passing it on to others. Forceful in presenting their ideas.

NOTE: I = Introversion; E = Extraversion; S = Sensing; N = Intuition; T = Thinking; F = Feeling; J = Judging; and P = Perceiving.

SOURCE: Modified and reproduced by special permission of the publisher, CPP, Inc., Palo Alto, CA 94303 from *Introduction to Type, Sixth Edition* by Isabel Briggs-Myers.

The Sixteen Types

The preferences combine to form sixteen distinct types, as shown in Table 3.3. For example, let's examine ESTJ. This type has Extraversion, Sensing, Thinking, and Judging preferences. ESTJs see the world as it is (S); make decisions objectively (T); and like structure, schedules, and order (J). Combining these qualities with their preference for interacting with others makes them natural managers. ESTJs are seen by others as dependable, practical, and able to get any job done. They are conscious of the chain of command and see work as a series of goals to be reached by following rules and regulations. They may have little tolerance for disorganization and have a high need for control. Research results from the *MBTI Atlas* show that most of the 7,463 managers studied were ESTJs.[67]

There are no good and bad types, and each type has its own strengths and weaknesses. There is a growing volume of research on type theory. The MBTI instrument has been found to have good reliability and validity as a measurement instrument for identifying type.[68, 69] Type has been found to be related to learning style, teaching style, and choice of occupation. For example, the MBTI types of engineering students at Georgia Tech were studied in order to see who was attracted to engineering and who was likely to leave the major. STs and NTs were more attracted to engineering. Es and Fs were more likely to withdraw from engineering courses.[70] Type has also been used to determine an individual's decision-making style and management style.

Recent studies have begun to focus on the relationship between type and specific managerial behaviors. The Introverted type (I) and the Feeling type (F), for example, have been shown to be more effective at participative management than their counterparts, the Extraverted type and the Thinking type.[71] Companies like AT&T, ExxonMobil, and Honeywell use the MBTI instrument in their management development programs to help employees understand the different viewpoints of others in the organization. The MBTI instrument can also be used for team building. Hewlett-Packard and Armstrong World Industries use the MBTI instrument to help teams realize that diversity and differences lead to successful performance.

Type theory is valued by managers for its simplicity and accuracy in depicting personalities. It is a useful tool for helping managers develop interpersonal skills. Managers also use type theory to build teams that capitalize on individuals' strengths and to help individual team members appreciate differences.

It should be recognized that there is the potential for individuals to misuse the information from the MBTI instrument in organizational settings.[72] Some inappropriate uses include labeling one another, providing a convenient excuse that they simply can't work with someone else, and avoiding responsibility for their own personal development with respect to working with others and becoming more flexible. One's type is not an excuse for inappropriate behavior.

We turn now to another psychological process that forms the basis for individual differences. Perception shapes the way we view the world, and it varies greatly among individuals.

SOCIAL PERCEPTION

7 Define *social perception* and explain how characteristics of the perceiver, the target, and the situation affect it.

Perception involves the way we view the world around us. It adds meaning to information gathered via the five senses of touch, smell, hearing, vision, and taste. Perception is the primary vehicle through which we come to understand ourselves and our surroundings. *Social perception* is the process of interpreting information about another person. Virtually all management activities rely on perception. In appraising performance, managers use their perceptions of an employee's behavior as a basis for the evaluation.

One work situation that highlights the importance of perception is the selection interview. The consequences of a bad match between an individual and the organization can be devastating for both parties, so it is essential that the data gathered be accurate. Typical first interviews are brief, and the candidate is usually one of many seen by an interviewer during a day. How long does it take for the interviewer to reach a decision about a candidate? In the first four to five minutes, the interviewer often makes an accept or reject decision based on his or her perception of the candidate.[73]

social perception
The process of interpreting information about another person.

In one study amongst CEOs and top management teams, it was found that perceptions of dissimilarity in values amongst CEOs and top management teams can lead to increased conflict. More interestingly, even if in reality there were no differences in values, just the perception thereof led to such increased conflict. This study highlights the importance of perception in organizations by recommending that managers pay attention to how their employees perceive organizational decisions because this (more than reality) might have an impact on behavior.[73a]

Perception is also culturally determined. Based on our cultural backgrounds, we tend to perceive things in certain ways. Read the following sentence:

> *Finished files are the result of years of scientific study combined with the experience of years.*

Now quickly count the number of *f*s in the sentence. Individuals for whom English is their second language see all six *f*s. Most native English speakers report that there are three *f*s. Because of cultural conditioning, *of* is not an important word and is ignored.[74] Culture affects our interpretation of the data we gather, as well as the way we add meaning to it.

Valuing diversity, including cultural diversity, has been recognized as a key to international competitiveness.[75] This challenge and others make social perception skills essential to managerial success.

Three major categories of factors influence our perception of another person: characteristics of ourselves, as perceivers; characteristics of the target person we are perceiving; and characteristics of the situation in which the interaction takes place. Figure 3.2 shows a model of social perception.

FIGURE 3.2 A Model for Social Perception

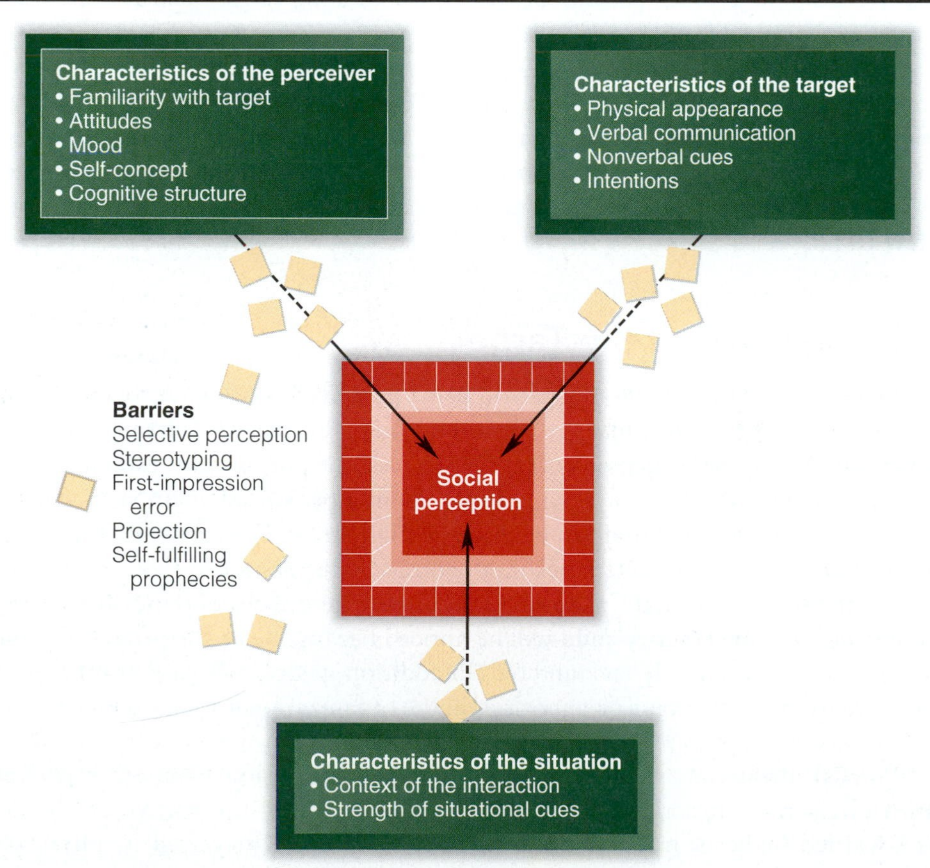

Characteristics of the Perceiver

Several characteristics of the perceiver can affect social perception. One such characteristic is *familiarity* with the target (the person being perceived). When we are familiar with a person, we have multiple observations on which to base our impression of him or her. If the information we have gathered during these observations is accurate, we may have an accurate perception of the other person. Familiarity does not always mean accuracy, however. Sometimes, when we know a person well, we tend to screen out information that is inconsistent with what we believe the person is like. This is a particular danger in performance appraisals where the rater is familiar with the person being rated.

The perceiver's *attitudes* also affect social perception. Suppose you are interviewing candidates for a very important position in your organization—a position that requires negotiating contracts with suppliers, most of whom are male. You may feel that women are not capable of holding their own in tough negotiations. This attitude will doubtless affect your perceptions of the female candidates you interview. Read all about how Steve Jobs's perception of his life events has affected the success of Apple in the Real World feature.

Mood can have a strong influence on the way we perceive someone.[76] We think differently when we are happy than we do when we are depressed. In addition, we remember information that is consistent with our mood state better than information that is inconsistent with our mood state. When in a positive mood, we form more favorable impressions of others. When in a negative mood, we tend to evaluate others unfavorably.

Another factor that can affect social perception is the perceiver's *self-concept*. An individual with a positive self-concept tends to notice positive attributes in another person. In contrast, a negative self-concept can lead a perceiver to pick out negative traits in another person. Greater understanding of self provides more accurate perceptions of others.

Cognitive structure, an individual's pattern of thinking, also affects social perception. Some people have a tendency to perceive physical traits, such as height, weight, and appearance, more readily. Others tend to focus more on central traits, or personality dispositions. Cognitive complexity allows a person to perceive multiple characteristics of another person rather than attending to just a few traits.

Characteristics of the Target

Characteristics of the target—the person being perceived—influence social perception. *Physical appearance* plays a big role in our perception of others. The perceiver will notice the target's physical features like height, weight, estimated age, race, and gender. Clothing says a great deal about a person. Blue pin-striped suits, for example, are decoded to mean banking or Wall Street. Perceivers tend to notice physical appearance characteristics that contrast with the norm, that are intense, or that are new or unusual.[77] A loud person, one who dresses outlandishly, a very tall person, or a hyperactive child will be noticed because he or she provides a contrast to what is commonly encountered. In addition, people who are novel can attract attention. Newcomers or minorities in the organization are examples of novel individuals.

Physical attractiveness often colors our entire impression of another person. Interviewers rate attractive candidates more favorably, and attractive candidates are awarded higher starting salaries.[78, 79] People who are perceived as physically

THE REAL WORLD 3.2

Steve Jobs: Managerial Genius or Micromanager?

© JUSTIN SULLIVAN/GETTY IMAGES

After a number of life-changing events, including being fired from his own company, Steve Jobs' management style has softened.

Steve Jobs is the cofounder and CEO of Apple and was the CEO of Pixar until it was acquired by Disney. Some have accused Jobs of being an egomaniac and very temperamental. Stories abound of his rash leadership style in which he recruited great talent yet belittled employees on a routine basis. Finally, the man he had hired to run Apple, John Sculley, fired Jobs from his own creation in 1984. In a recent commencement address at Stanford University, Jobs described this event as one of the best things that could have ever happened to him. He started another computer company called NeXT. This company was bought by Apple in 1996 and Jobs returned triumphantly to the helm of Apple.

Jobs's early life is a case in point for how individuals' life experiences shape personality and perception. Jobs dropped out of college but took calligraphy classes that eventually helped him design proportionally spaced fonts for the Mac. Jobs also backpacked around India in search of enlightenment and then returned to the States with a shaved head and wearing Indian clothing. In his Stanford commencement address, Jobs described his pancreatic cancer scare and battle as one of his most profound life lessons.

These experiences and Jobs's perception and attributions have changed his management style. Apple executives say that he is much calmer and more thoughtful. Perceiving a major crisis like being fired from your own company as a positive and life changing event is certainly unusual. However, that perception is what makes Steve Jobs one of the most enduring leaders in the business world today.

SOURCES: "Steve Jobs' Magic Kingdom: How Apple's Demanding Visionary Will Shake Up Disney and the World of Entertainment," http://www.businessweek.com/magazine/content/06_06/b3970001.htm; The Apple Museum, "Biography: Steve Jobs," by Darren Vader, http://www.theapplemuseum.com/index.php?id=49.

attractive face stereotypes as well. We will discuss these and other stereotypes later in this chapter.

Verbal communication from targets also affects our perception of them. We listen to the topics they speak about, their tone of voice, and their accent and make judgments based on this input.

Nonverbal communication conveys a great deal of information about the target. Eye contact, facial expressions, body movements, and posture all are deciphered by the perceiver in an attempt to form an impression of the target. It is interesting that some nonverbal signals mean very different things in different cultures. The "okay" sign in the United States (forming a circle with the thumb and forefinger) is an insult in South America. Facial expressions, however, seem to have universal meanings.

Individuals from different cultures are able to recognize and decipher such expressions the same way.[80]

The *intentions* of the target are inferred by the perceiver based on observation. We may see our boss appear in our office doorway and think, "Oh no! She's going to give me more work to do." Or we may perceive that her intention is to congratulate us on a recent success. In any case, the perceiver's interpretation of the target's intentions affects the way the perceiver views the target.

Characteristics of the Situation

The situation in which the interaction between the perceiver and the target takes place also influences the perceiver's impression of the target. The *social context* of the interaction is a major influence. Meeting a professor in his or her office affects your impression in a certain way that may contrast with the impression you would form had you met the professor in a local restaurant. In Japan, social context is very important. Business conversations after working hours or at lunch are taboo. If you try to talk business during these times, you may be perceived as rude.[81]

The *strength of situational cues* also affects social perception. As we discussed earlier in the chapter, some situations provide strong cues as to appropriate behavior. In these situations, we assume that the individual's behavior can be accounted for by the situation, and that it may not reflect her or his disposition. This is the *discounting principle* in social perception.[82] For example, you may encounter an automobile salesperson who has a warm and personable manner, asks about your work and hobbies, and seems genuinely interested in your taste in cars. Can you assume that this behavior reflects the salesperson's personality? You probably cannot, because of the influence of the situation. This person is trying to sell you a car, and in this particular situation he or she probably treats all customers in this manner.

You can see that characteristics of the perceiver, the target, and the situation all affect social perception. It would be wonderful if all of us had accurate social perception skills. Unfortunately, barriers often prevent us from perceiving another person accurately.

Barriers to Social Perception

(8) Identify five common barriers to social perception.

discounting principle
The assumption that an individual's behavior is accounted for by the situation.

selective perception
The process of selecting information that supports our individual viewpoints while discounting information that threatens our viewpoints.

stereotype
A generalization about a group of people.

Several factors lead us to form inaccurate impressions of others. Five of these barriers to social perception are selective perception, stereotyping, first-impression error, projection, and self-fulfilling prophecies.

We receive a vast amount of information. *Selective perception* is our tendency to choose information that supports our viewpoints. Individuals often ignore information that makes them feel uncomfortable or threatens their viewpoints. Suppose, for example, that a sales manager is evaluating the performance of his employees. One employee does not get along well with colleagues and rarely completes sales reports on time. This employee, however, generates the most new sales contracts in the office. The sales manager may ignore the negative information, choosing to evaluate the salesperson only on contracts generated. The manager is exercising selective perception.

A *stereotype* is a generalization about a group of people. Stereotypes reduce information about other people to a workable level, and they are efficient for compiling and using information. Stereotypes become even stronger when they are shared with and validated by others.[83] Stereotypes can be accurate; when they are accurate, they can be useful perceptual guidelines. Sometimes, however, stereotypes are inaccurate. They harm individuals when inaccurate impressions of them are inferred and are never tested or changed.[84]

In multicultural work teams, members often stereotype foreign coworkers rather than getting to know them before forming an impression. Team members from less developed countries are often assumed to have less knowledge simply because their homeland is economically or technologically less developed.[85] Stereotypes like these can deflate the productivity of the work team, as well as create low morale.

Attractiveness is a powerful stereotype. We assume that attractive individuals are also warm, kind, sensitive, poised, sociable, outgoing, independent, and strong. Are attractive people really like this? Certainly, all of them are not. A study of romantic relationships showed that most attractive individuals do not fit the stereotype, except for possessing good social skills and being popular.[86]

Some individuals may seem to us to fit the stereotype of attractiveness because our behavior elicits from them behavior that confirms the stereotype. Consider, for example, a situation in which you meet an attractive fellow student. Chances are that you respond positively to this person, because you assume he or she is warm, sociable, and so on. Even though the person may not possess these traits, your positive response may bring out these behaviors in the person. The interaction between the two of you may be channeled such that the stereotype confirms itself.[87]

Stereotyping pervades work life. When there is a contrast against a stereotype, the member of the stereotyped group is treated more positively (given more favorable comments or pats on the back). For example, a female softball player may be given more applause for a home run hit than a male teammate. This occurs because some people may stereotype women as less athletic than men, or because they hold female players to a lower standard. Either way, the contrast is still part of stereotyping.[88]

First impressions are lasting impressions, so the saying goes. Individuals place a good deal of importance on first impressions, and for good reason. We tend to remember what we perceive first about a person, and sometimes we are quite reluctant to change our initial impressions.[89] *First-impression error* occurs when we observe a very brief bit of a person's behavior in our first encounter and infer that this behavior reflects what the person is really like. Primacy effects can be particularly dangerous in interviews, given that we form first impressions quickly and that they may be the basis for long-term employment relationships.

What factors do interviewers rely on when forming first impressions? Perceptions of the candidate, such as whether they like the person, whether they trust the person, and whether or not the person seems credible, all influence the interviewer's decision. Something seemingly as unimportant as the pitch of your voice can leave a lasting impression. Speakers with higher vocal pitch are believed to be more competent, more dominant, and more assertive than those with lower voices. This belief can be carried too far; men whose voices are high enough that they sound feminine are judged the least favorably of all by interviewers. This finding is ironic, given that research has found that students with higher vocal pitch tend to earn better grades.[90]

Projection, also known as the false-consensus effect, is a cause of inaccurate perceptions of others. It is the misperception of the commonness of our own beliefs, values, and behaviors such that we overestimate the number of others who share these things. We assume that others are similar to us, and that our own values and beliefs are appropriate. People who are different are viewed as unusual and even

first-impression error
The tendency to form lasting opinions about an individual based on initial perceptions.

projection
Overestimating the number of people who share our own beliefs, values, and behaviors.

deviant. Projection occurs most often when you surround yourself with others similar to you. You may overlook important information about others when you assume everyone is alike and in agreement.[91]

Self-fulfilling prophecies are also barriers to social perception. Sometimes our expectations affect the way we interact with others such that we get what we wish for. Self-fulfilling prophecy is also known as the Pygmalion effect, named for the sculptor in Greek mythology who prayed that a statue of a woman he had carved would come to life, a wish that was granted by the gods.

Early studies of self-fulfilling prophecy were conducted in elementary school classrooms. Teachers were given bogus information that some of their pupils had high intellectual potential. These pupils were chosen randomly; there were really no differences among the students. Eight months later, the "gifted" pupils scored significantly higher on an IQ test. The teachers' expectations had elicited growth from these students, and the teachers had given them tougher assignments and more feedback on their performance.[92] Self-fulfilling prophecy has been studied in many settings, including at sea. The Israeli Defense Forces told one group of naval cadets that they probably wouldn't experience seasickness, and even if they did, it wouldn't affect their performance. The self-fulfilling prophecy worked! These cadets were rated better performers than other groups, and they also had less seasickness. The information improved the cadets' self-efficacy—they believed they could perform well even if they became seasick.[93]

The Pygmalion effect has been observed in work organizations as well.[94] A manager's expectations of an individual affect both the manager's behavior toward the individual and the individual's response. For example, suppose your initial impression is that an employee has the potential to move up within the organization. Chances are you will spend a great deal of time coaching and counseling the employee, providing challenging assignments, and grooming him or her for success.

Managers can harness the power of the Pygmalion effect to improve productivity in the organization. It appears that high expectations of individuals come true. Can a manager extend these high expectations to an entire group and have similar positive results? The answer is yes. When a manager expects positive things from a group, the group delivers.[95]

Impression Management

Most people want to make a favorable impression on others. This is particularly true in organizations, where individuals compete for jobs, favorable performance evaluations, and salary increases. The process by which people try to control the impressions others have of them is called *impression management*. Individuals use several techniques to control others' impressions of them.[96]

Some impression management techniques are self-enhancing. These techniques focus on enhancing others' impressions of the person using the technique. Name-dropping, which involves mentioning an association with important people in the hopes of improving one's image, is often used. Managing one's appearance is another technique for impression management. Individuals dress carefully for interviews because they want to "look the part" in order to get the job. Self-descriptions, or statements about one's characteristics, are used to manage impressions as well.

Another group of impression management techniques are *other-enhancing*. These techniques focus on the individual one is trying to impress rather than on one's self. Flattery is a common other-enhancing technique whereby compliments

self-fulfilling prophecy
The situation in which our expectations about people affect our interaction with them in such a way that our expectations are confirmed.

impression management
The process by which individuals try to control the impressions others have of them.

are given to an individual in order to win his or her approval. Favors are also used to gain the approval of others. Agreement with someone's opinion is a technique often used to gain a positive impression. People with disabilities, for example, often use other-enhancing techniques. They may feel that they must take it upon themselves to make others comfortable interacting with them. Impression management techniques are used by individuals with disabilities as a way of dealing with potential avoidance by others.[97]

Are impression management techniques effective? Most research on this topic has focused on employment interviews; the results indicate that candidates who engage in impression management by self-promoting performed better in interviews, were more likely to obtain site visits with potential employers, and were more likely to get hired.[98,99] In addition, employees who engage in impression management are rated more favorably in performance appraisals than those who do not.[100]

Impression management seems to have an impact on others' impressions. As long as the impressions conveyed are accurate, this process can be beneficial to organizations. If the impressions are found to be false, however, a strongly negative overall impression may result. Furthermore, excessive impression management can lead to the perception that the user is manipulative or insincere.[101] We have discussed the influences on social perception, the potential barriers to perceiving another person, and impression management. Another psychological process that managers should understand is attribution.

ATTRIBUTION IN ORGANIZATIONS

As human beings, we are innately curious. We are not content merely to observe the behavior of others; rather, we want to know why they behave the way they do. We also seek to understand and explain our own behavior. *Attribution theory* explains how we pinpoint the causes of our own behavior and that of other people.[102]

The attributions, or inferred causes, we provide for behavior have important implications in organizations. In explaining the causes of our performance, good or bad, we are asked to explain the behavior that was the basis for the performance.

Internal and External Attributions

9 Explain the attribution process and how attributions affect managerial behavior.

Attributions can be made to an internal source of responsibility (something within the individual's control) or an external source (something outside the individual's control). Suppose you perform well on an exam in this course. You might say you aced the test because you are smart or because you studied hard. If you attribute your success to ability or effort, you are making an *internal attribution*.

Alternatively, you might make an *external attribution* for your performance. You might say it was an easy test (you would attribute your success to degree of task difficulty) or that you had good luck. In this case, you are attributing your performance to sources beyond your control, or external sources. You can see that internal attributions include such causes as ability and effort, whereas external attributions include causes like task difficulty or luck.

Attribution patterns differ among individuals.[103] Achievement-oriented individuals attribute their success to ability and their failures to lack of effort, both internal causes. Failure-oriented individuals attribute their failures to lack of ability, and they may develop feelings of incompetence as a result of their attributional pattern.

attribution theory
A theory that explains how individuals pinpoint the causes of their own behavior and that of others.

Evidence indicates that this attributional pattern also leads to depression.[104] Women managers, in contrast to men managers, are less likely to attribute their success to their own ability. This may be because they are adhering to social norms that compel women to be more modest about their accomplishments or because they believe that success has less to do with ability than with hard work.[105]

Attribution theory has many applications in the workplace. The way you explain your own behavior affects your motivation. For example, suppose you must give an important presentation to your executive management group. You believe you have performed well, and your boss tells you that you've done a good job. To what do you attribute your success? If you believe careful preparation and rehearsal were the cause, you're likely to take credit for the performance and to have a sense of self-efficacy about future presentations. If, however, you think you were just lucky, you may not be motivated to repeat the performance because you believe you had little influence on the outcome.

One situation in which a lot of attributions are made is the employment interview. Candidates are often asked to explain the causes of previous performance ("Why did you perform poorly in math classes?") to interviewers. In addition, candidates often feel they should justify why they should be hired ("I work well with people, so I'm looking for a managerial job"). Research shows that successful and unsuccessful candidates differ in the way they make attributions for negative outcomes. Successful candidates are less defensive and make internal attributions for negative events. Unsuccessful candidates attribute negative outcomes to things beyond their control (external attributions), which gives interviewers the impression that the candidate failed to learn from the event. In addition, interviewers fear that the individuals would be likely to blame others when something goes wrong in the workplace.[106]

Attributional Biases

10 Evaluate the accuracy of managerial attributions from the standpoint of attribution biases and errors.

The attribution process may be affected by two very common errors: the fundamental attribution error and the self-serving bias. The tendency to make attributions to internal causes when focusing on someone else's behavior is known as the *fundamental attribution error*.[107] The other error, *self-serving bias*, occurs when focusing on one's own behavior. Individuals tend to make internal attributions for their own successes and external attributions for their own failures.[108] In other words, when we succeed, we take credit for it; when we fail, we blame it on other people.

Both of these biases were illustrated in a study of health care managers who were asked to cite the causes of their employees' poor performance.[109] The managers claimed that internal causes (their employees' lack of effort or lack of ability) were the problem. This is an example of the fundamental attribution error. When the employees were asked to pinpoint the cause of their own performance problems, they blamed a lack of support from the managers (an external cause), which illustrates self-serving bias.

fundamental attribution error
The tendency to make attributions to internal causes when focusing on someone else's behavior.

self-serving bias
The tendency to attribute one's own successes to internal causes and one's failures to external causes.

There are cultural differences in these two attribution errors. As described previously, these biases apply to people from the United States. In more fatalistic cultures, such as India's, people tend to believe that fate is responsible for much that happens. People in such cultures tend to emphasize external causes of behavior.[110]

In China, people are taught that hard work is the route to accomplishment. When faced with either a success or a failure, Chinese individuals first introspect about whether they tried hard enough or whether their attitude was correct. In a study of attributions for performance in sports, Chinese athletes attributed both their successes and failures to internal causes. Even when the cause of poor athletic performance was clearly external, such as bad weather, the Chinese participants made internal attributions. In terms of the Chinese culture, this attributional pattern is a reflection of moral values that are used to evaluate behavior. The socialistic value of selfless morality dictates that individual striving must serve collective interests. Mao Zedong stressed that external causes function only through internal causes; therefore, the main cause of results lies within oneself. Chinese are taught this from childhood and form a corresponding attributional tendency. In analyzing a cause, they first look to their own effort.[111]

© AP PHOTO/LEE JIN-MAN

In a study of attributions for performance in sports, Chinese athletes attributed both their successes and failures to internal causes.

The way individuals interpret the events around them has a strong influence on their behavior. People try to understand the causes of behavior in order to gain predictability and control over future behavior. Managers use attributions in all aspects of their jobs. In evaluating performance and rewarding employees, managers must determine the causes of behavior and a perceived source of responsibility. One tough call managers often make is whether allegations of sexual harassment actually resulted from sexual conduct, and if harassment did occur, what should be done about it. To make such tough calls, managers use attributions.

Attribution theory can explain how performance evaluation judgments can lead to differential rewards. A supervisor attributing an employee's good performance to internal causes, such as effort or ability, may give a larger raise than a supervisor attributing the good performance to external causes, such as help from others or good training. Managers are often called on to explain their own actions as well, and in doing so they make attributions about the causes of their own behavior. We continue our discussion of attributions in Chapter 6 in terms of how they are used in managing employee performance by presenting Kelley's attribution theory.

MANAGERIAL IMPLICATIONS: USING PERSONALITY, PERCEPTION, AND ATTRIBUTION AT WORK

Managers need to know as much as possible about individual differences in order to understand themselves and those with whom they work. An understanding of personality characteristics can help a manager appreciate differences in employees. With the increased diversity of the workforce, tools like the MBTI can be used to help employees see someone else's point of view. These tools can also help make communication among diverse employees more effective.

Managers use social perception constantly on the job. Knowledge of the forces that affect perception and the barriers to accuracy can help the manager form more accurate impressions of others.

Determining the causes of job performance is a major task for the manager, and attribution theory can be used to explain how managers go about determining causality. In addition, knowledge of the fundamental attribution error and self-serving bias can help a manager guard against these biases in the processes of looking for causes of behavior on the job.

In this chapter, we have explored the psychological processes of personality, perception, and attribution as individual differences. In the next chapter, we will continue our discussion of individual differences in terms of attitudes, values, and ethics.

LOOKING BACK: SERGEY BRIN'S PERSONALITY AND GOOGLE'S IDENTITY

Like all corporations, Google has its set of catchphrases. However, unlike other corporations that have catchphrases designed to sell their product, Google's catchphrases are reflective of the life and personality of founders Sergey Brin and Larry Page. For example, one saying is "Don't Be Evil." Speculation abounds that this phrase is important at Google as a result of Brin's exposure to the atrocities of the Soviet Union against Jews and his natural dislike for set corporate dictums. In fact, his reputation at Stanford was that of a bright young man who at times appeared arrogant. He had a natural penchant for a variety of outdoor activities and focused on taking classes that interested him (such as advanced swimming) rather than what was required. To this day, he hasn't finished his doctorate at Stanford but holds a master's degree from the school.

Brin's youthful brashness has translated into several innovative policies at Google, where engineers are encouraged to devote 20 percent of their work time (one day per week) on projects that interest them. One senior vice president at Google stated that about half of their new products originated from this concept of 20 percent time.

Also, the "Don't Be Evil" principle had translated into numerous worker-friendly practices such as free laundry services, separate areas for nursing mothers, video games, foosball, and so on. Such practices have catapulted Google to number one in *Fortune's* 2007 list of the best places to work in America. Brin's personality and his perception of the business world have played a huge role in Google's success.[112, 113]

Chapter Summary

1. Individual differences are factors that make individuals unique. They include personalities, perceptions, skills and abilities, attitudes, values, and ethics.
2. The trait theory and integrative approach are two personality theories.
3. Managers should understand personality because of its effect on behavior. Several characteristics affect behavior in organizations, including locus of control, self-esteem, self-monitoring, and positive/negative affect.
4. Personality has a stronger influence in weak situations, where there are few cues to guide behavior.
5. One useful framework for understanding individual differences is type theory, developed by Carl Jung and measured by the Myers-Briggs Type Indicator (MBTI).
6. Social perception is the process of interpreting information about another person. It is influenced by characteristics of the perceiver, the target, and the situation.
7. Barriers to social perception include selective perception, stereotyping, first-impression error, projection, and self-fulfilling prophecies.
8. Impression management techniques such as name-dropping, managing one's appearance, self-descriptions, flattery, favors, and agreement are used by individuals to control others' impressions of them.
9. Attribution is the process of determining the cause of behavior. It is used extensively by managers, especially in evaluating performance.

Key Terms

attribution theory (p. 103)
behavioral measures (p. 90)
discounting principle (p. 100)
extraversion (p. 92)
Feeling (p. 93)
first-impression error (p. 101)
fundamental attribution error (p. 104)
general self-efficacy (p. 87)
impression management (p. 102)
individual differences (p. 82)
integrative approach (p. 85)
interactional psychology (p. 83)
introversion (p. 92)
intuition (p. 92)
Judging Preference (p. 94)
locus of control (p. 86)
Myers-Briggs Type Indicator (MBTI) (p. 91)
negative affect (p. 89)
Perceiving Preference (p. 94)
personality (p. 83)
positive affect (p. 89)
projection (p. 101)
projective test (p. 90)
selective perception (p. 100)
self-esteem (p. 87)
self-fulfilling prophecy (p. 102)
self-monitoring (p. 88)
self-report questionnaire (p. 91)
self-serving bias (p. 104)
sensing (p. 92)
social perception (p. 96)
stereotype (p. 100)
strong situation (p. 90)
Thinking (p. 93)
trait theory (p. 84)

Review Questions

1. What are individual differences, and why should managers understand them?
2. Define *personality* and describe its origins.
3. Describe two theories of personality and explain what each contributes to our knowledge of personality.
4. Describe the eight preferences of the Myers-Briggs Type Indicator. How does this instrument measure Carl Jung's ideas?
5. What factors influence social perception? What are the barriers to social perception?
6. Describe the errors that affect the attribution process.

Discussion and Communication Questions

1. What contributions can high self-monitors make in organizations? Low self-monitors?
2. How can managers improve their perceptual skills?
3. Which has the stronger impact on personality: heredity or environment?
4. How can managers make more accurate attributions?
5. How can managers encourage self-efficacy in employees?
6. How can self-serving bias and the fundamental attribution error be avoided?
7. *(communication question)* You have been asked to develop a training program for interviewers. An integral part of this program focuses on helping interviewers develop better social perception skills. Write an outline for this section of the training program. Be sure to address barriers to social perception and ways to avoid them.
8. *(communication question)* Form groups of four to six; then split each group in half. Debate the origins of personality, with one half taking the position that personality is inherited and the other half that personality is formed by the environment. Each half should also discuss the implications of its position for managers.

Ethical Dilemma

Alice loves to hire new people. As manager of the Medicare Reimbursement department of a large hospital, she sees it as a great responsibility to aggressively pursue and hire the best people. She has already experienced the challenges of hiring the wrong person. She knows a bad personality match could undermine the culture she has worked so hard to build. Alice plans to do everything in her power to never repeat the mistake of a bad hire.

Her latest hire, however, is proving to be a bigger challenge than she had expected. The problem is that the position requires a good deal of specialized knowledge. Alice needs someone who knows the current Medicare regulations and can decipher new ones. The pool of candidates with this knowledge is extremely small. Truthfully, she has interviewed only one person with the skills and knowledge that she needs.

Jana had interviewed two weeks ago. She knew the regulations better than anyone Alice has ever met. Every question Alice asked, Jana answered. What an asset Jana would be to the department. The dilemma is that Jana seems to be extremely extroverted, needing and wanting a lot of social involvement. This job would not offer that opportunity. Even worse, Mike, the main person with whom Jana would be working, is an extreme introvert. He rarely speaks to anyone and prefers that people speak to him as little as possible. Alice can see nothing but problems between these two employees.

Alice does not know what to do. She values Mike a great deal and does not want to do anything to make him unhappy in his job. But she desperately needs someone in this vacant position. She has been depending on everyone to pitch in and cover the workload for weeks now. She knows that has to stop. But is it fair to bring in someone she feels sure would be unhappy in the job and would ultimately quit? She may even end up losing both Jana and Mike. She has no idea what to do.

Questions

1. Who are the stakeholders affected by Alice's decisions?
2. How much importance should Alice place on Mike's needs and wants?
3. Using consequential, rule-based, and character theories, evaluate Alice's decision alternatives.

Experiential Exercises

3.1 MBTI Types and Management Styles

Part I. This questionnaire will help you determine your preferences. For each item, circle either a or b. If you feel both a and b are true, decide which one is more like you, even if it is only slightly more true.

1. I would rather
   a. solve a new and complicated problem.
   b. work on something I have done before.
2. I like to
   a. work alone in a quiet place.
   b. be where the action is.
3. I want a boss who
   a. establishes and applies criteria in decisions.
   b. considers individual needs and makes exceptions.
4. When I work on a project, I
   a. like to finish it and get some closure.
   b. often leave it open for possible changes.
5. When making a decision, the most important considerations are
   a. rational thoughts, ideas, and data.
   b. people's feelings and values.
6. On a project, I tend to
   a. think it over and over before deciding how to proceed.
   b. start working on it right away, thinking about it as I go along.
7. When working on a project, I prefer to
   a. maintain as much control as possible.
   b. explore various options.
8. In my work, I prefer to
   a. work on several projects at a time and learn as much as possible about each one.
   b. have one project that is challenging and keeps me busy.
9. I often
   a. make lists and plans whenever I start something and may hate to seriously alter my plans.
   b. avoid plans and just let things progress as I work on them.
10. When discussing a problem with colleagues, it is easy for me to
    a. see "the big picture."
    b. grasp the specifics of the situation.
11. When the phone rings in my office or at home, I usually
    a. consider it an interruption.
    b. do not mind answering it.
12. Which word describes you better?
    a. Analytical
    b. Empathetic
13. When I am working on an assignment, I tend to
    a. work steadily and consistently.
    b. work in bursts of energy with "downtime" in between.
14. When I listen to someone talk on a subject, I usually try to
    a. relate it to my own experience and see if it fits.
    b. assess and analyze the message.
15. When I come up with new ideas, I generally
    a. "go for it."
    b. like to contemplate the ideas some more.
16. When working on a project, I prefer to
    a. narrow the scope so it is clearly defined.
    b. broaden the scope to include related aspects.
17. When I read something, I usually
    a. confine my thoughts to what is written there.
    b. read between the lines and relate the words to other ideas.
18. When I have to make a decision in a hurry, I often
    a. feel uncomfortable and wish I had more information.
    b. am able to do so with available data.
19. In a meeting, I tend to
    a. continue formulating my ideas as I talk about them.
    b. only speak out after I have carefully thought the issue through.

20. In work, I prefer spending a great deal of time on issues of
    a. ideas.
    b. people.
21. In meetings, I am most often annoyed with people who
    a. come up with many sketchy ideas.
    b. lengthen meetings with many practical details.
22. I am a
    a. morning person.
    b. night owl.
23. What is your style in preparing for a meeting?
    a. I am willing to go in and be responsive.
    b. I like to be fully prepared and usually sketch an outline of the meeting.
24. In a meeting, I would prefer for people to
    a. display a fuller range of emotions.
    b. be more task oriented.
25. I would rather work for an organization where
    a. my job is intellectually stimulating.
    b. I am committed to its goals and mission.
26. On weekends, I tend to
    a. plan what I will do.
    b. just see what happens and decide as I go along.
27. I am more
    a. outgoing.
    b. contemplative.
28. I would rather work for a boss who is
    a. full of new ideas.
    b. practical.

In the following, choose the word in each pair that appeals to you more:

29. a. Social
    b. Theoretical
30. a. Ingenuity
    b. Practicality
31. a. Organized
    b. Adaptable
32. a. Active
    b. Concentration

Scoring Key

Count one point for each item listed below that you have circled in the inventory.

Score for I	Score for E	Score for S	Score for N
2a	2b	1b	1a
6a	6b	10b	10a
11a	11b	13a	13b
15b	15a	16a	16b
19b	19a	17a	17b
22a	22b	21a	21b
27b	27a	28b	28a
32b	32a	30b	30a
Total			

Circle the one with more points—I or E.

Circle the one with more points—S or N.

Score for T	Score for F	Score for J	Score for P
3a	3b	4a	4b
5a	5b	7a	7b
12a	12b	8b	8a
14b	14a	9a	9b
20a	20b	18b	18a
24b	24a	23b	23a
25a	25b	26a	26b
29b	29a	31a	31b
Total			

Circle the one with more points—T or F.

Circle the one with more points—J or P.

Your score is

I or E ____ T or F ____

S or N ____ J or P ____

Part II. The purpose of this part of the exercise is to give you experience in understanding some of the individual differences that were proposed by Carl Jung and are measured by the MBTI.

Step 1. Your instructor will assign you to a group.

Step 2. Your group is a team of individuals who want to start a business. You are to develop a mission statement and a name for your business.

Step 3. After you have completed Step 2, analyze the decision process that occurred within the group. How did you decide on your company's name and mission?

Step 4. Your instructor will have each group report to the class the name and mission of the company, and then the decision process used. Your instructor will also give you some additional information about the exercise and provide some interesting insights about your management style.

SOURCE: "MBTI Types and Management Styles" from D. Marcic and P. Nutt, "Personality Inventory," in D. Marcic, ed., *Organizational Behavior: Experiences and Cases* (St. Paul, Minn.: West, 1989), 9–16. Reprinted by permission.

3.2 Stereotypes in Employment Interviews

Step 1. Your instructor will give you a transcript that records an applicant's interview for a job as a laborer. Your task is to memorize as much of the interview as possible.

Step 2. Write down everything you can remember about the job candidate.

Step 3. Your instructor will lead you in a discussion.

SOURCE: Adapted from D. A. Sachau and M. Hussang, "How Interviewers' Stereotypes Influence Memory: An Exercise," *Journal of Management Education* 16 (1992): 391–396. Copyright © 1992 by Sage Publications. Reprinted with permission of Sage Publications, Inc.

TAKE 2

Biz Flix | The Breakfast Club

John Hughes's careful look at teenage culture in a suburban Chicago high school focuses on a group of teenagers from the school's different subcultures. They start their Saturday detention with nothing in common, but over the course of a day, they learn each other's innermost secrets. The highly memorable characters—the Athlete, the Princess, the Criminal, the Basket Case, and the Brain—leave lasting impressions. If you have seen the film, try to recall which actor or actress played each character.

The scene from *The Breakfast Club* is an edited version of the "Lunchtime" sequence that appears in the first third of the film. Carefully study each character's behavior to answer the following questions. The rest of the film shows the growing relationships among the detainees as they try to understand each other's personality.

What to Watch for and Ask Yourself:

- Which Big Five personality dimensions describe each character in this scene?
- Which characters show positive affect? Which show negative affect?
- Refer to the Myers-Briggs Type Indicator (MBTI) section in this chapter. Which of the sixteen types shown in Table 3.3 best describes each character? Why?

Workplace Video | Managing Small Business Start-ups, Featuring The Little Guys

For many years David and Evie Wexler worked in a home-electronics store where their talents were not being utilized fully. Frustrated at not seeing their ideas put into action, the couple decided to leave the company and start a home-theater business with longtime associate Paul Gerrity. In just twelve years, the three partners grew their new venture, The Little Guys Home Electronics, into a thriving small business with $10 million in annual sales.

Like many entrepreneurs, the Wexlers felt limited by their former positions and wanted to strike out on their own. They had confidence that they could do things better than their previous employer, and they had a vision for opening an electronics business that could provide hands-on, personalized customer service. Above all, they believed in doing things differently from "the big guys"—hence the name.

The Wexlers and Gerrity possess a range of personality characteristics common to successful entrepreneurs. The partners are achievement-oriented extraverts who seek creative, rewarding enterprises. They thrive on overcoming the day-to-day challenges of operating a small business and demonstrate a high tolerance for ambiguity. Most importantly, they possess great confidence in their own abilities. "I knew we could pull it off," says cofounder David Wexler. "I was confident in our ability to succeed at some level. Failure was never something we accepted." Wexler's self-confidence was put to the test on numerous occasions—such as when the company moved up its grand opening a week

TAKE 2

ahead of schedule due to an advertising mistake—but the cofounders always found a way to keep The Little Guys on track.

Starting a new business is a risky venture, but the Wexlers and Gerrity had the personality, the openness to experience new things, and the internal motivation necessary to be successful. And while The Little Guys Home Electronics has already achieved enormous success, the company's owners don't rest on their laurels. Instead, they look forward to the next big challenge.

Discussion Questions

1. Describe the Wexlers' personality characteristics in terms of the partners' core self-evaluations (CSE).
2. Which of the Big Five personality traits do you consider the most important for small-business owners like the Wexlers? Explain.
3. Describe the three cofounders' social perceptions of each other, and explain how the characteristics of the perceiver, the target, and the situation influence those perceptions.

CASE

Sir Richard Branson: Development of an Entrepreneur

Virgin is one of the most respected brands in Great Britain and is rapidly becoming an important global brand as well. The Virgin brand was started in the 1970s with a small mail-order record company that grew out of a student magazine.[1] Since then, Richard Branson has developed the Virgin brand into a veritable entrepreneurial empire, with businesses in travel and tourism (e.g., Virgin Atlantic Airways, Virgin Trains, Virgin Balloon Flights, Virgin Galactic, and Virgin Holidays); leisure and pleasure (e.g., Virgin Games, V2 Music, and Virgin Comics); social and environmental (e.g., Virgin Fuels and Virgin Earth); shopping (e.g., Virgin Books, Virgin Megastore, and Virgin Wines); media and telecommunications (e.g., Virgin Media, Virgin Mobile, and Virgin Radio); finance and money (Virgin Money); and health (Virgin Active and Virgin Health Bank).[2]

Branson: The Background

In the first chapter of his autobiography, Branson reminisces about some of his childhood experiences—ones that would have a profound effect on his development as an adult and an entrepreneur. He writes that his parents, especially his mother, continually set challenges for him and his sisters, Vanessa and Lindi, in order to make them independent. These challenges were physical in nature rather than academic. According to Branson, he and his sisters were soon setting physical challenges for themselves.[3]

A loving family played an important role in Branson's development. "We were a family that would have killed for each other—and we still are," he says.[4] Teamwork was also a hallmark of the family. Branson's parents treated him and his two sisters as equals. They valued their children's opinions and only provided advice when the children asked for it. Branson's mother was very entrepreneurial, as was his Aunt Clare. Each developed several different ways of making money.[5]

Despite his enormous entrepreneurial success, Branson still lacks a high school diploma.[6] In school, he was a mediocre student but a superb athlete. Although he was dyslexic and had vision problems, his inability to read, write, and spell, and his poor performance on tests, were blamed on stupidity or laziness. In commenting on Branson's academic miseries as a child in relation to his athletic and future entrepreneurial successes, one observer noted: "In the end, it was the tests that failed. They totally missed his ability and passion for sports. They had no means to identify ambition, the fire inside that drives people to find a path to success that zigzags around the maze of standard doors that won't open. They never identified the most important talent of all. It's the ability to connect with people, mind to mind, soul to soul. It's that rare power to energize the ambitions of others so that they, too, rise to the level of their dreams."[7]

A passion for sports, adventure, family, and entrepreneurship define Sir Richard's life. Branson has broken several air and land speed and distance records while racing boats and hot air balloons in his pursuit of adventure. He structures his work schedule to leave ample time to spend with his family and friends. Indeed, Branson's efforts to synthesize work, play, and life seem to be the hallmark of his business model and business success.[8]

Branson: The Entrepreneur

Branson began building his entrepreneurial empire in his teenage years. At the age of 17, he became frustrated with the rules and regulations of schools. Brimming with activism, he and a friend, Jonny Gems, started a magazine called *Student*. The magazine tied many schools together and focused on the students themselves rather than the schools. After publishing the first issue, Branson received a note from the headmaster of the school that he and Gems attended. It read: "Congratulations, Branson. I predict that you will either go to prison or become a millionaire."[9]

Branson dropped out of school and continued to pursue his entrepreneurial interests. His next venture was a discount music business called Virgin Records. Then entrepreneurial venture after entrepreneurial venture developed, culminating in extraordinary success. Sir Richard—knighted by the Queen of England in 2000—has mostly majority stakes in over 200 companies that constitute his multibillion-dollar entrepreneurial empire.[10] Global revenues were approximately $20 billion in 2006.[11]

Branson is not a conventional businessperson—and he never intended to be one. In fact, he is about as far removed from the stereotypical CEO as one can imagine. "He continues to be a corporate iconoclast, defying conventional wisdom, pushing the envelope, poking fun at the big guys, saying exactly what he thinks and doing exactly what he wants."[12] Branson has irreverence for authority that he claims to have inherited from both parents. He relishes becoming involved in "industries that charge too much (music) or hold consumers hostage (cellular) or treat them badly and bore them to tears (airlines)."[13] His aim is to upset the status quo in such industries.

Branson also relishes teamwork and brings it into play in his entrepreneurial ventures. He has an "advisory team, whose job it is to capture his entrepreneurial ideas and wrestle them into some kind of corporate structure that is both attractive to investors and palatable to him."[14] He also gives others opportunities to develop their ideas into business ventures that he backs.

Sir Richard's entrepreneurial ventures and work pique his intellectual curiosity and provide the education he was never able to get in school. "What really sets him apart from other CEOs is that he doesn't mind surprises. He thrives on them. Startup problems don't bother him at all. Neither do unforeseen battles."[15]

Discussion Questions

1. Using the various personality characteristics discussed in this chapter, how would you describe Sir Richard Branson's personality?
2. What perceptions have you formed of Branson? How do you think your perceptions are affected by characteristics of you as the perceiver and Branson as the perceptual target? To what extent have the barriers to social perception influenced your view of him?
3. How do attributions factor into understanding the background of Branson's entrepreneurial development?

SOURCE: This case was written by Michael K. McCuddy, The Louis S. and Mary L. Morgal Chair of Christian Business Ethics and Professor of Management, College of Business Administration, Valparaiso University.

© TIM BOYLE/GETTY IMAGES

CHAPTER 4

Attitudes, Emotions, and Ethics

LEARNING OBJECTIVES

After reading this chapter, you should be able to do the following:

1 Explain the ABC model of an attitude.

2 Describe how attitudes are formed.

3 Identify sources of job satisfaction and commitment and suggest tips for managers to help build these two attitudes among their employees.

4 Distinguish between organizational citizenship and workplace deviance behaviors.

5 Identify the characteristics of the source, target, and message that affect persuasion.

6 Discuss the definition and importance of emotions at work.

7 Justify the importance of emotional contagion at work.

8 Contrast the effects of individual and organizational influences on ethical behavior.

9 Discuss how value systems, locus of control, Machiavellianism, and cognitive moral development affect ethical behavior.

THINKING AHEAD: THE TIMBERLAND COMPANY TAKES ETHICAL BEHAVIOR TO THE NEXT LEVEL

The Timberland Company ranked 74th on *Fortune*'s "100 Best Companies to Work For" in 2007. Timberland was also ranked 8th among *CRO* magazine's "100 Best Corporate Citizens." *CRO* magazine is a publication of the organization for Corporate Responsibility Officers. In trying business times such as ours where more ethical scandals break out each day, how does Timberland do it?

The answer is building a strong culture based on ethical value systems. Timberland has a very clear set of values and corporate governance code of conduct. It also has set up a clear ethical guidelines section that employees and corporate officers can refer to when in doubt. In fact, Timberland's mission statement includes a statement of their values and emphasis on ethical behavior. The four values driving ethical behavior at the company are humility, humanity, integrity, and excellence.

Timberland's major competitor, Nike, faced criticism in the past for using child labor. In 2006, Timberland announced it would include a "nutritional label" on its products to create more awareness among its customers about their product. This label includes a manufacturing details section that describes the name and location of the factory where that product was produced. The environmental impact section describes how much energy was spent on manufacturing it, and the community involvement section assesses whether the shoe meets the Timberland code of conduct and whether any child labor was involved. While some organizations focus on product packaging and service only to market their products, companies like Timberland seem to derive success from their value systems as much as from the product itself. You'll find more on Timberland's values and ethics in the Looking Back feature at the end of the chapter.[1, 2, 3]

In this chapter, we continue the discussion of individual differences we began in Chapter 3 with personality, perception, and attribution. Persons and situations jointly influence behavior, and individual differences help us to better understand the influence of the person. Our focus now is on three other individual difference factors: attitudes, emotions, and ethics.

ATTITUDES

An *attitude* is a psychological tendency that is expressed by evaluating a particular entity with some degree of favor or disfavor.[4] We respond favorably or unfavorably toward many things: coworkers, our own appearance, and politics are some examples.

Attitudes are important because of their links to behavior. Attitudes are also an integral part of the world of work. Managers speak of workers who have a "bad attitude" and conduct "attitude adjustment" talks with employees. Often, poor performance attributed to bad attitude really stems from lack of motivation, minimal feedback, lack of trust in management, or other problems. These are areas that managers must explore.

It is important for managers to understand the antecedents to attitudes as well as their consequences. Managers also need to understand the different components of attitudes, how attitudes are formed, the major attitudes that affect work behavior, and how to use persuasion to change attitudes.

The ABC Model

(1) Explain the ABC model of an attitude.

attitude
A psychological tendency expressed by evaluating an entity with some degree of favor or disfavor.

affect
The emotional component of an attitude.

Attitudes develop on the basis of evaluative responding. An individual does not have an attitude until he or she responds to an entity (person, object, situation, or issue) on an affective, cognitive, or behavioral basis. To understand the complexity of an attitude, we can break it down into three components, as depicted in Table 4.1.

These components—affect, behavioral intentions, and cognition—compose what we call the ABC model of an attitude.[5] *Affect* is the emotional component of an attitude. It refers to an individual's feeling about something or someone. Statements such as "I like this" or "I prefer that" reflect the affective component of an attitude. Affect is measured by physiological indicators such as galvanic skin response (changes in electrical resistance of skin that indicate emotional arousal) and blood pressure. These indicators show changes in emotions by measuring physiological arousal. An individual's attempt to hide his or her feelings might be shown by a change in arousal.

The second component is the intention to behave in a certain way toward an object or person. Our attitudes toward women in management, for example, may be inferred

TABLE 4.1 The ABC Model of an Attitude

	Component	Measured By	Example
A	Affect	Physiological indicators Verbal statements about feelings	I don't like my boss.
B	Behavioral intentions	Observed behavior Verbal statements about intentions	I want to transfer to another department.
C	Cognition	Attitude scales Verbal statements about beliefs	I believe my boss plays favorites at work.

SOURCE: Adapted from M. J. Rosenberg and C. I. Hovland, "Cognitive, Affective, and Behavioral Components of Attitude," in M. J. Rosenberg, C. I. Hovland, W. J. McGuire, R. P. Abelson, and J. H. Brehm, *Attitude Organization and Change* (New Haven, Conn.: Yale University Press, 1960). Copyright 1960 Yale University Press. Used with permission.

from observing the way we behave toward a female supervisor. We may be supportive, passive, or hostile, depending on our attitude. The behavioral component of an attitude is measured by observing behavior or by asking a person about behavior or intentions. The statement "If I were asked to speak at commencement, I'd be willing to try to do so, even though I'd be nervous" reflects a behavioral intention.

The third component of an attitude, cognition (thought), reflects a person's perceptions or beliefs. Cognitive elements are evaluative beliefs and are measured by attitude scales or by asking about thoughts. The statement "I believe Japanese workers are industrious" reflects the cognitive component of an attitude.

The ABC model shows that to thoroughly understand an attitude, we must assess all three components. Suppose, for example, you want to evaluate your employees' attitudes toward flextime (flexible work scheduling). You would want to determine how they feel about flextime (affect), whether they would use flextime (behavioral intention), and what they think about the policy (cognition). The most common method of attitude measurement, the attitude scale, measures only the cognitive component.

As rational beings, individuals try to be consistent in everything they believe in and do. They prefer consistency (consonance) between their attitudes and behavior. Anything that disrupts this consistency causes tension (dissonance), which motivates individuals to change either their attitudes or their behavior to return to a state of consistency. The tension produced when there is a conflict between attitudes and behavior is *cognitive dissonance*.[6]

Suppose, for example, a salesperson is required to sell damaged televisions for the full retail price, without revealing the damage to customers. She believes, however, that doing so constitutes unethical behavior. This creates a conflict between her attitude (concealing information from customers is unethical) and her behavior (selling defective TVs without informing customers about the damage).

The salesperson, experiencing the discomfort from dissonance, will try to resolve the conflict. She might change her behavior by refusing to sell the defective TV sets. Alternatively, she might rationalize that the defects are minor and that the customers will not be harmed by not knowing about them. These are attempts by the salesperson to restore equilibrium between her attitudes and behavior, thereby eliminating the tension from cognitive dissonance.

Managers need to understand cognitive dissonance because employees often find themselves in situations in which their attitudes conflict with their behavior. They manage the tension by changing their attitudes or behavior. Employees who display

cognitive dissonance
A state of tension that is produced when an individual experiences conflict between attitudes and behavior.

sudden shifts in behavior may be attempting to reduce dissonance. Some employees find the conflicts between strongly held attitudes and required work behavior so uncomfortable that they leave the organization to escape the dissonance.

Attitude Formation

(2) Describe how attitudes are formed.

Attitudes are learned. Our responses to people and issues evolve over time. Two major influences on attitudes are direct experience and social learning.

Direct experience with an object or person is a powerful influence on attitudes. How do you know that you like biology or dislike math? You have probably formed these attitudes from experience in studying the subjects. Research has shown that attitudes that are derived from direct experience are stronger, held more confidently, and more resistant to change than attitudes formed through indirect experience.[7] One reason attitudes derived from direct experience are so powerful is their availability. This means that the attitudes are easily accessed and are active in our cognitive processes.[8] When attitudes are available, we can call them quickly into consciousness. Attitudes that are not learned from direct experience are not as available, so we do not recall them as easily.

In *social learning,* the family, peer groups, religious organizations, and culture shape an individual's attitudes in an indirect manner.[9] Children learn to adopt certain attitudes by the reinforcement they are given by their parents when they display behaviors that reflect an appropriate attitude. This is evident when very young children express political preferences similar to their parents'. Peer pressure molds attitudes through group acceptance of individuals who express popular attitudes and through sanctions, such as exclusion from the group, placed on individuals who espouse unpopular attitudes.

Substantial social learning occurs through *modeling,* in which individuals acquire attitudes by merely observing others. After overhearing other individuals expressing an opinion or watching them engaging in a behavior that reflects an attitude, the observer adopts the attitude.

For an individual to learn from observing a model, four processes must take place:

1. The learner must focus attention on the model.
2. The learner must retain what was observed from the model. Retention is accomplished in two basic ways. In one, the learner "stamps in" what was observed by forming a verbal code for it. The other way is through symbolic rehearsal, by which the learner forms a mental image of himself or herself behaving like the model.
3. Behavioral reproduction must occur; that is, the learner must practice the behavior.
4. The learner must be motivated to learn from the model.

Culture also plays a definitive role in attitude development. Consider, for example, the contrast in the North American and European attitudes toward vacation and leisure. The typical vacation in the United States is two weeks, and some workers do not use all of their vacation time. In Europe, the norm is longer vacations; and in some countries, *holiday* means everyone taking a month off. The European attitude is that an investment in longer vacations is important to health and performance.

Attitudes and Behavior

If you have a favorable attitude toward participative management, will your management style be participative? As managers, if we know an employee's attitude, to what extent can we predict her or his behavior? These questions illustrate the fundamental issue of attitude–behavior correspondence, that is, the degree to which an attitude predicts behavior.

social learning
The process of deriving attitudes from family, peer groups, religious organizations, and culture.

This correspondence has concerned organizational behaviorists and social psychologists for quite some time. Can attitudes predict behaviors like being absent from work or quitting your job? Some studies suggested that attitudes and behavior are closely linked, while others found no relationship at all or a weak relationship at best. Attention then became focused on when attitudes predict behavior and when they do not. Attitude–behavior correspondence depends on five things: attitude specificity, attitude relevance, timing of measurement, personality factors, and social constraints.

Individuals possess both general and specific attitudes. You may favor women's right to reproductive freedom (a general attitude) and prefer pro-choice political candidates (a specific attitude) but not attend pro-choice rallies or send money to Planned Parenthood. That you don't perform these behaviors may make the link between your attitude and behaviors on this issue seem weak. However, given a choice between a pro-choice and an anti-abortion political candidate, you will probably vote for the pro-choice candidate. In this case, your attitude seems quite predictive of your behavior. The point is that the greater the attitude specificity, the stronger its link to behavior.[10]

Another factor that affects the attitude–behavior link is relevance.[11] Attitudes that address an issue in which we have some self-interest are more relevant for us, and our subsequent behavior is consistent with our expressed attitude. Suppose there is a proposal to raise income taxes for those who earn $150,000 or more. If you are a student, you may not find the issue of great personal relevance. Individuals in that income bracket, however, might find it highly relevant; their attitude toward the issue would be strongly predictive of whether they would vote for the tax increase.

The timing of the measurement also affects attitude–behavior correspondence. The shorter the time between the attitude measurement and the observed behavior, the stronger the relationship. For example, voter preference polls taken close to an election are more accurate than earlier polls.

Personality factors also influence the attitude–behavior link. One personality disposition that affects the consistency between attitudes and behavior is self-monitoring. Recall from Chapter 3 that low self-monitors rely on their internal states when making decisions about behavior, while high self-monitors are more responsive to situational cues. Low self-monitors therefore display greater correspondence between their attitudes and behaviors.[12] High self-monitors may display little correspondence between their attitudes and behavior because they behave according to signals from others and from the environment.

Finally, social constraints affect the relationship between attitudes and behavior.[13] The social context provides information about acceptable attitudes and behaviors.[14, 15] New employees in an organization, for example, are exposed to the attitudes of their work group. Suppose a newcomer from Afghanistan holds a negative attitude toward women in management because in his country the prevailing attitude is that women should not be in positions of power. He sees, however, that his work group members respond positively to their female supervisor. His own behavior may therefore be compliant because of social constraints. This behavior is inconsistent with his attitude and cultural belief system.

Work Attitudes

Attitudes at work are important because, directly or indirectly, they affect work behavior. Chief among the things that negatively affect employees' work attitudes are jobs that are very demanding, combined with a lack of control on the part of the employee.[16] A positive psychological climate at work, on the other hand, can lead to positive attitudes and good performance.[17] A study found that when hotel employees offered helpful, concerned service, hotel customers developed a warmer, more positive attitude toward the hotel itself. This attitude resulted in greater customer loyalty,

YOU 4.1

Assess Your Job Satisfaction

Think of the job you have now or a job you've had in the past. Indicate how satisfied you are with each aspect of your job below, using the following scale:

1 = Extremely dissatisfied
2 = Dissatisfied
3 = Slightly dissatisfied
4 = Neutral
5 = Slightly satisfied
6 = Satisfied
7 = Extremely satisfied

1. The amount of job security I have.
2. The amount of pay and fringe benefits I receive.
3. The amount of personal growth and development I get in doing my job.
4. The people I talk to and work with on my job.
5. The degree of respect and fair treatment I receive from my boss.
6. The feeling of worthwhile accomplishment I get from doing my job.
7. The chance to get to know other people while on the job.
8. The amount of support and guidance I receive from my supervisor.
9. The degree to which I am fairly paid for what I contribute to this organization.
10. The amount of independent thought and action I can exercise in my job.
11. How secure things look for me in the future in this organization.
12. The chance to help other people while at work.
13. The amount of challenge in my job.
14. The overall quality of the supervision I receive on my work.

Now compute your scores for the facets of job satisfaction.

Pay satisfaction:

Q2 + Q9 = Divided by 2:

Security satisfaction:

Q1 + Q1 = Divided by 2:

Social satisfaction:

Q4 + Q7 + Q12 = Divided by 3:

Supervisory satisfaction:

Q5 + Q8 + Q14 = Divided by 3:

Growth satisfaction:

Q3 + Q6 + Q10 + Q13 = Divided by 4:

Scores on the facets range from 1 to 7. (Scores lower than 4 suggest there is room for change.)

This questionnaire is an abbreviated version of the Job Diagnostic Survey, a widely used tool for assessing individuals' attitudes about their jobs. Compare your scores on each facet to the following norms for a large sample of managers.

Pay satisfaction:	4.6
Security satisfaction:	5.2
Social satisfaction:	5.6
Supervisory satisfaction:	5.2
Growth satisfaction:	5.3

How do your scores compare? Are there actions you can take to improve your job satisfaction?

SOURCE: *Work Redesign* by Hackman/Oldham, © 1980. Reprinted by permission of Pearson Education, Inc., Upper Saddle River, N.J.

greater likelihood that the customers would stay at the hotel, and even a willingness to pay more for the same service. Customer attitudes were strongly influenced by employee gestures, facial expressions, and words. In this study, customer attitudes were crucial to the success of the firm, and employee behaviors were crucial in forming customer attitudes, meaning firms can "train" their employees to "train" customers to have better attitudes![18]

Although many work attitudes are important, two attitudes in particular have been emphasized. Job satisfaction and organizational commitment are key attitudes of interest to managers and researchers.

③ Identify sources of job satisfaction and commitment and suggest tips for managers to help build these two attitudes among their employees.

job satisfaction
A pleasurable or positive emotional state resulting from the appraisal of one's job or job experiences.

Job Satisfaction Most of us believe that work should be a positive experience. *Job satisfaction* is a pleasurable or positive emotional state resulting from the appraisal of one's job or job experiences.[19] It has been treated both as a general attitude and as satisfaction with five specific dimensions of the job: pay, the work itself, promotion opportunities, supervision, and coworkers.[20] You can assess your own job satisfaction by completing You 4.1.

An individual may hold different attitudes toward various aspects of the job. For example, an employee may like her job responsibilities but be dissatisfied with the opportunities for promotion. Personal characteristics also affect job satisfaction.[21] Those with high negative affectivity are more likely to be dissatisfied with their jobs. Challenging work, valued rewards, opportunities for advancement, competent supervision, and supportive coworkers are dimensions of the job that can lead to satisfaction.

There are several measures of job satisfaction. One of the most widely used measures comes from the Job Descriptive Index (JDI). This index measures the specific facets of satisfaction by asking employees to respond yes, no, or cannot decide to a series of statements describing their jobs. Another popular measure is the Minnesota Satisfaction Questionnaire (MSQ).[22] This survey also asks employees to respond to statements about their jobs, using a five-point scale that ranges from very dissatisfied to very satisfied. Figure 4.1 presents some sample items from each questionnaire.

Managers and employees hold a common belief that happy or "satisfied" employees are more productive at work. Most of us feel more satisfied than usual when we believe that we are performing better than usual.[23] Interestingly, the relationship between job satisfaction and performance is quite a bit more complex than that. Are satisfied workers more productive? Or are more productive workers more satisfied? The link between satisfaction and performance has been widely explored. One view holds that satisfaction causes good performance. If this were true, the manager's job would simply be to keep workers happy. Although this may be the case for certain individuals, job satisfaction for most people is one of several causes of good performance. Read about one important consequence of low job satisfaction and employee morale at Yahoo in the Real World 4.1 feature.

Another view holds that good performance causes satisfaction. If this were true, managers would need to help employees perform well, and satisfaction would follow. However, some employees who are high performers are not satisfied with their jobs.

The research shows modest support for both views, but no simple, direct relationship between satisfaction and performance has been found.[24] One reason for these results may be the difficulty of demonstrating the attitude–behavior links we described earlier in this chapter. Future studies using specific, relevant attitudes and measuring personality variables and behavioral intentions may be able to demonstrate a link between job satisfaction and performance.

Another reason for the lack of a clear relationship between satisfaction and performance is the intervening role of rewards. Employees who receive valued rewards are more satisfied. In addition, employees who receive rewards that are contingent on performance (the higher the performance, the larger the reward) tend to perform better. Rewards thus influence both satisfaction and performance. The key to influencing both satisfaction and performance through rewards is that the rewards are valued by employees and are tied directly to performance.

(4) Distinguish between organizational citizenship and workplace deviance behaviors.

Job satisfaction has been shown to be related to many other important personal and organizational outcomes. It is related to *organizational citizenship behavior*—behavior that is above and beyond the call of duty. Satisfied employees are more likely to make positive comments about the company, refrain from complaining when things at work do not go well, and help their coworkers.[25] Going beyond the call of duty is especially important to organizations using teams to get work done. Employees depend on extra help from each other to get things accomplished. When massive wildfires swept through California in 2003, most businesses in the San Diego

organizational citizenship behavior
Behavior that is above and beyond the call of duty.

FIGURE 4.1 Sample Items from Satisfaction Questionnaires

Job Descriptive Index

Think of the work you do at present. How well does each of the following words or phrases describe your work? In the blank beside each word given below, write

__Y__ for "Yes" if it describes your work
__N__ for "No" if it does NOT describe it
__?__ if you cannot decide

WORK ON YOUR PRESENT JOB:

______ Routine
______ Satisfying
______ Good

Think of the majority of the people that you work with now or the people you meet in connection with your work. How well does each of the following words or phrases describe these people? In the blank beside each word, write

__Y__ for "Yes" if it describes the people you work with
__N__ for "No" if it does NOT describe them
__?__ if you cannot decide

COWORKERS (PEOPLE):

______ Boring
______ Responsible
______ Intelligent

Minnesota Satisfaction Questionnaire

1 = Very dissatisfied
2 = Dissatisfied
3 = I can't decide whether I am satisfied or not
4 = Satisfied
5 = Very satisfied

On my present job, this is how I feel about:

______ The chance to work alone on the job (independence)
______ My chances for advancement on this job (advancement)
______ The chance to tell people what to do (authority)
______ The praise I get for a good job (recognition)
______ My pay and the amount of work I do (compensation)

SOURCES: The Job Descriptive Index is copyrighted by Bowling Green State University. The complete forms, scoring key, instructions, and norms can be obtained from Dr. Patricia C. Smith, Department of Psychology, Bowling Green State University, Bowling Green, OH 43403. Minnesota Satisfaction Questionnaire from D. J. Weiss, R. V. Davis, G. W. England, and L. H. Lofquist, *Manual for the Minnesota Satisfaction Questionnaire* (University of Minnesota Vocational Psychology Research, 1967).

area closed for one or more days as choking black smoke filled the air and thousands of homes were threatened. Aplus.net, an Internet service provider, chose to remain open; however, due to the danger involved, the company did not require its employees to report to work. Yet, in spite of thick smoke, most of the firm's employees came to work anyway, even though some were unsure if their homes would be waiting for them when they left work that evening.[26] Because of their willingness to go the extra mile, Aplus.net and its customers remained up and running throughout the fires. The firm reported in November that the massive fires had no negative impact on its financial results for the quarter.

Satisfied workers are more likely to want to give something back to the organization because they want to reciprocate their positive experiences.[27] Often, employees may feel that citizenship behaviors are not recognized because they occur outside the confines of normal job responsibilities. Organizational citizenship behaviors (OCBs) do, however, influence performance evaluations. Employees who exhibit behaviors such as helping others, making suggestions for innovations, and developing their skills receive higher performance ratings.[28] And different parts of

THE REAL WORLD 4.1

Yahoo: Down and Out?

Yahoo was recently plagued by rumors of takeovers by Microsoft or Google. It is consistently being outperformed by its rival Google and is reporting its worst revenues in years. Several industry analysts have started to speculate that if Yahoo doesn't cut costs or divest assets, there might indeed be a takeover.

These speculations fueled some negative behaviors within the organization, including turnover. Several top Yahoo executives and engineers who have been with the company for years have migrated to greener pastures at Google or Apple. Yahoo's troubles are manifested through three main symptoms: mass exodus of experienced executives from the company, taking with them years of knowledge and know-how; a bureaucratic organizational structure that slows down decision making; and employee complaints about the lack of passion from their CEO, Terry Semel.

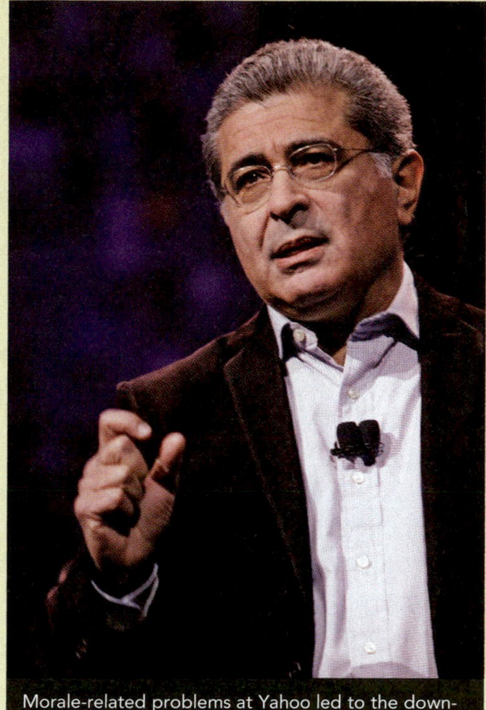

© AP PHOTO/DAMIAN DOVARGANES

Morale-related problems at Yahoo led to the downfall of former Yahoo CEO Terry Semel.

Such massive morale problems finally led to Semel's downfall at Yahoo. Now the company is headed by a woman president, Susan Decker, and a very young CEO, Jerry Yang, who is also its cofounder. Both executives are expected to bring a much-needed morale boost to Yahoo through their creative energy and expertise. For now, the rumors of a merger or takeover seem to have settled down. Only time will tell if Yahoo is able to pull itself out of its current morale problems.

SOURCES: R. D. Hof, "Even Yahoo! Gets the Blues." *Business Week* (2007): 37; M. Helft, "Can She Turn Yahoo into, Well, Google?" *The New York Times* (July 1, 2007), http://news.com.com/Can+she+turn+Yahoo+into%2C+well%2C+Google/2100-1024_3-6194437.html?tag=st.num.

an attitude relate to different targets of OCBs. Affect tends to direct OCBs toward other people, while job cognitions direct OCBs toward the organization.[29]

Individuals who identify strongly with the organization are more likely to perform OCBs.[30] High self-monitors, who base their behavior on cues from the situation, are also more likely to perform OCBs.[31] Good deeds, in the form of OCBs, can be contagious. One study found that when a person's close coworkers chose to perform OCBs, that person was more likely to reciprocate. When the norm among other team members was to engage in OCBs, the individual worker was more likely to offer them. The impact of one worker's OCBs can spread throughout an entire department.[32]

Although researchers have had a tough time demonstrating the link between job satisfaction and individual performance, this has not been the case for the link between job satisfaction and organizational performance. Companies with satisfied workers have better performance than companies with dissatisfied workers.[33] This may be due to the more intangible elements of performance, like organizational citizenship behavior, that contribute to organizational effectiveness but aren't necessarily captured by just measuring individual job performance.

Job satisfaction is related to some other important outcomes. People who are dissatisfied with their jobs are absent more frequently. The type of dissatisfaction that most often causes employee absenteeism is dissatisfaction with the work itself.

In addition, unhappy workers are more likely to quit their jobs, and turnover at work can be very costly to organizations. Such workers also report more psychological and medical problems than do satisfied employees.[34]

Researchers have consistently demonstrated a link between job satisfaction and turnover intentions; that is, unhappy employees tend to leave the organization. One thing that leads to dissatisfaction at work is a misfit between an individual's values and the organization's values, which is called a lack of person–organization fit. People who feel that their values don't mesh with the organization's experience job dissatisfaction and eventually leave the company when other job opportunities arise.[35]

Like all attitudes, job satisfaction is influenced by culture. American workers tend to hold to the "Protestant work ethic," which values work for its own sake and makes it a central part of their lives. Consistent with this basic view, American managers place a high value on outcomes such as autonomy, independence, and achievement. Koreans, in contrast to Americans, generally grow up in a more authoritarian system, which places greater value on family and less value on work for its own sake. Americans place greater value on and find greater job satisfaction through intrinsic job factors, whereas Koreans prefer extrinsic factors.[36]

This finding was echoed in a study comparing job satisfaction across 49 countries. Job characteristics and job satisfaction were more tightly linked in richer countries, more individualistic countries, and smaller power-distance countries. These findings suggest that cultural differences have strong influences on job satisfaction and the factors that produce it.[37]

Because organizations face the challenge of operating in the global environment, managers must understand that job satisfaction and other job attitudes are significantly affected by culture. Employees from different cultures may have differing expectations of their jobs; thus, there may be no single prescription for increasing the job satisfaction of a multicultural workforce. Researchers are currently studying job attitudes around the world. In China's hotel and restaurant industry, for example, researchers found that high-performance human resource practices led to service-oriented OCBs. Examples of such practices include promotions from within, flexibility in job assignments, long-term-results-oriented appraisals, and job security. Such OCBs were in turn linked to lower turnover and higher productivity at the organizational level.[38] So, it appears that high-performance human resource practices have very positive impacts in China.

Workplace deviance behavior (*WDB*)—counterproductive behavior that violates organizational norms and causes harm to others or the organization—is another outcome of attitudes at work.[39] Deviance is garnering attention due to negative events in the business world such as downsizing, technological insecurities, and other challenges being faced by many organizations. Layoffs, for example, may cause employees to develop negative attitudes and to feel anger and hostility toward the organization and to indulge in retaliatory behaviors. Even when an employee keeps his or her job but believes the procedure used to determine the layoff is unfair, workplace deviance such as bad-mouthing the employer or revenge against the manager may occur. [40, 41] Unfairness at work is a major cause of deviance, sabotage, and retaliation. Positive attitudes about the work environment lead to reduced deviance. Preventing and managing WDB is important because it harms department and organizational performance. You can assess your own workplace deviance behaviors with the questionnaire in You 4.2.

workplace deviance behavior
Any voluntary counterproductive behavior that violates organizational norms and causes some degree of harm to organizational functioning.

organizational commitment
The strength of an individual's identification with an organization.

Organizational Commitment The strength of an individual's identification with an organization is known as *organizational commitment*. There are three kinds of organizational commitment: affective, continuance, and normative.

YOU 4.2

Do You Engage in Workplace Deviance Behavior?

Think of the job you have now or a job you've had in the past. Indicate to what extent you engaged in the behaviors below. Use the following scale:

1 Very slightly or not at all
2 A little
3 Moderately
4 Quite a bit
5 Definitely

1. Worked on a personal matter instead of work for your employer.
2. Taken property from work without permission.
3. Spent too much time fantasizing or daydreaming instead of working.
4. Made fun of someone at work.
5. Falsified a receipt to get reimbursed for more money than you spent on business expenses.
6. Said something hurtful to someone at work.
7. Taken an additional or a longer break than is acceptable at your workplace.
8. Repeated a rumor or gossip about your company.
9. Made an ethnic, religious, or racial remark or joke at work.
10. Come in late to work without permission.
11. Littered your work environment.
12. Cursed at someone at work.
13. Called in sick when you were not.
14. Told someone about the lousy place where you work.
15. Lost your temper while at work.
16. Neglected to follow your boss's instructions.
17. Intentionally worked slower than you could have worked.
18. Discussed confidential company information with an unauthorized person.
19. Left work early without permission.
20. Played a mean prank on someone at work.
21. Left your work for someone else to finish.
22. Acted rudely toward someone at work.
23. Repeated a rumor or gossip about your boss or coworkers.
24. Made an obscene comment at work.
25. Used an illegal drug or consumed alcohol on the job.
26. Put little effort into your work.
27. Publicly embarrassed someone at work.
28. Dragged out work in order to get overtime.

SOURCE: R. J. Bennett and S. L. Robinson, S. L. "Development of a Measure of Workplace Deviance," *Journal of Applied Psychology* 85 (2000): 349–360.

Affective commitment is an employee's intention to remain in an organization because of a strong desire to do so. It consists of three factors:

- A belief in the goals and values of the organization.
- A willingness to put forth effort on behalf of the organization.
- A desire to remain a member of the organization.[42]

Affective commitment encompasses loyalty, but it is also a deep concern for the organization's welfare.

Continuance commitment is an employee's tendency to remain in an organization because he or she cannot afford to leave.[43] Sometimes employees believe that if they leave, they will lose a great deal of their investments in time, effort, and benefits and that they cannot replace these investments.

Normative commitment is a perceived obligation to remain with the organization. Individuals who experience normative commitment stay with the organization because they feel that they should.[44]

Certain organizational conditions encourage commitment. Participation in decision making and job security are two such conditions. Certain job characteristics also positively affect commitment. These include autonomy, responsibility, role clarity and interesting work.[45, 46]

affective commitment
A type of organizational commitment based on an individual's desire to remain in an organization.

continuance commitment
A type of organizational commitment based on the fact that an individual cannot afford to leave.

normative commitment
A type of organizational commitment based on an individual's perceived obligation to remain with an organization.

Affective and normative commitments are related to lower rates of absenteeism, higher quality of work, increased productivity, and several different types of performance.[47] Managers should encourage affective commitment because committed individuals expend more task-related effort and are less likely than others to leave the organization.[48]

Managers can increase affective commitment by communicating that they value employees' contributions, and that they care about employees' well-being.[49] Affective commitment also increases when the organization and employees share the same values, and when the organization emphasizes values like moral integrity, fairness, creativity, and openness.[50] Negative experiences at work can undoubtedly diminish affective commitment. One such experience is discrimination. Perceived age discrimination, whether for being too old or too young, can dampen affective commitment.[51]

Several researchers have examined organizational commitment in different countries. One study revealed that American workers displayed higher affective commitment than did Korean and Japanese workers.[52] Another study showed that Chinese workers place high value on social relationships at work and that those with stronger interpersonal relationships are more committed to their organizations.[53] The authors suggest that Chinese firms improve employee commitment and retention by organizing activities to help cultivate relationships among employees. This means that expatriate managers should be sensitive to the quality of relationships among their Chinese employees if they want to improve organizational commitment.

Job satisfaction and organizational commitment are two important work attitudes that managers can strive to improve among their employees. And these two attitudes are strongly related. Both affective and normative commitment are related to job satisfaction. Increasing job satisfaction is likely to increase commitment as well. To begin with, managers can use attitude surveys to reveal employees' satisfaction or dissatisfaction with specific facets of their jobs. Then they can take action to make the deficient aspects of the job more satisfying. Work attitudes are also important because they influence business outcomes. Job satisfaction and organizational citizenship behavior are linked to customer satisfaction and company profitability.[54]

Persuasion and Attitude Change

(5) Identify the characteristics of the source, target, and message that affect persuasion

To understand how attitudes can change, it is necessary to understand the process of persuasion. The days of command-and-control management, in which executives simply told employees what do to, are long gone. Modern managers must be skilled in the art of persuasion.[55] Through persuasion, one individual (the source) tries to change the attitude of another person (the target). Certain characteristics of the source, target, and message affect the persuasion process. There are also two cognitive routes to persuasion.

Source Characteristics Three major characteristics of the source affect persuasion: expertise, trustworthiness, and attractiveness.[56] A source who is perceived as an expert is particularly persuasive. Trustworthiness is also important. John Mack, head of Credit Suisse First Boston (CSFB), understands the importance of trust. When he came to CSFB, the investment bank was a huge mess, but in a short time Mack achieved amazing results by persuading his employees to trust him. First, he told CSFB's bankers that their pay packages were excessive and the firm could not afford them. The bankers gave back more than $400 million in cash bonuses. Next, he asked CSFB's executives to give up some of the richest pay packages in the business. Mack was able to convince them to give up amounts that sometimes exceeded $20 million, all so that younger executives could receive bonuses and remain with the firm. And when lawyers discovered an e-mail suggesting a top CSFB employee had covered up wrongdoing from federal regulators, Mack immediately alerted federal regulators. His employees trust him because he doesn't just talk about teamwork, integrity, and trust; he demonstrates them in his own career. This trustworthiness allowed him to persuade his employees to help him save the firm.[57] Finally, attractiveness and likeability play a role in persuasion. Attractive communicators have long been used in advertising to persuade consumers to buy certain products. As a source of persuasion, managers who are perceived as being experts, who are trustworthy, or who are attractive or likable will have an edge in changing employee attitudes.

Target Characteristics Some people are more easily persuaded than others. Individuals with low self-esteem are more likely to change their attitudes in response to persuasion than are those with high self-esteem. People who hold very extreme attitudes are more resistant to persuasion, and those who are in a good mood are easier to persuade.[58] Undoubtedly, individuals differ widely in their susceptibility to persuasion. Managers must recognize these differences and realize that their attempts to change attitudes may not receive universal acceptance.

Message Characteristics Suppose you must implement an unpopular policy at work. You want to persuade your employees that the policy is a positive change. Should you present one side of the issue or both sides? Given that your employees are already negatively inclined toward the policy, you will have more success in changing their attitudes if you present both sides. This shows support for one side of the issue while acknowledging that another side does exist. Moreover, refuting the other side makes it more difficult for the targets to hang on to their negative attitudes.

Messages that are obviously designed to change the target's attitude may be met with considerable negative reaction. In fact, undisguised, deliberate attempts at changing attitudes may cause attitude change in the opposite direction! This is most likely to occur when the target of the persuasive communication feels her or his freedom is threatened.[59] Less threatening approaches are less likely to elicit negative reactions. The emotional tone of the message is also important. Persuasion is more successful when messages are framed with the same emotion as that felt by the receiver.[60]

Cognitive Routes to Persuasion When are message characteristics more important, and when are other characteristics more important in persuasion? The elaboration likelihood model of persuasion, presented in Figure 4.2, proposes that persuasion occurs over two routes: the central route and the peripheral route.[61] The routes are differentiated by the amount of elaboration, or scrutiny, the target is motivated to give the message.

The *central route* to persuasion involves direct cognitive processing of the message's content. When an issue is personally relevant, the individual is motivated to think carefully about it. The listener may nod his/her head when the argument is strong and shake his or her head if the argument is weak.[62] In the central route, the content of the message is very important. If the arguments presented are logical and convincing, attitude change will follow.

In the *peripheral route* to persuasion, the individual is not motivated to pay much attention to the message's content. This is because the message may not be perceived as personally relevant, or the target may be distracted. Instead, the individual is persuaded by characteristics of the persuader—for example, expertise, trustworthiness, and attractiveness. In addition, he or she may be persuaded by statistics, the number of arguments presented, or the method of presentation—all of which are nonsubstantial aspects of the message.

The elaboration likelihood model shows that the target's level of involvement with the issue is important. That involvement also determines which route to

FIGURE 4.2 The Elaboration Likelihood Model of Persuasion

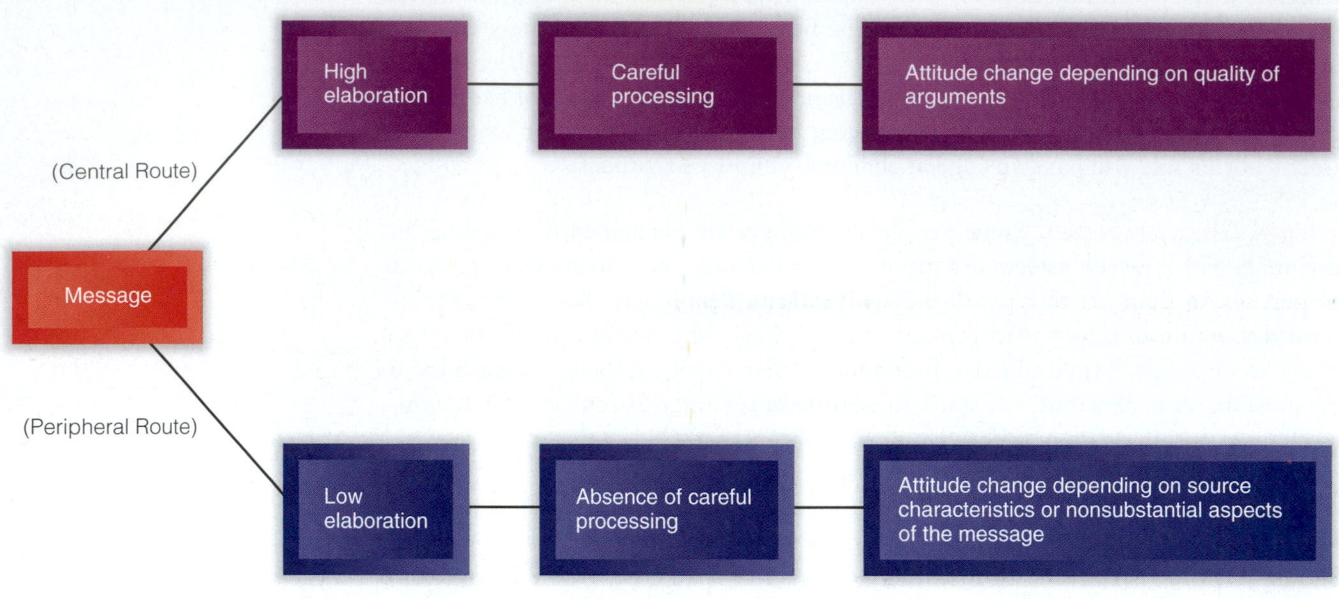

SOURCE: Adapted from R. E. Petty and J. T. Cacioppo, "The Elaboration Likelihood Model of Persuasion," in L. Berkowitz, ed., *Advances in Experimental Social Psychology*, vol. 19 (New York: Academic Press, 1986): 123–205.

persuasion will be more effective. In some cases, attitude change comes about through both the central and the peripheral routes. To cover all of the bases, managers should structure the content of their messages carefully, develop their own attributes that will help them be more persuasive, and choose a method of presentation that will be attractive to the audience.[63]

We have seen that the process of persuading individuals to change their attitudes is affected by the source, the target, the message, and the route. When all is said and done, however, managers are important catalysts for encouraging attitude change. This is a difficult process. Recently, researchers have proposed that people hold attitudes at two different levels.

EMOTIONS AT WORK

(6) Discuss the definition and importance of emotions at work

Traditional management theories did not place a premium on studying the effects of employee emotions at work. This was largely because emotions were thought to be "bad" for rational decision making. Ideas about management centered around the stereotypic ideal employee who kept her or his emotions in check and behaved in a totally rational rather than emotional manner. Because of recent research, we know that emotions and cognitions are intertwined and that both are normal parts of human functioning and decision making.

What are emotions? They are mental states that typically include feelings, physiological changes, and the inclination to act.[64]

emotions
Mental states that typically include feelings, physiological changes, and the inclination to act.

Emotions (e.g., anger, joy, pride, hostility) are short-lived, intense reactions to an event that affect work behaviors. Individuals differ in their capacity to experience both positive emotions (e.g. happiness, pride) and negative emotions (e.g., anger, fear, guilt).[65] Employees have to cope with both positive and negative events at work almost daily, and these events lead to moods and emotions. When events at work are positive and goals are being met, employees experience positive emotions.[66] Events that threaten or thwart the achievement of goals cause negative emotions,

The Inner Work Life and Impact of Emotions on Performance

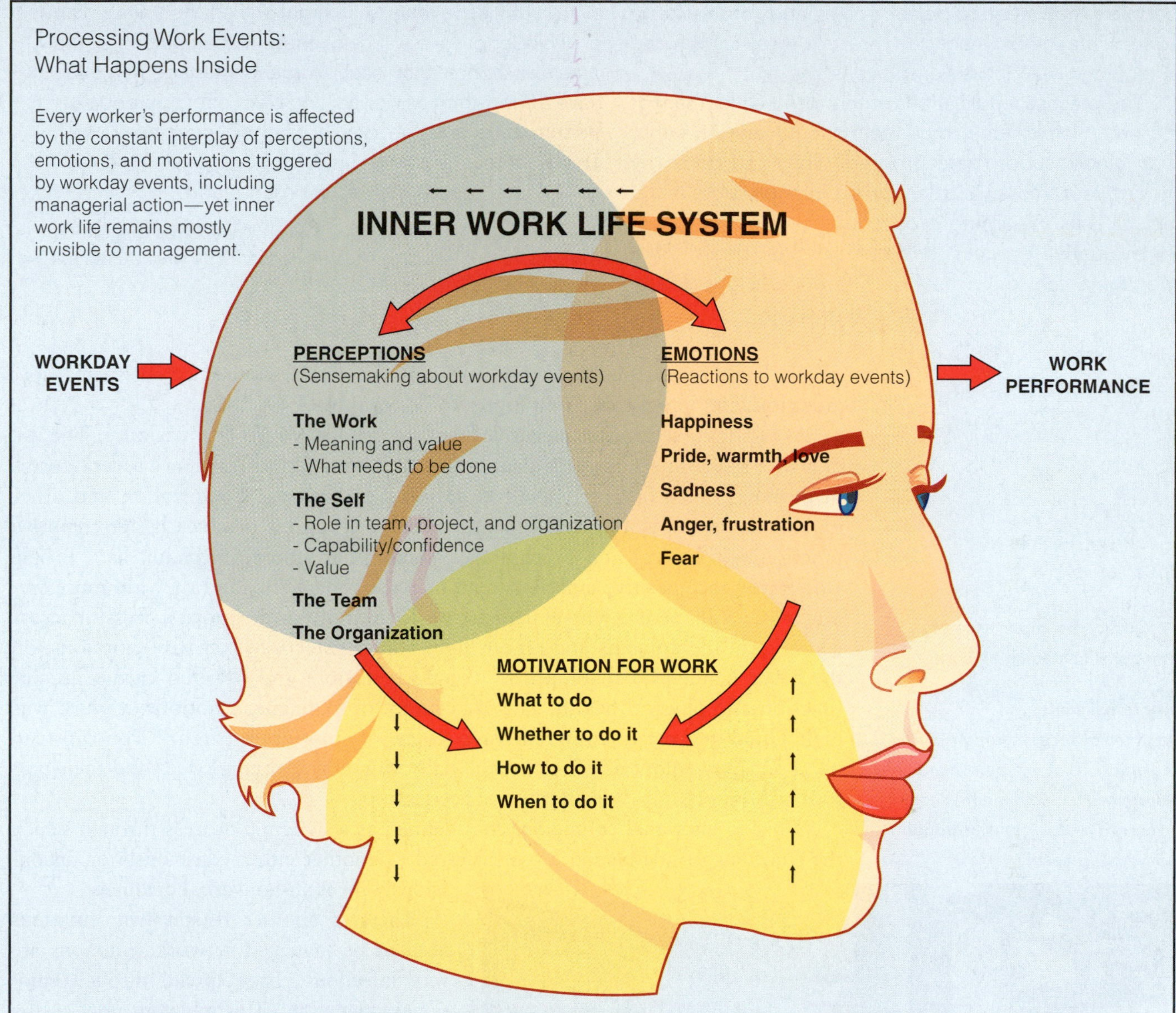

Do emotions matter to work life? This question led two researchers to explore the role of everyday emotion reactions in work behavior. In a comprehensive study involving 238 professionals from 28 project teams, these researchers uncovered the significant impact of emotions on team performance. They invited these knowledge professionals to keep diaries of their workday for the duration of a major project they were involved in. After 12,000 such diary entries later, these researchers were able to offer an insight into employees' inner work lives.

This study reveals that people perceive everyday work events (positive or negative) and immediately engage in a process of sense making. This sense making is affected by both the rational part of the brain responsible for logical decisions and the emotional part responsible for feelings. People's sense-making processes in turn evoke emotions, which impact what they do at work and their motivation to perform. For example, one diary entry revealed that a team was working on a project that was very important to their organization with huge financial implications ($145 million was at stake). As the team was working late hours and through Memorial Day when the rest of the country was on holiday, one employee reported positive emotions (e.g., happiness) in response to a top management official bringing them pizza and bottled water after-hours. This event caused the team to view top management as

(Continued)

supportive and caring. This in turn made them more confident in their project and led to better team performance. Similarly, layoffs announced after an acquisition caused immense fear and anger, which in turn affected people's motivation to perform. This study further highlighted that most managers are not in sync with the inner work lives of their employees.

The practical implications of this research for managers are twofold: one, managers should enable rather than hinder subordinate progress. They can do so by making resources available viewing work progress or the lack of it as a learning mechanism in addition to just an evaluative process, and setting clear goals. Two, managers can really make a difference to the quality of employees' inner work lives by managing with a human touch. People's progress in this research was vastly facilitated by perceptions of a supervisor that was appreciative and fair in interpersonal interactions. Focusing on trifling events that highlight shortcomings can only hinder progress. Finally, these researchers offer the practical advice that such humane management can have a short-term as well as long-term effect on people's performance and the quality of their inner work lives. That is ultimately why an understanding of such perceptions and emotions matters in organizations.

SOURCE: T. M. Amabile and S. J. Kamer, "Inner Work Life: Understanding the Subtext of Business Performance," *Harvard Business Review* 85 (5): (2007): 72–83.

which then threaten job satisfaction and commitment. Positive emotions such as joy, attention, and interest lead employees to perform more OCBs.[67]

As we discussed earlier, negative emotions lead to workplace deviance. The use of power and influence in organizations, even if it is routine, can spark several forms of deviance. Such deviance could be targeted at both the organization and other individuals in the work environment.[68] Positive emotions produce better cognitive functioning, physical and psychological health, and coping mechanisms.[69] People who experience positive emotions tend to do so repeatedly, and they are more creative.[70] Overall, people who experience positive emotions are more successful across a variety of life domains and report higher life satisfaction. Negative emotions, on the other hand, lead to unhealthy coping behaviors and lowered cardiovascular function and physical health. The importance of managing emotions at work was highlighted in a recent comprehensive review of emotion research.[71] You can read all about how emotions affect the the daily work lives of employees and their performance in organizations in the Science feature.

7 Justify the importance of emotional contagion at work.

emotional contagion
A dynamic process through which the emotions of one person are transferred to another either consciously or unconsciously through nonverbal channels.

What is emotional contagion? It is defined as a dynamic process through which the emotions of one person are transferred to another either consciously or unconsciously through nonverbal channels.

© DOUGLAS GRAHAM/CONGRESSIONAL QUARTERLY/GETTY IMAGES

An employee of Pike Place Fish, an open-air market in downtown Seattle, entertains customers by throwing a halibut to a co-worker for cleaning after selling the fish to a customer. Positive emotions that travel through a work group through emotional contagion produce cooperation and task performance.

There is another reason why emotions need to be managed at work: emotions are very infectious. They spread through emotional contagion. This phenomenon occurs primarily through nonverbal cues, and is affected through a basic human tendency of mimicry. We tend to mimic each other's facial expressions, body language, speech patterns, and vocal tones. Emotional contagion is an important work process because most jobs today require some degree of interpersonal interaction. Examples of such interactions could be dealing with a customer who is angry, a coworker who is fearful of a layoff decision, a leader who praises an employee's work, and so on. Emotional contagion could occur in many of these instances and travel throughout the work group. Positive emotions that spread through a work group through this process produce cooperation and task performance.[72] The opposite can occur as well. Negative emotions can permeate a work group and destroy morale and performance.

When organizations and their employees go through change and/or huge losses, the pain caused by such trauma is not always eased by reason. Good leaders learn how to use compassion to heal and rebuild employee morale.[73] You will recall the tragedy of September 11th in New York City. Examples abound of organizational leaders who stood by their people with strength and empathy in times of tragedy. Yet other companies there refused, for example, to give their employees the next day off. These organizations failed to create a comfortable place for their employees to share their grief and trauma. Undoubtedly, these are not issues that could be resolved by a sound business strategy alone but by compassionate leaders who are not afraid to let their emotions show appropriately and are not disdainful of employee feelings.

The impact of emotion is far-reaching in workplace behavior. Much of our decision-making is driven by emotions. Emotions play a particularly important role in heated negotiations wherein some parties might benefit from the experience of certain emotions.[74]

ETHICAL BEHAVIOR

Ethics is the study of moral values and moral behavior. *Ethical behavior* is acting in ways consistent with one's personal values and the commonly held values of the organization and society.[75]

There is evidence that paying attention to ethical issues pays off for companies. In the early 1990s, James Burke, then the CEO of Johnson & Johnson, put together a list of companies that devoted a great deal of attention to ethics. The group included Johnson & Johnson, Coca-Cola, Gerber, Kodak, 3M, and Pitney Bowes. Over a forty-year period, the market value of these organizations grew at an annual rate of 11.3 percent, as compared to 6.2 percent for the Dow Jones industrials as a whole.[76] Doing the right thing can have a positive effect on an organization's performance.[77]

Ethical behavior in firms can also lead to practical benefits, particularly in attracting new talent. Firms with better reputations are able to attract more applicants, creating a larger pool from which to hire, and evidence suggests that respected firms are able to choose higher-quality applicants.[78] For example, Timberland is built on a strong system of values as noted in the Thinking Ahead feature on pages 117–118. This continually helps them attract and recruit the best talent as well as maintain a solid reputation with investors.

Failure to handle situations in an ethical manner can cost companies. Employees who are laid off or terminated are very concerned about the quality of treatment they receive. Honestly explaining the reasons for the dismissal and preserving the dignity of the employee will reduce the likelihood that she or he will initiate a claim against the company. One study showed that less than 1 percent of employees who felt the company was being honest filed a claim; more than 17 percent of those who felt the company was being less than honest filed claims.[79]

Unethical behavior by employees can affect individuals, work teams, and even the organization. Organizations thus depend on individuals to act ethically. For this reason, more and more firms are starting to monitor their employees' Internet usage. "Little Brother" and "SurfControl Web Filter" are just two of several software packages that allow system administrators to easily monitor employee Web usage, flagging visits to specific Web sites by using neural network technology to classify URL content and block Web traffic.

ethical behavior
Acting in ways consistent with one's personal values and the commonly held values of the organization and society.

Although some employees have complained that this type of monitoring violates their privacy, the courts have generally disagreed, arguing that employees are using company hardware and software, hence the company is entitled to monitor what employees do with it. In one such case, Michael Smyth was fired from his job with Pillsbury Co. after company employees read inflammatory comments he made in several e-mails to his supervisor. Smyth sued for wrongful termination, claiming that his right to privacy was violated because the firm had told employees their e-mail would remain confidential. Despite these promises, the court ruled that Smyth had no reasonable expectation of privacy while using the firm's equipment; further, it said, Smyth's right to privacy was outweighed by the firm's need to conduct business in a professional manner. Only future court cases will clarify where a firm's effort to monitor potentially unethical behavior actually crosses its own ethical line.[80]

Today's high-intensity business environment makes it more important than ever to have a strong ethics program in place. In a survey of more than 4,000 employees conducted by the Washington, D.C.–based Ethics Resource Center, one-third of the employees said that they had witnessed ethical misconduct in the past year. If that many employees actually saw unethical acts, imagine how many unethical behaviors occurred behind closed doors! The most common unethical deeds witnessed were lying to supervisors (56 percent), lying on reports or falsifying records (41 percent), stealing or theft (35 percent), sexual harassment (35 percent), drug or alcohol abuse (31 percent), and conflicts of interest (31 percent).[81]

One of the toughest challenges managers face is aligning the ideal of ethical behavior with the reality of everyday business practices. Violations of the public's trust are costly. Since Jack in the Box restaurants' *E. coli* crisis, the company has faced image and financial problems. And Firestone Inc., after spending more than a third of a billion dollars replacing allegedly defective tires on Ford sport utility vehicles in 2000, still faces an uncertain future including billions of dollars in lawsuits. Studies show that firms experience lower accounting returns and slow sales growth for as long as five years after being convicted of a corporate illegality.[82]

The ethical issues that individuals face at work are complex. A review of articles appearing in *The Wall Street Journal* during just one week revealed more than sixty articles dealing with ethical issues in business.[83] As Table 4.2 shows, the themes

TABLE 4.2 Ethical Issues from One Week in *The Wall Street Journal*

1. **Stealing:** Taking things that don't belong to you.
2. **Lying:** Saying things you know aren't true.
3. **Fraud and deceit:** Creating or perpetuating false impressions.
4. **Conflict of interest and influence buying:** Bribes, payoffs, and kickbacks.
5. **Hiding versus divulging information:** Concealing information that another party has a right to know or failing to protect personal or proprietary information.
6. **Cheating:** Taking unfair advantage of a situation.
7. **Personal decadence:** Aiming below excellence in terms of work performance (e.g., careless or sloppy work).
8. **Interpersonal abuse:** Behaviors that are abusive of others (e.g., sexism, racism, emotional abuse).
9. **Organizational abuse:** Organizational practices that abuse members (e.g., inequitable compensation, misuses of power).
10. **Rule violations:** Breaking organizational rules.
11. **Accessory to unethical acts:** Knowing about unethical behavior and failing to report it.
12. **Ethical dilemmas:** Choosing between two equally desirable or undesirable options.

SOURCE: Kluwer Academic Publishers, by J. O. Cherrington and D. J. Cherrington, "A Menu of Moral Issues: One Week in the Life of *The Wall Street Journal*," *Journal of Business Ethics* 11 (1992): 255–265. Reprinted with kind permission of Springer Science and Business Media.

PepsiCo in India: The Impact of Cultural Differences in Perceptions of Ethical Behavior

PepsiCo recently named India as one of its topmost strategic priorities. Headed by a woman CEO with a Yale degree, this organization seems to be battling a strange and socially driven demon in India. Water is a scarce commodity in much of India, and PepsiCo CEO Indra K. Nooyi has firsthand experience in living with such scarcity. However, she might not have anticipated that this issue would resurface as one of the most important business challenges soon after she took over as the company's CEO last year.

© REUTERS/B MATHUR/LANDOV

There was a protest in India against PepsiCo and Coca-Cola after reports that products sold in India were contaminated with pesticides.

Driven by activist and social worker Sunita Narain, also a woman, the issue of water contamination in bottled beverages caused PepsiCo's sales to fall dramatically over the last year. Locals accused the multinational giant of exhausting their already scarce water resources and also that pesticides made their way into such bottled beverages. This accusation by a well-known and highly respected social activist and environmentalist caused public protests against PepsiCo's beverages and led to a ban of bottled soft drinks in several states.

Much of this protest seems to be entangled in the bigger issue of local Indian consumers' perception that such corporate giants pollute and use natural resources indiscriminately. To make matters worse, Narain called for a test of water samples used in both Pepsi and Coke's bottled beverages in India. They found contamination levels that would not be acceptable in the United States. Narain accused the two corporate giants of selling subpar products that would never be sold in the United States. PepsiCo subsequently lost corporate sponsors in India.

Recently, the company launched several efforts to address these perceptions of lack of concern for local communities by digging wells in villages. CEO Narain traveled through India trying to promote the image of PepsiCo as a company with a soul. She talks about investing in local communities and educating people about sustainable water harvesting techniques. Such practices seem to have diminished the intensity of this scandal in India, at least for now, as PepsiCo's sales continue to slowly climb.

SOURCE: D. Brady, "Pepsi: Repairing a Poisoned Reputation In India," *Business Week online* (June 11, 2007). http://www.businessweek.com/magazine/content/07_24/b4038064.htm?chan=search.

appearing throughout the articles were distilled into twelve major ethical issues. You can see that few of these issues are clear-cut. All of them depend on the specifics of the situation, and their interpretation depends on the characteristics of the individuals examining them. For example, look at issue 2: lying. We all know that "white lies" are told in business. Is this acceptable? The answer varies from person to person. Thus, the perception of what constitutes ethical versus unethical behavior in organizations varies among individuals. Check out Timberland's guidelines for ethical behavior at http://www.timberland.com/investorRelations/index.jsp. Moreover, corporate social responsibility might not be just a buzzword anymore. Check out the Real World 4.2 feature to learn about PepsiCo's troubles over water contamination in India.

Ethical behavior is influenced by two major categories of factors: individual characteristics and organizational factors.[84] This section looks at the individual influences. We examine organizational influences throughout the remainder of the

FIGURE 4.3 Individual/Organizational Model of Ethical Behavior

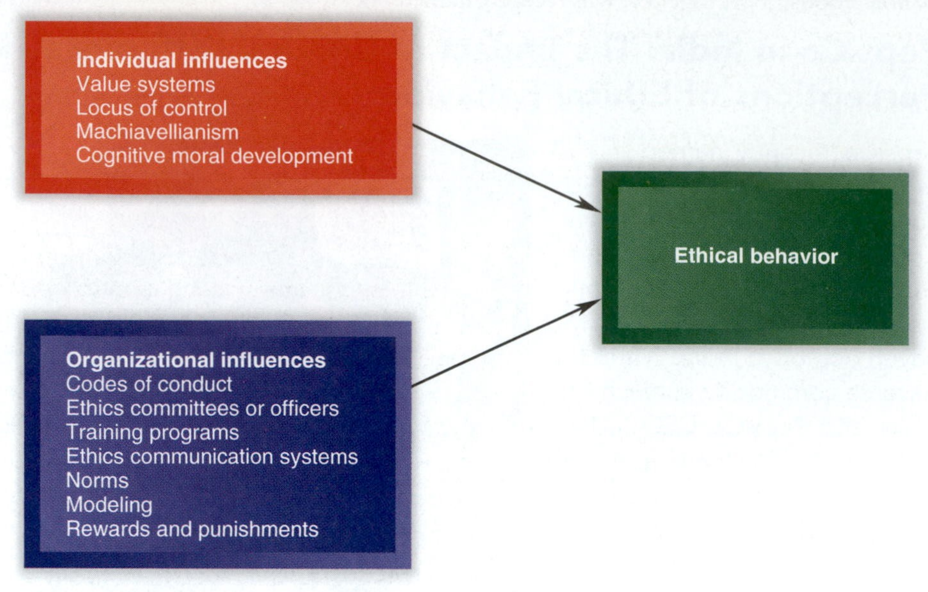

book—particularly in Chapter 15, where we focus on creating an organizational culture that reinforces ethical behavior.

8 Contrast the effects of individual and organizational influences on ethical behavior.

The model that guides our discussion of individual influences on ethical behavior is presented in Figure 4.3. It shows both individual and organizational influences.

Making ethical decisions is part of each manager's job. It has been suggested that ethical decision making requires three qualities of individuals:[85]

1. The competence to identify ethical issues and evaluate the consequences of alternative courses of action.
2. The self-confidence to seek out different opinions about the issue and decide what is right in terms of a particular situation.
3. Toughmindedness—the willingness to make decisions when all that needs to be known cannot be known and when the ethical issue has no established, unambiguous solution.

What are the individual characteristics that lead to these qualities? Our model presents four major individual differences that affect ethical behavior: value systems, locus of control, Machiavellianism, and cognitive moral development.

VALUES

9 Discuss how value systems, locus of control, Machiavellianism, and cognitive moral development affect ethical behavior.

values

Enduring beliefs that a specific mode of conduct or end state of existence is personally or socially preferable to an opposite or converse mode of conduct or end state of existence.

One important source of individual differences in ethical behavior is values. We use them to evaluate our own behavior and that of others. As such, they vary widely among individuals. *Values* are enduring beliefs that a specific mode of conduct or end state of existence is personally or socially preferable to an opposite or converse mode of conduct or end state of existence.[86] This definition was proposed by Rokeach, an early scholar of human values. As individuals grow and mature, they learn values, which may change over the life span as an individual develops a sense of self. Cultures, societies, and organizations shape values. Parents and others who are respected by the individual play crucial roles in value development by providing guidance about what is right and wrong. Because values are general beliefs about right and wrong, they form the basis for ethical behavior. For example, Whole Foods is committed to environmentally friendly causes

and has created a foundation for the compassionate treatment of animals. The CEO of Whole Foods, John Mackey, was recently named one of the top 30 corporate leaders in American businesses. Mackey has set an extraordinary example by ignoring conventional wisdom and refusing to compete with Wal-Mart. Instead he has led Whole Foods through five consecutive years of 21 percent sales gains by strongly adhering to what he believes in and being environmentally and socially responsible. Visit the wholefoods.com Web site to learn more about how being values driven can lead to success.

Instrumental and Terminal Values

Rokeach distinguished between two types of values: instrumental and terminal. *Instrumental values* reflect the means to achieving goals; that is, they represent the acceptable behaviors to be used in achieving some end state. Instrumental values identified by Rokeach include ambition, honesty, self-sufficiency, and courage. *Terminal values*, in contrast, represent the goals to be achieved or the end states of existence. Rokeach identified happiness, love, pleasure, self-respect, and freedom among the terminal values. A complete list of instrumental and terminal values is presented in Table 4.3. Terminal and instrumental values work in concert to provide individuals with goals to strive for and acceptable ways to achieve the goals.

This discussion of values is highlighted in our opening case of Timberland. The terminal values of Timberland include creating communities that are sustainable and manufacturing products that do not leave a footprint on the planet. Its instrumental values are concern for the environment and the communities that make its business happen. These instrumental values are shown in acts such as recruiting volunteers to engage in service in the communities in which they operate and displaying nutritional labels on their shoes.

Americans' rankings of instrumental and terminal values have shown remarkable stability over time.[87] The highest-ranked instrumental values were honesty, ambition, responsibility, forgiving nature, open-mindedness, and courage. The highest ranked terminal values were world peace, family security, freedom, happiness, self-respect, and wisdom.

TABLE 4.3 Instrumental and Terminal Values

	Instrumental Values	
Honesty	Ambition	Responsibility
Forgiving nature	Open-mindedness	Courage
Helpfulness	Cleanliness	Competence
Self-control	Affection/love	Cheerfulness
Independence	Politeness	Intelligence
Obedience	Rationality	Imagination
	Terminal Values	
World peace	Family security	Freedom
Happiness	Self-respect	Wisdom
Equality	Salvation	Prosperity
Achievement	Friendship	National security
Inner peace	Mature love	Social respect
Beauty in art and nature	Pleasure	Exciting, active life

SOURCE: Table adapted with the permission of The Free Press, a Division of Simon & Schuster, Inc., from *The Nature of Human Values* by Milton Rokeach. Copyright © 1973 by The Free Press.

instrumental values
Values that represent the acceptable behaviors to be used in achieving some end state.

terminal values
Values that represent the goals to be achieved or the end states of existence.

Age also affects values. Baby boomers' values contrast with those of the baby busters, who are beginning to enter the workforce. The baby busters value family life and time off from work and prefer a balance between work and home life. This contrasts with the more driven, work-oriented value system of the boomers. The baby boomers placed a huge emphasis on achievement values. Their successors in Generation X and Generation Y, however, are markedly different in what they value at work. For example, Generation X values self-reliance, individualism, and balance between family and work life. Generation Y, on the other hand, values freedom in scheduling so much that most are employed only part-time. Furthermore, they have a work-to-live mindset rather than the live-to-work philosophy of the baby boomers.[88]

Work Values

Work values are important because they affect how individuals behave on their jobs in terms of what is right and wrong.[89] Four work values relevant to individuals are achievement, concern for others, honesty, and fairness.[90] Achievement is a concern for the advancement of one's career. This is shown in such behaviors as working hard and seeking opportunities to develop new skills. Concern for others is shown in caring, compassionate behaviors such as encouraging other employees or helping others work on difficult tasks. These behaviors constitute organizational citizenship, as we discussed earlier. Honesty is providing accurate information and refusing to mislead others for personal gain. Fairness emphasizes impartiality and recognizes different points of view. Individuals can rank-order these values in terms of their importance in their work lives.[91] Although individuals' value systems differ, sharing similar values at work produces positive results. Employees who share their supervisor's values are more satisfied with their jobs and more committed to the organization.[92] Values also have profound effects on the choice of jobs. Traditionally, pay and advancement potential have been the strongest influences on job choice decisions. One study, however, found that three other work values—achievement, concern for others, and fairness—exerted more influence on job choice decisions than did pay and promotion opportunities.[93]

This means that organizations recruiting job candidates should pay careful attention to individuals' values and to the messages that organizations send about company values. A new "name and shame" report published in Australia by RepuTex is designed to embarrass companies that behave unethically. Nineteen groups graded each of Australia's top companies on corporate governance policies, environmental friendliness, and workplace practices. The 500-page report named Westpac, a major bank, as the most ethical firm in Australia. Westpac was the only company in the country's top 100 to receive the AAA rating.[94]

Cultural Differences in Values

As organizations face the challenges of an increasingly diverse workforce and a global marketplace, it becomes more important than ever for them to understand the influence of culture on values. Doing business in a global marketplace often means that managers encounter a clash of values among different cultures. Take the value of loyalty, for example. In Japan, loyalty means "compassionate overtime." Even though you have no work to do, you should stay late to give moral support to your peers who are working late.[95] In contrast, Koreans value loyalty to the person for whom one works.[96] In the United States, family and other personal loyalties are more highly valued than is loyalty to the company or one's supervisor.

Cultures differ in what they value in terms of an individual's contributions to work. Collectivist cultures such as China and Mexico value a person's contributions to relationships in the work team. In contrast, individualist cultures like the United States and the Netherlands value a person's contributions to task accomplishment. Both collectivist and individualist cultures value rewards based on individual performance.[97] Iran also represents a collectivist culture. Iranian managers' values, which include little tolerance for ambiguity, high need for structure, and willingness to sacrifice for the good of society, are greatly influenced by Islam. Belonging, harmony, humility, and simplicity are all values promoted by Islam.[98]

Values also affect individuals' views of what constitutes authority. French managers value authority as a right of office and rank. Their behavior reflects this value, as they tend to use power based on their position in the organization. In contrast, managers from the Netherlands and Scandinavia value group inputs to decisions and expect their decisions to be challenged and discussed by employees.[99]

Value differences between cultures must be acknowledged in today's global economy. We may be prone to judging the value systems of others, but we should resist the temptation to do so. Tolerating diversity in values can help us understand other cultures. Value systems of other nations are not necessarily right or wrong—merely different. The following suggestions can help managers understand and work with the diverse values that characterize the global environment:[100]

1. Learn more about and recognize the values of other peoples. They view their values and customs as moral, traditional, and practical.
2. Avoid prejudging the business customs of others as immoral or corrupt. Assume they are legitimate unless proved otherwise.
3. Find legitimate ways to operate within others' ethical points of view—do not demand that they operate within your value system.
4. Avoid rationalizing "borderline" actions with excuses such as the following:
   - "This isn't really illegal or immoral."
   - "This is in the organization's best interest."
   - "No one will find out about this."
   - "The organization will back me up on this."
5. Refuse to do business when stakeholder actions violate or compromise laws or fundamental organizational values.
6. Conduct relationships as openly and aboveboard as possible.

Locus of Control

Another individual influence on ethical behavior is locus of control. In Chapter 3, we introduced locus of control as a personality variable that affects individual behavior. Recall that people with an internal locus of control believe that they control events in their lives and that they are responsible for what happens to them. In contrast, people with an external locus of control believe that outside forces such as fate, chance, or other people control what happens to them.[101]

Internals are more likely than externals to take personal responsibility for the consequences of their ethical or unethical behavior. Externals are more apt to believe that external forces caused their ethical or unethical behavior. Research has shown that internals make more ethical decisions than do externals.[102] Internals also are more resistant to social pressure and are less willing to hurt another person, even if ordered to do so by an authority figure.[103]

Machiavellianism

Another individual difference that affects ethical behavior is Machiavellianism. Niccolò Machiavelli was a sixteenth-century Italian statesman. He wrote *The Prince*, a guide for acquiring and using power.[104] The primary method for achieving power that he suggested was manipulation of others. *Machiavellianism,* then, is a personality characteristic indicating one's willingness to do whatever it takes to get one's own way.

A high-Mach individual behaves in accordance with Machiavelli's ideas, which include the notion that it is better to be feared than loved. High-Machs tend to use deceit in relationships, have a cynical view of human nature, and have little concern for conventional notions of right and wrong.[105] They are skilled manipulators of other people, relying on their persuasive abilities. Low-Machs, in contrast, value loyalty and relationships. They are less willing to manipulate others for personal gain and are concerned with others' opinions.

High-Machs believe that the desired ends justify any means. They believe that manipulation of others is fine if it helps achieve a goal. Thus, high-Machs are likely to justify their manipulative behavior as ethical.[106] They are emotionally detached from other people and are oriented toward objective aspects of situations. And high-Machs are likelier than low-Machs to engage in behavior that is ethically questionable.[107] Employees can counter Machiavellian individuals by focusing on teamwork instead of on one-on-one relationships where high-Machs have the upper hand. It is also beneficial to make interpersonal agreements public and thus less susceptible to manipulation by high-Machs.

Cognitive Moral Development

An individual's level of *cognitive moral development* also affects ethical behavior. Psychologist Lawrence Kohlberg proposed that as individuals mature, they move through a series of six stages of moral development.[108] With each successive stage, they become less dependent on other people's opinions of right and wrong and less self-centered (acting in one's own interest). At higher levels of moral development, individuals are concerned with broad principles of justice and with their self-chosen ethical principles. Kohlberg's model focuses on the decision-making process and on how individuals justify ethical decisions. His model is a cognitive developmental theory about how people think about what is right and wrong and how the decision-making process changes through interaction with peers and the environment.

Cognitive moral development occurs at three levels, and each level consists of two stages. In Level I, called the premoral level, the person's ethical decisions are based on rewards, punishments, and self-interest. In Stage 1, the individual obeys rules to avoid punishment. In Stage 2, the individual follows the rules only if it is in his or her immediate interest to do so.

In Level II, the conventional level, the focus is on the expectations of others (parents, peers) or society. In Stage 3, individuals try to live up to the expectations of people close to them. In Stage 4, they broaden their perspective to include the laws of the larger society. They fulfill duties and obligations and want to contribute to society.

In Level III, the principled level, what is "right" is determined by universal values. The individual sees beyond laws, rules, and the expectations of other people. In Stage 5, individuals are aware that people have diverse value systems. They uphold their own values despite what others think. For a person to be classified as being in Stage 5, decisions must be based on principles of justice and rights. For example, a person who decides to picket an abortion clinic just because his religion says abortion is wrong is not a Stage 5 individual. A person who arrives at the same decision through a complex decision process based on justice and rights may be a Stage 5 individual. The key is the process rather than the decision itself. In Stage 6, the individual follows self-selected ethical principles. If there is a conflict between a law and a self-selected ethical principle, the individual acts according to the principle.

As people mature, their moral development passes through these stages in an irreversible sequence. Research suggests that most adults are in Stage 3 or 4. Most adults thus never reach the principled level of development (Stages 5 and 6).

Machiavellianism
A personality characteristic indicating one's willingness to do whatever it takes to get one's own way.

cognitive moral development
The process of moving through stages of maturity in terms of making ethical decisions.

Since it was proposed more than thirty years ago, Kohlberg's model of cognitive moral development has received a great deal of research support. Individuals at higher stages of development are less likely to cheat,[109] more likely to engage in whistle-blowing,[110] and more likely to make ethical business decisions.[111, 112]

Kohlberg's model has also been criticized. Gilligan, for example, has argued that the model does not take gender differences into account. Kohlberg's model was developed from a 20-year study of 84 boys.[113] Gilligan contends that women's moral development follows a different pattern—one that is based not on individual rights and rules but on responsibility and relationships. Women and men face the same moral dilemmas but approach them from different perspectives—men from the perspective of equal respect and women from the perspective of compassion and care. Researchers who reviewed the research on these gender differences concluded that the differences may not be as strong as originally stated by Gilligan. Some men use care reasoning, and some women may use justice reasoning when making moral judgments.[114]

There is evidence to support the idea that men and women view ethics differently. A large-scale review of 66 studies found that women were more likely than men to perceive certain business practices as unethical. Young women were more likely to see breaking the rules and acting on insider information as unethical. Both sexes agreed that collusion, conflicts of interest, and stealing are unethical. It takes about 21 years for the gender gap to disappear. Men seem to become more ethical with more work experience; the longer they are in the workforce, the more their attitudes become similar to those held by women. There is an age/experience effect for both sexes: experienced workers are more likely to think lying, bribing, stealing, and colluding are unethical.[115]

Individual differences in values, locus of control, Machiavellianism, and cognitive moral development are important influences on ethical behavior in organizations. Given that these influences vary widely from person to person, how can organizations use this knowledge to increase ethical behavior? One action would be to hire those who share the organization's values. Another would be to hire only internals, low-Machs, and individuals at higher stages of cognitive moral development. This strategy obviously presents practical and legal problems.

There is evidence that cognitive moral development can be increased through training.[116] Organizations could help individuals move to higher stages of moral development by providing educational seminars. However, values, locus of control, Machiavellianism, and cognitive moral development are fairly stable in adults.

The best way to use the knowledge of individual differences may be to recognize that they help explain why ethical behavior differs among individuals and to focus managerial efforts on creating a work situation that supports ethical behavior.

Most adults are susceptible to external influences; they do not act as independent ethical agents. Instead, they look to others and to the organization for guidance. Managers can offer such guidance by encouraging ethical behavior through codes of conduct, ethics committees, ethics communication systems, training, norms, modeling, and rewards and punishments, as shown in Figure 4.3. We discuss these areas further in Chapter 16.

MANAGERIAL IMPLICATIONS: ATTITUDES, VALUES, AND ETHICS AT WORK

Managers must understand attitudes because of their effects on work behavior. By understanding how attitudes are formed and how they can be changed, managers can shape employee attitudes. Attitudes are learned through observation of other employees and by the way they are reinforced. Job satisfaction and organizational commitment are important attitudes to encourage among employees, and participative management is an excellent tool for doing so.

Emotions are also important because of their influence on employee behaviors. Managers should be trained to perceive emotions in employees and manage them effectively. They should watch for burnout and emotional exhaustion, specifically in service occupations. Such emotion management can help foster organizational citizenship behaviors and prevent workplace deviance in the organization.

Ethical behavior at work is affected by individual and organizational influences. A knowledge of individual differences in value systems, locus of control, Machiavellianism, and cognitive moral development helps managers understand why individuals have diverse views about what constitutes ethical behavior.

This chapter concludes our discussion of individual differences that affect behavior in organizations. Attitudes, emotions, and ethics combine with personality, perception, and attribution to make people unique. Individual uniqueness is a major managerial challenge, and it is one reason there is no single best way to manage people.

LOOKING BACK: THE TIMBERLAND COMPANY

Walking the Talk and "Making It Better"

Jeffrey Schwartz, the CEO and president of the Timberland Company, seems to be adept at walking the talk. Since he took over in 1998, he has created a new corporate image for Timberland with renewed emphasis on ethical and environmental issues. Timberland employees recruited 9,000 volunteers to engage in about 54,000 hours of community service as a part of their Earth Day celebrations. Schwartz asserts that this is in line with the company's vision of becoming carbon neutral by the year 2010. Timberland also has a commitment to diversity and has a strong contingent of women and minorities on its board of directors. It also has several worker-friendly programs such as on-site childcare at its headquarters. Timberland's catchphrase "Make It Better" reflects such commitment to ethical standards in conduct of their business. They are also an industry leader in recruiting volunteers from the communities they operate in. Check out the following Web site to stay informed of the thousands of volunteer opportunities facilitated via Timberland.[117,118]

http://www.timberland.com/timberlandserve/timberlandserve_index.jsp

Chapter Summary

1. The ABC model of an attitude contends that an attitude has three components: affect, behavioral intentions, and cognition. Cognitive dissonance is the tension produced by a conflict between attitudes and behavior.
2. Attitudes are formed through direct experience and social learning. Direct experience creates strong attitudes because the attitudes are easily accessed and active in cognitive processes.
3. Attitude–behavior correspondence depends on attitude specificity, attitude relevance, timing of measurement, personality factors, and social constraints.
4. Two important work attitudes are job satisfaction and organizational commitment. There are cultural differences in these attitudes, and both attitudes can be improved by providing employees with opportunities for participation in decision making.

5. A manager's ability to persuade employees to change their attitudes depends on characteristics of the manager (expertise, trustworthiness, and attractiveness); the employees (self-esteem, original attitude, and mood); the message (one-sided versus two-sided); and the route (central versus peripheral).
6. Emotions can strongly affect an individual's behavior at work.
7. Instrumental values reflect the means to achieving goals; terminal values represent the goals to be achieved.
8. Ethical behavior is influenced by the individual's value system, locus of control, Machiavellianism, and cognitive moral development.

Key Terms

affect (p. 118)
affective commitment (p. 127)
attitude (p. 118)
cognitive dissonance (p. 119)
cognitive moral development (p. 140)
continuance commitment (p. 127)
emotions (p. 130)
emotional contagion (p. 132)
ethical behavior (p. 133)
instrumental values (p. 137)
job satisfaction (p. 122)
Machiavellianism (p. 140)
normative commitment (p. 127)
organizational citizenship behavior (p. 123)
organizational commitment (p. 126)
social learning (p. 120)
terminal values (p. 137)
values (p. 136)
workplace deviance behavior (p. 126)

Review Questions

1. How are attitudes formed? Which source is stronger?
2. Discuss cultural differences in job satisfaction and organizational commitment.
3. What are the major influences on attitude–behavior correspondence? Why do some individuals seem to exhibit behavior that is inconsistent with their attitudes?
4. What should managers know about the emotions at work?
5. Define *values*. Distinguish between instrumental values and terminal values. Are these values generally stable, or do they change over time?
6. What is the relationship between values and ethics?
7. How does locus of control affect ethical behavior?
8. What is Machiavellianism, and how does it relate to ethical behavior?
9. Describe the stages of cognitive moral development. How does this concept affect ethical behavior in organizations?

Discussion and Communication Questions

1. What jobs do you consider to be most satisfying? Why?
2. How can managers increase their employees' job satisfaction?
3. Suppose you have an employee whose lack of commitment is affecting others in the work group. How would you go about persuading the person to change this attitude?
4. In Rokeach's studies on values, the most recent data are from 1981. Do you think values have changed since then? If so, how?
5. What are the most important influences on an individual's perceptions of ethical behavior? Can organizations change these perceptions? If so, how?
6. How can managers encourage organizational citizenship?
7. *(communication question)* Suppose you are a manager in a customer service organization. Your group includes seven supervisors who report directly to you. Each supervisor manages a team of seven customer service representatives. One of your supervisors, Linda, has complained that Joe, one of her employees, has "an attitude problem." She has requested that Joe be transferred to another team. Write a memo to Linda explaining your position on this problem and what should be done.
8. *(communication question)* Select a company that you admire for its values. Use the resources of your university library to answer two questions. First, what are the company's values? Second, how do employees enact these values? Prepare an oral presentation to present in class.

9. *(communication question)* Think of a time when you have experienced cognitive dissonance. Analyze your experience in terms of the attitude and behavior involved. What did you do to resolve the cognitive dissonance? What other actions could you have taken? Write a brief description of your experience and your responses to the questions.

Ethical Dilemma

Sara, a manager in a large software development company, sits at her desk looking out the window. The challenge before her is to pick a project manager for a major new project just given to her department. She has narrowed her choice to two employees. Sara's first option is Paula, who is probably the most qualified candidate for this project. No one knows this area of software development better than Paula. She also has extensive knowledge of the client. Paula has one other attribute, which can be a positive or a negative factor: attitude. She is the best at her job and she knows it. She also lets everyone else know it. Because of this, she always gets the top projects. The problem is that Paula cares only about Paula and little else. She is not a team player and does little to contribute to the department as a whole. She can be arrogant and extremely self-centered.

Sara's other option is Mark. Mark is also talented with all the markings of becoming a great project manager if given the chance. In addition to his technical skills, Mark is an excellent coworker. He is a team player who cares as much about the success of the department as he does about his own personal success. He is well liked by everyone, especially Sara. As a manager, she always appreciates Mark's willingness to consider the department's needs and not just the work that would lead to personal success.

Sara's predicament needs to be resolved by the end of the day. She knows everyone expects her to again choose Paula to head this project. However, Sara really believes it is time to give Mark a chance. She realizes the fallout for not choosing Paula would be great, but she is really tired of doing what everyone, including Paula, expects her to do within her own department.

Questions

1. What is Sara's obligation to the client?
2. Does this obligation affect her decision?
3. Using consequential, rule-based, and character theories, evaluate Sara's decision options.

Experiential Exercises

4.1 Chinese, Indian, and American Values

Purpose

To learn some differences among Chinese, Indian, and American value systems.

Group size

Any number of groups of five to eight people.

Time required

50+ minutes

Exercise Schedule

1. **Complete rankings (preclass)**

   Students rank the fifteen values for either Chinese and American orientations or for Indian and American systems. If time permits, all three can be done.

	Unit time	Total time
2. Small groups (optional)	**15 min.**	**15 min.**
3. Group presentations (optional)	**15 min.**	**30 min.**
4. Discussion	**20+ min.**	**50 min.**

2. **Small groups (optional)** — Groups of five to eight members try to achieve consensus on the ranking values for both Chinese and American cultures.

3. **Group presentations (optional)** — Each group presents its rankings and discusses reasons for making those decisions.

4. **Discussion** — Instructor leads a discussion on the differences between Chinese and American value systems and presents the correct rankings.

Value Rankings

Rank each of the fifteen values below according to what you think they are in the Chinese, Indian (from India), and American cultures. Use "1" as the most important value for the culture and "15" as the least important value for that culture.

Value	American	Chinese	Indian
Achievement			
Deference			
Order			
Exhibition			
Autonomy			
Affiliation			
Intraception			
Succorance			

Dominance
Abasement
Nurturance
Change
Endurance
Heterosexuality
Aggression

Some Definitions

Intraception: The tendency to be governed by subjective factors, such as feelings, fantasies, speculations, and aspirations; the other side of extraception, where one is governed by concrete, clearly observable physical conditions.

Succorance: Willingness to help another or to offer relief.

Abasement: To lower oneself in rank, prestige, or esteem.

Internal/External Locus of Control

Consider American and Chinese groups. Which would tend to have more internal locus of control (tend to feel in control of one's destiny, that rewards come as a result of hard work, perseverance, and responsibility)? Which would be more external (fate, luck or other outside forces control destiny)?

Machiavellianism

This concept was defined by Christie and Geis as the belief that one can manipulate and deceive people for personal gain. Do you think Americans or Chinese would score higher on the Machiavellian scale?

Discussion Questions

1. What are some main differences among the cultures? Did any pattern emerge?
2. Were you surprised by the results?
3. What behaviors could you expect in business dealings with Chinese (or Indians) based on their value system?
4. How do American values dictate Americans' behaviors in business situations?

SOURCE: "Chinese, Indian, and American Values" by Dorothy Marcic, copyright 1993. Adapted from Michael Harris Bond, ed., *The Psychology of the Chinese People,* Hong Kong: Oxford University Press, 200 Madison Ave., NY 10016, 1986. The selection used here is a portion of "Chinese Personality and Its Change," by Kuo-Shu Yang, pp. 106–170. Reprinted by permission.

4.2 Is This Behavior Ethical?

The purpose of this exercise is to explore your opinions about ethical issues faced in organizations. The class should be divided into twelve groups. Each group will randomly be assigned one of the following issues, which reflect the twelve ethical themes found in *The Wall Street Journal* study shown in Table 4.3.

1. Is it ethical to take office supplies from work for home use? Make personal long-distance calls from the office? Use company time for personal business? Or do these behaviors constitute stealing?
2. If you exaggerate your credentials in an interview, is it lying? Is lying in order to protect a coworker acceptable?
3. If you pretend to be more successful than you are in order to impress your boss, are you being deceitful?
4. How do you differentiate between a bribe and a gift?
5. If there are slight defects in a product you are selling, are you obligated to tell the buyer? If an advertised "sale" price is really the everyday price, should you divulge the information to the customer?
6. Suppose you have a friend who works at the ticket office for the convention center where Shania Twain will be appearing. Is it cheating if you ask the friend to get you tickets so that you won't have to fight the crowd to get them? Is buying merchandise for your family at your company's cost cheating?
7. Is it immoral to do less than your best in terms of work performance? Is it immoral to accept workers' compensation when you are fully capable of working?
8. What behaviors constitute emotional abuse at work? What would you consider an abuse of one's position of power?
9. Are high-stress jobs a breach of ethics? What about transfers that break up families?
10. Are all rule violations equally important? Do employees have an ethical obligation to follow company rules?
11. To what extent are you responsible for the ethical behavior of your coworkers? If you witness unethical behavior and don't report it, are you an accessory?
12. Is it ethical to help one work group at the expense of another? For instance, suppose one group has excellent performance and you want to reward its members with an afternoon off. In that case, the other group will have to pick up the slack and work harder. Is this ethical?

Once your group has been assigned its issue, you have two tasks:

1. First, formulate your group's answer to the ethical dilemmas.
2. After you have formulated your group's position, discuss the individual differences that may have contributed to your position. You will want to discuss the individual differences presented in this chapter as well as any others that you feel affected your position on the ethical dilemma.

Your instructor will lead the class in a discussion of how individual differences may have influenced your positions on these ethical dilemmas.

SOURCE: Kluwer Academic Publishers, by J. O. Cherrington and D. J. Cherrington, "A Menu of Moral Issues: One Week in the Life of *The Wall Street Journal,*" *Journal of Business Ethics* 11 (1992): 255–265. Reprinted with kind permission of Springer Science and Business Media.

TAKE 2

Biz Flix | The Emperor's Club

William Hundert (Kevin Kline), a professor at Saint Benedict's Academy for Boys, believes in teaching his students about living a principled life. He also wants them to learn his beloved classical literature. New student Sedgewick Bell (Emile Hirsch) challenges Hundert's principled ways. Bell's behavior during the 73rd annual Mr. Julius Caesar Contest causes Hundert to suspect that Bell leads a less than principled life, a suspicion reinforced years later during a repeat of the competition.

This scene appears at the end of the film. It is an edited portion of the Mr. Julius Caesar Contest reenactment at former student Sedgewick Bell's (Joel Gretsch) estate. Bell wins the competition, but Hundert notices Bell's earpiece. Earlier in the film, Hundert had suspected that young Bell also wore an earpiece during the original competition. Bell announced his candidacy for the U.S. Senate just before talking to Hundert in the bathroom. In his announcement, he described his commitment to specific values he would pursue if elected.

What to Watch for and Ask Yourself:

- Does William Hundert describe a specific type of life that one should lead? If so, what are its elements?
- Does Sedgewick Bell lead that type of life? Is he committed to any specific ethics view or theory?
- What consequences or effects do you predict for Sedgewick Bell because of the way he chooses to live his life?

Workplace Video | Organizational Behavior at Zingerman's

For over 25 years Zingerman's has delighted its customers with traditionally made breads, cheeses, oils, vinegars, and other gourmet foods. While connoisseurs and everyday customers alike rave about the upscale-food retailer's flavorful menu items, cofounders Ari Weinzweig and Paul Saginaw know that a committed, enthusiastic staff is the key ingredient of great-tasting specialty foods at Zingerman's. The duo in charge of the deli, bakehouse, and other eateries in Zingerman's Community of Businesses foster a high level of job satisfaction among employees, and this has earned Zingerman's a reputation as "The Coolest Small Company in America," according to *Inc.* magazine.

Employees at Zingerman's have a positive attitude about the company and its leadership. "I wanted to come to work at Zingerman's," says ZingNet Marketing Manager Pete Sickman-Garner, "because I really wanted to work for a place where I respected the people above me and respected their ability to organize people and get them all to do what needed to be done." Human Resources Manager Pat McGraw claims that Zingerman's takes attitude to a new level: "People are excited about their jobs, and it is each person's enthusiasm for the job that creates that experience."

TAKE 2

Zingerman's has many organizational qualities that interest workers and motivate them to do a great job. Some employees like what the company stands for; others admire the founders' focus on organizational citizenship—work behavior that goes beyond one's job requirements and contributes to the organization's success. "In many firms," says Ron Maurer, VP of administration, "you wait for somebody else to make a decision and then you implement it. In this particular organization, you have a chance to actually influence the decision that is being made about what you're going to do." Such employee empowerment creates a positive work environment—one that in turn influences the cognitive thoughts, affective feelings, and behavioral intentions of each individual staff member.

Above all, management's commitment to delivering outstanding service—both to internal and external customers—lies at the core of the Zingerman's experience. "Our mission," says Weinzweig, "is to bring a great experience to everybody that we interact with, whether that's customers, coworkers, the community, or even just people walking down the street."

Discussion Questions

1. What is "servant leadership," and what impact do you think this managerial approach has on organizational commitment at Zingerman's?
2. What are some ways in which Zingerman's promotes job satisfaction among employees?
3. What personal qualities and values does Zingerman's look for in a candidate who is interviewing for a job?

CASE

Canine Companions for Independence: Enhancing People's Lives

Founded in July 1975 in Santa Rosa, California, "Canine Companions for Independence [CCI] is a nonprofit organization that enhances the lives of people with [physical or developmental] disabilities by providing highly trained assistance dogs and ongoing support to ensure quality partnerships."[1] These assistance dogs, called Canine Companions, help enhance the independence or quality of life of disabled people.

CCI operates nationwide with centers in Santa Rosa and Oceanside, California; Delaware, Ohio; Farmingdale, New York; and Orlando, Florida; and satellite offices in Chicago, Illinois, and Colorado Springs, Colorado. Private contributions, donations from civic groups, service clubs, and businesses, and fundraising through special events and mailings cover all of the costs associated with breeding, raising, and training Canine Companions. CCI does not receive any governmental funding, and participants in the program do not absorb any of the breeding, raising, or training costs. However, participants are responsible for the feeding, housing, proper care, and medical needs of their Canine Companion after they become partnered.[2]

The breed stock for Canine Companions consists of golden retrievers, Labrador retrievers, or a crossbreed between the two. Participants in the CCI program complete a mandatory two-week training session wherein the human user is matched with a Canine Companion and both are prepared to work well with each other. People with physical or developmental disabilities who want an assistance dog must complete an application process, and if selected for the CCI program, they attend the Team Training course. Professionals who work for organizations that provide physical or mental health care to clients may also apply to the program. To be eligible, the professional must demonstrate that clients would benefit from having a Canine Companion in the facility where they care for disabled clients.[3]

Types of CCI Assistance Teams

CCI trains four types of assistance teams: service teams, skilled companion teams, facility teams, and hearing teams. A service team consists of a child or adult with physical disabilities and a Canine Companion that performs physical tasks, such as picking up dropped items, turning light switches on or off, pulling a wheelchair, or opening doors and drawers, on behalf of the disabled person. The skilled companion team consists of an adolescent or adult with physical, emotional, or developmental disabilities as well as a human primary caretaker and a Canine Companion. The role of the Canine Companion is to help the disabled person with physical tasks and to provide companionship and affection.[4] A facility team links a Canine Companion with a rehabilitation professional or caregiver to help improve the physical, mental, or emotional health of people for whom the professional provides care in a facility setting.[5] A hearing team utilizes a Canine Companion to alert deaf or hard-of-hearing adults to everyday sounds like alarm clocks, smoke alarms, telephones, and doorbells.[6]

Just over 2,500 teams have been developed and placed between CCI's founding in 1975 and late August 2007. The first Canine Companion teams were placed with program participants in 1978. In the summer of 2007, approximately 1,200 active teams were operating nationwide.[7]

CCI Volunteers

Many volunteers are involved in raising puppies for the Canine Companions program. Indeed, in mid-2007, there were 623 active puppy raisers.[8] The puppy raisers care for the CCI puppies, take them to puppy classes, and train them in appropriate behaviors and house manners. Upon reaching the required age, the CCI puppies enter a formal training program at one of the five regional CCI centers.

Famed former professional basketball player Bill Walton and his wife, Lori, are puppy raiser volunteers. For fourteen months they raised, trained, and socialized a puppy named Loma. At fourteen months of age, Loma was placed in advanced training for nine months at one of CCI's regional training centers. During this time the Waltons could not have any contact with Loma. Turning her over to the Oceanside,

California, regional training center was an emotional time for the Waltons, given the relationship they had established with the dog. Loma was destined to be the Canine Companion for David Grucca, a quadriplegic. Upon Loma's completion of the advanced training, the Waltons ceremonially presented Loma to David Grucca and began a friendship with him that is likely to be permanent. The Waltons are now raising another CCI puppy.[9]

Two other volunteers, both employees of Perot Systems Corp. in Plano, Texas, also raised puppies to become Canine Companions. Amy Witherel and Karissa White gave their puppies, Hilani and Orenda, lots of love and affection while training them to be well mannered and housebroken. To become effectively socialized, the puppies went everywhere with their raisers, including the grocery store, sporting events, restaurants, movies theaters, the beauty parlor, and even work. Neither Witherel nor White relished the thought of parting with their beloved puppies, but they recognized that ultimately they will help people who really need the Canine Companions.[10]

Joyce and Gordon Spainhower raised Hovan, a retriever mix breed, for CCI. They became hooked on the program when they attended a graduation ceremony for the two-week training program and saw how delighted children were with their service dogs. The Spainhowers' motto now is: "Price of raising a service puppy: $3,000. Seeing a smile on a child's face: priceless."[11]

Volunteerism for CCI is not limited to adults or to those interested in raising puppies. Consider, for example, Kyle Orent, an eight-year-old boy from Northport, New York, who in 2005 asked his parents for a lemonade stand so he could raise money for charity. Kyle knew he wanted to help some charity but didn't know which one. A family friend who knew Kyle liked animals suggested that he visit the Northeast Regional Center of CCI. He did and was impressed. When Kyle saw the pictures of smiling people in wheelchairs, he knew he had found his charity. Since then he has raised over $20,000 on behalf of CCI.[12]

Discussion Questions

1. Using the five attributes of attitude-behavior correspondence that are discussed in the chapter, explain the linkage between the CCI volunteers' attitudes and their behaviors.
2. How can the concept of emotional contagion help in understanding the attitudes and behaviors of the CCI volunteers?
3. What instrumental values and terminal values become evident through the activities of Canine Companions for Independence? For the CCI volunteers?
4. What impact might the instrumental and terminal values of CCI volunteers have on their propensity to behave ethically or unethically?

SOURCE: This case was written by Michael K. McCuddy, The Louis S. and Mary L. Morgal Chair of Christian Business Ethics and Professor of Management, College of Business Administration, Valparaiso University.

CHAPTER 5

Motivation at Work

LEARNING OBJECTIVES

After reading this chapter, you should be able to do the following:

1. Define motivation.
2. Explain how Theory X and Theory Y relate to Maslow's hierarchy of needs.
3. Discuss the needs for achievement, power, and affiliation.
4. Describe the two-factor theory of motivation.
5. Explain two new ideas in human motivation.
6. Describe how inequity influences motivation and can be resolved.
7. Describe the expectancy theory of motivation.
8. Describe the cultural differences in motivation.

THINKING AHEAD: AMERICAN EXPRESS COMPANY

The Working Mother Hall of Fame

Fewer than 20 companies have landed a spot on the *Working Mother* list of 100 Best Companies for 15 years or more. These very select companies constitute the Working Mother Hall of Fame, and 2006 saw three new honorees added to the roster: GlaxoSmith-Kline, Northern Trust, and The Phoenix Company. American Express is one of the established members of the Hall of Fame because of its family-friendly policies.[1] These include flextime, compressed weeks, telecommuting, job sharing, childcare, maternity leave, fitness centers, massage and physical therapy, and career counseling. The company even allows its employees to bring along their children when traveling on business to cities with available emergency childcare centers. These work/life benefits require an investment by the company, but the returns include attracting and retaining top talent while propelling profits.

American Express chairman and CEO Kenneth Chenault believes that having an inspired and engaged workforce is key to providing customers with exceptional products and service. He emphasizes the importance of acknowledging employee needs, both in the workplace and in their personal lives. Some American Express employees are earning advanced degrees, some are raising children, while others are caring for an elderly relative. Still others volunteer in their communities. With this wide variance in gifts, talents, and needs, Chenault believes the company needs to look for ways to support every one of its employees. That support begins with understanding employees' needs and is followed by providing the resources and opportunities to meet them.

What about the numbers? American Express has a lot of women workers. Of their 28,627 employees, 19,245 are women, which is approximately 68 percent. Of those 19,245 women, 4,822 are women leaders. Therefore, 25 percent of women are in leadership positions. One hundred percent of the company's women receive career counseling, and 54 percent receive management or leadership training. Of the 19,245 women in the company, 2,519 are in the top 20 percent by pay. That means that 13 percent of the women are in this top 20 percent. The 14-member board of directors includes 2 women, or 14 percent. These numbers tell a story about women at American Express—but not the whole story. What about the faces and people behind these numbers? In the Looking Back feature on page 173, we profile the people behind the numbers.

This is the first of two chapters about motivation, behavior, and performance at work. A comprehensive approach to understanding these topics must consider three elements of the work situation—the individual, the job, and the work environment—and how these elements interact.[2] This chapter emphasizes internal and process theories of motivation. It begins with individual need theories of motivation, turns to the two-factor theory of motivation, and finishes by examining two individual–environment interaction or process theories of motivation. Chapter 6 emphasizes external theories of motivation and focuses on factors in the environment to help understand good or bad performance.

MOTIVATION AND WORK BEHAVIOR

(1) Define *motivation.*

Motivation is the process of arousing and sustaining goal-directed behavior. It is one of the more complex topics in organizational behavior. *Motivation* comes from the Latin root word *movere,* which means "to move."

Motivation theories attempt to explain and predict observable behavior. The wide range and variety of motivation theories result from the great diversity of people and the complexity of their behavior in organizations. Motivation theories may be broadly classified into internal, process, and external theories of motivation. Internal theories of motivation give primary consideration to variables within the individual that give rise to motivation and behavior. The hierarchy of needs theory exemplifies the internal theories. Process theories of motivation emphasize the nature of the interaction between the individual and the environment. Expectancy theory exemplifies the process theories. External

motivation
The process of arousing and sustaining goal-directed behavior.

theories of motivation focus on the elements in the environment, including the consequences of behavior, as the basis for understanding and explaining people's behavior at work. Any single motivation theory explains only a small portion of the variance in human behavior. Therefore, alternative theories have developed over time in an effort to account for the unexplained portions of the variance in behavior.

Internal Needs

Philosophers and scholars have theorized for centuries about human needs and motives. During the past century, attention narrowed to understanding motivation in businesses and other organizations.[3] Max Weber, an early German organizational scholar, argued that the meaning of work lay not in the work itself but in its deeper potential for contributing to a person's ultimate salvation.[4] From this Calvinistic perspective, the Protestant ethic was the fuel for human industriousness. The Protestant ethic said people should work hard because those who prospered at work were more likely to find a place in heaven. You 5.1 lets you evaluate how strongly you have a pro-Protestant versus a non-Protestant ethic. Although Weber, and later Blood, both used the term *Protestant ethic,* many see the value elements of this work ethic in the broader Judeo-Christian tradition. We concur.

A more complex motivation theory was proposed by Sigmund Freud. For him, a person's organizational life was founded on the compulsion to work and the power of love.[5] He saw much of human motivation as unconscious by nature. *Psychoanalysis* was Freud's method for delving into the unconscious mind to better understand a person's motives and needs. Freud's psychodynamic theory offers explanations for irrational and self-destructive behavior, such as suicide or workplace violence. The motives underlying such traumatic work events may be understood by analyzing a person's unconscious needs and motives. The psychoanalytic approach also helps explain deviant workplace behavior, which can have a negative impact on business unit performance.[6] Freud's theorizing is important as the basis for subsequent need theories of motivation. Research suggests that people's deeper feelings may transcend culture, with most people caring deeply about the same few things.[7]

Internal needs and external incentives both play an important role in motivation. Although extrinsic motivation is important, so too is intrinsic motivation, which varies by the individual.[8] Intrinsic work motivation is linked to spillover effects from work to home, with mothers transmitting the emotions of happiness, anger, and anxiety from work to home.[9] Interestingly, fathers who have high intrinsic work motivation tended to report greater overall anxiety at home after the workday. Therefore, it is important for managers to consider both internal needs and external incentives when attempting to motivate their employees. Further, managers who are more supportive and less controlling appear to elicit more intrinsic motivation from their employees.

External Incentives

Early organizational scholars made economic assumptions about human motivation and developed differential piece-rate systems of pay that emphasized external incentives. They assumed that people were motivated by self-interest and economic gain. The Hawthorne studies confirmed the positive effects of pay incentives on productivity and also found that social and interpersonal motives were important.[10] However, there are those who raise the question about where self-interest ends

psychoanalysis
Sigmund Freud's method for delving into the unconscious mind to better understand a person's motives and needs.

YOU 5.1

Protestant Ethic

Rate the following statements from 1 (for *disagree completely*) to 6 (for *agree completely*).

___ 1. When the workday is finished, people should forget their jobs and enjoy themselves.
___ 2. Hard work makes us better people.
___ 3. The principal purpose of people's jobs is to provide them with the means for enjoying their free time.
___ 4. Wasting time is as bad as wasting money.
___ 5. Whenever possible, a person should relax and accept life as it is rather than always striving for unreachable goals.
___ 6. A good indication of a person's worth is how well he or she does his or her job.
___ 7. If all other things are equal, it is better to have a job with a lot of responsibility than one with little responsibility.
___ 8. People who "do things the easy way" are the smart ones.

___ Total your score for the pro-Protestant ethic items (2, 4, 6, and 7).
___ Total your score for the non-Protestant ethic items (1, 3, 5, and 8).

A pro-Protestant ethic score of 20 or over indicates you have a strong work ethic; 15–19 indicates a moderately strong work ethic; 9–14 indicates a moderately weak work ethic; 8 or less indicates a weak work ethic.

A non-Protestant ethic score of 20 or over indicates you have a strong non-work ethic; 15–19 indicates a moderately strong non-work ethic; 9–14 indicates a moderately weak non-work ethic; 8 or less indicates a weak non-work ethic.

SOURCE: M. R. Blood, "Work Values and Job Satisfaction," *Journal of Applied Psychology* 53 (1969): 456–459.

and the public interest begins. The Real World 5.1 looks at this interesting question.

Those who made economic assumptions about human motivation emphasized financial incentives for behavior. The Scottish political economist and moral philosopher Adam Smith argued that a person's *self-interest* was God's providence, not the government's.[11] More recently, executives have focused on "enlightened" self-interest. Self-interest is what is in the best interest and benefit to the individual; enlightened self-interest additionally recognizes the self-interest of other people. Adam Smith laid the cornerstone for the free enterprise system of economics when he formulated the "invisible hand" and the free market to explain the motivation for individual behavior. The "invisible hand" refers to the unseen forces of a free market system that shape the most efficient use of people, money, and resources for productive ends. Smith's basic assumption was that people are motivated by self-interest for economic gain to provide the necessities and conveniences of life. Thus, employees are most productive when motivated by self-interest.

Technology is an important concept in Smith's view, because he believed that a nation's wealth is determined primarily by the productivity of its labor force. Therefore, a more efficient and effective labor force yields greater abundance for the nation. Technology is important as a force multiplier for the productivity of labor.[12]

self-interest
What is in the best interest and benefit to an individual.

Frederick Taylor, the founder of scientific management, was also concerned with labor efficiency and effectiveness.[13] His central concern was to change the relationship between management and labor from one of conflict to one of cooperation.[14] Taylor believed the basis of their conflict was the division of the profits. Instead of

THE REAL WORLD 5.1

Whose Interests?

Increasingly philanthropists and donors are combining charitable giving with their profit-making enterprises. This creates a challenge to determine where the self-interest of the donor ends and the public interest of the community begins. A case in point was that of Wade Dokken, whose 11,000-acre Ameya Preserve in Paradise Valley, Montana, is about 45 miles from Yellowstone Park. Dokken bought the land in 2005 for $23.3 million. He plans 301 luxury homes and related commercial development. What is unusual is that he promises in addition a package of donations that he claims have a value of more than $70 million. This package includes a $2 million homesite given to a benefit auction for the high-powered Robin Hood Foundation in New York, an earmark of $10 million for local nonprofits, a payment for low-cost Habitat for Humanity housing, and $1 million for the country's "social needs" as well as other charitable gifts. Some do not want the Ameya land developed at all. Dokken sees both a business opportunity and a chance to turn his development plan into an engine for charity. Thus, all land sales would be assessed a 0.5 percent donation to a nonprofit "community stewardship organization" dedicated to the environment, arts, and sciences. This initiative, which did receive the county commissioners' blessing, ignores traditional constituencies and challenges the line between the interests of the individual and the public.

Wade Dokken's purchase of the Ameya Preserve in Paradise Valley, Montana, challenges the line between the interests of the individual and of the public.

SOURCE: S. Beatty, "Giving Back: Developer Blends Charity, Profit," *The Wall Street Journal* (May 11, 2007): W2.

continuing this conflict over the division of profits, labor and management should form a cooperative relationship aimed at enlarging the total profits.

Employee Recognition and Ownership

Modern management practices—such as employee recognition programs, flexible benefit packages, and stock ownership plans—build on Smith's and Taylor's original theories. These practices emphasize external incentives, which may take either strictly economic form or more material form, such as "outstanding employee" plaques, gold watches, and other organizational symbols of distinction. Whataburger has developed the WhataGames in which the best employees compete for bragging rights as well as cash, prizes, and even medals.[15] This corporate Olympics is a training-and-loyalty exercise that helps significantly reduce turnover and build commitment. One bridge approach to employee motivation that considers both psychological needs and external incentives is psychological ownership. An increasing number of scholars and managers emphasize the importance of "feelings of ownership" for the organization. One study of 800 managers and employees in three different organizations found that psychological ownership increased organizational citizenship behavior, a key contextual performance beyond the call of duty as discussed in Chapter 3.[16]

MASLOW'S NEED HIERARCHY

Psychologist Abraham Maslow proposed a theory of motivation emphasizing psychological and interpersonal needs in addition to physical needs and economic necessity. His theory was based on a need hierarchy later applied through Theory X and Theory Y, two sets of assumptions about people at work. In addition, his need hierarchy was reformulated in an ERG theory of motivation using a revised classification scheme for basic human needs.

The Hierarchy of Needs

The core of Maslow's theory of human motivation is a hierarchy of five need categories.[17] Although he recognized that there were factors other than one's needs (for example, culture) that were determinants of behavior, he focused his theoretical attention on specifying people's internal needs. Maslow labeled the five hierarchical categories as physiological needs, safety and security needs, love (social) needs, esteem needs, and the need for self-actualization. Maslow's *need hierarchy* is depicted in Figure 5.1, which also shows how the needs relate to Douglas McGregor's assumptions about people, which will be discussed next.

Maslow conceptually derived the five need categories from the early thoughts of William James[18] and John Dewey,[19] coupled with the psychodynamic thinking of Sigmund Freud and Alfred Adler.[20] Maslow's need theory was later tested in research with working populations. For example, one study reported that middle managers and lower-level managers had different perceptions of their need deficiencies and the importance of their needs.[21] One distinguishing feature of Maslow's need hierarchy is the following progression hypothesis. Although some research has challenged the assumption, the theory says that only ungratified needs motivate

FIGURE 5.1 Human Needs, Theory X, and Theory Y

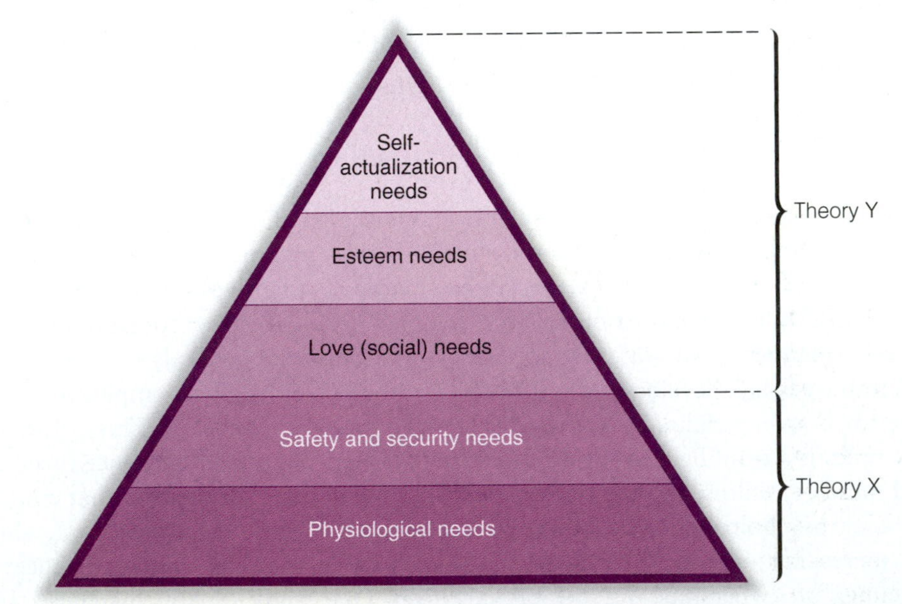

need hierarchy
The theory that behavior is determined by a progression of physical, social, and psychological needs, including lower-order needs and higher-order needs.

behavior.[22] Further, it is the lowest level of ungratified needs in the hierarchy that motivates behavior. As one level of need is met, a person progresses to the next higher level of need as a source of motivation. Hence, people progress up the hierarchy as they successively gratify each level of need.

Theory X and Theory Y

2 Explain how Theory X and Theory Y relate to Maslow's hierarchy of needs.

One important organizational implication of the need hierarchy concerns how to manage people at work (see Figure 5.1). Douglas McGregor understood people's motivation using Maslow's need theory. He grouped the physiological and safety needs as "lower order" needs and the social, esteem, and self-actualization needs as "higher order" needs, as shown in Figure 5.1. McGregor proposed two alternative sets of assumptions about people at work based on which set of needs were the motivators.[23] His *Theory X* and *Theory Y* assumptions are included in Table 5.1. McGregor saw the responsibility of management as the same under both sets of assumptions. Specifically, "management is responsible for organizing the elements of productive enterprise—money, materials, equipment, people—in the interest of economic ends."[24]

McGregor believed that Theory X assumptions are appropriate for employees motivated by lower order needs. Theory Y assumptions, in contrast, are appropriate for employees motivated by higher order needs. Employee participation programs are one consequence of McGregor's Theory Y assumptions. Therefore, *Fortune* 1000 corporations use employee involvement as one motivation strategy for achieving high performance.[25] Whole Foods founder and CEO John Mackey relies on Maslow's hierarchy of needs in leading the company.[26]

Gordon Forward, founding CEO of world-class Chaparral Steel Company, considered the assumptions made about people central to motivation and management.[27] He viewed employees as resources to be developed. Using Maslow's need hierarchy and Theory Y assumptions about people, he cultivated and developed a productive, loyal workforce in TXI's Chaparral Steel unit.

Theory X
A set of assumptions of how to manage individuals who are motivated by lower-order needs.

Theory Y
A set of assumptions of how to manage individuals who are motivated by higher-order needs.

TABLE 5.1 McGregor's Assumptions about People

Theory X	Theory Y
▪ People are by nature indolent. That is, they work as little as possible. ▪ People lack ambition, dislike responsibility, and prefer to be led. ▪ People are inherently self-centered and indifferent to organizational needs. ▪ People are by nature resistant to change. ▪ People are gullible and not very bright, the ready dupes of the charlatan and the demagogue.	▪ People are not by nature passive or resistant to organizational needs. They have become so as a result of experience in organizations. ▪ The motivation, the potential for development, the capacity for assuming responsibility, and the readiness to direct behavior toward organizational goals are all present in people. Management does not put them there. It is a responsibility of management to make it possible for people to recognize and develop these human characteristics for themselves. ▪ The essential task of management is to arrange conditions and methods of operation so that people can achieve their own goals best by directing their own efforts toward organizational objectives.

SOURCE: From "The Human Side of Enterprise" by Douglas M. McGregor; reprinted from *Management Review*, November 1957. http://www.amanet.org.

ERG Theory

Clayton Alderfer recognized Maslow's contribution to understanding motivation, but believed that the original need hierarchy was not quite accurate in identifying and categorizing human needs.[28] As an evolutionary step, Alderfer proposed the ERG theory of motivation, which grouped human needs into only three basic categories: existence, relatedness, and growth.[29] Alderfer classified Maslow's physiological and physical safety needs in an existence need category; Maslow's interpersonal safety, love, and interpersonal esteem needs in a relatedness need category; and Maslow's self-actualization and self-esteem needs in a growth need category.

In addition to the differences in categorizing human needs, ERG theory added a regression hypothesis to go along with the progression hypothesis originally proposed by Maslow. Alderfer's regression hypothesis helped explain people's behavior when frustrated at meeting needs at the next higher level in the hierarchy. Specifically, the regression hypothesis states that people regress to the next lower category of needs and intensify their desire to gratify these needs. Hence, ERG theory explains both progressive need gratification and regression when people face frustration.

MCCLELLAND'S NEED THEORY

(3) Discuss the needs for achievement, power, and affiliation.

A second major need theory of motivation focuses on personality and learned needs. Henry Murray developed a long list of motives and manifest needs in his early studies of personality.[30] David McClelland was inspired by Murray's early work.[31] McClelland identified three learned or acquired needs, called *manifest needs.* These were the needs for achievement, for power, and for affiliation. Some individuals have a high need for achievement, whereas others have a moderate or low need for achievement. The same is true for the other two needs. Hence, it is important to emphasize that different needs are dominant in different people. American Express has recognized the importance of diverse employees needs through its family-friendly policies, as we saw in the Thinking Ahead feature on page 151. For example, a manager may have a strong need for power, a moderate need for achievement, and a weak need for affiliation. Each need has quite different implications for people's behavior. The Murray Thematic Apperception Test (TAT) was used as an early measure of the achievement motive and was further developed by McClelland and his associates.[32] The TAT is a projective test, and projective tests were discussed in Chapter 3.

Need for Achievement

The *need for achievement* concerns issues of excellence, competition, challenging goals, persistence, and overcoming difficulties.[33] A person with a high need for achievement seeks excellence in performance, enjoys difficult and challenging goals, and is persevering and competitive in work activities. Example questions that address the need for achievement are: Do you enjoy difficult, challenging work activities? Do you strive to exceed your performance objectives? Do you seek out new ways to overcome difficulties?

need for achievement
A manifest (easily perceived) need that concerns individuals' issues of excellence, competition, challenging goals, persistence, and overcoming difficulties.

McClelland found that people with a high need for achievement perform better than those with a moderate or low need for achievement, and he has noted national differences in achievement motivation. Individuals with a high need for achievement have three unique characteristics. First, they set goals that are moderately difficult yet achievable. Second, they like to receive feedback on their progress toward these goals. Third, they do not like having external events or other people interfere with their progress toward the goals.

High achievers often hope and plan for success. They may be quite content to work alone or with other people—whichever is more appropriate to their task. High achievers like being very good at what they do, and they develop expertise and competence in their chosen endeavors. Research shows that need for achievement generalizes well across countries with adults who are employed full-time.[34] In addition, international differences in the tendency for achievement have been found. Specifically, achievement tendencies are highest for the United States, an individualistic culture, and lowest for Japan and Hungary, collectivistic societies.[35]

Need for Power

The *need for power* is concerned with the desire to make an impact on others, influence others, change people or events, and make a difference in life. The need for power is interpersonal, because it involves influence with other people. Individuals with a high need for power like to control people and events. McClelland makes an important distinction between socialized power, which is used for the benefit of many, and personalized power, which is used for individual gain. The former is a constructive force, whereas the latter may be a very disruptive, destructive force.

A high need for power was one distinguishing characteristic of managers rated the "best" in McClelland's research. Specifically, the best managers had a very high need for socialized power, as opposed to personalized power.[36] These managers are concerned for others; have an interest in organizational goals; and have a desire to be useful to the larger group, organization, and society.

While successful managers have the greatest upward velocity in an organization and rise to higher managerial levels more quickly than their contemporaries, they benefit their organizations most if they have a high socialized power need.[37] The need for power is discussed further in Chapter 11, on power and politics.

Need for Affiliation

The *need for affiliation* is concerned with establishing and maintaining warm, close, intimate relationships with other people.[38] Those with a high need for affiliation are motivated to express their emotions and feelings to others while expecting them to do the same in return. They find conflicts and complications in their relationships disturbing and are strongly motivated to work through any such barriers to closeness. The relationships they have with others are therefore close and personal, emphasizing friendship and companionship.

Over and above these three needs, Murray's manifest needs theory included the need for autonomy. This is the desire for independence and freedom from any constraints. People with a high need for autonomy prefer to work alone and to control the pace of their work. They dislike bureaucratic rules, regulations, and procedures. The need for relationships is important in each theory. A study of 555 nurses in specialized units found that intrinsic motivation increased with supportive relationships on the job.[39] Figure 5.2 summarizes Maslow's hierarchy of needs with its two extensions in the work of McGregor and Alderfer. The figure also summarizes McClelland's need theory of motivation. The figure shows the parallel structures of these four motivational theories.

need for power
A manifest (easily perceived) need that concerns an individual's need to make an impact on others, influence others, change people or events, and make a difference in life.

need for affiliation
A manifest (easily perceived) need that concerns an individual's need to establish and maintain warm, close, intimate relationships with other people.

FIGURE 5.2 Need Theories of Motivation

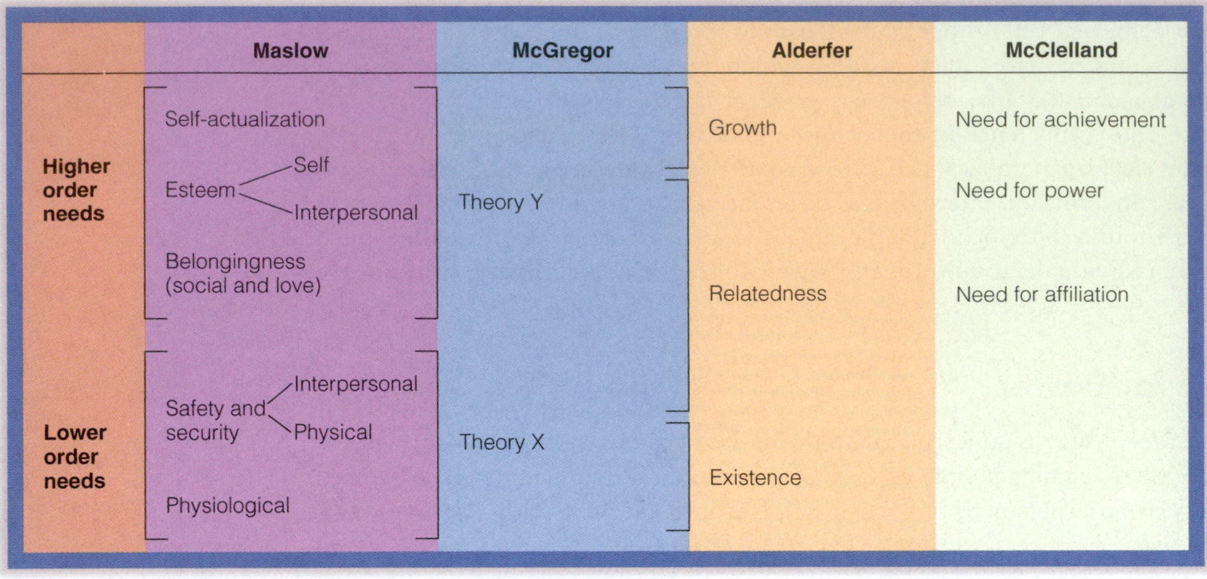

HERZBERG'S TWO-FACTOR THEORY

4 Describe the two-factor theory of motivation.

Frederick Herzberg departed from the need theories of motivation and examined the experiences that satisfied or dissatisfied people at work. This motivation theory became known as the two-factor theory.[40] Herzberg's original study included 200 engineers and accountants in western Pennsylvania during the 1950s. Herzberg asked these people to describe two important incidents at their jobs: one that was very satisfying and made them feel exceptionally good at work, and another that was very dissatisfying and made them feel exceptionally bad at work.

Herzberg and his colleagues believed that people had two sets of needs—one related to the avoidance of pain and one related to the desire for psychological growth. Conditions in the work environment would affect one or the other of these needs. Work conditions related to satisfaction of the need for psychological growth were labeled *motivation factors*. Work conditions related to dissatisfaction caused by discomfort or pain were labeled *hygiene factors*. Each set of factors related to one aspect of what Herzberg identified as the human being's dual nature regarding the work environment. Thus, motivation factors relate to job satisfaction, and hygiene factors relate to job dissatisfaction,[41] as shown in Figure 5.3.

Motivation Factors

motivation factor
A work condition related to satisfaction of the need for psychological growth.

hygiene factor
A work condition related to dissatisfaction caused by discomfort or pain.

Job satisfaction is produced by building motivation factors into a job, according to Herzberg. This process is known as job enrichment. In the original research, the motivation factors were identified as responsibility, achievement, recognition, advancement, and the work itself. When these factors are present, they lead to superior performance and effort on the part of job incumbents. As we saw in Thinking Ahead, American Express has clearly created growth and advancement opportunities for its women employees. Figure 5.3 also shows that salary is a motivational factor in some studies. Many organizational reward systems now include other financial benefits,

FIGURE 5.3 The Motivation–Hygiene Theory of Motivation

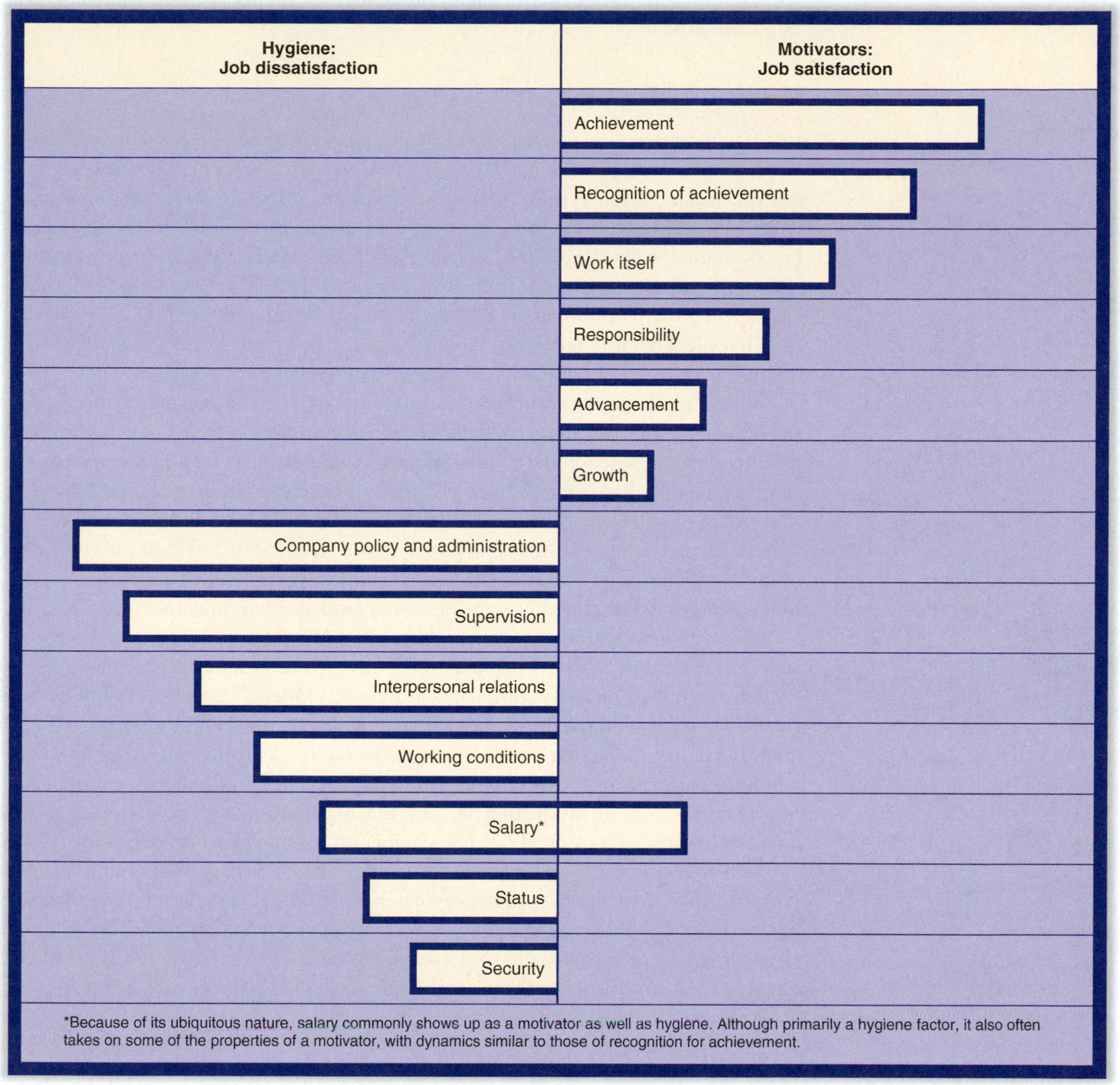

*Because of its ubiquitous nature, salary commonly shows up as a motivator as well as hygiene. Although primarily a hygiene factor, it also often takes on some of the properties of a motivator, with dynamics similar to those of recognition for achievement.

SOURCE: Reprinted from Frederick Herzberg, *The Managerial Choice: To Be Efficient or to Be Human* (Salt Lake City: Olympus, 1982). Reprinted by permission.

such as stock options, as part of an employee's compensation package. A long-term study of young men in the United States and West Germany found job satisfaction positively linked to earnings and changes in earnings, as well as voluntary turnover.[42]

Motivation factors lead to positive mental health and challenge people to grow, contribute to the work environment, and invest themselves in the organization. According to the theory and original research, the absence of these factors does not lead to dissatisfaction. Rather, it leads to the lack of satisfaction. The motivation factors are the more important of the two sets of factors, because they directly affect a person's motivational drive to do a good job. When they are absent, the person is demotivated to perform well and achieve excellence. The hygiene factors are a completely distinct set of factors unrelated to the motivation to achieve and do excellent work.

Hygiene Factors

Job dissatisfaction occurs when the hygiene factors are either not present or not sufficient. In the original research, the hygiene factors were company policy and administration; technical supervision; salary; interpersonal relations with one's supervisor; working conditions; and status. These factors relate to the context of the job and may be considered support factors. They do not directly affect a person's motivation to work but influence the extent of the person's discontent. They cannot stimulate psychological growth or human development but may be thought of as maintenance factors. Excellent hygiene factors result in employees' being *not dissatisfied* and contribute to the absence of complaints about these contextual considerations.

When these hygiene factors are poor or absent, the person complains about "poor supervision," "poor medical benefits," or whatever hygiene factor is poor. Employees experience a deficit and are dissatisfied when the hygiene factors are not present. Many companies have initiated formal flextime policies as a way to reduce dissatisfaction and persuade women leaders to come back to work.[43] Even in the absence of good hygiene factors, employees may still be very motivated to perform their jobs well if the motivation factors are present. Although this may appear to be a paradox, it is not, because the motivation and hygiene factors are independent of each other.

The combination of motivation and hygiene factors can result in one of four possible job conditions. First, a job high in both motivation and hygiene factors leads to high motivation and few complaints among employees. Second, a job low in both factors leads to low motivation and many complaints among employees. Third, a job high in motivation factors and low in hygiene factors leads to high employee motivation to perform coupled with complaints about aspects of the work environment. Fourth, a job low in motivation factors and high in hygiene factors leads to low employee motivation to excel but few complaints about the work environment.

Two conclusions can be drawn at this point. First, hygiene factors are of some importance up to a threshold level, but beyond the threshold there is little value in improving them. Second, the presence of motivation factors is essential to enhancing employee motivation to excel at work. You 5.2 asks you to rank a set of ten job reward factors in terms of their importance to the average employee, to supervisors, and to you.

Critique of the Two-Factor Theory

Herzberg's two-factor theory has been critiqued. One criticism concerns the classification of the two factors. Data have not shown a clear dichotomization of incidents into hygiene and motivator factors. For example, employees almost equally classify pay as a hygiene factor and a motivation factor. A second criticism is the absence of individual differences in the theory. Specifically, individual differences such as age, sex, social status, education, or occupational level may influence the classification of factors. A third criticism is that intrinsic job factors, such as the work flow process, may be more important in determining satisfaction or dissatisfaction on the job. Finally, almost all of the supporting data for the theory come from Herzberg and his students using his peculiar critical-incident technique. These criticisms challenge and qualify, yet do not invalidate, the theory. Independent research found his theory valid in a government research and development environment.[44] Herzberg's two-factor theory has important implications for the design of work, as discussed in Chapter 14.

What's Important to Employees?

There are many possible job rewards that employees may receive. Listed below are ten possible job reward factors. Rank these factors three times. First, rank them as you think the average employee would rank them. Second, rank them as you think the average employee's supervisor would rank them for the employee. Finally, rank them according to what you consider important.

Your instructor has normative data for 1,000 employees and their supervisors that will help you interpret your results and put them in the context of Maslow's need hierarchy and Herzberg's two-factor theory of motivation.

Employee	Supervisor	You	
			1. job security
			2. full appreciation of work done
			3. promotion and growth in the organization
			4. good wages
			5. interesting work
			6. good working conditions
			7. tactful discipline
			8. sympathetic help with personal problems
			9. personal loyalty to employees
			10. a feeling of being in on things

SOURCE: "Crossed Wires on Employee Motivation," *Training and Development* 49 (1995): 59–60. American Society for Training and Development. Reprinted with permission.

TWO NEW IDEAS IN MOTIVATION

5 Explain two new ideas in human motivation.

While executives like Whole Foods' CEO John Mackey value traditional motivation theories such as Maslow's, others like PepsiCo's CEO Steve Reinemund use new motivational ideas with their employees. Two new ideas in motivation have emerged in the past decade. One centers on eustress, strength, and hope. This idea comes from the new discipline of positive organizational behavior. The accompanying Science feature looks at core confidence in this regard. A second new idea centers on positive energy and full engagement. This idea translates what was learned from high-performance athletes for *Fortune* 500 executives and managers, such as those at PepsiCo. Both new ideas concern motivation, behavior, and performance at work.

Eustress, Strength, and Hope

Our detailed discussion of stress and health at work will come in Chapter 7. The positive side of stress discussed in Chapter 7 concerns its value as a motivational force, as in eustress. *Eustress* is healthy, normal stress.[45] Aligned with eustress in the new discipline of positive organizational scholarship are investing in strengths, finding positive meaning in work, displaying courage and principled action, and drawing on positive emotions at work.[46] This new, positive perspective on organizational life encourages optimism, hope, and health for people at work. Rather than focusing on the individual's needs, or alternatively on the rewards or punishment meted out

eustress
Healthy, normal stress.

Core Confidence and Employee Motivation

This study develops a new concept of core confidence as a higher order construct that is helpful in better understanding employee motivation in today's rapidly changing organizations. Globalization, advanced information technology, global sourcing, and new work structures and power distributions are now the norm instead of the exception. This dramatic change in organizations calls for development of new work motivation theories that fit the next work context. The purpose of this study is to develop new theory using new ideas from positive organizational behavior, the key construct of which is core confidence. Core confidence is manifested by hope, self-efficacy, optimism, and resilience. These four positive self-constructs share a common confidence core and thus, taken together, form the larger, higher-order construct of core confidence. The theory is that confidence is especially important in light of the new demands of the rapidly changing workplace that can trigger worrisome uncertainties for employees, giving them cause for doubt and anxiety. The ability to achieve and maintain high levels of motivation can therefore become a real challenge. In this context, core confidence can provide employees inner strength and help enhance their motivation by reducing their emotional experience of doubt, anxiety, and uncertainty. This positive experience leads then to both improved performance and positive subjective well-being.

SOURCE: A. D. Stajkovic, "Development of a Core Confidence–Higher Order Construct," *Journal of Applied Psychology* 91 (2006): 1208–1224.

in the work environment, this new idea in motivation focuses on the individual's interpretation of events.

Eustress is one manifestation of this broad, positive perspective. People are motivated by eustress when they see opportunities rather than obstacles, experience challenges rather than barriers, and feel energized rather than frustrated by the daily experiences of organizational life. Thus, eustress is a healthy and positive motivational force for individuals who harness its energy for productive work and organizational contributions.

Positive Energy and Full Engagement

The second new idea in motivation takes lessons learned from professional athletes and applies them in order to develop corporate athletes.[47] Jim Loehr's central tenets are the management of energy rather than time and the strategic use of disengagement to balance the power of full activity engagement.[48] This approach to motivation suggests that individuals do not need to be activated by unmet needs but are already activated by their own physical, emotional, mental, and spiritual energy. A manager's task is to help individuals learn to manage their energy so that they can experience periodic renewal and recovery and thus build positive energy and capacity for work.

A key to positive energy and full engagement is the concept that energy recovery is equally important to, if not more important than, energy expenditure. Individuals may be designed more as sprinters than long-distance runners, putting forth productive energy for short periods and then requiring time for recovery to reenergize. This approach to motivation and work is based on a balanced approach to the human body's potential to build or enhance its capacity, thus enabling the individual to sustain a high level of performance in the face of increasing work demands.

SOCIAL EXCHANGE AND EQUITY THEORY

Equity theory is a social exchange process theory of motivation that focuses on the individual–environment interaction. In contrast to internal needs theories of motivation, equity theory is concerned with the social processes that influence motivation and behavior. Power and exchange are important considerations in understanding human behavior.[49] In the same vein, Amitai Etzioni developed three categories of exchange relationships that people have with organizations: committed, calculated, and alienated involvements.[50] The implications of these relationships for power are discussed in detail in Chapter 11. Etzioni characterized committed relations as moral ones of high positive intensity, calculated relationships as ones of low positive or low negative intensity, and alienated relationships as ones of high negative intensity. Committed relationships may characterize a person's involvement with a religious group, and alienated relationships may characterize a person's incarceration in a prison. Social exchange theory may be the best way to understand effort–reward relationships and the sense of fairness at work as seen in a Dutch study.[51] Moral principles in workplace fairness are important because failures in fairness, or unfairness, lead to such things as theft, sabotage, and even violence.[52]

Demands and Contributions

Calculated involvements are based on the notion of social exchange in which each party in the relationship demands certain things of the other and contributes accordingly to the exchange. Business partnerships and commercial deals are excellent examples of calculated involvements. When they work well and both parties to the exchange benefit, the relationship has a positive orientation. When losses occur or conflicts arise, the relationship has a negative orientation. A model for examining these calculated exchange relationships is set out in Figure 5.4. We use this model to examine the nature of the relationship between a person and his or her employing organization.[53] The same basic model can be used to examine the relationship between two individuals or two organizations.

FIGURE 5.4 The Individual–Organizational Exchange Relationship

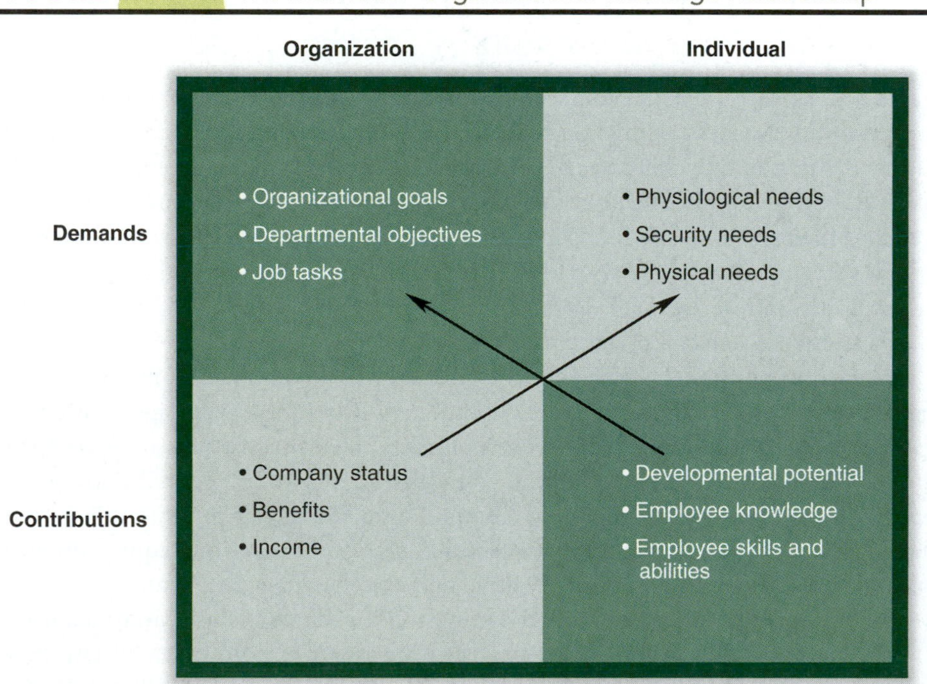

SOURCE: J. P. Campbell, M. D. Dunnette, E. E. Lawler III, and K. E. Weick, Jr., *Managerial Behavior, Performance, and Effectiveness* (New York: McGraw-Hill, Inc., 1970). Reproduced with permission from McGraw-Hill, Inc.

Demands Each party to the exchange makes demands upon the other. These demands express the expectations that each party has of the other in the relationship. The organization expresses its demands on the individual in the form of goal or mission statements, job expectations, performance objectives, and performance feedback. These are among the primary and formal mechanisms through which people learn about the organization's demands and expectations of them.

The organization is not alone in making demands of the relationship. The individual has needs to be satisfied as well, as we have previously discussed. These needs form the basis for the expectations or demands placed on the organization by the individual. Employee need fulfillment and the feeling of belonging are both important to a healthy exchange and to organizational membership.[54] These needs may be conceptualized from the perspective of Maslow, Alderfer, Herzberg, or McClelland. When employees are well taken care of by the company, then they take care of the business even in very difficult times, as discussed in The Real World 5.2.

Contributions Just as each party to the exchange makes demands upon the other, each also has contributions to make to the relationship. These contributions are the basis for satisfying the demands expressed by the other party in the relationship. Employees are able to satisfy organizational demands through a range of contributions, including their skills, abilities, knowledge, energy, professional contacts, and native talents. As people grow and develop over time, they are able to increasingly satisfy the range of demands and expectations placed upon them by the organization.

In a similar fashion, organizations have a range of contributions available to the exchange relationship to meet individual needs. These contributions include salary, benefits, advancement opportunities, security, status, and social affiliation. Some organizations are richer in resources and better able to meet employee needs than others. Thus, one of the concerns that individuals and organizations alike have is whether the relationship is a fair deal or an equitable arrangement for both members.

Adams's Theory of Inequity

(6) Describe how inequity influences motivation and can be resolved.

Blau's and Etzioni's ideas about social process and exchange provide a context for understanding fairness, equity, and inequity in work relationships. Stacy Adams explicitly developed the idea that *inequity* in the social exchange process is an important motivator. Adams's theory of inequity suggests that people are motivated when they find themselves in situations of inequity or unfairness.[55] Inequity occurs when a person receives more, or less, than the person believes is deserved based on effort and/or contribution. Inequity leads to the experience of tension, and tension motivates a person to act in a manner to resolve the inequity.

When does a person know that the situation is inequitable or unfair? Adams suggests that people examine the contribution portion of the exchange relationship just discussed. Specifically, individuals consider their inputs (their own contributions to the relationship) and their outcomes (the organization's contributions to the relationship). They then calculate an input/outcome ratio, which they compare with that of a generalized or comparison other. Figure 5.5 shows one equity situation and two inequity situations, one negative and one positive. For example, inequity in (b) could occur if the comparison other earned a higher salary, and inequity in (c) could occur if the person had more vacation time, in both cases all else being equal. Although not illustrated in the example, nontangible inputs, like emotional investment, and nontangible outcomes, like job satisfaction, may well enter into a person's equity equation.

inequity
The situation in which a person perceives he or she is receiving less than he or she is giving, or is giving less than he or she is receiving.

THE REAL WORLD 5.2

Be Nice . . . to Your Customers and Employees

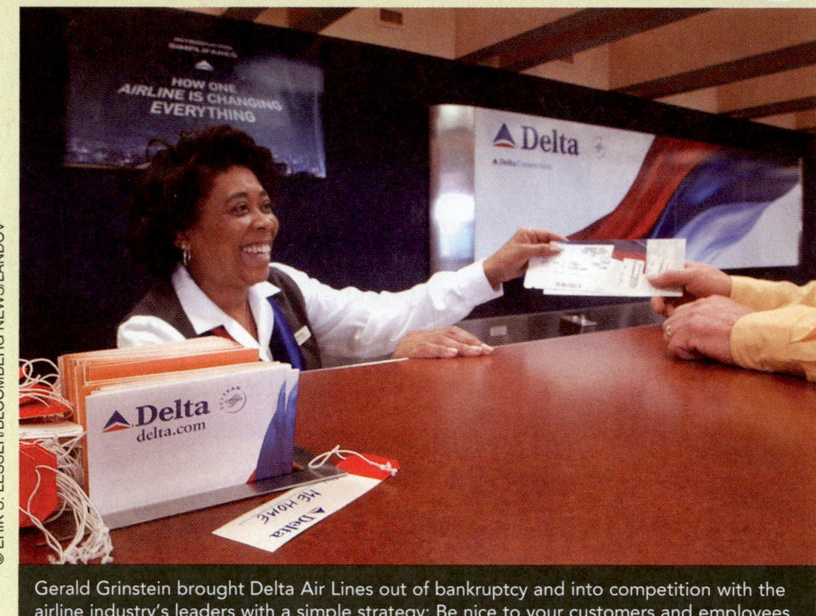

Gerald Grinstein brought Delta Air Lines out of bankruptcy and into competition with the airline industry's leaders with a simple strategy: Be nice to your customers and employees.

Gerald Grinstein brought Delta Air Lines out of bankruptcy and into competition with the leading airlines in the industry. The strategy he used was simple: Be nice to your customers and employees. Grinstein came out of retirement in 2004 to take on this turnaround challenge based on the chance that he could return the company to its glory days. Delta was weighed down by $21 billion in debts and gasping for air in 2005. The company emerged from bankruptcy with new routes, new planes, and new financing, which gave the number-three airline a chance to challenge industry leaders American Airlines and United while attempting to beat back low-fare rivals Southwest and JetBlue. Grinstein had to take drastic action that made a lot of people unhappy. He reduced the workforce to 47,000 from 70,000, slashed salaries, and dramatically cut executive incentives. Everyone was in the same boat. Once things began to turn around, he planned to plow money back into employee pockets if the company could meet its financial goals after coming out of bankruptcy. Was it ugly for employees? Absolutely! However, employees are now working together at Delta, and Grinstein knew that the company needed happy workers in the long run. As he gets ready to retire—again—he is leaving a legacy of happier and more productive Delta employees who came through a tough challenge successfully.

SOURCE: M. Tatge, "Out of the Woods," *Forbes* 179 (May 21, 2007): 44.

FIGURE 5.5 Equity and Inequity at Work

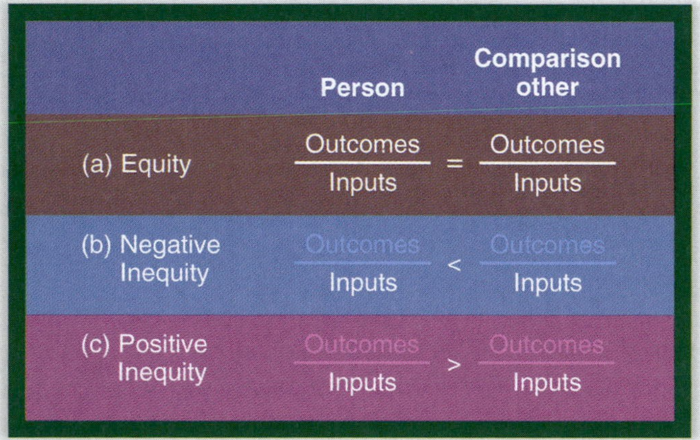

Person
Comparison other
(a) Equity
Outcomes / Inputs = Outcomes / Inputs
(b) Negative Inequity
Outcomes / Inputs < Outcomes / Inputs
(c) Positive Inequity
Outcomes / Inputs > Outcomes / Inputs

Pay inequity has been a particularly thorny issue for women in some professions and companies. Eastman Kodak and other companies have made real progress in addressing the problem through pay equity.[56] As organizations become increasingly international, it may be difficult to determine pay and benefit equity/inequity across national borders.

Adams would consider the inequity in Figure 5.5(b) to be a first level of inequity. A more severe, second level of inequity would occur if the comparison other's inputs were lower than the person's. Inequalities in one (inputs or outcomes) coupled with equality in the other (inputs or outcomes) are experienced as a less severe inequity than inequalities in both inputs and outcomes. Adams's theory, however, does not provide a way of determining if some inputs (such as effort or experience) or some outcomes are more important or weighted more than others, such as a degree or certification.

The Resolution of Inequity

Once a person establishes the existence of an inequity, a number of strategies can be used to restore equity to the situation. Adams's theory provides seven basic strategies: (1) alter the person's outcomes, (2) alter the person's inputs, (3) alter the comparison other's outcomes, (4) alter the comparison other's inputs, (5) change who is used as a comparison other, (6) rationalize the inequity, and (7) leave the organizational situation.

Within each of the first four strategies, a wide variety of tactics can be employed. For example, if an employee has a strategy to increase his or her income by $11,000 per year to restore equity, the tactic might be a meeting between the employee and his or her manager concerning the issue of salary equity. The person would present relevant data on the issue. Another tactic would be to work with the company's compensation specialists. A third tactic would be to bring the matter before an equity committee in the company. A fourth tactic would be to seek advice from the legal department.

The selection of a strategy and a set of tactics is a sensitive issue with possible long-term consequences. In this example, a strategy aimed at reducing the comparison other's outcomes may have the desired short-term effect of restoring equity while having adverse long-term consequences in terms of morale and productivity. Similarly, the choice of legal tactics may result in equity but have the long-term consequence of damaged relationships in the workplace. Therefore, as a person formulates the strategy and tactics to restore equity, the range of consequences of alternative actions must be taken into account. Hence, not all strategies or tactics are equally preferred. The equity theory does not include a hierarchy predicting which inequity reduction strategy a person will or should choose.

Field studies on equity theory suggest that it may help explain important organizational behaviors. For example, one study found that workers who perceived compensation decisions as equitable displayed greater job satisfaction and organizational commitment.[57] In addition, equity theory may play an important role in labor–management relationships with regard to union-negotiated benefits.

New Perspectives on Equity Theory

equity sensitive
An individual who prefers an equity ratio equal to that of his or her comparison other.

Since the original formulation of the theory of inequity, now usually referred to as equity theory, a number of revisions have been made in light of new theories and research. One important theoretical revision proposes three types of individuals based on preferences for equity.[58] *Equity sensitives* are those people who prefer equity based on the originally formed theory. Equity sensitivity contributes significantly to variation in free time spent working.[59] *Benevolents* are people who are comfortable with an equity ratio less than that of their comparison other, as exhibited in the Calvinistic heritage of the Dutch.[60] These people may be thought of as givers. *Entitleds* are people who are comfortable with an equity ratio greater than that of their comparison other, as exhibited by some offspring of the affluent who want and expect more.[61] These people may be thought of as takers. Females and minorities have not always been equitably treated in business and commerce.

Research on organizational justice has a long history.[62] One study suggests that a person's organizational position influences self-imposed performance expectations.[63] Specifically, a two-level move up in an organization with no additional pay creates a higher self-imposed performance expectation than a one-level move up with modest additional pay. Similarly, a two-level move down in an organization with no reduction in pay creates a lower self-imposed performance expectation than a one-level move down with a modest decrease in pay. This suggests that organizational position may be more important than pay in determining the level of a person's performance expectations.

One study on organizational justice suggests that a person's organizational position influences self-imposed performance expectations.

One of the unintended consequences of inequity and organizational injustice is dysfunctional behavior. Organizational injustice caused by payment inequity can even lead to insomnia, though the effects are reduced by training in interactional justice.[64] More seriously, workplace injustice can trigger aggressive reactions or other forms of violent and deviant behavior that do harm to both individuals and the organization. Fortunately, only a small number of individuals respond to such unfairness through dysfunctional behavior.[65]

Although most studies of equity theory take a short-term perspective, equity comparisons over the long term should be considered as well. Increasing, decreasing, or constant experiences of inequity over time may have very different consequences for people.[66] For example, do increasing experiences of inequity have a debilitating effect on people? In addition, equity theory may help companies implement two-tiered wage structures, such as the one used by American Airlines in the early 1990s. In a two-tiered system, one group of employees receives different pay and benefits than another group. A study of 1,935 rank-and-file members in one retail chain using a two-tiered wage structure confirmed the predictions of equity theory.[67] The researchers suggest that unions and management may want to consider work location and employment status (part-time versus full-time) prior to the implementation of a two-tiered system.

benevolent
An individual who is comfortable with an equity ratio less than that of his or her comparison other.

entitled
An individual who is comfortable with an equity ratio greater than that of his or her comparison other.

EXPECTANCY THEORY OF MOTIVATION

(7) Describe the expectancy theory of motivation.

Whereas equity theory focuses on a social exchange process, Vroom's expectancy theory of motivation focuses on personal perceptions of the performance process. His theory is founded on the basic notions that people desire certain outcomes of behavior and performance, which may be thought of as rewards or consequences of behavior, and that they believe there are relationships between the effort they put forth, the performance they achieve, and the outcomes they receive. Expectancy theory is a cognitive process theory of motivation.

The key constructs in the expectancy theory of motivation are the *valence* of an outcome, *expectancy*, and *instrumentality*.[68] Valence is the value or importance one places on a particular reward. Expectancy is the belief that effort leads to performance (for example, "If I try harder, I can do better"). Instrumentality is the belief that performance is related to rewards (for example, "If I perform better, I will get

valence
The value or importance one places on a particular reward.

expectancy
The belief that effort leads to performance.

instrumentality
The belief that performance is related to rewards.

FIGURE 5.6 An Expectancy Model for Motivation

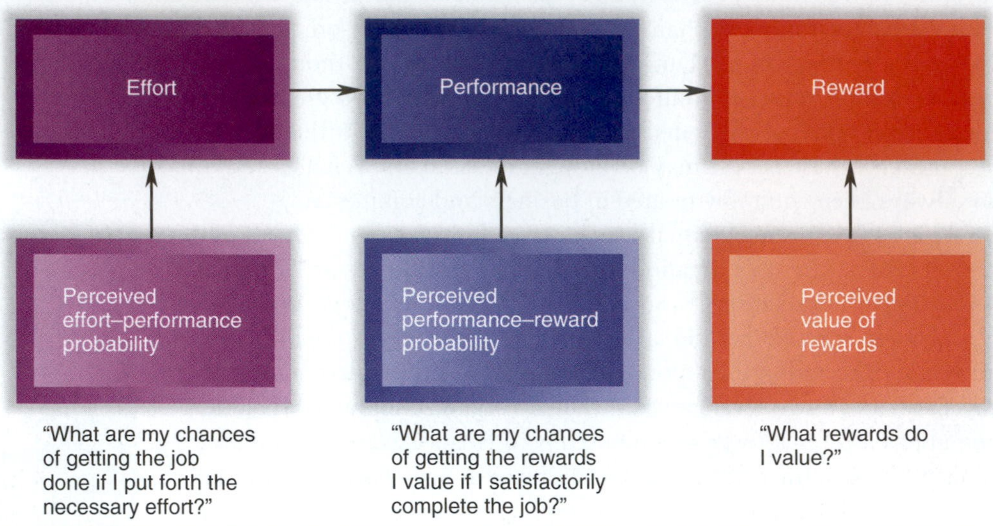

more pay"). A model for the expectancy theory notions of effort, performance, and rewards is depicted in Figure 5.6.

Valence, expectancy, and instrumentality are all important to a person's motivation. Expectancy and instrumentality concern a person's beliefs about how effort, performance, and rewards are related. For example, a person may firmly believe that an increase in effort has a direct, positive effect on performance and that a reduced amount of effort results in a commensurate reduction in performance. Another person may have a very different set of beliefs about the effort–performance link. The person might believe that regardless of the amount of additional effort put forth, no improvement in performance is possible. Therefore, the perceived relationship between effort and performance varies from person to person and from activity to activity.

In a similar fashion, people's beliefs about the performance–reward link vary. One person may believe that an improvement in performance has a direct, positive effect on the rewards received, whereas another person may believe that an improvement in performance has no effect on the rewards received. Again, the perceived relationship between performance and rewards varies from person to person and from situation to situation. From a motivation perspective, it is the person's belief about the relationships between these constructs that is important, not the actual nature of the relationship. During volatile times in business, the performance–reward linkage may be confusing.

Expectancy theory has been used by managers and companies to design motivation programs.[69] Sometimes called *performance planning and evaluation systems,* these motivation programs are designed to enhance a person's belief that effort would lead to better performance and that better performance would lead to merit pay increases and other rewards. Valence and expectancy are particularly important in establishing priorities for people pursuing multiple goals.[70]

A person's motivation increases along with his or her belief that effort leads to performance and that performance leads to rewards, assuming the person wants the rewards. This is the third key idea within the expectancy theory of motivation. It is the idea that the valence, or value, that people place on various rewards varies. One person prefers salary to benefits, whereas another person prefers the reverse. All people do not place the same value on each reward. Expectancy theory has been used in a wide variety of contexts, including test-taking motivation among students.[71]

Motivational Problems

Within the expectancy theory framework, motivational problems stem from three basic causes: disbelief in a relationship between effort and performance, disbelief in a relationship between performance and rewards, and lack of desire for the rewards offered.

If the motivational problem is related to the person's belief that effort will not result in performance, the solution lies in altering this belief. The person can be shown how an increase in effort, or an alteration in the kind of effort put forth, can be converted into improved performance. For example, the textbook salesperson who does not believe more calls (effort) will result in greater sales (performance) might be shown how to distinguish departments with high-probability sales opportunities from those with low-probability sales opportunities. Hence, more calls (effort) can be converted into greater sales (performance).

If the motivational problem is related to the person's belief that performance will not result in rewards, the solution lies in altering this belief. The person can be shown how an increase in performance or a somewhat altered form of performance will be converted into rewards. For example, the textbook salesperson who does not believe greater sales (performance) will result in overall higher commissions (rewards) might be shown computationally or graphically that a direct relationship does exist. Hence, greater sales (performance) are directly converted into higher commissions (rewards).

If the motivational problem is related to the value the person places on, or the preference the person has for, certain rewards, the solution lies in influencing the value placed on the rewards or altering the rewards themselves. For example, the textbook salesperson may not particularly want higher commissions, given the small incremental gain he would receive at his tax level. In this case, the company might establish a mechanism for sheltering commissions from being taxed or alternative mechanisms for deferred compensation.

Research results on expectancy theory have been mixed.[72] The theory has been shown to predict job satisfaction accurately.[73] However, the theory's complexity makes it difficult to test the full model, and the measures of instrumentality, valence, and expectancy have only weak validity.[74] In addition, measuring the expectancy constructs is time consuming, and the values for each construct change over time for an individual. Finally, a theory assumes the individual is totally rational and acts as a minicomputer, calculating probabilities and values. In reality, the theory may be more complex than people as they typically function.

Motivation and Moral Maturity

Expectancy theory would predict that people work to maximize their personal outcomes. This is consistent with Adam Smith's ideas of working for one's own self-interest. Ultimately, Smith and expectancy theories believe that people work to benefit themselves alone. Expectancy theory would not explain altruistic behavior for the benefit of others. Therefore, it may be necessary to consider an individual's *moral maturity* in order to better understand altruistic, fair, and equitable behavior. Moral maturity is the measure of a person's cognitive moral development, which was discussed in Chapter 4. Morally mature people act and behave based on universal ethical principles, whereas morally immature people act and behave based on egocentric motivations.[75]

moral maturity
The measure of a person's cognitive moral development.

Cultural Differences in Motivation

(8) Describe the cultural differences in motivation.

Most motivation theories in use today have been developed by, and are about, Americans.[76] When researchers have examined the universality of these theories, they have found cultural differences, at least with regard to Maslow's, McClelland's, and Herzberg's theories. For example, while self-actualization may be the pinnacle need for Americans in Maslow's need hierarchy, security may be the most important need for people in cultures such as Greece and Japan who have a high need to avoid uncertainty.[77] Although achievement is an important need for Americans, research noted earlier in the chapter suggested that other cultures do not value achievement as much as Americans do.

The two-factor theory has been tested in other countries as well. Results in New Zealand did not replicate the results found in the United States; supervision and interpersonal relationships were important motivators in New Zealand rather than hygienic factors as in America.[78] Equity theory is being examined in cross-cultural contexts, leading to a reexamination of equity preferences, selection of referent others, and reactions to inequity.[79] Finally, expectancy theory may hold up very nicely in cultures that value individualism but break down in more collectivist cultures that value cooperative efforts. In collectivist cultures, rewards are more closely tied to group and team efforts, thus rendering unnecessary the utility of expectancy theory.

MANAGERIAL IMPLICATIONS: MANY WAYS TO MOTIVATE PEOPLE

Managers must realize that all motivation theories are not equally good or equally useful. The later motivation theories, such as the equity and expectancy theories, may be more scientifically sound than earlier theories, such as the two-factor theory. Nevertheless, the older theories of motivation have conceptual value, show us the importance of human needs, and provide a basis for the later theories. The individual, internal theories of motivation and the individual–environment interaction process theories uniquely contribute to our overall understanding of human behavior and motivation at work.

Managers cannot assume they understand employees' needs. They should recognize the variety of needs that motivate employee behavior and ask employees for input to better understand their needs. Individual employees differ in their needs, and managers should be sensitive to ethnic, national, gender, and age differences in this regard. Employees with high needs for power must be given opportunities to exercise influence, and employees with high needs for achievement must be allowed to excel at work.

Managers can increase employee motivation by training (increased perceptions of success because of increased ability), coaching (increased confidence), and task assignments (increased perceptions of success because of more experience). Managers should ensure that rewards are contingent on good performance and that valued rewards, such as time off or flexible work schedules, are available. Managers must understand what their employees want.

Finally, managers should be aware that morally mature employees are more likely to be sensitive to inequities at work. At the same time, these employees are less likely to be selfish or self-centered and more likely to be concerned about equity issues for all employees. Morally mature employees will act ethically for the common good of all employees and the organization.

DIVERSITY DIALOGUE

Balance: Not Just for Working Moms Anymore

"Once upon a time—several decades ago—there was a clear divide between the roles of mothers and fathers. Mothers stayed home and took care of the kids and fathers went to work." That was the lead-in to an ABC television news story in June 2007. According to the story, the number of mothers working outside the home doubled to 80 percent in the past 40 years. This increase of women in the workforce has led many men to break from their traditional roles as the sole breadwinners of the family and embrace their new roles as "co-parents."

Bryan and Lisa Levey of Lexington, Massachusetts, are prime examples of how gender roles have converged. They both have careers yet they both share equally in the household duties—cooking, doing the laundry, helping with homework, and chauffeuring their two young children. Sharing the responsibilities takes the pressure off Lisa to be the primary caregiver and Bryan to be the primary breadwinner. Says Bryan, "Having the work/life balance is very critical to both of our [his and Lisa's] happiness."

Bryan's happiness has not come without a price, however. He has had to forgo at least one promotion in order to spend less time at the office and more time at home with his family. Bryan is fine with the choices that he's made. "Maybe I could have been at the top of a business at a young age, but I probably wouldn't have been very happy, so what's the point?"

1. What effect will gender convergence have on the ways in which companies motivate and reward its employees?
2. Do you think men who have chosen to spend more time at home will be stigmatized at work for the choice they've made? Why or why not? If so, how can they address such stigmatization?

SOURCE: B. Stark, "Dad: 'I Can't Stay for That Meeting,'" *ABC News*, June 16, 2007. http://abcnews.go.com.

LOOKING BACK: AMERICAN EXPRESS

Wanji Walcott, VP and Mother of Two

Wanji Walcott is an American Express Vice President and Chief Technology Counsel.[80] She is one of the company's many women leaders who has grown, developed, and advanced professionally. Walcott is a mother of two and lives in New York City. In addition to her professional and personal lives, she has a life of community service as well, whether coordinating pro bono corporate counsel services for those in need or fighting heart disease. She led American Express's 18-member team in the 2006–2007 Wall Street Run and Heart Walk, which made a contribution of $1,410,000 to fight heart disease, the leading cause of death for American women and men. She is an active, caring, contributing leader on many fronts. She did not start as a leader.

Walcott credits American Express's culture with providing the flexibility she needed to balance work and family, primarily through her telecommuting arrangements. In addition, the company's leadership development and talent assessment programs had a direct impact on her career advancement through the ranks. At American Express, women, including the company's general counsel, fill key executive positions. As a result, Walcott had lots of positive role models as she formed and advanced her career plan. Because the company encourages networking, she got involved in employee networks that afforded her valuable opportunities for informal mentoring and networking. While formal mentoring programs can add value to individual careers, informal mentoring has always been a powerful help for rising leaders in all industries and professions.

While informal mentoring and networking are essential, American Express works to ensure fairness and equity within its family-friendly systems. To do this, the company provides managers with detailed selection criteria, user guides, and a sample case study of successful flexible work arrangements. It's important to assess in determining whether a flexible schedule is the right fit for the employee and the company. The objective is to create a win-win dynamic through which employee needs are met and the company's goals are achieved. Because Walcott has two children, the company's child-care initiatives are important to her as well. American Express boasts eight free backup-care facilities throughout the United States while, as noted in Thinking Ahead, supporting appropriate business travel with children. In addition, new moms can take up to twelve weeks off after the birth of their child, receiving full pay for four weeks and partial pay for two.

Chapter Summary

1. Early economic theories of motivation emphasized extrinsic incentives as the basis for motivation and technology as a force multiplier.
2. Maslow's hierarchy of needs theory of motivation was the basis for McGregor's Theory X and Theory Y assumptions about people at work.
3. According to McClelland, the needs for achievement, power, and affiliation are learned needs that differ among diverse cultures.
4. The two-factor theory found that the presence of motivation factors led to job satisfaction, and the presence of hygiene factors prevented job dissatisfaction.
5. New ideas in motivation emphasize eustress, hope, positive energy, and full engagement.
6. Social exchange theory holds that people form calculated working relationships and expect fair, equitable, ethical treatment.
7. Expectancy theory says that effort is the basis for motivation and that people want their effort to lead to performance and rewards.
8. Theories of motivation are culturally bound, and differences occur among nations.

Key Terms

benevolent (p. 169)
entitled (p. 169)
equity sensitive (p. 168)
eustress (p. 163)
expectancy (p. 169)
hygiene factor (p. 160)
inequity (p. 166)
instrumentality (p. 169)
moral maturity (p. 171)
motivation (p. 152)
motivation factor (p. 160)
need for achievement (p. 158)
need for affiliation (p. 159)
need for power (p. 159)
need hierarchy (p. 156)
psychoanalysis (p. 153)
self-interest (p. 154)
Theory X (p. 157)
Theory Y (p. 157)
valence (p. 169)

Review Questions

1. How can knowledge of motivation theories help managers?
2. What are the five categories of motivational needs described by Maslow? Give an example of how each can be satisfied.
3. What are the Theory X and Theory Y assumptions about people at work? How do they relate to the hierarchy of needs?
4. What three manifest needs does McClelland identify?
5. How do hygiene and motivational factors differ? What are the implications of the two-factor theory for managers?
6. What are two new ideas in motivation that managers are using?
7. How is inequity determined by a person in an organization? How can inequity be resolved if it exists?
8. What are the key concepts in the expectancy theory of motivation?

Discussion and Communication Questions

1. What do you think are the most important motivational needs for the majority of people? Do you think your needs differ from those of most people?
2. At what level in Maslow's hierarchy of needs are you living? Are you basically satisfied at this level?
3. Assume you are leaving your current job to look for employment elsewhere. What will you look for that you do not have now? If you do not have a job, assume you will be looking for one soon. What are the most important factors you will seek?
4. If you were being inequitably paid in your job, which strategy do you think would be the most helpful to you in resolving the inequity? What tactics would you consider using?
5. Do you believe you can do a better job of working or studying than you are currently doing? Do you think you would get more pay and benefits or better grades if you did a better job? Do you care about the rewards (or grades) in your organization (or university)?
6. What important experiences have contributed to your moral and ethical development? Are you working to further your own moral maturity at this time?
7. *(communication question)* Prepare a memo describing the two employees you work with who most closely operate according to Theory X and Theory Y assumptions about human nature. Be as specific and detailed in your description as you can, using quotes and/or observational examples.
8. *(communication question)* Develop an oral presentation about the most current management practices in employee motivation. Find out what at least four different companies are doing in this area. Be prepared to compare these practices with the theory and research in the chapter.
9. *(communication question)* Interview a manager and prepare a memo summarizing the relative importance she or he places on the needs for achievement, power, and affiliation. Include (a) whether these needs have changed over time and (b) what job aspects satisfy these needs.

Ethical Dilemma

Mitch heard the alarm blaring. "It couldn't be 5:00 a.m. already," he thought. He sat on the edge of the bed wondering how he had gotten himself into this mess. Mitch graduated from a good school with a bachelor's degree in management and a good GPA. He had dreams of a great job and a wonderful life. Instead, he found himself working 60 or more hours per week and feeling constantly pressured to work more.

Mitch started working at Acme, an electronics retailer, right out of college. At the time, the company recruiter had painted a picture of great opportunity for the "right" people. Acme wanted employees who had a high need for achievement and a desire to attain positions of power and authority. It sounded perfect for Mitch. He knew he was executive material. The problem was that the company hired only people who were willing to go the extra mile.

Now, two years later, Mitch realized that the company was using his own personal needs against him. When he was hired by Acme, Mitch was told that the average workweek would be 50 hours. It was not the cushy job he had envisioned, but if it led to the advancement the company alluded to, it was well worth it. Although he was not required to go beyond the stated 50 hours, Mitch had never worked less than 60 hours and often approached 70. From day one, the company had pushed for full commitment. "The only way to advance is to prove yourself and your commitment to the company," was heard more than once. It was the mantra to every unit manager in the organization. Mitch was beginning to believe that the whole process had been a game. Acme hired employees who were highly motivated to achieve and then used that internal motivation against them to get as much productivity from them as possible. The company caused managers to burn out and simply hired new ones when they left. Mitch had never felt so deceived and used.

Questions

1. Did Acme mislead Mitch and the other managers?
2. Does Acme have an obligation to its shareholders to maximize productivity and profitability?
3. Using consequential, rule-based, and character theories, evaluate Acme's hiring practices.

Experiential Exercises

5.1 What Do You Need from Work?

This exercise provides an opportunity to discuss your basic needs and those of other students in your class. Refer back to You 5.2, and look over your ranking of the ten possible job reward factors. Think about basic needs you may have that are possibly work related and yet would not be satisfied by one or another of these ten job reward factors.

Step 1. The class will form into groups of approximately six members each. Each group elects a spokesperson and answers the following questions. The group should spend at least five minutes on the first question and make sure each member of the group makes a contribution. The second question will probably take longer for your group to answer, up to fifteen minutes. The spokesperson should be ready to share the group's answers.

a. *What important basic needs do you have that are not addressed by one or another of these ten job reward factors?* Members should focus on the whole range of needs discussed in the different need theories of motivation covered in Chapter 5. Develop a list of the basic needs overlooked by these ten factors.

b. *What is important to members of your group?* Rank-order all job reward factors (the original ten and any new ones your group came up with in Step 1) in terms of their importance for your group. If group members disagree about the rankings, take time to discuss the differences among group members. Work for consensus and also note points of disagreement.

Step 2. Each group will share the results of its answers to the questions in Step 1. Cross-team questions and discussion follow.

Step 3. If your instructor has not already shared the normative data for 1,000 employees and their supervisors mentioned in You 5.2, the instructor may do that at this time.

Step 4 (Optional). Your instructor may ask you to discuss the similarities and differences in your group's rankings with the employee and supervisory normative rankings. If so, spend some time addressing two questions.

a. *What underlying reasons do you think may account for the differences that exist?*

b. *How have the needs of employees and supervisors changed over the past 20 years? Are they likely to change in the future?*

5.2 What to Do?

According to Stacy Adams, the experience of inequity or social injustice is a motivating force for human behavior. This exercise provides you and your group with a brief scenario of an inequity at work. Your task is to consider feasible actions for redress of this inequity.

John and Mary are full professors in the same medical school department of a large private university. As a private institution, neither the school nor the university makes the salaries and benefits of its faculty a matter of public record. Mary has pursued a long-term (fourteen years) career in the medical school, rising through the academic ranks while married to a successful businessman with whom she has raised three children. Her research and teaching contributions have been broad ranging and award winning. John joined the medical school within the last three years and was recruited for his leading-edge contribution to a novel line of research on a new procedure. Mary thought he was probably attracted with a comprehensive compensation package, yet she had no details until an administrative assistant gave her some information about salary and benefits a month ago. Mary learned that John's base contract salary is 16 percent higher than hers ($250,000 versus $215,000), that he was awarded an incentive pay component for the commercialization of his new procedure, and that

he was given an annual discretionary travel budget of $35,000 and a membership in an exclusive private club. Mary is in a quandary about what to do. Given pressures from the board of trustees to hold down costs associated with public and private pressure to keep tuition increases low, Mary wonders how to begin to close this $70,000 inequity gap.

Step 1. Working in groups of six, discuss the equity issues in this medical school department situation using the text material on social exchange and equity theory. Do the outcome differences here appear to be based on gender, age, performance, or marital status? Do you need more information? If so, what would it be?

Step 2. Consider each of the seven strategies for the resolution of inequity as portrayed in this situation. Which ones are feasible to pursue based on what you know? Which ones are not feasible? Why? What are the likely consequences of each strategy or course of action? What would you advise Mary to do?

Step 3. Once your group has identified feasible resolution strategies, choose the best strategy. Next, develop a specific plan of action for Mary to follow in attempting to resolve the inequity so that she can achieve the experience and reality of fair treatment at work.

Step 4 (Optional). Your group may be asked to share its preferred strategy for this situation and your rationale for it.

TAKE 2

Biz Flix | For Love of the Game

Billy Chapel (Kevin Costner), a 20-year veteran pitcher for the Detroit Tigers, learns just before the season's last game that the team's new owners want to trade him. He also learns that his partner, Jane Aubrey (Kelly Preston), intends to leave him. Faced with these daunting blows, Chapel wants to pitch a perfect final game. Director Sam Raimi's love of baseball shines through in some striking visual effects.

The scene from *For Love of the Game* is a slightly edited version of the "Just Throw" sequence that begins the film's exciting closing scenes. In this scene, Tigers' catcher Gus Sinski (John C. Reilly) comes out to the pitching mound to talk to Chapel. It is the beginning of Chapel's last game.

What to Watch for and Ask Yourself:

- At what level are Billy Chapel's esteem needs at this point in the game?
- Do you expect Gus Sinski's talk to have any effect on Chapel? If it will, what effect do you expect it to have?
- What rewards potentially exist for Billy Chapel? Remember, this is the last baseball game of his career.

Workplace Video | Motivation, Featuring Washburn Guitar

Washburn Guitar has been making high-quality musical instruments since 1883. The Chicago-based manufacturer sells 50,000 acoustic and electric guitars each year, totaling $40 million in annual revenues. At the heart of Washburn's enduring success is a rich guitar-making tradition developed and maintained by the company's skilled craftsmen.

Manufacturing quality instruments is labor-intensive work, and crafting guitars that look, play, and sound just right is the job of Washburn's highly motivated production teams. Some employees in the guitar shop are motivated by a kind of rock 'n' roll "cool factor"—a personal satisfaction that comes from being connected to rock music culture. Other Washburn shop workers are passionate about their jobs because they, like their customers, play guitar and can appreciate well-made instruments. "I would say 95 percent of the employees play an instrument," states Kevin Lello, VP of marketing at Washburn. "It really improves the quality of all of our instruments because they have a passion for what they are doing."

Although many intrinsic and extrinsic factors motivate Washburn employees to give their all on the job, watching a guitar progress from the design phase to the manufacturing floor to the artist on stage may be the ultimate thrill for a guitar maker. "One of the biggest motivational factors for me," says Washburn Production Manager Gil Vasquez, "is when you're done with a guitar and have taken it from the drawing board to the manufacturing point and have given it to the artist. Watching him play it on stage, it's like validation."

Many well-known performing artists have played Washburn guitars over the years, including Greg Allman, George Harrison, and Robert Plant. More recent Washburn strummers include members of Weezer, The All-American Rejects, and Modest Mouse. Dan Donegan, the hard-rocking axe-player of Disturbed, plays his very own signature-series model, the Maya Pro DD75.

While Washburn guitars occupy an esteemed place in rock history, it's the behind-the-scenes effort from Washburn's dedicated craftsmen that makes the brand tops with customers. The company's custom shop output has grown from 20 guitars to 300 guitars per month, and a recent merger with Parker Guitars has added even more quality and volume to the production process. Washburn employees relish their role in the company's success. "It's a labor of love," says Vasquez.

Discussion Questions

1. What motivates Washburn's employees to produce high-quality guitars?
2. Do rock star endorsements of Washburn guitars constitute a motivation factor or a hygiene factor, according to Herzberg's two-factor theory of motivation?
3. Should managers at Washburn adopt Theory X assumptions or Theory Y assumptions when seeking new ways to motivate employees? Explain.

High Expectations for the Disney–Pixar Merger

On January 24, 2006, Pixar Animation Studios and The Walt Disney Company entered into a merger agreement to make Pixar a wholly owned subsidiary of Disney. The deal was consummated on May 5, 2006 for a purchase price of $7.4 billion.[1] Previously, the two companies had a business arrangement wherein Disney marketed and distributed Pixar's animated feature films, including *Toy Story 2*, *Finding Nemo*, *Cars*, *A Bug's Life*, and *The Incredibles*, among others.[2] As part of the merger agreement, Steve Jobs, Pixar's chairman and CEO, became Disney's largest stockholder and assumed a seat on Disney's board of directors. Another key part of the deal included installing two key Pixar executives into positions at Disney. John Lasseter, Pixar's top creative executive, now oversees development of movies at both Pixar's and Disney's animation studios, and Edwin Catmull, Pixar's president and technology chief, runs the business side for both studios.[3]

The merger is expected to have far-reaching results. Writing in *Business Week,* Peter Burrows and his colleagues observe that if Steve Jobs "can bring to Disney the same kind of industry-shaking, boundary-busting energy that has lifted Apple and Pixar sky-high, he could help the staid company become the leading laboratory for media convergence."[4] Jobs himself thinks the future will be very exciting for the Disney–Pixar merger.

What did Jobs, Lasseter, and Catmull accomplish at Pixar that brings so much excitement and high expectations to the merger? The three men are visionaries. In the mid-1980s, Jobs saw the potential when "Catmull and Lasseter believed they could use computer animation to create full-length movies, even though many in Hollywood and at Disney thought computers could never deliver the nuance and emotion of hand-drawn animation."[5] In continually achieving this vision, Pixar executives ensure that every movie gets the best efforts of the company's "brainy staff of animators, storytellers, and technologists."[6]

The creative staff is responsible for creating, writing, and animating all of Pixar's films. "Pixar strives to hire animators who have superior acting ability—those able to bring characters and inanimate objects to life, as though they have their own thought processes."[7] Lasseter, who guides the creative inspiration, maintains that good animated filmmaking is more about good storytelling than it is about innovative technology. Pixar makes films with a story that both make people laugh and grab their emotions. Technology helps to tell the story; it supports and enhances creativity. However, Lasseter maintains that animated film failures are never about bad technology but are always about bad storytelling.[8]

Pixar brings to the merger some very innovative proprietary technology that both reflects technical creativity and enables and supports animation creativity. With the technology side being led by Catmull, Pixar has developed several animation software packages including Marionette™, Ringmaster™, RenderMan®, and Luxo. Each is a proprietary software system that supports different aspects of computerized animation. RenderMan, for instance, is used to synthesize high-quality, photo-realistic images. Luxo allows fewer people to do more work, thus enhancing productivity. It also promotes creativity by automatically making adjustments to the animation environment when changes are made, for example, in the appearance of animated characters.[9]

Pixar's technological and creative genius has resulted in widespread acclaim and numerous film industry awards. The Academy of Motion Picture Arts and Sciences recognized the technical and creative advancements exemplified by RenderMan by awarding an Oscar to Catmull, Loren Carpenter, (senior scientist), and Rob Cook (vice president of software engineering). In total, Catmull has won three Scientific and Technical Engineering Awards. The Producer's Guild of America honored Pixar for achievement in new media and technology with its first Vanguard Award in 2002. Lasseter has won two Oscars for his direction of animated films. In 2004, the Art Directors Guild also honored Lasseter with its Outstanding Contribution to Cinematic Imagery award.[10] Over the years, "Pixar Animation Studios and its employees have received more than 100 awards and nominations for animated films, commercials and technical contributions."[11]

While Pixar's key employees receive significant financial incentives, this does not seem to be the force that drives them; rather, it is the creative freedom they are granted. Andrew Stanton, one of the cowriters and codirectors of *Finding Nemo*, is impressed with the creativity and quality of people at Pixar. He observes that people outside of Pixar "pale in comparison."[12] Pixar has created a working environment and working conditions that help to attract, motivate, and retain quality employees. "The enviably progressive working environment nurtures and sustains creativity, and the dividend has been a box-office winning streak that stands in notable contrast to the hit-and-miss model of almost every other movie studio."[13]

Discussion Questions

1. What needs does Pixar appeal to through its commitment to creative innovation and excellence?
2. What is important to you in terms of your personal work motivation? How do the things that motivate you fit with Pixar's approach to motivating employees?
3. Using the model of the individual–organizational exchange relationship shown in Figure 5.4, explain the relationship that Pixar seeks to develop with its employees. How might this exchange relationship influence the employees' perceptions of equity?

SOURCE: This case was written by Michael K. McCuddy, The Louis S. and Mary L. Morgal Chair of Christian Business Ethics and Professor of Management, College of Business Administration, Valparaiso University.

CHAPTER 6

Learning and Performance Management

LEARNING OBJECTIVES

After reading this chapter, you should be able to do the following:

1. Define *learning, reinforcement, punishment, extinction,* and *goal setting.*
2. Distinguish between classical and operant conditioning.
3. Explain the use of positive and negative consequences of behavior in strategies of reinforcement and punishment.
4. Identify the purposes of goal setting and five characteristics of effective goals.
5. Describe 360-degree feedback.
6. Compare individual and team-oriented reward systems.
7. Describe strategies for correcting poor performance.

THINKING AHEAD: TOYOTA

Details, Corrective Adjustment, and Frugality

In the first quarter of 2007, Toyota surpassed General Motors (GM) as the top seller of cars and trucks for the first time ever.[1] This was a ground-shifting, trend-breaking milestone for the Japanese automotive manufacturer, as it sold 2,350,000 vehicles worldwide during the period of January through March 2007, a 9 percent increase. This is compared to 2,260,000 vehicles for GM during the same period, a 3 percent gain. Thus, Toyota outsold GM by 90,000 vehicles. While GM CEO Rick Wagoner continuously vows that his company has no intention of ceding industry leadership to Toyota, the Japanese company pursues continuous improvement through its fanatical attention to detail, corrective adjustment, frugality, process redesign, and market adaptation. These learning-based principles have made the company very competitive and led to world-class performance in manufacturing. Toyota was not always so successful; it has earned and learned its way into its position of leadership.

Toyota's trajectory has not always been a smooth one. The company nearly went bankrupt in the early 1950s, and its first export to the United States (the Crown) was not well received. Toyota faced two hot blasts of protectionist sentiment in the late 1980s and mid-1990s. In this challenging context, the company's legendary production system leader

Taiichi Ohno established a set of in-house precepts that have paid off handsomely. Toyota's efficient and lean manufacturing system includes just-in-time delivery; continuous improvement (*kaizen*); mistake proofing (*pokayoke*); and *obeya,* or face-to-face brainstorming sessions between engineers, designers, marketing pros, and suppliers. These precepts helped to revolutionize car making in general, not just within Toyota but more broadly in global manufacturing. Quite a legacy!

Being number one is no guarantee of continuing success, as GM well knows and is still learning. The company is handicapped in its ability to engage in lean, rapid change and advancement by massive retiree pension obligations and a staggering health care tab. These are burdens that Toyota does not have. Toyota, however, is neither a flawless organization nor an untouchable one. The company knows this and does fear the "big-company disease" whose scariest symptom is complacency within the ranks. The disease includes a sense of satisfaction at becoming the industry leader and a sense of arrogance or entitlement from that success. Mindful of these risks associated with the successful culmination of its decades-long efforts, Toyota is concerned about losing its way. Safeguards include employing in-house gurus at its local plants and standardizing the act of immediately signaling superiors when things go wrong. Can Toyota keep learning and changing to ensure continuous advancement?

This is the second of two chapters addressing motivation and behavior. Chapter 5 emphasized internal and process theories of motivation. This chapter focuses on external theories of motivation and factors in the work environment that influence good and bad performance. The first section addresses learning theory and the use of reinforcement, punishment, and extinction at work. It also touches on Bandura's social learning theory and Jung's personality approach to learning. The second section presents theory, research, and practice related to goal setting in organizations. The third section addresses the definition and measurement of performance. The fourth section is concerned with rewarding performance. The fifth and concluding section addresses how to correct poor performance.

LEARNING IN ORGANIZATIONS

(1) Define *learning, reinforcement, punishment, extinction,* and *goal setting.*

learning
A change in behavior acquired through experience.

Learning is a change in behavior acquired through experience. Learning may begin with the cognitive activity of developing knowledge about a subject, which then leads to a change in behavior. Alternatively, the behaviorist approach to learning assumes that observable behavior is a function of its consequences. According to the behaviorists, learning has its basis in classical and operant conditioning. Learning helps guide and direct motivated behavior.

Classical Conditioning

(2) Distinguish between classical and operant conditioning.

Classical conditioning is the process of modifying behavior so that a conditioned stimulus is paired with an unconditioned stimulus and elicits an unconditioned response. It is largely the result of the research on animals (primarily dogs) by the Russian physiologist Ivan Pavlov.[2] Pavlov's professional exchanges with Walter B. Cannon and other American researchers during the early 1900s led to the application of his ideas in the United States.[3] Classical conditioning builds on the natural consequence of an unconditioned response to an unconditioned stimulus. In dogs, this might be the natural production of saliva (unconditioned response) in response to the presentation of meat (unconditioned stimulus). By presenting a conditioned stimulus (for example, a bell) simultaneously with the unconditioned stimulus (the meat), the researcher caused the dog to develop a conditioned response (salivation in response to the bell).

Classical conditioning may occur in a similar fashion in humans.[4] For example, a person working at a computer terminal may get lower back tension (unconditioned response) as a result of poor posture (unconditioned stimulus). If the person becomes aware of that tension only when the manager enters the work area (conditioned stimulus), then the person may develop a conditioned response (lower back tension) to the appearance of the manager.

Although this example is logical, classical conditioning has real limitations in its applicability to human behavior in organizations for at least three reasons. First, humans are more complex than dogs and less amenable to simple cause-and-effect conditioning. Second, the behavioral environments in organizations are complex and not very amenable to single stimulus–response manipulations. Third, complex human decision making makes it possible to override simple conditioning.

Operant Conditioning

Operant conditioning is the process of modifying behavior through the use of positive or negative consequences following specific behaviors. It is based on the notion that behavior is a function of its consequences,[5] which may be either positive or negative. The consequences of behavior are used to influence, or shape, behavior through three strategies: reinforcement, punishment, and extinction.

Organizational behavior modification (O.B. Mod., commonly known as OBM) is a form of operant conditioning used successfully in a variety of organizations to shape behavior by Luthans and his colleagues.[6] The three types of consequences used in OBM to influence behavior are financial reinforcement, nonfinancial reinforcement, and social reinforcement. A major review of the research on the influence of OBM in organizations found that it had significant and positive influence on task performance in both manufacturing and service organizations, but that the effects were most powerful in manufacturing organizations.[7] In a study of pay for performance, more productive employees chose pay for performance over fixed compensation when given a choice.[8] However, regardless of which pay scheme employees chose, all produced more under a pay for performance scheme.

classical conditioning
Modifying behavior so that a conditioned stimulus is paired with an unconditioned stimulus and elicits an unconditioned response.

operant conditioning
Modifying behavior through the use of positive or negative consequences following specific behaviors.

The Strategies of Reinforcement, Punishment, and Extinction

(3) Explain the use of positive and negative consequences of behavior in strategies of reinforcement and punishment.

Reinforcement is used to enhance desirable behavior, and punishment and extinction are used to diminish undesirable behavior. The application of reinforcement theory is central to the design and administration of organizational reward systems. Well-designed reward systems help attract and retain the very best employees. Strategic rewards help motivate behavior, actions, and accomplishments, which advance the organization toward specific business goals.[9] Strategic rewards go beyond cash to include training and educational opportunities, stock options, and recognition awards such as travel. Strategic rewards are important positive consequences of people's work behavior.

Reinforcement and punishment are administered through the management of positive and negative consequences of behavior. *Positive consequences* are the results of a person's behavior that he or she finds attractive or pleasurable. They might include a pay increase, a bonus, a promotion, a transfer to a more desirable geographic location, or praise from a supervisor. *Negative consequences* are the results of a person's behavior that she or he finds unattractive or aversive. They might include disciplinary action, an undesirable transfer, a demotion, or harsh criticism from a supervisor. Positive and negative consequences must be defined for the person receiving them. Therefore, individual, gender, and cultural differences may be important in their classification.

The use of positive and negative consequences following a specific behavior either reinforces or punishes that behavior.[10] Thorndike's law of effect states that behaviors followed by positive consequences are more likely to recur, and behaviors followed by negative consequences are less likely to recur.[11] Figure 6.1 shows how positive and negative consequences may be applied or withheld in the strategies of reinforcement and punishment.

Reinforcement *Reinforcement* is the attempt to develop or strengthen desirable behavior by either bestowing positive consequences or withholding negative consequences. Positive reinforcement results from the application of a positive consequence following a desirable behavior. Bonuses paid at the end of successful business years are an example of positive reinforcement. Marriott International provides positive reinforcement by honoring ten to twenty employees each year with its J. Willard Marriott Award of Excellence. Each awardee receives a medallion engraved with the words that express the basic values of the company: dedication, achievement, character, ideals, effort, and perseverance.

Negative reinforcement results from withholding a negative consequence when a desirable behavior occurs. For example, a manager who reduces an employee's

positive consequences
Results of a behavior that a person finds attractive or pleasurable.

negative consequences
Results of a behavior that a person finds unattractive or aversive.

reinforcement
The attempt to develop or strengthen desirable behavior by either bestowing positive consequences or withholding negative consequences.

FIGURE 6.1 Reinforcement and Punishment Strategies

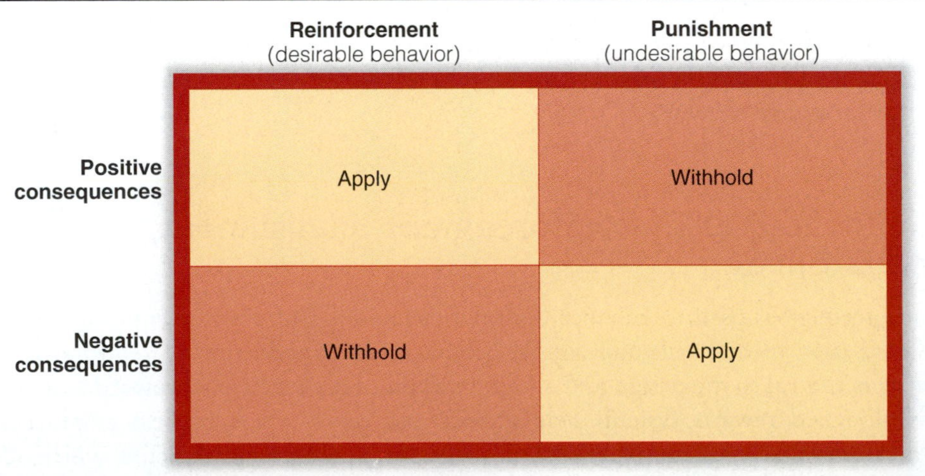

pay (negative consequence) if the employee comes to work late (undesirable behavior) and refrains from doing so when the employee is on time (desirable behavior) has negatively reinforced the employee's on-time behavior. The employee avoids the negative consequence (a reduction in pay) by exhibiting the desirable behavior (being on time to work).

Either continuous or intermittent schedules of reinforcement may be used. These reinforcement schedules are described in Table 6.1. When managers design organizational reward systems, they consider not only the type of reinforcement but also how often the reinforcement should be provided.

Punishment *Punishment* is the attempt to eliminate or weaken undesirable behavior. It is used in two ways. One way to punish a person is to apply a negative consequence following an undesirable behavior. For example, a professional athlete who is excessively offensive to an official (undesirable behavior) may be ejected from a game (negative consequence). The other way to punish a person is to withhold a positive consequence following an undesirable behavior. For example, a salesperson

punishment
The attempt to eliminate or weaken undesirable behavior by either bestowing negative consequences or withholding positive consequences.

TABLE 6.1 Schedules of Reinforcement

Schedule	Description	Effects on Responding
Continuous	Reinforcer follows every response.	1. Steady high rate of performance as long as reinforcement follows every response 2. High frequency of reinforcement may lead to early satiation 3. Behavior weakens rapidly (undergoes extinction) when reinforcers are withheld 4. Appropriate for newly emitted, unstable, low-frequency responses
Intermittent	Reinforcer does not follow every response.	1. Capable of producing high frequencies of responding 2. Low frequency of reinforcement precludes early satiation 3. Appropriate for stable or high-frequency responses
Fixed Ratio	A fixed number of responses must be emitted before reinforcement occurs.	1. A fixed ratio of 1:1 (reinforcement occurs after every response) is the same as a continuous schedule 2. Tends to produce a high rate of response that is vigorous and steady
Variable Ratio	A varying or random number of responses must be emitted before reinforcement occurs.	Capable of producing a high rate of response that is vigorous, steady, and resistant to extinction
Fixed Interval	The first response after a specific period of time has elasped is reinforced.	Produces an uneven response pattern varying from a very slow, unenergetic response immediately following reinforcement to a very fast, vigorous response immediately preceding reinforcement
Variable Interval	The first response after varying or random periods of time have elapsed is reinforced.	Tends to produce a high rate of response that is vigorous, steady, and resistant to extinction

SOURCE: Table from *Organizational Behavior Modification* by Fred Luthans and Robert Kreitner. Copyright © 1985, p. 58, by Scott Foresman and Company and the authors. Reprinted by permission of the authors.

who makes few visits to companies (undesirable behavior) and whose sales are well below the quota (undesirable behavior) is likely to receive a very small commission check (positive consequence) at the end of the month.

One problem with punishment is that it may have unintended results. Because punishment is discomforting to the individual being punished, the experience of punishment may result in negative psychological, emotional, performance, or behavioral consequences. For example, the person being punished may become angry, hostile, depressed, or despondent. From an organizational standpoint, this result becomes important when the punished person translates negative emotional and psychological responses into negative actions. Threat of punishment can elicit fear, a management tool used by some leaders but not at Southwest Airlines, a company that emphasizes positive relationships.[12] Some fears are legitimate, as seen in Thinking Ahead with Toyota's fear of "big-company disease."

Extinction An alternative to punishing undesirable behavior is *extinction*—the attempt to weaken a behavior by attaching no consequences (either positive or negative) to it. It is equivalent to ignoring the behavior. The rationale for using extinction is that a behavior not followed by any consequence is weakened. However, some patience and time may be needed for extinction to be effective.

Extinction may be practiced, for example, by not responding (no consequence) to the sarcasm (behavior) of a colleague. Extinction may be most effective when used in conjunction with the positive reinforcement of desirable behaviors. Therefore, in the example, the best approach might be to compliment the sarcastic colleague for constructive comments (reinforcing desirable behavior) while ignoring mocking comments (extinguishing undesirable behavior).

Extinction is not always the best strategy, however. In cases of dangerous behavior, punishment might be preferable to deliver a swift, clear lesson. It might also be preferable in cases of seriously undesirable behavior, such as employee embezzlement and other illegal or unethical behavior.

Bandura's Social Learning Theory

A social learning theory proposed by Albert Bandura is an alternative and complement to the behaviorist approaches of Pavlov and Skinner.[13] Bandura believes learning occurs through the observation of other people and the modeling of their behavior. Executives might teach their subordinates a wide range of behaviors, such as leader–follower interactions and stress management, by exhibiting these behaviors. Since employees look to their supervisors for acceptable norms of behavior, they are likely to pattern their own responses on the supervisor's.

Central to Bandura's social learning theory is the notion of *task-specific self-efficacy*, an individual's beliefs and expectancies about his or her ability to perform a specific task effectively. (Generalized self-efficacy was discussed in Chapter 3.) Individuals with high self-efficacy believe that they have the ability to get things done, that they are capable of putting forth the effort to accomplish the task, and that they can overcome any obstacles to their success. Self-efficacy is higher in a learning context than in a performance context, especially for individuals with a high learning orientation.[14] There are four sources of task-specific self-efficacy: prior experiences, behavior models (witnessing the success of others), persuasion from other people, and assessment of current physical and emotional capabilities.[15] Believing in one's own capability to get something done is an important facilitator of success. There is strong evidence that self-efficacy leads to high performance on a wide variety of physical and mental tasks.[16] High self-efficacy has also led to success in breaking addictions, increasing pain tolerance, and recovering from illnesses. Conversely,

extinction
The attempt to weaken a behavior by attaching no consequences to it.

task-specific self-efficacy
An individual's beliefs and expectancies about his or her ability to perform a specific task effectively.

success can enhance one's self-efficacy. For example, women who trained in physical self-defense increased their self-efficacy, both for specific defense skills and for coping in new situations.[17]

Alexander Stajkovic and Fred Luthans draw on Bandura's ideas of self-efficacy and social learning in expanding their original work in behavioral management and OBM into a more comprehensive framework for performance management.[18] Bandura saw the power of social reinforcement, recognizing that financial and material rewards often occur following or in conjunction with the approval of others, whereas undesirable experiences often follow social disapproval. Thus, self-efficacy and social reinforcement can be powerful influences over behavior and performance at work. A comprehensive review of 114 studies found that self-efficacy is positively and strongly related to work performance, especially for tasks that are not too complex.[19] Stajkovic and Luthans suggest that managers and supervisors can be confident that employees with high self-efficacy are going to perform well. The challenge managers face is how to select and develop employees so that they achieve high self-efficacy.

Managers can help employees in this process. The strongest way for an employee to develop self-efficacy is to succeed at a challenging task. Managers can help by providing job challenges, coaching and counseling for improved performance, and rewarding employees' achievements. Empowerment, or sharing power with employees, can be accomplished by interventions that help employees increase their self-esteem and self-efficacy. Given the increasing diversity of the workforce, managers may want to target their efforts toward women and minorities in particular. Research has indicated that these groups tend to have lower than average self-efficacy.[20] Counterintuitively in a training context, self-efficacy was negatively related to motivation and exam performance for students taking a series of five class exams despite a significant positive relationship with exam performance at the between-person level for these students.[21]

Learning and Personality Differences

The cognitive approach to learning mentioned at the beginning of the chapter is based on the *Gestalt* school of thought and draws on Jung's theory of personality differences (discussed in Chapter 3). Two elements of Jung's theory have important implications for learning and subsequent behavior.

The first element is the distinction between introverted and extraverted people. Introverts need quiet time to study, concentrate, and reflect on what they are learning. They think best when they are alone. Extraverts need to interact with other people, learning through the process of expressing and exchanging ideas with others. They think best in groups and while they are talking.

The second element is the personality functions of intuition, sensing, thinking, and feeling. These functions are listed in Table 6.2, along with their implications for learning by individuals. The functions of intuition and sensing determine the individual's preference for information gathering. The functions of thinking and feeling determine how the individual evaluates and makes decisions about newly acquired information.[22] Each person has a preferred mode of gathering information and a preferred mode of evaluating and making decisions about that information. For example, an intuitive thinker may want to skim research reports about implementing total quality programs and then, based on hunches, decide how to apply the research findings to the organization. A sensing feeler may prefer viewing videotaped interviews with people in companies that implemented total quality programs and then identify people in the organization most likely to be receptive to the approaches presented.

TABLE 6.2 Personality Functions and Learning

Personality Preference	Implications for Learning by Individuals
Information Gathering	
Intuitors	Prefer theoretical frameworks.
	Look for the meaning in material.
	Attempt to understand the grand scheme.
	Look for possibilities and interrelations.
Sensors	Prefer specific, empirical data.
	Look for practical applications.
	Attempt to master details of a subject.
	Look for what is realistic and doable.
Decision Making	
Thinkers	Prefer analysis of data and information.
	Work to be fair-minded and evenhanded.
	Seek logical, just conclusions.
	Do not like to be too personally involved.
Feelers	Prefer interpersonal involvement.
	Work to be tenderhearted and harmonious.
	Seek subjective, merciful results.
	Do not like objective, factual analysis.

SOURCE: O. Kroeger and J. M. Thuesen, *Type Talk: The 16 Personality Types That Determine How We Live, Love, and Work* (New York: Dell Publishing Co., 1989).

GOAL SETTING AT WORK

(4) Identify the purposes of goal setting and five characteristics of effective goals.

Goal setting is the process of establishing desired results that guide and direct behavior. Goal-setting theory is based on laboratory studies, field research experiments, and comparative investigations by Edwin Locke, Gary Latham, John M. Ivancevich, and others.[23] Goals help crystallize the sense of purpose and mission that is essential to success at work. Priorities, purpose, and goals are important sources of motivation for people at work, often leading to collective achievement, even in difficult times. Managing yourself and setting your own work goals can contribute to a productive U.S. government management career as we see in The Real World 6.1.

Characteristics of Effective Goals

Various organizations define the characteristics of effective goals differently. For the former Sanger-Harris, a retail organization, the acronym SMART communicated the approach to effective goals. SMART stands for *S*pecific, *M*easurable, *A*ttainable, *R*ealistic, and *T*ime-bound. Five commonly accepted characteristics of effective goals are specific, challenging, measurable, time-bound, and prioritized.

Specific and challenging goals serve to cue or focus the person's attention on exactly what is to be accomplished and to arouse the person to peak performance. In a wide range of occupations, people who set specific, challenging goals consistently outperform those who have easy or unspecified goals, as Figure 6.2 shows. The unconscious may have a positive effect here too. Two studies of subconscious goal motivation found that subconscious goals significantly enhanced task performance

goal setting
The process of establishing desired results that guide and direct behavior.

THE REAL WORLD 6.1

Set Work Goals and Manage Yourself

The U.S. government can provide a great career, but if it is to be a productive one, you cannot rely solely on your boss. You have to manage yourself, set your own work goals, reward yourself when you do well, and penalize yourself when you do a poor job. This is especially true for mid-level federal managers, one of the most challenging positions in any organization and one that often gets overlooked. Underperformance frequently triggers immediate negative feedback and punishment while there may be little or no response to good performance. If a manager helps her or his employees set goals and provides feedback on goal progress, why not do the same for herself or himself? Setting work goals provides the standards for job performance and the necessary clarity concerning the most important work to be done. Once you set your own work goals, you can set up measures and feedback systems that allow you to know if you are making positive progress toward these goals. Any performance problems related to your work goals are likely to come quickly and clearly. Therefore, do not be worried about being overly self-critical concerning performance problems; think more about rewarding yourself. When federal managers perform well, do a great job, and achieve their work goals, they are encouraged to praise themselves. Praise breeds confidence, which breeds better performance. It begins with work goals and good self-management.

SOURCE: B. Friel, "Manage Yourself," *Government Executive* (May 1, 2007), http://www.govexec.com/features/0507-01/0507-01admm.htm.

for conscious difficult and do-best goals, though not for easy goals.[24] How difficult and challenging are your work or school goals? You 6.1 gives you an opportunity to evaluate your goals for five dimensions.

Measurable, quantitative goals are useful as a basis for feedback about goal progress. Qualitative goals are also valuable. The Western Company of North America (now part of BJ Services Company) allowed about 15 percent of a manager's goals to be of a qualitative nature.[25] A qualitative goal might be to improve relationships with customers. Further work might convert the qualitative goal into quantitative measures such as number of complaints or frequency of complimentary letters. In this case, however, the qualitative goal may well be sufficient and most meaningful.

FIGURE 6.2 Goal Level and Task Performance

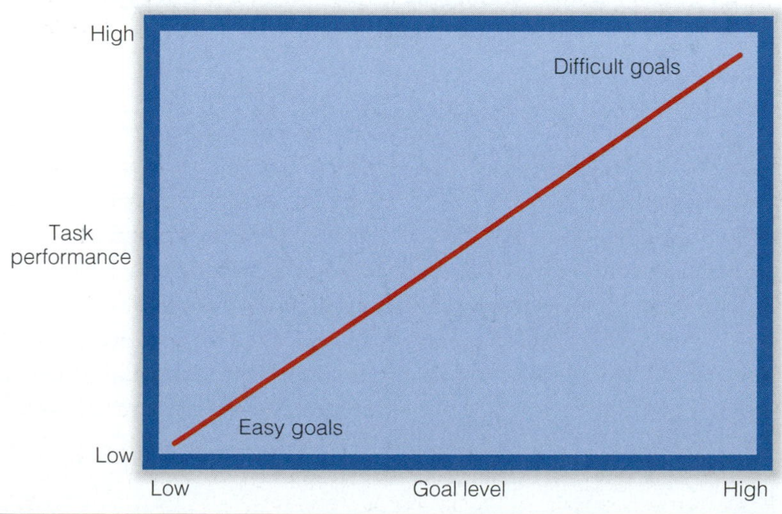

Task–Goal Attribute Questionnaire

Listed below is a set of statements that may or may not describe the job or school objectives toward which you are presently working. Please read each statement carefully and rate each on a scale from 1 (agree completely) to 7 (disagree completely) to describe your level of agreement or disagreement with the statement. *Please answer all questions.*

____ 1. I am allowed a high degree of influence in the determination of my work/school objectives.
____ 2. I should not have too much difficulty in reaching my work/school objectives; they appear to be fairly easy.
____ 3. I receive a considerable amount of feedback concerning my quantity of output on the job/in school.
____ 4. Most of my coworkers and peers try to outperform one another on their assigned work/school goals.
____ 5. My work/school objectives are very clear and specific; I know exactly what my job/assignment is.
____ 6. My work/school objectives will require a great deal of effort from me to complete them.
____ 7. I really have little voice in the formulation of my work/school objectives.
____ 8. I am provided with a great deal of feedback and guidance on the quality of my work.
____ 9. I think my work/school objectives are ambiguous and unclear.
____ 10. It will take a high degree of skill and know-how on my part to attain fully my work/school objectives.
____ 11. The setting of my work/school goals is pretty much under my own control.
____ 12. My boss/instructors seldom let(s) me know how well I am doing on my work toward my work/school objectives.
____ 13. A very competitive atmosphere exists among my peers and me with regard to attaining our respective work/school goals; we all want to do better than anyone else in attaining our goals.
____ 14. I understand fully which of my work/school objectives are more important than others; I have a clear sense of priorities on these goals.
____ 15. My work/school objectives are quite difficult to attain.
____ 16. My supervisor/instructors usually ask(s) for my opinions and thoughts when determining my work/school objectives.

Scoring:

Place your response (1 through 7) in the space provided. For questions 7, 12, 9, and 2, subtract your response from 8 to determine your adjusted score. For each scale (e.g., participation in goal setting), add the responses and divide by the number of questions in the scale.

Participation in Goal Setting:
- Question 1 ____
- Question 7 (8 − ____) = ____
- Question 11 ____
- Question 16 ____
- Total divided by 4 = ____

Feedback on Goal Effort:
- Question 3 ____
- Question 8 ____
- Question 12 (8 − ____) = ____
- Total divided by 3 = ____

Peer Competition:
- Question 4 ____
- Question 13 ____
- Total divided by 2 = ____

Goal Specificity:
- Question 5 ____
- Question 9 (8 − ____) = ____
- Question 14 ____
- Total divided by 3 = ____

Goal Difficulty:
- Question 2 (8 − ____) = ____
- Question 6 ____
- Question 10 ____
- Question 15 ____
- Total divided by 4 = ____

Interpreting your average scale scores:
6 or 7 is very high on this task–goal attribute.
4 is a moderate level on this task–goal attribute.
1 or 2 is very low on this task–goal attribute.

SOURCE: Adapted from R. M. Steers, "Factors Affecting Job Attitudes in a Goal-Setting Environment," *Academy of Management Journal* 19 (1976): 9. Permission conveyed through Copyright Clearance Center, Inc.

Time-bound goals enhance measurability. The time limit may be implicit in the goal, or it may need to be made explicit. For example, without the six-month time limit, an insurance salesperson might think the sales goal is for the whole year rather than for six months. Many organizations work on standardized cycles, such as quarters or years, where very explicit time limits are assumed. If there is any uncertainty about the time period of the goal effort, the time limit should be explicitly stated.

The priority ordering of goals allows for effective decision making about resource allocation.[26] As time, energy, or other resources become available, a person can move down the list of goals in descending order. The key concern is with achieving the top-priority goals. Priority helps direct a person's efforts and behavior. Although these characteristics help increase motivation and performance, that is not the only function of goal setting in organizations. One new study of goal setting suggests that it may be a theory of ability as well as a theory of motivation, especially in a learning context versus a performance context.[27]

Goal setting serves one or more of three functions. First, it can increase work motivation and task performance.[28] Second, it can reduce the role stress that is associated with conflicting or confusing expectations.[29] Third, it can improve the accuracy and validity of performance evaluation.[30]

Increasing Work Motivation and Task Performance

Goals are often used to increase employee effort and motivation, which in turn improve task performance. The higher the goal, the better the performance; that is, people work harder to reach difficult goals. The positive relationship between goal difficulty and task performance is depicted in Figure 6.2.

Three important behavioral aspects of enhancing performance motivation through goal setting are employee participation, supervisory commitment, and useful performance feedback. Employee participation in goal setting leads to goal acceptance by employees. Goal acceptance is thought to lead to goal commitment and then to goal accomplishment. Special attention has been given to factors that influence commitment to difficult goals, such as participation in the process of setting the difficult goals.[31] Even in the case of assigned goals, goal acceptance and commitment are considered essential prerequisites to goal accomplishment.

Supervisory goal commitment is a reflection of the organization's commitment to goal setting. Organizational commitment is a prerequisite for successful goal-setting programs, such as management by objectives (MBO) programs.[32] The organization must be committed to the program, and the employee and supervisors must be committed to specific work goals as well as to the program. (MBO is discussed in more detail later in the chapter.)

The supervisor plays a second important role by providing employees with interim performance feedback on progress toward goals. Performance feedback is most useful when the goals are specific, and specific goals improve performance most when interim feedback is given.[33] When done correctly, negative performance feedback can lead to performance improvement.[34] For example, assume an insurance salesperson has a goal of selling $500,000 worth of insurance in six months but has sold only $200,000 after three months. During an interim performance feedback session, the supervisor may help the salesperson identify his problem—that he is not focusing his calls on the likeliest prospects. This useful feedback coupled with the specific goal helps the salesperson better focus his efforts to achieve the goal. Feedback is most helpful when it is useful (helping the salesperson identify high-probability prospects) and timely (halfway through the performance period).

Reducing Role Stress, Conflict, and Ambiguity

A second function of goal setting is to reduce the role stress associated with conflicting and confusing expectations. This is done by clarifying the task–role expectations communicated to employees. Supervisors, coworkers, and employees are all important sources of task-related information. A fourteen-month evaluation of goal setting in reducing role stress found that conflict, confusion, and absenteeism were all reduced through the use of goal setting.[35]

The improved role clarity resulting from goal setting may be attributable to improved communication between managers and employees. An early study of the MBO goal-setting program at Ford Motor Company found an initial 25 percent lack of agreement between managers and their bosses concerning the definition of the managers' jobs. Through effective goal-setting activities, this lack of agreement was reduced to about 5 percent.[36] At FedEx, managers are encouraged to include communication-related targets in their annual MBO goal-setting process.[37]

Improving Performance Evaluation

The third major function of goal setting is improving the accuracy and validity of performance evaluation. One of the best methods of doing so is to use *management by objectives (MBO)*—a goal-setting program based on interaction and negotiation between employees and managers. MBO programs have been pervasive in organizations for nearly 30 years.[38]

According to Peter Drucker, who originated the concept, the objectives-setting process begins with the employee writing an "employee's letter" to the manager. The letter explains the employee's general understanding of the scope of the manager's job, as well as the scope of the employee's own job, and lays out a set of specific objectives to be pursued over the next six months or year. After some discussion and negotiation, the manager and the employee finalize these items into a performance plan.

Drucker considers MBO a participative and interactive process. This does not mean that goal setting begins at the bottom of the organization. It means that goal setting is applicable to all employees, with lower-level organizational members and professional staff having a clear influence over the goal-setting process.[39] (The performance aspect of goal setting is discussed in the next section of the chapter.)

Goal-setting programs have operated under a variety of names, including goals and controls at Purex (now part of Dial Corporation), work planning and review at Black & Decker and General Electric, and performance planning and evaluation at IBM. Most of these programs are designed to enhance performance,[40] especially when incentives are associated with goal achievement.

The two central ingredients in goal-setting programs are planning and evaluation. The planning component consists of organizational and individual goal setting. Organizational goal setting is an essential prerequisite to individual goal setting; the two must be closely linked for the success of both.[41] At FedEx, all individual objectives must be tied to the overall corporate objectives of people, service, and profit.

In planning, discretionary control is usually given to individuals and departments to develop operational and tactical plans to support the corporate objectives. The emphasis is on formulating a clear, consistent, measurable, and ordered set of goals to articulate *what* to do. It is also assumed that operational support planning helps determine *how* to do it. The concept of intention is used to encompass both the goal (*what*) and the set of pathways that lead to goal attainment (*how*), thus recognizing the importance of both what and how.[42]

management by objectives (MBO)

A goal-setting program based on interaction and negotiation between employees and managers.

The evaluation component consists of interim reviews of goal progress, conducted by managers and employees, and formal performance evaluation. The reviews are midterm assessments designed to help employees take self-corrective action. They are not designed as final or formal performance evaluations. The formal performance evaluation occurs at the close of a reporting period, usually once a year. To be effective, performance reviews need to be tailored to the business, capture what goes on in the business, and easily changed when the business changes.[43]

Because goal-setting programs are somewhat mechanical by nature, they are most easily implemented in stable, predictable industrial settings. Although most programs allow for some flexibility and change, they are less useful in organizations where high levels of unpredictability exist, as in basic research and development, or where the organization requires substantial adaptation or adjustment. Finally, individual, gender, and cultural differences do not appear to threaten the success of goal-setting programs.[44] Thus, goal-setting programs may be widely applied and effective in a diverse workforce.

PERFORMANCE: A KEY CONSTRUCT

Goal setting is designed to improve work performance, an important organizational behavior directly related to the production of goods or the delivery of services. Performance is most often thought of as task accomplishment, the term *task* coming from Taylor's early notion of a worker's required activity.[45] Some early management research found performance standards and differential piece-rate pay to be key ingredients in achieving high levels of performance, while other early research found stress helpful in improving performance up to an optimum point.[46] Hence, outcomes and effort are both important for good performance. That is not all that is needed to excel in talent management at General Electric, as we see in The Real World 6.2.

Predicting job performance has been a concern for over 100 years. Early theories around the time of World War I focused on the importance of intelligence and general mental ability (GMA). Research has found GMA highly predictive of job knowledge in both civilian and military jobs.[47] Equally important to predicting job performance is defining the term.

Performance Management

Performance management is a process of defining, measuring, appraising, providing feedback on, and improving performance.[48] The skill of defining performance in behavioral terms is an essential first step in the performance management process. Once defined, performance can be measured and assessed. This information about performance can then be fed back to the individual and used as a basis for setting goals and establishing plans for improving performance. Positive performance behaviors should be rewarded, and poor performance behaviors should be corrected. This section of the chapter focuses on defining, measuring, appraising, and providing feedback on performance. The last two sections of the chapter focus on rewarding, correcting, and improving performance.

Defining Performance

Performance must be clearly defined and understood by the employees who are expected to perform well at work. Performance in most lines of work is multidimensional. For example, a sales executive's performance may require administrative and financial skills along with the interpersonal skills needed to motivate a sales force. Or a medical doctor's performance may demand the positive interpersonal

performance management
A process of defining, measuring, appraising, providing feedback on, and improving performance.

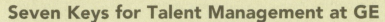

THE REAL WORLD 6.2

Seven Keys for Talent Management at GE

General Electric's legendary reputation for talent management owes much to one man, William J. Conaty, who retired in 2007 after 13 years as head of human resources and 40 years at GE. The company is known for having a deep bench of great leaders and emerging leaders as well as a relentless focus on continuous leadership development. Conaty has seven keys to share in nurturing leaders and achieving superior performance.

- Dare to differentiate the best from the rest by constantly judging, ranking, rewarding, and punishing employees for their performance.
- Constantly raise the bar to improve performance, which leaders do both among their own team members and for themselves.
- Do not be friends with the boss but establish your own trustworthiness and integrity as a confidant to all.
- Become easy to replace by developing great succession plans, especially when you do not need them, and mentoring the next generation.
- Be inclusive and do not favor people that you know because it can undermine your success.
- Free up others to do their jobs, especially by taking things off your boss' desk that are better done by you or others.
- Keep it simple by being consistent and straightforward because most organizations require simple, focused, and disciplined communications.

These seven keys are neither magic nor a panacea, yet they have served GE and Conaty well over the years.

SOURCE: D. Brady, "Secrets of an HR Superstar," *BusinessWeek* 4029 (April 9, 2007): 66.

skills of a bedside manner to complement the necessary technical diagnostic and treatment skills for enhancing the healing process. Each specific job in an organization requires the definition of skills and behaviors essential to excellent performance. Defining performance is a prerequisite to measuring and evaluating performance on the job.

Although different jobs require different skills and behaviors, organizational citizenship behavior (OCB) is one dimension of individual performance that spans many jobs. OCB was defined in Chapter 4 as behavior that is above and beyond the call of duty. OCB involves individual discretionary behavior that promotes the organization and is not explicitly rewarded; it includes helping behavior, sportsmanship, and civic virtue. According to supervisors, OCB is enhanced most through employee involvement programs aimed at engaging employees in the work organization rather than through employee involvement in employment decisions in nonunion operations.[49] OCB emphasizes collective performance in contrast to individual performance or achievement. OCB is just one of a number of performance dimensions to consider when defining performance for a specific job within an organization.

Performance appraisal is the evaluation of a person's performance once it is well defined. Accurate appraisals help supervisors fulfill their dual roles as evaluators and coaches. As a coach, a supervisor is responsible for encouraging employee growth and development. As an evaluator, a supervisor is responsible for making judgments that influence employees' roles in the organization. Although procedural justice is often thought of as a unidimensional construct, recent research shows that in the performance appraisal content it can be conceptualized as two-dimensional.[50]

performance appraisal
The evaluation of a person's performance.

Cross-cultural research has found that North American, Asian, and Latin American managers' perceptions of their employees' motivation are different and that their perceptions affect their appraisals of employee performance.[51]

The major purposes of performance appraisals are to give employees feedback on performance, identify the employees' developmental needs, make promotion and reward decisions, make demotion and termination decisions, and develop information about the organization's selection and placement decisions. For example, a review of 57,775 performance appraisals found higher ratings on appraisals done for administrative reasons and lower ratings on appraisals done for research or for employee development.[52]

© BLEND IMAGES/SUPERSTOCK

One major purpose of performance appraisals is to give employees feedback on performance. A supervisor is responsible for making judgments that influence employees' roles in the organization.

Measuring Performance

Ideally, actual performance and measured performance are the same. Practically, this is seldom the case. Measuring operational performance is easier than measuring managerial performance because of the availability of quantifiable data. Measuring production performance is easier than measuring research and development performance because of the reliability of the measures. Recent research has focused on measuring motivation for task performance and has found that wording and context may influence the validity of direct self-reports.[53]

Performance appraisal systems are intended to improve the accuracy of measured performance and increase its agreement with actual performance. The extent of agreement is called the true assessment, as Figure 6.3 shows. The figure also identifies the performance measurement problems that contribute to inaccuracy. These

FIGURE 6.3 Actual and Measured Performance

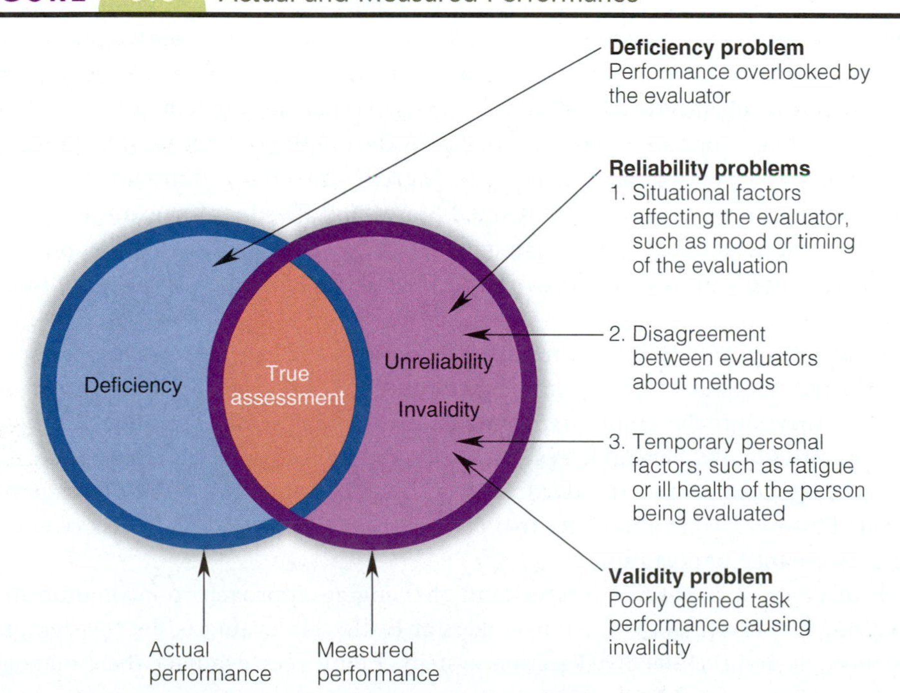

TABLE 6.3 Officer Effectiveness Reports, Circa 1813

Alexander Brown—Lt. Col., Comdg.—A good natured man.
Clark Crowell—first Major—A good man, but no officer.
Jess B. Wordsworth—2nd Major—An excellent officer.
Captain Shaw—A man of whom all unite in speaking ill. A knave despised by all.
Captain Thomas Lord—Indifferent, but promises well.
Captain Rockwell—An officer of capacity, but imprudent and a man of violent passions.
1st Lt. Jas. Kearns—Merely good, nothing promising.
1st Lt. Robert Cross—Willing enough—has much to learn—with small capacity.
2nd Lt. Stewart Berry—An ignorant unoffending fellow.
Ensign North—A good young man who does well.

SOURCE: Table from *The Air Officer's Guide,* 6th ed., Copyright © 1952 Stackpole Books. Used with permission.

include deficiency, unreliability, and invalidity. Deficiency results from overlooking important aspects of a person's actual performance. Unreliability results from poor-quality performance measures. Invalidity results from inaccurate definition of the expected job performance.

Early performance appraisal systems were often quite biased. See, for example, Table 6.3, which is a sample of officer effectiveness reports from an infantry company in the early 1800s. Even contemporary executive appraisals have a dark side, arousing managers' and executives' defenses. Addressing emotions and defenses is important to making appraisal sessions developmental.[54] Some performance review systems lead to forced rankings of employees, which may be controversial.

Performance-monitoring systems using modern electronic technology are sometimes used to measure the performance of vehicle operators, computer technicians, and customer service representatives. For example, such systems might record the rate of keystrokes or the total number of keystrokes for a computer technician. The people subject to this type of monitoring are in some cases unaware that their performance is being measured. What is appropriate performance monitoring? What constitutes inappropriate electronic spying on the employee? Are people entitled to know when their performance is being measured? The ethics of monitoring performance may differ by culture. The United States and Sweden, for example, respect individual freedom more than Japan and China do. The overriding issue, however, is how far organizations should go in using modern technology to measure human performance.

Goal setting and MBO are results-oriented methods of performance appraisal that do not necessarily rely on modern technology. Like performance-monitoring systems, they shift the emphasis from subjective, judgmental performance dimensions to observable, verifiable results. Goals established in the planning phase of goal setting become the standard against which to measure subsequent performance. However, rigid adherence to a results-oriented approach may risk overlooking performance opportunities.

FedEx has incorporated a novel and challenging approach to evaluation in its blueprint for service quality. All managers at FedEx are evaluated by their employees through a survey-feedback-action system. Employees evaluate their managers using a five-point scale on twenty-nine standard statements and ten local option ones. Low ratings suggest problem areas requiring management attention. For example, the following statement received low ratings from employees in 1990: "Upper management pays attention to ideas and suggestions from people at my level." CEO Fred Smith became directly involved in addressing this problem area. One of the actions he took to correct the problem was the development of a bi-weekly employee newsletter.

Performance Feedback: A Communication Challenge

Once clearly defined and accurate performance measures are developed, there is still the challenge of performance feedback. Feedback sessions are among the more stressful events for supervisors and employees. Early research at General Electric found employees responded constructively to positive feedback and were defensive over half the time in response to critical or negative feedback. Typical responses to negative feedback included shifting responsibility for the shortcoming or behavior, denying it outright, or providing a wide range of excuses for it.[55] In a study of 499 Chinese supervisor-subordinate dyads, supervisors responded positively to employees who sought performance feedback if their motive was performance enhancement or improvement.[56] However, if the employee's motive was impression management, supervisors responded less positively.

Both parties to a performance feedback session should try to make it a constructive learning experience, since positive and negative performance feedback has long-term implications for the employee's performance and for the working relationship. American Airlines follows three guidelines in providing evaluative feedback so that the experience is constructive for supervisor and employee alike.[57] First, refer to specific, verbatim statements and specific, observable behaviors displayed by the person receiving the feedback. This enhances the acceptance of the feedback while reducing the chances of denial. Second, focus on changeable behaviors, as opposed to intrinsic or personality-based attributes. People are often more defensive about who they are than about what they do. Third, plan and organize for the session ahead of time. Be sure to notify the person who will receive the feedback. Both the leader and the follower should be ready.

In addition to these ideas, many companies recommend beginning coaching and counseling sessions with something positive. The intent is to reduce defensiveness and enhance useful communication. There is almost always at least one positive element to emphasize. Once the session is underway and rapport is established, then the evaluator can introduce more difficult and negative material. Because people are not perfect, there is always an opportunity for them to learn and to grow through performance feedback sessions. Critical feedback is the basis for improvement and is essential to a performance feedback session. Specific feedback is beneficial for initial performance but discourages exploration and undermines the learning needed for later, more independent performance.[58]

360-degree feedback
A process of self-evaluation and evaluations by a manager, peers, direct reports, and possibly customers.

360-Degree Feedback

(5) Describe 360-degree feedback.

Many organizations use *360-degree feedback* as a tactic to improve the accuracy of performance appraisals because it is based on multiple sources of information. When self-evaluations are included in this process, there is evidence that the evaluation interviews can be more satisfying, more constructive, and less defensive.[59] One of the criticisms of self-evaluations is their low level of agreement with supervisory evaluations.[60] However, high levels of agreement may not necessarily be desirable if the

SCIENCE

360-Degree Feedback and Culture

An organization's capacity for sustainable growth hinges in part on the ability of its managers to learn better skills that improve performance. The 360-degree feedback process is one initiative used by companies to develop managerial skills in two ways: one, through its inherent ability to reinforce learning that has occurred through positive feedback and reinforcement; two, through the creation of actionable knowledge, which is scientifically rigorous knowledge that leads to implementing solutions to practical problems. Some global companies and multinationals have assumed that the 360-degree feedback process applies equally across cultures. These researchers have called this assumption into question and conducted a study with comparisons among five countries: Ireland, Israel, Malaysia, the Phillipines, and the U.S. The results revealed important differences among these countries. The study measured culture using the four work-related values that Hofstede's approach to culture proposed. The study results provided support for the overall effectiveness of the 360-degree feedback process. In addition, important between-group differences were found. Specifically, the 360-degree feedback process was found to be most effective in cultures with low power distance and individualistic values. These cultural context differences are important for managers and leaders to consider in the use of 360-degree feedback.

SOURCE: F. Shipper, R. C. Hoffman, and D. M. Rotondo, "Does the 360 Feedback Process Create Actionable Knowledge Equally Across Cultures?" *Academy of Management Learning & Education* 6 (2007): 33–50.

intent of the evaluation is to provide a full picture of the person's performance. This is a strength of the 360-degree feedback method, which provides a well-rounded view of performance from superiors, peers, followers, and customers.[61]

An example of a 360-degree feedback evaluation occurred in a large military organization for a mid-level civilian executive. The mid-level executive behaved very differently in dealing with superiors, peers, and followers. With superiors, he was positive, compliant, and deferential. With peers, he was largely indifferent, often ignoring them. With followers, he was tough and demanding, bordering on cruel and abusive. Without each of these perspectives, the executive's performance would not have been accurately assessed. When the executive received feedback, he was able to see the inconsistency in his behavior.

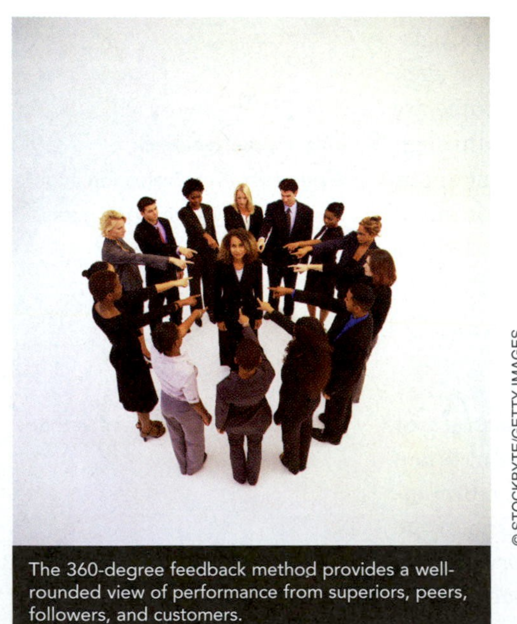

© STOCKBYTE/GETTY IMAGES

The 360-degree feedback method provides a well-rounded view of performance from superiors, peers, followers, and customers.

Two recommendations have been made to improve the effectiveness of the 360-degree feedback method. The first is to add a systematic coaching component to the 360-degree feedback.[62] By focusing on enhanced self-awareness and behavioral management, this feedback-coaching model can enhance performance as well as satisfaction and commitment, and reduce intent to turnover. The second is to separate the performance feedback component of the 360-degree appraisal from the management development component.[63] The feedback component should emphasize quantitative feedback and performance measures, while the management development component should emphasize qualitative feedback and competencies for development.

While 360-degree feedback generates actionable knowledge, its effectiveness has been found to vary across cultures. The accompanying Science feature examines one study of the importance of cultural context in the use of 360-degree feedback.

Developing People and Enhancing Careers

A key function of a good performance appraisal system is to develop people and enhance careers. Developmentally, performance appraisals should emphasize individual growth needs and future performance. If the supervisor is to coach and develop employees effectively, there must be mutual trust. The supervisor must be vulnerable and open to challenge from the subordinate while maintaining a position of responsibility for what is in the subordinate's best interests.[64] The supervisor must also be a skilled, empathetic listener who encourages the employee to talk about hopes and aspirations.[65]

The employee must be able to take active responsibility for future development and growth. This might mean challenging the supervisor's ideas about future development as well as expressing individual preferences and goals. Passive, compliant employees are unable to accept responsibility for themselves or to achieve full emotional development. Individual responsibility is a key characteristic of many organization work cultures that treat employees like adults and expect them to act and behave like adults. This contrasts with work cultures in which leaders treat employees more paternalistically.

Key Characteristics of an Effective Appraisal System

An effective performance appraisal system has five key characteristics: validity, reliability, responsiveness, flexibility, and equitability. Its validity comes from capturing multiple dimensions of a person's job performance. Its reliability comes from capturing evaluations from multiple sources and at different times over the course of the evaluation period. Its responsiveness allows the person being evaluated some input into the final outcome. Its flexibility leaves it open to modification based on new information, such as federal requirements. Its equitability results in fair evaluations against established performance criteria, regardless of individual differences.

REWARDING PERFORMANCE

One function of a performance appraisal system is to provide input for reward decisions. If an organization wants good performance, it must reward good performance. If it does not want bad performance, it must not reward bad performance. If companies talk "teamwork," "values," and "customer focus," they need to reward behaviors related to these ideas. Although this idea is conceptually simple, it can become very complicated in practice. Reward decisions are among the most difficult and complicated decisions made in organizations, and among the most important decisions. When leaders confront decisions about pay every day, they should know that it is a myth that people work for money.[66] While pay and rewards for performance have value, so too do trust, fun, and meaningful work. In addition, as we saw in The Real World 6.1, U.S. government managers are encouraged to reward themselves with self-praise when they know that they have performed well against their work goals.

A Key Organizational Decision Process

Reward and punishment decisions in organizations affect many people throughout the system, not just those being rewarded or punished. Reward allocation involves sequential decisions about which people to reward, how to reward them, and when to reward them. Taken together, these decisions shape the behavior of everyone in the organization because of the vicarious learning that occurs as people watch what happens to others, especially when new programs or initiatives are implemented.

People carefully watch what happens to peers who make mistakes or have problems with the new system; then they gauge their own behavior accordingly.

Individual versus Team Reward Systems

6 Compare individual and team-oriented reward systems.

One of the distinguishing characteristics of Americans is the value they place on individualism. Systems that reward individuals are common in organizations in the United States. One strength of these systems is that they foster autonomous and independent behavior that leads to creativity, to novel solutions to old problems, and to distinctive contributions to the organization. Individual reward systems directly affect individual behavior and encourage competitive striving within a work team. However, different types of employees may have different reward preferences. For example, award seekers may prefer travel awards, nesters may prefer days off, bottom-liners may prefer cash bonuses, freedom yearners may prefer flextime, praise cravers may prefer written praise, and upward movers may prefer status awards.[67] Motivation and reward systems outside the United States are often group focused.[68]

Too much competition within a work environment, however, may be dysfunctional. At the Western Company of North America (now part of BJ Services Company), individual success in the MBO program was tied too tightly to rewards, and individual managers became divisively competitive. For example, some managers took last-minute interdepartmental financial actions in a quarter to meet their objectives, but by doing so, they caused other managers to miss their objectives. Actions such as these raise ethical questions about how far individual managers should go in serving their own self-interest at the expense of their peers.

Team reward systems solve the problems caused by individual competitive behavior. These systems emphasize cooperation, joint efforts, and the sharing of information, knowledge, and expertise. The Japanese and Chinese cultures, with their collectivist orientations, place greater emphasis than Americans on the individual as an element of the team, not a member apart from the team. Digital Equipment Corporation (now part of Hewlett-Packard) used a partnership approach to performance appraisals. Self-managed work group members participated in their own appraisal process. Such an approach emphasizes teamwork and responsibility.

Some organizations have experimented with individual and group alternative reward systems.[69] At the individual level, these include skill-based and pay-for-knowledge systems. Each emphasizes skills or knowledge possessed by an employee over and above the requirements for the basic job. At the group level, gain-sharing plans emphasize collective cost reduction and allow workers to share in the gains achieved by reducing production or other operating costs. In such plans, everyone shares equally in the collective gain. Avnet, Inc. found that collective profit sharing improved performance.

The Power of Earning

The purpose behind both individual and team reward systems is to shape productive behavior. Effective performance management can be the lever of change that boosts individual and team achievements in an organization. So, if one wants the rewards available in the organization, one should work to earn them. Performance management and reward systems assume a demonstrable connection between performance and rewards. Organizations get the performance they reward, not the performance they say they want.[70] Further, when there is no apparent link between performance and rewards, people may begin to believe they are entitled to rewards regardless of how they perform. The concept of entitlement is very different

Correcting Poor Performance

At one time or another, each of us has had a poor performance of some kind. It may have been a poor test result in school, a poor presentation at work, or a poor performance in an athletic event. Think of a poor performance event that you have experienced and work through the following three steps.

Step 1. Briefly describe the specific event in some detail. Include why you label it a poor performance (bad score? someone else's evaluation?).

Step 2. Analyze the Poor Performance

a. List all the possible contributing causes to the poor performance. Be specific, such as the room was too hot, you did not get enough sleep, you were not told how to perform the task, etc. You might ask other people for possible ideas, too.

1. ____________________
2. ____________________
3. ____________________
4. ____________________
5. ____________________
6. ____________________
7. ____________________

b. Is there a primary cause for the poor performance? What is it?

Step 3. Plan to Correct the Poor Performance
Develop a step-by-step plan of action that specifies what you can change or do differently to improve your performance the next time you have an opportunity. Include seeking help if it is needed. Once your plan is developed, look for an opportunity to execute it.

from the concept of earning, which assumes a performance–reward link. Toyota's frugality, mentioned in Thinking Ahead, places underlying value on the power of earning.

The notion of entitlement at work is counterproductive when taken to the extreme because it counteracts the power of earning.[71] People who believe they are entitled to rewards regardless of their behavior or performance are not motivated to behave constructively. Merit raises in some organizations, for example, have come to be viewed as entitlements, thus reducing their positive value in the organizational reward system. People believe they have a right to be taken care of by someone, whether that is the organization or a specific person. Entitlement engenders passive, irresponsible behavior, whereas earning engenders active, responsible, adult behavior. If rewards depend on performance, people must perform responsibly to receive them. The power of earning rests on a direct link between performance and rewards.

CORRECTING POOR PERFORMANCE

(7) Describe strategies for correcting poor performance.

Often a complicated, difficult challenge for supervisors, correcting poor performance is a three-step process. First, the cause or primary responsibility for the poor performance must be identified. Second, if the primary responsibility is a person's, then the source of the personal problem must be determined. Third, a plan of action to correct the poor performance must be developed. You 6.2 gives you an opportunity to examine a poor performance you have experienced. As we saw in Thinking Ahead, Toyota is aggressive about making corrective adjustments when performance is not the best it can be.

Poor performance may result from a variety of causes, the more important being poorly designed work systems, poor selection processes, inadequate training and skills development, lack of personal motivation, and personal problems intruding

on the work environment. Not all poor performance is self-motivated; some is induced by the work system. Therefore, a good diagnosis should precede corrective action. For example, it may be that an employee is subject to a work design or selection system that does not allow the person to exhibit good performance. Identifying the cause of the poor performance comes first and should be done in communication with the employee. If the problem is with the system and the supervisor can fix it, everyone wins as a result.

If the poor performance is not attributable to work design or organizational process problems, then attention should be focused on the employee. At least three possible causes of poor performance can be attributed to the employee. The problem may lie in (1) some aspect of the person's relationship to the organization or supervisor, (2) some area of the employee's personal life, or (3) a training or developmental deficiency. In the latter two cases, poor performance may be treated as a symptom as opposed to a motivated consequence. In such cases, identifying financial problems, family difficulties, or health disorders may enable the supervisor to help the employee solve problems before they become too extensive. Employee assistance programs (EAPs) can be helpful to employees managing personal problems. These are discussed in Chapter 7 in relation to managing stress.

Poor performance may also be motivated by an employee's displaced anger or conflict with the organization or supervisor. In such cases, the employee may or may not be aware of the internal reactions causing the problem. In either event, sabotage, work slowdowns, work stoppages, and similar forms of poor performance may result from such motivated behavior. The supervisor may attribute the cause of the problem to the employee, and the employee may attribute it to the supervisor or organization. To solve motivated performance problems requires treating the poor performance as a symptom with a deeper cause. Resolving the underlying anger or conflict results in the disappearance of the symptom (poor performance).

Performance and Kelley's Attribution Theory

According to attribution theory, managers make attributions (inferences) concerning employees' behavior and performance.[72] The attributions may not always be accurate. For example, an executive with Capital Cities Communications/ABC (now part of the Disney Company) who had a very positive relationship with his boss was not held responsible for profit problems in his district. The boss blamed the problem on the economy. Supervisors and employees who share perceptions and attitudes, as in the Capital Cities situation, tend to evaluate each other highly.[73] Supervisors and employees who do not share perceptions and attitudes are more likely to blame each other for performance problems.

Harold Kelley's attribution theory aims to help us explain the behavior of other people. He also extended attribution theory by trying to identify the antecedents of internal and external attributions. Kelley proposed that individuals make attributions based on information gathered in the form of three informational cues: consensus, distinctiveness, and consistency.[74,75] We observe an individual's behavior and then seek out information in the form of these three cues. *Consensus* is the extent to which peers in the same situation behave the same way. *Distinctiveness* is the degree to which the person behaves the same way in other situations. *Consistency* refers to the frequency of a particular behavior over time.

consensus
An informational cue indicating the extent to which peers in the same situation behave in a similar fashion.

distinctiveness
An informational cue indicating the degree to which an individual behaves the same way in other situations.

consistency
An informational cue indicating the frequency of behavior over time.

We form attributions based on whether these cues are low or high. Figure 6.4 shows how the combination of these cues helps us form internal or external attributions. Suppose you have received several complaints from customers regarding one of your customer service representatives, John. You have not received complaints

FIGURE 6.4 Informational Cues and Attributions

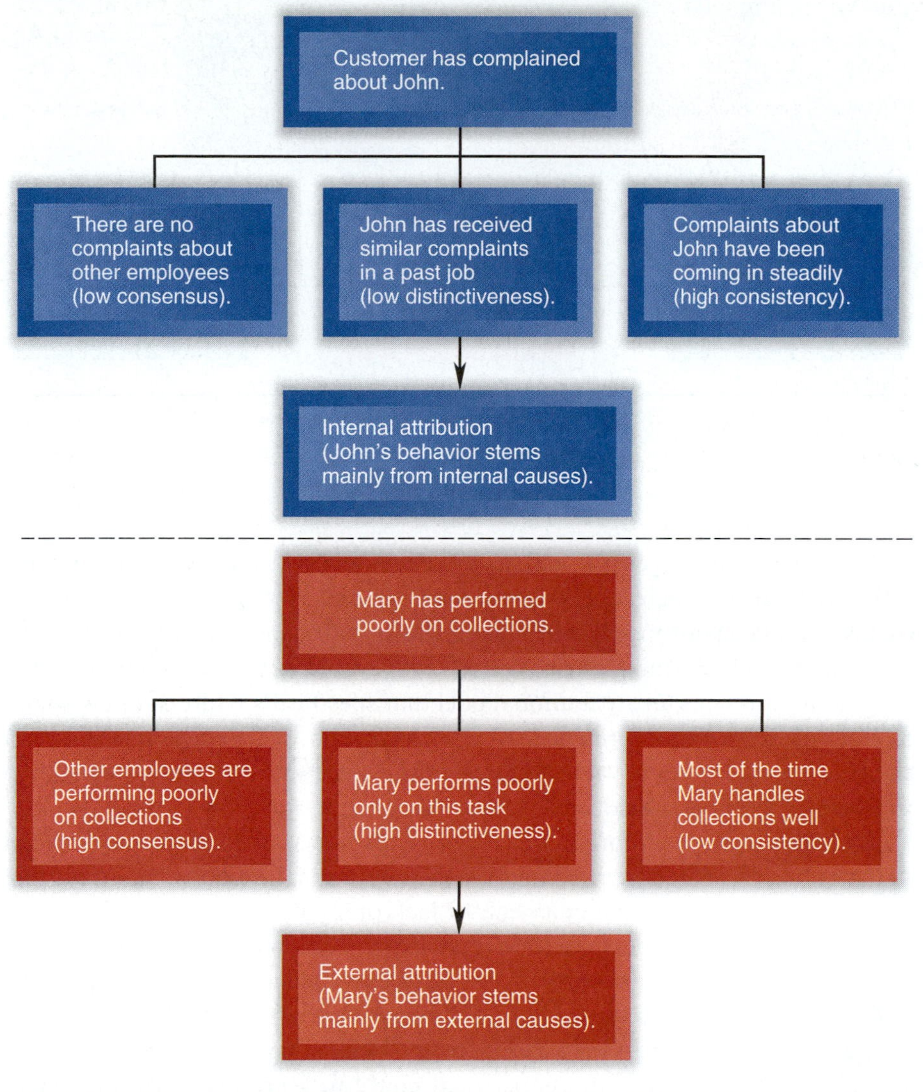

about your other service representatives (low consensus). Upon reviewing John's records, you note that he also received customer complaints during his previous job as a sales clerk (low distinctiveness). The complaints have been coming in steadily for about three months (high consistency). In this case, you would most likely make an internal attribution and conclude that the complaints must stem from John's behavior. The combination of low consensus, low distinctiveness, and high consistency leads to internal attributions.

Other combinations of these cues, however, produce external attributions. High consensus, high distinctiveness, and low consistency, for example, produce external attributions. Suppose one of your employees, Mary, is performing poorly on collecting overdue accounts. You find that the behavior is widespread within your work team (high consensus) and that Mary is performing poorly only on this aspect of the job (high distinctiveness), and that most of the time she handles this aspect of the job well (low consistency). You will probably decide that something about the work situation caused the poor performance—perhaps work overload or an unfair deadline.

FIGURE 6.5 Attribution Model

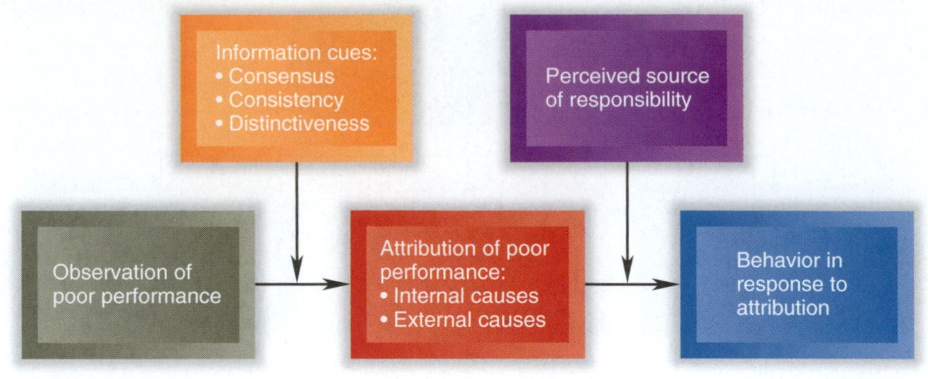

Consensus, distinctiveness, and consistency are the cues used to determine whether the cause of behavior is internal or external. The process of determining the cause of a behavior may not be simple and clear-cut, however, because of some biases that occur in forming attributions.

Figure 6.5 presents an attribution model that specifically addresses how supervisors respond to poor performance. A supervisor who observes poor performance seeks cues about the employee's behavior in the three forms discussed above: consensus, consistency, and distinctiveness.

On the basis of this information, the supervisor makes either an internal (personal) attribution or an external (situational) attribution. Internal attributions might include low effort, lack of commitment, or lack of ability. External attributions are outside the employee's control and might include equipment failure or unrealistic goals. The supervisor then determines the source of responsibility for the performance problem and tries to correct the problem.

Supervisors may choose from a wide range of responses. They can, for example, express personal concern, reprimand the employee, or provide training. Supervisors who attribute the cause of poor performance to a person (an internal cause) will respond more harshly than supervisors who attribute the cause to the work situation (an external cause). Supervisors should try not to make either of the two common attribution errors discussed in Chapter 3: the fundamental attribution error and the self-serving bias.

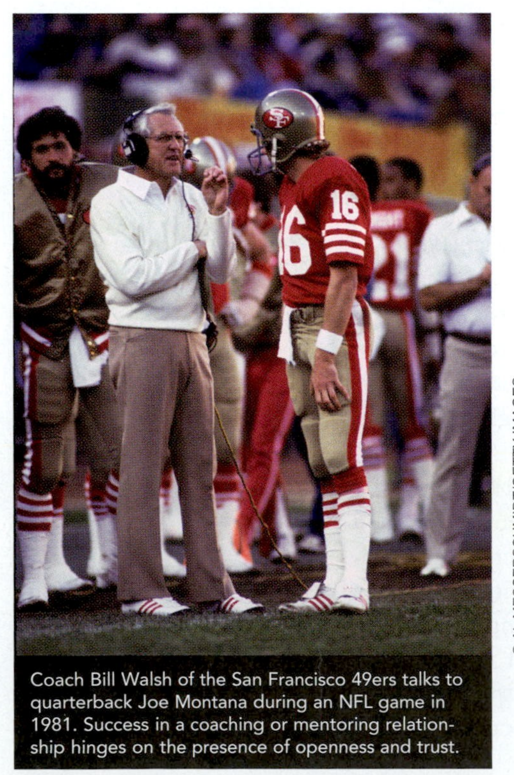

© AL MESSERSCHMIDT/GETTY IMAGES

Coach Bill Walsh of the San Francisco 49ers talks to quarterback Joe Montana during an NFL game in 1981. Success in a coaching or mentoring relationship hinges on the presence of openness and trust.

Coaching, Counseling, and Mentoring

Supervisors have important coaching, counseling, and mentoring responsibilities to their subordinates. Supervisors and coworkers have been found to be more effective in mentoring functions than assigned, formal mentors from higher up in the organizational hierarchy.[76] Success in the mentoring relationship also hinges on the presence of openness and trust.[77] This relationship may be one where performance-based deficiencies are addressed or one where personal problems that diminish employee performance, such as depression, are addressed.[78] In either case, supervisors can play a helpful role in employee problem-solving activities without accepting responsibility for the employees' problems. One important form of help is to refer the employee to trained professionals.

Coaching and counseling are among the career and psychosocial functions of a mentoring relationship.[79] *Mentoring* is a work relationship that encourages development and career enhancement for people moving through the career cycle. Mentor relationships typically go through four phases: initiation, cultivation, separation, and redefinition. For protégés, mentoring offers a number of career benefits.[80] The relationship can significantly enhance the early development of a newcomer and the midcareer development of an experienced employee. One study found that good performance by newcomers resulted in leaders giving more delegation.[81] Career development can be enhanced through peer relationships as an alternative to traditional mentoring relationships.[82] Executive coaching is increasingly being used as a way of outsourcing the business mentoring functions.[83] Informational, collegial, and special peers aid the individual's development through information sharing, career strategizing, job-related feedback, emotional support, and friendship. Hence, mentors and peers may both play constructive roles in correcting an employee's poor performance and in enhancing overall career development.

MANAGERIAL IMPLICATIONS: PERFORMANCE MANAGEMENT IS A KEY TASK

People in organizations learn from the consequences of their actions. Therefore, managers must exercise care in applying positive and negative consequences to ensure that they are connected to the behaviors the managers intend to reward or punish. Managers should also be judicious in the use of punishment and should consider extinction coupled with positive reinforcement as an alternative to punishment for shaping employee behavior. The strategic use of training and educational opportunities, stock options, and recognition awards is instrumental to successful organizational reward systems. Managers can serve as positive role models for employees' vicarious learning about ethical behavior and high-quality performance.

Goal-setting activities may be valuable to managers in bringing out the best performance from employees. Managers can use challenging, specific goals for this purpose and must be prepared to provide employees with timely, useful feedback on goal progress so that employees will know how they are doing. Goal-setting activities that are misused may create dysfunctional competition in an organization and lead to lower performance.

Good performance management systems are a valuable tool for providing employees with clear feedback on their actions. Managers who rely on valid and reliable performance measures may use them in employee development and to correct poor performance. Managers who use high-technology performance monitoring systems must remember that employees are humans, not machines. Managers are responsible for creating a positive learning atmosphere in performance feedback sessions, and employees are responsible for learning from these sessions. 360-degree feedback is especially effective when combined with coaching.

Finally, managers can use rewards as one of the most powerful positive consequences for shaping employee behavior. If rewards are to improve performance, managers must make a clear connection between specific performance and the rewards. Employees should be expected to earn the rewards they receive; they should expect rewards to be related to performance quality and skill development.

mentoring
A work relationship that encourages development and career enhancement for people moving through the career cycle.

LOOKING BACK: TOYOTA

Learning and Change at the University of Toyota

Toyota's learning principles have been a driving force in the company's continuous rise to the top of the automotive industry.[84] Its in-house training has served the company well. In 2006 the company began teaching its "lean thinking" to other businesses as well as to police and the U.S. military at its in-house training center, known as the University of Toyota. The school occupies the Toyota Plaza building in Gardena, California, and banners displaying key Toyota principles hang on the walls. These principles include *kaizen* (continuous improvement) and *genchi genbutsu* (go look, go see). Toyota has leapfrogged its competition yet done so through *kaizen*, which is progress made with a million incremental ideas. While it charges most organizations for its training and educational services, it provides these to police and the U.S. military as a public service.

The Los Angeles Police Department's Captain Patrick Findley is one of the beneficiaries of this public service. When he took over the LAPD's jails in 2005, incoming prisoners stood in line for hours waiting to be booked while officers spent valuable time heating up frozen dinners to feed them each evening. That is the way it had always been done, and Captain Findley did not think to question the process—until he took a two-day class at the University of Toyota. As a result, Captain Findley did away with serving dinner hot and began serving sandwiches with an apple and milk, thus freeing more officers during one of the jail's busiest times. This public service advancement occurs courtesy of knowledge transfer from lean manufacturing in the automotive industry to lean thinking in a whole different context. The improvements resulting from learning at Toyota will save the LAPD over $1 million annually.

Toyota began this process of expanding its teaching to non-auto businesses in the United States when it looked for a business that had already devised some lean thinking of its own. They found Quadrant Homes, a Seattle home builder owned by forest-products giant Weyerhaeuser Company. Quadrant had built homes with features based on market trends for years, selling the finished products. This build-first approach left them with unsold inventory. So Quadrant flipped the process, started taking orders, and then built to buyers' specifications. This cut prices, cut average construction time (to 54 from 120 days), and nearly tripled sales closings over a five-year period. Hoping to ingrain that thinking more deeply, Quadrant began sending teams of employees to the University of Toyota as soon as it opened its doors to outsider businesses. What works for cars may be translated to home improvements, jail improvements, and even innovative thinking in military combat operations.

Chapter Summary

1. Learning is a change in behavior acquired through experience.
2. The operant conditioning approach to learning states that behavior is a function of positive and negative consequences.
3. Reinforcement is used to develop desirable behavior; punishment and extinction are used to decrease undesirable behavior.
4. Bandura's social learning theory suggests that task-specific self-efficacy is important to effective learning.
5. Goal setting improves work motivation and task performance, reduces role stress, and improves the accuracy and validity of performance appraisal.
6. Performance management and 360-degree feedback can lead to improved performance.
7. Making accurate attributions about the behavior of others is an essential prerequisite to correcting poor performance.
8. High-quality performance should be rewarded, and poor performance should be corrected.
9. Mentoring is a relationship for encouraging development and career enhancement for people moving through the career cycle.

Key Terms

classical conditioning (p. 185)
consensus (p. 204)
consistency (p. 204)
distinctiveness (p. 204)
extinction (p. 188)
goal setting (p. 190)
learning (p. 184)
management by objectives (MBO) (p. 194)
mentoring (p. 207)
negative consequences (p. 186)
operant conditioning (p. 185)
performance appraisal (p. 196)
performance management (p. 195)
positive consequences (p. 186)
punishment (p. 187)
reinforcement (p. 186)
task-specific self-efficacy (p. 188)
360-degree feedback (p. 199)

Review Questions

1. Define the terms *learning, reinforcement, punishment*, and *extinction.*
2. What are positive and negative consequences in shaping behavior? How should they be managed? Explain the value of extinction as a strategy.
3. How can task-specific self-efficacy be enhanced? What are the differences in the way introverted and extraverted and intuitive and sensing people learn?
4. What are the five characteristics of well-developed goals? Why is feedback on goal progress important?
5. What are the purposes of conducting performance appraisals? What are the benefits of 360-degree feedback?
6. What are the two possible attributions of poor performance? What are the implications of each?
7. How can managers and supervisors best provide useful performance feedback?
8. How do mentors and peers help people develop and enhance their careers?

Discussion and Communication Questions

1. Which learning approach—the behavioral approach or Bandura's social learning theory—do you find more appropriate for people?
2. Given your personality type, how do you learn best? Do you miss learning some things because of how they are taught?
3. What goals do you set for yourself at work? In your personal life? Will you know if you achieve them?
4. If a conflict occurred between your self-evaluation and the evaluation given to you by your supervisor or instructor, how would you respond? What, specifically, would you do? What have you learned

from your supervisor or instructor during the last reporting period?

5. What rewards are most important to you? How hard are you willing to work to receive them?
6. *(communication question)* Prepare a memo detailing the consequences of behavior in your work or university environment (e.g., grades, awards, suspensions, and scholarships). Include in your memo your classification of these consequences as positive or negative. Should your organization or university change the way it applies these consequences?
7. *(communication question)* Develop an oral presentation about the most current management practices in employee rewards and performance management. Find out what at least four different companies are doing in this area. Be prepared to discuss their fit with the text materials.
8. *(communication question)* Interview a manager or supervisor who is responsible for completing performance appraisals on people at work. Ask the manager which aspects of performance appraisal and the performance appraisal interview process are most difficult and how he or she manages these difficulties.

Ethical Dilemma

Donna Hermann shuffled the papers on her desk. She was very surprised by what she read. On her desk sat the annual evaluations of Julie Stringer, an employee in Donna's department. Both worked for Telecom Solutions, a large call center in the Midwest where it was the policy to do 360-degree annual evaluation on all employees. Each individual was evaluated by his or her supervisor, peers, and subordinates if the person was in a management position. As Julie's supervisor, Donna was looking at the evaluations completed by three of Julie's peers and three of her subordinates.

Julie's peers' opinion of her performance closely matched Donna's. Working at Telecom was intense, and the managers had worked hard to create an environment where they supported each other. They felt that Julie was not supporting this environment. She never got in anyone's way, but she never pitched in to help either. Julie came to Telecom every day to work, nothing else. She never cared to make friends or to be a part of the team. Donna felt this was not good for the morale of her department and had hoped this annual evaluation would help her start the process of replacing Julie. The problem was that Julie's employees loved her. Donna had never seen such glowing reviews by anyone's subordinates. Obviously, Julie was not remote with her team. One of Julie's highest ratings from her team was her willingness to pitch in at any time for any reason. This was a very different perception from the management team.

Donna had no personal problem with Julie; she was concerned about her entire department. Since Julie joined the company, things had not been the same. However, was it more important for Julie's peers to be happy or her employees? Her group was always productive. Also, was it fair to punish someone for coming to the office to work? But, was it right to let Julie's behaviors continue chipping away at the culture that Donna and the other managers had worked so hard to achieve?

Questions

1. What is Donna's primary responsibility?
2. Does Donna have a greater responsibility to her direct reports or to those one level down?
3. Using consequential, rule-based, and character theories, evaluate Donna's decision regarding Julie.

Experiential Exercises

6.1 Positive and Negative Reinforcement

Purpose: To examine the effects of positive and negative reinforcement on behavior change.

1. Two or three volunteers are selected to receive reinforcement from the class while performing a particular task. The volunteers leave the room.
2. The instructor identifies an object for the student volunteers to locate when they return to the room. (The object should be unobtrusive but clearly visible to the class. Some that have worked well are a small triangular piece of paper that was left behind when a notice was torn off a classroom bulletin board, a

smudge on the chalkboard, and a chip in the plaster of a classroom wall.)

3. The instructor specifies the reinforcement contingencies that will be in effect when the volunteers return to the room. For negative reinforcement, students should hiss, boo, and throw things (although you should not throw anything harmful) when the first volunteer is moving away from the object; cheer and applaud when the second volunteer is getting closer to the object; and if a third volunteer is used, use both negative and positive reinforcement.
4. The instructor should assign a student to keep a record of the time it takes each of the volunteers to locate the object.
5. Volunteer number one is brought back into the room and is instructed: "Your task is to locate and touch a particular object in the room, and the class has agreed to help you. You may begin."
6. Volunteer number one continues to look for the object until it is found while the class assists by giving negative reinforcement.
7. Volunteer number two is brought back into the room and is instructed: "Your task is to locate and touch a particular object in the room, and the class has agreed to help you. You may begin."
8. Volunteer number two continues to look for the object until it is found while the class assists by giving positive reinforcement.
9. Volunteer number three is brought back into the room and is instructed: "Your task is to locate and touch a particular object in the room, and the class has agreed to help you. You may begin."
10. Volunteer number three continues to look for the object until it is found while the class assists by giving both positive and negative reinforcement.
11. In a class discussion, answer the following questions:
    a. How did the behavior of the volunteers differ when different kinds of reinforcement (positive, negative, or both) were used?
    b. What were the emotional reactions of the volunteers to the different kinds of reinforcement?
    c. Which type of reinforcement—positive or negative—is most common in organizations? What effect do you think this has on motivation and productivity?

6.2 Correcting Poor Performance

This exercise provides an opportunity for you to engage in a performance diagnosis role-play as either the assistant director of the Academic Computing Service Center or as a member of a university committee appointed by the president of the university at the request of the center director. The instructor will form the class into groups of five or six students and either ask the group to select who is to be the assistant director or assign one group member to be the assistant director.

Performance diagnosis, especially where some poor performance exists, requires making attributions and determining causal factors as well as formulating a plan of action to correct any poor performance.

Step 1. (5 minutes) Once the class is formed into groups, the instructor provides the assistant director with a copy of the role description and each university committee member with a copy of the role context information. Group members are to read through the materials provided.

Step 2. (15 minutes) The university committee is to call in the assistant director of the Academic Computing Service Center for a performance diagnostic interview. This is an information-gathering interview, not an appraisal session. The purpose is to gather information for the center director.

Step 3. (15 minutes) The university committee is to agree on a statement that reflects their understanding of the assistant director's poor performance and to include a specification of the causes. Based on this problem statement, the committee is to formulate a plan of action to correct the poor performance. The assistant director is to do the same, again ending with a plan of action.

Step 4. (10–15 minutes, optional) The instructor may ask the groups to share the results of their work in Step 3 of the role-play exercise.

TAKE 2

Biz Flix | Seabiscuit

Combine a jockey who is blind in one eye with an undersized, ill-tempered thoroughbred and an unusual trainer. The result: the Depression-era champion racehorse Seabiscuit. This engaging film shows the training and development of Seabiscuit by trainer "Silent" Tom Smith (Chris Cooper) and jockey Red Pollard (Tobey Maguire). The enduring commitment of owner Charles Howard (Jeff Bridges) ensures the ultimate success of Seabiscuit on the racing circuit. Based on *Seabiscuit: An American Legend,* the best selling book by Laura Hillenbrand, *Seabiscuit* received seven 2003 Academy Award nominations, including Best Picture.

The *Seabiscuit* scene is an edited composite from DVD Chapters 21 and 22 toward the end of the film. In earlier scenes, Red severely injured a leg and cannot ride Seabiscuit in the competition against War Admiral. Samuel Riddle (Eddie Jones), War Admiral's owner, described any new rider as immaterial to the race's result. The scene begins with Red giving George Wolff (Gary Stevens), Seabiscuit's new jockey, some tips about riding him. Red starts by saying to George, "He's got a strong left lead, Georgie. He banks like a frigg'n airplane." The film continues to its exciting and unexpected ending.

What to Watch for and Ask Yourself:

- Does Red set clear performance goals for George? If he does, what are they?
- Does Red help George reach those performance goals? How?
- Does Red give George any positive reinforcement while he tries to reach the performance goals?

Workplace Video | Managerial Planning and Goal Setting at Cold Stone Creamery

Donald and Susan Sutherland are serious about giving customers the "Ultimate Ice Cream Experience," as their slogan goes. In 1988, the couple turned their love of ice cream into the first Cold Stone Creamery in Tempe, Arizona, and today the franchise boasts more than 1,300 stores.

Cold Stone Creamery truly is "an experience." At every location, fresh ice cream is produced in a dizzying array of unusual flavors and mixed with tasty toppings—nuts, fruits, candy, cookies, and more. Crew members who serve up the gooey frozen treats offer an entertaining song and dance on the side—just for fun.

Careful planning and goal setting is the key to Cold Stone's success. The company's mission is to "make people happy around the world by selling the highest quality, most creative ice cream experience with passion, excellence, and innovation." Within that overarching mission, executives set a company-wide goal of becoming America's number-one-selling ice cream by 2010. Supporting this challenging goal is "Pyramid of Success 2010," a detailed strategic plan that informs employees at all levels of the organization about their role in achieving the companywide objective. By setting clear objectives and

TAKE 2

offering rewards for achievement, management lays the groundwork for top performance and unites all employees in the pursuit of a common cause.

In the race to be number one, Cold Stone Creamery remains true to the Sutherlands' original dream of providing the "Ultimate Ice Cream Experience." From the executive vice president to the first-line managers, all Cold Stone employees take pride in transforming ordinary ice cream into something extraordinary. In addition to signature creations like the Birthday Cake Remix and the ever-popular Founder's Favorite, Cold Stone experiments with new flavors, like French Toast and Cinnabon, while developing concepts such as Twinkie ice-cream sandwiches. Each new idea produces big smiles from ice cream lovers and moves the company ever closer to its 2010 target.

Discussion Questions

1. Do Cold Stone Creamery's goals possess the five characteristics of effective goals discussed in the chapter? Explain.
2. What makes the "Pyramid of Success 2010" graphic an effective tool for communicating Cold Stone Creamery's corporate mission and goals to all employees?
3. Should management at Cold Stone Creamery use the same reward system for employees in Japan as they do in the United States? Why or why not?

CASE

American Express: Challenges in Managing Learning and Performance

American Express (AMEX) was founded in 1850 to provide freight forwarding and delivery services. Over the past 150-plus years, it has evolved into a global financial services company, with operations in over 130 countries.[1]

Like other organizations, AMEX is concerned with enhancing the performance capabilities of employees. Developing and maintaining employee competencies and skills can be daunting, as two different challenges in managing learning and performance at the company illustrate.

Learning to Manage the Managers of Learning

Not only must the learning operations of an organization address the training and development needs of other units within the organization, but the organizational unit responsible for employee learning must also be concerned with developing the talents of its own staff members. In 2005, this lesson came to the forefront at American Express as the company's Learning Network evaluated its practices. The AMEX Learning Network discovered that it was not doing a satisfactory job of addressing the training and development needs of its own staff members—those AMEX employees directly charged with providing training and development experiences for the rest of the organization. The Learning Network subsequently took appropriate steps to improve its performance and craft a new vision and mission.[2]

A crucial problem was that it "had been so focused on the learning and development of others that its members had not devoted enough attention to their own knowledge and skills development."[3] Consequently, it began to focus efforts on the development of its own staff members. The Learning Network staff participated in various programs designed to elevate their skill levels. They also earned additional certifications from appropriate professional organizations. The Network also reviewed its compensation policies and practices to ensure they were in line with AMEX's pay-for-performance compensation model. Finally, to better link its own activities with the rest of the AMEX organization, the Learning Network also improved its measurement of training metrics. To better respond to the needs of AMEX's managers, the training metrics technology team developed what it called "metrics central," a Web-enabled tool that can be accessed by both Learning Network staffers and other AMEX managers.[4]

Mode of Leadership Development at AMEX

Another learning and performance management issue at American Express involved the Learning Network's efforts in the leadership development arena. AMEX was seeking to ascertain the most effective manner in which to conduct leadership training.

In 2006, the company implemented a new model of leadership development across the entire organization. Three groups of trainees (or learners) were formed, each exposed to a different training venue. One group had only online delivery of learning materials, which were studied through self-direction without any supporting events like peer discussion, formal meetings, or talks by senior organizational leaders. Another group of learners experienced traditional classroom training without any support of online materials or other formal events. The third group of learners experienced a *blended learning* approach that combined classroom or Web-based interaction with senior leaders, self-directed online learning, and encouragement of discussion among learners.[5]

In evaluating the three different approaches, AMEX assessed employee training responses—called *learner responses*—at five different levels. Level 1 measured learner reaction, wherein the trainees indicated the level of satisfaction they had with the learning experience. Level 2 focused on learner knowledge, or an assessment of the acquisition of new knowledge and skills. Level 3 addressed the learners' behavior by evaluating their observed improvement in leadership skills three months after the training sessions. Level 4 focused on the business impact of the training on the learners in terms of improved productivity of the learners' direct reports (i.e., those people for whom the learner has immediate supervisory responsibility). Level 5 targeted return on investment (ROI) via a cost/benefit analysis of the sales productivity of the learners' direct reports over the preceding three-month period. Assessments at levels 1 and 2 were based on the learner's self-report; at levels 3 and 4 the assessments were conducted via self-report from the learners and reports from the learners' supervisor and direct reports; and at level 5 it was based on objective data.[6]

Little difference was found among the three learning approaches—online self-directed, traditional classroom, and blended—for levels 1 and 2. However, blended learning proved to be the superior training approach at evaluation levels 3, 4, and 5.[7]

Challenges to Organizational Learning

How to effectively manage the managers of organizational learning and ascertaining the most effective mode of leadership development are only two of many challenges that can influence the effectiveness of learning and performance management activities in an organization. The manner in which an organization addresses these challenges can make a major impact on the effectiveness of organizational learning within a company.

Discussion Questions

1. How has the American Express Learning Network utilized learning theory, goal setting, and reward systems in addressing the challenge of its own staff members' training and development needs?
2. How is the use of learning theory and goal-setting theory evident in the design of AMEX's leadership development program?
3. Using relevant concepts from Chapter 6, explain why you think the blended learning approach to leadership development produced the best results for evaluation levels 3, 4, and 5.

SOURCE: This case was written by Michael K. McCuddy, The Louis S. and Mary L. Morgal Chair of Christian Business Ethics and Professor of Management, College of Business Administration, Valparaiso University.

CHAPTER 7

Stress and Well-Being at Work

LEARNING OBJECTIVES

After reading this chapter, you should be able to do the following:

1 Define *stress*, *distress*, and *strain*.

2 Compare four different approaches to stress.

3 Explain the psychophysiology of the stress response.

4 Identify work and nonwork causes of stress.

5 Describe the benefits of eustress and the costs of distress.

6 Discuss individual differences in the stress–strain relationship.

7 Distinguish the primary, secondary, and tertiary stages of preventive stress management.

8 Discuss organizational and individual methods of preventive stress management.

THINKING AHEAD: TIMBERLAND COMPANY

When the Going Gets Tough, Kick It Up a Notch

Every company has its ups and down, its successes and failures. Timberland reaches back to the early 1950s in its corporate history and in 2008 celebrates its thirty-fifth anniversary in its present form.[1] From some perspectives, 2007 was a very stressful and challenging year. Timberland is best known for superior boots and footwear, especially for rugged outdoor use. 2006 and 2007 have been problematic in that core part of the business, with sales declines in the boots and kids categories. In addition to sales declines, the COO and CFO left the company in early 2007. It would be fair to conclude that this period has been a demanding one for a very visible company with a strong brand name and successful track record for over a half century.

Timberland of all companies should know about stress and challenge. The company's brand and reputation were built on a rugged footwear model, for men, women, and children. From their popular yellow hiking boots to boat shoes as well as dress and outdoor casual footwear and sandals, the company got its traction from having its feet firmly planted on the ground. However, they did not stop there, adding both apparel and accessories to their bottom-line footwear. The apparel line of outerwear, shirts, pants, and socks are designed to offer customers stress-free protection in a wide range of environments while being comfortable all day long. Accessories include sunglasses, watches, and belts, again aimed at reducing the stress customers may experience outdoors. So, from the ground up, so to speak, Timberland has a strong array of high-quality products.

Great products are good for reducing customer stress, but how about for the company itself? Timberland faces strong competitors such as Patagonia, Merrill, and Columbia, who are all getting better. Boot sales declines in 2006 and 2007 challenged Timberland to find a secure basis for launching its next advance. While it has a large global footprint, with 220 company-owned and franchised stores in Asia, Canada, Europe, Latin America, the Middle East, and the United States, the expected 2007 decline in sales of boots and kids' products of $100 million globally was a worrying event. Could the company take more challenging, stressful, and/or bad news? Is there a silver lining in this dark cloud?

Stress is an important topic in organizational behavior, in part due to the increase in competitive pressures that take a toll on workers and managers alike. Poor leadership, work–family conflicts, and sexual harassment are among the leading causes of work stress.[2] This chapter has five major sections, each addressing one aspect of stress. The first section examines the question "What is stress?" The discussion includes four approaches to the stress response. The second section reviews the demands and stressors that trigger the stress response at work. The third section examines the performance and health benefits of stress and the individual and organizational forms of distress. The fourth section considers individual difference factors, such as gender and personality hardiness, that help moderate the stress–distress relationship. The fifth section presents a framework for preventive stress management and reviews a wide range of individual and organizational stress management methods.

(1) Define *stress, distress,* and *strain.*

stress
The unconscious preparation to fight or flee that a person experiences when faced with any demand.

stressor
The person or event that triggers the stress response.

distress
The adverse psychological, physical, behavioral, and organizational consequences that may arise as a result of stressful events.

strain
Distress.

WHAT IS STRESS?

Stress is one of the most creatively ambiguous words in the English language, with as many interpretations as there are people who use the word. In other languages, the term *stress* has a variety of meanings, and Spanish does not even have a direct translation of it. Even the stress experts do not agree on its definition. Stress carries a negative connotation for some people, as though it were something to be avoided. This is unfortunate, because stress is a great asset in managing legitimate emergencies and achieving peak performance. *Stress,* or the stress response, is the unconscious preparation to fight or flee that a person experiences when faced with any demand.[3] A *stressor,* or demand, is the person or event that triggers the stress response. *Distress* or *strain* refers to the adverse psychological, physical, behavioral, and organizational consequences that *may* occur as a result of stressful events. You 7.1 gives you an opportunity to examine how overstressed and angry you may be.

YOU 7.1

The Frazzle Factor

Read each of the following statements and rate yourself on a scale of 0 to 3, giving the answer that best describes how you generally feel (3 points for *always,* 2 points for *often,* 1 point for *sometimes,* and 0 points for *never*). Answer as honestly as you can, and do not spend too much time on any one statement.

Am I Overstressed?

____ 1. I have to make important snap judgments and decisions.
____ 2. I am not consulted about what happens on my job or in my classes.
____ 3. I feel I am underpaid.
____ 4. I feel that no matter how hard I work, the system will mess it up.
____ 5. I do not get along with some of my coworkers or fellow students.
____ 6. I do not trust my superiors at work or my professors at school.
____ 7. The paperwork burden on my job or at school is getting to me.
____ 8. I feel people outside the job or the university do not respect what I do.

Am I Angry?

____ 1. I feel that people around me make too many irritating mistakes.
____ 2. I feel annoyed because I do good work or perform well in school, but no one appreciates it.
____ 3. When people make me angry, I tell them off.
____ 4. When I am angry, I say things I know will hurt people.
____ 5. I lose my temper easily.
____ 6. I feel like striking out at someone who angers me.
____ 7. When a coworker or fellow student makes a mistake, I tell him or her about it.
____ 8. I cannot stand being criticized in public.

Scoring

To find your level of anger and potential for aggressive behavior, add your scores from both quiz parts.

40–48: The red flag is waving, and you had better pay attention. You are in the danger zone. You need guidance from a counselor or mental health professional, and you should be getting it now.

30–39: The yellow flag is up. Your stress and anger levels are too high, and you are feeling increasingly hostile. You are still in control, but it would not take much to trigger a violent flare of temper.

10–29: Relax, you are in the broad normal range. Like most people, you get angry occasionally, but usually with some justification. Sometimes you take overt action, but you are not likely to be unreasonably or excessively aggressive.

0–9: Congratulations! You are in great shape. Your stress and anger are well under control, giving you a laid-back personality not prone to violence.

SOURCE: Questionnaire developed by C. D. Spielberger. Appeared in W. Barnhill, "Early Warning," *The Washington Post* (August 11, 1992): B5.

Four Approaches to Stress

The stress response was discovered by Walter B. Cannon, a medical physiologist, early in the twentieth century.[4] Later researchers defined stress differently than Cannon. We will review four different approaches to defining stress: the homeostatic/medical, cognitive appraisal, person–environment fit, and psychoanalytic approaches. These four approaches will give you a more complete understanding of what stress really is.

② Compare four different approaches to stress.

The Homeostatic/Medical Approach When Walter B. Cannon originally discovered stress, he called it "the emergency response" or "the militaristic response," arguing that it was rooted in "the fighting emotions." His early writings provide the basis for calling the stress response the *fight-or-flight* response. According to Cannon, stress resulted when an external, environmental demand upset the person's natural steady-state balance.[5] He referred to this steady-state balance, or equilibrium, as *homeostasis*. Cannon believed the body was designed with natural defense mechanisms to keep it in homeostasis. He was especially interested in the role of the sympathetic nervous system in activating a person under stressful conditions.[6]

The Cognitive Appraisal Approach Richard Lazarus was more concerned with the psychology of stress. He de-emphasized the medical and physiological aspects, emphasizing instead the psychological and cognitive aspects of the response.[7] Like Cannon, Lazarus saw stress as a result of a person–environment interaction, and he emphasized the person's cognitive appraisal in classifying persons or events as stressful or not. Individuals differ in their appraisal of events and people. What is stressful for one person may not be stressful for another. Perception and cognitive appraisal are important processes in determining what is stressful. One study found culture-specific differences in perceptions of the causes of job stress between China and the United States.[8] For example, American employees reported lack of job control as a source of stress while Chinese employees reported job evaluations as a source. In addition to cognitive appraisal, Lazarus introduced problem-focused and emotion-focused coping. Problem-focused coping emphasizes managing the stressor, and emotion-focused coping emphasizes managing your response.

The Person–Environment Fit Approach Robert Kahn was concerned with the social psychology of stress. His approach emphasized how confusing and conflicting expectations of a person in a social role create stress for the person.[9] He extended the approach to examine a person's fit in the environment. A good person–environment fit occurs when a person's skills and abilities match a clearly defined, consistent set of role expectations. This results in a lack of stress for the person. Stress occurs when the role expectations are confusing and/or conflicting or when a person's skills and abilities are not able to meet the demands of the social role. After a period of this stress, the person can expect to experience strain, such as strain in the form of depression.

The Psychoanalytic Approach Harry Levinson defined stress based on Freudian psychoanalytic theory.[10] Levinson believes that two elements of the personality interact to cause stress. The first is the *ego-ideal*—the embodiment of a person's perfect self. The second is the *self-image*—how the person really sees himself or herself, both positively and negatively. Although not sharply defined, the ego-ideal encompasses admirable attributes of parental personalities, wished-for and/or imaginable qualities a person would like to possess, and the absence of any negative or distasteful qualities. Stress results from the discrepancy between the idealized self (ego-ideal) and the real self-image; the greater the discrepancy, the more stress a person experiences. More generally, psychoanalytic theory helps us understand the role of unconscious personality factors as causes of stress within a person.

homeostasis
A steady state of bodily functioning and equilibrium.

ego-ideal
The embodiment of a person's perfect self.

self-image
How a person sees himself or herself, both positively and negatively.

The Stress Response

③ Explain the psychophysiology of the stress response.

Whether activated by an ego-ideal/self-image discrepancy, a poorly defined social role, cognitive appraisal suggesting threat, or a lack of balance, the resulting stress response is characterized by a predictable sequence of mind and body events. The stress response begins with the release of chemical messengers, primarily adrenaline, into the bloodstream. These messengers activate the sympathetic nervous system and the endocrine (hormone) system. These two systems work together and trigger four mind–body changes to prepare the person for fight or flight:

1. The redirection of the blood to the brain and large-muscle groups and away from the skin, internal organs, and extremities.
2. Increased alertness by way of improved vision, hearing, and other sensory processes through the activation of the brainstem (ancient brain).
3. The release of glucose (blood sugar) and fatty acids into the bloodstream to sustain the body during the stressful event.
4. Depression of the immune system, as well as restorative and emergent processes (such as digestion).

This set of four changes shifts the person from a neutral, or naturally defensive, posture to an offensive posture. The stress response can be very functional in preparing a person to deal with legitimate emergencies and to achieve peak performance. It is neither inherently bad nor necessarily destructive.

SOURCES OF WORK STRESS

4 Identify work and nonwork causes of stress.

Work stress is caused both by factors in the work environment and by pressures from outside the workplace that have spillover effects into the workplace. For companies like Timberland, stress comes from the challenge of competitors, as we saw in Thinking Ahead. An example of the latter would be when a working mother or father is called at work to come pick up a sick child from the day-care center so that the child does not expose other children to a health risk. Therefore, the two major categories of sources of work stress are the work demands and nonwork demands shown in Table 7.1. As the table suggests, one of the most complex causes

TABLE 7.1 Work and Nonwork Demands

Work Demands	
Task Demands	**Role Demands**
Change	Role conflict:
Lack of control	Interrole
Career progress	Intrarole
New technologies	Person–role
Time pressure	Role ambiguity
Interpersonal Demands	**Physical Demands**
Emotional toxins	Extreme environments
Sexual harassment	Strenuous activities
Poor leadership	Hazardous substances
	Global travel
Nonwork Demands	
Home Demands	**Personal Demands**
Family expectations	Workaholism
Child-rearing/day-care arrangements	Civic and volunteer work
Parental care	Traumatic events

of work stress is role conflict. An innovative study by Pam Perrewé and her colleagues examined the dysfunctional physical and psychological consequences of role conflict.[11] The researchers found political skill to be an antidote for role conflict, one of a range of preventive stress management strategies discussed later in the chapter.

Work Demands

Role ambiguity is the second major role demand identified in Table 7.1 that causes work stress. In addition, role demands, task demands, interpersonal demands, and physical demands are shown in the table. The table does not present an exhaustive list of work demands but rather aims to show major causes of work stress in each of the four major domains of the work environment.

Task Demands Globalization is creating dramatic changes at work, causing on-the-job pressure and stress.[12] Change leads to uncertainty, a lack of predictability in a person's daily tasks and activities, and may be caused by job insecurity related to difficult economic times. Even as the U.S. economy recovered strongly in 2004, creating hundreds of thousands of jobs, nearly 80,000 U.S. workers continue to lose their jobs monthly. For those who do not lose their jobs, underemployment, monotony, and boredom may be problems. Technology and technological innovation create further change and uncertainty for many employees, requiring adjustments in training, education, and skill development. Intended to make life and work easier and more convenient, information technology may have a paradoxical effect and be a source of stress rather than a stress reliever.

Lack of control is a second major source of stress, especially in work environments that are difficult and psychologically demanding. The lack of control may be caused by inability to influence the timing of tasks and activities, to select tools or methods for accomplishing the work, to make decisions that influence work outcomes, or to exercise direct action to affect the work outcomes. One study found that male workers in occupations with low job autonomy (lack of control) and high job demands (heavy workloads) experienced more heart attacks than other male workers.[13]

Concerns over career progress, new technologies, and time pressures (or work overload) are three additional task demands triggering stress for the person at work. Career stress is related to the career gridlock that has occurred in many organizations as the middle-manager ranks have been thinned due to mergers, acquisitions, and downsizing during the past two decades.[14] Leaner organizations, unfortunately, often leave work overload for those who are still employed. Time pressure is a leading cause of stress and is often associated with work overload, but may result from poor time management skills. Challenge stressors that promote personal growth and achievement, however, are positively related to job satisfaction and organizational commitment.[15] New technologies create both career stress and "technostress" for people at work who wonder if "smart" machines will replace them.[16] Although they enhance the organization's productive capacity, new technologies may be viewed as the enemy by workers who must ultimately learn to use them. This creates a real dilemma for management.

Role Demands The social–psychological demands of the work environment may be every bit as stressful as task demands at work. People encounter two major categories of role stress at work: role conflict and role ambiguity.[17] Role conflict results from inconsistent or incompatible expectations being communicated. The conflict may be an interrole, intrarole, or person–role conflict.

Interrole conflict is caused by conflicting expectations related to two separate roles, such as employee and parent. For example, the employee with a major sales presentation on Monday and a sick child at home Sunday night is likely to experience interrole conflict. Work–family conflicts like these can lead individuals to withdrawal behaviors.[18]

Intrarole conflict is caused by conflicting expectations related to a single role, such as employee. For example, the manager who presses employees for both very fast *and* high-quality work may be viewed at some point as creating a conflict for employees.

Ethics violations are likely to cause person–role conflicts. Employees expected to behave in ways that violate personal values, beliefs, or principles experience conflict. The unethical acts of committed employees exemplify this problem. Organizations with high ethical standards, such as Johnson & Johnson, are less likely to create ethical conflicts for employees. Person–role conflicts and ethics violations create a sense of divided loyalty for an employee.

The second major cause of role stress is role ambiguity. Role ambiguity is the confusion a person experiences related to the expectations of others. Role ambiguity may be caused by not understanding what is expected, not knowing how to do it, or not knowing the result of failure to do it. For example, a new magazine employee asked to copyedit a manuscript for the next issue may experience confusion because of lack of familiarity with the magazine's copyediting procedures and conventions.

A 21-nation study of middle managers examined their experiences of role conflict, role ambiguity, and role overload. The results indicated that role stress varies more by country than it does by demographic and organizational factors. For example, non-Western managers experience less role ambiguity and more role overload than do their Western counterparts.[19] A study of U.S. military personnel found that when role clarity was high in a supportive work group, psychological strain was low.[20] A study of 2,273 Norwegian employees found that role conflict, role ambiguity, and conflict with coworkers actually increased under laissez-faire leadership, suggesting that this leadership style and behavior is destructive, even toxic.[21]

Interpersonal Demands Emotional toxins, sexual harassment, and poor leadership in the organization are interpersonal demands for people at work. Emotional toxins are often generated at work by abrasive personalities.[22] They can spread through a work environment and cause a range of disturbances. Even emotional dissonance can be a cause of work stress.[23] Organizations are increasingly less tolerant of sexual harassment, a gender-related interpersonal demand that creates a stressful working environment both for the person being harassed and for others. The vast majority of sexual harassment is directed at women in the workplace and is a chronic yet preventable workplace problem.[24] Poor leadership in organizations and excessive, demanding management styles are a leading cause of work stress for employees. Employees who feel secure with strong, directive leadership may be anxious with an open management style. Those comfortable with participative leaders may feel restrained by a directive style. Trust is an important characteristic of the leader–follower interpersonal relationship, and a threat to a worker's reputation with her or his supervisor may be especially stressful.[25] Functional diversity in project groups also causes difficulty in the establishment of trusting relationships, thus increasing job stress, which leads to lower cohesiveness within the group.[26]

Organizations are increasingly less tolerant of sexual harassment, a gender-related interpersonal demand that creates a stressful working environment both for the person being harassed and for others.

THE REAL WORLD 7.1

It May Not Kill You . . . but the Wear and Tear?

The World Health Organization (WHO) has a Special Programme on Health and Environment. The WHO aims to advance the health and well-being of people around the world—in developed countries such as Switzerland, where the WHO is headquartered in Geneva, and developing countries such as Afghanistan. Noise is one major concern, along with occupational health and air quality, of this Special Programme. According to the WHO, one of the most disturbing aspects of noise is the chronic exposure. For example, the ongoing din of construction sites, airports, and even leaf blowers takes a toll on health and happiness because it triggers the stress response with all of its associated "fight-or-flight" hormones. Urban, occupational, and everyday noise are often under the radar, yet they have a constant wear-and-tear effect on a person's mind and body. While the chronic exposure to noise is unlikely to be lethal, it does lead to fatigue, irritability, and poor concentration along with sleep disturbance. In addition to the WHO's concerns about this, even the U.S. Environmental Protection Agency notes that the idea that people get used to noise is a myth. While people may think they have become accustomed to noise, the body's reactions tell a different story. The fact that the WHO places noise on its list of important environmental concerns is something that everyone should think about.

SOURCE: R. Weiss, "Health," *The Washington Post* (June 5, 2007): F-1.

Physical Demands Extreme environments, strenuous activities, hazardous substances, and global travel create physical demands for people at work. Work environments that are very hot or very cold place differing physical demands on people and create unique risks. One cross-cultural study that examined the effects of national culture and ambient temperature on role stress concluded that ambient temperature does affect human well-being, leading to the term *sweatshop* for inhumane working conditions.[27] Dehydration is one problem of extremely hot climates, whereas frostbite is one problem of extremely cold climates. The strenuous job of a steelworker and the hazards associated with bomb disposal work are physically demanding in different ways. The unique physical demands of work are often occupation specific, such as the risk of gravitationally induced loss of consciousness for military pilots flying high-performance fighters[28] or jet lag and loss of sleep for globe-trotting CEOs like IBM's Samuel J. Palmisano and Carlos Ghosn, CEO of two auto companies, Renault and Nissan that are a half a world apart. The demands of business travel are increasingly recognized as sources of stress.[29] However, the positive aspects of business trips are also increasingly recognized.[30]

Office work has its physical hazards as well. Noisy, crowded offices, such as those of some stock brokerages, can prove stressful as well as harmful as suggested by the World Health Organization in The Real World 7.1. Working with a computer terminal can also be stressful, especially if the ergonomic fit between the person and machine is not correct. Eyestrain, neck stiffness, and arm and wrist problems can occur. Office designs that use partitions (cubicles) rather than full walls can create stress. These systems offer little privacy for the occupant (for example, to conduct employee counseling or performance appraisal sessions) and little protection from interruptions.

Nonwork Demands

Nonwork demands also create stress, which may carry over into the work environment, or vice versa.[31] Nonwork demands may be broadly identified as home demands from an individual's personal life environment and personal demands that are self-imposed.

Home Demands Not all workers are subject to family demands related to marriage, child rearing, and parental care. The wide range of home and family arrangements in contemporary American society has created great diversity in this arena. For those in traditional families, these demands may create role conflicts or overloads that are difficult to manage. For example, the loss of good day care for children may be especially stressful for dual-career and single-parent families.[32] The tension between work and family may lead to a struggle to achieve balance in life. This struggle led Rocky Rhodes, co-founder of Silicon Graphics, to establish four priorities for his life: God, family, exercise, and work.[33] These priorities helped him reallocate his time to achieve better balance in his life. As a result of the maturing of the American population, an increasing number of people face the added demand of parental care. Even when a person works to achieve an integrative social identity, combining many social roles into a "whole" identity for a more stress-free balance in work and nonwork identities, the process of integration is not an easy one.[34]

The loss of good day care for children may be stressful for dual-career and single-parent families.

Personal Demands Self-imposed, personal demands are the second major category of nonwork demands identified in Table 7.1. While self-imposed and personal, they can and do contribute to work stress on the job. *Workaholism* may be the most notable of these personal demands that causes stress at work and has been identified as a form of addiction.[35] Some of the early warning signs of workaholism include overcommitment to work, inability to enjoy vacations and respites from work, preoccupation with work problems when away from the workplace, and constantly taking work home on the weekend. Another type of personal demand comes from civic activities, volunteer work, and nonwork organizational commitments, such as in churches, synagogues, and public service organizations. These demands become more or less stressful depending on their compatibility with the person's work and family life and their capacity to provide alternative satisfactions for the person. Finally, traumatic events, such as 9/11, and their aftermath are stressful for people who experience them.[36] Not all traumatic events are as catastrophic as 9/11, however. Job loss, examination failures, and termination of romantic attachments are all traumatic, though less catastrophic, and may lead to distress if not addressed and resolved.

THE CONSEQUENCES OF STRESS

(5) Describe the benefits of eustress and the costs of distress.

Stress can be good or bad. Some managers and executives thrive under pressure because they practice what world-class athletes already know.[37] That is, to bring mind, body, and spirit to peak condition requires recovering energy, which is just as important as expending energy. Hence, world-class athletes and managers who practice what they know get high marks on any "stress test" because they use stress-induced energy in positive, healthy, and productive ways. The Science feature examines one study that found motivation as a mediator of the emotional exhaustion–job performance relationship. The consequences of healthy, normal stress (called *eustress*, for "euphoria + stress") include a number of performance and health benefits to be balanced against the more commonly known costs of individual and organizational distress.[38] The benefits of eustress and the costs of distress are listed

workaholism
An imbalanced preoccupation with work at the expense of home and personal life satisfaction.

Emotional Exhaustion, Motivation, and Job Performance

Burnout is a psychological response to job stress that Christina Maslach defined along three dimensions: emotional exhaustion, depersonalization, and reduced perceptions of personal accomplishment. Emotional exhaustion, which is an energy depletion condition, is at the heart of the burnout experience. The conventional suggestion is that burnout leads to reduced job performance, hence a direct burnout–performance link. This study questions this assumption and suggests that the influence of motivation has been overlooked in understanding the burnout–performance relationship. They understand motivation to be concerned with the psychological processes of the arousal, direction, intensity, and persistence of voluntary, goal-directed actions. Because motivation, with the emphasis on the goals people work toward, is considered a direct antecedent of performance, this study theorizes that motivation mediates the burnout–performance relationship. Hence, their model is burnout–motivation–performance. The investigators' use of two time-lagged samples allowed for a constructive replication of their model as well as greater occupational generalizability. The results did support the emotional exhaustion–motivation–performance model. In addition, participants in the studies appeared to target their investment of resources in response to emotional exhaustion so as to develop social support thorough social exchange, hence replenishing their emotional energy through positive interpersonal relationships. This study offers a deeper understanding of the stress, burnout, and emotional exhaustion processes with greater insights into the positive coping strategies that people may draw upon in times of need.

SOURCE: J. R. B. Halbesleben and W. M. Bowler, "Emotional Exhaustion and Job Performance: The Mediating Role of Motivation," *Journal of Applied Psychology* 92 (2007): 93–106.

in Table 7.2. An organization striving for high-quality products and services needs a healthy workforce to support the effort. Eustress is a characteristic of healthy people; distress is not.

Performance and Health Benefits

The Yerkes-Dodson law, shown in Figure 7.1, indicates that stress leads to improved performance up to an optimum point.[39] Beyond the optimum point, further stress and arousal have a detrimental effect on performance. Therefore, healthy amounts of eustress are desirable to improve performance by arousing a person to action. It is in the midrange of the curve that the greatest performance benefits from stress are

TABLE 7.2 Benefits of Eustress and Costs of Distress

Benefits of Eustress	
Performance	**Health**
Increased arousal	Cardiovascular efficiency
Bursts of physical strength	Balance in the nervous system
Full engagement	Enhanced focus in an emergency
Costs of Distress	
Individual	**Organizational**
Psychological disorders	Participation problems
Medical illnesses	Performance decrements
Behavioral problems	Compensation awards

FIGURE 7.1 Yerkes-Dodson Law

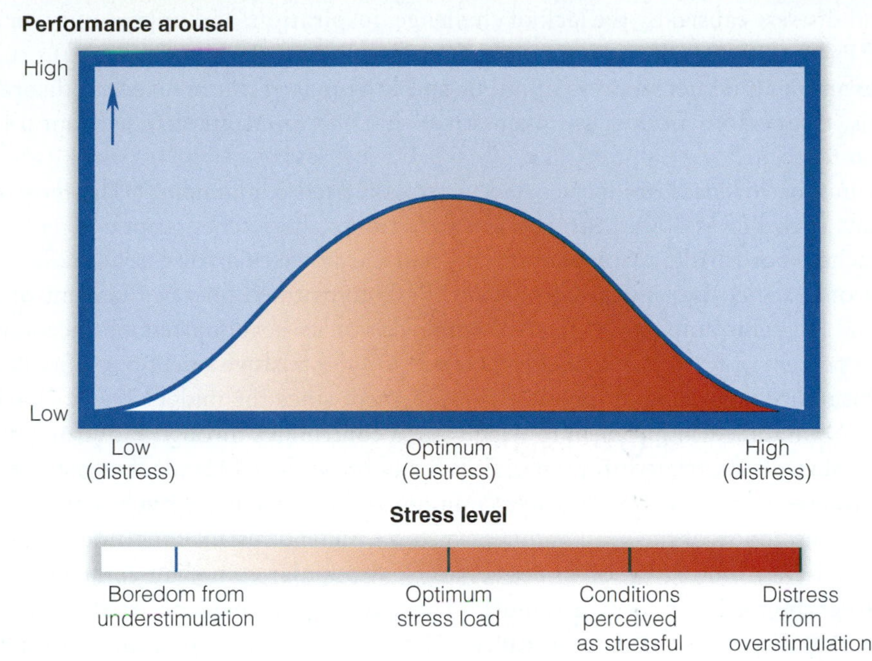

achieved. Joseph McGrath has suggested that performance declines beyond the midpoint in the Yerkes-Dodson curve because of the increasing difficulty of the task to be performed.[40] The stress response does provide momentary strength and physical force for brief periods of exertion, thus providing a basis for peak performance in athletic competition or other events. In addition, psychological well-being contributes positively to job performance.[41]

Specific stressful activities, including aerobic exercise, weight training, and flexibility training, improve health and enhance a person's ability to manage stressful demands or situations. Cannon argued that the stress response better prepares soldiers for combat[42] and Timberland prepares its customers for healthy outdoor living with its products. In the outdoors, in survival or in combat situations, stress provides one with the necessary energy boost to manage the situation successfully.

The stress response is not inherently bad or destructive. The various individual and organizational forms of distress often associated with the word *stress* are the result of prolonged activation of the stress response, mismanagement of the energy induced by the response, or unique vulnerabilities in a person. We next examine the forms of individual distress and then the forms of organizational distress.

Individual Distress

An extreme preoccupation with work may result in acute individual distress, such as the unique Japanese phenomenon of *karoshi,* or death by overwork.[43] In general, individual distress usually takes one of the three basic forms shown in Table 7.2. Work-related psychological disorders are among the ten leading health disorders and diseases in the United States, according to the National Institute for Occupational Safety and Health.[44] The most common types of psychological distress are depression, burnout, and psychosomatic disorders. Depression and burnout can lead to emotional exhaustion with its associated negative consequences.[45]

Emotional exhaustion may also be caused by the requirements for emotional expression on the job.[46] Burnout contrasts with rust-out, which is a form of psychological distress caused by the lack of challenge, inspiration, and opportunity on the job.[47] Psychosomatic disorders are physical disorders with a psychological origin. For example, the intense stress of public speaking may result in a speech disorder; that is, the person is under so much stress that the mind literally will not allow speech to occur.

A number of medical illnesses have a stress-related component.[48] The most significant such illnesses are heart disease and strokes, backaches, peptic ulcers, and headaches. Ford Motor Company found that cardiovascular diseases, the leading cause of death in the United States since 1910, constituted only 1.5 percent of the medical incidents among 800 salaried employees at its headquarters but accounted for 29 percent of the reported medical costs.[49] On the positive side, premature death and disability rates have dropped 24 to 36 percent since the mid-1970s. Backaches are a nonfatal medical problem to which stress contributes through the strong muscular contractions related to preparation for fight or flight. Headaches may be related to eyestrain or have a migraine component, but tension headaches are caused by the contraction of the head and neck muscles under stressful conditions. Finally, stress is a contributing factor to peptic ulcers. A popular comedian commented, "I don't get angry; I just grow a tumor!" There is no clear evidence that stress is a direct causal agent in the onset of cancer. However, stress may play an indirect role in the progression of the disease.[50]

Behavioral problems are the third form of individual distress. These problems include workplace aggression, substance abuse of various kinds, and accidents. Workplace aggression may be triggered by perceptions of injustice in the workplace.[51] Interpersonal conflicts can be a form of nonphysical aggression. One study found that conflicts with workmates, neighbors, and other "nonintimates" account for about 80 percent of our bad moods.[52] Ethnic and cultural differences are too often a basis for interpersonal conflicts and may escalate into physical violence in the workplace. For example, some U.S. employees of Arab descent experienced ethnic slurs at work during the War on Terror with Iraq, a largely Arab nation.

Substance abuse ranges from legal behaviors such as alcohol abuse, excessive smoking, and the overuse of prescription drugs to illegal behaviors such as heroin addiction. Former surgeon general C. Everett Koop's war on smoking was warranted based on health risk information reported by the American Heart Association. However, the war on smoking also raises an ethical debate about the restriction of individual behavior. How far can the government or society go in restricting individual behavior that has adverse health consequences for many? This is even more problematic in light of recent research results showing the adverse health effects nonsmokers experience as a result of secondhand smoke.

Accidents, both on and off the job, are another behavioral form of distress that can sometimes be traced to work-related stressors. For example, an unresolved problem at work may continue to preoccupy or distract an employee driving home and result in an automobile accident.

These three forms of individual distress—psychological disorders, medical illnesses, and behavioral problems—cause a burden of personal suffering. They also cause a collective burden of suffering reflected in organizational distress.

Organizational Distress

The University of Michigan studies on organizational stress identified a variety of indirect costs of mismanaged stress for the organization, such as low morale, dissatisfaction, breakdowns in communication, and disruption of working relationships.

Subsequent research at the Survey Research Center at Michigan established behavioral costing guidelines, which specify the direct costs of organizational distress.[53] New research suggests that even positive performance stereotypes can have an adverse effect on organizational health.[54]

Participation problems are the costs associated with absenteeism, tardiness, strikes and work stoppages, and turnover. In the case of absenteeism, the organization may compensate by hiring temporary personnel who take the place of the absentee, thus elevating personnel costs. When considering turnover, a distinction should be made between dysfunctional and functional turnover. Dysfunctional turnover occurs when an organization loses a valuable employee. It is costly for the organization. Replacement costs, including recruiting and retraining, for the valued employee range from five to seven months of the person's monthly salary. Functional turnover, in contrast, benefits the organization by creating opportunities for new members, new ideas, and fresh approaches. Functional turnover occurs when an organization loses an employee who has little or no value or is a problem. Functional turnover is good for the organization. The "up or out" promotion policy for members of some organizations is designed to create functional turnover.

Performance decrements are the costs resulting from poor quality or low quantity of production, grievances, and unscheduled machine downtime and repair. As in the case of medical illnesses, stress is not the only causal agent in these performance decrements. Stress does play a role, however, whether the poor quality or low quantity of production is motivated by distressed employees or by an unconscious response to stress on the job. In California, some employees have the option of taking a "stress leave" rather than filing a grievance against the boss.

participation problem
A cost associated with absenteeism, tardiness, strikes and work stoppages, and turnover.

Compensation awards are the organizational costs resulting from court awards for job distress.[55] One former insurance employee in Louisiana filed a federal suit against the company, alleging it created a high-strain job for him that resulted in an incapacitating depression.[56] A jury awarded him a $1.5 million judgment that was later overturned by the judge. Job stress–related claims have skyrocketed and threaten to bankrupt the workers' compensation system in some states, although claims and costs are down in other states.[57] However, employers need not panic because fair procedures go a long way toward avoiding legal liability, and legal rulings are setting realistic limits on employers' obligations.[58]

performance decrement
A cost resulting from poor quality or low quantity of production, grievances, and unscheduled machine downtime and repair.

compensation award
An organizational cost resulting from court awards for job distress.

INDIVIDUAL DIFFERENCES IN THE STRESS–STRAIN RELATIONSHIP

(6) Discuss individual differences in the stress–strain relationship.

The same stressful events may lead to distress and strain for one person and to excitement and healthy results for another. Individual differences play a central role in the stress–strain relationship. The weak organ hypothesis in medicine, also known as the Achilles' heel phenomenon, suggests that a person breaks down at his or her weakest point. Some individual differences, such as gender and Type A behavior pattern, enhance vulnerability to strain under stressful conditions. Other individual differences, such as personality hardiness and self-reliance, reduce vulnerability to strain under stressful conditions. One study of personality and emotional performance found that individuals high on extraversion experienced elevated heart rates when asked to express personality incongruent emotions, such as anger, and that neuroticism was associated with increased heart rate and poor performance more generally.[59] This suggests that extraversion and neuroticism affect the stress–strain relationship.

Gender Effects

While prevailing stereotypes suggest that women are the weaker sex, the truth is that the life expectancy for American women is approximately seven years longer than for American men. This implies that women may be stronger. The stereotype is challenged by research in public accounting, which finds that female public accountants have no higher turnover rates than males even though they report more stress, thus suggesting that women respond differently to stress.[60] This is further supported by research that finds women's behavioral responses to stress are in fact different from men's responses to stress.[61]

Some literature indicates that there are differences in the stressors to which the two sexes are subject.[62] For example, sexual harassment is a gender-related source of stress for many working women. There is also substantive evidence that the important differences in the sexes are in vulnerabilities.[63] Males, for instance, are more vulnerable at an earlier age to fatal health problems, such as cardiovascular disorders, whereas women report more nonfatal, but long-term and disabling, health problems. Although we can conclude that gender indeed creates a differential vulnerability between the two sexes, it may actually be more important to examine the differences *among* women or *among* men.

Type A Behavior Pattern

Type A behavior pattern, also labeled *coronary-prone behavior,*[64] is a complex of personality and behavioral characteristics, including competitiveness, time urgency, social status insecurity, aggression, hostility, and a quest for achievements. Table 7.3 lists four primary components of the Type A behavior pattern.

There are two primary hypotheses concerning the lethal part of the Type A behavior pattern. One hypothesis says that the problem is time urgency, whereas the other suggests that it is the hostility and aggression. The weight of evidence indicates the latter.[65] Look back at your result in You 7.1. Are you too angry and overstressed?

The alternative to the Type A behavior pattern is the Type B behavior pattern. People with Type B personalities are relatively free of the Type A behaviors and characteristics identified in Table 7.3. Type B people are less coronary prone, but if they do have a heart attack, they do not appear to recover as well as those with Type A personalities. Organizations can also be characterized as Type A or Type B.[66] Type A individuals in Type B organizations and Type B individuals in Type A organizations experience stress related to a misfit between their personality type and the predominant type of the organization. However, preliminary evidence suggests that Type A individuals in Type A organizations are most at risk of health disorders.

Type A behavior pattern
A complex of personality and behavioral characteristics, including competitiveness, time urgency, social status insecurity, aggression, hostility, and a quest for achievements.

TABLE 7.3 Type A Behavior Pattern Components

1. Sense of time urgency (a kind of "hurry sickness").
2. The quest for numbers (success is measured by the number of achievements).
3. Status insecurity (feeling unsure of oneself deep down inside).
4. Aggression and hostility expressed in response to frustration and conflict.

Type A behavior can be modified. The first step is recognizing that an individual is prone to this pattern. Another possible step is to spend time with Type B individuals. Type B people often recognize Type A behavior and can help them take hassles less seriously and see the humor in situations. Type A individuals can also pace themselves, manage their time well, and try not to do multiple things at once. Focusing only on the task at hand and its completion, rather than worrying about other tasks, can help them cope more effectively.

Personality Hardiness

People who have personality hardiness resist strain reactions when subjected to stressful events more effectively than do people who are not hardy.[67] The components of *personality hardiness* are commitment (versus alienation), control (versus powerlessness), and challenge (versus threat). Commitment is a curiosity and engagement with one's environment that leads to the experience of activities as interesting and enjoyable. Control is an ability to influence the process and outcomes of events that leads to the experience of activities as personal choices. Challenge is the viewing of change as a stimulus to personal development, which leads to the experience of activities with openness.

The hardy personality appears to use these three components actively to engage in transformational coping when faced with stressful events.[68] *Transformational coping* is the act of actively changing an event into something less subjectively stressful by viewing it in a broader life perspective, by altering the course and outcome of the event through action, and/or by achieving greater understanding of the process. The alternative to transformational coping is regressive coping, a much less healthy form of coping with stressful events characterized by a passive avoidance of events by decreasing interaction with the environment. Regressive coping may lead to short-term stress reduction at the cost of long-term healthy life adjustment.

Self-Reliance

There is increasing evidence that social relationships have an important impact on health and life expectancy.[69] *Self-reliance* is a personality attribute related to how people form and maintain supportive attachments with others. Self-reliance was originally based in attachment theory, a theory about normal human development.[70] The theory identifies three distinct patterns of attachment, and research suggests that these patterns extend into behavioral strategies during adulthood, in professional as well as personal relationships.[71] Self-reliance results in a secure pattern of attachment and interdependent behavior. Interpersonal attachment is emotional and psychological connectedness to another person. The two insecure patterns of attachment are counterdependence and overdependence.

Self-reliance is a healthy, secure, *interdependent* pattern of behavior. It may appear paradoxical, because a person appears independent while maintaining a host of supportive attachments.[72] Self-reliant people respond to stressful, threatening situations by reaching out to others appropriately. Self-reliance is a flexible, responsive strategy of forming and maintaining multiple, diverse relationships. Self-reliant people are confident, enthusiastic, and persistent in facing challenges.

Counterdependence is an unhealthy, insecure pattern of behavior that leads to separation in relationships with other people. When faced with stressful and threatening situations, counterdependent people draw into themselves, attempting to exhibit strength and power. Counterdependence may be characterized as a rigid, dismissing denial of the need for other people in difficult and stressful times. Counterdependent people exhibit a fearless, aggressive, and actively powerful response to challenges.

personality hardiness
A personality resistant to distress and characterized by commitment, control, and challenge.

transformational coping
A way of managing stressful events by changing them into less subjectively stressful events.

self-reliance
A healthy, secure, *interdependent* pattern of behavior related to how people form and maintain supportive attachments with others.

counterdependence
An unhealthy, insecure pattern of behavior that leads to separation in relationships with other people.

Overdependence is also an unhealthy, insecure pattern of behavior. Overdependent people respond to stressful and threatening situations by clinging to other people in any way possible. Overdependence may be characterized as a desperate, preoccupied attempt to achieve a sense of security through relationships. Overdependent people exhibit an active but disorganized and anxious response to challenges. Overdependence prevents a person from being able to organize and maintain healthy relationships and thus creates much distress. It is interesting to note that both counterdependence and overdependence are exhibited by some military personnel who are experiencing adjustment difficulties during the first thirty days of basic training.[73] In particular, basic military trainees who have the most difficulty have overdependence problems and find it difficult to function on their own during the rigors of training.

overdependence
An unhealthy, insecure pattern of behavior that leads to preoccupied attempts to achieve security through relationships.

You 7.2 gives you an opportunity to examine how self-reliant (interdependent), counterdependent, and/or overdependent you are.

PREVENTIVE STRESS MANAGEMENT

7 Distinguish the primary, secondary, and tertiary stages of preventive stress management.

Stress is an inevitable feature of work and personal life. It is neither inherently bad nor destructive. Stress can be managed. The following is the central principle of *preventive stress management:* Individual and organizational distress are not inevitable. Preventive stress management is an organizational philosophy about people and organizations taking joint responsibility for promoting health and preventing distress and strain. Preventive stress management is rooted in the public health notions of prevention, which were first used in preventive medicine. The three stages of prevention are primary, secondary, and tertiary prevention. A framework for understanding preventive stress management is presented in Figure 7.2, which includes the three stages of prevention in a preventive medicine context, as well as an organizational context.

preventive stress management
An organizational philosophy that holds that people and organizations should take joint responsibility for promoting health and preventing distress and strain.

FIGURE 7.2 A Framework for Preventive Stress Management

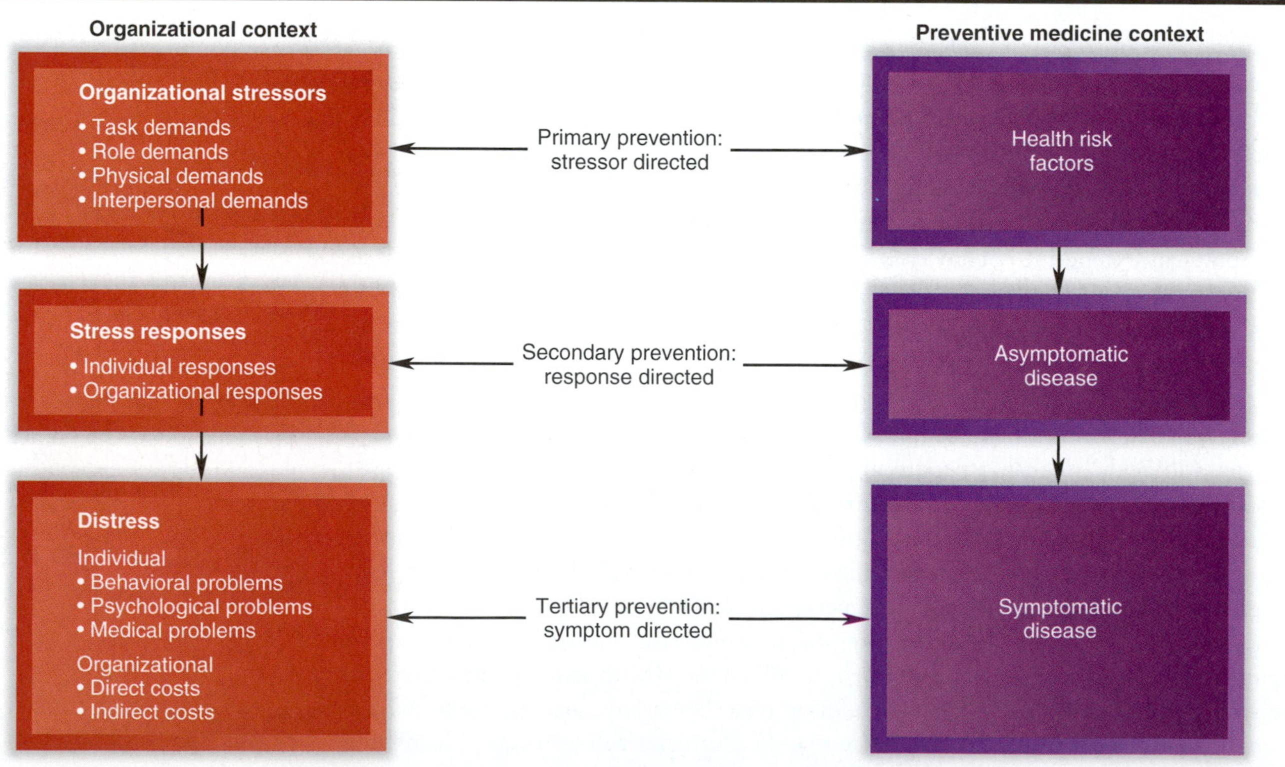

SOURCE: J. D. Quick, R. S. Horn, and J. C. Quick, "Health Consequences of Stress," *Journal of Organizational Behavior Management* 8, No. 2, figure 1 (Fall 1986): 21. Reprinted with permission of Haworth Press, Inc., 10 Alice Street, Binghamton, NY 13904. Copyright 1986.

YOU 7.2

Are You Self-Reliant?

Each of the following questions relates to how you form relationships with people at work, at home, and in other areas of your life. Read each statement carefully and rate each on a scale from 0 (strongly disagree) to 5 (strongly agree) to describe your degree of disagreement or agreement with the statement. *Answer all 15 questions.*

____ 1. It is difficult for me to delegate work to others.
____ 2. Developing close relationships at work will backfire on you.
____ 3. I avoid depending on other people because I feel crowded by close relationships.
____ 4. I am frequently suspicious of other people's motives and intentions.
____ 5. Asking for help makes me feel needy, and I do not like that.
____ 6. It is difficult for me to leave home or work to go to the other.
____ 7. People will always be there when I need them.
____ 8. I regularly and easily spend time with other people during the workday.
____ 9. I trust at least two other people to have my best interests at heart.
____ 10. I have a healthy, happy home life.
____ 11. I need to have colleagues or subordinates close in order to feel secure about my work.
____ 12. I become very concerned when I have conflict with family members at home.
____ 13. I get very upset and disturbed if I have conflicts in relationship(s) at work.
____ 14. I prefer very frequent feedback from my boss to know I am performing well.
____ 15. I always consult others when I make decisions.

Scoring:

Follow the instructions to determine your score for each subscale of the Self-Reliance Inventory. *Note: Question 6 is used twice in scoring.*

Self-Reliance/Counterdependence

Step 1: Total your responses to Questions 1–6 ______
Step 2: Total your responses to Questions 7–10 ______
Step 3: Subtract your Step 2 total from 20 (20 – ______) = ______
Step 4: Add your results in Steps 1 and 3 ______

Self-Reliance/Overdependence

Step 5: Total your responses to Questions 6 and 11–15 ______

A score lower than 16 in Step 4 or Step 5 indicates self-reliance on that particular subscale.

A score higher than 20 in Step 4 suggests possible counterdependence, and a score higher than 20 in Step 5 suggests possible overdependence.

SOURCE: Adapted from J. C. Quick, D. L. Nelson, and J. D. Quick, "The Self-Reliance Inventory," in J. W. Pfeiffer, ed., *The 1991 Annual: Developing Human Resources* (San Diego: Pfeiffer & Co., 1991), 149–161.

Primary prevention is intended to reduce, modify, or eliminate the demand or stressor causing stress. The idea behind primary prevention is to eliminate or ameliorate the source of a problem. True organizational stress prevention is largely primary in nature, because it changes and shapes the demands the organization

primary prevention
The stage in preventive stress management designed to reduce, modify, or eliminate the demand or stressor causing stress.

places on people at work. *Secondary prevention* is intended to alter or modify the individual's or the organization's response to a demand or stressor. People must learn to manage the inevitable, inalterable work stressors and demands so as to avert distress and strain while promoting health and well-being. *Tertiary prevention* is intended to heal individual or organizational symptoms of distress and strain. The symptoms may range from early warning signs (such as headaches or absenteeism) to more severe forms of distress (such as hypertension, work stoppages, and strikes). One innovative approach used by the computer company DriveSavers blends treatment and prevention with a full-time former grief counselor.[74] We discuss the stages of prevention in the context of organizational prevention, individual prevention, and comprehensive health promotion.

Organizational Stress Prevention

(8) Discuss organizational and individual methods of preventive stress management.

Some organizations are low-stress, healthy environments, whereas others are high-stress environments that may place their employees' health at risk. The experience of organizational justice and fairness is emerging as one contextual factor at work that leads to a positive low-stress work environment.[75] One comprehensive approach to organizational health and preventive stress management was pioneered in the U.S. Air Force by Colonel Joyce Adkins, who developed an Organizational Health Center (OHC) within the Air Force Materiel Command.[76] The OHC's goal is to keep people happy, healthy, and on the job, while increasing efficiency and productivity to their highest levels by focusing on workplace stressors, organizational and individual forms of distress, and managerial and individual strategies for preventive stress management. This comprehensive, organizational health approach addresses primary, secondary, and tertiary prevention. Most organizational prevention, however, is primary prevention, including job redesign, goal setting, role negotiation, and career management. Two organizational stress prevention methods, team building and social support at work, are secondary prevention. While we discuss team building in Chapter 9, we should note here that team structure under stress may influence team effectiveness. Specifically, teams experiencing quantitative demands are more effective when more tightly structured, while teams experiencing qualitative demands are more effective when more loosely structured.[77] Finally, companies such as Kraft Foods (a subsidiary of Altria Group, Inc.) and Hardee's Food Systems (part of CKE Restaurants, Inc.) have developed specific violence prevention programs to combat the rise in workplace violence. Violence in organizations is a category of dysfunctional behaviors that are often motivated by stressful events and whose negative consequences organizations want to prevent.[78]

Job Redesign The job strain model presented in Figure 7.3 suggests that the combination of high job demands and restricted job decision latitude or worker control leads to a high-strain job. A major concern in job redesign should be to enhance worker control. Increasing worker control reduces distress and strain without necessarily reducing productivity in many cases.

secondary prevention
The stage in preventive stress management designed to alter or modify the individual's or the organization's response to a demand or stressor.

tertiary prevention
The stage in preventive stress management designed to heal individual or organizational symptoms of distress and strain.

Job redesign to increase worker control is one strategy of preventive stress management. It can be accomplished in a number of ways, the most common being to increase job decision latitude. Increased job decision latitude might include greater decision authority over the sequencing of work activities, the timing of work schedules, the selection and sequencing of work tools, or the selection of work teams. A second objective of job redesign should be to reduce uncertainty and increase predictability in the workplace. Uncertainty is a major stressor.

FIGURE 7.3 Job Strain Model

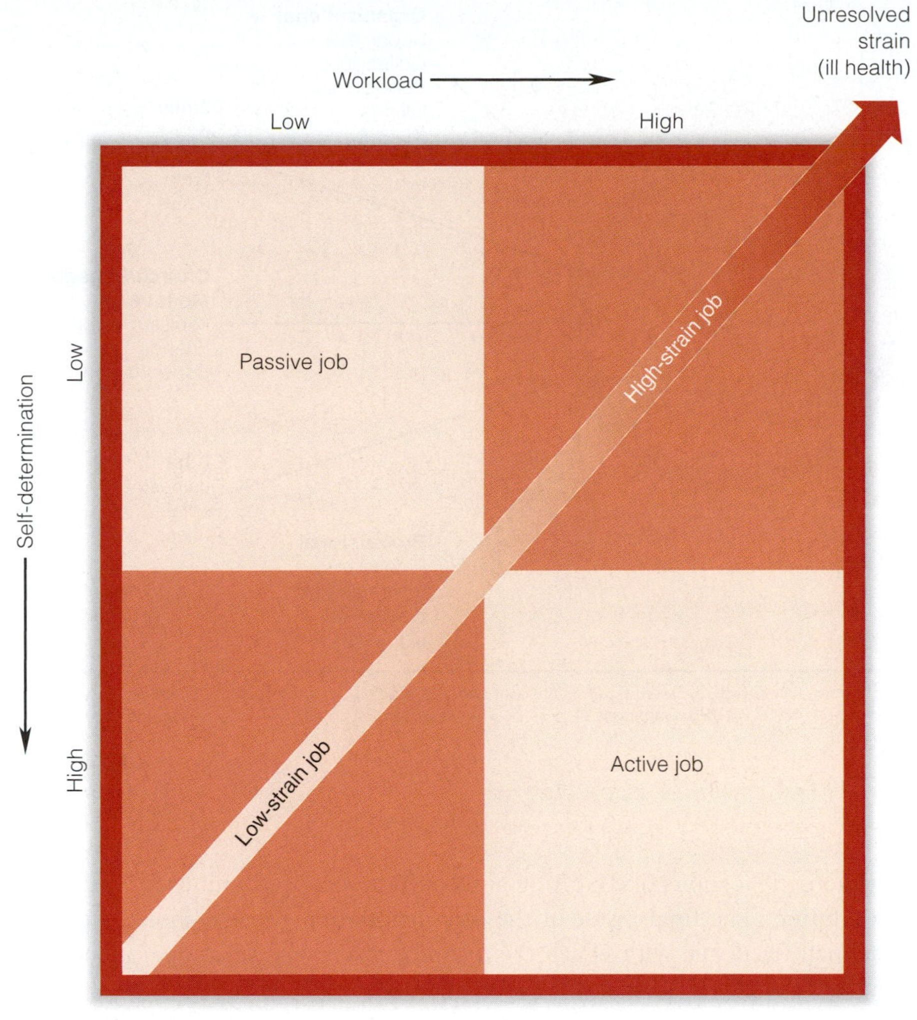

SOURCE: B. Gardell, "Efficiency and Health Hazards in Mechanized Work," in J. C. Quick, R. S. Bhagat, J. E. Dalton, and J. D. Quick, eds., *Work Stress: Health Care Systems in the Workplace*. Copyright © 1987. Reproduced with permission of Greenwood Publishing Group, Inc., Westport, CT.

Goal Setting Organizational preventive stress management can also be achieved through goal-setting activities. These activities are designed to increase task motivation, as discussed in Chapter 6, while reducing the degree of role conflict and ambiguity to which people at work are subject. Goal setting focuses a person's attention while directing energy into a productive channel. Implicit in much of the goal-setting literature is the assumption that people participate in, and accept, their work goals. Chapter 6 addressed goal setting in depth.

Role Negotiation The organizational development technique of role negotiation has value as a stress management method because it allows people to modify their work roles.[79] Role negotiation begins with the definition of a specific role, called the focal role, within its organizational context. The person in the focal role then identifies the expectations understood for that role, and key organizational members specify their expectations of the person in the focal role. The actual negotiation follows from the comparison of the role incumbent's expectations and key members'

FIGURE 7.4 Social Support at Work and Home

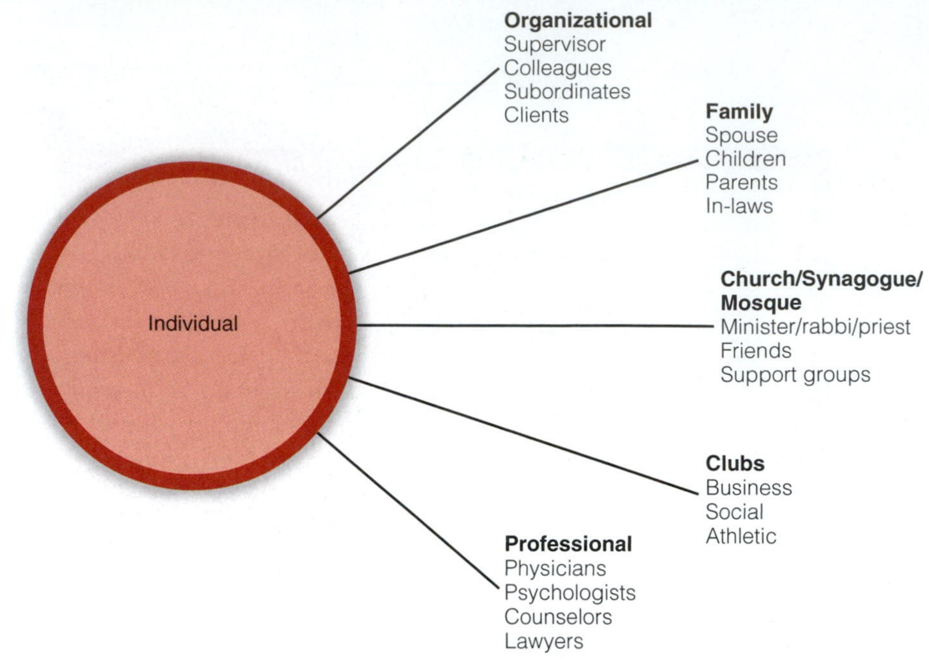

SOURCE: From J. C. Quick, J. D. Quick, D. L. Nelson, and J. J. Hurrell, Jr., in *Preventive Stress Management in Organizations,* 1997, p. 198. Copyright © 1997 by The American Psychological Association. Reprinted with permission.

expectations. The points of confusion and conflict are opportunities for clarification and resolution. The final result of the role negotiation process should be a clear, well-defined focal role with which the incumbent and organizational members are all comfortable.

Social Support Systems Team building, discussed in Chapter 9, is one way to develop supportive social relationships in the workplace. However, team building is primarily task oriented, not socioemotional, in nature. Although employees may receive much of their socioemotional support from personal relationships outside the workplace, such support within the workplace is also necessary for psychological well-being.

Social support systems can be enhanced through the work environment in a number of ways. Interpersonal communication is the key to unlocking social support for preventive stress management.[80] Figure 7.4 identifies key elements in a person's work and nonwork social support system. These relations provide emotional caring, information, evaluative feedback, modeling, and instrumental support.

Individual Prevention

Clinical research shows that individuals may use a number of self-directed interventions to help prevent distress and enhance positive well-being.[81] Individual prevention can be of a primary, secondary, or tertiary nature. The primary prevention activities we discuss are learned optimism, time management, and leisure-time activities. The secondary prevention activities we discuss are physical exercise, relaxation, and diet. The tertiary prevention activities we discuss are opening up and professional help. These eight methods and their benefits are summarized in Table 7.4.

TABLE 7.4 Individual Preventive Stress Management

Primary Prevention	
Positive thinking:	Optimistic, nonnegative self-talk that reduces depression.
Time management:	Improves planning and prioritizes activities.
Leisure-time activity:	Balances work and nonwork activities.
Secondary Prevention	
Physical exercise:	Improves cardiovascular function and muscular flexibility.
Relaxation training:	Lowers all indicators of the stress response.
Diet:	Lowers the risk of cardiovascular disease and improves overall physical health.
Tertiary Prevention	
Opening up:	Releases internalized traumas and emotional tensions.
Professional help:	Provides information, emotional support, and therapeutic guidance.

Positive Thinking Positive thinking is an optimistic approach used by people to explain the good and bad events in their lives to themselves.[82] It is a habit of thinking learned over time, though some people are predisposed to positive thinking. Pessimism is an alternative explanatory style leading to depression, physical health problems, and low levels of achievement. In contrast, positive thinking and optimism enhance physical health and achievement and avert susceptibility to depression. Positive thinking does not mean ignoring real stress and challenge, as we saw Timberland facing in Thinking Ahead.

Optimistic people avoid distress by viewing the bad events and difficult times in their lives as temporary, limited, and caused by something other than themselves. They face difficult times and adversity with hope. Optimistic people take more credit for the good events in their lives; they see these good events as more pervasive and generalized. Learned optimism begins with identifying pessimistic thoughts and then distracting oneself from these thoughts or disputing them with evidence and alternative thoughts. Learned optimism is nonnegative thinking. This is one of the five dimensions of positive organizational behavior (POB), the other four being confidence/self-efficacy, hope, subjective well-being/happiness, and emotional intelligence.[83]

Time Management Time pressure is one of the major sources of stress listed in Table 7.1 for both workers and students. The leading symptoms of poor time management include constant rushing, missed deadlines, work overload and the sense of being overwhelmed, insufficient rest time, and indecision. Good time managers are "macro" time managers who use a GP^3 method of time management.[84] This method includes (1) setting *goals* that are challenging yet attainable; (2) *prioritizing* these goals in terms of their relative importance; (3) *planning* for goal attainment through specific tasks, activities, scheduling, and even delegation; and (4) *praising* oneself for specific achievements along the way. Setting concrete goals and prioritizing them are the most important first steps in time management skills, ensuring that the most critical work and study activities receive enough time and attention. This system of time management enables a person to track his or her success over time and goes a long way toward reducing unnecessary stress and confusion.

THE REAL WORLD 7.2

Carl Camden, Off the Grid and Wireless

While many CEOs may give their spouses gifts that include luxury cars and objets d'art, Kelly Services' Carl Camden has given his wife the gift of time and attention. When they take one- to two-week vacations on a small island near Maui, they go off the grid and wireless. Technology has gone a long way to erode personal boundaries and to make CEOs like Camden available 24/7 anywhere in the world. However, being constantly available does not create peak performance. Vacation deprivation can lead to mistakes, anger, and resentment directed at coworkers and family members. Working for Air New Zealand in the Pacific, former NASA scientists have used testing tools normally reserved for astronauts and found that vacationers experienced an 82 percent increase in job performance post-trip. The micro-vacations of two or three days do not deliver the same stress-reduction benefits that Camden and his wife achieve in their one- or two-week annual trips to the Pacific. There are vacation risks for high-visibility executives like Camden, such as the press critiques that President George W. Bush gets when he heads to his Crawford ranch or that Wal-Mart CEO Lee Scott received when he took an entire month off in 2006. However, the space science seems to be on Camden's side, suggesting that his vacations are positive and beneficial respites that contribute to better performance on the job.

SOURCE: M. Conlin, "Do Us a Favor, Take a Vacation," *BusinessWeek* 4035 (May 21, 2007): 88.

Leisure-Time Activities Unremitted striving characterizes many people with a high need for achievement. Leisure-time activities provide employees an opportunity for rest and recovery from strenuous activities either at home or at work. Many individuals, when asked what they do with their leisure time, say that they clean the house or mow the lawn. These activities are fine, as long as they produce the stress-reducing benefit of pleasure. Some say our work ethic is a cultural barrier to pleasure. We work longer hours, and two-income families are the norm. Leisure is increasingly a luxury among working people. The key to the effective use of leisure time is enjoyment. Leisure time can be used for spontaneity, joy, and connection with others in our lives. The Real World 7.2 looks at a vacation approach used by Kelly Services CEO Carl Camden. While vacations can be a relief from job burnout, they may suffer fade-out effects.[85] Hence, leisure time and vacations must be periodic, recurring activities.

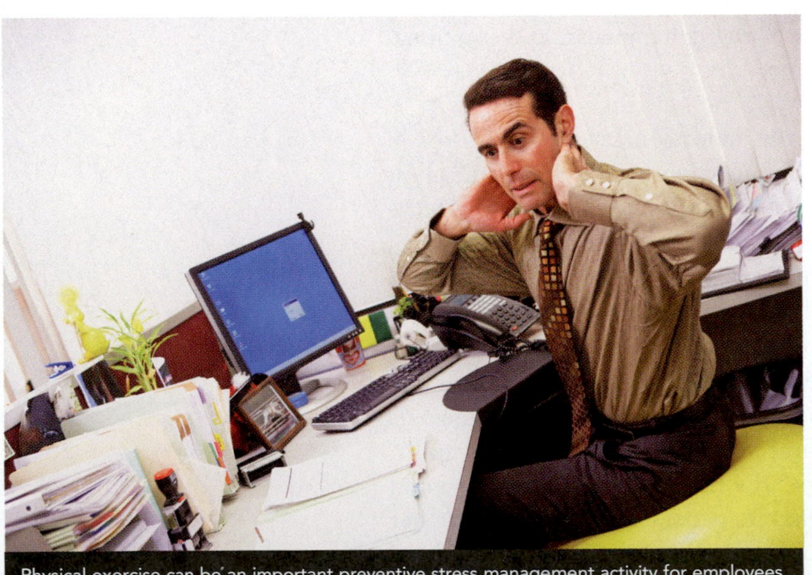

Physical exercise can be an important preventive stress management activity for employees.

© JUPITERIMAGES/BANANASTOCK/ALAMY

Physical Exercise Different types of physical exercise are important secondary stress prevention activities. Colleges and universities often implement physical exercise through phys ed classes, while military organizations implement it through physical fitness standards. Aerobic exercise improves a person's responsiveness to stressful activities. Kenneth Cooper has long advocated aerobic exercise.[86] Research at the Aerobics Center in Dallas has found that aerobically fit people (1) have lower levels of adrenaline in their blood at rest; (2) have a slower, stronger heart functioning; and (3) recover from stressful events more quickly.

Flexibility training is an important type of exercise because of the muscular contractions associated with the stress response. One component of the stress response is the contraction of the flexor muscles, which prepares a person to fight or flee. Flexibility training enables a person to stretch and relax these muscles to prevent the accumulation of unnecessary muscular tension.[87] Flexibility exercises help maintain joint mobility, increase strength, and play an important role in the prevention of injury.

Relaxation Training Herbert Benson was one of the first people to identify the relaxation response as the natural counterresponse to the stress response.[88] In studying Western and Eastern peoples, Benson found that Judeo-Christian people have elicited this response through their time-honored tradition of prayer, whereas Eastern people have elicited it through meditation. The relaxation response does not require a theological or religious component. If you have a practice of regular prayer or meditation, you may already elicit the relaxation response regularly. Keep in mind that digestion may interfere with the elicitation of the response, so avoid practicing relaxation shortly after eating.

Diet Diet may play an indirect role in stress and stress management. High sugar content in the diet can stimulate the stress response, and foods high in cholesterol can adversely affect blood chemistry. Good dietary practices contribute to a person's overall health, making her or him less vulnerable to distress. In his nonsurgical, nonpharmacological approach to reversing heart disease, Dean Ornish proposes a very stringent "reversal diet" for people with identifiable blockage of the arteries.[89] Ornish recommends a somewhat less stringent "prevention diet" as one of four elements for opening up the arteries. Another element in his program is being open in relationships with other people.

Opening Up Everyone experiences a traumatic, stressful, or painful event in life at one time or another. One of the most therapeutic, curative responses to such an event is to confide in another person.[90] Discussing difficult experiences with another person is not always easy, yet health benefits, immune system improvement, and healing accrue through self-disclosure. In one study comparing those who wrote once a week about traumatic events with those who wrote about nontraumatic events, significant health benefits and reduced absenteeism were found in the first group.[91] Confession need not be through a personal relationship with friends. It may occur through a private diary. For example, a lawyer might write each evening about all of his or her most troubling thoughts, feelings, and emotions during the course of the day. The process of opening up and confessing appears to counter the detrimental effects of stress.

Professional Help Confession and opening up may occur through professional helping relationships. People who need healing have psychological counseling, career counseling, physical therapy, medical treatment, surgical intervention, and other therapeutic techniques available. Employee assistance programs (EAPs) may be very helpful in referring employees to the appropriate caregivers. Even combat soldiers who experience battle stress reactions severe enough to take them out of action can heal and be ready for subsequent combat duty.[92] The early detection of distress and strain reactions, coupled with prompt professional treatment, can be instrumental in averting permanent physical and psychological damage.

Comprehensive Health Promotion

Whereas organizational stress prevention is aimed at eliminating health risks at work, comprehensive health promotion programs are aimed at establishing a "strong and resistant host" by building on individual prevention and lifestyle change.[93]

Physical fitness and exercise programs characterize corporate health promotion programs in the United States and Canada.[94] A health promotion and wellness survey of accredited medical schools in the United States, Canada, and Puerto Rico found that these programs place the most emphasis on physical well-being and the least emphasis on spiritual well-being.[95] A new approach to comprehensive health promotion places the focus on the organization and organizational wellness.[96] Still, social and cognitive processes are key considerations in the successful implementation of stress prevention programs.[97]

Johnson & Johnson developed a comprehensive health promotion program with a significant number of educational modules for individuals and groups. These modules addressed a specific topic, such as Type A behavior, exercise, diet (through cooperative activities with the American Heart Association), stress, and risk assessment (through regular risk assessments and health profiles for participants). Johnson & Johnson found that the health status of employees who are not participating in health promotion programs in the workplace improves if the worksite does have such a program.

MANAGERIAL IMPLICATIONS: STRESS WITHOUT DISTRESS

Stress is an inevitable result of work and personal life. Distress is not an inevitable consequence of stressful events, however; in fact, well-managed stress can improve health and performance. Managers must learn how to create healthy stress for employees to facilitate performance and well-being without distress. Managers can help employees by adjusting workloads, avoiding ethical dilemmas, being sensitive to diversity among individuals concerning what is stressful, and being sensitive to employees' personal life demands.

New technologies create demands and stress for employees. Managers can help employees adjust to new technologies by ensuring that their design and implementation are sensitive to employees and that employee involvement is strong.

Managers can be sensitive to early signs of distress at work, such as employee fatigue or changes in work habits, in order to avoid serious forms of distress. The serious forms of distress include violent behavior, psychological depression, and cardiovascular problems. Distress is important to the organization because of the costs associated with turnover and absenteeism, as well as poor-quality production.

Managers should be aware of gender, personality, and behavioral differences when analyzing stress in the workplace. Men and women have different vulnerabilities when it comes to distress. Men are at greater risk of fatal disorders, for example, and women are more vulnerable to nonfatal disorders, such as depression. Managers should be aware that even positive performance stereotypes may place undue stress on employees, leading to chronic disorders such as hypertension. Personality hardiness and self-reliance are helpful in managing stressful events.

Managers can use the principles and methods of preventive stress management to create healthier work environments. They can practice several forms of individual stress prevention to create healthier lifestyles for themselves, and they can encourage employees to do the same. Large organizations can create healthier workforces through the implementation of comprehensive health promotion programs. Setting an example is one of the best things a manager can do for employees when it comes to preventive stress management.

DIVERSITY DIALOGUE

When Domestic Violence "Goes to Work"

Rachel was assaulted by her partner when she was eight months pregnant. Not only did he assault her, he snatched the telephone out of the wall, leaving Rachel with no way to call for help. By the time she cleaned up her head wound and got to a pay phone to call in sick, her shift had already begun.

This wasn't the first time that Rachel had to miss work. She regularly called in sick due to the physical and emotional effects of the abuse she suffered at the hands of her partner. In fact, Rachel had become a pro at making excuses to explain away her cuts, strangle marks, and bruises to her colleagues. When the "I fell" and "I hurt myself in a sporting event" explanations wore thin, she began to cover up the telltale marks on her neck and arms with long sleeves and sweaters even during the summer. All of the other times, Rachel had gotten away with calling in sick so often, but this time was different. This time she lost her job.

Rachel is not alone. She is one of the 57 percent of women who have reported domestic abuse at some time in their lives. Although they struggle to keep their personal and professional lives separate, women who experience domestic trauma often find it very difficult if not impossible to concentrate at work. Because these women often suffer in silence, their employers may feel they have no other alternative but to fire them.

1. Is domestic violence a workplace issue?
2. What can employers do if they suspect an employee's poor performance is related to stress stemming from domestic abuse?

SOURCE: B. Pennings, "Domestic Violence: A Workplace Issue," *New Matilda* (June 6, 2007).

LOOKING BACK: TIMBERLAND COMPANY

A Healthy Balance Sheet Is One Secure Base . . .

When the competition is the severest and the bottom falls out of the market is not the time to panic. That is the time to kick it up a notch, and Timberland is a company that understands this. Challenging times require thinking optimistically as well as realistically. If your head is in the clouds, at least your feet need to be on the ground. In the face of the declining sales in its boots and kids business, Timberland cut its earnings estimate dramatically, from $1.69 to $1.22, based on current results and outlook. That move displays realistic attention to the market context and to the real challenges the company must meet in order to position itself for future growth and advancement.

One of Timberland's strengths is a very healthy balance sheet. Less robust companies are vulnerable to severe damage or, in the worst-case scenario, complete collapse. The competitive industrial and corporate landscape is littered through history with companies that failed to anticipate the difficult times that come to all companies, industries, and individuals. To weather the worst requires strong assets and secure anchors. A healthy balance sheet with strong assets is critical in this regard. In addition, in the midst of its challenges, Timberland faced the positive opportunity for margin improvement in its business.

Financial assets and a healthy balance sheet are not enough, however, and Timberland has an array of other assets on the human side of its ledger. In 2006, *Business Ethics* magazine honored the company as one of the 100 Best Corporate Citizens. Integrity and ethics go a long way in insuring a personal and a corporate reputation. The Committee to Encourage Corporate Philanthropy selected Timberland for its 2001 Annual Excellence in Corporate Philanthropy Award, signaling a giving and other-directed corporate culture. From 2004 through 2006, *Working Mother* annually named Timberland as one of the 100 Best Companies for Working Mothers. These are among the human and less tangible assets the company has that give it strength and security to weather the hard times. Good numbers and good people mean good protection in the face of stress.[98]

Chapter Summary

1. Stress is the unconscious preparation to fight or flee when faced with any demand. Distress is the adverse consequence of stress.
2. Four approaches to understanding stress are the homeostatic/medical approach, the cognitive appraisal approach, the person–environment fit approach, and the psychoanalytic approach.
3. The stress response is a natural mind–body response characterized by four basic mind–body changes.
4. Employees face task, role, interpersonal, and physical demands at work, along with nonwork demands. Globalization, international competition, and advanced technologies create new stresses at work.
5. Nonwork stressors, such as family problems and work–home conflicts, can affect an individual's work life and home life.
6. Stress has health benefits, including enhanced performance.
7. Distress is costly to both individuals and organizations.
8. Individual diversity requires attention to gender, Type A behavior, personality hardiness, and self-reliance in determining the links between stress and strain.
9. Preventive stress management aims to enhance health and reduce distress or strain. Primary prevention focuses on the stressor, secondary prevention focuses on the response to the stressor, and tertiary prevention focuses on symptoms of distress.

Key Terms

compensation award (p. 229)
counterdependence (p. 231)
distress (p. 218)
ego-ideal (p. 220)
homeostasis (p. 220)
overdependence (p. 232)
participation problem (p. 229)
performance decrement (p. 229)
personality hardiness (p. 231)
preventive stress management (p. 232)
primary prevention (p. 233)
secondary prevention (p. 234)
self-image (p. 220)
self-reliance (p. 231)
strain (p. 218)
stress (p. 218)
stressor (p. 218)
tertiary prevention (p. 234)
transformational coping (p. 231)
Type A behavior pattern (p. 230)
workaholism (p. 225)

Review Questions

1. Define *stress, distress,* and *strain.*
2. Describe four approaches to understanding stress. How does each add something new to our understanding of stress?
3. What are the four changes associated with the stress response?
4. List three demands of each type: task, role, interpersonal, and physical.
5. What is a nonwork demand? How does it affect an individual?
6. Describe the relationship between stress and performance.
7. What are the major medical consequences of distress? The behavioral consequences? The psychological consequences?
8. Why should organizations be concerned about stress at work? What are the costs of distress to organizations?
9. How do individual differences such as gender, Type A behavior, personality hardiness, and self-reliance moderate the relationship between stress and strain?
10. What is primary prevention? Secondary prevention? Tertiary prevention? Describe major organizational stress prevention methods.
11. Describe eight individual preventive stress management methods.
12. What is involved in comprehensive health promotion programs?

Discussion and Communication Questions

1. Why should organizations help individuals manage stress? Isn't stress basically the individual's responsibility?
2. Is there more stress today than in past generations? What evidence is available concerning this question?
3. Discuss the following statement: Employers should be expected to provide stress-free work environments.
4. If an individual claims to have job-related anxiety or depression, should the company be liable?
5. Do you use any stress prevention methods that are not discussed in the chapter? If so, what are they?
6. (*communication question*) Write a memo describing the most challenging demands and/or stressors at your workplace (or university). Be specific in describing the details of these demands and/or stressors. How might you go about changing them?
7. (*communication question*) Interview a medical doctor, a psychologist, or another health care professional about the most common forms of health problems and distress seen in their work. Summarize your interview and compare the results to the categories of distress discussed in the chapter.
8. (*communication question*) Do research on social support and diaries as ways to manage stressful and/or traumatic events. Develop an oral presentation for class that explains the benefits of each of these approaches for preventive stress management. Include guidelines on how to practice each.

Ethical Dilemma

Josh Newland is very excited about the proposal on his desk. If it is accepted, it could be the turning point in his career. Josh is an analyst for Barnes and Associates, a financial services company. He has been with the company for five years and is beginning to be noticed. He has put a lot of time and effort into this proposal in hopes of turning that attention into a promotion. He just wishes he felt better about turning it in.

Josh looked up from the proposal to the pictures on his desk. The eyes of his wife and two sons look back. They are the only drawbacks to the proposal being the success Josh is certain it will be. The promotion he wants so badly would allow even less time to spend with Mary and the kids. But he has worked very hard to get where he is. His parents had worked hard to send him to the best schools. It would be wrong to ignore everyone's efforts.

But Mary has worked hard too. She has career dreams as well. She is happy to take time off while the children are small, but she has definite plans to return to work. However, if Josh gets this promotion, there will be little time for him to support her career as she has supported his. He would not be able to watch the kids while Mary works late nights to get noticed. Nor would he be able to perform any other parental duties so that Mary would not have to ask for time off. Mary has so willingly put her career on hold so that they could have a family. Is it fair not to give her a chance to regain what she has lost? Is it right to allow his sons to grow up with a dad who is rarely there? But is it wrong for him to take advantage of the best career opportunity he may ever have? He only wants to provide the best life possible for his family.

Questions

1. Does Josh have a responsibility to question submitting this proposal?
2. Evaluate Josh's alternatives using consequential, rule-based, and character theories.

Experiential Exercises

7.1 Gender Role Stressors

The major sources of stress are not necessarily the same for men and women. This exercise will help you identify the similarities and differences in the stressors and perceptions of men and women.

Step 1. Individually list the major sources of stress for you because of your gender. Be as specific as possible, and within your list, prioritize your stressors.

Step 2. Individually list what you think are the major sources of stress for those of the opposite gender. Again, be as specific as possible, and prioritize your list.

Step 3. In teams of five or six members of the same sex, share your two lists of stressors. Discuss these stressors, and identify the top five sources of stress for your group because of your gender and the top five sources of stress for those of the opposite gender. Again, be as specific as possible, and prioritize your list.

Step 4. The class will then engage in a cross-team exchange of lists. Look for similarities and differences among the teams in your class as follows. Select one gender to be addressed first. If the females are first, for example, the male groups will post their predictions. This will be followed by the actual stressor lists from the female groups. Then do the same for the other gender.

7.2 Workplace Stress Diagnosis

The following exercise gives you an opportunity to work within a group to compare the work demands and job stressors found in different work settings. Intervention for preventive stress management should always be based on a good diagnosis. This exercise gives you a start in this direction.

Step 1. Rate the degree to which each of the following work demands is a source of stress for you and your coworkers at work. Use a 7-point rating scale for assigning the stressfulness of the work demand, with 7 = very high source of stress, 4 = moderate source of stress, and 1 = very little source of stress.

___ Uncertainty about various aspects of the work environment

___ Lack of control over people, events, or other aspects of work

___ Lack of career opportunities and progress

___ The implementation of new technologies

___ Work overload; that is, too much to do and not enough time

___ Conflicting expectations from one or more people at work

___ Confusing expectations from one or more people at work

___ Dangerous working conditions and/or hazardous substances

___ Sexual harassment by supervisors, coworkers, or others

___ Abrasive personalities and/or political conflicts

___ Rigid, insensitive, unresponsive supervisors or managers

Step 2. Write a brief description of the most stressful event that has occurred in your work environment during the past twelve-month period.

Step 3. The class will form into groups of approximately six members each. Each group elects a spokesperson and then compares the information developed by each person in Steps 1 and 2. In the process of this comparison, answer the following questions:

a. What are the similarities between work environments in terms of their most stressful work demands?

b. What are the differences among work environments in terms of their most stressful work demands?

c. Are there similarities in the descriptions of the most stressful events? If so, what are they?

Step 4. Each group will share the results of its answers to the questions in Step 3. Cross-team questions and discussion follow.

Step 5 (Optional). Your instructor may ask you to choose one or another of the work environments in which to develop some preventive stress management strategies. Complete parts a and b below in your group.

a. Identify one to three preventive stress management strategies that you think are the best to use in the work environment. Why have you chosen them?

b. How should the effectiveness of these strategies be evaluated?

TAKE 2

Biz Flix | Meet the Parents

Greg Focker (Ben Stiller) hopes his weekend visit to his girlfriend Pam's (Teri Polo) home will leave a positive impression on her parents. Unfortunately, Jack (Robert De Niro), Pam's father, immediately dislikes him. Jack's fondness does not improve after Greg accidentally breaks the urn holding Jack's mother's ashes. Other factors do not help the developing relationship: Greg is Jewish, while Jack is a WASP ex-CIA psychological profiler. These factors blend well to cause the continuous development of stress and stress responses of all parties involved.

The scene from *Meet the Parents* comes from the "Bomb's the Word" segment in the last quarter of the film. Greg has boarded his flight to return home after his excruciating weekend visit with Pam's family. By this time, he has experienced an almost endless stream of stressors: meeting Pam's parents for the first time, taking a polygraph test administered by Jack, adjusting to Jinx the Himalayan cat's odd behavior, and . . . the film continues to a predictable happy ending.

What to Watch for and Ask Yourself:

- Does Greg experience the stress response during this scene? What evidence appears in the scene?
- Does he experience distress or eustress?
- Why does Greg respond so harshly to the simple request to check his bag?

Workplace Video | Human Resource Management, Featuring Allstate

Successful businesses recognize that human capital is an organization's most valuable asset. At Allstate, recruiting qualified employees and helping them achieve their personal best is the focus of the company's human resource management program.

While pay is often the first thing that comes to mind when people think of human resources, companies are increasingly using non-pay-related benefits to attract and retain top talent. For example, Allstate offers flexible work arrangements and on-site childcare. In addition, the company encourages professional growth through training seminars, mentoring programs, college courses, and tuition reimbursement. Two popular learning programs at Allstate include the Talent Acceleration Program, which helps workers develop leadership abilities, and the Learning Resource Network, which offers thousands of activities aimed at boosting business, interpersonal, and technical skills.

Corporate benefits that reduce unhealthy stress and promote well-being on the job are especially desirable among today's younger professionals. Allstate offers many perks that help employees unwind. For example, professionals seeking to blow off steam can work out at the company's on-site fitness center. If relaxation is the need of the hour, however, workers can get a manicure at Allstate's on-site salon or sip lattes in the company's Starbucks kiosk. Unusual perks like on-site dry cleaning and oil change show special concern for the company's time-stressed personnel.

TAKE 2

"Free perks" are never free, however, and Allstate spares no expense in promoting employee well-being. In 2005, Allstate spent $3.3 billion on employee compensation and benefits. Despite the steep investment, management feels confident that money spent on developing human capital is money well spent. Such confidence is not misplaced: employee satisfaction at Allstate approaches 90 percent, according to some surveys. People really are in good hands with Allstate.

Discussion Questions

1. In what way is Allstate's benefits program a necessary response to the changing labor market?
2. How does Allstate's on-site childcare center help employees alleviate stress?
3. Identify a benefit at Allstate that demonstrates the company's commitment to "preventive stress management."

CASE

Promoting Employee Wellness at Genentech

Genentech, founded in 1976 by biochemist Dr. Herbert W. Boyer and venture capitalist Robert A. Swanson, has a "mission of discovering, developing, manufacturing and commercializing life-enhancing and life-saving medicines for patients with unmet medical needs."[1] The company markets biotherapeutic products in the areas of oncology, immunology, and disorders of tissue growth and repair.[2] Over the years, Genentech has become a leading biotechnology company, noted as much for its human resources programs as for its development and commercialization of new biotherapeutic products.

Genentech has "designed employee centered programs and services specifically to support employees in creating the kind of work environment and lifestyle that help them bring the best to the business and to their families."[3] As a result of this proactive approach, Genentech has been recognized repeatedly for being one of the top places to work in the United States. In 2007, for example, *Fortune* included Genentech on its list of the "100 Best Companies to Work For" for the ninth year in a row. In 2006, *Working Mother* identified it as one of the "100 Best Companies for Working Mothers" for the fourteenth time. Also in 2006, *Science* tagged Genentech as "the top employer and most admired company in the biotechnology and pharmaceutical industries" for the fifth consecutive year.[4]

What does Genentech do that makes it such a good place to work? Part of the answer lies in the company's conscious strategies for making the work environment exciting and challenging. Employees work hard and play hard—they are intensely serious when it comes to science, patients, and the pursuit of excellence, and equally intense in their ability to have fun.[5] Indeed, Genentech demands nothing less than the best from its more than 10,700 employees and rewards them accordingly. The rewards include an employee stock purchase plan, a paid sabbatical program, one of the largest corporate-sponsored day-care centers in the country, and health care benefits that are among the best in the industry.[6]

Genentech is in the business of protecting the health, safety, and wellness of its customers. This same philosophy extends to how the company treats its employees. As its Web site states, "Genentech recognizes that protecting the health, safety and wellness of our employees is a natural extension of our commitment to improving the state of human health. To this end, the company has developed extensive programs that promote a safe and healthy workplace."[7]

The company's varied wellness programs promote a safe and healthy workplace as well as healthy lifestyles for employees and their families. These programs include a generous health insurance package with medical, dental, vision, and wellness coverage; a variety of fitness options, including some on-site facilities; on-site Weight Watchers meetings; and reimbursement of employees' costs upon successful completion of treatment to stop smoking.[8] Many other wellness options also exist.

Of particular note among these options is Club Genentech, an on-site health club facility in the South San Francisco headquarters. This facility was developed in response to survey input from employees regarding the on-site services they valued the most. Covering 24,000 square feet, Club Genentech provides a wide variety of fitness and wellness program options for headquarters' employees. For instance, the club has a cycle room and basketball court as well as sauna and steam rooms. Massages are also available, and an extensive fitness program is offered, including but not limited to group exercise and yoga classes, personal training, and sports leagues. Membership in Club Genentech is free for Genentech employees and is available to families of employees for a small fee.[9]

Although Club Genentech is located at the South San Francisco headquarters, the company's commitment to employee fitness extends beyond this facility. Employees working at the company's other two main facilities—in Vacaville and Oceanside, California—enjoy company-paid memberships in local fitness facilities. In Vacaville, the company contracts with a sports club; in Oceanside, with a YMCA. Employees who work in other locations are not excluded from wellness benefits; they receive up to a $600 annual reimbursement for the cost of fitness activities.[10]

According to Diane Fuller, Senior Occupational Health Nurse at the company's South San Francisco facility, "[W]ellness programs such as Club Genentech, Weight Watchers, or the flu vaccination program help support our employees in staying healthy. Having such opportunities on-site encourages participation and demonstrates that Genentech's senior management understands the importance of a healthy, balanced lifestyle."[11]

Discussion Questions

1. Would you characterize Genentech's employees as experiencing distress or eustress?
2. How can the Yerkes–Dodson law be related to the impact of Genentech's wellness programs?
3. What might Genentech's wellness programs accomplish with respect to enabling employees to better deal with workplace stress or its consequences?
4. How could you personally benefit from wellness programs like those provided by Genentech?

SOURCE: This case was written by Michael K. McCuddy, The Louis S. and Mary L. Morgal Chair of Christian Business Ethics and Professor of Management, College of Business Administration, Valparaiso University.

BP: Safety and Public Relations in America (B)

Beginning in early 2005, BP, one of the world's largest oil companies, experienced a series of disasters and public relations debacles in its American operations. In March 2005, an explosion at the company's refinery in Texas City, Texas, claimed 15 lives and injured 180 people.[1] In March 2006, a large oil spill occurred on BP's Alaska pipeline due to neglected preventive maintenance.[2] In November 2006, U.S. health and safety regulators imposed a $384,000 fine on BP for deficient lights and wiring, wrongly set heat alarms, and untested fire hydrants at its refinery in Whiting, Indiana.[3] Then the following April, equipment failure caused a fire at the same refinery. The fire cut daily production in half and employees "complained of a 'run until it breaks' approach at the plant."[4] These various safety violations intensified BP's public relations problems. Also in the spring of 2007, in conjunction with a planned $3.8 billion expansion of the Whiting refinery, BP sought and received a permit from the Indiana Department of Environmental Management (IDEM) to discharge 54 percent more ammonia and 35 percent more suspended solids into Lake Michigan.[5] This further magnified both public criticism of BP and the company's public relations problems.

Public Perception of BP

Under CEO John Browne, BP rebranded itself—BP came to signify *Beyond Petroleum*.[6] This reflected the company's evolving commitment to protecting the environment and developing alternative energy sources. Indeed, in May 2006, a spokesperson for BP's Whiting refinery said, "We always want to do what is best for the environment. . . . We also want to stay ahead in the industry and keep being innovative. We try to create something that is sustainable and compatible and not just wait for the legislation."[7]

As *The Economist* observed, BP "has tried to portray itself as more considerate of the environment than other big oil firms, with slogans like '*Beyond Petroleum*.' But it has suffered from a series of embarrassing accidents. With each new incident it seems more likely that BP, long admired for the quality of its management, has a serious problem overseeing its global operations."[8]

Another observer of the oil industry, Rance Crain, argues that BP had lost its focus on the oil business as it had grown in recent years through various acquisitions, invested in developing alternative energies, and pursued its *Beyond Petroleum* strategy. Crain, writing in an editorial for *Advertising Age*, says, "I wish BP still believed it was in the oil business. If it did, maybe it would have paid a little more attention to its pipeline. But the company was way out there, beyond petroleum, and I guess the oil business just wasn't cutting-edge enough to warrant its attention."[9] Likewise, *New York Times* reporter Joe Nocera observes, "If BP hadn't been so 'holier than thou' in its marketing during the last few years," it probably wouldn't be getting criticized as much now. "And if there is one ironclad rule about marketing," Nocera adds, "it is that you had better be practicing internally what you are preaching to the world."[10]

This lesson became painfully apparent to BP executives in the summer of 2007 as Congress as well as citizens and politicians in the states surrounding Lake Michigan chastised BP for its plans to increase the amount of ammonia and suspended solid pollutants discharged by the Whiting refinery. In July 2007, the House of Representatives, by a vote of 387 to 266, approved a resolution urging IDEM to reconsider the permit it had granted to BP. Indiana's governor, Mitch Daniels, the Indiana Department of Environmental Management, the Federal Environmental Protection Agency, and BP asserted that the company was within the law with regard to the approved additional discharges into Lake Michigan. This, however, did not assuage the growing public and political concern. Thousands of people signed petitions, and numerous meetings were held to pressure both BP and the appropriate governmental agencies.[11]

At a meeting between BP executives and a bipartisan group of politicians in which they discussed IDEM's granting of a new discharge permit, no Indiana lawmakers were present. Indiana lawmakers "generally have been reluctant to criticize BP, at least in part because the refinery expansion [which would generate the additional pollutants] would add 80 new jobs."[12] However, the press secretary for Indiana's Senator Evan Bayh said, "We can't compromise Lake Michigan or any part of our environment for economic progress . . . but the refinery is vital to issues relating to the nation's energy supply and our economy."[13] Still, "In advertisements and e-mails . . . , BP has insisted the treated water it pumps into the lake is largely free of toxic waste. Federal records, though, show the refinery already is one of the largest sources of industrial pollution pumped directly into Lake Michigan."[14] On August 24, 2007, BP "announced that it was abandoning plans to discharge more pollution from its northwest Indiana refinery into Lake Michigan" but "denied the company was succumbing to intense public and political pressure, instead saying they changed their minds because of 'regulatory uncertainty.'"[15]

Despite the assertions of BP executives regarding the company's safety and environmental records, skepticism remains. "BP's recent safety and environmental record in the US diminishes its credibility as an industry leader in the field of corporate social responsibility (CSR) and project management. As such, it is a public-relations disaster for a company that has invested significant amounts of money and time in asserting its green credentials—from the branding gimmick of *Beyond Petroleum* to its admirable investments in renewables and its significant acceptance of global warming theory and support for carbon-reduction schemes."[16]

Roots of BP's American Problems: Emphasis on Cost Cutting and Performance

BP's problems with its Alaska pipeline and Texas City and Whiting refineries may be attributed to the company's aggressive emphasis on cost cutting and performance. Cost cutting was a key BP strategy under John Browne. For instance, when BP acquired Amoco in 1998, Browne pledged to cut expenses by $2 billion a year.[17] The Alaska pipeline leak has been linked to aggressive cost cutting. Contrary to an industry standard of once every five years, internal pipeline inspections with a smart-pig were not conducted in the 14-year period preceding the pipeline spill.[18] "Charles Hamel, who represents the interests of local oil workers [in Alaska], claims he has been warning BP about pipeline corrosion in Prudhoe Bay for years. He cites specific correspondence with senior BP officials in 2003 and 2004 in which he warned about the dangers."[19]

Questions regarding both cost cutting and performance accountability were raised in an internal report on the Texas City refinery explosion. The report, commissioned by BP, stated, "It should not be overlooked that serious mistakes and failures for which the ISOM staff [isomerization unit where the blast occurred] clearly is responsible. . . . BP's management, however, was ultimately responsible for assuring the appropriate priorities were in place, adequate resources were provided and clear accountabilities were established for the safe operation of the [Texas City] refinery."[20]

The emphasis on performance targets and performance accountability can be traced to the structural reorganization of BP subsequent to the company becoming fully privatized in 1987. A very aggressive style of management took hold that reflects a management structure less hierarchical than its competitors. Then in 1992 the company was split up into 150 business units and managers' pay was linked to their unit's profits.[21] Although this performance culture permeated BP for over a decade, in late 2005 John Browne outlined seven behavioral expectations that would increase emphasis on individual accountability among the company's top 600 executives. Under this performance measurement and reward system, 25 percent of an individual executive's annual bonus is tied to what is achieved in seven areas—strategic direction, prioritization, support/development of direct reports, external environment, internal/external relationships, values, and code of conduct—and how it is achieved.[22]

Given BP's emphasis on cost cutting and performance, can the company overcome the safety and environmental problems and the associated public relations debacle that it has endured in the recent past?

Discussion Questions

1. What insights can concepts regarding perception and attribution provide in helping BP executives understand the public's reaction to its series of safety problems and its proposal to increase the discharge of pollutants into Lake Michigan?
2. What emotional, attitudinal, and ethical concerns do BP's safety and public relations problems raise for the company? For the public?

3. How might BP's aggressive emphasis on cost cutting and achieving performance goals influence the motivation of the company' executives?
4. What impact might aggressive cost cutting and performance management have on the level of stress experienced by BP executives? How might the performance pressure on executives influence the stress levels experienced by lower-level organization members?

SOURCE: This case was written by Michael K. McCuddy, The Louis S. and Mary L. Morgal Chair of Christian Business Ethics and Professor of Management, College of Business Administration, Valparaiso University.

© DIGITAL VISION

PART 3

Interpersonal Processes and Behavior

CHAPTER 8

Communication

LEARNING OBJECTIVES

After reading this chapter, you should be able to do the following:

1 Understand the roles of the communicator, the receiver, perceptual screens, and the message in interpersonal communication.

2 Practice good reflective listening skills.

3 Describe the five communication skills of effective supervisors.

4 Explain five communication barriers and gateways through them.

5 Distinguish between defensive and nondefensive communication.

6 Explain positive, healthy communication.

7 Describe Information Communication Technology (ICT) used by managers.

THINKING AHEAD: CARIBOU COFFEE

Brewing Innovative Customer Service

Caribou makes coffee the old-fashioned way, by brewing it. But it also has an eye to the future. By teaming with American icon IBM, Caribou aims to improve customer experience through the seamless use of in-store technology. IBM, the world's largest information technology and business services company, is the leader in providing the retail industry with a full range of e-business solutions. These solutions include point-of-sale systems, automated self-checkout systems, additional hardware and software, IT strategy and planning, supply chain optimization, and consulting focused on business transformation. What better way to provide innovative customer service than using a great business partner like IBM's retail systems?

Caribou stays focused on its motto: "Guests are always our priority—Everything else waits." For the business side of their coffeehouses, the company is building a relationship with IBM as the information technology company to trust for the most reliable, integrated, and easy-to-use systems. Innovative IBM Anyplace Kiosks help Caribou enhance employee productivity. The Anyplace Kiosks are compact units located in the barista (coffee-making) stations within the coffeehouses. These units help employees to process orders quickly and easily using advanced infrared touch-screen display. Caribou pilot tested these all-in-one kiosks in 2006 as managers' workstations with an eye to possible customer-facing applications, such as for easy-to-read information on menu items, specials, and promotions. The company plans to have over 400 of these IBM Anytime Kiosks operational by 2008.

The Anytime Kiosks are just one of an array of information and communication technologies that IBM can deploy in support of Caribou's mission to be number one in customer experience. The IBM SurePOS 500 is another retail technology used by Caribou, which has purchased over 900 of these point-of-sale systems. The SurePOS 500 allows Caribou employees to "ring up" orders quickly and accurately while offering a space-saving footprint in the coffeehouses. IBM has created an elegant, retail-hardened design for this system that complements the Caribou coffeehouse environment. This IBM system is robust, thus eliminating the need for Caribou to have a separate back-office server in its stores. While Caribou is serving up the opportunity for its guests to spend time in joyful, deep, sad, happy, or otherwise emotionally rich interpersonal communication with each other—and maybe even Caribou employees—IBM is the technology powerhouse in the background providing the technology that facilitates this important human exchange. What else does Caribou have to offer?[1]

Communication is the evoking of a shared or common meaning in another person. *Interpersonal communication* occurs between two or more people in an organization. Reading, listening, managing and interpreting information, and serving clients are among the interpersonal communication skills identified by the Department of Labor as being necessary for successful functioning in the workplace.[2] In Chapter 7, we noted that interpersonal communication is the key to social support for preventive stress management.[3] Interpersonal communication is central to health and well-being.

This chapter addresses the interpersonal and technological dimensions of communication in organizations. The first section presents an interpersonal communication model and a reflective listening technique intended to improve communication. The next section of the chapter addresses the five communication skills that characterize effective supervisors. The third section examines five barriers to effective communication and gives suggestions for overcoming them. The fourth section compares defensive and nondefensive communication. The fifth section discusses kinds of nonverbal communication. The final section gives an overview of the latest technologies for information management in organizations.

communication
The evoking of a shared or common meaning in another person.

interpersonal communication
Communication between two or more people in an organization.

INTERPERSONAL COMMUNICATION

(1) Understand the roles of the communicator, the receiver, perceptual screens, and the message in interpersonal communication.

Interpersonal communication is important in building and sustaining human relationships at work. This kind of communication cannot be replaced by the advances in information technology and data management that have taken place during the past several decades. The model in this section of the chapter provides a basis for understanding the four key elements of interpersonal communication: the communicator, the receiver, the perceptual screens, and the message. Reflective listening is a valuable tool for improving interpersonal communication.

An Interpersonal Communication Model

Figure 8.1 presents an interpersonal communication model as a basis for the discussion of communication. The model has four basic elements: the communicator, the receiver, perceptual screens, and the message. The *communicator* is the person originating the message. The *receiver* is the person receiving the message. The receiver must interpret and understand the message. *Perceptual screens* are the windows through which we interact with people in the world. The communicator's and the receiver's perceptual screens influence the quality, accuracy, and clarity of the message. The screens influence whether the message sent and the message received are the same or whether distortion occurs in the message. Perceptual screens are composed of the personal factors each person brings to interpersonal communication, such as age, gender, values, beliefs, past experiences, cultural influences, and individual needs. The extent to which these screens are open or closed significantly influences both the sent and received messages.

The *message* contains the thoughts and feelings that the communicator intends to evoke in the receiver. The message has two primary components. The thought or conceptual component of the message (its content) is contained in the words, ideas, symbols, and concepts chosen to relay the message. The feeling or emotional component of the message (its affect) is contained in the intensity, force, demeanor, and sometimes the gestures of the communicator. Language and emotion expressed in initial claims were both important to the likelihood of online dispute resolution.[4] This component of the message adds the emotional overtones, such as joy, anger, fear, or pain, to the conceptual component. This addition often enriches and clarifies the message. The feeling component gives the message its full meaning.

Feedback may or may not be activated in the model. Feedback occurs when the receiver provides the communicator with a response to the message. More broadly, it occurs when information is fed back that completes two-way communication. At Caribou Coffee, as we saw in Thinking Ahead, great information technology stands behind the important two-way communication between guest and employee, which is a key to the success of the business.

The *language* of the message is increasingly important because of the multinational nature of many organizations. Language is the words, their pronunciation,

communicator
The person originating a message.

receiver
The person receiving a message.

perceptual screen
A window through which we interact with people that influences the quality, accuracy, and clarity of the communication.

message
The thoughts and feelings that the communicator is attempting to elicit in the receiver.

feedback
Information fed back that completes two-way communication.

language
The words, their pronunciation, and the methods of combining them used and understood by a group of people.

FIGURE 8.1 A Basic Interpersonal Communication Model

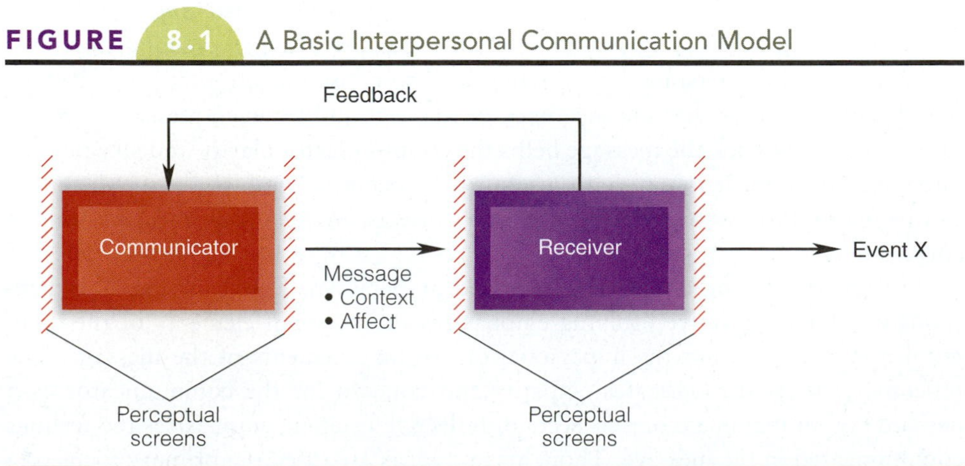

TABLE 8.1 Communication Media: Information Richness and Data Capacity

Medium	Information Richness	Data Capacity
Face-to-face discussion	Highest	Lowest
Telephone	High	Low
Electronic mail	Moderate	Moderate
Individualized letter	Moderate	Moderate
Personalized note or memo	Moderate	Moderate
Formal written report	Low	High
Flyer or bulletin	Low	High
Formal numeric report	Lowest	Highest

SOURCE: Created by E. A. Gerloff from "Information Richness: A New Approach to Managerial Behavior and Organizational Design" by Richard L. Daft and R. H. Lengel in *Research in Organizational Behavior* 6 (1984): 191–233. Reprinted by permission of JAI Press Inc.

data
Uninterpreted and unanalyzed facts.

information
Data that have been interpreted, analyzed, and have meaning to some user.

richness
The ability of a medium or channel to elicit or evoke meaning in the receiver.

and the methods of combining them used by a community of people. Language will be addressed as a possible barrier to communication. For example, special language barriers arise for non–Japanese-speaking Americans who work with Japanese employees and for non–Spanish-speaking Canadians who work with Spanish-speaking employees.

Data are the uninterpreted, unanalyzed elements of a message. *Information* is data with meaning to some person who has interpreted or analyzed them. Messages are conveyed through a medium, such as a telephone or face-to-face discussion. Messages differ in *richness,* the ability of the medium to convey the meaning.[5] Table 8.1 compares different media with regard to data capacity and information richness. Attributes of communication media affect how influence-seeking behavior is generated and perceived in organizations.[6]

Reflective Listening

(2) Practice good reflective listening skills.

Reflective listening is the skill of carefully listening to another person and repeating back to the speaker the heard message to correct any inaccuracies or misunderstandings. This kind of listening emphasizes the role of the receiver or audience in interpersonal communication. Managers use it to understand other people and help them solve problems at work.[7] Reflective listening enables the listener to understand the communicator's meaning, reduce perceptual distortions, and overcome interpersonal barriers that lead to communication failures. Reflective listening ensures that the meanings of the sent and received messages are the same. Reflecting back the message helps the communicator clarify and sharpen the intended meaning. It is especially useful in problem solving. Reflective listening can be learned in a short time with positive effects on behaviors and emotions in corporate settings.[8]

reflective listening
A skill intended to help the receiver and communicator clearly and fully understand the message sent.

Reflective listening can be characterized as personal, feeling oriented, and responsive.[9] First, reflective listening emphasizes the personal elements of the communication process, not the impersonal or abstract elements of the message. The reflective listener demonstrates empathy and concern for the communicator as a person, not an inanimate object. Second, reflective listening emphasizes the feelings communicated in the message. Thoughts and ideas are often the primary focus of a receiver's response, but that is not the case in reflective listening. The receiver should pay special attention to the feeling component of the message. Third, reflective listening emphasizes responding to, not leading, the communicator. Receivers should distinguish their own feelings and thoughts from those of the speaker so as not to confuse the two. The focus must be on the speaker's feelings and thoughts in order to respond to them. A good reflective listener does not lead the speaker according to the listener's own thoughts and feelings.

Four levels of verbal response by the receiver are part of active reflective listening: affirming contact, paraphrasing expressed thoughts and feelings, clarifying implicit thoughts and feelings, and reflecting "core" feelings not fully expressed. Nonverbal behaviors also are useful in reflective listening. Specifically, silence and eye contact are responses that enhance reflective listening.

Each reflective response is illustrated through the case of a software engineer and her supervisor. The engineer has just discovered a major problem, which is not yet fully defined, in a large information system she is building for a very difficult customer.

Affirming Contact The receiver affirms contact with the communicator by using simple statements such as "I see," "Uh-huh," and "Yes, I understand." The purpose of an affirmation response is to communicate attentiveness, not necessarily agreement. In the case of the software engineer, the supervisor might most appropriately use several affirming statements as the engineer begins to talk through the problem. Affirming contact is especially reassuring to a speaker in the early stages of expressing thoughts and feelings about a problem, particularly when there may be some associated anxiety or discomfort. As the problem is more fully explored and expressed, it is increasingly useful for the receiver to use additional reflective responses.

Paraphrasing the Expressed After an appropriate time, the receiver might paraphrase the expressed thoughts and feelings of the speaker. Paraphrasing is useful because it reflects back to the speaker the thoughts and feelings as the receiver heard them. This verbal response enables the receiver to build greater empathy, openness, and acceptance into the relationship while ensuring the accuracy of the communication process.

In the case of the software engineer, the supervisor may find paraphrasing the engineer's expressed thoughts and feelings particularly useful for both of them in developing a clearer understanding of the system problem. For example, the supervisor might say, "I hear you saying that you are very upset about this problem and that you are not yet clear about what is causing it." It is difficult to solve a problem until it is clearly understood.

Clarifying the Implicit People often communicate implicit thoughts and feelings about a problem in addition to their explicitly expressed thoughts and feelings. Implicit thoughts and feelings are not clearly or fully expressed. The receiver may or may not assume that the implicit thoughts and feelings are within the awareness of the speaker. For example, the software engineer may be anxious about how to talk with a difficult customer concerning the system problem. This may be implicit in her discussion with her supervisor because of the previous discussions about this customer. If her anxiety feelings are not expressed, the supervisor may want to clarify them. For example, the supervisor might say, "I hear that you are feeling very upset about the problem and may be worried about the customer's reaction when you inform him." This would help the engineer shift the focus of her attention from the main problem, which is in the software, to the important and related issue of discussing the matter with the customer.

Reflecting "Core" Feelings Next, the receiver should go beyond the explicit or implicit thoughts and feelings that the speaker is expressing. The receiver, in reflecting the core feelings that the speaker may be experiencing, is reaching beyond the immediate awareness level of the speaker. "Core" feelings are the deepest and most important ones from the speaker's perspective. For example, if the software engineer had not been aware of any anxiety in her relationship with the difficult customer, her supervisor's ability to sense the tension and bring it to the engineer's awareness would exemplify reflecting core feelings.

The receiver runs a risk of overreaching in reflecting core feelings if a secure, empathetic relationship with the speaker does not already exist or if strongly repressed feelings are reflected back. Even if the receiver is correct, the speaker may not want those feelings brought to awareness. Therefore, it is important to exercise caution and care in reflecting core feelings to a speaker.

Silence Long, extended periods of silence may cause discomfort and be a sign or source of embarrassment, but silence can help both speaker and listener in reflective listening. From the speaker's perspective, silence may be useful in moments of thought or confusion about how to express difficult ideas or feelings. The software engineer may need some patient, silent response as she thinks through what to say next. Listeners can use brief periods of silence to sort out their own thoughts and feelings from those of the speaker. Reflective listening focuses only on the latter. In the case of the software engineer's supervisor, any personal, angry feelings toward the difficult customer should not intrude on the engineer's immediate problem. Silence provides time to identify and isolate the listener's personal responses and exclude them from the dialogue.

Eye Contact Eye contact is a nonverbal behavior that may help open up a relationship and improve communication between two people. The absence of any direct eye contact during an exchange tends to close communication. Cultural and individual differences influence what constitutes appropriate eye contact. For example, some cultures, such as in India, place restrictions on direct eye contact initiated by women or children. Too much direct eye contact, regardless of the individual or culture, has an intimidating effect.

Moderate direct eye contact, therefore, communicates openness and affirmation without causing either speaker or listener to feel intimidated. Periodic aversion of the eyes allows for a sense of privacy and control, even in intense interpersonal communication.

One-Way versus Two-Way Communication Reflective listening encourages two-way communication. *Two-way communication* is an interactive form of communication in which there is an exchange of thoughts, feelings, or both and through which shared meaning often occurs. Problem solving and decision making are often examples of two-way communication. *One-way communication* occurs when a person sends a message to another person and no feedback, questions, or interaction follow. Giving instructions or giving directions are examples of one-way communication. One-way communication occurs whenever a person sends a one-directional message to a receiver with no reflective listening or feedback in the communication.

two-way communication
A form of communication in which the communicator and receiver interact.

one-way communication
Communication in which a person sends a message to another person and no feedback, questions, or interaction follow.

One-way communication is faster, although how much faster depends on the amount and complexity of information communicated and the medium chosen. Even though it is faster, one-way communication is often less accurate than two-way communication. This is especially true for complex tasks where clarifications and iterations may be required for task completion. Where time and accuracy are both important to the successful completion of a task, such as in combat or emergency situations, extensive training prior to execution enhances accuracy and

efficiency of execution without two-way communication.[10] Firefighters and military combat personnel engage extensively in such training to minimize the need for communication during emergencies. These highly trained professionals rely on fast, abbreviated, one-way communication as a shorthand for more complex information. However, this communication only works within the range of situations for which the professionals are specifically trained.

It is difficult to draw general conclusions about people's satisfaction with one-way versus two-way communication. For example, communicators with a stronger need for feedback or who are not uncomfortable with conflicting or confusing questions may find two-way communication more satisfying. In contrast, receivers who believe that a message is very straightforward may be satisfied with one-way communication and dissatisfied with two-way communication because of its lengthy, drawn-out nature.

FIVE KEYS TO EFFECTIVE SUPERVISORY COMMUNICATION

(3) Describe the five communication skills of effective supervisors.

Interpersonal communication, especially between managers and employees, is a critical foundation for effective performance in organizations, as well as for health and well-being as seen later in the chapter. As we see in The Real World 8.1, effective communication with employees was a key to US Airways' successful restructuring. Language and power are intertwined in the communication that occurs between managers and their employees.[11] This is especially critical when leaders are articulating vision and achieving buy-in from employees.[12] One large study of managers in a variety of jobs and industries found that managers with the most effective work units engaged in routine communication within their units, whereas the managers with the highest promotion rates engaged in networking activities with superiors.[13] Another study of male and female banking managers suggested that higher-performing managers are better and less apprehensive communicators than lower-performing managers.[14] Oral communication (voice) and cooperative behaviors are important contextual performance skills that have positive effects on the psychosocial quality of the work environment.[15]

A review of the research on manager–employee communication identified five communication skills that distinguish "good" from "bad" supervisors.[16] These skills include being expressive speakers, empathetic listeners, persuasive leaders, sensitive people, and informative managers. Some supervisors are effective without possessing each of these skills, and some organizations value one or another skill over the others. Thus, dyadic (two-person) relationships are at the core of much organization-based communication.[17]

Expressive Speakers

Better supervisors express their thoughts, ideas, and feelings and speak up in meetings. They are comfortable expressing themselves. They tend toward extraversion. Supervisors who are not talkative or who tend toward introversion may at times leave their employees wondering what their supervisors are thinking or how they feel about certain issues. Supervisors who speak out let the people they work with know where they stand, what they believe, and how they feel.

Empathetic Listeners

In addition to being expressive speakers, the better supervisors are willing, empathetic listeners. They use reflective listening skills; they are patient with, and

THE REAL WORLD 8.1

Effective Communication and Employee Engagement

Christopher Chiames was senior vice president for corporate affairs at US Airways when the company needed to seriously restructure in the midst of the airline industry fallout from 9/11. US Airways was in a death spiral, and the company needed some deep sacrifices from its workers and employees if it was going to survive. Rather than an afterthought, the company used effective communication as a primary means of increasing employee engagement and reaching all of its constituencies quickly about what it was attempting to accomplish and why. This strategy gave everyone with a stake in US Airways a context in which to understand the essential need for shared sacrifice for the survival of the company. Employees were not asked to make sacrifices for the sake of making sacrifices. Senior management provided a vision of where the company was going to be and which airline was as an attractive merger partner, and in the process was able to preserve more jobs than were eliminated. Did employees like it? Certainly not; major restructuring inevitably causes real pain and loss for some people. However, the entire company was not lost as was the case with Pan American and Eastern Airlines, both of which went out of business and all employees including senior management lost their jobs. Thus, effective communication enabled US Airways employees to stay engaged and contribute to the survival of the airline, albeit a very different one post-restructuring.

SOURCE: C. Chiames (interview), "Effective Employee Communication," *Workforce Management* 86 (April 23, 2007): 6.

responsive to, problems that employees, peers, and others bring to them about their work. They respond to and engage the concerns of other people. For example, the president of a health care company estimated that he spent 70 percent of his interpersonal time at work listening to others.[18] He listens empathetically to personal and work dilemmas without taking responsibility for others' problems. Empathetic listeners are able to hear the feelings and emotional dimensions of the messages people send them, as well as the content of the ideas and issues. Better supervisors are approachable and willing to listen to suggestions and complaints. In the case of physicians, those with high perceived control were more open in their communication and patients found them more empathetic.[19] You 8.1 gives you an opportunity to evaluate how active a listener you are. Active listening is one key communication skill that closes the feedback gap between managers and employees.[20]

Persuasive Leaders (and Some Exceptions)

Better supervisors are persuasive leaders rather than directive, autocratic ones. All supervisors and managers must exercise power and influence in organizations if they are to ensure performance and achieve results. These better supervisors are distinguished by their use of persuasive communication when influencing others. Specifically, they encourage others to achieve results instead of telling others what to do. They are not highly directive or manipulative in their influence attempts. Patience may be a virtue in this context because the sleeper effect, or delayed influence, may be active in some situations.[21]

The exceptions to this pattern of communication occur in emergency or high-risk situations, such as life-threatening traumas in medical emergency rooms or in oil rig firefighting. In these cases, the supervisor must be directive and assertive.

YOU 8.1

Are You an Active Listener?

Reflective listening is a skill that you can practice and learn. Here are ten tips to help you become a better listener.

1. Stop talking. You cannot listen if your mouth is moving.
2. Put the speaker at ease. Break the ice to help the speaker relax. Smile!
3. Show the speaker you want to listen. Put away your work. Do not look at your watch. Maintain good eye contact.
4. Remove distractions. Close your door. Do not answer the telephone.
5. Empathize with the speaker. Put yourself in the speaker's shoes.
6. Be patient. Not everyone delivers messages at the same pace.
7. Hold your temper. Do not fly off the handle.
8. Go easy on criticism. Criticizing the speaker can stifle communication.
9. Ask questions. Paraphrase and clarify the speaker's message.
10. Stop talking. By this stage, you are probably very tempted to start talking, but do not. Be sure the speaker has finished.

Think of the last time you had a difficult communication with someone at work or school. Evaluate yourself in that situation against each of the ten items. Which one(s) do you need to improve on the most?

SOURCE: From "Steps to Better Listening" by C. Hamilton and B. H. Kleiner. Copyright © February 1987. Reprinted with permission, *Personnel Journal*, all rights reserved.

Sensitivity to Feelings

Better supervisors are also sensitive to the feelings, self-image, and psychological defenses of their employees. Although the supervisor is capable of giving criticism and negative feedback to employees, he or she does it confidentially and constructively. Care is taken to avoid giving critical feedback or reprimanding employees in public. Those settings are reserved for the praise of employees' accomplishments, honors, and achievements. In this manner, the better supervisors are sensitive to the self-esteem of others. They work to enhance that self-esteem as appropriate to the person's real talents, abilities, and achievements.

Informative Managers

Finally, better supervisors keep those who work for them well informed and appropriately and selectively disseminate information. This role involves receiving large volumes of information through a wide range of written and verbal communication media and filtering it before distributing it. The failure to do so can lead to either information overload for the employees or a lack of sufficient information for performance and task accomplishment. Better supervisors favor giving advance notice of organizational changes and explaining the rationale for organizational policies.

A person may become a good supervisor even in the absence of one of these communication skills. For example, a person with special talents in planning and organizing or in decision making may compensate for a shortcoming in expressiveness or sensitivity. Further, when supervisors and employees engage in overt behaviors of communication and forward planning, they have a greater number of agreements about the employee's performance and behavior.[22] Overall, interpersonal communication is a key foundation for human relationships.

BARRIERS AND GATEWAYS TO COMMUNICATION

④ Explain five communication barriers and gateways through them.

Barriers to communication are factors that block or significantly distort successful communication. About 20 percent of communication problems that cause organizational problems and drain profitability can be prevented or solved by communication policy guidelines.[23] *Gateways to communication* are pathways through these barriers and serve as antidotes to the problems caused by communication barriers. These barriers may be temporary and can be overcome. Awareness and recognition are the first steps in formulating ways to overcome them. Five communication barriers are physical separation, status differences, gender differences, cultural diversity, and language. The discussion of each concludes with one or two ways to overcome it.

Physical Separation

The physical separation of people in the work environment poses a barrier to communication. Telephones and technology, such as electronic mail, often help bridge the physical gap. We address a variety of new technologies in the closing section of the chapter. Although telephones and technology can be helpful, they are not as information rich as face-to-face communication (see Table 8.1).

Periodic face-to-face interactions is one antidote to physical separation problems, because the communication is much richer, largely because of nonverbal cues. The richer the communication, the lower the potential for confusion or misunderstandings. Another gateway through the barrier of physical separation is regularly scheduled meetings for people who are organizationally interrelated.

Status Differences

barriers to communication
Aspects of the communication content and context that can impair effective communication in a workplace.

gateways to communication
Pathways through barriers to communication and antidotes to communication problems.

Status differences related to power and the organizational hierarchy pose another barrier to communication among people at work, especially within manager–employee pairs.[24] Because the employee is dependent on the manager as the primary link to the organization, the employee is more likely to distort upward communication than either horizontal or downward communication.

Effective supervisory skills, discussed at the beginning of the chapter, make the supervisor more approachable and remedy the problems related to status differences. In addition, when employees feel secure, they are more likely to be straightforward in upward communication. The absence of status, power, and hierarchical differences, however, is not a cure-all. New information technologies provide another way to overcome status-difference barriers because they encourage the formation of nonhierarchical working relationships.[25]

Men and women have different conversational styles, which may pose a communication barrier between those of opposite sexes.

© INSADCO PHOTOGRAPHY/ALAMY

Gender Differences

Communication barriers can be explained in part by differences in conversational styles.[26] Thus, when people of different ethnic or class backgrounds talk to one another, what the receiver understands may not be the same as what the speaker meant. In a similar way, men and women have different conversational styles, which may pose a communication barrier between those of opposite sexes. For example, women prefer to converse face to face, whereas men are comfortable sitting side by side and concentrating on some focal point in front of them. Hence, conversation style differences may result in a failure to communicate between men and women. Again, what is said by one may be understood to have an entirely different meaning by the other. Male–female conversation is really cross-cultural communication. In a work context, one study found that female employees sent less information to their supervisors and experienced less information overload than did male employees.[27]

An important gateway through the gender barrier to communication is developing an awareness of gender-specific differences in conversational style. These differences can enrich organizational communication and empower professional relationships.[28] A second gateway is to actively seek clarification of the person's meaning rather than freely interpreting meaning from one's own frame of reference.

Cultural Diversity

Cultural values and patterns of behavior can be very confusing barriers to communication. Important international differences in work-related values exist among people in the United States, Germany, the United Kingdom, Japan, and other nations.[29] These value differences have implications for motivation, leadership, and teamwork in work organizations.[30] Habitual patterns of interaction within a culture often substitute for communication. Outsiders working in a culture foreign to them often find these habitual patterns confusing and at times bizarre. For example, the German culture places greater value on authority and hierarchical differences. It is therefore more difficult for German workers to engage in direct, open communication with their supervisors than it is for U.S. workers.[31]

These types of cultural stereotypes can be confusing and misleading in cross-cultural communications. When people from one culture view those in another culture through the lens of stereotypes, they in effect are discounting the individual differences within the other culture. For example, an Asian stereotype of Americans may be that they are aggressive and arrogant and, thus, insensitive and unapproachable. Or an American may stereotype the Chinese and Japanese as meek and subservient, unable to be appropriately strong and assertive. Individuals who depend on the accuracy of these forms of cultural stereotypes may be badly misled in communicating with those in other cultures.

One gateway through cultural diversity as a communication barrier is increasing awareness and sensitivity. In addition, companies can provide seminars for expatriate managers as part of their training for overseas assignments. Bernard Isautier, chairman, president, and CEO of PetroKazakhstan, believes that understanding and communication are two keys to success with workplace diversity, which is an essential ingredient for success in international markets.[32] A second gateway is developing or acquiring a guide, map, or beacon for understanding and interacting with members of other cultures. One approach to doing this is to describe a nation in terms of a suitable and complex metaphor.[33] For example, Irish conversations, the Spanish bullfight, and American football are consensually derived metaphors that can enable those outside the culture to understand its members.

Language

Language is a central element in communication. It may pose a barrier if its use obscures meaning and distorts intent. Although English is the international language of aviation, it is not the international language of business. Where the native languages of supervisors and employees differ, the risk of barriers to communication exists. However, increasing numbers of businesspeople are bilingual or multilingual. For example, Honeywell former CEO Michael Bonsignore's ability to speak four languages helped him conduct business around the world more fluently. Less obvious are subtle distinctions in dialects within the same language, which may cause confusion and miscommunication. For example, the word *lift* means an elevator in Great Britain and a ride in the United States. In a different vein, language barriers are created across disciplines and professional boundaries by technical terminology. Acronyms may be very useful to those on the inside of a profession or discipline as means of shorthand communication. Technical terms can convey precise meaning between professionals. However, acronyms and technical terms may only confuse, obscure, or derail any attempt at clear understanding for people unfamiliar with their meaning and usage. For example, while *probable* is a meaningful word for the forecaster, *likely* is a better term for the layperson to avoid miscommunication.[34] Use simple, direct, declarative language. Speak in brief sentences and use terms or words you have heard from your audience. As much as possible, speak in the language of the listener. Do not use jargon or technical language except with those who clearly understand it.

DEFENSIVE AND NONDEFENSIVE COMMUNICATION

(5) Distinguish between defensive and nondefensive communication.

Defensive communication in organizations also can create barriers between people, whereas nondefensive communication helps open up relationships.[35] *Defensive communication* includes both aggressive, attacking, angry communication and passive, withdrawing communication. *Nondefensive communication* is an assertive, direct, powerful form of communication. It is an alternative to defensive communication. Although aggressiveness and passiveness are both forms of defensive communication, assertiveness is nondefensive communication. Organizations are increasingly engaged in courtroom battles and media exchanges, which are especially fertile settings for defensive communication. Catherine Crier had extensive experience as a trial lawyer and judge in dealing with defensive people. She carried this knowledge over into her position as a news anchor for CNN, ABC, Fox News, and during her years on Court TV. Her four basic rules are (1) define the situation, (2) clarify the person's position, (3) acknowledge the person's feelings, and (4) bring the focus back to the facts.

Defensive communication in organizations leads to a wide range of problems, including injured feelings, communication breakdowns, alienation in working relationships, destructive and retaliatory behaviors, nonproductive efforts, and problem-solving failures. When such problems arise in organizations, everyone is prone to blame everyone else for what is not working.[36] The defensive responses of counterattack or sheepish withdrawal derail communication. Such responses tend to lend heat, not light, to the communication. An examination of eight defensive tactics follows the discussion of the two basic patterns of defensiveness in the next section.

Nondefensive communication, in contrast, provides a basis for asserting and defending oneself when attacked, without being defensive. There are appropriate ways to defend oneself against aggression, attack, or abuse. An assertive, nondefensive style restores order, balance, and effectiveness in working relationships. A discussion of nondefensive communication follows the discussion of defensive communication.

Defensive Communication at Work

defensive communication
Communication that can be aggressive, attacking, and angry, or passive and withdrawing.

nondefensive communication
Communication that is assertive, direct, and powerful.

Defensive communication often elicits defensive communication in response. The two basic patterns of defensiveness are dominant defensiveness and subordinate defensiveness. One must be able to recognize various forms of defensive communication before learning to engage in constructive, nondefensive communication. You 8.2 helps you examine your defensive communication. Complete it before reading the following text material.

What Kind of a Defender Are You?

Not all of our communication is defensive, but each of us has a tendency to engage in either subordinate or dominant defensiveness. The following table presents twelve sets of choices that will help you see whether you tend to be more subordinate or dominant when you communicate defensively.

Complete the questionnaire by allocating 10 points between the two alternatives in each of the twelve rows. For example, if you never ask permission when it is not needed, but you do give or deny permission frequently, you may give yourself 0 and 10 points, respectively, in the third row. However, if you do each of these behaviors about equally, though at different times, you may want to give yourself 5 points for each alternative.

Add your total points for each column. Whichever number is larger identifies your defensive style.

Subordinate Defensiveness	Dominant Defensiveness
____ Explain, prove, justify your actions, ideas, or feelings more than is required for results wanted.	____ Prove that you're right. *I told you so. Now see, that proves my point.*
____ Ask why things are done the way they are, when you really want to change them. *Why don't they . . . ?*	____ Give patient explanations but few answers. *It's always been done this way. We tried that before, but . . .*
____ Ask permission when not needed. *Is it okay with you if . . . ?*	____ Give or deny permission. *Oh, I couldn't let you do that.*
____ Give away decisions, ideas, or power when it would be appropriate to claim them as your own. *Don't you think that . . . ?*	____ Make decisions or take power as your natural right. *The best way to do it is . . . Don't argue, just do as I say.*
____ Apologize, feel inadequate, say *I'm sorry* when you're not.	____ Prod people to get the job done. *Don't just stand there . . .*
____ Submit or withdraw when it's not in your best interest. *Whatever you say . . .*	____ Take over a situation or decision even when it's delegated; get arbitrary. *My mind is made up.*
____ Lose your cool, lash out, cry where it's inappropriate (turning your anger toward yourself).	____ Lose your cool, yell, pound the desk where it's inappropriate (turning your anger toward others).
____ Go blank, click off, be at a loss for words just when you want to have a ready response. *I should've said . . .* (afterwards)	____ Shift responsibility for something you should have taken care of yourself. *You've always done it before. What're you all of a sudden upset for now?*
____ Use coping humor, hostile jocularity, or put yourself down when "buying time" or honest feedback would get better results. *Why don't you lay off?*	____ Use coping humor, baiting, teasing, hostile jocularity, mimicry to keep other people off balance so you don't have to deal with them. *What's the matter, can't you take it?*
____ Use self-deprecating adjectives and reactive verbs. *I'm just a . . . I'm just doing what I was told.*	____ Impress others with how many important people you know. *The other night at Bigname's party when I was talking to . . .*
____ Use the general *you* and *they* when *I* and personal names would state the situation more clearly. *They really hassle you here.*	____ Don't listen: interpret. Catch the idea of what they're saying, then list rebuttals or redefine their point. *Now what you really mean is . . .*
____ Smile to cover up feelings or put yourself down since you don't know what else to do and it's nice.	____ Use verbal dominance, if necessary, to make your point. Don't let anyone interrupt what you have to say.
____ TOTAL Subordinate Points	____ TOTAL Dominant Points

Subordinate Defensiveness Subordinate defensiveness is characterized by passive, submissive, withdrawing behavior. The psychological attitude of the subordinately defensive person is "You are right, and I am wrong." People with low self-esteem may be prone to this form of defensive behavior, as well as people at lower organizational levels. When people at lower levels fear sending bad news up the organization, information that is sensitive and critical to organizational performance may be lost.[37] People who are subordinately defensive do not adequately assert their thoughts and feelings in the workplace. Passive-aggressive behavior is a form of defensiveness that begins as subordinate defensiveness and ends up as dominant defensiveness. It is behavior that appears very passive but, in fact, masks underlying aggression and hostility.

Dominant Defensiveness Dominant defensiveness is characterized by active, aggressive, attacking behavior. It is offensive in nature: "The best defense is a good offense." The psychological attitude of the dominantly defensive person is "I am right, and you are wrong." People who compensate for low self-esteem may exhibit this pattern of behavior, as well as people who are in higher-level positions within the organizational hierarchy.

Junior officers in a regional banking organization described such behavior in the bank chairman, euphemistically called "The Finger." When giving orders or admonishing someone, he would point his index finger in a domineering, intimidating, emphatic manner that caused defensiveness on the part of the recipient.

Defensive Tactics

Unfortunately, defensive tactics are all too common in work organizations. Eight major defensive tactics are summarized in Table 8.2. They might be best understood in the context of a work situation: Joe is in the process of completing a critical report for his boss, and the deadline is drawing near. Mary, one of Joe's peers at work, is to

TABLE 8.2 Defensive Tactics

Defensive Tactic	Speaker	Work Example
Power play	The boss	"Finish this report by month's end or lose your promotion."
Put-down	The boss	"A capable manager would already be done with this report."
Labeling	The boss	"You must be a slow learner. Your report is still not done?"
Raising doubts	The boss	"How can I trust you, Joe, if you can't finish an easy report?"
Misleading	Joe	"Mary has not gone over with me the information I need from her for the report." (She left him a copy.)
Scapegoating	Joe	"Mary did not give me her input until just today."
Hostile jokes	Joe	"You can't be serious! The report isn't that important."
Deception	Joe	"I gave it to the secretary. Did she lose it?"

provide him with some input for the report, and the department secretary is to prepare a final copy of it. Each work example in the table is related to this situation.

Until defensiveness and defensive tactics are recognized for what they are, it is difficult either to change them or to respond to them in nondefensive ways. Defensive tactics are how defensive communication is acted out. In many cases, such tactics raise ethical dilemmas and issues for those involved. For example, is it ethical to raise doubts about another person's values, beliefs, or sexuality? At what point does simple defensiveness become unethical behavior?

Power plays are used by people to control and manipulate others through the use of choice definition (defining the choice another person is allowed to make), either/or conditions, and overt aggression. The underlying dynamic in power plays is that of domination and control.

A put-down is an effort by the speaker to gain the upper hand in the relationship. Intentionally ignoring another person or pointing out his or her mistakes in a meeting are kinds of put-downs.

Labeling is often used to portray another person as abnormal or deficient. Psychological labels are often used out of context for this purpose, such as calling a person "paranoid," a word that has a specific, clinical meaning.

Raising doubts about a person's abilities, values, preferential orientations, or other aspects of her or his life creates confusion and uncertainty. This tactic tends to lack the specificity and clarity present in labeling.

Giving misleading information is the selective presentation of information designed to leave a false and inaccurate impression in the listener's mind. It is not the same as lying or misinforming. Giving misleading information is one form of deception.

Scapegoating and its companion, buck-passing, are methods of shifting responsibility to the wrong person. Blaming other people is another form of scapegoating or buck-passing.

Hostile jokes should not be confused with good humor, which is both therapeutic and nondefensive. Jokes created at the expense of others are destructive and hostile.

Deception may occur through a variety of means, such as lying or creating an impression or image that is at variance with the truth. Deception can be very useful in military operations, but it can be a destructive force in work organizations.

Nondefensive Communication

Nondefensive communication is a constructive, healthy alternative to defensive communication in working relationships. The person who communicates nondefensively may be characterized as centered, assertive, controlled, informative, realistic, and honest. Nondefensive communication is powerful, because the speaker is exhibiting self-control and self-possession without rejecting the listener. Converting defensive patterns of communication to nondefensive ones enhances relationship building at work. Relationship building behaviors and communication help reduce adverse responses, such as blame and anger, following negative events at work.[38]

The subordinately defensive person needs to learn to be more assertive. This can be done in many ways, of which two examples follow. First, instead of asking for permission to do something, report what you intend to do and invite confirmation. Second, instead of using self-deprecating words, such as "I'm just following orders," drop the *just,* and convert the message into a self-assertive, declarative statement. Nondefensive communication should be self-affirming without being self-aggrandizing. Some people overcompensate for subordinate defensiveness and inadvertently become domineering.

The person prone to be domineering and dominantly defensive needs to learn to be less aggressive. This may be especially difficult because it requires overcoming the person's sense of "I am right." People who are working to overcome dominant

Cross Your Arms . . . and Get the Job Done

Nonverbal behaviors play an integral role in the way individuals convey their thoughts, feelings, and intentions to others; evidence of this dates back as far as the work of Charles Darwin in the late 1870s. This research focused on the behavior of arm crossing and its effect on persistence and subsequent performance. For example, think of the posture of seven-time basketball championship titleholder Pat Riley who paced the National Basketball Association's Miami Heat sidelines as coach. His highly distinctive pose included arms crossed tightly around his chest, his chin jutting outward, and his shoulders spread wide. His posture sends the clear message: "I am going to persevere." The investigators in this research conducted two experiments to test the effect of arm crossing on persistence and performance. In Experiment 1, inducing participants to cross their arms led to greater persistence on an unsolvable anagram. In Experiment 2, inducing participants to cross their arms led to better performance on solvable anagrams and the better performance was mediated by persistence. Hence, arm crossing does lead to persistence that in turn leads to better performance. An interesting side note in this research was the fact that participants appeared to be unaware of the effect of their arm-crossing behavior. The authors conclude that one's body posture and position do inform internal subjective experience and consequently influence behavior. Riley's message was clear and the effects evident in the seven championship titles.

Miami Heat Head Coach Pat Riley has a highly distinctive pose, with arms crossed tightly around his chest and chin jutting outward. His posture says, 'I am going to persevere.'

SOURCE: R. Friedman and A. J. Elliott, "The Effect of Arm Crossing on Persistence and Performance," *European Journal of Social Psychology* (in press).

defensiveness should be particularly sensitive to feedback from others about their behavior. There are many ways to change this pattern of behavior. Here are two examples. First, instead of giving and denying permission, give people free rein except in situations where permission is essential as a means of clearing approval or ensuring the security of the task. Second, instead of becoming inappropriately angry, provide information about the adverse consequences of a particular course of action.

NONVERBAL COMMUNICATION

Much defensive and nondefensive communication focuses on the language used. However, most of the meaning in a message (an estimated 65 to 90 percent) is conveyed through nonverbal communication.[39] *Nonverbal communication* includes all elements of communication, such as gestures and the use of space, that do not involve words or language.[40] The four basic kinds of nonverbal communication are proxemics, kinesics, facial and eye behavior, and paralanguage. They are important topics for managers attempting to understand the types and meanings of nonverbal signals from employees. Nonverbal communication is influenced by both psychological and physiological processes.[41]

nonverbal communication
All elements of communication that do not involve words.

Some of the scientific research in nonverbal communication is interesting, as we see in the Science feature. In any case, the interpretation of nonverbal communication is specific to the context of the interaction and the actors. That is, nonverbal cues only give meaning in the context of the situation and the interaction of the actors. For example, some federal and state judges attempt to curb nonverbal communication in the courtroom. The judges' primary concern is that nonverbal behavior may unfairly influence jurors' decisions. It is also important to note that nonverbal behavior is culturally bound. Gestures, facial expressions, and body locations have different meanings in different cultures. The globalization of business means managers should be sensitive to the nonverbal customs of other cultures in which they do business.

Proxemics

The study of an individual's perception and use of space, including territorial space, is called *proxemics*.[42] *Territorial space* refers to bands of space extending outward from the body. These bands constitute comfort zones. In each comfort zone, different cultures prefer different types of interaction with others. Figure 8.2 presents four zones of territorial space based on U.S. culture.

The first zone, intimate space, extends outward from the body to about 1½ feet. In this zone, we interact with spouses, significant others, family members, and others with whom we have an intimate relationship. The next zone, the personal distance zone, extends from 1½ feet outward to 4 feet. Friends typically interact within this distance. The third zone, the social distance zone, spans the distance from 4 to 12 feet. We prefer that business associates and acquaintances interact with us in this zone. The final zone is the public distance zone, extending 12 feet from the body outward. Most of us prefer that strangers stay at least 12 feet from us, and we become uncomfortable when they move closer.

FIGURE 8.2 Zones of Territorial Space in U.S. Culture

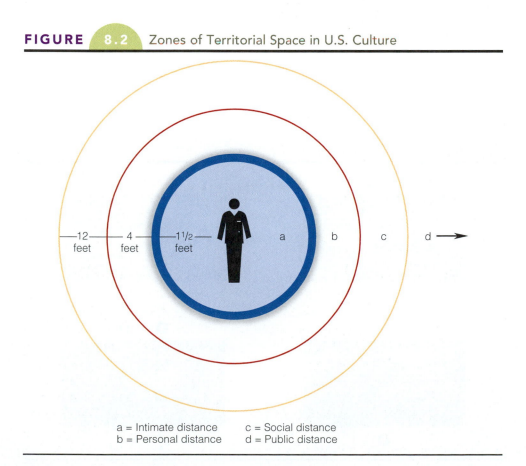

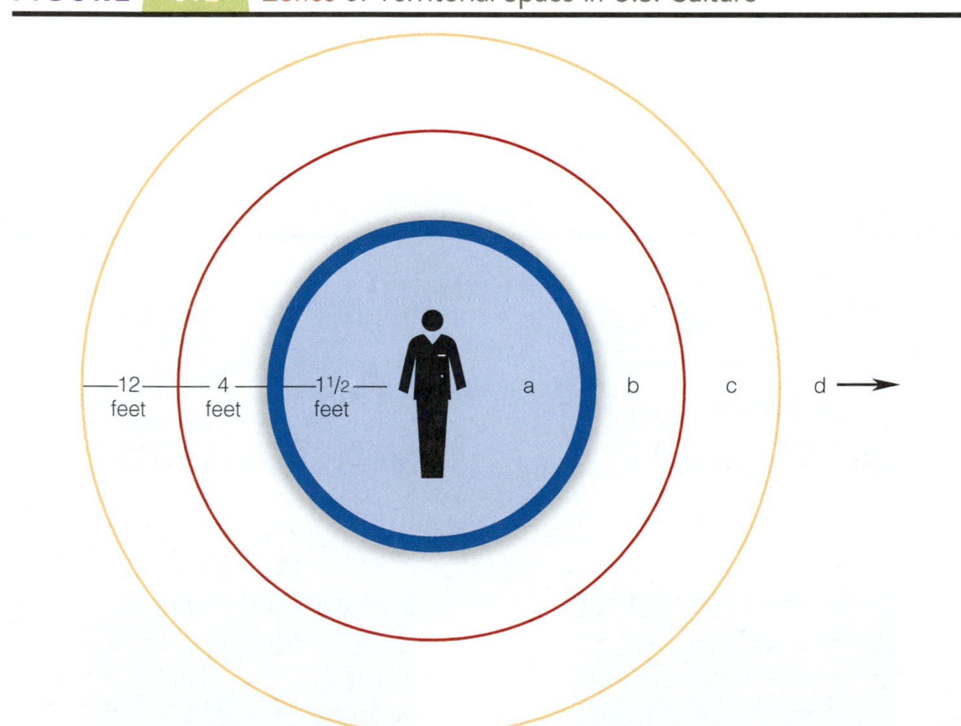

Territorial space varies greatly across cultures. People often become uncomfortable when operating in territorial spaces different from those with which they are familiar. Edward Hall, a leading proxemics researcher, says Americans working in the Middle East tend to back away to a comfortable conversation distance when interacting with Arabs. Because Arabs' comfortable conversation distance is closer than that of Americans, Arabs perceive Americans as cold and aloof. One Arab wondered, "What's the matter? Does he find me somehow offensive?"[43] Personal space tends to be larger in cultures with cool climates, such as the United States, Great Britain, and northern Europe, and smaller in cultures with warm climates, such as southern Europe, the Caribbean, India, or South America.[44]

Our relationships shape our use of territorial space. For example, we hold hands with, or put an arm around, significant others to pull them into intimate space. Conversely, the use of territorial space can shape people's interactions. A 4-foot-wide business desk pushes business interactions into the social distance zone. An exception occurred for one SBC manager who met with her seven first-line supervisors around her desk. Being elbow to elbow placed the supervisors in one another's intimate and personal space. They appeared to act more like friends and frequently talked about their children, favorite television shows, and other personal concerns. When the manager moved the staff meeting to a larger room and the spaces around each supervisor were in the social distance zone, the personal exchanges ceased, and they acted more like business associates again.

Seating dynamics, another aspect of proxemics, is the art of seating people in certain positions according to their purpose in communication. Caribou Coffee takes advantage of this through the use of their adaptable table designs, noted earlier. Figure 8.3 depicts some common seating dynamics. To encourage cooperation, you should seat the other party beside you, facing the same direction. To facilitate direct and open communication, seat the other party across a corner of your desk from you or in another place where you will be at right angles. This allows for more honest disclosure. To take a competitive stand with someone, position the person directly across from you. Suppose you hold a meeting around a conference table, and two of the attendees are disrupting it. Where should you seat them? If you place one on each side of yourself, it should stifle the disruptions (unless one is so bold as to lean in front of you to keep chatting).

FIGURE 8.3 Seating Dynamics

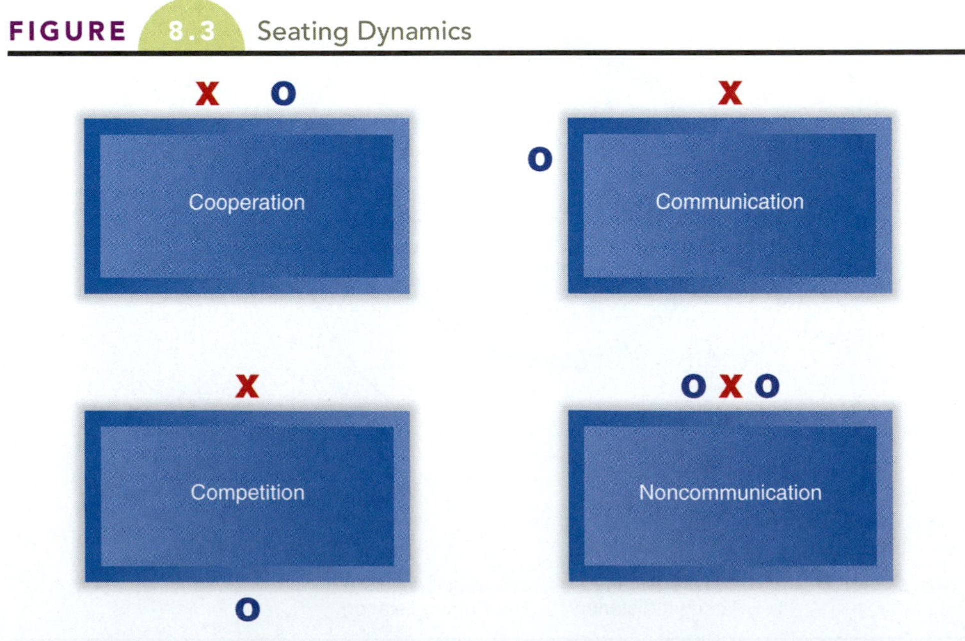

Kinesics

Kinesics is the study of body movements, including posture.[45] Like proxemics, kinesics is culturally bound; there is no single universal gesture. For example, the U.S. hand signal for "okay" is an insult in other countries. With this in mind, we can interpret some common U.S. gestures. Rubbing one's hands together or exhibiting a sharp intake of breath indicates anticipation. Stress is indicated by a closed hand position (that is, tight fists), hand wringing, or rubbing the temples. Nervousness may be displayed through drumming fingers, pacing, or jingling coins in the pocket. Perhaps most fun to watch is preening behavior, seen most often in couples on a first date. Preening communicates "I want to look good for you" to the other party and consists of smoothing skirts, straightening the tie, or arranging the hair. No discussion of gestures would be complete without mention of insult gestures—some learned at an early age, much to the anxiety of parents. Sticking out one's tongue while waving fingers with one's thumbs in the ears is a common childhood insult gesture.

Facial and Eye Behavior

The face is a rich source of nonverbal communication. Facial expression and eye behavior are used to add cues for the receiver. The face may give unintended clues to emotions the sender is trying to hide. Dynamic facial actions and expressions in a person's appearance are key clues of truthfulness, especially in deception situations.[46] In legal proceedings, laypeople and professionals alike assume nonverbal behaviors, such as avoiding eye contact, are displayed while lying. However, research found support for only three nonverbal behaviors in regard to lying: nodding, foot and leg movements, and hand movements.[47]

Although smiles have universal meaning, frowns, raised eyebrows, and wrinkled foreheads must all be interpreted in conjunction with the actors, the situation, and the culture. One study of Japanese and U.S. students illustrates the point. The students were shown a stress-inducing film, and their facial expressions were videotaped. When alone, the students had almost identical expressions. However, the Japanese students masked their facial expressions of unpleasant feelings much better than did the American students when another person was present.[48]

As mentioned earlier, eye contact can enhance reflective listening and, along with smiling, is one good way of displaying positive emotion.[49] However, eye contact must be understood in a cultural context. A direct gaze indicates honesty, truthfulness, and forthrightness in the United States. This may not be true in other cultures. For example, Barbara Walters was uncomfortable interviewing Muammar al-Qaddafi in Libya because he did not look directly at her. However, in Libya, it is a serious offense to look directly at a woman.[50] In Asian cultures it is considered good behavior to bow the head in deference to a superior rather than to look in the supervisor's eyes.

Paralanguage

Paralanguage consists of variations in speech, such as pitch, loudness, tempo, tone, duration, laughing, and crying.[51] People make attributions about the sender by deciphering paralanguage cues. A high-pitched, breathy voice in a female may contribute to the stereotype of the "dumb blonde." Rapid, loud speech may be taken as a sign of nervousness or anger. Interruptions such as "mmm" and "ah-hah" may be used to speed up the speaker so that the receiver can get in a few words. Clucking of the tongue or the "tsk-tsk" sound is used to shame someone. All these cues relate to how something is said.

How Accurately Do We Decode Nonverbal Cues?

People's confidence in their ability to decode nonverbal communication is greater than their accuracy in doing so. Judges with several years' experience in interviewing were asked in one study to watch videotapes of job applicants and to rate the

TABLE 8.3 Common Nonverbal Cues from Manager to Employee

Nonverbal Communication	Signal Received	Reaction from Receiver
Manager looks away when talking to the employee.	Divided attention	My supervisor is too busy to listen to my problem or simply does not care.
Manager fails to acknowledge greeting from fellow employee.	Unfriendliness	This person is unapproachable.
Manager glares ominously (i.e., gives the evil eye).	Anger	Reciprocal anger, fear, or avoidance, depending on who is sending the signal in the organization.
Manager rolls the eyes.	Not taking person seriously	This person thinks he or she is smarter or better than I am.
Manager sighs deeply.	Disgust or displeasure	My opinions do not count. I must be stupid or boring to this person.
Manager uses heavy breathing (sometimes accompanied by hand waving).	Anger or heavy stress	Avoid this person at all costs.
Manager does not maintain eye contact when communicating.	Suspicion or uncertainty	What does this person have to hide?
Manager crosses arms and leans away.	Apathy or closed-mindedness	This person already has made up his or her mind; my opinions are not important.
Manager peers over glasses.	Skepticism or distrust	He or she does not believe what I am saying.
Manager continues to read a report when employee is speaking.	Lack of interest	My opinions are not important enough to get the supervisor's undivided attention.

SOURCE: From "Steps to Better Listening" by C. Hamilton and B. H. Kleiner.

applicants' social skills and motivation levels.[52] The judges were fairly accurate about the social skills, but not about motivation. They relied on smiling, gesturing, and speaking as cues to motivation, yet none of these cues are motivation indicators. Thus, incorrectly interpreting nonverbal codes leads to inaccuracy.

Studies of deception emphasize how to use nonverbal cues to interpret whether someone is lying. In one simulation study, customers were asked to detect whether or not automobile salespeople were lying. The customers' ability to detect lies in this study was no better than chance. Does this suggest that salespeople are skilled deceivers who control nonverbal behaviors to prevent detection?[53]

Paul Ekman, a psychologist who has trained judges, Secret Service agents, and polygraphers to detect lies, says that the best way to detect lies is to look for inconsistencies in the nonverbal cues. Rapidly shifting facial expressions and discrepancies between the person's words and body, voice, or facial expressions are some clues.[54]

Nonverbal communication is important for managers because of its impact on the meaning of the message. However, a manager must consider the total message and all media of communication. A message can only be given meaning in context, and cues are easy to misinterpret. Table 8.3 presents common nonverbal behaviors exhibited by managers and how employees may interpret them. Nonverbal cues can give others the wrong signal.

(6) Explain positive, healthy communication.

POSITIVE, HEALTHY COMMUNICATION

communicative disease
The absence of heartfelt communication in human relationships leading to loneliness and social isolation.

The absence of heartfelt communication in human relationships leads to loneliness and social isolation and has been labeled *communicative disease* by James Lynch.[55] Communicative disease has adverse effects on the heart and cardiovascular system and can ultimately lead to premature death. According to Lynch, heartfelt communication is a healing dialogue and central antidote for communicative disease. Positive, healthy communication is central to health and well-being. While communication may often be thought of as a cognitive activity of the head, Lynch suggests that the heart may be more important in the communications process.

Positive, healthy communication is one important aspect of working together when the term *working together* is taken for its intrapersonal meaning as well as its interpersonal meaning.[56] The balance between head and heart is achieved when a person displays positive emotional competence and is able to have a healthy internal conversation between his or her thoughts and feelings, ideas, and emotions. In addition, working together occurs when there are cooperative work behaviors between people based on positive, healthy, and open communication that is in turn based on trust and truthfulness. Honest competition within the workplace is not inconsistent with this notion of working together; forthright, well-managed, honest competition can bring out the best in all those involved.

Positive, healthy communication is at the core of personal integrity as displayed by healthy executives.[57] Former President Ronald Reagan was a great communicator who displayed strong ethical character, personal integrity, and simplicity in his communication. He exemplified communication from the heart in the sense that his messages came from his core values, beliefs, and aspirations for himself and others. His optimism shone through from the core of his person, displaying a continuing positive attitude that drew even his opponents to like him. Communication from core values and beliefs is communication anchored in personal integrity and ethical character.

Personal integrity in positive, healthy communication is achieved through emotional competence and the head-to-heart dialogue mentioned earlier. In addition to the public self, as is familiar in the case of Ronald Reagan, all executives have a private self. Karol Wasylyshyn has shown that one dimension of coaching star executives is to enhance their emotional competence and capacity to talk through challenging issues, both personally and professionally.[58] Quick and Macik-Frey focus on the private-self aspect of positive, healthy communication in developing their model of executive coaching through deep interpersonal communication.[59] This model relies on what Lynch might call a healing dialogue between executive and coach. However, their model of deep interpersonal communication is one that can enhance positive, healthy communication in a wider range of human relationships.

COMMUNICATING THROUGH NEW TECHNOLOGIES

7 Describe Information Communication Technology (ICT) used by managers.

Nonverbal behaviors can be important in establishing trust in working relationships, but modern technologies may challenge our ability to maintain that trust. In Thinking Ahead, we saw that Caribou Coffee took advantage of IBM's power in information technology in part because they trusted them. Many organizations around the world are now plugging into the Internet, which allows for the easy transfer of information and data across continents. The Real World 8.2 presents three corporate models of alternative e-mail management to improve employee communication. Managers in today's business world have access to more communication tools than ever before. All of these new technologies are, surprisingly, having relatively little impact on work culture. In addition, security concerns since 9/11 have complicated wireless access. An understanding of the use of these new technologies facilitates effective, successful communication. In addition, it is important to understand how these new technologies affect others' communication and behavior. Finally, information technology can encourage or discourage moral dialogue, and moral conversations are central to addressing ethical issues at work.[60]

THE REAL WORLD 8.2

E-mail is Dead . . . at Capital One, at Union Bank, at Reuters

In the beginning, it was exciting to receive new e-mails, but those days are long gone for most employees. Because of the glut of e-mails in so many inboxes, corporations are seeking ways to minimize the waste of resources associated with it. The Capital One model for addressing the e-mail problem is to teach employees, who receive an average of 40 or 50 messages per day, how to write better messages and subject lines. Over 3,000 employees have gone through a specially designed workshop for writing better e-mail messages, and the company estimates an eleven-day per year savings per employee as a result. Union Bank in California has used a different model. Rather than carpet-bombing all 10,000 employees with all kinds of informational e-mails, the bank has developed a targeting strategy that employs RSS Web feeds. The new system is called KnowNow and aims to send information only to the employees in jobs and locations that need it. Union's conservative savings estimate with KnowNow is in excess of $750,000 annually. The third model, developed by Reuters, supplements e-mail messaging with Instant Messaging (IM). By using IM in the appropriate context and for the right issues, such as scheduling meetings or places, Reuters has found that a whole string of back-and-forth e-mails never happen. Each of these three corporate models for e-mail management improves communication and reduces inbox clutter.

SOURCE: D. Beizer, "Email Is Dead," *Fast Company* 117 (July/August 2007): 46.

Written Communication

Many organizations are working toward paperless offices and paperless interfaces with their customers. Some written communication is still required, however. Forms are one category of written communication. Manuals are another. Policy manuals are important in organizations because they set out guidelines for decision making and rules of actions for organizational members. Operations and procedures manuals explain how to perform various tasks and resolve problems that may occur at work. Reports are a third category of written communication; company annual reports are an example. Reports may summarize the results of a committee's or department's work or provide information on progress toward certain objectives.

Letters and memorandums are briefer, more frequently used categories of written communication in organizations. Letters are a formal means of communication—often with people outside the organization—and may vary substantially in length. Memorandums are another formal means of communication, often to constituencies within the organization. Memos are sometimes used to create a formal, historical record of a specific event or occurrence to which people in the organization may want to refer at some future date. Looking back at Table 8.1, we can conclude that written communication has the advantage of high to moderate data capacity and the possible disadvantage of moderate to low information richness.

An understanding of the use of new technologies, such as the Apple iPhone, influences effective, successful communication.

© AP PHOTO/MANUEL BALCE CENETA

Communication Technologies

Computer-mediated communication was once used only by technical specialists but now influences virtually all managers' behavior in the work environment. Informational databases are becoming more commonplace. These databases provide a tremendous amount of information with the push of a button. Another example of an informational database is the type of system used in many university libraries, in which books and journals are available through an electronic card catalog.

Electronic mail systems represent another technology; users can leave messages via the computer to be accessed at any time by the receiver. This eliminates the time delay of regular mail and allows for immediate reply. Research comparing e-mail to face-to-face communication on choices individuals make found that the effects vary with the nature of the decisions and may depend on the complexity and content of what needs to be communicated.[61] Thus, e-mail has strengths and advantages in communication as well as limitations with which to exercise caution. Unfortunately, some people feel much less inhibited when using e-mail and end up sending caustic messages they would never consider saying in person. The MoodWatch software system helps guard against "flaming" e-mails by notifying users if their message contains hostile, abusive, or bullying content (flames). The bottom line is that people cannot communicate as effectively over e-mail as they think.[62] In addition and on a positive note, there are also devices that enable international e-mail users to have their messages translated to and from French, German, Spanish, Portuguese, and English.

Voice mail systems are another widely used communication mode, especially in sales jobs where people are away from the office. Voice behavior influences the quality of the work environment. This has implications for the quality of voice mail as well. Some voice mail systems allow the user to retrieve messages from remote locations. Timely retrieval of messages is important. One manager in the office furniture industry had a problem with her voice mail when first learning to use it. She would forget to check it until late in the day. Employees with problems early in the day felt frustrated with her slow response time. When using voice mail, it is important to remember that the receiver may not retrieve the messages in a timely manner. Urgent messages must be delivered directly.

Facsimile (fax) machine systems allow the immediate transmission of documents. This medium allows the sender to communicate facts, graphs, and illustrations very rapidly. Fax machines are used in cars as well as offices and remote locations.

Cell phones are also commonplace, permitting communication while away from the office and on the commute to and from work. They are used extensively in sales jobs involving travel. Not all reactions to car phones are positive. For example, one oil producer did not want his thinking time while driving disturbed by a cell phone. Using a cell phone while driving is also risky, with some estimates suggesting it is as risky as driving under the influence of alcohol. For this reason, some states have outlawed the use of cell phones while driving a motor vehicle.

How Do Communication Technologies Affect Behavior?

Information Communication Technology (ICT) offers faster, more immediate access to information than was available in the past. It provides instant exchange of information in minutes or seconds across geographic boundaries and time zones. Schedules and office hours become irrelevant. The normal considerations of time and distance become less important in the exchange. Hence, these technologies have important influences on people's behavior.

One aspect of computer-mediated communication is its impersonal nature. The sender interacts with a machine, not a person. As mentioned earlier, studies show that using these technologies results in an increase in flaming, or making rude or obscene outbursts by computer.[63] Interpersonal skills like tact and graciousness diminish, and managers are more blunt when using electronic media. People who participate in discussions quietly and politely when face to face may become impolite, more intimate, and uninhibited when they communicate using computer conferencing or e-mail.[64]

Information Communication Technology (ICT)
The various new technologies, such as e-mail, voice mail, teleconferencing, and wireless access, which are used for interpersonal communication.

Another effect of the new technologies is that the nonverbal cues we rely on to decipher a message are absent. Gesturing, touching, facial expressions, and eye contact are not available, so the emotional element of the message is difficult to access. In addition, clues to power, such as organizational position and departmental membership, may not be available, so the social context of the exchange is altered.

Communication via technologies also changes group interaction. It tends to equalize participation, because group members participate more equally, and charismatic or higher-status members may have less power.[65] Studies of groups that make decisions via computer interaction (computer-mediated groups) have shown that the computer-mediated groups took longer to reach consensus than face-to-face groups. In addition, they were more uninhibited, and there was less influence from any one dominant person. It appears that groups that communicate by computer experience a breakdown of social and organizational barriers.

The potential for overload is particularly great with the new communication technologies. Not only is information available more quickly, the sheer volume of information at the manager's fingertips also is staggering. An individual can easily become overwhelmed by information and must learn to be selective in accessing it.

A paradox created by the new, modern communication technology lies in the danger it may pose for managers. The danger is that managers cannot get away from the office as much as in the past, because they are more accessible to coworkers, subordinates, and the boss via telecommunications. Interactions are no longer confined to the 9 to 5 work hours.

In addition, the use of new technologies encourages polyphasic activity (that is, doing more than one thing at a time). Managers can simultaneously make phone calls, send computer messages, and work on memos. Polyphasic activity has its advantages in terms of getting more done—but only up to a point. Paying attention to more than one task at a time splits a person's attention and may reduce effectiveness. Constantly focusing on multiple tasks can become a habit, making it psychologically difficult for a person to let go of work.

Finally, the new technologies may make people less patient with face-to-face communication. The speed advantage of the electronic media may translate into an expectation of greater speed in all forms of communication. However, individuals may miss the social interaction with others and may find their social needs unmet. Communicating via computer means an absence of small talk; people tend to get to the point right away.

With many of these technologies, the potential for immediate feedback is reduced, and the exchange can become one-way. Managers can use the new technologies more effectively by keeping the following hints in mind:

1. Strive for completeness in your message.
2. Build in opportunities for feedback.
3. Do not assume you will get an immediate response.
4. Ask yourself if the communication is really necessary.
5. "Disconnect" yourself from the technology at regular intervals.
6. Provide opportunities for social interaction at work.

MANAGERIAL IMPLICATIONS: COMMUNICATE WITH STRENGTH AND CLARITY

Interpersonal communication is important for the quality of working relationships in organizations. Managers who are sensitive and responsive in communicating with employees encourage the development of trusting, loyal relationships. Managers and

DIVERSITY DIALOGUE

Don Imus: Cross-Cultural Miscommunication or Insensitivity?

When Don Imus referred to members of the Rutgers University women's basketball team as "nappy-headed hos," he ignited a firestorm of criticism from a wide variety of sources including the NAACP and the National Organization for Women—culminating in his dismissal from the *Imus in the Morning* radio show.

As a result of Imus's remarks, six of ten of the nation's largest advertisers pulled their support from the show, putting MSNBC's $163 million-plus in total annual advertising revenue at risk. As the owners of the radio station that originated the Imus broadcast, NBC and CBS were responsible for taking any disciplinary action against the host. First NBC, then CBS fired Imus and yanked his program off the air. According to NBC CEO Jeff Zucker, this was done to preserve the organization's strong reputation for integrity, not due to pressure from advertisers.

By the time he was fired in 2007, the 66-year-old Imus had been no stranger to pushing the envelope. In fact, former *60 Minutes* host Mike Wallace termed *Imus in the Morning* as "dirty and sometimes racist" back in 1998. Similar to those of other radio shock jocks such as Howard Stern and Opie & Andy, the show regularly included talk that seemed to some like social satire but to others more like racism and sexism. Many wondered why it took his employers so long to discipline him.

1. Should organizations be held responsible for their employees' communications? Discuss any factors that might enhance or diminish their level of responsibility.
2. Were NBC and CBS justified in ending *Imus in the Morning*? Why or why not?

SOURCE: B. Steinberg, B. Barnes, and E. Steel, "Facing Ad Defection, NBC Takes Don Imus Show Off TV," *The Wall Street Journal* (April 12, 2007): B1; A. Neuharth, "Does Imus' Trash Talk Hurt First Amendment?," *USA Today* (April 12, 2007), http://www.usatoday.com/news/opinion/columnist/neuharth/2007-04-12-imus_N.htm.

employees alike benefit from secure working relations. Managers who are directive, dictatorial, or overbearing with employees, in contrast, are likely to find such behavior counterproductive, especially in periods of change.

Encouraging feedback and practicing reflective listening skills at work can open up communication channels in the work environment. Open communication benefits decision-making processes, because managers are better informed and more likely to base decisions on complete information. Open communication encourages nondefensive relationships, as opposed to defensive relationships, among people at work. Defensive relationships create problems because of the use of tactics that trigger conflict and division among people.

Managers benefit from sensitivity to employees' nonverbal behavior and territorial space, recognizing that understanding individual and cultural diversity is important in interpreting a person's nonverbal behavior. Seeking verbal clarification on nonverbal cues improves the accuracy of the communication and helps build trusting relationships. In addition, managers benefit from an awareness of their own nonverbal behaviors. Seeking employee feedback about their own nonverbal behavior helps managers provide a message consistent with their intentions.

Managers may complement good interpersonal contact with the appropriate use of new information technology. New information technologies' high data capacity is an advantage in a global workplace. The high information richness of interpersonal contacts is an advantage in a culturally diverse workforce. Therefore, managers benefit from both interpersonal and technological media by treating them as complementary modes of communication, not as substitutes for each other.

LOOKING BACK: CARIBOU COFFEE

A Cup of Coffee . . . and Wandering Wi-Fi

Caribou Coffee aims to do more than deliver a cup of coffee and the accoutrements; it also hopes to build and deepen relationships with its customers. One way to achieve this is though advanced communication technology, and in particular, Wi-Fi. Caribou designed its Wi-Fi program to accommodate the needs of the vast majority of its customers who average less than one hour per user session. The company's participating coffeehouses offer connectivity without the complicated hassle of a lengthy login or credit card process, thus recognizing its customers' desire for convenience. The program is about simplicity and privacy, with the intention of making each experience in one of their coffeehouses a memorable one. In addition, it is intended to deepen the customer relationship by using a Caribou Coffee–branded network page where customers can register, receive coupons, and purchase premium items.

Caribou Coffee chose Wandering WiFi as the partner to provide this service. Wandering WiFi, which was founded "by wanderers for wanderers," is one of the leading wireless HotSpot and corporate wireless infrastructure solution providers in the United States. The company deploys customized wireless solutions for over 500 corporate customers across the country, with locations including airports, cafes, hotels, condos and resorts, retail outlets, and corporate offices. Their strategy is a turnkey one that encompasses hardware, industry-leading software, technical support, and individualized customer experiences. As in the case of the partnership with IBM, Caribou sought a partner for its Wi-Fi program that was technically on the cutting edge while being trustworthy in its relationships.

Trustworthiness is important and "free" is not always free. Many locations worldwide offer wireless access yet are more dangerous than users might imagine. Some risks are as simple as the inconvenience and challenge of connecting or sending e-mails. More serious problems include viruses that may be communicated across the Internet via systems that are not well protected. Wandering WiFi distinguishes itself with safe and secure Internet access that offers convenient and easy access and use. Caribou's Wi-Fi program is additionally geared to the needs of its customers by providing free access during the first hour of use in a coffeehouse. If guests want another hour, Caribou gives them a Wi-Fi access code for the minimum store purchase of $1.50, or about the price of a small cup of coffee.[66]

Chapter Summary

1. The perceptual screens of communicators and listeners either help clarify or distort a message that is sent and received. Age, gender, and culture influence the sent and received messages.
2. Reflective listening involves affirming contact, paraphrasing what is expressed, clarifying the implicit, reflecting "core" feelings, and using appropriate nonverbal behavior to enhance communication.
3. The best supervisors talk easily with diverse groups of people, listen empathetically, are generally persuasive and not directive, are sensitive to a person's self-esteem, and are communication minded.
4. Physical separation, status differences, gender differences, cultural diversity, and language are potential communication barriers that can be overcome.
5. Active or passive defensive communication destroys interpersonal relationships, whereas assertive, nondefensive communication leads to clarity.
6. Nonverbal communication includes the use of territorial space, seating arrangements, facial gestures, eye contact, and paralanguage. Nonverbal communication varies by nation and culture around the world.
7. Communicative disease is the absence of heartfelt communication in human relationship and can lead to loneliness and social isolation.
8. Information Communication Technology (ICT) includes e-mail, voice mail, and cell phones. High-tech innovations require high-touch responses.

Key Terms

barriers to communication (p. 264)
communication (p. 256)
communicative disease (p. 274)
communicator (p. 257)
data (p. 258)
defensive communication (p. 266)
feedback (p. 257)
gateways to communication (p. 264)
information (p. 258)
Information Communication Technology (ICT) (p. 277)
interpersonal communication (p. 256)
language (p. 257)
message (p. 257)
nondefensive communication (p. 266)
nonverbal communication (p. 270)
one-way communication (p. 260)
perceptual screen (p. 257)
receiver (p. 257)
reflective listening (p. 258)
richness (p. 258)
two-way communication (p. 260)

Review Questions

1. What different components of a person's perceptual screens may distort communication?
2. What are the three defining features of reflective listening?
3. What are the four levels of verbal response in reflective listening?
4. Compare one-way and two-way communication.
5. What are the five communication skills of effective supervisors and managers?
6. Describe dominant and subordinate defensive communication. Describe nondefensive communication.
7. What four kinds of nonverbal communication are important in interpersonal relationships?
8. What are helpful nonverbal behaviors in the communication process? Unhelpful behaviors?
9. What is communicative disease?
10. Describe at least five new communication technologies in terms of data richness.

Discussion and Communication Questions

1. Who is the best communicator you know? Why do you consider that person to be so?
2. Who is the best listener you have ever known? Describe what that person does that makes him or her so good at listening.
3. What methods have you found most helpful in overcoming barriers to communication that are physical? Status-based? Cultural? Linguistic?
4. Who makes you the most defensive when you talk with that person? What does the person do that makes you so defensive or uncomfortable?

5. With whom are you the most comfortable and nondefensive in conversation? What does the person do that makes you so comfortable or nondefensive?
6. What nonverbal behaviors do you find most helpful in others when you are attempting to talk with them? When you try to listen to them?
7. *(communication question)* Identify a person at work or at school who is difficult to talk to and arrange an interview in which you practice good reflective listening skills. Ask the person questions about a topic you think may interest her or him. Pay particular attention to being patient, calm, and nonreactive. After the interview, summarize what you learned.
8. *(communication question)* Go to the library and read about communication problems and barriers. Write a memo categorizing the problems and barriers you find in current literature (last five years). What changes do organizations or people need to make to solve these problems?
9. *(communication question)* Develop a role-playing activity for class that demonstrates defensive (dominant or subordinate) and nondefensive communication. Write brief role descriptions that classmates can act out.
10. *(communication question)* Read everything you can find in the library about a new communication technology. Write a two-page memo summarizing what you have learned and the conclusions you draw about the new technology's advantages and disadvantages.

Ethical Dilemma

Pat Williams sat at her desk listening to the conversation in the next cubicle. She didn't want to listen, but it was impossible to miss. The discussion was between a coworker, Jake Timmons, and their supervisor, Mark Andersen. They were in a heated discussion about one of the company's biggest clients, Patel Manufacturing.

An executive from Patel had contacted Mark to tell him that Jake had not been giving them the attention such a large client deserved. He claimed that Jake did not return phone calls and often missed appointments. Mark was furious about the situation and was demanding an explanation. Jake tried to explain that he was doing everything he could to effectively manage the account, but the breakdown was on the other end. John, his contact at Patel, was the problem. He rarely responded to any of Jake's calls or e-mail. Jake had thought about reporting him but didn't want to get him in trouble with his manager.

Mark seemed not to hear a word Jake was saying. He simply continued to accuse Jake of endangering their most important customer. As Pat listened to this conversation, she considered whether or not she should get involved. It was obvious that Mark was not listening to anything Jake said. She had overheard Jake on several occasions trying to reach John without success. She could testify to that. But she had worked with John herself and had never experienced any problems. Also, she had only Jake's word for just how bad things were. She really didn't know Jake very well, and what if he was really slacking on his end and using John as an excuse? She didn't want to add to the disparaging comments about John if they weren't true. But she also didn't think it was fair that Mark was not giving any credit to what Jake was trying to explain. She didn't want to get Mark angry at her but felt she needed to support Jake in some way.

Questions

1. Does Pat have a duty to support Jake?
2. Does she have a responsibility to John?
3. Evaluate Pat's decision using consequential, rule-based, and character theories.

Experiential Exercises

8.1 Communicate, Listen, Understand

The following exercise gives you an opportunity to work within a three-person group to do a communication skill-building exercise. You can learn to apply some of the reflective listening and two-way communication materials from the early sections of the chapter, as well as some of the lessons managing difficult communication in a nondefensive manner.

Step 1. The class is formed into three-person groups and each group designates its members "A," "B," and "C." There will be three 5- to 7-minute conversations among the group members: first, between A and B; second, between B and C; third, between C and A. During each conversation, the nonparticipating group member is to observe and make notes about two communicating group members.

Step 2. Your instructor will give you a list of controversial topics and ask A to pick a topic. A is then asked to discuss her or his position on this topic, with the rationale for the position, with B. B is to practice reflective listening and engage in listening checks periodically by paraphrasing what he or she understands to be A's position. C should observe whether B is practicing good listening skills or becoming defensive. C should also observe whether A is becoming dominantly defensive in the communication. This should be a two-way communication.

Step 3. Repeat Step 2 with B as communicator, C as listener, and A as observer.

Step 4. Repeat Step 2 with C as communicator, A as listener, and B as observer.

Step 5. After your instructor has had all groups complete Steps 1 through 4, your three-person group should answer the following questions.

a. *Did either the listener or the communicator become visibly (or internally) angry or upset during the discussion?*

b. *What were the biggest challenges for the listeners in the controversial communication? For the communicator?*

c. *What are the most important skill improvements (e.g., better eye contact or more patience) the listener and communicator could have made to improve the quality of understanding achieved through the communication process?*

8.2 Preparing for an Employment-Selection Interview

The purpose of this exercise is to help you develop guidelines for an employment-selection interview. Such interviews are one of the more important settings in which supervisors and job candidates use applied communication skills. There is always the potential for defensiveness and confusion as well as lack of complete information exchange in this interview. This exercise allows you to think through ways to maximize the value of an employment-selection interview, whether you are the supervisor or the candidate, so that it is a productive experience based on effective applied communication.

Your instructor will form your class into groups of students. Each group should work through Steps 1 and 2 of the exercise.

Step 1. *Guidelines for the Supervisor*

Develop a set of guidelines for the supervisor in preparing for and then conducting an employment-selection interview. Consider the following questions in developing your guidelines.

a. What should the supervisor do before the interview?

b. How should the supervisor act and behave during the interview?

c. What should the supervisor do after the interview?

Step 2. *Guidelines for the Employee*

Develop another set of guidelines for the employee in preparing for and then being involved in an employment-selection interview. Consider the following questions in developing your guidelines.

a. What should the employee do before the interview?

b. How should the employee act and behave during the interview?

c. What should the employee do after the interview?

Once each group has developed the two sets of guidelines, the instructor will lead the class in a general discussion in which groups share and compare their guidelines. Consider the following questions during this discussion.

1. What similarities are there among the groups for each set of guidelines?
2. What unique or different guidelines have some of the groups developed?
3. What are essential guidelines for conducting an employment-selection interview?

TAKE 2

Biz Flix | Patch Adams

Hunter "Patch" Adams (Robin Williams), a maverick medical student, believes that laughter is the best medicine. The rest of the medical community believes that medicine is the best medicine. Unlike traditional physicians who remain aloof, Patch Adams prefers closeness to his patients. Williams's wackiness comes through clearly in this film, which is based on a true story.

The scene from *Patch Adams* comes from an early sequence, "The Experiment," which takes place after the students' medical school orientation. Patch Adams and fellow medical student Truman Schiff (Daniel London) leave the University Diner. They begin Patch's experiment for changing the programmed responses of people they meet on the street. Along the way, they stumble upon a meat packer's convention where this scene occurs. The film continues with the convention and then returns to the medical school.

What to Watch for and Ask Yourself:

- What parts of the communication process appear in this scene? Note each part of the process that you see in the scene.
- What type of communication does this scene show? Small group, large audience, or persuasive?
- Is Patch Adams an effective communicator? Why or why not?

Workplace Video | Corporate Communication, Featuring Navistar International

Miscommunication can be costly to a business, especially when it results in errors and wasted effort. Assuring the highest quality of communication is a task that Navistar International takes seriously throughout its truck, engine, and financial services divisions.

Formerly known as International Harvester and founded by famed inventor Cyrus McCormick, Navistar is a respected icon of quality American manufacturing. The Warrenville, Illinois-based corporation is a leading producer of medium and heavy trucks, midrange diesel engines, and associated parts. The company's V-8 diesel engines are especially popular with auto manufacturers, providing powerful muscle for many vans and pickups on the road today.

Corporate message strategy at Navistar requires careful coordination, as each of the company's three business units—truck, engine, and financial—operates as a separate division. The Department of Communication, led by Communications Director Karen Denning, organizes the formulation and dissemination of messages across all divisions. Underneath that central department are communications managers of each division who work closely with Denning to ensure that message strategy is unified throughout all business segments. The decision to appoint communications managers to the separate divisions was a major development in Navistar's corporate communications. "What we did a few years ago," says Denning, "was deploy communications managers and directors into our business units so that they could have a seat at the table when business strategy is developed."

As is the case in other organizations, communications at Navistar may be vertical or horizontal, and messages flow across a variety of channels. Important personal messages require the rich, two-way interaction of face-to-face discussions and telephone conversations; informal and impersonal messages are disseminated through e-mail, memos, bulletins, and business reports. Some communication scenarios require careful preplanning, such as when a shooting at one of Navistar's plants a few years ago led to multiple fatalities. The company's communications team, led by Denning, performed flawlessly. "I believe it's only because we had our plan in place and were ready to respond to the crisis that we responded as well as we did," Denning remarks.

In every situation, whether in crisis or daily routine, Navistar's team of professional communicators delivers timely, effective messages that are highly relevant to internal and external stakeholders.

Discussion Questions

1. What enables Navistar to meet the communication needs of its separate business divisions?
2. Explain why the communication channels used to send messages within a Navistar division may not be well suited to transmitting messages across the company's business units.
3. Why is it important for businesses to have a crisis communications plan ready at all times? What should an effective crisis communications plan entail?

CASE

Rahodeb (or John Mackey): Internet Postings about Whole Foods and Wild Oats

Started as one small store in Austin, Texas, in 1980, Whole Foods Market has grown into the world's leading retailer of natural and organic foods, with more than 270 locations in North America and the United Kingdom as of September 2007.[1] The company was founded by Craig Weller, Mark Skiles, and John Mackey, who serves as the company's CEO. Whole Foods has expanded through the acquisition of numerous companies, including but not limited to Wellspring Grocery, Fresh Fields, Bread of Life, Merchant of Vino, Allegro Coffee, Nature's Heartland, and Harry's Farmers Market, among others. The most recent acquisition was Wild Oats Markets.[2]

However, the acquisition of Wild Oats was not without its problems. The Federal Trade Commission (FTC) filed suit in June 2007 to block Whole Foods' acquisition of rival grocer Wild Oats on antitrust grounds.[3] Then in late August 2007, a federal appeals court rejected the FTC's request to overturn a federal district court ruling allowing Whole Foods to complete its purchase.[4]

Interestingly, while conducting its antitrust review, the FTC discovered that, over a period of eight years, John Mackey had posted comments about Whole Foods and its competitors in the online stock forums of Yahoo Finance. Mackey used the screen name "Rahodeb"—an anagram of Deborah, the name of Mackey's wife—to conceal his true identity as CEO of Whole Foods.[5] At least 240 of Rahodeb's 1,300 or so posts mentioned Wild Oats, a company with which Mackey had an increasingly bitter rivalry.[6]

The acrimony between Mackey and Perry Odak, CEO of Wild Oats, can be traced to the first time the two men met six years ago at a retailing conference in Manhattan in 2001. "I'm going to destroy you," Mackey shouted at Odak. Whole Foods' officials tell a different version of the story—with milder language—but the confrontation has persisted as a food-industry legend.[7]

In some of his pseudonymous postings, Mackey lauded Whole Foods' stock, cheered its financial results, and castigated Wild Oats.[8] In January 2005, Rahodeb posted this opinion: "No company would want to buy Wild Oats Markets Inc." He continued, "Would Whole Foods buy OATS? Almost surely not at current prices. What would they gain? OATS locations are too small. . . . [Wild Oats management] clearly doesn't know what it is doing . . . OATS has no value and no future."[9] Other comments that Mackey posted under the Rahodeb alias included the following: "While I'm not a Mackey groupie . . . I do admire what the man has accomplished." "I love the company and I'm in it for the long haul. I shop at Whole Foods. I own a great deal of its stock. I'm aligned with the mission and the values of the company . . . is there something wrong with this?"[10]

Mackey asserts that his online comments were personal, not professional. However, Mackey's friends and colleagues say there is little distinction between his personal and professional sides,[11] and that he is straightforward and transparent.[12] Mackey's defenders also say, "his anonymous comments—though boastful, provocative, and impulsive—were no different from his public ones, and were never intended to disclose insider information or move stock prices."[13]

In a statement published in mid-July 2007 on the Whole Foods' Web site, Mackey "said his anonymous statements didn't reflect his or the company's policies or beliefs. Some of the views Rahodeb expressed, Mr. Mackey said, didn't match his own beliefs." Mackey further stated that he made the anonymous comments on Yahoo Finance because he "had fun doing it."[14]

As of mid-August 2007, Rahodeb's (or Mackey's) online postings were being investigated through an informal Securities and Exchange Commission (SEC) inquiry and an internal probe by Whole Foods' board.[15] Whole Foods has asserted that

Mackey's online postings from 1999 to 2006 under the screen name Rahodeb were designed to "avoid having his comments associated with the Company and to avoid others placing too much emphasis on his remarks."[16]

The whole saga of Rahodeb's online postings is intriguing as well as perplexing in light of Whole Foods' corporate vision, which is captured in its *Declaration of Interdependence*. In part, the Whole Foods *Declaration of Interdependence* states, "[o]ur ability to instill a clear sense of interdependence among our various stakeholders . . . is contingent upon our efforts to communicate more often, more openly, and more compassionately. Better communication equals better understanding and more trust."[17]

How should Mackey's postings under the screen name Rahodeb be viewed in light of the communications provision of the Whole Foods *Declaration of Interdependence*?

Discussion Questions

1. Can the basic interpersonal communication model that is presented in Figure 8.1 be applied to the impersonal nature of an online forum? If so, how?
2. How does defensive communication enter into this case?
3. How is the Internet transforming the way people communicate?
4. What ethical problems are revealed by examining John Mackey's online postings in relation to the communications provision of the Whole Foods *Declaration of Interdependence*?

SOURCE: This case was written by Michael K. McCuddy, The Louis S. and Mary L. Morgal Chair of Christian Business Ethics and Professor of Management, College of Business Administration, Valparaiso University.

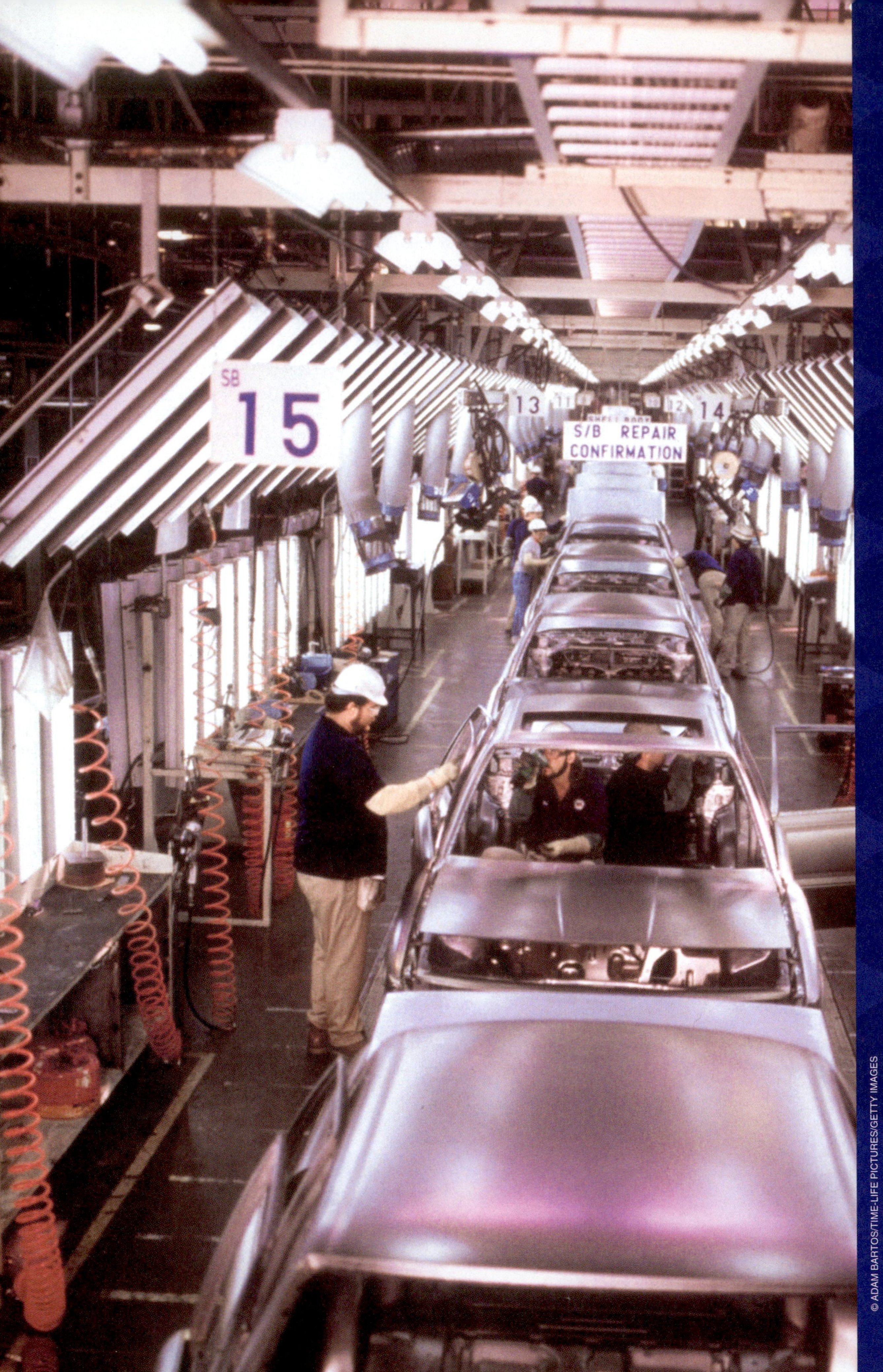
SB
15
13
14
S/B REPAIR
CONFIRMATION

CHAPTER 9

Work Teams and Groups

LEARNING OBJECTIVES

After reading this chapter, you should be able to do the following:

1 Define *group* and *work team*.

2 Explain four important aspects of group behavior.

3 Describe group formation, the four stages of a group's development, and the characteristics of a mature group.

4 Explain the task and maintenance functions in groups.

5 Identify the social benefits of group and team membership.

6 Discuss diversity and creativity in teams.

7 Discuss empowerment, teamwork, and self-managed teams.

8 Explain the importance of upper echelons and top management teams.

THINKING AHEAD: TOYOTA

Trust Is Job One for Toyota

The Toyota Way to number one was not necessarily an easy one for the Japanese-based corporation.[1] The trend line that took the company past General Motors in worldwide sales globally in 2007 is likely to hold up over the coming years. As is often the case for a lead runner, Toyota is not complacent about its position. Being number two is often more comfortable because it allows a company to benchmark efforts, progress, and success against its more successful competitor. Being number one allows a company to set the standards and lead the way, but puts it risk by making it more vulnerable to change. The Toyota Way is constant improvement. While the company does not have a monopoly on this idea, it certainly exemplifies it.

In addition to constant striving for improvement, teamwork is a hallmark of both the Japanese way and the Toyota Way. At the heart of great teamwork is trust; trust in team members, in oneself, and in the system. Trust is more important than price for Toyota, though price is important as well. Trust is the basis of long-lasting relationships, it drives the teamwork that Toyota has with its suppliers, and it leads to win-win outcomes for all concerned. One supplier of axles for Toyota pickup trucks, for example, was flabbergasted when there was no mention of price during the negotiations. Toyota's entire focus was on the supplier's processes and quality. Were they acceptable to Toyota?

Much has been made of an uneven playing field between Toyota and General Motors, with key comparisons focusing on the cost structures. GM workers have enjoyed some of the best retirement and medical benefits in the American workforce. These benefits drive up the cost of GM cars. It is not all in the cost structure, however. Toyota has had its own challenges in overcoming the cultural barriers to understanding Americans and American needs. For example, the Camry's chief engineer is a Japanese man, and while the car does not sell well in Japan, it is a huge success in America. Why? Because the chief engineer and his team apply themselves to understanding American customer desires. Will Toyota always be a "Japanese" company?

(1) Define *group* and *work team*.

Northrop Grumman was able to achieve teamwork among employees, customers, and partners through knowledge sharing in integrated product teams.[2] Not all teams and groups work face to face. In today's information age, advanced computer and telecommunications technologies enable organizations to be more flexible through the use of virtual teams.[3] Virtual teams also address new workforce demographics, enabling companies to access expertise and the best employees who may be located anywhere in the world. Whether a traditional group or a virtual team, groups and teams continue to play a vital role in organizational behavior and performance at work.

A *group* is two or more people having common interests, objectives, and continuing interaction. Table 9.1 summarizes the characteristics of a well-functioning, effective group.[4] A *work team* is a group of people with complementary skills who are committed to a common mission, performance goals, and approach for which they hold themselves mutually accountable.[5] All work teams are groups, but not all groups are work teams. Groups emphasize individual leadership, individual accountability, and individual work products. Work teams emphasize shared leadership, mutual accountability, and collective work products.

group
Two or more people with common interests, objectives, and continuing interaction.

work team
A group of people with complementary skills who are committed to a common mission, performance goals, and approach for which they hold themselves mutually accountable.

TABLE 9.1 Characteristics of a Well-Functioning, Effective Group

- The atmosphere tends to be relaxed, comfortable, and informal.
- The group's task is well understood and accepted by the members.
- The members listen well to one another; most members participate in a good deal of task-relevant discussion.
- People express both their feelings and their ideas.
- Conflict and disagreement are present and centered around ideas or methods, not personalities or people.
- The group is aware and conscious of its own operation and function.
- Decisions are usually based on consensus, not majority vote.
- When actions are decided, clear assignments are made and accepted by members of the group.

The chapter begins with a traditional discussion of group behavior and group development in the first two sections. The third section discusses teams. The final two sections explore the contemporary team issues of empowerment, self-managed teams, and upper echelon teams.

GROUP BEHAVIOR

Group behavior has been a subject of interest in social psychology for a long time, and many different aspects of group behavior have been studied over the years. We now look at four topics relevant to groups functioning in organizations: norms of behavior, group cohesion, social loafing, and loss of individuality. Group behavior topics related to decision making, such as polarization and groupthink, are addressed in Chapter 10.

(2) Explain four important aspects of group behavior.

Norms of Behavior

The standards that a work group uses to evaluate the behavior of its members are its *norms of behavior*. These norms may be written or unwritten, verbalized or not, implicit or explicit. As long as individual members of the group understand them, the norms can be effective in influencing behavior. Norms may specify what members of a group should do (such as a stated dress code for men and women), or they may specify what members of a group should not do (such as executives not behaving arrogantly with employees).

Norms may exist in any aspect of work group life. They may evolve informally or unconsciously within a group, or they may arise in response to challenges, such as the norm of disciplined behavior by firefighters in responding to a three-alarm fire to protect the group.[6] Performance norms are among the most important group norms from the organization's perspective. Even when group members work in isolation on creative projects, they display conformity to group norms.[7] Group norms of cooperative behavior within a teams can lead to members working for mutual benefit, which in turn facilitate team performance.[8] We discuss performance standards further in a later section of this chapter. Organizational culture and corporate codes of ethics, such as Johnson & Johnson's credo (see Chapter 2), reflect behavioral norms expected within work groups. Finally, norms that create awareness of, and help regulate, emotions are critical to groups' effectiveness.[9]

Group Cohesion

The "interpersonal glue" that makes the members of a group stick together is *group cohesion*. Group cohesion can enhance job satisfaction for members and improve organizational productivity.[10] Highly cohesive groups are able to control and manage their membership better than work groups low in cohesion. In one study of 381 banking teams in Hong Kong and the United States, increased job complexity and task autonomy led to increased group cohesiveness, which translated into better performance.[11] In addition to performance, highly cohesive groups are strongly motivated to maintain good, close relationships among the members. We examine group cohesion in further detail, along with factors leading to high levels of it, when discussing the common characteristics of well-developed groups.

norms of behavior
The standards that a work group uses to evaluate the behavior of its members.

group cohesion
The "interpersonal glue" that makes members of a group stick together.

social loafing
The failure of a group member to contribute personal time, effort, thoughts, or other resources to the group.

Social Loafing

Social loafing occurs when one or more group members rely on the efforts of other group members and fail to contribute their own time, effort, thoughts, or other

resources to a group.[12] This may create a drag on the group's efforts and achievements. Some scholars argue that, from the individual's standpoint, social loafing, or free riding, is rational behavior in response to an experience of inequity or when individual efforts are hard to observe. However, it shortchanges the group, which loses potentially valuable resources possessed by individual members.[13]

A number of methods for countering social loafing exist, such as having identifiable individual contributions to the group product and member self-evaluation systems. For example, if each group member is responsible for a specific input to the group, a member's failure to contribute will be noticed by everyone. If members must formally evaluate their contributions to the group, they are less likely to loaf.

Loss of Individuality

Social loafing may be detrimental to group achievement, but it does not have the potentially explosive effects of *loss of individuality*. Loss of individuality, or deindividuation, is a social process in which individual group members lose self-awareness and its accompanying sense of accountability, inhibition, and responsibility for individual behavior.[14]

When individuality is lost, people may engage in morally reprehensible acts and even violent behavior as committed members of their group or organization. For example, loss of individuality was one of several contributing factors in the violent and aggressive acts that led to the riot that destroyed sections of Los Angeles following the Rodney King verdict in the early 1990s. Loss of individuality is not always negative or destructive, however. The loosening of normal ego control mechanisms in the individual may lead to prosocial behavior and heroic acts in dangerous situations.[15] A group that successfully matures may not encounter problems with loss of individuality.

GROUP FORMATION AND DEVELOPMENT

(3) Describe group formation, the four stages of a group's development, and the characteristics of a mature group.

After its formation, a group goes through predictable stages of development. If successful, it emerges as a mature group. One logical group development model proposes four stages following the group's formation:[16] mutual acceptance, decision making, motivation and commitment, and control and sanctions. To become a mature group, each of the stages in development must be successfully negotiated.

According to this group development model, a group addresses three issues: interpersonal issues, task issues, and authority issues.[17] The interpersonal issues include matters of trust, personal comfort, and security. As we saw in the Thinking Ahead feature, trust is a key issue for Toyota in its working relationships. The task issues include the mission or purpose of the group, the methods the group employs, and the outcomes expected of the group. The authority issues include decisions about who is in charge, how power and influence are managed, and who has the right to tell whom to do what. This section addresses group formation, each stage of group development, and the characteristics of a mature group.

Group Formation

loss of individuality
A social process in which individual group members lose self-awareness and its accompanying sense of accountability, inhibition, and responsibility for individual behavior.

Formal and informal groups form in organizations for different reasons. Formal groups are sometimes called official or assigned groups, and informal groups may be called unofficial or emergent groups. Formal groups gather to perform various tasks and include an executive and staff, standing committees of the board of directors, project task forces, and temporary committees. An example of a formal group was the task force assembled by the University of Texas at Arlington (UTA), whose mission was to design the Goolsby Leadership Academy that bridges academics and practice. Chaired by the associate dean of business, the task force was composed of seven members with diverse academic expertise and business experience. The task force envisioned a five-year developmental plan to create a national center of excellence in preparing Goolsby Scholars for authentic leadership in the twenty-first century.

© AP PHOTO/MANISH SWARUP

Diversity is important in the workplace. PepsiCo President and CEO Indra Nooyi was born in India.

Diversity is an important consideration in the formation of groups. For example, Monsanto Agricultural Company, now simply Monsanto Company, created a task force titled "Valuing Diversity" to address subtle discrimination resulting from workforce diversity.[18] The original task force was titled "Eliminating Subtle Discrimination (ESD)" and was composed of fifteen women, minorities, and white males. Subtle discrimination might include the use of gender- or culture-specific language. Monsanto and the task force's intent was to build on individual differences—whether in terms of gender, race, or culture—in developing a dominant heterogeneous culture. Diversity can enhance group performance. One study of gender diversity among U.S. workers found that men and women in gender-balanced groups had higher job satisfaction than those in homogeneous groups.[19]

Ethnic diversity has characterized many industrial work groups in the United States since the 1800s. This was especially true during the early years of the 1900s, when waves of immigrant workers arrived from Germany, Yugoslavia, Italy, Poland, Scotland, the Scandinavian countries, and many other nations. Organizations were challenged to blend these culturally and linguistically diverse peoples into effective work groups.

In addition to ethnic, gender, and cultural diversity, there is interpersonal diversity. Highly effective work groups achieve compatibility through interpersonal diversity. Successful interpersonal relationships are the basis of group effort, a key foundation for business success. Effective, productive work groups often differ in their needs for inclusion in activities, control of people and events, and interpersonal affection from others. Although diverse in their interpersonal needs, the work group thus finds strength through balance and complementarity.

Informal groups evolve in the work setting to gratify a variety of member needs not met by formal groups. For example, organizational members' inclusion and affection needs might be satisfied through informal athletic or interest groups. Athletic teams representing a department, unit, or company may achieve semiofficial status, such as the AT&T National Running Team that uses the corporate logo on its race shirts.

Stages of Group Development

All groups, formal and informal, go through stages of development, from forming interpersonal relationships among the members to becoming a mature and productive unit. Mature groups are able to work through the necessary interpersonal, task, and authority issues to achieve at high levels. Demographic diversity and group fault lines (i.e., potential breaking points in a group) are two possible predictors of the sense-making process, subgroup formation patterns, and nature of group conflict at various stages of group development.[20] Hence, group development through these stages may not always be smooth.

There are a number of group development models in the literature and we look at two of these models in particular. These two well-known models are Tuckman's

FIGURE 9.1 Tuckman's Five-Stage Model of Group Development

and Gersick's. Each of these models looks at the evolution of behavior in teams, and Tuckman's model also focuses on leadership.

The Five-Stage Model Bruce Tuckman's five-stage model of group development proposes that team behavior progresses through five stages: forming, storming, norming, performing, and adjourning.[21] These stages and the emphasis on relationships and leadership styles in each are shown in Figure 9.1.

Dependence on guidance and direction is the defining characteristic in the *forming* stage. Team members are unclear about individual roles and responsibilities and tend to rely heavily on the leader to answer questions about the team's purpose, objectives, and external relationships. Moving from this stage requires that team members feel they are part of the team.

Team members compete for position in the *storming* stage. As the name suggests, this is a stage of considerable conflict as power struggles, cliques, and factions within the group begin to form. Clarity of purpose increases, but uncertainties still exist. This is also the stage when members assess one another with regard to trustworthiness, emotional comfort, and evaluative acceptance. For the "Valuing Diversity" task force at Monsanto, trust was one of the early issues to be worked through. A coaching style by the leader is key during this stage of group development as team members may challenge him or her.

Agreement and consensus are characteristic of team members in the *norming* stage. It is in this stage that roles and responsibilities become clear and accepted with big decisions being made by group agreement. The focus turns from interpersonal relations to decision-making activities related to the group's task accomplishment. Small decisions may be delegated to individuals or small teams within the group. The group addresses authority questions like these: Who is responsible for what aspects of the group's work? Does the group need one primary leader and spokesperson? Wallace Supply Company, an industrial distributor of pipes, valves, and fittings, has found employee teams particularly valuable in this aspect of work life.[22] Leadership is facilitative with some leadership responsibilities being shared by the team.

As a team moves into the *performing* stage, it becomes more strategically aware and clear about its mission and purpose. In this stage of development, the group has successfully worked through the necessary interpersonal, task, and authority issues and can stand on its own with little interference from the leader. Primarily, the team makes decisions, and disagreements are resolved positively with necessary changes to structure and processes attended to by the team. A mature group is able to control its members through the judicious application of specific positive and negative sanctions based on the evaluation of specific member behaviors. Recent research shows that evaluation biases stemming from liking someone operate in face-to-face groups but not in electronic groups, such as virtual teams.[23] Members at this stage do not need to be instructed but may ask for assistance from the leader with personal or interpersonal development. The team requires a leader who delegates and oversees.

The final stage of group development is the *adjourning* stage. When the task is completed, everyone on the team can move on to new and different things. Team members have a sense of accomplishment and feel good knowing that their purpose is fulfilled. The leader's role is primarily one of recognition of the group's achievements. Unless the group is a task force or other informal team, most groups in organizations remain at the performing stage and do not disband as the adjourning stage suggests.

Punctuated Equilibrium Model Although it is still highly cited in team and group research, Tuckman's "forming–norming–storming–performing–adjourning" model may be unrealistic from an organizational perspective. In fact, research has shown that many teams experience relational conflicts at different times and in different contexts. Connie Gersick proposes that groups do not necessarily progress linearly from one step to another in a predetermined sequence but alternate between periods of inertia with little visible progress toward goal achievement *punctuated* by bursts of energy as work groups develop. It is in these periods of energy that the majority of a group's work is accomplished.[24] For example, a task force given nine months to complete a task may use the first four months to choose its norms, explore contextual issues, and determine how it will communicate.

Characteristics of a Mature Group

The description of a well-functioning, effective group in Table 9.1 characterizes a mature group. Such a group has four distinguishing characteristics: a clear purpose and mission, well-understood norms and standards of conduct, a high level of group cohesion, and a flexible status structure.

Purpose and Mission The purpose and mission may be assigned to a group (as in the previous example of the Goolsby Leadership Academy task force of UTA) or emerge from within the group (as in the case of the AT&T National Running Team). Even in the case of an assigned mission, the group may reexamine, modify, revise, or question the mission. It may also embrace the mission as stated. The importance of mission is exemplified in IBM's Process Quality Management, which requires that a process team of not more than twelve people develop a clear understanding of mission as the first step in the process.[25] The IBM approach demands that all members agree to go in the same direction. The mission statement is converted into a specific agenda, clear goals, and a set of critical success factors. Stating the purpose and mission in the form of specific goals enhances productivity over and above any performance benefits achieved through individual goal setting.[26]

Behavioral Norms Behavioral norms, which evolve over a period of time, are well-understood standards of behavior within a group.[27] They are benchmarks against which team members are evaluated and judged by other team members. Some behavioral norms become written rules, such as an attendance policy or an ethical code for a team. Other norms remain informal, although they are no less understood by team members. Dress codes and norms about after-hours socializing may fall into this category. Behavioral norms also evolve around performance and productivity.[28] Productivity norms even influence the performance of sports teams.[29] The group's productivity norm may or may not be consistent with, and supportive of, the organization's productivity standards. A high-performance team sets productivity standards above organizational expectations with the intent to excel. Average teams set productivity

THE REAL WORLD 9.1

Taking Care of All Concerned

Former Chairman Bill Greehey spun Valero Energy off of Coastal Corporation in 1980, and then worked to set a standard within the company of compassion and community service that has led to great market as well as human resource results. Valero Energy was ranked number three in the *Fortune* list of "100 Best Companies to Work For 2006." This success comes from hundreds of groups and teams throughout the company and the compassion of human resources professionals like Robert K. (Bob) Grimes. Grimes was encouraged by Greehey to take his message of compassion, caring, and community service to Corpus Christi from the headquarters in San Antonio, heading up human resources at their south Texas refinery. Grimes did just that and then took on public relations responsibilities too. He led by example, becoming president of the Rotary Club of Corpus Christi, being recognized for his committed community service as a Paul Harris Fellow for living the Rotary test: "Will it be beneficial to all concerned?" From a small group of caring and committed professionals, Valero has grown since 2002 into the largest refining company in North America. Bob Grimes' and other Valero leaders' challenge is to extend the norms of caring, compassion, and community service throughout the thousands of new employees who now make up 80 percent of the company.

COURTESY OF VALERO ENERGY CORPORATION

Valero Energy was ranked No. 3 on the list of "*Fortune* 100 Best Companies to Work For 2006," due in part to the compassion of human resource professionals like Robert Grimes, pictured here.

SOURCE: B. Leonard, "Taking Care of Their Own," *HR Magazine* (June 2006): 112–115.

standards based on, and consistent with, organizational expectations. Noncompliant or counterproductive teams may set productivity standards below organizational expectations with the intent of damaging the organization or creating change. On the positive side, behavioral norms can permeate an entire organizational culture for the benefit of all, as we see in The Real World 9.1 discussion of Valero Energy.

Group Cohesion Group cohesion was earlier described as the interpersonal attraction binding group members together. It enables a group to exercise effective control over its members in relation to its behavioral norms and standards. Goal conflict, unpleasant experiences, and domination of a subgroup are among the threats to a group's cohesion. Groups with low levels of cohesion have greater difficulty exercising control over their members and enforcing their standards of behavior. A classic study of cohesiveness in 238 industrial work groups found cohesion to be an important factor influencing anxiety, tension, and productivity within the groups.[30] Specifically, work-related tension and anxiety were lower in teams high in cohesion, and they were higher in teams low in cohesion, as depicted in Figure 9.2. This suggests that cohesion has a calming effect on team members, at least concerning work-related tension and anxiety. In addition, actual productivity was found to vary significantly less in highly cohesive teams, making these teams much more predictable with regard to their productivity. The actual productivity levels were primarily determined by the productivity norms within each work group. That is, highly cohesive groups with

FIGURE 9.2 Cohesiveness and Work-Related Tension*

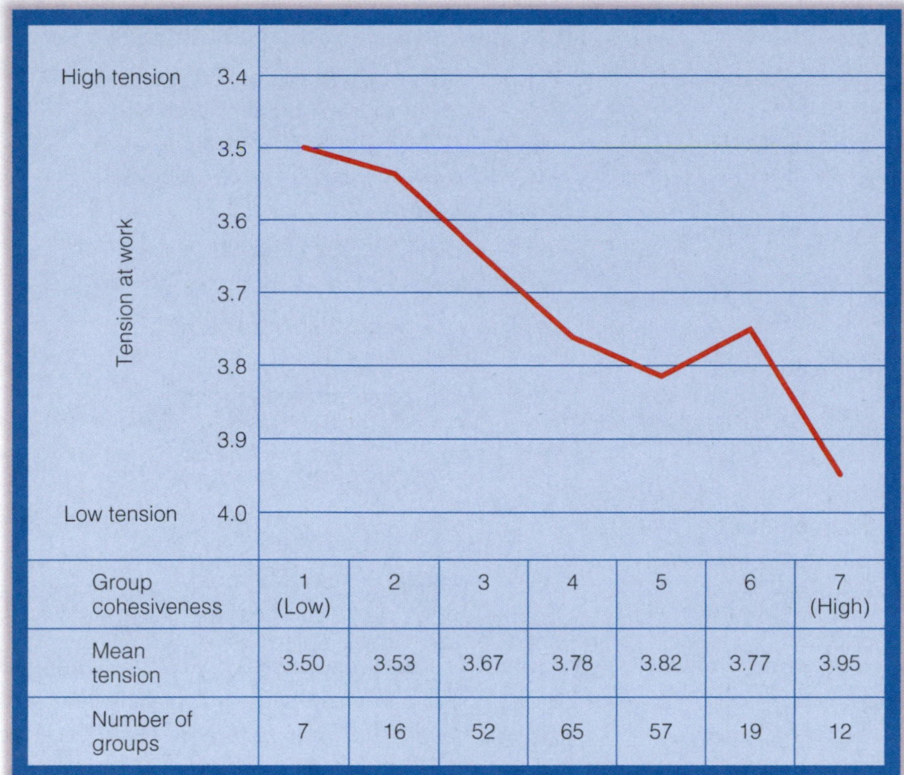

Group cohesiveness	1 (Low)	2	3	4	5	6	7 (High)
Mean tension	3.50	3.53	3.67	3.78	3.82	3.77	3.95
Number of groups	7	16	52	65	57	19	12

Note: Product–moment correlation is 0.28, and critical ratio is 4.20; the group cohesion–tension relationship is highly significant at the .001 level.

*The measure of tension at work is based on group mean response to the question "Does your work ever make you feel 'jumpy' or nervous?" A low numerical score represents relatively high tension.

SOURCE: From S. E. Seashore, *Group Cohesiveness in the Industrial Work Group*, 1954. Research conducted by Stanley E. Seashore at the Institute for Social Research, University of Michigan. Reprinted by permission.

high production standards are very productive. Similarly, highly cohesive groups with low productivity standards are unproductive. Member satisfaction, commitment, and communication are better in highly cohesive groups. Groupthink may be a problem in highly cohesive groups and is discussed in Chapter 10. You 9.1 includes the three group cohesion questions from this research project. Complete You 9.1 to determine the level of cohesion in a group of which you are a member.

Group cohesion is influenced by a number of factors, most notably time, size, the prestige of the team, external pressure, and internal competition. Group cohesion evolves gradually over time through a group's normal development. Smaller groups—those of five or seven members, for example—are more cohesive than those of more than twenty-five, although cohesion does not decline much with size after forty or more members. Prestige or social status also influences a group's cohesion, with more prestigious groups, such as the U.S. Air Force Thunderbirds or the U.S. Navy Blue Angels, being highly cohesive. However, even groups of very low prestige may be highly cohesive in how they stick together. Finally, external pressure and internal competition influence group cohesion. Although the mechanics' union, pilots, and other internal constituencies at Eastern Airlines had various differences of opinion, they all pulled together in a cohesive fashion in resisting Frank Lorenzo when he came in to reshape the airline before its demise. Whereas external pressures tend to enhance cohesion, internal competition usually decreases cohesion within a team. One study found that company-imposed work pressure disrupted group cohesion by increasing internal competition and reducing cooperative interpersonal activity.[31]

YOU 9.1

How Cohesive Is Your Group?

Think about a group of which you are a member. Answer each of the following questions in relation to this group by circling the number next to the alternative that most reflects your feelings.

1. Do you feel that you are really a part of your group?
   5—Really a part of the group.
   4—Included in most ways.
   3—Included in some ways, but not in others.
   2—Do not feel I really belong.
   1—Do not work with any one group of people.
2. If you had a chance to do the same activities in another group, for the same pay if it is a work group, how would you feel about moving?
   1—Would want very much to move.
   2—Would rather move than stay where I am.
   3—Would make no difference to me.
   4—Would rather stay where I am than move.
   5—Would want very much to stay where I am.
3. How does your group compare with other groups that you are familiar with on each of the following points?
   - The way people get along together.
     5—Better than most.
     3—About the same as most.
     1—Not as good as most.
   - The way people stick together.
     5—Better than most.
     3—About the same as most.
     1—Not as good as most.
   - The way people help one another on the job.
     5—Better than most.
     3—About the same as most.
     1—Not as good as most.

Add up your circled responses. If you have a number of 20 or above, you view your group as highly cohesive. If you have a number between 10 and 19, you view your group's cohesion as average. If you have a number of 7 or less, you view your group as very low in cohesion.

SOURCE: From S. E. Seashore, *Group Cohesiveness in the Industrial Work Group*, University of Michigan, 1954. Reprinted by permission.

Status Structure *Status structure* is the set of authority and task relations among a group's members. The status structure may be hierarchical or egalitarian (i.e., democratic), depending on the group. Successful resolution of the authority issue within a team results in a well-understood status structure of leader–follower relationships. Where leadership problems arise, it is important to find solutions and build team leader effectiveness.[32] Whereas groups tend to have one leader, teams tend to share leadership. For example, one person may be the team's task master who sets the agenda, initiates much of the work activity, and ensures that the team meets its deadlines. Another team member may take a leadership role in maintaining effective interpersonal relationships in the group. Hence, shared leadership is very feasible in teams. An effective status structure results in role interrelatedness among group members,[33] such as that displayed by Bill Perez and Bill Wrigley. Their tag-team style of cooperation in leading Wm. Wrigley Jr. Company has served the company well.

status structure
The set of authority and task relations among a group's members.

Diversity in a group is healthy, and members may contribute to the collective effort through one of four basic styles:[34] the contributor, the collaborator, the communicator, and the challenger. The contributor is data driven, supplies necessary information, and adheres to high performance standards. The collaborator sees the big picture and is able to keep a constant focus on the mission and urge other

members to join efforts for mission accomplishment. The communicator listens well, facilitates the group's process, and humanizes the collective effort. The challenger is the devil's advocate who questions everything from the group's mission, purpose, and methods to its ethics. Members may exhibit one or more of these four basic styles over a period of time. In addition, an effective group must have an integrator.[35] This can be especially important in cross-functional teams, where different perspectives carry the seeds of conflict. However, cross-functional teams are not necessarily a problem. Effectively managing cross-functional teams of artists, designers, printers, and financial experts enabled Hallmark Cards to cut its new-product development time in half.[36]

Emergent leadership in groups was studied among sixty-two men and sixty women.[37] Groups performed tasks not classified as either masculine or feminine, that is, "sex-neutral" tasks. Men and women both emerged as leaders, and neither gender had significantly more emergent leaders. However, group members who described themselves in masculine terms were significantly more likely to emerge as leaders than group members who described themselves in feminine, androgynous (both masculine and feminine), or undifferentiated (neither masculine nor feminine) terms. Hence, gender stereotypes may play a role in emergent leadership.

Task and Maintenance Functions

An effective group or team carries out various task functions to perform its work successfully and various maintenance functions to ensure member satisfaction and a sense of team spirit.[38] Teams that successfully fulfill these functions afford their members the potential for psychological intimacy and integrated involvement. Table 9.2 presents nine task and nine maintenance functions in teams or groups.

(4) Explain the task and maintenance functions in groups.

Task functions are those activities directly related to the effective completion of the team's work. For example, the task of initiating activity involves suggesting ideas, defining problems, and proposing approaches and/or solutions to problems. The task of seeking information involves asking for ideas, suggestions, information, or facts. Effective teams have members who fulfill various task functions as they are required.

Some task functions are more important at one time in the life of a group, and other functions are more important at other times. For example, during the engineering test periods for new technologies, the engineering team needs members who focus on testing the practical applications of suggestions and those who diagnose problems and suggest solutions.

TABLE 9.2 Task and Maintenance Functions in Teams or Groups

Task Functions	Maintenance Functions
Initiating activities	Supporting others
Seeking information	Following others' leads
Giving information	Gatekeeping communication
Elaborating concepts	Setting standards
Coordinating activities	Expressing member feelings
Summarizing ideas	Testing group decisions
Testing ideas	Consensus testing
Evaluating effectiveness	Harmonizing conflict
Diagnosing problems	Reducing tension

task function
An activity directly related to the effective completion of a team's work.

The effective use of task functions leads to the success of the group, and the failure to use them may lead to disaster. For example, the successful initiation and coordination of an emergency room (ER) team's activities by the senior resident saved the life of a knife wound victim.[39] The victim was stabbed one-quarter inch below the heart, and the ER team acted quickly to stem the bleeding, begin intravenous fluids, and monitor the victim's vital signs.

Maintenance functions are those activities essential to the effective, satisfying interpersonal relationships within a group or team. For example, following another group member's lead may be as important as leading others. Communication gatekeepers within a group ensure balanced contributions from all members. Because task activities build tension into teams and groups working together, tension-reduction activities are important to drain off negative or destructive feelings. For example, in a study of twenty-five work groups over a five-year period, humor and joking behavior were found to enhance the social relationships in the groups.[40] The researchers concluded that performance improvements in the twenty-five groups indirectly resulted from improved relationships attributable to the humor and joking behaviors. Maintenance functions enhance togetherness, cooperation, and teamwork, enabling members to achieve psychological intimacy while furthering the success of the team. Jody Grant's supportive attitude and comfortable demeanor as chairman and CEO of Texas Capital Bancshares enabled him to build a vibrant bank in the aftermath of the great Texas banking crash of 1982–1992. Grant was respected for his expertise *and* his ability to build relationships. Both task and maintenance functions are important for successful groups and teams.

WORK TEAMS IN ORGANIZATIONS

Work teams are task-oriented groups, though in some organizations the term *team* has a negative connotation for unions and union members. Work teams make important and valuable contributions to the organization and are important to the member need satisfaction. For example, an idea to implement a simple change in packaging from a work team at Glenair, a UK-based aerospace and defense contractor, saved the company twenty-five minutes of packaging time per unit. Additionally, a job that used to take one worker half an hour to complete was reduced to only five minutes, freeing the worker to perform other work in the factory.[41]

Several kinds of work teams exist. One classification scheme uses a sports analogy. Some teams work like baseball teams with set responsibilities, other teams work like football teams through coordinated action, and still others work like doubles tennis teams with primary yet flexible responsibilities. In addition, crews are a distinct type of work team that can be studied using the concept of "crewness."[42] Although each type of team may have a useful role in the organization, the individual expert should not be overlooked.[43] That is, at the right time and in the right context, individual members must be allowed to shine.

Why Work Teams?

Teams are very useful in performing work that is complicated, complex, interrelated, and/or more voluminous than one person can handle. Harold Geneen, while chairman of ITT, said, "If I had enough arms and legs and time, I'd do it all myself." Obviously, people working in organizations cannot do everything because of the limitations of arms, legs, time, expertise, knowledge, and other resources. Individual limitations are overcome and problems are solved through teamwork and collaboration. World-class U.S. corporations, such as Motorola, Inc., are increasingly deploying work teams in their global affiliates to meet the competition and gain an

maintenance function
An activity essential to effective, satisfying interpersonal relationships within a team or group.

advantage.[44] Motorola's "Be Cool" team in the Philippines has a family atmosphere and may even begin a meeting with a prayer, yet is committed to improving individual and team performance. As we saw in Thinking Ahead, Toyota uses teamwork more broadly in its relationship with suppliers and customers too.

Teams make important contributions to organizations in work areas that lend themselves to teamwork. *Teamwork* is a core value at Hewlett-Packard. Complex, interdependent work tasks and activities that require collaboration particularly lend themselves to teamwork. Teams are appropriate where knowledge, talent, skills, and abilities are dispersed across organizational members and require integrated effort for task accomplishment. The recent emphasis on team-oriented work environments is based on empowerment with collaboration, not on power and competition. Teams with experience working together may produce valuable innovations, and individual contributions are valuable as well.[45] Larry Hirschhorn labels this "the new team environment" founded on a significantly more empowered workforce in the industrial sectors of the American economy. This new team environment is compared with the old work environment in Table 9.3. Beyond the new team environment is the emergence of virtual teams, such as those at BP PLC, Nokia Corporation, and Ogilvy & Mather as we see in The Real World 9.2.

That teams are necessary is a driving principle of total quality efforts in organizations. Total quality efforts often require the formation of teams—especially cross-functional teams composed of people from different functions, such as manufacturing and design, who are responsible for specific organizational processes. Former Eastman Kodak CEO George Fisher believed in the importance of participation and cooperation as foundations for teamwork and a total quality program. In a study of forty machine crews in a northeastern U.S. paper mill, organizational citizenship behaviors, specifically helping behavior and sportsmanship, contributed significantly to the quantity and quality of work group performance.[46]

Work Team Structure and Work Team Process

Work team effectiveness in the new team environment requires attention by management to both work team structure and work team process.[47] The primary structural issues for work teams are goals and objectives, operating guidelines,

TABLE  9.3 A Comparison of the New Team Environment versus the Old Work Environment

New Team Environment	Old Work Environment
Person comes up with initiatives.	Person follows orders.
Team has considerable authority to chart its own steps.	Team depends on the manager to chart its course.
Members form a team because people learn to collaborate in the face of their emerging right to think for themselves. People both rock the boat and work together.	Members were a team because people conformed to direction set by the manager. No one rocked the boat.
People cooperate by using their thoughts and feelings. They link up through direct talk.	People cooperated by suppressing their thoughts and feelings. They wanted to get along.

SOURCE: *Managing in the New Team Environment*, by L. Hirschhorn, © 1991. Reprinted by permission of Prentice-Hall, Inc., Upper Saddle River, N.J.

teamwork
Joint action by a team of people in which individual interests are subordinated to team unity.

THE REAL WORLD 9.2

Rule of the Game in Virtual Teams at BP PLC, Nokia, and Ogilvy & Mather

BP PLC, Nokia, and Ogilvy & Mather are among the global companies that are benefiting from virtual teams. David Ogilvy, the late founder of advertising company Ogilvy & Mather, set the stage early for virtual teams with his investment in sharing knowledge through an internal IT-based community within the company. The in-depth case studies of successful virtual teams at Ogilvy & Mather, BP, and Nokia have led to ten golden rules.

1. Invest in an online resource where members can learn quickly about one another.
2. Choose a few team members who already know each other.
3. Identify "boundary spanners" and ensure that they make up at least 15 percent of the team.
4. Cultivate boundary spanners as a regular part of companywide practices and processes.
5. Break the team's work into modules so that progress in one location is not overly dependent on progress in another.
6. Create an online site where a team can collaborate, exchange ideas, and inspire one another.
7. Encourage frequent communication.
8. Assign only tasks that are challenging and interesting.
9. Ensure the task is meaningful to the team and the company.
10. When building a virtual team, solicit volunteers as much as possible.

These rules come from successful experience and any company implementing virtual teams should monitor the success and problems within their own work context.

SOURCE: L. Gratton, "Working Together . . . When Apart," *The Wall Street Journal* (June 16, 2007): R4.

performance measures, and the specification of roles. A work team's goals and objectives specify what must be achieved, while the operating guidelines set the organizational boundaries and decision-making limits within which the team must function. The goal-setting process was discussed in Chapter 6 and has applicability for work teams, too. In addition to these two structural elements, the work team needs to know what performance measures are being used to assess its task accomplishment. For example, a medical emergency team's performance measures might include the success rate in saving critically injured patients and the average number of hours a patient is in the emergency room before being transferred to a hospital bed. Finally, work team structure requires a clearly specified set of roles for the executives and managers who oversee the work of the team, for the work team leaders who exercise influence over team members, and for team members. These role specifications should include information about required role behaviors, such as decision making and task performance, as well as restrictions or limits on role behaviors, such as the limitations on managerial interventions in work team activities and decision making. Expectations as well as experience may be especially important for newcomer role performance in work teams.[48]

Work team process is the second important dimension of effectiveness. Two of the important process issues in work teams are the managing of cooperative behaviors and the managing of competitive behaviors. Both sets of behaviors are helpful in task accomplishment, and they should be viewed as complementary sets of behaviors. Cooperative teamwork skills include open communication, trust, personal integrity, positive interdependence, and mutual support. On the other hand, positive competitive teamwork skills include the ability to enjoy competition, play fair, be a good winner or loser; to have access to information for monitoring where the team and members are in the competition; and not to overgeneralize or exaggerate the results of any specific competition. In a study of reward structures in 75 four-member teams, competitive rewards enhanced speed of performance, while cooperative rewards enhanced accuracy of performance.[49]

Work team process issues have become more complex in the global workplace with teams composed of members from many cultures and backgrounds. This is enhanced by the presence of virtual work teams operating on the global landscape. Our discussions of diversity earlier in the text have particular relevance to multicultural work teams. In addition to the process issues of cooperation, competition, and diversity, three other process issues are related to topics we discuss elsewhere in the text. These are empowerment, discussed in the next major section of this chapter; team decision making, discussed in Chapter 10; and conflict management and resolution, discussed in Chapter 13.

Quality Teams and Circles

Quality teams and quality circles are part of a total quality program. Decision making in *quality teams* is discussed in detail in Chapter 10. Quality teams are different from QCs in that they are more formal and are designed and assigned by upper-level management. Quality teams are not voluntary and have formal power, whereas quality circles have less formal power and decision authority. Although less commonly used than a decade ago, quality circle principles continue to have value.

Quality circles (QCs) are small groups of employees who work voluntarily on company time—typically one hour per week—to address work-related problems such as quality control, cost reduction, production planning and techniques, and even product design. Membership in a QC is typically voluntary and is fixed once a circle is formed, although some changes may occur as appropriate. QCs are trained in various problem-solving techniques and use them to address the work-related problems.

QCs were popularized as a Japanese management method when an American, W. Edwards Deming, exported his thinking about QCs to Japan following World War II.[50] QCs became popular in the United States in the 1980s, when companies such as Ford, Hewlett-Packard, and Eastman Kodak implemented them. The Camp Red Cloud Garrison in South Korea saved $2 million by implementing the Six Sigma quality program that involved all garrison supervisors and looked at efficiencies from the customer's perspective. Some of the money saved from technology improvements has gone back to employees in an effort to improve safety equipment, work facilities, and employee recreation.

Quality teams and quality circles must deal with substantive issues if they are to be effective; otherwise, employees begin to believe the quality effort is simply a management ploy. QCs do not necessarily require final decision authority to be effective if their recommendations are always considered seriously and implemented when appropriate. One study found that QCs are effective for a period of time, and then their contributions begin to diminish.[51] This may suggest that quality teams and QCs must be reinforced and periodically reenergized to maintain their effectiveness over long periods of time.

quality team
A team that is part of an organization's structure and is empowered to act on its decisions regarding product and service quality.

quality circle (QC)
A small group of employees who work voluntarily on company time, typically one hour per week, to address work-related problems such as quality control, cost reduction, production planning and techniques, and even product design.

Social Benefits

(5) Identify the social benefits of group and team membership.

Two sets of social benefits are available to team or group members. One set accrues from achieving psychological intimacy. The other comes from achieving integrated involvement.[52]

Psychological intimacy is emotional and psychological closeness to other team or group members. It results in feelings of affection and warmth, unconditional

psychological intimacy
Emotional and psychological closeness to other team or group members.

positive regard, opportunity for emotional expression, openness, security and emotional support, and giving and receiving nurturance. Failure to achieve psychological intimacy results in feelings of emotional isolation and loneliness. This may be especially problematic for chief executives who experience loneliness at the top. Although psychological intimacy is valuable for emotional health and well-being, it need not necessarily be achieved in the work setting.

Integrated involvement is closeness achieved through tasks and activities. It results in enjoyable and involving activities, social identity and self-definition, being valued for one's skills and abilities, opportunity for power and influence, conditional positive regard, and support for one's beliefs and values. Failure to achieve integrated involvement results in social isolation. Whereas psychological intimacy is more emotion based, integrated involvement is more behavior and activity based. Integrated involvement contributes to social psychological health and well-being.

Psychological intimacy and integrated involvement each contribute to overall health. It is not necessary to achieve both in the same team or group. For example, while chief executive at Xerox Corporation, David Kearns was also a marathon runner; he found integrated involvement with his executive team and psychological intimacy with his athletic companions on long-distance runs.

Teams and groups have two sets of functions that operate to enable members to achieve psychological intimacy and integrated involvement. These are task and maintenance functions.

DIVERSITY AND CREATIVITY IN TEAMS

(6) Discuss diversity and creativity in teams.

Diversity and creativity are important, emerging issues in the study of teams and teamwork. Recent research in diversity has focused on the issue of dissimilarity and its effect within the team itself. This is often studied based on social identity theory and self-categorization theory. Later in the chapter, we specifically address the issue of multicultural diversity in upper echelons, or top management teams, in the global workplace. Creativity concerns new and/or dissimilar ideas or ways of doing things within teams. Novelty and innovation are creativity's companions. While creativity is developed in some detail in Chapter 10, we treat it briefly here in the context of teams.

Dissimilarity

We defined diversity in Chapter 1 in terms of individual differences. Recent relational demography research finds that demographic dissimilarity influences employees' absenteeism, commitment, turnover intentions, beliefs, workgroup relationships, self-esteem, and organizational citizenship behavior (OCB).[53] Thus, dissimilarity may have positive or negative effects in teams and on team members. In the accompanying Science feature, we see how structural diversity can enhance team performance. While value dissimilarity may be positively related to task and relationship conflict, it is negatively related to team involvement.[54] This highlights the importance of managing dissimilarity in teams, being open to diversity, and turning conflicts over ideas into positive outcomes.

Functional background is one way to look at dissimilarity in teams. One study of 262 professionals in thirty-seven cross-functional teams found that promoting functional background social identification helped individuals perform better as team members.[55] Another study of multifunctional management teams in a *Fortune* 100 company found that functional background predicted team involvement.[56] Finally, in a slightly different study of 129 members on twenty multidisciplinary project teams, informational dissimilarity had no adverse effects when there was member task and goal congruence.[57] Where there was incongruence, dissimilarity adversely affected team identification and OCBs.

integrated involvement
Closeness achieved through tasks and activities.

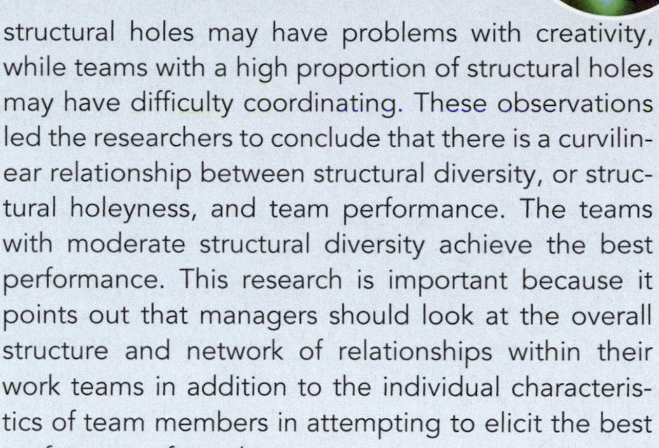

Structural "Holeyness" in Teams

This research examined diversity and performance of nineteen teams in a wood products company. The investigators were interested in demographic diversity among team members as well as the structural diversity of the team. Structural diversity concerns the number of structural holes within a work team. A structural hole in a team is a disconnection between two of its members. Is this disconnection good or bad for the team? What are the consequences of having more or fewer structural holes between team members? Neither race nor gender was a demographic factor that influenced the proportion of structural holes within a work team. However, age diversity significantly reduced the extent of structural holeyness. Hence, greater variance in age within a team leads to more member-to-member connections and fewer member-to-member disconnections. Teams with few structural holes may have problems with creativity, while teams with a high proportion of structural holes may have difficulty coordinating. These observations led the researchers to conclude that there is a curvilinear relationship between structural diversity, or structural holeyness, and team performance. The teams with moderate structural diversity achieve the best performance. This research is important because it points out that managers should look at the overall structure and network of relationships within their work teams in addition to the individual characteristics of team members in attempting to elicit the best performance from these teams.

SOURCE: F. Balkundi, M. Kilduff, Z. I. Barsness, and J. H. Michael, "Demographic Antecedents and Performance Consequences of Structural Holes in Work Teams," *Journal of Organizational Behavior* 28 (2007): 241–260.

Creativity

Creativity is often thought of in an individual context rather than a team context. However, there is such a thing as team creativity. In a study of fifty-four research and development teams, one study found that team creativity scores would be explained by aggregation processes across both people and time.[58] The investigators concluded that it is important to consider aggregation across time as well as across individuals when one is attempting to understand team creativity. In another study of creative behavior, a Korean electronics company found that individual dissimilarity in age and performance as well as functional diversity within the team positively affect individual employees' creative behavior.

Some think that the deck is stacked against teams as agents of creativity. Leigh Thompson disagrees and suggests that team creativity and divergent thinking can be enhanced through greater diversity in teams, brainwriting, training facilitators, membership change in teams, electronic brainstorming, and building a playground.[59] These practices can overcome social loafing, conformity, and downward norm setting in teams and organizations. Team members might exercise care in timing the insertion of their novel ideas into the team process so as to maximize the positive impact and benefits.[60]

EMPOWERMENT AND SELF-MANAGED TEAMS

7 Discuss empowerment, teamwork, and self-managed teams.

Quality teams and quality circles, as we discussed earlier, are one way to implement teamwork in organizations. Self-managed teams are broad-based work teams that deal with issues beyond quality. Decision making in self-managed teams is also discussed in Chapter 10. On a dysfunctional note, employee resistance behavior can emerge in self-managed work teams. It is influenced by cultural values and can affect employee attitudes.[61] However, self-managed teams have an overall positive history and are increasingly used by U.S. multinational corporations in global operations.

Empowerment may be thought of as an attribute of a person or of an organization's culture.[62] As an organizational culture attribute, empowerment encourages participation, an essential ingredient for teamwork.[63] Quality action teams (QATs) at FedEx are the primary quality improvement process (QIP) technique used by the company to engage management and hourly employees in four- to ten-member problem-solving teams.[64] The teams are empowered to act and solve problems as specific as charting the best route from the Phoenix airport to the local distribution center or as global as making major software enhancements to the online package-tracking system.

Empowerment may give employees the power of a lightning strike, but empowered employees must be properly focused through careful planning and preparation before they strike.[65]

You 9.2 includes several items from FedEx's survey-feedback-action (SFA) survey related to employee empowerment. Complete You 9.2 to see if you are empowered.

Empowerment Skills

Empowerment through employee self-management is an alternative to empowerment through teamwork.[66] Whether through self-management or teamwork, empowerment requires the development of certain skills if it is to be enacted effectively. Competence skills are the first set of skills required for empowerment. Mastery and experience in one's chosen discipline and profession provide an essential foundation for empowerment. This means that new employees and trainees should experience only limited empowerment until they demonstrate the capacity to accept more responsibility, a key aspect of empowerment.

Empowerment also requires certain process skills. The most critical process skills for empowerment include negotiating skills, especially with allies, opponents, and adversaries.[67] Allies are the easiest people to negotiate with because they agree with you about the team's mission, and you can trust their actions and behavior. Opponents require a different negotiating strategy; although you can predict their actions and behavior, they do not agree with your concept of the team's mission. Adversaries are dangerous, difficult people to negotiate with because they do not agree with your concept of the team's mission, and you cannot predict their actions or behaviors.

A third set of empowerment skills involves the development of cooperative and helping behaviors.[68] Cooperative people are motivated to maximize the gains for everyone on the team; they engage in encouraging, helpful behavior to bring about that end. The alternatives to cooperation are competitive, individualistic, and egalitarian orientations. Competitive people are motivated to maximize their personal gains regardless of the expense to other people. This can be very counterproductive from the standpoint of the team. Individualistic people are motivated to act autonomously, though not necessarily to maximize their personal gains. They are less prone to contribute to the efforts of the team. Egalitarian people are motivated to equalize the outcomes for each team member, which may or may not be beneficial to the team's well-being. Actually, the team members who need the most help often get the least because helping behaviors are frequently targeted to the most "expert" team members, a dynamic that actually compromises overall team performance.[69]

Communication skills are a final set of essential empowerment skills.[70] These include skills in self-expression and reflective listening. Empowerment cannot occur in a team unless members are able to express themselves effectively and listen carefully to one another.

Self-Managed Teams

Self-managed teams make decisions that were once reserved for managers. They are also called *self-directed teams* or *autonomous work groups*. Self-managed teams are one way to implement empowerment in organizations. Even so, managers have an important role in providing leadership and influence.[71] In doing so, there is strong support for the use of soft influence tactics in managers' communication with self-directed

self-managed team

A team that makes decisions that were once reserved for managers.

YOU 9.2

Are You an Empowered Employee?*

Read each of the following statements carefully. Then, to the right, indicate which answer best expresses your level of agreement (5 = strongly agree, 4 = agree, 3 = sometimes agree/sometimes disagree, 2 = disagree, 1 = strongly disagree, and 0 = undecided/do not know). Mark only one answer for each item, and respond to all items.

____	1. I feel free to tell my manager what I think.	5	4	3	2	1	0
____	2. My manager is willing to listen to my concerns.	5	4	3	2	1	0
____	3. My manager asks for my ideas about things affecting our work.	5	4	3	2	1	0
____	4. My manager treats me with respect and dignity.	5	4	3	2	1	0
____	5. My manager keeps me informed about things I need to know.	5	4	3	2	1	0
____	6. My manager lets me do my job without interfering.	5	4	3	2	1	0
____	7. My manager's boss gives us the support we need.	5	4	3	2	1	0
____	8. Upper management (directors and above) pays attention to ideas and suggestions from people at my level.	5	4	3	2	1	0

Scoring

To determine if you are an empowered employee, add your scores.

32–40: You are empowered! Managers listen when you speak, respect your ideas, and allow you to do your work.

24–31: You have *some* power! Your ideas are considered sometimes, and you have some freedom of action.

16–23: You must exercise caution! You cannot speak or act too boldly, and your managers appear to exercise close supervision.

8–15: Your wings are clipped! You work in a powerless, restrictive work environment.

*If you are not employed, discuss these questions with a friend who is employed. Is your friend an empowered employee?
SOURCE: *Survey-Feedback-Action (SFA)*, FedEx Corporation, Memphis, TN.

teams, which yields more positive results.[72] A one-year study of self-managed teams suggests that they have a positive impact on employee attitudes but not on absenteeism or turnover.[73] Evaluative research is helpful in achieving a better understanding of this relatively new way of approaching teamwork and the design of work. Research can help in establishing expectations for self-managed teams. For example, one study of autonomous work teams found that a key ingredient to enhancing organizational commitment and job satisfaction involves the perception that one has the required skills and abilities to perform well.[74] Further, there are risks, such as groupthink, in self-managing teams that must be prevented or managed if the team is to achieve full development and function.[75] Finally, one evaluation of empowerment, teams, and TQM programs found that companies associated with these popular management techniques did not have higher economic performance.[76]

Other evaluations of self-managed teams are more positive. Southwest Industries, a high-technology aerospace manufacturing firm, embarked on a major internal reorganization in the early 1990s that included the creation of self-managed teams to fit its high-technology production process. Southwest's team approach resulted in a 30 percent increase in shipments, a 30 percent decrease in lead time, a 40 percent decrease in total inventory, a decrease in machinery downtime, and almost a one-third decrease in production costs.[77] Self-managed teams were also the foundation for the miraculous resurrection of the former Chrysler (now DaimlerChrysler) Corporation's oldest plant in New Castle, Indiana, as the United Auto Workers' union and company management forged a partnership for success.[78]

A game called Learning Teams is available to help people create self-directed teams, learn cooperatively, and master factual information.[79] With no outside help, an engineering team in the Defense Systems and Electronics Group (DSEG), now part of Raytheon, developed themselves into a highly effective, productive, self-managed team. They then helped DSEG in its successful effort to win a Malcolm Baldrige National Quality Award.

UPPER ECHELONS: TEAMS AT THE TOP

(8) Explain the importance of upper echelons and top management teams.

Self-managed teams at the top of the organization—top-level executive teams—are referred to as *upper echelons*. Organizations are often a reflection of these upper echelons.[80] Upper echelon theory argues that the background characteristics of the top management team can predict organizational characteristics. Furthermore, upper echelons are one key to the strategic success of the organization.[81] Thus, the teams at the top are instrumental in defining the organization over time such that the values, competence, ethics, and unique characteristics of the top management team are eventually reflected throughout the organization. This ability to exert organization-wide power and influence makes the top management team a key to the company's success. This ability may be compromised if the top team sends mixed signals about teamwork and if executive pay systems foster competition, politics, and individualism.[82]

For example, when Lee Iacocca became CEO at the former Chrysler Corporation, his top management team was assembled to bring about strategic realignment within the corporation by building on Chrysler's historical engineering strength. The dramatic success of Chrysler during the early 1980s was followed by struggle and accommodation during the late 1980s. This raises the question of how long a CEO and the top management team can sustain organizational success.

upper echelon

A top-level executive team in an organization.

Hambrick and Fukutomi address this question by examining the dynamic relationship between a CEO's tenure and the success of the organization.[83] They found five seasons in a CEO's tenure: (1) response to a mandate, (2) experimentation, (3) selection of an enduring theme, (4) convergence, and (5) dysfunction. A summary of each season is shown in Table 9.4. All else being equal, this seasons model has significant implications for organizational performance. Specifically, organizational performance increases during a CEO's tenure to a peak, after which performance declines. This relationship is depicted in Figure 9.3. The peak has been found to come at about seven years—somewhere in the middle of the executive's seasons. As indicated by the dotted lines in the figure, the peak may be extended, depending on several factors, such as diversity in the executive's support team.

© KIMBERLY WHITE/REUTERS/LANDOV

Top-level executive teams are referred to as upper echelons. Google executives pictured here (L-R): Chief Executive Officer Eric Schmidt, Vice President of Global Communications and Public Affairs Elliot Schrage, Co-Founder & President of Products Larry Page, Co-Founder & President of Technology Sergey Brin, and Senior Vice President of Corporate Development David Drummond.

TABLE 9.4 The Five Seasons of a CEO's Tenure

Critical CEO Characteristics	1 Response to Mandate	2 Experimentation	3 Selection of an Enduring Theme	4 Convergence	5 Dysfunction
Commitment to a Paradigm	Moderately strong	Could be strong or weak	Moderately strong	Strong; increasing	Very strong
Task Knowledge	Low but rapidly increasing	Moderate; somewhat increasing	High; slightly increasing	High; slightly increasing	High; slightly increasing
Information Diversity	Many sources; unfiltered	Many sources but increasingly filtered	Fewer sources; moderately filtered	Few sources; highly filtered	Very few sources; highly filtered
Task Interest	High	High	Moderately high	Moderately high but diminishing	Moderately low and diminishing
Power	Low; increasing	Moderate; increasing	Moderate; increasing	Strong; increasing	Very strong; increasing

SOURCE: D. Hambrick and G. D. S. Fukutomi, "The Seasons of a CEO's Tenure," *Academy of Management Review*, 1991, p. 729. Permission conveyed through Copyright Clearance Center, Inc.

Diversity at the Top

From an organizational health standpoint, diversity and depth in the top management team enhance the CEO's well-being.[84] From a performance standpoint, the CEO's top management team can influence the timing of the performance peak, the degree of dysfunction during the closing season of the CEO's tenure, and the rate of decline in organizational performance. Diversity and heterogeneity in the top management team help sustain high levels of organizational performance at the peak and help maintain

FIGURE 9.3 Executive Tenure and Organizational Performance

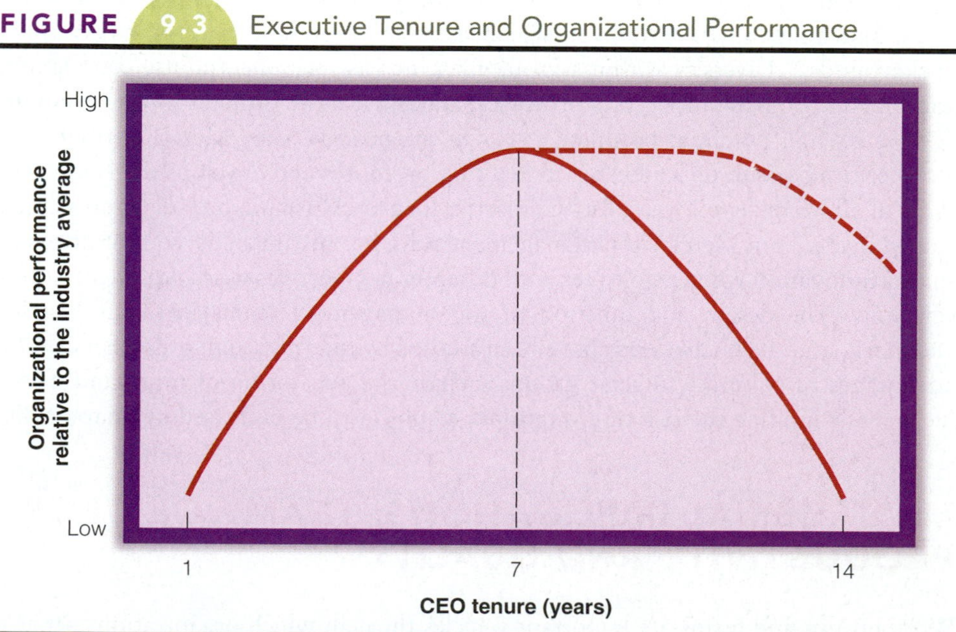

SOURCE: D. Hambrick, The Seasons of an Executive's Tenure, keynote address, the Sixth Annual Texas Conference on Organizations, Lago Vista, Texas, April 1991.

the CEO's vitality. The presence of a "wild turkey" in the top management team can be a particularly positive force. The wild turkey is a devil's advocate who challenges the thinking of the CEO and other top executives and provides a counterpoint during debates. If not shouted down or inhibited, the wild turkey helps the CEO and the team sustain peak performance and retard the CEO's dysfunction and decline. For example, President George W. Bush had his administration enhanced by the independent voice of Secretary of State Colin Powell. Often taking a more moderate position on policy issues than either the secretary of defense or the vice president, Powell brought variance and value to the voice of President Bush's administration. As we see in the Looking Back feature, Toyota is enhancing the diversity of its top management team.

No organization can succeed without a senior team that, collectively, captures a diversity of attributes: vision, task mastery, stewardship, and facilitation.[85] Leaders must evolve communication strategies to bring together a team that is functionally diverse, intellectually diverse, demographically diverse, temperamentally diverse, and so on, in order to complement each other. Dissimilarity develops strength, while similarity builds connections.

We can conclude that the leadership, composition, and dynamics of the top management team have an important influence on the organization's performance. In some cases, corporations have eliminated the single CEO. Current research has shown a dramatic increase in the number of co-CEO arrangements in both public and private corporations.[86] While more common in Europe than in the United States in the past, historical U.S. examples exist as well, such as when Walter Wriston created a three-member team when he was chairman at Citicorp (now part of Citigroup). At Southwest Airlines, the new top management team is emerging from the long shadow of legendary founder Herb Kelleher. This new top team led Southwest successfully through the terrorist crisis of September 2001.

Multicultural Top Teams

The backgrounds of group members may be quite different in the global workplace. Homogeneous groups in which all members share similar backgrounds are giving way to token groups in which all but one member come from the same background, bicultural groups in which two or more members represent each of two distinct cultures, and multicultural groups in which members represent three or more ethnic backgrounds.[87] Diversity within a group may increase the uncertainty, complexity, and inherent confusion in group processes, making it more difficult for the group to achieve its full, potential productivity.[88] On the positive side, Merck attributes its long-term success to its leadership model that promotes and develops the leadership skills of all Merck employees. Ray Gilmartin, former chairman, president, and CEO, valued diversity in Merck's top management team because he believed that diversity sparks innovation when employees with different perspectives work together to offer solutions. The design and function of top management teams in Great Britian, Denmark, and the Netherlands have been studied by international researchers.[89] The advantages of culturally diverse groups include the generation of more and better ideas while limiting the risk of groupthink, a subject to be discussed in Chapter 10.

MANAGERIAL IMPLICATIONS: TEAMWORK FOR PRODUCTIVITY AND QUALITY

Work groups and teams are important vehicles through which organizations achieve high-quality performance. The current emphasis on the new team environment, shown in Table 9.3, places unique demands on managers, teams, and individuals in leading,

FIGURE 9.4 The Triangle for Managing in the New Team Environment

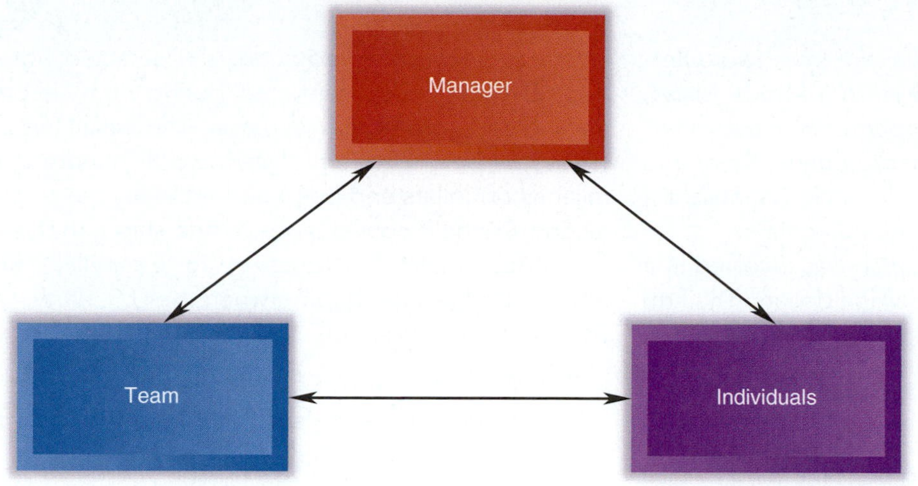

SOURCE: *Managing in the New Team Environment,* by L. Hirschhorn, © 1991. Reprinted by permission of Prentice-Hall, Inc., Upper Saddle River, N.J.

working, and managing. Managing these demands requires an understanding of individual diversity and the interrelationships of individuals, teams, and managers, as depicted in the triangle in Figure 9.4. Expectations associated with these three key organizational roles for people at work are different. The first role is as an individual, empowered employee. The second is as an active member of one or more teams. The third is the role of manager or formal supervisor. Earlier in the chapter, we discussed the foundations for teamwork, empowerment, and working in the new team environment. Individual empowerment must be balanced with collaborative teamwork.

The manager in the triangle is responsible for creating a receptive organizational environment for work groups and teams. This requires that she or he achieve a balance between setting limits (so that individuals and teams do not go too far afield) and removing barriers (so that empowered individuals and self-managed teams can accomplish their work). In addition, the manager should establish a flexible charter for each team. Once the charter is established, the manager continues to be available to the team as a coaching resource, as necessary. The manager establishes criteria for evaluating the performance effectiveness of the team, as well as the individuals, being supervised. In an optimum environment, this involves useful and timely performance feedback to teams that carries a sense of equity and fairness with it. The manager's responsibilities are different from the team leader's.

Effective team leaders may guide a work group or share leadership responsibility with their teams, especially self-managed teams. Team leaders are active team members with responsibility for nurturing the development and performance of the team.[90] They require skills different from those of the manager. Whereas the manager establishes the environment in which teams flourish, the team leader teaches, listens, solves problems, manages conflict, and enhances the dynamics of team functioning to ensure its success. It is the team leader's task to bring the team to maturity; help it work through interpersonal, task, and authority issues; and be skilled in nurturing a cohesive, effective team. A team leader requires the hands-on skills of direct involvement and full membership in the team. Flexibility, delegation, and collaboration are characteristics of healthy teams and their leaders. Increasing globalization requires team leaders to be skilled at forging teamwork among diverse individuals, whereas managers must be skilled at forging collaboration among diverse groups.

Diverse Duo Seals the Deal

Kerry Cannella and Selma Bueno are from two different worlds—literally. Cannella is from Rhode Island, while Bueno is from Brazil. Although they have different geographic and cultural backgrounds, Kerry and Selma are both bankers at Merrill Lynch; Cannella is a managing director; Bueno, a junior associate.

Earlier in the year, Merrill Lynch was involved in a deal potentially worth several million dollars. The firm had been representing Brazilian investors who were selling their stake in a multibillion-dollar Latin American company to potential U.S. investors. The deal was in process, but each side was moving slowly and cautiously. Merrill Lynch needed to do something to step up the pace of negotiations and close the deal.

Enter the team of Cannella and Bueno. The two bankers made frequent trips between New York and Brazil. Bueno analyzed financial papers and put together an offering document for investors in her native Portuguese. In addition, she selected hotels and restaurants and translated during negotiations, making both sides feel at ease. The result was a successful deal for Merrill Lynch worth hundreds of millions of dollars and one that met everyone's satisfaction. Cannella considers his partnership with Bueno "a perfect match." According to Cannella, "She [Bueno] bridged the gap between the U.S. party, the Brazilian party, and me."

1. Could Merrill Lynch have achieved similar success without having someone on the team with Selma Bueno's cultural background? Explain.
2. What risks and rewards can employers expect by placing representatives with diverse backgrounds on work groups and teams?

SOURCE: E. Iwata, "Companies Find Gold inside Melting Pot," *USA Today* (July 9, 2007): B1.

LOOKING BACK: TOYOTA

Diversity at the Top

James E. Press became the first non-Japanese member of Toyota's board of directors at age 60 while serving as president of the company's North American operations. He thus became a senior managing director of the corporation. The North American market is a large and important part of Toyota's overall business. About 34 percent of the company's overall sales volume, and 43 percent of its operating profit, comes from North America. In addition, Toyota exported about 50 percent of the cars it manufactures in Japan during 2007, an increase from the 38 percent that it exported during 2005. While the Japanese domestic car market—only one-third the size of the U.S. market—has remained flat, Toyota has enjoyed rising sales in the U.S. market, in part due to a spike in demand for its fuel-efficient cars.

There has been a deeper trend in diversity within Toyota that is apparently reflected in the new board appointment of Mr. Press. His appointment may be the tip of the iceberg. Other Americans hold top positions in Toyota divisions, such as in plant management and product development. There are also thousands of foreign employees within the company, so many that it opened a "Toyota Institute" outside Toyota City in order to teach them its corporate values. This initiative aims at establishing norms of behavior and building cohesion throughout the workforce. This deeper-level diversity trend within the employee population has increased to the extent that four foreigners held managing-officer positions by 2007. These key positions are just below the board level of the company.

At the top of every company or corporation sits its board of directors. Toyota had been publicly criticized for not having a non-Japanese executive on its 25-member board. The appearance was one of a glass ceiling for foreign employees, similar to the barriers many women have encountered within American companies and corporations. Toyota is now doing some top management team shuffling and expanding its board from 25 to 30 members, opening opportunities for outside senior-level executives. Diversity within this key team affords Toyota some distinct opportunities, advantages, and insights because it brings more direct and personal understanding into its important North American operations from a fellow board member. The key to taking advantage of this strategic opportunity is how fellow board members relate to their new and first non-Japanese member.[91]

Chapter Summary

1. Groups are often composed of diverse people at work. Teams in organizations are key to enhancing quality and achieving success.
2. Important aspects of group behavior include norms of behavior, group cohesion, social loafing, and loss of individuality.
3. Once a group forms, it generally goes through five stages of development. If successful, the group can function independently, with little interference from its leader.
4. Quality circles, originally popularized in Japan, and quality teams contribute to solving technological and quality problems in the organization.
5. Teams provide social benefits for team members, as well as enhancing organizational performance.
6. Functional and value dissimilarity may have positive or negative effects on teams. Managing dissimilarity in teams and being open to diversity are highly important for promoting creativity.
7. Empowerment and teamwork require specific organizational design elements and individual psychological characteristics and skills.
8. Upper echelons and top management teams are key to the strategy and performance of an organization. Diversity and a devil's advocate in the top team enhance performance.
9. Managing in the new team environment places new demands on managers, teams, and individuals. Managers must create a supportive and flexible environment for collaborative teams and empowered individuals. Team leaders must nurture the team's development.

Key Terms

group (p. 290)
group cohesion (p. 291)
integrated involvement (p. 304)
loss of individuality (p. 292)
maintenance function (p. 300)
norms of behavior (p. 291)
psychological intimacy (p. 303)
quality circle (QC) (p. 303)
quality team (p. 303)
self-managed team (p. 306)
social loafing (p. 291)
status structure (p. 298)
task function (p. 299)
teamwork (p. 301)
upper echelon (p. 308)
work team (p. 290)

Review Questions

1. What is a group? A work team?
2. Explain four aspects of group behavior. How can each aspect help or hinder the group's functioning?
3. Describe what happens in each stage of a group's development according to Tuckman's Five-Stage Model. What are the leadership requirements in each stage?

4. Describe the four characteristics of mature groups.
5. Why are work teams important to organizations today? How and why are work teams formed?
6. Describe at least five task and five maintenance functions that effective work teams must perform.
7. Discuss diversity and creativity in teams.
8. Describe the necessary skills for empowerment and teamwork.
9. What are the benefits and potential drawbacks of self-managed teams?
10. What is the role of the manager in the new team environment? What is the role of the team leader?

Discussion and Communication Questions

1. Which was the most effective group (or team) of which you have been a member? What made that group (or team) so effective?
2. Have you ever felt peer pressure to act more in accordance with the behavioral norms of a group? Have you ever engaged in a little social loafing? Have you ever lost your head and been caught up in a group's destructive actions?
3. Name a company that successfully uses teamwork and empowerment. What has that company done that makes it so successful in this regard? Has its team approach made a difference in its performance? How?
4. Name a person you think is a particularly good team member. What makes him or her so? Name someone who is a problem as a team member. What makes this person a problem?
5. Think about your current work environment. Does it use quality circles or self-managed teams? What are the barriers to teamwork and empowerment in that environment? What elements of the environment enhance or encourage teamwork and empowerment? (If you do not work, discuss this question with a friend who does.)
6. (*communication question*) Prepare a memo describing your observations about work teams and groups in your workplace or university. Where have you observed teams or groups to be most effective? Why? What changes might be made at work or in the university to make teams more effective?
7. (*communication question*) Develop an oral presentation about what the most important norms of behavior should be in an academic community and workplace. Be specific. Discuss how these norms should be established and reinforced.
8. (*communication question*) Interview an employee or manager about what he or she believes contributes to cohesiveness in work groups and teams. Ask the person what the conclusions are based on. Be prepared to discuss what you have learned in class.
9. Do you admire the upper echelons in your organization or university? Why or why not? Do they communicate effectively with groups and individuals throughout the organization?

Ethical Dilemma

Greg Towns and Michele Brown sat chatting. Michele had come to Greg's office to discuss the first meeting of the strategic planning team. Michele had found out only last week that she would be the team leader for this very important project. Recently, upper management discovered that many of their employees didn't feel that their needs, desires, or capabilities were being considered in the formation of company goals. In response, the president requested that a team of employees be formed to provide employee input for the new plan.

This would be Michele's first time in a leadership position. She was excited, especially since she had been handpicked by the president. She had come to Greg's office to ask for his support in the meetings. Michele did not have confidence in her leadership skills and wanted to know that she could count on someone to back her. Greg confidently assured Michele that she could count on him.

Everyone was excited as the meeting began. They were all happy to be working for a company that cared enough about its employees to create this committee. Michele began the meeting by reminding everyone why they were called together. She felt this was their time to shine for management. People began offering suggestions. Michele dismissed the first two as too broad. The third she called juvenile. The room fell silent. Michele was surprised by the silence and asked if everyone was out of suggestions. Allen Jamison finally spoke up. He told Michele that no one wanted to make suggestions if she was just going to shoot down every idea. Michele denied that she was discounting the others' ideas. She just wanted to be sure that they sent management their very best suggestions. Michele looked to Greg, waiting for the promised support.

Greg felt trapped. He agreed with Allen. Michele's behavior did not encourage input. She was acting like a dictator, not a team leader. He had promised to support her, but he never dreamt that she would act this way. Supporting her behavior went against his beliefs. But he had promised.

Questions

1. How would Greg's promise to support Michele still hold given her behavior?
2. Evaluate Greg's decision using consequential, rule-based, and character theories.

Experiential Exercises

9.1 Tower Building: A Group Dynamics Activity

This exercise gives you an opportunity to study group dynamics in a task-oriented situation. Each group must bring materials to class for building a tower. All materials must fit in a box no greater than eight cubic feet (i.e., 2 ft. × 2 ft. × 2 ft. or 1 ft. × 2 ft. × 4 ft.).

Step 1. Each group is assigned a meeting place and a workplace. One or two observers should be assigned in each group. The instructor may assign a manager to each group.

Step 2. Each group plans for the building of the paper tower (no physical construction is allowed during this planning period). Towers will be judged on the basis of height, stability, beauty, and meaning. (Another option is to have the groups do the planning outside of class and come prepared to build the tower.)

Step 3. Each group constructs its tower.

Step 4. Groups inspect other towers, and all individuals rate towers other than their own. See the evaluation sheet at the right. Each group turns in its point totals (i.e., someone in the group adds up each person's total for all groups rated) to the instructor, and the instructor announces the winner.

Step 5. Group dynamics analysis. Observers report observations to their own groups, and each group analyzes the group dynamics that occurred during the planning and building of the tower.

Step 6. Groups report on major issues in group dynamics that arose during the tower planning and building. Complete the tower building aftermath questionnaire as homework if requested by your instructor.

	GROUPS							
CRITERIA	1	2	3	4	5	6	7	8
Height								
Stability/Strength Beauty								
Meaning/ Significance								
TOTALS								

Rate each criterion on a scale of 1–10, with 1 being lowest or poorest, and 10 being highest or best.

SOURCE: From *Organizational Behavior and Performance*, 5/e by Szilagyi/Wallace, © 1997. Reprinted by permission of Prentice-Hall, Inc., Upper Saddle River, N.J.

9.2 Design a Team

The following exercise gives you an opportunity to design a team. Working in a six-person group, address the individual characteristics, team composition, and norms for an effective group whose task is to make recommendations on improving customer relations. The president of a small clothing manufacturer is concerned that his customers are not satisfied enough with the company's responsiveness, product quality, and returned-orders process. He has asked your group to put together a team to address these problems.

Step 1. The class will form into groups of approximately six members each. Each group elects a spokesperson and answers the following questions. The group should spend an equal amount of time on each question.

a. *What characteristics should the individual members of the task team possess?* Members may consider professional competence, skills, department, and/or personality and behavioral characteristics in the group's discussion.

b. *What should the composition of the task team be?* Once your group has addressed individual characteristics, consider the overall composition of the task team. Have special and/or unique competencies, knowledge, skills, and abilities been considered in your deliberations?

c. *What norms of behavior do you think the task team should adopt?* A team's norms of behavior may evolve, or they may be consciously discussed and agreed upon. Take the latter approach.

Step 2. Each group will share the results of its answers to the questions in Step 1. Cross-team questions and discussion follow.

TAKE 2

Biz Flix | Apollo 13

This superb film dramatically shows the NASA mission to the moon that had an in-space disaster. Innovative problem solving and decision making amid massive ambiguity saved the crew. *Apollo 13* has many examples of problem solving and decision making.

The scene from the film shows day 5 of the mission, about two-thirds of the way through *Apollo 13*. Earlier in the mission, Jack Swigert (Kevin Bacon) stirred the oxygen tanks at mission control's request. An explosion in the spacecraft happened shortly after this procedure, causing unknown damage to the command module. Before this scene takes place, the damage has forced the crew to move into the LEM (Lunar Exploration Module), which becomes their lifeboat for return to earth.

What to Watch for and Ask Yourself:

- What triggers the conflict in this scene?
- Is this intergroup conflict or intragroup conflict? What effects can such conflict have on the group dynamics on board *Apollo 13*?
- Does mission commander Jim Lovell (Tom Hanks) successfully manage the group dynamics to return the group to a normal state?

Workplace Video | Teamwork, Featuring Cold Stone Creamery

Freshly baked brownies and cones, handmade ice cream in an array of flavors, colorful tasty toppings—that's the "Ultimate Ice Cream Experience" at Cold Stone Creamery, and it's winning over customers in the United States and around the world.

Delivering Cold Stone's fun, flavorful "experience" to millions of customers takes teamwork, and the Scottsdale, Arizona-based ice-cream franchise uses many different kinds of teams to ensure that operations are as smooth as its cold, velvety treats. The company's vertical teams, which include members from the executive suite all the way down to the local managers, create plans and strategies that set the company in motion. Horizontal teams, which are comprised of employees of the same hierarchical level, work on daily prep, baking, and entertainment-oriented tasks. Special-purpose teams come together for a time to work on specific projects, such as boosting same-store sales. Self-directed teams form when multiskilled workers make group decisions normally reserved for managers.

Widespread excitement about Cold Stone Creamery has led to the development of another important team: the global team. Global teams collaborate across international boundaries to bring the Ultimate Ice Cream Experience to Japan, South Korea, China, and elsewhere. Because of the challenges of working across great distances, these groups function as virtual teams, relying on advanced telecommunications technologies to coordinate efforts.

All teams need effective leadership, and Cold Stone CEO Doug Ducey provides both the vision and resources necessary for his teams to succeed. Ducey and other top executives have set an ambitious company-wide goal that gives focus to the work of every employee: make Cold Stone Creamery the number-one-selling ice cream in the United States by 2010. The bar is high, but Ducey is confident that his franchisees can meet expectations if first-line managers and crew members are united in their efforts.

TAKE 2

Finally, while group-led initiative is helping Cold Stone achieve organizational success, it also is having a positive impact on individual workers. Teamwork at Cold Stone has increased employee satisfaction, expanded job knowledge, and augmented worker productivity. Most importantly, teams have created a culture of fun. Who would expect anything less from the maker of the ever-popular Birthday Cake Remix and the deliciously dirty Mud Pie Mojo?

Discussion Questions

1. What norms of behavior would you expect to find among team members working in a Cold Stone Creamery ice cream store?
2. What are some of the challenges involved in creating a global team at Cold Stone?
3. What characteristics of a team may influence group effectiveness, and what role does diversity play in team success?

CASE

Stryker's Use of Teamwork in Redesigning Surgical Equipment

The Stryker Corporation was built on innovation. "When Dr. Homer Stryker, an orthopedic surgeon from Kalamazoo, Michigan, found that certain medical products were not meeting his patients' needs, he invented new ones. As interest in these products grew, Dr. Stryker started a company in 1941 to produce them. The company's goal was to help patients lead healthier, more active lives through products and services that make surgery and recovery simpler, faster and more effective."[1]

Homer Stryker started Orthopedic Frame Company to sell devices for moving patients with spinal injuries.[2] A short time later he invented the first power tool for removing plaster casts after patients' broken bones had healed. After that the company began providing hospital beds. These early initiatives, but especially the oscillating cast saw, formed the foundation of what is now the Stryker Corporation, one of the leading companies in the worldwide market for orthopedic devices.[3] Stryker, headquartered in Kalamazoo, Michigan, employs over 15,000 people, with most of its operations being in the United States, Europe, and Japan. As a leading medical technology company and one of the largest in the $28.6 billion worldwide orthopedic market, Stryker manufactures replacement joints such as shoulders, knees, and hips; high-tech tools like imaging systems that help surgeons reconstruct body parts; and a variety of other medical devices and products, including surgical tools and hospital beds.[4]

One of Stryker's recent orthopedic innovations was a navigation system for hip replacement surgery that permitted surgeons to observe via a computer screen the precise positioning of a hip replacement prosthesis. Due to the nature of hip replacement, the navigation system had to have the capability of withstanding the various physical stresses put on the equipment, including pounding with a surgical hammer. In addition, the navigation system—especially its sophisticated electronics—had to survive repeated sterilization under 270-degree-Fahrenheit steam pressure. However, shortly after field testing of the hip replacement navigation system began, significant problems were discovered. Numerous complaints were received from surgeons, and the systems were returned to Stryker. Examination of the returned units revealed that the precision electronics of the system frequently failed and metal parts were broken or damaged.[5]

Finding a solution to the navigation system problems was assigned to Klaus Welte, vice president and plant manager for Stryker's Freiburg, Germany facility, which was acquired in 1998. Under its previous owner, Leibinger, the Freiburg facility had developed a magnetic imaging navigation system for use in neurosurgery. After the acquisition by Stryker, the Freiburg facility applied its navigation system technology and expertise to developing other surgical tools, including ones for orthopedics. Thus, the Freiburg facility was given the responsibility for solving the problems with the hip replacement navigation system.[6]

Welte's first challenge was assembling a team to work on solving the navigation system problem. Welte believed that the team's success "would require both a clear view of what had to be accomplished and a deep understanding of each team member's abilities."[7] Welte assembled a team of the best people at Freiburg in operations, computer-aided design, engineering, and research. One team member was talented in structural analysis, communication, and follow-through. Another member provided the "social glue" for the team and would never stop until all tasks were complete. Still another was an organizer who helped keep the team on task and from rushing ahead before it was ready. Yet another member was especially knowledgeable regarding how a product design will successfully survive the manufacturing process. Another person was noted for highly innovative—indeed visionary—product design ideas.[8]

Although each team member's abilities were important, how those abilities fit together was equally important. According to Welte, "Creating an effective team requires more than just filling all the job descriptions with someone who has the right talent and experience. . . . By no means can you substitute one engineer for another. There are really very, very specific things that they are good at . . . and how well the team members' abilities combine is as important as the abilities themselves."[9] How well the Stryker team jelled became evident in their approach to problem solving.

Due to the number of problems with the hip replacement navigation system, the Freiburg team addressed each problem separately, beginning with the most crucial issue and working down to the relatively minor problems. The solution for each problem was thoroughly tested before moving on to the next issue. Consequently, the team did not have a fully assembled prototype until all the problems were addressed. This approach proved successful, both in terms of the ultimate success of the prototype design and the team working effectively together as problem solvers. In the first nine months after the redesigned hip replacement navigation system was released, the company did not receive a single complaint from surgeons—an incredible achievement for complex surgical equipment.[10]

Discussion Questions

1. Using Table 9.1, discuss the extent to which the characteristics of well-functioning, effective groups accurately describe the Freiburg hip replacement navigation system team.
2. Explain why teamwork is important to effectively solve the problems revealed by field testing of the hip replacement navigation system.
3. Using Table 9.2, describe how the task functions and maintenance functions are operating within the Freiburg team.
4. Explain why diversity and creativity are important to the effective functioning of the Freiburg team.

SOURCE: This case was written by Michael K. McCuddy, The Louis S. and Mary L. Morgal Chair of Christian Business Ethics and Professor of Management, College of Business Administration, Valparaiso University.

CHAPTER 10

Decision Making by Individuals and Groups

LEARNING OBJECTIVES

After reading this chapter, you should be able to do the following:

1. Explain the assumptions of bounded rationality.
2. Describe Jung's cognitive styles and how they affect managerial decision making.
3. Describe and evaluate the role of intuition and creativity in decision making.
4. Critique your own level of creativity and list ways of improving it.
5. Compare and contrast the advantages and disadvantages of group decision making.
6. Discuss the symptoms of groupthink and ways to prevent it.
7. Evaluate the strengths and weaknesses of several group decision-making techniques.
8. Explain the emerging role of virtual decision making in organizations.
9. Utilize an "ethics check" for examining managerial decisions.

THINKING AHEAD: GENENTECH, INC.

Good Decision Making Against All Odds

Genentech is the leading biotechnology firm in the pharmaceutical industry. As its competitors such as Pfizer continue to struggle, Genentech has repeatedly proven its ability to successfully develop and market drugs designed to fight a variety of diseases.

Recently, Genentech reported an increase in its earnings by 65 percent thanks to two new cancer-fighting drugs: Avastin and Tarceva. Genentech's CEO Arthur Levinson knows that the odds are one in 350 million that a new drug will be successful. Yet Genentech seems to be able to consistently beat those odds.

So, how does this biotechnology giant do it? They take a simple yet effective approach to decision making under great uncertainty. First, they have clearly defined short- and long-term goals that help everyone in the company rally around the same overarching objectives. Second, they let good science, rather than political behavior, drive all their decision making. Third, they have created a high employee involvement culture driven by team-based decision making. Finally, and perhaps most critically, Genentech is constantly seeking new domains of discovery. For example, they were investing money in research and development in cancer-fighting drugs some 25 years ago, when such investments were not even feasible for other companies. At the moment, they are embarking on ambitious research into immunology-related drugs even though it is entirely new territory for them.[1,2] In the Looking Back feature, you can read about Genentech's challenge one of their cancer drugs and their hope for the future.

THE DECISION-MAKING PROCESS

Decision making is a critical activity in the lives of managers. The decisions a manager faces can range from very simple, routine matters for which she or he has an established decision rule (*programmed decisions*) to new and complex decisions that require creative solutions (*nonprogrammed decisions*).[3] Scheduling lunch hours for one's work group is a programmed decision. The manager performs the decision activity on a daily basis, using an established procedure with the same clear goal in mind. In contrast, decisions like buying out another company are nonprogrammed. Genentech's decisions about which markets to penetrate and what areas to invest in for R&D purposes are examples of nonprogrammed decisions. The decision to acquire a company is another situation that is unique and unstructured and requires considerable judgment. Regardless of the type of decision made, it is helpful to understand as much as possible about how individuals and groups make decisions.

Decision making is a process involving a series of steps, as shown in Figure 10.1. The first step is recognition of the problem; that is, the manager realizes that a decision must be made. Identification of the real problem is important; otherwise, the manager may be reacting to symptoms and firefighting rather than dealing with the root cause of the problem. Next, a manager must identify the objective of the decision—in other words, determine what is to be accomplished by it.

programmed decision
A simple, routine matter for which a manager has an established decision rule.

nonprogrammed decision
A new, complex decision that requires a creative solution.

The third step in the decision-making process is gathering information relevant to the problem. The manager must pull together sufficient information about why the problem occurred. This involves conducting a thorough diagnosis of the situation and going on a fact-finding mission.

The fourth step is listing and evaluating alternative courses of action. During this step, a thorough "what-if" analysis should also be conducted to determine the various factors that could influence the outcome. It is important to generate a wide range of options and creative solutions in order to be able to move on to the fifth step.

© MICHAEL HALSBAND/LANDOV

The Blue Man Group has a history of making effective decisions. They have grown famous and successful by making sound business choices, even though none of the founders has any formal training in music, acting, or business.

Next, the manager selects the alternative that best meets the decision objective. If the problem has been diagnosed correctly and sufficient alternatives have been identified, this step is much easier.

Finally, the solution is implemented. The situation must then be monitored to see whether the decision met its objective. Consistent monitoring and periodic feedback are essential parts of the follow-up process.

Decision making can be stressful. Managers must make decisions with significant risk and uncertainty, and often without full information. They must trust and rely on others in arriving at their decisions, but they are ultimately responsible. Sometimes the decisions are painful and involve exiting businesses, firing people, and

FIGURE 10.1 The Decision-Making Process

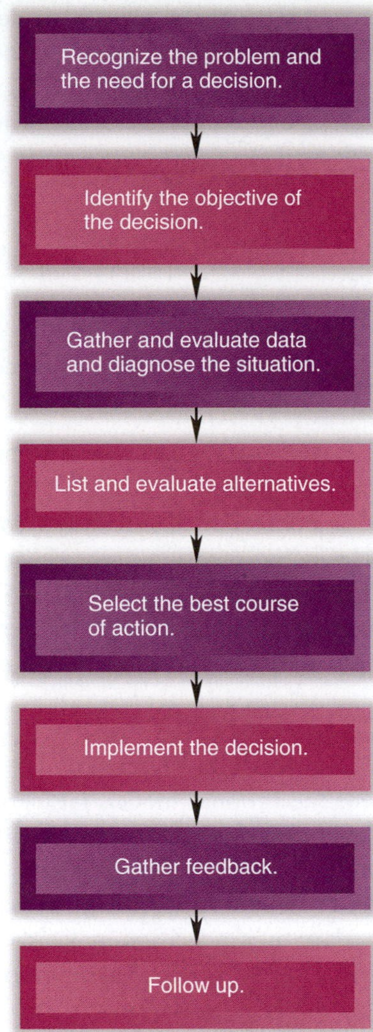

admitting wrong. Blue Man Group has a history of making effective decisions. Their theatrical productions are a creative combination of comedy, music, and multimedia in a type of entertainment that is totally unique. They have grown wildly famous and successful by making sound business choices, even though none of the founders has any formal training in music, acting, or business. The group turned down offers to sell credit cards, soft drinks, breath mints, and paint, all of course related to the color blue. With each new opportunity, the three founders use the same evaluation: "Okay, that's all well and good, that's a nice thought—but is it Blue Man?" They also have achieved what a lot of businesses want to do but never complete: a detailed 132-page operating manual. The founders make decisions by unanimous agreement.[4]

MODELS OF DECISION MAKING

The success of any organization depends on managers' abilities to make *effective decisions*. An effective decision is timely, is acceptable to the individuals affected by it, and meets the desired objective.[5] This section describes three models of decision making: the rational model, the bounded rationality model, and the garbage can model.

effective decision
A timely decision that meets a desired objective and is acceptable to those individuals affected by it.

Rational Model

Rationality refers to a logical, step-by-step approach to decision making, with a thorough analysis of alternatives and their consequences. The rational model of decision making comes from classic economic theory and contends that the decision maker is completely rational in his or her approach. The rational model has the following important assumptions:

1. The outcome will be completely rational.
2. The decision maker has a consistent system of preferences, which is used to choose the best alternative.
3. The decision maker is aware of all the possible alternatives.
4. The decision maker can calculate the probability of success for each alternative.[6]

In the rational model, the decision maker strives to optimize, that is, to select the best possible alternative.

Given its assumptions, the rational model is unrealistic. There are time constraints and limits to human knowledge and information-processing capabilities. In addition, a manager's preferences and needs change often. The rational model is thus an ideal that managers strive for in making decisions. It captures the way a decision should be made but does not reflect the reality of managerial decision making.[7]

Bounded Rationality Model

(1) Explain the assumptions of bounded rationality.

Recognizing the deficiencies of the rational model, Herbert Simon suggested that there are limits on how rational a decision maker can actually be. His decision theory, the bounded rationality model, earned a Nobel Prize in 1978.

Simon's model, also referred to as the "administrative man" theory, rests on the idea that there are constraints that force a decision maker to be less than completely rational. The bounded rationality model has four assumptions:

1. Managers select the first alternative that is satisfactory.
2. Managers recognize that their conception of the world is simple.
3. Managers are comfortable making decisions without determining all the alternatives.
4. Managers make decisions by rules of thumb or heuristics.

Bounded rationality assumes that managers *satisfice;* that is, they select the first alternative that is "good enough," because the costs of optimizing in terms of time and effort are too great.[8] Further, the theory assumes that managers develop shortcuts, called *heuristics*, to make decisions in order to save mental activity. Heuristics are rules of thumb that allow managers to make decisions based on what has worked in past experiences.

Does the bounded rationality model more realistically portray the managerial decision process? Research indicates that it does.[9] One of the reasons managers face limits to their rationality is that they must make decisions under risk and time pressure. The situation they find themselves in is highly uncertain, and the probability of success is not known.

rationality
A logical, step-by-step approach to decision making, with a thorough analysis of alternatives and their consequences.

bounded rationality
A theory that suggests there are limits to how rational a decision maker can actually be.

satisfice
To select the first alternative that is "good enough," because the costs in time and effort are too great to optimize.

heuristics
Shortcuts in decision making that save mental activity.

garbage can model
A theory that contends that decisions in organizations are random and unsystematic.

Garbage Can Model

Sometimes the decision-making process in organizations appears to be haphazard and unpredictable. In the *garbage can model,* decisions are random and unsystematic.[10]

FIGURE 10.2 The Garbage Can Model

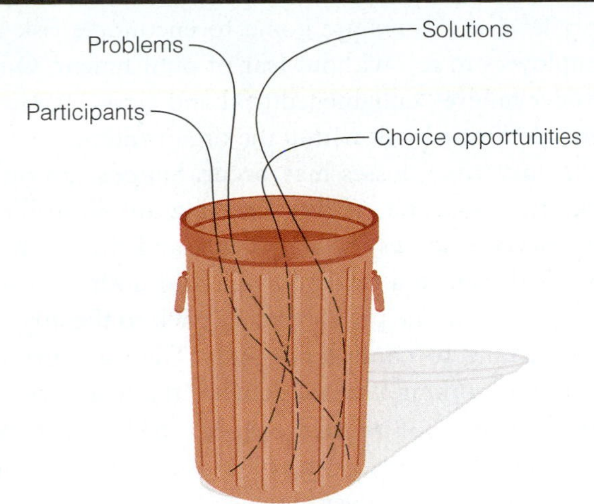

SOURCE: From M. D. Cohen, J. G. March, and J. P. Olsen in *Administrative Science Quarterly* 17 (March 1972): 1–25. Reprinted by permission of the *Administrative Science Quarterly*.

Figure 10.2 depicts the garbage can model. In this model, the organization is a garbage can in which problems, solutions, participants, and choice opportunities are floating around randomly. If the four factors happen to connect, a decision is made.[11] The quality of the decision depends on timing. The right participants must find the right solution to the right problem at the right time.

The garbage can model illustrates the idea that not all organizational decisions are made in a step-by-step, systematic fashion. Especially under conditions of high uncertainty, the decision process may be chaotic. Some decisions appear to happen out of sheer luck.

On the high-speed playing field of today's businesses, managers must make critical decisions quickly, with incomplete information, and must also involve employees in the process.

DECISION MAKING AND RISK

Many decisions involve some element of risk. For managers, hiring decisions, promotions, delegation, acquisitions and mergers, overseas expansions, new product development, and other decisions make risk a part of the job.

Risk and the Manager

Individuals differ in terms of their willingness to take risks. Some people experience *risk aversion*. They choose options that entail fewer risks, preferring familiarity and certainty. Other individuals are risk takers; that is, they accept greater potential for loss in decisions, tolerate greater uncertainty, and in general are more likely to make risky decisions. Risk takers are also more likely to take the lead in group discussions.[12]

Research indicates that women are more averse to risk taking than men and that older, more experienced managers are more risk averse than younger managers. There is also some evidence that successful managers take more risks than unsuccessful ones.[13] However, the tendency to take risks or avoid them is only part of behavior toward risk. Risk taking is influenced not only by an individual's tendency but also by organizational factors. In commercial banks, loan decisions that require the assessment of risk are made every day.

risk aversion
The tendency to choose options that entail fewer risks and less uncertainty.

Upper-level managers face a tough task in managing risk-taking behavior. By discouraging lower-level managers from taking risks, they may stifle creativity and innovation. If upper-level managers are going to encourage risk taking, however, they must allow employees to fail without fear of punishment. One way to accomplish this is to consider failure "enlightened trial and error."[14] The key is establishing a consistent attitude toward risk within the organization.

When individuals take risks, losses may occur. Suppose an oil producer thinks there is an opportunity to uncover oil by reentering an old drilling site. She gathers a group of investors and shows them the logs, and they chip in to finance the venture. The reentry is drilled to a certain depth, and nothing is found. Convinced they did not drill deep enough, the producer goes back to the investors and requests additional financial backing to continue drilling. The investors consent, and she drills deeper, only to find nothing. She approaches the investors, and after lengthy discussion, they agree to provide more money to drill deeper. Why do decision makers sometimes throw good money after bad? Why do they continue to provide resources to what looks like a losing venture?

Escalation of Commitment

Continuing to support a failing course of action is known as *escalation of commitment*.[15] In situations characterized by escalation of commitment, individuals who make decisions that turn out to be poor choices tend to hold fast to them, even when substantial costs are incurred.[16] An example of escalation is the price wars that often occur between airlines. The airlines reduce their prices in response to competitors until at a certain stage, both airlines are in a "no-win" situation. Yet they continue to compete despite the heavy losses they are incurring. The desire to win is a motivation to continue to escalate, and each airline continues to reduce prices (lose money) based on the belief that the other airline will pull out of the price war. Another example of escalation of commitment is NASA's enormous International Space Station. Originally estimated to cost $8 billion, the Space Station has been redesigned five times and remains unfinished. Its estimated cost topped $30 billion, and some pundits speculate that the total bill may reach $130 billion for what physicist Robert Park describes as "the biggest technological blunder in history." Despite the station's drain on virtually every other NASA program, it remains a focal point of NASA's work and continues to consume vast resources.[17]

In the Real World 10.1, you can read about IBM's recent risky decision making that seemed like escalation of commitment at first, and how it seems to have paid off for the company.

Why does escalation of commitment occur? One explanation is offered by cognitive dissonance theory, as we discussed in Chapter 4. This theory assumes that humans dislike inconsistency, and that when there is inconsistency among their attitudes or between their attitudes and behavior, they strive to reduce the dissonance.[18]

Other reasons why people maintain a losing course of action are optimism and control. Some people are overly optimistic and overestimate the likelihood that positive things will happen to them. Other people operate under an illusion of control—that they have special skills to control the future that other people don't have.[19] In addition, sunk costs may encourage escalation. Individuals think, "Well, I've already invested this much . . . what's a few dollars more?" And the closer a project is to completion, the more likely escalation is to occur.[20]

escalation of commitment
The tendency to continue to support a failing course of action.

Clinging to a poor decision can be costly to organizations. While most U.S. airlines (including United, American, and TWA) originally placed orders for the prestigious Mach 2 Concorde airliner during the 1960s, all U.S. orders for the plane were

IBM Corporation: Challenging the Boundaries of Collaborative Research

IBM has long been a leading innovator in the computer hardware industry. Given the fierce competition and narrower profit margins, IBM has faced some rough times. In the latter half of 2003, IBM's chip-making division was in trouble. The company had pumped millions of dollars into research and development and the division was losing millions of dollars every year with no hope for the future.

This situation called for one of two decisions: IBM could either quit this course of action or it could take a novel approach to R&D. John Kelly, then head of the semiconductor division, called a meeting of top executives at IBM and suggested that they open the doors of their R&D division to key R&D partners. This proposal was met with fierce opposition as many feared it would reflect escalation of commitment. They also feared that almost ten years of their research might be in jeopardy if such open R&D collaborations went into effect. This decision also would mark a radical departure from IBM's usual strategy with R&D, which was that if IBM couldn't build it, it probably wasn't good enough.

Yet after two hours of debate, Kelly convinced his executives that in the changing business environment, there would be great minds working outside IBM and it would help the company to collaborate. As a result, IBM adopted an open R&D collaboration with nine key partners including big names like Toshiba and Sony.

This decision paid off for IBM. Its partners have helped with the R&D costs, supplied much-needed brainpower, and IBM's chip-making division is turning a profit. This story reveals that it is sometimes very difficult to determine whether a risky decision will eventually pay off or not. IBM's decision highlighted key principles of innovative, outside-the-box decision making.

SOURCE: S. Hamm, "Radical Collaboration, Lessons from IBM's Innovation Factory," Special Report, *Business Week Online* (August 30, 2007), http://www.businessweek.com/innovate/content/aug2007/id20070830_258824.htm?chan=search.

eventually cancelled, leaving only British Airways and Air France as customers. While these two firms doggedly held onto their marginally profitable Concorde operations for almost three decades, a crash in 2000 led to closer scrutiny of the aging fleet, which was eventually retired in 2003. Industry insiders estimate that every customer who took the Concorde rather than a 747 cost British Airways more than $1,200 in profits.[21] Organizations can deal with escalation of commitment in several ways. One is to split the responsibility for decisions about projects. One individual can make the initial decision, and another can make subsequent decisions. Companies have also tried to eliminate escalation of commitment by closely monitoring decision makers.[22] Another suggestion is to provide individuals with a graceful exit from poor decisions so that their images are not threatened. One way of accomplishing this is to reward people who admit to poor decisions before escalating their commitment to them. A study also suggested that having groups, rather than individuals, make an initial investment decision would reduce escalation. Support has been found for this idea. Participants in group decision making may experience a diffusion of responsibility for the failed decision rather than feeling personally responsible; thus, they can pull out of a bad decision without threatening their image.[23]

We have seen that there are limits to how rational a manager can be in making decisions. Most managerial decisions involve considerable risk, and individuals react differently to risk situations.

JUNG'S COGNITIVE STYLES

(2) Describe Jung's cognitive styles and how they affect managerial decision making.

In Chapter 3 we introduced Jungian theory as a way of understanding and appreciating differences among individuals. This theory is especially useful in pointing out that individuals have different styles of making decisions. Carl Jung's original theory identified two styles of information gathering (sensing and intuiting) and two styles of making judgments (thinking and feeling). You already know what each individual preference means. Jung contended that individuals prefer one style of perceiving and one style of judging.[24] The combination of a perceiving style and a judging style is called a *cognitive style*. There are four cognitive styles: sensing/thinking (ST), sensing/feeling (SF), intuiting/thinking (NT), and intuiting/feeling (NF). Each of the cognitive styles affects managerial decision making.[25]

STs rely on facts. They conduct an impersonal analysis of the situation and then make an analytical, objective decision. The ST cognitive style is valuable in organizations because it produces a clear, simple solution. STs remember details and seldom make factual errors. Their weakness is that they may alienate others because of their tendency to ignore interpersonal aspects of decisions. In addition, they tend to avoid risks.

SFs also gather factual information, but they make judgments in terms of how they affect people. They place great importance on interpersonal relationships but also take a practical approach to gathering information for problem solving. The SFs' strength in decision making lies in their ability to handle interpersonal problems well and to take calculated risks. SFs may have trouble accepting new ideas that break the organization's rules.

NTs focus on the alternative possibilities in a situation and then evaluate them objectively and impersonally. NTs love to initiate ideas, and they like to focus on the long term. They are innovative and will take risks. This makes NTs good at things like new business development.[26] Weaknesses of NTs include their tendencies to ignore arguments based on facts and to ignore the feelings of others.

NFs also search out alternative possibilities, but they evaluate the possibilities in terms of how they will affect the people involved. They enjoy participative decision making and are committed to developing their employees. However, NFs may be prone to making decisions based on personal preferences rather than on more objective data. They may also become too responsive to the needs of others.

Research supports the existence of these four cognitive styles and their influences on managerial decision making.[27] One study asked managers to describe their ideal organization, and the researchers found strong similarities in the descriptions of managers with the same cognitive style.[28] STs wanted an organization that relied on facts and details and that exercised impersonal methods of control. SFs focused on facts, too, but they did so in terms of the relationships within the organization. NTs emphasized broad issues and described impersonal, idealistic organizations. NFs described an organization that would serve humankind well and focused on general, humanistic values.

All four cognitive styles have much to contribute to organizational decision making.[29] Isabel Briggs Myers, creator of the MBTI, also developed the Z problem-solving model, which capitalizes on the strengths of the four separate preferences (sensing, intuiting, thinking, and feeling). By using this model, managers can use both their preferences and nonpreferences to make decisions more effectively. The Z model is presented in Figure 10.3.

According to this model, good problem solving has four steps:

1. *Examine the facts and details.* Use sensing to gather information about the problem.
2. *Generate alternatives.* Use intuiting to develop possibilities.
3. *Analyze the alternatives objectively.* Use thinking to logically determine the effects of each alternative.
4. *Weigh the impact.* Use feeling to determine how the people involved will be affected.

cognitive style
An individual's preference for gathering information and evaluating alternatives.

FIGURE 10.3 The Z Problem-Solving Model

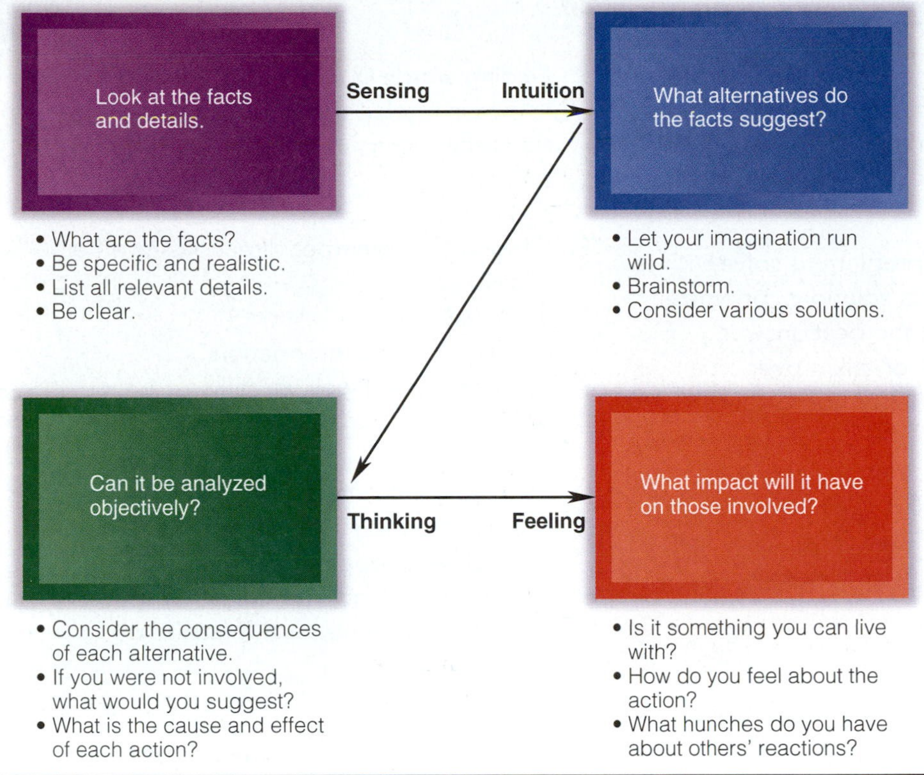

Look at the facts and details.
Sensing
Intuition
What alternatives do the facts suggest?
• What are the facts?
• Be specific and realistic.
• List all relevant details.
• Be clear.
• Let your imagination run wild.
• Brainstorm.
• Consider various solutions.
Can it be analyzed objectively?
Thinking
Feeling
What impact will it have on those involved?
• Consider the consequences of each alternative.
• If you were not involved, what would you suggest?
• What is the cause and effect of each action?
• Is it something you can live with?
• How do you feel about the action?
• What hunches do you have about others' reactions?

SOURCE: Excerpted from *Type Talk at Work* by Otto Kroeger and Janet M. Thuesen, 1992, Delacorte Press. Reprinted by permission of Otto Kroeger Associates.

Using the Z model can help an individual develop his or her nonpreferences. Another way to use the Z model is to rely on others to perform the nonpreferred activities. For example, an individual who is an NF might want to turn to a trusted NT for help in analyzing alternatives objectively.

OTHER INDIVIDUAL INFLUENCES ON DECISION MAKING

In addition to the cognitive styles just examined, many other individual differences affect a manager's decision making. Other personality characteristics, attitudes, and values, along with all of the individual differences variables that were discussed in Chapters 3 and 4, have implications for managerial decision making. Managers must use both their logic and their creativity to make effective decisions. Most of us are more comfortable using either logic or creativity, and we show that preference in everyday decision making. You 10.1 is an activity that will tell you which process, logic or creativity, is your preferred one. Take You 10.1 now, and then read on to interpret your score.

Brain hemispheric dominance is related to students' choices of college majors. Left-brained students gravitate toward business, engineering, and sciences, whereas right-brained students are attracted to education, nursing, communication, and literature.[30]

Our brains have two lateral halves (Figure 10.4). The right side is the center for creative functions, while the left side is the center for logic, detail, and planning. There are advantages to both kinds of thinking, so the ideal situation is to be "brain-lateralized" or to be able to use either logic or creativity or both, depending

Which Side of Your Brain Do You Favor?

There are no "right" or "wrong" answers to this questionnaire. It is more of a self-assessment than a test. Do not read the questions more than once. Don't overanalyze. Merely circle "a" or "b" to indicate which answer is more typical of you.

1. Typically, when I have a problem to solve,
   a. I make a list of possible solutions, prioritize them, and then select the best answer.
   b. I "let it sit" for a while or talk it over with someone before I attempt to reach a solution.
2. When I sit with my hands clasped in my lap (FOLD YOUR HANDS THAT WAY RIGHT NOW BEFORE GOING ON, THEN LOOK AT YOUR HANDS), the thumb that is on top is
   a. my right thumb.
   b. my left thumb.
3. I have hunches
   a. sometimes, but do not place much faith in them.
   b. frequently and I usually follow them.
4. If I am at a meeting or lecture, I tend to take extensive notes.
   a. True
   b. False
5. I am well organized, have a system for doing things, have a place for everything and everything in its place, and can assimilate information quickly and logically.
   a. True
   b. False
6. I am good with numbers.
   a. True
   b. False
7. Finding words in a dictionary or looking up names in a telephone book is something I can do easily and quickly.
   a. True
   b. False
8. If I want to remember directions or other information,
   a. I make notes.
   b. I visualize the information.
9. I express myself well verbally.
   a. True
   b. False
10. To learn dance steps or athletic moves,
    a. I try to understand the sequence of the steps and repeat them mentally.
    b. I don't think about it; I just try to get the feel of the game or the music.

Interpretation: b = 6 a = 4

- Four, five, or six "a" answers indicate lateralization—an ability to use either hemisphere easily and to solve problems according to their nature rather than according to a favored manner.
- One, two, or three "a" answers indicate right-hemisphere dominance; corresponding traits include inventiveness, creativity, innovation, risk taking, whimsy, and an ability to see the "big picture."
- Seven, eight, or nine "a" answers indicate a left-hemisphere dominance—a tendency toward attention to detail, the use of logic, and traits of thoroughness and accuracy.

SOURCE: "Which Side of the Brain Do You Favor?" from *Quality Driven Designs.* Copyright 1992 Pfeiffer/Jossey-Bass. Reprinted by permission of Jossey-Bass, Inc., a subsidiary of John Wiley & Sons, Inc.

on the situation. There are ways to develop the side of the brain you are not accustomed to using. To develop your right side, or creative side, you can ask "what-if" questions, engage in play, and follow your intuition. To develop the left side, you can set goals for completing tasks and work to attain these goals. For managers, it is important to see the big picture, craft a vision, and plan strategically—all of which require right-brain skills. It is equally important to be able to understand day-to-day operations and flow chart work processes, which are left-hemisphere brain skills.

FIGURE 10.4 Functions of the Left and Right Brain Hemispheres

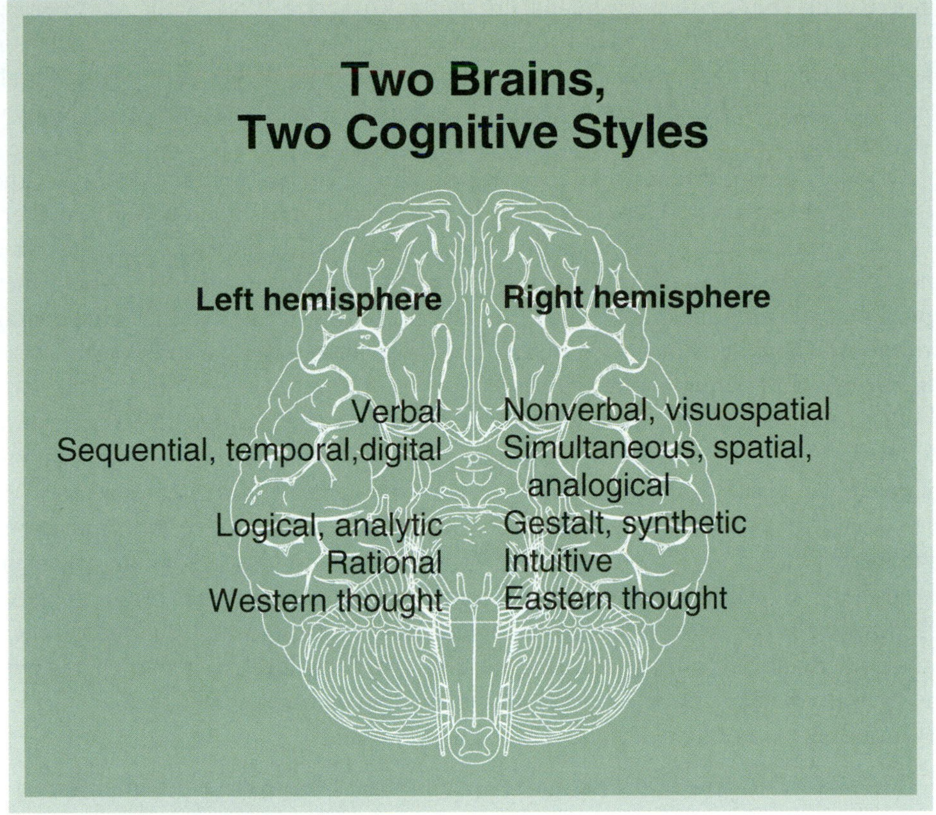

SOURCES: Created based on ideas from *Left Brain, Right Brain* by Springer and Deutsch, p. 272. © 1993 by Sally P. Springer and Georg Deutsch (New York: W. H. Freeman and Company, 1993). DILBERT reprinted by permission of United Feature Syndicate, Inc.

Two particular individual influences that can enhance decision-making effectiveness will be highlighted next: intuition and creativity.

(3) Describe and evaluate the role of intuition and creativity in decision making.

The Role of Intuition

intuition
A fast, positive force in decision making that is utilized at a level below consciousness and involves learned patterns of information.

There is evidence that managers use their *intuition* to make decisions.[31] Henry Mintzberg, in his work on managerial roles, found that in many cases managers do not appear to use a systematic, step-by-step approach to decision making. Rather, Mintzberg argued, managers make judgments based on "hunches."[32] Daniel Isenberg studied the way senior managers make decisions and found that intuition was used extensively, especially as a mechanism to evaluate decisions made more rationally.[33] Robert Beck studied the way managers at BankAmerica (now Bank of America) made decisions about the future direction of the company following the deregulation of the banking industry. Beck described their use of intuition as an antidote to "analysis paralysis," or the tendency to analyze decisions rather than developing innovative solutions.[34]

Dr. Gary Klein, a renowned cognitive psychologist, has written a book on the power of intuition. Dr. Klein and his colleagues insist that skilled decision makers rely on patterns of learned information in making quick and efficient decisions. In a series of studies conducted with the U.S. Navy, firefighters, and the U.S. Army, they found that decision makers normally relied on intuition in unfamiliar, challenging situations. These decisions were superior to those made after careful evaluation of information and potential alternatives.[35]

Just what is intuition? In Jungian theory, intuiting (N) is one preference used to gather data. This is only one way that the concept of intuition has been applied to managerial decision making, and it is perhaps the most widely researched form of the concept of intuition. There are, however, many definitions of *intuition* in the managerial literature. Chester Barnard, one of the early influential management researchers, argued that intuition's main attributes were speed and the inability of the decision maker to determine how the decision was made.[36] Other researchers have contended that intuition occurs at an unconscious level, and that this is why the decision maker cannot verbalize how the decision was made.[37]

Intuition has been variously described as follows:

> The ability to know or recognize quickly and readily the possibilities of a situation.[38]
> Smooth automatic performance of learned behavior sequences.[39]
> Simple analyses frozen into habit and into the capacity for rapid response through recognition.[40]

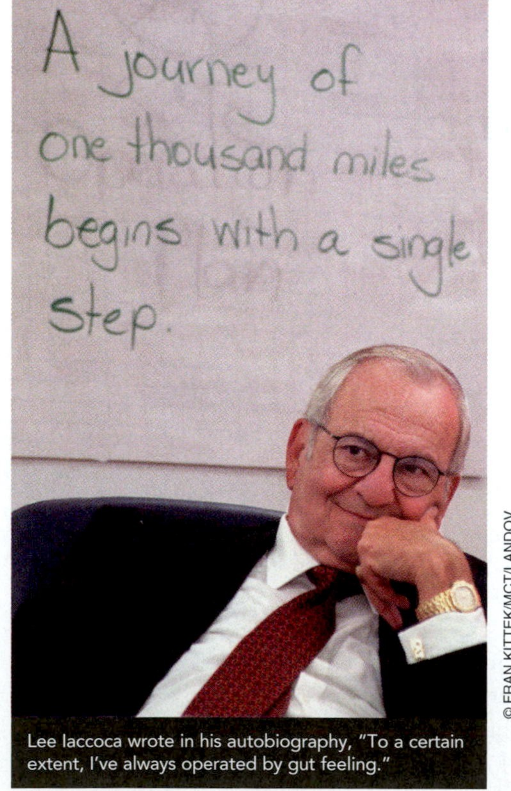

Lee Iaccoca wrote in his autobiography, "To a certain extent, I've always operated by gut feeling."

These definitions share some common assumptions. First, there seems to be a notion that intuition is fast. Second, intuition is utilized at a level below consciousness. Third, there seems to be agreement that intuition involves learned patterns of information. Fourth, intuition appears to be a positive force in decision making.

The use of intuition may lead to more ethical decisions. Intuition allows an individual to take on another's role with ease, and role taking is a fundamental part of developing moral reasoning. You may recall from Chapter 4 the role of cognitive moral development in ethical decision making. One study found a strong link between cognitive moral development and intuition. The development of new perspectives through intuition leads to higher moral growth, and thus to more ethical decisions.[41]

One question that arises is whether managers can be taught to use their intuition. Weston Agor, who has conducted workshops on developing intuitive skills in managers, has attained positive results in organizations such as the city of Phoenix and entertainment powerhouse Walt Disney Enterprises. After giving intuition tests to more than 10,000 executives, he has concluded that in most cases, higher management positions are held by individuals with higher levels of intuition. Just as the brain needs both hemispheres to work, Agor cautions that organizations need both analytical and intuitive minds to function at their peak. Consider Grant Tinker, former head of NBC. "Sometimes the boss has to go by his gut, hold his nose, and jump," Tinker writes in *Tinker in Television*. Lee Iacocca, in his autobiography, spends pages extolling intuition: "To a certain extent, I've always operated by gut feeling."[42] Agor suggests relaxation techniques, using images to guide the mind, and taking creative pauses before making a decision.[43] A review of the research on intuition suggests that although intuition itself cannot be taught, managers can be trained to rely more fully on the promptings of their intuition.[44]

Intuition is an elusive concept, and one with many definitions. There is an interesting paradox regarding intuition. Some researchers view "rational" methods as preferable to intuition, yet satisfaction with a rational decision is usually determined by how the decision feels intuitively.[45] Intuition appears to have a positive effect on managerial decision making, but it is not without controversy. Some writers argue that intuition has its place and that instincts should be trusted, but not as a substitute for reason. With new technologies, managers can analyze a lot more information in a lot less time, making the rational method less time-consuming than it once was.[46]

Creativity at Work

Creativity is a process influenced by individual and organizational factors that results in the production of novel and useful ideas, products, or both.[47] The social and technological changes that organizations face require creative decisions.[48] Managers of the future need to develop special competencies to deal with the turbulence of change, and one of these is the ability to promote creativity in organizations.[49]

Creativity is a process that is at least in part unconscious. The four stages of the creative process are preparation, incubation, illumination, and verification.[50] Preparation means seeking out new experiences and opportunities to learn, because creativity grows from a base of knowledge. Travel and educational opportunities of all kinds open the individual's mind. Incubation is a process of reflective thought and is often conducted subconsciously. During incubation, the individual engages in other pursuits while the mind considers the problem and works on it. Illumination occurs when the individual senses an insight for solving the problem. Finally, verification is conducted to determine if the solution or idea is valid. This is accomplished by thinking through the implications of the decision, presenting it to another person, or trying it out. Sleep is an important contributor to creative problem solving. Momentary quieting of the brain through relaxation can also increase "coherence" or the ability of different parts of the brain to work together.[51,52] Both individual and organizational influences affect the creative process.

Individual Influences

Several individual variables are related to creativity. One group of factors involves the cognitive processes that creative individuals tend to use. One cognitive process is divergent thinking, meaning the individual's ability to generate several potential solutions to a problem.[53] In addition, associational abilities and the use of imagery are associated with creativity.[54] Unconscious processes such as dreams are also essential cognitive processes related to creative thinking.[55]

Personality factors have also been related to creativity in studies of individuals from several different occupations. These characteristics include intellectual and artistic values, breadth of interests, high energy, concern with achievement, independence of judgment, intuition, self-confidence, and a creative self-image.[56] Tolerance of ambiguity, intrinsic motivation, risk taking, and a desire for recognition are also associated with creativity.[57]

creativity
A process influenced by individual and organizational factors that results in the production of novel and useful ideas, products, or both.

There is also evidence that people who are in a good mood are more creative.[58] Positive affect is related to creativity in work teams because being in a positive mood allows team members to explore new ways of thinking.[59] Positive emotions enhance creativity by broadening one's cognitive patterns and resources. For example, repeated experiences of love, interest, courage, and gratitude cause one to discard old theories and automatic ways of doing things. Instead, these positive emotions initiate thoughts and actions that are novel and unscripted.[60, 61] Moreover, it is a cyclical process, because creative thoughts and incidents lead to more positive affect. You might say that thinking positively makes us more creative, and being more creative makes us think positively.[62] In tasks involving considerable cognitive demands, however, it has been found that people in negative moods perform better. When an individual experiences negative moods or emotions, it is a signal that all is not well, which leads to more attention and vigilance in cognitive activity. Positive moods signal that all is well with the status quo, which can lead to decreased performance on some decision-making tasks involving complex mental activity.[63,64]

Organizational Influences The organizational environment people work in can either support or impede creativity. Creativity killers include focusing on how work is going to be evaluated, being closely monitored while you are working, and competing with other people in win–lose situations. In contrast, creativity facilitators include feelings of autonomy, being part of a team with diverse skills, and having creative supervisors and coworkers.[65] High-quality, supportive relationships with supervisors are related to creativity.[66] High-quality social networks that are cohesive can have a positive impact on creative decision making. Such social networks encourage creative decision making by facilitating shared sense-making of relevant information and consensus building.[67] Flexible organizational structures and participative decision making have also been associated with creativity. An organization can also present impediments to creativity. These barriers include internal political problems, harsh criticism of new ideas, destructive internal competition, and avoidance of risk.[68] The physical environment can also hamper creativity. Companies like Oticon, a Danish hearing-aid manufacturer, and Ethicon Endo-Surgery, a division of Johnson & Johnson, use open-plan offices that eliminate office walls and cubicles so that employees interact more frequently. When people mix, ideas mix as well.[69]

Studies of the role of organizational rewards in encouraging creativity have mixed results. Some studies have shown that monetary incentives improve creative performance, whereas others have found that is not the case.[70] Still other studies have indicated that explicitly contracting to obtain a reward led to lower levels of creativity when compared with contracting for no reward, being presented with just the task, or being presented with the task and receiving the reward later.[71] Organizations can therefore enhance individuals' creative decision making by providing a supportive environment, participative decision making, and a flexible structure.

Individual/Organization Fit Research has indicated that creative performance is highest when there is a match, or fit, between the individual and organizational influences on creativity. For example, when individuals who desire to be creative are matched with an organization that values creative ideas, the result is more creative performance.[72]

A common mistaken assumption regarding creativity is that either you have it or you do not. Research refutes this myth and has shown that individuals can be trained to be more creative.[73] The Disney Institute features a wide range of programs offered to companies, and one of their best-sellers is creativity training. You 10.2 allows you to determine whether you prefer creative or logical problem solving.

Creative or Logical Problem Solving: What Is Your Preference?

Try the following creative problem-solving challenge.

Each of the following problems is an equation that can be solved by substituting the appropriate words for the letters. Have fun with them!

Examples: 3F = 1Y (3 feet = 1 yard.)
4LC = GL (4 leaf clover = Good luck.)

1. M + M + NH + V + C + RI = NE.
2. "1B in the H = 2 in the B."
3. 8D − 24H = 1W.
4. 3P = 6.
5. HH & MH at 12 = N or M.
6. 4J + 4Q + 4K = All the FC.
7. S & M & T & W & T & F & S are D of W.
8. A + N + AF + MC + CG = AF.
9. T = LS State.
10. 23Y − 3Y = 2D.
11. E − 8 = Z.
12. Y + 2D = T.
13. C + 6D = NYE.
14. Y − S − S − A = W.
15. A & E were in the G of E.
16. My FL and South P are both MC.
17. "NN = GN."
18. N − P + SM = S of C.
19. 1 + 6Z = 1M.
20. "R = R = R."
21. AL & JG & WM & JK were all A.
22. N + V + P + A + A + C + P + I = P of S.
23. S + H of R = USC.

SOURCE: From *A Whack on the Side of the Head* by Roger Von Oech. Copyright © 1983, 1990, 1998 by Roger Von Oech. By permission of Warner Books.

Now try the following logical problem-solving exercise, entitled "Who Owns the Fish?", which is attributed to Albert Einstein.

There are five houses in a row and in five different colors. In each house lives a person from a different country. Each person drinks a certain drink, plays a certain game, and keeps a certain pet. No two people drink the same drink, play the same game, or keep the same pet.

- The Brit lives in a red house.
- The Swede keeps dogs.
- The Dane drinks tea.
- The green house is on the left of the white house.
- The green house owner drinks coffee.
- The person who plays tennis rears birds.
- The owner of the yellow house plays chess.
- The man living in the house right in the center drinks milk.
- The Norwegian lives in the first house.
- The man who plays poker lives next to the man who keeps cats.
- The man who keeps horses lives next to the one who plays chess.
- The man who plays billiards drinks beer.
- The German plays golf.
- The Norwegian lives next to the blue house.
- The man who plays poker has a neighbor who drinks water.

Question: Who owns the fish?

Answer: Your instructor can provide the solutions to this exercise.

SOURCE: By E. O. Welles, © 2004 Gruner + Jahr USA Publishing. "The Billionaire Next Door," first published in *Inc. Magazine*, 23 (6) (May 2001): pp. 80–85. Reprinted with permission.

Part of creativity training involves learning to open up mental locks that keep us from generating creative alternatives to a decision or problem. The following are some mental locks that diminish creativity:

- Searching for the "right" answer.
- Trying to be logical.
- Following the rules.
- Avoiding ambiguity.
- Striving for practicality.
- Being afraid to look foolish.
- Avoiding problems outside our own expertise.
- Fearing failure.
- Believing we are not really creative.
- Not making play a part of work.[74]

4 Critique your own level of creativity and list ways of improving it.

Note that many of these mental locks stem from values within organizations. Organizations can facilitate creative decision making in many ways. Rewarding creativity, allowing employees to fail, making work more fun, and providing creativity training are a few suggestions. Also, companies can encourage creativity by exposing employees to new ideas. This can be done in several ways, including job rotation, which moves employees through different jobs and gives them exposure to different information, projects, and teams. Employees can also be assigned to work with groups outside the company, such as suppliers or consultants. Finally, managers can encourage employees to surround themselves with stimuli that they have found to enhance their creative processes. These may be music, artwork, books, or anything else that encourages creative thinking.[75]

We have seen that both individual and organizational factors can produce creativity. Creativity can also mean finding problems as well as fixing them. Recently, four different types of creativity have been proposed, based on the source of the trigger (internal or external) and the source of the problem (presented versus discovered). Responsive creativity means responding to a problem that is presented to you by others because it is part of your job. Expected creativity is discovering problems because you are expected to by the organization. Contributory creativity is responding to problems presented to you because you want to be creative. Proactive creativity is discovering problems because you want to be creative.[76]

3M consistently ranks among the top ten in *Fortune*'s annual list of most admired corporations. It earned this reputation through innovation: More than one-quarter of 3M's sales are from products less than four years old. Post-It Notes, for example, were created by a worker who wanted little adhesive papers to mark hymns for church service. He thought of another worker who had perfected a light adhesive, and the two spent their free time developing Post-It Notes. 3M has continued its tradition of innovation with Post-It Flags, Pop-Up Tape Strips, and Nexcare Ease-Off Bandages.

Leaders can play key roles in modeling creative behavior. Sir Richard Branson, founder and chairman of UK-based Virgin Group, believes that if you do not use your employees' creative potential, you are doomed to failure. At Virgin Group, the culture encourages risk taking and rewards innovation. Rules and regulations are not over-valued, nor is analyzing ideas to death. Branson says an employee can have an idea in the morning and implement it in the afternoon.[77]

Creativity is a global concern. Poland, for example, is undergoing a major shift from a centrally planned economy and monoparty rule to a market economy and Western-style democracy. One of the major concerns for Polish managers is creativity. Finding ingenious solutions and having the ability to think creatively can be a question of life or death for Polish organizations, which are making the transition to a faster pace of learning and change.[78]

Both intuition and creativity are important influences on managerial decision making. Both concepts require additional research so that managers can better understand how to use them, as well as how to encourage employees to use them to make more effective decisions.

PARTICIPATION IN DECISION MAKING

Effective management of people can improve a company's economic performance. Firms that capitalize on this fact share several common practices. Chief among them is participation of employees in decision making.[79] Many companies do this through highly empowered self-managed teams like the ones we discussed in Chapter 9. Even in situations where formal teams are not feasible, decision authority can be handed down to front-line employees who have the knowledge and skills to make a difference. At Hampton Inn hotels, for example, guest services personnel are empowered to do whatever is necessary to make guests happy—without consulting their superiors.

The Effects of Participation

Participative decision making occurs when individuals who are affected by decisions influence the making of those decisions. Participation buffers employees from the negative experiences of organizational politics.[80] In addition, participative management has been found to increase employee creativity, job satisfaction, and productivity.[81]

GE Capital believes in participation. Each year it holds dreaming sessions, and employees from all levels of the company attend strategy and budget meetings to discuss where the company is heading. As a result, young employees came up with e-commerce ideas like http://www.financiallearning.com and http://www.gefn.com, which were highly successful.[82]

As our economy becomes increasingly based on knowledge work, and as new technologies make it easier for decentralized decision makers to connect, participative decision making will undoubtedly increase.[83] Consider the city and county of San Francisco, a combined city/county government organization. When the city and county of San Francisco needed to adopt a single messaging system to meet the needs of more than 20,000 users, it faced a huge challenge in getting all the users to provide input into the decision. Technology helped craft a system that balanced the needs of all the groups involved, and IT planners developed a twenty-eight-page spreadsheet to pull together the needs and desires of all sixty departments into a focused decision matrix. Within two years, 90 percent of the users had agreed on and moved to a single system, reducing costs and complexity.[84]

Foundations for Participation and Empowerment

Organizational and individual foundations underlie empowerment that enhances task motivation and performance. The organizational foundations for empowerment include a participative, supportive organizational culture and a team-oriented work design. A supportive work environment is essential because of the uncertainty

participative decision making
Decision making in which individuals who are affected by decisions influence the making of those decisions.

that empowerment can cause within the organization. Empowerment requires that lower-level organizational members be able to make decisions and take action on them. As operational employees become empowered to make decisions, fear, anxiety, or even terror can be created among middle managers in the organization.[85] Senior leadership must create an organizational culture that is supportive and reassuring for these middle managers as the power dynamics of the system change. If not supported and reassured, the middle managers can become a restraining, disruptive force to participative decision-making efforts.

A second organizational foundation for empowerment concerns the design of work. The old factory system relied on work specialization and narrow tasks with the intent of achieving routinized efficiency.[86] This approach to the design of work had some economic advantages, but it also had some distressing disadvantages leading to monotony and fatigue. This approach to the design of work is inconsistent with participation, because the individual feels absolved of much responsibility for a whole piece of work. Team-oriented work designs are a key organizational foundation because they lead to broader tasks and a greater sense of responsibility. For example, Volvo builds cars using a team-oriented work design in which each person does many different tasks, and each person has direct responsibility for the finished product.[87] These work designs create a context for effective participation as long as the empowered individuals meet necessary individual prerequisites.

The three individual prerequisites for participation and empowerment are (1) the capability to become psychologically involved in participative activities, (2) the motivation to act autonomously, and (3) the capacity to see the relevance of participation for one's own well-being.[88] First, people must be psychologically equipped to become involved in participative activities if they are to be empowered and become effective team members. Not all people are so predisposed. For example, Germany has an authoritarian tradition that runs counter to participation and empowerment at the individual and group level. General Motors encountered significant difficulties implementing quality circles in its German plants, because workers expected to be directed by supervisors, not to engage in participative problem solving. The German initiatives to establish supervisory/worker boards in corporations are intended to change this authoritarian tradition.

A second individual prerequisite is the motivation to act autonomously. People with dependent personalities are predisposed to be told what to do and to rely on external motivation rather than internal, intrinsic motivation.[89] These dependent people are not effective contributors to decision making.

Finally, if participative decision making is to work, people must be able to see how it provides a personal benefit to them. The personal payoff for the individual need not be short term. It may be a long-term benefit that results in people receiving greater rewards through enhanced organizational profitability.

What Level of Participation?

Participative decision making is complex, and one of the things managers must understand is that employees can be involved in some, or all, of the stages of the decision-making process. For example, employees could be variously involved in identifying problems, generating alternatives, selecting solutions, planning implementations, or evaluating results. Research shows that greater involvement in all five of these stages has a cumulative effect. Employees who are involved in all five processes have higher satisfaction and performance levels. And all decision processes are not created equal. If employees can't be provided with full participation in all stages, the highest payoffs seem to come with involvement in generating alternatives, planning implementations, and evaluating results.[90] Styles of participation in decision making may need to change as the company grows or as its culture changes.

THE GROUP DECISION-MAKING PROCESS

Managers use groups to make decisions for several reasons. One is *synergy,* which occurs when group members stimulate new solutions to problems through the process of mutual influence and encouragement within the group. Another reason for using a group is to gain commitment to a decision. Groups also bring more knowledge and experience to the problem-solving situation.

Group decisions can sometimes be predicted by comparing the views of the initial group members with the final group decision. These simple relationships are known as *social decision schemes.* One social decision scheme is the majority-wins rule, in which the group supports whatever position is taken by the majority of its members. Another scheme, the truth-wins rule, predicts that the correct decision will emerge as an increasing number of members realize its appropriateness. The two-thirds-majority rule means that the decision favored by two-thirds or more of the members is supported. Finally, the first-shift rule states that members support a decision represented by the first shift in opinion shown by a member.

Research indicates that these social decision schemes can predict a group decision as much as 80 percent of the time.[91] Current research is aimed at discovering which rules are used in particular types of tasks. For example, studies indicate that the majority-wins rule is used most often in judgment tasks (that is, when the decision is a matter of preference or opinion), whereas the truth-wins rule predicts decisions best when the task is an intellective one (that is, when the decision has a correct answer).[92]

Advantages and Disadvantages of Group Decision Making

(5) Compare and contrast the advantages and disadvantages of group decision making.

Both advantages and disadvantages are associated with group decision making. The advantages include (1) more knowledge and information through the pooling of group member resources; (2) increased acceptance of, and commitment to, the decision, because the members had a voice in it; and (3) greater understanding of the decision, because members were involved in the various stages of the decision process. The disadvantages of group decision making include (1) pressure within the group to conform and fit in; (2) domination of the group by one forceful member or a dominant clique, who may ramrod the decision; and (3) the amount of time required, because a group makes decisions more slowly than an individual.[93]

Given these advantages and disadvantages, should an individual or a group make a decision? Substantial empirical research indicates that whether a group or an individual should be used depends on the type of task involved. For judgment tasks requiring an estimate or a prediction, groups are usually superior to individuals because of the breadth of experience that multiple individuals bring to the problem.[94] On tasks that have a correct solution, other studies have indicated that the most competent individual outperforms the group.[95] This finding has been called into question, however. Much of the previous research on groups was conducted in the laboratory, where group members interacted only for short periods of time. Researchers wanted to know how a longer experience in the group would affect

synergy
A positive force that occurs in groups when group members stimulate new solutions to problems through the process of mutual influence and encouragement within the group.

social decision schemes
Simple rules used to determine final group decisions.

decisions. Their study showed that groups who worked together for longer periods of time outperformed the most competent member 70 percent of the time. As groups gained experience, the best members became less important to the group's success.[96] This study demonstrated that experience in the group is an important variable to consider when evaluating the individual versus group decision-making question.

Research is just beginning on the role of trust and trustworthiness in team decision making. One study was conducted for six weeks on student teams that were involved in designing an information systems project. The teams' trust of each other and risk-taking actions were cyclical. When teams saw the other team as trustworthy, they took a risk; then the other team, based on their perception of the first team's trustworthiness, decided whether or not to take a risk, and so on. The study showed that the trust process works between teams much the same as it does between individuals.[97]

Given the emphasis on teams in the workplace, many managers believe that groups produce better decisions than do individuals, yet the evidence is mixed. It is clear that more research needs to be conducted in organizational settings to help answer this question.

Two potential liabilities are found in group decision making: groupthink and group polarization. These problems are discussed in the following sections.

Groupthink

(6) Discuss the symptoms of groupthink and ways to prevent it.

One liability of a cohesive group is its tendency to develop *groupthink*, a dysfunctional process. Irving Janis, the originator of the groupthink concept, describes groupthink as "a deterioration of mental efficiency, reality testing, and moral judgment" resulting from pressures within the group.[98]

Certain conditions favor the development of groupthink. One of the conditions is high cohesiveness. Cohesive groups tend to favor solidarity because members identify strongly with the group.[99] High-ranking teams that make decisions without outside help are especially prone to groupthink because they are likely to have shared mental models; that is, they are more likely to think alike.[100] And homogeneous groups (ones with little to no diversity among members) are more likely to suffer from groupthink.[101] Two other conditions that encourage groupthink are having to make a highly consequential decision and time constraints.[102] A highly consequential decision is one that will have a great impact on the group members and on outside parties. When group members feel that they have a limited time in which to make a decision, they may rush through the process. These antecedents cause members to prefer concurrence in decisions and to fail to evaluate one another's suggestions critically. A group suffering from groupthink shows recognizable symptoms. Table 10.1 presents these symptoms and makes suggestions on how to avoid groupthink.

An incident cited as a prime example of groupthink is the 1986 *Challenger* disaster, in which the shuttle exploded and killed all seven crew members. A presidential commission concluded that flawed decision making was the primary cause of the accident. Sadly, organizations often struggle to learn from their mistakes. In 2003, the shuttle *Columbia* exploded over Texas upon reentering the earth's atmosphere, killing all seven crew members. Within days of the *Columbia* disaster, questions began to surface about the decision-making process that led flight engineers to assume that damage caused to the shuttle upon take-off was minor and to continue the mission. Subsequent investigation led observers to note that NASA's decision-making process appears just as flawed today as it was in 1986, exhibiting all the classic symptoms of groupthink. The final accident report

groupthink
A deterioration of mental efficiency, reality testing, and moral judgment resulting from pressures within the group.

TABLE 10.1 Symptoms of Groupthink and How to Prevent It

Symptoms of Groupthink

- *Illusions of invulnerability.* Group members feel that they are above criticism. This symptom leads to excessive optimism and risk taking.
- *Illusions of group morality.* Group members feel they are moral in their actions and therefore above reproach. This symptom leads the group to ignore the ethical implications of their decisions.
- *Illusions of unanimity.* Group members believe there is unanimous agreement on the decisions. Silence is misconstrued as consent.
- *Rationalization.* Group members concoct explanations for their decisions to make them appear rational and correct. The results are that other alternatives are not considered, and there is an unwillingness to reconsider the group's assumptions.
- *Stereotyping the enemy.* Competitors are stereotyped as evil or stupid. This leads the group to underestimate its opposition.
- *Self-censorship.* Members do not express their doubts or concerns about the course of action. This prevents critical analysis of the decisions.
- *Peer pressure.* Any members who express doubts or concerns are pressured by other group members who question their loyalty.
- *Mindguards.* Some members take it upon themselves to protect the group from negative feedback. Group members are thus shielded from information that might lead them to question their actions.

Guidelines for Preventing Groupthink

- Ask each group member to assume the role of the critical evaluator who actively voices objections or doubts.
- Have the leader avoid stating his or her position on the issue prior to the group decision.
- Create several groups that work on the decision simultaneously.
- Bring in outside experts to evaluate the group process.
- Appoint a devil's advocate to question the group's course of action consistently.
- Evaluate the competition carefully, posing as many different motivations and intentions as possible.
- Once consensus is reached, encourage the group to rethink its position by reexamining the alternatives.

SOURCE: Irving L. Janis, *Groupthink: Psychological Studies of Policy Decisions and Fiascoes*, Second Edition.

blamed the NASA culture that downplayed risk and suppressed dissent for the decision.[103,104]

Consequences of groupthink include an incomplete survey of alternatives, failure to evaluate the risks of the preferred course of action, biased information processing, and a failure to work out contingency plans. The overall result of groupthink is defective decision making. This was evident in the *Challenger* situation. The group considered only two alternatives: launch or no launch. They failed to consider the risks of their decision to launch the shuttle, and they did not develop any contingency plans.

Table 10.1 presents Janis's guidelines for avoiding groupthink. Many of these suggestions center around the notion of ensuring that decisions are evaluated completely, with opportunities for discussion from all group members. This strategy helps encourage members to evaluate one another's ideas critically. Groups that are educated about the value of diversity tend to perform better at decision-making tasks. On the other hand, groups that are homogenous and are not educated about the value of diversity do not accrue such benefits in decision making.[105]

Janis has used the groupthink framework to conduct historical analyses of several political and military fiascoes, including the Bay of Pigs invasion, the Vietnam War, and Watergate. One review of the decision situation in the *Challenger* incident proposed that two variables, time and leadership style, are important to include.[106] When a decision must be made quickly, there is more potential for groupthink. Leadership style can either promote groupthink (if the leader makes his or her opinion known up-front) or avoid groupthink (if the leader encourages open and frank discussion).

There are few empirical studies of groupthink, and most of these involved students in a laboratory setting. More applied research may be seen in the future, however, as a questionnaire has been developed to measure the constructs associated with groupthink.[107] Janis's work on groupthink has led to several interdisciplinary efforts at understanding policy decisions.[108] The work underscores the need to examine multiple explanations for failed decisions. Teams that experience cognitive (task-based) conflict are found to make better decisions than teams that experience affective (emotion-based) conflict. As such, one prescription for managers has been to encourage cognitive conflict while minimizing affective conflict. However, these two forms of conflict can also occur together, and more research is needed on how one can be encouraged while minimizing the other.[109]

Group Polarization

Another group phenomenon was discovered by a graduate student. His study showed that groups made riskier decisions; in fact, the group and each individual accepted greater levels of risk following a group discussion of the issue. Subsequent studies uncovered another shift—toward caution. Thus, group discussion produced shifts both toward more risky positions and toward more cautious positions.[110] Further research revealed that individual group member attitudes simply became more extreme following group discussion. Individuals who were initially against an issue became more radically opposed, and individuals who were in favor of the issue became more strongly supportive following discussion. These shifts came to be known as *group polarization*.[111]

The tendency toward polarization has important implications for group decision making. Groups whose initial views lean a certain way can be expected to adopt more extreme views following interaction.

Several ideas have been proposed to explain why group polarization occurs. One explanation is the social comparison approach. Prior to group discussion, individuals believe they hold better views than the other members. During group discussion, they see that their views are not so far from average, so they shift to more extreme positions.[112] A second explanation is the persuasive arguments view. It contends that group discussion reinforces the initial views of the members, so they take a more extreme position.[113] Both explanations are supported by research. It may be that both processes, along with others, cause the group to develop more polarized attitudes.

group polarization
The tendency for group discussion to produce shifts toward more extreme attitudes among members.

Group polarization leads groups to adopt extreme attitudes. In some cases, this can be disastrous. For instance, if individuals are leaning toward a dangerous decision, they are likely to support it more strongly following discussion. Both groupthink and group polarization are potential liabilities of group decision making, but several techniques can be used to help prevent or control these two liabilities.

TECHNIQUES FOR GROUP DECISION MAKING

Once a manager has determined that a group decision approach should be used, he or she can determine the technique that is best suited to the decision situation. Seven techniques will be briefly summarized: brainstorming, nominal group technique, Delphi technique, devil's advocacy, dialectical inquiry, quality circles and quality teams, and self-managed teams.

(7) Evaluate the strengths and weaknesses of several group decision-making techniques.

Brainstorming

Brainstorming is a good technique for generating alternatives. The idea behind *brainstorming* is to generate as many ideas as possible, suspending evaluation until all of the ideas have been suggested. Participants are encouraged to build on the suggestions of others, and imagination is emphasized. One company that benefits from brainstorming is Toyota. Despite its success with the baby-boomer generation, Toyota's executives realized that they were failing to connect with younger buyers, who viewed the firm as stodgy. In response, the company assembled a group of younger employees to brainstorm new products for this market. The result was the Toyota Echo, as well as the Scion, an entirely new line of boxy crossover vehicles aimed at young drivers.[114, 115, 116] Evidence suggests, however, that group brainstorming is less effective than a comparable number of individuals working alone. In groups, participants engage in discussions that can make them lose their focus.[117]

One recent trend is the use of electronic rather than verbal brainstorming in groups. Electronic brainstorming overcomes two common problems that can produce group brainstorming failure: production blocking and evaluation apprehension. In verbal brainstorming, individuals are exposed to the inputs of others. While listening to others, individuals are distracted from their own ideas.[118] This is referred to as production blocking. When ideas are recorded electronically, participants are free from hearing the interruptions of others; thus, production blocking is reduced. Some individuals suffer from evaluation apprehension in brainstorming groups. They fear that others might respond negatively to their ideas. In electronic brainstorming, input is anonymous, so evaluation apprehension is reduced. Studies indicate that anonymous electronic brainstorming groups outperform face-to-face brainstorming groups in the number of ideas generated.[119]

brainstorming
A technique for generating as many ideas as possible on a given subject, while suspending evaluation until all the ideas have been suggested.

Nominal Group Technique

A structured approach to decision making that focuses on generating alternatives and choosing one is called *nominal group technique (NGT)*. NGT involves the following discrete steps:

1. Individuals silently list their ideas.
2. Ideas are written on a chart one at a time until all ideas are listed.
3. Discussion is permitted but only to clarify the ideas. No criticism is allowed.
4. A written vote is taken.

nominal group technique (NGT)
A structured approach to group decision making that focuses on generating alternatives and choosing one.

NGT is a good technique to use in a situation where group members fear criticism from others.[120]

Delphi Technique

The *Delphi technique*, which originated at the Rand Corporation, involves gathering the judgments of experts for use in decision making. Experts at remote locations respond to a questionnaire. A coordinator summarizes those responses, and the summary is sent back to the experts. The experts then rate the various alternatives generated, and the coordinator tabulates the results. The Delphi technique is valuable in its ability to generate a number of independent judgments without the requirement of a face-to-face meeting.[121]

Devil's Advocacy

In the *devil's advocacy* decision method, a group or individual is given the role of critic. This devil's advocate has the task of coming up with the potential problems of a proposed decision. This helps organizations avoid costly mistakes in decision making by identifying potential pitfalls in advance.[122] As we discussed in Chapter 9, a devil's advocate who challenges the CEO and top management team can help sustain the vitality and performance of the upper echelon.

Dialectical Inquiry

Dialectical inquiry is a debate between two opposing sets of recommendations. Although it sets up a conflict, it is a constructive approach, because it brings out the benefits and limitations of both sets of ideas.[123] When using this technique, it is important to guard against a win–lose attitude and to concentrate on reaching the most effective solution for all concerned. Research has shown that the way a decision is framed (that is, win–win versus win–lose) is very important. A decision's outcome could be viewed as a gain or a loss, depending on the way the decision is framed.[124]

Quality Circles and Quality Teams

As you recall from Chapter 9, quality circles are small groups that voluntarily meet to provide input for solving quality or production problems. Quality circles are also a way of extending participative decision making into teams. Managers often listen to recommendations from quality circles and implement the suggestions. The rewards for the suggestions are intrinsic—involvement in the decision-making process is the primary one.

Quality circles are often generated from the bottom up; that is, they provide advice to managers, who still retain decision-making authority. As such, quality circles are not empowered to implement their own recommendations. They operate in parallel fashion to the organization's structure, and they rely on voluntary participation.[125] In Japan, quality circles have been integrated into the organization instead of added on. This may be one reason for Japan's success with this technique. In contrast, the U.S. experience is not as positive. It has been estimated that 60 to 75 percent of the quality circles have failed. Reasons for the failures have included lack of top management support and lack of problem-solving skills among quality circle members.[126]

Quality teams, in contrast, are included in total quality management and other quality improvement efforts as part of a change in the organization's structure.

Delphi technique
Gathering the judgments of experts for use in decision making.

devil's advocacy
A technique for preventing groupthink in which a group or individual is given the role of critic during decision making.

dialectical inquiry
A debate between two opposing sets of recommendations.

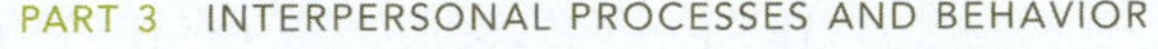

Quality teams are generated from the top down and are empowered to act on their own recommendations. Whereas quality circles emphasize the generation of ideas, quality teams make data-based decisions about improving product and service quality. Various decision-making techniques are employed in quality teams. Brainstorming, flow charts, and cause-and-effect diagrams help pinpoint problems that affect quality.

Some organizations have moved toward quality teams, but Toyota has stuck with quality circles. The company has used them since 1963 and was the second company in the world to do so. Toyota's quality circles constitute a limited form of empowerment—and they like it that way. The members want to participate but not be self-directed. They would rather leave certain decisions to managers who are trusted to take good care of them. Toyota attributes its success with quality circles to the longevity of their use and to its view of them as true methods of participation.[127]

Quality circles and quality teams are methods for using groups in the decision-making process. Self-managed teams take the concept of participation one step further.

Self-Managed Teams

Another group decision-making method is the use of self-managed teams, which we also discussed in Chapter 9. The decision-making activities of self-managed teams are more broadly focused than those of quality circles and quality teams, which usually emphasize quality and production problems. Self-managed teams make many of the decisions that were once reserved for managers, such as work scheduling, job assignments, and staffing. Unlike quality circles, whose role is an advisory one, self-managed teams are delegated authority in the organization's decision-making process.

Many organizations have claimed success with self-managed teams. At Northern Telecom (now Nortel Networks), revenues rose 63 percent and sales increased 26 percent following the implementation of self-managed teams.[128] Research evidence shows that such teams can lead to higher productivity, lower turnover among employees, and flatter organization structure.[129]

Self-managed teams, like any cohesive group, can fall victim to groupthink. The key to stimulating innovation and better problem solving in these groups is welcoming dissent among members. Dissent breaks down complacency and sets in motion a process that results in better decisions. Team members must know that dissent is permissible so that they won't fear embarrassment or ridicule.[130] Before choosing a group decision-making technique, the manager should carefully evaluate the group members and the decision situation. Then the best method for accomplishing the objectives of the group decision-making process can be selected. If the goal is generating a large number of alternatives, for example, brainstorming would be a good choice. If group members are reluctant to contribute ideas, the nominal group technique would be appropriate. The need for expert input would be best facilitated by the Delphi technique. To guard against groupthink, devil's advocacy or dialectical inquiry would be effective. Decisions that concern quality or production would benefit from the advice of quality circles or the empowered decisions of quality teams. Moreover, recent research suggests that if individuals within a team are made accountable for the process of decision making (rather than for the end decision itself), then such teams are more likely to gather diverse information, share information, and eventually make better decisions.[131] Finally, a manager who wants to provide total empowerment to a group should consider self-managed teams.

DIVERSITY AND CULTURE IN DECISION MAKING

Styles of decision making vary greatly among cultures. Many of the dimensions proposed by Hofstede that were presented in Chapter 2 affect decision making. Uncertainty avoidance, for example, can affect the way people view decisions. In the United States, a culture with low uncertainty avoidance, decisions are seen as opportunities for change. In contrast, cultures such as those of Indonesia and Malaysia attempt to accept situations as they are rather than to change them.[132] Power distance also affects decision making. In more hierarchical cultures, such as India, top-level managers make decisions. In countries with low power distance, lower-level employees make many decisions. The Swedish culture exemplifies this type.

The individualist/collectivist dimension has implications for decision making. Japan, with its collectivist emphasis, favors group decisions. The United States has a more difficult time with group decisions because it is an individualistic culture. Time orientation affects the frame of reference of the decision. In China, with its long-term view, decisions are made with the future in mind. In the United States, many decisions are made considering only the short term.

The masculine/feminine dimension can be compared to the Jungian thinking/feeling preferences for decision making. Masculine cultures, as in many Latin American countries, value quick, assertive decisions. Feminine cultures, as in many Scandinavian countries, value decisions that reflect concern for others.

Managers should learn as much as possible about the decision processes in other cultures. NAFTA, for example, has eliminated many barriers to trade with Mexico. In Mexican organizations, decision-making authority is centralized, autocratic, and retained in small groups of top managers. As a consequence, Mexican employees are reluctant to participate in decision making and often wait to be told what to do rather than take a risk. Significant differences exist amongst Hispanic work-related ethics and non-Hispanic work-related ethics as well. These differences need be managed effectively by managers to help individuals make decisions that are aligned with organizational values and ethics.[133] In addition, joint ventures with family-owned *grupos* (large groups of businesses) can be challenging. It may be difficult to identify the critical decision maker in the family and to determine how much decision-making authority is held by the *grupo's* family board.[134] Mexican managers may be more likely to engage in escalation of commitment or continue to invest in a losing venture. However, because lower-level managers in Mexico have control over smaller amounts of resources, they tend to invest in smaller increments than do U.S. managers.[135]

Recent research examining the effects of cultural diversity on decision making has found that when individuals in a group are racially dissimilar, they engage in more open information sharing, encourage dissenting perspectives, and arrive at better decisions than racially similar groups.[136] Other kinds of diversity such as functional background have been studied as well. Top management teams that have members who come from a variety of functional backgrounds (for example, marketing, accounting, information systems) engage in greater debate in decision making that top management teams in which the members come from similar backgrounds. This diversity results in better financial performance for the firm.[137] Research also indicates than strategic decision making in firms can vary widely by culture. For example, one such source of variation stems from the differential emphasis placed on environmental scanning in different cultures. Furthermore, strategic decision making might appear rational but is also informed by firm level and national characteristics.[138]

TECHNOLOGICAL AIDS TO DECISION MAKING

Many computerized decision tools are available to managers. These systems can be used to support the decision-making process in organizations.

Expert Systems

Artificial intelligence is used to develop an expert system, which is a programmed decision tool. The system is set up using decision rules, and the effectiveness of the expert system is highly dependent on its design. Because expert systems are sources of knowledge and experience and not just passive software, the organization must decide who is responsible for the decisions made by expert systems. Organizations must therefore be concerned about the liability for using the recommendations of expert systems.

TriPath Imaging has found a way to automate a critical but tedious process: screening Pap smears for signs of cancer. Programmers developing this software, called FocalPoint, met with numerous pathologists to learn which criteria they look for, such as the color of a cell's nucleus. They then allowed the software to learn by "practicing" on slides that had already been examined by experts. Today, FocalPoint software screens about 10 percent of all Pap smear slides in the United States.[139]

Expert systems hold great potential for affecting managerial decisions. Thus, managers must carefully scrutinize the expert system rather than simply accepting its decisions.

Decision Support Systems

Managers use decision support systems (DSS) as tools to enhance their ability to make complex decisions. DSS are computer and communication systems that process incoming data and synthesize pertinent information for managers to use. One example is the Fire Management Information System (FMIS) developed by a team of five partners from companies representing four European countries. Fire managers who are in charge of emergencies are bombarded with information and stress as situations change. The team sought to design a system that would help the fire managers in their decision-making tasks during forest fires. Although emergencies can take different forms, managers do not require radically different plans for dealing with them. This makes it possible to develop and store skeletal plans that can be accessed using the DSS instead of starting from scratch with each forest fire.

The team combined five decision support services in putting together the system:

- Weather monitoring synthesized information from remote meteorological stations.
- Fire risk rating assessed risk using an expert system.
- Fighting adviser proposed plans for preventing and fighting the fire.
- Fire detection used a network of imaging sensors for early detection of fires.
- Fire modeling simulated the fire's pattern and spread, taking into account vegetation, topography, and weather.

The fire manager uses the system in two modes. In standby mode, the system constantly updates databases and maps. In operational mode, the fire manager navigates through different functions when an emergency arises. In this way, the FMIS integrates all the decision support tools the manager needs to make the quick decisions needed to fight forest fires.[140]

Group Decision Support Systems

Another tool for decision making focuses on helping groups make decisions. A group decision support system (GDSS) uses computer support and communication facilities to support group decision-making processes in either face-to-face meetings or dispersed meetings. The GDSS has been shown to affect conflict management within a group by depersonalizing the issue and by forcing the group to discuss its conflict management process.[141] Team decisions often improve by using a GDSS because members share information more fully when they use a GDSS.[142]

Shell Oil realized several years ago that its engineers were wasting time and money finding answers to questions when other people in the firm already had the solutions. To help leverage its internal knowledge, Shell devised a massive but simple system based on the familiar model of Web discussion groups. Within these "communities," engineers can pose questions to experts in other segments of the business. But perhaps more important, Shell indexes and archives the discussions from these boards, creating a living, growing knowledge base that future generations of engineers will rely on even more heavily. To date, Shell estimates that it has saved $200 for every dollar invested in the project.[143]

Northrop Grumman, a major defense contractor, works with a dazzling array of advanced technologies. But what happens when an aircraft engineer faces a decision involving an area with which he is unfamiliar, even though he is fairly sure that one of Grumman's other 10,000 employees probably knows the answer? Today, he can use a piece of decision support software called ActiveNet. ActiveNet digs through mountains of data, including employee profiles and internal documents—from e-mail to PowerPoint slides—to identify individuals whose interests or backgrounds might match the need. In some cases, the key people may be just down the hall; in others, they might be on another continent. By bringing workers together with other experts, ActiveNet helps them broaden their decision-making abilities by tapping the resources already present around them.[144]

The success of GDSS as an aid to decision making depends on a number of factors. Organizations in which people are open to change and in which managers attach importance to flexible and creative decision-making processes are more likely to benefit. Evidence also shows that a GDSS that encourages full participation and promotes raising questions and expressing concerns is more likely to be successful. Further, managers should carefully consider the group's size and the type of task in planning for a GDSS. In the initial stages of decision making, such as generating alternatives, larger groups may work well with a GDSS. For more complex problem solving and choice making, however, small groups (fifteen members or fewer) are more effective.[145]

The effects of GDSS need further investigation. In a study that involved making investment decisions, minority opinion holders expressed their views most frequently using a GDSS. However, these minority views were more influential under face-to-face communication. This means that GDSS may facilitate the expression of minority viewpoints, but GDSS may also diminish their influence on group decisions.[146]

DECISION MAKING IN THE VIRTUAL WORKPLACE

(8) Explain the emerging role of virtual decision making in organizations.

Managers today are working in flexible organizations—so flexible in fact that many workplaces are unconstrained by geography, time, and organizational boundaries. Virtual teams are emerging as a new form of working arrangement. Virtual teams are groups of geographically dispersed coworkers who work together using a combination of telecommunications and information technologies to

SCIENCE

Virtual Goal Setting

Although technologies advance and offer several new media for communication, concerns associated with the effectiveness of such media have also arisen. For example, one common criticism of electronic communication is that it lacks the richness offered by face-to-face contact such as eye contact, gesturing, and body language.

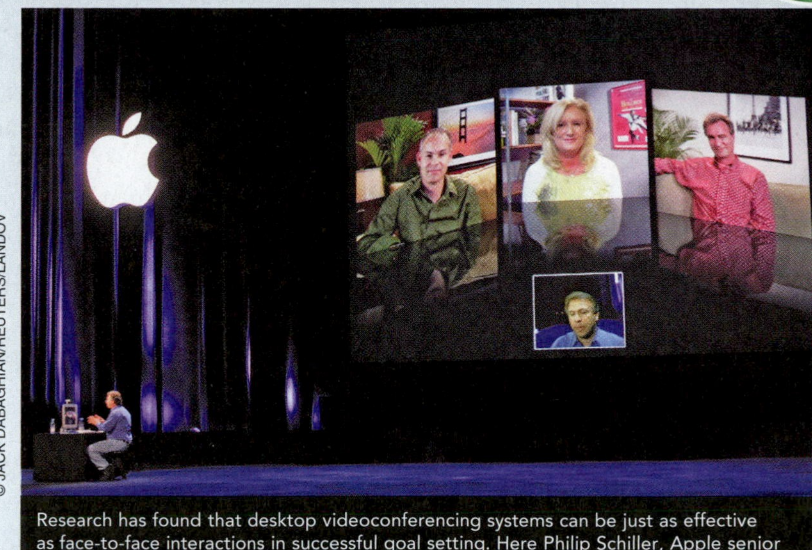

© JACK DABAGHIAN/REUTERS/LANDOV

Research has found that desktop videoconferencing systems can be just as effective as face-to-face interactions in successful goal setting. Here Philip Schiller, Apple senior vice president of worldwide product marketing, chats with three colleagues via multi-video conference.

Researchers in Germany conducted two experiments meant to contrast the effectiveness of face-to-face (FTF) goal-setting procedures with desktop videoconferencing systems (DCVS) goal setting. They hypothesized that FTF goal setting would result in better performance on a series of brainstorming tasks. The context of the study was a simulated advertising company, and participants were exposed to one of two forms of goal setting: do your best (DYB) versus setting specific difficult goals. Furthermore, they were also assigned to conditions of goal-setting interaction with their supervisor using either FTF or DCVS.

Researchers found that DCVS are just as effective as, if not more effective than, FTF interactions in successful goal setting. They also indicated that participative goal setting in the DCVS condition was the most effective technique of goal setting. In other words, when supervisors used a directive goal setting style in which DCVS was only used to communicate goals, they were not as effective as when they allowed workers to participate in setting the goals.

This research offers initial evidence for the use of DCVS as an effective managerial tool in participative goal-setting programs in organizations.

SOURCE: J. Wegge, T. Bipp, and U. Kleinbeck, "Goal Setting via Videoconferencing," *European Journal of Work & Organizational Psychology* 16 (2) (2007): 169–194.

accomplish a task. Virtual teams seldom meet face-to-face, and membership often shifts according to the project at hand.

How are decisions made in virtual teams? These teams require advanced technologies for communication and decision making. Many technologies aid virtual teams in decision making: desktop videoconferencing systems (DVCS), group decision support systems (GDSS), Internet/intranet systems, expert systems, and agent-based modeling.[147]

Desktop videoconferencing systems are the major technologies that form the basis for other virtual team technologies. DVCS recreate the face-to-face interactions of teams and go one step beyond by supporting more complex levels of communication among virtual team members. Small cameras on top of computer monitors provide video feeds, and voice transmissions are made possible through earpieces and microphones. High-speed data connections are used for communication. All team members can be connected, and outside experts can even be added. A local group can connect with up to fifteen different individuals or groups. Users can simultaneously work on documents, analyze data, or map out ideas. In the Science feature, you can read about the benefits of DVCS for goal setting as discussed in Chapter 5.

Managers use decision support systems (DSS) as tools to enhance their ability to make complex decisions. DSS are computer and communication systems that process incoming data and synthesize pertinent information for managers to use. Another tool for decision making focuses on helping groups make decisions. A group decision support system (GDSS) uses computer support and communication facilities to support group decision-making processes in either face-to-face meetings or dispersed meetings. The GDSS has been shown to affect conflict management within a group by depersonalizing the issue and by forcing the group to discuss its conflict management process.[148] Team decisions often improve by using a GDSS because members share information more fully when they use a GDSS.[149]

GDSS make real-time decision making possible in the virtual team. They are ideal systems for brainstorming, focus groups, and group decisions. By using support tools within the GDSS, users can turn off their individual identities and interact with anonymity, and can poll participants and assemble statistical information relevant to the decision being made. GDSS are thus the sophisticated software that makes collaboration possible in virtual teams.

Internal internets, or intranets, are adaptations of internet technologies for use within a company. For virtual teams, the Internet and intranets can be rich communication and decision-making resources. These tools allow virtual teams to archive text, video, audio, and data files for use in decision making. They permit virtual teams to inform other organization members about the team's progress and enable the team to monitor other projects within the organization.

By using DVCS, GDSS, and Internet/intranet technologies, virtual teams can capitalize on a rich communications environment for decision making. It is difficult, however, to duplicate the face-to-face environment. The effectiveness of a virtual team's decision making depends on its members' ability to use the tools that are available. Collaborative systems can enhance virtual teams' decision quality if they are used well.[150]

Agent-based modeling (ABM) is an agent-based simulation in which a computer creates thousands, even millions, of individual actors known as agents. Each of these virtual agents makes virtual decisions, thus providing an estimate of how each decision type might affect outcomes.[151]

Several organizations have adopted agent-based modeling to evaluate potential consequences of important decisions. For example, when Macy's was considering a major remodeling of their store space, they enlisted the services of PricewaterhouseCoopers to develop an ABM system that virtually modeled the changes in floor plans and consumer's responses to these changes. This simulation helped Macy's experiment with differing layout plans in cyberspace, thus predicting consumer behavior before it risked costly changes in the real world. You can see that for organizations like Macy's, ABM is a software simulation that can be very useful in making complex, nonroutine decisions involving some degree of uncertainty.

Decision making in the virtual workplace is characterized by the use of sophisticated technologies to assist in decision making. Some of these technologies, like videoconferencing, DSS, and GDSS, simply assist humans in making the decision. Others, like expert systems and some forms of agent-based modeling, play a greater role in making the decision. Regardless of the degree to which they play a role, all of these technologies make decision making in today's virtual workplace easier.

ETHICAL ISSUES IN DECISION MAKING

9 Utilize an "ethics check" for examining managerial decisions.

One criterion that should be applied to decision making is the ethical implications of the decision. Ethical decision making in organizations is influenced by many factors, including individual differences and organizational rewards and punishments.

Kenneth Blanchard and Norman Vincent Peale proposed an "ethics check" for decision makers in their book *The Power of Ethical Management.*[152] They contend that the decision maker should ponder three questions:

1. *Is it legal?* (Will I be violating the law or company policy?)
2. *Is it balanced?* (Is it fair to all concerned in the short term and long term? Does it promote win–win relationships?)
3. *How will it make me feel about myself?* (Will it make me proud of my actions? How will I feel when others become aware of the decision?)

General Dynamics, a major defense contractor that builds weapons ranging from submarines to fighter jets, faced charges of defrauding the government out of more than $2 billion on the Los Angeles class submarine project. While the company ultimately admitted no guilt, the scandal cost Admiral Hyman Rickover his career. And audiotapes of the firm's CEO and CFO discussing their plans to "screw the Navy," combined with revelations that a company vice president billed the Navy for the cost of kenneling his dog while he was out of town, started a long downhill slide that ultimately cost the two executives their jobs and cost General Dynamics its reputation.[153,154]

In summary, all decisions, whether made by individuals or by groups, must be evaluated for their ethics. Organizations should reinforce ethical decision making among employees by encouraging and rewarding it. Socialization processes should convey to newcomers the ethical standards of behavior in the organization. Groups should use devil's advocates and dialectical methods to reduce the potential for groupthink and the unethical decisions that may result. Effective and ethical decisions are not mutually exclusive. In recent times, almost all major businesses are paying attention to social and environmental issues in their decision-making processes. However, one major oil company and its CEO seem to take a different stand on such green business practices. Read about ExxonMobil CEO Rex Tillerson's viewpoints and decision-making strategy on such ethical issues in the Real World 10.2.

MANAGERIAL IMPLICATIONS: DECISION MAKING IS A CRITICAL ACTIVITY

Decision making is important at all levels of every organization. At times managers may have the luxury of optimizing (selecting the best alternative), but more often they are forced to satisfice (select the alternative that is good enough). And, at times, the decision process can even seem unpredictable and random.

Individuals differ in their preferences for risk, as well as in their styles of gathering information and making judgments. Understanding individual differences can help managers maximize strengths in employee decision styles and build teams that capitalize on strengths. Creativity is one such strength. It can be encouraged by providing employees with a supportive environment that nourishes innovative ideas. Creativity training has been used in some organizations with positive results.

Some decisions are best made by individuals and some by teams or groups. The task of the manager is to diagnose the situation and implement the appropriate level of participation. To do this effectively, managers should know the advantages and disadvantages of various group decision-making techniques and should minimize the potential for groupthink. Finally, decisions made by individuals or groups should be analyzed to see whether they are ethical.

THE REAL WORLD 10.2

ExxonMobil: Smarter Decision Making or Just Plain Profit Driven?

ExxonMobil is the largest energy company in the world. In an economy driven by concerns about global climate change and introduction of cleaner fuels and hybrid vehicles, one CEO stands tall—and alone—in his views on "greener" fuels. In his address at a major energy conference in 2007, Rex Tillerson reiterated Exxon's skepticism about global climate change issues. He commented that he wasn't 100 percent sure how global warming could or should affect industry activity. Some industry insiders speculate that such a stand could eventually hurt ExxonMobil, but for now, the tall Texan CEO is responding in a unique, and potentially risky, way.

He has invested in cutting down carbon dioxide emissions at Exxon's global facilities, an initiative claims has helped reduce carbon dioxide emissions equivalent to taking two million cars off the road. Exxon is also partnered with researchers at Stanford University to investigate complex biofuels. Thus, his strategy seems to be that Exxon will continue to invest in technological breakthroughs rather than adopting any other forms of green initiatives.

In spite of these initiatives, it is public knowledge that Tillerson does not yet support the idea that fossil fuels contribute to global warming or that alternative energy fuels are the answer. This position stands in stark opposition to other energy companies such as British Petroleum that are actively involved in reducing their footprint on the ecosystem. Only time will tell if Tillerson and ExxonMobil are truly ahead of the game and actually care about environmental issues. For now, there is a lot of speculation that the initiatives described above do not point in that direction and that they are just lip service to industry concerns with such issues.

SOURCE: C. Palmeri, "Exxon's Boss Is Cool on Green Policies," *Business Week Online* (February 14, 2007), http://www.businessweek.com/bwdaily/dnflash/content/feb2007/db20070214_217175.htm.

DIVERSITY DIALOGUE

Functional Diversity Comes Through in a Pinch

Jim Amoss is the editor of the *Times-Picayune* in New Orleans. Ordinarily, the newspaper's staffers would look to him or the senior editors to make the decisions. As the publication's leader, Amoss would be the most likely person to know what to do in case of an emergency. But on the morning of August 30, 2005, he did not know what to do. That was no ordinary day. It was the day that Hurricane Katrina struck New Orleans.

Like most organizations in the area, the staff at the *Times* had prepared for natural disasters. Extra generators were in place, and the staff had practiced emergency drills many times. In fact, the *Times* had even written articles detailing what to expect during a major hurricane. Unfortunately, all that planning literally went out the window during Hurricane Katrina. Water had flooded the generators and phones weren't working so no one could communicate. But this was the biggest story of their lives, and it had to be covered.

The staffers responded quickly without waiting for Amoss to hand out assignments. A functionally diverse team of about a dozen journalists, which included an editorial page editor, an art critic, and a religion writer, made the decision to return to the city's downtown area to gather supplies. They then went door to door searching for phone lines. The members of the team had never worked together before, but each of them went outside their comfort zones to make a decision that Amoss referred to as "an extraordinary moment of spontaneous leadership."

1. Discuss the effect of the team's functional heterogeneity on their decision to cover the Hurricane Katrina story.
2. What was Amoss' role in the team's ultimate decision?

SOURCE: J. Alexander, "Out of Disaster, Power in Numbers," *U.S. News & World Report* 141 (16), (October 30, 2006): 75–77.

LOOKING BACK: GENENTECH, INC.

Hope for the Future

Genentech recently added new research avenues to its existing R&D efforts and invested in eight new strategic collaborations. The biotech giant continues to surge forward, and its CEO Arthur Levinson remains committed to scientific excellence. He envisions a very hopeful future for Genentech based on new drug trials that have indicated positive results.

Genentech continues to build on its strategy of pioneering research in treatment of diseases that are scarcely researched in the industry. The road has not always been easy. In its published trials of the new cancer-fighting drug, Avastin, Genentech fared so poorly that stock analysts predicted the demise of the biotech superpower. However, through persistence in its R&D efforts, the company managed to turn the tide and now the investment in Avastin is paying off. This story shows how innovation and creative decisions might not always succeed in the short term, but there might be long-term benefits. In fact, one of Genentech's core strategies driving its decision making is a long-term focus on projects rather than blockbuster short-term miracle drugs. For now, this strategy seems to be working.[155, 156]

Chapter Summary

1. Bounded rationality assumes that there are limits to how rational managers can be.
2. The garbage can model shows that under high uncertainty, decision making in organizations can be an unsystematic process.
3. Jung's cognitive styles can be used to help explain individual differences in gathering information and evaluating alternatives.
4. Intuition and creativity are positive influences on decision making and should be encouraged in organizations.
5. Empowerment and teamwork require specific organizational design elements and individual characteristics and skills.
6. Techniques such as brainstorming, nominal group technique, Delphi technique, devil's advocacy, dialectical inquiry, quality circles and teams, and self-managed teams can help managers reap the benefits of group methods while limiting the possibilities of groupthink and group polarization.
7. Technology is providing assistance to managerial decision making, especially through expert systems and group decision support systems. More research is needed to determine the effects of these technologies.
8. Managers should carefully weigh the ethical issues surrounding decisions and encourage ethical decision making throughout the organization.

Key Terms

bounded rationality (p. 324)
brainstorming (p. 343)
cognitive style (p. 328)
creativity (p. 333)
Delphi technique (p. 344)
devil's advocacy (p. 344)
dialectical inquiry (p. 344)
effective decision (p. 323)
escalation of commitment (p. 326)
garbage can model (p. 324)
group polarization (p. 342)
groupthink (p. 340)
heuristics (p. 324)
intuition (p. 331)
nominal group technique (NGT) (p. 343)
nonprogrammed decision (p. 322)
participative decision making (p. 337)
programmed decision (p. 322)
rationality (p. 324)
risk aversion (p. 325)
satisfice (p. 324)
social decision schemes (p. 339)
synergy (p. 339)

Review Questions

1. Compare the garbage can model with the bounded rationality model. Compare the usefulness of these models in today's organizations.
2. List and describe Jung's four cognitive styles. How does the Z problem-solving model capitalize on the strengths of the four preferences?
3. What are the individual and organizational influences on creativity?
4. What are the organizational foundations of empowerment and teamwork? The individual foundations?
5. Describe the advantages and disadvantages of group decision making.
6. Describe the symptoms of groupthink, and identify actions that can be taken to prevent it.
7. What techniques can be used to improve group decisions?

Discussion and Communication Questions

1. Why is identification of the real problem the first and most important step in the decision-making process? How does attribution theory explain mistakes that can be made as managers and employees work together to explain why the problem occurred?
2. How can organizations effectively manage both risk taking and escalation of commitment in the decision-making behavior of employees?
3. How will you most likely make decisions based on your cognitive style? What might you overlook using your preferred approach?
4. How can organizations encourage creative decision making?
5. What are some organizations that use expert systems? Group decision support systems? How will these two technologies affect managerial decision making?
6. How do the potential risks associated with participating in quality circles differ from those associated with participating in quality teams? If you were a member of a quality circle, how would management's decisions to reject your recommendations affect your motivation to participate?
7. *(communication question)* Form a team of four persons. Find two examples of recent decisions made in organizations: one that you consider a good decision, and one that you consider a bad decision. Two members should work on the good decision, and two on the bad decision. Each pair should write a brief description of the decision. Then write a summary of what went right, what went wrong, and what could be done to improve the decision process. Compare and contrast your two examples in a presentation to the class.
8. *(comunication question)* Reflect on your own experiences in groups with groupthink. Describe the situation in which you encountered groupthink, the symptoms that were present, and the outcome. What remedies for groupthink would you prescribe? Summarize your answers in a memo to your instructor.

Ethical Dilemma

Slowly the managers of Beckman Services began arriving. An unexpected meeting had been called for 8:30 this morning and not everyone anticipated the news they were about to hear. Beckman was a financial services company that sold their services to individuals and companies. Since the terrorists' attacks on 9/11, Beckman had been experiencing financial difficulties. In order to boost sales, an incentive plan had been rolled out last December that management hoped would solve the problem. The plan challenged the sales force to increase sales by 15 percent. A daunting task, but the generous incentives made the challenge well worth the endeavor.

CEO Frank May opened the meeting by welcoming everyone to "one of the most difficult meetings he has ever had to call." Frank explained that although the incentive plan seemed to be working very well, the company's cash reserves were not as strong as they had hoped and delivering the promised bonuses would be more difficult than they had anticipated. He realized this was not going to be a popular decision, but he felt sure the salespeople would understand.

Richard Johnson, VP of human recourses sat quietly in the meeting. He could not believe what was happening. It was now early November, and the salespeople had been working hard for the last ten months. He knew many of the salespeople well, and they were counting on the promised bonuses. What message was the company sending if they cancelled this program at the last minute? He also knew he should say something, but disagreeing with Frank was never a good idea, especially when everyone else seemed to agree with the plan. Richard looked up and realized that the meeting was coming to an end. To challenge his boss in front of the team could be the end of his career at Beckman. But it couldn't be possible that everyone really agreed with Frank, could they? "Any questions or concerns about proceeding?" Frank asked. Richard needed to make a decision and make it fast.

Questions

1. Who are the stakeholders in Beckman Services and what is Frank May's responsibility to them?
2. To whom does Richard Johnson have a responsibility?
3. Evaluate Johnson's decision using consequential, rule-based, and character theories.

Experiential Exercises

10.1 Making a Layoff Decision

Purpose

In this exercise, you will examine how to weigh a set of facts and make a difficult personnel decision about laying off valued employees during a time of financial hardship. You will also examine your own values and criteria used in the decision-making process.

The Problem

Walker Space Institute (WSI) is a medium-sized firm located in Connecticut. The firm essentially has been a subcontractor on many large space contracts that have been acquired by firms like Alliant Techsystems and others.

With the cutback in many of the National Aeronautics and Space Administration programs, Walker has an excess of employees. Stuart Tartaro, the head of one of the sections, has been told by his superior that he must reduce his section of engineers from nine to six. He is looking at the following summaries of their vitae and pondering how he will make this decision.

1. *Roger Allison*, age twenty-six, married, two children. Allison has been with WSI for a year and a half. He is a very good engineer, with a degree from Rensselaer Polytech. He has held two prior jobs and lost both of them because of cutbacks in the space program. He moved to Connecticut from California to take this job. Allison is well liked by his coworkers.
2. *Dave Jones*, age twenty-four, single. Jones is an African American, and the company looked hard to get him because of affirmative action pressure. He is not very popular with his coworkers. Because he has been employed less than a year, not much is known about his work. On his one evaluation (which was average), Jones accused his supervisor of bias against African Americans. He is a graduate of the Detroit Institute of Technology.
3. *William Foster*, age fifty-three, married, three children. Foster is a graduate of "the school of hard knocks." After serving in the Vietnam War, he started to go to school but dropped out because of high family expenses. Foster has worked at the company for twenty years. His ratings were excellent for fifteen years. The last five years they have been average. Foster feels his supervisor grades him down because he does not "have sheepskins covering his office walls."
4. *Donald Boyer*, age thirty-two, married, no children. Boyer is well liked by his coworkers. He has been at WSI five years, and he has a B.S. and M.S. in engineering from Purdue University. Boyer's ratings have been mixed. Some supervisors rated him high and some average. Boyer's wife is an M.D.
5. *Ann Shuster*, age twenty-nine, single. Shuster is a real worker, but a loner. She has a B.S. in engineering from the University of California. She is working on her M.S. at night, always trying to improve her technical skills. Her performance ratings have been above average for the three years she has been at WSI.
6. *Sherman Soltis*, age thirty-seven, divorced, two children. He has a B.S. in engineering from Ohio State University. Soltis is very active in community affairs: Scouts, Little League, and United Way. He is a friend of the vice president through church work. His ratings have been average, although some recent ones indicate that he is out of date. He is well liked and has been employed at WSI for fourteen years.
7. *Warren Fortuna*, age forty-four, married, five children. He has a B.S. in engineering from Georgia Tech. Fortuna headed this section at one time. He worked so hard that he had a heart attack. Under doctor's orders, he resigned from the supervisory position. Since then he has done good work, though because of his health, he is a bit slower than the others. Now and then he must spend extra time on a project because he did get out of date during the eight years he headed the section. His performance evaluations for the last two years have been above average. He has been employed at WSI for fourteen years.

8. *Robert Treharne*, age forty-seven, single. He began an engineering degree at MIT but had to drop out for financial reasons. He tries hard to stay current by regular reading of engineering journals and taking all the short courses the company and nearby colleges offer. His performance evaluations have varied, but they tend to be average to slightly above average. He is a loner, and Tartaro thinks this has negatively affected Treharne's performance evaluations. He has been employed at WSI for sixteen years.
9. *Sandra Rosen*, age twenty-two, single. She has a B.S. in engineering technology from the Rochester Institute of Technology. Rosen has been employed less than a year. She is enthusiastic, a very good worker, and well liked by her coworkers. She is well regarded by Tartaro.

Tartaro does not quite know what to do. He sees the good points of each of his section members. Most have been good employees. They all can pretty much do one another's work. No one has special training.

He is fearful that the section will hear about the downsizing and morale will drop. Work would fall off. He does not even want to talk to his wife about it, in case she would let something slip. Tartaro has come to you, Edmund Graves, personnel manager at WSI, for some guidelines on this decision—legal, moral, and best personnel practice.

Assignment

You are Edmund Graves. Write a report with your recommendations for termination and a careful analysis of the criteria for the decision. You should also carefully explain to Tartaro how you would go about the terminations and what you would consider reasonable termination pay. You should also advise him about the pension implications of this decision. Generally, fifteen years' service entitles you to at least partial pension.

SOURCE: W. F. Glueck, *Cases and Exercises in Personnel* (Dallas: Business Publications, 1978), 24–26.

10.2 Dilemma at 29,000 Feet

Purpose

Making ethical decisions often requires taking decisive actions in ambiguous situations. Making these decisions entails not just weighing options and making rational choices but making choices between competing but equally important demands. Managers must not only take action, they must also provide compelling reasons that make their choices rationally accountable to others. This exercise requires you to think through an ethical situation, take an action, and create a convincing justification for your action. The exercise is designed to encourage critical thinking about complex problems and to encourage thinking about how you might resolve a dilemma outside your area of expertise.

The Problem

Imagine you are the sole leader of a mountain-climbing expedition and have successfully led a group of three climbers to the mountain summit. However, on your descent, trouble sets in as a fierce storm engulfs the mountain and makes progression down nearly impossible. One climber collapses from exhaustion at 24,000 feet and cannot continue down the mountain. The two stronger climbers insist on continuing down without you because they know if they stay too long at high altitude death is certain. No one has ever survived overnight on the mountain. A rescue attempt is impossible because helicopters cannot reach you above 18,000 feet.

As the leader, you are faced with a difficult choice: abandon your teammate and descend alone or stay with your dying teammate and face almost certain death. On one hand, you might stay with your dying teammate in hopes that the storm might clear and a rescue party will be sent. However, you know that if you stay both of you will most likely die. On the other hand, you are still strong and may be able to make it down to safety, abandoning your teammate to die alone on the mountain.

Assignment

Your assignment is to make an argument for one of the actions: staying with your teammate or descending alone. The technical aspects of mountain climbing are not important, nor is it good enough to state that you would not get in this situation in the first place! What is important is that you provide a well-reasoned argument for your action. A good argument might address the following points:

1. A discussion of the pros and cons of each action: staying with your teammate or descending alone.
2. A discussion of the underlying values and assumptions of each action. For example, staying with the teammate implies that you have a particular obligation as the leader of a team; descending alone suggests that you may place a higher value on your own life.
3. A discussion of your own values and viewpoints on the topic. In other words, take a stand and justify your position. How, for example, might you justify to the family of the abandoned climber your decision to descend alone? How might you justify to

your own family your decision to stay with the ailing climber?

4. What prior experience, knowledge, or beliefs lead you to your conclusion?
5. How might this situation be similar to or different from the dilemmas faced in more typical organizations? For example, do leaders need to take actions that require them to make similar difficult decisions? Have you experienced any similar dilemmas that had no easy answer in the workplace, and how did you resolve them?

Final Thoughts

Remember, there is no right or wrong answer to this case. The point is to consider and make clear your own ethical choices by evaluating all relevant information, evaluating the underlying assumptions of each, and creating a clear and convicing argument for action. A quote by philosopher Martha Craven Nussbaum might act as a starting point for your study. She writes,

"Both alternatives make a serious claim on your practical attention. You might sense that no matter how you choose, you will be left with some regret that you did not do the other thing. Sometimes you may be clear about which is the better choice and yet feel pain over the frustration of the other significant concerns. It is extremely important to realize that the problem is not just one difficult decision but that conflicts arise when the final decision itself is perfectly obvious."

Good luck in your decision!

SOURCE: D. C. Kayes, "Dilemma at 29,000 Feet: An Exercise in Ethical Decision Making Based on the 1996 Mt. Everest Climbing Disaster," *Journal of Management Education* 26 (2002): 307–321. Reprinted by permission of Sage Publications.

TAKE 2

Biz Flix | Dr. Seuss' How the Grinch Stole Christmas

Readers and lovers of the Dr. Seuss original tale may feel put off by Ron Howard's loose adaptation of the story. Whoville, a magical, mythical land, features the Whos who love Christmas and the Grinch (Jim Carrey) who hates it. Cindy Lou Who (Taylor Momsen) tries to bring the Grinch back to the Yuletide celebrations, an effort that backfires on all involved. Sparkling special effects will dazzle most viewers and likely distract them from the film's departures from the original story.

The selected scene is an edited version of the "Second Thoughts" sequence early in the film. Just before this scene, fearless Cindy Lou entered the Grinch's lair to invite him to be the Holiday Cheermeister at the Whobilation One-Thousand celebration. In typical Grinch fashion, he pulls the trap door on Cindy Lou, who unceremoniously slides out of his lair to land on a snowy Whoville street. The Grinch now must decide whether to accept the invitation. The film continues with the Cheermeister award ceremony.

What to Watch for and Ask Yourself:

- What are the Grinch's decision alternatives or options?
- What decision criteria does the Grinch use to choose from the alternatives?
- Describe the steps in the Grinch's decision-making process.

Workplace Video | Managerial Decision Making, Featuring McDonald's

McDonald's is the most recognized fast-food franchise in the world. In the sixty years since Dick and Mac McDonald first introduced the "Speedee Service System" at their San Bernardino, California, restaurant, the burger giant has grown to more than 30,000 locations in 118 countries, serving 50 million people daily.

The McDonald's story, which gained legendary status under the leadership of Ray Kroc and Fred Turner, weaves together many themes of business success—visionary leadership, mass-marketing genius, and groundbreaking business models. Yet one theme in the McDonald's success story is often overlooked: good decision making in turbulent times.

In 2001, cracks began appearing in the famed Golden Arches. Customer guest counts were down, profitability was on the decline, and rapid expansion of new stores wasn't producing financial results. As these internal problems raged, McDonald's found itself at the center of a politically charged obesity debate. The company finally hit bottom in 2004 when two consecutive CEOs died—a bizarre tragedy that made James Skinner the company's third chief in a single year.

To halt the slide, senior management began rethinking the company's decision-making process. First, McDonald's launched a formal probe to identify problems. Next, as part of its quantitative analysis, the company conducted market research aimed at identifying ongoing customer concerns. In addition, the company adopted a system of interdepartmental collaboration that encouraged managers from different areas of the organization to provide input and to propose fresh solutions.

TAKE 2

After a period of evaluation and introspection, executives determined that short-term thinking was at the root of the company's sluggish growth. In particular, the company had spent too much time opening new restaurants and too little time improving existing ones. To remedy the situation, McDonald's created long-term plans and rallied leaders to promote comprehensive buy-in at the corporate, franchise, and customer levels.

Today McDonald's is back on top. Customers are responding positively to changes in the company's brand image, and gutsy decisions have refreshed the company mission. Even shareholders are feeling good again. Instead of expressing worries that franchises like Subway and Burger King will soon dominate the industry, McDonald's stakeholders are again feeling confident that the future of fast food lies beneath the Golden Arches.

Discussion Questions

1. Cite at least two ways in which McDonald's management followed the decision-making process during the company's big turnaround.
2. Were the decisions made by McDonald's management programmed or nonprogrammed? Explain.
3. What common decision-making errors could have caused even greater problems for McDonald's?

CASE

3M's Conundrum of Efficiency and Creativity

Innovative, successful companies, like Minnesota Mining and Manufacturing (3M), share at least four fundamental characteristics: (1) putting people and ideas at the heart of the management philosophy; (2) giving people opportunities and latitude to develop, try new things, and learn from their mistakes; (3) building a strong sense of openness, trust, and community throughout the organization; and (4) facilitating the mobility of talent within the organization.[1] 3M believes in the power of ideas and individual initiative, and "recognizes that entrepreneurial behavior will continue to flourish only if management is willing to accept and even applaud 'well-intentioned failure.'"[2] Innovation, the traditional hallmark of 3M's business operations and success, is "a process that thrives on multiple, diverse, independent and rapid experimentation, in a failure-tolerant environment that values and accommodates constructive conflict."[3]

The creative and innovative orientation of 3M—and in particular its tolerance for failure or defects or errors—came under serious attack in late 2000. When former General Electric executive James McNerney took over as CEO of 3M in December 2000, he immediately began implementing Six Sigma.[4] Management programs such as Six Sigma are designed to identify problems in work processes, and then use rigorous measurement to reduce variation, eliminate defects, and increase efficiency. When initiatives such as Six Sigma become embedded in a company's culture, as they did at 3M, creativity and innovation can easily get squelched.[5] In mid-2005, when McNerney departed 3M to take the CEO's job at Boeing, he left his successors with the difficult question of "whether the relentless emphasis on efficiency had made 3M a less creative company."[6]

According to management guru Tom Peters, McNerney's implementation of Six Sigma at 3M "more or less closed the lid on entrepreneurial behavior."[7] Vijay Govindarajan, a professor at Dartmouth's Tuck School of Business, observes that when more emphasis is placed on programs such as Six Sigma and Total Quality Management, the more likely it is that breakthrough innovations will be harmed.[8] Art Fry, the inventor of 3M's Post-It notes, says, "[y]ou have to go through 5,000 to 6,000 raw ideas to find one successful business," but the Six Sigma program would ask "why not eliminate all that waste and just come up with the right idea the first time?"[9] However, others have contended that Six Sigma should not be criticized indiscriminately. The program, they say, is very useful in reducing waste in virtually all processes where there is a known result that must be achieved.

Unfortunately, at 3M Six Sigma was deployed in an environment of innovation where the target was unknown.[10] "The problem is not with the methodology itself but rather with how it is applied and what specifically it is applied to . . . if managed effectively, Six Sigma can absolutely co-exist with innovation."[11] Six Sigma can eliminate mundane, repetitive, and tedious tasks that impede creative thinking and innovation.[12]

Six Sigma focuses on efficiency and quality in order to enhance profits, but the lifeblood of long-term profitability for most, if not all, businesses is innovation. Indeed, "to compete in the coming decades, creativity is one process that can't be left for later."[13] Still, "[t]urning ideas into commercial reality requires persistence and discipline, and overall effectiveness ultimately depends on top management being able to find the right balance between corporate creativity and efficiency."[14] Effective innovation "requires a delicate balancing act between play and discipline, practice and process, creativity and efficiency, where firms need to 'learn how to walk the fine line between rigidity—which smothers creativity—and chaos—where creativity runs amok and nothing ever gets to market.'"[15]

Robert Carter, a consultant at Raytheon, indicates that the Six Sigma process of define, measure, analyze, improve, control (DMAIC) can lead to overanalyzing the situation, which can be very detrimental when an idea begins to germinate.[16] "Six Sigma tries to replace subjectivity with objectivity and intuition with data wherever possible. While this is appropriate for some operations—like administration, logistics, and manufacturing—it's detrimental to exploratory research and design, which depend on subjectivity and intuition."[17] Creativity is seldom a logical process, and Six Sigma is not a panacea.[18]

Discussion Questions

1. How would you describe 3M's efficiency and creativity conundrum in terms of programmed and nonprogrammed decisions?
2. How would you describe 3M's efficiency and creativity conundrum in terms of the rational, bounded rationality, and garbage can models of decision making?
3. What role do intuition and creativity play in the decision making that is evident in 3M's efficiency and creativity conundrum?

SOURCE: This case was written by Michael K. McCuddy, The Louis S. and Mary L. Morgal Chair of Christian Business Ethics and Professor of Management, College of Business Administration, Valparaiso University.

CHAPTER 11

Power and Political Behavior

LEARNING OBJECTIVES

After reading this chapter, you should be able to do the following:

1 Distinguish among power, influence, and authority.
2 Compare the interpersonal and intergroup sources of power.
3 Understand the ethical use of power.
4 Explain power analysis, an organizational-level theory of power.
5 Identify symbols of power and powerlessness in organizations.
6 Define organizational politics and understand the role of political skill and major influence tactics.
7 Develop a plan for managing employee–boss relationships.
8 Discuss how managers can empower others.

THINKING AHEAD: GOOGLE NAVIGATES POWER AND POLITICS

Google is one of the most successful firms in the technology world today. Every time stock analysts speculate that the company might crash, it has come out stronger than before. And it seems to be continuing in its ascent to the position of industry leader.

Yet Google's rapid rise has also brought its share of concerns and challenges for the Internet giant. For example, the company was involved in a major controversy with the Chinese government that restricted the kind of information Google could process in searches. As a result, in China Google now has to filter information and can only make publicly available information that does not violate government guidelines. In addition, Google has drawn considerable criticism for imitating Microsoft in certain monopolistic behaviors. The company plans to create and acquire software that profiles Internet users so that it can better customize its search services to individual preferences. This move is alarming to many because it enables Google to acquire and store massive amounts of personal data on Internet users—information that could be misused.

Some people even question whether actions such as signing a deal consenting to censorship by the Chinese government and monitoring Internet users are part of founders

Larry Page and Sergey Brin's monster ambitions to be the most powerful people on the Internet. Some also wonder how acts such as these square with Google's famous corporate mission, "Do No Evil."[1,2] We'll continue to examine Google's power controversy at the end of the chapter.

THE CONCEPT OF POWER

(1) Distinguish among power, influence, and authority.

Power is the ability to influence someone else. As an exchange relationship, it occurs in transactions between an agent and a target. The agent is the person using the power, and the target is the recipient of the attempt to use power.[3]

Because power is an ability, individuals can learn to use it effectively. *Influence* is the process of affecting the thoughts, behavior, and feelings of another person. *Authority* is the right to influence another person.[4] It is important to understand the subtle differences among these terms. For instance, a manager may have authority but no power. She may have the right, by virtue of her position as boss, to tell someone what to do. But she may not have the skill or ability to influence other people.

In a relationship between the agent and the target, there are many influence attempts that the target considers legitimate. Working forty hours per week, greeting customers, solving problems, and collecting bills are actions that, when requested by the manager, are considered legitimate by a customer service representative. Requests such as these fall within the employee's *zone of indifference*—the range in which attempts to influence the employee are perceived as legitimate and are acted on without a great deal of thought.[5] The employee accepts that the manager has the authority to request such behaviors and complies with the requests. Some requests, however, fall outside the zone of indifference, so the manager must work to enlarge the employee's zone of indifference. Enlarging the zone is accomplished with power (an ability) rather than with authority (a right).

Suppose the manager asks the employee to purchase a birthday gift for the manager's wife or to overcharge a customer for a service call. The employee may think the manager has no right to ask these things. These requests fall outside the zone of indifference; they're viewed as extraordinary, and the manager has to operate from outside the authority base to induce the employee to fulfill them. In some cases, no power base is enough to induce the employee to comply, especially if the employee considers the behaviors requested by the manager unethical.

Failures to understand power and politics can be costly in terms of your career. In the wake of the attacks on September 11, 2001, American Airlines CEO Donald Carty managed to wrest over a billion dollars from unions in concessions to keep the company from having to file bankruptcy. Unfortunately, on the same day the agreement was announced, it was disclosed that special pension trust funding and huge retention bonuses were given to American Airlines executives, including Carty—despite the fact that union workers had agreed to the steep pay cuts. Carty spent the next three-and-a-half weeks apologizing, even giving the money back, before falling on his sword. He may have lost his job because he lost the trust of his employees. This example illustrates that managers must learn as much as possible about power and politics to be able to use them effectively and to manage the inevitable political behavior in organizations.[6]

power
The ability to influence another person.

influence
The process of affecting the thoughts, behavior, and feelings of another person.

authority
The right to influence another person.

zone of indifference
The range in which attempts to influence a person will be perceived as legitimate and will be acted on without a great deal of thought.

FORMS AND SOURCES OF POWER IN ORGANIZATIONS

Individuals have many forms of power to use in their work settings. Some of them are interpersonal—used in interactions with others. One of the earliest and most influential theories of power comes from French and Raven, who tried to determine the sources of power managers use to influence other people.

(2) Compare the interpersonal and intergroup sources of power.

Interpersonal Forms of Power

French and Raven identified five forms of interpersonal power that managers use: reward, coercive, legitimate, referent, and expert power.[7]

reward power
Power based on an agent's ability to control rewards that a target wants.

Reward power is based on the agent's ability to control rewards that a target wants. For example, managers control the rewards of salary increases, bonuses, and promotions. Reward power can lead to better performance, but only as long as the employee sees a clear and strong link between performance and rewards. To use reward power effectively, then, the manager should be explicit about the behavior being rewarded and should make the connection clear between the behavior and the reward.

coercive power
Power that is based on an agent's ability to cause an unpleasant experience for a target.

Coercive power is based on the agent's ability to cause the target to have an unpleasant experience. To coerce someone into doing something means to force the person to do it, often with threats of punishment. Managers using coercive power may verbally abuse employees or withhold support from them.

Legitimate power, which is similar to authority, is based on position and mutual agreement. The agent and target agree that the agent has the right to influence the target. It doesn't matter that a manager thinks he has the right to influence his employees; for legitimate power to be effective, the employees must also believe the manager has the right to tell them what to do. In some Native American societies, the chief has legitimate power; tribe members believe in his right to influence the decisions in their lives.

© PICTORIAL PRESS/ALAMY

Coercive power is based on the agent's ability to cause the target to have an unpleasant experience. In the 1972 film *The Godfather,* Marlon Brando's character used the threat of punishment to get others to do as he wished.

Referent power is based on interpersonal attraction. The agent has referent power over the target because the target identifies with or wants to be like the agent. Charismatic individuals are often thought to have referent power. Interestingly, the agent need not be superior to the target in any way. People who use referent power well are most often individualistic and respected by the target.

legitimate power
Power that is based on position and mutual agreement; agent and target agree that the agent has the right to influence the target.

referent power
An elusive power that is based on interpersonal attraction.

expert power
The power that exists when an agent has specialized knowledge or skills that the target needs.

Expert power exists when the agent has specialized knowledge or skills that the target needs. For expert power to work, three conditions must be in place. First, the target must trust that the expertise given is accurate. Second, the knowledge involved must be relevant and useful to the target. Third, the target's perception of the agent as an expert is crucial. Using easy-to-understand language signals the target that the expert has an appreciation for real-world concerns and increases the target's trust in the expert.[8]

Which type of interpersonal power is most effective? Research has focused on this question since French and Raven introduced their five forms of power. Some of the results are surprising. Reward power and coercive power have similar effects.[9] Both lead to compliance. That is, employees will do what the manager asks them to, at least temporarily, if the manager offers a reward or threatens

The Power of Age and Experience

Several CEOs of successful organizations are young entrepreneurs like Sergey Brin and Larry Page of Google, and this might create the perception that young leaders can best lead firms. However, a comprehensive research study conducted among manufacturing and service firms might prove otherwise. This study included 632 small to medium-sized firms and reveals some interesting findings.

CEOs have a lot of power and influence within organizational settings, yet they have to gain approval from the board of directors or top management team (TMT) on key strategic decisions. One avenue for improving an organization's performance is through pursuit of new business directions, but this represents a certain level of risk for the firm. This study highlights the effects of CEO tenure with the firm as a key ingredient in determining their influence in persuading the TMT to adopt risks. Specifically, researchers found that CEOs with 30-plus years of experience with the same firm have the most influence on the TMT in persuading them to take risks. This risk taking in turn led to better firm performance. The reason that CEOs with tenure are more influential is because they have in-depth knowledge of the technical aspects of the firm's products and capabilities, understand business contingencies, and develop deep social connections with members of the TMT. These results highlight the significance of expert power and legitimacy in the organization.

SOURCE: Z. Simsek, "CEO Tenure and Organizational Performance: An Intervening Model," *Strategic Management Journal* 28 (6) (2007): 653–662.

them with punishment. Reliance on these sources of power is dangerous, however, because it may require the manager to be physically present and watchful in order to apply rewards or punishment when the behavior occurs. Constant surveillance creates an uncomfortable situation for managers and employees and eventually results in a dependency relationship. Employees will not work unless the manager is present.

Legitimate power also leads to compliance. When told "Do this because I'm your boss," most employees will comply. However, the use of legitimate power has not been linked to organizational effectiveness or to employee satisfaction.[10] In organizations where managers rely heavily on legitimate power, organizational goals are not necessarily met.

Referent power, such as that of Oprah Winfrey, is based on interpersonal attraction.

Referent power is linked with organizational effectiveness. It is the most dangerous power, however, because it can be too extensive and intensive in altering the behavior of others. Charismatic leaders need an accompanying sense of responsibility for others. The late disabled actor Christopher Reeve's referent power made him a powerful spokesperson for research on spinal injuries and stem cell research.

Expert power has been called the power of the future.[11] Of the five forms of power, it has the strongest relationship with performance and satisfaction. It is through expert power that vital skills, abilities, and knowledge are passed on within the organization. Employees internalize what they observe and learn from managers they perceive to be experts.

The results on the effectiveness of these five forms of power pose a challenge in organizations. The least effective power bases—legitimate, reward, and coercive—are the ones most likely to be used by managers.[12]

Managers inherit these power bases as part of the position when they take a supervisory job. In contrast, the most effective power bases—referent and expert—are ones that must be developed and strengthened through interpersonal relationships with employees. Marissa Mayer, vice president of search products and user experience at Google, is well respected and liked by her colleagues. She is described as someone with a lot of technical knowledge, and she is comfortable in social environments. This represents her expert power and referent power—she has an advanced degree in computer science from Stanford University and is known for her ability to connect with people. At 33 years old, she has had a very successful career at Google and is one of the most powerful female executives in the country.[13] Expert power and social networks help CEOs influence their top management teams in ways that are profitable for the firm, as you can see in the Science feature.

Using Power Ethically

(3) Understand the ethical use of power.

Managers can work at developing all five of these forms of power for future use. The key to using them well is using them ethically, as Table 11.1 shows. Coercive power, for example, requires careful administration if it is to be used in an ethical manner. Employees should be informed of the rules in advance, and any punishment should be used consistently, uniformly, and privately. The key to using all five types of interpersonal power ethically is to be sensitive to employees' concerns and to communicate well.

To French and Raven's five power sources, we can add a source that is very important in today's organizations. *Information power* is access to and control over important information. Consider, for example, the CEO's administrative assistant. He or she has information about the CEO's schedule that people need if they are going to get in to see the CEO. Central to the idea of information power is the person's position in the communication networks in the organization, both formal and informal. Also important is the idea of framing, which is the "spin" that managers put on information. Managers not only pass information on to subordinates; they interpret this information and influence the subordinates' perceptions of it. Information power occurs not only in the downward direction; it may also flow upward from subordinates to managers. In manufacturing plants, database operators often control information about plant metrics and shipping performance that is vital to managerial decision making. Information power can also flow laterally. Salespersons convey information from the outside environment (their customers) that is essential for marketing efforts.

Determining whether a power-related behavior is ethical is complex. Another way to look at the ethics surrounding the use of power is to ask three questions that show the criteria for examining power-related behaviors:[14]

1. *Does the behavior produce a good outcome for people both inside and outside the organization?* This question represents the criterion of *utilitarian outcomes*. The behavior should result in the greatest good for the greatest number of people. If the power-related behavior serves only the individual's self-interest and fails to help the organization reach its goals, it is considered unethical. A salesperson might be tempted to discount a product deeply in order to make a sale that would win a contest. Doing so would be in her self-interest but would not benefit the organization.
2. *Does the behavior respect the rights of all parties?* This question emphasizes the criterion of *individual rights*. Free speech, privacy, and due process are individual rights that are to be respected, and power-related behaviors that violate these rights are considered unethical.

information power
Access to and control over important information.

TABLE 11.1 Guidelines for the Ethical Use of Power

Form of Power	Guidelines for Use
Reward power	Verify compliance. Make feasible, reasonable requests. Make only ethical requests. Offer rewards desired by subordinates. Offer only credible rewards.
Coercive power	Inform subordinates of rules and penalties. Warn before punishing. Administer punishment consistently and uniformly. Understand the situation before acting. Maintain credibility. Fit punishment to the infraction. Punish in private.
Legitimate power	Be cordial and polite. Be confident. Be clear and follow up to verify understanding. Make sure request is appropriate. Explain reasons for request. Follow proper channels. Exercise power consistently. Enforce compliance. Be sensitive to subordinates' concerns.
Referent power	Treat subordinates fairly. Defend subordinates' interests. Be sensitive to subordinates' needs and feelings. Select subordinates similar to oneself. Engage in role modeling.
Expert power	Maintain credibility. Act confident and decisive. Keep informed. Recognize employee concerns. Avoid threatening subordinates' self-esteem.

SOURCE: *Leadership in Organizations* by Gary A. Yukl. Copyright © 1981. Reprinted by permission of Prentice-Hall, Upper Saddle River, N.J.

3. *Does the behavior treat all parties equitably and fairly?* This question represents the criterion of *distributive justice*. Power-related behavior that treats one party arbitrarily or benefits one party at the expense of another is unethical. Granting a day of vacation to one employee in a busy week in which coworkers must struggle to cover for him might be considered unethical.

To be considered ethical, power-related behavior must meet all three criteria. If the behavior fails to meet the criteria, then alternative actions should be considered. Unfortunately, most power-related behaviors are not easy to analyze. Conflicts may exist among the criteria; for example, a behavior may maximize the greatest good for the

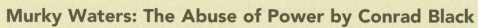

Murky Waters: The Abuse of Power by Conrad Black

People in positions of power are constantly faced with the pull of making decisions that benefit themselves and their own agendas rather than the organization's. The business world is replete with examples of such leaders, but the latest fall in ethical standards comes in the form of Conrad Black, a wealthy publisher and owner of Hollinger Inc. His company once owned newspapers such as the *Chicago Sun-Times*, the *National Post*, and the *Daily Telegraph* of London. The allegations against Black included charges of mail fraud, obstruction of justice, and pocketing money that should have gone to his shareholders.

Black sold major portions of his businesses starting in 1998 and entered into deals with the new owners which stated that his company would not compete against them. He diverted money from these deals to his personal account rather than paying shareholders. Furthermore, he was videotaped removing documents from his office that could potentially serve as evidence despite a court order against such actions. It was corrupt use of his position power that led to his conviction and he faces 35 years in prison and a penalty of $1 million.

The conviction of Conrad Black reflects a growing business concern with abuse of power. The justice system and the government have heightened their efforts in going after corporate offenders like Conrad Black with the hope that such convictions could serve as deterrents to the misuse of power within organizational settings.

SOURCE: Associated Press, "Ex-Media Mogul Black Convicted of Fraud," *MSNBC News*, http://www.msnbc.msn.com/id/19745657/.

greatest number of people but may not treat all parties equitably. Individual rights may need to be sacrificed for the good of the organization. A CEO may need to be removed from power for the organization to be saved. Still, these criteria can be used on a case-by-case basis to sort through the complex ethical issues surrounding the use of power. The ethical use of power is one of the hottest topics in the current business arena, due to the abuse of power by top executives at several firms such as Enron and Tyco International. Read about Conrad Black's fall from glory in The Real World 11.1.

Two Faces of Power: One Positive, One Negative

personal power
Power used for personal gain.

We turn now to a theory of power that takes a strong stand on the "right" versus "wrong" kind of power to use in organizations. David McClelland has spent a great deal of his career studying the need for power and the ways managers use power. As was discussed in Chapter 5, he believes there are two distinct faces of power, one negative and one positive.[15] The negative face of power is *personal power*—power used for personal gain. Managers who use personal power are commonly described as "power hungry." Dennis Koslowski's tenure as CEO of Tyco was marked by one of the most massive strings of acquisitions by any American firm, earning him the nickname "Deal-a-Month Dennis." But as questions began to mount about why Tyco continued to expand when many of its existing divisions were not profitable, Kozlowski simply dismissed them. Only later would it come to light that not only had Kozlowski mismanaged the firm, but he had also looted it for more than $240 million, which he spent on artwork, houses, yachts, and a $2 million birthday party for his wife.[16] People who approach

Personal power is power used for personal gain. During Dennis Koslowski's tenure as CEO of Tyco, he mismanaged the firm and looted more than $240 million, which he spent on personal items.

relationships with an exchange orientation often use personal power to ensure that they get at least their fair share—and often more—in the relationship. They are most concerned with their own needs and interests. One way to encourage ethical behavior in organizations is to encourage principled dissent. This refers to valid criticism that can benefit the organization rather than mere complaints about working conditions. Much like whistle-blowers who can serve as checks on powerful people within the organization, dissenters can pinpoint wrongdoings, encourage employee voice in key issues, and create a climate conducive to the ethical use of power.[17]

Individuals who rely on personal power at its extreme might be considered Machiavellian—willing to do whatever it takes to get one's own way. Niccolo Machiavelli was an Italian statesman during the sixteenth century who wrote *The Prince,* a guide for acquiring and using power.[18] Among his methods was manipulating others, believing that it was better to be feared than loved. Machiavellians (or high Machs) are willing to manipulate others for personal gain, and are unconcerned with others' opinions or welfare.

The positive face of power is *social power*—power used to create motivation or to accomplish group goals. McClelland clearly favors the use of social power by managers. People who approach relationships with a communal orientation focus on the needs and interests of others. They rely on social power.[19] McClelland has found that managers who use power successfully have four power-oriented characteristics:

1. *Belief in the authority system.* They believe that the institution is important and that its authority system is valid. They are comfortable influencing and being influenced. The source of their power is the authority system of which they are a part.
2. *Preference for work and discipline.* They like their work and are very orderly. They have a basic value preference for the Protestant work ethic, believing that work is good for a person over and beyond its income-producing value.
3. *Altruism.* They publicly put the company and its needs before their own needs. They are able to do this because they see their own well-being as integrally tied to the corporate well-being.
4. *Belief in justice.* They believe justice is to be sought above all else. People should receive what they are entitled to and what they earn.

McClelland takes a definite stand on the proper use of power by managers. When power is used for the good of the group, rather than for individual gain, it is positive.

Intergroup Sources of Power

Groups or teams within an organization can also use power from several sources. One source of intergroup power is control of *critical resources.*[20] When one group controls an important resource that another group desires, the first group holds power. Controlling resources needed by another group allows the power-holding group to influence the actions of the less powerful group. This process can continue in an upward spiral. Groups seen as powerful tend to be given more resources from top management.[21]

Groups also have power to the extent that they control *strategic contingencies*—activities that other groups depend on in order to complete their tasks.[22] The dean's office, for example, may control the number of faculty positions to be filled in each department of a college. The departmental hiring plans are thus contingent on approval from the dean's office. In this case, the dean's office controls the strategic contingency of faculty hiring, and thus has power.

social power
Power used to create motivation or to accomplish group goals.

strategic contingencies
Activities that other groups depend on in order to complete their tasks.

Three factors can give a group control over a strategic contingency.[23] One is the *ability to cope with uncertainty*. If a group can help another group deal with uncertainty, it has power. One organizational group that has gained power in recent years is the legal department. Faced with increasing government regulations and fears of litigation, many other departments seek guidance from the legal department.

Another factor that can give a group control power is a *high degree of centrality* within the organization. If a group's functioning is important to the organization's success, it has high centrality. The sales force in a computer firm, for example, has power because of its immediate effect on the firm's operations and because other groups (accounting and servicing groups, for example) depend on its activities.

The third factor that can give a group power is *nonsubstitutability*—the extent to which a group performs a function that is indispensable to an organization. A team of computer specialists may be powerful because of its expertise with a system. It may have specialized experience that another team cannot provide.

The strategic contingencies model thus shows that groups hold power over other groups when they can reduce uncertainty, when their functioning is central to the organization's success, and when the group's activities are difficult to replace.[24] The key to all three of these factors, as you can see, is dependency. When one group controls something that another group needs, it creates a dependent relationship—and gives one group power over the other.

POWER ANALYSIS: A BROADER VIEW

(4) Explain power analysis, an organizational-level theory of power.

Amitai Etzioni takes a more sociological orientation to power. Etzioni has developed a theory of power analysis.[25] He says that there are three types of organizational power and three types of organizational involvement, or membership, that will lead to either congruent or incongruent uses of power. The three types of organizational power are the following:

1. *Coercive power*—influencing members by forcing them to do something under threat of punishment or through fear and intimidation.
2. *Utilitarian power*—influencing members by providing them with rewards and benefits.
3. *Normative power*—influencing members by using the knowledge that they want very much to belong to the organization and by letting them know that what they are expected to do is the "right" thing to do.

Along with these three types of organizational power, Etzioni proposes that we can classify organizations by the type of membership they have:

1. *Alienative membership*. The members have hostile, negative feelings about being in the organization. They don't want to be there. Prisons are a good example of alienative memberships.
2. *Calculative membership*. Members weigh the benefits and limitations of belonging to the organization. Businesses are good examples of organizations with calculative memberships.
3. *Moral membership*. Members have such positive feelings about organizational membership that they are willing to deny their own needs. Organizations with many volunteer workers, such as the American Heart Association, are examples of moral memberships. Religious groups are another.

Etzioni argues that the type of organizational power should be matched to the type of membership in the organization in order to achieve congruence. Figure 11.1 shows the matches in his power analysis theory.

FIGURE 11.1 Etzioni's Power Analysis

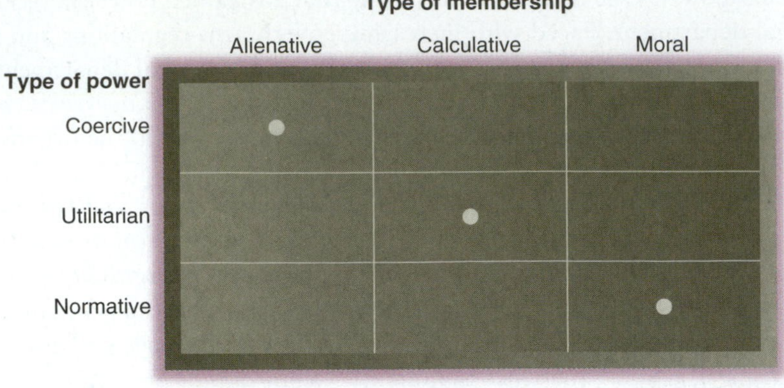

SOURCE: Adapted from Amitai Etzioni, *Modern Organizations* (Upper Saddle River, N.J.: Prentice-Hall, 1964), 59–61. Reprinted by permission of Pearson Education, Inc., Upper Saddle River, N.J.

In an alienative membership, members have hostile feelings. In prisons, for example, Etzioni would contend that coercive power is the appropriate type to use.

A calculative membership is characterized by an analysis of the good and bad aspects of being in the organization. In a business partnership, for example, each partner weighs the benefits from the partnership against the costs entailed in the contractual arrangement. Utilitarian or reward-based power is the most appropriate type to use.

In a moral membership, the members have strong positive feelings about the particular cause or goal of the organization. Normative power is the most appropriate to use because it capitalizes on the members' desires to belong.

Etzioni's power analysis is an organizational-level theory. It emphasizes that the characteristics of an organization play a role in determining the type of power appropriate for use in it. Etzioni's theory is controversial in its contention that a single type of power is appropriate in any organization.

SYMBOLS OF POWER

(5) Identify symbols of power and powerlessness in organizations.

Organization charts show who has authority but reveal little about who has power. We'll now look at two very different ideas about the symbols of power. The first comes from Rosabeth Moss Kanter. It is a scholarly approach to determining who has power and who feels powerless. The second is a semiserious look at the tangible symbols of power by Michael Korda.

Kanter's Symbols of Power

Kanter provides several characteristics of powerful people in organizations:[26]

1. *Ability to intercede for someone in trouble.* An individual who can pull someone out of a jam has power.
2. *Ability to get placements for favored employees.* Getting a key promotion for an employee is a sign of power.
3. *Exceeding budget limitations.* A manager who can go above budget limits without being reprimanded has power.
4. *Procuring above-average raises for employees.* One faculty member reported that her department head distributed 10 percent raises to the most productive

faculty members although the budget allowed for only 4 percent increases. "I don't know how he did it; he must have pull," she said.

5. *Getting items on the agenda at meetings.* If a manager can raise issues for action at meetings, it's a sign of power.
6. *Access to early information.* Having information before anyone else does is a signal that a manager is plugged into key sources.
7. *Having top managers seek out their opinion.* When top managers have a problem, they may ask for advice from lower-level managers. The managers they turn to have power.

A theme that runs through Kanter's list is doing things for others: for people in trouble, for employees, for bosses. There is an active, other-directed element in her symbols of power.

You can use Kanter's symbols of power to identify powerful people in organizations. They can be particularly useful in finding a mentor who can effectively use power.

Kanter's Symbols of Powerlessness

Kanter also wrote about symptoms of *powerlessness*—a lack of power—in managers at different levels of the organization. First-line supervisors, for example, often display three symptoms of powerlessness: overly close supervision, inflexible adherence to the rules, and a tendency to do the job themselves rather than training their employees to do it. Staff professionals such as accountants and lawyers display different symptoms of powerlessness. When they feel powerless, they tend to resist change and try to protect their turf. Top executives can also feel powerless. They show symptoms such as focusing on budget cutting, punishing others, and using dictatorial, top-down communication. Acting in certain ways can lead employees to believe that a manager is powerless. By making external attributions (blaming others or circumstances) for negative events, a manager looks as if he or she has no power.[27]

What can you do when you recognize that employees are feeling powerless? The key to overcoming powerlessness is to share power and delegate decision-making authority to employees.

Korda's Symbols of Power

Michael Korda takes a different look at symbols of power in organizations.[28] He discusses three unusual symbols: office furnishings, time power, and standing by.

Furniture is not just physically useful; it also conveys a message about power. Locked file cabinets are signs that the manager has important and confidential information in the office. A rectangular (rather than round) conference table enables the most important person to sit at the head of the table. The size of one's desk may convey the amount of power. Most executives prefer large, expensive desks.

Time power means using clocks and watches as power symbols. Korda says that the biggest compliment a busy executive can pay a visitor is to remove his watch and place it face down on the desk, thereby communicating "my time is yours." He also notes that the less powerful the executive, the more intricate the watch. Moreover, managers who are really secure in their power wear no watch at all, since they believe nothing important can happen without them. A full calendar is also proof of power. Personal planners are left open on the desk to display busy schedules.

Standing by is a game in which people are obliged to keep their cell phones, pagers, etc. with them at all times so executives can reach them. The idea is that

powerlessness
A lack of power.

the more you can impose your schedule on other people, the more power you have. In fact, Korda defines *power* as follows: There are more people who inconvenience themselves on your behalf than there are people on whose behalf you would inconvenience yourself. Closely tied to this is the ability to make others perform simple tasks for you, such as getting your coffee or fetching the mail.

While Kanter's symbols focus on the ability to help others, Korda's symbols focus on status—a person's relative standing in a group based on prestige and having other people defer to him or her.[29] By identifying powerful people and learning from their modeled behavior, you can determine the keys to power use in the organization.

POLITICAL BEHAVIOR IN ORGANIZATIONS

(6) Define organizational politics and understand the role of political skill and major influence tactics.

Like power, the term *politics* in organizations may conjure up a few negative images. However, *organizational politics* is not necessarily negative; it is the use of power and influence in organizations. Organizations are arenas in which people have competing interests, which effective managers must reconcile. Organizational politics are central to managing. As people try to acquire power and expand their power base, they use various tactics and strategies. Some are sanctioned (acceptable to the organization); others are not. *Political behavior* refers to actions not officially sanctioned by an organization that are taken to influence others in order to meet one's personal goals.[30] Sometimes personal goals are aligned with team or organizational goals, and they can be achieved in support of others' interests. But other times personal goals and the interests of others collide, and individuals pursue politics at the expense of others' interests.[31]

Politics is a controversial topic among managers. Some managers take a favorable view of political behavior; others see it as detrimental to the organization. Some workers who perceive their workplace as highly political actually find the use of political tactics more satisfying and report greater job satisfaction when they engage in political behavior. Some people may therefore thrive in political environments, while others may find office politics distasteful and stressful.[32]

Most people are also amazingly good at recognizing political behavior at all levels of the firm. Employees are not only keenly aware of political behavior at their level but can also spot political behavior at both their supervisor's level and the topmost levels of the organization.[33]

Many organizational conditions encourage political activity. Among them are unclear goals, autocratic decision making, ambiguous lines of authority, scarce resources, and uncertainty.[34] Even supposedly objective activities may involve politics. One such activity is the performance appraisal process. A study of sixty executives who had extensive experience in employee evaluation indicated that political considerations were nearly always part of the performance appraisal process.[35]

Marissa Mayer of Google is charged with the key task of approving new ideas at Google to be presented to founders Sergey Brin and Larry Page. She takes several steps to ensure that politicking does not occur in choice of ideas that move forward. For this purpose she has very clear criteria for objectively evaluating new ideas, holds meetings that allow ten minutes per idea with a timer ticking down, and has someone transcribe everything that is said in the meeting. She is also personally involved in the hiring process and conducts a summer trip abroad to stimulate creativity and build relationships with her design engineers.[36]

organizational politics
The use of power and influence in organizations.

political behavior
Actions not officially sanctioned by an organization that are taken to influence others in order to meet one's personal goals.

The effects of political behavior in organizations can be quite negative when such behavior is strategically undertaken to maximize self-interest. If people within the organization are competitively pursuing selfish ends, they're unlikely to be attentive to the concerns of others. The workplace can seem less helpful, more threatening, and more unpredictable. People focus on their own concerns rather than on organizational goals. This represents the negative face of power described earlier by David McClelland as personal power. If employees view the organization's political climate as extreme, they experience more anxiety, tension, fatigue, and burnout. They are also dissatisfied with their jobs and are more likely to leave.[37] Not all political behavior is destructive. Constructive political behavior is selfless, rather than selfish, in nature. In this respect, it is similar to David McClelland's concept of social power. Constructive organizational politicians see the difference between ethical and unethical behavior, understand that relationships drive the political process, and use power with a sense of responsibility.[38]

Influence Tactics

Influence is the process of affecting the thoughts, behavior, or feelings of another person. That other person could be the boss (upward influence), an employee (downward influence), or a coworker (lateral influence). There are eight basic types of influence tactics. They are listed and described in Table 11.2.[39]

Research has shown that the four tactics used most frequently are consultation, rational persuasion, inspirational appeals, and ingratiation. Upward appeals and coalition tactics are used moderately. Exchange tactics are used least often, while pressure is the least effective tactic.

Influence tactics are used for impression management, which was described in Chapter 3. In impression management, individuals use influence tactics to control others' impressions of them. One way in which people engage in impression management is through image building. Another way is to use impression management to get support for important initiatives or projects.

Ingratiation is an example of a tactic often used for impression management. Ingratiation can take many forms, including flattery, opinion conformity, and subservient behavior.[40] Exchange is another influence tactic that may be used for impression management. Offering to do favors for someone in an effort to create a favorable impression is an exchange tactic.

Which influence tactics are most effective? It depends on the target of the influence attempt and the objective. Individuals use different tactics for different purposes, and for different people. Influence attempts with subordinates, for example, usually involve assigning tasks or changing behavior. With peers, the objective is often to request help. With superiors, influence attempts are often made to request approval, resources, political support, or personal benefits. Rational persuasion and coalition tactics are used most often to get support from peers and superiors to change company policy. Consultation and inspirational appeals are particularly effective for gaining support and resources for a new project.[41] Overall, the most effective tactic in terms of achieving objectives is rational persuasion. Pressure is the least effective tactic.

Influence tactics are often used on bosses in order to get them to evaluate the employee more favorably or to give the employee a promotion. Two tactics, rational persuasion and ingratiation, appear to work effectively. Employees who use these tactics receive higher performance evaluations than employees who don't.[42] When supervisors believe an employee's motive for doing favors for the boss is simply to be a good citizen, they are likely to reward that employee. However, when the motive is seen as brownnosing (ingratiation), supervisors respond negatively.[43] And, as it becomes more obvious that the employee has something to gain by impressing the boss, the likelihood that ingratiation will succeed decreases. So, how does one use ingratiation effectively? A study conducted among supervisors and subordinates of

TABLE 11.2 Influence Tactics Used in Organizations

Tactics	Description	Examples
Pressure	The person uses demands, threats, or intimidation to convince you to comply with a request or to support a proposal.	If you don't do this, you're fired. You have until 5:00 to change your mind, or I'm going without you.
Upward appeals	The person seeks to persuade you that the request is approved by higher management or appeals to higher management for assistance in gaining your compliance with the request.	I'm reporting you to my boss. My boss supports this idea.
Exchange	The person makes an explicit or implicit promise that you will receive rewards or tangible benefits if you comply with a request or support a proposal or reminds you of a prior favor to be reciprocated.	You owe me a favor. I'll take you to lunch if you'll support me on this.
Coalition	The person seeks the aid of others to persuade you to do something or uses the support of others as an argument for you to agree also.	All the other supervisors agree with me. I'll ask you in front of the whole committee.
Ingratiation	The person seeks to get you in a good mood or to think favorably of him or her before asking you to do something.	Only you can do this job right. I can always count on you, so I have another request.
Rational persuasion	The person uses logical arguments and factual evidence to persuade you that a proposal or request is viable and likely to result in the attainment of task objectives.	This new procedure will save us $150,000 in overhead. It makes sense to hire John; he has the most experience.
Inspirational appeals	The person makes an emotional request or proposal that arouses enthusiasm by appealing to your values and ideals or by increasing your confidence that you can do it.	Being environmentally conscious is the right thing. Getting that account will be tough, but I know you can do it.
Consultation	The person seeks your participation in making a decision or planning how to implement a proposed policy, strategy, or change.	This new attendance plan is controversial. How can we make it more acceptable? What do you think we can do to make our workers less fearful of the new robots on the production line?

SOURCE: First two columns from G. Yukl and C. M. Falbe, "Influence Tactics and Objectives in Upward, Downward, and Lateral Influence Attempts," *Journal of Applied Psychology* 75 (1990): 132–140.

a large state agency indicates that subordinates with higher scores on political skill used ingratiation regularly and received higher performance ratings, whereas individuals with lower scores on political skill who used ingratiation frequently received lower performance ratings.[44] Additionally, another research study demonstrated that supervisors rated subordinate ingratiation behavior as less manipulative if the subordinate was highly politically skilled.[45] These results indicate that political skill might be one factor that enables people to use ingratiation effectively. We'll describe political skill in more detail in the section of the chapter that follows.

Still, a well-disguised ingratiation is hard to resist. Attempts that are not obvious usually succeed in increasing the target's liking for the ingratiator.[46] Most people have trouble remaining neutral when someone flatters them or agrees with them. However, witnesses to the ingratiation are more likely to question the motive behind it. Observers are more skeptical than the recipients of the ingratiation.

There is evidence that men and women view politics and influence attempts differently. Men tend to view political behavior more favorably than do women. When both men and women witness political behavior, they view it more positively if the agent is of their gender and the target is of the opposite gender.[47] Women executives often view politics with distaste and expect to be recognized and promoted only on the merit of their work. A lack of awareness of organizational politics is a barrier that holds women back in terms of moving into senior executive ranks.[48] Women may have fewer opportunities to develop political skills because of a lack of mentors and role models and because they are often excluded from informal networks.[49]

Different cultures prefer different influence tactics at work. One study found that American managers dealing with a tardy employee tended to rely on pressure tactics such as "If you don't start reporting on time for work, I will have no choice but to start docking your pay." In contrast, Japanese managers relied on influence tactics that either appealed to the employee's sense of duty ("It is your duty as a responsible employee of this company to begin work on time.") or emphasized a consultative approach ("Is there anything I can do to help you overcome the problems that are preventing you from coming to work on time?").[50]

It is important to note that influence tactics do have some positive effects. When investors form coalitions and put pressure on firms to increase their research and development efforts, it works.[51] However, some influence tactics, including pressure, coalition building, and exchange, can have strong ethical implications. There is a fine line between being an impression manager and being seen as a manipulator.

How can a manager use influence tactics well? First, she or he can develop and maintain open lines of communication in all directions: upward, downward, and lateral. Then the manager can treat the targets of influence attempts—whether managers, employees, or peers—with basic respect. Finally, the manager can understand that influence relationships are reciprocal—they are two-way relationships. As long as the influence attempts are directed toward organizational goals, the process of influence can be advantageous to all involved.

Political Skill

Researchers at Florida State University have generated an impressive body of research on political skill.[52] *Political skill* is the ability to get things done through positive interpersonal relationships outside the formal organization. Researchers suggest that it should be considered in hiring and promotion decisions. They found that leader political skill has a positive effect on team performance and on trust and support for the leader.[53,54] Furthermore, it buffers the negative effects of stressors such as role conflict in work settings. These findings point to the importance of developing political skill for managerial success.[55] Politically skilled individuals have the ability to accurately understand others and use this knowledge to influence them in order to meet personal or organizational goals. Political skill is made up of four key dimensions: social astuteness, interpersonal influence, networking ability, and sincerity.

Political skill
The ability to get things done through favorable interpersonal relationships outside of formally prescribed organizational mechanisms.

1. *Social astuteness* refers to accurate perception and evaluation of social situations. Socially astute individuals manage social situations in ways that present them in the most favorable light.
2. *Interpersonal influence* refers to a subtle and influential personal style that is effective in getting things done. Individuals with interpersonal influence are

very flexible in adapting their behavior to differing targets of influence or differing contexts in order to achieve their goals.

3. *Networking ability* is an individual's capacity to develop and retain diverse and extensive social networks. People who have networking ability are effective in building successful alliances and coalitions, thus making them skilled at negotiation and conflict resolution.
4. *Sincerity* refers to an individual's ability to portray forthrightness and authenticity in all of their dealings. Individuals who can appear sincere inspire more confidence and trust, thus making them very successful in influencing other people.[56]

These four dimensions of political skill can each be learned. Several organizations now offer training to help develop this ability in their employees. And political skill is important at all levels of the organization. The biggest cause of failure among top executives is lack of social effectiveness.[57] High self-monitors and politically savvy individuals score higher on an index of political skill, as do individuals who are emotionally intelligent. You 11.1 helps you assess your political skill.

Military settings are particularly demanding in their need for leaders who can adapt to changing situations and maintain a good reputation. In such an environment, politically skilled leaders are seen as more sincere in their motives, can more readily perceive and adapt to work events, and can thus build a strong positive reputation among followers. In fact, political skill can be acquired through a social learning process and by having a strong mentor. Such a mentor then serves as a role model and helps the protégé navigate organizational politics and helps him/her learn the informal sources of power and politics in the organization.[58]

Managing Political Behavior in Organizations

Politics cannot and should not be eliminated from organizations. Managers can, however, take a proactive stance and manage the political behavior that inevitably occurs.[59]

Open communication is one key to managing political behavior. Uncertainty tends to increase such behavior, and communication that reduces the uncertainty is important. One helpful form of communication is to clarify the sanctioned and nonsanctioned political behaviors in the organization. For example, you may want to encourage social power as opposed to personal power.[60]

Another key is to clarify expectations regarding performance. This can be accomplished through the use of clear, quantifiable goals and the establishment of a clear connection between goal accomplishment and rewards.[61]

Participative management is yet another key. Often, people engage in political behavior when they feel excluded from decision-making processes in the organization. By including such people, you will encourage positive input and eliminate behind-the-scenes maneuvering.

Encouraging cooperation among work groups is another strategy for managing political behavior. Managers can instill a unity of purpose among work teams by rewarding cooperative behavior and by implementing activities that emphasize the integration of team efforts toward common goals.[62]

Managing scarce resources well is also important. An obvious solution to the problem of scarce resources is to increase the resource pool, but few managers have this luxury. Clarifying the resource allocation process and making the connection

YOU 11.1

Using the following 7-point scale, choose the number that best describes how much you agree with each statement about yourself.

1 = *strongly disagree*
2 = *disagree*
3 = *slightly disagree*
4 = *neutral*
5 = *slightly agree*
6 = *agree*
7 = *strongly agree*

1. _____ I spend a lot of time and effort at work networking with others.
2. _____ I am able to make most people feel comfortable and at ease around me.
3. _____ I am able to communicate easily and effectively with others.
4. _____ It is easy for me to develop good rapport with most people.
5. _____ I understand people very well.
6. _____ I am good at building relationships with influential people at work.
7. _____ I am particularly good at sensing the motivations and hidden agendas of others.
8. _____ When communicating with others, I try to be genuine in what I say and do.
9. _____ I have developed a large network of colleagues and associates at work who I can call on for support when I really need to get things done.
10. _____ At work, I know a lot of important people and am well connected.
11. _____ I spend a lot of time at work developing connections with others.
12. _____ I am good at getting people to like me.
13. _____ It is important that people believe I am sincere in what I say and do.
14. _____ I try to show a genuine interest in other people.
15. _____ I am good at using my connections and I network to make things happen at work.
16. _____ I have good intuition or savvy about how to present myself to others.
17. _____ I always seem to instinctively know the right things to say or do to influence others.
18. _____ I pay close attention to people's facial expressions.

A higher score indicates better political skill than a lower score.

between performance and resources explicit can help discourage dysfunctional political behavior.

Providing a supportive organizational climate is another way to manage political behavior effectively. A supportive climate allows employees to discuss controversial issues promptly and openly. This prevents the issue from festering and potentially causing friction among employees.[63]

Managing political behavior at work is important. The perception of dysfunctional political behavior can lead to dissatisfaction.[64] When employees perceive that there are dominant interest groups or cliques at work, they are less satisfied with pay and promotions. When they believe that the organization's reward practices are influenced by who you know rather than how well you perform, they are less satisfied.[65] In addition, when employees believe that their coworkers are exhibiting increased political behavior, they are less satisfied with their coworkers. Open communication, clear expectations about performance and rewards, participative decision-making practices, work group cooperation, effective management of scarce resources, and a supportive organizational climate can help managers prevent the negative consequences of political behavior.

MANAGING UP: MANAGING THE BOSS

(7) Develop a plan for managing employee–boss relationships.

One of the least discussed aspects of power and politics is the relationship between you and your boss. This is a crucial relationship, because your boss is your most important link with the rest of the organization.[66] The employee–boss relationship is one of mutual dependence; you depend on your boss to give you performance feedback, provide resources, and supply critical information. She depends on you for performance, information, and support. Because it's a mutual relationship, you should take an active role in managing it. Too often the management of this relationship is left to the boss; but if the relationship doesn't meet your needs, chances are you haven't taken the responsibility to manage it proactively.

Table 11.3 shows the basic steps to take in managing your relationship with your boss. The first step is to try to understand as much as you can about her. What are his goals and objectives? What kind of pressures does he face in the job? Many individuals naively expect the boss to be perfect and are disappointed when they find that this is not the case. What are the boss's strengths, weaknesses, and blind spots? Because this is an emotionally charged relationship, it is difficult to be objective; but this is a critical step in forging an effective working relationship. What is the boss's preferred work style? Does he prefer everything in writing or hate detail? Does he prefer that you make appointments or is dropping in at his office acceptable? The point is to gather as much information about your boss as you can and to try to put yourself in his shoes.

The second step in managing this important relationship is to assess yourself and your own needs in the same way you analyzed your boss's. What are your strengths, weaknesses, and blind spots? What is your work style? How do you normally relate to authority figures? Some of us have tendencies toward counterdependence; that

TABLE  11.3 Managing Your Relationship with Your Boss

Make Sure You Understand Your Boss and Her Context, Including:
Her goals and objectives.
The pressures on her.
Her strengths, weaknesses, and blind spots.
Her preferred work style.

Assess Yourself and Your Needs, Including:
Your own strengths and weaknesses.
Your personal style.
Your predisposition toward dependence on authority figures.

Develop and Maintain a Relationship That:
Fits both your needs and styles.
Is characterized by mutual expectations.
Keeps your boss informed.
Is based on dependability and honesty.
Selectively uses your boss's time and resources.

SOURCE: Reprinted by permission of *Harvard Business Review*. From "Managing Your Boss," by J. J. Gabarro and J. P. Kotter, (May–June 1993): p. 155. Copyright © 1993 by the Harvard Business School Publishing Corporation; all rights reserved.

is, we rebel against the boss as an authority and view him or her as a hindrance to our performance. Or, in contrast, we might take an overdependent stance, passively accepting the employee–boss relationship and treating him or her as an all-wise, protective parent. What is your tendency? Knowing how you react to authority figures can help you understand your interactions with your boss.

Once you have done a careful self-analysis and tried to understand your boss, the next step is to work to develop an effective relationship. Both parties' needs and styles must be accommodated. A fundraiser for a large volunteer organization related a story about a new boss, describing him as cold, aloof, unorganized, and inept. She made repeated attempts to meet with him and clarify expectations, and his usual reply was that he didn't have the time. Frustrated, she almost looked for a new job. "I just can't reach him!" was her refrain. Then she stepped back to consider her boss's style and her own. Being an intuitive-feeling type of person, she prefers constant feedback and reinforcement from others. Her boss, an intuitive thinker, works comfortably without feedback from others and has a tendency to fail to praise or reward others. She sat down with him and cautiously discussed the differences in their needs. This discussion became the basis for working out a comfortable relationship. "I still don't like him, but I understand him better," she said.

Another aspect of managing the relationship involves working out mutual expectations. One key activity is to develop a plan for work objectives and have the boss agree to it.[67] It is important to do things right, but it is also important to do the right things. Neither party to the relationship is a mind reader, and clarifying the goals is a crucial step.

Keeping the boss informed is also a priority. No one likes to be caught off guard, and there are several ways to keep the boss informed. Give the boss a weekly to-do list as a reminder of the progress towards goals. When you read something pertaining to your work, clip it out for the boss. Most busy executives appreciate being given materials they don't have time to find for themselves. Give the boss interim reports, and let the boss know if the work schedule is slipping. Don't wait until it's too late to take action.

The employee–boss relationship must be based on dependability and honesty. This means giving and receiving positive and negative feedback. Most of us are reluctant to give any feedback to the boss, but positive feedback is welcomed at the top. Negative feedback, while tougher to initiate, can clear the air. If given in a problem-solving format, it can even bring about a closer relationship.[68]

Finally, remember that the boss is on the same team you are. The golden rule is to make the boss look good, because you expect the boss to do the same for you.

SHARING POWER: EMPOWERMENT

(8) Discuss how managers can empower others.

Another positive strategy for managing political behavior is *empowerment*—sharing power within an organization. As modern organizations grow flatter, eliminating layers of management, empowerment becomes more and more important. Jay Conger defines *empowerment* as "creating conditions for heightened motivation through the development of a strong sense of personal self-efficacy."[69] This means sharing power in such a way that individuals learn to believe in their ability to do the job. The driving idea of empowerment is that the individuals closest to the work and to the customers should make the decisions and that this makes the best use of employees' skills and talents. You can empower yourself by developing your sense of self-efficacy. You 11.2 helps you assess your progress in terms of self-empowerment.

empowerment
Sharing power within an organization.

Are You Self-Empowered?

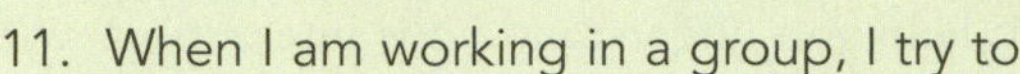

Circle to indicate how you usually are in these situations:

1. If someone disagrees with me in a class or a meeting, I
   a. immediately back down.
   b. explain my position further.
2. When I have an idea for a project, I
   a. typically take a great deal of time to start it.
   b. get going on it fairly quickly.
3. If my boss or teacher tells me to do something that I think is wrong, I
   a. do it anyway, telling myself he or she is "the boss".
   b. ask for clarification and explain my position.
4. When a complicated problem arises, I usually tell myself
   a. I can take care of it.
   b. I will not be able to solve it.
5. When I am around people of higher authority, I often
   a. feel intimidated and defer to them.
   b. enjoy meeting important people.
6. As I awake in the morning, I usually feel
   a. alert and ready to conquer almost anything.
   b. tired and have a hard time getting myself motivated.
7. During an argument I
   a. put a great deal of energy into "winning".
   b. try to listen to the other side and see if we have any points of agreement.
8. When I meet new people, I
   a. always wonder what they are "really" up to.
   b. try to learn what they are about and give them the benefit of the doubt until they prove otherwise.
9. During the day I often
   a. criticize myself on what I am doing or thinking.
   b. think positive thoughts about myself.
10. When someone else does a great job, I
    a. find myself picking apart that person and looking for faults.
    b. often give a sincere compliment.
11. When I am working in a group, I try to
    a. do a better job than the others.
    b. help the group function more effectively.
12. If someone pays me a compliment, I typically
    a. try not to appear boastful and I downplay the compliment.
    b. respond with a positive "thank you" or similar response.
13. I like to be around people who
    a. challenge me and make me question what I do.
    b. give me respect.
14. In love relationships I prefer the other person to
    a. have his/her own selected interests.
    b. do pretty much what I do.
15. During a crisis I try to
    a. resolve the problem.
    b. find someone to blame.
16. After seeing a movie with friends, I
    a. wait to see what they say before I decide whether I liked it.
    b. am ready to talk about my reactions right away.
17. When work deadlines are approaching, I typically
    a. get flustered and worry about completion.
    b. buckle down and work until the job is done.
18. If a job comes up I am interested in, I
    a. go for it and apply.
    b. tell myself I am not qualified enough.
19. When someone treats me unkindly or unfairly, I
    a. try to rectify the situation.
    b. tell other people about the injustice.
20. If a difficult conflict situation or problem arises, I
    a. try not to think about it, hoping it will resolve itself.
    b. look at various options and may ask others for advice before I figure out what to do.

Scoring:

Score one point for each of the following circled: 1b, 2b, 3b, 4a, 5b, 6a, 7b, 8b, 9b, 10b, 11b, 12b, 13a, 14a, 15a, 16b, 17b, 18a, 19a, 20b.

Analysis of Scoring

16–20 You are a take-charge person and generally make the most of opportunities. When others tell you something cannot be done, you may take this as a challenge and do it anyway. You see the world as an oyster with many pearls to harvest.

11–15 You try hard, but sometimes your negative attitude prevents you from getting involved in productive projects. Many times you take responsibility, but there are situations where you look to others to take care of problems.

0–10 You complain too much and are usually focused on the "worst case scenario." To you the world is controlled by fate, and no matter what you do, it seems to get you nowhere, so you let other people develop opportunities. You need to start seeing the positive qualities in yourself and in others and see yourself as the "master of your fate."

SOURCE: "Are You Self-Empowered?" by Dorothy Marcic.

Four dimensions comprise the essence of empowerment: meaning, competence, self-determination, and impact.[70]

- *Meaning* is a fit between the work role and the employee's values and beliefs. It is the engine of empowerment that energizes employees about their jobs. If employees' hearts are not in their work, they cannot feel empowered.
- *Competence* is the belief that one has the ability to do the job well. Without competence, employees will feel inadequate and lack a sense of empowerment.
- *Self-determination* is having control over the way one does his or her work. Employees who feel they're just following orders from the boss cannot feel empowered.
- *Impact* is the belief that one's job makes a difference within the organization. Without a sense of contributing to a goal, employees cannot feel empowered.

Employees need to experience all four of the empowerment dimensions in order to feel truly empowered. Only then will organizations reap the hoped-for rewards from empowerment efforts. The rewards sought are increased effectiveness, higher job satisfaction, and less stress.

Empowerment is easy to advocate but difficult to put into practice. Conger offers some guidelines on how leaders can empower others.

First, managers should express confidence in employees and set high performance expectations. Positive expectations can go a long way toward enabling good performance, as the Pygmalion effect shows (Chapter 3).

Second, managers should create opportunities for employees to participate in decision making. This means participation in the forms of both voice and choice. Employees should not just be asked to contribute their opinions about any issue; they should also have a vote in the decision that is made. One method for increasing participation is using self-managed teams, as we discussed in Chapter 9.

Third, managers should remove bureaucratic constraints that stifle autonomy. Often, companies have antiquated rules and policies that prevent employees from managing themselves. An example is a collection agency where a manager's signature was once required to approve long-term payment arrangements for delinquent customers. Collectors, who spoke directly with customers, were the best judges of

FIGURE 11.2 Employee Empowerment Grid

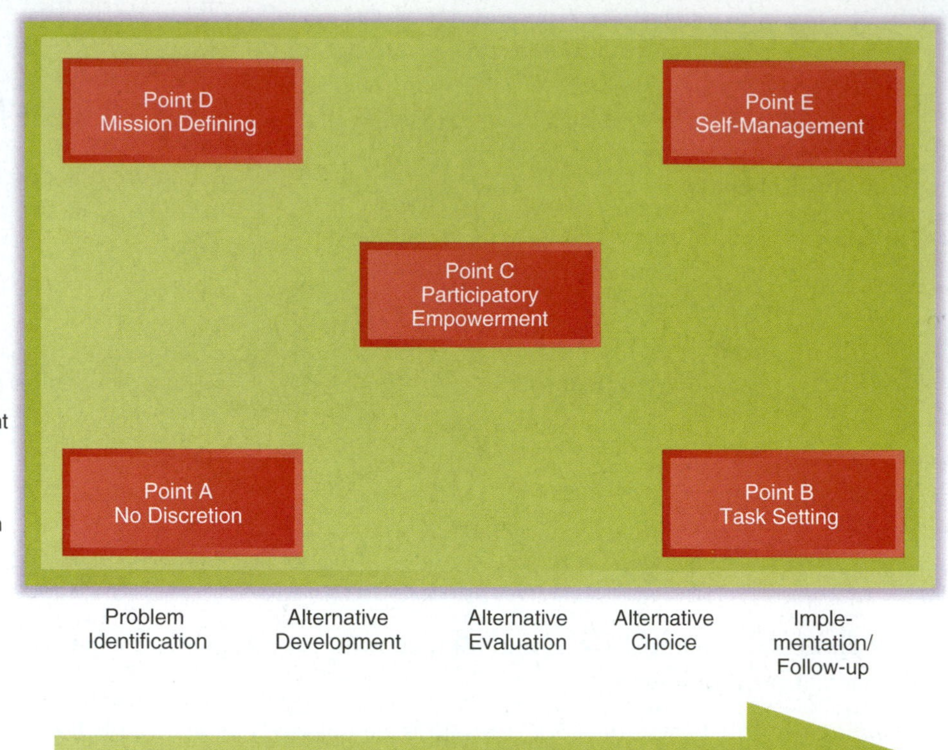

whether the payment arrangements were workable, and having to consult a manager made them feel closely supervised and powerless. The rule was dropped and collections increased.

Fourth, managers should set inspirational or meaningful goals. When individuals feel they "own" a goal, they are more willing to take personal responsibility for it.

Empowerment is a matter of degree. Jobs can be thought of in two dimensions: job content and job context. Job content consists of the tasks and procedures necessary for doing a particular job. Job context is broader. It is the reason the organization needs the job and includes the way the job fits into the organization's mission, goals, and objectives. These two dimensions are depicted in Figure 11.2, the employee empowerment grid.

Both axes of the grid contain the major steps in the decision-making process. As shown on the horizontal axis, decision-making authority over job content increases in terms of greater involvement in the decision-making process. Similarly, the vertical axis shows that authority over job context increases with greater involvement in that decision-making process. Combining job content and job context authority in this way produces five points that vary in terms of the degree of empowerment.[71]

No Discretion (point A) represents the traditional, assembly-line job: highly routine and repetitive, with no decision-making power. Recall from Chapter 7 that if these jobs have a demanding pace and if workers have no discretion, distress will result.

Task Setting (point B) is the essence of most empowerment programs in organizations today. In this case, the worker is empowered to make decisions about the best way to get the job done but has no decision responsibility for the job context.

Participatory Empowerment (point C) represents a situation that is typical of autonomous work groups that have some decision-making power over both job content and job context. Their involvement is in problem identification, developing alternatives, and evaluating alternatives, but the actual choice of alternatives is often beyond their power. Participatory empowerment can lead to job satisfaction and productivity.

Mission Defining (point D) is an unusual case of empowerment and is seldom seen. Here, employees have power over job context but not job content. An example would be a unionized team that is asked to decide whether their jobs could be better done by an outside vendor. Deciding to outsource would dramatically affect the mission of the company but would not affect job content, which is specified in the union contract. Assuring these employees of continued employment regardless of their decision would be necessary for this case of empowerment.

Self-Management (point E) represents total decision-making control over both job content and job context. It is the ultimate expression of trust. One example is TXI Chaparral Steel (part of Texas Industries), where employees redesign their own jobs to add value to the organization.

Empowerment should begin with job content and proceed to job context. Because the workforce is so diverse, managers should recognize that some employees are more ready for empowerment than others. Managers must diagnose situations and determine the degree of empowerment to extend to employees. Recently, the management of change in organizations was identified as another area wherein empowerment can have a strong effect. Empowered employees are more likely to participate in and facilitate change processes in organizations as they feel more committed to the organizations' success.[72]

Robert Polet, the CEO of Gucci, seems to know how to get empowerment right. Read about his management style using empowerment in The Real World 11.2.

The empowerment process also carries with it a risk of failure. When you delegate responsibility and authority, you must be prepared to allow employees to fail; and failure is not something most managers tolerate well. At Merck, some say the CEO Ray Gilmartin empowered scientists too much and that their failures cost Merck its profitability and reputation as one of *Fortune*'s Most Admired Companies. One example of this empowerment involved a diabetes drug that early research showed caused tumors in mice. Scientists argued that despite early studies showing the drug wasn't viable, research should continue, and it did—until the drug was finally axed, costing the company considerably in terms of time and money.[73]

MANAGERIAL IMPLICATIONS: USING POWER EFFECTIVELY

Sydney Finkelstein, a professor at Dartmouth University, spends his time studying why executives fail. Interestingly, most of these failures involve the misuse of power and organizational politics. Here are several reasons why executives fail:

- *They see themselves and their companies as dominating their environments.* While confidence is helpful, the perception that a company is without peer is a recipe for failure. On a more personal level, CEOs who see themselves as uniquely gifted in comparison to their competitors and coworkers are generally ripe for a fall.

THE REAL WORLD 11.2

Gucci: Fine Fashion, Finer Management

When he took over as CEO of the Gucci Group, industry analysts wondered how Robert Polet, whose previous experience was in ice cream and frozen foods at Unilever, could handle the world of fine fashion and expensive leather. Besides, he was stepping into the uncomfortable role of having to manage Gucci's top designers and creative geniuses who are known for their temperamental personalities. Yet Gucci has done exceptionally well under Polet: income increased by 44 percent and some of the company's unprofitable brands are making a turnaround. So, what is the key to Polet's success?

Polet made changes to the management structure and style at Gucci. He strongly believes in empowering his design teams. Under his reign, each brand that Gucci owns operates largely autonomously. Each team is headed by a creative director who oversees the creative process of design, while a CEO for each team oversees the packaging and advertising part of the business. In addition, Polet set out a clear road map for where he expects Gucci to be in the future. This vision translated into clearly defined roles and responsibilities for key organizational players and roles, along with empowerment to carry out the responsibilities effectively. More than anything else, Polet seems adept at emphasizing the importance of the brand over the people associated with it, so that employees never lose sight of organizational goals. These acts of cooperation and empowerment have propelled Gucci towards success.

SOURCE: J. L. Yang, "Managing Top Talent at Gucci Group," *Fortune* (July 17, 2007). http://money.cnn.com/magazines/fortune/fortune_archive/2007/07/23/100135662/?postversion=2007071710

- *They think they have all the answers.* While decisive leadership and vision often lead to the executive suite, an unwillingness to admit ignorance or seek others' input is may trigger disaster. A reluctance to empower others leads to failure.
- *They ruthlessly eliminate anyone who isn't 100 percent behind them.* Business history is replete with leaders who culled the ranks of those who were willing to voice different opinions, only to find themselves blundering down the road to catastrophe without anyone to yell "Stop!"
- *They stubbornly rely on what worked for them in the past.* Like most of us, business leaders tend to fall back on what has worked before. Unfortunately, yesterday's solution is rarely an ideal fit for today's challenge, and successes of the past may well inhibit success in the future.
- *They have no clear boundaries between their personal interests and corporate interests.* As a top leader invests more time and effort in a firm, it's easy for him or her to become convinced that the firm is simply a reflection of his or her own enormous ego. Ironically, leaders who fail to make this distinction tend to be far less careful about spending corporate resources, leading to often embarrassing revelations of executive excess at employee and stockholder expense.[74]

While Finkelstein is quick to point out that corporate executives are, almost without exception, amazingly bright and talented individuals, they also tend to succumb to the same temptations as lesser mortals. Given the extreme power they wield, their failures tend to be much more visible, painful, and far-reaching than most. Corporate executives need accountability to help them avoid these mistakes.

In addition to learning from failure, there is research on how to use power successfully. John Kotter argues that managers need to develop power strategies

to operate effectively.[75] Kotter offers the following guidelines for managing dependence on others and for using power successfully:

- *Use power in ethical ways.* People make certain assumptions about the use of power. One way of using the various forms of power ethically is by applying the criteria of utilitarian outcomes, individual rights, and distributive justice.
- *Understand and use all of the various types of power and influence.* Successful managers diagnose the situation, understand the people involved, and choose a compatible influence method.
- *Seek jobs that allow you to develop your power skills.* Recognize that managerial positions are dependent ones, and look for positions that allow you to focus on a critical issue or problem.
- *Use power tempered by maturity and self-control.* Power for its own sake should not be a goal, nor should power be used for self-aggrandizement.
- *Accept that influencing people is an important part of the management job.* Power means getting things accomplished; it is not a dirty word. Acquiring and using power well is a key to managerial success.

You can use these guidelines to enhance your own power skills. Mastering the power and politics within an organization takes respect and patience. When all people are empowered, the total amount of power within the organization will increase.

LOOKING BACK: IS GOOGLE "DOING NO EVIL"?

Google has recently suffered intense backlash from industry competitors for its wide-ranging power and influence. It has expanded from being an Internet search engine to being a giant in the advertising industry, thus scaring television and the print media. It has stepped on Microsoft's toes by offering an online office software package for a portion of Microsoft's Office software package. It also acquired the widely popular YouTube. Viacom sued Google for a whopping $1 billion for copyright infringements as users uploaded clips of popular TV shows like *The Colbert Report* and *South Park* on YouTube. Skeptics worry that Google has too much power in an industry where anything is possible thanks to the freedoms afforded by the Internet. One author even speculated that the company might pose a defense concern due to the vast amounts of information it has access to.

Yet Google seems to be navigating such allegations of a monopoly fairly well. It has done so by creating a strong company culture of employee commitment, empowerment, and cooperation. Ultimately, analysts point out, Google could survive concerns about its growing power and far-reaching influence by following its corporate mantra, "Do No Evil." Time will tell if Google can do so, but right now the outlook is good.[76]

Chapter Summary

1. Power is the ability to influence others. Influence is the process of affecting the thoughts, behavior, and feelings of others. Authority is the right to influence others.
2. French and Raven's five forms of interpersonal power are reward, coercive, legitimate, referent, and expert power. Information power is another form of interpersonal power.
3. The key to using all of these types of power well is to use them ethically.
4. McClelland believes personal power is negative and social power is positive.
5. Intergroup power sources include control of critical resources and strategic contingencies.
6. According to Etzioni's power analysis, the characteristics of the organization are an important factor in deciding the type of power to use.
7. Recognizing symbols of both power and powerlessness is a key diagnostic skill for managers.
8. Organizational politics is an inevitable feature of work life. Political behavior consists of actions not officially sanctioned that are taken to influence others in order to meet personal goals. Managers should take a proactive role in managing politics. Political skill is the ability to get things done through favorable interpersonal relationships outside of formally prescribed organizational mechanisms.
9. The employee–boss relationship is an important political relationship. Employees can use their skills to develop more effective working relationships with their bosses.
10. Empowerment is a positive strategy for sharing power throughout the organization.

Key Terms

authority (p. 364)
coercive power (p. 365)
empowerment (p. 381)
expert power (p. 365)
influence (p. 364)
information power (p. 367)
legitimate power (p. 365)
organizational politics (p. 374)
personal power (p. 369)
political behavior (p. 374)
political skill (p. 377)
power (p. 364)
powerlessness (p. 373)
referent power (p. 365)
reward power (p. 365)
social power (p. 370)
strategic contingencies (p. 370)
zone of indifference (p. 364)

Review Questions

1. What are the five types of power according to French and Raven? What are the effects of these types of power? What is information power?
2. What are the intergroup sources of power?
3. Distinguish between personal and social power. What are the four power-oriented characteristics of the best managers?
4. According to Rosabeth Moss Kanter, what are the symbols of power? The symptoms of powerlessness?
5. How do organizations encourage political activity?
6. Which influence tactics are most effective?
7. What are some of the characteristics of an effective relationship between you and your boss?
8. What are some ways to empower people at work?

Discussion and Communication Questions

1. Who is the most powerful person you know personally? What is it that makes the person so powerful?
2. Why is it hard to determine if power has been used ethically?
3. What kinds of membership (alienative, calculative, moral) do you currently have? Is the power used in these relationships congruent?

4. As a student, do you experience yourself as powerful, powerless, or both? On what symbols or symptoms are you basing your perception?
5. How does attribution theory explain the reactions supervisors can have to influence tactics? How can managers prevent the negative consequences of political behavior?
6. Are people in your work environment empowered? How could they become more empowered?
7. Chapter 2 discussed power distance as a dimension of cultural differences. How would empowerment efforts be different in a country with high power distance?
8. *(communication question)* Think of a person you admire. Write a newspaper feature analyzing the person's use of power in terms of the ideas presented in the chapter.

Ethical Dilemma

James Allen, a manager for a large retail department store, sat at his desk remembering how this whole thing began. He had called a meeting of his team in early June in which he had laid out his plan to increase productivity over the next six months. Between back to school and the holidays, July through December was always a busy time in retail, but this year needed to be exceptional. Just weeks before that meeting, James had been informed that the store manager was retiring and his successor would be appointed from within the organization. Specifically, the manager whose department was the most productive and efficient through the end of the year would be named the new general manager.

It was now October, and the evaluation period was half over. James felt confident that things were going well in his department. His concern at the moment was Tom Sharp's department. One of Tom's employees had confided that Tom was promising favors to his employees who helped him gain this promotion. Once promoted, he would be in a position to give raises or even promote those who had helped him advance. To help Tom accomplish his goals, the department employees were willing to do just about anything, even work overtime off the clock to reduce labor costs.

James knew that these practices were wrong and against the company's mission and policies. His concern was how to handle it. He felt confident that his department would be the best, so Tom's unethical practices would not affect the outcome. And if he were the new general manager, he could handle the problem then. However, was it right to let these behaviors continue for another three months? Was James sending the wrong signal to his own employees by keeping quiet? Was it enough to say that fair and just practices win in the end? If he did blow the whistle, would the people he would soon supervise think badly of him for being a snitch? James really wanted to do the right thing, but he just was not sure what that was.

Questions

1. Who are the stakeholders that would be affected by James's decision?
2. Does James have a responsibility to come forward with this information?
3. Using consequential, rule-based, and character theories, evaluate James's decision options.

Experiential Exercises

11.1 Social Power Role Plays

1. Divide the class into five groups of equal size, each of which is assigned one of the French and Raven types of power.
2. Read the following paragraph and prepare an influence plan using the type of power that has been assigned to your group. When you have finished your planning, select one member to play the role of instructor. Then choose from your own or another group a "student" who is to be the recipient of the "instructor's" efforts.

You are an instructor in a college class and have become aware that a potentially good student has been repeatedly absent from class and sometimes is unprepared when he is there. He seems to be satisfied with the grade he is getting, but you would like to see him attend regularly, be better prepared, and thus do better in the class. You even feel that the student might get really turned on to pursuing a career in this field, which is an exciting one for you. You are respected and liked by your students, and it irritates you that this person treats your dedicated teaching with such a cavalier attitude. You want to influence the student to start attending regularly.

3. Role-playing.
   a. Each group role-plays its influence plan.
   b. During the role-playing, members in other groups should think of themselves as the student being influenced. Fill out the following "Reaction to Influence Questionnaire" for each role-playing episode, including your own.
4. Tabulate the results of the questionnaire within your group. For each role-playing effort, determine how many people thought the power used was reward, coercive, and so on; then add up each member's score for item 2, then for items 3, 4, and 5.
5. Group discussion.
   a. As a class, discuss which influence strategy is the most effective in compliance, long-lasting effect, acceptable attitude, and enhanced relationships.
   b. What are the likely side effects of each type of influence strategy?

Reaction to Influence Questionnaire

Role-Play #1

1. Type of power used (mark one):

   Reward—Ability to influence because of potential reward.

   Coercive—Ability to influence because of capacity to coerce or punish.

   Legitimate—Stems from formal position in organization.

   Referent—Comes from admiration and liking.

   Expert—Comes from superior knowledge or ability to get things done.

Role-Plays

1	2	3	4	5

Think of yourself on the receiving end of the influence attempt just described and record your own reaction with an "X" in the appropriate box.

2. As a result of this influence attempt I will . . .
   definitely not comply definitely comply
   1 2 3 4 5
3. Any change that does come about will be . . .
   temporary long-lasting
   1 2 3 4 5
4. My own personal reaction is . . .
   resistant accepting
   1 2 3 4 5
5. As a result of this influence attempt, my relationship with the instructor will probably be . . .
   worse better
   1 2 3 4 5

Role-Plays

1	2	3	4	5

SOURCE: Gib Akin, *Exchange* 3, No. 4 (1978): 38–39. Reprinted by permission of Gib Akin, McIntire School of Commerce, University of Virginia.

11.2 Empowerment in the Classroom

1. Divide the class into groups of six people.
2. Each group is to brainstorm ways in which students might be more empowered in the classroom. The ideas do not have to be either feasible or reasonable. They can be as imaginative as possible.
3. Each group should now analyze each of the empowerment ideas for feasibility, paying attention to administrative or other constraints that may hamper implementation. This feasibility discussion might include ideas about how the college or university could be altered.
4. Each group should present its empowerment ideas along with its feasibility analysis. Questions of clarification for each group should follow each presentation.
5. Discuss the following questions as a class:
   a. Who is threatened by the power changes caused by empowerment?
   b. Are there unintended or adverse consequences of empowerment? Explain.

TAKE 2

Biz Flix | Scarface

Cuban refugee Antonio "Tony" Montana (Al Pacino) comes to Miami to pursue the American dream. He quickly rises in power within the Miami drug world until life turns against him. This lengthy, punishing film will leave unforgettable images and thoughts with almost any viewer. It is a remake of the 1931 *Scarface*, a classic gangster film starring Paul Muni that set an early standard for films of this type.

The scene from *Scarface* comes from the "Shakedown" sequence that occurs about halfway through the film. The sequence takes place at a disco before Tony's confrontation with his sister Gina (Mary Elizabeth Mastrantonio) about the man she is dating.

Chief Detective of Narcotics Mel Bernstein (Harris Yulin) and Tony Montana discuss Mel's proposal to protect Tony's drug operation. After Mel says, "Thank you for the drink" and leaves, Tony goes to Elvira's (Michelle Pfeiffer) table. The film continues through more of Tony Montana's complex drug deals and to its well-known violent ending.

What to Watch for and Ask Yourself:

- What are Mel's sources or bases of power in this interaction with Tony Montana?
- What are Tony Montana's sources or bases of power?
- What type of power relationship forms between the two men?

Workplace Video | Managing in Turbulent Times, Featuring The Second City Theater

Since 1959, The Second City has been the nation's premier source of improvisational and sketch comedy. Originally founded as a cabaret revue staged by University of Chicago undergraduates, the theater troupe rose to fame in 1975 when owner Andrew Alexander produced the acclaimed comedy television series *SCTV*. Today Second City operates multiple entertainment divisions, including comedy clubs, improvisational training centers, national touring companies, and corporate communication workshops. The company's stage performances are a main attraction of big-city nightlife, delighting audiences from Chicago to Los Angeles.

From the beginning, Second City has been a launching pad for comedians, actors, directors, and others in show business. Mike Myers, Tina Fey, Bill Murray, and John Candy are just a few of the big stars whose careers developed under the watchful eye of Andrew Alexander and his Second City management team.

Planning, leading, and controlling a business based around creative talent requires creative leadership. Inartful leaders who use power coercively or merely for personal gain don't stand a chance in the theater world. For years Second City's managers have used authority and influence to forge creative partnerships with their diverse staff. Taking cues from the art form they promote, managers embrace improv's "yes-and" approach—an acting method in which one performer plays off another performer's ideas and adds to them. Like skilled improvisational actors on a stage, management at Second City

TAKE 2

encourage feedback from front-line employees and spontaneously parlay that information into new business opportunities.

The Second City has what it takes to direct a talented, diverse group of people. In a world of abusive bosses, Alexander and his team represent the positive face of power and authority. The chief's adroit use of social power to accomplish goals is fitting for a company whose product is people. As producer Robin Hammond says, the company is "all about the people on the stages—they are the heart and soul of The Second City."

Discussion Questions

1. Who has authority at Second City, and what forms of interpersonal power do these individuals possess by virtue of their formal positions?
2. Give an example of power in action at Second City.
3. In what ways does Second City's improvisational "yes-and" approach to management empower employees?

CASE

Power and Politics in the Fall and Rise of John Lasseter

John Lasseter grew up in a family heavily involved in artistic expression. Lasseter was drawn to cartoons as a youngster. Then as a freshman in high school he read *The Art of Animation*, a book about the making of the Disney animated film *Sleeping Beauty*. This proved to be a revelation for Lasseter. He discovered that people could earn a living by making cartoons. Lasseter started writing letters to The Walt Disney Company Studios regarding his interest in creating cartoons. Studio representatives, who corresponded with Lasseter many times, told him to get a great art education, after which they would teach him animation.[1]

When Disney started a Character Animation Program at the California Institute of Arts film school, the Disney Studio contacted Lasseter and he enrolled in the program. Classes were taught by extremely talented Disney animators who also shared stories about working with Walt Disney. During summer breaks, jobs at Disneyland further fueled Lasseter's passion for working as an animator for Disney Studios. Full of excitement, he joined the Disney animation staff in 1979 after graduation, but he was met with disappointment. According to Lasseter, "[T]he animation studio wasn't being run by these great Disney artists like our teachers at Cal Arts, but by lesser artists and businesspeople who rose through attrition as the grand old men retired." Lasseter was told, "[Y]ou put in your time for 20 years and do what you're told, and then you can be in charge." He continues, "I didn't realize it then, but I was beginning to be perceived as a loose cannon. All I was trying to do was make things great, but I was beginning to make some enemies."[2]

In the early 1980s, Lasseter became enthralled with the potential of using computer graphics technology for animation but found little interest among Disney Studio executives for the concept. Nonetheless, a young Disney executive, Tom Willhite, eventually allowed Lasseter and a colleague to develop a 30-second test film that combined "hand-drawn, two-dimensional Disney-style character animation with three-dimensional computer-generated backgrounds." Lasseter found a story that would fit the test and could be developed into a full movie. When he presented the test clip and feature movie idea to the Disney Studio head, the only question the studio head asked concerned the cost of production. Lasseter told him the cost of production with computer animation would be about the same as a regular animated feature, and Lasseter was informed, "I'm only interested in computer animation if it saves money or time."[3]

Lasseter subsequently discovered that his idea was doomed before he ever presented it to the studio head. Says Lasseter, "[W]e found out later that others poked holes in my idea before I had even pitched it. In our enthusiasm, we had gone around some of my direct superiors, and I didn't realize how much of an enemy I had made of one of them. I mean, the studio head had made up his mind before we walked in. We could have shown him anything and he would have said the same thing." Shortly after the studio head left the room, Lasseter received a call from the superior who didn't like him, informing him that his employment at Disney was being terminated immediately.[4]

Despite being fired, Lasseter did not speak negatively of the Disney organization, nor did he let others know anything other than that the project on which he was working had ended. His personal admiration and respect for Walt Disney and animation were too great to allow him to do otherwise.[5]

Lasseter was recruited to Lucasfilm by Ed Catmull to work on a project that "turned out to be the very first character-animation cartoon done with a computer."[6] Not long afterwards, Steve Jobs bought the animation business from George Lucas for $10 million and Pixar Animation Studios was born.[7] Lasseter became the chief creative genius behind Pixar's subsequent animated feature film successes like *Toy Story, Toy Story 2, A Bug's Life,* and *The Incredibles,* among others.[8]

In 2006, Disney CEO Robert Iger and Pixar CEO Steve Jobs consummated a deal for Pixar to become a wholly-owned subsidiary of Disney. Iger wanted to reinvigorate animation at Disney, and as the top creative executive at Pixar, John Lasseter was viewed a key figure in achieving this objective.[9] Lasseter ". . . is regarded by Hollywood executives as the modern Walt [Disney] himself [with capabilities]. . . that have made Pixar a sure thing in the high stakes animated world."[10] Former Disney Studios head Peter Schneider says Lasseter "is a kid who has never grown up and continues to show the wonder and joy that you need in this business."[11] Current Disney Studio chief Dick Cook says that Lasseter is like the famous professional basketball player Michael Jordan: "He makes all the players around him better."[12]

Lasseter now oversees development of movies at both Pixar's and Disney's animation studios.[13] Says Lasseter, "I can't tell you how thrilled I am to have all these new roles. I do what I do in life because of Walt Disney—his films and his theme park and his characters and his joy in entertaining. The emotional feeling that his creations gave me is something that I want to turn around and give to others."[14]

Discussion Questions

1. What forms of interpersonal power are evident in the case?
2. In what ways do the two faces of power appear in this case?
3. Do the firing of John Lasseter from Disney Studios and the events leading up to his firing demonstrate the ethical use of power? Explain your answer.
4. Did the firing of John Lasseter indicate the existence of political behavior in the Disney organization?

SOURCE: This case was written by Michael K. McCuddy, The Louis S. and Mary L. Morgal Chair of Christian Business Ethics and Professor of Management, College of Business Administration, Valparaiso University.

CHAPTER 12

Leadership and Followership

LEARNING OBJECTIVES

After reading this chapter, you should be able to do the following:

1. Define *leadership* and *followership*.
2. Discuss the differences between leadership and management and between leaders and managers.
3. Evaluate the effectiveness of autocratic, democratic, and laissez-faire leadership styles.
4. Explain initiating structure and consideration, leader behaviors, and the Leadership Grid.
5. Evaluate the usefulness of Fiedler's contingency theory of leadership.
6. Compare and contrast the path–goal theory, Vroom–Yetton–Jago theory, the Situational Leadership® model, leader–member exchange, and the Substitutes for Leadership model.
7. Distinguish among transformational, charismatic, and authentic leaders.
8. Discuss the characteristics of effective and dynamic followers.

THINKING AHEAD: AMERICAN EXPRESS

Ken Chenault: Leading with Kindness and Compassion

Ken Chenault is among the most unlikely competitors for the topmost position of a powerful American company. He is known as much for his kindness and gentlemanly side as he is for his business acumen. In a world crippled by ethical scandals, he is known for his honesty, integrity, and likeability. He has a law degree from Harvard and is known for his extremely good negotiating skills. More importantly, though, Chenault has consistently driven change at American Express, thus preparing it for changing business markets. In his reign at AMEX, Chenault has had to make several tough decisions, including cutting 16 percent of the workforce in order to survive in a post-9/11 environment. However, he succeeded in turning this tragic event into a defining learning moment for him personally and for AMEX. Through all the tough decisions, Chenault has received praise for his candor and fearlessness. He is also seen as a very charismatic leader who has helped the company survive several financial downswings and still come out on the top.[1]

In the Looking Back feature, we will focus on the key principles that drive this powerful and influential leader.

1 Define *leadership* and *followership.*

Leadership in organizations is the process of guiding and directing the behavior of people in the work environment. The first section of this chapter distinguishes leadership from management. *Formal leadership* occurs when an organization officially bestows on a leader the authority to guide and direct others in the organization. *Informal leadership* occurs when a person is unofficially accorded power by others in the organization and uses influence to guide and direct their behavior. Leadership is among the most researched but least understood social processes in organizations.

Leadership has a long, rich history in organizational behavior. In this chapter, we explore many of the theories and ideas that have emerged along the way in that history. To begin, we examine the differences between leaders and managers. Next, we explore the earliest theories of leadership, the trait theories, which tried to identify a set of traits that leaders have in common. Following the trait theories came behavioral theories, which proposed that leader behaviors, not traits, are what counts. Contingency theories followed soon after. These theories argue that appropriate leader behavior depends on the situation and the followers. Next, we present some exciting contemporary theories of leadership, followed by the exciting new issues that are arising in leadership. We end by discussing *followership* and offering some guidelines for using this leadership knowledge.

LEADERSHIP AND MANAGEMENT

2 Discuss the differences between leadership and management and between leaders and managers.

leadership
The process of guiding and directing the behavior of people in the work environment.

formal leadership
Officially sanctioned leadership based on the authority of a formal position.

informal leadership
Unofficial leadership accorded to a person by other members of the organization.

followership
The process of being guided and directed by a leader in the work environment.

John Kotter suggests that leadership and management are two distinct yet complementary systems of action in organizations.[2] Specifically, he believes that effective leadership produces useful change in organizations and that good management controls complexity in the organization and its environment. Fred Smith, who founded Federal Express (FedEx) in 1971, has been producing constant change since the company's start. FedEx began with primarily high-dollar medical and technology shipments. The company recently bought Kinko's to extend its reach from the back office to the front.[3] Bill Gates has successfully controlled complexity—Microsoft has grown exponentially from early times when his company's sole product was DOS. Healthy organizations need both effective leadership and good management.

For Kotter, the management process involves (1) planning and budgeting, (2) organizing and staffing, and (3) controlling and problem solving. The management process reduces uncertainty and stabilizes an organization. Alfred P. Sloan's integration and stabilization of General Motors after its early growth years are an example of good management.

In contrast, the leadership process involves (1) setting a direction for the organization; (2) aligning people with that direction through communication; and (3) motivating people to action, partly through empowerment and partly through basic need gratification. The leadership process creates uncertainty and change in an organization. Donald Peterson's championing of a quality revolution at Ford Motor Company is an example of effective leadership. As noted in the opening feature, one reason why Ken Chenault is seen as a powerful business leader is that he has championed change at AMEX. Effective leaders not only control the future of the organization but also act as enablers of change. They disturb existing patterns of behaviors, promote novel ideas, and help organizational members makes sense of the change process.[4]

Abraham Zaleznik proposes that leaders have distinct personalities that stand in contrast to the personalities of a manager.[5] Zaleznik suggests that both leaders and managers make a valuable contribution to an organization and that each one's contribution is different. Whereas *leaders* agitate for change and new approaches, *managers* advocate stability and the status quo. There is a dynamic tension between leaders and managers that makes it difficult for each to understand the other. Leaders and managers differ along four separate dimensions of personality: attitudes toward goals, conceptions of work, relationships with other people, and sense of self. The differences between these two personality types are summarized in Table 12.1. Zaleznik's distinction between leaders and managers is similar to the distinction made between transactional and transformational leaders, or between leadership and supervision. Transactional leaders use formal rewards and punishment to engage in deal making and contractual obligations, which you will read about later in this chapter.

It has been proposed that some people are strategic leaders who embody both the stability of managers and the visionary abilities of leaders. Thus, strategic leaders combine the best of both worlds in a synergistic way. The unprecedented success of both Coca-Cola and Microsoft suggests that their leaders, the late Roberto Goizueta (of Coke) and Bill Gates, were strategic leaders.[6]

TABLE 12.1 Leaders and Managers

Personality Dimension	Manager	Leader
Attitudes toward goals	Has an impersonal, passive, functional attitude; believes goals arise out of necessity and reality	Has a personal and active attitude; believes goals arise from desire and imagination
Conceptions of work	Views work as an enabling process that combines people, ideas, and things; seeks moderate risk through coordination and balance	Looks for fresh approaches to old problems; seeks highrisk positions, especially with high payoffs
Relationships with others	Avoids solitary work activity, preferring to work with others; avoids close, intense relationships; avoids conflict	Is comfortable in solitary work activity; encourages close, intense working relationships; is not conflict averse
Sense of self	Is once born; makes a straightforward life adjustment; accepts life as it is	Is twice born; engages in a struggle for a sense of order in life; questions life

SOURCE: Reprinted by permission of *Harvard Business Review*. From "Managers and Leaders: Are They Different?" by A. Zaleznik (January 2004).

leader
An advocate for change and new approaches to problems.

manager
An advocate for stability and the status quo.

EARLY TRAIT THEORIES

The first studies of leadership attempted to identify what physical attributes, personality characteristics, and abilities distinguished leaders from other members of a group.[7] The physical attributes considered have been height, weight, physique, energy, health, appearance, and even age. This line of research yielded some interesting findings. However, very few valid generalizations emerged from this line of inquiry. Therefore, there is insufficient evidence to conclude that leaders can be distinguished from followers on the basis of physical attributes.

Leader personality characteristics that have been examined include originality, adaptability, introversion–extraversion, dominance, self-confidence, integrity, conviction, mood optimism, and emotional control. There is some evidence that leaders may be more adaptable and self-confident than the average group member.

With regard to leader abilities, attention has been devoted to such constructs as social skills, intelligence, scholarship, speech fluency, cooperativeness, and insight. In this area, there is some evidence that leaders are more intelligent, verbal, and cooperative and have a higher level of scholarship than the average group member.

These conclusions suggest traits leaders possess, but the findings are neither strong nor uniform. For each attribute or trait claimed to distinguish leaders from followers, there were always at least one or two studies with contradictory findings. For some, the trait theories are invalid, though interesting and intuitively of some relevance. The trait theories have had very limited success in being able to identify the universal, distinguishing attributes of leaders. Recent research investigated the effects of heritability among 178 fraternal and 214 identical female twins. Results indicated that genetic factors contribute to the motivation to occupy leadership positions among women leaders. Similarly, prior work experience also has a significant impact on the motivation to lead. Thus it seems that both personal factors and experience affect a person's desire to become a leader.[8]

BEHAVIORAL THEORIES

(3) Evaluate the effectiveness of autocratic, democratic, and laissez-faire leadership styles.

autocratic style
A style of leadership in which the leader uses strong, directive, controlling actions to enforce the rules, regulations, activities, and relationships in the work environment.

democratic style
A style of leadership in which the leader takes collaborative, responsive, interactive actions with followers concerning the work and work environment.

laissez-faire style
A style of leadership in which the leader fails to accept the responsibilities of the position.

Behavioral theories emerged as a response to the deficiencies of the trait theories. Trait theories told us what leaders were like, but didn't address how they behaved. Three theories are the foundations of many modern leadership theories: the Lewin, Lippitt, and White studies; the Ohio State studies; and the Michigan studies.

Lewin Studies

The earliest research on leadership style, conducted by Kurt Lewin and his students, identified three basic styles: autocratic, democratic, and laissez-faire.[9] Each leader uses one of these three basic styles when approaching a group of followers in a leadership situation. The specific situation is not an important consideration, because the leader's style does not vary with the situation. The *autocratic style* is directive, strong, and controlling in relationships. Leaders with an autocratic style use rules and regulations to run the work environment. Followers have little discretionary influence over the nature of the work, its accomplishment, or other aspects of the work environment. The leader with a *democratic style* is collaborative, responsive, and interactive in relationships and emphasizes rules and regulations less than the autocratic leader. Followers have a high degree of discretionary influence, although the leader has ultimate authority and responsibility. The leader with a *laissez-faire style* leads through nonleadership. A laissez-faire leader abdicates the authority and responsibility of the position, which often results in chaos.

Laissez-faire leadership also causes role ambiguity for followers by the leader's failure to clearly define goals, responsibilities, and outcomes. It leads to higher interpersonal conflict at work.[10]

Ohio State Studies

The leadership research program at The Ohio State University also measured specific leader behaviors. The initial Ohio State research studied aircrews and pilots.[11] The aircrew members, as followers, were asked a wide range of questions about their lead pilots using the Leader Behavior Description Questionnaire (LBDQ). The results using the LBDQ suggested that there were two important underlying dimensions of leader behaviors.[12] These were labeled initiating structure and consideration.

(4) Explain initiating structure and consideration, leader behaviors, and the Leadership Grid.

Initiating structure is leader behavior aimed at defining and organizing work relationships and roles, as well as establishing clear patterns of organization, communication, and ways of getting things done. *Consideration* is leader behavior aimed at nurturing friendly, warm working relationships, as well as encouraging mutual trust and interpersonal respect within the work unit. These two leader behaviors are independent of each other. That is, a leader may be high on both, low on both, or high on one while low on the other. The Ohio State studies were intended to describe leader behavior, not to evaluate or judge it.[12]

Michigan Studies

Another approach to the study of leadership, developed at the University of Michigan, suggests that the leader's style has very important implications for the emotional atmosphere of the work environment and, therefore, for the followers who work under that leader. Two styles of leadership were identified: production oriented and employee oriented.[14]

A production-oriented style leads to a work environment characterized by constant influence attempts on the part of the leader, either through direct, close supervision or through the use of many written and unwritten rules and regulations for behavior. The focus is clearly on getting work done.

In comparison, an employee-oriented leadership style leads to a work environment that focuses on relationships. The leader exhibits less direct or less close supervision and establishes fewer written or unwritten rules and regulations for behavior. Employee-oriented leaders display concern for people and their needs.

These three groups of studies—Lewin, Lippitt, and White; Ohio State; and Michigan—taken together form the building blocks of many recent leadership theories. What the studies have in common is that two basic leadership styles were identified, with one focusing on tasks (autocratic, production oriented, initiating structure) and one focusing on people (democratic, employee oriented, consideration). Use You 12.1 to assess your supervisor's task- versus people-oriented styles.

initiating structure
Leader behavior aimed at defining and organizing work relationships and roles, as well as establishing clear patterns of organization, communication, and ways of getting things done.

consideration
Leader behavior aimed at nurturing friendly, warm working relationships, as well as encouraging mutual trust and interpersonal respect within the work unit.

Leadership Grid
An approach to understanding a leader's or manager's concern for results (production) and concern for people.

The Leadership Grid: A Contemporary Extension

Robert Blake and Jane Mouton's *Leadership Grid*, originally called the Managerial Grid, was developed with a focus on attitudes.[15] The two underlying dimensions of the grid are labeled Concern for Results and Concern for People. These two attitudinal dimensions are independent of each other and in different combinations form various leadership styles. Blake and Mouton originally identified five distinct managerial styles, and further development of the grid has led to the seven distinct leadership styles shown in Figure 12.1.

YOU 12.1

How Does Your Supervisor Lead?

Answer the following sixteen questions concerning your supervisor's (or professor's) leadership behaviors using the seven-point Likert scale. Then complete the summary to examine your supervisor's behaviors.

	Not at All						Very Much
1. Is your superior strict about observing regulations?	1	2	3	4	5	6	7
2. To what extent does your superior give you instructions and orders?	1	2	3	4	5	6	7
3. Is your superior strict about the amount of work you do?	1	2	3	4	5	6	7
4. Does your superior urge you to complete your work by the time he or she has specified?	1	2	3	4	5	6	7
5. Does your superior try to make you work to your maximum capacity?	1	2	3	4	5	6	7
6. When you do an inadequate job, does your superior focus on the inadequate way the job was done instead of on your personality?	1	2	3	4	5	6	7
7. Does your superior ask you for reports about the progress of your work?	1	2	3	4	5	6	7
8. Does your superior work out precise plans for goal achievement each month?	1	2	3	4	5	6	7
9. Can you talk freely with your superior about your work?	1	2	3	4	5	6	7
10. Generally, does your superior support you?	1	2	3	4	5	6	7
11. Is your superior concerned about your personal problems?	1	2	3	4	5	6	7
12. Do you think your superior trusts you?	1	2	3	4	5	6	7
13. Does your superior give you recognition when you do your job well?	1	2	3	4	5	6	7
14. When a problem arises in your workplace, does your superior ask your opinion about how to solve it?	1	2	3	4	5	6	7
15. Is your superior concerned about your future benefits like promotions and pay raises?	1	2	3	4	5	6	7
16. Does your superior treat you fairly?	1	2	3	4	5	6	7

Add up your answers to Questions 1 through 8. This total indicates your supervisor's performance orientation:

Task orientation = _______

Add up your answers to Questions 9 through 16. This total indicates your supervisor's maintenance orientation:

People orientation = _______

A score above 40 is high, and a score below 20 is low.

SOURCE: Reprinted from "The Performance-Maintenance Theory of Leadership: Review of a Japanese Research Program" by J. Misumi and M. F. Peterson, published in *Administrative Science Quarterly* 30 (1985): 207. By permission of Administrative Science Quarterly © 1985.

organization man manager (5,5)
A middle-of-the-road leader.

authority-compliance manager (9,1)
A leader who emphasizes efficient production.

The *organization man manager (5,5)* is a middle-of-the-road leader who has a medium concern for people and production. This leader attempts to balance a concern for both people and production without a commitment to either.

The *authority-compliance manager (9,1)* has great concern for production and little concern for people. This leader desires tight control in order to get tasks done efficiently and considers creativity and human relations unnecessary. Authority-compliance managers may become so focused on running an efficient organization that they actually use tactics such as bullying. Some authority-compliance managers may intimidate, verbally and mentally attack, and otherwise mistreat subordinates. This form of abuse is quite common, with one in six U.S. workers reporting that

FIGURE 12.1 The Leadership Grid

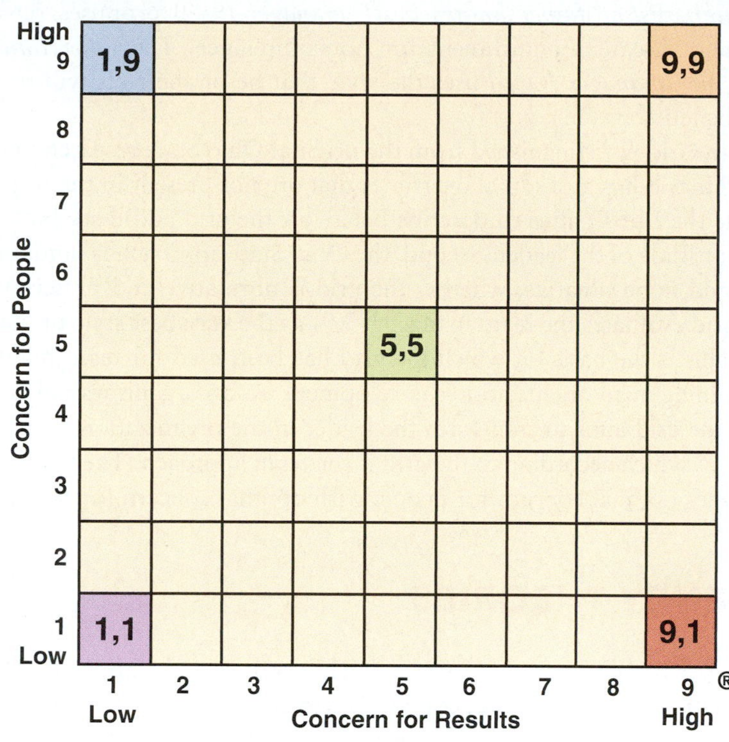

1,9 Country Club Management:
Thoughtful attention to the needs of the people for satisfying relationships leads to a comfortable, friendly organization atmosphere and work tempo.

9,9 Team Management:
Work accomplishment is from committed people; interdependence through a "common stake" in organization purpose leads to relationships of trust and respect.

5,5 Middle-of-the-Road Management:
Adequate organization performance is possible through balancing the necessity to get work out while maintaining morale of people at a satisfactory level.

1,1 Impoverished Management:
Exertion of minimum effort to get required work done is appropriate to sustain organization membership.

9,1 Authority-Compliance Management:
Efficiency in operations results from arranging conditions of work in such a way that human elements interfere to a minimum degree.

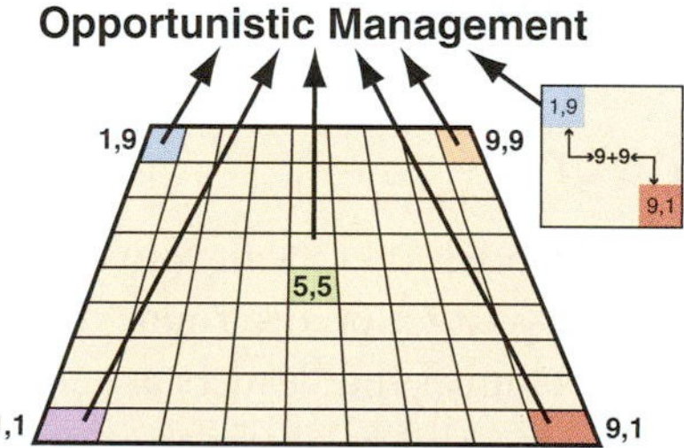

In Opportunisitic Management, people adapt and shift to any grid style needed to gain the maximum advantage. Performance occurs according to a system of selfish gain. Effort is given only for an advantage for personal gain.

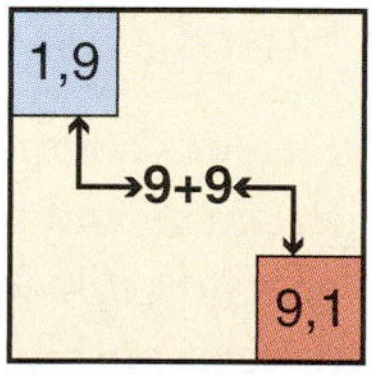

9+9: Paternalism/Maternalism Management:
Reward and approval are bestowed to people in return for loyalty and obedience; failure to comply leads to punishment.

SOURCE: "The Leadership Grid®" figure, Paternalism figure, and Opportunism from *Leadership Dilemmas—Grid Solutions,* by Robert R. Blake and Anne Adams McCanse (formerly *The Managerial Grid* by Robert R. Blake and Jane S. Mouton). Houston: Gulf Publishing Company (Grid Figure: p. 29; Paternalism Figure: p. 30; Opportunism Figure: p. 31). Copyright 1991 by Blake and Mouton, and Scientific Methods, Inc. Reproduced by permission of the owners.

they have been bullied by a manager.[16] The *country club manager (1,9)* has great concern for people and little concern for production, attempts to avoid conflict, and seeks to be well liked. This leader's goal is to keep people happy through good interpersonal relations, which are more important to him or her than the task. (This style is not a sound human relations approach but rather a soft Theory X approach.)

The *team manager (9,9)* is considered ideal and has great concern for both people and production. This leader works to motivate employees to reach their highest levels of accomplishment, is flexible, responsive to change, and understands the need for change. The *impoverished manager (1,1)* is often referred to as a

country club manager (1,9)
A leader who creates a happy, comfortable work environment.

team manager (9,9)
A leader who builds a highly productive team of committed people.

impoverished manager (1,1)
A leader who exerts just enough effort to get by.

laissez-faire leader. This leader has little concern for people or production, avoids taking sides, and stays out of conflicts; he or she does just enough to get by. Two new leadership styles have been added to these five original leadership styles within the grid. The *paternalistic "father knows best" manager (9+9)* promises reward for compliance and threatens punishment for noncompliance. The *opportunistic "what's in it for me" manager (Opp)* uses the style that he or she feels will return the greatest self-benefits.

The Leadership Grid is distinguished from the original Ohio State research in two important ways. First, it has attitudinal overtones that are not present in the original research. Whereas the LBDQ aims to describe behavior, the grid addresses both the behavior and the attitude of the leader. Second, the Ohio State approach is fundamentally descriptive and nonevaluative, whereas the grid is normative and prescriptive. Specifically, the grid evaluates the team manager (9,9) as the very best style of managerial behavior. This is the basis on which the grid has been used for team building and leadership training in an organization's development. As an organizational development method, the grid aims to transform the leader in the organization to lead in the "one best way," which according to the grid is the team approach. The team style is one that combines optimal concern for people with optimal concern for results.

CONTINGENCY THEORIES

Contingency theories involve the belief that leadership style must be appropriate for the particular situation. By their nature, contingency theories are "if–then" theories: If the situation is ____, then the appropriate leadership behavior is ____. We examine four such theories, including Fiedler's contingency theory, path–goal theory, normative decision theory, and situational leadership theory.

Fiedler's Contingency Theory

5 Evaluate the usefulness of Fiedler's contingency theory of leadership.

Fiedler's contingency theory of leadership proposes that the fit between the leader's need structure and the favorableness of the leader's situation determine the team's effectiveness in work accomplishment. This theory assumes that leaders are either task oriented or relationship oriented, depending on how the leaders obtain their primary need gratification.[17] Task-oriented leaders are primarily gratified by accomplishing tasks and getting work done. Relationship-oriented leaders are primarily gratified by developing good, comfortable interpersonal relationships. Accordingly, the effectiveness of both types of leaders depends on the favorableness of their situation. The theory classifies the favorableness of the leader's situation according to the leader's position power, the structure of the team's task, and the quality of the leader–follower relationships.

paternalistic "father knows best" manager (9+9)
A leader who promises reward and threatens punishment.

opportunistic "what's in it for me" manager (Opp)
A leader whose style aims to maximize self-benefit.

least preferred coworker (LPC)
The person a leader has least preferred to work with over his or her career.

The Least Preferred Coworker Fiedler classifies leaders using the Least Preferred Coworker (LPC) Scale.[18] The LPC Scale is a projective technique through which a leader is asked to think about the person with whom he or she can work least well (the *least preferred coworker*, or *LPC*).

The leader is asked to describe this coworker using sixteen eight-point bipolar adjective sets. Two of these sets follow (the leader marks the blank most descriptive of the least preferred coworker):

Efficient : : : : : : : : : Inefficient
Cheerful : : : : : : : : : Gloomy

Leaders who describe their least preferred coworker in positive terms (that is, pleasant, efficient, cheerful, and so on) are classified as high LPC, or relationship-oriented, leaders. Those who describe their least preferred coworker in negative terms (that is, unpleasant, inefficient, gloomy, and so on) are classified as low LPC, or task-oriented, leaders.

The LPC score is a controversial element in contingency theory.[19] It has been critiqued conceptually and methodologically because it is a projective technique with low measurement reliability.

Situational Favorableness The leader's situation has three dimensions: task structure, position power, and leader–member relations. Based on these three dimensions, the situation is either favorable or unfavorable for the leader. *Task structure* refers to the number and clarity of rules, regulations, and procedures for getting the work done. *Position power* refers to the leader's legitimate authority to evaluate and reward performance, punish errors, and demote group members.

The quality of *leader–member relations* is measured by the Group-Atmosphere Scale, composed of nine eight-point bipolar adjective sets. Two of these bipolar adjective sets follow:

Friendly : : : : : : : : : Unfriendly
Accepting : : : : : : : : : Rejecting

A favorable leadership situation is one with a structured task for the work group, strong position power for the leader, and good leader–member relations. In contrast, an unfavorable leadership situation is one with an unstructured task, weak position power for the leader, and moderately poor leader–member relations. Between these two extremes, the leadership situation has varying degrees of moderate favorableness for the leader.

Leadership Effectiveness The contingency theory suggests that low and high LPC leaders are each effective if placed in the right situation.[20] Specifically, low LPC (task-oriented) leaders are most effective in either very favorable or very unfavorable leadership situations. In contrast, high LPC (relationship-oriented) leaders are most effective in situations of intermediate favorableness. Figure 12.2 shows the nature of these relationships and suggests that leadership effectiveness is determined by the degree of fit between the leader and the situation. Recent research has shown that relationship-oriented leaders encourage team learning and innovativeness, which helps products get to market faster. This means that most relationship-oriented leaders perform well in leading new product development teams. In short, the right team leader can help get creative new products out the door faster, while a mismatch between the leader and the situation can have the opposite effect.[21]

What, then, is to be done if there is a misfit? That is, what happens when a low LPC leader is in a moderately favorable situation or when a high LPC leader is in a highly favorable or highly unfavorable situation? It is unlikely that the leader can be changed, according to the theory, because the leader's need structure is an enduring trait that is hard to change. Fiedler recommends that the leader's situation be changed to fit the leader's style.[22] A moderately favorable situation would be reengineered to be more favorable and therefore more suitable for the low LPC leader. A highly favorable or highly unfavorable situation would be changed to one that is moderately favorable and more suitable for the high LPC leader.

Fiedler's theory makes an important contribution in drawing our attention to the leader's situation. The following Science feature illustrates the importance of aligning leadership training with the context of the organization.

task structure
The degree of clarity, or ambiguity, in the work activities assigned to the group.

position power
The authority associated with the leader's formal position in the organization.

leader–member relations
The quality of interpersonal relationships among a leader and the group members.

FIGURE 12.2 Leadership Effectiveness in the Contingency Theory

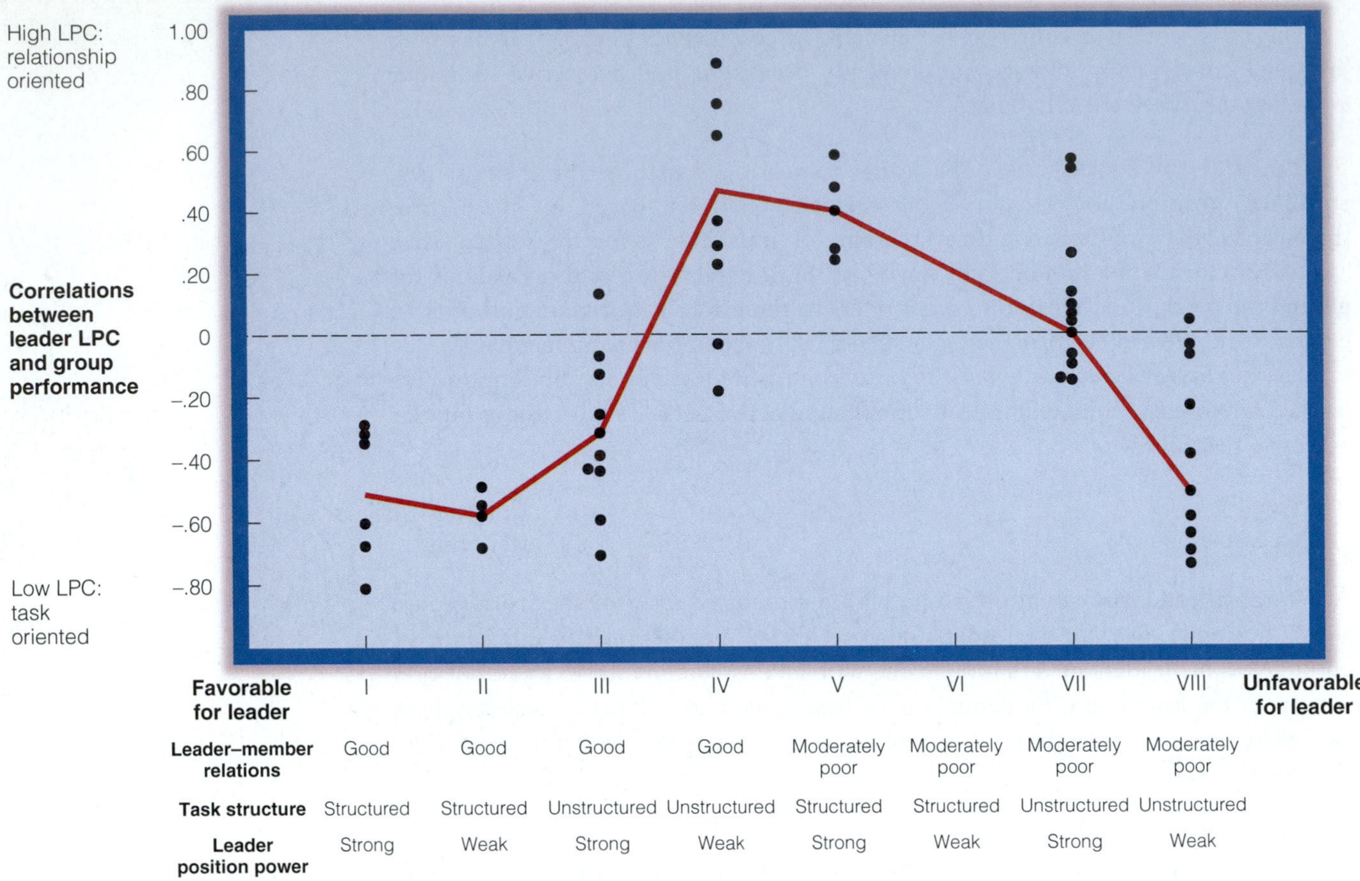

SOURCE: F. E. Fiedler, *A Theory of Leader Effectiveness* (New York: McGraw-Hill, 1964). Reprinted with permission of the author.

Path–Goal Theory

6 Compare and contrast the path–goal theory, Vroom–Yetton–Jago theory, the Situational Leadership model, leader–member exchange, and the Substitutes for Leadership model.

Robert House developed a path–goal theory of leader effectiveness based on an expectancy theory of motivation.[23] From the perspective of path–goal theory, the basic role of the leader is to clear the follower's path to the goal. The leader uses the most appropriate of four leader behavior styles to help followers clarify the paths that lead them to work and personal goals. The key concepts in the theory are shown in Figure 12.3.

A leader selects from the four leader behavior styles, shown in Figure 12.3, the one that is most helpful to followers at a given time. The *directive style* is used when the leader must give specific guidance about work tasks, schedule work, and let followers know what is expected. The *supportive style* is used when the leader needs to express concern for followers' well-being and social status. The *participative style* is used when the leader must engage in joint decision-making activities with followers. The *achievement-oriented style* is used when the leader must set challenging goals for followers and show strong confidence in those followers.

In selecting the appropriate leader behavior style, the leader must consider both the followers and the work environment. A few characteristics are included in Figure 12.3. Let us look at two examples. In Example 1, the followers are

SCIENCE

America's Leadership Factories: How They Do It

America's best-known companies seem to have perfected the art of grooming and producing exceptional leaders. Companies like General Electric, Johnson & Johnson, PepsiCo, and several others have strong leadership development programs in place that help them identify and groom employees for leadership positions. These leaders in turn are instrumental in guiding the organization to the goal of delivering on its promises. For example, Lexus is known for its tagline "The Pursuit of Perfection." Customers expect a certain degree of quality with a Lexus. The company's leadership translates this promise into reality by a strong emphasis on quality programs such as Six Sigma.

One research study examined the internal processes of leadership development across 150 of the top leader-producing firms and identified five key principles that were common to all the organizations. First, they identify leaders who are proficient at setting organizational strategy and identifying talent within the company. Second, they focus on customer expectations of the firm and ensure that leadership never loses sight of those expectations. Third, leader performance and effectiveness are evaluated against these customer expectations. Fourth, leadership training at these firms includes skill development that is specific to meeting customer expectations. Fifth, the success of leadership development is periodically evaluated. An important aspect of this last principle is that customers are used for feedback and evaluation of company leadership. For example, this study illustrated a case in which the board of directors called on shareholders, important customers, and community leaders to evaluate and give feedback on CEO actions and accomplishments.

In sum, many organizations invest millions of dollars in leadership development, but many of these programs fail because they are very broad based and not tailored to the particular organization. By keeping the specific needs and characteristics of the organization in mind, these leadership development programs can produce high-quality, effective leaders.

SOURCE: D. Ulrich and N. Smallwood, "Building a Leadership Brand," *Harvard Business Review* 85 (7, 8) (2007): 92–100.

inexperienced and working on an ambiguous, unstructured task. The leader in this situation might best use a directive style. In Example 2, the followers are highly trained professionals, and the task is a difficult yet achievable one. The leader in this situation might best use an achievement-oriented style. The leader always chooses the leader behavior style that helps followers achieve their goals.

FIGURE 12.3 The Path–Goal Theory of Leadership

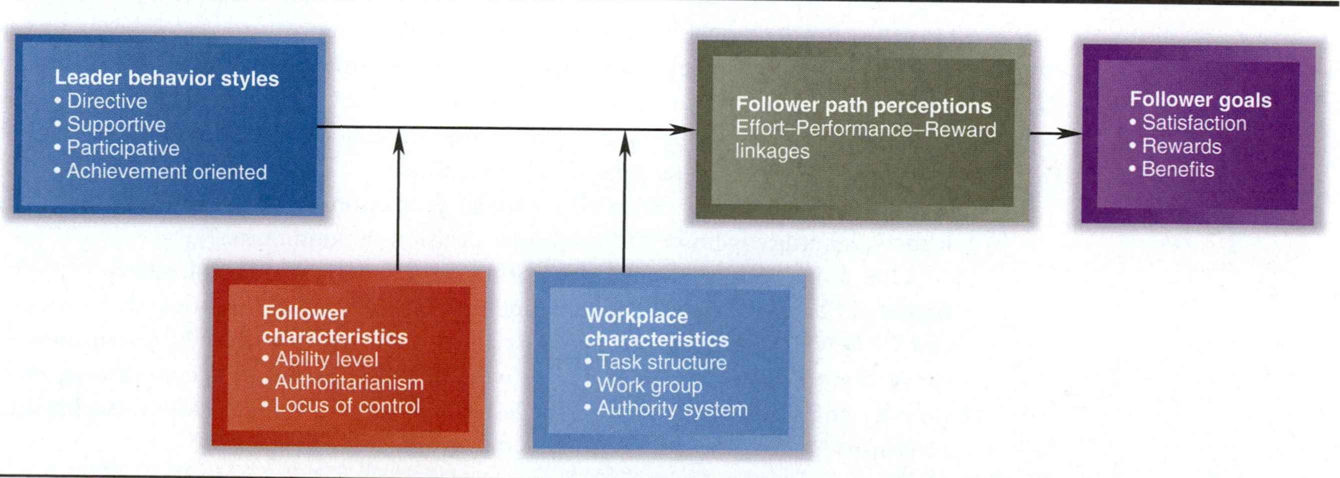

The path–goal theory assumes that leaders adapt their behavior and style to fit the characteristics of the followers and the environment in which they work. Actual tests of the path–goal theory and its propositions provide conflicting evidence.[24] The path–goal theory does have intuitive appeal and reinforces the idea that the appropriate leadership style depends on both the work situation and the followers. Research is focusing on which style works best in specific situations. For example, in small organizations, leaders who used visionary, transactional, and empowering behaviors, while avoiding autocratic behaviors, were most successful.[25]

Vroom–Yetton–Jago Normative Decision Model

The Vroom–Yetton–Jago normative decision model helps leaders and managers know when to have employees participate in the decision-making process. Victor Vroom, Phillip Yetton, and Arthur Jago developed and refined the normative decision model, which helps managers determine the appropriate decision-making strategy to use. The model recognizes the benefits of authoritative, democratic, and consultive styles of leader behavior.[26] Five forms of decision making are described in the model:

- *Decide.* The manager makes the decision alone and either announces it or "sells" it to the group.
- *Consult individually.* The manager presents the problem to the group members individually, gets their input, and then makes the decision.
- *Consult group.* The manager presents the problem to the group members in a meeting, gets their inputs, and then makes the decision.
- *Facilitate.* The manager presents the problem to the group in a meeting and acts as a facilitator, defining the problem and the boundaries that surround the decision. The manager's ideas are not given more weight than any other group member's ideas. The objective is to get concurrence.
- *Delegate.* The manager permits the group to make the decision within the prescribed limits, providing needed resources and encouragement.[27]

The key to the normative decision model is that a manager should use the decision method most appropriate for a given decision situation. The manager arrives at the proper method by working through matrices like the one in Figure 12.4. The factors across the top of the model (decision significance, commitment, leader expertise, etc.) are the situational factors in the normative decision model. This matrix is for decisions that must be made under time pressure, but other matrices are also available. For example, there is a different matrix managers can use when their objective is to develop subordinates' decision-making skills. Vroom has also developed a Windows-based computer program called Expert System that can be used by managers to determine which style to use.

Although the model offers very explicit predictions as well as prescriptions for leaders, its utility is limited to the leader decision-making tasks.

One unique study applied the normative decision model of leadership to the battlefield behavior of ten commanding generals in six major battles of the American Civil War. When the commanders acted consistently with the prescriptions of the Vroom–Yetton–Jago model, they were more successful in accomplishing their military goals. The findings also suggested that a lack of information sharing and consensus building resulted in serious disadvantages.[28]

FIGURE 12.4 Time-Driven Model (Reprinted from a Model of Leadership Style by Victor Vroom 1999)

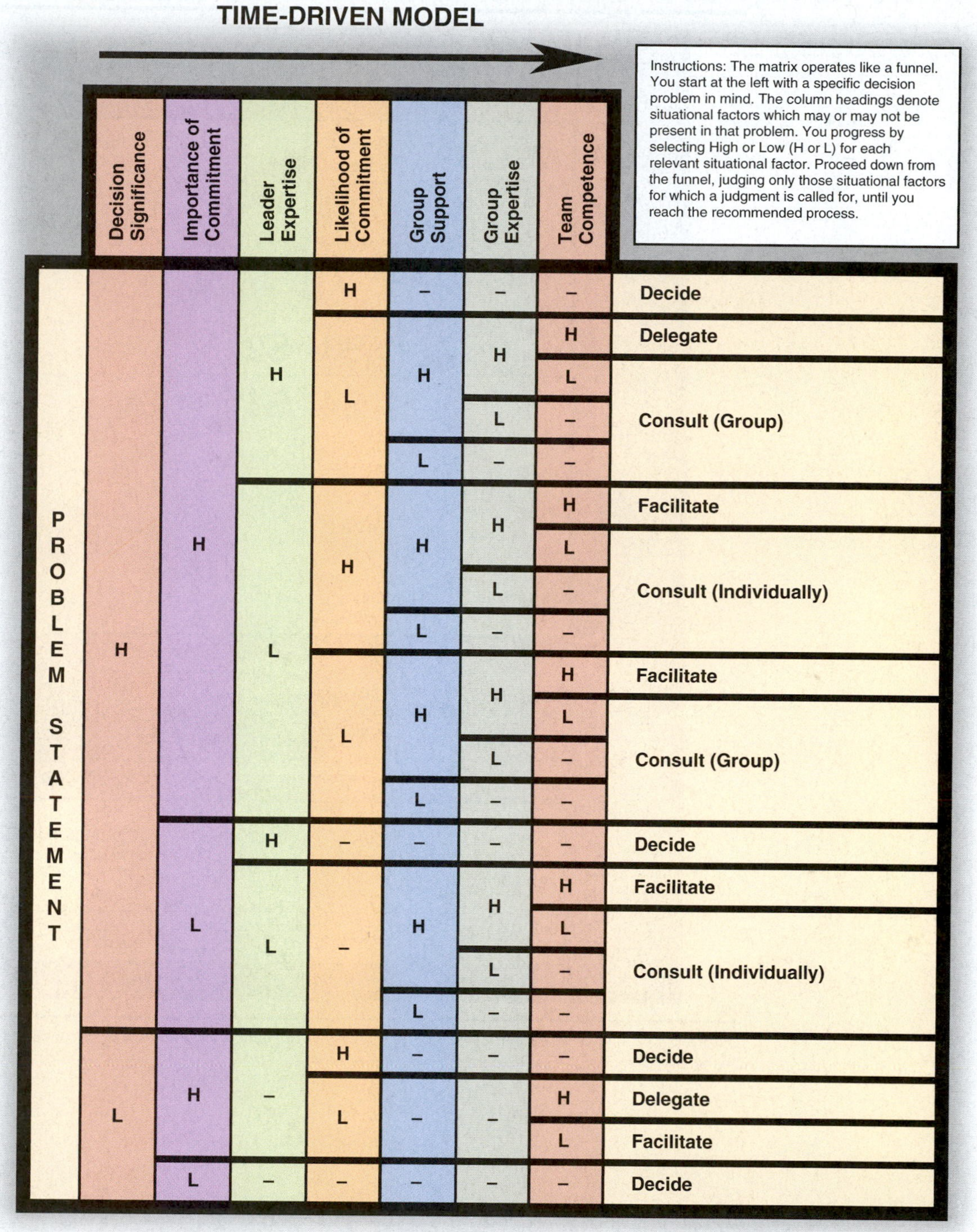

TIME-DRIVEN MODEL

Instructions: The matrix operates like a funnel. You start at the left with a specific decision problem in mind. The column headings denote situational factors which may or may not be present in that problem. You progress by selecting High or Low (H or L) for each relevant situational factor. Proceed down from the funnel, judging only those situational factors for which a judgment is called for, until you reach the recommended process.

PROBLEM STATEMENT	Decision Significance	Importance of Commitment	Leader Expertise	Likelihood of Commitment	Group Support	Group Expertise	Team Competence	
	H	H	H	H	–	–	–	Decide
				L	H	H	H	Delegate
							L	Consult (Group)
						L	–	
					L	–	–	
			L	H	H	H	H	Facilitate
							L	Consult (Individually)
						L	–	
					L	–	–	
				L	H	H	H	Facilitate
							L	Consult (Group)
						L	–	
					L	–	–	
		L	H	–	–	–	–	Decide
			L	–	H	H	H	Facilitate
							L	Consult (Individually)
						L	–	
					L	–	–	
	L	H	–	H	–	–	–	Decide
				L	–	–	H	Delegate
							L	Facilitate
		L	–	–	–	–	–	Decide

SOURCE: Reprinted from *Organizational Dynamics*, 28, by V. H. Vroom, "Leadership and the Decision-Making Process," 82–94 (Spring 2000) with permission from Elsevier.

The Situational Leadership Model

The Situational Leadership model, developed by Paul Hersey and Kenneth Blanchard, suggests that the leader's behavior should be adjusted to the maturity level of the followers.[29] The model employs two dimensions of leader behavior as

FIGURE 12.5 The Situational Leadership Model: The Hersey–Blanchard Model

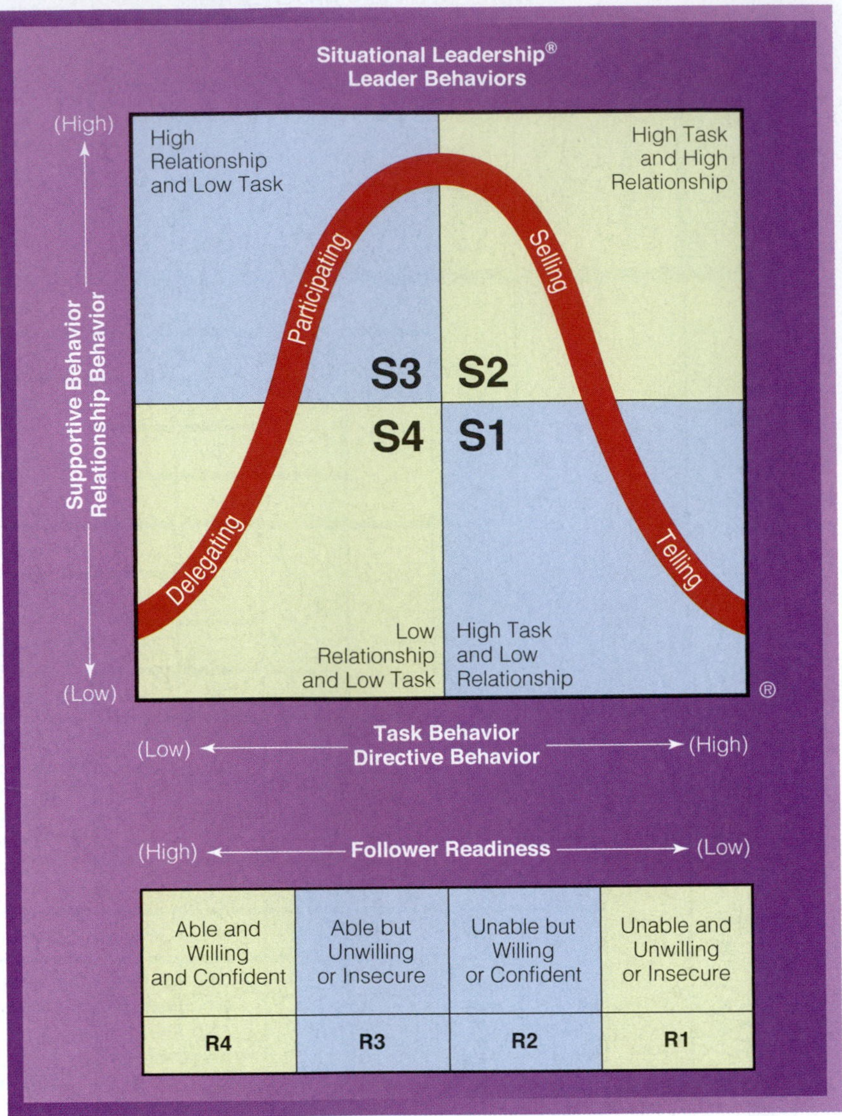

SOURCE: © 2006 Reprinted with permission of the Center for Leadership Studies, Inc., Escondido, CA 92025. All rights reserved.

used in the Ohio State studies; one dimension is task oriented, and the other is relationship oriented. Follower maturity is categorized into four levels, as shown in Figure 12.5. Follower readiness is determined by the follower's ability and willingness to complete a specific task. Readiness can therefore be low or high depending on the particular task. In addition, readiness varies within a single person according to the task. One person may be willing and able to satisfy simple requests from customers (high readiness) but less able or willing to give highly technical advice to customers (low readiness). It is important that the leader be able to evaluate the readiness level of each follower for each task. The four styles of leader behavior associated with the four readiness levels are depicted in the figure as well.

According to the Situational Leadership model, a leader should use a telling style (S1) when a follower is unable and unwilling to do a certain task. This style involves providing instructions and closely monitoring performance. As such, the telling style involves considerable task behavior and low relationship behavior. When a follower is unable but willing and confident to do a task, the leader can use the selling style (S2) in which there is high task behavior and high relationship behavior. In this case, the leader explains decisions and provides opportunities for the employee to seek clarification or help. Sometimes a follower will be able to complete a task but may seem unwilling or insecure about doing so. In these cases, a participating style (S3) is warranted, which involves high relationship but low task behavior. The leader in this case encourages the follower to participate in decision making. Finally, for tasks in which a follower is able and willing, the leader is able to use a delegating style (S4), characterized by low task behavior and low relationship behavior. In this case, follower readiness is high, and low levels of leader involvement (task or relationship) are needed.

One key limitation of the Situational Leadership model is the absence of central hypotheses that could be tested, which would make it a more valid, reliable theory of leadership.[30] However, the theory has intuitive appeal and is widely used for training and development in corporations. In addition, the theory focuses attention on follower maturity as an important determinant of the leadership process.

Leader–Member Exchange

Leader–member exchange theory, or LMX, recognizes that leaders may form different relationships with followers. The basic idea behind LMX is that leaders form two groups of followers: in-groups and out-groups. In-group members tend to be similar to the leader and given greater responsibilities, more rewards, and more attention. They work within the leader's inner circle of communication. As a result, in-group members are more satisfied, have lower turnover, and have higher organizational commitment. In contrast, out-group members are outside the circle and receive less attention and fewer rewards. They are managed by formal rules and policies.[31]

Research on LMX is supportive. In-group members are more likely to engage in organizational citizenship behavior, while out-group members are more likely to retaliate against the organization.[32] And the type of stress varies by the group to which a subordinate belongs. In-group members' stress comes from the additional responsibilities placed on them by the leader, whereas out-group members' stress comes from being left out of the communication network.[33] One surprising finding is that more frequent communication with the boss may either help or hurt a worker's performance ratings, depending on whether the worker is in the in-group or the out-group. Among the in-group, more frequent communication generally leads to higher performance ratings, while members of the out-group who communicate more often with the superior tend to receive lower performance ratings. Perhaps the out-group members get to talk to the boss only when something has gone wrong![34]

Employees who enjoy more frequent contact with the boss also have a better understanding of what the boss's expectations are. Such agreement tends to lead to better performance by the employee and fewer misunderstandings between employer and employee.[35]

In-group members are also more likely to support the values of the organization and to become models of appropriate behavior. If the leader, for example, wants to promote safety at work, in-group members model safe work practices, which leads to a climate of workplace safety.[36]

Substitutes for Leadership

Sometimes situations can neutralize or even replace leader behavior. This is the central idea behind the substitutes for leadership theory.[37] When a task is very satisfying and employees get feedback about performance, leader behavior is irrelevant, because the employee's satisfaction comes from the interesting work and the feedback. Other things that can substitute for leadership include high skill on the part of the employee, team cohesiveness, and formal controls on the part of the organization. Research on this idea is generally supportive, and other factors that act as substitutes are being identified.[38] Even a firm's customers can be a substitute for leadership. In service settings, employees with lots of customer contact actually receive significant leadership and direction from customer demands, allowing the firm to provide less formal supervision to these employees than to workers with little customer contact. This finding adds new weight to the old adage about the customer being boss.[39]

THE EMERGENCE OF INSPIRATIONAL LEADERSHIP THEORIES

Leadership is an exciting area of organizational behavior, one in which new research is constantly emerging. Three new developments are important to understand. These are transformational leadership, charismatic leadership, and authentic leadership. These three theories can be called inspirational leadership theories because in each one, followers are inspired by the leader to perform well.

Transformational Leadership

(7) Distinguish among transformational, charismatic, and authentic leaders.

As we indicated earlier in the chapter, transactional leaders are those who use rewards and punishment to strike deals with followers and shape their behavior. In contrast, transformational leaders inspire and excite followers to high levels of performance.[40] They rely on their personal attributes instead of their official position to manage followers. There is some evidence that transformational leadership can be learned.[41] Transformational leadership consists of the following four sub dimensions: charisma, individualized consideration, inspirational motivation, and intellectual stimulation. We describe charisma in detail below. Individualized consideration refers to how much the leader displays concern for each follower's individual needs, and acts as a coach or a mentor. Inspirational motivation is the extent to which the leader is able to articulate a vision that is appealing to followers.[42] An extensive research study shows that transformational leadership predicts several criteria such as follower job satisfaction, leader effectiveness ratings, group or organizational performance, and follower motivation.[43] Transformational leadership research conducted in China, Kenya, and Thailand also showed that it had positive effects on employee commitment and negative effects on employee work withdrawal.[44]

As U.S. corporations increasingly operate in a global economy, there is a greater demand for leaders who can practice transformational leadership by converting their visions into reality[45] and by inspiring followers to perform "above and beyond the call of duty."[46] Howard Schultz, founder and chairman of Starbucks Coffee, is the transformational leader and visionary heart of Starbucks. He has grown his firm from a small specialty coffee bar into one of the best-known brands in the world. With the firm hoping to continue its rapid growth pace of 25–30 percent per year, Schultz's ability to develop new leaders within the firm (which helped Starbucks get where it is today) will be sorely tested. But given the enormous market for coffee worldwide (Starbucks currently has less than 10 percent of the market), the potential for further growth exists if the company can develop the people to tap it.[47]

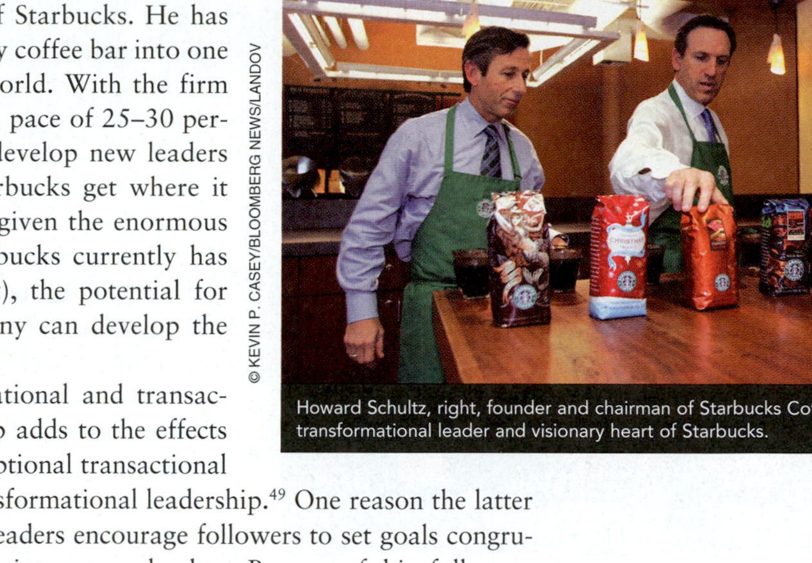

Howard Schultz, right, founder and chairman of Starbucks Coffee, is the transformational leader and visionary heart of Starbucks.

Leaders can be both transformational and transactional.[48] Transformational leadership adds to the effects of transactional leadership, but exceptional transactional leadership cannot substitute for transformational leadership.[49] One reason the latter is effective is that transformational leaders encourage followers to set goals congruent with the followers' own authentic interests and values. Because of this, followers see their work as important and their goals as aligned with who they are.[50]

There is some evidence that transformational leadership may work in military organizations. One study showed that military leaders who practiced transformational leadership produced both greater development and better performance among their subordinates than leaders who used other leadership styles.[51]

Charismatic Leadership

Steve Jobs, the pioneer behind the Macintosh computer and the growing music download market, has an uncanny ability to create a vision and convince others to become part of it. This was evidenced by Apple's continual overall success despite its major blunders in the desktop computer wars. Jobs's ability is so powerful that Apple employees coined a term in the 1980s for it, the *reality-distortion field*. This expression is used to describe the persuasive ability and peculiar charisma of managers like Steve Jobs. This reality-distortion field allows Jobs to convince even skeptics that his plans are worth supporting, no matter how unworkable they may appear. Those close to these managers become passionately committed to seemingly impossible projects, without regard to the practicality of their implementation or competitive forces in the marketplace.[52] Similarly, people who have worked with Ken Chenault note that they admire him immensely and would do anything for him. He is known for chatting with executives and secretaries alike and is seen as someone who is free from the normal trappings of power.

Charismatic leadership results when a leader uses the force of personal abilities and talents to have profound and extraordinary effects on followers.[53] Some scholars see transformational leadership and charismatic leadership as very similar, but others believe they are different. *Charisma* is a Greek word meaning "gift"; the charismatic leader's unique and powerful gifts are the source of his or her great influence with followers.[54] In fact, followers often view the charismatic leader as one who possesses superhuman, or even mystical, qualities.[55] Charismatic leaders rely heavily on referent power, discussed in Chapter 11, and charismatic leadership is especially effective in times of uncertainty.[56] Charismatic leadership falls to those who are "chosen" (born with the "gift" of charisma) or who cultivate that gift. Some say charismatic leaders are born, and others say they are taught.

charismatic leadership
A leader's use of personal abilities and talents in order to have profound and extraordinary effects on followers.

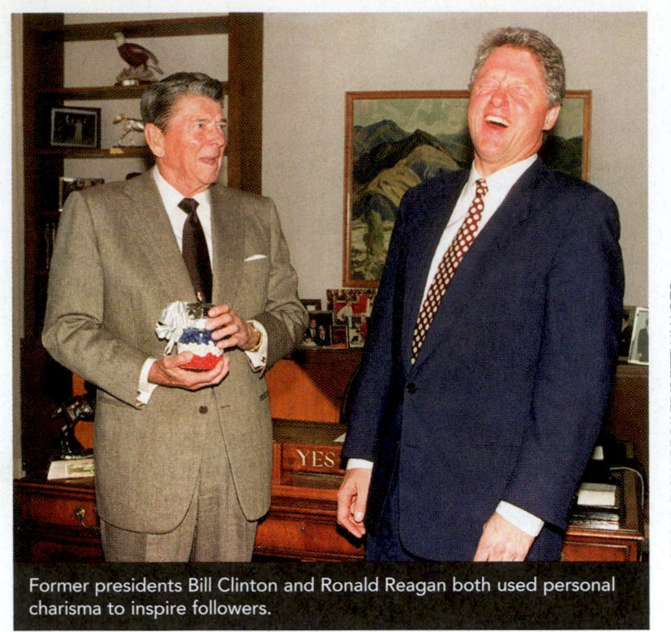

© PAUL RICHARDS/AFP/GETTY IMAGES

Former presidents Bill Clinton and Ronald Reagan both used personal charisma to inspire followers.

Some charismatic leaders rely on humor as a tool for communication. Charismatic leadership carries with it not only great potential for high levels of achievement and performance on the part of followers but also shadowy risks of destructive courses of action that might harm followers or other people. Several researchers have attempted to demystify charismatic leadership and distinguish its two faces.[57] The ugly face of charisma is revealed in the personalized power motivations of Adolf Hitler in Nazi Germany and David Koresh of the Branch Davidian cult in Waco, Texas. Both men led their followers into struggle, conflict, and death. The brighter face of charisma is revealed in the socialized power motivations of U.S. President Franklin D. Roosevelt. Former presidents Bill Clinton and Ronald Reagan, while worlds apart in terms of their political beliefs, were actually quite similar in their use of personal charisma to inspire followers and motivate them to pursue the leader's vision. In each case, followers perceived the leader as imbued with a unique vision for America and unique abilities to lead the country there.

Authentic Leadership

Recently, a new form of leadership has started to garner attention thanks to the ethical scandals rocking the business world. In response to concerns about the potential negative side of inspirational forms of leadership, researchers have called for authentic leadership.[58] *Authentic leadership* includes transformational, charismatic, or transactional leadership as the situation demands. However, it differs from the other kinds in that authentic leaders have a conscious and well-developed sense of values. They act in ways that are consistent with their value systems, so authentic leaders have a highly evolved sense of moral right and wrong. Their life experiences (often labeled "moments that matter") lead to authentic leadership development, and allow authentic leaders to be their true selves.[59] Read about how such life experiences can lead to effective authentic leadership in The Real World 12.1. Authentic leaders arouse and motivate followers to higher levels of performance by building a workforce characterized by high levels of hope, optimism, resiliency, and self-efficacy.[60] Followers also experience more positive emotions and trust leadership as a result of transparency and a collective caring climate engendered by the leader. Researchers contend that this is the kind of leadership embodied by Gandhi, Nelson Mandela, and others like them throughout history. Only time and solid management research will tell if this approach can yield results for organizational leadership. One recent development in the identification of authentic leaders stems from the area of emotions. Emotions act as checks and balances that not only keep the ugly side of charisma in check but also provide certain cues to followers. For example, a leader who espouses benevolence (as a value) and does not display compassion (an emotion) might not be very authentic in followers' eyes.[61] Similarly, a leader who displays compassion when announcing a layoff may be seen by followers as more morally worthy and held in higher regard.[62]

authentic leadership
A style of leadership that includes transformational, charismatic, or transactional approaches as the situation demands.

THE REAL WORLD 12.1

View from the Top: Authentic Anne Mulcahy at Xerox

Leadership is an acquired skill. Organizations offer several leadership development and training programs to help groom employees for top positions. However, themes among all great business leaders are their willingness to step outside of their comfort zone and the ability to turn travesty into opportunity.

© STEFAN ZAKLIN/GETTY IMAGES

The perception that Anne Mulcahy, chairman and CEO of Xerox, is an authentic leader, as well as her reputation as a consensus leader, has helped her overcome challenges at Xerox.

One such business leader is Anne Mulcahy, chairman and CEO of Xerox. When she took over Xerox in 2000, the company was drowning in debt to the tune of $18 million, and she was advised to file for bankruptcy. She had no background in finance and reached out to people in the company to tutor her. She started to ride with field salespeople to understand the business better. More than anything else, Mulcahy showed herself to be a consensus leader, seeking out several opinions and making decisions on the basis of consensus. Such tenacity, combined with a perception of Mulcahy as an authentic leader, has helped her overcome several challenges at Xerox. She managed to avert bankruptcy by cutting operating expenses.

Fortune magazine featured Mulcahy as one of the brightest minds and leaders in America in 2007. She has climbed the heights of the corporate world by staying true to the company's core values that stress employee engagement and citizenship toward employees, customers, and suppliers. Today, all her business decisions are guided by the same core values that were a part of Xerox almost thirty years ago when she first joined the company.

SOURCE: B. George, "What Is Your True North?" An excerpt from *True North* by Bill George, *Fortune* (March 19, 2007): 125–130.

CNNMoney.com, "How to Succeed in 2007?" http://money.cnn.com/popups/2006/biz2/howtosucceed/7.html

Despite the warm emotions charismatic leaders can evoke, some of them are narcissists who listen only to those who agree with them.[63] Whereas charismatic leaders with socialized power motivation are concerned about the collective well-being of their followers, charismatic leaders with a personalized power motivation are driven by the need for personal gain and glorification.[64]

Charismatic leadership styles are associated with several positive outcomes. One study reported that firms headed by more charismatic leaders outperformed other firms, particularly in difficult economic times. Perhaps even more important, charismatic leaders were able to raise more outside financial support for their firms than noncharismatic leaders, meaning that charisma at the top may translate to greater funding at the bottom.[65]

EMERGING ISSUES IN LEADERSHIP

Along with the recent developments in theory, some exciting issues have emerged of which leaders must be aware. These include emotional intelligence, trust, women leaders, and servant leadership.

Emotional Intelligence

It has been suggested that effective leaders possess emotional intelligence, which is the ability to recognize and manage emotion in oneself and in others. In fact, some researchers argue that emotional intelligence is more important for effective leadership than either IQ or technical skills.[66] Emotional intelligence is made up of several competencies, including self-awareness, empathy, adaptability, and self-confidence. While most people gain emotional intelligence as they age, not everyone starts with an equal amount. Fortunately, emotional intelligence can be learned. With honest feedback from coworkers and ongoing guidance, almost any leader can improve emotional intelligence, and with it, the ability to lead in times of adversity.[67]

Emotional intelligence affects the way leaders make decisions. Under high stress, leaders with higher emotional intelligence tend to keep their cool and make better decisions, while leaders with low emotional intelligence make poor decisions and lose their effectiveness.[68] Joe Torre, former manager of the New York Yankees, got the most out of his team, worked for a notoriously tough boss, and kept his cool. He was a model of emotional intelligence: compassionate, calm under stress, and a great motivator. He advocated "managing against the cycle," which means staying calm when situations are tough, but turning up the heat on players when things are going well.[69]

Trust

Trust is an essential element in leadership. Trust is the willingness to be vulnerable to the actions of another.[70] This means that followers believe that their leader will act with the followers' welfare in mind. Trustworthiness is also one of the competencies in emotional intelligence. Trust among top management team members facilitates strategy implementation; this means that if team members trust each other, they have a better chance of getting "buy-in" from employees on the direction of the company.[71] And if employees trust their leaders, they will buy in more readily.

How would you go about leading a team of people in different organizations, in different geographic locations around the world, who had never met? They would not have shared understandings of problems, norms, work distribution, roles, or responsibilities. This is a challenge that is becoming more common, and one that Boeing-Rocketdyne faced. What Boeing-Rocketdyne learned is that the leader of such teams needs to be the "spoke in the center of the wheel" in terms of coordination. The leader also needs to help the team create a common language and document results for the entire team.[72] Not surprisingly, Boeing's largest rival—Airbus Industries of Europe—has developed its own virtual teams. Called Elab, this network helps Airbus coordinate work by aerospace firms all over Europe, including British Aerospace, Rolls Royce, and Snecma. Using complex communications tools, including high-quality video, Elab allows these member firms to create complete working environments for groups of engineers scattered throughout the continent.[73] Leading virtual teams requires trust, because face-to-face interaction that is the hallmark of leadership is not possible. Leaders must not only come to trust their subordinates, but they must also express that trust. Research has shown that workers who believe their boss trusts them (called "felt trustworthiness") enjoy their work more, are more productive, and are more likely to "go the extra mile" at work and perform organizational citizenship behaviors.[74]

Effective leaders also understand both *who* to trust and *how* to trust. At one extreme, leaders often trust a close circle of advisors, listening only to them and gradually cutting themselves off from dissenting opinions. At the opposite extreme, lone-wolf leaders may trust nobody, leading to preventable mistakes. Wise leaders carefully evaluate both the competence and the position of those they trust, seeking out a variety of opinions and input.[75]

Gender and Leadership

An important, emergent leadership question is this: Do women and men lead differently? Historical stereotypes persist, and people characterize successful managers as having more male-oriented attributes than female-oriented attributes.[76] Although legitimate gender differences may exist, the same leadership traits may be interpreted differently in a man and a woman because of stereotypes. The real issue should be leader behaviors that are not bound by gender stereotypes.

Early evidence shows that women tend to use a more people-oriented style that is inclusive and empowering. Women managers excel in positions that demand strong interpersonal skills.[77] More and more women are assuming positions of leadership in organizations. Donna Dubinsky, founder and CEO of palmOne, co-founded Palm and Handspring and is known as the mother of the handheld computer. She wants to change the world so that PDAs outsell PCs. Interestingly, much of what we know about leadership is based on studies that were conducted on men. We need to know more about the ways women lead. Interestingly, recent research reports on the phenomenon of the *glass cliff* (as opposed to the *glass ceiling* effect discussed in Chapter 2). The *glass cliff* represents a trend in organizations of placing more women in difficult leadership situations. Women perceive these assignments as necessary due to difficulty in attaining leadership positions and lack of alternate opportunities combined with male in-group favoritism. On the other hand, men perceive that women are better suited to difficult leadership positions due to better decision making.[78]

Servant Leadership

Robert Greenleaf was director of management research at AT&T for many years. He believed that leaders should serve employees, customers, and the community, and his essays are the basis for today's view called servant leadership. His personal and professional philosophy was that leaders lead by serving others. Other tenets of servant leadership are that work exists for the person as much as the person exists for work, and that servant leaders try to find out the will of the group and lead based on that. Servant leaders are also stewards who consider leadership a trust and desire to leave the organization in better shape for future generations.[79] Although Greenleaf's writings were completed thirty years ago, many have now been published and are becoming more popular.

FOLLOWERSHIP

In contrast to leadership, the topic of followership has not been extensively researched. Much of the leadership literature suggests that leader and follower roles are highly differentiated. The traditional view casts followers as passive, whereas a more contemporary view casts the follower role as an active one with potential for leadership.[80] The follower role has alternatively been cast as one of self-leadership in which the follower assumes responsibility for influencing his or her own performance.[81] This approach emphasizes the follower's individual responsibility and self-control. Self-led followers perform naturally motivating tasks and do work that must be done but that is not naturally motivating. Self-leadership enables followers to be disciplined and effective, essential first steps if one is to become a leader.

THE REAL WORLD 12.2

An Engaged Workforce through Emotionally Intelligent Leadership

Johnson & Johnson (J&J) Medical Products in Canada is in the business of sales, marketing, and distribution of medical devices and diagnostic products. In this market, competition is intense and J&J implemented a leadership development program known as the "talent pool" to identify and develop leaders who could build a more engaged workforce. This initiative was driven by J&J's philosophy that an engaged workforce could help them outperform the competition. It was also directed at creating a culture of individual behavioral change and a shared language.

This program has resulted in several tangible benefits for the company and created a sustainable competitive advantage that is difficult for competitors to imitate. On the individual front, employee engagement increased from 29 percent to 59 percent since the inception of the program. These numbers are far higher than the average workforce engagement prevalent in the industry. J&J also reaped rewards related to organizational performance. For example, the market growth rate at J&J is three times the industry norm. Thus, individual engagement is tied to better organizational performance. J&J achieved these successes by assessing leaders using a 360-degree emotional intelligence inventory and by offering training in areas where managers were lacking. Moreover, this cycle of improvement is a continuous one at J&J with several short- and long-term action steps in place for employee development.

SOURCE: C. Cameron. "Johnson & Johnson Canada's Design, Development, and Business Impact of a Local Leadership Development Program," *Organization Development Journal* 25 (2) (2007): 65–70.

Organizational programs such as empowerment and self-managed work teams may be used to further activate the follower role.[82]

Types of Followers

8 Discuss the characteristics of effective and dynamic followers.

Contemporary work environments are ones in which followers recognize their interdependence with leaders and learn to challenge them while at the same time respecting the leaders' authority.[83] Effective followers are active, responsible, and autonomous in their behavior and critical in their thinking without being insubordinate or disrespectful—in essence, they are highly engaged at work. Johnson & Johnson Medical Products instituted a leadership development program aimed at increasing engagement among followers. Read about it in The Real World 12.2.

Effective followers and four other types of followers are identified based on two dimensions: (1) activity versus passivity and (2) independent, critical thinking versus dependent, uncritical thinking.[84] Figure 12.6 shows these follower types.

Alienated followers think independently and critically, yet are very passive in their behavior. As a result, they become psychologically and emotionally distanced from their leaders. Alienated followers are potentially disruptive and a threat to the health of the organization. "Sheep" are followers who do not think independently or critically and are passive in their behavior. They simply do as they are told by their leaders. "Yes people" are followers who also do not think independently or critically, yet are very active in their behavior. They uncritically reinforce the thinking and ideas of their leaders with enthusiasm, never questioning or challenging the wisdom of the leaders' ideas and proposals. Yes people are the most dangerous to a leader because they are the most likely to give a false positive reaction and give no warning of potential pitfalls. Survivors are the least disruptive and the lowest risk followers in an organization. They perpetually sample the wind, and their motto is "better safe than sorry."

FIGURE 12.6 Five Types of Followers

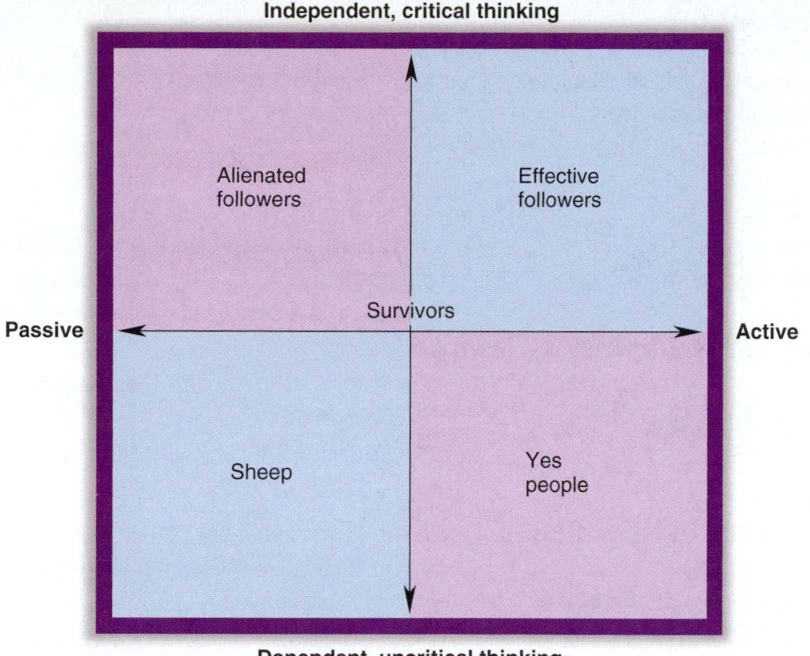

SOURCE: Reprinted by permission of *Harvard Business Review*. From "In Praise of Followers" by R. E. Kelley, (November–December 1988), p. 145. Copyright © 1988 by Harvard Business School Publishing Corporation; all rights reserved.

Effective followers are the most valuable to a leader and an organization because of their active contributions. Effective followers share four essential qualities. First, they practice self-management and self-responsibility. A leader can delegate to an effective follower without anxiety about the outcome. Second, they are committed to both the organization and a purpose, principle, or person outside themselves. Effective followers are not self-centered or self-aggrandizing. Third, effective followers invest in their own competence and professionalism and focus their energy for maximum impact. Effective followers look for challenges and ways in which to add to their talents or abilities. Fourth, they are courageous, honest, and credible. You 12.2 gives you an opportunity to consider your effectiveness as a follower.

Effective followers might be thought of as self-leaders who do not require close supervision.[85] The notion of self-leadership, or superleadership, blurs the distinction between leaders and followers. Caring leaders are able to develop dynamic followers.

The Dynamic Follower

The traditional stereotype of the follower or employee is of someone in a powerless, dependent role rather than in a potent, active, significant role. The latter, in which the follower is dynamic, is a more contemporary, healthy role.[86] The *dynamic follower* is a responsible steward of his or her job, is effective in managing the relationship with the boss, and practices responsible self-management.

dynamic follower
A follower who is a responsible steward of his or her job, is effective in managing the relationship with the boss, and practices self-management.

The dynamic follower becomes a trusted adviser to the boss by keeping the supervisor well informed and building trust and dependability into the relationship. He or she is open to constructive criticism and solicits performance feedback. The dynamic follower shares needs and is responsible.

Are You an Effective Follower?

To determine whether you are an effective follower, read the text section on "Types of Followers," look back at your self-reliance results in You 7.2, and work through the following four steps. Answer each question in the four steps yes or no.

Step 1. Self-Management and Self-Responsibility

_____ Do you take the initiative at work?
_____ Do you challenge the system at work when appropriate?
_____ Do you ask questions when you need more information?
_____ Do you successfully bring your projects to completion?

Step 2. Commitment beyond Yourself

_____ Are you committed to your boss's and company's success?
_____ Is there a higher purpose in life that you value deeply?
_____ Is there a principle(s) that you will not compromise?
_____ Is there a person at work or elsewhere you admire greatly?

Step 3. Self-Development

_____ Do you attend a professional development class annually?
_____ Do you have a program of self-study or structured learning?
_____ Do you take at least one class each semester in the year?
_____ Have you identified new skills to learn for your job?

Step 4. Courage and Honesty

_____ Have you disagreed with your boss twice this year?
_____ Have you taken two unpopular positions at work this year?
_____ Have you given critical feedback to someone, kindly?
_____ Have you taken one risk at work to do a better job?

Scoring:

Count the number of "yes" answers in Steps 1 through 4: _____

If you have 10 to 16 "yes" answers, this would suggest that you are an effective follower. If you have 7 or fewer "yes" answers, this may suggest that you fall into one of the other four categories of followers.

People who are self-reliant may also be effective followers, and effective followers may also be self-reliant. If you are an effective follower, were you also self-reliant in You 7.2? If you were not self-reliant in You 7.2, did you fall into a category other than the effective follower category?

SOURCE: Reprinted by permission of *Harvard Business Review.* From "In Praise of Followers" by R. E. Kelley, (November–December 1988).

It takes time and patience to nurture a good relationship between a follower and a supervisor. Once this relationship has been developed, it is a valuable resource for both.

CULTURAL DIFFERENCES IN LEADERSHIP

The situational approaches to leadership would lead to the conclusion that a leader must factor in culture as an important situational variable when exercising influence and authority. Thus, global leaders should expect to be flexible enough to alter their approaches when crossing national boundaries and working with people from foreign cultures.[87]

We are beginning to learn more about how perspectives on effective leadership vary across cultures. You might assume that most Europeans view leadership in the same way. Research tells us instead that there are many differences among European countries. In Nordic countries like Finland, leaders who are direct and close to subordinates are viewed positively, while in Turkey, Poland, and Russia this is not the case. And leaders who give subordinates autonomy are viewed more positively in Germany and Austria than in the Czech Republic and Portugal.[88] There are even differences between the American view of transformational leadership and that found in the United Kingdom. The UK approach to transformational leadership is much closer to what we in the United States refer to as servant leadership. It involves more connectedness between leaders and followers and more vulnerability on the part of the leader.[89]

Ten years ago, a lot of people were talking about Denny's and race, as Denny's name became almost synonymous with racial tension. Today, people are still talking about Denny's and race, but in a different way. *Fortune* named Denny's one of the Best Companies for Minorities. What brought about the change?

Somebody had to lead the change. Former CEO of Denny's Jim Adamson believed that he had to find someone with a passion for diversity and the fire to make it happen. He knew that Ray Hood-Phillips had led Burger King toward an inclusive workplace, so he called her and asked for help. She agreed to consult for two or three days a week, getting up at 3:00 a.m. to commute from her home in Miami to Denny's headquarters in Spartanburg. After a few months of working eighteen-hour days, Hood-Phillips agreed to join Denny's.

Hood-Phillips's passion is diversity and inclusion. She led big changes at Denny's but was also a dynamic follower who didn't hesitate to challenge the boss (Adamson). Speaking to a group of executives, Adamson remarked, "You know, we need to be color-blind; we can't see color." Once they were out the door, Hood-Phillips pulled the CEO aside and took him to the woodshed. She told him that all humans have differences and that people from different racial and ethnic backgrounds also have different cultural and social references—people shouldn't be expected to think or act in the same ways. Adamson listened and credits Hood-Phillips with helping him see that Denny's could not pretend that everyone in the United States is the same. This distinction made all the difference.

Hood-Phillips has helped Denny's get diversity right. She monitors diversity progress in every area of the company's operations, including purchasing contracts, management positions, training and education, philanthropy, performance evaluations, and trade partnerships with minority groups. She has led the diversity charge at Denny's and is not afraid to be a dynamic follower in terms of challenging authority. Today, she is the company's chief diversity officer and also consults with other *Fortune* 500 firms that seek advice on diversity at work.[90, 91]

To be effective, leaders must understand other cultures. U.S. executives often perceive specific global regions as being made up of relatively homogenous individuals. For example, some U.S. leaders think that most of Latin America is populated with people of similar values and beliefs. But a recent study of more than 1,000 small-business owners in the region demonstrated that despite similarities, these business leaders are quite diverse in terms of their individual goals. Mexican and Brazilian leaders had values that were very different from leaders in other countries in the region. This means that we cannot stereotype people from Latin America as being totally similar.[92]

Whereas most American workers follow traditional Protestant work values, workers from other countries base their work values on very different sets of beliefs, drawing in some cases from multiple philosophies. China, for instance, draws from not one but three perspectives, as Buddhism, Taoism, and Confucianism harmonize to create work values such as trust, hierarchy, loyalty, and networks.[93] Across cultures, leaders vary widely in their orientation towards the future. This translates into focus on either short-term benefits or longer-term orientation toward employee development. For example, Singapore was the most future oriented of all cultures that were studied. This implies that leaders in Singapore are more focused on longer-term benefits such as delayed gratification, long-term planning, and investing in employee development with longer-term payoffs.[94]

GUIDELINES FOR LEADERSHIP

Leadership is a key to influencing organizational behavior and achieving organizational effectiveness. Studies of leadership succession show a moderately strong leader influence on organizational performance.[95] With this said, it is important to recognize that other factors also influence organizational performance. These include environmental factors (such as general economic conditions) and technological factors (such as efficiency).

Corporate leaders play a central role in setting the ethical tone and moral values for their organizations. While many corporate leaders talk about ethics, many never have to actually risk the firm's fortune on an ethical decision. In 1976, when James Burke, head of Johnson & Johnson, challenged his management team to reaffirm the company's historic commitment to ethical behavior, he had no idea he would be asked to demonstrate that commitment in action. But six years later, when poisoned packages of Tylenol appeared on store shelves, Burke did not hesitate to act on what he had pledged. The company pulled the product from the shelves at a cost of $100 million. It also offered a reward and revamped the product's packaging. In the end, Tylenol recovered and is once again the leading pain medication in the United States. Burke was recently recognized by *Fortune* as one of the ten greatest CEOs of all time, and Johnson & Johnson continues to be rated one of the best companies for which to work.[96]

Five useful guidelines have emerged from the extensive leadership research of the past sixty years:

- First, leaders and organizations should appreciate the unique attributes, predispositions, and talents of each leader. No two leaders are the same, and there is value in this diversity.
- Second, although there appears to be no single best style of leadership, there are organizational preferences in terms of style. Leaders should be chosen who challenge the organizational culture, when necessary, without destroying it.
- Third, participative, considerate leader behaviors that demonstrate a concern for people appear to enhance the health and well-being of followers in the work environment. This does not imply, however, that a leader must ignore the team's work tasks.
- Fourth, different leadership situations call for different leadership talents and behaviors. This may result in different individuals taking the leader role, depending on the specific situation in which the team finds itself.
- Fifth, good leaders are likely to be good followers. Although there are distinctions between their social roles, the attributes and behaviors of leaders and followers may not be as distinct as is sometimes thought.

DIVERSITY DIALOGUE

White Males: Diversity Programs' Newest Leaders?

Keith Ruth was very surprised when he was approached by PricewaterhouseCoopers' chief diversity officer, Chris Simmons, to help lead the firm's corporate diversity effort. Why was he so surprised? Because Ruth is a white male, and it is common knowledge that diversity programs aren't designed for white males, right? Not according to Simmons.

When he became PwC's chief diversity officer in 2004, Simmons was given a directive by the U.S. chairman to move diversity "off the sidelines" and "into the mainstream." That meant fully integrating diversity into the firm's daily operations including client assignments and employee promotions. At the same time, diversity leaders were being named for PwC's four business units. Although Simmons is African American, he was concerned that none of the diversity leaders being named as a business unit diversity leader was a white male. He believed that having a Caucasian male champion diversity would be instrumental in helping to bring other white males on board. After all, he reasoned, they are still the majority of workers in most large firms. Frank McCloskey, Georgia Power's first white male head of diversity, insists that it would be difficult to create a sustainable diversity initiative if the majority of the workforce felt there was nothing in it for them.

Since becoming a PwC diversity leader, Keith Ruth has had much success reaching many people Chris Simmons admits he had had a difficult time reaching.

1. Do you believe recruiting white males to lead diversity programs is a good strategy for garnering support for diversity? Why or why not?
2. What leadership skills must Keith Ruth and other Caucasians use in order to be effective diversity leaders? Contrast them with skills that minority leaders must use.

SOURCE: E. White, "Diversity Programs Look to Involve White Males as Leaders," *The Wall Street Journal* (May 7, 2007): B4.

LOOKING BACK: AMERICAN EXPRESS

Ken Chenault addressed the Wharton Business School and talked about the driving principles of American Express. He noted that the key to success is adaptability through good leadership. He admits he has made mistakes in his career and is not afraid to correct them. He also noted that while compassion is an important part of being a good leader, one must also act decisively. Six attributes stand out in Chenault's mind while envisioning good leadership: integrity, courage, being a team player, emotional intelligence (as opposed to general intelligence), helping others succeed, and being proactive instead of reactive. These driving principles have taken American Express to the pinnacle of success in the corporate world while also creating a niche for Chenault as one of the most influential business leaders.[97]

Chapter Summary

1. Leadership is the process of guiding and directing the behavior of followers in organizations. Followership is the process of being guided and directed by a leader. Leaders and followers are companions in these processes.
2. A leader creates meaningful change in organizations, whereas a manager controls complexity. Charismatic leaders have a profound impact on their followers.
3. Autocratic leaders create high pressure for followers, whereas democratic leaders create healthier environments for followers.
4. The five styles in the Leadership Grid are manager, authority-compliance manager, country club manager, team manager, and impoverished manager.
5. According to Fiedler's contingency theory, task-oriented leaders are most effective in highly favorable or highly unfavorable leadership situations, and relationship-oriented leaders are most effective in moderately favorable leadership situations.
6. The path–goal theory, Vroom–Yetton–Jago theory, and Situational Leadership model say that a leader should adjust his or her behavior to the situation and should appreciate diversity among followers.
7. There are many developments in leadership. Emerging issues include emotional intelligence, trust, women leaders, and servant leadership.
8. Effective, dynamic followers are competent and active in their work, assertive, independent thinkers, sensitive to their bosses' needs and demands, and responsible self-managers. Caring leadership and dynamic followership go together.

Key Terms

authentic leadership (p. 414)
authority-compliance manager (9,1) (p. 402)
autocratic style (p. 400)
charismatic leadership (p. 413)
consideration (p. 401)
country club manager (1,9) (p. 403)
democratic style (p. 400)
dynamic follower (p. 419)
followership (p. 398)
formal leadership (p. 398)
impoverished manager (1,1) (p. 403)
informal leadership (p. 398)
initiating structure (p. 401)
laissez-faire style (p. 400)
leader (p. 399)
leader–member relations (p. 405)
leadership (p. 398)
Leadership Grid (p. 401)
least preferred coworker (LPC) (p. 404)
manager (p. 399)
opportunistic "what's in it for me" manager (Opp) (p. 404)
organization man manager (5,5) (p. 402)
paternalistic "father knows best" manager (9 + 9) (p. 404)
position power (p. 405)
task structure (p. 405)
team manager (9,9) (p. 403)

Review Questions

1. Define *leadership* and *followership*. Distinguish between formal leadership and informal leadership.
2. Discuss transformational, charismatic, and authentic leadership. Would you expect these styles of leadership to exist in all cultures? Differ across cultures?
3. Describe the differences between autocratic and democratic work environments. How do they differ from a laissez-faire workplace?
4. Define *initiating structure* and *consideration* as leader behaviors.
5. Describe the middle-of-the-road manager, authority-compliance manager, country club manager, team manager, and impoverished manager.
6. How does the LPC scale measure leadership style? What are the three dimensions of the leader's situation?
7. Describe the alternative decision strategies used by a leader in the Vroom–Yetton–Jago normative decision theory.
8. Compare House's path–goal theory of leadership with the Situational Leadership model.
9. Describe alienated followers, sheep, yes people, survivors, and effective followers.

Discussion and Communication Questions

1. Do you (or would you want to) work in an autocratic, democratic, or laissez-faire work environment? What might be the advantages of each? The disadvantages?
2. Is your supervisor or professor someone who is high in concern for production? High in concern for people? What is his or her Leadership Grid style?
3. What decision strategies does your supervisor use to make decisions? Are they consistent or inconsistent with the Vroom–Yetton–Jago model?
4. Discuss the similarities and differences between effective leadership and dynamic followership. Are you dynamic?
5. Describe the relationship you have with your supervisor or professor. What is the best part of the relationship? The worst part? What could you do to make the relationship better?
6. *(communication question)* Who is the leader you admire the most? Write a description of this person's characteristics and attributes that you admire. Note any aspects of this leader's behavior that you find less than wholly admirable.
7. *(communication question)* Refresh yourself on the distinction between leaders (also called transformational leaders) and managers (also called transactional leaders) in the text. Then read about four contemporary business leaders. Prepare a brief summary of each and classify them as leaders or managers.
8. *(communication question)* Interview a supervisor or manager about the best follower the supervisor or manager has worked with. Ask questions about the characteristics and behaviors that made this person such a good follower. Note in particular how this follower responds to change. Be prepared to present your interview results in class.

Ethical Dilemma

Sam Bennett has been president of Chateau Bank for the past thirty-five years. Next to his family, running the bank has been the focus of his life. When Sam took over as president, the bank was small and poorly run. Today, there are fifty branch offices across three counties, an accomplishment in which Sam takes great pride. Now Sam is almost seventy and is ready to retire. He has been preparing for this event for some time. Grooming his replacement is very important and something he has been working on for years.

For several years, Chris Hollister has been the heir apparent. Chris had caught Sam's eye when he first joined the bank. Sam has watched with great interest as Chris rose through the ranks. As Chris began moving into the upper echelons, Sam made it well known that Chris was his choice to succeed him as president. The problem Sam now faces is that Chateau is not the same bank. It has, and rightly so, become a bank of the twenty-first century. Computers run everything. But Chris is from the old school. He understands computers well enough, but moving the company into the future requires someone who understands that technology is the catalyst to do that.

Dana Heart might just be that person. Dana joined the company at the management level twelve years ago, straight from graduate school. She grew up in the technology era and knows how to use technology to her and the bank's advantage. Dana is not only good at what she does, but she also has a vision for the future. Sam likes Dana, but how can he turn his back on Chris?

Should his loyalty be with the man he has been grooming for so long or with the growth needs of the organization? Sam is sure that Chris could get the job done, but Dana would move the company forward.

Questions

1. Does Sam have an obligation to appoint Chris as the next president?
2. Evaluate each of Sam's alternatives, choosing Chris or Dana, using consequential, rule-based, and character theories.

Experiential Exercises

12.1 National Culture and Leadership

Effective leadership often varies by national culture, as Hofstede's research has shown. This exercise gives you the opportunity to examine your own and your group's leadership orientation compared to norms from ten countries, including the United States.

Exercise Schedule

1. Preparation (before class)
Complete the 29-item questionnaire.

2. Individual and Group Scoring
Your instructor will lead you through the scoring of the questionnaire, both individually and as a group.

3. Comparison of Effective Leadership Patterns by Nation
Your instructor leads a discussion on Hofstede's value system and presents the culture dimension scores for the ten countries.

In the questionnaire below, indicate the extent to which you agree or disagree with each statement. For example, if you strongly agree with a particular statement, circle the 5 next to the statement.

1 = strongly disagree
2 = disagree
3 = neither agree nor disagree
4 = agree
5 = strongly agree

QUESTIONNAIRE	STRONGLY DISAGREE				STRONGLY AGREE
1. It is important to have job instructions spelled out in detail so that employees always know what they are expected to do.	1	2	3	4	5
2. Managers expect employees to closely follow instructions and procedures.	1	2	3	4	5
3. Rules and regulations are important because they inform employees what the organization expects of them.	1	2	3	4	5
4. Standard operating procedures are helpful to employees on the job.	1	2	3	4	5
5. Instructions for operations are important for employees on the job.	1	2	3	4	5
6. Group welfare is more important than individual rewards.	1	2	3	4	5
7. Group success is more important than individual success.	1	2	3	4	5
8. Being accepted by the members of your work group is very important.	1	2	3	4	5
9. Employees should pursue their own goals only after considering the welfare of the group.	1	2	3	4	5
10. Managers should encourage group loyalty even if individual goals suffer.	1	2	3	4	5
11. Individuals may be expected to give up their goals in order to benefit group success.	1	2	3	4	5
12. Managers should make most decisions without consulting subordinates.	1	2	3	4	5
13. Managers should frequently use authority and power when dealing with subordinates.	1	2	3	4	5
14. Managers should seldom ask for the opinions of employees.	1	2	3	4	5
15. Managers should avoid off-the-job social contacts with employees.	1	2	3	4	5
16. Employees should not disagree with management decisions.	1	2	3	4	5
17. Managers should not delegate important tasks to employees.	1	2	3	4	5
18. Managers should help employees with their family problems.	1	2	3	4	5
19. Managers should see to it that employees are adequately clothed and fed.	1	2	3	4	5
20. A manager should help employees solve their personal problems.	1	2	3	4	5

(continued)

QUESTIONNAIRE	STRONGLY DISAGREE				STRONGLY AGREE
21. Management should see that all employees receive health care.	1	2	3	4	5
22. Management should see that children of employees have an adequate education.	1	2	3	4	5
23. Management should provide legal assistance for employees who get into trouble with the law.	1	2	3	4	5
24. Managers should take care of their employees as they would their children.	1	2	3	4	5
25. Meetings are usually run more effectively when they are chaired by a man.	1	2	3	4	5
26. It is more important for men to have a professional career than it is for women to have a professional career.	1	2	3	4	5
27. Men usually solve problems with logical analysis; women usually solve problems with intuition.	1	2	3	4	5
28. Solving organizational problems usually requires an active, forceful approach, which is typical of men.	1	2	3	4	5
29. It is preferable to have a man, rather than a woman, in a high-level position.	1	2	3	4	5

SOURCES: By Peter Dorfman, *Advances in International Comparative Management,* vol. 3, pages 127–150, 1988. Reprinted by permission of JAI Press Inc. D. Marcic and S. M. Puffer, "Dimensions of National Culture and Effective Leadership Patterns: Hofstede Revisited," *Management International* (Minneapolis/St. Paul: West Publishing, 1994), 10–15.

12.2 Leadership and Influence

To get a better idea of what your leadership style is and how productive it would be, fill out the following questionnaire. If you are currently a manager or have been a manager, answer the questions considering "members" to be your employees. If you have never been a manager, think of situations when you were a leader in an organization and consider "members" to be people working for you.

Response choices for each item:

A = always B = often C = occasionally
D = seldom E = never

	A	B	C	D	E
1. I would act as the spokesperson of the group.					
2. I would allow the members complete freedom in their work.					
3. I would encourage overtime work.					
4. I would permit the members to use their own judgment in solving problems.					
5. I would encourage the use of uniform procedures.					
6. I would needle members for greater effort.					
7. I would stress being ahead of competing groups.					

	A	B	C	D	E
8. I would let the members do their work the way they think best.					
9. I would speak as the representative of the group.					
10. I would be able to tolerate postponement and uncertainty.					
11. I would try out my ideas in the group.					
12. I would turn the members loose on a job, and let them go on it.					
13. I would work hard for a promotion.					
14. I would get swamped by details.					
15. I would speak for the group when visitors are present.					
16. I would be reluctant to allow the members any freedom of action.					
17. I would keep the work moving at a rapid pace.					

	A	B	C	D	E
18. I would let some members have authority that I should keep.					
19. I would settle conflicts when they occur in the group.					
20. I would allow the group a high degree of initiative.					
21. I would represent the group at outside meetings.					
22. I would be willing to make changes.					
23. I would decide what will be done and how it will be done.					
24. I would trust the members to exercise good judgment.					
25. I would push for increased production.					
26. I would refuse to explain my actions.					

	A	B	C	D	E
27. Things usually turn out as I predict.					
28. I would permit the group to set its own pace.					
29. I would assign group members to particular tasks.					
30. I would act without consulting the group.					
31. I would ask the members of the group to work harder.					
32. I would schedule the work to be done.					
33. I would persuade others that my ideas are to their advantage.					
34. I would urge the group to beat its previous record.					
35. I would ask that group members follow standard rules and regulations.					

Scoring

People oriented: Place a check mark by the number if you answered either A or B to any of these questions:

Question # 2 ____ 10 ____ 22 ____
4 ____ 12 ____ 24 ____
6 ____ 18 ____ 28 ____
8 ____ 20 ____

Place a check mark by the number if you answered either D or E to any of these questions:

14 ____ 16 ____ 26 ____ 30 ____

Count your check marks to get your total people-oriented score. ____

Task oriented: Place a check mark by the number if you answered either A or B to any of these questions:

3 ____ 7 ____ 11 ____ 13 ____
17 ____ 25 ____ 29 ____ 31 ____
34 ____

Place a check mark by the number if you answered C or D to any of these questions:

1 ____ 5 ____ 9 ____ 15 ____
19 ____ 21 ____ 23 ____ 27 ____
32 ____ 33 ____ 35 ____

Count your check marks to get your total task-oriented score. ____

Range	Range		
People 0–7;	Task 0–10	You are not involved enough in either the task or the people.	Uninvolved
People 0–7;	Task 10–20	You tend to be autocratic, a whip-snapper. You get the job done, but at a high emotional cost.	Task-oriented
People 8–15;	Task 0–10	People are happy in their work, but sometimes at the expense of productivity.	People-oriented
People 8–15;	Task 10–20	People enjoy working for you and are productive. They naturally expend energy because they get positive reinforcement for doing a good job.	Balanced

As a leader, most people tend to be more task oriented or more people oriented. Task orientation is concerned with getting the job done, while people orientation focuses on group interactions and the needs of individual workers.

Effective leaders, however, are able to use both styles, depending on the situation. There may be times when a rush job demands great attention placed on task completion. During a time of low morale, though, sensitivity to workers' problems would be more appropriate. The best managers are able to balance both task and people concerns. Therefore, a high score on both would show this balance. Ultimately, you will gain respect, admiration, and productivity from your workers.

Exercise Schedule

1. Preparation (before class)

Complete and score inventory.

2. Group discussion

The class should form four groups based on the scores on the Leadership Style Inventory. Each group will be given a separate task.

Uninvolved: Devise strategies for developing task-oriented and people-oriented styles.

Task-oriented: How can you develop a more people-oriented style? What problems might occur if you do not do so?

People-oriented: How can you develop a more task-oriented style? What problems might occur if you do not do so?

Balanced: Do you see any potential problems with your style? Are you a fully developed leader?

SOURCE: From Thomas Sergiovanni, Richard Metzcus, and Larry Burden, "Toward a Particularistic Approach to Leadership Style: Some Findings," *American Educational Research Journal,* vol. 6 (1), January 1969.

TAKE 2

Biz Flix | U-571

This action-packed World War II thriller shows a U.S. submarine crew's efforts to retrieve an Enigma encryption device from a disabled German submarine. After the crew gets the device, a German vessel torpedoes and sinks their submarine. The survivors must now use the disabled German submarine to escape from the enemy with their prize.

The *U-571* scene is an edited composite of the "To Be a Captain" sequence early in the film and the "A Real Sea Captain" sequence in about the middle of the film. A "chalkboard" (title screen) that reads, "Mr. Tyler, permission to speak freely?" separates the two parts. You can pause and separately study each part of the scene.

The first part occurs before the crew boards the disabled German U-boat. The second part occurs after the crew of survivors board the U-boat and try to return to England. Andrew Tyler (Matthew McConaughey), formerly the executive officer, is now the submarine's commander following the drowning death of Mike Dahlgren (Bill Paxton), the original commander. Just before this part of the scene, Tyler overheard some crewmen questioning his decision about taking a dangerous route to England. They also question why Chief Petty Officer Henry Klough (Harvey Keitel) is not the commander. The film continues with a German reconnaissance airplane circling their submarine and a crewman challenging Tyler's authority.

What to Watch for and Ask Yourself:

- What aspects of leadership does Dahlgren describe as important for a submarine commander?
- Which leadership behaviors or traits does Klough emphasize?
- Are these traits or behaviors right for this situation? Why or why not?

Workplace Video | Leadership, Featuring McDonald's

"Would you like to Supersize that?" This familiar phrase is heard by nearly 50 million people in more than 119 countries each day. Indeed McDonald's has become one of the most recognizable franchises in the world. The company's storied history, which gained legendary status under the leadership of Ray Kroc, weaves together many enduring themes of business success: visionary leadership, mass marketing, and groundbreaking business models.

Kroc, the iconic businessman credited with the rapid expansion of the McDonald's Corporation, was a franchising pioneer. The one-time distributor of Multimixer milkshake makers was first to see the potential in replicating the McDonald's restaurant across the country. While visiting a McDonald's hamburger stand in California one day, Kroc noticed that the restaurant used eight Multimixers to serve a record number of customers. Knowing a good idea when he saw one, the young entrepreneur proposed opening several such restaurants. In 1955, Kroc opened the first McDonald's chain location in Des Plaines, Illinois. The rest is history.

Kroc is remembered as a leader who inspired many with his personal charisma and vision. Even so, he also was a methodical supervisor who possessed strong initiating

TAKE 2

structure. Kroc's clever quip "If you've got time to lean, you've got time to clean" reveals a goal-oriented approach that continues to guide managerial strategy at McDonald's today.

Although good leadership is concerned with goals and results, effective leaders must also show consideration for people. Top leaders at McDonald's demonstrate concern for their employees in various ways. "Plan-to-Win," the company's global strategy, lays out a comprehensive commitment to people that involves employee training, flexible scheduling, and career development. Moreover, managers promote job satisfaction by recognizing and rewarding the good effort of all employees. On the interpersonal level, supervisors treat subordinates as they themselves would want to be treated, acting more like coaches than chieftains.

Like many industry-leading corporations, McDonald's has achieved its greatness by showing equal concern for people and performance. That balance, though difficult to maintain, is as vital to the company's ongoing success as it was when Ray Kroc transformed a small hamburger stand into a franchising wonder.

Discussion Questions

1. Where does leadership at McDonald's fall on the Leadership Grid discussed in this chapter? Explain.
2. Which contingency model of leadership is utilized at McDonald's, according to the video?
3. Would you describe Ray Kroc as a transformational, charismatic leader? Why or why not?

CASE

Triumvirate Leadership at Google

In 1998, while they were doctoral students at Stanford University, Sergey Brin and Larry Page founded Google. In 2001, Brin and Page recruited Eric Schmidt to be Google's chief executive officer. Schmidt was charged with providing the organizational and operational expertise and leadership for Google, while Brin and Page provided the engineering, technological, and product development leadership.[1] As some pundits have said, Page and Brin knew they weren't professional managers or marketers or masters of strategy, so they brought in a "grown-up," Eric Schmidt, to operate the company.[2]

Google's success can be attributed to its triumvirate leadership of Brin, Page, and Schmidt, "who have managed to beat back rivals from Yahoo! to Microsoft."[3] However, one of Google's biggest mysteries is its three-man leadership and how it functions.[4] Page is president for products and is acknowledged as the company's thought leader and someone who gets involved in projects to make sure things get done. Brin is president of technology and assumes responsibility for advertising initiatives, which is the money-making part of Google.[5] "Conventional wisdom is that Schmidt's job is to break ties between Page and Brin and to communicate with Wall Street and the news media. Insiders say that underplays his role. He sets the company's overall agenda, gives direction on workaday issues the founders don't care to address, and more than occasionally reminds Page and Brin to behave themselves."[6] Schmidt is a skilled big-company executive, having had substantial experience at Novell and Sun Microsystems before being recruited to Google. He is a seasoned marketer and a renowned technology expert as well.[7] In April 2007, Schmidt was elected board chairman in addition to being CEO. Google had not had a chairman since it went public in 2004, although Schmidt effectively served in that role.[8] In commenting on the role Schmidt has played in Google's success, David Nadler, a renowned business consultant, says, "Page and Brin's handoff to Schmidt can be seen as a classic case of redesigning the management structure to complement the strengths of the top people."[9]

Nonetheless, Brin and Page seem to be the dominant forces in the company because their stock shares carry ten times as many votes as the ordinary stock shares. Moreover, Brin and Page "give themselves carte blanche to do what they like, buy what they like, diversify wherever they like and pay no dividends."[10]

The leadership triumvirate also has high expectations for Google employees. Google hires only class-A talent because Brin, Page, and Schmidt believe that hiring just one B-level person initiates a slide into mediocrity. The company has generous reward and award programs in order to ensure that employees with great ideas don't launch their own entrepreneurial ventures.[11] Moreover, Google essentially lets engineers run the show. Every Google employee divides his or her work time into three parts: 70 percent is devoted to Google's core businesses of search and advertising; 20 percent is targeted toward off-budget projects related to the core businesses; and 10 percent is allocated to the pursuit of far-out ideas.[12] The time allocation for off-budget projects and far-out ideas is more than a perk; "it's Google's seed corn for the future."[13]

Brin and Page do not see themselves as "infallible seers with a divine right to dictate Google's next strategy and the one after that." Instead, they have "created a Darwinian environment in which every idea must compete on its merits, not on the grandeur of its sponsor's title."[14] Encouraging creativity and innovation is a Google hallmark, and the company has implemented many policies, processes, and procedures to foster creativity and innovation. For instance, mechanisms are in place to share ideas, get input from peers, recruit people to work on project ideas, and generate support for change. This makes Google a highly transparent organization for insiders.[15]

But Google is not highly transparent for outsiders! The company seems to relish being secretive and opaque and confusing the competition.[16] This is nowhere more apparent than in the leadership triumvirate's deliberately confusing comments on transparency and corporate strategy. In describing the need for transparency in business, Schmidt says, "[w]ith all the headlines we're making, we don't want our announcements to surprise or confuse anyone. We don't want our partners to think we're competing against them." Schmidt continues, "[w]e try very hard to look like we're out of control. But in fact the company is very measured. And that's part of our secret."[17] Page adds, "[w]e don't generally talk about strategy . . . because it's strategic. I would rather have people think we're confused than let our competitors know what we're going to do."[18] Schmidt also says that he "intentionally propagated the perception of Google as a wacky place to allow the company to build up its business under the radar."[19]

Along with not being transparent to outsiders, Google has created some disharmony with them. By taking on Microsoft (desktop software), phone companies (a San Francisco Wi-Fi plan for free wireless Internet service), eBay (classified advertising), and others, Google has not been making friends.[20] The company even seems to be offending its paying customers, and in some "parts of the business community, it is acquiring the image of a somewhat sanctimonious bully."[21] This is an interesting anomaly, particularly given Google's famous slogan—"Don't Be Evil"—and its pro-consumer stance. Rather than creating disharmony, Google should have been winning friends.[22]

Discussion Questions

1. In what ways are Sergey Brin, Larry Page, and Eric Schmidt managers? In what ways are they leaders?
2. Describe the nature of followership that Brin, Page, and Schmidt have sought to develop at Google.
3. Using the Leadership Grid and its underlying leader behaviors of initiating structure and consideration, explain the leadership orientations of Google's triumvirate.
4. Use the concepts of transactional, transformational, charismatic, and authentic leaders to describe the leadership of Brin, Page, and Schmidt.
5. What skills would you personally need to develop to become a leader like Brin, Page, and Schmidt? What could you do to develop or refine those skills?

SOURCE: This case was written by Michael K. McCuddy, The Louis S. and Mary L. Morgal Chair of Christian Business Ethics and Professor of Management, College of Business Administration, Valparaiso University.

CHAPTER 13

Conflict and Negotiation

LEARNING OBJECTIVES

After reading this chapter, you should be able to do the following:

1 Diagnose functional versus dysfunctional conflict.

2 Identify the causes of conflict in organizations.

3 Identify the different forms of conflict.

4 Understand the defense mechanisms that individuals exhibit when they engage in interpersonal conflict.

5 Describe effective and ineffective techniques for managing conflict.

6 Understand five styles of conflict management, and diagnose your own preferred style.

THINKING AHEAD: GENENTECH, INC.

Conflict within One of the "Best Companies"

Only a select few ever make *Fortune*'s list of "100 Best Companies to Work For." For Genentech, making the esteemed list has become something of an annual tradition. In fact, the company's place on the 2007 list was number two—a slight drop from its 2006 ranking of number one. While all seems well inside the company, Genentech is in the business of pharmaceutical innovation, which brings with it some disputes and conflicts from time to time.

For example, Genentech has been hit by legal action for using research from another source without full permission. One such case came to light when a jury ordered it to hand over $300 million in unpaid royalties to City of Hope for the use of some of their patented methods of developing protein-based drugs that they had licensed to Genentech in 1976. City of Hope claimed that Genentech licensed these methods to other companies. City of Hope should have received royalties from this, but they claimed that Genentech had intentionally cheated them of their money. Ultimately, Genentech announced that they had been honest in all their transactions and had to take the hit for this one decision.[1]

In the Looking Back feature, we will examine how Genentech CEO Arthur Levinson made the most of such mistakes and conflicts. Today, the company has a program in place to avoid this type of conflict with other organizations.

THE NATURE OF CONFLICTS IN ORGANIZATIONS

All of us have experienced conflict of various types, yet we probably fail to recognize the variety of conflicts that occur in organizations. *Conflict* is defined as any situation in which incompatible goals, attitudes, emotions, or behaviors lead to disagreement or opposition between two or more parties.[2]

Today's organizations may face greater potential for conflict than ever before in history. The marketplace, with its increasing competition and globalization, magnifies differences among people in terms of personality, values, attitudes, perceptions, languages, cultures, and national backgrounds.[3] With the increasing diversity of the workforce, furthermore, comes the potential for incompatibility and conflict.

Importance of Conflict Management Skills for the Manager

Estimates show that managers spend about 21 percent of their time dealing with conflict.[4] That is the equivalent of one day every week. And conflict management skills are a major predictor of managerial success.[5] Emotional intelligence (EI) relates to the ability to manage conflict. It is the power to control one's emotions and perceive emotions in others, adapt to change, and manage adversity. Conflict management skills may be more a reflection of EI than of IQ. People who lack emotional intelligence, especially empathy or the ability to see life from another person's perspective, are more likely to be causes of conflict than managers of conflict.[6] EI seems to be valid across cultures. It is common among successful people not only in North America, but also in Nigeria, India, Argentina, and France.

Functional versus Dysfunctional Conflict

(1) Diagnose functional versus dysfunctional conflict.

Not all conflict is bad. In fact, some types of conflict encourage new solutions to problems and enhance creativity in the organization. In these cases, managers will want to encourage the conflicts. Thus, the key to conflict management is to stimulate functional conflict and prevent or resolve dysfunctional conflict. The difficulty, however, is distinguishing between dysfunctional and functional conflicts. The consequences of conflict can be positive or negative, as shown in Table 13.1.

Functional conflict is a healthy, constructive disagreement between two or more people. Functional conflict can produce new ideas, learning, and growth among individuals. When individuals engage in constructive conflict, they develop a better awareness of themselves and others. In addition, functional conflict can improve working relationships; when two parties work through their disagreements, they feel they have accomplished something together. By releasing tensions and solving problems in working together, morale is improved.[7] Functional conflict can lead to innovation and positive change for the organization.[8] Because it tends to encourage creativity among individuals, this positive form of conflict can translate into increased productivity.[9] A key to recognizing functional conflict is that it is often cognitive in origin; that is, it arises from someone challenging old policies or thinking of new ways to approach problems.

conflict
Any situation in which incompatible goals, attitudes, emotions, or behaviors lead to disagreement or opposition for two or more parties.

functional conflict
A healthy, constructive disagreement between two or more people.

TABLE 13.1 Consequences of Conflict

Positive Consequences	Negative Consequences
• Leads to new ideas	• Diverts energy from work
• Stimulates creativity	• Threatens psychological well-being
• Motivates change	• Wastes resources
• Promotes organizational vitality	• Creates a negative climate
• Helps individuals and groups establish identities	• Breaks down group cohesion
• Serves as a safety valve to indicate problems	• Can increase hostility and aggressive behaviors

Dysfunctional conflict is an unhealthy, destructive disagreement between two or more people. Its danger is that it shifts the focus from the work to be done to the conflict itself and the parties involved. Excessive conflict drains energy that could be used more productively. A key to recognizing a dysfunctional conflict is that its origin is often emotional or behavioral. Disagreements that involve personalized anger and resentment directed at specific individuals rather than specific ideas are dysfunctional.[10] Individuals involved in dysfunctional conflict tend to act before thinking, and they often rely on threats, deception, and verbal abuse to communicate. In dysfunctional conflict, the losses to both parties may exceed any potential gain from the conflict.

Diagnosing conflict as good or bad is not easy. The manager must look at the issue, the context of the conflict, and the parties involved. The following questions can be used to diagnose the nature of the conflict a manager faces:

- Are the parties approaching the conflict from a hostile standpoint?
- Is the outcome likely to be a negative one for the organization?
- Do the potential losses of the parties exceed any potential gains?
- Is energy being diverted from goal accomplishment?

If the majority of the answers to these questions are yes, the conflict is probably dysfunctional. Once the manager has diagnosed the type of conflict, he or she can work either to resolve it (if it is dysfunctional) or to stimulate it (if it is functional).

It is easy to make mistakes in diagnosing conflicts. Sometimes task conflict, which is functional, can be misattributed as being personal, and dysfunctional conflict can follow. Developing trust within the work group can keep this misattribution from occurring.[11] A study of group effectiveness found that American decision-making groups made up of friends were able to more openly engage in disagreement than groups made up of strangers, allowing the friends' groups to make more effective decisions. When group members (friends) felt comfortable and trusting enough to express conflicting opinions, optimal performance resulted. But similar groups made up of Chinese friends and strangers exhibited both high levels of conflict *and* low levels of performance, suggesting that open disagreement in these groups was not helpful. This finding should serve as a cautionary tale for managers trying to apply one country's management style and techniques in another cultural setting.[12]

One occasion when managers should work to stimulate conflict is when they suspect their group is suffering from groupthink, discussed in Chapter 10.[13] When a group fails to consider alternative solutions and becomes stagnant in its thinking, it might benefit from healthy disagreements. Teams exhibiting symptoms of groupthink should be encouraged to consider creative problem solving and should

dysfunctional conflict
An unhealthy, destructive disagreement between two or more people.

appoint a devil's advocate to point out opposing perspectives. These actions can help stimulate constructive conflict in a group.

CAUSES OF CONFLICT IN ORGANIZATIONS

(2) Identify the causes of conflict in organizations.

Conflict is pervasive in organizations. To manage it effectively, managers should understand the many sources of conflict. They can be classified into two broad categories: structural factors, which stem from the nature of the organization and the way in which work is organized, and personal factors, which arise from differences among individuals. Figure 13.1 summarizes the causes of conflict within each category.

Structural Factors

The causes of conflict related to the organization's structure include specialization, interdependence, common resources, goal differences, authority relationships, status inconsistencies, and jurisdictional ambiguities.

Specialization When jobs are highly specialized, employees become experts at certain tasks. For example, one software company has one specialist for databases, one for statistical packages, and another for expert systems. Highly specialized jobs can lead to conflict, because people often have little awareness of the tasks that others perform.

A classic conflict of specialization may occur between salespeople and engineers. Engineers are technical specialists responsible for product design and quality. Salespeople are marketing experts and liaisons with customers. Salespeople are often accused of making delivery promises to customers that engineers cannot keep because the sales force lacks the technical knowledge necessary to develop realistic delivery deadlines.

Interdependence Work that is interdependent requires groups or individuals to depend on one another to accomplish goals.[14] Depending on other people to get work done is fine when the process works smoothly. When there is a problem, however, it becomes very easy to blame the other party, and conflict escalates. In a garment manufacturing plant, for example, when the fabric cutters get behind in their work, the workers who sew the garments are delayed as well. Considerable frustration may result when the workers at the sewing machines feel their efforts are being blocked by the cutters' slow pace, and their pay is affected because they are paid piece-rate.

FIGURE 13.1 Causes of Conflict in Organizations

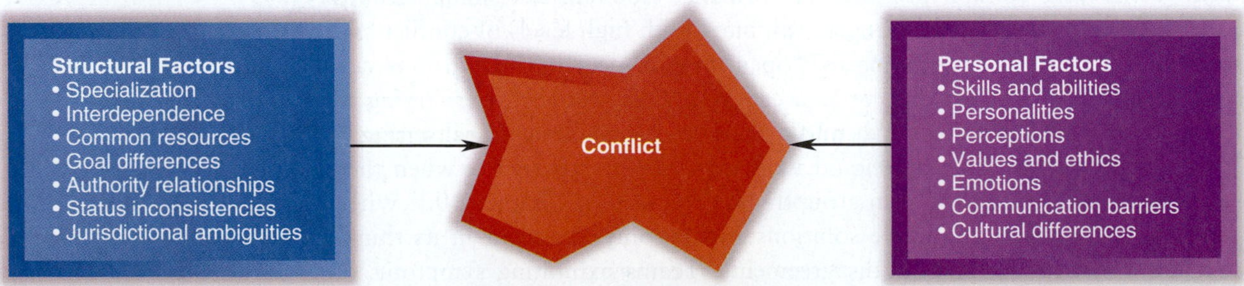

Common Resources Any time multiple parties must share resources, there is potential for conflict.[15] This potential is enhanced when the shared resources become scarce. For example, managers often share secretarial support. Not uncommonly, one secretary supports ten or more managers, each of whom believes his or her work is most important. This puts pressure on the secretary and leads to potential conflicts in prioritizing and scheduling work.

Goal Differences When work groups have different goals, these goals may be incompatible. For example, in one cable television company, the salesperson's goal was to sell as many new installations as possible. This created problems for the service department, because its goal was timely installations. With increasing sales, the service department's workload became backed up, and orders were delayed. Often these types of conflicts occur because individuals do not have knowledge of another department's objectives.

Authority Relationships A traditional boss–employee relationship is hierarchical in nature with a boss who is superior to the employee. For many employees, such a relationship is not a comfortable one, because another individual has the right to tell them what to do. Some people resent authority more than others, and obviously this creates conflicts. In addition, some bosses are more autocratic than others; this compounds the potential for conflict in the relationship. As organizations move toward the team approach and empowerment, there should be less potential for conflict from authority relationships.

Status Inconsistencies Some organizations have a strong status difference between management and nonmanagement workers. Managers may enjoy privileges—such as flexible schedules, reserved parking spaces, and longer lunch hours—that are not available to nonmanagement employees. This may result in resentment and conflict.

Jurisdictional Ambiguities Have you ever telephoned a company with a problem and had your call transferred through several different people and departments? This situation illustrates *jurisdictional ambiguity*—that is, unclear lines of responsibility within an organization.[16] The classic situation here involves the hardware/software dilemma. You call the company that made your computer, and they inform you that the problem is caused by the software. You call the software division, and they tell you it's the hardware . . . you get the idea.

The factors just discussed are structural in that they arise from the ways in which work is organized. Other conflicts come from differences among individuals.

Personal Factors

The causes of conflict that arise from individual differences include skills and abilities, personalities, perceptions, values and ethics, emotions, communication barriers, and cultural differences.

Skills and Abilities The workforce is composed of individuals with varying levels of skills and ability. Diversity in skills and abilities may be positive for the organization, but it also holds potential for conflict, especially when jobs are interdependent. Experienced, competent workers may find it difficult to work alongside new and unskilled recruits. Workers can become resentful when their new boss, fresh from college, knows a lot about managing people but is unfamiliar with the technology with which they are working.

jurisdictional ambiguity
The presence of unclear lines of responsibility within an organization.

Personalities Individuals do not leave their personalities at the doorstep when they enter the workplace. Personality conflicts are realities in organizations. To expect that you will like all of your coworkers, or vice versa, may be naive.

One personality trait that many people find difficult to deal with is abrasiveness.[17] An abrasive person ignores the interpersonal aspects of work and the feelings of colleagues. Abrasive individuals are often achievement oriented and hardworking, but their perfectionist, critical style often leaves others feeling unimportant. This style creates stress and strain for those around the abrasive person.[18]

Perceptions Differences in perception can also lead to conflict. For example, managers and workers may not have a shared perception of what motivates people. In this case, the reward system can create conflicts if managers provide what they think employees want rather than what employees really want.

Values and Ethics Differences in values and ethics can be sources of disagreement. Older workers, for example, value company loyalty and probably would not take a sick day when they were not really ill. Younger workers, valuing mobility, like the concept of "mental health days," or calling in sick to get away from work. This may not be true for all workers, but it illustrates that differences in values can lead to conflict.

Most people have their own sets of values and ethics. The extent to which they apply these ethics in the workplace varies. Some people have a strong desire for approval from others and will work to meet others' ethical standards. Some people are relatively unconcerned about approval from others and strongly apply their own ethical standards. Still others operate seemingly without regard to ethics or values.[19] When conflicts about ethics or values do arise, heated disagreement is common because of the personal nature of the differences.

Emotions The emotions of others can be a source of conflict in the workplace. Problems at home often spill over into the work arena, and the related moods can be hard for others to deal with.

Conflict by its nature is an emotional interaction,[20] and the emotions of the parties involved in conflict play a pivotal role in how they perceive the negotiation and respond to one another. In fact, emotions are now considered critical elements of any negotiation that must be included in any examination of the process and how it unfolds.[21]

One important research finding has been that emotion can play a problematic role in negotiations. In particular, when negotiators begin to act based on emotions rather than on cognitions, they are much more likely to reach an impasse.[22]

Communication Barriers Communication barriers such as physical separation and language can create distortions in messages, and these can lead to conflict. Another communication barrier is value judgment, in which a listener assigns a worth to a message before it is received. For example, suppose a team member is a chronic complainer. When this individual enters the manager's office, the manager is likely to devalue the message before it is even delivered. Conflict can then emerge.

Cultural Differences Although cultural differences are assets in organizations, sometimes they can be seen as sources of conflict. Often, these conflicts stem from a lack of understanding of another culture. In one MBA class, for example, Indian students were horrified when American students challenged the professor. Meanwhile, the American students thought the students from India were too passive. Subsequent discussions revealed that professors in India expected to be treated deferentially and with great respect. While students might challenge an idea vigorously, they would rarely challenge the professor. Diversity training that emphasizes education on cultural differences can make great strides in preventing misunderstandings.

GLOBALIZATION AND CONFLICT

Large transnational corporations employ many different ethnic and cultural groups. In these multiethnic corporations, the widely differing cultures represent vast differences among individuals, so the potential for conflict increases.[23] As indicated in Chapter 2, Hofstede has identified five dimensions along which cultural differences may emerge: individualism/collectivism, power distance, uncertainty avoidance, masculinity/femininity, and long-term/short-term orientation.[24] These cultural differences have many implications for conflict management in organizations.

Individualism means that people believe that their individual interests take priority over society's interests. Collectivism, in contrast, means that people put the good of the group first. For example, the United States is a highly individualistic culture, whereas Japan is a very collectivist culture. The individualism/collectivism dimension of cultural differences strongly influences conflict management behavior. People from collectivist cultures tend to display a more cooperative approach to managing conflict.[25]

Hofstede's second dimension of cultural differences is power distance. In cultures with high power distance, individuals accept that people in organizations have varying levels of power. In contrast, in cultures with low power distance, individuals do not automatically respect those in positions of authority. For example, the United States is a country of low power distance, whereas Brazil is a country with a high power distance. Differences in power distance can lead to conflict. Imagine a U.S. employee managed by a Brazilian supervisor who expects deferential behavior. The supervisor would expect automatic respect based on legitimate power. When this respect is not given, conflict would arise.

Uncertainty avoidance also varies by culture. In the United States, employees can tolerate high levels of uncertainty, whereas employees in Israel tend to prefer certainty in their work settings. A U.S.-based multinational firm might run into conflicts operating in Israel. Suppose such a firm is installing a new technology. Its expatriate workers from the United States would tolerate the uncertainty of the technological transition better than would their Israeli coworkers, and this might lead to conflicts among the employees.

Masculinity versus femininity illustrates the contrast between preferences for assertiveness and material goods versus preferences for human capital and quality of life. The United States is a masculine society, whereas Sweden is considered a feminine society. Adjustment to the assertive interpersonal style of U.S. workers may be difficult for Swedish coworkers.

Conflicts can also arise between cultures that vary in their time orientation of values. China, for example, has a long-term orientation; the Chinese prefer values that focus on the future, such as saving and persistence. The United States and Russia, in contrast, have short-term orientations. These cultures emphasize values in the past and present, such as respect for tradition and fulfillment of social obligations. Conflicts can arise when managers fail to understand the nature of differences in values.

An organization whose workforce consists of multiple ethnicities and cultures holds potential for many types of conflict because of the sheer volume of individual differences among workers. The key to managing conflict in a multicultural workforce is understanding cultural differences and appreciating their value.

FORMS OF CONFLICT IN ORGANIZATIONS

(3) Identify the different forms of conflict.

Conflict can take on any of several different forms in an organization, including interorganizational, intergroup, intragroup, interpersonal, and intrapersonal conflicts. It is important to note that the prefix *inter* means "between," whereas the prefix *intra* means "within."

Interorganizational Conflict

Conflict that occurs between two or more organizations is called *interorganizational conflict*. Competition can heighten interorganizational conflict. Corporate takeovers, mergers, and acquisitions can also produce interorganizational conflict. What about the interorganizational conflict between major league baseball's players' union and management, which is sometimes characterized as a battle between millionaires and multimillionaires. The players regularly go on strike to extract more of the profits from management, while management cries that it is not making a dime.

Conflicts among organizations abound. Some of these conflicts can be functional, as when firms improve the quality of their products and services in the spirit of healthy competition. Other interorganizational conflicts can have dysfunctional results.

Intergroup Conflict

When conflict occurs between groups or teams, it is known as *intergroup conflict*. Conflict between groups can have positive effects within each group, such as increased group cohesiveness, increased focus on tasks, and increased loyalty to the group. There are, however, negative consequences as well. Groups in conflict tend to develop an "us against them" mentality whereby each sees the other team as the enemy, becomes more hostile, and decreases its communication with the other group. Groups are even more competitive and less cooperative than individuals. The inevitable outcome is that one group gains and the other group loses.[26]

Competition between groups must be managed carefully so that it does not escalate into dysfunctional conflict. Research has shown that when groups compete for a goal that only one group can achieve, negative consequences like territoriality, aggression, and prejudice toward the other group can result.[27] Managers should encourage and reward cooperative behaviors across groups. Some effective ways of doing this include modifying performance appraisals to include assessing intergroup behavior and using an external supervisor's evaluation of intergroup behavior. Group members will be more likely to help other groups when they know that the other group's supervisor will be evaluating their behavior, and that they will be rewarded for cooperation.[28] In addition, managers should encourage social interactions across groups so that trust can be developed. Trust allows individuals to exchange ideas and resources with members of other groups and results in innovation when members of different groups cooperate.[29] Conflict often results when older employees fear that younger new-hires may take over their jobs. Social interaction can help reduce these perceived threats, creating trust and reducing the intergroup conflict in the process.[30] An emerging challenge identified by research in conflict management points at the intergenerational conflict brought about by the diversity in age in the U.S. workforce as discussed in Chapter 2. This type of intergenerational conflict can stem from the design of employee benefit packages that might appeal more to one age group than another. Organizations should design flexible employee benefit systems that

interorganizational conflict
Conflict that occurs between two or more organizations.

intergroup conflict
Conflict that occurs between groups or teams in an organization.

The Effects of Conflict on Trust in Self-Managed Teams

Task-focused conflict occurs when group members cannot agree on ideas, opinions, and decisions about group goal achievement. On the other hand, relationship conflict is based on interpersonal conflict driven by incompatibilities, and it shows up as annoyance, tension in the group, and other such behaviors.

One research study investigated the effects of task and relationship conflict on trust among team members. The participants in the study were MBA students who were organized as self-managed teams and worked together on a variety of projects and case simulations across eight courses in a four-month period. Each team was constructed to maximize diversity (gender, cultural, and functional background) and had total discretion in how they completed assigned tasks.

The results from this study indicated that relationship conflict reduced trust among team members. Reduced trust levels led to less individual autonomy. Both types of conflict reduced the team members' interdependence on each other. Most importantly, this study revealed that high levels of each form of conflict led to lower team performance.

In summary, this research raises several interesting implications for the management of conflict in self-managed teams. One prescription is that perhaps organizations can impose restrictions on the structural factors in teams so that individual autonomy and team interdependence are preserved. Another prescription is that self-managed teams should be coached on prevention of conflict and how to implement resolution strategies. Otherwise, self-managed teams can fall prey to dysfunctional behaviors that hurt team performance.

SOURCE: C. W. Langfred, "The Downside of Self-Management: A Longitudinal Study of Conflict on Trust, Autonomy, and Task Interdependence in Self-Managing Teams," *Academy of Management Journal* 50 (4) (2007): 885–900.

have a broader appeal to a diverse age group to curtail this type of intergenerational conflict.[31]

Intragroup Conflict

Conflict that occurs within groups or teams is called *intragroup conflict*. Some conflict within a group is functional. It can help the group avoid groupthink, as we discussed in Chapter 10. Furthermore, recall that self-managed teams have a high degree of decision-making and implementation authority. One recent study reported in the Science feature above describes how conflict within a self-managed team can change its structure and lead to dysfunctional behaviors.

Even the newest teams, virtual teams, are not immune to conflict. The nuances and subtleties of face-to-face communication are often lacking in these teams, and misunderstandings can result. To avoid dysfunctional conflicts, virtual teams should make sure their tasks fit their methods of interacting. Complex strategic decisions may require face-to-face meetings rather than e-mails or threaded discussions. Face-to-face and telephone interactions early on can eliminate later conflicts and allow virtual teams to move on to use electronic communication because trust has been developed.[32]

Teams can experience many types of conflict. Using You 13.1, you can assess the types of conflict in a team you belong to, as well as design ways to manage those conflicts.

Interpersonal Conflict

Conflict between two or more people is *interpersonal conflict*. Conflict between people can arise from many individual differences, including personalities, attitudes, values, perceptions, and the other differences we discussed in Chapters 3 and 4. Later in this chapter, we look at defense mechanisms that individuals exhibit in interpersonal conflict and at ways to cope with difficult people.

intragroup conflict
Conflict that occurs within groups or teams.

interpersonal conflict
Conflict that occurs between two or more individuals.

YOU 13.1

Assess Your Team's Conflict

Think of a team you're a member of or one you were part of in the past. Answer the following eight questions regarding that team.

1. How much emotional tension was there in your team?

   No tension — Lots of tension

   1 2 3 4 5

2. How much conflict of ideas was there in your team?

   No idea conflict — Lots of idea conflict

   1 2 3 4 5

3. How often did people get angry while working in your team?

   Never — Often

   1 2 3 4 5

4. How different were your views on the content of your project?

   Very similar views — Very different views

   1 2 3 4 5

5. How much were personality clashes evident in your team?

   No clashes evident — Personality clashes very evident

   1 2 3 4 5

6. How much did you talk through disagreements about your team projects?

   Never talked through disagreements — Always talked through disagreements

   1 2 3 4 5

7. How much interpersonal friction was there in your team?

   No friction — Lots of friction

   1 2 3 4 5

8. How much disagreement was there about task procedure in your team?

   No disagreement about procedure — Lots of disagreement about procedure

   1 2 3 4 5

Total for items 2, 4, 6, and 8 =__________ indicating task conflict.

Total for items 1, 3, 5, and 7 = __________ indicating relationship conflict.

- Did your team experience higher relationship or task conflict?
- What actions can you take to better manage task conflict? Relationship conflict?
- Was there an absence of both, or either, types of conflict in your team? What does this indicate?

SOURCE: Adapted from K. Jehn, "A Multimethod Examination of the Benefits and Detriments of Intragroup Conflict," *Administrative Science Quarterly* 40 (1995): 256–282.

Advances in information technology, which allow employees to use office communications after hours, is associated with increased work-life conflict.

© DIGITAL RAILROAD

Intrapersonal Conflict

When conflict occurs within an individual, it is called *intrapersonal conflict*. There are several types of intrapersonal conflict, including interrole, intrarole, and person–role conflicts. A role is a set of expectations placed on an individual by others.[33] The person occupying the focal role is the role incumbent, and the individuals who place expectations on the person are role senders. Figure 13.2 depicts a set of role relationships.

Interrole conflict occurs when a person experiences conflict among the multiple roles in his or her life. One interrole conflict that many employees experience is work/home conflict, in which their role as worker clashes with their role as spouse or parent.[34] Work/home conflict has become even more common

FIGURE 13.2 An Organization Member's Role Set

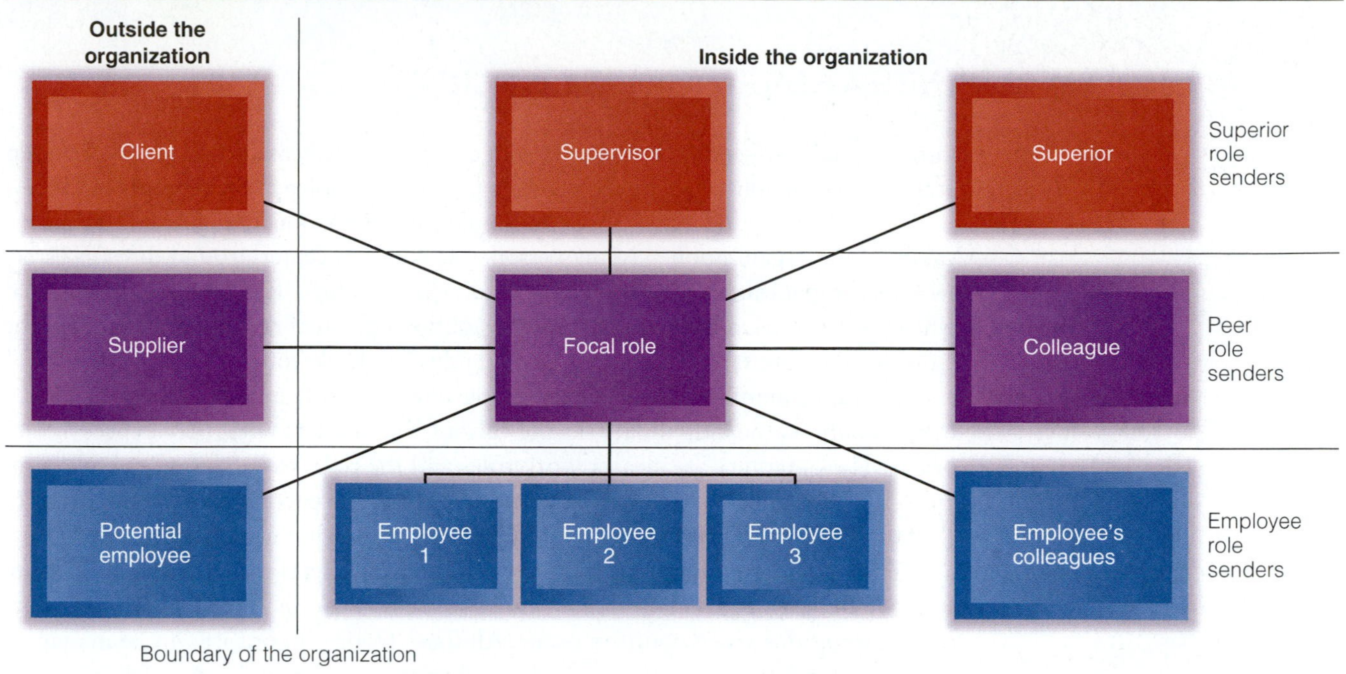

SOURCE: J. C. Quick, J. D. Quick, D. L. Nelson, and J. J. Hurrell, Jr., *Preventive Stress Management in Organizations,* 1997. Copyright © 1997 by the American Psychological Association. Reprinted with permission.

with the rise of work-at-home professionals and telecommuting because the home becomes the office, blurring the boundary between work and family life.[35] Recently, organizations are leveraging their use of information technology to gain a competitive edge. This has translated into ambitious and highly involved employees using office communications (for example, voice mail, e-mail, etc.) even after-hours. Such after-hours communication usage is associated with increased work-life conflict as reported by the employee and a significant other.[36]

Intrarole conflict is conflict within a single role. It often arises when a person receives conflicting messages from role senders about how to perform a certain role. Suppose a manager receives counsel from her department head that she needs to socialize less with the nonmanagement employees. She also is told by her project manager that she needs to be a better team member, and that she can accomplish this by socializing more with the other nonmanagement team members. This situation is one of intrarole conflict.

Person–role conflict occurs when an individual in a particular role is expected to perform behaviors that clash with his or her values.[37] Salespeople, for example, may be required to offer the most expensive item in the sales line first to the customer, even when it is apparent that the customer does not want or cannot afford the item. A computer salesman may be required to offer a large, elaborate system to a student he knows is on a tight budget. This may conflict with the salesman's values, and he may experience person–role conflict.

Intrapersonal conflicts can have positive consequences. Often, professional responsibilities clash with deeply held values. A budget shortfall may force you to lay off a loyal, hardworking employee. Your daughter may have a piano recital on the same day your largest client is scheduled to be in town visiting the office. In such conflicts, we often have to choose between right and right; that is, there's no correct response. These may be thought of as *defining moments* that challenge us to choose between two or more things in which we believe.[38] Character is formed in defining

intrapersonal conflict
Conflict that occurs within an individual.

interrole conflict
A person's experience of conflict among the multiple roles in his or her life.

intrarole conflict
Conflict that occurs within a single role, such as when a person receives conflicting messages from role senders about how to perform a certain role.

person–role conflict
Conflict that occurs when an individual is expected to perform behaviors in a certain role that conflict with his or her personal values.

moments because they cause us to shape our identities. They help us crystallize our values and serve as opportunities for personal growth.

INTRAPERSONAL CONFLICT

Intrapersonal conflict can be managed with careful self-analysis and diagnosis of the situation. Three actions in particular can help prevent or resolve intrapersonal conflicts.

First, when seeking a new job, you should find out as much as possible about the values of the organization.[39] Many person–role conflicts center around differences between the organization's values and the individual's values. Research has shown that when there is a good fit between the values of the individual and the organization, the individual is more satisfied and committed and is less likely to leave the organization.[40]

Second, to manage intrarole or interrole conflicts, role analysis is a good tool.[41] In role analysis, the individual asks the various role senders what they expect of him or her. The outcomes are clearer work roles and the reduction of conflict and ambiguity.[42] Role analysis is a simple tool that clarifies the expectations of both parties in a relationship and reduces the potential for conflict within a role or between roles.

Third, political skills can help buffer the negative effects of stress that stem from role conflicts. Effective politicians, as we discussed in Chapter 11, can negotiate role expectations when conflicts occur. All these forms of conflict can be managed. An understanding of the many forms is a first step. The next section focuses more extensively on interpersonal conflict because of its pervasiveness in organizations.

INTERPERSONAL CONFLICT

When a conflict occurs between two or more people, it is known as interpersonal conflict. To manage interpersonal conflict, it is helpful to understand power networks in organizations, defense mechanisms exhibited by individuals, and ways to cope with difficult people.

Power Networks

According to Mastenbroek, individuals in organizations are organized in three basic types of power networks.[43] Based on these power relationships, certain kinds of conflict tend to emerge. Figure 13.3 illustrates three basic kinds of power relationships in organizations.

The first relationship is equal versus equal, in which there is a horizontal balance of power among the parties. An example of this type of relationship would be a conflict between individuals from two different project teams. The behavioral tendency is toward suboptimization; that is, the focus is on a win–lose approach to problems, and each party tries to maximize its power at the expense of the other party. Conflict within this type of network can lead to depression, low self-esteem, and other distress symptoms. Interventions like improving coordination between the parties and working toward common interests can help manage these conflicts.

The second power network is high versus low, or a powerful versus a less powerful relationship. Conflicts that emerge here take the basic form of the powerful individuals trying to control others, with the less powerful people trying to become more autonomous. Conflict in this network can lead to job dissatisfaction, low organizational commitment, and turnover.[44] Organizations typically respond to these conflicts by tightening the rules. However, the more successful ways of managing these conflicts are to try a different style of leadership, such as a coaching and counseling style, or to change the structure to a more decentralized one.

FIGURE 13.3 Power Relationships in Organizations

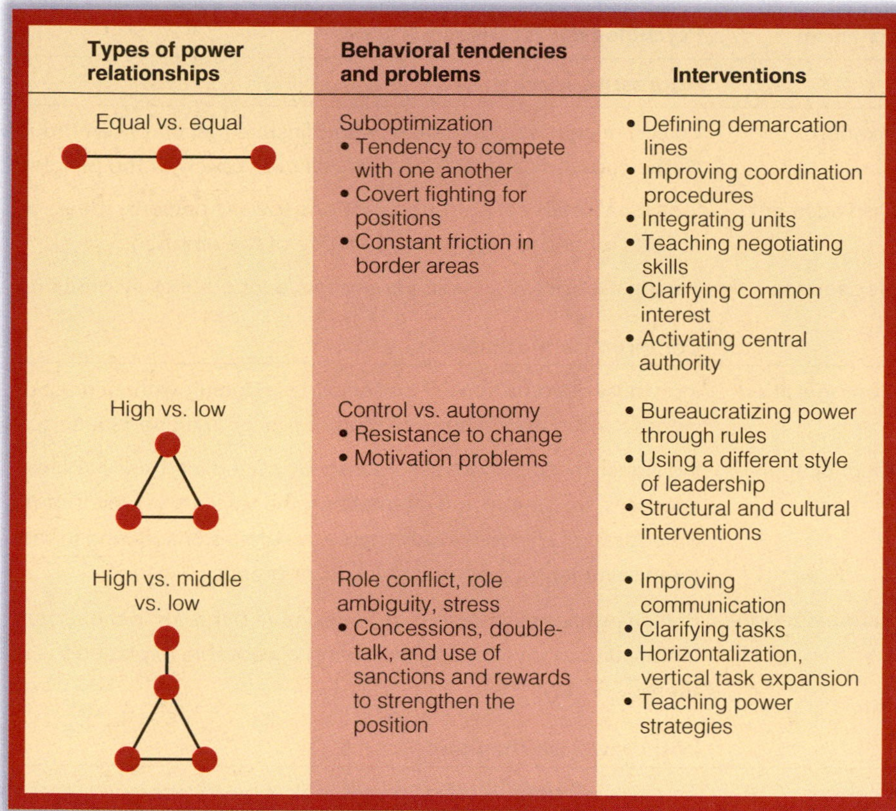

Types of power relationships	Behavioral tendencies and problems	Interventions
Equal vs. equal	Suboptimization • Tendency to compete with one another • Covert fighting for positions • Constant friction in border areas	• Defining demarcation lines • Improving coordination procedures • Integrating units • Teaching negotiating skills • Clarifying common interest • Activating central authority
High vs. low	Control vs. autonomy • Resistance to change • Motivation problems	• Bureaucratizing power through rules • Using a different style of leadership • Structural and cultural interventions
High vs. middle vs. low	Role conflict, role ambiguity, stress • Concessions, double-talk, and use of sanctions and rewards to strengthen the position	• Improving communication • Clarifying tasks • Horizontalization, vertical task expansion • Teaching power strategies

SOURCE: W. F. G. Mastenbroek, *Conflict Management and Organization Development,* 1987. Copyright John Wiley & Sons Limited. Reproduced with permission.

The third power network is high versus middle versus low. This power network illustrates the classic conflicts felt by middle managers. Two particular conflicts are evident for middle managers: role conflict, in which conflicting expectations are placed on the manager from bosses and employees, and role ambiguity, in which the expectations of the boss are unclear. Improved communication among all parties can reduce role conflict and ambiguity. In addition, middle managers can benefit from training in positive ways to influence others.

Knowing the typical kinds of conflicts that arise in various kinds of relationships can help a manager diagnose conflicts and devise appropriate ways to manage them.

Defense Mechanisms

(4) Understand the defense mechanisms that individuals exhibit when they engage in interpersonal conflict.

When individuals are involved in conflict with another human being, frustration often results.[45] Conflicts can often arise within the context of a performance appraisal session. Most people do not react well to negative feedback, as was illustrated in a classic study.[46] In this study, when employees were given criticism about their work, over 50 percent of their responses were defensive.

When individuals are frustrated, as they often are in interpersonal conflict, they respond by exhibiting defense mechanisms.[47] Defense mechanisms are common reactions to the frustration that accompanies conflict. Table 13.2 describes several defense mechanisms seen in organizations.

fixation
An aggressive mechanism in which an individual keeps up a dysfunctional behavior that obviously will not solve the conflict.

Aggressive mechanisms, such as fixation, displacement, and negativism, are aimed at attacking the source of the conflict. In *fixation,* an individual fixates on

TABLE 13.2 Common Defense Mechanisms

Defense Mechanism	Psychological Process
	Aggressive Mechanisms
• Fixation	Person maintains a persistent, nonadjustive reaction even though all the cues indicate the behavior will not cope with the problem.
• Displacement	Individual redirects pent-up emotions toward persons, ideas, or objects other than the primary source of the emotion.
• Negativism	Person uses active or passive resistance, operating unconsciously.
	Compromise Mechanisms
• Compensation	Individual devotes himself or herself to a pursuit with increased vigor to make up for some feeling of real or imagined inadequacy.
• Identification	Individual enhances own self-esteem by patterning behavior after another's, frequently also internalizing the values and beliefs of the other person; also vicariously shares the glories or suffering in the disappointments of other individuals or groups.
• Rationalization	Person justifies inconsistent or undesirable behavior, beliefs, statements, and motivations by providing acceptable explanations for them.
	Withdrawal Mechanisms
• Flight or withdrawal	Through either physical or psychological means, person leaves the field in which frustration, anxiety, or conflict is experienced.
• Conversion	Emotional conflicts are expressed in muscular, sensory, or bodily symptoms of disability, malfunctioning, or pain.
• Fantasy	Person daydreams or uses other forms of imaginative activity to obtain an escape from reality and obtain imagined satisfactions.

SOURCE: Timothy W. Costello and Sheldon S. Zalkind, adapted table from "Psychology in Administration: A Research Orientation" from *Journal of Conflict Resolution* III 1959, pp. 148–149. Reprinted by permission of Sage Publications, Inc.

displacement
An aggressive mechanism in which an individual directs his or her anger toward someone who is not the source of the conflict.

negativism
An aggressive mechanism in which a person responds with pessimism to any attempt at solving a problem.

compensation
A compromise mechanism in which an individual attempts to make up for a negative situation by devoting himself or herself to another pursuit with increased vigor.

identification
A compromise mechanism whereby an individual patterns his or her behavior after another's.

the conflict, or keeps up a dysfunctional behavior that obviously will not solve the conflict. An example of fixation occurred in a university, where a faculty member became embroiled in a battle with the dean because the faculty member felt he had not received a large enough salary increase. He persisted in writing angry letters to the dean, whose hands were tied because of a low budget allocation to the college. *Displacement* means directing anger toward someone who is not the source of the conflict. For example, a manager may respond harshly to an employee after a telephone confrontation with an angry customer. Another aggressive defense mechanism is *negativism,* which is active or passive resistance. Negativism is illustrated by a manager who, when appointed to a committee on which she did not want to serve, made negative comments throughout the meeting.

Compromise mechanisms, such as compensation, identification, and rationalization, are used by individuals to make the best of a conflict situation. *Compensation* occurs when an individual tries to make up for an inadequacy by putting increased energy into another activity. Compensation can be seen when a person makes up for a bad relationship at home by spending more time at the office. *Identification* occurs when one individual patterns his or her behavior after another's. One supervisor at a construction firm, not wanting to acknowledge consciously that she was not likely to be promoted, mimicked the behavior of her boss, even going so far as to buy a car just like the boss's. *Rationalization* is trying to justify one's behavior by constructing bogus reasons for it. Employees may rationalize unethical behavior like padding their expense accounts because "everyone else does it."

Withdrawal mechanisms are exhibited when frustrated individuals try to flee from a conflict using either physical or psychological means. Flight, withdrawal, conversion, and fantasy are examples of withdrawal mechanisms. Physically escaping a conflict is *flight*. When an employee takes a day off after a blowup with the boss is an example. *Withdrawal* may take the form of emotionally leaving a conflict, such as exhibiting an "I don't care anymore" attitude. *Conversion* is a process whereby emotional conflicts are expressed in physical symptoms. Most of us have experienced the conversion reaction of a headache following an emotional exchange with another person. *Fantasy* is an escape by daydreaming. In the Internet age, fantasy as an escape mechanism has found new meaning. A study conducted by International Data Corporation (IDC) showed that 30 to 40 percent of all Internet surfing at work is nonwork-related and that more than 70 percent of companies have had sex sites accessed from their networks, suggesting that employees' minds aren't always focused on their jobs.[48]

When employees exhibit withdrawal mechanisms, they often fake it by pretending to agree with their bosses or coworkers in order to avoid facing an immediate conflict. Many employees fake it because the firm informally rewards agreement and punishes dissent. The long-term consequence of withdrawal and faking it is emotional distress for the employee.[49]

Knowledge of these defense mechanisms can be extremely beneficial to a manager. By understanding the ways in which people typically react to interpersonal conflict, managers can be prepared for employees' reactions and help them uncover their feelings about a conflict.

rationalization
A compromise mechanism characterized by trying to justify one's behavior by constructing bogus reasons for it.

flight/withdrawal
A withdrawal mechanism that entails physically escaping a conflict (flight) or psychologically escaping (withdrawal).

conversion
A withdrawal mechanism in which emotional conflicts are expressed in physical symptoms.

fantasy
A withdrawal mechanism that provides an escape from a conflict through daydreaming.

CONFLICT MANAGEMENT STRATEGIES AND TECHNIQUES

The overall approach (or strategy) you use in a conflict is important in determining whether the conflict will have a positive or negative outcome.

These overall strategies are competitive versus cooperative strategies. Table 13.3 depicts the two strategies and four different conflict scenarios. The competitive strategy is founded on assumptions of win–lose and entails dishonest communication, mistrust, and a rigid position from both parties.[50] The cooperative strategy is founded on different assumptions: the potential for win–win outcomes, honest communication, trust, openness to risk and vulnerability, and the notion that the whole may be greater than the sum of the parts.

To illustrate the importance of the overall strategy, consider the case of two groups competing for scarce resources. Suppose budget cuts have to be made at an

TABLE 13.3 Win–Lose versus Win–Win Strategies

Strategy	Department A	Department B	Organization
Competitive	Lose	Lose	Lose
	Lose	Win	Lose
	Win	Lose	Lose
Cooperative	Win–	Win–	Win

insurance company. The claims manager argues that the sales training staff should be cut, because agents are fully trained. The sales training manager argues that claims personnel should be cut, because the company is processing fewer claims. This could turn into a dysfunctional brawl, with both sides refusing to give ground. This would constitute a win–lose, lose–win, or lose–lose scenario. Personnel cuts could be made in only one department, or in both departments. In all three cases, with the competitive approach the organization winds up in a losing position.

Even in such intense conflicts as those over scarce resources, a win–win strategy can lead to an overall win for the organization. In fact, conflicts over scarce resources can be productive if the parties have cooperative goals—a strategy that seeks a winning solution for both parties. To achieve a win–win outcome, the conflict must be approached with open-minded discussion of opposing views. Through open-minded discussion, both parties integrate views and create new solutions that facilitate productivity and strengthen their relationship; the result is feelings of unity rather than separation.[51]

In the example of the conflict between the claims manager and the sales training manager, open-minded discussion might reveal that there are ways to achieve budget cuts without cutting personnel. Sales support might surrender part of its travel budget, and claims might cut out overtime. This represents a win–win situation for the company. The budget has been reduced, and relationships between the two departments have been preserved. Both parties have given up something (note the "win–" in Table 13.3), but the conflict has been resolved with a positive outcome.

You can see the importance of the broad strategy used to approach a conflict. We now move from broad strategies to more specific techniques.

Ineffective Techniques

(5) Describe effective and ineffective techniques for managing conflict.

There are many specific techniques for dealing with conflict. Before turning to techniques that work, it should be recognized that some actions commonly taken in organizations to deal with conflict are not effective.[52]

Nonaction is doing nothing in hopes that the conflict will disappear. Generally, this is not a good technique, because most conflicts do not go away, and the individuals involved in the conflict react with frustration.

nonaction
Doing nothing in hopes that a conflict will disappear.

Secrecy, or trying to keep a conflict out of view of most people, only creates suspicion. An example is an organizational policy of pay secrecy. In some organizations, discussion of salary is grounds for dismissal. When this is the case, employees suspect that the company has something to hide. In The Real World 13.1, you can read about the drama between Hewlett-Packard and a former employee. This feature illustrates some of the potential harmful effects of secrecy. Secrecy may result in surreptitious political activity by employees who hope to uncover the secret![53]

secrecy
Attempting to hide a conflict or an issue that has the potential to create conflict.

Administrative orbiting is delaying action on a conflict by buying time, usually by telling the individuals involved that the problem is being worked on or that the boss is still thinking about the issue. Like nonaction, this technique leads to frustration and resentment.

administrative orbiting
Delaying action on a conflict by buying time.

Due process nonaction is a procedure set up to address conflicts that is so costly, time-consuming, or personally risky that no one will use it. Some companies' sexual harassment policies are examples of this technique. To file a sexual harassment complaint, detailed paperwork is required, the accuser must go through appropriate channels, and the accuser risks being branded a troublemaker. Thus, the company has a procedure for handling complaints (due process), but no one uses it (nonaction).

due process nonaction
A procedure set up to address conflicts that is so costly, time-consuming, or personally risky that no one will use it.

Character assassination is an attempt to label or discredit an opponent. Character assassination can backfire and make the individual who uses it appear dishonest

character assassination
An attempt to label or discredit an opponent.

THE REAL WORLD 13.1

Karl Kamb versus Hewlett-Packard

Karl Kamb Jr. was one of HP's wonder boys in 2002. In 2003, he made a presentation that convinced former CEO Carly Fiorina that HP should enter the lucrative flat panel television market. Fiorina liked the idea and a few months later, she announced that HP would indeed act on Kamb's suggestion. Just over a year later, Kamb was fired along with ten senior executives. HP sued him for $100 million, alleging he stole trade secrets and company funds to start his own flat panel television business.

In January 2007, Kamb filed a countersuit that was even more dramatic. He claimed that the money that HP was claiming went into his business was actually used to conduct illegal spying on its competitor Dell's upcoming business decisions in the printer market. He claimed that HP knew this money had gone there and even accused HP of pretexting or secretly reviewing his personal phone records.

While the legal decision on this saga as of 2007 is pending, analysts wonder why HP would bother spending so much in court costs in going after a case that might not even help them recover attorney fees if HP did win. HP states that going after past employees who might have violated company trust is a lesson in ethics and integrity and thus is important. The bigger question becomes: Why would a respected company like HP engage in questionable business practices, and why the secrecy?

SOURCE: N. Varchaver, "A Pretext for Revenge," *Fortune* (May 31, 2007), http://money.cnn.com/magazines/fortune/fortune_archive/2007/06/11/100060613/index.htm.

and cruel. It often leads to name-calling and accusations by both parties, both ending up losers in the eyes of those who witness the conflict.

Effective Techniques

Fortunately, there are effective conflict management techniques. These include appealing to superordinate goals, expanding resources, changing personnel, changing structure, and confronting and negotiating.

Superordinate Goals An organizational goal that is more important to both parties in a conflict than their individual or group goals is a *superordinate goal*.[54] Superordinate goals cannot be achieved by an individual or by one group alone. The achievement of these goals requires cooperation by both parties.

One effective technique for resolving conflict is to appeal to a superordinate goal—in effect, to focus the parties on a larger issue on which they both agree. This helps them realize their similarities rather than their differences.

In the conflict between service representatives and cable television installers that was discussed earlier, appealing to a superordinate goal would be an effective technique for resolving the conflict. Both departments can agree that superior customer service is a goal worthy of pursuit and that this goal cannot be achieved unless cables are installed properly and in a timely manner, and customer complaints are handled effectively. Quality service requires that both departments cooperate to achieve the goal.

Expanding Resources One conflict resolution technique is so simple that it may be overlooked. If the conflict's source is scarce resources, providing more resources may be a solution. Of course, managers working with tight budgets may not have this luxury. Nevertheless, it is a technique to be considered. In the example earlier in this chapter, one solution to the conflict among managers over secretarial support would be to hire more secretaries.

superordinate goal
An organizational goal that is more important to both parties in a conflict than their individual or group goals.

Changing Personnel In some cases, long-running severe conflict may be traced to a specific individual. For example, managers with lower levels of emotional intelligence have been demonstrated to have more negative work attitudes, to exhibit less altruistic behavior, and to produce more negative work outcomes. A chronically disgruntled manager who exhibits low EI may not only frustrate his employees but also impede his department's performance. In such cases, transferring or firing an individual may be the best solution, but only after due process.[55]

Changing Structure Another way to resolve a conflict is to change the structure of the organization. One way of accomplishing this is to create an integrator role. An integrator is a liaison between groups with very different interests. In severe conflicts, it may be best that the integrator be a neutral third party.[56] Creating the integrator role is a way of opening dialogue between groups that have difficulty communicating.

Using cross-functional teams is another way of changing the organization's structure to manage conflict. In the old methods of designing new products in organizations, many departments had to contribute, and delays resulted from difficulties in coordinating the activities of the various departments. Using a cross-functional team made up of members from different departments improves coordination and reduces delays by allowing many activities to be performed at the same time rather than sequentially.[57] The team approach allows members from different departments to work together and reduces the potential for conflict. However, recent research also suggests that such functional diversity can lead to slower informational processing in teams due to differences in members' perceptions of what might be required to achieve group goals. When putting together cross-functional teams, organizations should emphasize superordinate goals and train team members on resolving conflict. One such training technique could involve educating individual members in other functional areas so that everyone in the team can have a shared language.[58] In teamwork, it is helpful to break up a big task so that it becomes a collection of smaller, less complex tasks, and to have smaller teams work on the smaller tasks. This helps to reduce conflict, and organizations can potentially improve the performance of the overall team by improving the outcomes in each subteam.[59]

Confronting and Negotiating Some conflicts require confrontation and negotiation between the parties. Both these strategies require skill on the part of the negotiator and careful planning before engaging in negotiations. The process of negotiating involves an open discussion of problem solutions, and the outcome often is an exchange in which both parties work toward a mutually beneficial solution.

Negotiation is a joint process of finding a mutually acceptable solution to a complex conflict. Negotiating is a useful strategy under the following conditions:

> There are two or more parties. Negotiation is primarily an interpersonal or intergroup process.
> There is a conflict of interest between the parties such that what one party wants is not what the other party wants.
> The parties are willing to negotiate because each believes it can use its influence to obtain a better outcome than by simply taking the side of the other party.
> The parties prefer to work together rather than to fight openly, give in, break off contact, or take the dispute to a higher authority.

distributive bargaining
A negotiation approach in which the goals of the parties are in conflict, and each party seeks to maximize its resources.

There are two major negotiating approaches: distributive bargaining and integrative negotiation.[60] *Distributive bargaining* is an approach in which the goals of one party are in direct conflict with the goals of the other party. Resources are limited, and

Deutsche Telekom (DT): When Everyone Wants a Bigger Piece of the Pie

Deutsche Telekom is the largest telecom company in Germany. Recently there was a major dispute between the unionized workforce of DT and management. DT was planning on assigning 50,000 of its employees to work in subsidiary firms as a cost-cutting measure. The move would have resulted in these employees making substantially less money than they were making with DT. In response, the union threatened a strike, and 11,000 employees actually walked off the job in May 2007. Union negotiations leader Lothar Schröder said the strike was entirely due to management's refusal to consider any compromises offered by the union. Ironically, the man that he was up against in these negotiations was CEO René Obermann, whom he had helped into the top slot.

© OIVER BERG/DPA/LANDOV

A strike between the unionized workforce and management at Deutsche Telekom, a German telecom company, ended only after major stakeholders and the German government got involved.

This strike and the impasse between DT and the union were seen as a massive showdown in the telecom industry. Analysts feared that the recovering German economy and the telecom industry in general would feel severe repercussions if the union carried out its strike for a long period. Obermann insisted that the union was just interested in gaining all their demands and did not really care about the future of the company. DT employs about 160,000 employees and was also planning on major cutbacks in the future.

The strike ended after six weeks with major stakeholders and the German government getting involved. The union completely gave in to the demands of management and accepted pay cuts and longer working hours as a part of the settlement. Many analysts speculate that this was an unscrupulous power game as the German government controls 15 percent of DT's stocks. The union called the solution a "compromise" but some observers declared it a complete sellout.

SOURCE: *F. Dohmen, K. Kerbusk*, and J. Tietz , "DT Strikes a Battle for the Ages," *Business Week Online* (May 16, 2007), http://www.businessweek.com/globalbiz/content/may2007/gb20070516_600514.htm. Editorial Board Statement, "Germany: Union Sells Out Deutsche Telekom Strike—Agrees to Wage Cuts and Longer Working Hours" (June 25, 2007), http://www.wsws.org/articles/2007/jun2007/tele-j25.shtml.

each party wants to maximize its share of the resources (get its part of the pie). It is a competitive or win–lose approach to negotiations. Sometimes distributive bargaining causes negotiators to focus so much on their differences that they ignore their common ground. In these cases, distributive bargaining can become counterproductive. The reality is, however, that some situations are distributive in nature, particularly when the parties are interdependent. If a negotiator wants to maximize the value of a single deal and is not worried about maintaining a good relationship with the other party, distributive bargaining may be an option. The Real World 13.2 illustrates the effects of such a tactic in one major German telecom company.

In contrast, *integrative negotiation* is an approach in which the parties' goals are not seen as mutually exclusive and in which the focus is on making it possible for both sides to achieve their objectives. Integrative negotiation focuses on the merits of the issues and is a win–win approach. (How can we make the pie bigger?) For integrative negotiation to be successful, certain preconditions must be present. These

integrative negotiation
A negotiation approach that focuses on the merits of the issues and seeks a win–win solution.

include having a common goal, faith in one's own problem-solving abilities, a belief in the validity of the other party's position, motivation to work together, mutual trust, and clear communication.[61]

Cultural differences in negotiation must be acknowledged. Japanese negotiators, for example, when working with American negotiators, tend to see their power as coming from their role (buyer versus seller). Americans, in contrast, view their power as their ability to walk away from the negotiations.[62] Neither culture understands the other very well, and the negotiations can resemble a dance in which one person is waltzing and the other doing a samba. The collectivism–individualism dimension (discussed in Chapter 2) has a great bearing on negotiations. Americans, with their individualism, negotiate from a position of self-interest; Japanese focus on the good of the group. Cross-cultural negotiations can be more effective if you learn as much about other cultures as possible.

Gender may also play a role in negotiation. There appears to be no evidence that men are better negotiators than women or vice versa. The differences lie in how negotiators are treated. Women have historically been discriminated against in terms of the offers made to them in negotiations.[63] Gender stereotypes also affect the negotiating process. Women may be seen as accommodating, conciliatory, and emotional (negatives in negotiations), and men may be seen as assertive, powerful, and convincing (positive for negotiations) in accordance with traditional stereotypes. Sometimes, when women feel they're being stereotyped, they exhibit stereotype reactance, which is a tendency to display behavior inconsistent with (or opposite of) the stereotype. This means they become more assertive and convincing. Alternatively, men may hesitate when they're expected to fulfill the stereotype, fearing that they might not be able to live up to the stereotype.

One way to help men and women avoid stereotyping each other is to promote shared, positive identities between the negotiators. This means recognizing similarities between the two parties; for example, recognizing each other as highly successful professionals. This results in more cooperation because of shared and equal status, as opposed to more competition because of gender stereotypes.[64]

CONFLICT MANAGEMENT STYLES

(6) Understand five styles of conflict management, and diagnose your own preferred style.

Managers have at their disposal a variety of conflict management styles: avoiding, accommodating, competing, compromising, and collaborating. One way of classifying styles of conflict management is to examine the styles' assertiveness (the extent to which you want your goals met) and cooperativeness (the extent to which you want to see the other party's concerns met).[65] Figure 13.4 graphs the five conflict management styles using these two dimensions. Table 13.4 lists appropriate situations for using each conflict management style.

Avoiding

Avoiding is a style low on both assertiveness and cooperativeness. Avoiding is a deliberate decision to take no action on a conflict or to stay out of a conflict situation. In recent times, Airbus, a European manufacturer of aircraft, has faced massive intra-organizational conflict stemming from major expansions that included French, German, Spanish, and British subsidiaries within the same parent company. Power struggles among executives, combined with massive changes in organizational structure, are believed to have led to this type of conflict. Airbus seems to be adopting the avoidance strategy in an effort to let these conflicts subside on their own.[66] Some relationship conflicts, such as those involving political norms and personal tastes, may

FIGURE 13.4 Conflict Management Styles

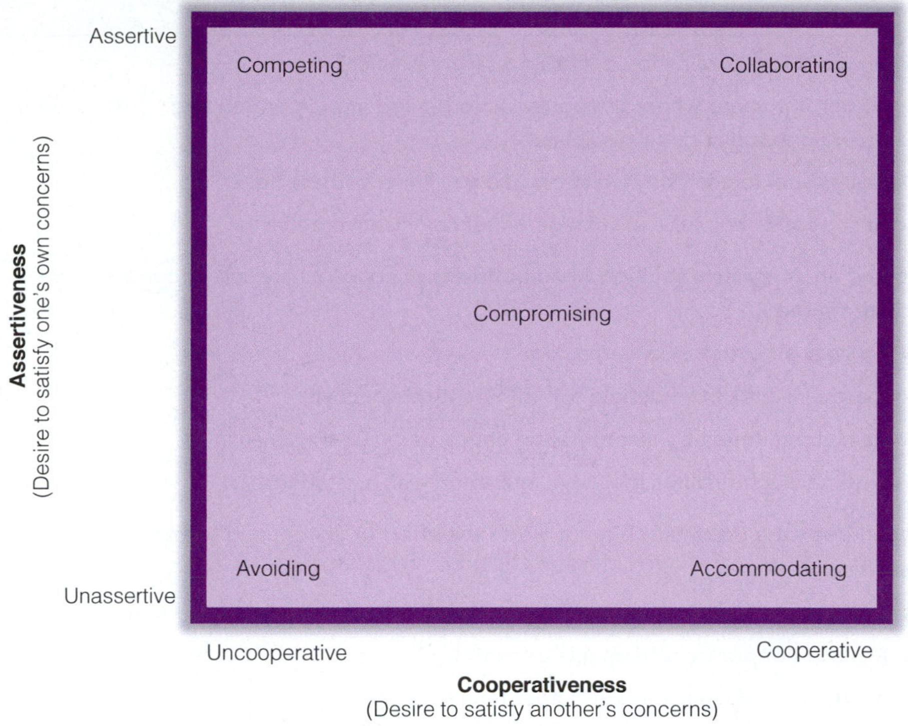

SOURCE: K. W. Thomas, "Conflict and Conflict Management," in M. D. Dunnette, *Handbook of Industrial and Organizational Psychology* (Chicago: Rand McNally, 1976), 900. Used with permission of M. D. Dunnette.

distract team members from their tasks and avoiding may be an appropriate strategy.[67] When the parties are angry and need time to cool down, it may be best to use avoidance. There is a potential danger in using an avoiding style too often, however. Research shows that overuse of this style results in negative evaluations from others in the workplace.[68]

Accommodating

Accommodating is a style in which you are concerned that the other party's goals be met but relatively unconcerned with getting your own way. It is cooperative but unassertive. Appropriate situations for accommodating include times when you find you are wrong, when you want to let the other party have his or her way so that that individual will owe you similar treatment later, or when the relationship is important. Overreliance on accommodating has its dangers. Managers who constantly defer to others may find that others lose respect for them. In addition, accommodating managers may become frustrated because their own needs are never met, and they may lose self-esteem.[69]

Competing

Competing is a style that is very assertive and uncooperative. You want to satisfy your own interests and are willing to do so at the other party's expense. In an emergency or in situations where you know you are right, it may be appropriate to put your foot down. For example, environmentalists forced Shell Oil Company (part of Royal Dutch/Shell Group) to scrap its plans to build a refinery in Delaware after a bitter "To Hell with Shell" campaign.[70] Relying solely on competing strategies is dangerous, though. Managers who do so may become reluctant to admit when they

TABLE 13.4 Uses of Five Styles of Conflict Management

Conflict-Handling Style	Appropriate Situation
Competing	1. When quick, decisive action is vital (e.g., emergencies). 2. On important issues where unpopular actions need implementing (e.g., cost cutting, enforcing unpopular rules, discipline). 3. On issues vital to company welfare when you know you are right. 4. Against people who take advantage of noncompetitive behavior.
Collaborating	1. To find an integrative solution when both sets of concerns are too important to be compromised. 2. When your objective is to learn. 3. To merge insights from people with different perspectives. 4. To gain commitment by incorporating concerns into a consensus. 5. To work through feelings that have interfered with a relationship.
Compromising	1. When goals are important but not worth the effort or potential disruption of more assertive modes. 2. When opponents with equal power are committed to mutually exclusive goals. 3. To achieve temporary settlements to complex issues. 4. To arrive at expedient solutions under time pressure. 5. As a backup when collaboration or competition is unsuccessful.
Avoiding	1. When an issue is trivial or more important issues are pressing. 2. When you perceive no chance of satisfying your concerns. 3. When potential disruption outweighs the benefits of resolution. 4. To let people cool down and regain perspective. 5. When gathering information supersedes immediate decision. 6. When others can resolve the conflict more effectively. 7. When issues seem tangential or symptomatic of other issues.
Accommodating	1. When you find you are wrong—to allow a better position to be heard, to learn, and to show your reasonableness. 2. When issues are more important to others than to yourself—to satisfy others and maintain cooperation. 3. To build social credits for later issues. 4. To minimize loss when you are outmatched and losing. 5. When harmony and stability are especially important. 6. To allow employees to develop by learning from mistakes.

SOURCE: K. W. Thomas, "Toward Multidimensional Values in Teaching: The Example of Conflict Behaviors," *Academy of Management Review* 2 (1977): 309–325.

are wrong and may find themselves surrounded by people who are afraid to disagree with them. In team settings, it has been noted earlier that task conflict and relationship conflict could occur together although task conflict is seen as functional, whereas relationship conflict is seen as dysfunctional for the team. In a recent study, pairs of participants were exposed to task-based conflict. One of the two members of the pairs was trained on using either the competing conflict handling style or the collaborative style. Results indicated that the competing style led to the most relationship

conflict, whereas the collaborative style led to the least relationship conflict after the task conflict was resolved.[71]

Compromising

Compromising style is an intermediate style in both assertiveness and cooperativeness, because each party must give up something to reach a solution to the conflict. Compromises are often made in the final hours of union–management negotiations, when time is of the essence. Compromise may be an effective backup style when efforts toward collaboration are not successful.[72]

It is important to recognize that compromises are not optimal solutions. Compromise means partially surrendering one's position for the sake of coming to terms. Often, when people compromise, they inflate their demands to begin with. The solutions reached may only be temporary, and often compromises do nothing to improve relationships between the parties in the conflict.

Collaborating

Collaborating is a win–win style that is high on both assertiveness and cooperativeness. Working toward collaborating involves an open and thorough discussion of the conflict and arriving at a solution that is satisfactory to both parties. Situations where collaboration may be effective include times when both parties need to be committed to a final solution or when a combination of different perspectives can be formed into a solution. Collaborating requires open, trusting behavior and sharing information for the benefit of both parties. Long term, it leads to improved relationships and effective performance.[73]

Research on the five styles of conflict management indicates that although most managers favor a certain style, they have the capacity to change styles as the situation demands.[74] A study of project managers found that managers who used a combination of competing and avoiding styles were seen as ineffective by the engineers who worked on their project teams.[75] In another study of conflicts between R&D project managers and technical staff, competing and avoiding styles resulted in more frequent conflict and lower performance, whereas the collaborating style resulted in less frequent conflict and better performance.[76] Use You 13.2 to assess your dominant conflict management style.

Cultural differences also influence the use of different styles of conflict management. For example, one study compared Turkish and Jordanian managers with U.S. managers. All three groups preferred the collaborating style. Turkish managers also reported frequent use of the competing style, whereas Jordanian and U.S. managers reported that it was one of their least used styles.[77]

The human resources manager of one U.S. telecommunications company's office in Singapore engaged a consultant to investigate the conflict in the office.[78] Twenty-two expatriates from the United States and Canada and thirty-eight Singaporeans worked in the office. The consultant used the Thomas model (Figure 13.4) and distributed questionnaires to all managers to determine their conflict management styles. The results were not surprising: The expatriate managers preferred the competing, collaborating, and compromising styles, while the Asians preferred the avoiding and accommodating styles.

Workshops were conducted within the firm to develop an understanding of the differences and how they negatively affected the firm. The Asians interpreted the results as reflecting the tendency of Americans to "shout first and ask questions later." They felt that the Americans had an arrogant attitude and could not handle having their ideas rejected. The Asians attributed their own styles to their

What Is Your Conflict-Handling Style?

Instructions:

For each of the fifteen items, indicate how often you rely on that tactic by circling the appropriate number.

	Rarely Always
1. I argue my case with my coworkers to show the merits of my position.	1—2—3—4—5
2. I negotiate with my coworkers so that a compromise can be reached.	1—2—3—4—5
3. I try to satisfy the expectations of my coworkers.	1—2—3—4—5
4. I try to investigate an issue with my coworkers to find a solution acceptable to us.	1—2—3—4—5
5. I am firm in pursuing my side of the issue.	1—2—3—4—5
6. I attempt to avoid being "put on the spot" and try to keep my conflict with my coworkers to myself.	1—2—3—4—5
7. I hold on to my solution to a problem.	1—2—3—4—5
8. I use "give and take" so that a compromise can be made.	1—2—3—4—5
9. I exchange accurate information with my coworkers to solve a problem together.	1—2—3—4—5
10. I avoid open discussion of my differences with my coworkers.	1—2—3—4—5
11. I accommodate the wishes of my coworkers.	1—2—3—4—5
12. I try to bring all our concerns out in the open so that the issues can be resolved in the best possible way.	1—2—3—4—5
13. I propose a middle ground for breaking deadlocks.	1—2—3—4—5
14. I go along with the suggestions of my coworkers.	1—2—3—4—5
15. I try to keep my disagreements with my coworkers to myself in order to avoid hard feelings.	1—2—3—4—5

Scoring Key:

Collaborating		Accommodating		Competing		Avoiding		Compromising	
Item	**Score**	**Item**	**Score**	**Item**	**Score**	**Item**	**Score**	**Item**	**Score**
4.	____	3.	____	1.	____	6.	____	2.	____
9.	____	11.	____	5.	____	10.	____	8.	____
12.	____	14.	____	7.	____	15.	____	13.	____
Total =	____	Total =	____	Total =	____	Total =	____	Total =	____

Your primary conflict-handling style is: ______
(The category with the highest total.)

Your backup conflict-handling style is: ______
(The category with the second highest total.)

SOURCE: Reprinted with permission of Academy of Management, PO Box 3020, Briar Cliff Manor, NY 10510-8020. *A Measure of Styles of Handling Interpersonal Conflict* (adaptation), M. A. Rahim, *Academy of Management Journal*, June 1983. Reproduced by permission of the publisher via Copyright Clearance Center, Inc.

cultural background. The Americans attributed the results to the stereotypical view of Asians as unassertive and timid, and they viewed their own results as reflecting their desire to "get things out in the open."

The process opened a dialogue between the two groups, who began to work on the idea of harmony through conflict. They began to discard the traditional stereotypes in favor of shared meanings and mutual understanding.

China is one of the biggest marketplaces in the world, and negotiating with the Chinese is very frustrating for Americans due to a lack of understanding of Chinese conflict management styles. One study indicated that compromising and avoiding are the most preferred conflict handling styles among the Chinese. Interestingly, the Chinese reported the most satisfaction with a business negotiation when accommodating and competing approaches were used by both parties.[79]

It is important to remember that preventing and resolving dysfunctional conflict is only half the task of effective conflict management. Stimulating functional conflict is the other half.

© CHINA NEWSPHOTO/REUTERS/CORBIS

Chinese and American businesspersons have begun to discard the traditional stereotypes in favor of shared meanings and mutual understandings.

MANAGERIAL IMPLICATIONS: CREATING A CONFLICT-POSITIVE ORGANIZATION

Dean Tjosvold argues that well-managed conflict adds to an organization's innovation and productivity.[80] He discusses procedures for making conflict positive. Too many organizations take a win–lose, competitive approach to conflict or avoid conflict altogether. These two approaches view conflict as negative. A positive view of conflict, in contrast, leads to win–win solutions. Figure 13.5 illustrates these three approaches to conflict management.

Four interrelated steps are involved in creating a conflict-positive organization:

1. *Value diversity and confront differences.* Differences should be seen as opportunities for innovation, and diversity should be celebrated. Open and honest confrontations bring out differences, and they are essential for positive conflict.
2. *Seek mutual benefits and unite behind cooperative goals.* Conflicts have to be managed together. Through conflict, individuals learn how much they depend on one another. Even when employees share goals, they may differ on how to accomplish the goals. The important point is that they are moving toward the same objectives. Joint rewards should be given to the whole team for cooperative behavior.

FIGURE 13.5 Three Organization Views of Conflict

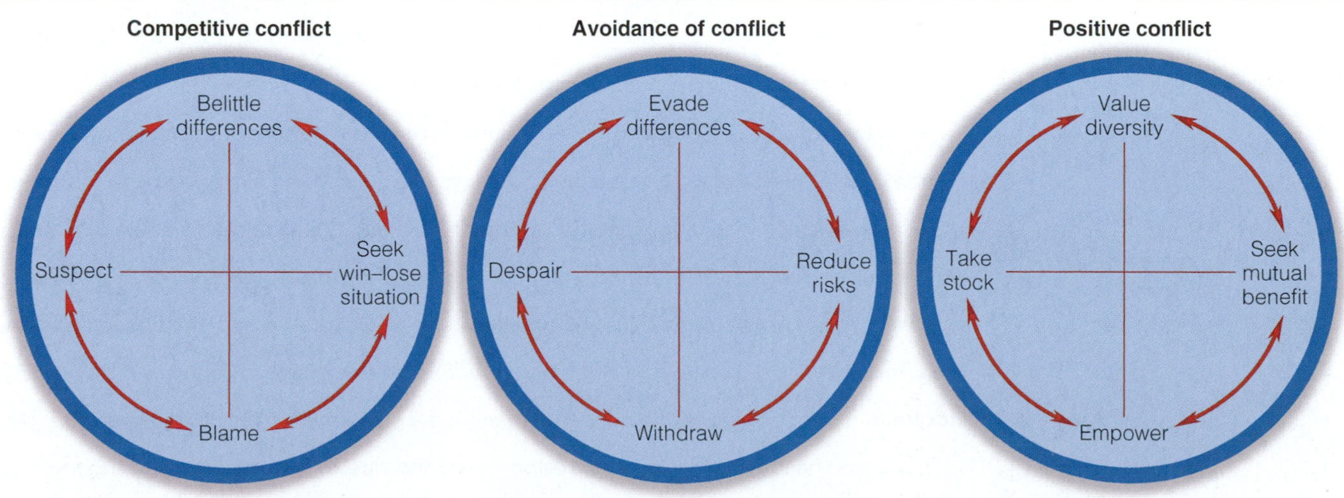

SOURCE: *The Conflict Positive Organization*, by Dean Tjosvold, © 1991. Reprinted by permission of Prentice-Hall, Inc., Upper Saddle River, N.J.

3. *Empower employees to feel confident and skillful.* People must be made to feel that they control their conflicts and that they can deal with their differences productively. When they do so, they should be recognized.
4. *Take stock to reward success and learn from mistakes.* Employees should be encouraged to appreciate one another's strengths and weaknesses and to talk directly about them. They should celebrate their conflict managment successes and work out plans for ways they can improve in the future.

Tjosvold believes that a conflict-positive organization has competitive advantages for the future.

A complimentary perspective comes from Peter J. Frost, who proposed that over time, organizational practices like poor conflict management can "poison" the organization as well as those who work within it. He describes how compassionate leaders can help reduce the effects of organizational toxins on their coworkers and how these toxin handlers should be rewarded for this crucial role in maintaining organizational health. Frost's position echoes Tjosvold's, as he calls for firms to become emotionally healthy workplaces for the good of their employees as well as for the good of their stockholders.[81]

Finally, don't overlook the importance of high emotional intelligence in the work of a good conflict manager. The ability to influence your own and others' emotions is not just a practical tool, but it can also serve as an important tactical asset, making you a better negotiator in a variety of situations and helping reduce conflict and increase productivity in your organization.[82]

LOOKING BACK: GENENTECH, INC.

Genentech: Lessons Learned from Many Conflicts

In Looking Ahead, we profiled the legal woes of Genentech and the huge fines it had to pay for unauthorized use of a patented protein drug development system. That was not the end of its legal troubles. In 1995, when current CEO Arthur Levinson took over, Genentech was in financial trouble and had just pleaded guilty to federal criminal charges of marketing a human growth hormone for uses not approved by the FDA. Genentech ended up paying $50 million in fines for this charge.

Next, in the 2002–2004 period, when its major cancer treatment drug Avastin was failing clinical trials, Levinson had to face crowds of angry investors urging him to suspend further research on Avastin. They also wanted Genentech to change its strategy of going after high-impact niche drugs such as cancer treatments and target mass medicinal drugs. Levinson, however, stood his ground because he believed in the power of Avastin in helping to fight cancer. Today, Avastin is one of the company's blockbuster drugs, already approved by the FDA for treatment of two types of cancer and awaiting decision on the treatment of breast cancer.

Levinson handled conflicts with investors by staying true to his values and staying involved with the R&D process. He also made sure that Genentech was less exposed to legal wrangling by requiring examination of all their sales information by their legal and regulatory departments.[83]

Chapter Summary

1. Conflict management skills are keys to management success. The manager's task is to stimulate functional conflict and prevent or resolve dysfunctional conflict.
2. Structural causes of conflict include specialization, interdependence, common resources, goal differences, authority relationships, status inconsistencies, and jurisdictional ambiguities.
3. Personal factors that lead to conflict include differences in skills and abilities, personalities, perceptions, or values and ethics; emotions; communication barriers; and cultural differences. The increasing diversity of the workforce and globalization of business have potential to increase conflict arising from these differences.
4. The levels of conflict include interorganizational, intergroup, interpersonal, and intrapersonal.
5. Individuals engaged in interpersonal conflict often display aggressive, compromise, or withdrawal defense mechanisms.
6. Ineffective techniques for managing conflict include nonaction, secrecy, administrative orbiting, due process nonaction, and character assassination.
7. Effective techniques for managing conflict include appealing to superordinate goals, expanding resources, changing personnel, changing structure, and confronting and negotiating.
8. In negotiating, managers can use a variety of conflict management styles, including avoiding, accommodating, competing, compromising, and collaborating.
9. Managers should strive to create a conflict-positive organization—one that values diversity, empowers employees, and seeks win–win solutions to conflicts.

Key Terms

administrative orbiting (p. 450)
character assassination (p. 450)
compensation (p. 448)
conflict (p. 436)
conversion (p. 449)
displacement (p. 448)
distributive bargaining (p. 452)
due process nonaction (p. 450)
dysfunctional conflict (p. 437)
fantasy (p. 449)
fixation (p. 447)
flight/withdrawal (p. 449)
functional conflict (p. 436)
identification (p. 448)
integrative negotiation (p. 453)
intergroup conflict (p. 442)
interorganizational conflict (p. 442)
interpersonal conflict (p. 443)
interrole conflict (p. 445)
intragroup conflict (p. 443)
intrapersonal conflict (p. 445)
intrarole conflict (p. 445)
jurisdictional ambiguity (p. 439)
negativism (p. 448)
nonaction (p. 450)
person–role conflict (p. 445)
rationalization (p. 449)
secrecy (p. 450)
superordinate goal (p. 451)

Review Questions

1. Discuss the differences between functional and dysfunctional conflict. Why should a manager understand conflict?
2. Identify the structural and personal factors that contribute to conflict.
3. Discuss the four major forms of conflict in organizations.
4. What defense mechanisms do people use in interpersonal conflict?
5. What are the most effective techniques for managing conflict at work? What are some ineffective techniques?
6. Identify and discuss five styles of conflict management.

Discussion and Communication Questions

1. What causes you the most conflict at work or school?
2. Identify the different intragroup, interrole, intrarole, and person–role conflicts that you experience.
3. Which defense mechanism do you see people exhibiting most frequently? Why do you think this is the case? How can you manage this type of reaction to a conflict?
4. Are you comfortable with your preferred conflict management style? Would you consider modifying it?
5. *(communication question)* Think of a person with whom you have had a recent conflict. Write a letter to this person, attempting to resolve the conflict. Use the concepts from the chapter to accomplish your objective. Be sure to address whether the conflict is functional or dysfunctional, what styles each party has used, effective strategies for resolving the conflict, and ineffective strategies that should be avoided.

Ethical Dilemma

Scott Davis sat at his desk anxiously waiting for the next few minutes to pass. It was almost time for the meeting he had scheduled between Debra Cronin and Ken Brown. Scott knew this meeting would be challenging for everyone. Debra and Ken had been at odds for quite some time. The problems started soon after Ken joined the company. At first Scott thought the conflict was healthy and would bring some much-needed change to the department. Scott soon learned that the disputes between Debra and Ken were more personal than professional.

Debra had been with the company for seven years. Scott had no complaints about her performance. She was a hard worker who got the job done. Unfortunately, Debra was also the source of a lot of conflict in the department. She always felt she knew the best way to do everything and freely shared that opinion with everyone, whether they wanted it or not. Scott has spent many hours listening to employees' complaints about Debra's insistence on showing them the "proper" way to do their jobs. Debra's interference had caused a fair amount of discontent in the department, but Scott never felt it was enough to consider termination. The meeting today might well change that opinion.

Ken Brown was new to the company. He had joined Scott's department just four months ago. He was young, with a lot of fresh ideas. Scott liked everything about Ken and thought he would be great for the department and the company. But like those before him, Ken found working with Debra difficult. She was set in her ways and was not going to change. Worse, she was undermining the other employees' interest in changing. Scott felt that he had done everything he could to resolve the conflict between the two, without success. He felt sure that today's meeting would end with one person leaving the company. His decision was which one: Debra, the longtime employee, or Ken, the newcomer with a vision for the future?

Questions

1. Does Scott have a greater responsibility to Debra than to Ken?
2. To whom does Scott owe the greatest responsibility?
3. Evaluate Scott's decision alternatives using consequential, rule-based, and character theories.

Experiential Exercises

13.1 Conflicts over Unethical Behavior

Many conflicts in work organizations arise over differences in beliefs concerning what constitutes ethical versus unethical behavior. The following questionnaire provides a list of behaviors that you or your coworkers might engage in when working for a company. Go over each item, and circle the number that best indicates the frequency with which you personally would (or do, if you work now) engage in that behavior. Then put an *X* over the number you think represents how often your coworkers would (or do) engage in that behavior. Finally, put a check mark beside the item (in the "Needs Control" column) if you believe that management should control that behavior.

	At Every Opportunity	Often	About Half the Time	Seldom	Never	Needs Control
1. Passing blame for errors to an innocent coworker.	5	4	3	2	1	____
2. Divulging confidential information.	5	4	3	2	1	____
3. Falsifying time/quality/quantity reports.	5	4	3	2	1	____
4. Claiming credit for someone else's work.	5	4	3	2	1	____
5. Padding an expense account by over 10 percent.	5	4	3	2	1	____
6. Pilfering company materials and supplies.	5	4	3	2	1	____
7. Accepting gifts/favors in exchange for preferential treatment.	5	4	3	2	1	____
8. Giving gifts/favors in exchange for preferential treatment.	5	4	3	2	1	____
9. Padding an expense account by up to 10 percent.	5	4	3	2	1	____
10. Authorizing a subordinate to violate company rules.	5	4	3	2	1	____

	At Every Opportunity	Often	About Half the Time	Seldom	Never	Needs Control
11. Calling in sick to take a day off.	5	4	3	2	1	____
12. Concealing one's errors.	5	4	3	2	1	____
13. Taking longer than necessary to do a job.	5	4	3	2	1	____
14. Using company services for personal use.	5	4	3	2	1	____
15. Doing personal business on company time.	5	4	3	2	1	____
16. Taking extra personal time (lunch hour, breaks, early departure, and so forth).	5	4	3	2	1	____
17. Not reporting others' violations of company policies and rules.	5	4	3	2	1	____
18. Overlooking a superior's violation of policy to prove loyalty to the boss.	5	4	3	2	1	____

Discussion Questions

1. Would (do) your coworkers seem to engage in these behaviors more often than you would (do)? Why do you have this perception?
2. Which behaviors tend to be most frequent?
3. How are the most frequent behaviors different from the behaviors engaged in less frequently?
4. What are the most important items for managers to control? How should managers control these behaviors?
5. Select a particular behavior from the list. Have two people debate whether the behavior is ethical or not.
6. What types of conflicts could emerge if the behaviors in the list occurred frequently?

13.2 The World Bank Game: An Intergroup Negotiation

The purposes of this exercise are to learn about conflict and trust between groups and to practice negotiation skills. In the course of the exercise, money will be won or lost. Your team's objective is to win as much money as it can. Your team will be paired with another team, and both teams will receive identical instructions. After reading these instructions, each team will have ten minutes to plan its strategy.

Each team is assumed to have contributed $50 million to the World Bank. Teams may have to pay more or may receive money from the World Bank, depending on the outcome.

Each team will receive twenty cards. These cards are the weapons. Each card has a marked side (*X*) and an unmarked side. The marked side signifies that the weapon is armed; the unmarked side signifies that the weapon is unarmed.

At the beginning, each team will place ten of its twenty weapons in their armed position (marked side up) and the remaining ten in their unarmed position (marked side down). The weapons will remain in the team's possession and out of sight of the other team at all times.

The game will consist of *rounds* and *moves*. Each round will be composed of seven moves by each team. There will be two or more rounds in the game, depending on the time available. Payoffs will be determined and recorded after each round. The rules are as follows:

1. A move consists of turning two, one, or none of the team's weapons from armed to unarmed status, or vice versa.
2. Each team has one-and-a-half minutes for each move. There is a thirty-second period between each move. At the end of the one-and-a-half minutes, the team must have turned two, one, or none of its weapons from armed to unarmed status or from unarmed to armed status. If the team fails to move in the allotted time, no change can be made in weapon status until the next move.
3. The two-minute length of the period between the beginning of one move and the beginning of the next is unalterable.

Finances:

The funds each team has contributed to the World Bank are to be allocated in the following manner: $30 million will be returned to each team to be used as the team's treasury during the course of the game, and $20 million will be retained for the operation of the World Bank.

Payoffs:

1. If there is an attack:
   a. Each team may announce an attack on the other team by notifying the banker during the thirty seconds following any minute-and-a-half period used to decide upon the move (including the

seventh, or final, decision period in any round). The choice of each team during the decision period just ended counts as a move. An attack may not be made during negotiations.

b. If there is an attack by one or both teams, two things happen: (1) the round ends, and (2) the World Bank assesses a penalty of $2.5 million on each team.

c. The team with the greater number of armed weapons wins $1.5 million for each armed weapon it has over and above the number of armed weapons of the other team. These funds are paid directly from the treasury of the losing team to the treasury of the winning team. The banker will manage the transfer of funds.

2. If there is no attack:

   At the end of each round (seven moves), each team's treasury will receive from the World Bank $1 million for each of its weapons that is at that point unarmed; and each team's treasury will pay to the World Bank $1 million for each of its weapons remaining armed.

Negotiations:

Between moves, each team will have the opportunity to communicate with the other team through its negotiations. Either team may call for negotiations by notifying the banker during any of the thirty-second periods between decisions. A team is free to accept or reject any invitation to negotiate.

Negotiators from both teams are required to meet after the third and sixth moves (after the thirty-second period following the move, if there is no attack).

Negotiations can last no longer than three minutes. When the two negotiators return to their teams, the minute-and-a-half decision period for the next move will begin once again.

Negotiators are bound only by (1) the three-minute time limit for negotiations and (2) their required appearance after the third and sixth moves. They are always free to say whatever is necessary to benefit themselves or their teams. The teams are not bound by agreements made by their negotiators, even when those agreements are made in good faith.

Special Roles:

Each team has ten minutes to organize itself and plan team strategy. During this period, before the first round begins, each team must choose persons to fill the following roles:

- A *negotiator*—activities stated above.
- A *representative*—to communicate the team's decisions to the banker.
- A *recorder*—to record the moves of the team and to keep a running balance of the team's treasury.
- A *treasurer*—to execute all financial transactions with the banker.

The instructor will serve as the banker for the World Bank and will signal the beginning of each of the rounds.

At the end of the game, each participant should complete the following questionnaire, which assesses reactions to the World Bank Game.

World Bank Questionnaire:

1. To what extent are you satisfied with your team's strategy?

   Highly dissatisfied 1 2 3 4 5 6 7 Highly satisfied

2. To what extent do you believe the other team is trustworthy?

   Highly untrustworthy 1 2 3 4 5 6 7 Highly trustworthy

3. To what extent are you satisfied with the performance of your negotiator?

   Highly dissatisfied 1 2 3 4 5 6 7 Highly satisfied

4. To what extent was there a consensus on your team regarding its moves?

   Very little 1 2 3 4 5 6 7 A great deal

5. To what extent do you trust the other members of your team?

   Very little 1 2 3 4 5 6 7 A great deal

6. Select one word that describes how you feel about your team: ______________________.

7. Select one word that describes how you feel about the other team: ____________________.

Negotiators only:

How did you see the other team's negotiator?

Phony and insincere 1 2 3 4 5 6 7 Authentic and sincere

At the end of the game, the class will reconvene and discuss team members' responses to the World Bank Questionnaire. In addition, the following questions are to be addressed:

1. What was each team's strategy for winning? What strategy was most effective?
2. Contrast the outcomes in terms of win–win solutions to conflict versus win–lose solutions.

SOURCE: Adapted by permission from N. H. Berkowitz and H. A. Hornstein, "World Bank: An Intergroup Negotiation," in J. W. Pfeiffer and J. E. Jones, eds., *The 1975 Handbook for Group Facilitators* (San Diego: Pfeiffer), 58–62.

WORLD BANK RECORD SHEET

	Round One		Round Two		Round Three		Round Four	
	Armed	Unarmed	Armed	Unarmed	Armed	Unarmed	Armed	Unarmed
Move	10	10	10	10	10	10	10	10
1								
2								
3								
Required Negotiation								
4								
5								
6								
Required Negotiation								
7								

Funds in Team Treasury	$30 million				
Funds of Other Treasury	$30 million				
Funds in World Bank	$40 million				

TAKE 2

Biz Flix | The Guru

"Deepak Chopra meets Dr. Ruth" is a possible alternate title or subtitle for this film. The film follows Ramu Gupta's (Jimi Mistry) journey from India to the United States where he wants to become a film star. Unlucky at keeping a job, Ramu is fired from a waiter's job and a pornographic film role. By closely following the advice of Sharrona (Heather Graham), his ex-pornographic co-star, Ramu becomes a highly acclaimed though mystical sex therapist.

The scene from *The Guru* appears in the final quarter of the film. It occurs after Ramu starts his performance at the Broadway Playhouse to a packed, enthusiastic audience. By this time in the film, he has become a renowned sex therapist who has moved from individual therapy to public performances. The film continues after this scene with self-appointed manager Vijay (Emil Marwa) bringing several beautiful women to Ramu's new apartment.

What to Watch for and Ask Yourself:

> What is the latent conflict (cause of conflict) that triggered this conflict event or episode?

> What conflict management style do Ramu and Sharrona use during this episode?

> Do they end the conflict with a clear conflict aftermath? Do you expect the conflict to continue? Why or why not?

Workplace Video | Managing in a Global Environment, Featuring Yahoo

Yahoo is a global-business success story. Launched as the hobby of two Stanford University graduate students in 1995, the search-engine portal has become one of the most trafficked Web sites in the world. Millions of netizens visit Yahoo for headline news and entertainment, and the site's loyal account members log on daily to check e-mail and use community services like Yahoo Groups and Yahoo Personals.

Attracting international audiences is a daunting task, and Yahoo uses various strategies to reach the world's billion-plus Internet users. For example, the company translates its Web properties and services into thirteen languages. In addition, the Sunnyvale, California-based company garners international interest through globally produced online events, such as Yahoo Time Capsule—a Web-based repository of personal musings posted by individuals in over 200 countries.

While access to billions of people creates enormous opportunity, having a global reach also puts strain on an organization. Managing conflict and overcoming international barriers is the job of Yahoo's offices in Europe, Asia-Pacific, Latin America, and Canada. These regional offices are generally effective in situating Yahoo's business within a local context outside the United States. They do not resolve all conflict, however, as opening offices overseas presents economic, political, and sociocultural challenges. Increasingly Yahoo looks to experienced global managers and teams to deal with such conflicts.

Despite its prestigious past, Yahoo maintains a forward-looking focus. Competitors like Google and MySpace threaten the relevance of Yahoo's services, and managing 11,000 employees worldwide requires twenty-first-century managerial thinking. Nevertheless, the

TAKE 2

continued strength of Yahoo's brand long after the dot-com bust seems a harbinger of future success. The company's management have shown they have both the global savvy and conflict-resolution skills necessary to lead the Internet to its next phase of growth.

Discussion Questions

1. What structural factors can lead to conflict at Yahoo and other global corporations?
2. What personal factors can lead to conflict at Yahoo?
3. How might Yahoo's managers diagnose if a specific conflict is functional or dysfunctional?

CASE

Molson Coors Brewing Company: Conflict Resolution in the Aftermath of a Merger

In the mid-1990s a dispute developed between rival factions of the Molson family for control of its business empire, including the Molson brewing business. Cousins Eric Molson and Ian Molson were pitted against one another in this struggle for control.[1] They clashed at board meetings, with their differences becoming increasingly intense and embittered. At a January 2003 board meeting, Eric announced a review of Molson's corporate governance. While a surprise to the board, the review was nonetheless conducted. The governance report recommended eliminating Ian's position as deputy chairman. Ian confronted Eric but nothing was resolved. At the following November board meeting, the recommendation to eliminate Ian's position was defeated. At the May 2004 meeting, three board members, including Ian, resigned in protest over Eric's leadership of the company. The remainder of the board chose to reaffirm Eric's status as chairman. At the company's annual meeting the following month, Ian and four other members of the family-controlled board refused to stand for re-election.[2]

Meanwhile, Molson Inc. and Adolph Coors Co. initiated merger talks. The two companies had been working together since 1998, with each distributing the other's products in its home territory. The major hurdle to the proposed merger was the feud between the two factions of the Molson family. Eric, who along with allied family members controlled more than half the voting shares, favored the merger. Ian, with approximately 10 percent of the voting shares, was against the merger. A shareholder agreement between Ian and Eric prevented either one from transferring or selling his voting shares without the consent of the other.[3] Eric maintained that he had found a legal way to circumvent the agreement. Ian, on the other hand, was preparing to offer as much as $4 billion to acquire Molson Inc. in order to prevent the merger with Coors.[4] On July 22, 2004, the two companies jointly announced the merger of Molson and Coors.[5] As a result, Molson Coors became the third-largest brewer in the United States and the fifth largest in the world, operating primarily in three mature markets—Canada, the United States, and the United Kingdom.[6]

"At the time of the merger, bringing together the Molson and Coors families seemed like a recipe for disaster. One was Canadian. One was American. One was east. One was west. And they both built their businesses in different ways."[7] Even nearly three years afterwards, ". . . the merger is still a sore point with some, including Eric's cousin Ian Molson, who saw the 'merger of equals' as an outright takeover—and not an advantageous one for shareholders at that."[8] Nonetheless, just "[t]wo years after the highly publicized merger . . . the management problems anticipated by many analysts—most notably a power struggle between two long standing brewing families—have yet to come to pass. In fact, Molson Coors Brewing Co . . . is leveraging the strength of its family-based culture to strategically focus on brand building and growing its domestic and international beer business."[9]

How has Molson Coors Brewing avoided being decimated by conflict? CEO Leo Kiely, in describing how they were able to successfully merge two companies with strong cultures and traditions, cited two key factors. One factor involved investing local teams with the responsibility for their markets since the markets of the pre-merger Molson and Coors did not overlap much. The second factor was celebrating the two companies' common features—a strong family heritage and a passion for brewing beer.[10]

According to Kiely, the first priority after the merger was to get "a good balanced team in place."[11] After the merger of Molson and Coors, the senior management team was reorganized by drawing in people from both companies and both families and by establishing executive headquarters in both Denver and Montreal. Eric Molson serves as chairman of the board, and Peter Coors serves as vice chairman. Eric Molson works from Montreal, Canada, and CEO Kiely, from the Coors side, runs the merged company from Denver.[12] Other members of both the Molson and Coors families play active roles in the business.[13]

Another major factor in avoiding debilitating conflict was the similar business interests and heritage of the two companies. Geoff Molson, a seventh-generation family member working in the business, says "the thing outsiders don't understand is that the families' passion for brewing was 'really the essential ingredient' in getting the deal done." Molson continues, "In the past two years, we've had differences, identified them, and figured out a way to address them together with the interests of building the beer business at the same time."[14]

Although the merged company reflects twenty-first-century globalization and consolidation within the brewing industry, "each of the two companies is fighting to keep its identity, which is rooted in the past."[15] Regarding the Canadian side of the merger, Eric Molson says, "Since 1786, playing a part in the community has been the Molson tradition—a tradition that is woven into the cultural fabric of Molson and our family, and continues to thrive today. We are very proud to be part of this country, from coast to coast."[16] A similar perspective applies to the Coors traditions. Indeed, the family aspect and community involvement of both Molson and Coors define the separate histories of the companies as well as the present times of the merged Molson Coors Brewing.[17]

Will the two families of Molson Coors Brewing be able to continue working together amiably as they face an increasingly globalized and consolidated brewing industry? Addressing this dilemma became increasing more complicated on October 9, 2007 when Molson Coors and SABMiller PLC announced plans to merge their United States operations. The Molson and Coors families did not want to sell the entire brewing company to SABMiller, and consequently the company's operations in Canada and the United Kingdom will remain independent of SABMiller.[18]

Discussion Questions

1. From your perspective, were the consequences of the conflict between Eric Molson and Ian Molson positive or negative?
2. What *ineffective* techniques for managing conflict are evident in the case?
3. What *effective* techniques for managing conflict are evident in the case?

SOURCE: This case was written by Michael K. McCuddy, The Louis S. and Mary L. Morgal Chair of Christian Business Ethics and Professor of Management, College of Business Administration, Valparaiso University.

BP: The Dynamics of Leading a Large Global Organization

From its humble beginnings just over a century ago, BP has developed into a global energy giant employing over 96,000 people. On a daily basis, the company serves approximately 13 million customers in over 100 nations around the world.[1] BP has become the second-largest oil company in the world behind ExxonMobil.[2] A good deal of this phenomenal growth can be attributed to the leadership of John P. Browne, from his appointment as CEO in 1995 until his resignation from that position on May 1, 2007. At that time, Tony Hayward assumed the mantle of leadership as BP's CEO.

John Browne: CEO, 1995 to May 2007

John P. Browne, educated at Cambridge University in the United Kingdom, joined BP as a university apprentice in 1966. He eventually became head of BP's exploration unit, and then in 1995 became CEO.[3] Not long after that, Browne embarked on a strategic path that would significantly alter BP's stature in the oil industry. He reasoned that a limited world supply of oil and gas reserves meant that the best alternative for BP's future growth would be through the acquisition other oil companies.[4] This logic, coupled with the fact that world oil market prices were hovering close to $10 a barrel in the late 1990s, enabled Browne to convince BP's board of directors that acquisition of other oil companies and cost cutting were the only ways to survive.

The first acquisition occurred in 1998 when BP and Chicago-based Amoco Corporation merged. Interestingly, this merger set off numerous copycat deals within the oil industry.[5] The Amoco deal, worth $52 billion, turned BP, a midsize British company, into one of the world's energy giants. The deal put BP in a league with Royal Dutch/Shell and ExxonMobil. In conjunction with the Amoco acquisition, Browne promised he would slash $2 billion a year from expenses, half of which would come from the information technology area where there were overlapping systems and staffs.[6]

Subsequent to the Amoco merger, Browne engineered acquisitions of ARCO in 1999 and Burmah Castrol in 2000.[7] He also formed a partnership with the Russian company TNK to develop energy resources in Eastern Siberia.[8] BP's initiatives, as well as those of other oil companies, led to considerable consolidation within the oil industry. All these successes gave Browne his reputation as "an oilman's oilman."[9] In recent years, however, "critics have blamed the big spending cuts that accompanied the industry's consolidation for curtailing supply and contributing to today's super-high oil prices."[10]

Browne has also received accolades for being the first oilman to embrace the concept of global warming and emphasize environmental concerns. "As early as 1997, in a speech at Stanford Business School, he acknowledged the problem of climate change, the first leader of the oil industry to do so."[11] BP also became engaged in significant efforts to develop alternative energy sources, including biofuels, solar energy, and hydrogen fuels.[12] Then by 2003, BP had rebranded itself, with its initials now signifying *Beyond Petroleum*.[13]

After the Texas City, Texas, refinery explosion and fire, an investigative panel headed by James Baker found fault with the cost-cutting mentality associated with BP's culture. The Baker panel "determined that BP's management did not devote enough money or effort to ensuring safety at its American refineries."[14] Additionally, they commented on Browne's reputation as an advocate of reducing carbon dioxide emissions and promoting alternative fuels. In comparing his leadership on environmental and safety issues, the Baker panel observed, "[i]f Browne had demonstrated comparable leadership on and commitment to process safety, that leadership and commitment would likely have resulted in a higher level of process safety performance in BP's US refineries.'"[15] The Baker panel also noted that BP has "not adequately established process safety as a core value."[16]

Browne, however, "insists that there is no pattern to BP's various problems and no over-arching failure of management."[17] Yet other people believe BP's management is not assertive enough. Neil McMahon, with the Sanford Bernstein financial services firm, argues that BP should be reorganized in order to reduce the decentralized autonomy of its multiple units and to ensure more consistent policies and standards.[18]

Shortly before the Baker Panel's report was issued, Browne said that he would accelerate his scheduled retirement by seventeen months, to the end of July 2007. This announcement reinforced the growing perception "that something had gone badly wrong at BP and that a fresh start was needed to set the firm to rights."[19] Then on May 1, 2007, Browne abruptly resigned as BP's CEO.[20] Nigel Davis, a longtime observer of the oil industry, commented: "BP has lost its most influential leader and one of the most respected businessmen of his generation. Browne succeeded in areas where others could not. He transformed BP, indeed the oil world, with ground breaking deals with Amoco, Arco, Burmah Castrol, Veba Oel and Russia's TNK. The value of the company rocketed under his tenure. He has been called a businessman of intuition, vision and foresight. Yet those qualities appeared to leave him in his latter days as BP CEO."[21]

Tony Hayward: CEO, May 2007 to . . .

Browne's abrupt resignation did not catch the company unprepared. BP and the board of directors already had a succession plan in place for Tony Hayward. These preparations reflected, in part, efforts to deal with the accumulated safety and environmental problems from the past few years. As one observer noted, "the company seems to be gearing down and taking a close look at its operations, some of which have been troubled. BP may even be trying to ease the pressure on Hayward by lowering expectations."[22] Hayward probably will not change BP's strategy—at least very quickly. However, he has indicated he will put a new emphasis on safety given the series of operational problems that have occurred over the past two years.[23] Indeed, Hayward believes that in dealing with these operational problems, "BP's top brass were too imperious and failed to heed the concerns of the lower ranks."[24]

Hayward "spent his entire career at BP, much of it as . . . Browne's protégé, so he is steeped in its culture."[25] His knowledge of that culture can help him institute change. Yet he may be less inclined to initiate cultural—and structural—change *because* he has been so much a part of BP.

Initial indications are that Hayward may lead BP a bit differently than Browne did. Browne remained aloof from most BP staff members. Hayward is operating differently—for example, stopping by the basement cafeteria of BP's London headquarters. Moreover, "[o]n recent visits to the company's U.S. refineries, he spent hours talking to equipment operators rather than huddled with senior managers."[26]

Will the new leadership at the top of BP help in addressing the company's multiple challenges?

Discussion Questions

1. How would you describe John Browne's approach to leadership?
2. How would you describe Tony Hayward's approach to leadership?
3. How did Browne's approach to leadership affect communications and decision making at BP? How did his leadership approach reflect the use of power?
4. How might Tony Hayward's leadership approach affect work group dynamics within BP? How might his approach impact the resolution of conflict?

SOURCE: This case was written by Michael K. McCuddy, The Louis S. and Mary L. Morgal Chair of Christian Business Ethics and Professor of Management, College of Business Administration, Valparaiso University.

© DIGITAL VISION

PART 4

Organizational Processes and Structure

CHAPTER 14

Jobs and the Design of Work

LEARNING OBJECTIVES

After reading this chapter, you should be able to do the following:

1 Define the term *job* and identify six patterns of defining *work.*

2 Discuss the four traditional approaches to job design.

3 Describe the Job Characteristics Model.

4 Compare the social information-processing (SIP) model with traditional job design approaches.

5 Explain ergonomics and the interdisciplinary framework for the design of work.

6 Compare Japanese, German, and Scandinavian approaches to work.

7 Explain how job control, uncertainty, and conflict can be managed for employee well-being.

8 Discuss five contemporary issues in the design of work.

THINKING AHEAD: TOYOTA MOTOR CORPORATION

Back to Basics, Strengths in Teams

Toyota is in one of the most competitive industries worldwide today. There is direct, head-to-head competition between automotive manufacturers headquartered in the United States and North America, in European countries such as Germany, and in Japan. This competition cannot be won just in dollars and cents or in capital equipment differences between the companies. Ultimately the competition comes down to people and to high-quality manufacturing. In 2007, Toyota was afraid of losing its competitive edge. While the company was reaping huge profits and saw sales soar, a deeper look by Seiichi Sudo, the CEO for North America, revealed that labor costs as a percentage of sales in North America were increasing faster than profit margin. At its present rate, this would add $900 million in labor cost by fiscal year 2011.

Toyota put a plan into place to retrain all of its 30,000 workers in the United States, Canada, and Mexico. Investment in people is the company's strategy for maintaining its competitive edge in manufacturing. Because constant improvement and change are at the heart of the company culture, complacency is not an affordable luxury given the competition.

While some might have said, "I've been working here for 20 years; I don't need to do this," everyone was retrained in the "Back to Basics" program, aimed at refreshing all employees' ability to perform the standard steps learned when they were first hired into their job. Toyota wants to take this investment global. Every plant is looking at how to do this retraining. This includes extending the retraining plan to cover workers in Japan as well.[1]

Even though Toyota's roots in Japanese culture mean that it emphasizes collective effort, the company understands that individuals are not interchangeable parts. "Back to Basics" provides standardized training that helps workers do their jobs more uniformly, more efficiently, and more effectively, thus creating a high-competency workforce that can excel in a wide range of jobs. Individuals may have hidden skills, abilities, and interests beyond the standardized ones. To identify these skills, Toyota reached out to The Gallup Organization and its StrengthsFinder program. These individual strengths complement the standardized base from "Back to Basics." What can well-trained Toyota workers achieve in their jobs and for the company?

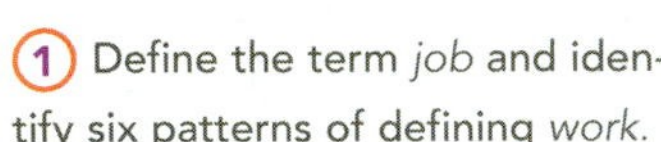

(1) Define the term *job* and identify six patterns of defining *work*.

A *job* is defined as an employee's specific work and task activities in an organization. A job is not the same as an organizational position or a career. *Organizational position* identifies a job in relation to other parts of the organization; career refers to a sequence of job experiences over time.

This chapter focuses on jobs and the design of work as elements of the organization's structure. Jobs help people define their work and become integrated into the organization. The first section in the chapter examines the meaning of work in organizations. The second section addresses four traditional approaches to job design developed between the late 1800s and the 1970s. The third section examines four alternative approaches to job design developed over the past couple of decades. The final section addresses emerging issues in job design.

WORK IN ORGANIZATIONS

Work is effortful, productive activity resulting in a product or a service. It is one important reason why organizations exist. A job is composed of a set of specific tasks, each of which is an assigned piece of work to be done in a specific time period. Work is an especially important human endeavor because it has a powerful effect in binding a person to reality. Through work, people become securely attached to reality and securely connected in human relationships. This was especially important to Metropolitan Police officer Paula Craig after her paralyzing injury, as we see in The Real World 14.1. *Work* has different meanings for different people. For all people, work is organized into jobs, and jobs fit into the larger structure of an organization. The structure of jobs is the concern of this chapter, and the structure of the organization is the concern of the next chapter. Both chapters emphasize organizations as sets of task and authority relationships through which people get work done.

job
A set of specified work and task activities that engage an individual in an organization.

work
Mental or physical activity that has productive results.

THE REAL WORLD 14.1

From Detective Constable to Detective Inspector with a Murder Team

Paula Craig was a detective constable with London's Metropolitan Police with aspirations to become a member of the Flying Squad after five years of service with the national crime squad. Then it happened! While cycling, she was knocked off her bike and broke her thoracic vertebrae, left wrist, shoulder blade, fibula, and two ribs. Sir John Stevens, the Met's chief executive, assured her that she would have a job when she recovered. His reasoning was that it would be tragic to throw away twenty years of policing experience. The Disability Discrimination Act (DDA) 2005 placed a duty on public-sector organizations, including police forces, to actively promote disability equality. This is more than simply accommodating an individual. The DDA 2005 has important implications for infrastructure and for job design, meaning that the organization must actively anticipate the employment of disabled people and ensure that obstacles are removed in advance. This is a cultural challenge for police forces whose stereotype is the able-bodied man tackling physically challenging villains and fighting crime. Hence, this transition required a major change in mindset and in self-image. Stevens could not work miracles for Paula Craig, nor could he make choices for her. However, he could create opportunities and alternatives. Her job as an officer with a beat ended with her injury, but her job as a detective inspector investigating homicides as part of a murder team began.

SOURCE: L. Polluck, "A Different Beat," *People Management* 12 (24) (December 7, 2006): 40–42.

The Meaning of Work

The *meaning of work* differs from person to person, and from culture to culture. In an increasingly global workplace, it is important to understand and appreciate differences among individuals and cultures with regard to the meaning of work. One study found six patterns people follow in defining *work*, and these help explain the cultural differences in people's motivation to work.[2]

> *Pattern A* people define *work* as an activity in which value comes from performance and for which a person is accountable. It is generally self-directed and devoid of negative affect.
>
> *Pattern B* people define *work* as an activity that provides a person with positive personal affect and identity. Work contributes to society and is not unpleasant.
>
> *Pattern C* people define *work* as an activity from which profit accrues to others by its performance, and that may be done in various settings other than a working place. Work is usually physically strenuous and somewhat compulsive.
>
> *Pattern D* people define *work* as primarily a physical activity a person must do that is directed by others and generally performed in a working place. Work is usually devoid of positive affect and is unpleasantly connected to performance.
>
> *Pattern E* people define *work* as a physically and mentally strenuous activity. It is generally unpleasant and devoid of positive affect.
>
> *Pattern F* people define *work* as an activity constrained to specific time periods that does not bring positive affect through its performance.

These six patterns were studied in six different countries: Belgium, Germany, Israel, Japan, the Netherlands, and the United States. Table 14.1 summarizes the percentage of workers in each country who defined work according to each of the six patterns. An examination of the table shows that a small percentage of workers in all six countries used either Pattern E or Pattern F to define *work*. Furthermore, there are significant differences among countries in how *work* is defined. In the Netherlands,

meaning of work
The way a person interprets and understands the value of work as part of life.

TABLE 14.1 Work Definition Patterns by Nation

Sample	Pattern* A	B	C	D	E	F
Total Sample ($N \times$ 4,950)	**11%**	**28%**	**18%**	**22%**	**11%**	**12%**
Nation						
Belgium	8%	40%	13%	19%	11%	9%
Germany	8%	26%	13%	28%	11%	14%
Israel	4%	22%	33%	23%	9%	9%
Japan	21%	11%	13%	29%	10%	17%
The Netherlands	15%	43%	12%	11%	9%	9%
United States	8%	30%	19%	19%	12%	11%

Note: X^2 = 680.98 (25 degrees of freedom). <.0001 Significance level

*In Pattern A, work is valued for its performance. The person is accountable and generally self-directed. In Pattern B, work provides a person with positive affect and identity. It contributes to society. In Pattern C, work provides profit to others by its performance. It is physical and not confined to a working place. In Pattern D, work is a required physical activity directed by others and generally unpleasant. In Pattern E, work is physically and mentally strenuous. It is generally unpleasant. In Pattern F, work is constrained to specific time periods. It does not bring positive affect through performance.

SOURCE: From G. W. England and I. Harpaz, "How Working Is Defined: National Contexts and Demographic and Organizational Role Influences," from *Journal of Organizational Behavior*, 11, 1990. Copyright John Wiley & Sons, Limited. Reproduced with permission.

it is defined most positively and with the most balanced personal and collective reasons for doing it. *Work* is defined least positively and with the most collective reason for doing it in Germany and Japan. Belgium, Israel, and the United States represent a middle position between these two. Future international studies should include Middle Eastern countries, India, Central and South American countries, and other Asian countries to better represent the world's cultures.

In another international study, 5,550 people across ten occupational groups in twenty different countries completed the Work Value Scales (WVS).[3] The WVS is composed of thirteen items measuring various aspects of the work environment, such as responsibility and job security. The study found two common basic work dimensions across cultures. Work content is one dimension, measured by items such as "the amount of responsibility on the job." Job context is the other dimension, measured by items such as "the policies of my company." This finding suggests that people in many cultures distinguish between the nature of the work itself and elements of the context in which work is done. This supports Herzberg's two-factor theory of motivation (see Chapter 5) and his job enrichment method discussed later in this chapter. Although the meaning of work differs among countries, new theorizing about crafting a job also suggests that individual employees can alter work meaning and work identity by changing task and relationship configurations in their work.[4]

Jobs in Organizations

Task and authority relationships define an organization's structure. Jobs are the basic building blocks of this task–authority structure and are considered the microstructural element to which employees most directly relate. Jobs are usually designed to complement and support other jobs in the organization. Isolated jobs are rare, although one was identified at Coastal Corporation during the early 1970s. Shortly after Oscar Wyatt moved the company from Corpus Christi, Texas, to Houston, Coastal developed organizational charts and job descriptions because the company had grown so large. In the process of charting the organization's structure, it was discovered that the beloved corporate economist reported to no one. Everyone assumed he worked for someone else. Such peculiarities are rare, however.

Jobs in organizations are interdependent and designed to make a contribution to the organization's overall mission and goals. For salespeople to be successful, the production people must be effective. For production people to be effective, the material department must be effective. These interdependencies require careful planning and design so that all of the "pieces of work" fit together into a whole. For example, an envelope salesperson who wants to take an order for one million envelopes from John Hancock Financial Services must coordinate with the production department to establish an achievable delivery date. The failure to incorporate this interdependence into his planning could create conflict and doom the company to failure in meeting John Hancock's expectations. The central concerns of this chapter are designing work and structuring jobs to prevent such problems and to ensure employee well-being. Inflexible jobs that are rigidly structured have an adverse effect and lead to stressed-out employees.

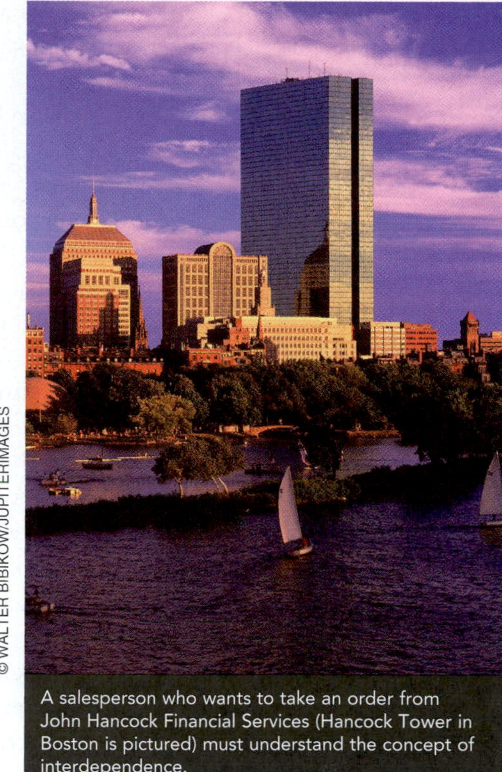

A salesperson who wants to take an order from John Hancock Financial Services (Hancock Tower in Boston is pictured) must understand the concept of interdependence.

Chapter 15 addresses the larger issues in the design of organizations. In particular, it examines the competing processes of differentiation and integration in organizations. Differentiation is the process of subdividing and departmentalizing the work of an organization. Jobs result from differentiation, which is necessary because no one can do it all (contrary to the famous statement made by Harold Geneen, former chairman of ITT: "If I had enough arms and legs and time, I'd do it all myself"). Even small organizations must divide work so that each person is able to accomplish a manageable piece of the whole. At the same time the organization divides up the work, it must also integrate those pieces back into a whole. Integration is the process of connecting jobs and departments into a coordinated, cohesive whole. For example, if the envelope salesperson had coordinated with the production manager before finalizing the order with John Hancock, the company could have met the customer's expectations, and integration would have occurred.

TRADITIONAL APPROACHES TO JOB DESIGN

(2) Discuss the four traditional approaches to job design.

Failure to differentiate, integrate, or both may result in badly designed jobs, which in turn cause a variety of performance problems in organizations. Good job design helps avoid these problems, improves productivity, and enhances employee well-being. Four approaches to job design that were developed during the twentieth century are scientific management, job enlargement/job rotation, job enrichment, and the job characteristics theory. Each approach offers unique benefits to the organization, the employee, or both, but each also has limitations and drawbacks. Furthermore, an unthinking reliance on a traditional approach can be a serious problem in any company. The later job design approaches were developed to overcome the limitations of traditional job design approaches. For example, job enlargement was intended to overcome the problem of boredom associated with scientific management's narrowly defined approach to jobs.

Scientific Management

work simplification
Standardization and the narrow, explicit specification of task activities for workers.

Scientific management, an approach to work design first advocated by Frederick Taylor, emphasized work simplification. *Work simplification* is the standardization and the narrow, explicit specification of task activities for workers.[5] Jobs designed through scientific management have a limited number of tasks, and each task is scientifically specified so that the worker is not required to think or deliberate. According to Taylor, the role of management and the industrial engineer is to calibrate and define each task carefully. The role of the worker is to execute the task. The elements of scientific management, such as time and motion studies, differential piece-rate systems of pay, and the scientific selection of workers, all focus on the efficient use of labor to the economic benefit of the corporation. Employees who are satisfied with various aspects of repetitive work may like scientifically designed jobs.

Two arguments supported the efficient and standardized job design approach of scientific management in the early days of the American Industrial Revolution. The first argument was that work simplification allowed individuals of diverse ethnic and skill backgrounds to work together in a systematic way. This was important during the first great period of globalization in the late 1800s during which Germans, Scots, Hungarians, Poles, and other immigrants came to work in America.[6] Taylor's unique approach to work standardization allowed diverse individuals to be blended into a functional workforce.

The second argument for scientific management was that work simplification led to production efficiency in the organization and, therefore, to higher profits. This economic argument for work simplification tended to treat labor as a means of production and dehumanized it. Toyota's "Back to Basics" aims to enhance efficiency and effectiveness for collective gain, as we saw in Thinking Ahead.

A fundamental limitation of scientific management is that it undervalues the human capacity for thought and ingenuity. Jobs designed through scientific management use only a portion of a person's capabilities. This underutilization makes work boring, monotonous, and understimulating. The failure to fully utilize the workers' capacity in a constructive fashion may cause a variety of work problems. Contemporary approaches to enhancing motivation through pay and compensation work to overcome these problems through modern job designs that retain talent and reduce turnover.[7]

Job Enlargement/Job Rotation

Job enlargement is a traditional approach to overcome the limitations of overspecialized work, such as boredom.[8] *Job enlargement* is a method of job design that increases the number of tasks in a job. *Job rotation*, a variation of job enlargement, exposes a worker to a variety of specialized job tasks over time. The reasoning behind these approaches to the problems of overspecialization is as follows.

First, the core problem with overspecialized work was believed to be lack of variety. That is, jobs designed by scientific management were too narrow and limited in the number of tasks and activities assigned to each worker. Second, a lack of variety led to understimulation and underutilization of the worker. Third, the worker would be more stimulated and better utilized by increasing the variety in the job. Variety could be increased by increasing the number of activities or by rotating the worker through different jobs. For example, job enlargement for a lathe operator in a steel plant might include selecting the steel pieces to be turned and performing all of the maintenance work on the lathe. As an example of job rotation, an employee at a small bank might take new accounts one day, serve as a cashier another day, and process loan applications on a third day.

job enlargement

A method of job design that increases the number of activities in a job to overcome the boredom of overspecialized work.

job rotation

A variation of job enlargement in which workers are exposed to a variety of specialized jobs over time.

One of the first studies of the problem of repetitive work was conducted at IBM after World War II. The company implemented a job enlargement program during the war and evaluated the effort after six years.[9] The two most important results were a significant increase in product quality and a reduction in idle time, both for people and for machines. Less obvious and measurable are the benefits of job enlargement to IBM through enhanced worker status and improved manager–worker communication. IBM concluded that job enlargement countered the problems of work specialization. A contemporary study in a Swedish electronics assembly plant used physiological measures of muscle tension.[10] Job enlargement had a positive effect on mechanical exposure variability.

A later study examined the effects of mass production jobs on assembly-line workers in the automotive industry.[11] Mass production jobs have six characteristics: mechanically controlled work pace, repetitiveness, minimum skill requirements, predetermined tools and techniques, minute division of the production process, and a requirement for surface mental attention, rather than thoughtful concentration. The researchers conducted 180 private interviews with assembly-line workers and found generally positive attitudes toward pay, security, and supervision. They concluded that job enlargement and job rotation would improve other job aspects, such as repetition and a mechanical work pace.

Job rotation and *cross-training* programs are variations of job enlargement. Pharmaceutical company Eli Lilly has found that job rotation can be a proactive means for enhancing work experiences for career development and can have tangible benefits for employees in the form of salary increases and promotions.[12] In cross-training, workers are trained in different specialized tasks or activities. All three kinds of programs horizontally enlarge jobs; that is, the number and variety of an employee's tasks and activities are increased. Graphic Controls Corporation (now a subsidiary of Tyco International) used cross-training to develop a flexible workforce that enabled the company to maintain high levels of production.[13]

Job Enrichment

Whereas job enlargement increases the number of job activities through horizontal loading, job enrichment increases the amount of job responsibility through vertical loading. Both approaches to job design are intended, in part, to increase job satisfaction for employees. A study to test whether job satisfaction results from characteristics of the job or of the person found that an interactionist approach is most accurate and that job redesign can contribute to increased job satisfaction for some employees. Another two-year study found that intrinsic job satisfaction and job perceptions are reciprocally related to each other.[14]

Job enrichment is a job design or redesign method aimed at increasing the motivational factors in a job. Job enrichment builds on Herzberg's two-factor theory of motivation, which distinguished between motivational and hygiene factors for people at work. Whereas job enlargement recommends increasing and varying the number of activities a person does, job enrichment recommends increasing the recognition, responsibility, and opportunity for achievement. For example, enlarging the lathe operator's job means adding maintenance activities, and enriching the job means having the operator meet with customers who buy the products.

Herzberg believes that only certain jobs should be enriched and that the first step is to select the jobs appropriate for job enrichment.[15] He recognizes that some people prefer simple jobs. Once jobs are selected for enrichment, management should brainstorm about possible changes, revise the list to include only specific changes related to motivational factors, and screen out generalities and suggestions that would simply increase activities or numbers of tasks. Those whose jobs are to be enriched should not participate in this process because of a conflict of interest. Two key problems can arise in the implementation of job enrichment. First, an initial drop in performance can be expected as workers accommodate to the change. Second, first-line supervisors may experience some anxiety or hostility as a result of employees' increased responsibility.

cross-training
A variation of job enlargement in which workers are trained in different specialized tasks or activities.

job enrichment
Designing or redesigning jobs by incorporating motivational factors into them.

A seven-year implementation study of job enrichment at AT&T found the approach beneficial.[16] Job enrichment required a big change in management style, and AT&T found that it could not ignore hygiene factors in the work environment just because it was enriching existing jobs. Although the AT&T experience with job enrichment was positive, a critical review of job enrichment did not find that to be the case generally.[17] One problem with job enrichment as a strategy for work design is that it is based on an oversimplified motivational theory. Another problem is the lack of consideration for individual differences among employees. Job enrichment, like scientific management's work specialization and job enlargement/job rotation, is a universal approach to the design of work and thus does not differentiate among individuals.

Job Characteristics Theory

(3) Describe the Job Characteristics Model.

The job characteristics theory, which was initiated during the mid-1960s, is a traditional approach to the design of work that makes a significant departure from the three earlier approaches. It emphasizes the interaction between the individual and specific attributes of the job; therefore, it is a person–job fit model rather than a universal job design model. It originated in a research study of 470 workers in forty-seven different jobs across eleven industries.[18] The study measured and classified relevant task characteristics for these forty-seven jobs and found four core job characteristics: job variety, autonomy, responsibility, and interpersonal interaction. The study also found that core job characteristics did not affect all workers in the same way. A worker's values, religious beliefs, and ethnic background influenced how the worker responded to the job. Specifically, workers with rural values and strong religious beliefs preferred jobs high in core characteristics, and workers with urban values and weaker religious beliefs preferred jobs low in core characteristics.

Richard Hackman and his colleagues modified the original model by including three critical psychological states of the individual and refining the measurement of core job characteristics. The result is the *Job Characteristics Model* shown in Figure 14.1.[19] The *Job Diagnostic Survey (JDS)*, the most commonly used job design measure, was developed to diagnose jobs by measuring the five core job characteristics and three critical psychological states shown in the model. The core job characteristics stimulate the critical psychological states in the manner shown in Figure 14.1. This results in varying personal and work outcomes, as identified in the figure.

The five core job characteristics are defined as follows:

1. *Skill variety.* The degree to which a job includes different activities and involves the use of multiple skills and talents of the employee.
2. *Task identity.* The degree to which the job requires completion of a whole and identifiable piece of work—that is, doing a job from beginning to end with a tangible outcome.
3. *Task significance.* The degree to which the job has a substantial impact on the lives or work of other people, whether in the immediate organization or in the external environment.
4. *Autonomy.* The degree to which the job provides the employee with substantial freedom, independence, and discretion in scheduling the work and in determining the procedures to be used in carrying it out.
5. *Feedback from the job itself.* The degree to which carrying out the work activities results in the employee's obtaining direct and clear information about the effectiveness of his or her performance.

Job Characteristics Model
A framework for understanding person–job fit through the interaction of core job dimensions with critical psychological states within a person.

Job Diagnostic Survey (JDS)
The survey instrument designed to measure the elements in the Job Characteristics Model.

FIGURE 14.1 The Job Characteristics Model

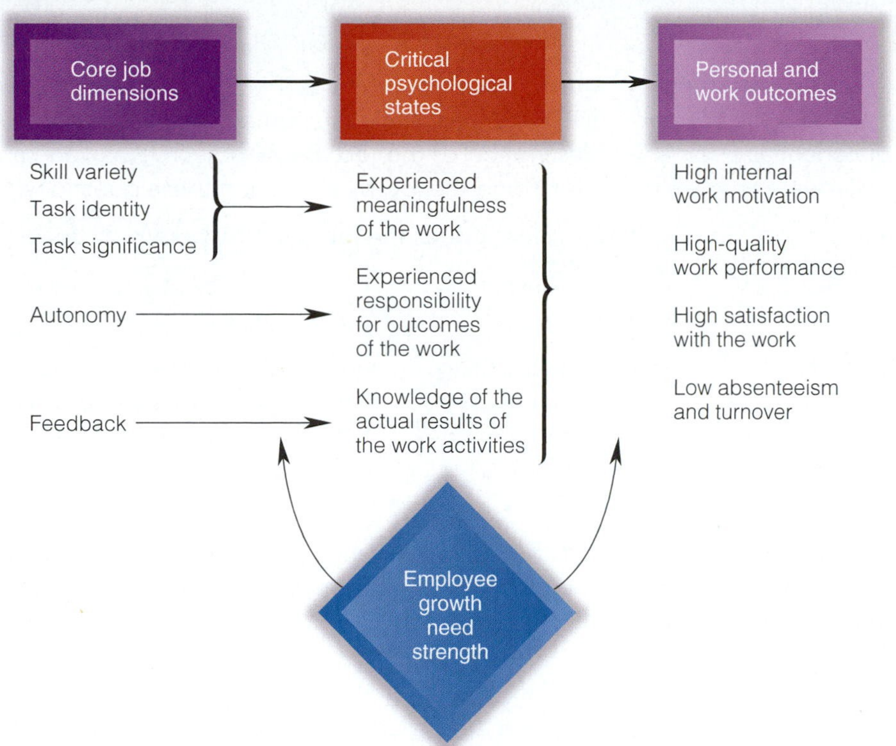

SOURCE: J. R. Hackman and G. R. Oldham, "The Relationship Among Core Job Dimensions, the Critical Psychological States, and On-the-Job Outcomes," *The Job Diagnostic Survey: An Instrument for the Diagnosis of Jobs and the Evaluation of Job Redesign Projects*, 1974. Reprinted by permission of Greg R. Oldham.

Hackman and his colleagues say that the five core job characteristics interact to determine an overall Motivating Potential Score (MPS) for a specific job. The MPS indicates a job's potential for motivating incumbents. An individual's MPS is determined by the following equation:

$$\text{MPS} = \frac{\left[\begin{array}{c}\text{Skill}\\\text{variety}\end{array}\right] + \left[\begin{array}{c}\text{Task}\\\text{identity}\end{array}\right] + \left[\begin{array}{c}\text{Task}\\\text{significance}\end{array}\right]}{3} \times [\text{Autonomy}] \times [\text{Feedback}].$$

You 14.1 enables you to answer five questions from the JDS short form to get an idea about the motivating potential of your present job or any job you have held.

The Job Characteristics Model includes *growth-need strength* (the desire to grow and fully develop one's abilities) as a moderator. People with a high growth need strength respond favorably to jobs with high MPSs, and individuals with low growth need strength respond less favorably to such jobs. The job characteristics theory further suggests that core job dimensions stimulate three critical psychological states according to the relationships specified in the model. These critical psychological states are defined as follows:

1. *Experienced meaningfulness of the work*, or the degree to which the employee experiences the job as one that is generally meaningful, valuable, and worthwhile.
2. *Experienced responsibility for work outcomes*, or the degree to which the employee feels personally accountable and responsible for the results of the work he or she does.
3. *Knowledge of results*, or the degree to which the employee knows and understands, on a continuous basis, how effectively he or she is performing the job.

Diagnosing Your Job

This questionnaire challenges you to examine the motivating potential in your job. If you are not currently working, complete the questionnaire for any job you have ever held for which you want to examine the motivating potential. For each of the following five questions, circle the number of the most accurate description of the job. Be as objective as you can in describing the job by answering these questions.

1. How much *autonomy* is there in the job? That is, to what extent does the job permit a person to decide *on his or her own* how to go about doing the work?

   1 2 3 4 5 6 7

1–2	3–5	6–7
Very little; the job gives a person almost no personal say about how and when the work is done.	Moderate autonomy; many things are standardized and not under the control of the person, but he or she can make some decisions about the work.	Very much; the job gives the person almost complete responsibility for deciding how and when the work is done.

2. To what extent does the job involve doing a *"whole"* and *identifiable piece of work*? That is, is the job a complete piece of work that has an obvious beginning and end? Or is it a small part of the overall piece of work, which is finished by other people or by automatic machines?

   1 2 3 4 5 6 7

1–2	3–5	6–7
The job is only a tiny part in the overall piece of work; the results of the person's activities cannot be seen in the final product or service.	The job is a moderate-sized "chunk" of the overall piece of work; the person's own contribution can be seen in the final outcome.	The job involves doing the whole piece of work, from start to finish; the results of the person's activities are easily seen in the final product or service.

3. How much *variety* is there in the job? That is, to what extent does the job require a person to do many different things at work, using a variety of his or her skills and talents?

   1 2 3 4 5 6 7

1–2	3–5	6–7
Very little; the job requires the person to do the same routine things over and over again.	Moderate variety.	Very much; the job requires the person to do many different things, using a number of different skills and talents.

4. In general, how *significant* or *important* is the job? That is, are the results of the person's work likely to affect significantly the lives or well-being of other people?

   1 2 3 4 5 6 7

1–2	3–5	6–7
Not at all significant; the outcome of the work is *not* likely to affect anyone in any important way.	Moderately significant.	Highly significant; the outcome of the work can affect other people in very important ways.

5. To what extent *does doing the job itself* provide the person with information about his or her work performance? That is, does the actual work itself provide clues about how well the person is doing—aside from any feedback coworkers or supervisors may provide?

   1 2 3 4 5 6 7

1–2	3–5	6–7
Very little; the job itself is set up so a person could work forever without finding out how well he or she is doing.	Moderately; sometimes doing the job provides feedback to the person; sometimes it does not.	Very much; the job is set up so that a person gets almost constant feedback as he or she works about how well he or she is doing.

(continued)

To score your questionnaire, place your responses to Questions 3, 2, 4, 1, and 5, respectively, in the blank spaces in the following equation:

$$\text{Motivating Potential Score (MPS)} = \frac{[\ \ ]_{Q\#3} + [\ \ ]_{Q\#2} + [\ \ ]_{Q\#4}}{3} \times [\ \ ]_{Q\#1} \times [\ \ ]_{Q\#5} = \underline{\qquad}.$$

If the MPS for the job you rated is between

- 200 and 343, it is high in motivating potential.
- 120 and 199, it is moderate in motivating potential.
- 0 and 119, it is low in motivating potential.

SOURCE: J. R. Hackman and G. R. Oldham, "The Job Diagnostic Survey: An Instrument for the Diagnosis of Jobs and the Evaluation of Job Redesign Projects," *Technical Report No. 4,* 1974, 2–3 of the Short Form. Reprinted by permission of Greg R. Oldham.

In one early study, Hackman and Oldham administered the JDS to 658 employees working on sixty-two different jobs in seven business organizations.[20] The JDS was useful for job redesign efforts through one or more of five implementing concepts: (1) combining tasks into larger jobs, (2) forming natural work teams to increase task identity and task significance, (3) establishing relationships with customers, (4) loading jobs vertically with more responsibility, and/or (5) opening feedback channels for the job incumbent. For example, if an automotive mechanic received little feedback on the quality of repair work performed, one redesign strategy would be to solicit customer feedback one month after each repair.

A more recent sequence of two studies conducted in Egypt aimed to disaggregate work autonomy, one important component in job design theory.[21] Study 1 included 534 employees in two Egyptian organizations. Study 2 involved 120 managers in four organizations. The results indicated that separate work method, work schedule, and work criteria autonomy were three separate facets of work autonomy. In an extension of job characteristics theory, the accompanying Science feature looks at the development of the Work Design Questionnaire (WDQ).

In another international study, the Job Characteristics Model was tested in a sample of fifty-seven jobs from thirty-seven organizations in Hong Kong.[22] Job incumbents and their supervisors both completed questionnaires about the incumbents' jobs.[23] The supervisory version asked the supervisor to rate the employee's job. The study supported the model in general. However, task significance was not a reliable core job dimension in Hong Kong, which suggests either national differences in the measurement of important job dimensions or cultural biases about work. This result also suggests that value differences may exist between American and Asian people with regard to jobs.

An alternative to the Job Characteristics Model is the Job Characteristics Inventory (JCI) developed by Henry Sims and Andrew Szilagyi.[24] The JCI primarily measures core job characteristics. It is not as comprehensive as the JDS or the new WDQ because it does not incorporate critical psychological states, personal and work outcomes, or employee needs. The JCI does give some consideration to structural and individual variables that affect the relationship between core job characteristics and the individual.[25] One comparative analysis of the JCI and JDS found similarities in the measures and in the models' predictions.[26] The comparative analysis also found two differences. First, the variety scales in the two models appear to have different effects on performance. Second, the autonomy scales in the two models appear to have different effects on employee satisfaction. Overall, the JCI, JDS, and new

Assessing Job Design and the Nature of Work

This study was intended to provide a more comprehensive measure of job design and the nature of work by building on the strong tradition of previous, more narrowly focused lines of research. The resulting Work Design Questionnaire (WDQ) measures twenty-one distinct work characteristics in three categories. These are motivational work characteristics such as skill variety and task identity, social characteristics such as interdependence and social support, and work context characteristics such as physical demands and work conditions. Work outcomes of concern in this research included satisfaction, efficiency, and workload. The WDQ was validated with 540 incumbents, many of whom were managers, in 243 distinct jobs, and the results showed excellent reliability as well as convergent and discriminant validity. While the results found that motivational work characteristics do predict satisfaction, social support was a strong incremental predictor of satisfaction beyond the motivational work characteristics. Thus, enhancing social support in the work may yield both motivational and training benefits for job incumbents. In addition, while many work redesign efforts often require trade-offs between satisfaction and training and compensation requirements, the range of design choices is much greater with the WDQ. Therefore, the WDQ offers the potential to avoid the trade-offs commonly encountered in earlier work redesign efforts. The study concludes that the WDQ holds promise for scholars studying work design theory and practitioners redesigning jobs and work in organizations.

SOURCE: F. P. Morgeson and S. E. Humphrey, "The Work Design Questionnaire (WDQ): Developing and Validating a Comprehensive Measure for Assessing Job Design and the Nature of Work," *Journal of Applied Psychology* 91 (2006): 1321–1329.

WDQ all support the usefulness of a person–job fit approach to the design of work over the earlier, universal theories.

Engagement

Psychological conditions related to job design features are a particular concern of the Job Characteristics Model.[27] One study of over 200 managers and employees in a Midwestern insurance company found that meaningfulness, safety, and availability were three important psychological conditions that affected employees' *engagement* in their jobs and work roles. Engagement at work is important for its positive individual and organizational outcomes. Engagement is the harnessing of organizational members to their work roles. When engaged, people employ and express themselves physically, cognitively, and emotionally as they perform their jobs and their work roles. For example, Gallup's Q was used to improve engagement for a clinical nutrition group at St. Mary's/Duluth Clinic Health System.[28]

Full engagement requires the strategic management of one's energy in response to the environment.[29] Being fully engaged in one's work role and job can be highly appropriate and yet demand energy, time, and effort. To achieve balance and afford opportunity for recovery, there is a commensurate need to strategically and appropriately disengage from one's job and work role on a periodic basis. The effective management of energy in response to one's job and work role leads to both high performance and personal renewal. Thus, while the design of work is important, the human spirit's response to job characteristics and work design features is equally important.

ALTERNATIVE APPROACHES TO JOB DESIGN

engagement
The expression of oneself as one performs in work or other roles.

Because each of the traditional job design approaches has limitations, several alternative approaches to job design have emerged over the past couple of decades. This section examines four of these alternatives that are in the process of being tried and tested. First, it examines the social information-processing model. Second, it reviews ergonomics and the interdisciplinary framework of Michael Campion and Paul Thayer. Their framework builds on the traditional job design approaches. Third, this section examines the international perspectives of the Japanese, Germans, and Scandinavians. Finally, it focuses on the health and well-being aspects of work design. Healthy work enables individuals to adapt, function well, and balance work with private life activities.[30] An emerging fifth approach to the design of work through teams and autonomous work groups was addressed in Chapter 9.

Social Information Processing

(4) Compare the social information-processing (SIP) model with traditional job design approaches.

The traditional approaches to the design of work emphasize objective core job characteristics. In contrast, the *social information-processing (SIP) model* emphasizes the interpersonal aspects of work design. Specifically, the SIP model says that what others tell us about our jobs is important.[31] The SIP model has four basic premises about the work environment.[32] First, other people provide cues we use to understand the work environment. Second, other people help us judge what is important in our jobs. Third, other people tell us how they see our jobs. Fourth, other people's positive and negative feedback helps us understand our feelings about our jobs. This is very consistent with the dynamic model of the job design process that views it as a social one involving job-holders, supervisors, and peers.[33]

People's perceptions and reactions to their jobs are shaped by information from other people in the work environment.[34] In other words, what others believe about a person's job may be important to understanding the person's perceptions of, and reactions to, the job. This does not mean that objective job characteristics are unimportant; rather, it means that others can modify the way these characteristics affect us. For example, one study of task complexity found that the objective complexity of a task must be distinguished from the subjective task complexity experienced by the employee.[35] While objective task complexity may be a motivator, the presence of others in the work environment, social interaction, or even daydreaming may be important additional sources of motivation. The SIP model makes an important contribution to the design of work by emphasizing the importance of other people and the social context of work. For example, relational job design may motivate employees to take prosocial action and make a positive difference in other people's lives.[36] In addition, the relational aspects of the work environment may be more important than objective core job characteristics. Therefore, the subjective feedback of other people about how difficult a particular task is may be more important to a person's motivation to perform than an objective estimate of the task's difficulty.

(5) Explain ergonomics and the interdisciplinary framework for the design of work.

Ergonomics and Interdisciplinary Framework

Michael Campion and Paul Thayer use *ergonomics* based on engineering, biology, and psychology to develop an interdisciplinary framework for the design of work. Actually, they say that four approaches—the mechanistic, motivational, biological, and perceptual/motor approaches—are necessary because no one approach can solve all performance problems caused by poorly designed jobs. Each approach has its benefits as well as its limitations. One ergonomics study of eighty-seven administrative municipal employees found lower levels of upper body pain along with other positive outcomes of the workstation redesign.[37]

The interdisciplinary framework allows the job designer or manager to consider trade-offs and alternatives among the approaches based on desired outcomes. If a manager finds poor performance a problem, for example, she or he should analyze the job to ensure a design aimed at improving performance. The interdisciplinary

social information-processing (SIP) model
A model that suggests that the important job factors depend in part on what others tell a person about the job.

ergonomics
The science of adapting work and working conditions to the employee or worker.

TABLE 14.2 Summary of Outcomes from Various Job Design Approaches

Job Design Approach (Discipline)	Positive Outcomes	Negative Outcomes
Mechanistic Approach (mechanical engineering)	Decreased training time Higher personnel utilization levels Lower likelihood of error Less chance of mental overload Lower stress levels	Lower job satisfaction Lower motivation Higher absenteeism
Motivational Approach (industrial psychology)	Higher job satisfaction Higher motivation Greater job involvement Higher job performance Lower absenteeism	Increased training time Lower personnel utilization levels Greater chance of errors Greater chance of mental overload and stress
Biological Approach (biology)	Less physical effort Less physical fatigue Fewer health complaints Fewer medical incidents Lower absenteeism Higher job satisfaction	Higher financial costs because of changes in equipment or job environment
Perceptual Motor Approach (experimental psychology)	Lower likelihood of error Lower likelihood of accidents Less chance of mental stress Decreased training time Higher personnel utilization levels	Lower job satisfaction Lower motivation

SOURCE: Reprinted from *Organizational Dynamics*, Winter/1987 Copyright © 1987, with permission from Elsevier Science.

framework is important because badly designed jobs cause far more performance problems than managers realize.[38]

Table 14.2 summarizes the positive and negative outcomes of each job design approach. The mechanistic and motivational approaches to job design are very similar to scientific management's work simplification and to the Job Characteristics Model, respectively. Because these were discussed earlier in the chapter, they are not further elaborated here.

The biological approach to job design emphasizes the person's interaction with physical aspects of the work environment and is concerned with the amount of physical exertion, such as lifting and muscular effort, required by the position. For example, an analysis of medical claims within TXI's steel operating company identified lower back problems as the most common physical problem experienced by steelworkers and managers alike. As a result, the company instituted an education and exercise program under expert guidance to improve care of the lower back. Program graduates received back cushions for their chairs with "Chaparral Steel Company" embossed on them. Herman Miller designed an office chair to support the lower back and other parts of the human body.[39] The chair was tested in several offices including that of the director of human resources for Valero Energy Corporation prior to large-scale production. Lower back problems associated with improper lifting may be costly, but they are not fatal. Campion describes the potentially catastrophic problem that occurred at Three Mile Island, when nuclear materials contaminated the surrounding area and threatened disaster. Campion concluded that poor design of the control room operator's job caused the problem.

The perceptual/motor approach to job design also emphasizes the person's interaction with physical aspects of the work environment and is based on engineering that considers human factors such as strength or coordination, ergonomics, and experimental psychology. It places an important emphasis on human interaction with computers, information, and other operational systems. This approach addresses how people mentally process information acquired from the physical work environment through perceptual and motor skills. The approach emphasizes perception and fine motor skills as opposed to the gross motor skills and muscle strength emphasized in the mechanistic approach. The perceptual/motor approach is more likely to be relevant to operational and technical work, such as keyboard operations and data entry jobs, which may tax a person's concentration and attention, than to managerial, administrative, and custodial jobs, which are less likely to strain concentration and attention.

One study using the interdisciplinary framework to improve jobs evaluated 377 clerical, 80 managerial, and 90 analytical positions.[40] The jobs were improved by combining tasks and adding ancillary duties. The improved jobs provided greater motivation for the incumbents and were better from a perceptual/motor standpoint. The jobs were poorly designed from a mechanical engineering standpoint, however, and they were unaffected from a biological standpoint. Again, the interdisciplinary framework considers trade-offs and alternatives when evaluating job redesign efforts.

International Perspectives on the Design of Work

(6) Compare Japanese, German, and Scandinavian approaches to work.

Each nation or ethnic group has a unique way of understanding and designing work.[41] As organizations become more global and international, an appreciation of the perspectives of other nations is increasingly important. The Japanese, Germans, and Scandinavians in particular have distinctive perspectives on the design and organization of work.[42] Each country's perspective is forged within its unique cultural and economic system, and each is distinct from the approaches used in North America.

The Japanese Approach The Japanese began harnessing their productive energies during the 1950s by drawing on the product quality ideas of W. Edwards Deming.[43] In addition, the central government became actively involved in the economic resurgence of Japan, and it encouraged companies to conquer industries rather than merely to maximize profits.[44] Such an industrial policy, which built on the Japanese cultural ethic of collectivism, has implications for how work is done. Whereas Frederick Taylor and his successors in the United States emphasized the job of an individual worker, the Japanese work system emphasizes the strategic level and encourages collective and cooperative working arrangements.[45] As Table 14.1 shows, the Japanese emphasize performance, accountability, and other- or self-directedness in defining work, whereas Americans emphasize the positive affect, personal identity, and social benefits of work.

The Japanese success with lean production has drawn the attention of managers. *Lean production* methods are similar to the production concept of *sociotechnical systems (STS)*, although there are some differences.[46] In particular, STS gives greater emphasis to teamwork and self-managed and autonomous work groups, to the ongoing nature of the design process, and to human values in the work process. The approaches are similar, however, in that both differ from Taylor's scientific management and both emphasize job variety, feedback to work groups and teams,

lean production
Using committed employees with ever-expanding responsibilities to achieve zero waste, 100 percent good product, delivered on time, every time.

sociotechnical systems (STS)
Giving equal attention to technical and social considerations in job design.

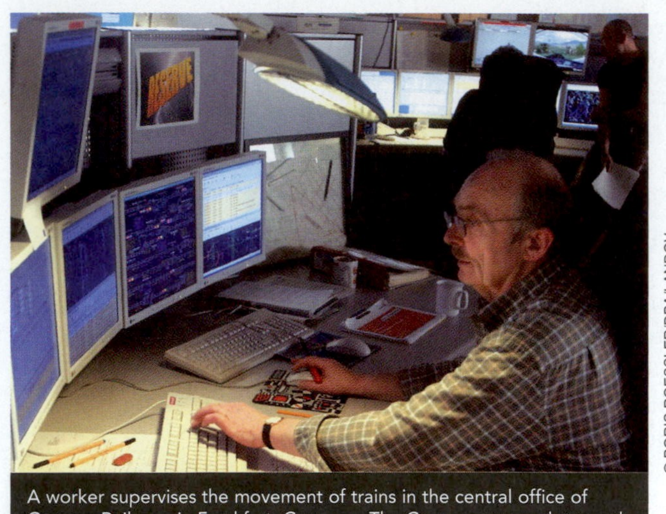
© BORIS ROESSLER/DPA/LANDOV

A worker supervises the movement of trains in the central office of German Railways in Frankfurt, Germany. The German approach to work has been shaped by Germany's unique educational system, including a multitrack design with technical and university alternatives.

support of human resources, and control of production variance close to the point of origin. One three-year evaluation of lean teams, assembly lines, and workflow formalization as lean production practices was conducted in Australia.[47] Employees in all lean production groups were negatively affected, and the assembly-line employees the worst.

The German Approach The German approach to work has been shaped by Germany's unique educational system, cultural values, and economic system. The Germans are a highly educated and well-organized people. For example, their educational system has a multitrack design with technical and university alternatives. The German economic system puts a strong emphasis on free enterprise, private property rights, and management–labor cooperation. A comparison of voluntary and mandated management–labor cooperation in Germany found that productivity was superior under voluntary cooperation.[48] The Germans value hierarchy and authority relationships and, as a result, are generally disciplined.[49] Germany's workers are highly unionized, and their discipline and efficiency have enabled Germany to be highly productive while its workers labor substantially fewer hours than do Americans.

The traditional German approach to work design was *technocentric*, an approach that placed technology and engineering at the center of job design decisions. Recently, German industrial engineers have moved to a more *anthropocentric* approach, which places human considerations at the center of job design decisions. The former approach uses a natural scientific process in the design of work, whereas the latter relies on a more humanistic process, as shown in Figure 14.2. In the anthropocentric approach, work is evaluated using the criteria of practicability and worker satisfaction at the individual level and the criteria of endurability and acceptability at the group level. Figure 14.2 also identifies problem areas and disciplines concerned with each aspect of the work design.

technocentric
Placing technology and engineering at the center of job design decisions.

anthropocentric
Placing human considerations at the center of job design decisions.

The Scandinavian Approach The Scandinavian cultural values and economic system stand in contrast to the German system. The social democratic tradition in Scandinavia has emphasized social concern rather than industrial efficiency. The Scandinavians place great emphasis on a work design model that encourages a high degree of worker control and good social support systems for workers.[50] Lennart Levi believes that circumstantial and inferential scientific evidence provides a sufficiently strong basis for legislative and policy actions for redesigns aimed at enhancing worker well-being. An example of such an action for promoting good working environments and occupational health was Swedish Government Bill 1976/77:149, which stated, "Work should be safe both physically and mentally *but also* provide opportunities for involvement, job satisfaction, and personal development." In 1991, the Swedish Parliament set up the Swedish Working Life Fund to finance research, intervention programs, and demonstration projects in work design. For example, a study of Stockholm police on shift schedules found that going from a daily, counterclockwise rotation to a clockwise rotation was more compatible with human biology and resulted in improved sleep, less fatigue, lower systolic blood pressure, and lower blood levels of triglycerides and glucose.[51] Hence, the work redesign improved the police officers' health.

FIGURE 14.2 Hierarchical Model of Criteria for the Evaluation of Human Work

Scientific approaches of labor sciences	Levels of evaluation of human work	Problem areas and assignment to disciplines
View from natural science ←	Practicability	Technical, anthropometric, and psychophysical problems (ergonomics)
	Endurability	Technical, physiological, and medical problems (ergonomics and occupational health)
Primarily oriented to individuals ← Primarily oriented to groups ←	Acceptability	Economical and sociological problems (occupational psychology and sociology, personnel management)
View from cultural studies ←	Satisfaction	Sociopsychological and economic problems (occupational psychology and sociology, personnel management)

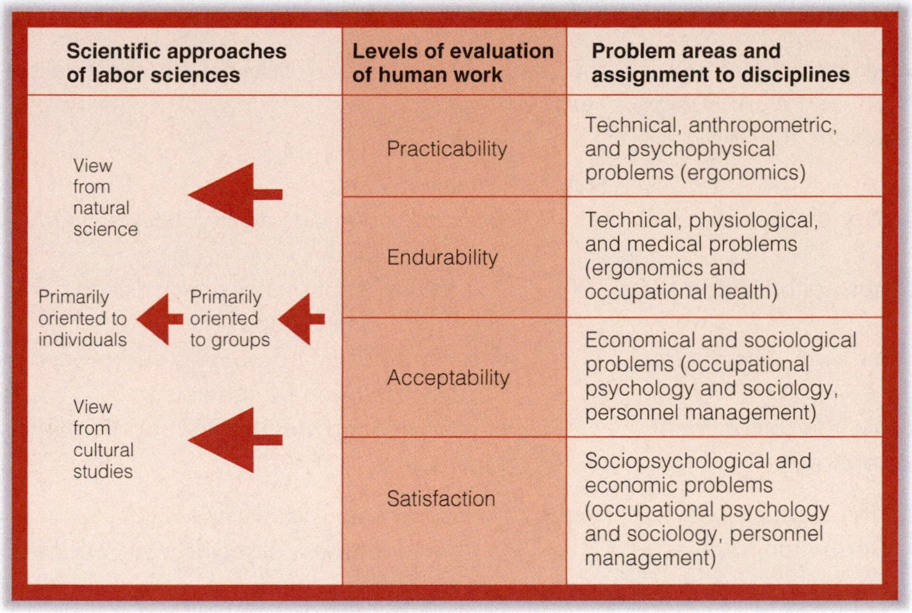

SOURCE: H. Luczak, "'Good Work' Design: An Ergonomic, Industrial Engineering Perspective," in J. C. Quick, L. R. Murphy, and J. J. Hurrell, eds., *Stress and Well-Being at Work* (Washington, D.C.). Copyright ©1997 by the American Psychological Association. Reprinted with permission.

Work Design and Well-Being

⑦ Explain how job control, uncertainty, and conflict can be managed for employee well-being.

An international group of scholars, including American social scientists, has been concerned about designing work and jobs that are both healthy and productive.[52] This issue was discussed briefly in Chapter 7. Economic and industry-specific upheavals in the United States during the 1990s led to job loss and unemployment, and the adverse health impact of these factors has received attention.[53] The Japanese have been instrumental in this global initiative and Toyota has a concern for individual strengths, as we saw in Thinking Ahead. Attention has also been devoted to the effects of specific work design parameters on psychological health.[54] For example, by mixing cognitively challenging and "mindless" work throughout the day, one may reduce pressures for chronic overwork and enhance creativity. Frank Landy believes that organizations should redesign jobs to increase worker control and reduce worker uncertainty, while at the same time managing conflict and task/job demands. These objectives can be achieved in several ways.

Control in work organizations can be increased by (1) giving workers the opportunity to control several aspects of the work and the workplace; (2) designing machines and tasks with optimal response times and/or ranges; and (3) implementing performance-monitoring systems as a source of relevant feedback to workers. Uncertainty can be reduced by (1) providing employees with timely and complete information needed for their work; (2) making clear and unambiguous work assignments; (3) improving communication at shift change time; and (4) increasing employee access to information sources. Conflict at work can be managed through (1) participative decision making to reduce conflict; (2) using supportive supervisory styles to resolve conflict; and (3) having sufficient resources available to meet work demands, thus preventing conflict. Task/job design can be improved by enhancing core job characteristics and not patterning service work after assembly-line work.

YOU 14.2

Is Your Work Environment a Healthy One?

To determine whether your work environment is a healthy one, read the text section on "Work Design and Well-Being," and then complete the following four steps. Answer each question in the five steps "yes" or "no."

Step 1. Control and Influence

____ Do you have influence over the pace of your work?

____ Are system response times neither too fast nor too slow?

____ Do you have a say in your work assignments and goals?

____ Is there an opportunity for you to comment on your performance appraisal?

Step 2. Information and Uncertainty

____ Do you receive timely information to complete your work?

____ Do you receive complete information for your work assignments?

____ Is there adequate planning for changes that affect you at work?

____ Do you have access to all the information you need at work?

Step 3. Conflict at Work

____ Does the company apply policies clearly and consistently?

____ Are job descriptions and task assignments clear and unambiguous?

____ Are there adequate policies and procedures for the resolution of conflicts?

____ Is your work environment an open, participative one?

Step 4. Job Scope and Task Design

____ Is there adequate variety in your work activities and/or assignments?

____ Do you receive timely, constructive feedback on your work?

____ Is your work important to the overall mission of the company?

____ Do you work on more than one small piece of a big project?

Scoring

Count the number of "yes" answers in Steps 1 through 4: ______

If you have 10 to 16 "yes" answers, this suggests that your work environment is a psychologically healthy one.

If you have 7 or fewer "yes" answers, this may suggest that your work environment is not as psychologically healthy as it could be.

Task uncertainty was shown to have an adverse effect on morale in a study of 629 employment security work units in California and Wisconsin.[55] More important, the study showed that morale was better predicted by considering both the overall design of the work unit and the task uncertainty. This study suggests that if one work design parameter, such as task uncertainty, is a problem in a job, its adverse effects on people may be mitigated by other work design parameters. For example, higher pay may offset an employee's frustration with a difficult coworker, or a friendly, supportive working environment may offset frustration with low pay. You 14.2 provides you with an opportunity to evaluate how psychologically healthy your work environment is.

CONTEMPORARY ISSUES IN THE DESIGN OF WORK

(8) Discuss five contemporary issues in the design of work.

A number of contemporary issues related to specific aspects of the design of work have an effect on increasing numbers of employees. Rather than addressing job design or worker well-being in a comprehensive way, these issues address one or another aspect of a job. The issues include telecommuting, alternative work patterns, technostress,

Telecommuting and Leadership

© AP PHOTO/CHARLES KRUPA

Jack and Suzy Welch have faced the challenge of achieving the necessary amount of face time to lead while telecommuting.

Telecommuting can be ideal for writers like Jack and Suzy Welch and for individuals responsible for writing code, analyzing legal documents, designing marketing materials, or selling financial services. The expansion of intellectual commerce and e-commerce has considerably increased the number and kinds of jobs and work ideally suited to telecommuting. However, there is a real cost that comes with telecommuting as well—face time. The telecommuter engaged in that aspect of her or his work is not face-to-face with coworkers and bosses. Therefore, telecommuting and leadership may be antithetical and intractable. When Jack Welch and his team were climbing the corporate GE ladder and building the businesses, they needed face time. Leaders do not just show up for photo ops and retreats. They are in the trenches with the people they lead. Followers must see how calm the leader is in a PR crisis, how decent he or she is to the new employee who does not yet have the hang of the job, how much the leader sweats during a tough deal, and how hard he or she works on a deadline without complaining. Leadership is personal and interpersonal, requiring human interaction and face time. Followers need leaders to be there, to lead, and that cannot be done through telecommuting.

SOURCE: J. Welch and S. Welch, "The Importance of Being There," *Business Week* (April 16, 2007): 92.

task revision, and skill development. One study found that employees stay motivated when their work is relationally designed to provide opportunities for respectful contact with those critical to their work.[56] Telecommuting and alternative work patterns such as job sharing can increase flexibility for employees. Companies use these and other approaches to the design of work as ways to manage a growing business while contributing to a better balance of work and family life for employees.

Telecommuting

Telecommuting, as noted in Chapter 2, is when employees work at home or in other locations geographically separate from their company's main location. Telecommuting may entail working in a combination of home, satellite office, and main office locations. This flexible arrangement is designed to achieve a better fit between the needs of the individual employee and the organization's task demands. Cisco Systems manager Christian Renaud moved from California and began telecommuting from Johnston, Iowa, when he and his wife began their family. Based on years of experience leading GE, Jack Welch concludes that telecommuting can be an ideal situation for some but not for leaders, as we see in the accompanying The Real World 14.2.

Telecommuting has been around since the 1970s but was slower to catch on than some expected.[57] This was due to the inherent paradoxes associated with telecommuting.[58] Actually, with a greater emphasis on managing the work rather than the worker, managers can enhance control, effectively decentralize, and even encourage teamwork through telecommuting. A number of companies, such as AT&T in Phoenix and Bell Atlantic (now part of Verizon Communications), have programs in telecommuting for a wide range of employees. These flexible arrangements help some companies respond to changing demographics and a shrinking labor pool. The Travelers Group (now part of Citigroup) was one of the first companies to try telecommuting and was considered an industry leader in telecommuting. Because of its confidence in its employees, Travelers reaped rewards from telecommuting, including higher productivity, reduced absenteeism, expanded opportunities for workers with disabilities, and an increased ability to attract and retain talent.[59]

Pacific Bell (now part of AT&T) tried telecommuting on a large scale.[60] Pacific Bell had 1,500 managers who telecommuted. For example, an employee might work at home four days a week as an information systems designer and spend one day a week at the main office location in meetings, work exchanges, and coordination with others. Of 3,000 Pacific Bell managers responding to a mail survey, 87 percent said telecommuting would reduce employee stress, 70 percent said it would increase job satisfaction while reducing absenteeism, and 64 percent said it would increase productivity.

Telecommuting is neither a cure-all nor a universally feasible alternative. Many telecommuters feel a sense of social isolation. Some executives are concerned that while such workers are more productive, their lack of visibility may hold back their careers. Furthermore, not all forms of work are amenable to telecommuting. For example, firefighters and police officers must be at their duty stations to be successful in their work. Employees for whom telecommuting is not a viable option within a company may feel jealous of those able to telecommute. In addition, telecommuting may have the potential to create the sweatshops of the twenty-first century. Thus, it is a novel, emerging issue.

Alternative Work Patterns

Job sharing is an alternative work pattern in which more than one person occupies a single job. It may be an alternative to telecommuting for addressing demographic and labor pool concerns. Job sharing is found throughout a wide range of managerial and professional jobs, as well as in production and service jobs. It is not common among senior executives.

The *four-day workweek* is a second type of alternative work schedule. Information systems personnel at the United Services Automobile Association (USAA) in San Antonio, Texas, work four ten-hour days and enjoy a three-day weekend. This arrangement provides the benefit of more time for those who want to balance work and family life through weekend travel. However, the longer workdays may be a drawback for employees with many family or social activities on weekday evenings. Hence, the four-day workweek has both benefits and limitations.

job sharing
An alternative work pattern in which more than one person occupies a single job.

flextime
An alternative work pattern that enables employees to set their own daily work schedules.

Flextime, in which employees can set their own daily work schedules, is a third alternative work pattern. It has been applied in numerous ways in work organizations and can lead to reduced absenteeism. Companies in highly concentrated urban areas, like Houston, Los Angeles, and New York City, may allow employees to set their own daily work schedules as long as they start their eight hours at any thirty-minute interval from 6:00 a.m. to 9:00 a.m. This arrangement is designed to ease traffic and commuting pressures. It also is responsive to individual biorhythms, allowing early risers to go to work early and nighthawks to work late. Typically,

9:00 a.m. to 3:00 p.m. is the required core working time for everyone in the company. Even in companies without formal flextime programs, flextime may be an individual option arranged between supervisor and subordinate. For example, a first-line supervisor who wants to complete a college degree may negotiate a work schedule accommodating both job requirements and course schedules at the university. Flextime options may be more likely for high performers who assure their bosses that work quality and productivity will not suffer.[61] On the cautionary side, one study found that a woman on a flexible work schedule was perceived to have less job–career dedication and less advancement motivation, though no less ability.[62]

Technology at Work

New technologies and electronic commerce are here to stay and are changing the face of work environments, dramatically in some cases. Many government jobs expect to change, and even disappear, with the advent of e-government using Internet technology. As forces for change, new technologies are a double-edged sword that can be used to improve job performance or to create stress. On the positive side, modern technologies are helping to revolutionize the way jobs are designed and the way work gets done. The *virtual office* is a mobile platform of computer, telecommunication, and information technology and services that allows mobile workforce members to conduct business virtually anywhere, anytime, globally. While virtual offices have benefits, they may also lead to a lack of social connection or to technostress.

Technostress is stress caused by new and advancing technologies in the workplace, most often information technologies.[63] For example, the widespread use of electronic bulletin boards as a forum for rumors of layoffs may cause feelings of uncertainty and anxiety—technostress. However, the same electronic bulletin boards can be an important source of information and thus *reduce* uncertainty for workers.

New information technologies enable organizations to monitor employee work performance, even when the employee is not aware of the monitoring.[64] These new technologies also allow organizations to tie pay to performance because performance is electronically monitored.[65] Three guidelines can help make electronic workplace monitoring, especially of performance, less distressful. First, workers should participate in the introduction of the monitoring system. Second, performance standards should be seen as fair. Third, performance records should be used to improve performance, not to punish the performer. In the extreme, new technologies that allow for virtual work in remote locations take employees beyond such monitoring.[66]

Task Revision

A new concept in the design of work is *task revision*.[67] Task revision is an innovative way to modify an incorrectly specified role or job. Task revision assumes that organizational roles and job expectations may be correctly or incorrectly defined. Furthermore, a person's behavior in a work role has very different performance consequences depending on whether the role is correctly or incorrectly defined. Table 14.3 sets out the performance consequences of three categories of role behaviors based on the definition of the role or job. As indicated in the table, standard role behavior leads to good performance if the role is correctly defined, and it leads to poor performance if the role is incorrectly defined. These performances go to the extreme when incumbents exhibit extreme behavior in their jobs.[68] Going to extremes leads one to exceed expectations and display extraordinary behavior (extrarole behavior); this results in either excellent or poor performance, depending on the accuracy of the defined role.

virtual office
A mobile platform of computer, telecommunication, and information technology and services.

technostress
The stress caused by new and advancing technologies in the workplace.

task revision
The modification of incorrectly specified roles or jobs.

TABLE  Performance Consequences of Role Behaviors

Role Characteristics	Standard Role Behavior (Meets Expectations)	Extra Role Behavior (Goes Beyond Expectations)	Counter-Role Behavior (Differs From Expected)
Correctly specified role	Ordinary good performance	Excellent performance (organizational citizenship and prosocial behavior)	Poor performance (deviance, dissent, and grievance)
Incorrectly specified role	Poor performance (bureaucratic behavior)	Very poor performance (bureaucratic zeal)	Excellent performance (task revision and redirection, role innovation)

SOURCE: Republished with permission of Academy of Management, PO Box 3020, Briar Cliff Manor, NY 10510-8020. "Task Revision: A Neglected Form of Work Performance," (Table), R. M. Staw & R. D. Boettger, *Academy of Management Journal*, 1990, Vol. 33. Reproduced by permission of the publisher via Copyright Clearance Center, Inc.

Counter-role behavior is when the incumbent acts contrary to the expectations of the role or exhibits deviant behavior. This is a problem if the role is correctly defined. For example, poor performance occurred on a hospital ward when the nursing supervisor failed to check the administration of all medications for the nurses she was supervising, resulting in one near fatality because a patient was not given required medication by a charge nurse. The nursing supervisor exhibited counter-role behavior in believing she could simply trust the nurses and did not have to double-check their actions. The omission was caught on the next shift. When a role or task is correctly defined (for example, double-checking medication administration), counter-role behavior leads to poor performance.

Task revision is counter-role behavior in an incorrectly specified role and is a useful way to correct the problem in the role specification (see Table 14.3). Task revision is a form of role innovation that modifies the job to achieve a better performance. Task revision is the basis for long-term adaptation when the current specifications of a job are no longer applicable.[69] For example, the traditional role for a surgeon is to complete surgical procedures in an accurate and efficient manner. Based on this definition, socio-emotional caregiving is counter-role behavior on the part of the surgeon. However, if the traditional role were to be labeled incorrect, the surgeon's task revision through socio-emotional caregiving would be viewed as leading to much better medical care for patients.

Skill Development

Problems in work system design are often seen as the source of frustration for those dealing with technostress.[70] However, system and technical problems are not the only sources of technostress in new information technologies. Some experts see a growing gap between the skills demanded by new technologies and the skills possessed by employees in jobs using these technologies.[71] Although technical skills are important and are emphasized in many training programs, the largest sector of the economy is actually service oriented, and service jobs require interpersonal skills. Managers also need a wide range of nontechnical skills to be effective in their work.[72] Therefore, any discussion of jobs and the design of work must recognize the importance of incumbent skills and abilities to meet the demands of the work. Organizations must consider the talents and skills of their employees when they engage in job design efforts. The two issues of employee skill development and job design are interrelated. The knowledge and information requirements for jobs of the future are especially high—hence Toyota's investment in "Back to Basics" training discussed in Thinking Ahead.

counter-role behavior
Deviant behavior in either a correctly or incorrectly defined job or role.

MANAGERIAL IMPLICATIONS: THE CHANGING NATURE OF WORK

Work is an important aspect of a healthy life. The two central needs in human nature are to engage in productive work and to form healthy relationships with others. Work means different things to different ethnic and national groups. Therefore, job design efforts must be sensitive to cultural values and beliefs.

In crafting work tasks and assignments, managers should make an effort to fit the jobs to the people who are doing them. There are no universally accepted ways to design work, and early efforts to find them have been replaced by a number of alternatives. Early approaches to job design were valuable for manufacturing and administrative jobs of the mid-1900s. Now, however, the changing nature of work in the United States and the Americans with Disabilities Act (ADA) challenge managers to find new ways to define work and design jobs.

The distinguishing feature of job design in the foreseeable future is flexibility. Dramatic global, economic, and organizational changes dictate that managers be flexible in the design of work in their organizations. Jobs must be designed to fit the larger organizational structures discussed in Chapter 15. Organizations must ask, does the job support the organization's mission? Employees must ask, does the job meet my short- and long-term needs?

Technology is one of the distinguishing features of the modern workplace. Advances in information, mechanical, and computer technology are transforming work into a highly scientific endeavor demanding employees who are highly educated, knowledgeable workers. American workers can expect these technological advances to continue during their lifetimes and should expect to meet the challenge through continuous skill development and enhancement.

LOOKING BACK: TOYOTA MOTOR CORPORATION

Well-Trained Workers Meet the Competition

An organization can design the most efficient production system in the world with jobs that support that system in grand elegance. However, it is ultimately about the people and their ability to do the work. One of the huge challenges that organizations like Toyota face is the expected shortfall of well-trained workers as baby boomers started retiring in 2007. Well-trained workers are essential to the maintenance of a high quality manufacturing organization like an automotive company. In addition to the competitive pressures that Toyota faces from other car makers, it must address the increasing impact of countries around the world raising environmental standards and safety requirements. These competitive pressures require great leadership from those filling the top jobs in the company and great performance from well-trained workers.

Toyota's automotive assembly lines have traditionally been able to produce just two or three models of cars. However, the company is aiming for a line that can produce eight different models. This requires well-trained workers and a well-designed production system for efficient and effective work. The company plans to spend ¥30 billion (about $2.5 billion) to install a production line at its key Takaoka Plant in Aichi Prefecture to achieve this objective. In 2007, the line was manufacturing the Corolla and other models. The redesign will add sublines for assembling parts and use robots for conveying car bodies. A completed car will be rolled off every 50 seconds, down from every 60 seconds. This raises the production line's efficiency by around 20 percent. After increasing completion rates at the Takaoka factory, Toyota will study installing the production line at its North American and Asian plants.

Toyota may be number one in the world, but it is not standing still. The company is investing in its people and in its way of doing work. This inevitably pushes its competition. For example, Nissan Motor Company is aiming to leverage information technology and automate parts conveyance along with other routine steps at its Oppama Plant in Kanagawa Prefecture, hoping to save 10 percent. Honda Motor Company will overhaul its car assembly methods at its Yorii, Saitama Prefecture plant as a way of staying competitive. Suzuki Motor Company is implementing labor-intensive, state-of-the-art methods used in Japan in its emerging-nation factories. The competition cannot, and does not, stand still. So too, Toyota must look ahead to stay on top while at the same time looking back to see what the competition is doing. Investing in people, in work processes, and in the latest technology are key elements to maintain quality and remain competitive.[73]

Chapter Summary

1. Different countries have different preferences for one or more of six distinct patterns of defining work.
2. Scientific management, job enlargement/job rotation, job enrichment, and the job characteristics theory are traditional American approaches to the design of work and the management of workforce diversity.
3. The social information-processing (SIP) model suggests that information from others and the social context are important in a job.
4. Ergonomics and the interdisciplinary framework draw on engineering, psychology, and biology in considering the advantages and disadvantages of job and work design efforts.
5. The cultural values and social organizations in Japan, Germany, and Scandinavia lead to unique approaches to the design of work.
6. Control, uncertainty, conflict, and job/task demands are important job design parameters to consider when designing work for the well-being of the workers.
7. Telecommuting, alternative work patterns, technostress, task revision, and skill development are emerging issues in the design of work and the use of information technology.

Key Terms

anthropocentric (p. 490)
counter-role behavior (p. 496)
cross-training (p. 481)
engagement (p. 486)
ergonomics (p. 487)
flextime (p. 494)
job (p. 476)
Job Characteristics Model (p. 482)
Job Diagnostic Survey (JDS) (p. 482)
job enlargement (p. 480)
job enrichment (p. 481)
job rotation (p. 480)
job sharing (p. 494)
lean production (p. 489)
meaning of work (p. 477)
social information-processing (SIP) model (p. 487)

sociotechnical systems (STS) (p. 489)
task revision (p. 495)
technocentric (p. 490)
technostress (p. 495)
virtual office (p. 495)
work (p. 476)
work simplification (p. 479)

Review Questions

1. Define a job in its organizational context.
2. Describe six patterns of working that have been studied in different countries.
3. Describe four traditional approaches to the design of work in America.
4. Identify and define the five core job dimensions and the three critical psychological states in the Job Characteristics Model.
5. What are the salient features of the social information-processing (SIP) model of job design?
6. List the positive and negative outcomes of the four job design approaches considered by the interdisciplinary framework.
7. How do the Japanese, German, and Scandinavian approaches to work differ from one another and from the American approach?
8. Describe the key job design parameters considered when examining the effects of work design on health and well-being.
9. What are five emerging issues in jobs and the design of work?

Discussion and Communication Questions

1. Is there ever one best way to design a particular job?
2. What should managers learn from the traditional approaches to the design of work used in the United States?
3. It is possible for American companies to apply approaches to the design of work that were developed in other countries?
4. What is the most important emerging issue in the design of work?
5. *(communication question)* Read about new approaches to jobs, such as job sharing. Prepare a memo comparing what you have learned from your reading with one or more approaches to job design discussed in the chapter. What changes in approaches to jobs and job design do you notice from this comparison?
6. *(communication question)* Interview an employee in your organization or another organization and develop an oral presentation about how his or her job could be enriched. Make sure you ask questions about all aspects of the employee's work (e.g., what specific tasks are done and with whom the employee interacts on the job).
7. *(communication question)* Based on the materials in the chapter, prepare a memo detailing the advantages and disadvantages of flextime job arrangements. In a second part of the memo, identify the specific conditions and characteristics required for a successful flextime program. Would you like to work under a flextime arrangement?

Ethical Dilemma

Bill Rider is the manager for the medical records department of a large university-based hospital. He loves his job, but there are times when it stretches his tolerance. He has been dealing with one such challenge for the last several weeks. Bill is trying to hire someone for a key position in his department. The hospital is in a large city that usually offers a great applicant pool from which to fill openings. But this position has always been different. It is a very demanding job and one that is often extremely stressful. Bill has tried everything he knows to restructure the position, but it remains one of the most difficult jobs in his department.

The position has been open for two months now, and the pressure to hire someone is increasing. Bill has interviewed many people. Only one person stands out in Bill's mind: Elizabeth Murry. She is smart and has plenty of medical records experience. She would be perfect for the job except for Bill's concerns about putting her in such a stressful position.

During the interview process, Bill and Elizabeth had chatted about her life as a single mom. Bill had respected Elizabeth's honesty. He also recognized how badly she needs this job. The position comes with a generous pay raise and a much shorter commute. Both things would allow Elizabeth to better provide for her children.

Bill's concern is that Elizabeth does not realize just how demanding this job could be. He also realizes that she does not fully understand the dynamics of the job.

Bill had not lied, but he had not been completely honest either. He is afraid she will not accept the position if she really understands what she is getting into. No job is perfect, but this one has some real flaws. Bill is unsure what to do. He could be honest and chance losing Elizabeth, or he could just be quiet and hope she is willing to live with the negatives of the position.

Questions

1. Where does Bill's primary responsibility lie?
2. Will his responsibilities to his employer be met if he hires Elizabeth under these conditions?
3. Evaluate Bill's decision using consequential, rule-based, and character theories.

Experiential Exercises

14.1 Chaos and the Manager's Job

Managers' jobs are increasingly chaotic as a result of high rates of change, uncertainty, and turbulence. Some managers thrive on change and chaos, but others have a difficult time responding to high rates of change and uncertainty in a positive manner. This questionnaire gives you an opportunity to evaluate how you would react to a manager's job that is rather chaotic.

Exercise Schedule

1. Preparation (preclass)

   Complete the questionnaire.

2. Individual Scoring

   Give yourself 4 points for each A, 3 points for each B, 2 points for each C, 1 point for each D, and 0 points for each E. Compute the total, divide by 24, and round to one decimal place.

3. Group Discussion

   Your instructor may have you discuss your scores in groups of six students. The higher your score, the more you respond positively to change and chaos; the lower your score, the more difficulty you would have responding to this manager's job in a positive manner. In addition, answer the following questions.

   a. If you could redesign this manager's job, what are the two or three aspects of the job that you would change first?

   b. What are the two or three aspects of the job that you would feel no need to change?

SOURCE: "Chaos and the Manager's Job" in D. Marcic, "Option B. Quality and the New Management Paradigm," *Organizational Behavior: Experiences and Cases*, 4th ed. (Minneapolis/St. Paul: West Publishing, 1995): 296–297. Reprinted by permission.

A Manager's Job*

Listed below are some statements a thirty-seven-year-old manager made about his job at a large and successful corporation. If your job had these characteristics, how would you react to them? After each statement are five letters, A–E. Circle the letter that best describes how you would react according to the following scale:

A. I would enjoy this very much; it's completely acceptable.

B. This would be enjoyable and acceptable most of the time.

C. I'd have no reaction one way or another, or it would be about equally enjoyable and unpleasant.

D. This feature would be somewhat unpleasant for me.

E. This feature would be very unpleasant for me.

1. I regularly spend 30–40 percent of my time in meetings. A B C D E
2. A year and a half ago, my job did not exist, and I have been essentially inventing it as I go along. A B C D E
3. The responsibilities I either assume or am assigned consistently exceed the authority I have for discharging them. A B C D E
4. At any given moment in my job, I average about a dozen phone calls to be returned. A B C D E
5. There seems to be very little relation in my job between the quality of my performance and my actual pay and fringe benefits. A B C D E
6. I need about two weeks of management training a year to stay current in my job. A B C D E
7. Because we have very effective equal employment opportunity in my company and because it is thoroughly multinational, my job consistently brings me into close contact at a professional level with people of many races, ethnic groups, and nationalities and of both sexes. A B C D E
8. There is no objective way to measure my effectiveness. A B C D E

9. I report to three different bosses for different aspects of my job, and each has an equal say in my performance appraisal. A B C D E
10. On average, about a third of my time is spent dealing with unexpected emergencies that force all scheduled work to be postponed. A B C D E
11. When I need to meet with the people who report to me, it takes my secretary most of a day to find a time when we are all available, and even then I have yet to have a meeting where everyone is present for the entire meeting. A B C D E
12. The college degree I earned in preparation for this type of work is now obsolete, and I probably should return for another degree. A B C D E
13. My job requires that I absorb about 100–200 pages a week of technical material. A B C D E
14. I am out of town overnight at least one night a week. A B C D E
15. My department is so interdependent with several other departments in the company that all distinctions about which department is responsible for which tasks are quite arbitrary. A B C D E
16. I will probably get a promotion in about a year to a job in another division that has most of these same characteristics. A B C D E
17. During the period of my employment here, either the entire company or the division I worked in has been reorganized every year or so. A B C D E
18. While I face several possible promotions, I have no real career path. A B C D E
19. While there are several possible promotions I can see ahead of me, I think I have no realistic chance of getting to the top levels of the company. A B C D E
20. While I have many ideas about how to make things work better, I have no direct influence on either the business policies or the personnel policies that govern my division. A B C D E
21. My company has recently put in an "assessment center" where I and other managers must go through an extensive battery of psychological tests to assess our potential. A B C D E
22. My company is a defendant in an antitrust suit, and if the case comes to trial, I will probably have to testify about some decisions that were made a few years ago. A B C D E
23. Advanced computer and other electronic office technology is continually being introduced into my division, necessitating constant learning on my part. A B C D E
24. The computer terminal and screen I have in my office can be monitored in my boss's office without my knowledge. A B C D E

* "A Manager's Job" by Peter B. Vaill in *Managing as a Performing Art: New Ideas for a World of Chaotic Change*, 1989. Reprinted by permission of Jossey-Bass Inc., Publishers.

14.2 A Job Redesign Effort

This activity will help you consider ways in which work can be redesigned to improve its impact on people and its benefit to the organization. Consider the following case:

> Eddie is a quality control inspector for an automotive manufacturer. His job is to inspect the body, interior, and engine of cars as they roll off the assembly line. Eddie's responsibility is to identify quality problems that either hinder the functioning of these parts of the car or noticeably mar the car's appearance. He is to report the problem so that it can be corrected. Sometimes late in the day, especially on Thursdays and Fridays, Eddie lets assembly problems slip past him. In addition, his back feels sore at the end of the day, and sometimes he is very stiff in the morning. There are times when he is not sure whether he is seeing a serious problem or just a glitch.

As part of a five-person team, your job is to evaluate two alternative approaches to redesigning Eddie's job using theories presented in the chapter. Answer the following questions as a team. Your team should be prepared to present its recommendations to the class as a whole.

Discussion Questions

Your instructor will lead a class discussion of each of the following questions:

1. For this particular job, which are the two best models to use in a redesign effort? Why?
2. Does your team need any additional information before it begins to redesign Eddie's job? If so, what information do you need?
3. Using the two models you chose in Question 1, what would your team specifically recommend to redesign Eddie's job?

TAKE 2

Biz Flix | Reality Bites

Four Generation X'ers meet life's realities after their college graduation. Life's realities play cruel tricks on them as they continue developing together. Lelaina Pierce (Winona Ryder) records their reality interactions in an almost endless documentary video. Ben Stiller, in his directorial debut with this film, tries to make penetrating observations on this generation's growth, development, and shared life expectations.

This scene from *Reality Bites* is the "Wienerdude" segment that appears about one-third of the way through the film. Lelaina, her class's valedictorian, desperately seeks a job after her termination as a TV morning show production assistant. She has had three unsuccessful job interviews before the one shown in this scene at a local Wienerschnitzel. Just before this scene, Lelaina asked her mother (Susan Norfleet) for a loan. Lelaina's mother noted that times are hard, and Lelaina should perhaps find a job at a fast-food restaurant. The film continues with Lelaina trying to escape her depression by chain-smoking cigarettes, watching mindless television programs, and talking to a psychic telephone partner (voiced by Amy Stiller).

What to Watch for and Ask Yourself:

- Assess the proposed job using the core job characteristics of the Job Characteristics Model. Is each job characteristic high or low?
- Do you expect the job described by Wienderdude (David Spade, uncredited) to induce high levels of internal work motivation and work satisfaction? Why or why not?
- Would you expect the work context (working conditions, supervision, coworkers) to positively or negatively affect a person's motivation and satisfaction?

Workplace Video | The Evolution of Management Thinking

The world is a very different place than it was 100 years ago. The offices and factories of yesteryear look very little like the tech-driven businesses of today. Times have changed, and so has labor. However, then as now, managers have taken on the task of creating jobs and motivating employees to accomplish organizational goals.

Maximizing worker potential is an important responsibility of management, and managers of the past century have taken different approaches to designing work. The leaders of the American Industrial Revolution believed that standardizing job design was the best way to turn workers and businesses into efficient operating machines. The narrow work simplification of the factory system was deemed monotonous, however, and managers began looking for new ways to improve the experience of work.

As a correction to overspecialized work, other traditional and contemporary methods of job design emerged. Rotating employees through different jobs and increasing the tasks individuals perform were two ways managers used to add variety to workers' daily routines. Other approaches saw person–job fit as the key to job satisfaction. One such approach, the job characteristics theory, emphasized the role of skill variety, task

TAKE 2

significance, and autonomy in heightening workers' sense of meaning and personal responsibility while on the job. These perspectives, though different in their methodologies, shared the view that managers must design jobs that appeal to employees' higher needs.

As managers throughout the century shaped the design of work from within, forces from outside the organization also began changing the way people work. Technology, in particular, had a revolutionary impact on jobs. Because information and ideas have become more important than physical capital in today's world, employers now look to computer systems and mobile telecommunications technologies to achieve new efficiencies. And though the digital age is changing how and where managers interact with their subordinates, rapid innovation associated with new technology is adding to the stress that people feel at work.

As history shows, management theories evolve and are shaped by the times. By learning the various approaches to work that have come before, today's managers can become better equipped to create satisfying, engaging jobs—ones that reduce stress and increase employee well-being.

Discussion Questions

1. How might managers at Peet's Coffee & Tea utilize job rotation and why?
2. Using the Job Characteristics Model, explain why American Apparel's implementation of self-directed teams led to quality work performance and high worker satisfaction.
3. While technology has enabled Zingerman's to develop an e-commerce component to its gourmet-food business, how might technology change the way the company designs jobs for employees throughout its seven Ann Arbor, Michigan, locations?

CASE

What Employees of The Coca-Cola Company Say about Their Jobs

The Coca-Cola Company, headquartered in Atlanta, Georgia, produces approximately 400 beverage brands in over 200 nations around the world. It is the world's largest nonalcoholic beverage company. In 2006, net operating revenue was just over $24 billion, up 4 percent from the preceding year, and operating income was $6.3 billion, also up 4 percent from 2005.[1]

The Coca-Cola Company describes itself as "a local employer, with responsibility to enable our people to tap into their full potential; working at their innovative best and representing the diversity of the world we serve."[2] Encouraging performance excellence by creating meaningful and involving jobs seems to be a hallmark of Coca-Cola's approach to employee motivation throughout its global operations. According to the company's Web site, "[e]ach employee of The Coca-Cola Company helps lead our success in the beverage industry by committing to benefit and refresh everyone who is touched by our business."[3] Coca-Cola's Web site also states, "[w]hen pride, passion and drive come together, you get the professionals of The Coca-Cola Company. We're looking for individuals who want to make a difference, develop and inspire others, drive innovative ideas and deliver results, and who live our values."[4]

In recruiting prospective employees, Coca-Cola encourages people to "[b]ecome one of the secret ingredients that make our company so refreshing."[5] When the question—"What are the secret ingredients that make your job at The Coca-Cola Company so refreshing?"—was posed to a group of current employees, several responded with answers that provide insight into how jobs are designed at the company. Here is what seven of these employees said, in their own words.

Hector, Supply Chain General Management

"Professionally, I feel rewarded as there are many new challenges, which allow me to grow, learn and explore."[6]

Joycelyn, Brand Management

"Based on my background, they [Coca-Cola recruiters and managers] were convinced I had the cultural understanding and sensitivity, as well as the specific marketing expertise, required to deliver against the Hispanic marketing department's business objectives and goals."[7]

Mary Page, Strategic Planning

"My job at The Coca-Cola Company is to facilitate development of the strategy of a global, *Fortune* 100 company. By definition, there are very few places where one can do that, and it is fascinating. I can say without a doubt—I love my job. . . . The bar is set high at The Coca-Cola Company. We attract the best and brightest from all over the world. I feel privileged to work with so many smart people from such diverse backgrounds. They show me many different ways of thinking about not only our business, but the world. . . . Having the ability, and the willingness, to learn from each local market—to scale the best ideas globally and to capture the learnings from less successful experiences—gives us a truly unique competitive advantage. . . . You have the opportunity to explore, learn and grow, all within the system that is Coca-Cola."[8]

Rebecca, Global Marketing

"Our work makes people happy. We provide optimism through our brands, and we refresh many different people every day. The work I do gives a framework that connects people around the world. . . . I have had an opportunity to help the Company regain its leadership position as the most respected marketing company worldwide. . . . My experience at The Coca-Cola Company has probably changed my life. It has helped me develop as an individual, opened my mind to cultures and perspectives and has exposed me to life-changing experiences."[9]

Tor, Sales Director

"There are even broader opportunities for personal and professional growth. In this environment, I feel that it is my responsibility to take on where my passions lie. I can in fact, create my own career destiny."[10]

Tania, Information Technology General Management

"We work at a real level that connects directly with billions of people around the globe each and every day. . . . The ideas, the markets, the portfolio of brands and approach, it's like a small company where you can make an impact and see the difference. It's where a little gem of an idea can and has turned into something extraordinary. The company encourages and supports you being 'fluid.' You can look beyond your job description to other ideas you might have. You're not just doing a j-o-b. You have the freedom to innovate and execute your ideas. It's really like a big and small company all in one."[11]

Vikram, Strategic Growth

"I've been with The Coca-Cola Company for a short time and I can already see the meaningful significance that The Coca-Cola Company makes in the world. Many of our products are sold at small 'mom and pop' stores. The margins the owners receive on our products often impacts their ability to support their family, and gives them an opportunity to send their kids to college. . . . The value that we create and share is more than just providing a refreshing beverage. We truly have global impact and are making a difference."[12]

From a job design perspective, how would you interpret what these seven employees of The Coca-Cola Company say about the secret ingredients that make their jobs so refreshing?

Discussion Questions

1. What information contained in the seven employees' comments about their jobs relates to the core job characteristics of *skill variety*?
2. What information contained in the comments relates to the core job characteristics of *task identity*?
3. What information relates to the core job characteristics of *task significance*?
4. What information relates to the core job characteristics of *autonomy*?
5. What information relates to the core job characteristics of *feedback from the job itself*?
6. How can the social information-processing model be applied to understanding The Coca-Cola Company's approach to creating jobs that are refreshing?

SOURCE: This case was written by Michael K. McCuddy, The Louis S. and Mary L. Morgal Chair of Christian Business Ethics and Professor of Management, College of Business Administration, Valparaiso University.

CHAPTER 15

Organizational Design and Structure

LEARNING OBJECTIVES

After reading this chapter, you should be able to do the following:

1 Define *differentiation* and *integration* as organizational design processes.

2 Discuss six basic design dimensions of an organization.

3 Briefly describe five structural configurations for organizations.

4 Describe four contextual variables for an organization.

5 Explain the four forces reshaping organizations.

6 Discuss emerging organizational structures.

7 Identify two cautions about the effect of organizational structures on people.

THINKING AHEAD: TIMBERLAND

Strategic Goal and Organizational Structure

Timberland's principal strategic goal is to become the authentic outdoor brand of choice globally. In pursuit of this goal, the company drives progress on key strategic fronts. These include enhancing the company's leadership position in its core footwear business; capturing the opportunity in outdoor-inspired apparel; extending enterprise reach through development of new brand platforms and brand-building licensing agreements; expanding geographically throughout America and around the world; and driving operational and financial excellence while setting the standard for commitment to the community. In harmony with Timberland's strategic goal is the company's aspiration to be the global employer of choice and to reinforce the premium positioning of the Timberland brand. Strategy leads and the company's structure follows.

With its clear strategic goal in mind, Timberland engaged in a global restructuring initiative in December 2006 that involved making a series of organizational changes to support its goal while aligning the organizational structure with the company's consumers. Therefore, Timberland examined its organizational structure in the context of its environment with its strategic goal in mind. The result of the examination was a new go-to-market infrastructure that was seen as an essential means of supporting its goal. The restructuring involved assessing its business segment definitions, which led to the establishment of four new consumer categories: Authentic Youth, Casual Gear, Outdoor Group, and Industrial. Each business segment organization has dedicated resources for merchandising, design, sales planning, marketing within the consumer category, and global sales.

While it has a new organizational structure, Timberland is extending and building on its past success, not changing directions. The clearly articulated strategic goal and new organizational structure aim toward the future while at the same time honoring the past. The company continues to develop a diverse portfolio of footwear, apparel, and accessories that reinforce the functional performance, benefits, and classic styling of its products. Consumers have come to expect these high-quality marks from the Timberland brand. The company continues to sell its products to consumers who embrace an outdoor-inspired lifestyle through high-quality distribution channels. These channels include the company's own retail stores.[1] With a clear strategic goal and a new organizational structure, the question becomes: What about the people?

Organizational design is the process of constructing and adjusting an organization's structure to achieve its goals. The design process begins with the organization's goals. These goals are broken into tasks as the basis for jobs, as discussed in Chapter 14. Jobs are grouped into departments, and departments are linked to form the *organizational structure*. Chapter 15 builds on Chapter 14 by examining the macro structure of the organization in a parallel fashion to how Chapter 14 examines the micro structure of the organization.

The first section of the chapter examines the design processes of differentiation and integration. The second section addresses the six basic design dimensions of an organization's structure. The organization's structure gives it the form to fulfill its function in the environment. As Louis Sullivan, the father of the skyscraper, said, "Form ever follows function." The third section of the chapter presents five structural configurations for organizations. Based on its mission and purpose, an organization determines the best structural configuration for its unique situation. Boeing had to create a global organizational structure for the design and construction of its 787 Dreamliner, as we see in The Real World 15.1. The fourth section examines size, technology, environment, and strategy and goals as *contextual variables* influencing organizational design. When these variables change, the organization must redesign itself to meet new demands and functions. The fifth section examines five forces shaping organizations today. The final section notes several areas where managers should be cautious with regard to structural weaknesses and dysfunctional structural constellations.

organizational design
The process of constructing and adjusting an organization's structure to achieve its goals.

organizational structure
The linking of departments and jobs within an organization.

contextual variables
A set of characteristics that influence the organization's design processes.

Boeing Designs around the Clock . . . and the World

Boeing Commercial Airplanes is designing and building the 787 Dreamliner as an American midsized, wide-body, twin-engine jet that can carry between 210 and 330 passengers depending on configuration. The company enlisted global partners to deliver this next generation of aircraft into service during 2008. Boeing created a unique organizational structure for the design and production of the Dreamliner. Dozens of direct suppliers—including Mitsubishi, Kawasaki Heavy Industries, Alenia in Italy, and Spirit in Wichita—contributed to the effort. Coordination happened early in the process at Boeing's Seattle headquarters, and a single design system was used. Everyone used this system in real time from every point around the world. Any design change was done in real time so that everyone involved would see it.

Boeing Commercial Airplanes worked with global partners from around the world to design and build the 787 Dreamliner, an American midsized, wide-body, twin-engine jet.

For production, Boeing set up an organizational structure of Life Cycle Product Teams (LCPT). The two categories of LCPTs were vertical and horizontal teams. The vertical LCPTs each had a structural component, such as the fuselage, the wing and landing gear, and propulsion. The horizontal LCPTs each address a service, such as systems and production operations, across the structural component teams. Some teams, such as the wing and landing gear team, had hundreds of members. To design and produce the Dreamliner, Boeing truly created a global organizational structure spanning the United States, Europe, and Asia.

SOURCE: J. Dodge, "Designing Around the Clock, and the World," *Design News* 62 (June 4, 2007): 97–100.

KEY ORGANIZATIONAL DESIGN PROCESSES

1 Define *differentiation* and *integration* as organizational design processes.

Differentiation is the design process of breaking the organizational goals into tasks. Integration is the design process of linking the tasks together to form a structure that supports goal accomplishment. These two processes are the keys to successful organizational design. The organizational structure is designed to prevent chaos through an orderly set of reporting relationships and communication channels. Understanding the key design processes and organizational structure helps a person understand the larger working environment and may prevent confusion in the organization.

The organization chart is the most visible representation of a company's structure and underlying components. Figure 15.1 is the organizational chart for the World Trade Organization (WTO). Most organizations have a series of such charts showing reporting relationships throughout the system. The underlying components are (1) formal lines of authority and responsibility (the organizational structure designates reporting relationships by the way jobs and departments are grouped) and (2) formal systems of communication, coordination, and integration (the organizational structure designates the expected patterns of formal interaction among employees).[2]

FIGURE  15.1 Organization Chart for the World Trade Organization

WTO Structure

All WTO members may participate in all councils, committees, etc., except Appellate Body, Dispute Settlement panels, Textiles Monitoring Body, and plurilateral committees.

Ministerial Conference

General Council meeting as **Dispute Settlement Body**

General Council

General Council meeting as **Trade Policy Review Body**

Appellate Body
Dispute Settlement panels

Committees on
- Trade and Environment
- Trade and Development
  - *Subcommittee on Least-Developed Countries*
- Regional Trade Agreements
- Balance of Payments Restrictions
- Budget, Finance and Administration

Working parties on
- Accession

Working groups on
- Relationship between Trade and Investment
- Interaction between Trade and Competition Policy
- Transparency in Government Procurement
- Trade, Debt, and Finance
- Trade and Technology Transfer

Plurilaterals
- Information Technology Agreement Committee

Council for Trade in Goods

Committees on
- Market Access
- Agriculture
- Sanitary and Phytosanitary Measures
- Technical Barriers to Trade
- Subsidies and Countervailing Measures
- Anti-Dumping Practices
- Customs Valuation
- Rules of Origin
- Import Licensing
- Trade-Related Investment Measures
- Safeguards

Textiles Monitoring Body

Working party on
- State-Trading Enterprises

Council for Trade-Related Aspects of Intellectual Property Rights

Council for Trade in Services

Committees on
- Trade in Financial Services
- Specific Commitments

Working parties on
- Domestic Regulation
- GATS Rules

Plurilaterals
- Trade in Civil Aircraft Committee
- Government Procurement Committee

Doha Development Agenda: TNC and its bodies

Trade Negotiations Committee

Special Sessions of
- Services Council / TRIPS Council / Dispute Settlement Body / Agriculture Committee / Trade and Development Committee / Trade and Environment Committee

Negotiating groups on
- Market Access / Rules

Key
- (blue line) Reporting to General Council (or a subsidiary)
- (purple line) Reporting to Dispute Settlement Body
- (red squares) Plurilateral committees inform the General Council or Goods Council of their activities, although these agreements are not signed by all WTO members
- (purple dots) Trade Negotiations Committee reports to General Council

The General Council also meets as the Trade Policy Review Body and Dispute Settlement Body

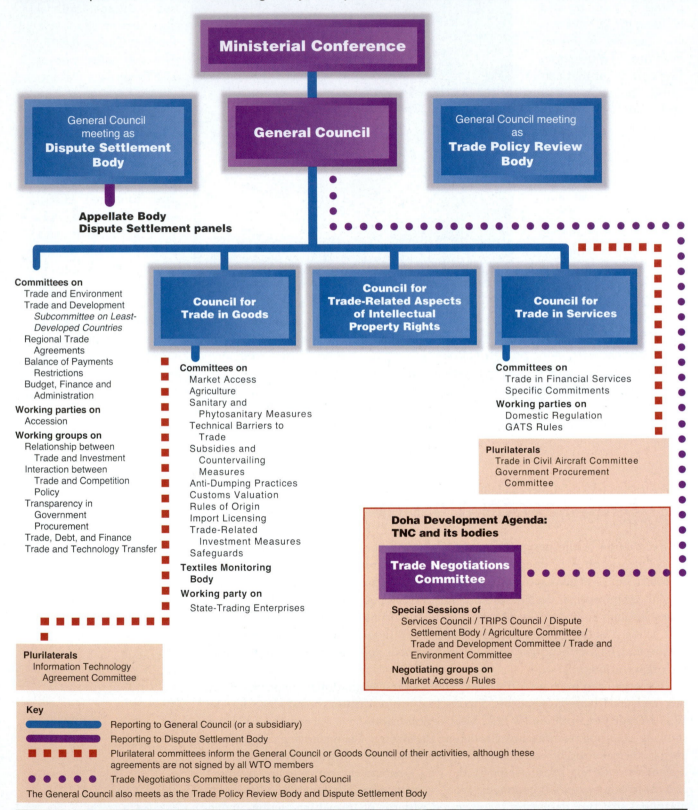

SOURCE: WTO Organization Chart http://www.wto.org/english/thewto_e/whatis_e/tif_e/org2_e.htm

Differentiation

Differentiation is the process of deciding how to divide the work in an organization.[3] Differentiation ensures that all essential organizational tasks are assigned to one or more jobs and that the tasks receive the attention they need. Many dimensions of differentiation have been considered in organizations. Lawrence and Lorsch found four dimensions of differentiation in one study: (1) manager's goal orientation, (2) time orientation, (3) interpersonal orientation, and (4) formality of structure.[4] Table 15.1 shows some typical differences in orientation for various functional areas of an organization. Three different forms of differentiation are horizontal, vertical, and spatial.

Horizontal differentiation is the degree of differentiation between organizational subunits and is based on employees' specialized knowledge, education, or training. For example, two university professors who teach specialized subjects in different academic departments are subject to horizontal differentiation. Horizontal differentiation increases with specialization and departmentation.

Specialization refers to the particular grouping of activities performed by an individual.[5] The degree of specialization or the division of labor in the organization gives an indication of how much training is needed, what the scope of a job is, and what individual characteristics are needed for jobholders. Specialization can also lead to the development of a specialized vocabulary, as well as other behavioral norms. As the two college professors specialize in their subjects, abbreviations or acronyms take on unique meanings. For example, OB means "organizational behavior" to a professor of management but "obstetrics" to a professor of medicine.

Usually, the more specialized the jobs within an organization, the more departments are differentiated within that organization (the greater the departmentation). Departmentation can be by function, product, service, client, geography, process, or some combination of these. A large organization may departmentalize its structure using all or most of these methods at different levels of the organization.

Vertical differentiation is the difference in authority and responsibility in the organizational hierarchy. Vertical differentiation occurs, for example, between a chief executive and a maintenance supervisor. Tall, narrow organizations have greater vertical differentiation, and flat, wide organizations have less vertical differentiation. The height of the organization is also influenced by level of horizontal differentiation and span of control. The span of control refers to and defines the number of subordinates a manager can and should supervise.[6]

Tall structures—those with narrow spans of control—tend to be characterized by closer supervision and tighter controls. In addition, the communication becomes more burdensome, since directives and information must be passed through more layers. The banking industry has often had tall structures. Flat structures—those with wider spans of control—have simpler communication chains and reduced promotion opportunities due to fewer levels of management. Sears is an example of an organization that has gone to a flat structure. With the loss of more than a million

differentiation
The process of deciding how to divide the work in an organization.

TABLE 15.1 Differentiation between Marketing and Engineering

Basis for Difference	Marketing	Engineering
Goal orientation	Sales volume	Design
Time orientation	Long run	Medium run
Interpersonal orientation	People oriented	Task oriented
Structure	Less formal	More formal

middle-management positions, many organizations are now flatter. The degree of vertical differentiation affects organizational effectiveness, but there is no consistent finding that flatter or taller organizations are better.[7] Organizational size, type of jobs, skills and personal characteristics of employees, and degree of freedom must all be considered in determining organizational effectiveness.[8]

Spatial differentiation is the geographic dispersion of an organization's offices, plants, and personnel. A salesperson in New York and one in Portland experience spatial differentiation. An increase in the number of locations increases the complexity of organizational design but may be necessary for organizational goal achievement or organizational protection. For example, if an organization wants to expand into a different country, it may be best to form a separate subsidiary that is partially owned and managed by citizens of that country. Few U.S. citizens think of Shell Oil Company as being a subsidiary of Royal Dutch/Shell Group, a company whose international headquarters is in the Netherlands.

Spatial differentiation may give an organization political and legal advantages in a country because it is identified as a local company. Distance is as important as political and legal issues in making spatial differentiation decisions. For example, a salesperson in Lubbock, Texas, would have a hard time servicing accounts in Beaumont, Texas (over 500 miles away), whereas a salesperson in Delaware might be able to cover all of that state, as well as parts of one or two others.

Horizontal, vertical, and spatial differentiation indicate the amount of width, height, and breadth an organizational structure needs. Just because an organization is highly differentiated along one of these dimensions does not mean it must be highly differentiated along the others. The university environment, for example, is generally characterized by great horizontal differentiation but relatively little vertical and spatial differentiation. A company such as Coca-Cola is characterized by a great deal of all three types of differentiation. The more structurally differentiated an organization is, the more complex it is.[9]

Complexity refers to the number of activities, subunits, or subsystems within the organization. Lawrence and Lorsch suggest that an organization's complexity should mirror the complexity of its environment. As the complexity of an organization increases, its need for mechanisms to link and coordinate the differentiated parts also increases. If these links do not exist, the departments or differentiated parts of the organization can lose sight of its larger mission, and the organization runs the risk of chaos. Designing and building linkage and coordination mechanisms is known as *integration*.

Integration

Integration is the process of coordinating the different parts of an organization. Integration mechanisms are designed to achieve unity among individuals and groups in various jobs, departments, and divisions in the accomplishment of organizational goals and tasks.[10] Integration helps keep the organization in a state of dynamic equilibrium, a condition in which all the parts of the organization are interrelated and balanced.

Vertical linkages are used to integrate activities up and down the organizational chain of command. A variety of structural devices can be used to achieve vertical linkage. These include hierarchical referral, rules and procedures, plans and schedules, positions added to the structure of the organization, and management information systems.[11]

integration
The process of coordinating the different parts of an organization.

The vertical lines on an organization chart indicate the lines of hierarchical referral up and down the organization. When employees do not know how to solve a problem, they can refer it up the organization for consideration and resolution.

Work that needs to be assigned is usually delegated down the chain of command as indicated by the vertical lines.

Rules and procedures, as well as plans and schedules, provide standing information for employees without direct communication. These vertical integrators, such as an employee handbook, communicate to employees standard information or information that they can understand on their own. These integrators allow managers to have wider spans of control, because the managers do not have to inform each employee of what is expected and when it is expected. Vertical integrators encourage managers to use management by exception—to make decisions when employees bring problems up the hierarchy. Military organizations depend heavily on vertical linkages. The army, for example, has a well-defined chain of command. Certain duties are expected to be carried out, and proper paperwork is to be in place. In times of crisis, however, much more information is processed, and the proper paperwork becomes secondary to "getting the job done." Vertical linkages help individuals understand their roles in the organization, especially in times of crisis.

Adding positions to the hierarchy is used as a vertical integrator when a manager becomes overloaded by hierarchical referral or problems arise in the chain of command. Positions such as "assistant to" may be added, as may another level. Adding levels to the hierarchy often reflects growth and increasing complexity. This action tends to reduce the span of control, thus allowing more communication and closer supervision.

Management information systems that are designed to process information up and down the organization also serve as a vertical linkage mechanism. With the advent of computers and network technology, it has become easier for managers and employees to communicate through written reports that are entered into a network and then electronically compiled for managers in the hierarchy. Electronic mail systems allow managers and employees greater access to one another without having to be in the same place at the same time or even attached by telephone. These types of systems make information processing up and down the organization more efficient.

Generally, the taller the organization, the more vertical integration mechanisms are needed. This is because the chains of command and communication are longer. Additional length requires more linkages to minimize the potential for misunderstandings and miscommunications.

Horizontal integration mechanisms provide the communication and coordination that are necessary for links across jobs and departments in the organization. The need for horizontal integration mechanisms increases as the complexity of the organization increases. The horizontal linkages are built into the design of the organization by including liaison roles, task forces, integrator positions, and teams.

A liaison role is created when a person in one department or area of the organization has the responsibility for coordinating with another department (for example, a liaison between the engineering and production departments). Task forces are temporary committees composed of representatives from multiple departments who assemble to address a specific problem affecting these departments.[12]

A stronger device for integration is to develop a person or department designed to be an integrator. In most organizations, the integrator has a good deal of responsibility but not much authority. Such an individual must have the ability to get people together to resolve differences within the perspective of organizational goals.[13]

The strongest method of horizontal integration is through teams. Horizontal teams cut across existing lines of organizational structure to create new entities that make organizational decisions. An example of this may occur in product development with the formation of a team that includes marketing, research, design, and production personnel. Ford used such a cross-functional team to develop the Taurus automobile, which was designed to regain market share in the United States. The information exchanged by such a product development team should lead to a product that is acceptable to a wider range of organizational groups, as well as to customers.[14]

The use of these linkage mechanisms varies from one organization to another, as well as within areas of the same organization. In general, the flatter the organization, the more necessary are horizontal integration mechanisms.

BASIC DESIGN DIMENSIONS

Differentiation, then, is the process of dividing work in the organization, and integration is the process of coordinating work in the organization. From a structural perspective, every manager and organization look for the best combination of differentiation and integration for accomplishing the goals of the organization. There are many ways to approach this process. One way is to establish a desired level of each structural dimension on a high to low continuum and then develop a structure that meets the desired configuration. These structural dimensions include the following:[15]

2 Discuss six basic design dimensions of an organization.

formalization
The degree to which the organization has official rules, regulations, and procedures.

centralization
The degree to which decisions are made at the top of the organization.

specialization
The degree to which jobs are narrowly defined and depend on unique expertise.

standardization
The degree to which work activities are accomplished in a routine fashion.

complexity
The degree to which many different types of activities occur in the organization.

hierarchy of authority
The degree of vertical differentiation across levels of management.

1. *Formalization:* The degree to which an employee's role is defined by formal documentation (procedures, job descriptions, manuals, and regulations).
2. *Centralization:* The extent to which decision-making authority has been delegated to lower levels of an organization. An organization is centralized if the decisions are made at the top of the organization and decentralized if decision making is pushed down to lower levels.
3. *Specialization:* The degree to which organizational tasks are subdivided into separate jobs. The division of labor and the degree to which formal job descriptions spell out job requirements indicate the level of specialization in the organization.
4. *Standardization:* The extent to which work activities are described and performed routinely in the same way. Highly standardized organizations have little variation in the defining of jobs.
5. *Complexity:* The number of activities within the organization and the amount of differentiation needed within the organization.
6. *Hierarchy of authority:* The degree of vertical differentiation through reporting relationships and the span of control within the structure of the organization.

An organization that is high on formalization, centralization, specialization, standardization, and complexity and has a tall hierarchy of authority is said to be highly bureaucratic. Bureaucracies are not in themselves bad; however, they are often tainted by abuse and red tape.

An organization that is on the opposite end of each of these continua is very flexible and loose. Control is very hard to implement and maintain in such an organization, but at certain times such an organization is appropriate. The research and development departments in many organizations are often more flexible than other departments in order to stimulate creativity. An important organizational variable, which is not included in the structural dimensions, is trust.

Another approach to the process of accomplishing organizational goals is to describe what is and is not important to the success of the organization rather than worry about specific characteristics. Henry Mintzberg feels that the following

questions can guide managers in designing formal structures that fit each organization's unique set of circumstances:[16]

1. How many tasks should a given position in the organization contain, and how specialized should each task be?
2. How standardized should the work content of each position be?
3. What skills, abilities, knowledge, and training should be required for each position?
4. What should be the basis for the grouping of positions within the organization into units, departments, divisions, and so on?
5. How large should each unit be, and what should the span of control be (that is, how many individuals should report to each manager)?
6. How much standardization should be required in the output of each position?
7. What mechanisms should be established to help individuals in different positions and units adjust to the needs of other individuals?
8. How centralized or decentralized should decision-making power be in the chain of authority? Should most of the decisions be made at the top of the organization (centralized) or be made down in the chain of authority (decentralized)?

(3) Briefly describe five structural configurations for organizations.

The manager who can answer these questions has a good understanding of how the organization should implement the basic structural dimensions. These basic design dimensions act in combination with one another and are not entirely independent characteristics of an organization. You 15.1 gives you (or a friend) an opportunity to consider how decentralized your company is.

FIVE STRUCTURAL CONFIGURATIONS

Differentiation, integration, and the basic design dimensions combine to yield various structural configurations. Very early organization structures were often based on either product or function. The matrix organization structure crossed these two ways of organizing.[17] Mintzberg moved beyond these early approaches and proposed five structural configurations: the simple structure, the machine bureaucracy, the professional bureaucracy, the divisionalized form, and the adhocracy.[18] Table 15.2 summarizes the prime coordinating mechanism, the key part of the organization, and the type of decentralization for each of these structural

TABLE 15.2 Five Structural Configurations of Organizations

Structural Configuration	Prime Coordinating Mechanism	Key Part of Organization	Type of Decentralization
Simple structure	Direct supervision	Upper echelon	Centralization
Machine bureaucracy	Standardization of work processes	Technical staff	Limited horizontal decentralization
Professional bureaucracy	Standardization of skills	Operating level	Vertical and horizontal decentralization
Divisionalized form	Standardization of outputs	Middle level	Limited vertical decentralization
Adhocracy	Mutual adjustment	Support staff	Selective decentralization

SOURCE: H. Mintzberg, *The Structuring of Organizations*, ©1979, 301. Reprinted by permission of Prentice-Hall, Inc., Upper Saddle River, N.J.

FIGURE 15.2 Mintzberg's Five Basic Parts of an Organization

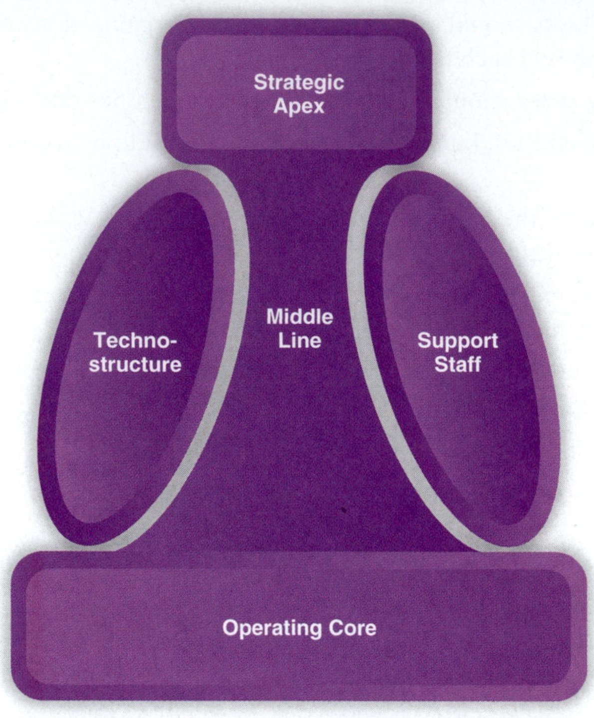

SOURCE: From H. Mintzberg, *The Structuring of Organizations*, © 1979, 20. Reprinted by permission of Pearson Education, Inc., Upper Saddle River, N.J.

configurations. The five basic parts of the organization, for Mintzberg, are the upper echelon or strategic apex; the middle level; the operating core, where work is accomplished; the technical staff; and the support staff. Figure 15.2 depicts these five basic parts with a small strategic apex, connected by a flaring middle line to a large, flat operating core. Each configuration affects people in the organization somewhat differently and all organizational structures should support the firm's strategic goals, as we saw in the case of Timberland in Thinking Ahead.

Simple Structure

The *simple structure* is an organization with little technical and support staff, strong centralization of decision making in the upper echelon, and a minimal middle level. This structure has a minimum of vertical differentiation of authority and minimal formalization. It achieves coordination through direct supervision, often by the chief executive in the upper echelon. An example of a simple structure is a small, independent landscape practice in which one or two landscape architects supervise the vast majority of work with no middle-level managers. Even an organization with as few as thirty people can become dysfunctional as a simple structure after an extended period.

simple structure
A centralized form of organization that emphasizes the upper echelon and direct supervision.

Machine Bureaucracy

The *machine bureaucracy* is an organization with a well-defined technical and support staff differentiated from the line operations of the organization, limited horizontal decentralization of decision making, and a well-defined hierarchy of authority. The technical staff is powerful in a machine bureaucracy. There is strong formalization through policies, procedures, rules, and regulations. Coordination is

machine bureaucracy
A moderately decentralized form of organization that emphasizes the technical staff and standardization of work processes.

YOU 15.1

How Decentralized Is Your Company?

Decentralization is one of the key design dimensions in an organization. It is closely related to several behavioral dimensions of an organization, such as leadership style, degree of participative decision making, and the nature of power and politics within the organization.

The following questionnaire allows you to get an idea about how decentralized your organization is. (If you do not have a job, have a friend who does work complete the questionnaire to see how decentralized his or her organization is.) Which level in your organization has the authority to make each of the following eleven decisions? Answer the questionnaire by circling one of the following:

0 = The board of directors makes the decision.
1 = The CEO makes the decision.
2 = The division/functional manager makes the decision.
3 = A subdepartment head makes the decision.
4 = The first-level supervisor makes the decision.
5 = Operators on the shop floor make the decision.

Decision Concerning:	**Circle Appropriate Level**					
a. The number of workers required.	0	1	2	3	4	5
b. Whether to employ a worker.	0	1	2	3	4	5
c. Internal labor disputes.	0	1	2	3	4	5
d. Overtime worked at shop level.	0	1	2	3	4	5
e. Delivery dates and order priority.	0	1	2	3	4	5
f. Production planning.	0	1	2	3	4	5
g. Dismissal of a worker.	0	1	2	3	4	5
h. Methods of personnel selection.	0	1	2	3	4	5
i. Method of work to be used.	0	1	2	3	4	5
j. Machinery or equipment to be used.	0	1	2	3	4	5
k. Allocation of work among workers.	0	1	2	3	4	5

Scoring

Add up all your circled numbers.
Total = _______.
The higher your number (for example, 45 or more), the more decentralized your organization. The lower your number (for example, 25 or less), the more centralized your organization.

SOURCE: From D. Miller and C. Droge, "Psychological and Traditional Determinants of Structure," *Administrative Science Quarterly* 31 (1986): 558. Reprinted by permission of the *Administrative Science Quarterly*.

achieved through the standardization of work processes. An example of a machine bureaucracy is an automobile assembly plant with routinized operating tasks. The strength of the machine bureaucracy is efficiency of operation in stable, unchanging environments. The weakness of the machine bureaucracy is its slow responsiveness to external changes and to individual employee preferences and ideas.

Professional Bureaucracy

The *professional bureaucracy* emphasizes the expertise of the professionals in the operating core of the organization. The technical and support staffs serve the

NASA, which is composed of many talented experts who work in small teams on a wide range of projects, is an adhocracy.

© AP PHOTO/UNITED LAUNCH ALLIANCE, CARLETON BAILIE

professionals. There is both vertical and horizontal differentiation in the professional bureaucracy. Coordination is achieved through the standardization of the professionals' skills. Examples of professional bureaucracies are hospitals and universities. The doctors, nurses, and professors are given wide latitude to pursue their work based on professional training and indoctrination through professional training programs. Large accounting firms may fall into the category of professional bureaucracies.

Divisionalized Form

The *divisionalized form* is a loosely coupled, composite structural configuration.[19] It is a configuration composed of divisions, each of which may have its own structural configuration. Each division is designed to respond to the market in which it operates. There is vertical decentralization from the upper echelon to the middle of the organization, and the middle level of management is the key part of the organization. This form of organization may have one division that is a machine bureaucracy, one that is an adhocracy, and one that is a simple structure. An example of this form of organization is Valero Energy Corporation, headquartered in San Antonio, Texas, with oil refining operations throughout the country. The divisionalized organization uses standardization of outputs as its coordinating mechanism.

Adhocracy

The *adhocracy* is a highly open and decentralized, rather than highly structured, configuration with minimal formalization and order. It is designed to fuse interdisciplinary experts into smoothly functioning ad hoc project teams. Liaison devices are the primary mechanism for integrating the project teams through a process of mutual adjustment. There is a high degree of horizontal specialization based on formal training and expertise. Selective decentralization of the project teams occurs within the adhocracy. An example of this form of organization is the National Aeronautics and Space Administration (NASA), which is composed of many talented experts who work in small teams on a wide range of projects related to America's space agenda. New high-technology businesses also often select an adhocracy design. Once a highly decentralized organization, the FBI is in the process of transformation for the twenty-first century, as we see in The Real World 15.2.

professional bureaucracy
A decentralized form of organization that emphasizes the operating core and standardization of skills.

divisionalized form
A moderately decentralized form of organization that emphasizes the middle level and standardization of outputs.

adhocracy
A selectively decentralized form of organization that emphasizes the support staff and mutual adjustment among people.

CONTEXTUAL VARIABLES

The basic design dimensions and the resulting structural configurations play out in the context of the organization's internal and external environments. Four contextual variables influence the success of an organization's design: size, technology, environment, and strategy and goals. These variables provide a manager with key considerations for the right organizational design, although they do not determine the structure. The amount of change in the contextual variables throughout the life of the organization influences the amount of change needed in the basic dimensions of its structure.[20] For example, competitive pressures in many industries have led to outsourcing, one of the greatest shifts in organization structure in a century.[21]

THE REAL WORLD 15.2

The FBI in the Age of Technology and Terrorism

The FBI was designed to solve crimes after the fact and has thrived on a compartmentalized, highly decentralized organization. The single field agent's talent, instinct, and effort were the key to either stopping drug traffickers or sniffing out political corruption in this federal crime-fighting system. However, that all changed dramatically after 9/11, when international terrorists attacked America. The FBI had to shift gears from solving crimes after they are committed to stopping them before they occur. This latter mission requires a very different form of organization and functioning, one that relies on the latest information technology and the systemic capacity to place single events or occurrences into a broader and emerging pattern. The FBI is one of the world's best-known crime-fighting organizations, with storied successes such as its capture of gangster John Dillinger. The agency now has an urgent need to achieve "Mission Impossible" and become a twenty-first-century leader in fighting counterterrorism. The two biggest challenges the agency has faced in its transformation are implementing advanced information technology and transforming the skills and training of its human resources. While the FBI has made several key strides in the shift to a counterterrorism posture, this transformation has not yet been fully institutionalized. Organization designs that worked in the past cannot necessarily be relied on in today's environment, as the FBI has come to understand.

SOURCE: J. J. Brazil, "Mission: Impossible?" *Fast Company* 114 (April 2007): 92–109.

Size

(4) Describe four contextual variables for an organization.

The total number of employees is the appropriate definition of size when discussing the design of organizational structure. This is logical, because people and their interactions are the building blocks of structure. Other measures, such as net assets, production rates, and total sales, are usually highly correlated with the total number of employees but may not reflect the actual number of interpersonal relationships that are necessary to effectively structure an organization.

Electronic Data Systems (EDS) began as an entrepreneurial venture of H. Ross Perot and had grown into an internationally prominent provider of information technology services when it was bought by General Motors Corporation (GM) in the early 1980s. Nearly half of EDS's revenues came from GM at the time of the buyout. The early culture of EDS placed a premium on technical competence, high achievement drive, an entrepreneurial attitude, and a maverick spirit. EDS grew well after the acquisition because GM exploited EDS's technological capability in a coordinated way while protecting EDS' autonomy as an information technology leader.[22] In 1996, it was spun off by GM and became an autonomous company once again.[23] However, following the spin-off, the company has struggled to find a clear focus and identity and has lost two chairmen (Les Alberthal and Dick Brown) in the process.

Although there is some argument over the degree of influence that size has on organizational structure, there is no question that it influences design options. In one study, Meyer found size to be the most important of all variables considered in influencing the organization's structure and design, whereas other researchers argue that the decision to expand the organization's business causes an increase in size as the structure is adjusted to accommodate the planned growth.[24] Downsizing is a planned strategy to reduce the size of an organization, and is often accompanied by related restructuring and revitalization activities.[25] Organizational size is one key predictor—along with industry type, firm diversification strategy, and network effects—of the likelihood of women on corporate boards.[26]

TABLE 15.3 Relationship between Organizational Size and Basic Design Dimensions

Basic Design Dimensions	Small Organizations	Large Organizations
Formalization	Less	More
Centralization	High	Low
Specialization	Low	High
Standardization	Low	High
Complexity	Low	High
Hierarchy of authority	Flat	Tall

How much influence size exerts on the organization's structure is not as important as the relationship between size and the design dimensions of structure. In other words, when exploring structural alternatives, what should the manager know about designing structures for large and small organizations?

Table 15.3 illustrates the relationships among each of the design dimensions and organizational size. Formalization, specialization, and standardization all tend to be greater in larger organizations because they are necessary to control activities within the organization. For example, larger organizations are more likely to use documentation, rules, written policies and procedures, and detailed job descriptions than to rely on personal observation by the manager. The more relationships that have to be managed by the structure, the more formalized and standardized the processes need to be. McDonald's has several volumes that describe how to make all its products, how to greet customers, how to maintain the facilities, and so on. This level of standardization, formalization, and specialization helps McDonald's maintain the same quality of product no matter where a restaurant is located. In contrast, at a small, locally owned café, your hamburger and french fries may taste a little different every time you visit. This is evidence of a lack of standardization.

Formalization and specialization also help a large organization decentralize decision making. Because of the complexity and number of decisions in a large organization, formalization and specialization are used to set parameters for decision making at lower levels. Can you imagine the chaos if the President of the United States, commander-in-chief of all U.S. military forces, had to make operational-level decisions in the war on terrorism? By decentralizing decision making, the larger organization adds horizontal and vertical complexity, but not necessarily spatial complexity. However, it is more common for a large organization to have more geographic dispersion.

Another dimension of design, hierarchy of authority, is related to complexity. As size increases, so does complexity; thus, more levels are added to the hierarchy of authority. This keeps the span of control from getting too large. However, there is a balancing force, because formalization and specialization are added. The more formalized, standardized, and specialized the roles within the organization, the wider the span of control can be.

Although some contend that the future belongs to small, agile organizations, others argue that size continues to be an advantage. To take advantage of size, organizations must become centerless corporations with a global core.[27] These concepts are pioneered by Booz Allen Hamilton based on its worldwide technology and management consulting. The global core provides strategic leadership, helps distribute and provide access to the company's capabilities and knowledge, creates the corporate identity, ensures access to low-cost capital, and exerts control over the enterprise as a whole.

Technology

An organization's technology is an important contextual variable in determining its structure, as noted in Chapter 2.[28] Technology is defined as the tools, techniques, and actions used by an organization to transform inputs into outputs.[29] The inputs of the organization include human resources, machines, materials, information, and money. The outputs are the products and services the organization offers to the external environment. Determining the relationship between technology and structure is complicated, because different departments may employ very different technologies. As organizations become larger, there is greater variation in technologies across its units. Joan Woodward, Charles Perrow, and James Thompson have developed ways to understand traditional organizational technologies. More work is needed to better understand the contemporary engineering, research and development, and knowledge-based technologies of the information age.

Woodward introduced one of the best-known classification schemes for technology, identifying three types: unit, mass, or process production. Unit technology is small-batch manufacturing technology and, sometimes, made-to-order production. Examples include Smith & Wesson's arms manufacture and the manufacture of fine furniture. Mass technology is large-batch manufacturing technology. Examples include American automotive assembly lines and latex glove production. Process production means continuous production. Examples include oil refining and beer making. Woodward classified unit technology as the least complex, mass technology as more complex, and process technology as the most complex. The more complex the organization's technology, the more complex the administrative component or structure of the organization needs to be.

Perrow proposed an alternative to Woodward's scheme based on two variables: task variability and problem analyzability. Task variability considers the number of exceptions encountered in doing the tasks within a job. Problem analyzability examines the types of search procedures followed to find ways to respond to task exceptions. For example, for some exceptions encountered while doing a task, the appropriate response is easy to find. If you are driving down a street and see a sign that says, "Detour—Bridge Out," it is very easy to respond to the task variability. When Thomas Edison was designing the first electric light bulb, however, the problem analyzability was very high for his task.

Perrow went on to identify the four key aspects of structure that could be modified to the technology. These structural elements are (1) the amount of discretion that an individual can exercise to complete a task, (2) the power of groups to control the unit's goals and strategies, (3) the level of interdependence among groups, and (4) the extent to which organizational units coordinate work using either feedback or planning. Figure 15.3 summarizes Perrow's findings about types of technology and basic design dimensions.[30]

Thompson offered yet another view of technology and its relationship to organizational design. This view is based on the concept of *technological interdependence* (that is, the degree of interrelatedness of the organization's various technological elements) and the pattern of an organization's work flows. Thompson's research suggests that greater technological interdependence leads to greater organizational complexity and that the problems of this greater complexity may be offset by decentralized decision making.[31]

technological interdependence
The degree of interrelatedness of the organization's various technological elements.

The research of these three early scholars on the influence of technology on organizational design can be combined into one integrating concept—routineness in the process of changing inputs into outputs in an organization. This routineness has a very strong relationship with organizational structure. The more routine

FIGURE 15.3 Summary of Perrow's Findings about the Relationship between Technology and Basic Design Dimensions

Problem Analyzability \ Task Variability	Few Exceptions	Many Exceptions
Ill-Defined and Unanalyzable	Craft 1. Moderate 2. Moderate 3. Moderate 4. Low-moderate 5. High 6. Low	Nonroutine 1. Low 2. Low 3. Low 4. Low 5. High 6. Low
Well-Defined and Analyzable	Routine 1. High 2. High 3. Moderate 4. High 5. Low 6. High	Engineering 1. Moderate 2. Moderate 3. High 4. Moderate 5. Moderate 6. Moderate

Key:
1. Formalization
2. Centralization
3. Specialization
4. Standardization
5. Complexity
6. Hierarchy of authority

SOURCE: Built from C. Perrow, "A Framework for the Comparative Analysis of Organizations," *American Sociological Review* (April 1967): 194–208.

and repetitive the tasks of the organization, the higher the degree of formalization that is possible; the more centralized, specialized, and standardized the organization can be; and the more hierarchical levels with wider spans of control that are possible.

Since the work of Woodward, Perrow, and Thompson, however, an important caveat to the discussion of technology has emerged: the advance of information technology has influenced how organizations transform inputs into outputs. The introduction of computer-integrated networks, CAD/CAM systems, and computer-integrated manufacturing has broadened the span of control, flattened the organizational hierarchy, decentralized decision making, and lowered the amount of specialization and standardization.[32] Advances in information technology have allowed for other advances in manufacturing, such as mass customization. Hewlett-Packard has found a key to mass customization in postponing the task of differentiating a product for a specific customer until the latest possible time.[33]

Further, the emergence of new digital technologies along with the globalization of the economy are major forces for change. These two forces affect all organizations throughout the economy, ushering in a new economy that has four characteristics. Stanley M. Davis describes these as (1) *any time*—customers can get their goods and services 24/7; (2) *any place*—customers can order from anywhere if they have Internet access; (3) *no matter*—intangibles are adding value to products, such as through digital photography; and (4) *mass customization*—technology and information allow for rapid, responsive customization of products.[34] Thus, digital technology and economic change have resulted in downsizing and restructuring activities in the private sector.

Environment

The third contextual variable for organizational design is *environment*. The environment of an organization is most easily defined as anything outside the boundaries of that organization. Different aspects of the environment have varying degrees of influence on the organization's structure. In one study of 318 CEOs between 1996 and 2000, strategic decision speed was found to moderate the relationship between the environment and the organization structure and performance.[35] For example, in response to the 9/11 terrorist attack on the World Trade Center, President George W. Bush acted swiftly to restructure the U.S. federal government and create the Department of Homeland Security. The general environment includes all conditions that may have an impact on the organization. These conditions could include economic factors, political considerations, ecological changes, sociocultural demands, and governmental regulation.

Task Environment When aspects of the general environment become more focused in areas of direct interest to the organization, those aspects become part of the *task environment*, or specific environment. The task environment is that part of the environment that is directly relevant to the organization. Typically, it includes stakeholders such as unions, customers, suppliers, competitors, government regulatory agencies, and trade associations. A key element of Timberland's task environment is its consumers, a key to its reorganization as described in Thinking Ahead.

The domain of the organization refers to the area the organization claims for itself with respect to how it fits into its relevant environments. The domain is particularly important because it is defined by the organization, and it influences how the organization perceives and acts within its environments.[36] For example, Wal-Mart and Neiman Marcus both sell clothing apparel, but their domains are very different.

The organization's perceptions of its environment and the actual environment may not be the same. The environment that the manager perceives is the one that the organization responds to and organizes for.[37] Therefore, two organizations may be in relatively the same environment from an objective standpoint, but if the managers perceive differences, the organizations may enact very different structures to deal with this same environment. For example, one company may decentralize and use monetary incentives for managers that lead it to be competitively aggressive, while another company may centralize and use incentives for managers that lead it to be less intense in its rivalry.[38]

Environmental Uncertainty The perception of *environmental uncertainty* or the perception of the lack of it is how the contextual variable of environment most influences organizational design. Some organizations have relatively static environments with little uncertainty, whereas others are so dynamic that no one is sure what tomorrow may bring. Binney & Smith, for example, has made relatively the same product for more than fifty years with very few changes in the design or packaging. The environment for its Crayola products is relatively static. In fact, customers rebelled when the company tried to get rid of some old colors and add new ones. In contrast, in the last two decades, competitors in the airline industry have encountered deregulation, mergers, bankruptcies, safety changes, changes in cost and price structures, changes in customer and employee demographics, and changes in global competition. In such uncertain conditions, fast-response organizations must use expertise coordination practices to ensure that distributed expertise is managed and applied in a timely manner.[39]

The amount of uncertainty in the environment influences the structural dimensions. Burns and Stalker labeled two structural extremes that are appropriate for

environment
Anything outside the boundaries of an organization.

task environment
The elements of an organization's environment that are related to its goal attainment.

environmental uncertainty
The amount and rate of change in the organization's environment.

TABLE 15.4 Mechanistic and Organic Organizational Forms

Basic Design Dimensions	Mechanistic	Organic
Formalization	High	Low
Centralization	High	Low
Specialization	High	Low
Standardization	High	Low
Complexity	Low	High
Hierarchy of authority	Strong, tall	Weak, flat

the extremes of environmental uncertainty—*mechanistic structure* and *organic structure*.[40] Table 15.4 compares the structural dimensions of these two extremes. The mechanistic and organic structures are opposite ends of a continuum of organizational design possibilities. Although the general premise of environmental uncertainty and structural dimensions has been upheld by research, the organization must make adjustments for the realities of its perceived environment when designing its structure.[41]

The question for those trying to design organizational structures is how to determine environmental uncertainty. Dess and Beard defined three dimensions of environment that should be measured in assessing the degree of uncertainty: capacity, volatility, and complexity.[42] The *capacity* of the environment reflects the abundance or scarcity of resources. If resources abound, the environment supports expansion, mistakes, or both. In contrast, in times of scarcity, the environment demands survival of the fittest. *Volatility* is the degree of instability. The airline industry is in a volatile environment. This makes it difficult for managers to know what needs to be done. The *complexity* of the environment refers to the differences and variability among environmental elements.

If the organization's environment is uncertain, dynamic, and complex and resources are scarce, the manager needs an organic structure that is better able to adapt to its environment. Such a structure allows the manager to monitor the environment from a number of internal perspectives, thus helping the organization maintain flexibility in responding to environmental changes.[43]

Strategy and Goals

The fourth contextual variable that influences how the design dimensions of structure should be enacted is the strategies and goals of the organization. Strategies and goals provide legitimacy to the organization, as well as employee direction, decision guidelines, and criteria for performance.[44] In addition, they help the organization fit into its environment.

As more understanding of the contextual influence of strategies and goals has developed, several strategic dimensions that influence structure have been defined. One of these definitions was put forth by Danny Miller.[45] His framework for these strategic dimensions and their implications for organizational structure are shown in Table 15.5.

For example, when Apple Computer introduced personal computers to the market, its strategies were very innovative. The structure of the organization was relatively flat and very informal. Apple had Friday afternoon beer and popcorn discussion sessions, and eccentric behavior was easily accepted. As the personal computer market became more competitive, however, the structure of Apple changed to help it differentiate its products and to help control costs. The innovative strategies and

mechanistic structure
An organizational design that emphasizes structured activities, specialized tasks, and centralized decision making.

organic structure
An organizational design that emphasizes teamwork, open communication, and decentralized decision making.

TABLE 15.5 Miller's Integrative Framework of Structural and Strategic Dimensions

Strategic Dimension	Predicted Structural Characteristics
Innovation—to understand and manage new processes and technologies	Low formalization Decentralization Flat hierarchy
Market differentiation—to specialize in customer preferences	Moderate to high complexity Moderate to high formalization Moderate centralization
Cost control—to produce standardized products efficiently	High formalization High centralization High standardization Low complexity

SOURCE: D. Miller, "The Structural and Environmental Correlates of Business Strategy," *Strategic Management Journal* 8 (1987): 55–76. Copyright © John Wiley & Sons Limited. Reproduced with permission.

structures devised by Steve Jobs, one of Apple's founders, were no longer appropriate. The board of directors recruited John Scully, a marketing expert from PepsiCo, to help Apple better compete in the market it had created. In 1996 and 1997, Apple reinvented itself again and brought back Jobs to try to restore its innovative edge. Since his return, Apple has become a major player in the digital music market with its introduction of the iPod, selling over 200,000 units in one quarter.

© NOAH BERGER/BLOOMBERG NEWS/LANDOV

Steve Jobs returned to Apple in the mid-1990s to help restore its innovative edge.

Limitations exist, however, on how much strategies and goals influence structure. Because the structure of the organization includes the formal information-processing channels in the organization, it stands to reason that the need to change strategies may not be communicated throughout the organization. In such a case, the organization's structure influences its strategic choice. Changing that structure may not unlock value but rather drive up costs and difficulties. Therefore, strategic success may hinge on choosing an organization design that works reasonably well, and then fine-tuning the structure through a strategic system.[46]

The inefficiency of the structure in perceiving environmental changes may even lead to organizational failure. In the airline industry, several carriers failed to adjust quickly enough to deregulation and the highly competitive marketplace. Only those airlines that were generally viewed as lean structures with good information-processing systems have flourished in the turbulent years since deregulation. Examples of how different design dimensions can affect the strategic decision process are listed in Table 15.6.

The four contextual variables—size, technology, environment, and strategy and goals—combine to influence the design process. However, the existing structure of the organization influences how it interprets and reacts to information about each of the variables. Each of the contextual variables has management researchers who claim that it is the most important variable in determining the best structural design. Because of the difficulty in studying the interactions of the four contextual dimensions and the complexity of organizational structures, the argument about which variable is most important continues.

TABLE  15.6 Examples of How Structure Affects the Strategic Decision Process

Formalization
As the level of formalization increases, so does the probability of the following:
1. The strategic decision process will become reactive to crisis rather than proactive through opportunities.
2. Strategic moves will be incremental and precise.
3. Differentiation in the organization will not be balanced with integrative mechanisms.
4. Only environmental crises that are in areas monitored by the formal organizational systems will be acted upon.
Centralization
As the level of centralization increases, so does the probability of the following:
1. The strategic decision process will be initiated by only a few dominant individuals.
2. The decision process will be goal oriented and rational.
3. The strategic process will be constrained by the limitations of top managers.
Complexity
As the level of complexity increases, so does the probability of the following:
1. The strategic decision process will become more politicized.
2. The organization will find it more difficult to recognize environmental opportunities and threats.
3. The constraints on good decision processes will be multiplied by the limitations of each individual within the organization.

SOURCE: Republished with permission of Academy of Management, PO Box 3020, Briar Cliff Manor, NY 10510–8020. "The Strategic Decision Process and Organizational Structure" (table), J. Fredrickson, *Academy of Management Review* (1986): 284. Reproduced by permission of the publisher via Copyright Clearance Center, Inc.

What is apparent is that there must be some level of fit between the structure and the contextual dimensions of the organization. The better the fit, the more likely the organization will achieve its short-run goals. In addition, the better the fit, the more likely the organization will process information and design appropriate organizational roles for long-term prosperity, as indicated in Figure 15.4.

FORCES RESHAPING ORGANIZATIONS

(5) Explain the four forces reshaping organizations.

Managers and researchers traditionally examine organizational design and structure within the framework of basic design dimensions and contextual variables. Several forces reshaping organizations are causing managers to go beyond the traditional frameworks and to examine ways to make organizations more responsive to customer needs. Some of these forces include shorter life cycles within the organization, globalization, and rapid changes in information technology. These forces together increase the demands on process capabilities within the organization and emerging organizational structures. To successfully retain their health and vitality, organizations must function as open systems, as discussed in Chapter 1, that are responsive to their task environment.[47]

Life Cycles in Organizations

Organizations are dynamic entities. As such, they ebb and flow through different stages. Usually, researchers think of these stages as *organizational life cycles*. The total organization has a life cycle that begins at birth, moves through growth and maturity to decline, and possibly experiences revival.[48]

organizational life cycle
The differing stages of an organization's life from birth to death.

Organizational subunits may have very similar life cycles. Because of changes in technology and product design, many such subunits, especially those that are product based, are experiencing shorter life cycles. Hence, the subunits that

FIGURE 15.4 The Relationship among Key Organizational Design Elements

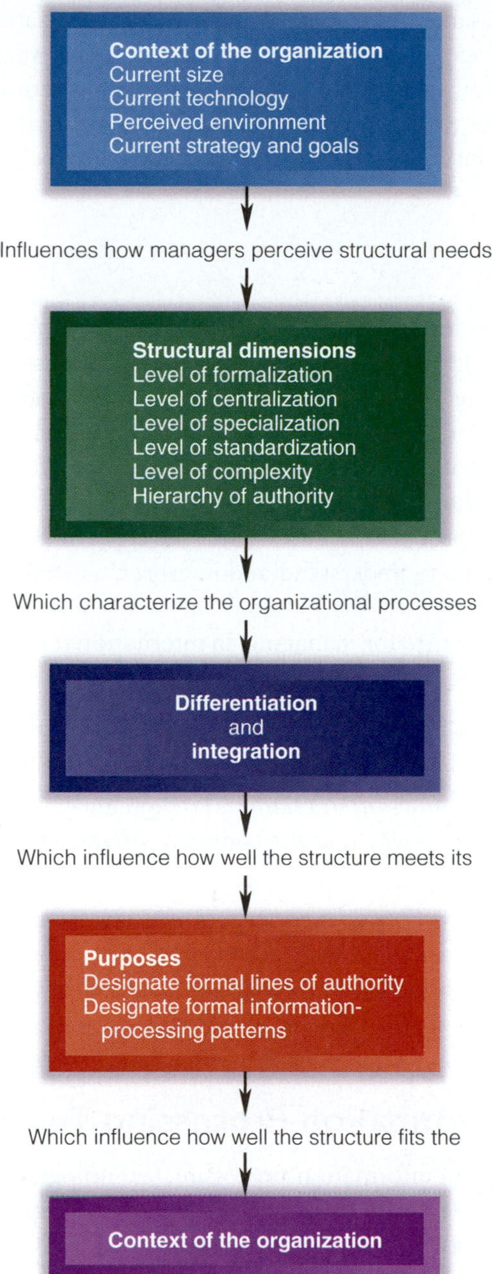

compose the organization are changing more rapidly than in the past. These shorter life cycles enable the organization to respond quickly to external demands and changes.

When a new organization or subunit is born, the structure is organic and informal. If the organization or subunit is successful, it grows and matures. This usually leads to formalization, specialization, standardization, complexity, and a more mechanistic structure. If the environment changes, however, the organization must be able to respond. A mechanistic structure is not able to respond to a dynamic environment as well as an organic one. If the organization or subunit does respond, it becomes more organic and revives; if not, it declines and possibly dies.

Shorter life cycles put more pressure on the organization to be both flexible and efficient at the same time. Further, as flexible organizations use design to their competitive advantage, discrete organizational life cycles may give way to a kaleidoscope of continuously emerging, efficiency-seeking organizational designs.[49] The manager's challenge in this context becomes one of creating congruency among various organizational design dimensions to fit continuously changing markets and locations.

Globalization

Another force that is reshaping organizations is globalization. In other words, organizations operate worldwide rather than in just one country or region. Global corporations can become pitted against sovereign nations when rules and laws conflict across national borders. Globalization makes spatial differentiation even more of a reality for organizations. Besides the obvious geographic differences, there may be deep cultural and value system differences. This adds another type of complexity to the structural design process and necessitates the creation of integrating mechanisms so that people are able to understand and interpret, as well as coordinate with, one another.

The choice of structure for managing an international business is generally based on the following three factors:

1. *The level of vertical differentiation.* A hierarchy of authority must be created that clarifies the responsibilities of both domestic and foreign managers.
2. *The level of horizontal differentiation.* Foreign and domestic operations should be grouped in such a way that the company effectively serves the needs of all customers.
3. *The degree of formalization, specialization, standardization, and centralization.* The global structure must allow decisions to be made in the most appropriate area of the organization. However, controls must be in place that reflect the strategies and goals of the parent firm.[50]

Changes in Information-Processing Technologies

Many of the changes in information-processing technologies have allowed organizations to move into new product and market areas more quickly. However, just as shorter life cycles and globalization have caused new concerns for designing organizational structures, so has the increased availability of advanced information-processing technologies.

Organizational structures are already feeling the impact of advanced information-processing technologies. More integration and coordination are evident, because managers worldwide can be connected through computerized networks. The basic design dimensions have also been affected as follows:

1. The hierarchy of authority has been flattened.
2. The basis of centralization has been changed. Now managers can use technology to acquire more information and make more decisions, or to push information and decision making lower in the hierarchy and thus decrease centralization.
3. Less specialization and standardization are needed, because people using advanced information-processing technologies have more sophisticated jobs that require a broader understanding of how the organization gets work done.[51]

Advances in information processing are leading to knowledge-based organizations, the outlines of which are now only seen dimly. Some of the hallmarks of these new organizational forms are virtual enterprising, dynamic teaming, and knowledge networking.[52] This fifth generation of management thought and practice leads to co-creation of products and services. Future organizations may well be defined by networks of overlapping teams.

Demands on Organizational Processes

Because of the forces reshaping organizations, managers find themselves trying to meet what seem to be conflicting goals: an efficiency orientation that results in on-time delivery *and* a quality orientation that results in customized, high-quality goods or services.[53] Traditionally, managers have seen efficiency and customization as conflicting demands.

To meet these conflicting demands, organizations need to become "dynamically stable."[54] To do so, an organization must have managers who see their roles as architects who clearly understand the "how" of the organizing process. Managers must combine long-term thinking with flexible and quick responses that help improve process and know-how. The organizational structure must help define, at least to some degree, roles for managers who hope to successfully address the conflicting demands of dynamic stability. The differences between the structural roles of managers today and managers of the future are illustrated in Table 15.7. You 15.2 allows you to examine the ways managers in your organization currently operate on the job.

Emerging Organizational Structures

The demands on managers and on process capabilities place demands on structures. The emphasis in organizations is shifting to organizing around processes. This

(6) Discuss emerging organizational structures.

TABLE  15.7 Structural Roles of Managers Today versus Managers of the Future

Roles of Managers Today

1. Strictly adhering to boss–employee relationships.
2. Getting things done by giving orders.
3. Carrying messages up and down the hierarchy.
4. Performing a prescribed set of tasks according to a job description.
5. Having a narrow functional focus.
6. Going through channels, one by one by one.
7. Controlling subordinates.

Roles of Future Managers

1. Having hierarchical relationships subordinated to functional and peer relationships.
2. Getting things done by negotiating.
3. Solving problems and making decisions.
4. Creating the job by developing entrepreneurial projects.
5. Having broad cross-functional collaboration.
6. Emphasizing speed and flexibility.
7. Coaching their workers.

SOURCE: Reprinted by permission of the publisher, from *Management Review*, January 1991 © 1991. Thomas R. Horton. American Management Association, New York. All rights reserved.

Virtuality, Innovation, and Psychologically Safe Communication

Innovation is a critical means of competitive advantage for firms in a variety of industries because it allows organizations to diversify, adapt, and even reinvent themselves to meet evolving markets and technologies. Virtual organizations often have virtual teams as their key structural building block, and virtual is often an implied single concept. This research breaks down virtuality into four interlocking components: geographic dispersion, electronic interdependence, dynamic structure, and national diversity. The core hypothesis for the research is that virtual design strategies used by organizations to foster innovation in fact do the reverse. The researchers conducted 177 in-depth qualitative interviews across a variety of industries. This interview study was followed by survey data collection from 266 members of 56 aerospace design teams. The results concluded that the four characteristics of virtuality are not highly intercorrelated. In addition, each of the characteristics of virtuality has independent and differential effects on innovation, primarily adverse effects. The research yielded one very positive result as well, which was the importance of a psychologically safe communication climate. Specifically, the presence of a psychologically safe communication climate acts to mitigate any adverse effects of geographic dispersion, electronic interdependence, dynamic structure, and national diversity on innovation. Organizational design strategies should therefore encourage psychologically safe communication.

SOURCE: C. B. Gibson and J. L. Gibbs, "Unpacking the Concept of Virtuality: Geographic Dispersion, Electronic Dependence, Dynamic Structure, and National Diversity on Team Innovation," *Administrative Science Quarterly* 51 (2006): 451–495.

process orientation emerges from the combination of three streams of applied organizational design: high-performance, self-managed teams; managing processes rather than functions; and the evolution of information technology. Information technology and advanced communication systems have led to internetworking. In a study of 469 firms, deeply internetworked firms were found to be more focused and specialized, less hierarchical, and more engaged in external partnering.[55] Three emerging organizational structures associated with these changes are network organizations, virtual organizations, and the circle organization. The accompanying Science feature unpacks the concept of virtuality in organization design and innovation.

Network organizations are weblike structures that contract some or all of their operating functions to other organizations and then coordinate their activities through managers and other employees at their headquarters. Information technology is the basis for building the weblike structure of the network organization and business unit managers that are essential to the success of these systems. This type of organization has arisen in the age of electronic commerce and brought into practice transaction cost economics, interorganizational collaborations, and strategic alliances. Network organizations can be global in scope.[56]

Virtual organizations are temporary network organizations consisting of independent enterprises. Many dot-coms were virtual organizations designed to come together swiftly to exploit an apparent market opportunity. They may function much like a theatrical troupe that comes together for a "performance."[57] Trust can be a challenge for virtual organizations because it is a complex phenomenon involving ethics, morals, emotions, values, and natural attitudes. However, trust and trustworthiness are important connective issues in virtual environments. Three key ingredients for the development of trust in virtual organizations are technology that can communicate emotion; a sharing of values, vision, and organizational identity; and a high standard of ethics.[58]

The circle organization is a third emerging structure crafted by Harley-Davidson in its drive to achieve teamwork without teams.[59] The company evolved the circle form of organization shown in Figure 15.5. The three organizational parts are those that (1) create demand, (2) produce product, and (3) provide support. As the figure

YOU 15.2

Managers of Today and the Future

Are the roles for managers in your organization more oriented toward today or toward the future? (If you do not work, think of an organization where you have worked or talk with a friend about managerial roles in his or her organization.)

Step 1. Reread Table 15.7 and check which orientation (today or future) predominates in your organization for each of the following seven characteristics:

	Today	Future
1. Boss–employee relationships.	______	______
2. Getting work accomplished.	______	______
3. Messenger versus problem solver.	______	______
4. Basis for task accomplishment.	______	______
5. Narrow versus broad functional focus.	______	______
6. Adherence to channels of authority.	______	______
7. Controlling versus coaching subordinates.	______	______

Step 2. Examine the degree of consistency across all seven characteristics. Could the organization make one or two structural changes to achieve a better alignment of the manager's role with today or with the future?

Step 3. Identify one manager in your organization who fits very well into the organization's ideal manager's role. What does this manager do that creates a good person–role fit?

Step 4. Identify one manager in your organization who does not fit very well into the organization's ideal manager's role. What does this manager do that creates a poor person–role fit?

indicates, these three parts are linked by the leadership and strategy council (LSC). The circle organization is a more open system and an organic structure for customer responsiveness. One innovation in this organizational scheme is the "circle coach," who possesses acute communication, listening, and influencing skills that make him or her highly respected by circle members and the company's president.

FIGURE 15.5 Harley-Davidson's Circle Organization

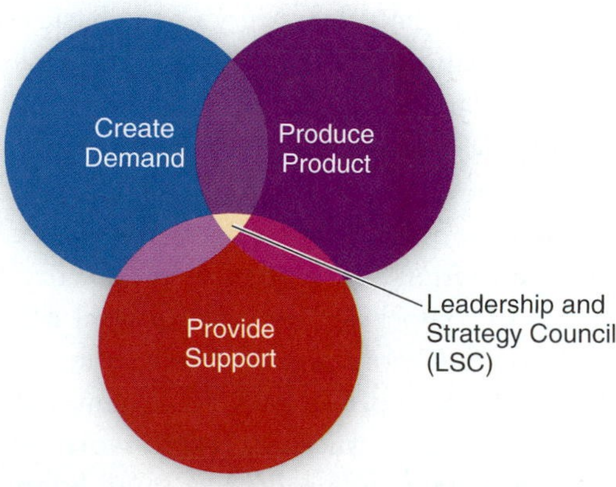

SOURCE: Reprinted by permission of Harvard Business School Press from *More than a Motorcycle: The Leadership Journey at Harley-Davidson*, by R. Teerlink and L. Ozley, Boston, MA, 2000, p. 139.

CAUTIONARY NOTES ABOUT STRUCTURE

(7) Identify two cautions about the effect of organizational structures on people.

This chapter has identified the purposes of structure, the processes of organizational design, and the dimensions and contexts that must be considered in structure. In addition, it has looked at forces and trends in organizational design. Two cautionary notes are important for the student of organizational behavior. First, an organizational structure may be weak or deficient. In general, if the structure is out of alignment with its contextual variables, one or more of the following four symptoms appears. First, decision making is delayed because the hierarchy is overloaded and too much information is being funneled through one or two channels. Second, decision making lacks quality because information linkages are not providing the correct information to the right person in the right format. Third, the organization does not respond innovatively to a changing environment, especially when coordinated effort is lacking across departments. Fourth, a great deal of conflict is evident when departments are working against one another rather than working for the strategies and goals of the organization as a whole; the structure is often at fault here.

The second caution is that the personality of the chief executive may adversely affect the structure of the organization.[60] Managers' personal, cognitive biases and political ideologies affect their good judgment and decision making.[61] Five dysfunctional combinations of personality and organization have been identified: the paranoid, the depressive, the dramatic, the compulsive, and the schizoid.[62] Each of these personality–organization constellations can create problems for the people who work in the organization. For example, in a paranoid constellation, people are suspicious of each other, and distrust in working relationships may interfere with effective communication and task accomplishment. For another example, in a depressive constellation, people feel depressed and inhibited in their work activities, which can lead to low levels of productivity and task accomplishment. The chief executive's personality is not always harmful. In the Looking Back feature, we meet the new president of Timberland's four new global consumer category segments. Each is essential to the health and productivity of his organization.

MANAGERIAL IMPLICATIONS: FITTING PEOPLE AND STRUCTURES TOGETHER

Organizations are complex social systems composed of numerous interrelated components. They can be complicated to understand. Managers who design, develop, and improve organizations must have a mastery of the basic concepts related to the anatomy and processes of organizational functioning. It is essential for executives at the top to have a clear concept of how the organization can be differentiated and then integrated into a cohesive whole.

People can work better in organizations if they understand how their jobs and departments relate to other jobs and departments in the organization. An understanding of the whole organization enables people to better relate their contribution to its overall mission and to compensate for its structural deficiencies.

Different structural configurations place unique demands on the people who work within them. The diversity of people in work organizations suggests that some people are best suited to a simple structure, others work better in a professional bureaucracy, and still others are most productive in an adhocracy. Organizational structures are not independent of the people who work within them. This is especially true for organizations operating in a global work environment.

Managers must pay attention to the technology of the organization's work, the amount of change occurring in its environment, and the regulatory pressures created by governmental agencies as the managers design effective organizations and subunits to meet emerging international demands and a diverse, multicultural workforce.

LOOKING BACK: TIMBERLAND

Four New Organizations, Four New Presidents

Timberland's restructuring to create four new consumer category organizations with dedicated resources and support required the selection of four new presidents to lead them. The company chose a traditional reporting structure in which each of the four presidents reports directly to the company's CEO. Timberland's previous organizational structure was designed around geography and products, and the reorganization has a clearly more consumer-focused structure aimed to better serve the trade and consumer in each business segment. Aligning structure with strategy is important, but that must be accompanied by the selection and empowerment of the right leaders to insure that the organizational structure supports the strategic goal.[63]

Mike Harrison is president of Casual Gear and responsible for men's, women's, and kids' footwear and apparel around the world in both retail and wholesale distribution channels. Harrison came to the position with a strong showing as senior vice president of Timberland's international business, which expanded in revenues and operating profits at double-digit rates for three successive years under his leadership. Scott Thresher is president of Industrial and is responsible for product development, sales, and marketing for Timberland's industrial business. Thresher was responsible for the launch of the company's e-commerce business as senior director for strategic initiatives and later as group vice president of North America, a position that included responsibility for Timberland PRO series products. These are two of the four new Timberland presidents.

Gene McCarthy is president of Authentic Youth and is responsible for serving Timberland's youth consumers on a global basis, from merchandising and product execution to developing innovations and providing strategic direction. Relatively new to Timberland, McCarthy came with a strong history with global footwear leader Reebok and before that with Nike. He held both marketing and management positions in both organizations. Gary Smith is president of Outdoor Group and is responsible worldwide for the entire Outdoor Performance portfolio that includes Timberland Outdoor Performance, SmartWool, GoLite, and Miôn. Smith has a five-year track record with the company, including senior vice president of supply chain management and general manager of Outdoor Performance. The creation of the four senior positions for presidents of these newly designed consumer-focused organizations led to corresponding internal appointments. It's important to note that Timberland did not go outside the company for a single one of its four presidential appointments.

Chapter Summary

1. Three basic types of differentiation occur in organizations: horizontal, vertical, and spatial.
2. The greater the complexity of an organization because of its degree of differentiation, the greater the need for integration.
3. Formalization, centralization, specialization, standardization, complexity, and hierarchy of authority are the six basic design dimensions in an organization.
4. Simple structure, machine bureaucracy, professional bureaucracy, divisionalized form, and adhocracy are five structural configurations of an organization.
5. The contextual variables important to organizational design are size, technology, environment, and strategy and goals.
6. Life cycles, globalization, changes in information-processing technologies, and demands on process capabilities are forces reshaping organizations today.
7. Network organizations, virtual organizations, and the circle organization are emerging organizational structures.
8. Organizational structures may be inherently weak, or chief executives may create personality–organization constellations that adversely affect employees.

Key Terms

adhocracy (p. 518)
centralization (p. 514)
complexity (p. 514)
contextual variables (p. 508)
differentiation (p. 511)
divisionalized form (p. 518)
environment (p. 523)
environmental uncertainty (p. 523)
formalization (p. 514)
hierarchy of authority (p. 514)
integration (p. 512)
machine bureaucracy (p. 516)
mechanistic structure (p. 524)
organic structure (p. 524)
organizational design (p. 508)
organizational life cycle (p. 526)
organizational structure (p. 508)
professional bureaucracy (p. 518)
simple structure (p. 516)
specialization (p. 514)
standardization (p. 514)
task environment (p. 523)
technological interdependence (p. 521)

Review Questions

1. Define the processes of differentiation and integration.
2. Describe the six basic dimensions of organizational design.
3. Discuss five structural configurations from the chapter.
4. Discuss the effects of the four contextual variables on the basic design dimensions.
5. Identify four forces that are reshaping organizations today.
6. Discuss the nature of emerging organizational structures.
7. List four symptoms of structural weakness and five unhealthy personality–organization combinations.

Discussion and Communication Questions

1. How would you describe the organization you work for (or your college) on each of the basic design dimensions? For example, is it a very formal organization or an informal organization?
2. Do the size, technology, and mission of your organization directly affect you? How?
3. Who are your organization's competitors? What changes do you see in information technology where you work?
4. Does your company show any one or more of the four symptoms of structural deficiency discussed at the end of the chapter?
5. *(communication question)* Write a memo classifying and describing the structural configuration of your university based on the five choices in Table 15.2. Do you need more information than you have to be comfortable with your classification and description? Where could you get the information?
6. *(communication question)* Interview an administrator in your college or university about possible changes in size (Will the college or university get bigger? Smaller?) and technology (Is the college or university making a significant investment in information technology?). What effects does the administrator anticipate from these changes? Be prepared to present your results orally to the class.

Ethical Dilemma

Kate Brown was a human resource manager for Summit Maintenance, a national commercial janitorial service company. She worked hard to represent the employees' best interest to management. Kate worked at one of Summit's regional headquarters. She had four regional human resource representatives who worked in the field to cover her region. Like many large, older companies, Summit was very bureaucratic with several levels of managers. Kate directly reported to the regional human resources vice president, but she also reported to the general manager for her regional office.

At the moment, Kate was feeling the burden of reporting to two different people. She had just left a meeting with Terry Beck, the general manager. Terry had explained that he wanted to make some small changes in the way they interpreted some of the company policies. Terry understood that these policies had been created for a lot of good reasons but were not really appropriate for the more rural area their region covered. He went on to explain that he wasn't asking Kate to break the rules, just enforce them differently and more effectively for their employees.

After listening to Terry, Kate had to agree that his ideas would work much better in their area. Terry was most concerned with some of the safety policies that were developed for people working in large high-rise buildings or in high-crime areas. Their employees worked in neither. They mostly worked in small, rural family businesses. The need to follow policies regarding terrorist attacks or escaping a high-rise fire seemed extremely remote. Yet day after day, employees were forced to carry extra equipment or go through extra procedures to ensure their safety against these dangers. Money, time, and space were wasted following policies that would probably never affect them.

Kate's only concern was her primary supervisor, Vernon Miller, the regional vice president. He would never go for this idea. He was a stickler for rules whether they made sense or not. Kate knew her first duty was to the HR executive, but she saw the value in easing the safety policies for their employees.

Questions

1. Does Kate have the right to interpret the policies they way she believes to be best?
2. Evaluate Kate's decision using consequential, rule-based, and character theories.

Experiential Exercises

15.1 Words-in-Sentences Company

Purpose: To design an organization for a particular task and carry through to production; to compare design elements with effectiveness.

Group Size: Any number of groups of six to fourteen persons.

Time Required: Fifty to ninety minutes.

Related Topics: Dynamics within groups and work motivation.

Background

You are a small company that manufactures words and then packages them in meaningful English-language sentences. Market research has established that sentences of at least three words but not more than six words are in demand. Therefore, packaging, distribution, and sales should be set up for three- to six-word sentences.

The "words-in-sentences" (WIS) industry is highly competitive; several new firms have recently entered what appears to be an expanding market. Since raw materials, technology, and pricing are all standard for the industry, your ability to compete depends on two factors: (1) volume and (2) quality.

Your Task

Your group must design and participate in running a WIS company. You should design your organization to be as efficient as possible during each ten-minute production run. After the first production run, you will have an opportunity to reorganize your company if you want.

Raw Materials

For each production you will be given a "raw material word or phrase." The letters found in the word or phrase serve as raw materials available to produce new words in sentences. For example, if the raw material word is "organization," you could produce the words and sentence: "Nat ran to a zoo."

Production Standards

Several rules must be followed in producing "words-in-sentences." If these rules are not followed, your output will not meet production specifications and will not pass quality-control inspection.

1. The same letter may appear only as often in a manufactured word as it appears in the raw material word or phrase; for example, "organization" has two o's.

Thus, "zoo" is legitimate, but not "zoonosis." It has too many o's and s's.

2. Raw material letters can be used again in different manufactured words.
3. A manufactured word may be used only once in a sentence and in only one sentence during a production run; if a word—for example, "a"—is used once in a sentence, it is out of stock.
4. A new word may not be made by adding "s" to form the plural of an already manufactured word.
5. A word is defined by its spelling, not its meaning.
6. Nonsense words or nonsense sentences are unacceptable.
7. All words must be in the English language.
8. Names and places are acceptable.
9. Slang is not acceptable.

Measuring Performance

The output of your WIS company is measured by the total number of acceptable words that are packaged in sentences. The sentences must be legible, listed on no more than two sheets of paper, and handed to the Quality Control Review Board at the completion of each production run.

Delivery

Delivery must be made to the Quality Control Review Board thirty seconds after the end of each production run, or else all points are lost.

Quality Control

If any word in a sentence does not meet the standards set forth above, all the words in the sentence will be rejected. The Quality Control Review Board (composed of one member from each company) is the final arbiter of acceptability. In the event of a tie on the Review Board, a coin toss will determine the outcome.

Exercise Schedule

	Unit Time	Total Time
1. Form groups, organizations, and assign workplaces Groups should have between six and fourteen members (if there are more than eleven or twelve persons in a group, assign one or two observers). Each group is a company.	**2–5 min.**	**2–5 min.**
2. Read "Background" Ask the instructor about any points that need clarification.	**5 min.**	**10 min.**
3. Design organizations Design your organizations using as many members as you see fit to produce your "words-in-sentences." You may want to consider the following. a. What is your objective? b. What technology would work here? c. What type of division of labor is effective? Assign one member of your group to serve on the Quality Review Board. This person may also take part in production runs.	**7–15 min.**	**14–25 min.**
4. Production Run #1 The instructor will hand each WIS company a sheet with a raw material word or phrase. When the instructor announces "Begin production," you are to manufacture as many words as possible and package them in sentences for delivery to the Quality Control Review Board. You will have ten minutes. When the instructor announces "Stop production," you will have thirty seconds to deliver your output to the Quality Control Review Board. Output received after thirty seconds does not meet the delivery schedule and will not be counted.	**7–10 min.**	**21–35 min.**
5. Quality Review Board meets, evaluates output While that is going on, groups discuss what happened during the previous production run.	**5–10 min.**	**26–45 min.**

6. **Companies evaluate performance and type of organization** Groups may choose to restructure and reorganize for the next production run.	**5–10 min.**	**31–55 min.**
7. **Production Run #2 (same as Production Run #1)**	**7–10 min.**	**38–65 min.**
8. **Quality Review Board meets** Quality Review Board evaluates output while groups draw their organization charts (for Runs #1 and #2) on the board.	**5–10 min.**	**43–75 min.**
9. **Class discussion** Instructor leads discussion of exercise as a whole. Discuss the following questions: a. What were the companies' scores for Runs #1 and #2? b. What type of structure did the "winning" company have? Did it reorganize for Run #2? c. What type of task was there? Technology? Environment? d. What would Joan Woodward, Henry Mintzberg, Frederick Taylor, Lawrence and Lorsch, or Burns and Stalker say about WIS Company organization?	**7–15 min.**	**50–90 min.**

SOURCE: "Words-in-Sentences Company" in Dorothy Marcic, *Organizational Behavior: Experiences and Cases*, 4th ed. (St. Paul: West, 1995), 303–305. Reprinted by permission.

15.2 Design and Build a Castle

This exercise is intended to give your group an opportunity to design an organization and produce a product.

Your group is one of three product-development teams working within the research and development division of the GTM (General Turret and Moat) Corporation. GTM has decided to enter new markets by expanding the product line to include fully designed and produced castles, rather than selling components to other companies, as it has in the past.

Each of the three teams has been asked to design a castle for the company to produce and sell. Given its limited resources, GTM cannot put more than one design on the market. Therefore, it will have to decide which of the three designs it will use and will discard the other two designs.

Your task is to develop and design a castle. You will have forty-five minutes to produce a finished product. At the end of this period, several typical consumers, picked by scientific sampling techniques, will judge which is the best design. Before the consumers make their choice, each group will have one to two minutes to make a sales presentation.

Step 1. Each group is designated either 1, 2, or 3. The instructor will provide group members a memorandum appropriate for their group. One observer (or two for larger groups) is selected for each group. Observers read their materials.

Step 2. Groups design their organization in order to complete their goal.

Step 3. Each group designs its own castle and draws it on newsprint.

Step 4. "Typical consumers" (may be observers) tour building locations and hear sales pitches. Judges caucus to determine winner.

Step 5. Groups meet again and write up their central goal statement. They also write the organization chart on newsprint with the goal written beneath. These are posted around the room.

Step 6. Instructor leads a class discussion on how the different memos affected organization design. Which design seemed most effective for this task?

NOTE: Your instructor may allow more time and actually have you *build* the castles.

SOURCE: "Design and Build a Castle" from Dorothy Marcic and Richard C. Housley, *Organizational Behavior: Experiences and Cases* (St. Paul: West, 1989), 221–225. Reprinted by permission.

TAKE 2

Biz Flix | Casino

Martin Scorcese's lengthy, complex, and beautifully photographed study of 1970s' Las Vegas gambling casinos and their organized crime connections completes his trilogy that includes *Mean Streets* (1973) and the 1990 *Goodfellas*. Ambition, greed, drugs, and sex destroy the mob's gambling empire. The film includes strong performances by Robert De Niro, Joe Pesci, and Sharon Stone. The violence and expletive-filled dialogue give *Casino* its R rating.

The *Casino* scene is part of "The Truth about Las Vegas" sequence early in the film. It follows the scenes of deceiving the Japanese gambler. It starts with a close-up of Sam "Ace" Rothstein (Robert De Niro) standing between his two casino executives (Richard Amalfitano, Richard F. Strafella). His voice-over says, "In Vegas, everybody's gotta watch everybody else." The scene ends after Sam Rothstein describes the excheaters who monitor the gambling floor with binoculars. The film continues with the introduction of Ginger (Sharon Stone).

What to Watch for and Ask Yourself:

- Which type or form of organizational design does this scene show?
- Does this scene show the results of the differentiation and integration organizational design processes?
- Does this scene show any behavioral demands of organizational design? What are they?

Workplace Video | Designing Adaptive Organizations, Featuring Boyne Mountain & Boyne Highlands

In 1947, Everett Kircher started his career with little more than a dream and a $1 down payment on a piece of land. From that humble beginning the Detroit native would go on to launch a ski-resort network that would change the shape of the industry.

Kircher's dream, now known as Boyne USA Resorts, is the largest privately owned ski-and-golf corporation, and third largest resort network, in North America. Boyne resort locations offer an array of sport-and-leisure activities for all seasons, from skiing and golf to indoor water parks and scenic chairlifts. Many amenities at Boyne resorts, such as snowmaking, snow-grooming, and ski lifts, were pioneered by Kircher, and have since become standard features at ski resorts everywhere.

At the beginning, Boyne USA operated with a vertical organizational structure in which strategic decisions came from Kircher's centralized command—from the top down. Kircher wore many hats in those days: CEO, chief engineer, head chef, and director of marketing and finance. However, as Boyne's business grew during the 1950s and 1960s, Kircher found it necessary to appoint general managers to carry out his roles and responsibilities. The shift marked the beginning of an ongoing decentralization at Boyne, where decision-making authority was delegated to lower levels in the organizational hierarchy.

TAKE 2

After 2000, Boyne USA split into two divisions: Boyne East and Boyne West. Each division operates as an autonomous business serving its own geographic market. To handle the increasing complexity of operations, as well as the broadening of Boyne's business to include golf, retail, food, and waterparks, the two divisions began appointing "subject-matter experts" to top management. By hiring managers who possess knowledge of highly specialized areas of the business, Boyne is able to deliver a higher level of customer satisfaction.

Structural change has paid off for Kircher and his skilled management teams. Boyne USA Resorts has grown from $40 million in revenues in 1990 to over $200 million in 2005. Moreover, the natural beauty and premium amenities at each resort attract guests from all over the world. Although Kircher died in 2002 at the age of 85, his legacy lives on. His smart management practices have produced a network of thriving getaways where sport and leisure enthusiasts go to embrace the "Boyne way of life."

Discussion Questions

1. Why was decentralization essential to Boyne's continued growth, despite the company's early success with Everett Kircher at the helm of a vertical structure?
2. What would have happened if Kircher had been unwilling to delegate authority and decision making to general managers as the business grew and became more complicated?
3. Discuss the impact of environment and technology on Boyne USA's organizational structure.

NASA: Organizational Design Frontiers for Exploring Space Frontiers

With the increasingly complex and unstable external environments encountered by nearly all types of organizations in the twenty-first century, the best way to design those organizations has become a prominent concern for executives and managers. Effective organization design requires executives and managers to make numerous decisions about complex, interrelated variables such as how specialization should be used to maximize output, how specialists' work should be integrated, who makes decisions, and how communication should occur within work teams and with management.[1] For an increasing number of organizations, these decisions result in some sort of *network* organization design, or *lattice* design. Some of the key features of a lattice design are crucial elements of organizations that are designed to achieve success in the twenty-first century. These key features include process differentiation rather than functional differentiation; process champions in place of multilevel management pyramids; activity teams instead of specialized departments; curtailing hierarchy to enable empowerment; and multidirectional flow of information among process teams.[2]

Among the many organizations that are viable candidates for utilizing a network or lattice design is the United States' National Aeronautics and Space Administration (NASA). In mid-2004, Sean O'Keefe, NASA's head administrator, announced a transformation of the agency's organization structure. This massive transformation effort was in response to the President's Commission on Implementation of U.S. Space Exploration Policy, which found that "NASA needs to transform itself into a leaner, more focused agency by developing an organizational structure that recognizes the need for a more integrated approach to science requirements, management, and implementation of systems development and exploration missions."[3] O'Keefe said, "[o]ur task is to . . . . promote synergy across the agency, and support the long-term exploration vision in a way that is sustainable and affordable. . . . We need to take these critical steps to streamline the organization and create a structure that affixes clear authority and accountability."[4] The new structure revolved around four mission directorates—Aeronautics Research, Science, Exploration Systems, and Space Operations—and some headquarters support functions.[5] The new organization structure was "a large matrix between projects (managed by Exploration Systems) and functional areas (overseen by Space Operations, Science, and Aeronautics Research)."[6]

In concert with the overall structural transformation of NASA, a comprehensive organizational design effort was undertaken in the Systems Analysis Integrated Discipline Team (SAIDT), one of several teams charged with carrying out NASA's Vision for Space Exploration.[7] In creating the organization design for SAIDT, "[t]he larger organization and environment constrained the design, and the design needed to coordinate SAIDT work tasks involving personnel from geographically distributed centers." The design process was conducted using three different simulation packages: Design Structure Matrix, OrgCon™, and SimVision™. The organizational design challenge was "to create a high-performing organization characterized by wide-open communication across the many interfaces, strong motivation to cooperate in spite of competing profit motives, and strong goal orientation to ensure astronaut safety and mission success."[8]

The Design Structure Matrix (DSM) analysis approach was used to establish a *baseline* model for the organizational design of the SAIDT. This approach required the chairperson of SAIDT and his core leadership team "to identify the personnel requirements, estimate the resources required for the team, and scope the roles and responsibilities of individual team members." The DSM analysis was supplemented with information regarding the internal division of work, coordination mechanisms, and the likelihood of meeting project goals—all of which were organizational design aspects at a level of detail beyond the capability of the DSM design simulation.[9]

The next design step used OrgCon, an approach that "provides a top-down assessment of the fits and misfits between contingencies such as the organization's strategy, structure, incentives, management style, climate, and environment. This enabled the SAIDT chairperson and other members of the SAIDT design team to evaluate alternative organization designs relative to the baseline model.[10]

The third major design step utilized SimVision. This analytical tool relies on information about project parameters, task features and task flows, and the skills and characteristics of individuals to further explore variations on the baseline organization design. In contrast to the top-down analytical approach of OrgCon, SimVision provides a bottom-up, task-oriented analysis.[11]

By employing the three complementary analytical approaches, could the SAIDT design team create an effective lattice organizational design?

Discussion Questions

1. What is a network (or lattice) organization, and how does it differ from more traditional organization structures?
2. Why have network (or lattice) organizations come into existence?
3. How does the network (or lattice) organization relate to NASA's overall structural transformation and to the organization design for the Systems Analysis Integrated Discipline Team (SAIDT)?
4. How does contingency thinking relate to the contextual factors of organization design for the Systems Analysis Integrated Discipline Team (SAIDT)?
5. What do the analytical simulations—Design Structure Matrix, OrgCon, and SimVision—contribute to NASA's ability to create an effective organization design?
6. What advantages and disadvantages do you think arise from utilizing a network (or lattice) organization?

SOURCE: This case was written by Michael K. McCuddy, The Louis S. and Mary L. Morgal Chair of Christian Business Ethics and Professor of Management, College of Business Administration, Valparaiso University.

CHAPTER 16

© TIM BOYLE/GETTY IMAGES

Organizational Culture

LEARNING OBJECTIVES

After reading this chapter, you should be able to do the following:

1 Describe organizational culture.
2 Critically evaluate the roles of the three levels of culture.
3 Evaluate the four functions of culture within an organization.
4 Explain the relationship between organizational culture and performance.
5 Contrast the characteristics of adaptive and nonadaptive cultures.
6 Describe five ways leaders reinforce organizational culture.
7 Describe the three stages of organizational socialization and the ways culture is communicated in each step.
8 Identify ways of assessing organizational culture.
9 Explain actions managers can take to change organizational culture.

THINKING AHEAD: CARIBOU COFFEE

A Culture of Shared Dreams

Caribou Coffee was born out of a simple dream that its founders shared: to create something that inspired people and made the day better. It happened in 1990 when newlyweds Kim and John Puckett were hiking through the Alaskan wilderness. When they reached the top of the mountain, they were captivated by the sensational view. This experience lit their entrepreneurial ambitions and led to their realization that true achievement takes hard work but is worth striving for.[1]

Caribou has maintained its cultural identity by staying true to the Pucketts' dreams. All their stores are designed in the fashion of Alaskan wilderness lodges. The company takes pride in creating a unique experience for their customers. They feature mountain-style furnishings, open ceilings with wooden beams, and pictures of the founders in the mountains. This strategy is designed to reflect their company and its mantra, "Life is short, stay awake for it."[2] As a continuing theme of these beginnings, Caribou has a set of core values in place that reflect its culture: "Blaze new trails," "Be excellent not average," and "Make a difference to our community." In addition, Caribou labels all its hourly team members "vice presidents of smiles and service" as a way of recognizing their contribution as the face of Caribou Coffee to its customers. They encourage employees to chat with each other over a cup of coffee rather than sending e-mails to each other. Moreover, they take pride in displaying pictures of employees on vacation throughout their stores and offices as they believe such adventures lead to creativity and encourage entrepreneurial thinking. Caribou's culture has also led to awards and recognition. In the Looking Back feature at the end of the chapter, you can see how the company's values, a part of its culture, translate into actions.

THE KEY ROLE OF ORGANIZATIONAL CULTURE

The concept of organizational culture has its roots in cultural anthropology. As in larger human society, there are cultures within organizations. These cultures are similar to societal cultures. They are shared, communicated through symbols, and passed down from generation to generation of employees.

The concept of cultures in organizations was alluded to as early as the Hawthorne studies, which described work group culture. The topic came into its own during the early 1970s, when managers and researchers alike began to search for keys to survival for organizations in a competitive and turbulent environment. Then, in the early 1980s, several books on corporate culture were published, including Deal and Kennedy's *Corporate Cultures*,[3] Ouchi's *Theory Z*,[4] and Peters and Waterman's *In Search of Excellence*.[5] These books found wide audiences, and research began in earnest on the elusive topic of organizational cultures. Executives indicated that these cultures were real and could be managed.[6]

Culture and Its Levels

(1) Describe organizational culture.

Many definitions of *organizational culture* have been proposed. Most of them agree that there are several levels of culture and that these levels differ in terms of their visibility and their ability to be changed. The definition adopted in this chapter is that *organizational (corporate) culture* is a pattern of basic assumptions that are considered valid and that are taught to new members as the way to perceive, think, and feel in the organization.[7]

Edgar Schein, in his comprehensive book on organizational culture and leadership, suggests that organizational culture has three levels. His view of culture is presented in Figure 16.1. The levels range from visible artifacts and creations to testable values to invisible and even preconscious basic assumptions. To achieve a complete understanding of an organization's culture, all three levels must be studied.

(2) Critically evaluate the roles of the three levels of culture.

organizational (corporate) culture
A pattern of basic assumptions that are considered valid and that are taught to new members as the way to perceive, think, and feel in the organization.

artifacts
Symbols of culture in the physical and social work environment.

Artifacts

Symbols of culture in the physical and social work environment are called *artifacts*. They are the most visible and accessible level of culture. The key to understanding culture through artifacts lies in figuring out what they mean. Artifacts are also the most frequently studied manifestation of organizational culture, perhaps because of their accessibility. Among the artifacts of culture are personal enactment, ceremonies and rites, stories, rituals, and symbols.[8]

FIGURE 16.1 Levels of Organizational Culture

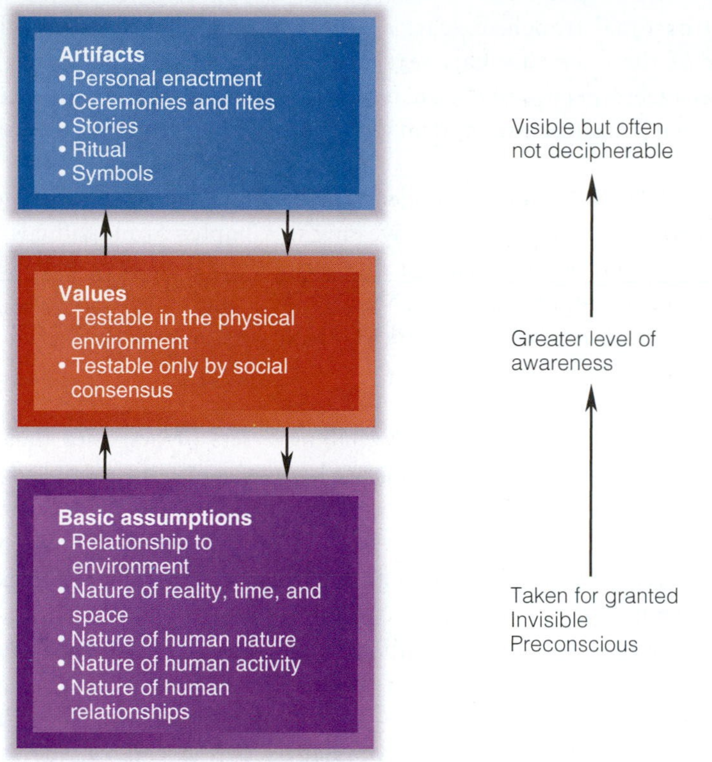

SOURCE: From Edgar H. Schein, *Organizational Culture and Leadership: A Dynamic View.* Copyright © 1985 Jossey-Bass Inc. Reprinted by permission of Jossey-Bass, Inc., a subsidiary of John Wiley & Sons, Inc.

As noted in Looking Ahead, photos on the walls of all Caribou cafes feature the founders hiking in the wilderness. These images of the outdoors and recreation serve as an artifact of Caribou's culture, representing the belief that all good things in life are worth working hard for. Similarly, the corporate culture of Google is apparent in the offices of its headquarters in Mountain View, California. The lobby is replete with lava lamps, pianos, and live searches on the Google search engine from around the world. The hallways house bikes and exercise machines, while office spaces are laid-back, featuring couches and occupied by dogs who go with their owners to work.[9] The artifacts at Google reinforce the notion that the company cares about employees and wants them to be creative and comfortable.

Personal Enactment Culture can be understood, in part, through an examination of the behavior of organization members. Personal enactment is behavior that reflects the organization's values. In particular, personal enactment by the top managers provides insight into these values. Steve Irby is the founder and CEO of Stillwater Designs, the company that created Kicker audio speakers. He values good relationships and believes that people are the most important part of his company. Irby builds trust with his employees by sharing the financial results of the business each month. The employees know that if monthly sales are higher than the sales in the same month of the previous year, Irby will hold a cookout for the employees on the following Friday. Irby and the general manager always do the cooking. Eskimo Joe's, a Stillwater, Oklahoma, restaurant chain and one of the largest t-shirt sellers in the United States, could probably have become a national franchise years ago. But founder Stan Clark, who began as co-owner of the once-tiny bar, says his intent is to become better, not bigger. Clark still meets personally with new hires for the restaurant's serving staff, ensuring that they receive a firm grounding in his philosophy of food and fun.[10]

Modeled behavior is a powerful learning tool for employees, as Bandura's social learning theory demonstrated.[11] As we saw in Chapter 5, individuals learn vicariously by observing others' behavior and patterning their own behavior similarly. Culture can be an important leadership tool. Managerial behavior can clarify what is important and coordinate the work of employees, in effect negating the need for close supervision.[12]

Ceremonies and Rites Relatively elaborate sets of activities that are enacted time and again on important occasions are known as organizational ceremonies and rites.[13] These occasions provide opportunities to reward and recognize employees whose behavior is congruent with the values of the company. Ceremonies and rites send a message that individuals who both espouse and exhibit corporate values are heroes to be admired.

The ceremonies also bond organization members together. Southwestern Bell (now part of SBC Communications) emphasized the importance of management training to the company. Training classes were kicked off by a high-ranking executive (a rite of renewal), and completion of the classes was signaled by a graduation ceremony (a rite of passage). Six kinds of rites in organizations have been identified:[14]

1. *Rites of passage* show that an individual's status has changed. Retirement dinners are an example.
2. *Rites of enhancement* reinforce the achievement of individuals. An example is the awarding of certificates to sales contest winners.
3. *Rites of renewal* emphasize change in the organization and commitment to learning and growth. An example is the opening of a new corporate training center.
4. *Rites of integration* unite diverse groups or teams within the organization and renew commitment to the larger organization. Company functions such as annual picnics fall into this category.
5. *Rites of conflict reduction* focus on dealing with conflicts or disagreements that arise naturally in organizations. Examples are grievance hearings and the negotiation of union contracts.
6. *Rites of degradation* are used by some organizations to visibly punish persons who fail to adhere to values and norms of behavior. Some CEOs, for example, are replaced quite publicly for unethical conduct or for failure to achieve organizational goals. In some Japanese organizations, employees who perform poorly are given ribbons of shame as punishment.

The Berkshire Hathaway Inc. annual meeting is a ceremony of celebration and appears more like a music festival than a corporate meeting. Here Chairman Warren Buffett plays with a bluegrass band before the 2007 meeting.

Berkshire Hathaway Inc. is an Omaha-based company that owns and operates a number of insurance firms and several other subsidiaries. Its chairman and CEO is Warren Buffett, known for his business acumen and for ensuring good returns on shareholder investments. Berkshire's annual meeting is a ceremony of celebration and appears more like a rock music festival than a corporate meeting. In 2007 Jimmy Buffett sang "Margaritaville" at the meeting with some of the lyrics changed to "wasting away in Berkshire-Hathaway-a-ville"! The meeting started at 7 am with Pink Floyd's song "Money" and turned into a six-hour party that included games like ping-pong and cards. Bill Gates, who is on the board of directors at Berkshire Hathaway, made it to the meeting as well and was seen socializing with Warren Buffett. Over 20,000 shareholders, employees, and Warren Buffett relatives braved thunderstorms to attend this event.[15]

Stories Some researchers have argued that the most effective way to reinforce organizational values is through stories.[16] As they are told and retold, stories give meaning and identity to organizations and are especially helpful in orienting new employees. Part of the strength of organizational stories is that the listeners are left to draw their own conclusions—a powerful communication tool.[17]

Some corporate stories even transcend cultural and political boundaries. Visit the Web site of Wal-Mart China, and you will read the true story of Jeff, a pharmacist in Harrison, Arkansas, a small town deep in the Ozarks. When Jeff received an early morning weekend call telling him that a diabetic patient needed insulin, he quickly opened his pharmacy and filled the prescription.[18] While Arkansas and Beijing are worlds apart, stories such as this one help transfer Wal-Mart's corporate "personality" to its new Asian associates. Research by Joanne Martin and her colleagues has indicated that certain themes recur in stories across different types of organizations:[19]

1. *Stories about the boss.* These stories may reflect whether the boss is "human" or how the boss reacts to mistakes.
2. *Stories about getting fired.* Events leading to employee firings are recounted.
3. *Stories about how the company deals with employees who have to relocate.* These stories relate to the company's actions toward employees who have to move—whether the company is helpful and takes family and other personal concerns into account.
4. *Stories about whether lower-level employees can rise to the top.* Often, these stories describe a person who started out at the bottom and eventually became the CEO.
5. *Stories about how the company deals with crisis situations.* Johnson & Johnson's employees' response to the Tylenol crisis has become legendary in business circles as an example of doing the right thing.
6. *Stories about how status considerations work when rules are broken.* When Tom Watson, Sr., was CEO of IBM, he was once confronted by a security guard because he was not wearing an ID badge.

These are the themes that can emerge when stories are passed down. The information from these stories serves to guide the behavior of organization members.

To be effective cultural tools, stories must be credible. You can't tell a story about your flat corporate hierarchy and then have reserved parking spaces for managers. Stories that aren't backed by reality can lead to cynicism and mistrust. For example, Steve Jobs, the founder and current CEO of Apple, made a commencement address at Stanford University and told stories relating his successful battle with cancer, his struggles with keeping Apple afloat, and his being fired and getting back on top. These stories were meant to reinforce his lesson that one should work towards whatever his or her passion might be.[20]

Effective stories can also reinforce culture and create renewed energy. Lucasfilm is the home of director and producer George Lucas and the birthplace of such blockbusters as *Star Wars* and *Forrest Gump*. Stories of the company's legendary accomplishments are used to reinforce the creative culture and to rally the troops. When Gail Currey, former head of the company's digital division, found her 300 designers were grumbling, she reminded them of how they did *Gump* when everyone else said it was impossible and what a hit the film was. The designers would then head back to their computers to contribute to the company's success.[21]

Rituals Everyday organizational practices that are repeated over and over are rituals. They are usually unwritten, but they send a clear message about "the way we do things around here." While some companies insist that people address each other by their titles (Mr., Mrs., Ms., Miss) and surnames to reinforce a professional image, others prefer that employees operate on a first-name basis—from the top manager on down. Hewlett-Packard values open communication, so its employees address one another by first names only.

In the fast-paced world of automotive manufacturing, the endless grind of the assembly line makes it tough for workers to imagine the person who will actually drive the car they are building. But at Saturn's Tennessee assembly plant, each car travels down the assembly line with the customer's name attached to it. And upon delivery, the customer is handed the keys and photographed by the dealer in a small ceremony commemorating the event. Not surprisingly, Saturn owners are among the most loyal in the industry.[22]

As everyday practices, rituals reinforce the organizational culture. Insiders who commonly practice the rituals may be unaware of their subtle influence, but outsiders recognize it easily.

Symbols Symbols communicate organizational culture by unspoken messages. Southwest Airlines has used symbols in several ways. During its early years, the airline emphasized its customer service value by using the heart symbol (the "love" airline) and "love bites" (peanuts). More recently, the airline has taken on the theme of fun. Flight attendants wear casual sports clothes in corporate colors. Low fares are "fun fares," and weekend getaways are "fun packs." Some aircraft are painted to resemble Shamu the whale, underscoring the fun image. Symbols are representative of organizational identity and membership to employees. Nike's trademark "swoosh" is proudly tattooed above the ankles of some Nike employees. Apple Computer employees readily identify themselves as "Apple People." Symbols are used to build solidarity in the organizational culture.[23]

Personal enactment, rites and ceremonies, stories, rituals, and symbols serve to reinforce the values that are the next level of culture.

Values

Values are the second, and deeper, level of culture. They reflect a person's underlying beliefs of what should be or should not be. Values are often consciously articulated, both in conversation and in a company's mission statement or annual report. However, there may be a difference between a company's *espoused values* (what the members say they value) and its *enacted values* (values reflected in the way the members actually behave).[24] Values also may be reflected in the behavior of individuals, which is an artifact of culture. One study investigating the gender gap in a Canadian sports organization found that coaches and athletes believed that inequities resulting from this gap were normal or natural or completely denied such inequities existed even though they were widespread. This was because even though the organization espoused gender equity as a value, its practices did not demonstrate and support gender equity.[25]

espoused values
What members of an organization say they value.

enacted values
Values reflected in the way individuals actually behave.

Ritz-Carlton: Storytelling for Better Service

The Ritz-Carlton chain of hotels is well known for its quality service and helpful employees in a world where customer service is at a premium. Think back to your last five hotel stays and ask yourself if you would want to return. The Ritz-Carlton chain believes in creating customers for life and prides itself on training its employees not every month or every year but every day on the value of service.

Employees at these hotels are encouraged to make an emotional connection with their guests because people are more likely to go back to a place they feel connected to. Furthermore, they have everyday fifteen-minute training sessions, called "lineups." In these sessions, employees are encouraged to share one "wow" story for the day in which someone in their workforce went above and beyond the call of duty. The remarkable thing about these stories is that the same story is shared across all the Ritz-Carlton locations across the world! These stories reinforce organizational service and teamwork values. They create a sense of identity and recognition of outstanding workers. Undoubtedly, the Ritz-Carlton is investing thousands of hours in training employees in its culture and values through storytelling. This is driven by the belief that stories appeal to both reason and emotion in their workforce and can hence serve as powerful learning tools.

SOURCE: C. Gallo, "How Ritz-Carlton Maintains Its Mystique," *Business Week* (February 13, 2007), http://www.businessweek.com/print/smallbiz/content/feb2007/sb20070213_171606.htm.

A firm's values and how it promotes and publicizes them can also affect how workers feel about their jobs and themselves. A study of 180 managers looked at their employers' effectiveness in communicating concern for employees' welfare. Managers in organizations that consistently communicated concern for workers' well-being and that focused on treating employees fairly reported feeling better about themselves and their role in the organization.[26] The lesson? *Treat* employees like valuable team members, and they are more likely to *feel* like valuable team members. Read about how one of the classiest hotel chains in the world, Ritz-Carlton, uses storytelling to reinforce company service values on a daily basis in the Real World 16.1.

Values underlie the adaptable and innovative culture at Levi Strauss. As guides for behavior, they are reinforced in the aspirations statement and in the reward system of the organization. Workforce diversity is valued at Levi Strauss. A former strong supporter of the Boy Scouts of America, the company discontinued its funding after the Scouts were shown to discriminate on the basis of sexual orientation. Mary Gross, a Levi Strauss spokesperson, expressed the company's position on valuing diversity: "One of the family values of this company is treating people who are different from you the same as you'd like to be treated. Tolerance is a pretty important family value."[27]

Some organizational cultures are characterized by values that support healthy lifestyle behaviors. When the workplace culture values worker health and psychological needs, there is enhanced potential for high performance and improved well-being.[28] Clif Bar, the energy bar maker, even has a twenty-two-foot rock-climbing wall in its corporate office.

When Harley-Davidson hires new customer service employees, they had better be ready to do more than just answer telephones. Working at Harley-Davidson is not only a job, it's about an entire subculture that revolves around Harleys. New employees are immersed in this culture, typically through working at a Harley owners' rally and taking demonstration rides. Over time, most employees become Harley riders or owners, which helps them provide better service to other Harley lovers.[29]

Charles Schwab Corporation, a financial services firm, is a model of a values-driven business. Its core organizational values are as follows:

- Be fair, empathetic, and responsive in serving our clients.
- Respect and reinforce our fellow employees and the power of teamwork.
- Strive relentlessly to innovate what we do and how we do it.
- Always earn and be worthy of our clients' trust.[30]

Assumptions

Assumptions are the deeply held beliefs that guide behavior and tell members of an organization how to perceive and think about things. As the deepest and most fundamental level of an organization's culture, according to Edgar Schein, they are the essence of culture. They are so strongly held that a member behaving in any fashion that would violate them would be unthinkable. Another characteristic of assumptions is that they are often unconscious. Organization members may not be aware of their assumptions and may be reluctant or unable to discuss them or change them.

While unconscious assumptions often guide a firm's actions and decisions, some companies are quite explicit in their assumptions about employees. Earthlink, an Internet service provider, includes several of these assumptions on its Web site. The firm assumes that people who are treated with respect will respond by giving their best. It also assumes that because life is about more than work, its employees will have fun. And the firm sees competition as a normal, even healthy part of work, due in part to its assumption that competition helps individuals, teams, and firms raise their level of performance. Earthlink is so confident of these assumptions, it encourages visitors who believe it is not living up to these values to "call us on it."[31]

Now that you understand Schein's three levels of culture, you can use You 16.1 to assess a culture you'd like to learn more about.

FUNCTIONS AND EFFECTS OF ORGANIZATIONAL CULTURE

(3) Evaluate the four functions of culture within an organization.

assumptions
Deeply held beliefs that guide behavior and tell members of an organization how to perceive and think about things.

In an organization, culture serves four basic functions. First, culture provides a sense of identity to members and increases their commitment to the organization.[32] When employees internalize the values of the company, they find their work intrinsically rewarding and identify with their fellow workers. Motivation is enhanced, and employees are more committed.[33]

Second, culture is a sense-making device for organization members. It provides a way for employees to interpret the meaning of organizational events.[34] Leaders can use organizational symbols like corporate logos as sense-making devices to help employees understand the changing nature of their organizational identity. This is specifically so in an environment that is constantly changing.[35] Sometimes symbols can remain the same to ensure that some things stay constant despite changing conditions; other times symbols may have to change to reflect the new culture in the organization. For example, McDonald's is known worldwide for its golden arches that have remained the same since its inception in 1955.[36] In contrast, Southwest Airlines changed its logo in 2002 to mark its leadership in the airline industry as the "fun"

Southwest Airlines changed its logo in 2002 to mark its leadership in the airline industry as the fun airline and to capitalize on one of its most important trademarks, being "the love airline."

YOU 16.1

Analyzing the Three Levels of Culture

Select an organization you respect. Analyze its culture using the following dimensions.

The artifacts of _______________'s culture are as follows:

Personal enactment:

Rites and ceremonies:

Stories:

Rituals:

Symbols:

The values embedded in _______________'s culture are as follows:

The assumptions of _______________'s culture are as follows:

1. On what information did you base your analysis?
2. How complete is your view of this organization's culture?

airline and to capitalize on one of its most important trademarks, being "the love airline."

Third, culture reinforces the values in the organization. The culture at SSM Health Care emphasizes patient care and continuous improvement. The St. Louis-based company, which owns and manages twenty-one acute-care hospitals in four states, values compassionate, holistic, high-quality care. SSM was the first health care organization to win the Malcolm Baldrige National Quality Award.

Finally, culture serves as a control mechanism for shaping behavior. Norms that guide behavior are part of culture. If the norm the company wants to promote is teamwork, its culture must reinforce that norm. The company's culture must be characterized by open communication, cooperation between teams, and integration of teams.[37] Culture can also be used as a powerful tool to discourage dysfunctional and deviant behaviors in organizations. Norms can send clear messages that certain behaviors are unacceptable.[38] For example, the workgroup that an employee is involved with can have an impact her or his absenteeism behavior. That is, if the workgroup does not have explicit norms in place discouraging absenteeism, members are more likely to be engage in excessive absenteeism.[39]

The effects of organizational culture are hotly debated by organizational behaviorists and researchers. Managers attest strongly to the positive effects of culture in organizations, but it is difficult to quantify these effects. John Kotter and James Heskett have reviewed three theories about the relationship between organizational culture and performance and the evidence that either supports or refutes these theories.[40] The three are the strong culture perspective, the fit perspective, and the adaptation perspective.

(4) Explain the relationship between organizational culture and performance.

strong culture
An organizational culture with a consensus on the values that drive the company and with an intensity that is recognizable even to outsiders.

The Strong Culture Perspective

The strong culture perspective states that organizations with "strong" cultures perform better than other organizations.[41] A *strong culture* is an organizational culture with a consensus on the values that drive the company and with an intensity that is

recognizable even to outsiders. Thus, a strong culture is deeply held and widely shared. It also is highly resistant to change. One example of a strong culture is IBM's. Its culture is one we are all familiar with: conservative, with a loyal workforce and an emphasis on customer service.

Strong cultures are thought to facilitate performance for three reasons. First, they are characterized by goal alignment; that is, all employees share common goals. Second, they create a high level of motivation because of the values shared by the members. Third, they provide control without the oppressive effects of a bureaucracy.

To test the strong culture hypothesis, Kotter and Heskett selected 207 firms from a wide variety of industries. They used a questionnaire to calculate a culture strength index for each firm, and they correlated that index with the firm's economic performance over a twelve-year period. They concluded that strong cultures were associated with positive long-term economic performance, but only modestly.

There are also two perplexing questions about the strong culture perspective. First, what can be said about evidence showing that strong economic performance can create strong cultures, rather than the reverse? Second, what if the strong culture leads the firm down the wrong path? Sears, for example, is an organization with a strong culture, but in the 1980s, it focused inward, ignoring competition and consumer preferences and damaging its performance. Changing Sears' strong but stodgy culture has been a tough task, with financial performance only recently showing an upward trend.[42]

The Fit Perspective

The fit perspective argues that a culture is good only if it "fits" the industry or the firm's strategy. For example, a culture that values a traditional hierarchical structure and stability would not work well in the computer manufacturing industry, which demands fast response and a lean, flat organization. Three particular characteristics of an industry may affect culture: the competitive environment, customer requirements, and societal expectations.[43] In the computer industry, firms face a highly competitive environment, customers who require highly reliable products, and a society that expects state-of-the-art technology and high-quality service.

A study of twelve large U.S. firms indicated that cultures consistent with industry conditions help managers make better decisions. It also indicated that cultures need not change as long as the industry doesn't change. If the industry does change, however, many cultures change too slowly to avoid negative effects on firms' performance.[44]

The fit perspective is useful in explaining short-term performance but not long-term performance. It also indicates that it is difficult to change culture quickly, especially if the culture is widely shared and deeply held. But it doesn't explain how firms can adapt to environmental change.

The Adaptation Perspective

adaptive culture
An organizational culture that encourages confidence and risk taking among employees, has leadership that produces change, and focuses on the changing needs of customers.

The third theory about culture and performance is the adaptation perspective. Its theme is that only cultures that help organizations adapt to environmental change are associated with excellent performance. An *adaptive culture* is one that encourages confidence and risk taking among employees,[45] has leadership that produces change,[46] and focuses on the changing needs of customers.[47] 3M is a company with an adaptive culture in that it encourages new product ideas from all levels within the company.

TABLE 16.1 Adaptive versus Nonadaptive Organizational Cultures

	Adaptive Organizational Cultures	Nonadaptive Organizational Cultures
Core values	Most managers care deeply about customers, stockholders, and employees. They also strongly value people and processes that can create useful change (e.g., leadership up and down the management hierarchy).	Most managers care mainly about themselves, their immediate work group, or some product (or technology) associated with that work group. They value the orderly and risk-reducing management process much more highly than leadership initiatives.
Common behavior	Managers pay close attention to all their constituencies, especially customers, and initiate change when needed to serve their legitimate interests, even if that entails taking some risks.	Managers tend to behave somewhat insularly, politically, and bureaucratically. As a result, they do not change their strategies quickly to adjust to or take advantage of changes in their business environments.

SOURCE: Reprinted with the permission of The Free Press, a Division of Simon & Schuster, Inc. from *Corporate Culture and Performance* by John P. Kotter and James L. Heskett. Copyright © 1992 by Kotter Associates, Inc. and James L. Heskett.

To test the adaptation perspective, Kotter and Heskett interviewed industry analysts about the cultures of twenty-two firms. The contrast between adaptive cultures and nonadaptive cultures was striking. The results of the study are summarized in Table 16.1.

(5) Contrast the characteristics of adaptive and nonadaptive cultures.

Adaptive cultures facilitate change to meet the needs of three groups of constituents: stockholders, customers, and employees. Nonadaptive cultures are characterized by cautious management that tries to protect its own interests. Adaptive firms showed significantly better long-term economic performance in Kotter and Heskett's study. One contrast that can be made is between Hewlett-Packard (HP), a high performer, and Xerox, a lower performer. The analysts viewed HP as valuing excellent leadership more than Xerox did and as valuing all three key constituencies more than Xerox did. Economic performance from 1977 through 1988 supported this difference: HP's index of annual net income growth was 40.2, as compared to Xerox's 13.1. Kotter and Heskett concluded that the cultures that promote long-term performance are those that are most adaptive.

Given that high-performing cultures are adaptive ones, it is important to know how managers can develop adaptive cultures. Would you think that the military is an adaptive culture or nonadaptive? In the Science feature, discover how West Point Military Academy is struggling with implementing change due to a gap between its cultural artifacts and espoused values.

In the next section, we will examine the leader's role in managing organizational culture.

THE LEADER'S ROLE IN SHAPING AND REINFORCING CULTURE

(6) Describe five ways leaders reinforce organizational culture.

According to Edgar Schein, leaders play crucial roles in shaping and reinforcing culture.[48] The five most important elements in managing culture are (1) what leaders pay attention to; (2) how leaders react to crises; (3) how leaders behave; (4) how leaders allocate rewards; and (5) how leaders hire and fire individuals.

The United States Military Academy at West Point: Challenges to Changing a Strong Culture

Laws passed in 1993 required the three wings of the U.S. defense learning academies to add civilians to the faculty team. It mandated that there be a 75 percent (military) and 25 percent (civilian) ratio at these academies in order to promote diverse learning techniques. In response to this legislation, the United States Military Academy at West Point engaged in an aggressive civilian faculty drive because they believed that civilians could bring diversity to perspectives at West Point. Today, the Academy has reached its quota and has now officially integrated civilian faculty into its system.

© TIMOTHY FADEK/BLOOMBERG NEWS/LANDOV

West Point engaged in an aggressive civilian faculty drive when laws were passed mandating there be a 75 percent military to 25 percent civilian ratio in the teaching staff at military academies in order to promote diverse learning techniques.

So did this initiative go down well with the military faculty at West Point? Did the military manage to truly integrate these civilians into their system? A recent scientific study assessed the impact of organizational culture at West Point on such a change initiative. This comprehensive study found that the integration is far from complete and that the civilian faculty members' perceptions of their status, leadership, and departmental value were mostly far from satisfactory.

The interesting aspect of this study is that most of these perceptions were driven by cultural artifacts and rites. For example, when a military officer is promoted there is considerable fanfare and rituals to celebrate the occasion, but there is no such process in place for recognition and celebration of civilian accomplishments. Another informal symbol of status was the departmental directory listing various personnel. Civilians are listed after almost all military officers (regardless of their official status) and sometimes even after civilian secretarial staff. This study concluded that there was a clear gap between the stated goals of the military (espoused values) and what translates into actual behaviors. Recommendations to correct this situation included clearly defining the specific meaning of integration as not everyone at West Point had the same ideas about what it encompassed. Subtle signals are sent to organizational members about what is really valued in the organization through its symbols, rituals, language, and resource allocation decisions. Finally, this study highlighted the importance of leadership's role in clearly defining a vision and walking the talk consistent with that vision. Leaders should be receptive to outside perceptions as a way of reevaluating cultural inconsistencies in the organization.

Although many action steps might be in place officially, members pay attention to informal cultural symbols and rules to make sense of the change process.

SOURCE: C. M. Ruvolo, "The Organizational Culture of Diversity: An Assessment of West Point's Faculty," *Consulting Psychology Journal: Practice and Research* 59(1) (2007): 54–67.

The Enron Corporation fiasco illustrates each of these roles. "Enron ethics" is the term applied to the gap between words and deeds, and it illustrates that leader behavior deeply affects organizational culture.[49] Enron created deceptive partnerships and used questionable accounting practices to maintain its investment-grade rating. Employees recorded earnings before they were realized; they thought this was merely recording them early, not wrongly. Enron's culture was shaping the ethical boundaries of its employees, and Enron executives bent the rules for personal gain.

What Leaders Pay Attention To

Leaders in an organization communicate their priorities, values, and beliefs through the themes that consistently emerge from what they focus on. These themes are reflected in what they notice, comment on, measure, and control. If leaders are consistent in what they pay attention to, measure, and control, employees receive clear signals about what is important in the organization. If, however, leaders are inconsistent, employees spend a lot of time trying to decipher and find meaning in the inconsistent signals.

Enron leader Jeffrey Skilling paid attention to money and profit at all costs. Employees could take as much vacation as they wanted as long as they were delivering results; they could deliberately break company rules as long as they were making money.

How Leaders React to Crises

The way leaders deal with crises communicates a powerful message about culture. Emotions are heightened during a crisis, and learning is intense. With mergers and acquisitions, the way in which the leader reacts to change, transparency of the procedures used, and communication quality affect how followers perceive change and ultimately acceptance of any associated changes in the organizational culture.[50]

Difficult economic times present crises for many companies and illustrate their different values. Some organizations do everything possible to prevent laying off workers. Others may claim that employees are important but quickly institute major layoffs at the first signal of an economic downturn. Employees may perceive that the company shows its true colors in a crisis and thus may pay careful attention to the reactions of their leaders.

When the Enron crisis became public, managers quickly shifted blame and pointed fingers. Before bankruptcy was declared, managers began systematically firing any employee they could lay blame on, while denying that there was a problem with accounting irregularities. During the crisis, managers responded with anonymous whistle-blowing, hiding behind the Fifth Amendment and shredding documents.

How Leaders Behave

Through role modeling, teaching, and coaching, leaders reinforce the values that support the organizational culture. Employees often emulate leaders' behavior and look to the leaders for cues to appropriate behavior. Many companies are encouraging employees to be more entrepreneurial—to take more initiative and be more innovative in their jobs. A study showed that if managers want employees to be more entrepreneurial, they must demonstrate such behaviors themselves.[51] This is the case with any cultural value. Employees observe the behavior of leaders to find out what the organization values.

The behavior of Enron's managers spoke volumes; they broke the law as they created fake partnerships. They ignored and then denied that problems existed. While employees were unable to dump their Enron stocks, managers were hastily getting rid of their shares, all the while telling employees that the company would be fine.

How Leaders Allocate Rewards

To ensure that values are accepted, leaders should reward behavior that is consistent with the values. Some companies, for example, may claim that they use a pay-for-performance system that distributes rewards on the basis of performance.

When the time comes for raises, however, the increases are awarded according to length of service with the company. Imagine the feelings of a high-performing newcomer who has heard leaders espouse the value of rewarding individual performance and then receives only a tiny raise.

Some companies may value teamwork. They form cross-functional teams and empower them to make important decisions. However, when performance is appraised, the criteria for rating employees focus on individual performance. This sends a confusing signal to employees about the company's culture: Is individual performance valued, or is teamwork the key?

At Enron, employees were rewarded only if they produced consistent results, with little regard for ethics. Managers were given extremely large bonuses to keep the stock price up at any cost. Performance reviews were done in public, and poor performers were ridiculed.

How Leaders Hire and Fire Individuals

A powerful way that leaders reinforce culture is through the selection of newcomers to the organization. With the advent of electronic recruitment practices, applicant perceptions of organizational culture are shaped by what the organization advertises on their recruitment Web site. Typical perception-shaping mechanisms are organizational values, policies, awards, and goals.[52] Leaders often unconsciously look for individuals who are similar to current organizational members in terms of values and assumptions. Some companies hire individuals on the recommendation of a current employee; this tends to perpetuate the culture because the new employees typically hold similar values. Jeffrey Swartz, CEO of Timberland, has a unique way of hiring people. He has his recruiter call the applicant in advance and have them wear anything they feel passionately about other than Timberland shoes. Senior applicants go through a day of community service with Timberland executives because Swartz claims that anyone can be smarter than him in an interview, but service brings out the real person and this is who they try to hire.[53]

The way a company fires an employee and the rationale behind the firing also communicate the culture. Some companies deal with poor performers by trying to find a place within the organization where they can perform better and make a contribution. Other companies seem to operate under the philosophy that those who cannot perform are out quickly.

The reasons for terminations may not be directly communicated to other employees, but curiosity leads to speculation. An employee who displays unethical behavior and is caught may simply be reprimanded even though such behavior is clearly against the organization's values. Other employees may view this as a failure to reinforce the values within the organization.

Enron hired employees who had aggressiveness, greed, a desire to win at all costs, and a willingness to break rules. It fired nonproductive employees, using a "rank and yank" system whereby the bottom 15–20 percent of employees were let go each year. Peers were required to rank each other, which led to cutthroat competition and extreme distrust among employees.

In summary, leaders play a critical role in shaping and reinforcing organizational culture. The Enron case illustrates how powerful, and potentially damaging, that influence can be. The lesson for future managers is to create a positive culture through what they pay attention to, how they react to crises, how they behave, the way they allocate rewards, and how they hire and fire employees. Research results from a study of finance professionals in Greece supports this

FIGURE 16.2 The Organizational Socialization Process: Stages and Outcomes

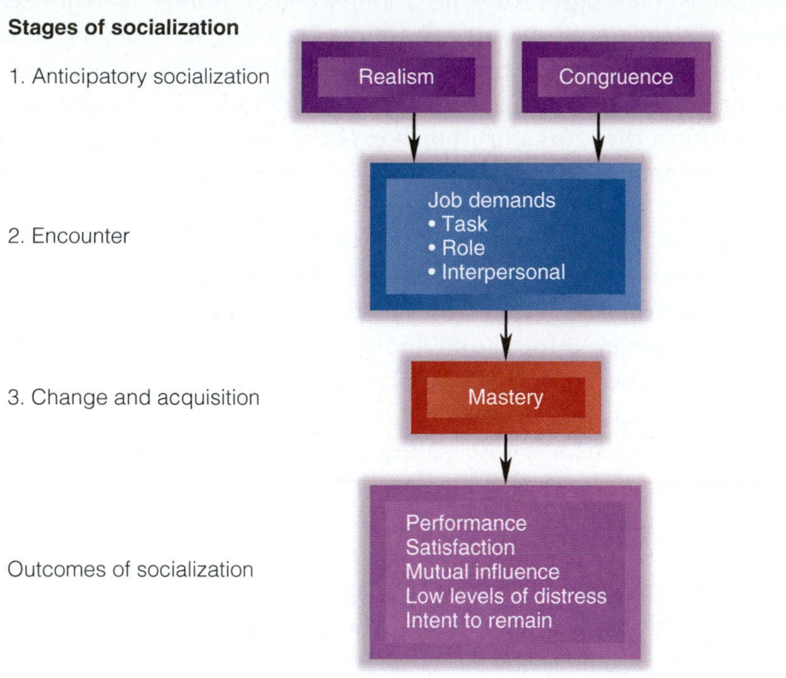

SOURCE: Reprinted from *Organizational Dynamics,* Autumn 1989, "An Ethical Weather Report: Assessing the Organization's Ethical Climate" by John B. Cullen, et al. Copyright © 1989, with permission from Elsevier Science.

view. Transformational leaders create a more adaptive culture, which in turn increases business unit performance.[54]

ORGANIZATIONAL SOCIALIZATION

We have seen that leaders play key roles in shaping an organization's culture. Another process that perpetuates culture is the way it is handed down from generation to generation of employees. Newcomers learn the culture through *organizational socialization*—the process by which newcomers are transformed from outsiders to participating, effective members of the organization.[55] The process is also a vehicle for bringing newcomers into the organizational culture. As we saw earlier, cultural socialization begins with the careful selection of newcomers who are likely to reinforce the organizational culture.[56] Once selected, newcomers pass through the socialization process.

(7) Describe the three stages of organizational socialization and the ways culture is communicated in each step.

The Stages of the Socialization Process

The organizational socialization process is generally described as having three stages: anticipatory socialization, encounter, and change and acquisition. Figure 16.2 presents a model of the process and the key concerns at each stage of it.[57] It also describes the outcomes of the process, which will be discussed in the next section of the chapter.

organizational socialization
The process by which newcomers are transformed from outsiders to participating, effective members of the organization.

anticipatory socialization
The first socialization stage, which encompasses all of the learning that takes place prior to the newcomer's first day on the job.

Anticipatory Socialization *Anticipatory socialization*, the first stage, encompasses all of the learning that takes place prior to the newcomer's first day on the job. It includes the newcomer's expectations. The two key concerns at this stage are realism and congruence.

Realism is the degree to which a newcomer holds realistic expectations about the job and about the organization. One thing newcomers should receive information about during entry into the organization is the culture. Information about values at this stage can help newcomers begin to construct a scheme for interpreting their organizational experiences. A deeper understanding of the organization's culture will be possible through time and experience in the organization.

There are two types of *congruence* between an individual and an organization: congruence between the individual's abilities and the demands of the job, and the fit between the organization's values and the individual's values. Organizations disseminate information about their values through their Web pages, annual reports, and recruitment brochures.[58] Value congruence is particularly important for organizational culture. It is also important in terms of newcomer adjustment. Newcomers whose values match the company's values are more satisfied with their new jobs, adjust more quickly, and say they intend to remain with the firm longer.[59]

Encounter The second stage of socialization, *encounter*, is when newcomers learn the tasks associated with the job, clarify their roles, and establish new relationships at work. This stage commences on the first day at work and is thought to encompass the first six to nine months on the new job. Newcomers face task demands, role demands, and interpersonal demands during this period.

Task demands involve the actual work performed. Learning to perform tasks is related to the organization's culture. In some organizations, newcomers are given considerable latitude to experiment with new ways to do the job, and creativity is valued. In others, newcomers are expected to learn the established procedures for their tasks. Early experiences with trying to master task demands can affect employees' entire careers. Auditors, for example, are often forced to choose between being thorough, on the one hand, and being fast in completing their work, on the other. By pressuring auditors in this way, firms often set themselves up for problems later, when these pressures may lead auditors to make less-than-ethical decisions.

Role demands involve the expectations placed on newcomers. Newcomers may not know exactly what is expected of them (role ambiguity) or may receive conflicting expectations from other individuals (role conflict). The way newcomers approach these demands depends in part on the culture of the organization. Are newcomers expected to operate with considerable uncertainty, or is the manager expected to clarify the newcomers' roles? Some cultures even put newcomers through considerable stress in the socialization process, including humility-inducing experiences, so newcomers will be more open to accepting the firm's values and norms. Long hours, tiring travel schedules, and an overload of work are part of some socialization practices.

Interpersonal demands arise from relationships at work. Politics, leadership style, and group pressure are interpersonal demands. All of them reflect the values and assumptions that operate within the organization. Most organizations have basic assumptions about the nature of human relationships. The Korean chaebol (business conglomerate) LG Group strongly values harmony in relationships and in society, and its decision-making policy emphasizes unanimity.

In the encounter stage, the expectations formed in anticipatory socialization may clash with the realities of the job. It is a time of facing the task, role, and interpersonal demands of the new job.

encounter

The second socialization stage in which the newcomer learns the tasks associated with the job, clarifies roles, and establishes new relationships at work.

Change and Acquisition In the third and final stage of socialization, *change and acquisition,* newcomers begin to master the demands of the job. They become proficient at managing their tasks, clarifying and negotiating their roles, and engaging in relationships at work. The time when the socialization process is completed varies widely, depending on the individual, the job, and the organization. The end of the process is signaled by newcomers being considered by themselves and others as organizational insiders.

Outcomes of Socialization

Newcomers who are successfully socialized should exhibit good performance, high job satisfaction, and the intention to stay with the organization. In addition, they should exhibit low levels of distress symptoms.[60] High levels of organizational commitment are also marks of successful socialization.[61] This commitment is facilitated throughout the socialization process by the communication of values that newcomers can buy into. Successful socialization is also signaled by mutual influence; that is, the newcomers have made adjustments in the job and organization to accommodate their knowledge and personalities. Newcomers are expected to leave their mark on the organization and not be completely conforming.

When socialization is effective, newcomers understand and adopt the organization's values and norms. This ensures that the company's culture, including its central values, survives. It also provides employees a context for interpreting and responding to things that happen at work, and it ensures a shared framework of understanding among employees.[62]

Newcomers adopt the company's norms and values more quickly when they receive positive support from organizational insiders. Sometimes this is accomplished through informal social gatherings.[63]

Socialization as Cultural Communication

Socialization is a powerful cultural communication tool. While the transmission of information about cultural artifacts is relatively easy, the transmission of values is more difficult. The communication of organizational assumptions is almost impossible, since organization members themselves may not be consciously aware of them.

The primary purpose of socialization is the transmission of core values to new organization members.[64] Newcomers are exposed to these values through the role models they interact with, the training they receive, and the behavior they observe being rewarded and punished. Newcomers are vigilant observers, seeking clues to the organization's culture and consistency in the cultural messages they receive. If they are expected to adopt these values, it is essential that the message reflect the underlying values of the organization.

One company known for its culture is The Walt Disney Company. Disney transmits its culture to employees though careful selection, socialization, and training. The Disney culture is built around customer service, and its image serves as a filtering process for applicants. Peer interviews are used to learn how applicants interact with each other. Disney tries to secure a good fit between employee values and the organization's culture. To remind employees of the image they are trying to project, employees are referred to as "cast members" and they occupy a "role." They work either "on stage" or "backstage" and wear "costumes" rather than uniforms. Disney operates its own "universities," which are attended by all new employees. Once trained at a Disney university, cast members are paired with role models to continue their learning on-site.

change and acquisition
The third socialization stage, in which the newcomer begins to master the demands of the job.

Companies such as Disney use the socialization process to communicate messages about organizational culture. Both individuals and organizations can take certain actions to ensure the success of the socialization process.

ASSESSING ORGANIZATIONAL CULTURE

8 Identify ways of assessing organizational culture.

Although some organizational scientists argue for assessing organizational culture with quantitative methods, others say qualitative methods yield better results.[65] Quantitative methods, such as questionnaires, are valuable because of their precision, comparability, and objectivity. Qualitative methods, such as interviews and observations, are valuable because of their detail, descriptiveness, and uniqueness.

Two widely used quantitative assessment instruments are the Organizational Culture Inventory (OCI) and the Kilmann-Saxton Culture-Gap Survey. Both assess the behavioral norms of organizational cultures, as opposed to the artifacts, values, or assumptions of the organization.

Organizational Culture Inventory

The OCI focuses on behaviors that help employees fit into the organization and meet the expectations of coworkers. Using Maslow's motivational need hierarchy as its basis, it measures twelve cultural styles. The two underlying dimensions of the OCI are task/people and security/satisfaction. There are four satisfaction cultural styles and eight security cultural styles.

A self-report instrument, the OCI contains 120 questions. It provides an individual assessment of culture and may be aggregated to the work group and to the organizational level.[66] It has been used in firms throughout North America, Western Europe, New Zealand, and Thailand, as well as in U.S. military units, the Federal Aviation Administration, and nonprofit organizations.

Kilmann-Saxton Culture-Gap Survey

The Kilmann-Saxton Culture-Gap Survey focuses on what actually happens and on the expectations of others in the organization.[67] Its two underlying dimensions are technical/human and time (the short term versus the long term). With these two dimensions, the actual operating norms and the ideal norms in four areas are assessed. The areas are task support (short-term technical norms), task innovation (long-term technical norms), social relationships (short-term human orientation norms), and personal freedom (long-term human orientation norms). Significant gaps in any of the four areas are used as a point of departure for cultural change to improve performance, job satisfaction, and morale.

A self-report instrument, the Gap Survey provides an individual assessment of culture and may be aggregated to the work group. It has been used in firms throughout the United States and in nonprofit organizations.

Triangulation

triangulation
The use of multiple methods to measure organizational culture.

A study of a rehabilitation center in a 400-bed hospital incorporated *triangulation* (the use of multiple methods to measure organizational culture) to improve inclusiveness and accuracy in measuring the organizational culture.[68] Triangulation has been used by anthropologists, sociologists, and other behavioral scientists to study organizational culture. Its name comes from the navigational technique of using multiple reference points to locate an object. In the rehabilitation center study, the three methods used to triangulate on the culture were (1) obtrusive observations by eight trained observers, which provided an outsider perspective; (2) self-administered questionnaires, which provided quantitative insider information; and (3) personal interviews with the center's staff, which provided qualitative contextual information.

The study showed that each of the three methods made unique contributions toward the discovery of the rehabilitation center's culture. The complete picture could not have been drawn with just a single technique. Triangulation can lead to a better understanding of the phenomenon of culture and is the best approach to assessing organizational culture.

CHANGING ORGANIZATIONAL CULTURE

Changing situations may require changes in the existing culture of an organization. With rapid environmental changes such as globalization, workforce diversity, and technological innovation, the fundamental assumptions and basic values that drive the organization may need to be altered. One particular situation that may require cultural change is a merger or acquisition. The blending of two distinct organizational cultures may prove difficult.

Despite good-faith efforts, combining cultures is difficult. When established media giant Time Warner merged with Internet upstart America Online in 2001, few could imagine the fireworks that would result when these two "oil and water" firms tried to mix. Typical of the conflicts that followed was a client dinner in which AOL executive Neil Davis horrified Time Warner executives by describing how AOL preferred to handle weakened competitors. Taking a steak knife from the table, Davis raised his arm and drove the knife into the table top, explaining that, "What we like to do to a competitor that is damaged is drive the knife in their heart." The shocked client ultimately declined to buy ads on AOL, and the entire merger was eventually deemed a multibillion-dollar failure due, at least in part, to the culture clash between the two partners.[69]

Prior to the Daimler-Chrysler merger, both automotive giants enjoyed good performance. After the merger, however, it was a different story. The Chrysler division started losing money and instituted major, unanticipated layoffs. Differences in culture were cited as responsible for this failure. Daimler-Benz had a culture that was formal, with a very structured management style. Chrysler, in contrast, had a relaxed management style that accounted for its premerger success. The two divisions had vastly different views on pay scales and travel expenses. Chrysler executives and engineers began leaving in great numbers, and Chrysler employees believed that Daimler was trying to control the company and impose its culture on Chrysler. The stock price after the merger fell to half of its previous value following the initial postmerger high.[70, 71]

Alterations in culture may also be required when an organization employs people from different countries. Research indicates that some organizational cultures actually enhance differences in national cultures.[72] One study compared foreign employees working in a multinational organization with employees working in different organizations within their own countries. The assumption was that the employees from various countries working for the same multinational organization would be more similar than employees working in diverse organizations in their native countries. The results were surprising, in that there were significantly greater differences among the employees of the multinational than among managers working for different companies within their native countries. In the multinational, Swedes became more Swedish, Americans became more American, and so forth. It appears that employees enhance their national culture traditions even when working within a single organizational culture.[73] This is more likely to occur when diversity is moderate. When diversity is very high, employees are more likely to develop a shared identity in the organization's culture instead of relying on their own national culture.[74]

9 Explain actions managers can take to change organizational culture.

Changing an organization's culture is feasible but difficult.[75] One reason for the difficulty is that assumptions—the deepest level of culture—are often unconscious. As such, they are often nonconfrontable and nondebatable. Another reason for the difficulty is that culture is deeply ingrained and behavioral norms and rewards are well learned.[76] In a sense, employees must unlearn the old norms before they can learn new ones. Managers who want to change the culture should look first to the ways culture is maintained. Research among hospitals found that change was welcomed in private hospitals with a collaborative culture, whereas change was met with opposition in public hospitals with an autocratic culture.[77]

A model for cultural change that summarizes the interventions managers can use is presented in Figure 16.3. In this model, the numbers represent the actions managers can take. There are two basic approaches to changing the existing culture: (1) helping current members buy into a new set of values (actions 1, 2, and 3); or (2) adding newcomers and socializing them into the organization and removing current members as appropriate (actions 4 and 5).[78]

The first action is to change behavior in the organization. Even if behavior does change, however, this is not sufficient for cultural change to occur. Behavior is an artifact (level 1) of culture. Individuals may change their behavior but not the values that drive it. They may rationalize, "I'm only doing this because my manager wants me to."

FIGURE 16.3 Interventions for Changing Organizational Culture

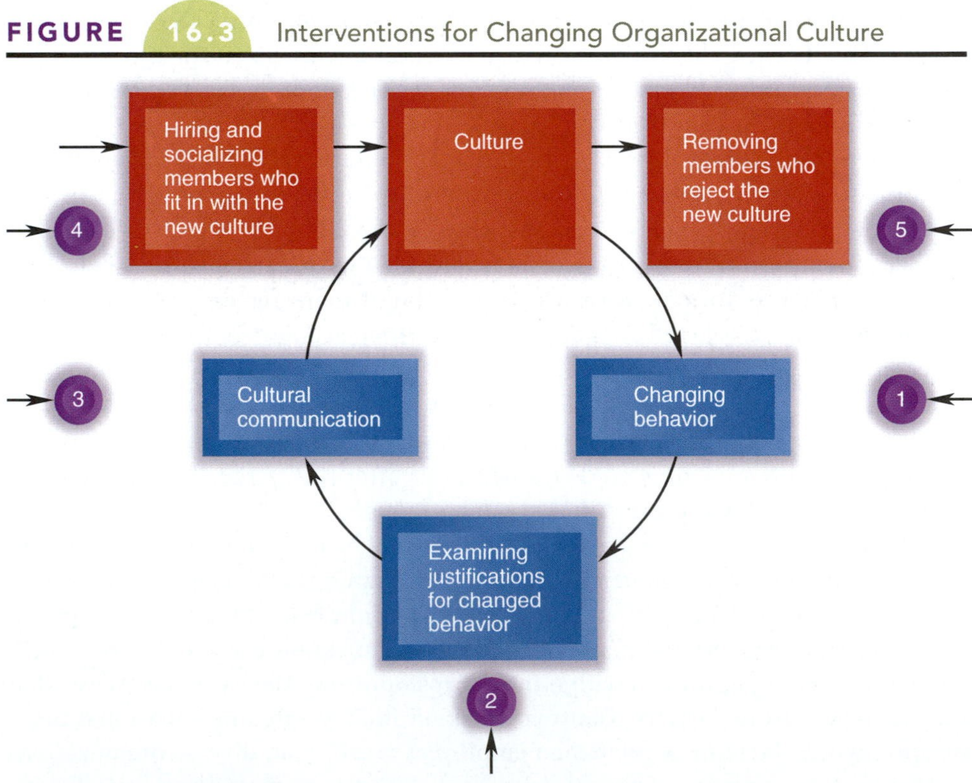

SOURCE: From Vijay Sathe, "How to Decipher and Change Corporate Culture," Chap. 13 in *Gaining Control of the Corporate Culture* (R. H. Kilmann et al., eds.), Fig. 1, p. 245. Copyright © 1985 Jossey-Bass, Inc. Reprinted by permission of Jossey-Bass, Inc., a subsidiary of John Wiley & Sons, Inc.

Therefore, managers must use action 2, which is to examine the justifications for the changed behavior. Are employees buying into the new set of values, or are they just complying?

The third action, cultural communication, is extremely important. All of the artifacts (personal enactment, stories, rites and ceremonies, rituals, and symbols) must send a consistent message about the new values and beliefs. It is crucial that the communication be credible; that is, managers must live the new values and not just talk about them. Leaders should pay attention to the informal social networks rather than just structural positions in leading organizational change. These informal network communication channels, combined with employee's values and the belief that managers are highly committed to the change effort, can go a long way in making the change a success.[79]

The two remaining actions (4 and 5) involve shaping the workforce to fit the intended culture. First, the organization can revise its selection strategies to more accurately reflect the new culture. Second, the organization can identify individuals who resist the cultural change or who are no longer comfortable with the values in the organization. Reshaping the workforce should not involve a ruthless pursuit of nonconforming employees; it should be a gradual and subtle change that takes considerable time. Changing personnel in the organization is a lengthy process; it cannot be done effectively in a short period of time without considerable problems.

Evaluating the success of cultural change may be best done by looking at behavior. Cultural change can be assumed to be successful if the behavior is intrinsically motivated—on "automatic pilot." If the new behavior would persist even if rewards were not present, and if the employees have internalized the new value system, then the behavior is probably intrinsically motivated. If employees automatically respond to a crisis in ways consistent with the corporate culture, then the cultural change effort can be deemed successful.

One organization that has changed its culture is AT&T. In 1984, the courts ordered the breakup of the company. Prior to the breakup, AT&T operated in a stable environment with low levels of uncertainty. The organization was a highly structured bureaucracy. The culture emphasized lifetime employment, promotion from within, and loyalty. AT&T faced minimal competition, and it offered individual security. When the courts ordered AT&T to divest its Bell operating companies, the old culture was no longer effective. The company had to move toward a culture that holds individuals accountable for their performance. Change at AT&T was painful and slow, but it was necessary for the company to be able to operate in the new competitive environment.[80] Changing environments may bring about changes in organizational culture.

Given the current business environment, managers may want to focus on three particular cultural modifications: (1) support for a global view of business, (2) reinforcement of ethical behavior, and (3) empowerment of employees to excel in product and service quality.

Developing a Global Organizational Culture

The values that drive the organizational culture should support a global view of the company and its efforts. To do so, the values should be clear to everyone involved so that everyone understands them. The values should also be strongly supported at the top. Management should embody the shared values and reward employees who support the global view. Finally, the values should be consistent over time. Consistent values give an organization a unifying theme that competitors may be unable to emulate.[81]

Global corporations suffer from the conflicting pressures of centralization and decentralization. An overarching corporate culture that integrates the decentralized subsidiaries in locations around the world can be an asset in the increasingly competitive global marketplace.

Following are six specific guidelines for managers who want to create a global culture:[82]

1. Create a clear and simple mission statement. A shared mission can unite individuals from diverse cultural backgrounds.
2. Create systems that ensure an effective flow of information. Coordination councils and global task forces can be used to ensure that information flows throughout the geographically dispersed organization are consistent.
3. Create "matrix minds" among managers; that is, broaden managers' minds to allow them to think globally. IBM does this through temporary overseas assignments. Managers with international experience share that experience when they return to the home organization.
4. Develop global career paths. This means ensuring not only that home country executives go overseas but also that executives from other countries rotate into service in the home office.
5. Use cultural differences as a major asset. The former Digital Equipment Corporation (now part of Hewlett-Packard), for example, transferred its research and development functions to Italy to take advantage of the free-flowing Italian management style that encouraged creativity. Its manufacturing operations went to Germany, which offered a more systematic management style.
6. Implement worldwide management education and team development programs. Unified training efforts that emphasize corporate values can help establish a shared identity among employees.

These guidelines are specifically aimed at multinational organizations that want to create a global corporate culture, but other organizations can also benefit from them. Companies that want to broaden employees' views or to use the diversity of their workforce as a resource will find several of these recommendations advantageous.

Developing an Ethical Organizational Culture

While a majority of U.S. firms have rushed to create and publicize codes of ethics in an effort to help their employees discern right from wrong, the impact of these codes is not always as positive as might be expected. While the implementation of formal ethics guidelines might be expected to improve ethical behavior, some studies have shown the exact opposite, with institution of formal ethics codes actually leading to less ethical behavior among employees. While the reasons for this are not clear, it appears that in some cases employees see the code of ethics as simply a management showpiece, leading to cynicism and resentment. In other cases, a heavy reliance on a strict set of rules may reduce the perceived need for employees to think about and be involved in ethical decision making, leading to inferior choices in the long run.[83]

The organizational culture, however, can have profound effects on the ethical behavior of organization members.[84] When a company's culture promotes ethical norms, individuals behave accordingly. Managers can encourage ethical behavior by being good role models for employees. They can institute the philosophy that ethical behavior makes good business sense and puts the company in congruence with the larger values of society.[85] Managers can also communicate that rationalizations for unethical behavior are not tolerated. For example, some salespersons justify padding their expense accounts because everyone else does it. Declaring these justifications illegitimate sends a clear message about the lack of tolerance for such behavior. Leaders can also use storytelling as a tool to build an ethical culture and create a sense of identity for organizational members with a higher purpose or goal within the organization.[86] For example, Cisco's CEO John Chambers is known for his ability to give inspiring speeches. Yet Cisco is in the business of selling routers and switches—items that are crucial for Internet connectivity but that most users don't even see. Chambers tells stories of how such connectivity can change lives and make the world a better place and thus creates a sense of identity and higher purpose for his investors as well as employees.[87]

Trust is another key to effectively managing ethical behavior, especially in cultures that encourage whistle-blowing (as we saw in Chapter 2). Employees must trust that whistle-blowers will be protected, that procedures used to investigate ethical problems will be fair, and that management will take action to solve problems that are uncovered.

At John Deere & Company, a simple idea guides the firm's ethics and decision making: "No smoke, no mirrors, no tricks: just right down the middle of the field," as Robert Lane, chairman and CEO, puts it. John Deere's decision to donate a multimillion-dollar parcel of land to a university, rather than selling it to a developer, demonstrates its values and is one of the reasons the firm made the top ten in *Business Ethics* magazine's list of the "100 Best Corporate Citizens for 2004."[88]

The reasons most often cited for unethical corporate conduct are interesting.[89] They include the belief that a behavior is not really unethical, that it is in the organization's best interest, that it will not be discovered, and that the organization will support it because it offers a good outcome for the organization. An ethical corporate culture can eliminate the viability of these excuses by clearly communicating the boundaries of ethical conduct, selecting employees who support the ethical culture, rewarding organization members who exhibit ethical behavior, and conspicuously punishing members who engage in unethical behavior.

Organizations that seek to encourage ethical behavior can do so by using their organizational culture. By completing You 16.2, you can assess the ethical culture of an organization you're familiar with.

Developing a Culture of Empowerment and Quality

Throughout this book, we have seen that successful organizations promote a culture that empowers employees and excels in product and service quality. Empowerment serves to unleash employees' creativity and productivity. It requires eliminating traditional hierarchical notions of power. Cultures that emphasize empowerment and quality are preferred by employees. Companies that value empowerment and continuous improvement have cultures that promote high product and service quality.[90]

Corporate culture can also support values that help firms compete. In The Real World 16.2, you can learn about Wegmans and how it uses corporate values and employee development to leverage success in the highly competitive grocery business. New Balance Athletic Shoe competes with low-wage suppliers in Asia (where the average wage is less than $2 per hour), even though one-fourth of its products are produced in the United States. Part of the firm's success comes from its willingness to empower its employees by sharing information with them. For instance, the firm often shares cost data with employees, pointing out that a competitor's shoe can be made overseas for $15 and challenging them to meet that cost point. Today, New Balance workers in the United States receive twenty-two hours of training when they are hired and continual training on the factory floor. The result is that New Balance's U.S. workers can produce a pair of shoes in twenty-four minutes, compared to almost three hours in Asia.[91, 92]

Harley-Davidson might well be the ultimate old-line manufacturing firm trying to develop a culture of quality. From 1985, with the firm literally minutes from bankruptcy, to today, with demand for its high-quality cycles at an all-time high,

Organizational Culture and Ethics

Think about the organization you currently work for or one you know something about and complete the following Ethical Climate Questionnaire.

Use the scale below and write the number that best represents your answer in the space next to each item.

To what extent are the following statements true about your company?

Completely false	Mostly false	Somewhat false	Somewhat true	Mostly true	Completely true
0	1	2	3	4	5

____ 1. In this company, people are expected to follow their own personal and moral beliefs.
____ 2. People are expected to do anything to further the company's interests.
____ 3. In this company, people look out for each other's good.
____ 4. It is very important here to follow the company's rules and procedures strictly.
____ 5. In this company, people protect their own interests above other considerations.
____ 6. The first consideration is whether a decision violates any law.
____ 7. Everyone is expected to stick by company rules and procedures.
____ 8. The most efficient way is always the right way in this company.
____ 9. Our major consideration is what is best for everyone in the company.
____ 10. In this company, the law or ethical code of the profession is the major consideration.
____ 11. It is expected at this company that employees will always do what is right for the customer and the public.

To score the questionnaire, first add up your responses to questions 1, 3, 6, 9, 10, and 11. This is subtotal number 1. Next, reverse the scores on questions 2, 4, 5, 7, and 8 (5 = 0, 4 = 1, 3 = 2, 2 = 3, 1 = 4, 0 = 5). Add the reverse scores to form subtotal number 2. Add subtotal number 1 to subtotal number 2 for an overall score.

Subtotal 1 ______ + Subtotal 2 ______ = Overall Score ______.

Overall scores can range from 0 to 55. The higher the score, the more the organization's culture encourages ethical behavior.

SOURCE: Reprinted from *Organizational Dynamics*, Autumn 1989, "An Ethical Weather Report: Assessing the Organization's Ethical Climate" by John B. Cullen, et al.

Harley-Davidson has gone from the valley to the mountaintop. Like many other old manufacturing firms, Harley tried to compete in the 1970s with techniques developed in the 1950s. Huge forklifts wandered the shop floor, shuffling millions of dollars worth of components among workstations; quality was poor—in short, Harley was fat and inefficient. Over the last two decades, Harley has reinvented itself. Manufacturing has been streamlined to reflect more modern thinking on efficiency. Product quality has improved immensely, and the firm's workforce continues to improve, with close to half the company's employees taking training courses in any given year.

Harley's high level of quality is not merely an artifact of better shop practices. The company's management has worked to foster a unique congenial relationship with its unions, ensuring that continuous improvement is an organizational priority rather than simply the latest management fad. Today's Harley "hog" costs less to make and is more reliable than any before it, due in large part to the firm's incessant drive to make a better product.[93]

Medrad, Inc., won the 2003 Malcolm Baldrige Award for quality in manufacturing. Medrad makes devices that allow doctors to see through you; using diagnostic

THE REAL WORLD 16.2

Wegmans: Leveraging Values and Human Capital to Succeed

Wegmans is a large supermarket chain headquartered in Rochester, New York. It has been a family owned and operated business ever since its founding in 1931, although the founders owned grocery stores before then starting in 1916. In 2006, the company had annual sales of $4.6 billion, operating about 70 stores mainly on the East Coast and employing 36,000 people.

Wegmans has consistently ranked on *Fortune*'s "100 Best Companies to Work For," ranking number one in 2005 and number three in 2007. It has differentiated itself from most retailers by offering great quality and a wide selection of foods. For example, the company offers about 400 different kinds of gourmet cheese in any of its stores. Wegmans is also well known for placing value on its human capital. It has some of the best human resource practices and benefits in the country and thus consistently attracts employees who wish to stay and provide high-quality customer service. One of its innovations is the Work-Scholarship program, which focuses on helping young adults and equipping them with skills they need to stay in school and hold a job. The company has invested $63 million in scholarships for 20,000 employees attending universities while they work at Wegmans.

In addition, Wegmans is active in contributing to the communities they operate in. They are engaged in several local giving programs, including those that provide food for the needy. Such strong corporate values focused on the development of its internal workforce as well as the local communities have earned Wegmans several national awards and have contributed to its success.

SOURCE: Wegmans corporate Web site, http://www.wegmans.com/about/pressRoom/overview.asp#whatwebelieve

imaging technology, doctors get an inside view of the human body. It sells these products to hospitals and imaging centers around the world. CEO John Friel is committed to continuous improvement and quality, as well as employee empowerment. He spends at least one day a month in company shop floor operations—including customer service, tech support, and even sweeping the floor in maintenance. Friel's employees are committed to him, to Medrad, and to quality.[94]

Managers can learn from the experiences of New Balance, Harley-Davidson, and Medrad that employee empowerment is a key to achieving quality. Involving employees in decision making, removing obstacles to their performance, and communicating the value of product and service quality reinforce the values of empowerment and quality in the organizational culture.

MANAGERIAL IMPLICATIONS: THE ORGANIZATIONAL CULTURE CHALLENGE

Managing organizational culture is a key challenge for leaders in today's organizations. With the trend toward downsizing and restructuring, maintaining an organizational culture in the face of change is difficult. In addition, such challenges as globalization, workforce diversity, technology, and managing ethical behavior often require that an organization change its culture. Adaptive cultures that can respond to changes in the environment can lead the way in terms of organizational performance.

Managers have at their disposal many techniques for managing organizational culture. These techniques range from manipulating the artifacts of culture, such as ceremonies and symbols, to communicating the values that guide the organization. The socialization process is a powerful cultural communication process. Managers are models who communicate the organizational culture to employees through personal enactment. Their modeled behavior sets the norms for the other employees to follow. Their leadership is essential for developing a culture that values diversity, supports empowerment, fosters innovations in product and service quality, and promotes ethical behavior.

Culture Change Ordered for Cola Giant

Coca-Cola was given five years to change its corporate culture and treatment of people of color as part of a $192.5 million discrimination lawsuit settlement, the largest in U.S. history. For years, the cola giant highlighted its commitment to African Americans outside the company: consumers, suppliers, and members of the community. However many believed the organization did not show the same level of commitment to its employees *inside* the firm.

The case began when African American Linda Ingram's manager made derogatory remarks to her, calling her the N-word to her face. Says Ingram, "She did it around some other peers . . . I was so appalled and shocked that something of that nature would happen at that company in that day and time." Ingram's manager was subsequently fired for her remarks, but the investigation increased tension between Ingram and her coworkers (all of whom were white) so much that she requested a transfer to another department. After her requests were continually ignored by the company's human resource manager, Ingram felt she had no other recourse but to seek relief outside of the firm.

Ingram did not sue Coca-Cola because her former manager called her the N-word. She brought legal action against Coca-Cola as a result of the company's culture of indifference after the fact. Cyrus Mehri, the attorney who won a landmark $176 million judgment in the 1997 Texaco discrimination case, took on Ingram's case, charging Coca-Cola with engaging in systematic race discrimination that extended throughout its employment policies and practices.

1. Why do you believe Coca-Cola was ordered to change its culture and not only its treatment of employees of color?
2. What are the first steps you would you take to initiate such a culture change?

SOURCE: S. Spruell, "Coca-Cola: From Discrimination Suit to Diversity Leader," *DiversityInc* (January/February 2007): 21–30.

LOOKING BACK: CARIBOU COFFEE

The Corporate Green Globe Award

The Rainforest Alliance, a New York–based nonprofit, certifies farms that use responsible ecological and social farming practices. It also awards the prestigious Corporate Green Globe award to firms that engage in such environmentally friendly practices. At a recent gala in New York City, the Rainforest Alliance recognized business leaders who promote sustainable agriculture and practices. This year, Caribou Coffee won the Green Globe Award for its commitment to buying its coffee from Rainforest-certified farms. Caribou has indicated that by the year 2008, its goal is to ensure that 50 percent of all its coffee be purchased from such farms. This award highlights Caribou's strong commitment to an ethical culture not just within its company but also in the communities that its suppliers are drawn from.[95]

Caribou's commitment to its values and ethical culture is further evidenced in its community giving programs. The company is currently supporting causes focusing on breast cancer, children's literacy, and the environment. This last commitment is evidenced by investment in coffee-growing communities to help promote socially and agriculturally responsible practices. Caribou also invested in a medical clinic in one of the poorest coffee-growing communities in the Huehuetenango region of Guatemala. Farmers there had struggled to secure a clinic since the 1970s, and the generosity of Caribou helped make it happen. Farmers previously had to walk half a day to get to the nearest health care facility. These initiatives affirm Caribou's commitment to its value of promoting quality of life in coffee-producing communities.[96]

Chapter Summary

1. Organizational (corporate) culture is a pattern of basic assumptions that are considered valid and that are taught to new members as the way to perceive, think, and feel in the organization.
2. The most visible and accessible level of culture is artifacts, which include personal enactment, ceremonies and rites, stories, rituals, and symbols.
3. Organizational culture has four functions: giving members a sense of identity and increasing their commitment, serving as a sense-making device for members, reinforcing organizational values, and serving as a control mechanism for shaping behavior.
4. Three theories about the relationship between culture and performance are the strong culture perspective, the fit perspective, and the adaptation perspective.
5. Leaders shape and reinforce culture by what they pay attention to, how they react to crises, how they behave, how they allocate rewards, and how they hire and fire individuals.
6. Organizational socialization is the process by which newcomers become participating, effective members of the organization. Its three stages are anticipatory socialization, encounter, and change and acquisition. Each stage plays a unique role in communicating organizational culture.
7. The Organizational Culture Inventory and Kilmann-Saxton Culture-Gap Survey are two quantitative instruments for assessing organizational culture. Triangulation, using multiple methods for assessing culture, is an effective measurement strategy.
8. It is difficult but not impossible to change organizational culture. Managers can do so by helping current members buy into a new set of values, by adding newcomers and socializing them into the organization, and by removing current members as appropriate.

Key Terms

adaptive culture (p. 552)
anticipatory socialization (p. 557)
artifacts (p. 544)
assumptions (p. 550)
change and acquisition (p. 559)
enacted values (p. 548)
encounter (p. 558)
espoused values (p. 548)
organizational (corporate) culture (p. 544)
organizational socialization (p. 557)
strong culture (p. 551)
triangulation (p. 560)

Review Questions

1. Explain the three levels of organizational culture. How can each level be measured?
2. Describe five artifacts of culture and give an example of each.
3. Explain three theories about the relationship between organizational culture and performance. What does the research evidence say about each one?
4. Contrast adaptive and nonadaptive cultures.
5. How can leaders shape organizational culture?
6. Describe the three stages of organizational socialization. How is culture communicated in each stage?
7. How can managers assess the organizational culture? What actions can they take to change the organizational culture?
8. How does a manager know that cultural change has been successful?
9. What can managers do to develop a global organizational culture?

Discussion and Communication Questions

1. Name a company with a visible organizational culture. What do you think are the company's values? Has the culture contributed to the organization's performance? Explain.
2. Name a leader you think manages organizational culture well. How does the leader do this? Use Schein's description of how leaders reinforce culture to analyze the leader's behavior.
3. Suppose you want to change your organization's culture. What sort of resistance would you expect from employees? How would you deal with this resistance?
4. Given Schein's three levels, can we ever truly understand an organization's culture? Explain.
5. To what extent is culture manageable? Changeable?
6. *(communication question)* Select an organization that you might like to work for. Learn as much as you can about that company's culture, using library resources, online sources, contacts within the company, and as many creative means as you can. Prepare a brief presentation to the class summarizing the culture.

Ethical Dilemma

Jean Miller is the managing director of housekeeping at a large, upscale hotel. She feels good about working for an organization that cares about its employees. The hotel respects its employees and does everything possible to create a culture of loyalty and commitment. Throughout Jean's twenty years, the hotel's strong commitment is among the most positive aspects of her job. Lately, Jean feels this loyalty is going too far, especially when it comes to Mary, one of the housekeeping supervisors.

Housekeeping is a very physical job that Mary excelled at for many years. Now Mary is ready to retire, but she is not in a financial position to do so. This greatly affects her attitude, and unrest is beginning to spread among the people who work for her. There are three openings in Mary's department already and more are expected. The biggest obstacle, from Jean's perspective, is that she feels any new hires sent to Mary would end up quitting. Jean has recently hired a very promising new person, Pat. Jean had even warned her about Mary's department. Within the first few weeks, Pat had been socialized into the negativity of the department. Jean tried to relocate Pat to a different department when she saw what was happening, but it was too late. Even in the new environment, Pat has retained the mindset she had already developed.

The most pressing challenge is what to do about the open positions. Jean is sure that any new person would react as Pat had to Mary, but it isn't fair to those who have to carry a great number of rooms every day until the positions are filled. Jean has tried to move people from other departments, but everyone has threatened to quit if they are transferred. Jean could also go to management and ask that Mary's retirement be enforced, but she doesn't want to do that either, given Mary's financial situation. Jean is unsure how to proceed but knows that she has to do something.

Questions

1. Is it Jean's responsibility to resolve this conflict?
2. Evaluate Jean's decision using consequential, rule-based, and character theories.

Experiential Exercises

16.1 Identifying Behavioral Norms

This exercise asks you to identify campus norms at your university. Every organization or group has a set of norms that help determine individuals' behavior. A norm is an unwritten rule for behavior in a group. When a norm is not followed, negative feedback is given. It may include negative comments, stares, harassment, and exclusion.

1. As a group, brainstorm all the norms you can think of in the following areas:

   Dress
   Classroom behavior
   Studying
   Weekend activities
   Living arrangements
   Campus activities
   Dating (who asks whom)
   Relationships with faculty
   Eating on campus versus off campus
   Transportation

2. How did you initially get this information?
3. What happens to students who don't follow these norms?
4. What values can be inferred from these norms?

SOURCE: "Identifying Behavioral Norms" by Dorothy Marcic, *Organizational Behavior: Experiences and Cases* (St. Paul, Minn.: West Publishing, 1989). Reprinted by permission.

16.2 Contrasting Organizational Cultures

To complete this exercise, groups of four or five students should be formed. Each group should select one of the following pairs of organizations:

American Airlines and Northwest Airlines
Anheuser-Busch and Coors
Hewlett-Packard and Xerox
Albertsons and Winn-Dixie
Dayton-Hudson (Target) and J. C. Penney Company

Use your university library's resources to gather information about the companies' cultures. Contrast the cultures of the two organizations using the following dimensions:

- Strength of the culture.
- Fit of the culture with the industry's environment.
- Adaptiveness of the culture.

Which of the two is the better performer? On what did you base your conclusion? How does the performance of each relate to its organizational culture?

SOURCE: Adapted with the permission of The Free Press, a Division of Simon & Schuster, Inc., from *Corporate Culture and Performance* by John P. Kotter and James L. Heskett. Copyright © 1992 by Kotter Associates, Inc., and James L. Heskett.

T A K E 2

Biz Flix | Backdraft

Two brothers follow their late father, a legendary Chicago firefighter, and join the department. Stephen "Bull" McCaffrey (Kurt Russell) joins first and rises to the rank of lieutenant. Younger brother Brian (William Baldwin) joins later and becomes a member of Bull's Company 17. Sibling rivalry tarnishes their work relationships, but they continue to successfully fight Chicago fires. Add a plot element about a mysterious arsonist, and you have the basis for an extraordinary film. The intense, unprecedented special effects give the viewer an unparalleled experience of what it is like to fight a fire.

The scene appears early in *Backdraft* as part of the sequence called "The First Day." Brian McCaffrey has graduated from the fire academy, and the fire department has assigned him to his brother's company. This scene shows Company 17 preparing to fight a garment factory fire. The film continues with Brian receiving some harsh first-day lessons as Company 17 successfully fights the fire.

What to Watch for and Ask Yourself:

- What parts of the Chicago fire department culture does this scene show? Does the scene show any cultural artifacts or symbols? If it does, what are they?
- Does the scene show any values or norms that guide the firefighters' behavior? If it does, what are they?
- What does Brian McCaffrey learn on his first workday?

Workplace Video | The Environment and Corporate Culture, Featuring Caterpillar

In recent years, Caterpillar Inc. has encountered a variety of growth-related challenges, from globalization and conducting business in China to learning how to be a good corporate citizen. Since its establishment in 1925, the Peoria, Illinois–based industrial-goods manufacturer has expanded operations into 40 countries, and today Caterpillar is the world's leading producer of construction and mining equipment, diesel and natural gas engines, and industrial gas turbines.

Despite many decades of success, leadership at CAT had become convinced that big changes were necessary if the company was to keep in step with the societal, political, and natural climates of today's global village. Led by CEO James Owens, senior management at Caterpillar analyzed the situation and reached an intriguing conclusion: the best way to prepare the company for the future was to make changes to the company's corporate culture. In particular, Owens and his teams envisioned a culture at Caterpillar that reflected the company's status not only as a market leader but also as an ambassador of good will and social responsibility.

To redirect his company, Owens launched a project aimed at establishing a vision of social responsibility throughout the organization. As a first action item, the CAT communications team published "Our Values in Action: Caterpillar's Worldwide Code of

TAKE 2

Conduct," an ethics-oriented guide that spelled out the values and beliefs management deemed necessary for taking on the future. Supplementing that guide was "The Cat Manifesto," a print booklet that linked company efforts with corporate philanthropy and sustainability initiatives around the globe. Management's enthusiasm about the green side of CAT's new image eventually led to "The World: In Progress," a global ad campaign that proclaimed Caterpillar's mission to make the world a better place.

While these integrated marketing communications were successful in broadcasting Caterpillar's new vision, getting deep values to resonate with employees in forty countries required more than print manifestos and ad campaigns. To promote buy-in among Caterpillar's 100,000-person workforce, management launched a mission-related Web site, translated the Cat Manifesto and Code of Conduct into eleven different languages, and began circulating stories about Caterpillar's role in the economic and social progress of developing nations. Most importantly, managers at all levels of the organization—starting at the top with CEO Jim Owens and the group presidents—began reinforcing behaviors that moved the company in a new direction.

Management's message was clear: the only organizational culture capable of achieving high performance while showing world concern over the long term was one in which all employees were united around shared values and invested personally in meaningful work. Without shared values, CAT's progress would stall. As Ali Bahaj, vice president of corporate auditing, remarked, "Values are foundational to everything we do. Without those values of integrity, commitment, excellence, and teamwork, it is impossible for us to achieve our vision and goals."

Discussion Questions

1. How can Caterpillar's corporate culture, which springs from the organization's internal environment, impact the external environment?
2. What "story" does management at Caterpillar recount as a way of communicating the company's redesigned values, according to the video? Why are such stories important?
3. What role do leaders play in shaping Caterpillar's organizational culture? Why is it difficult to change a company's organizational culture, and how can management know when a permanent change has successfully occurred?

CASE

Developing Chinks in the Vaunted "Toyota Way"

"There is the world car industry, and then there is Toyota. Since 2000 the output of the global industry has risen by about 3m [3 million] vehicles to some 60m [60 million]: of that increase, half came from Toyota alone."[1] Toyota has enjoyed a dramatic growth spurt around the globe, and it is on the verge of making more cars abroad than at home.[2] As of March 2007, Toyota marketed vehicles in more than 170 countries and employed approximately 299,400 people worldwide. In addition to its parts manufacturing and vehicle assembly facilities in Japan, Toyota has 52 manufacturing companies in 26 nations and regions.[3]

Toyota's strong corporate culture is the "glue" that holds these far-flung "operations together and makes them part of a single entity."[4] "Spend some time with Toyota people and . . . you realize there is something different about them. The rest of the car industry raves about engines, gearboxes, acceleration, fuel economy, handling, ride quality and sexy design. Toyota's people talk about 'The Toyota Way' and about customers."[5] Toyota's customer focus is legendary. Jim Press, head of the company's North America sales, says, "[t]he Toyota culture is inside all of us. Toyota is a customer's company. . . . Everything is done to make . . . [the customer's] life better."[6]

Toyota's culture, labeled "The Toyota Way," has five distinct components: *kaizen, genchi genbutsu,* challenge, teamwork, and respect. *Kaizen* refers to the process of continuous improvement, and it is as much a frame of mind as it is a business process. *Genchi genbutsu* focuses on going to the source of a problem, finding the facts, and building consensus through arguments that are well supported. *Challenge* encourages Toyota employees to view problems as a way to help them improve their performance rather than as something undesirable. *Teamwork* puts the company's interests before those of any individual, and promotes sharing knowledge with other employees. Toyota's employees exhibit *respect* for other people and their skills and special knowledge.[7]

Toyota's culture has served the company very well for many years. Indeed, competitors marvel at that culture and its ongoing success. As one General Motors planner observed privately, ". . . the only way to stop Toyota would be the business equivalent of germ warfare, finding a 'poison pill' or 'social virus' that could be infiltrated into the company to destroy its culture."[8]

Over the years, "Toyota has adapted well to changes facing the automotive industry by establishing sound processes and procedures. It has made continuous change and improvement the essence of its business philosophy: each year thousands of improvements are suggested by employees and many are implemented. . . . It has built its success with products that are made according to the all-embracing 'Toyota Way.' In fact, so confident is Toyota of its quality and reliability record, that it allows rival companies to visit its factories all over the world."[9]

Recently, however, some chinks seem to be developing in the armor of the company's vaunted culture. An internal Toyota study compared its products against those of its competitors—component by component, car by car—and found Toyota's products to be superior in just over half of hundreds of components and vehicle systems. Toyota judged such quality performance to be unacceptably mediocre.[10] In reference to the U.S. market, some business analysts say the company's rapid growth is one cause of its growing quality-control problems. For example, in 2005 "Toyota recalled 2.38 million vehicles in the U.S., more than the 2.26 million vehicles it sold—a sign that indicates Toyota is troubled not only by manufacturing problems but also by design flaws."[11]

Toyota CEO Katsuaki Watanabe "thinks Toyota is losing its competitive edge as it expands around the world. He frets that quality, the foundation of its U.S. success, is slipping. He grouses that Toyota's factories and engineering practices aren't efficient enough. Within the company, he has even questioned a core tenet of Toyota's corporate culture—kaizen, the relentless focus on incremental improvement."[12] Tetsuo Agata, one of Toyota's manufacturing experts, points out that the company needs to depart from its history of steady, incremental improvement and develop radical new ways of manufacturing vehicle components more economically.[13] Watanabe also argues that "The Toyota Way" of the future needs to embrace *kakushin*—revolutionary change in Toyota's design of factories and cars. Watanabe wants Toyota to reduce by half the number of components that it uses in a typical vehicle, and to create new fast and flexible plants for assembling these simplified cars.[14]

How will Toyota's global organizational culture change as the company embraces *kakushin*?

Discussion Questions

1. Describe Toyota's culture from the perspective of *espoused values* and *enacted values*.
2. Using the perspective of the *functions* of organizational culture, explain the impact of "The Toyota Way."
3. Using the perspective of the *effects* of organizational culture, explain the impact of "The Toyota Way."
4. What challenges does Toyota face as it embarks on transforming its global organizational culture from *kaizen* to *kakushin*?

SOURCE: This case was written by Michael K. McCuddy, The Louis S. and Mary L. Morgal Chair of Christian Business Ethics and Professor of Management, College of Business Administration, Valparaiso University.

CHAPTER 17

Google
Dessert Menu
Tiramisu Cake
Mini Napoleon
Oatmeal Raspberry Squares
Organic Fruits

Career Management

LEARNING OBJECTIVES

After reading this chapter, you should be able to do the following:

1 Define *career* and *career management*.

2 Explain occupational and organizational choice decisions.

3 Describe the four stages of the career model.

4 Explain the psychological contract.

5 Describe how mentors help organizational newcomers.

6 Describe ways to manage conflicts between work and home.

7 Explain how career anchors help form a career identity.

THINKING AHEAD: GOOGLE

View from the Top of the Mountain

Google is number one on *Fortune* magazine's list of 100 best places to work in America. It gets an estimated 1,300 new résumés every day. So what makes Google such a great place to work? The benefits of being a Googler seem unending. And that is what attracts most tech people to it. For example, the company offers on-site doctors, swimming spas, and free food at its Mountain View, California, campus. This last aspect is driven by founders Larry Page and Sergey Brin's belief that one should never be more than 100 feet away from a food source!

Engineers at Google get to spend 20 percent of their workweek on any project that is their own and develop their own ideas. This helps keep the creative fires burning inside the innovation giant. Google has a projected job growth rate of 67 percent in the upcoming year, a very good sign for a technology-driven company.[1, 2] Interestingly enough, while Google ranks as the best place to work, it does not appear on the top ninety companies that pay the most in America. Google has recently been moving into the office software market to compete with Yahoo and Microsoft, which rank respectively twelfth and fourteenth on the list of America's best-paying companies. This shows that people who want to work for Google are attracted more to the careers at Google than just to the financial package. Google's approach is focused on keeping employees happy and developing them into well-rounded, healthy individuals.[3]

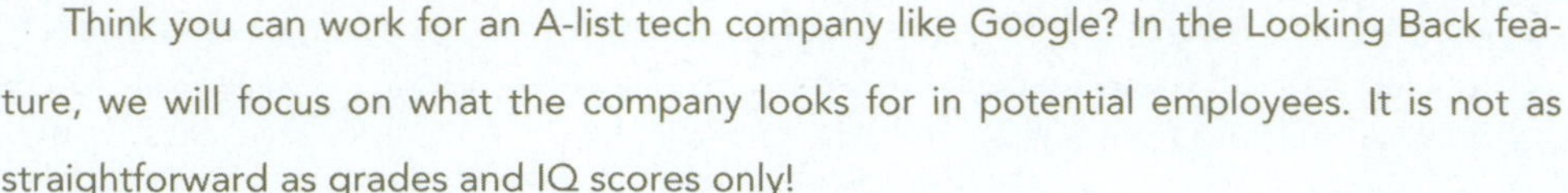

Think you can work for an A-list tech company like Google? In the Looking Back feature, we will focus on what the company looks for in potential employees. It is not as straightforward as grades and IQ scores only!

CAREERS AS JOINT RESPONSIBILITIES

(1) Define *career* and *career management*.

Career management is an integral activity in our lives. There are three reasons why it is important to understand careers. First, if we know what to look forward to over the course of our careers, we can take a proactive approach to planning and managing them. Second, as managers, we need to understand the experiences of our employees and colleagues as they pass through the various stages of careers over their life spans. Third, career management is good business. It makes good financial sense to have highly trained employees keep up with their fields so that organizations can protect valuable investments in human resources.

A *career* is a pattern of work-related experiences that span the course of a person's life.[4] The two elements in a career are the objective element and the subjective element.[5] The objective element of the career is the observable, concrete environment. For example, you can manage a career by getting training to improve your skills. In contrast, the subjective element involves your perception of the situation. Rather than getting training (an objective element), you might change your aspirations (a subjective element). Thus, both objective events and the individual's perception of those events are important in defining a career.

Career management is a lifelong process of learning about self, jobs, and organizations; setting personal career goals; developing strategies for achieving the goals; and revising the goals based on work and life experiences.[6] Whose responsibility is career management? It is tempting to place the responsibility on individuals, and it is appropriate. However, it is also the organization's duty to form partnerships with individuals in managing their careers. Careers are made up of exchanges between individuals and organizations. Inherent in these exchanges is the idea of reciprocity, or give and take.

The balance between individuals and organizations in terms of managing careers has shifted in recent times. With restructuring and reengineering has come a new perspective of careers and career management.

THE NEW CAREER

career
The pattern of work-related experiences that span the course of a person's life.

career management
A lifelong process of learning about self, jobs, and organizations; setting personal career goals; developing strategies for achieving the goals, and revising the goals based on work and life experiences.

The time of the fast track to the top of the hierarchical organization is past. Also gone is the idea of lifetime employment in a single organization. Today's environment demands leaner organizations. The paternalistic attitude that organizations take care of employees no longer exists. Individuals now take on more responsibility for managing their own careers. The concept of the career is undergoing a paradigm shift, as shown in Table 17.1. The old career is giving way to a new career characterized by discrete exchange, occupational excellence, organizational empowerment, and project allegiance.[7] Moreover, one recent study found that both individuals and organizations are actively involved in the management of the new career of employees. As such, the new career involves a type of participatory management technique on the part of the individual, but the organization responds to each individual's needs and thus is more flexible in its career development programs.[8]

TABLE 17.1 The New versus Old Career Paradigms

New Career Paradigm	Old Career Paradigm
Discrete exchange means:	**The mutual loyalty contract meant:**
• explicit exchange of specified rewards in return for task performance	• implicit trading of employee compliance in return for job security
• basing job rewards on the current market value of the work being performed	• allowing job rewards to be routinely deferred into the future
• engaging in disclosure and renegotiation on both sides as the employment relationship unfolds	• leaving the mutual loyalty assumptions as a political barrier to renegotiation
• exercising flexibility as each party's interests and market circumstances change	• assuming employment and career opportunities are standardized and prescribed by the firm
Occupational excellence means:	**The one-employer focus meant:**
• performance of current jobs in return for developing new occupational expertise	• relying on the firm to specify jobs and their associated occupational skill base
• employees identifying with and focusing on what is happening in their adopted occupation	• employees identifying with and focusing on what is happening in their particular firm
• emphasizing occupational skill development over the local demands of any particular firm	• forgoing technical or functional development in favor of firm-specific learning
• getting training in anticipation of future job opportunities; having training lead jobs	• doing the job first to be entitled to new training: making training follow jobs
Organizational empowerment means:	**The top-down firm meant:**
• strategic positioning is dispersed to separate business units	• strategic direction is subordinated to "corporate headquarters"
• everyone is responsible for adding value and improving competitiveness	• competitiveness and added value are the responsibility of corporate experts
• business units are free to cultivate their own markets	• business unit marketing depends on the corporate agenda
• new enterprise, spinoffs, and alliance building are broadly encouraged	• independent enterprise is discouraged, and likely to be viewed as disloyalty
Project allegiance means:	**Corporate allegiance meant:**
• shared employer and employee commitment to the overarching goal of the project	• project goals are subordinated to corporate policy and organizational constraints
• a successful outcome of the project is more important than holding the project team together	• being loyal to the work group can be more important than the project itself
• financial and reputational rewards stem directly from project outcomes	• financial and reputational rewards stem from being a "good soldier" regardless of results
• upon project completion, organization and reporting arrangements are broken up	• social relationships within corporate boundaries are actively encouraged

Discrete exchange occurs when an organization gains productivity while a person gains work experience. It is a short-term arrangement that recognizes that job skills change in value and that renegotiation of the relationship must occur as conditions change. This contrasts sharply with the mutual loyalty contract of the old career paradigm in which employee loyalty was exchanged for job security.

Occupational excellence means continually honing skills that can be marketed across organizations. The individual identifies more with the occupation (I am an engineer) than the organization (I am an IBMer). In contrast, the old one-employer focus meant that training was company specific rather than preparing the person for future job opportunities. A recent research study that focused on ethnographic data (interviews and stories) was conducted among software engineers in three European firms and two U.S. firms. Software engineers did not have much respect for their immediate supervisors, the organization, or formal dress codes. The only thing they did believe in was occupational excellence so that they could be better at what they do. In this regard, the authors of the study note that software engineers represent a unique group in terms of career development, and that they fit well within the model of the "new career."[9]

Organizational empowerment means that power flows down to business units and in turn to employees. Employees are expected to add value and help the organization remain competitive by being innovative and creative. The old top-down approach meant that control and strategizing were only done by the top managers, and individual initiative might be viewed as disloyalty or disrespect.

Project allegiance means that both individuals and organizations are committed to the successful completion of a project. The firm's gain is the project outcome; the individual's gain is experience and shared success. On project completion, the project team breaks up as individuals move on to new projects. Under the old paradigm, corporate allegiance was paramount. The needs of projects were overshadowed by corporate policies and procedures. Work groups were long term, and keeping the group together was often a more important goal than project completion.

While spending an entire career in one company was the old career model, times have changed, and job hopping and company hopping are becoming more the norm. You can expect to change jobs many times in your career. College graduates typically change jobs four times in their first ten years of work, a number that is projected to increase. At that rate, you could easily hold twenty different jobs in a typical career. In fact, the stigma associated with frequent job changes has largely disappeared. Some recruiters now view a résumé littered with different companies and locations as a sign of a smart self-promoter. The key is to know *why* you are making each job move, including both what it will cost and gain for you. By presenting your job-hopping career path as a growth process rather than a series of impulsive changes, you may set yourself apart in the minds of recruiters.[10] Individuals must prepare for the new career and manage their careers with change in mind. In The Real World 17.1, you can read about the drastic changes in career choices and attitudes towards work that Generation Y brings to the current workplace.

Becoming Your Own Career Coach

The best way to stay employed is to see yourself as being in business for yourself, even if you work for someone else. Know what skills you can package for other employers and what you can do to ensure that your skills are state of the art. Organizations need employees who have acquired multiple skills and are adept at more than one job. Employers want employees who have demonstrated competence in dealing with change.[11] To be successful, think of organizational change not as a disruption to your work but as its central focus. You will also need to develop self-reliance, as we discussed in Chapter 7, to deal effectively with the stress of change. Self-reliant individuals take an interdependent approach to relationships and are comfortable both giving and receiving support from others.

THE REAL WORLD 17.1

Bye-Bye 60-Hour Workweek, Hello Nonfat Milk, No Ice, No Caffeine, Iced Mocha Latte!

The current workforce is facing a new kind of invasion—that of Generation Y. Companies are clamoring to hire these new college graduates born between roughly 1977 and 1995 as they will soon represent a bigger proportion of the workforce than the baby boomers. Moreover, a massive chunk of the baby boomers are retiring or have already retired, creating room for this different kind of worker profile.

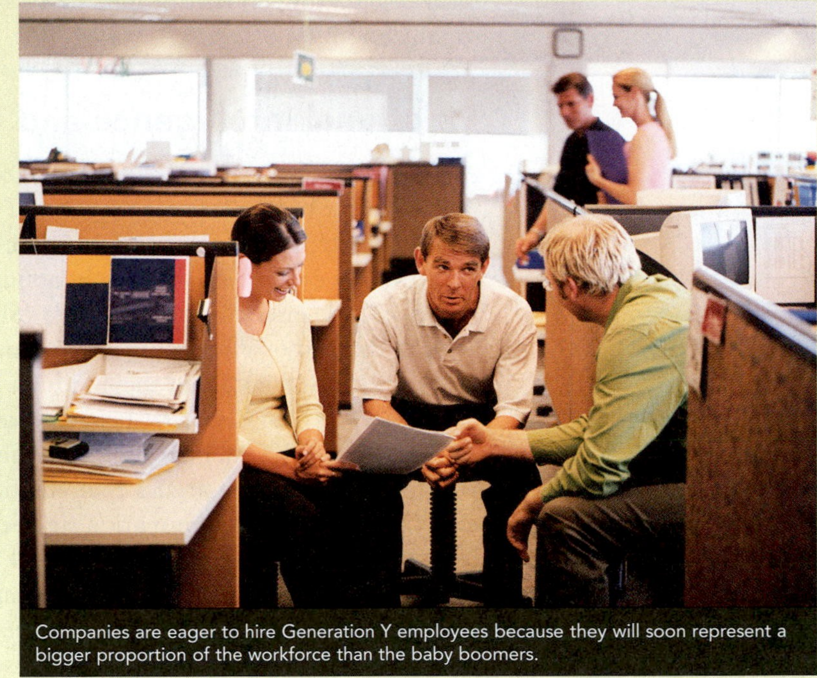
© BANANASTOCK/JUPITERIMAGES

Companies are eager to hire Generation Y employees because they will soon represent a bigger proportion of the workforce than the baby boomers.

Gen Yers are different in almost every aspect from prior generations that employers are used to. They tend to question everything and put other things (family, friends, time off) above work. They refuse to work longer workweeks. In fact, one high-profile attorney in this generation took a pay cut and went to work for a firm in which the secretarial staff had windows in their offices but lawyers did not! She felt this made sense because secretaries spent more time at their desks than did lawyers and thus were more deserving of windows.

From an employer standpoint, the things to keep in mind are that Gen Yers like to be given meaningful tasks and performance-related information on a regular basis. The good news for employers is they are predicted to be the highest-performing workforce in history since they have access to, and familiarity with, unlimited amounts of information (helped along by tools like the Blackberry); are very comfortable with diversity in all its forms; are not afraid to innovate; and are extremely sociable.

SOURCE: N. A. Hira, "Attracting the Twentysomething Worker," *CNNmoney.com*, May 15, 2007, http://money.cnn.com/magazines/fortune/fortune_archive/2007/05/28/100033934/index.htm.

The people who will be most successful in the new career paradigm are those who are flexible, team oriented (rather than hierarchical), energized by change, and tolerant of ambiguity. The people who will become frustrated in the new career are those who are rigid in their thinking and learning styles and who have high needs for control. A commitment to continuous, lifelong learning will prevent you from becoming a professional dinosaur.[12] An intentional and purposeful commitment to taking charge of your professional life will be necessary in managing the new career.

In the current business environment of ethical scandals, behaving in an ethical manner, standing by your values and building a professional image of integrity is very important. Major corporations such as Google conduct extensive reference checks on their applicants—not just with the references supplied by the applicants but also with friends of friends of such references. Recall that we mentioned earlier in this book that managing ethical behavior is one of the most significant challenges facing managers today. Ever wonder why highly respected and well-paid top management executives engage in fraud and endanger their careers? One study suggests that this happens as top executives feel the pressure to keep up with inflated expectations and changes in cultural norms, short-term versus long-term orientations, board of directors' composition, and senior leadership in the organization.[13]

Emotional Intelligence and Career Success

Almost 40 percent of new managers fail within the first eighteen months on the job. What are the reasons for the failure? Newly hired managers flame out because they fail to build good relationships with peers and subordinates (82 percent of failures), are confused or uncertain about what their bosses expect (58 percent of failures), lack internal political skills (50 percent of failures), and are unable to achieve the two or three most important objectives of the new job (47 percent of failures).[14] You'll note that these failures are all due to a lack of human skills.

COURTESY OF DANIEL GOLEMAN INFO

Daniel Goleman, pictured, says that emotional intelligence is a constellation of the qualities that mark a star performer at work.

In Chapter 13, we introduced the concept of emotional intelligence (EI) as an important determinant of conflict management skills. Daniel Goleman argues that emotional intelligence is a constellation of the qualities that mark a star performer at work. These attributes include self-awareness, self-control, trustworthiness, confidence, and empathy, among others. Goleman's belief is that emotional competencies are twice as important to people's success today as raw intelligence or technical know-how. He also argues that the further up the corporate ranks you go, the more important emotional intelligence becomes.[15, 16] Employers, either consciously or unconsciously, look for emotional intelligence during the hiring process. In addition to traditionally recognized competencies such as communication and social skills, interns with higher levels of emotional intelligence are rated as more hireable by their host firms than those with lower levels of EI.[17] Neither gender seems to have cornered the market on EI. Both men and women who can demonstrate high levels of EI are seen as particularly gifted and may be promoted more rapidly.[18]

Emotional intelligence is important to career success in many cultures. A recent study in Australia found that high levels of emotional intelligence are associated with job success. EI improves one's ability to work with other team members and to provide high-quality customer service, and workers with high EI are more likely to take steps to develop their skills. This confirms U.S. studies that portray high emotional intelligence as an important attribute for the upwardly mobile worker.[19] You can assess your own emotional intelligence using You 17.1.

L'Oreal has found emotional intelligence to be a profitable selection tool. Salespeople selected on the basis of emotional competence outsold those selected using the old method by an average of $91,370 per year. As an added bonus for the firm, these salespeople also had 63 percent less turnover during the first year than those selected in the traditional way.[20]

The good news is that emotional intelligence can be developed and does tend to improve throughout life. Some companies are providing training in EI competencies. American Express began sending managers through an emotional competence training program. It found that trained managers outperformed those who lacked this training. In the year after completing the course, managers trained in emotional

What's Your EI at Work?

Answering the following 25 questions will allow you to rate your social skills and self-awareness.

EI, the social equivalent of IQ, is complex in no small part because it depends on some pretty slippery variables—including your innate compatibility, or lack thereof, with the people who happen to be your coworkers. But if you want to get a rough idea of how your EI stacks up, this quiz will help.

As honestly as you can, estimate how you rate in the eyes of peers, bosses, and subordinates on each of the following traits, on a scale of 1 to 4, with 4 representing strong agreement, and 1, strong disagreement.

____ 1. I usually stay composed, positive, and unflappable even in trying moments.

____ 2. I can think clearly and stay focused on the task at hand under pressure.

____ 3. I am able to admit my own mistakes.

____ 4. I usually or always meet commitments and keep promises.

____ 5. I hold myself accountable for meeting my goals.

____ 6. I'm organized and careful in my work.

____ 7. I regulary seek out fresh ideas from a wide variety of sources.

____ 8. I'm good at generating new ideas.

____ 9. I can smoothly handle multiple demands and changing priorities.

____ 10. I'm results-oriented, with a strong drive to meet my objectives.

____ 11. I like to set challenging goals and take calculated risks to reach them.

____ 12. I'm always trying to learn how to improve my performance, including asking advice from people younger than I am.

____ 13. I readily make sacrifices to meet an important organizational goal.

____ 14. The company's mission is something I understand and can identify with.

____ 15. The values of my team—or of our division or department, or the company—influence my decisions and clarify the choices I make.

____ 16. I actively seek out opportunities to further the overall goals of the organization and enlist others to help me.

____ 17. I pursue goals beyond what's required or expected of me in my current job.

____ 18. Obstacles and setbacks may delay me a little, but they don't stop me.

____ 19. Cutting through red tape and bending outdated rules are sometimes necessary.

____ 20. I seek fresh perspectives, even if that means trying something totally new.

____ 21. My impulses or distressing emotions don't often get the best of me at work.

____ 22. I can change tactics quickly when circumstances change.

____ 23. Pursuing new information is my best bet for cutting down on uncertainty and findings ways to do things better.

____ 24. I usually don't attribute setbacks to a personal flaw (mine or someone else's).

____ 25. I operate from an expectation of success rather than a fear of failure.

A score below 70 indicates a problem. If your total is somewhere in the basement, don't despair: EI is not unimprovable. "Emotional intelligence can be learned, and in fact we are each building it, in varying degrees, throughout life. It's sometimes called maturity," says Daniel Goleman. "EI is nothing more or less than a collection of tools that we can sharpen to help ensure our own survival."

SOURCE: A. Fisher, "Success Secret: A High Emotional IQ." Reprinted from the October 26, 1998, issue of *Fortune* by special permission;

competence grew their businesses by an average of 18.1 percent compared to 16.2 percent for those businesses whose managers were untrained.[21]

Before turning to the stages of an individual's career, we will examine the process of preparation for the world of work. Prior to beginning a career, individuals must make several important decisions.

Preparing for the World of Work

(2) Explain occupational and organizational choice decisions.

When viewed from one perspective, you might say that we spend our youth preparing for the world of work. Educational experiences and personal life experiences help an individual develop the skills and maturity needed to enter a career. Preparation for work is a developmental process that gradually unfolds over time.[22] As the time approaches for beginning a career, individuals face two difficult decisions: the choice of occupation and the choice of organization.

Occupational Choice

In choosing an occupation, individuals assess their needs, values, abilities, and preferences and attempt to match them with an occupation that provides a fit. Personality plays a role in the selection of occupation. John Holland's theory of occupational choice contends that there are six types of personalities and that each is characterized by a set of interests and values.[23] Holland's six types are as follows:

1. *Realistic:* stable, persistent, and materialistic.
2. *Artistic:* imaginative, emotional, and impulsive.
3. *Investigative:* curious, analytical, and independent.
4. *Enterprising:* ambitious, energetic, and adventurous.
5. *Social:* generous, cooperative, and sociable.
6. *Conventional:* efficient, practical, and obedient.

Holland also states that occupations can be classified using this typology. For example, realistic occupations include mechanic, restaurant server, and mechanical engineer. Artistic occupations include architect, voice coach, and interior designer. Investigative occupations include physicist, surgeon, and economist. Real estate agent, human resource manager, and lawyer are enterprising occupations. The social occupations include counselor, social worker, and member of the clergy. Conventional occupations include word processor, accountant, and data entry operator.

Holland's typology has been used to predict career choices with a variety of international participants, including Mexicans, Australians, Indians, New Zealanders, Taiwanese, Pakistanis, South Africans, and Germans.[24]

An assumption that drives Holland's theory is that people choose occupations that match their own personalities. People who fit Holland's social types are those who prefer jobs that are highly interpersonal in nature. They may see careers in physical and math sciences, for example, as not affording the opportunity for interpersonal relationships.[25] To fulfill the desire for interpersonal work, they may instead gravitate toward jobs in customer service or counseling in order to better match their personalities.

Although personality is a major influence on occupational choice, it is not the only influence. There are a host of other ones, including social class, parents' occupations, economic conditions, and geography.[26] Once a choice of occupation has been made, another major decision individuals face is the choice of organizations.

Organizational Choice and Entry

Several theories of how individuals choose organizations exist, ranging from those that postulate very logical and rational choice processes to those that offer seemingly irrational processes. Expectancy theory, which we discussed in Chapter 5, can be applied to organizational choice.[27] According to the expectancy theory view, individuals choose organizations that maximize positive outcomes and avoid negative outcomes. Job candidates calculate the probability that an organization will provide a certain outcome and then compare the probabilities across organizations.

Other theories propose that people select organizations in a much less rational fashion. Job candidates may satisfice—that is, select the first organization that meets one or two important criteria—and then justify their choice by distorting their perceptions.[28]

The method of selecting an organization varies greatly among individuals and may reflect a combination of the expectancy theory and theories that postulate less rational approaches. Entry into an organization is further complicated by the conflicts that occur between individuals and organizations during the process. Figure 17.1 illustrates these potential conflicts. The arrows in the figure illustrate four types of conflicts that can occur as individuals choose organizations and organizations choose individuals. The first two conflicts (1 and 2) occur between individuals and organizations. The first is a conflict between the organization's effort to attract candidates and the individual's choice of an organization. The individual needs complete and accurate information to make a good choice, but the organization may not provide it. The organization is trying to attract a large number of qualified candidates, so it presents itself in an overly attractive way.

The second conflict is between the individual's attempt to attract several organizations and the organization's need to select the best candidate. Individuals want good offers, so they do not disclose their faults. They describe their preferred job in terms of the organization's opening instead of describing a job they would really prefer.

Conflicts 3 and 4 are internal to the two parties. The third is a conflict between the organization's desire to recruit a large pool of qualified applicants and the organization's need to select and retain the best candidate. In recruiting, organizations tend to give only positive information, which results in mismatches between the individual and the organization. The fourth conflict is internal to the individual; it

FIGURE 17.1 Conflicts during Organizational Entry

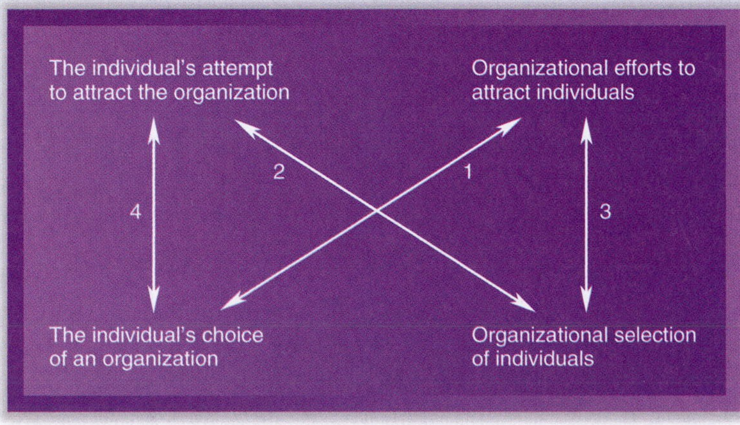

SOURCE: Figure in L. W. Porter, E. E. Lawler III, and J. R. Hackman, *Behavior in Organizations*, New York: McGraw-Hill, Inc., 1975, page 134. Reproduced with permission of The McGraw-Hill Companies.

is between the individual's desire for several job offers and the need to make a good choice. When individuals present themselves as overly attractive, they risk being offered positions that are poor fits in terms of their skills and career goals.[29]

The organizational choice and entry process is very complex due to the nature of these conflicts. Partial responsibility for preventing these conflicts rests with the individual. Individuals should conduct thorough research of the organization through published reports and industry analyses. They also should conduct a careful self-analysis and be as honest as possible with organizations to ensure a good match. The job interview process can be stressful, but also fun.

Partial responsibility for good matches also rests with the organization. One way of avoiding the conflicts and mismatches is to utilize a realistic job preview.

Realistic Job Previews

The conflicts just discussed may result in unrealistic expectations on the part of the candidate. People entering the world of work may expect, for example, that they will receive explicit directions from their boss, only to find that they are left with ambiguity about how to do the job. They may expect that promotions will be based on performance and find that in fact they are based mainly on political considerations. Some new hires expect to be given managerial responsibilities right away; however, this is not often the case.

Giving potential employees a realistic picture of the job they are applying for is known as a *realistic job preview (RJP)*. When candidates are given both positive and negative information, they can make more effective job choices. Traditional recruiting practices produce unrealistically high expectations, which produce low job satisfaction when these unrealistic expectations hit the reality of the job situation. RJPs tend to create expectations that are much closer to reality, and they increase the numbers of candidates who withdraw from further consideration.[30] This occurs because candidates with unrealistic expectations tend to look for employment elsewhere. The Idaho State Police Department's online employment site provides an RJP, which begins with these words: "[Y]ou should put aside the images you have seen on television or in the movies and read carefully about the tasks an Idaho State Police Trooper performs."[31] It then goes on to provide an exhaustive list of tasks ranging from the exciting (manhunts and serving warrants) to the mundane (inspecting heavy trucks), as well as noting that troopers currently work rotating ten-hour shifts. While the site concludes with a summary of the rewards that accompany the job, it clearly notes that the work is at times tedious and far less glamorous than might be expected.

RJPs can also be thought of as inoculation against disappointment. If new recruits know what to expect in the new job, they can prepare for the experience. Newcomers who are not given RJPs may find that their jobs don't measure up to their expectations. They may then believe that their employer was deceitful in the hiring process, become unhappy and mishandle job demands, and ultimately leave the organization.[32]

Job candidates who receive RJPs view the organization as honest and also have a greater ability to cope with the demands of the job.[33] RJPs perform another important function: uncertainty reduction.[34] Knowing what to expect, both good and bad, gives a newcomer a sense of control that is important to job satisfaction and performance.

realistic job preview (RJP)
Both positive and negative information given to potential employees about the job they are applying for, thereby giving them a realistic picture of the job.

With today's emphasis on ethics, organizations need to do all they can to be seen as operating consistently and honestly. Realistic job previews are one way companies can provide ethically required information to newcomers. Ultimately, RJPs result in more effective matches, lower turnover, and higher organizational commitment and job satisfaction.[35] There is much to gain, and little to risk, in providing realistic job information.[36]

In summary, the needs and goals of individuals and organizations can clash during entry into the organization. To avoid potential mismatches, individuals should conduct a careful self-analysis and provide accurate information about themselves to potential employers. Organizations should present realistic job previews to show candidates both the positive and negative aspects of the job, along with the potential career paths available to the employee.

After entry into the organization, individuals embark on their careers. A person's work life can be traced through successive stages, as we see in the career stage model.

THE CAREER STAGE MODEL

(3) Describe the four stages of the career model.

A common way of understanding careers is viewing them as a series of stages through which individuals pass during their working lives.[37] Figure 17.2 presents the career stage model, which will form the basis for our discussion in the remainder of this chapter.[38] The career stage model shows that individuals pass through four stages in their careers: establishment, advancement, maintenance, and withdrawal. It is important to note that the age ranges shown are approximations; that is, the timing of the career transitions varies greatly among individuals.

Establishment is the first stage of a person's career. The activities that occur in this stage center around learning the job and fitting into the organization and occupation. *Advancement* is a high-achievement-oriented stage in which people focus on increasing their competence. The *maintenance* stage finds the individual trying to maintain productivity while evaluating progress toward career goals. The *withdrawal* stage involves contemplation of retirement or possible career change.

Along the horizontal axis in Figure 17.2 are the corresponding life stages for each career stage. These life stages are based on the pioneering research on adult development conducted by Levinson and his colleagues. Levinson conducted extensive biographical interviews to trace the life stages of men and women. He interpreted his research in two books, *The Seasons of a Man's Life* and *The Seasons of*

establishment
The first career stage in which the person learns the job and begins to fit into the organization and occupation.

advancement
The second, high-achievement-oriented career stage in which the individual focuses on increasing competence.

maintenance
The third career stage in which the individual tries to maintain productivity while evaluating progress toward career goals.

withdrawal
The final career stage in which the individual contemplates retirement or possible career changes.

FIGURE 17.2 The Career Stage Model

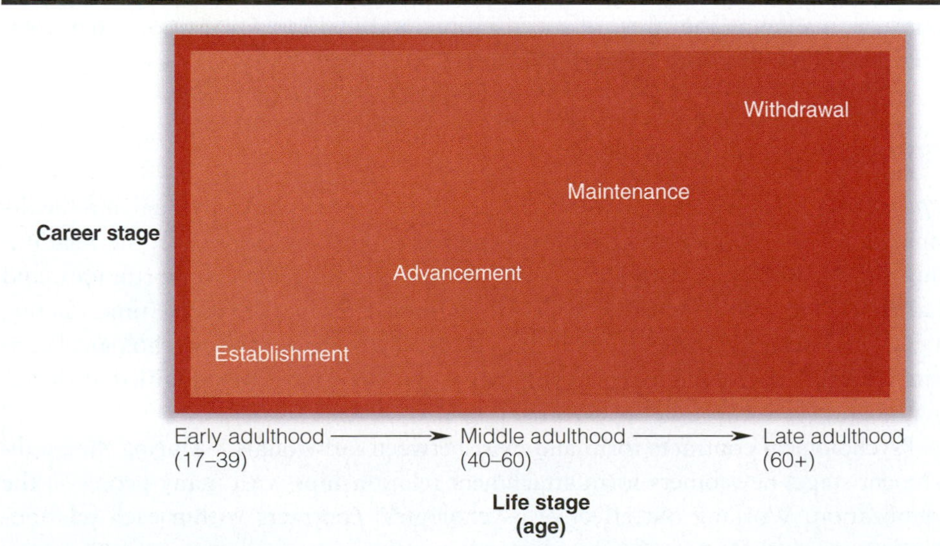

a Woman's Life.[39] Levinson's life stages are characterized by an alternating pattern of stability and transition.[40] Throughout the discussion of career stages that follows, we weave in the transitions of Levinson's life stages. Work and personal life are inseparable, and to understand a person's career experiences, we must also examine the unfolding of her or his personal experiences.

You can see that adult development provides unique challenges for the individual and that there may be considerable overlap between the stages. Now let us examine each career stage in detail.

THE ESTABLISHMENT STAGE

During the establishment stage, the individual begins a career as a newcomer to the organization. This is a period of great dependence on others, as the individual is learning about the job and the organization. The establishment stage usually occurs during the beginning of the early adulthood years (ages eighteen to twenty-five). During this time, Levinson notes, an important personal life transition into adulthood occurs: the individual begins to separate from his or her parents and becomes less emotionally and financially dependent. Following this period is a fairly stable time of exploring the adult role and settling down.

The transition from school to work is a part of the establishment stage. Many graduates find the transition a memorable experience. The following description was provided by a newly graduated individual who went to work at a large public utility:

> We all tried to one-up each other about jobs we had just accepted . . . bragging that we had the highest salary, the best management training program, the most desirable coworkers, the most upward mobility . . . and believed we were destined to become future corporate leaders. . . . Every Friday after work we met for happy hour to visit and relate the events of the week. It is interesting to look at how the mood of those happy hours changed over the first few months . . . at first, we jockeyed for position in terms of telling stories about how great these new jobs were, or how weird our bosses were. . . . Gradually, things quieted down at happy hour. The mood went from "Wow, isn't this great?" to "What in the world have we gotten ourselves into?" There began to be general agreement that business wasn't all it was cracked up to be.[41]

Establishment is thus a time of big transitions in both personal and work life. At work, three major tasks face the newcomer: negotiating effective psychological contracts, managing the stress of socialization, and making a transition from organizational outsider to organizational insider.

Psychological Contracts

(4) Explain the psychological contract.

A *psychological contract* is an implicit agreement between the individual and the organization that specifies what each is expected to give and receive in the relationship.[42] Individuals expect to receive salary, status, advancement opportunities, and challenging work to meet their needs. Organizations expect to receive time, energy, talents, and loyalty in order to meet their goals. Working out the psychological contract with the organization begins with entry, but the contract is modified as the individual proceeds through the career.

psychological contract
An implicit agreement between an individual and an organization that specifies what each is expected to give and receive in the relationship.

Psychological contracts form and exist between individuals.[43] During the establishment stage, newcomers form attachment relationships with many people in the organization. Working out effective psychological contracts within each relationship is important. Newcomers need social support in many forms and from many

TABLE 17.2 Newcomer–Insider Psychological Contracts for Social Support

Type of Support	Function of Supportive Attachments	Newcomer Concern	Examples of Insider Response/Action
Protection from stressors	Direct assistance in terms of resources, time, labor, or environmental modification	What are the major risks/threats in this environment?	*Supervisor* cues newcomer to risks/threats.
Informational	Provision of information necessary for managing demands	What do I need to know to get things done?	*Mentor* provides advice on informal political climate in organization.
Evaluative	Feedback on both personal and professional role performances	How am I doing?	*Supervisor* provides day-to-day performance feedback during first week on new job.
Modeling	Evidence of behavioral standards provided through modeled behavior	Whom do I follow?	Newcomer is apprenticed to *senior colleague*.
Emotional	Empathy, esteem, caring, or love	Do I matter? Who cares if I'm here or not?	*Other newcomers* empathize with and encourage individual when reality shock sets in.

SOURCE: Table from D. L. Nelson, J. C. Quick, and J. R. Joplin, "Psychological Contracting and Newcomer Socialization: An Attachment Theory Foundation," from *Journal of Social Behavior and Personality* 6 (1991): 65. Reprinted with permission.

sources. Table 17.2 shows the type of psychological contracts, in the form of social support, that newcomers may work out with key insiders in the organization.

One common newcomer concern, for example, is whose behavior to watch for cues to appropriate behavior. Senior colleagues can provide modeling support by displaying behavior that the newcomer can emulate. This is only one of many types of support that newcomers need. Newcomers should contract with others to receive each of the needed types of support so that they can adjust to the new job. Organizations should help newcomers form relationships early and should encourage the psychological contracting process between newcomers and insiders. The influence of a broken psychological contract is often felt even after an employee leaves a job. Laid-off employees who feel that a psychological contract breach has occurred are not only unhappy with their former firms but may also be both more cynical and less trusting of their new employers.[44]

The Stress of Socialization

In Chapter 16, we discussed three phases that newcomers go through in adjusting to a new organization: anticipatory socialization, encounter, and change and acquisition. (You may want to review Figure 16.2.) Another way to look at these three phases is to examine the kinds of stress newcomers experience during each stage.[45]

In anticipatory socialization, the newcomer is gathering information from various sources about the job and organization. The likely stressor in this stage is ambiguity, so the provision of accurate information is important. During this stage, the psychological contract is formed. It is essential that both parties go into it with good intentions of keeping up their end of the agreement.

The Effects of Socialization Tactics on Newcomer Adjustment and Job Outcomes

Individuals and organizations both have their own techniques for easing the transition into a new position. It is estimated that 25 percent of the U.S. workforce is currently undergoing socialization to help employees adjust to new jobs. Results from a meta-analysis of a large group of research studies showed that socialization is a joint responsibility of both the organization and the newcomer. From the organization's standpoint, six distinct dimensions of socialization tactics were identified. These six dimensions refer to differences in the ways organizations choose to socialize their newcomers. For example, some organizations hire in cohorts and emphasize a group socialization program, whereas others focus on individual socialization. Other dimensions include whether the program is formal or informal, the use of sequential or randomly spaced meetings, and whether there are fixed timetables for completion or not. Sometimes role models are used, and other times not; sometimes insiders encourage newcomers to forge their own identities, and sometimes not.

From the individual's standpoint, seeking out new information was the critical predictor of adjustment. Taken together, organizational tactics and individual tactics had a positive effect on the newcomer's role clarity, self-efficacy, and social acceptance within the organization. These three individual newcomer adjustment metrics (role clarity, self-efficacy, and social acceptance) in turn positively affected job performance, job satisfaction, organizational commitment, intention to remain with that organization, and negatively impacted turnover.

This study highlights the importance of socialization in helping manage the career of new employees. Furthermore, it highlights the importance of both the organization and the individual being actively involved in the process consistent with the earlier perspective on the new career.

SOURCE: T. N. Bauer, T. Bodner, B. Erdogan, D. M. Truxillo, and J. S. Tucker, "Newcomer Adjustment During Organizational Socialization: A Meta-Analytic Review of Antecedents, Outcomes, and Methods," *Journal of Applied Psychology* 92(3): 707–721.

In the encounter phase, the demands of the job in terms of the role, task, interpersonal relationships, and physical setting become apparent to the newcomer. The expectations formed in anticipatory socialization may clash with the realities of organizational life, and reality shock can occur.[46] This very predictable "surprise" reaction may find the new employee thinking, "What have I gotten myself into?"[47] The degree of reality shock depends on the expectations formed in the anticipatory socialization stage. If these expectations are unrealistic or unmet, reality shock may be a problem.

While most organizations allow some time for newcomers to adapt, as little as two to three months may be allotted for new hires to reach some level of independence. This unwritten rule will mean that new hires who cannot quickly get up to speed on the organization's and their workgroup's norms and procedures will quickly find themselves experiencing negative feedback from coworkers.[48]

In the change and acquisition phase, the newcomer begins to master the demands of the job. Newcomers need to feel that they have some means of control over job demands.

Easing the Transition from Outsider to Insider

Being a newcomer in an organization is stressful. The process of becoming a functioning member of the organization takes time, and the newcomer needs support in making the transition. A successful transition from outsider to insider can be ensured if both the newcomer and the organization work together to smooth the way. In the Science feature you can read about specific tactics used by both individuals and organizations in easing this transition.

Individual Actions Newcomers should ask about the negative side of the job if they were not given a realistic job preview. In particular, newcomers should ask about the stressful aspects of the job. Other employees are good sources of this information. Research has shown that newcomers who underestimate the stressfulness of job demands do not adjust well.[49] In addition, newcomers should present honest and accurate information about their own weaknesses. Both actions can promote good matches.

During the encounter phase, newcomers must prepare for reality shock. Realizing that slight depression is natural when adjusting to a new job can help alleviate the distress. Newcomers can also plan ways to cope with job stress ahead of time. If, for example, long assignments away from home are typical, newcomers can plan for these trips in advance. Part of the plan for dealing with reality shock should include ways to seek support from others. Networking with other newcomers who empathize can help individuals cope with the stress of the new job.

In the change and acquisition stage of adjusting to a new organization, newcomers should set realistic goals and take credit for the successes that occur as they master the job. Newcomers must seek feedback on job performance from their supervisors and coworkers. Organizations also can assist newcomers in their transition from outsiders to insiders.

Organizational Actions Realistic job previews start the relationship between the newcomer and the organization with integrity and honesty. Careful recruitment and selection of new employees can help ensure good matches.

During the encounter phase, organizations should provide early job assignments that present opportunities for the new recruit to succeed. Newcomers who experience success in training gain increased self-efficacy and adjust to the new job more effectively.[50] Newcomers who face early job challenges successfully tend to be higher performers later in their careers.[51] Providing encouragement and feedback to the newcomer during this stage is crucial. The immediate supervisor, peers, other newcomers, and support staff are important sources of support during encounter.[52] Otis Elevator has experimented with a program in which new hires, regardless of their specific job function (sales, manufacturing, finance, etc.), all complete a six-week training course covering all aspects of the elevator industry. During this program, they not only visit Otis's manufacturing and headquarters sites, they also visit construction sites to experience the gritty world of elevator installation.[53]

In contrast, some firms do little to help newcomers adjust. A recent survey of information technology firms found that only 38 percent have formal company policies regarding training for new employees. The remaining 62 percent answered that when it comes to new-hire training, they simply "wing it."[54]

During the change and acquisition phase, rewards are important. Organizations should tie the newcomers' rewards as explicitly as possible to performance.[55] Feedback is also crucial. Newcomers should receive daily, consistent feedback. This communicates that the organization is concerned about their progress and wants to help them learn the ropes along the way.

The establishment stage marks the beginning of an individual's career. Its noteworthy transitions include the transition from school to work, from dependence on parents to dependence on self, from organizational outsider to organizational insider. Individuals who successfully complete the establishment stage go through many positive changes, including increased self-confidence, interpersonal skills, and self-knowledge.[56] Once they have met their need to fit in, individuals move on to the advancement stage of their careers.

THE ADVANCEMENT STAGE

The advancement stage is a period when individuals strive for achievement. They seek greater responsibility and authority and strive for upward mobility. Usually around age thirty, an important life transition occurs.[57] Individuals reassess their goals and feel the need to make changes in their career dreams. The transition at age thirty is followed by a period of stability during which the individual tries to find a role in adult society and wants to succeed in the career. During this stage, several issues are important: exploring career paths, finding a mentor, working out dual-career partnerships, and managing conflicts between work and personal life.

Career Paths and Career Ladders

Career paths are sequences of job experiences along which employees move during their careers.[58] At the advancement stage, individuals examine their career dreams and the paths they must follow to achieve them. For example, suppose a person dreams of becoming a top executive in the pharmaceutical industry. She majors in chemistry in undergraduate school and takes a job with a nationally recognized firm. After she has adjusted to her job as a quality control chemist, she reevaluates her plan and decides that further education is necessary. She plans to pursue an MBA degree part-time, hoping to gain expertise in management. From there, she hopes to be promoted to a supervisory position within her current firm. If this does not occur within five years, she will consider moving to a different pharmaceutical company. An alternate route would be to try to transfer to a sales position, from which she might advance into management.

The career paths of many women have moved from working in large organizations to starting their own businesses. Currently, there are 10.6 million women-owned firms in the United States, comprising almost half of all privately held firms in the country. What is the motivation for this exodus to entrepreneurship? The main reasons are to seek additional challenge and self-fulfillment and to have more self-determination and freedom.[59]

A *career ladder* is a structured series of job positions through which an individual progresses in an organization. For example, at Southwestern Bell, it is customary to move through a series of alternating line and staff supervisory assignments to advance toward upper management. Supervisors in customer service might be assigned next to the training staff and then rotate back as line supervisors in network services to gain experience in different departments.

Some companies use the traditional concept of career ladders to help employees advance in their careers. Other organizations take a more contemporary approach to career advancement. Sony encourages creativity in its engineers by using nontraditional career paths. At Sony, individuals have the freedom to move on to interesting and challenging job assignments without notifying their supervisors. If they join a new project team, their current boss is expected to let them move on. This self-promotion philosophy at Sony is seen as a key to high levels of innovation and creative new product designs. There has been heightened interest in international assignments by multinational corporations in response to globalization and global staffing issues. One challenge in this regard has been that most expatriate assignments are not successful, and organizations have been facing the challenge of properly training and preparing individuals for such assignments. Alternative international work assignments (e.g., commuter work assignments, virtual assignments, short-term assignments, etc.) can be used to help individuals gain international work experience in preparation for higher levels in the organization.[60]

career path

A sequence of job experiences that an employee moves along during his or her career.

career ladder

A structured series of job positions through which an individual progresses in an organization.

Another approach used by some companies to develop skills is the idea of a "career lattice"—an approach to building competencies by moving laterally through different departments in the organization or by moving through different projects. Top management support for the career lattice is essential, because in traditional terms an employee who has made several lateral moves might not be viewed with favor. However, the career lattice approach is an effective way to develop an array of skills to ensure one's employability.[61]

Exploring career paths is one important activity in advancement. Another crucial activity during advancement is finding a mentor.

Finding a Mentor

5 Describe how mentors help organizational newcomers.

A *mentor* is an individual who provides guidance, coaching, counseling, and friendship to a protégé. Mentors are important to career success because they perform both career and psychosocial functions.[62]

The career functions provided by a mentor include sponsorship, facilitating exposure and visibility, coaching, and protection. Sponsorship means actively helping the individual get job experiences and promotions. Facilitating exposure and visibility means providing opportunities for the protégé to develop relationships with key figures in the organization in order to advance. Coaching involves providing advice in both career and job performance. Protection is provided by shielding the protégé from potentially damaging experiences. Career functions are particularly important to the protégé's future success. One study found that the amount of career coaching received by protégés was related to more promotions and higher salaries four years later.[63]

The mentor also performs psychosocial functions. Role modeling occurs when the mentor displays behavior for the protégé to emulate. This facilitates social learning. Acceptance and confirmation is important to both the mentor and protégé. When the protégé feels accepted by the mentor, it fosters a sense of pride. Likewise, positive regard and appreciation from the junior colleague provide a sense of satisfaction for the mentor. Counseling by a mentor helps the protégé explore personal issues that arise and require assistance. Friendship is another psychosocial function that benefits both mentor and protégé alike.

There are characteristics that define good mentoring relationships. In effective mentoring relationships, there is regular contact between mentor and protégé that has clearly specified purposes. Mentoring should be consistent with the corporate culture and the organization's goals. Both mentors and protégés alike should be trained in ways to manage the relationship. Mentors should be held accountable and rewarded for their role. Mentors should be perceived (accurately) by protégés as having considerable influence within the organization.[64] While it may be tempting to go after the "top dog" as your mentor, personality compatibility is also an important factor in the success or failure of a mentoring relationship. Mentors who are similar to their protégés in terms of personality traits like extraversion, and whose expectations are largely met by the relationship, are more likely to show interest in continuing the arrangement.[65] Cigna Financial Advisors takes a proactive approach to integrating new employees. As part of the company's Partnership Program, all new hires work for up to twenty-seven months under the oversight of an experienced, successful mentor. This relationship provides the new hires with hands-on instruction in how to sell more effectively, as well as increasing sales levels for the mentors themselves. Cigna demonstrates its commitment to this approach by hiring no more new producers than it can assign to individual mentors.[66]

mentor
An individual who provides guidance, coaching, counseling, and friendship to a protégé.

Mentoring programs are also effective ways of addressing the challenge of workforce diversity. The mentoring process, however, presents unique problems, including the availability of mentors, issues of language and acculturation, and cultural sensitivity, for minority groups such as Hispanic Americans. Negative stereotypes can limit minority members' access to mentoring relationships and the benefits associated with mentoring.[67] To address this problem, companies can facilitate access to mentors in organizations. Informal mentoring programs identify pools of mentors and protégés, give training in the development of effective mentoring and diversity issues, and then provide informal opportunities for the development of mentoring relationships. Network groups are another avenue for mentoring. Network groups help members identify with those few others who are like them within an organization, build relationships with them, and build social support. Network groups enhance the chance that minorities will find mentors.[68] Lucent Technologies, for example, has several Employee Business Partner groups that serve networking functions. Some of these groups are HISPA, for Hispanic Americans; 4A, for Asian Americans; ABLE, for African Americans; LUNA, for Native Americans; and Equal!, for gay, lesbian, and bisexual individuals. These groups serve as links to their respective communities within Lucent. Networks also increase the likelihood that individuals have more than one mentor. Employees with multiple mentors, such as those gained from mentoring networks, have even greater career success than those with only one mentor.[69]

Some companies have formal mentoring programs. PricewaterhouseCoopers (PWC) also uses the mentoring model to help its interns. Each intern is assigned both a peer mentor to help with day-to-day questions and an experienced mentor to help with larger issues such as career path development. As an international firm, PWC also employs similar methods overseas. In PWC's Czech Republic operations, a team of two mentors—one of whom is called a "counselor"—fills the same guidance role as the two mentors generally fill for U.S. employees.[70]

Mentoring has had a strong impact in shaping the identities of the Big Four accounting firms. In one study, every partner who was interviewed reported having at least one mentor who played a critical role in his or her attainment of the partnership and beyond. Protégés' identities are shaped through mentoring, and their work goals, language, and even lifestyles reflect the imperatives of the Big Four firm.[71] Protégés are schooled on partners' "hot buttons" (what not to talk about), what to wear, to "tuck in the tie," and not to cut the grass without wearing a shirt.

Although some companies have formal mentoring programs, junior employees more often are left to negotiate their own mentoring relationships. The barriers to finding a mentor include lack of access to mentors, fear of initiating a mentoring relationship, and fear that supervisors or coworkers might not approve of the mentoring relationship. Individuals may also be afraid to initiate a mentoring relationship because it might be misconstrued as a sexual advance by the potential mentor or others. This is a fear of potential mentors as well. Some are unwilling to develop a relationship because of their own or the protégé's gender. Women report more of these barriers than men, and individuals who lack previous experience report more barriers to finding a mentor.[72]

Organizations can encourage junior workers to approach mentors by providing opportunities for them to interact with senior colleagues. The immediate supervisor is not always the best mentor for an individual, so exposure to other senior workers is important. Seminars, multilevel teams, and social events can serve as vehicles for bringing together potential mentors and protégés.

Mentoring relationships go through a series of phases: initiation, cultivation, separation, and redefinition. There is no fixed time length for each phase, because each relationship is unique. In the *initiation* phase, the mentoring relationship begins to take on significance for both the mentor and the protégé. In the *cultivation* phase, the relationship becomes more meaningful, and the protégé shows rapid progress because of the career and psychosocial support provided by the mentor. Protégés influence mentors as well.

In the *separation* phase, the protégé feels the need to assert independence and work more autonomously. Separation can be voluntary, or it can result from an involuntary change (the protégé or mentor may be promoted or transferred). The separation phase can be difficult if it is resisted, either by the mentor (who is reluctant to let go of the relationship) or by the protégé (who resents the mentor's withdrawal of support). Separation can proceed smoothly and naturally or can result from a conflict that disrupts the mentoring relationship.

The *redefinition* phase occurs if separation has been successful. In this phase, the relationship takes on a new identity as both parties consider themselves colleagues or friends. The mentor feels pride in the protégé, and the protégé develops a deeper appreciation for the support from the mentor.

Why are mentors so important? Aside from the support they provide, the research shows that mentors are vital to the protégé's future success. For example, studies have demonstrated that individuals with mentors have higher promotion rates and higher incomes than individuals without them.[73] Professionals who have mentors earn between $5,600 and $22,000 more per year than those who do not.[74] Individuals with mentors also are better decision makers.[75] And it is not just the presence of the mentor that yields these benefits. The quality of the relationship is most important.[76]

During the advancement stage, many individuals face another transition: They settle into a relationship with a life partner. This lifestyle transition requires adjustment in many respects: learning to live with another person, being concerned with someone besides yourself, dealing with an extended family, and many other demands. The partnership can be particularly stressful if both members are career oriented.

Dual-Career Partnerships

The two-career lifestyle has increased in recent years due in part to the need for two incomes to maintain a preferred standard of living. *Dual-career partnerships* are relationships in which both people have important career roles. This type of partnership can be mutually beneficial, but it can also be stressful. Often these stresses center around stereotypes that providing income is a man's responsibility and taking care of the home is the woman's domain. Among married couples, working women's satisfaction with the marriage is affected by how much the husband helps with childcare. Men who adhere to traditional gender beliefs may be threatened when the wife's income exceeds their own. Beliefs about who should do what in the partnership complicate the dual-career issue.[77]

One stressor in a dual-career partnership is time pressure. When both partners work outside the home, there may be a time crunch in fitting in work, family, and leisure time. Another potential problem is jealousy. When one partner's career blooms before the other's, the less successful partner may feel threatened.[78] Another issue to work out is whose career takes precedence. For example, what happens if one partner is transferred to another city? Must the other partner make a move that might threaten his or her own career in order to be with the individual who was transferred? Who, if anyone, will stay home and take care of a new baby?

Working out a dual-career partnership takes careful planning and consistent communication between the partners. Each partner must serve as a source of social support for the other. Couples can also turn to other family members, friends, and professionals for support if the need arises.

dual-career partnership
A relationship in which both people have important career roles.

Work–Home Conflicts

(6) Describe ways to manage conflicts between work and home.

An issue related to dual-career partnerships that is faced throughout the career cycle, but often first encountered in the advancement phase, is the conflicts that occur between work and personal life. Experiencing a great deal of work–home conflict negatively affects an individual's overall quality of life. Such conflicts can lead to emotional exhaustion. Dealing with customer complaints all day, failed sales calls, and missed deadlines can magnify negative events at home, and vice versa.[79] Responsibilities at home can clash with responsibilities at work, and these conflicts must be planned for. For example, suppose a child gets sick at school. Who will pick up the child and stay home with him or her? Couples must work together to resolve these conflicts. Even at Eli Lilly and Company, only 36 percent of workers said it is possible to get ahead in their careers and still devote sufficient time to family. This is surprising, because Lilly has a reputation as one of the world's most family-friendly workplaces.[80]

Work–home conflicts are particular problems for working women.[81] Women have been quicker to share the provider role than men have been to share responsibilities at home.[82] When working women experience work–home conflict, their performance declines, and they suffer more strain. Work–home conflict is a broad topic. It can be narrowed further into work–family conflict, in which work interferes with family, versus family–work conflict, in which family or home life interferes with work.[83] Cultural differences arise in these types of conflicts. One study showed that while Americans experience more family–work conflict, Chinese experience more work–family conflict.[84] For example, women in management positions in China were very positive about future advancements and carried a strong belief in their ability to succeed. This, in turn, caused them to reevaluate their personal and professional identities. Such an identity transformation is marked by happiness associated with career advancement, even though many women foresaw emotional costs with such career advancement. This study indicated that female Chinese managers experience work–family conflict in part because the Chinese culture emphasizes close social close ties and guanxi, or personalized networks of influence.[85]

To help individuals deal with work–home conflict, some companies offer on-site day-care centers. Here Kirstie Foster of General Mills visits her daughter in the day-care facility at the company's headquarters.

To help individuals deal with work–home conflict, companies can offer *flexible work schedules*.[86] These programs, such as flextime, which we discussed in Chapter 14, give employees freedom to take care of personal concerns while still getting their work done. Company-sponsored childcare is another way to help. Companies with on-site day-care centers include Johnson & Johnson, Perdue Farms, and Campbell Soup. Mitchell Gold, an award-winning furniture maker, believes that treating people right must come first. Its 2,700-square-foot on-site day-care center is education based rather than activity based and operates at break-even rates to make it more accessible. The day-care facility was named the county's "Provider of the Year" in 2003.[87] Whereas large companies may offer corporate day care, small companies can also assist their workers by providing referral services for locating the type of childcare the workers need. For smaller organizations, this is a cost-effective alternative.[88] At the very least, companies can be sensitive to work–home conflicts and handle them on a case-by-case basis with flexibility and concern. In The Real World 17.2, you can read about how Netflix is managing its employees in a completely different way to ensure that the best talent is recruited and retained.

flexible work schedule
A work schedule that allows employees discretion in order to accommodate personal concerns.

THE REAL WORLD 17.2

Netflix: Combating Competition through Innovation

Netflix founder Reed Hastings is no stranger to success. His first job was at a start-up called Pure that specialized in writing debugging software and was very successful. In fact, it was so successful that it eventually ended up as a part of IBM. However, Hastings learned a few lessons from that job. He claimed that Pure started out as a very exciting place to work but soon became boring due to bureaucratic shackles. When he founded Netflix, he swore that it would never turn into a company like that. As a result, his management style is rather unorthodox to say the least.

One of the striking things about his system is that newcomers can design their compensation system; there is no upper limit on how Netflix will pay for the brightest minds in the industry. In fact, they regularly collect data on newcomer salaries and set their salaries substantially higher than what the market pays. This has helped them attract some of the best minds in the software business to help them stay ahead of the curve in writing code for movie recommendations and other Neflix tasks.

So that's how they attract people—but how do they keep them? By doing away with formal performance reviews, by offering raises that have no limits if people produce, and a severance package if they do not. Netflix doesn't give a warning or a write-up; they simply let people go if they do not perform.

In addition, employees are free to take as much vacation time as they like, but while at work they are expected to produce the work equivalent to that of four people in similar firms! Many employees liken the atmosphere at Netflix to that of the movie *Oceans 11* with Reed Hastings as the influential leader who drives everyone to do their best using unconventional means. Industry analysts believe that these competitive edges in terms of brainpower and unique company culture will help Netflix compete against Blockbuster and similar companies.

SOURCE: M. Conlin, "Netflix: Recruiting and Retaining the Best Talent," *BusinessWeek Online* (September 13, 2007), http://www.businessweek.com/managing/content/sep2007/ca20070913_564868.htm?chan=careers_managing+index+page_managing+your+team.

A program of increasing interest that organizations can provide is *eldercare*. Often workers find themselves part of the sandwich generation: They are expected to care for both their children and their elderly parents. This extremely stressful role is reported more often by women than men.[89] The impact of caring for an aging loved one is often underestimated. But 17 percent of those who provide care eventually quit their jobs due to time constraints, and another 15 percent cut back their work hours for the same reason.[90] Caring for an elderly dependent at home can create severe work–home conflicts for employees and also takes a toll on the employee's own well-being and performance at work. This is especially true if the organization does not provide a supportive climate for discussion of eldercare issues.[91] Harvard University has taken steps to help its faculty and staff deal with eldercare issues by contracting with Parents in a Pinch, a firm that specializes in nanny services and now also offers eldercare.[92]

eldercare
Assistance in caring for elderly parents and/or other elderly relatives.

John Beatrice is one of a handful of men making work fit their family, rather than trying to fit family around career. John remembers his father working most of the night so he could be at John's athletic events during the day, and John wants the same for his family. So while job sharing, flexible scheduling, and telecommuting have traditionally been viewed as meeting the needs of working mothers, John and other men are increasingly taking advantage of such opportunities. In John's case, flexible work hours at Ernst & Young allow him to spend part of his mornings and afternoons coaching a high school hockey team. In John's assessment, flexible work hours actually lead him to work more hours than he would otherwise, and he's happier about doing it. Not surprisingly, John's employer also benefits from the arrangement; after nineteen years, John is more loyal than ever and still loves what he does.[93]

Alternative work arrangements such as flextime, compressed workweeks, work-at-home arrangements, part-time hours, job sharing, and leave options can help employees manage work–home conflicts. Managers must not let their biases get in the way of these benefits. Top managers may be less willing to grant alternative work arrangements to men than to women, to supervisors than to subordinates, and to employees caring for elderly parents rather than children. It is important that family-friendly policies be applied fairly.[94]

The advancement stage is filled with the challenges of finding a mentor, balancing dual-career partnerships, and dealing with work–home conflicts. Developmental changes that occur in either the late advancement stage or the early maintenance stage can prove stressful, too. The midlife transition, which takes place approximately between ages forty and forty-five, is often a time of crisis. Levinson points out three major changes that contribute to the midlife transition. First, people realize that their lives are half over and that they are mortal. Second, age forty is considered by people in their twenties and thirties to be "over the hill" and not part of the youth culture. Finally, people reassess their dreams and evaluate how close they have come to achieving those dreams. All of these factors make up the midlife transition.

THE MAINTENANCE STAGE

Maintenance may be a misnomer for this career stage because some people continue to grow in their careers, although the growth is usually not at the rate it was earlier. A career crisis at midlife may accompany the midlife transition. A senior product manager at Borden found himself in such a crisis and described it this way: "When I was in college, I had thought in terms of being president of a company. . . . But at Borden I felt used and cornered. Most of the guys in the next two rungs above me had either an MBA or fifteen to twenty years of experience in the food business. My long-term plans stalled."[95]

Some individuals who reach a career crisis are burned out, and a month's vacation will help, according to Carolyn Smith Paschal, who owns an executive search firm. She recommends that companies give employees in this stage sabbaticals instead of bonuses. This would help rejuvenate them.

Some individuals reach the maintenance stage with a sense of achievement and contentment, feeling no need to strive for further upward mobility. Whether the maintenance stage is a time of crisis or contentment, however, there are two issues to grapple with: sustaining performance and becoming a mentor.

Sustaining Performance

Remaining productive is a key concern for individuals in the maintenance stage. This becomes challenging when one reaches a *career plateau*, a point where the probability of moving further up the hierarchy is low. Some people handle career plateauing fairly well, but others may become frustrated, bored, and dissatisfied with their jobs.

To keep employees productive, organizations can provide challenges and opportunities for learning. Lateral moves are one option. Another option is to involve the employee in project teams that provide new tasks and skill development. The key is keeping the work stimulating and involving. Individuals at this stage also need continued affirmation of their value to the organization. They need to know that their contributions are significant and appreciated.[96]

career plateau

A point in an individual's career in which the probability of moving further up the hierarchy is low.

Becoming a Mentor

During maintenance, individuals can make a contribution by sharing their wealth of knowledge and experience with others. Opportunities to be mentors to new employees can keep senior workers motivated and involved in the organization. It is important for organizations to reward mentors for the time and energy they expend. Some employees adapt naturally to the mentor role, but others may need training on how to coach and counsel junior workers.

Kathy Kram notes that there are four keys to the success of a formal mentoring program. First, participation should be voluntary. No one should be forced to enter a mentoring relationship, and careful matching of mentors and protégés is important. Second, support from top executives is needed to convey the intent of the program and its role in career development. Third, training should be provided to mentors so they understand the functions of the relationship. Finally, a graceful exit should be provided for mismatches or for people in mentoring relationships that have fulfilled their purpose.[97]

Maintenance is a time of transition, like all career stages. It can be managed by individuals who know what to expect and plan to remain productive, as well as by organizations that focus on maximizing employee involvement in work. According to Levinson, during the latter part of the maintenance stage, another life transition occurs. The age fifty transition is another time of reevaluating the dream and working further on the issues raised in the midlife transition. Following the age fifty transition is a fairly stable period. During this time, individuals begin to plan seriously for withdrawing from their careers.

THE WITHDRAWAL STAGE

The withdrawal stage usually occurs later in life and signals that a long period of continuous employment will soon come to a close. Older workers may face discrimination and stereotyping. They may be viewed by others as less productive, more resistant to change, and less motivated. However, older workers are one of the most undervalued groups in the workforce. They can provide continuity in the midst of change and can serve as mentors and role models to younger generations of employees.

Discrimination against older workers is prohibited under the Age Discrimination in Employment Act.[98] Organizations must create a culture that values older workers' contributions. With their level of experience, strong work ethic, and loyalty, these workers have much to contribute. In fact, older workers have lower rates of tardiness and absenteeism, are more safety conscious, and are more satisfied with their jobs than are younger workers.[99]

Planning for Change

The decision to retire is an individual one, but the need for planning is universal. A retired sales executive from Boise Cascade said that the best advice is to "plan no unplanned retirement."[100] This means carefully planning not only the transition but also the activities you will be involved in once the transition is made. All options should be open for consideration. One recent trend is the need for temporary top-level executives. Some companies are hiring senior managers from the outside on a temporary basis. The qualities of a good temporary executive include substantial high-level management experience, financial security that allows the executive to choose only assignments that really interest him or her, and a willingness to relocate.[101] Some individuals at the withdrawal stage find this an attractive option.

Planning for retirement should include not only financial planning but also a plan for psychologically withdrawing from work. The pursuit of hobbies and travel, volunteer work, or more time with extended family can all be part of the plan. The key is to plan early and carefully, as well as to anticipate the transition with a positive attitude and a full slate of desirable activities.

Retirement

There are several retirement trends right now, ranging from early retirement to phased retirement to never retiring. Some adults are choosing a combination of these options, leaving their first career for some time off before reentering the workforce either part-time or full-time doing something they enjoy. For more and more Americans, the idea of a retirement spent sitting beside the swimming pool lacks appeal. Factors that influence the decision of when to retire include company policy, financial considerations, family support or pressure, health, and opportunities for other productive activities.[102]

During the withdrawal stage, the individual faces a major life transition that Levinson refers to as the late adulthood transition (ages sixty to sixty-five). One's own mortality becomes a major concern and the loss of one's family members and friends becomes more frequent. The person works to achieve a sense of integrity—that is, the encompassing meaning and value—in life.

Some retirement-agers may go through a second midlife crisis. People are living longer and staying more active. Vickie Ianucelli, for example, bought a condo on a Mexican beach, celebrated a birthday in Paris, bought herself a 9.5-karat ring, and got plastic surgery. And it's her second midlife crisis. She's a psychologist who is also a 60-plus grandmother of two.[103]

Retirement need not be a complete cessation of work. Many alternative work arrangements can be considered, and many companies offer flexibility in these options. *Phased retirement* is a popular option for retirement-age workers who want to gradually reduce their hours and/or responsibilities. There are many forms of phased retirement, including reduced workdays or workweeks, job sharing, and consulting and mentoring arrangements. Many organizations cannot afford the loss of large numbers of experienced employees at once. In fact, although 50 percent of all U.S. workers are officially retired by age sixty, only 11 percent fully withdraw from work. This means there is an increase in *bridge employment*, which takes place after a retirement from a full-time position but before permanent withdrawal from the workforce. Bridge employment is related to retirement satisfaction and overall life satisfaction.[104]

Some companies are helping employees transition to retirement in innovative ways. Retired individuals can continue their affiliation with the organization by serving as mentors to employees who are embarking on retirement planning or other career transitions. This helps diminish the fear of loss some people have about retirement, because the retiree has an option to serve as a mentor or consultant to the organization.

Lawrence Livermore National Labs (LLNL) employs some of the best research minds in the world. And when these great minds retire from full-time work, they have numerous opportunities to continue contributing. LLNL's retiree program Web site lists a wide variety of requests, ranging from leading tours and making phone calls to providing guidance on current research and helping researchers make contact with other researchers.[105] Programs like this help LLNL avoid the typical knowledge drain that takes place when seasoned veteran employees retire.

Now that you understand the career stage model, you can begin to conduct your own career planning. It is never too early to start.

phased retirement
An arrangement that allows employees to reduce their hours and/or responsibilities in order to ease into retirement.

bridge employment
Employment that takes place after retiring from a full-time position but before permanent withdrawal from the workforce.

Career Anchors

7 Explain how career anchors help form a career identity.

Much of an individual's self-concept rests on a career. Over the course of a person's work life, career anchors are developed. *Career anchors* are self-perceived talents, motives, and values that guide an individual's career decisions.[106] Edgar Schein developed the concept of career anchors based on a twelve-year study of MBA graduates from the Massachusetts Institute of Technology (MIT). Schein found great diversity in the graduates' career histories but great similarities in the way they explained the career decisions they had made.[107] From extensive interviews with the graduates, Schein developed five career anchors:

1. *Technical/functional competence.* Individuals who hold this career anchor want to specialize in a given functional area (for example, finance or marketing) and become competent. The idea of general management does not interest them.
2. *Managerial competence.* Adapting this career anchor means individuals want general management responsibility. They want to see their efforts have an impact on organizational effectiveness.
3. *Autonomy and independence.* Freedom is the key to this career anchor, and often these individuals are uncomfortable working in large organizations. Autonomous careers such as writer, professor, or consultant attract these individuals.
4. *Creativity.* Individuals holding this career anchor feel a strong need to create something. They are often entrepreneurs.
5. *Security/stability.* Long-term career stability, whether in a single organization or in a single geographic area, fits people with this career anchor. Some government jobs provide this type of security.

Career anchors emerge over time and may be modified by work or life experiences.[108] The importance of knowing your career anchor is that it can help you find a match between yourself and an organization. For example, individuals with creativity as an anchor may find themselves stifled in bureaucratic organizations. Textbook sales may not be the place for an individual with a security anchor because of the frequent travel and seasonal nature of the business.

MANAGERIAL IMPLICATIONS: MANAGING YOUR CAREER

The challenges of globalization, diversity, technology, and ethics have provided unique opportunities and threats for career management. The ongoing restructuring of American organizations with its accompanying downsizing has resulted in a reduction of 25 percent of the jobs held in the *Fortune* 500 companies.[109] The flattening of the organizational hierarchy has resulted in fewer opportunities for promotion. Forty-year careers with one organization, a phenomenon baby boomers saw their parents experience, are becoming less and less the norm. Negotiating the turbulent waters of the U.S. employment market will be a challenge in the foreseeable future.

Many industries are experiencing sinking employment, but there are some bright spots. According to Labor Department projections, the U.S. economy will add approximately 21.3 million jobs by the year 2012, most of them in service industries. Figure 17.3 shows where the new jobs will be found. Of all the occupations expected to have faster-than-average employment growth, above-average earnings, and below-average unemployment, the ones shown in this chart have the largest number of projected openings. These occupations will account for 5 million new jobs, or 27 percent of all job growth. Most of these jobs require at least a bachelor's degree.

career anchors
A network of self-perceived talents, motives, and values that guide an individual's career decisions.

FIGURE 17.3 High-Paying Occupations with Many Openings, Projected 2002–2012

Over the 2002–2012 decade, career choices abound for those seeking high earnings and lots of opportunities. High-paying occupations that are projected to have many openings are varied. This diverse group includes teachers, managers, and construction trades workers.

The job openings shown in the chart represent the total that are expected each year for workers who are entering these occupations for the first time. The job openings result from each occupation's growth and from the need to replace workers who retire or leave the occupation permanently for some other reason. Not included among these openings are ones that are created when workers move from job to job within an occupation.

Median earnings, such as those listed below, indicate that half of the workers in an occupation made more than that amount, and half made less. The occupations in the chart ranked in the highest or second-highest earnings quartiles for 2002 median earnings. This means that median earnings for workers in these occupations were higher than the earnings for at least 50 percent of all occupations in 2002.

Most of these occupations had another thing going for them in 2002: low or very low unemployment. Workers in occupations that had higher levels of unemployment—truck drivers, carpenters, and electricians—were more dependent on a strong economy or seasonal employment.

	Annual average job openings due to growth and net replacement needs, projected 2002–2012	Median annual earnings, 2002
Registered nurses	110,119	$48,090
Postsecondary teachers	95,980	49,090
General and operations managers	76,245	68,210
Sales representatives, wholesale and manufacturing, except technical and scientific products	66,239	42,730
Truck drivers, heavy and tractor-trailer	62,517	33,210
Elementary school teachers, except special education	54,701	41,780
First-line supervisors or managers of retail sales workers	48,645	29,700
Secondary school teachers, except special and vocational education	45,761	43,950
General maintenance and repair workers	44,978	29,370
Executive secretaries and administrative assistants	42,444	33,410
First-line supervisors or managers of office and administrative support workers	40,909	38,820
Accountants and auditors	40,465	47,000
Carpenters	31,917	34,190
Automotive service technicians and mechanics	31,887	30,590
Police and sheriff's patrol officers	31,290	42,270
Licensed practical and licensed vocational nurses	29,480	31,440
Electricians	28,485	41,390
Management analysts	25,470	60,340
Computer systems analysts	23,735	62,890
Special education teachers	23,297	43,450

SOURCE: Bureau of Labor Statistics, "High-Paying Occupations with Many Openings, Projected 2002–2012," *Occupational Outlook Quarterly* 48 (Spring 2004), http://www.bls.gov/opub/ooq/2004/spring/oochart.pdf.

Andy Grove, chairman of Intel Corporation, suggests that as a general rule, you must accept that no matter where you work, you are not an employee. Instead, you are in a business with one employee: yourself. You face tremendous competition with millions of other businesses. You own your career as a sole proprietor. Grove poses three key questions that are central to managing your career. Continually ask:

1. *Am I adding real value?* You add real value by continually looking for ways to make things truly better in your organization. In principle, every hour of your workday should be spent increasing the value of the output of the people for whom you're responsible.
2. *Am I plugged into what's happening around me?* Inside the company? The industry? Are you a node in a network of plugged-in people, or are you floating around by yourself?
3. *Am I trying new ideas, new techniques, and new technologies?* Try them personally—don't just read about them.[110]

The key to survival is to add more value every day and to be flexible. You can use You 17.2 to assess the current state of your flexibility skills.

YOU 17.2

Assess Your Flexibility Skills

Use the following scale to rate the frequency with which you perform the behaviors described in each question. Place the corresponding number (1–7) in the blank preceding the statement.

Rarely	Irregularly	Occasionally	Usually	Frequently	Almost Always	Consistently
1	2	3	4	5	6	7

____ 1. I manage a variety of assignments with varying demands and complexities.

____ 2. I adjust work plans to account for new circumstances.

____ 3. I modify rules and procedures in order to meet operational needs and goals.

____ 4. I work with ambiguous assignments when necessary and use these when possible to further my goals and objectives.

____ 5. I rearrange work or personal schedules to meet deadlines.

____ 6. In emergencies, I respond to the most pressing needs first.

____ 7. I change my priorities to accommodate unexpected events.

____ 8. I manage my personal work overload by seeking assistance or by delegating responsibility to others.

____ 9. I vary the way I deal with others according to their needs and personalities.

____ 10. I help others improve their job performance, or I assign tasks that will further their development.

____ 11. I accept the authority of my manager but continue to demonstrate my initiative and assertiveness.

____ 12. I work well with all types of personalities.

____ 13. I measure my performance on the job against the feedback I receive.

(Continued)

____ 14. I correct performance deficits that have been brought to my attention.

____ 15. When I disagree with my manager's appraisal of my work, I discuss our differences.

____ 16. I seek training and assignments that can help me improve my job-related skills.

____ 17. In disagreements concerning work-related issues, I look at matters impersonally and concentrate on the facts.

____ 18. I make compromises to get problems moving toward resolution.

____ 19. I look for new and better ways to accomplish my duties and responsibilities.

____ 20. I offer to negotiate all areas of disagreement.

FIGURE A
Flexible Behaviors Questionnaire (FBQ) Scoring

Skill Area	Items	Score
Working with new, changing, and ambiguous situations	1, 2, 3, 4	
Working under pressure	5, 6, 7, 8	
Dealing with different personal styles	9, 10, 11, 12	
Handling feedback	13, 14, 15, 16	
Resolving conflicts	17, 18, 19, 20	
TOTAL SCORE		

FIGURE B
Flexible Behaviors Questionnaire (FBQ) Evaluation

Total Score

Lowest score — Highest score

20 50 80 110 40

Category Scores

Working with new, changing, and ambiguous situations
4 10 16 22 28

Working under pressure
4 10 16 22 28

Dealing with different personality styles
4 10 16 22 28

Handling feedback
4 10 16 22 28

Resolving conflicts
4 10 16 22 28

FBQ Scoring

The scoring sheet in Figure A summarizes your responses for the FBQ. It will help you identify your existing strengths and pinpoint areas that need improvement.

FBQ Evaluation

Figure B shows score lines for your total score and for each category measured on the FBQ. Each line shows a continuum from the lowest score to the highest.

The score lines in Figure B show graphically where you stand with regard to the five flexible behaviors. If you have been honest with yourself, you now have a better idea of your relative strengths and weaknesses in the categories that make up the skills of flexibility.

SOURCE: "Assess Your Flexibility Skills" by Fandt, from *Management Skills, Learning Through Practice and Experience, 1e*. pp. 431–433.

DIVERSITY DIALOGUE

Retirees Find New Careers Working for Their Children

Robert Shipman is a 64-year-old retired CEO of a clothing manufacturing company who carries pink business cards with a picture of a pug on them. Why does he do that? Because his daughter told him he had to. After Shipman retired, he began working for his then-28-year-old daughter at her cosmetics firm. The pug is the company mascot and as for the color of the business card, well . . . his daughter likes pink. Shipman retired from a company that boasted $130 million in annual sales, and though he is fond of neither pugs nor pink, he carries the business cards anyway as a condition of his employment.

Shipman is not alone. Working for their children is a growing trend among retirees, with many notable parents having worked for their children at some point in their careers. For example, after helping him find an attorney to defend Microsoft in a government lawsuit, William H. Gates, Sr., was hired by Bill Gates as the chairman of the Gates Foundation. After G. Harry Huizenga retired, he was hired to oversee the real estate for his son H. Wayne Huizenga's company, Blockbuster Entertainment.

Shipman, Gates, and Huizenga are reminders about the changing nature of retirement. Many retirees are no longer satisfied to withdraw to the golf course or trade in their business suits and ties for shorts and sandals. Instead, more and more retirement-age executives are using their knowledge and expertise to fill important roles in new companies—in many cases where their children are their bosses.

1. Imagine you are hiring your retired parent in an executive position in your firm. What issues should you address to ensure the partnership is a healthy one?
2. Older workers are the most undervalued groups in the workforce, often the target of age discrimination. Can working for their children help change this perception? How?

SOURCE: T. Demos, "Hiring Parents," *Fortune* 155(12) (June 25, 2007): 134; A. Fisher, "Working for Your Kids," *Fortune* 155(12) (June 25, 2007): 130–138.

LOOKING BACK: GOOGLE

Do You Have What It Takes?

Most young people dream about working for a great place like Google. As noted in the Looking Ahead feature, it was honored as the best place to work in America in 2007. However, what makes an employee attractive to Google? How does the company screen and pick the people it thinks belong there? The process is not as straightforward as you might think.

Think about this: How many golf balls can you fit in a school bus, or how much would you charge for washing all the windows in Seattle? These are the kinds of questions you should be ready for if interviewing with a major tech company like Google. What does washing windows have to do with writing code or coming up with the next big innovation in search engine technologies? Google has achieved notoriety for using unusual techniques to find the best and the brightest. For example, they recruited many engineers by posting complex mathematical problems on a major highway and asking passing drivers to submit their answers on a Web site that was part of the solution. They could only get to the Web site if they had the correct solution!

The answer is that Google looks for people who can think on their feet, can constantly adapt to change, and can come up with creative ideas and solutions to problems. So, even if you did not have the right answers to any of these questions, you might still qualify for employment at Google if you are creative and exhibit a quality thought process.[111]

Chapter Summary

1. Career management is a joint responsibility of individuals and organizations.
2. Good matches between individuals and organizations can be promoted with a realistic job preview (RJP).
3. The four stages in an individual's career are establishment, advancement, maintenance, and withdrawal. Each stage has unique challenges.
4. Psychological contracts are implicit agreements between individuals and organizations.
5. Mentoring is crucial to both the career success of young workers and the needs of older workers.
6. Childcare, eldercare, and flexible work schedules can help employees manage work–home conflicts.
7. Career anchors help an individual form a career identity and formulate an effective career plan.

Key Terms

advancement (p. 587)
bridge employment (p. 600)
career (p. 578)
career anchors (p. 601)
career ladder (p. 592)
career management (p. 578)
career path (p. 592)
career plateau (p. 598)
dual-career partnership (p. 595)
eldercare (p. 597)
establishment (p. 587)
flexible work schedule (p. 596)
maintenance (p. 587)
mentor (p. 593)
phased retirement (p. 600)
psychological contract (p. 588)
realistic job preview (RJP) (p. 586)
withdrawal (p. 587)

Review Questions

1. What is career management?
2. What is the new career, and how does it differ from older notions about careers?
3. What are the sources of potential conflict during organizational entry? How can they be avoided?
4. What is a realistic job preview, and why is it important?
5. What are psychological contracts?
6. What stressors are associated with socialization?
7. What are the career functions provided by a mentor?
8. What are some of the most likely causes of home–work conflicts?
9. What are the two key issues to deal with during the maintenance career stage?
10. What is the key to career survival?

Discussion and Communication Questions

1. What are the realities of the new career? How can developing your emotional intelligence help you turn these realities into opportunities to improve your career?
2. What do you think will be the most stressful career stage? What type of stressors led you to make this choice?
3. Does the career stage model have exceptions? In other words, can it be applied to all careers? If not, what are the exceptions?
4. Do men and women have different expectations of a dual-career partnership? How do these expectations differ?
5. Given the downsizing and restructuring in many organizations, how can organizations help employees with career management if there are fewer opportunities for promotion?
6. How has each of the four challenges (globalization, diversity, technology, and ethics) affected career management in recent years?
7. *(communication question)* Contact the human resources manager of a local business. Ask if he or she would take a few minutes to discuss some issues about résumés with you. Structure your discussion around the following questions:
   a. How often do you encounter "padded" résumés? What is the most common padding, and how do you react to it?
   b. Do you verify the information on résumés? How do you do this? How long does it take for you to be sure that an applicant has been honest about his or her qualifications?
   c. What would you do if you found that a productive, loyal employee had lied on a résumé when applying for a job? Is "résumé fraud" an offense that warrants firing?

   Summarize the findings from your interview in a memo to your instructor.
8. *(communication question)* Select an individual in the field you want to work in or in a company you might want to work for. Contact the individual and ask if you might take a minute of her or his time for some career advice. Ask the following two questions, along with others you design yourself. First, how has the idea of a "career" changed over the past few years? Second, what advice would the person give to college students just beginning a new career? Be prepared to present your interview results in class.

Ethical Dilemma

Allen Jamison is manager of the information technology department of a small manufacturing firm. Allen's job is to ensure that everyone's computer systems work well. Allen is also responsible for the well-being of his employees. He knows only too well the challenges of being an IT employee. Everyone depends on their computers to do their jobs, and when a computer is down, no one wants to hear excuses. Allen's employees are often on the receiving end of the frustration many people feel in these situations. Because of this, he feels it is his responsibility to create an environment of support in his department. He always makes it clear to everyone in the department what he expects from them. Allen frequently assures his employees that they can count on his support: "Do your best in every situation and I will always watch your back."

The problem now is that the organization has just experienced a serious network malfunction that has resulted in a 24-hour shutdown. Allen feels sure that his department has played a role in creating this situation, but this certainly is not the only cause. Allen is willing for his department to accept part of the blame, but he has just left a meeting in which he has been asked to take more of the responsibility than he feels his people deserve. The president described how critical it is that the organization gains buy-in for the new software platform by everyone. The president readily admitted that the new platform is in large part the reason for the shutdown. His concern is that this early failure will bias the employees against the equipment. He asked Allen if he would be willing to accept a larger part of the responsibility for the problem to keep dissatisfaction for the new system as low as possible.

Allen feels certain that his employees can handle the added criticism, but why should they? They have dealt with enough customer service problems already. But Allen also knows how critical acceptance of the software platform is to its success.

Questions

1. Does Allen have a responsibility to do what the president is asking him to do?
2. Using consequential, rule-based, and character theories, evaluate Allen's decision.

Experiential Exercises

17.1 The Individual–Organizational Dialogue

The purpose of this exercise is to help you gain experience in working out a psychological contract from both perspectives—the individual's and the organization's.

Students should form groups of six to eight members. Within each group, half of the students will be job candidates, and half will represent organization members (insiders).

Step 1. Each half should make two lists as follows:

List 1, candidate version. What information should you, as a job candidate, provide the organization to start an effective psychological contract?

List 2, candidate version. What information should you, as a job candidate, seek from the organization?

List 1, insider version. What information should you, as an organization insider, seek from potential employees?

List 2, insider version. What information should you, as an organization insider, provide to potential employees to start an effective psychological contract?

Step 2. Within each group, compare lists by matching the two versions of List 1. What were the similarities and differences in your lists? Then compare List 2 from each half of the group. What were the similarities and differences in these lists?

Step 3. Review the lists, and select the most difficult information to obtain from the candidate and the organization. Select one person to play the candidate and one to play the insider. First, have the candidate role-play an interaction with the insider in which the candidate tries to get the difficult information from the organization. Then have the insider try to obtain the difficult information from the candidate.

Step 4. Reconvene as a class, and discuss the following questions:

1. What did you find to be the most difficult questions asked by candidates?
2. What did you find to be the most difficult questions asked by insiders?
3. What information is necessary for an effective psychological contract?
4. What keeps each party from fully disclosing the information needed for a good psychological contract?
5. What can organizations do to facilitate the process of forming good psychological contracts?
6. What can individuals do to facilitate the process?

17.2 The Ethics of Résumés and Recommendations

The purpose of this exercise is to explore ethical issues concerning résumés and recommendations. First, read the following brief introductory scenario.

Jason Eckerle returned to his desk from lunch with a single mission in mind: to select the half-dozen best candidates for a regional customer service manager's position. As he hung up his suit jacket, Eckerle sized up the stack of résumés and recommendations he'd been dealing with all morning—more than 100 of them.

The work had been slow but steady, gradually forming into three distinct piles: one contained absolute rejects (not enough work experience, wrong academic credentials, or poor recommendations from former employers), the second contained a few definite candidates for personal interviews, while the third held the applications of those about whom he still had questions or reservations.

His task for the afternoon—selecting three more applicants to bring to the company headquarters for interviews—was complicated by the résumés and recommendation letters themselves. Some questions were obvious: "This guy lists five years' full time sales and marketing experience, yet he's only twenty-two years old. How can he go to school full-time and have that kind of experience?" Here's another: "This young lady says she went to school at the Sorbonne in Paris for two years; yet on the application form, under the heading 'Foreign Languages' she's checked 'none.'" Here's one more: "This fella says he has a degree from the University of Texas, yet nowhere on his résumé does he say he lived or spent time there. Did he get that diploma by correspondence?"

Other issues are even more mysterious: "This young lady's résumé lists education and work experience, but there's a three-year gap from 1989 to 1992. What's that all about? Is she trying to conceal something, or just absentminded?" As Eckerle thumbed through another résumé, he noticed the application form declaring "fluency in Japanese, French, and Spanish." "How do you get to be *fluent* in a language unless you've lived where it's spoken?" he wondered. The résumé didn't list any of those languages as native, nor did the application mention living abroad.

"Some of this stuff is outright fraud," he observed. As he sifted through the "reject" pile, Eckerle pulled out one application with an education block that lists a degree the applicant didn't have. "When we checked," he said, "they told us he was close to finishing a master's degree, but he hadn't yet finished his thesis. The applicant said he had the degree in hand." Another listed work experience no one could verify. "This guy's résumé says he was a client service representative for Litiplex, Inc., of Boston, but the phone book doesn't list any firm by that name, no one in our business has ever heard of it, and we can't check out his claims. I asked the applicant about the company, and he says, 'Maybe they went out of business.'"

Résumés weren't Eckerle's only problem. Recommendations were almost as bad. "Letters of recommendation aren't particularly useful," he said. "In the first place, almost no one is dumb enough to ask for a recommendation from someone who'll give them a bad one. Second, most recommenders write in broad, general, vague terms that don't tell me much about an applicant's work history, aptitude, or potential. They use glowing, nonspecific words that tell me the applicant's a marvelous human being but don't say whether the guy's had any comparable work experience that I could use to help make a decision."

Eckerle mentioned one other recommendation problem. "Most of the people who write letters in support of a job applicant are fairly close friends of the applicant. They'll often say things that are laudatory, but just aren't true. By the time you're done reading the letter, you'd think the young man in question could walk on water. When he comes for an interview, he can't get his own name straight." Excessive praise in letters of recommendation, Eckerle noted, can be expensive for a firm when the recommendation just doesn't reflect the applicant's true potential. "It costs us nearly $1,000 to bring in an entry-level management candidate for interviews," he said, "and it's my job to make sure we don't bring in someone who's just not competitive." Inflated recommendations, he thought, can make that job much more difficult.

Next, the class should be divided into ten groups. Each group will be assigned one ethical issue. The group should formulate an answer to the dilemma and be ready to present the group's solution to the class.

1. Is a job applicant obligated to list *all employment* or *every work experience* on a résumé? What about jobs in which an applicant has had a bad relationship with a supervisor? Is it fair to "load up" a résumé only with positive work experience?
2. What if an applicant has been fired? Is a résumé *required* to reveal the exact circumstances under which he or she left the job?
3. Is it ethical to list educational institutions or degree programs that an applicant has attended but not completed? How much detail is necessary? Should an applicant explain *why* he or she left a degree program or school without finishing?
4. Is a job applicant *obliged* to list offenses against the law on a résumé? What about convictions or incarceration—say, 90 days' jail time for DWI?
5. Under such résumé categories as "Foreign Languages," how does an applicant determine whether he or she is "fluent," "conversant," or merely "familiar with" a language? Do the same general rules apply to listing technical skills, such as computer languages and software applications?
6. In a letter of recommendation, is it ethical to lavish praise on a young man or woman just because you know the person is in need of a job? Conversely, does faint praise mean that a job applicant will likely be refused?
7. Is it better to turn away a student for asking for a letter of recommendation, or should you do what's *honest* and tell a graduate school (or potential employer) exactly what you think of the person?
8. Is a résumé something like a *certificate of authenticity*, listing specifics and details with absolute adherence to honesty and accuracy? Or is it more like a *sales brochure*, offering the best possible picture of a person in search of employment?
9. How well do you have to know someone before you can write an authentic, honest letter of recommendation? Is there a minimum time requirement before you can do so in good conscience?
10. Is the author of a letter of recommendation required to reveal *everything relevant* that he or she knows about an applicant? What about character or integrity flaws that may stand in the way of a job applicant's success? To whom is the author of such letters obligated—the potential employer or the applicant?

SOURCE: J. S. O'Rourke, "The Ethics of Résumés and Recommendations: When Do Filler and Fluff Become Deceptions and Lies?" *Business Communication Quarterly* 58 (1995): 54–56. Reprinted with permission by the author.

TAKE 2

Biz Flix | The Secret of My Success

College graduate Brantley Foster (Michael J. Fox) leaves his Kansas home and goes to New York to look for a job. He is continually frustrated in his quest but eventually lands a mailroom job. An entertaining look at corporate life, this film features power, negotiation, and sexual shenanigans.

The scene from *The Secret of My Success* appears early in the film following Brantley's layoff from a job he never started. He looks up at a building while saying, "O.K., New York. If that's the way you want it, O.K." The scene ends after Ms. Miller (Judith Malina) says to Brantley, "Can you be a minority woman?" The film continues with Brantley talking to his mother on a public telephone.

What to Watch for and Ask Yourself:

- What do these scenes suggest about the job seeking process?
- Does Brantley behave ethically during his job interviews?
- What do these scenes suggest about career management?

Workplace Video | Operations and Service Management, Featuring Gil Vasquez and Washburn Guitar

Washburn Guitar has been making high-quality musical instruments since 1883. The Chicago-based manufacturer sells 50,000 acoustic and electric guitars each year, totaling $40 million in annual revenues. At the heart of Washburn's enduring success is a rich guitar-making tradition developed and maintained by the company's skilled craftspeople.

Making quality instruments is labor-intensive work, and crafting guitars that look, play, and sound just right is the job of Washburn's highly motivated production teams. Chief among Washburn's production staff is Gil Vasquez, head manager of Washburn's U.S. production facility. Known for his creative managerial style and eye for perfection, Vasquez has been instrumental in boosting quality on the production floor. From the drafting board to the assembly shop, every station along the production line upholds Vasquez's high standards for instruments stamped with the Washburn label.

Prior to winning his current position, Vasquez made high-end guitars for other guitar companies. Intent on securing top talent, headhunters at Washburn recruited the respected craftsman to broaden the company's expertise. "One of the major things we've done in the last few years that has really stepped it up for us," says one Washburn supervisor, "is bring in Gil Vasquez, a master builder who's been building guitars for years out on the West Coast."

A veteran of his trade, Vasquez exemplifies the shift from the old career model to the new. Unlike workers of past generations who expected to work for only one company, new-career employees like Vasquez job-hop their way up the career ladder, taking jobs at numerous companies to obtain the best growth opportunities. Although Vasquez currently sits atop the managerial hierarchy of Washburn USA, his career path has included

TAKE 2

key positions at Fender, Baker Guitars, and Ernie Ball—all prominent companies in the guitar manufacturing industry.

Although Washburn guitars occupy an esteemed place in rock history—stars from George Harrison to members of Modest Mouse rock out on the instruments—it is the behind-the-scenes efforts of dedicated craftspeople like Vasquez that make the brand tops with customers. Under his watch, the company's custom shop output has grown from 20 to 300 guitars per month. Vasquez relishes his team's success. "It's a labor of love," he says.

Discussion Questions

1. At what stage of the career stage model is manager Gil Vasquez? Explain your answer.
2. Has working numerous jobs with many different companies made Vasquez more valuable in the eyes of today's employers? Why or why not?
3. In your view, what are Vasquez's career anchors?

Developing Store Managers at Caribou Coffee

Caribou Coffee, the second-largest specialty coffee retailer in America, opened its first store in 1992 in Minnesota. Headquartered in Minneapolis, the company now has hundreds of stores and over 5,000 employees in eighteen states and the District of Columbia.[1] Caribou tries to be different—it tries to be everything that Starbucks, its number-one competitor, isn't![2] Unlike Starbucks' hip, urbane sophistication that is "an extension of the hustle and bustle of a city street," Caribou Coffee is designed in a fashion reminiscent of a rustic Alaskan cabin or a ski lodge. Also unlike Starbucks, Caribou provides its customers with one free refill on regular coffee during each visit.[3]

Caribou Coffee describes itself as "a fabulous place to work." The company's Web site states, "[w]hether you're young or old, on your way to college or retirement—or somewhere in-between, we invite you to explore our upscale lodge setting as an exceptional place to work."[4] Moreover, the company emphasizes that "[a]ttracting and retaining good people is critical to Caribou Coffee's success."[5] The company also invites prospective employees to live its core values. These values are succinct and straightforward: "Blaze new trails. Be excellent, not average. Enjoy what you do. Respect diversity. Teamwork builds success. Success and profit create opportunities. Make a difference in our community."[6]

Store Managers play a key role in implementing these core values. They also are crucial to the success of Caribou Coffee. Their responsibilities and expectations include:

- Acting as business owners of their stores.
- Commanding high personal standards and working for the greater good of Caribou Coffee.
- Meeting and exceeding sales goals.
- Growing sales by delivering top-quality products through timely and friendly service in clean, pleasant surroundings.
- Recruiting and hiring efficient and friendly employees, who are called team members.
- Training and developing team members, through regular feedback and coaching, to deliver excellent guest service.
- Leading by example, and dividing time equally among team members and guests.
- Developing successful sales and marketing efforts with local communities.
- Developing and maintaining relationships with vendors.
- Working 55 hours per week, including nights and weekends.
- Committing to three years in a Store Manager role.
- Making a positive impact on their communities.[7]

The path to Store Manager follows one of two different routes: individuals who are hired from the outside and then undergo an intensive training program; and employees who are capable and desire to move up in the company. Outside hires participate in the Manager-In-Training Program. These people, known as Manager-in-Training (MIT) candidates, typically have experience with another restaurant or retail company. Usually, they also have some experience in balancing the multiple responsibilities of managing people, products, and profits. MITs start their training by working in a store under the guidance of a designated Store Manager trainer. The eight-week training program combines in-store, classroom, and self-study training modules to impart the necessary skills, knowledge, and experience needed to be a successful Store Manager. Upon completion of the eight-week program, MITs are prepared to assume that position.[8]

Employees who desire to advance in the company through the Store Manager route can enter the Manager Apprentice Program (MAP). MAP candidates typically are employees who have succeeded as both a team member and a shift supervisor. Unlike the MIT program, there is no set time frame for MAP training. The progress of MAPs depends on how quickly and thoroughly they master the skills needed for effective store management.[9]

Once the MITs and MAPs become Store Managers, they "are treated like owners of their own businesses."[10] The Store Managers hire, train, and develop team members to meet the store's goals for people, profit, sales, and quality.[11] To help ensure that new Store Managers are successful, Caribou Coffee provides various forms of support. Store Managers are mentored by a District Manager, each of whom oversees six to ten stores. The main goal of the District Managers is to share their knowledge and experience with their Store Managers.[12] Within a given district, Store Managers also have the opportunity to interact with one another on a monthly basis. At these monthly district meetings, financial results, business trends, and upcoming initiatives are discussed. These meetings also provide an opportunity to discuss important issues and to benefit from the knowledge and experience of others.[13]

Other than a challenging job, what does Caribou Coffee offer its Store Managers? "Along with a healthy work culture comes a competitive, comprehensive compensation and benefits package that includes medical, dental, 401(k), life insurance, pooled leave, short- and long-term disability, discounts on drinks and merchandise, and other perks. Many of these benefits are contingent on position, number of hours worked, and time with the company."[14]

Although the Store Managers are expected to make a three-year commitment to that role, they can advance in the company. Store Managers have been promoted to positions in District Management, Marketing, Training, Human Resources, and Customer Service, among others.[15]

Discussion Questions

1. Using the facts of the case, along with the career stage model shown in Figure 17.2, describe the stage of career development likely occupied by Manager-in-Training (MIT) candidates and Manager Apprentice Program (MAP) candidates.
2. How can the MIT and MAP programs be explained from the perspective of socialization?
3. Using the psychological contract concept, explain the exchange between Caribou Coffee and its Store Managers.
4. How does mentoring factor into Caribou's development of Store Managers?

SOURCE: This case was written by Michael K. McCuddy, The Louis S. and Mary L. Morgal Chair of Christian Business Ethics and Professor of Management, College of Business Administration, Valparaiso University.

CHAPTER 18

Managing Change

LEARNING OBJECTIVES

After reading this chapter, you should be able to do the following:

1. Examine the major external and internal forces for change in organizations.
2. Understand *incremental change, strategic change, transformational change,* and *change agent.*
3. Evaluate the reasons for resistance to change, and discuss methods organizations can use to manage resistance.
4. Apply force field analysis to a problem.
5. Explain Lewin's organizational change model.
6. Describe the use of organizational diagnosis and needs analysis as a first step in organizational development.
7. Discuss the major organization development interventions.
8. Identify the ethical issues that must be considered in organization development efforts.

THINKING AHEAD: AMERICAN EXPRESS

Taking You Wherever You Want to Be in the World

Think American Express is a credit card company only? Think again! American Express has diversified into a number of areas over the years to maintain its competitive edge in the changing business environment. It partnered with airlines to provide its card members access to airport lounges and with the PGA to support golf memberships and ticket acquisitions. In its recent foray into the travel industry, the company has introduced the American Express Business Travel division. In the first 100 days of 2007 alone, this division grossed more than $1 billion from global usage of its programs.[1] American Express has achieved this success by capitalizing on two important business-related changes in globalization and the technology revolution. It introduced a commerce platform known as AXIOM (the American Express Intelligent Online Marketplace) that serves as a one-stop shop for corporate consumers traveling globally to make all their business travel plans in one place. This service allows customers to make air, hotel, ground transportation, dining, and local events bookings in one place.[2] In addition, American Express partnered with Regus, a provider of virtual office space, to offer Business Platinum customers access to virtual offices and business services around the world.[3] Moreover, they offer a Global Assist

Hotline with English-speaking customer service representatives. This is a service customers can use anywhere in the world to get help for legal, medical, emergency cash situations, lost luggage, and passport issues. *Accenture,* a study commissioned by American Express but conducted by an external consulting firm, revealed that the use of this business travel program reduced air travel expenses by 19 percent as compared to other business travel management companies. Similarly, the savings in hotel and rental car expenses were 13 percent and 15 percent respectively as compared to other agencies. Thus, American Express is making global business travel easier and cheaper.[4]

FORCES FOR CHANGE IN ORGANIZATIONS

Change has become the norm in most organizations. Plant closings, business failures, mergers and acquisitions, and downsizing are experiences common to American companies. *Adaptiveness*, *flexibility*, and *responsiveness* are characteristics of the organizations that will succeed in meeting the competitive challenges that businesses face.[5] In the past, organizations could succeed by claiming excellence in one area—quality, reliability, or cost, for example—but this is not the case today. The current environment demands excellence in all areas and vigilant leaders. A recent survey of CEOs who were facing crises found that 50 percent said they believed the problems arrived "suddenly" and that they had not prepared adequately for them. More than 10 percent said they were, in fact, the last to know about the problems.[6]

As we saw in Chapter 1, change is what's on managers' minds. The pursuit of organizational effectiveness through downsizing, restructuring, reengineering, productivity management, cycle-time reduction, and other efforts is paramount. Organizations are in a state of tremendous turmoil and transition, and all members are affected. Continued downsizings may have left firms leaner but not necessarily richer. Although downsizing can increase shareholder value by better aligning costs with revenues, firms may suffer from public criticism for their actions. Laying off employees may be accompanied by increases in CEO pay and stock options, linking the misery of employees with the financial success of owners and management.[7]

Organizations must also deal with ethical, environmental, and other social issues. Competition is fierce, and companies can no longer afford to rest on their laurels. American Airlines has developed a series of programs to constantly reevaluate and change its operating methods to prevent the company from stagnating. General Electric holds off-site WorkOut sessions with groups of managers and employees whose goal is to make GE a faster, less complex organization that can respond effectively to change. In the WorkOut sessions, employees recommend specific changes, explain why they are needed, and propose ways the changes can be implemented. Top management must make an immediate response: an approval, a disapproval (with an explanation), or a request for more information. The GE WorkOut sessions eliminate the barriers that keep employees from contributing to change.

planned change
Change resulting from a deliberate decision to alter the organization.

unplanned change
Change that is imposed on the organization and is often unforeseen.

There are two basic forms of change in organizations. *Planned change* is change resulting from a deliberate decision to alter the organization. Companies that wish to move from a traditional hierarchical structure to one that facilitates self-managed teams must use a proactive, carefully orchestrated approach. Not all change is planned, however. *Unplanned change* is imposed on the organization and is often unforeseen. Changes in government regulations and in the economy, for example, are often unplanned. Responsiveness to unplanned change requires tremendous flexibility and adaptability on the part of organizations. Managers must be prepared to handle both planned and unplanned forms of change in organizations.

Forces for change can come from many sources. Some of these are external, arising from outside the company, whereas others are internal, arising from sources within the organization.

External Forces

The four major managerial challenges we have described throughout the book—globalization, workforce diversity, technological change, and managing ethical behavior—are significant external forces that precipitate change in organizations.

(1) Examine the major external and internal forces for change in organizations.

Globalization The power players in the global market are the multinational and transnational organizations. NAFTA's impact has been felt across numerous industries. American agriculture has been a tremendous beneficiary, with annual U.S. exports of fruits and vegetables to Mexico climbing by more than $1 billion since 1993. This expanded market has been a tremendous windfall for U.S. producers, but trouble may be looming. Mexican farm leaders have accused the United States of unfairly dumping fruits and vegetables into the Mexican market.[8] They also claim that small Mexican farms cannot compete with large industrialized U.S. operations, and they have asked the Mexican government to renegotiate NAFTA to give them greater protection.[9] Because global business implicitly involves multiple governments and legal systems, it carries unique risks not found by firms competing within a single nation.

The United States is but one nation in the drive to open new markets. Japan and Germany are responding to global competition in powerful ways, and the emergence of the European Union as a powerful trading group will have a profound impact on world markets. By joining with their European neighbors, companies in smaller countries will begin to make major progress in world markets, thus increasing the fierce competition that already exists.

Coca-Cola faced a crisis when it introduced its Dasani bottled water in Great Britain. Coke had chosen a particularly compelling theme for its advertising, touting Dasani as more pure than other bottled waters. After Coke had invested more than £7 million in this project, government regulators found that the water contained illegally high levels of bromate, a potentially cancer-causing chemical. To make matters worse, Coke was forced to admit that the contamination was introduced by its own production process. Coke's response was swift: it quickly pulled half a million bottles of Dasani from London shelves and postponed plans for product launches in France and Germany. Some British writers rank Coke's introduction of Dasani among the worst marketing disasters in Britain's history.[10]

All of these changes, along with others, have led companies to rethink the borders of their markets and to encourage their employees to think globally. Jack Welch, former CEO of GE, was among the first to call for a boundaryless company, in which there are no mental distinctions between domestic and foreign operations or between managers and employees.[11] GE has locations in 160 countries across the globe and has become a truly multinational corporation. The thought that drives the boundaryless company is that barriers that get in the way of people's working together should be removed. Globalizing an organization means rethinking the most efficient ways to use resources, disseminate and gather information, and develop people. It requires not only structural changes but also changes in the minds of employees. Microsoft, for example, has become a global leader by acquiring leading software solutions providers across the globe. In 2002, they acquired Navision, a Denmark-based business software solutions provider. By doing so, they combined the power of Navision's reach in the European markets with their own and now have a stronghold in providing global business solutions in the software industry.[12] In 2006 and the first half of 2007 alone, Microsoft had acquired seventeen new businesses both in the United States and elsewhere to stay ahead of the competition resulting from globalization.[13]

Workforce Diversity Related to globalization is the challenge of workforce diversity. As we have seen throughout this book, workforce diversity is a powerful force for change in organizations. Let us recap the demographic trends contributing to workforce diversity that we discussed at length in Chapter 2. First, the workforce will see increased participation from females, because the majority of new workers will be female.[14] Second, the workforce will be more culturally diverse than ever. Part of this is attributable to globalization, but in addition, U.S. demographics are changing. The participation of African Americans and Hispanic Americans is increasing in record numbers. Third, the workforce is aging. There will be fewer young workers and more middle-aged Americans working.[15]

A few years ago, Denny's, the restaurant chain, was a name synonymous with racism. In 1994, the company paid $54.4 million to settle two lawsuits brought by black customers who claimed some restaurants refused to seat or serve them. In 1995, Denny's undertook radical changes led by a blunt-talking CEO and a determined diversity officer. Performance appraisals are now based on valuing diversity. A top manager who doesn't do so can have up to 25 percent of his or her bonus withheld. The company's response to a recent incident demonstrates that it takes this issue seriously: a cook and a waiter accused of racist behavior toward an African American customer in Florida were fired within twenty-four hours of the complaint. Almost half of Denny's 1,011 franchises are owned by minorities, 255 of them by Asian Indians, while one-third of restaurant managers and one-fifth of executives are also minorities. Denny's ranked fifth on *Fortune*'s list of the "50 Best Companies for Minorities in 2004."[16] And, more recently, it reported that over 50 percent of its board of directors and senior management committees are composed of women and minorities. The company has trained over one million employees in its diversity training program and emphasizes diversity as a core value.[17] Because Denny's responded quickly, decisively, and sincerely, it weathered the crisis.

Technological Change Rapid technological innovation is another force for change in organizations, and those who fail to keep pace can quickly fall behind. *Smart tags*, for example, are replacing bar codes for tracking and scanning products. Bar codes are passive identification markers whose stripes are unchangeable, and items must be lined up individually for scanning (like in a grocery store checkout line). Manufacturers are starting to use radio-frequency identification (RFID) tags that are as small as two matches laid side by side, and hold digital memory chips the size of a pinhead. RFIDs are also used in show dogs and cats. The tags are injected under a pet's skin with a syringe.

RFIDs contain a lot more information than bar codes, and users can alter that information. As many as fifty tags per second can be read—forty times faster than bar-code scanners. Ford uses RFIDs to track parts. Data such as a unique ID, part type, plant location, and time/date stamps are included on the tag. Because RFIDs are reusable, the long-term costs are about the same as bar codes.[18] American Express Business Travel Program has gained widespread popularity in the corporate world, but American Express has not lost sight of the fact that competing through technology also should be coupled with excellent customer service. It invests in employee engagement, skill training, and leadership development programs. Furthermore, it emphasizes quality of customer care through what it calls the Great

Call Experience. Employees are trained on a standard set of protocols to enhance customer satisfaction.[19]

Technological innovations bring about profound change because they are not just changes in the way work is performed. Instead, the innovation process promotes associated changes in work relationships and organizational structures.[20] The team approach adopted by many organizations leads to flatter structures, decentralized decision making, and more open communication between leaders and team members.

Managing Ethical Behavior Recent ethical scandals have brought ethical behavior in organizations to the forefront of public consciousness. Ethical issues, however, are not always public and monumental. Employees face ethical dilemmas in their daily work lives. The need to manage ethical behavior has brought about several changes in organizations. Most center around the idea that an organization must create a culture that encourages ethical behavior.

All public companies issue annual financial reports. Gap Inc. has gone a step further by issuing an annual ethical report. The clothing industry is almost synonymous with the use of sweatshops—low-paying overseas factories in which third-world workers (including children) labor for fifty to sixty hours each week for a few dollars in pay. Gap is hardly alone in facing these issues. What sets the company apart is its candor, beginning with its open admission that none of its 3,000 suppliers fully complies with the firm's ethical code of conduct. But rather than run from these problems, Gap has chosen to work with its suppliers to improve conditions overseas. The firm has more than ninety full-time employees charged with monitoring supplier operations around the world.[21]

The annual report includes extensive descriptions of these workers' activities, including which factories were monitored, what violations were found, and which factories are no longer used by Gap because of violations. It also addresses media reports critical of Gap and its operations.

Gap tries to improve worker conditions by providing training and encouraging suppliers to develop their own conduct codes. For example, in China it has encouraged lunchtime sessions in which workers are advised of their rights. While most facilities respond positively to these efforts, some don't, and Gap pulled its business from 136 factories it concluded were not going to improve. It also terminated contracts with two factories that had verifiable use of child labor. Gap's approach to overseas labor offers a model for other garment firms.[22]

Society expects organizations to maintain ethical behavior both internally and in relationships with other organizations. Ethical behavior is expected in relationships with customers, the environment, and society. These expectations may be informal, or they may come in the form of increased legal requirements. In The Real World 18.1, we profile McDonald's Europe's efforts in successfully dealing with a changing market base focused on healthier food and environmentally responsible business practices.

These four challenges are forces that place pressures to change on organizations. There are other forces as well. Legal developments, changing stakeholder expectations, and shifting consumer demands can also lead to change.[23] And some companies change simply because others are changing.[24] Other powerful forces for change originate from within the organization.

Internal Forces

Pressures for change that originate inside the organization are generally recognizable in the form of signals indicating that something needs to be altered. A declining effectiveness is a pressure to change. A company that experiences its third quarterly loss within a fiscal year is undoubtedly motivated to do something about it. Some

THE REAL WORLD 18.1

McDonald's Europe: A Greener Way to the Bank

Corporate social responsibility is a growing concern in business. More and more investors choose to put their money where their values and ethics lie. Thus, businesses cannot ignore the demands of socially responsible business practices anymore. One unlikely fast food giant has taken a proactive approach to managing such change in the business environment.

McDonald's Europe has started investing in "greener" business practices in order to beat market pressures in Europe. The company buys all of its coffee from the poorest farmers in the world and from farms sanctioned by the Rainforest Alliance, a nonprofit involved in promoting sustainable farming. It also buys most of its beef locally, thus supporting the communities it operates in.

© ADAM BERRY/BLOOMBERG NEWS/LANDOV

An employee takes orders in a McDonald's restaurant in Berlin, Germany. McDonald's Europe has started investing in "greener" business practices in order to beat market pressures in Europe.

Because of health concerns and scares such as mad cow disease, it has introduced more organic products to its menu and only buys meat that is not genetically altered. The boldest move for McDonald's came in the form of its pledge to drastically cut trans fats from its menu offering and making a $7 million gift to the American Heart Association. You might be interested to learn that a large meal of chicken nuggets and French fries in the United States contains almost ten times more trans fats than the same meal in Denmark! McDonald's Europe has committed to matching Denmark's trans fat content by 2008.

Such proactive strategies to addressing change have made McDonald's Europe very profitable, contributing 40 percent to profits at McDonald's worldwide in 2006.

SOURCE: K. Capell, "McDonald's Offers Ethics with Those Fries," *Business Week* (January 9, 2007), http://www.businessweek.com/globalbiz/content/jan2007/gb20070109_958716.htm.

companies react by instituting layoffs and massive cost-cutting programs, whereas others look at the bigger picture, view the loss as symptomatic of an underlying problem, and seek the cause of the problem.

A crisis may also stimulate change in an organization. Strikes or walkouts may lead management to change the wage structure. The resignation of a key decision maker may cause the company to rethink the composition of its management team and its role in the organization. A much-publicized crisis that led to change at Exxon (now ExxonMobil) was the oil spill caused by the *Exxon Valdez* oil tanker. The accident brought about many changes in Exxon's environmental policies.

Changes in employee expectations can also trigger change in organizations. A company that hires a group of young newcomers may find that their expectations are very different from those expressed by older workers. The workforce is more educated than ever before. Although this has its advantages, workers with more education demand more of employers. Today's workers are also concerned with career and family balance issues, such as dependent care. The many sources of workforce diversity hold potential for a host of differing expectations among employees.

Changes in the work climate at an organization can also stimulate change. A workforce that seems lethargic, unmotivated, and dissatisfied must be addressed. These symptoms are common in organizations that have experienced layoffs. Workers

who have escaped a layoff may grieve for those who have lost their jobs and may find it hard to continue to be productive. They may fear they will be laid off as well.

CHANGE IS INEVITABLE

We have seen that organizations face substantial pressures to change from both external and internal sources. Change in organizations is inevitable, but change is a process that can be managed. The scope of change can vary from small to quantum.

The Scope of Change

(2) Understand *incremental change, strategic change, transformational change,* and *change agent.*

Change can be of a relatively small scope, such as a modification in a work procedure (an *incremental change*). Such changes, in essence, are a fine-tuning of the organization, or the making of small improvements. Intel and other chip producers must continually upgrade their manufacturing equipment just to stay competitive. Intel's new Arizona chip-making plant opened in 2007 and cost $3 billion; it is so large that more than 17 football fields can fit inside it.[25] While radical change is more exciting and interesting to discuss, most research on change has focused on evolutionary (incremental) rather than revolutionary change.[26] Change can also be of a larger scale, such as the restructuring of an organization (a *strategic change*).[27] In strategic change, the organization moves from an old state to a known new state during a controlled period of time. Strategic change usually involves a series of transition steps. AT&T, the granddaddy of long distance companies, made a strategic decision in 2004 to get out of the residential long distance market entirely. When eBay purchased Skype, whose software allows people to make phone calls via the Internet, it departed from its core business, but it opened up huge potential in e-commerce. Only time will tell whether the strategic change paid off. [28]

The most massive scope of change is *transformational change*, in which the organization moves to a radically different, and sometimes unknown, future state.[29] In transformational change, the organization's mission, culture, goals, structure, and leadership may all change dramatically.[30] Just over a century ago, two successful bicycle makers decided to leave the safety of the bike business to devote their time to building and selling an amazing new invention—the airplane. This invention would transform travel, warfare, communications, and indeed the entire world. Of all the tasks a leader undertakes, many say that changing the form and nature of the organization itself may be the most difficult, an observation supported by research.[31]

One of the toughest decisions faced by leaders is the proper "pace" of change. Some scholars argue that rapid change is more likely to succeed, since it creates momentum,[32] while others argue that these short, sharp changes are actually rare and not experienced by most firms.[33] Still others observe that change in a large organization may occur incrementally in parts of the firm and quickly in others.[34] In summary, researchers agree that the pace of change is important, but they can't quite agree on which pace of change is most beneficial.

Very little long-term research has looked at change over a significant time period. One twelve-year study examined change in the structure of Canadian National Sports Organizations (NSOs). It found that within NSOs, radical transition did not always require a fast pace of change. It also found that successful transitions often involve changing the high-impact elements of an organization (in this case, their decision-making structures) early in the process.[35]

incremental change
Change of a relatively small scope, such as making small improvements.

strategic change
Change of a larger scale, such as organizational restructuring.

transformational change
Change in which the organization moves to a radically different, and sometimes unknown, future state.

change agent
The individual or group that undertakes the task of introducing and managing a change in an organization.

The Change Agent's Role

The individual or group that undertakes the task of introducing and managing a change in an organization is known as a *change agent*. Change agents can be internal, such as managers or employees who are appointed to oversee the change process. In her book *The Change Masters*, Rosabeth Moss Kanter notes that at companies like Hewlett-Packard and Polaroid, managers and employees alike are developing the needed skills to produce change and innovation in the organization.[36] Change agents can also be external, such as outside consultants.

Internal change agents have certain advantages in managing the change process. They know the organization's past history, its political system, and its culture. Because they must live with the results of their change efforts, internal change agents are likely to be very careful about managing change. There are disadvantages, however, to using internal change agents. They may be associated with certain factions within the organization and may easily be accused of favoritism. Furthermore, internal change agents may be too close to the situation to have an objective view of what needs to be done.

Change leaders within organizations tend to be young, in the twenty-five to forty age range. They are more flexible than ordinary general managers and much more people oriented. A high number of change leaders are women. The change leaders have a balance of technical and interpersonal skills. They are tough decision makers who focus on performance results. They also know how to energize people and get them aligned in the same direction. They get more out of people than ordinary managers can. In addition, they have the ability to operate in more than one leadership style and can shift from a team mode to command and control, depending on the situation. They are also comfortable with uncertainty.[37]

If change is large scale or strategic in nature, it may take a team of leaders to make change happen. A team assembling leaders with a variety of skills, expertise, and influence that can work together harmoniously may be needed to accomplish change of large scope.[38]

External change agents bring an outsider's objective view to the organization. They may be preferred by employees because of their impartiality. External change agents face certain problems, however; not only is their knowledge of the organization's history limited, but they may also be viewed with suspicion by organization members. External change agents have more power in directing changes if employees perceive the change agents as being trustworthy, possessing important expertise, having a track record that establishes credibility, and being similar to them.[39]

Different change agent competencies are required at different stages of the change process. Leadership, communication, training, and participation have varying levels of impact as the change proceeds, meaning change agents must be flexible in how they work through the different phases of the process.[40] Effective change leaders build strong relationships within their leadership team, between the team and organizational members, and between the team and key environmental players. Maintaining all three relationships simultaneously is quite difficult, so successful leaders are continually "coupling" and "uncoupling" with the different groups as the change process proceeds. Adaptability is a key skill for both internal and external change leaders.[41]

THE PROCESS OF CHANGE IN ORGANIZATIONS

Organizations tend to respond to change by continuing to do what they are good at. After all, these strategies have been successful in the past. After periods of success, organizations can lose the ability to recognize when it is necessary to give up past strategies and try something new. Once an organization has made the decision to change, careful planning and analysis must take place. Change processes such as business process reengineering cannot ensure the success of the change. The people aspects of change are the most critically important for successful transformations.[42]

Even Michael Hammer, who launched the reengineering movement, admits that he forgot about the "human aspects" of change. "I was reflecting on my engineering background and was insufficiently appreciative of the human dimension. I've learned that it's critical."[43] If people are not taken into account, a change process will be negatively affected or may even fail. Like organizations, people tend to cling to what has worked in the past, especially if they have been successful and they see no need for change.[44] One major aspect that change agents need to consider is the altered psychological contracts that employees perceive with their employers after a merger or acquisition. Change agents can typically help people adjust to these corporate culture changes by working with them to enhance their coping abilities.[45]

The challenge of managing the change process involves harnessing the energy of diverse individuals who hold a variety of views of change. It is important to recognize that most changes will be met with varying degrees of resistance and to understand the basis of resistance to change.

Resistance to Change

(3) Evaluate the reasons for resistance to change, and discuss methods organizations can use to manage resistance.

People often resist change in a rational response based on self-interest. However, there are countless other reasons people resist change. Many of these center around the notion of reactance—that is, a negative reaction that occurs when individuals feel that their personal freedom is threatened.[46] Some of the major reasons for resisting change follow.

Fear of the Unknown Change often brings with it substantial uncertainty. Employees facing a technological change, such as the introduction of a new computer system, may resist the change simply because it introduces ambiguity into what was once a comfortable situation for them. This is especially a problem when there has been little communication about the change.

Fear of Loss When a change is impending, some employees may fear losing their jobs; this fear is particularly acute when an advanced technology like robotics is introduced. Employees may also fear losing their status because of a change.[47] Computer systems experts, for example, may feel threatened when they believe their expertise is eroded by the installation of a more user-friendly networked information system. Another common fear is that changes may diminish the positive qualities the individual enjoys in the job. Computerizing the customer service positions at Southwestern Bell (now part of AT&T), for example, threatened the autonomy that representatives previously enjoyed.

Fear of Failure Some employees fear changes because they fear their own failure. Employees may fear that changes will result in increased workloads or increased task difficulty, and they may question their own competencies for handling these. They may also fear that performance expectations will be elevated following the change, and that they may not measure up.[48] Resistance can also stem from a fear that the change itself will not really take place. In one large library that was undergoing a major automation effort, employees were doubtful that the vendor could really deliver the state-of-the-art system that was promised. In this case, the implementation never became a reality—the employees' fears were well founded.[49]

Disruption of Interpersonal Relationships Employees may resist change that threatens to limit meaningful interpersonal relationships on the job. Librarians facing the automation effort described previously feared that once the computerized system was implemented, they would not be able to interact as they did when they had to go to another floor of the library to get help finding a resource. In the new system, with the touch of a few buttons on the computer, they would get their information without consulting another librarian.

Personality Conflicts When the change agent's personality engenders negative reactions, employees may resist the change. A change agent who appears insensitive to employee concerns and feelings may meet considerable resistance, because employees perceive that their needs are not being taken into account.

Politics Organizational change may also shift the existing balance of power in the organization. Individuals or groups who hold power under the current arrangement may be threatened with losing these political advantages in the advent of change.

Cultural Assumptions and Values Sometimes cultural assumptions and values can be impediments to change, particularly if the assumptions underlying the change are alien to employees. Other times, employees might interpret strategic change initiatives from the standpoint of the organization's value system and ideologies of the management team. In fact, research indicates that employees pay attention to the informal sense-making process prevalent in organizations, and hence top-down change initiatives often fail.[50] This form of resistance can be very difficult to overcome, because some cultural assumptions are unconscious. As we discussed in Chapter 2, some cultures tend to avoid uncertainty. In Mexican and Greek cultures, for example, change that creates a great deal of uncertainty may be met with great resistance.

Some individuals are more tolerant of ambiguity than others. You can assess your own attitude toward ambiguity in You 18.1.

We have described several sources of resistance to change. The reasons for resistance are as diverse as the workforce itself and vary with different individuals and organizations. The challenge for managers is introducing change in a positive manner and managing employee resistance.

Managing Resistance to Change

The traditional view of resistance to change treated it as something to be overcome, and many organizational attempts to reduce the resistance have only intensified it. The contemporary view holds that resistance is simply a form of feedback and that this feedback can be used very productively to manage the change process.[51] One key to managing resistance is to plan for it and to be ready with a variety of strategies for using the resistance as feedback and helping employees negotiate the transition. Three key strategies for managing resistance to change are communication, participation, and empathy and support.[52]

Communication about impending change is essential if employees are to adjust effectively.[53] The details of the change should be provided, but equally important is the rationale behind the change. Employees want to know why change is needed. If there is no good reason for it, why should they favor the change? Providing accurate and timely information about the change can help prevent unfounded fears and potentially damaging rumors from developing. Delaying the announcement of a change and handling information in a secretive fashion can fuel the rumor mill. Open communication in a culture of trust is a key ingredient for successful change.[54] It is also beneficial to inform people about the potential consequences of the change. Managers should pay attention to the informal communication networks in an organization because they can serve as power channels of disseminating change-related information.[55] Educating employees on new work procedures is often helpful. In addition, mentors and mentees both derive benefits from going through the process

Tolerance for Ambiguity

Tolerance for Ambiguity Survey Form

Read each of the following statements carefully. Then rate each of them in terms of the extent to which you either agree or disagree with the statement using the following scale:

Completely Disagree			Neither Agree nor Disagree			Completely Agree
1	2	3	4	5	6	7

Place the number that best describes your degree of agreement or disagreement in the blank to the left of each statement.

____ 1. An expert who doesn't come up with a definite answer probably doesn't know much.

____ 2. I would like to live in a foreign country for a while.

____ 3. The sooner we all acquire similar values and ideals, the better.

____ 4. A good teacher is one who makes you wonder about your way of looking at things.

____ 5. I like parties where I know most of the people more than ones where all or most of the people are complete strangers.

____ 6. Teachers or supervisors who hand out vague assignments give a chance for one to show initiative and originality.

____ 7. A person who leads an even, regular life in which few surprises or unexpected happenings arise really has a lot to be grateful for.

____ 8. Many of our most important decisions are based upon insufficient information.

____ 9. There is really no such thing as a problem that can't be solved.

____ 10. People who fit their lives to a schedule probably miss most of the joy of living.

____ 11. A good job is one where what is to be done and how it is to be done are always clear.

____ 12. It is more fun to tackle a complicated problem than to solve a simple one.

____ 13. In the long run, it is possible to get more done by tackling small, simple problems rather than large and complicated ones.

____ 14. Often the most interesting and stimulating people are those who don't mind being different and original.

____ 15. What we are used to is always preferable to what is unfamiliar.

Scoring: For even-numbered questions, add the total points.
For odd-numbered questions, use reverse scoring and add the total points.
Your score is the total of the even- and odd-numbered questions.

Norms Using the Tolerance for Ambiguity Scale

SOURCE: The Tolerance for Ambiguity Scale

Basis: The survey asks 15 questions about personal and work-oriented situations with ambiguity. You were asked to rate each situation on a scale from one (tolerant) to seven (intolerant). (Alternating questions have the response scale reversed.) The index scores the items. A perfectly tolerant person would score 15 and a perfectly intolerant person 105. Scores between 20 and 80 are reported, with means of 45. The responses to the even-numbered questions with 7 minus the score are added to the response for the odd-numbered questions.

(continued)

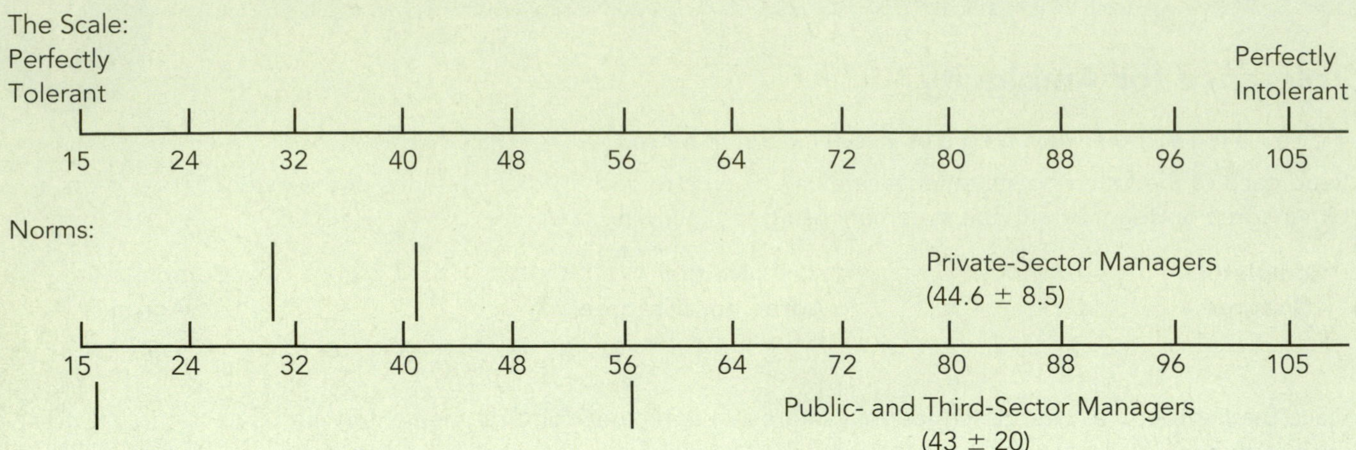

SOURCE: "Tolerance for Ambiguity" from D. Marcic, *Organizational Behavior: Experiences and Cases* (St. Paul, Minn.: West Publishing, 1992), 339–340. Adapted from Paul Nutt. Used with permission.

of organizational change together. Mentees are assisted by mentors who help them make sense of the change, and mentors experience satisfaction in having helped the mentee through the change process.[56] Studies on the introduction of computers in the workplace indicate that providing employees with opportunities for hands-on practice helps alleviate fears about the new technology. Employees who have experience with computers display more positive attitudes and greater efficacy—a sense that they can master their new tasks.[57] Another key ingredient that can help employees adjust to change is a supervisor they can trust. When employees trust their supervisors, it serves as a social support mechanism, making them more committed to the organization even if they feel they can't control the change process.[58]

There is substantial research support underscoring the importance of participation in the change process. Employees must be engaged and involved in order for change to work—as evidenced by the notion "That which we create, we support." Participation helps employees become involved in the change and establish a feeling of ownership in the process. Mergers and Acquisitions (M&A) are widely prevalent in the current business environment. In the Science feature, discover how employees' psychological contracts with their employers are altered after such an M&A. When employees are allowed to participate, they are more committed to the change.

Designer retailer Prada, famous for its extravagant clothing, decided to create an equally remarkable retail location. The company opened perhaps the world's most sophisticated boutique in New York City, spending one-fourth of its IT budget on the experiment. Wireless networks linked each item in inventory to a single database, allowing staff to walk the floor armed with wireless PDAs to check inventory. Automated dressing rooms with touchscreens offered additional information to customers. But within three years, most of the technology sat abandoned, some of it malfunctioning, some of it simply too difficult to use. Like many firms before it, Prada appears to have fallen in love with the idea of going high tech without bothering to get the actual users (its employees) onboard.[59] Prada fell victim to the utopian idea of going high tech without doing a due diligence reality check—convincing employees to buy into the idea.

Another strategy for managing resistance is providing empathy and support to employees who have trouble dealing with the change. Active listening is an excellent tool for identifying the reasons behind resistance and for uncovering fears. An expression of concerns about the change can provide important feedback that managers can use

Psychological Contract Volations after a Merger and Acquisition in Greece

Mergers and acquisitions (M&As) represent major changes in an organization. Employees fear mergers or acquisitions because they worry about the security of their jobs, changes in culture, breaches of their psychological contract with the current employer, and changes in working conditions. A psychological contract is an employee's expectation that the organization will behave in certain ways both at the present time and in the future.

Companies undertake M&As in order to grow or enter new product markets, or simply to cut costs. Yet close to 50 percent of all mergers fail, and the numbers keep rising.

Researchers suspected that a major contributor to M&A failures is lack of employee buy-in and commitment to the change. Research conducted among 255 employees across a variety of industries in Greece (who had all gone through a merger or acquisition) found that employees perceive breaches of psychological contracts in M&As because they feel that the post-merger organization will not fulfill its obligations and provide job security in the same way the pre-merger organization did. Employees perceived that one party to the contract (the employer) changed without the explicit approval of the other party. Thus, it is important to involve employees in the process and decision making during M&As. Another conclusion of this study was that post-merger organizations should communicate with employees in detail about their future with the company and iron out expectations of both parties. This means working out a new psychological contract, which would build acceptance rather than engender resistance to a major organizational change.

SOURCE: V. Bellou, "Psychological Contract Assessment after a Major Organizational Change: The Case of Mergers and Acquisitions," *Employee Relations* 29 (2007): 68–88.

to improve the change process. Emotional support and encouragement can help an employee deal with the anxiety that is a natural response to change. Employees who experience severe reactions to change can benefit from talking with a counselor. Some companies provide counseling through their employee assistance plans.

Open communication, participation, and emotional support can go a long way toward managing resistance to change. Managers must realize that some resistance is inevitable, however, and should plan ways to deal with it early in the change process.

The Hartford Financial Services Group encountered resistance to change in going global. When the company attempted to enter the lucrative British and Dutch insurance markets by acquiring British and Dutch companies, the overseas staff resisted changes suggested by Hartford, such as using laptops and introducing new financial products. The introduction of such U.S. business practices is often referred to as "economic imperialism" by employees who feel they are being forced to substitute corporate values for personal or national values.

Hartford needed its European staff to understand that they were part of a transnational company. Its solution was to offer a stock ownership plan that tied the personal fortunes of the staff to the company. This gave employees a considerable interest in Hartford's success and helped them identify with the company.[60]

Behavioral Reactions to Change

In spite of attempts to minimize the resistance to change in an organization, some reactions to change are inevitable. Negative reactions may be manifested in overt behavior or through more passive resistance to change. People show four basic, identifiable reactions to change: disengagement, disidentification, disenchantment, and disorientation.[61] Managers can use interventions to deal with these reactions, as shown in Table 18.1.

TABLE 18.1 Reactions to Change and Managerial Interventions

Reaction	Expression	Managerial Intervention
Disengagement	Withdrawal	Confront, identify
Disidentification	Sadness, worry	Explore, transfer
Disenchantment	Anger	Neutralize, acknowledge
Disorientation	Confusion	Explain, plan

SOURCE: Table adapted from H. Woodward and S. Buchholz, *Aftershock: Helping People through Corporate Change*, p. 15. Copyright © 1987 John Wiley & Sons, Inc. Reprinted by permission of John Wiley & Sons, Inc.

Disengagement is psychological withdrawal from change. The employee may appear to lose initiative and interest in the job. Employees who disengage may fear the change but approach it by doing nothing and simply hoping for the best. Disengaged employees are physically present but mentally absent. They lack drive and commitment, and they simply comply without real psychological investment in their work. Disengagement can be recognized by behaviors such as being hard to find or doing only the basics to get the job done. Typical disengagement statements include "No problem" or "This won't affect me."

One oil and gas company that started ventures in Russia found that the very idea of change was alien to Russian managers. These managers felt that their task was to establish procedures and ensure continuity. When Western managers tried to institute change, the Russian managers disengaged, believing that their job was to secure stability rather than change.[62]

The basic managerial strategy for dealing with disengaged individuals is to confront them with their reaction and draw them out so that they can identify the concerns that need to be addressed. Disengaged employees may not be aware of the change in their behavior, and they need to be assured of your intentions. Drawing them out and helping them air their feelings can lead to productive discussions. Disengaged people seldom become cheerleaders for the change, but they can be brought closer to accepting and working with a change by open communication with an empathetic manager who is willing to listen.

Another reaction to change is *disidentification*. Individuals reacting in this way feel that their identity has been threatened by the change, and they feel very vulnerable. Many times they cling to a past procedure because they had a sense of mastery over it, and it gave them a sense of security. "My job is completely changed" and "I used to . . ." are verbal indications of disidentification. Disidentified employees often display sadness and worry. They may appear to be sulking and dwelling on the past by reminiscing about the old ways of doing things.

Because disidentified employees are so vulnerable, they often feel like victims in the change process. Managers can help them through the transition by encouraging them to explore their feelings and helping them transfer their positive feelings into the new situation. One way to do this is to help them identify what they liked in the old situation and then show them how it is possible to have the same positive experience in the new situation. Disidentified employees need to see that work itself and emotion are separable—that is, that they can let go of old ways and experience positive reactions to new ways of performing their jobs.

Disenchantment is also a common reaction to change. It is usually expressed as negativity or anger. Disenchanted employees realize that the past is gone, and they are mad about it. They may try to enlist the support of other employees by forming coalitions. Destructive behaviors like sabotage and backstabbing may result. Typical verbal signs of disenchantment are "This will never work" and "I'm getting out of this company as soon as I can." The anger of a disenchanted person may be

disengagement
Psychological withdrawal from change.

disidentification
Feeling that one's identity is being threatened by a change.

disenchantment
Feeling negativity or anger toward a change.

directly expressed in organizational cultures where it is permissible to do so. This behavior tends to get the issues out in the open. More often, however, cultures view the expression of emotion at work as improper and unbusinesslike. In these cultures, the anger is suppressed and emerges in more passive-aggressive ways, such as badmouthing and starting rumors. One of the particular dangers of disenchantment is that it is quite contagious in the workplace. Managers should try to bring the employee to a more neutral emotion state and acknowledge that her or his anger is valid.

It is often difficult to reason with disenchanted employees. Thus, the first step in managing this reaction is to bring these employees from their highly negative, emotionally charged state to a more neutral state. To neutralize the reaction does not mean to dismiss it; rather, it means to allow the individuals to let off the necessary steam so that they can come to terms with their anger. The second part of the strategy for dealing with disenchanted employees is to acknowledge that their anger is normal and that you do not hold it against them. Sometimes disenchantment is a mask for one of the other three reactions, and it must be worked through to get to the core of the employee's reaction. Employees may also become cynical about change and lose faith in the leaders of change.

A final reaction to change is *disorientation*. Disoriented employees are lost and confused, and often unsure of their feelings. They waste energy trying to figure out what to do instead of how to do things. Disoriented individuals ask a lot of questions and become very detail oriented. They may appear to need a good deal of guidance and may leave their work undone until all of their questions have been answered. "Analysis paralysis" is characteristic of disoriented employees. They feel that they have lost touch with the priorities of the company, and they may want to analyze the change to death before acting on it. Disoriented employees may ask questions like "Now what do I do?" or "What do I do first?"

Disorientation is a common reaction among people who are used to clear goals and unambiguous directions. When change is introduced, it creates uncertainty and a lack of clarity. The managerial strategy for dealing with this reaction is to explain the change in a way that minimizes the ambiguity that is present. The information about the change needs to be put into a framework or an overall vision so that the disoriented individual can see where he or she fits into the grand scheme of things.[63] Once the disoriented employee sees the broader context of the change, you can plan a series of steps to help him or her adjust. The employee needs a sense of priorities to work on.

Managers need to be able to diagnose these four reactions to change. Because each reaction brings with it significant and different concerns, no single universal strategy can help all employees adjust. By recognizing each reaction and applying the appropriate strategy, it is possible to help even strong resisters work through a transition successfully.

Lewin's Change Model

Kurt Lewin developed a model of the change process that has stood the test of time and continues to influence the way organizations manage planned change. Lewin's model is based on the idea of force field analysis.[64] Figure 18.1 shows a force field analysis of a decision to engage in exercise behavior.

(4) Apply force field analysis to a problem.

This model contends that a person's behavior is the product of two opposing forces; one force pushes toward preserving the status quo, and the other force pushes for change. When the two opposing forces are approximately equal, current behavior is maintained. For behavioral change to occur, the forces maintaining the status quo must be overcome. This can be accomplished by increasing the

disorientation

Feelings of loss and confusion due to a change.

FIGURE 18.1 Force Field Analysis of a Decision to Engage in Exercise

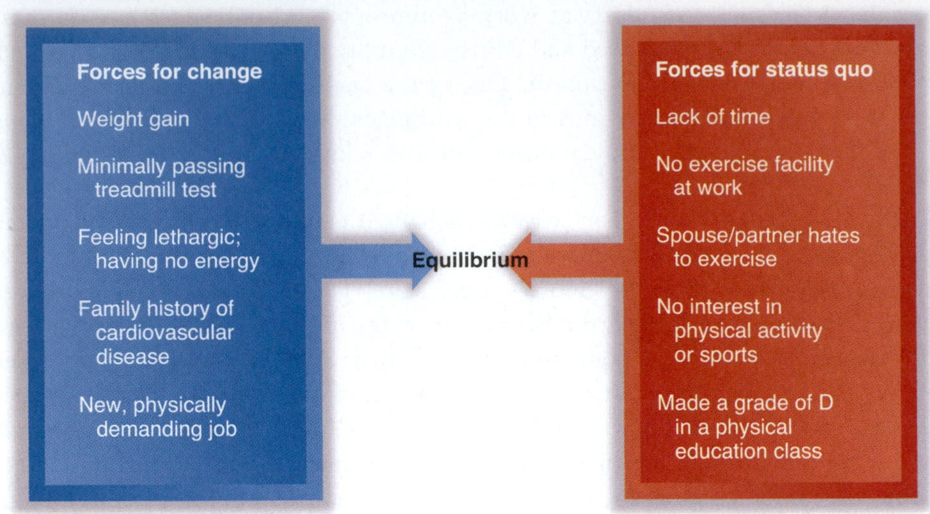

forces for change, by weakening the forces for the status quo, or by a combination of these actions. You 18.2 asks you to apply force field analysis to a problem in your life.

(5) Explain Lewin's organizational change model.

Lewin's change model is a three-step process, as shown in Figure 18.2. The process begins with *unfreezing*, which is a crucial first hurdle in the change process. Unfreezing involves encouraging individuals to discard old behaviors by shaking up the equilibrium state that maintains the status quo. Change management literature has long advocated that certain individuals have personalities that make them more resistant to change. However, recent research indicates that only a small portion of a study's respondents (23 percent) displayed consistency in their reactions to three different kinds of change: structural, technological, and office relocation. The majority of respondents (77 percent) reacted differently to these various kinds of change, suggesting that reactions to change might be more situationally driven than was previously thought.[65] Organizations often accomplish unfreezing by eliminating the rewards for current behavior and showing that current behavior is not valued. By unfreezing, individuals accept that change needs to occur. In essence, individuals surrender by allowing the boundaries of their status quo to be opened in preparation for change.[66]

The second step in the change process is *moving*. In the moving stage, new attitudes, values, and behaviors are substituted for old ones. Organizations accomplish moving by initiating new options and explaining the rationale for the change, as well as by providing training to help employees develop the new skills they need. Employees should be given the overarching vision for the change so that they can establish their roles within the new organizational structure and processes.[67]

unfreezing
The first step in Lewin's change model, in which individuals are encouraged to discard old behaviors by shaking up the equilibrium state that maintains the status quo.

moving
The second step in Lewin's change model, in which new attitudes, values, and behaviors are substituted for old ones.

FIGURE 18.2 Lewin's Change Model

Unfreezing	Moving	Refreezing
Reducing forces for status quo	Developing new attitudes, values, and behaviors	Reinforcing new attitudes, values, and behaviors

YOU 18.2

Applying Force Field Analysis

Think of a problem you are currently facing. An example would be trying to increase the amount of study time you devote to a particular class.

1. Describe the problem, as specifically as possible.
2. List the forces driving change on the arrows at the left side of the diagram.
3. List the forces restraining change on the arrows at the right side of the diagram.
4. What can you do, specifically, to remove the obstacles to change?
5. What can you do to increase the forces driving change?
6. What benefits can be derived from breaking a problem down into forces driving change and forces restraining change?

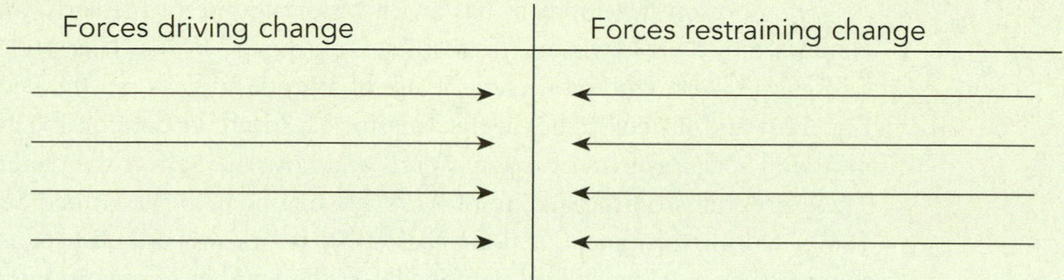

Refreezing is the final step in the change process. In this step, new attitudes, values, and behaviors are established as the new status quo. The new ways of operating are cemented in and reinforced. Managers should ensure that the organizational culture and formal reward systems encourage the new behaviors and avoid rewarding the old ways of operating. Changes in the reward structure may be needed to ensure that the organization is not rewarding the old behaviors and merely hoping for the new behaviors. A study by Exxon Research and Engineering showed that framing and displaying a mission statement in managers' offices may eventually change the behavior of 2 percent of the managers. In contrast, changing managers' evaluation and reward systems will change the behavior of 55 percent of the managers almost overnight.[68]

The approach used by Monsanto to increase opportunities for women within the company is an illustration of how to use Lewin's model effectively. First, Monsanto emphasized unfreezing by helping employees debunk negative stereotypes about women in business. This also helped overcome resistance to change. Second, Monsanto moved employees' attitudes and behaviors by diversity training in which differences were emphasized as positive, and supervisors learned ways of training and developing female employees. Third, Monsanto changed its reward system so that managers were evaluated and paid according to how they coached and promoted women, which helped refreeze the new attitudes and behaviors.

One frequently overlooked issue is whether or not the change is consistent with the company's deeply held core values. Value consistency is critical to making a change "stick." Organizations whose members perceive the changes to be consistent with the firm's values adopt the changes much more easily and fully. Conversely, organizations whose members' values conflict with the changes may display "superficial conformity," in which members pay lip service to the changes but ultimately revert to their old behaviors.[69]

Organizations that wish to change can select from a variety of methods to make a change become reality. Organization development is a method that consists of various programs for making organizations more effective.

refreezing
The final step in Lewin's change model, in which new attitudes, values, and behaviors are established as the new status quo.

ORGANIZATION DEVELOPMENT INTERVENTIONS

Organization development (OD) is a systematic approach to organizational improvement that applies behavioral science theory and research in order to increase individual and organizational well-being and effectiveness.[70] This definition implies certain characteristics. First, OD is a systematic approach to planned change. It is a structured cycle of diagnosing organizational problems and opportunities and then applying expertise to them. Second, OD is grounded in solid research and theory. It involves the application of our knowledge of behavioral science to the challenges that organizations face. Third, OD recognizes the reciprocal relationship between individuals and organizations. It acknowledges that for organizations to change, individuals must change. Finally, OD is goal oriented. It is a process that seeks to improve both individual and organizational well-being and effectiveness.

Organization development has a rich history. Some of the early work in OD was conducted by Kurt Lewin and his associates during the 1940s. This work was continued by Rensis Likert, who pioneered the use of attitude surveys in OD. During the 1950s, Eric Trist and his colleagues at the Tavistock Institute in London focused on the technical and social aspects of organizations and how they affect the quality of work life. These programs on the quality of work life migrated to the United States during the 1960s. During this time, a 200-member OD network was established, and it has grown to more than 4,100 members worldwide. As the number of practitioners has increased, so has the number of different OD methods. One compendium of organizational change methods estimates that more than 300 different methods have been used.[71]

Organization development is also being used internationally. OD has been applied in Canada, Sweden, Norway, Germany, Japan, Australia, Israel, and Mexico, among others. Some OD methods are difficult to implement in other cultures. As OD becomes more internationally widespread, we will increase our knowledge of how culture affects the success of different OD approaches.

organization development (OD)
A systematic approach to organizational improvement that applies behavioral science theory and research in order to increase individual and organizational well-being and effectiveness.

Prior to deciding on a method of intervention, managers must carefully diagnose the problem they are attempting to address. Diagnosis and needs analysis is a critical first step in any OD intervention. Following this, an intervention method is chosen and applied. Finally, a thorough follow-up of the OD process is conducted. Figure 18.3 presents the OD cycle, a continuous process of moving the organization and its employees toward effective functioning.

6 Describe the use of organizational diagnosis and needs analysis as a first step in organizational development.

Diagnosis and Needs Analysis

Before any intervention is planned, a thorough organizational diagnosis should be conducted. Diagnosis is an essential first step for any organization development

FIGURE 18.3 The Organization Development Cycle

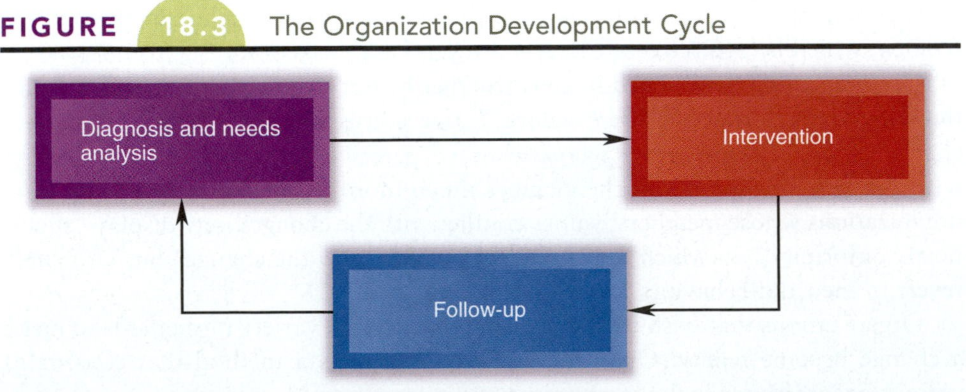

intervention.[72] The term *diagnosis* comes from *dia* (through) and *gnosis* (knowledge of). Thus, the diagnosis should pinpoint specific problems and areas in need of improvement. Problems can arise in any part of the organization. Six areas to examine carefully are the organization's purpose, structure, reward system, support systems, relationships, and leadership.[73]

Harry Levinson's diagnostic approach asserts that the process should begin by identifying where the pain (the problem) in the organization is, what it is like, how long it has been happening, and what has already been done about it.[74] Then a four-part, comprehensive diagnosis can begin. The first part of the diagnosis involves achieving an understanding of the organization's history. In the second part, the organization as a whole is analyzed to obtain data about its structure and processes. In the third part, interpretive data about attitudes, relationships, and current organizational functioning are gathered. In the fourth part of the diagnosis, the data are analyzed and conclusions are reached. In each stage of the diagnosis, the data can be gathered using a variety of methods, including observation, interviews, questionnaires, and archival records.

The diagnostic process may yield the conclusion that change is necessary. As part of the diagnosis, it is important to address the following issues:

- What are the forces for change?
- What are the forces preserving the status quo?
- What are the most likely sources of resistance to change?
- What are the goals to be accomplished by the change?

This information constitutes a force field analysis, as discussed earlier in the chapter.

A needs analysis is another crucial step in managing change. This is an analysis of the skills and competencies that employees must have to achieve the goals of the change. A needs analysis is essential because interventions such as training programs must target these skills and competencies.

Hundreds of alternative OD intervention methods exist. One way of classifying these methods is by the target of change. The target of change may be the organization, groups within the organization, or individuals.

Organization- and Group-Focused Techniques

Some OD intervention methods emphasize changing the organization itself or changing the work groups within the organization. Intervention methods in this category include survey feedback, management by objectives, product and service quality programs, team building, and process consultation.

(7) Discuss the major organization development interventions.

Survey Feedback *Survey feedback* is a widely used intervention method whereby employee attitudes are solicited using a questionnaire. Once the data are collected, they are analyzed and fed back to the employees to diagnose problems and plan other interventions. Survey feedback is often used as an exploratory tool and then is combined with some other intervention. The effectiveness of survey feedback in actually improving outcomes (absenteeism or productivity, for example) increases substantially when this method is combined with other interventions.[75] The effectiveness of this technique is contingent on trust between management and subordinates, and this can be reinforced through the anonymity and confidentiality of survey responses.

For survey feedback to be an effective method, certain guidelines should be used. Unless the assurance of confidentiality and anonymity is given, employee responses may not be honest. Feedback should be reported in a group format; that is, no individual responses should be identified. Employees must be able to trust that there

survey feedback
A widely used method of intervention whereby employee attitudes are solicited using a questionnaire.

will be no negative repercussions from their responses. They should be informed of the purpose of the survey. Failing to do this can set up unrealistic expectations about the changes that might come from the surveys. One recent study found that the personality characteristic *change-specific self-efficacy,* which reflects an individual's belief that she or he can successfully cope with change, had a positive impact on employees' attitudes toward and commitment to change. Thus, managers could help build employee change efficacy by presenting them with smaller changes and helping them succeed. Providing positive feedback and rewarding efforts directed at coping with change can further build change self-efficacy. In addition, role-playing related to managing change, mentoring, and coaching can also help build change self-efficacy. Leaders might focus on developing this trait among employees while implementing major changes.[76]

In addition, management must be prepared to follow up on the survey results. If some things cannot be changed, the rationale (for example, prohibitive cost) must be explained to employees. Without appropriate follow-through, employees will not take the survey process seriously the next time.

Management by Objectives As an organization-wide technique, *management by objectives (MBO)* involves joint goal setting between employees and managers. The MBO process includes the setting of initial objectives, periodic progress reviews, and problem solving to remove any obstacles to goal achievement.[77] All these steps are joint efforts between managers and employees.

MBO is a valuable intervention because it meets three needs. First, it clarifies what is expected of employees. This reduces role conflict and ambiguity. Second, MBO provides knowledge of results, an essential ingredient in effective job performance. Finally, MBO provides an opportunity for coaching and counseling by the manager. The problem-solving approach encourages open communication and discussion of obstacles to goal achievement.[78]

Companies that have used MBO successfully include the former Tenneco, Mobil (now part of ExxonMobil), and General Electric. The success of MBO in effecting organizational results hinges on the linking of individual goals to the goals of the organization.[79] MBO programs should be used with caution, however. An excessive emphasis on goal achievement can result in cutthroat competition among employees, falsification of results, and striving for results at any cost. In The Real World 18.2, we profile the woes of Wal-Mart and how its nonadaptive business strategy might be getting the retail giant in trouble. Moreover, it highlights the perils of centralized decision making that ignores knowledge distributed at lower levels in the organization.

Product and Service Quality Programs *Quality programs*—programs that embed product and service quality excellence in the organizational culture—are assuming key roles in the organization development efforts of many companies. For example, the success or failure of a service company may depend on the quality of customer service it provides.[80]

The Ritz-Carlton Hotel Company (now part of Marriott International) integrated its comprehensive service quality program into marketing and business objectives. The Atlanta-based company, which managed twenty-eight luxury hotels, won the Malcolm Baldrige Award for service quality. Key elements of Ritz-Carlton's quality program included participatory executive leadership, thorough information gathering, coordinated execution, and employees who were empowered to "move heaven and earth" to satisfy customers.[81]

At Ritz-Carlton, the company president and thirteen senior executives made up the senior quality management team, which met weekly to focus on service

management by objectives (MBO)
An organization-wide intervention technique that involves joint goal setting between employees and managers.

quality program
A program that embeds product and service quality excellence in the organizational culture.

THE REAL WORLD 18.2

Wal-Mart: Price Cuts Might Not Always Be the Answer

In an increasingly competitive retail market, Wal-Mart has been struggling to identify itself beyond being a low-price alternative. In fact, the company recently reported the worst performance in its business history and falling share prices. In response to these performance concerns, Wal-Mart CEO H. Lee Scott made some striking changes to its strategy. One such initiative was to enter a higher-end retail market by offering more upscale goods in contrast to its usual strategy of being entirely cost focused. However, this strategy seems to have thus far hurt the corporate giant more than helping it.

Some analysts believe Scott should use the knowledge dispersed among Wal-Mart's store managers to get it right. The centralized decision-making system at the company uses computers to make decisions on product availability. Sometimes the computer system goes against the judgment of local store managers, and they claim it hurts their business. For example, Wal-Mart is slowly trying to eliminate baked goods like doughnuts because they have low returns and high costs to sell. However, store managers claim this hurts business because doughnuts get customers inside a Wal-Mart and while there, they make other, unplanned purchases. There are several such short-term decisions that have seriously hurt the business. Another change opposed by store managers is Wal-Mart's decision to transform its workforce to 40 percent part-timers in an effort to save money. Managers believe that this seriously hurts the day-to-day operations and service provided to customers.

So the Wal-Mart saga continues. Thus far, it's a lesson in listening to employees and making sure they participate in the change process if a change in strategy is to succeed.

SOURCE: P. Gogoi, "How to Fix Wal-Mart? Ask Its Managers," *Business Week* (August 21, 2007), http://www.businessweek.com/bwdaily/dnflash/content/aug2007/db20070820_358861.htm

quality. Quality goals were established at all levels of the company. The crucial product and service requirements of travel consumers were translated into Ritz-Carlton Gold Standards, which included a credo, a motto, three steps of service, and twenty Ritz-Carlton Basics. These standards guided service quality throughout the organization.

Employees were required to act on a customer complaint at once and were empowered to provide "instant pacification," no matter what it took. Quality teams set action plans at all levels of the company. Each hotel had a quality leader, who served as a resource to the quality teams. Daily quality production reports provided an early warning system for identifying areas that needed quality improvement.

After celebrating an award as the best hotel in the world, Ritz-Carlton did not stop its quality improvement process. At one hotel, the chief complaint was that room service was always late. A quality team was put together, including a cook, a waiter, and a room service order taker. They studied how the process flowed. When they discovered that the service elevator was slow, they added an engineer and a representative from the elevator company to the team. They found that the elevators worked fine. Next, they posted a team member in the elevator twenty-four hours a day for a week. Every time the door opened, the team member had to find out why. Finally, a team member noticed that housemen who helped the maids got on the elevator a lot. It turned out that the housemen were taking towels from other floors because their maids needed more. The problem with room service was that the hotel didn't own enough towels. Ritz-Carlton bought more towels, and room service complaints fell 50 percent.[82] Toyota Motor Corporation, like Ritz-Carlton, constantly finds ways to integrate cutting-edge technological innovations with the growing pains of global expansion. The famed "Toyota Way" of doing business is based on two key principles: continuous improvement focused on innovation and respect for people.[83]

Team Building *Team building* programs can improve the effectiveness of work groups. Team building usually begins with a diagnostic process through which team members identify problems, and it continues with the team's planning actions to take in order to resolve those problems. The OD practitioner in team building serves as a facilitator, and the work itself is completed by team members.[84]

Team building is a very popular OD method. A survey of *Fortune* 500 companies indicated that human resource managers considered team building the most successful OD technique.[85] Managers are particularly interested in building teams that can learn. To build learning teams, members must be encouraged to seek feedback, discuss errors, reflect on successes and failures, and experiment with new ways of performing. Mistakes should be analyzed for ways to improve, and a climate of mutual support should be developed. Leaders of learning teams are good coaches who promote a climate of psychological safety so that team members feel comfortable discussing problems.[86]

One popular technique for team building is the use of outdoor challenges. Participants go through a series of outdoor activities, such as climbing a fourteen-foot wall. Similar physical challenges require the participants to work as a team and focus on trust, communication, decision making, and leadership. GE and Weyerhaeuser use outdoor challenges at the beginning of their team-building courses, and later in the training, team members apply what they have learned to actual business situations.[87] Now that adventure courses, paintball, and even high-powered go-karting have become common corporate training exercises, what's the next big thing? One innovative firm called Teambuilding Inc. uses rowing as team-building exercise. It enlisted the services of an Olympic gold medalist, Dan Lyons, to design a seminar focused on team building using rowing as the central organizing theme. This activity encourages participants to practice leadership, communication, goal setting, conflict management, and motivation. GE Healthcare, ING Direct, and Wyeth Corporate Communications have all used this technique for their team-building programs.[88, 89] Preliminary studies indicate that team building can improve group processes.[90]

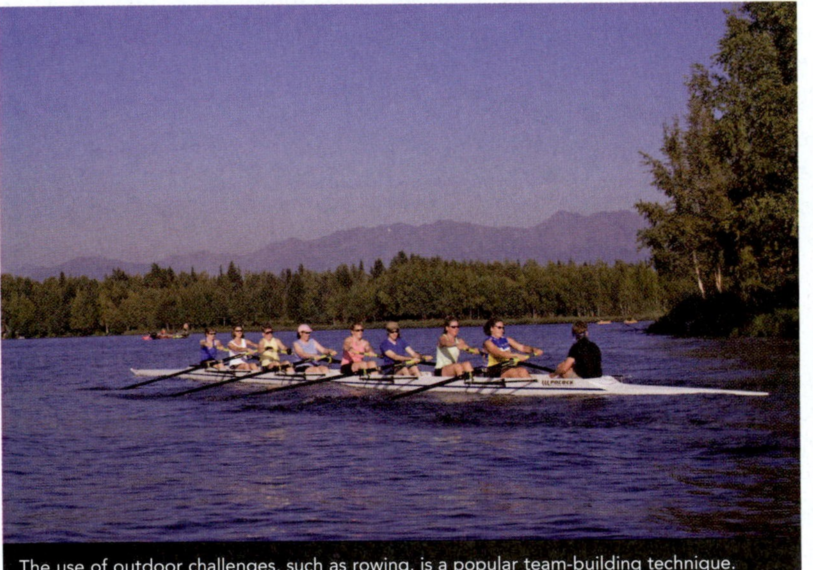
The use of outdoor challenges, such as rowing, is a popular team-building technique.

© JIM R. KOHL/PHOTOLIBRARY

Process Consultation Pioneered by Edgar Schein, *process consultation* is an OD method that helps managers and employees improve the processes that are used in organizations.[91] The processes most often targeted are communication, conflict resolution, decision making, group interaction, and leadership.

One of the distinguishing features of the process consultation approach is that an outside consultant is used. The role of the consultant is to help employees help themselves. In this way, the ownership of a successful outcome rests with the employees.[92] The consultant guides the organization members in examining the processes in the organization and in refining them. The steps in process consultation are entering the organization, defining the relationship, choosing an approach, gathering data and diagnosing problems, intervening, and gradually leaving the organization.

Process consultation is an interactive technique between employees and an outside consultant, so it is seldom used as a sole OD method. Most often, it is used in combination with other OD interventions.

team building
An intervention designed to improve the effectiveness of a work group.

process consultation
An OD method that helps managers and employees improve the processes that are used in organizations.

All the preceding OD methods focus on changing the organization or the work group. Other OD methods are aimed at facilitating change within individuals.

Individual-Focused Techniques

Organization development efforts that are targeted toward individuals include skills training, leadership training and development, executive coaching, role negotiation, job redesign, health promotion programs, and career planning.

Skills Training The key question addressed by *skills training* is "What knowledge, skills, and abilities are necessary to do this job effectively?" Skills training is accomplished either in formal classroom settings or on the job. The challenge of integrating skills training into organization development is the rapid change that most organizations face. The job knowledge in most positions requires continual updates to keep pace with rapid change.

FedEx depends on more than 218,000 full- and part-time employees in 215 countries to deliver 100 percent customer satisfaction. The company is constantly changing its products and services, sometimes at the rate of 1,700 changes per year. FedEx decided to accomplish its mission using Web-based training and job skills testing. Employees find the training easy to use, convenient, and individualized. FedEx has found it to be economical as well because it eliminates travel expenses and the need for instructors. In job skills testing, every customer service employee takes a test every six months via computer. The test generates a unique prescription that informs employees what they do well and how they need to improve. It also directs employees to the interactive video lesson they need to practice to improve their skills.[93]

Leadership Training and Development Companies invest millions of dollars in *leadership training and development*, a term that encompasses a variety of techniques designed to enhance individuals' leadership skills. One popular technique is sending future leaders to off-site training classes. Research shows that this type of education experience can have some impact, but participants' enthusiastic return to work may be short-lived due to the challenges and realities of work life. Classroom learning alone thus has a limited effect on leadership skills.

The best leadership training and development programs combine classroom learning with on-the-job experiences. One way of accomplishing development is through the use of action learning, a technique that was pioneered in Europe.[94] In action learning, leaders take on unfamiliar problems or familiar problems in unfamiliar settings. The leaders work on the problems and meet weekly in small groups made up of individuals from different organizations. The outcome of action learning is that leaders learn about themselves through the challenges of their comrades. Other techniques that provide active learning for participants are simulation, business games, role-playing, and case studies.[95]

Eli Lilly has an action learning program that pulls together eighteen future company leaders and gives them a strategic business issue to resolve. For six weeks, the trainees meet with experts, best-practices organizations, and customers and then present their recommendations to top brass. One action learning team was charged with coming up with an e-business strategy; their plan was so good that executives immediately implemented it. At Eli Lilly and other firms, action learning programs provide developmental experiences for leaders and result in useful initiatives for the company.[96]

Leadership training and development is an ongoing process that takes considerable time and effort. There are no quick fixes. At IBM, managers are strongly

skills training
Increasing the job knowledge, skills, and abilities that are necessary to do a job effectively.

leadership training and development
A variety of techniques that are designed to enhance individuals' leadership skills.

held accountable for leadership development. In fact, IBM's managers will not be considered for promotion into senior executive positions unless they have a record of developing leaders. Top management must be committed to the process of leadership training and development if they want to create a pipeline of high-potential employees to fill leadership positions.[97]

Executive Coaching *Executive coaching* is a technique in which managers or executives are paired with a coach in a partnership to help the executive perform more effectively at work and, sometimes, even in personal life. Although coaching is usually done in a one-on-one manner, it is sometimes done in groups. The popularity of executive coaching has increased dramatically in recent years. In just two years of existence, the International Coach Federation, a group that trains and accredits executive coaches, doubled its membership, which is now at 7,000 members in thirty-five countries.

Coaching is typically a special investment in top-level managers. Coaches provide another set of eyes and ears and help executives see beyond their own blinders. They elicit solutions and ideas from the client rather than making suggestions; thus, they enhance the talents and capabilities within the client, in addition to developing new ones. Many coaching arrangements focus on developing the emotional intelligence of the client executive and may use a 360-degree assessment in which the executive, his or her boss, peers, subordinates, and even family members rate the executive's emotional competencies.[98, 99] This information is then fed back to the executive, and along with the coach, a development plan is put in place.

Good coaches form strong connections with clients, exhibit professionalism, and deliver forthright, candid feedback. The top reasons executives seek out coaches are to make personal behavior changes, enhance their effectiveness, and foster stronger relationships. Does executive coaching pay off? Evidence suggests that successful coaching can result in sustained changes in executives' behavior, increased self-awareness and understanding, and more effective leadership competencies.[100] In one study, for example, executives who worked with executive coaches were more likely to set specific goals, ask for feedback from their supervisors, and were rated as better performers by their supervisors and subordinates when compared to executives who simply received feedback from surveys.[101] Effective coaching relationships depend on a professional, experienced coach, an executive who is motivated to learn and change, and a good fit between the two.

Role Negotiation Individuals who work together sometimes have differing expectations of one another within the working relationship. *Role negotiation* is a simple technique whereby individuals meet and clarify their psychological contract. In doing this, the expectations of each party are clarified and negotiated. The outcome of role negotiation is a better understanding between the two parties of what each can be expected to give and receive in the reciprocal relationship. When both parties have a mutual agreement on expectations, there is less ambiguity in the process of working together.

Job Redesign As an OD intervention method, *job redesign* emphasizes the fit between individual skills and the demands of the job. Chapter 14 outlined several approaches to job design. Many of these methods are used as OD techniques for realigning task demands and individual capabilities or for redesigning jobs to fit new techniques or organizational structures better.

Ford Motor Company has redesigned virtually all of its manufacturing jobs, shifting workers from individual to team-based roles in which they have greater control of their work and can take the initiative to improve products and production techniques. Ford began trying this technique more than a decade ago and found that it improved

executive coaching
A technique in which managers or executives are paired with a coach in a partnership to help the executive perform more efficiently.

role negotiation
A technique whereby individuals meet and clarify their psychological contract.

job redesign
An OD intervention method that alters jobs to improve the fit between individual skills and the demands of the job.

not only employee job satisfaction but also productivity and product quality.

Another form of job redesign is telecommuting, in which employees perform some or all of their work from home. Companies including American Express, AT&T, and Merrill Lynch have significant numbers of employees who work this way. When AT&T surveyed its managers to assess the impact of telecommuting, 76 percent were happier with their jobs, and 79 percent were happier with their careers in general since they began telecommuting.[102]

© ALYSONG/REUTERS/LANDOV

Ford redesigned virtually of its manufacturing jobs, shifting workers from individual to team-based roles.

Health Promotion Programs As organizations have become increasingly concerned with the costs of distress in the workplace, health promotion programs have become a part of larger organization development efforts. In Chapter 7, we examined stress and strain at work. Companies that have successfully integrated health promotion programs into their organizations include AT&T, Caterpillar, Kimberly-Clark, and Johnson & Johnson.

The American Psychological Association recently began recognizing companies for innovative programs that support psychologically healthy work environments. Winners in 2007 included *El Nuevo Dia* and Green Mountain Coffee Roasters, among others. *El Nuevo Dia* is the most popular newspaper in Puerto Rico and offers its employees no-cost health care benefits, after-work workout programs, and quarterly health publications designed to prevent stress and maintain a healthy lifestyle. Green Mountain Coffee Roasters has in place yoga, meditation, and physical therapy programs to reduce work-related stress and injury. It pays for 90 percent of health care costs of its full-time employees. Furthermore, the company reimburses each employee up to $400 per year for participation in wellness programs, health club memberships, or smoking cessation programs [103]

Although companies have long recognized the importance of maintenance on their machinery, many are only recently learning that their human assets need maintenance as well, in the form of employee wellness and health promotion activities. The components of these programs can include education about stress and coping, relaxation training, company-sponsored exercise, and employee assistance programs. All are focused on helping employees manage their stress and health in a preventive manner.

Career Planning Matching an individual's career aspirations with the opportunities in the organization is *career planning*. This proactive approach to career management is often part of an organization's development efforts. Career planning is a joint responsibility of organizations and individuals. Companies like IBM, Travelers Life & Annuity (part of Citigroup), and 3M have implemented career-planning programs.

Career-planning activities benefit the organization as well as its workers. Through counseling sessions, employees identify their skills and skill deficiencies. The organization then can plan its training and development efforts based on this information. In addition, the process can be used to identify and nurture talented employees for potential promotion.

Managers can choose from a host of organization development techniques to facilitate organizational change. Some of these techniques are aimed toward organizations or groups, and others focus on individuals. Large-scale changes in organizations require the use of multiple techniques. For example, implementing a new technology like robotics may require simultaneous changes in the structure of the organization, the configuration of work groups, and individual attitudes.

We should recognize at this point that the organization development methods just described are means to an end. Programs do not drive change; business needs do. The OD methods are merely vehicles for moving the organization and its employees in a more effective direction.

ETHICAL CONSIDERATIONS IN ORGANIZATION DEVELOPMENT

(8) Identify the ethical issues that must be considered in organization development efforts.

Organization development is a process of helping organizations improve. It may involve resistance to change, shifts in power, losses of control, and redefinition of tasks.[104] These are all sensitive issues. Further, the change agent, whether a manager from within the organization or a consultant from outside, is in a position of directing the change. Such a position carries the potential for misuse of power. The ethical concerns surrounding the use of organization development center around four issues.[105]

The first issue is the *selection* of the OD method to be used. Every change agent has inherent biases about particular methods, but these biases must not enter into the decision process. The OD method used must be carefully chosen in accordance with the problem as diagnosed, the organization's culture, and the employees concerned. All alternatives should be given fair consideration in the choice of a method. In addition, the OD practitioner should never use a method he or she is not skilled in delivering. Using a method you are not an expert in is unethical, because the client assumes you are.

The second ethical issue is *voluntary participation.* No employee should be forced to participate in any OD intervention.[106] To make an informed decision about participation, employees should be given information about the nature of the intervention and what will be expected of them. They should also be afforded the option to discontinue their participation at any time they choose.

The third issue of ethical concern is *confidentiality.* Change agents gather a wealth of information during organizational diagnoses and interventions. Successful change agents develop a trusting relationship with employees. They may receive privileged information, sometimes unknowingly. It is unethical for a change agent to reveal information in order to give some group or individual political advantage or to enhance the change agent's own standing. Consultants should not reveal information about an organization to its competitors. The use of information gathered from OD efforts is a sensitive issue and presents ethical dilemmas.

A final ethical concern in OD is the potential for *manipulation* by the change agent. Because any change process involves influence, some individuals may feel manipulated. The key to alleviating the potential for manipulation is open communication. Participants should be given complete knowledge of the rationale for change, what they can expect of the change process, and what the intervention will entail. No actions should be taken that limit the participants' freedom of choice.[107]

ARE ORGANIZATION DEVELOPMENT EFFORTS EFFECTIVE?

Because organization development is designed to help organizations manage change, it is important to evaluate the effectiveness of these efforts. The success of any OD intervention depends on a host of factors, including the technique used, the

competence of the change agent, the organization's readiness for change, and top management commitment. No single method of OD is effective in every instance. Instead, multiple-method OD approaches are recommended because they allow organizations to capitalize on the benefits of several approaches.[108]

Evaluations of OD efforts have focused on outcomes such as productivity. One review of more than 200 interventions indicated that worker productivity improved in 87 percent of the cases.[109] A separate analysis of ninety-eight of these interventions revealed impressive productivity gains.[110] We can conclude that when properly applied and managed, organization development programs have positive effects on performance.[111]

MANAGERIAL IMPLICATIONS: MANAGING CHANGE

Several guidelines can be used to facilitate the success of management change efforts.[112] First, managers should recognize the forces for change. These forces can come from a combination of sources both internal and external to the organization.

A shared vision of the change should be developed that includes participation by all employees in the planning process. Top management must be committed to the change and should visibly demonstrate support, because employees look to these leaders to model appropriate behavior. A comprehensive diagnosis and needs analysis should be conducted. The company then must ensure that there are adequate resources for carrying out the change.

Resistance to change should be planned for and managed. Communication, participation, and empathetic support are ways of helping employees adjust. The reward system within the organization must be carefully evaluated to ensure that new behaviors, rather than old ones, are being reinforced. Participation in the change process should also be recognized and rewarded.

The organization development technique used should be carefully selected to meet the goals of the change. Finally, organization development efforts should be managed in an ethical manner and should preserve employees' privacy and freedom of choice. Employees must be treated fairly, and management's explanations for change must be congruent with their actions. The congruence between talk and actions, or "walking the talk," is critical in managing organizational change.[113] By using these guidelines, managers can meet the challenges of managing change while enhancing productivity in their organizations.

LOOKING BACK: AMERICAN EXPRESS

A Model Corporate Citizen

In the Looking Ahead feature, we examined how American Express has managed to leverage globalization and technology to its advantage. Here we spotlight its successful handling of social responsibility in business. American Express is involved in a number of corporate giving programs to bolster its reputation in the communities it operates in globally. Three main giving themes are supported currently. First, "Partners in Preservation" explores ways to preserve cultural heritages. This program has led to a collaboration between American Express, the World Monuments Fund (WMF), and the National

Trust for Historic Preservation. American Express has donated $10 million over the last ten years to help preserve endangered historic monuments. Second, the relatively new "Leadership Development" focuses on methodologies for developing global leaders This program's first initiative was to sponsor a New York–based nonprofit "Bridge Span" aimed at recruiting like-minded nonprofits. Eventually these organizations will combine their expertise to develop leaders who can meet significant social challenges in the metropolitan New York area. Finally, "Community Service" includes volunteer work by its employees in mentoring, providing food and shelter, and furthering environmental awareness in local communities. In addition, American Express has committed $5.6 million over twelve years to the American Red Cross to help bring relief to disaster-struck areas such as New Orleans, Pakistan, the Philippines, and Indonesia. In addition, it has awarded grants to several nonprofits such as Big Brothers and Big Sisters of New York City and Project Angel, a meal delivery program, in Los Angeles.

By engaging in such programs, American Express has built a strong reputation as a good corporate citizen in the face of the changing business ethics landscape.[114]

Chapter Summary

1. Organizations face many pressures to change. Some forces are external, including globalization, workforce diversity, technological innovation, and ethics. Other forces are internal, such as declining effectiveness, crises, changing employee expectations, and a changing work climate.
2. Organizations face both planned and unplanned change. Change can be of an incremental, strategic, or transformational nature. The individual who directs the change, known as a change agent, can be internal or external to the organization.
3. Individuals resist change for many reasons, and many of these reasons are rooted in fear. Organizations can help manage resistance by educating workers and openly communicating the change, encouraging worker participation in the change efforts, and providing empathy and support to those who have difficulty dealing with change.
4. Reactions to change may be manifested in behaviors reflecting disengagement, disidentification, disenchantment, and disorientation. Managers can use separate interventions targeted toward each reaction.
5. Force field analysis states that when the forces for change are balanced by the forces restraining change, an equilibrium state exists. For change to occur, the forces for change must increase or the restraining forces must decrease.
6. Lewin's change model proposes three stages of change: unfreezing, moving, and refreezing.
7. A thorough diagnosis and needs analysis is a critical first step in any organization development (OD) intervention.
8. OD interventions targeted toward organizations and groups include survey feedback, management by objectives, product and service quality programs, team building, and process consultation.
9. OD interventions that focus on individuals include skills training, leadership training and development, executive coaching, role negotiation, job redesign, health promotion programs, and career planning.
10. OD efforts should be managed ethically and should preserve individual freedom of choice and privacy.
11. When properly conducted, organization development can have positive effects on performance.

Key Terms

change agent (p. 621)
disenchantment (p. 628)
disengagement (p. 628)
disidentification (p. 628)
disorientation (p. 629)
executive coaching (p. 638)
incremental change (p. 621)
job redesign (p. 638)
leadership training and development (p. 637)
management by objectives (MBO) (p. 634)
moving (p. 630)
organization development (OD) (p. 632)
planned change (p. 616)
process consultation (p. 636)
quality program (p. 634)
refreezing (p. 631)
role negotiation (p. 638)
skills training (p. 637)
strategic change (p. 621)
survey feedback (p. 633)
team building (p. 636)
transformational change (p. 621)
unfreezing (p. 630)
unplanned change (p. 616)

Review Questions

1. What are the major external and internal forces for change in organizations?
2. Contrast incremental, strategic, and transformational change.
3. What is a change agent? Who plays this role?
4. What are the major reasons individuals resist change? How can organizations deal with resistance?
5. Name the four behavioral reactions to change. Describe the behavioral signs of each reaction, and identify an organizational strategy for dealing with each reaction.
6. Describe force field analysis and its relationship to Lewin's change model.
7. What is organization development? Why is it undertaken by organizations?
8. Name six areas to be critically examined in any comprehensive organizational diagnosis.
9. What are the major organization-focused and group-focused OD intervention methods? The major individual-focused methods?
10. Which OD intervention is most effective?

Discussion and Communication Questions

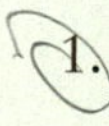

1. What are the major external forces for change in today's organizations?
2. What are the advantages of using an external change agent? An internal change agent?
3. Review You 18.1. What can you learn from this challenge about how individuals' tolerance for ambiguity can lead to resistance?
4. Can organizations prevent resistance to change? If so, how?
5. What organization development techniques are the easiest to implement? The most difficult to implement? Why?
6. Suppose your organization experiences a dramatic increase in turnover. How would you diagnose the underlying problem?
7. Downsizing has played a major role in changing U.S. organizations. Analyze the internal and external forces for change regarding downsizing an organization.
8. If you were in charge of designing the ideal management development program, what topics would you include? Why?
9. *(communication question)* Find an article that describes an organization that has gone through change and managed it well. Develop a Real World feature of your own about the example you find using the format in this book. Prepare a brief oral presentation of your Real World feature for your class.
10. *(communication question)* Think of a change you would like to make in your life. Using Figure 18.1 as a guide, prepare your own force field analysis for that change. How will you overcome the forces for the status quo? How will you make sure to "refreeze" following the change? Summarize your analysis in an action plan.

Ethical Dilemma

Tom Wood cannot contain his feelings of sadness. He is sitting at his desk considering the dismissal of his best department supervisor: Liz Williams. Liz has always been one of his best employees. She ran an efficient department and was always well within budget. Best of all, her employees were the happiest and most productive in the company. Tom had spent many days wishing he had several more supervisors like Liz Williams working for him.

But that was the old Liz. Since the merger, Liz has become a very different employee. She has resented some of the changes that have taken place since the company merged with a large multinational corporation. Tom has spoken with Liz on several occasions about the changes that have taken place. He knows she is struggling with the new management philosophy, and he does not want to lose her. Liz liked the way the previous company operated and is not making the necessary adjustments to become part of the new organization. She disagrees with the new company's procedures, and she is not afraid to let people know it. On more than one occasion in the last six months, Tom has had to defend his decision to keep Liz as part of the team.

Recently, Tom believed things were getting better for Liz. She seemed to be settling down and adjusting to the new culture. At least that is what he thought until yesterday when she had a major dispute with her counterpart at the home office in Germany. It was the last straw for upper management. Tom had gotten the phone message this morning that Liz needs to go. He needs to decide if he is pushing his luck too far by going to bat for Liz one more time. He isn't sure how much more his superiors are willing to listen to him defend her. Even he agrees that she is beginning to be a real problem. But she is also a good friend and under normal circumstances a very good worker. Does she deserve another chance?

Questions

1. How long does Tom need to defend Liz's behaviors?
2. What is Liz's responsibility to Tom?
3. Using consequential, rule-based, and character theories, evaluate Tom's decision.

Experiential Exercises

18.1 Organizational Diagnosis of the University

The purpose of this exercise is to give you experience in organizational diagnosis. Assume that your team has been hired to conduct a diagnosis of problem areas in your university and to make preliminary recommendations for organization development interventions.

Each team member should complete the following University Profile. Then, as a team, evaluate the strengths and weaknesses within each area (academics, teaching, social, cultural, and administrative) using the accompanying University Diagnosis form. Finally, make recommendations concerning organization development interventions for each area. Be as specific as possible in both your diagnosis and your recommendations. Each team should then present its diagnosis to the class.

University Profile

Not True 1 2 3 4 5 Very True

I. Academics

1 2 3 4 5 1. There is a wide range of courses to choose from.

1 2 3 4 5 2. Classroom standards are too easy.

1 2 3 4 5 3. The library is adequate.

1 2 3 4 5 4. Textbooks are helpful.

II. Teachers

1 2 3 4 5 1. Teachers here are committed to quality instruction.

1 2 3 4 5 2. We have a high-quality faculty.

III. Social

1 2 3 4 5 1. Students are friendly to one another.

1 2 3 4 5 2. It is difficult to make friends.

1 2 3 4 5 3. Faculty get involved in student activities.

1 2 3 4 5 4. Too much energy goes into drinking and goofing off.

IV. Cultural Events

1 2 3 4 5 1. There are ample activities on campus.

1 2 3 4 5 2. Student activities are boring.

1 2 3 4 5 3. The administration places a high value on student activities.

1 2 3 4 5 4. Too much emphasis is placed on sports.

1 2 3 4 5 5. We need more "cultural" activities.

V. Organizational/Management

1 2 3 4 5 1. Decision making is shared at all levels of the organization.

1 2 3 4 5 2. There is unity and cohesiveness among departments and units.

1 2 3 4 5 3. Too many departmental clashes hamper the organization's effectiveness.

1 2 3 4 5 4. Students have a say in many decisions.

1 2 3 4 5 5. The budgeting process seems fair.

1 2 3 4 5 6. Recruiting and staffing are handled thoughtfully with student needs in mind.

University Diagnosis

	STRENGTH	WEAKNESS	INTERVENTION
1. Academic			
2. Teaching			
3. Social			
4. Cultural			
5. Administrative			

SOURCE: "Organizational Diagnosis of the University" by D. Marcic, *Organizational Behavior: Experiences and Cases* (St. Paul, Minn.: West Publishing Company, 1989), 326–329. Reprinted by permission.

18.2 Team Building for Team Effectiveness

This exercise will allow you and your team to engage in an organization development activity for team building. The two parts of the exercise are diagnosis and intervention.

Part 1. Diagnosis

Working as a team, complete the following four steps:

1. Describe how you have worked together this semester as a team.
2. What has your team done especially well? What has enabled this?
3. What problems or conflicts have you had as a team? (Be specific.) What was the cause of the problems your team experienced? Have the conflicts been over ideas, methods, or people?
4. Would you assess the overall effectiveness of your team as excellent, good, fair, poor, or a disaster? Explain your effectiveness rating.

Part 2. Intervention

A diagnosis provides the basis for intervention and action in organization development. Team building is a way to improve the relationships and effectiveness of teams at work. It is concerned with the results of work activities and the relationships among the members of the team. Complete the following three steps as a team.

Step 1. Answer the following questions with regard to the relationships within the team:

a. How could conflicts have been handled better?

b. How could specific relationships have been improved?

c. How could the interpersonal atmosphere of the team have been improved?

Step 2. Answer the following questions with regard to the results of the team's work:

a. How could the team have been more effective?

b. Are there any team process changes that would have improved the team's effectiveness?

c. Are there any team structure changes that would have improved the team's effectiveness?

Step 3. Answer the following questions with regard to the work environment in your place of employment:

a. What have you learned about team building that you can apply there?

b. What have you learned about team building that would not be applicable there?

TAKE 2

Biz Flix | Field of Dreams

Ray Kinsella (Kevin Costner) hears a voice while working in his Iowa cornfield that says, "If you build it, he will come." Ray concludes that "he" is legendary "Shoeless Joe" Jackson (Ray Liotta), a 1919 Chicago White Sox player suspended for rigging the 1919 World Series. With the support of his wife Annie (Amy Madigan), Ray jeopardizes his farm by replacing some corn fields with a modern baseball diamond. "Shoeless Joe" soon arrives, followed by the rest of the suspended players. This charming fantasy film, based on W. P. Kinsella's novel *Shoeless Joe*, shows the rewards of pursuing a dream.

The scene is part of the "People Will Come" sequence toward the end of *Field of Dreams*. By this time in the story, Ray has met Terrence Mann (James Earl Jones). They have traveled together from Boston to Minnesota to find A. W. "Moonlight" Graham (Burt Lancaster). At this point, the three are at Ray's Iowa farm.

This scene follows Mark's (Timothy Busfield) arrival to discuss the foreclosure of Ray and Annie's mortgage. Mark, who is Annie's brother, cannot see the players on the field. Ray and Annie's daughter Karin (Gaby Hoffman) has proposed that people will come to Iowa City and buy tickets to watch a baseball game. Mark does not understand her proposal. The film continues to its end.

What to Watch for and Ask Yourself:

> Who is the target of change in this scene?

> What are the forces for change? Are the forces for change internal or external to the change target?

> Does the scene show the role of leadership in organizational change? If it does, who is the leader? What does this person do to get desired change?

Workplace Video | Managing Change and Innovation, Featuring Hard Rock International

Founded by rock music devotees in London during the early 1970s, Hard Rock Cafe took off worldwide in the 1980s and went on to become one of the most popular theme restaurants in the business. Today the chain boasts 120 locations in forty-three countries and showcases over 70,000 pieces of authentic rock 'n' roll memorabilia. The company has flourished for more than thirty years in the rough-and-tumble world of the hospitality industry.

Over the years, management has guided the company through major changes such as standardizing its brand identity, downsizing after 9/11, adjusting to shifting technology, and implementing top-down reengineering moves. Through it all, Hard Rock has maintained its free-spirited culture and outpaced competing theme restaurants.

At the close of 2006, British gaming company Rank Group sold its Hard Rock business to the Seminole Tribe of Florida for $965 million. The deal transferred ownership of the Hard Rock brand, 124 Hard Rock Cafes and stores around the world, eight hotels, and two live concert venues. The acquisition marked the first time that a Native American

TAKE 2

tribe had purchased such a large international corporation. It was not the first time the Seminole tribe made history, however. Despite efforts in the early 1800s by U.S. Army and militia forces to destroy the tribe or force them to yield, they never surrendered. The Seminoles went on to become the first tribe to win the right to build a tax-free gambling hall on Indian land, a move that changed the economic landscape for Native American tribes forever. Ownership of Hard Rock now gives the savvy tribe a full-blown international presence.

The Hard Rock Cafe stands to benefit from its many changes. The new owners intend to expand operations and will look into adding casinos to existing Hard Rock hotels. Now under new management, this casual dining restaurant and living museum of rock history is positioned to offer up good food and great music to a new generation.

Discussion Questions

1. What sort of resistance might Hard Rock's new owners face when initiating organizational change?
2. What measures can Hard Rock's new owners take to reassure staff and investors that change is good?
3. What innovative ideas or changes could Hard Rock implement to appeal to the next generation of music lovers?

CASE

Into the Future: Forces for Change at Cisco Systems

Cisco Systems was founded in 1984 by Len Bosack and Sandy Lerner, two computer scientists from Stanford University. Adapting its name from San Francisco, gateway to the Pacific Rim, the company was geared toward enabling disparate computer networks to communicate with each other and share information.[1] Cisco has grown into the worldwide sales leader of "networking equipment and software technology for routing, switching, and fiber- and Internet Protocol (IP)-based solutions" with "more than 35,000 employees in five theaters worldwide," covering the United States, Africa, the non-U.S. Americas, Asia/Pacific Rim, and Europe.[2] Cisco has been recognized by *Fortune* as the one of the "100 Best Companies to Work For" and by *Working Mother* magazine as one of the "100 Best Companies for Working Mothers." Cisco has also been cited by *Business Ethics* magazine as being among the "100 Best Corporate Citizens."[3]

According to its Web site, "Cisco has long led the market for Internet routers and switches, both in market share and innovation; and more recently expanded its presence into six advanced technology markets—wireless, home networking, security, optical, IP telephony and storage. Combined, these core and advanced technologies comprise Cisco's vision of the Intelligent Information Network. Cisco is the number one or two player in almost every market in which it competes, and continues to deliver innovations that extend its Intelligent Information Network."[4]

On the occasion of Cisco System's twentieth business anniversary in 2004, president and CEO John Chambers observed: "There are a lot of market transitions going on in the industry and it is the key to prioritize where we are going to go. It's now about the future. The company that brought you the routers to make the Internet work 20 years ago is now innovating and allowing people to enable the power of the Internet by a factor of 100, opening up new ideas that were previously unimaginable. This is truly the end of the beginning."[5]

Cisco focuses its technology on where the market is going—on the future. What does the future hold for it and other companies? A recent study conducted by *The Economist Intelligence Unit* and sponsored by Cisco identifies five key trends that will likely influence businesses through 2020.[6] These trends are in the areas of globalization, demographics, atomization, personalization, and knowledge management.

In terms of *globalization*, emerging markets—especially India and China—will become more dominant in the world economy. Countries that are not members of the Organization for Economic Cooperation and Development (OECD) will account for more market growth than will OECD-member nations. Moreover, lower-cost, lower-wage economies will continue to experience a massive influx of labor-intensive production processes.[7]

With respect to *demographics*, the aging population will have a significant impact on economic growth, as more products and services are targeted at that growing demographic. Mature markets will have workforces that are older and have a higher proportion of women in them. The changing racial and ethnicity demographics of the United States are likely to mitigate the impact of aging to some degree, and indeed will encourage economic growth. In Europe, however, the aging population is likely to inhibit economic growth.[8]

Globalization and networking technologies enable *atomization*, wherein businesses and their processes, customers, and supply chains will fragment with overseas expansion as information is digitized and work flows to where it is best accomplished. The boundaries between different industries and business, and functions within individual businesses, will become indistinct, and consequently effective collaboration will become increasingly important. Moreover, data formats and technologies will become standardized.[9]

Personalization of products and services will assume an increasingly prominent role in customers' preferences and decision making. Price and quality will still matter as much as ever to customers, but personalization or customization will be added to the customers' decision-making mix. This will affect the design and manufacturing of products, as well as relationships with customers and suppliers.[10]

Knowledge management will become an increasingly important source of competitive advantage for businesses. More attention will be focused on those business areas "where personal chemistry or creative insight matter more than rules or processes." In addition, improving knowledge workers' productivity, through training, technology, and organizational change, will be a major challenge for businesses.[11]

How is Cisco Systems positioning itself to capitalize on these trends? According to its CEO, the company will continue to draw on it traditional strengths of making routers and switchers for electronic networks while also vigorously developing Cisco into a consumer-technology company. Chambers says, "[w]e were an enterprise company that moved into selling equipment to phone and cable companies. We went from there into selling equipment to small and medium businesses, and now we're moving into [the] consumer" market.[12] By combining its core strength of Internet Protocol with intelligence, Cisco is leading the transition to a network-centric technology environment by "creating a powerful communications platform that will serve as the basis for the convergence of data, voice, video and mobile communications in a secure, integrated architecture."[13]

Three recent acquisitions—Linksys, Scientific Atlanta, and WebEx—provide some additional clues regarding how Cisco is positioning itself for the future.[14] The company "extended its networking technology expertise in the enterprise and service provider markets into the high-growth consumer networking market" with the acquisition of Linksys in June 2003. Linksys has a home networking product line with over seventy products that span a variety of wired and wireless home applications including, but not limited to, sharing of digital music, photo, and video media files.[15] "Linksys specializes in products and solutions that provide effortless and economical sharing of broadband Internet connections, files, printers, digital music, videos, photos and gaming over a wired or wireless network. These reliable, easy-to-use, world-class products are backed with award-winning technical support, setting the standard for excellence in the consumer and small business."[16]

Cisco's acquisition of Scientific Atlanta in February 2006 provides entry into consumers' homes via set-top cable TV boxes that receive television programming from cable and phone companies. This acquisition also strengthened Cisco's relationships with content providers.[17] Scientific Atlanta is "a leading global provider of set-top boxes, end-to-end video distribution networks and video systems integration. The acquisition allows Cisco to offer a world class, end-to-end data, voice, video, and mobility solution for carrier networks and the digital home."[18]

Cisco completed acquisition of WebEx in May 2007. "WebEx's service portfolio includes technologies and services that allow companies to engage in real-time and asynchronous data conferences over the Internet as well as share web-based documents and workspaces that help improve productivity, performance and efficiency of workers in any size organization. WebEx's subscription-based services strategy has been [the] key to its success, and Cisco plans to preserve this business model going forward."[19]

CEO Chambers says, "Fifteen years ago we said we would change the way the world works, lives, plays and learns. Today, the company has the ability to understand and adapt to change, with a balance of leadership in four key customer segments. We have the courage to change, are setting the pace for change in our industry that's never been seen before, and have the vision to take our customers into the future. We are truly redefining the industry, with the network becoming the platform for all communications and IT. What this really means is that we are the company that will enable all of life's experiences, both personal and business, for the future."[20]

Discussion Questions

1. Describe the *external* forces for change that seem to be affecting Cisco Systems.
2. Describe the *internal* forces for change that seem to be affecting Cisco Systems.
3. Using force-field analysis, explain Cisco's development as a business enterprise.
4. Explain the development of Cisco from the perspectives of incremental change, strategic change, and transformational change.

SOURCE: This case was written by Michael K. McCuddy, The Louis S. and Mary L. Morgal Chair of Christian Business Ethics and Professor of Management, College of Business Administration, Valparaiso University.

BP: A Tale of Two Careers Wrapped in a Strong Corporate Culture (D)

BP, the London-based energy giant, is facing various challenges regarding refinery safety, environmental pollution, and access to global oil resources. These challenges have arisen, in part, from BP's corporate culture. They have also ensnared the careers of two top BP executives—John Browne and Tony Hayward.

BP's Culture

Under Browne's leadership, BP's culture rapidly evolved into one that can be characterized as aggressive, results oriented, and environmentally conscious. This culture also emphasizes the assumption of risk and the adoption of an entrepreneurial perspective.

A key element of BP's culture is the results orientation promulgated by Browne. Although he grilled his managers every quarter in extremely tough, detailed reviews, the company operated with a relatively decentralized structure. This decentralized approach was intended to reward individual initiative, and managers are expected to exercise their own judgment in running their organizational units.[1] The decentralized approach and the associated reward structure also encouraged entrepreneurial behavior.

Assumption of risk appears to have been a major element of BP's culture and strategy. John Leggate, BP's Chief Information Officer, has argued that risk is an integral part of BP's strategy.[2] Such an emphasis on risk assumption, in conjunction with the strong desire to obtain results, created a high-pressure performance culture at BP. Indeed, Matthew Simmons, a veteran energy banker, says, "[t]he whole culture at BP has made it a ruthless place to work."[3] According to Gordon Picchi, an analyst at Wall Street Access, "BP is a financial culture gone wild. . . . The company has been doing deals for the sake of doing deals with . . . a maniacal focus on the bottom line, to the [detriment] of normal operating standards."[4]

Sacrifice of normal operating standards may have contributed, in large part, to the challenges detailed in *BP: Facing Multiple Challenges (Part I)*. These challenges include oil refinery safety issues, an oil pipeline spill in Alaska, manipulation of the propane market, public opposition to additional pollutant discharges into Lake Michigan, and energy exploration and development operations in Russia and Venezuela. "Browne's intense drive for results combined with BP's entrepreneurial culture may have also played a role in the company's woes. . . . One source says Browne may have been guilty of 'naiveté' in trusting that managers in Texas and Alaska could achieve his demanding financial goals without compromising operations."[5]

Although BP has committed financial resources to addressing safety problems, critics have questioned whether the company's culture will usurp the commitment of resources. In commenting on BP's $7 billion safety budget, Jerry Laws, editor of *Occupational Health & Safety*, writes, ". . . cash can't buy a world-class safety culture. Money alone won't make a supervisor who reveres production above all else change his outlook, nor will it sober up a hard-drinking or drug-using worker whose habits endanger those around him."[6]

Another element of BP's culture that could create difficulty in solving the safety problems is the concern about managerial actions toward workers taking the initiative to report safety violations. For instance, in its report on the Texas City, Texas, refinery explosion, the U.S. Chemical Safety Board "wants BP to work with the United Steelworkers International Union to report promoting of incidents and near misses 'without fear of reprisals.'"[7]

Still another important element of BP's culture stems from John Browne's push for the company to move *Beyond Petroleum*. Under Browne's guidance BP began focusing explicitly on its responsibilities with respect to environmental concerns and the development of alternative energy sources.[8] Unfortunately, this element of the organization's culture may have been subordinated to the emphasis on cost cutting and financial results (see *BP: Safety and Public Relations in America (Part II)* for details).

BP's culture is one legacy of Browne's tenure as CEO; he—as much as any BP executive or manager—was instrumental in developing and maintaining it.

John Browne's Career

Browne's career with BP spanned four decades, starting in 1966 when he joined the company as a university apprentice. At the time he was studying physics at Cambridge University in the United Kingdom. Soon after he graduated, BP sent Browne to Alaska. This was a time of turmoil in the oil industry, with shortages and price hikes becoming routine occurrences in the 1970s and 1980s. Major oil discoveries in Alaska during this period helped Western countries survive the oil industry turmoil.[9] Undoubtedly, Browne's experiences in Alaska would influence his future decisions as he rose in BP's managerial ranks.

Browne, who became a key player in the worldwide oil industry, provided a sharp contrast to the Americans who had dominated the industry for most of the twentieth century. Whereas the American oil barons were rough-hewn, Browne presented a much more sophisticated public image as an art collector and opera buff. For many years, Browne, who remained single, lived with his mother, a Holocaust survivor from Hungary. Before her death in 2000, she accompanied Browne to various BP events.[10]

In recognition of Browne's achievements and leadership of BP, Queen Elizabeth II knighted him in 1998. Then in 2001 the British government awarded him a life peerage, and thereafter he was entitled to be called Lord Browne of Madingley.[11]

At that time, life appeared to be exceptionally good for Browne. He was well respected, both personally and professionally. Matthew Simmons, a veteran energy banker, characterized him as "the best cost cutter in the industry."[12] Another writer called him a brilliant business titan.[13] And BP was doing well as a major player in the global oil industry.

Soon, however, life—both professionally and personally—began to unravel for Browne. The various challenges described in *BP: Facing Multiple Challenges (Part I)* began taking their toll. The safety and environmental challenges were especially daunting. BP was being assailed as a company that failed to practice what it preached. As described in *BP: Safety and Public Relations in America (Part II)*, the public increasingly perceived the company's *Beyond Petroleum* branding to be at loggerheads with its growing safety and environmental problems.

Interestingly, however, "[a]mid the problems, Lord Browne's view toward his coming retirement started puzzling some board members according to people familiar with the situation. At a speech early last year [2006], he blasted statutory retirement limits. Newspaper articles mentioned the idea of an extended tenure. Directors started wondering if Browne or his allies were floating trial balloons" to delay his retirement.[14]

On the personal side, an alleged homosexual relationship came to light and Browne tried to conceal it, even lying to a British court in a lawsuit filed to prevent the British media from publishing accounts of his relationship. Although Browne's proclivities apparently escaped the attention of the British media for some time previous to this, his sexual orientation did not seem to surprise BP executives.[15] Some observers argue that the revelation of Browne's homosexuality brought about his rapid downfall as BP's CEO. Others maintain that the growing stable of safety and environmental problems at BP were the real reasons for Browne's sooner-than-expected retirement. According to this view, Browne's "fall likely is due to the conflict between how he actually managed the company and the public principles he claimed were the essence of BP's corporate character. Tragic mishaps in safety, environmental lapses, and questionable competitive maneuvers—not his lifestyle—eroded the company's self-righteous advertising image and Browne's legitimacy to lead."[16]

Tony Hayward's Career

Tony Hayward, with a 25-year career at BP, was selected in early January 2007 to be John Browne's successor as CEO. During his years at BP, Hayward worked closely with Browne and learned a great deal from him. One lesson Hayward says he learned from Browne was not to promise too much. Also like his mentor, Hayward led BP's exploration and production unit before being named BP's CEO.[17]

In a speech to BP employees in December 2006, Hayward said, the "mantra of more-for-less holds that we can get 100% of the task completed with 90% of the resources. But it needs to be deployed with great judgment and wisdom. Otherwise you run into trouble."[18] After being tapped as Browne's successor, "Hayward didn't give many clues about where he will be taking BP. He indicated he would continue to follow Browne's strategy of seeking out giant discoveries that offer economies of scale. On the issue of mergers, Hayward said that he learned from Browne that M&A was just a tool for implementing strategy. He said that thanks to recent high prices, there has 'been more value in selling than in purchasing' assets."[19] Hayward did indicate, however, that BP would adopt a more cautious approach and reduce production targets.[20]

On May 1, 2007, Browne unexpectedly resigned as BP's CEO and Hayward immediately assumed that position. As reported in the July 23, 2007 issue of *Business Week*, Hayward now has a four-item to-do list as he embarks on the next stage of his career:

- *Safety*: Hayward must make BP an industry leader after the various safety mishaps.
- *Culture*: Hayward must reconnect management with frontline workers in refineries and on drilling platforms.
- *Performance*: Hayward must get key refineries back into full service and start pumping oil from new fields.
- *Focus*: Hayward must concentrate on the company's best projects and facilities while selling marginal assets.[21]

Can Hayward, as BP's new CEO, effectively implement the organizational changes required by this list?

Discussion Questions

1. What concepts from Chapter 16 are helpful in describing and understanding BP's organizational culture? Explain your answer.
2. What insights about BP's organization design can you derive from the description of its culture?
3. How can BP's organizational culture be linked with John Browne's career progression?
4. How might BP's organizational culture affect Tony Hayward's actions as BP's new CEO?
5. What future competitive challenges await Tony Hayward and BP? Do you think BP will be able to effectively address these competitive challenges, given its culture?

SOURCE: This case was written by Michael K. McCuddy, The Louis S. and Mary L. Morgal Chair of Christian Business Ethics and Professor of Management, College of Business Administration, Valparaiso University.

Appendix A

A Brief Historical Perspective

Organizational behavior may be traced back thousands of years, as noted in Sterba's analysis of the ancient Mesopotamian temple corporations. However, we will focus on the modern history of organizational behavior, which dates to the late 1800s. One of the more important series of studies conducted during this period was the Hawthorne studies. As these and other studies have unfolded, the six disciplines discussed in Chapter 1 of the text have contributed to the advancement of organizational behavior. An overview of the progress during the past century is presented in Table A.1 and the accompanying text. This is followed by a discussion of the Hawthorne studies.

TABLE A.1 One Hundred Years of Progress in Organizational Behavior

1890s	• Frederick Taylor's development of scientific management
1900s	• Max Weber's concept of bureaucracy and the Protestant ethic
1910s	• Walter Cannon's discovery of the "emergency (stress) response"
1920s	• Elton Mayo's illumination studies in the textile industry • The Hawthorne studies at Western Electric Company
1930s	• Kurt Lewin's, Ronald Lippitt's, and Ralph White's early leadership studies
1940s	• Abraham Maslow's need hierarchy motivation theory • B. F. Skinner's formulation of the behavioral approach • Charles Walker's and Robert Guest's studies of routine work
1950s	• Ralph Stogdill's Ohio State leadership studies • Douglas McGregor's examination of the human side of enterprise • Frederick Herzberg's two-factor theory of motivation and job enrichment
1960s	• Arthur Turner's and Paul Lawrence's studies of diverse industrial jobs • Robert Blake's and Jane Mouton's Leadership Grid • Patricia Cain Smith's studies of satisfaction in work and retirement • Fred Fiedler's contingency theory of leadership
1970s	• J. Richard Hackman's and Greg Oldham's job characteristics theory • Edward Lawler's approach to pay and organizational effectiveness • Robert House's path–goal and charismatic theories of leadership
1980s	• Peter Block's political skills for empowered managers • Charles Manz's approach to self-managed work teams • Edgar Schein's approach to leadership and organizational culture
1990s	• Robert Solomon's personal integrity, character, and virtue ethics • Martin Seligman's positive psychology of hope and strength
2000s	• Fred Luthan's new framework of positive organzational behavior (POB) • Bruce Avolio's approach to authentic leadership

ONE HUNDRED YEARS OF PROGRESS

Progress in any discipline, practice, or field of study is measured by significant events, discoveries, and contributions over time. The history of organizational behavior begins, as noted in Table A.1, with the work of Frederick Taylor in scientific management at Midvale Steel Company, Bethlehem Steel Company, and elsewhere.[1] Taylor applied engineering principles to the study of people and their behavior at work. He pioneered the use of performance standards for workers, set up differential piece-rate systems of pay, and argued for the scientific selection of employees. He hoped to ultimately improve labor–management relationships in American industry. Taylor's lasting contributions include organizational goal-setting programs, incentive pay systems, and modern employee selection techniques.

The late 1800s also saw the United States make the transition from an agricultural society to an industrial one, and Taylor was part of this transformation process. About the same time Taylor was developing a uniquely American approach to the design of work, Max Weber was undertaking a classic work on religion and capitalism in Germany.[2] Weber's lasting legacies to management and organizational behavior are found in his notions of bureaucracies and the Protestant ethic, the latter an important feature of Chapter 5 in the text. Another major event of this era, as noted in Table A.1, was Walter Cannon's discovery of the stress response in about 1915. This discovery laid a foundation for psychosomatic medicine, industrial hygiene, and an understanding of the emotional components of health at work and play.[3] Finally, the first quarter of the twentieth century saw the initiation of the Hawthorne studies, a major research advancement in understanding people at work.[4] The Hawthorne studies are discussed in some depth in the second half of this brief history.

From the end of the 1930s through the 1950s, major contributions were made to the understanding of leadership, motivation, and behavior in organizations, as noted in Table A.1.[5] Lewin, Lippitt, and White's early examination of autocratic, democratic, and laissez-faire leadership styles was followed over a decade later by Ralph Stogdill's extensive studies at The Ohio State University focusing on leader behaviors. This marked a point of departure from earlier leadership studies, which had focused on the traits of the leader. Abraham Maslow proposed a need hierarchy of human motivation during the early 1940s, which served as a foundation for Douglas McGregor's theorizing in the 1950s about assumptions concerning the human side of a business enterprise. The 1950s was the decade in which Frederick Herzberg developed a new theory of motivation, which he later translated into an approach to job design, called *job enrichment*. This is quite different from the approach to designing work that Charles Walker and Robert Guest formulated a decade earlier in response to the problems they found with routine work. Attention was also given to group dynamics during this era in an effort to explain small group behavior.[6]

The 1960s and 1970s saw continued attention to theories of motivation, leadership, the design of work, and job satisfaction.[7] For example, Arthur Turner and Paul Lawrence's studies of diverse industrial jobs in various industries was a forerunner for the research program of Richard Hackman and Greg Oldham, which led to their job characteristics theory a decade later. Robert Blake and Jane Mouton's Leadership Grid was a variation on the Ohio State leadership studies of a decade earlier, while Fred Fiedler's contingency theory of leadership was an entirely new approach to leadership that emerged during the 1960s. Robert House proposed path–goal and charismatic theories of leadership during this era, and Edward Lawler drew attention to the importance of pay in performance and organizational effectiveness.

The 1980s saw attention shift to organizational culture, teamwork, and political skills in organizations. Peter Block drew our attention to the political skills required to empower managers in increasingly challenging work environments, while Charles Manz directed attention to teamwork and self-managed teams. Leadership continued to be an important topic, and Edgar Schein formulated a framework for understanding how leaders created, embedded, and maintained an organizational culture. Throughout the changing and unfolding story of the study of organizational behavior during the twentieth century there has been a common theme: How do we understand people, their psychology, and their behavior in the workplace?[8]

The 1990s saw an emerging concern for personal integrity, character, and virtue ethics as well as the new domain of positive psychology. The political scandals and impeachment hearings during the Clinton administration led to discussions in corporate boardrooms and college campuses about personal integrity and character. Robert Solomon framed an approach to personal virtues using an Aristotelian approach to business ethics.[9] Solomon extends his philosophy of personal integrity and character by articulating how they can lead to corporate success.[10] A second important development during the 1990s was the emergence of positive psychology, which Martin Seligman suggested was an underdeveloped aspect of the science of human behavior. The focus of positive psychology is building upon human strength and encouraging hope and optimism.[11] One early dissertation study in the management field linked positive psychology with eustress at work.[12] Since the year 2000, Fred Luthans has extended positive psychology with his emphasis on positive organizational behavior (POB), which emphasizes confidence, hope, optimism, and other positive attributes at work[13] Bruce Avolio draws upon POB research in his approach to authentic leadership.[14]

The intention of this brief historical review and time line in Table A.1 is to give you a sense of perspective on the drama of unfolding research programs, topics, and investigators who have brought us to the present state of knowledge and practice in organizational behavior. Although the text addresses the field in a topical manner by chapter, we think it is important that students of organizational behavior have a sense of historical perspective of the whole field. We now turn to the Hawthorne studies, one of the seminal research programs from the early part of the twentieth century.

THE HAWTHORNE STUDIES

Initiated in 1925 with a grant from Western Electric, the Hawthorne studies were among the most significant advances in the understanding of organizational behavior during the past century. They were preceded by a series of studies of illumination conducted by Elton Mayo in the textile industry of Philadelphia. The research at the Hawthorne Works (an industrial manufacturing facility in Cicero, Illinois) was directed by Fritz Roethlisberger and consisted of four separate studies throughout a seven-year period.[15] These studies included (1) experiments in illumination, (2) the relay assembly test room study, (3) experiments in interviewing workers, and (4) the bank wiring room study. We will briefly examine this research program.

Experiments in Illumination

The experiments in illumination were a direct follow-up to Mayo's earlier work in the textile industry. At Hawthorne, the experiments in illumination consisted of a series of studies of test groups, in which the researchers varied illumination levels, and control groups, in which conditions were held constant. The purpose was to examine the relation of the quality and quantity of illumination to the efficiency of industrial workers. The experiments began in 1925 and extended over several years.

The researchers were surprised to discover that productivity increased to roughly the same rate in both test and control groups. It was only in the final experiment, where they decreased illumination levels to 0.06 footcandle (roughly moonlight intensity), that an appreciable decline in output occurred. The anticipated finding of a positive, linear relationship between illumination and industrial efficiency was simply not found. The researchers concluded that the results were "screwy" in the absence of this simple, direct cause-and-effect relationship.

It is from these first experiments that the term *Hawthorne Effect* was coined, referring originally to the fact that people's knowledge that they are being studied leads them to modify their behavior. A closer consideration of the Hawthorne Effect reveals that it is poorly understood and has taken on different meanings with the passage of time.[16] Hence, it has become somewhat an imprecise concept.

Relay Assembly Test Room Study

The researchers next set out to study workers segregated according to a range of working condition variables, such as workroom temperature and humidity, work schedule, rest breaks, and food consumption. The researchers chose five women in the relay assembly test room and kept careful records of the predictor variables, as well as output (measuring the time it took each woman to assemble a telephone relay of approximately forty parts).

Again, there was little the researchers were able to conclude from the actual data in this study in terms of a relationship between the predictor variables and industrial efficiency. However, they began to suspect that employee attitudes and sentiments were critically important variables not previously taken into account. Therefore, the researchers underwent a radical change of thought.

Experiments in Interviewing Workers

In 1928, a number of the researchers began a program of going into the workforce, without their normal tools and equipment, for the purpose of getting the workers to talk about what was important to them. Nearly 20,000 workers were interviewed over a period of two years, and in this interviewing process a major breakthrough occurred. The interview study was a form of research in which the investigators did not have a set of preconceptions concerning what they would find, as was the case in the two earlier phases of research. Rather, they set out to sympathetically and skillfully listen to what each worker was saying. As the interviewing progressed, the researchers discovered that the workers would open up and talk freely about what were the most important, and at times problematic, issues on their minds. The researchers discovered a rich and intriguing world previously unexamined within the Hawthorne Works.

Ultimately, Roethlisberger and his colleagues formulated guidelines for the conduct of interviews, and these guidelines became the basis for contemporary interviewing and active listening skills.[17] The discovery of the informal organization and its relationship to the formal organization began during the interview study. This led to a richer understanding of the social, interpersonal dynamics of people at work.

The Bank Wiring Room Study

The concluding study at Hawthorne was significant because it confirmed the importance of one aspect of the informal organization on worker productivity.

Specifically, the researchers studied workers in the bank wiring room and found that the behavioral norms set by the work group had a powerful influence over the productivity of the group. The higher the norms, the greater the productivity. The lower the norms, the lower the productivity. The power of the peer group and the importance of group influence on individual behavior and productivity were confirmed in the bank wiring room.

The Hawthorne studies laid a foundation for understanding people's social and psychological behavior in the workplace. Some of the methods used at Hawthorne, such as the experimental design methods and the interviewing technique, are used today for research in organizations. However, the discipline of organizational behavior is more than the psychology of people at work and more than the sociology of their behavior in organizations. Organizational behavior emerges from a wide range of interdisciplinary influences.

Appendix B

How Do We Know What We Know about Organizational Behavior?

By Uma Sekaran

This book has examined the skills and knowledge that managers need to be successful in their jobs. But how do you know how much faith to put in all the information you acquire from textbooks and management journals? Are some theories and statements more applicable than others? Even when applicable, will they apply at all times and under all circumstances? You can find answers to these important questions once you know the foundation on which theories and assertions rest. This appendix provides that foundation. It first examines why managers need to know about research and then discusses the basis for knowledge in this field. It then looks at the research process and research design and ends with a discussion of how research knowledge affects you.

WHY MANAGERS SHOULD KNOW ABOUT RESEARCH

Why is it necessary for you to know about research? First, this knowledge helps you determine how much of what is offered in textbooks is of practical use to you as a manager. Second, a basic understanding of how good empirical research is done can make you an effective manager by helping you to make intelligent decisions about research proposals and reports that reach your desk. Third, it enables you to become an informed and discriminating consumer of research articles published in the management journals that you need to read to keep up with new ideas and technology. For your convenience, a list of the current academic and practitioner-oriented journals that frequently publish articles on organizational behavior is provided in Table B.1.

Understanding scientific research methods enables you to differentiate between good and appropriate research, which you can apply in your setting, and flawed or inappropriate research, which you cannot use. Moreover, knowledge of techniques such as sampling design enables you to decide whether the results of a study using a particular type of sample in certain types of organizations is applicable to your setting.

Managers need to understand, predict, and control the research-oriented problems in their environment. Some of these problems may be relatively simple and can be solved through simple data gathering and analysis. Others may be relatively

TABLE B.1 Journals with Organizational Behavior Articles

Academic Journals	Practitioner-Oriented Journals
Academy of Management Journal	Academy of Management Executive
Academy of Management Review	Business Horizons
Administrative Science Quarterly	California Management Review
Advances in International Comparative Management	Columbia Journal of World Business
Group and Organization Studies	Harvard Business Review
Human Relations	Human Resource Development Quarterly
Human Resource Management	Industrial Relations
Human Resource Management Review	Industry Week
Human Resource Planning	Organizational Dynamics
Industrial and Labor Relations Review	Personnel Journal
International Journal of Human Resource Management	SAM Advanced Management Journal
International Journal of Management	Sloan Management Review
Journal of Applied Behavioral Science	Supervision
Journal of Applied Business Research	Training
Journal of Applied Psychology	Training and Development Journal
Journal of Business	
Journal of Business Ethics	
Journal of Business Research	
Journal of International Business Studies	
Journal of Management	
Journal of Management Studies	
Journal of Occupational Psychology	
Journal of Organizational Behavior	
Journal of Organizational Behavior Management	
Journal of Vocational Behavior	
Organizational Behavior and Human Decision Processes	
Personnel Administrator	
Sex Roles	
Women in Business	

complex, needing the assistance of researchers or consultants. In either case, without some basic knowledge of scientific research, managers will be unable to solve the problems themselves or to work effectively with consultants.

Managers need to discuss their problems with consultants in a useful way. This includes informing the problem solvers right at the start of the consulting process of any constraints (such as company records that are off limits to outsiders) or of types of recommendations that will not be considered (such as laying off or hiring more people). Such discussions not only save time but also help the managers and researchers start off on the right foot. Managers who don't understand the important aspects of research will not be equipped to anticipate and forestall the inevitable hurdles in manager–researcher interactions. Also, paying a consultant handsomely for a research report will not help the company unless the manager is capable of determining how much scientific value can be placed on the findings. For these and other reasons, a working knowledge of the scientific research process and research design is necessary.

OUR BASIS FOR KNOWLEDGE

Observation and scientific data gathering have led to some of our knowledge about management. For instance, very early on, Frederick Winslow Taylor observed, studied, experimented, and demonstrated how coal-mining operations could be managed more efficiently by changing the way men shoveled coal—changing how the shovel was handled, how the body movements were made, and so on. The era of scientific management that Taylor's work ushered in provided much knowledge about how management could improve efficiency. This type of knowledge is not easy to come by, however, when we are examining employees' feelings, attitudes, and behaviors. Our knowledge of organizational behavior stems instead from armchair theories, case studies, and scientific research.

Armchair Theories

In trying to understand organizational behavior, management experts and scholars initially resorted to *armchair theorizing*—theorizing based on the observation of various phenomena and behaviors in the workplace. For instance, Douglas McGregor, through observation and experience, theorized that managers have two different world views of employees. Some managers (Theory X) assume that employees are, by nature, lazy and not very bright, that they dislike responsibility and prefer to be led rather than to lead, and that they resist change. Other managers (Theory Y) assume that employees have the opposite characteristics. McGregor's concept of Theory X and Theory Y managers has become a classic armchair theory.

Few people either totally accept or totally dispute this theory because of the lack of hard data to either substantiate or negate this interesting notion. Armchair theories are based on natural observation with no systematic experimentation and hence are not very useful for application in organizations.

Case Studies

Case studies—studies that examine the environment and background in which events occur in specific organizations in a particular period of time—help us to understand behavior in those organizations at that time. For example, we could study a particular organization in depth to determine the contributing factors that led to its fast recovery after a prolonged recession. We might find several factors, including price reductions, the offering of good incentives to a highly motivated workforce, and the taking of big risks. However, the findings from this one-time study of an organization offer only limited knowledge about fast recovery from recessions, because the findings may not hold true for other organizations or for even the same organization at another time. The replication of case studies is almost impossible, since environmental and background factors are rarely the same from organization to organization. Most of the companies whose problems you have been asked to solve are from real cases written by management scholars who studied the companies. The solutions they found may not work for other organizations experiencing similar problems, since differences in size, technology, environment, labor force, clientele, and other internal and external factors may exist. However, through case studies, we do gather information and gain insights and knowledge that might help us to develop theories and test them later.

Scientific Research

Empirical or data-based *scientific research* identifies a problem and solves it after a systematic gathering and analysis of the relevant data. This type of research offers in-depth understanding, confidence in the findings, and the capability of applying the knowledge gained to similar organizations. Scientific research is the main focus of this appendix.

SCIENTIFIC INQUIRY

Scientific inquiry involves a well-planned and well-organized systematic effort to identify and solve a problem. It encompasses a series of well-thought-out and carefully executed activities that help to solve the problem—as opposed to the symptoms—that is identified.

Purposes of Scientific Research: Applied and Basic Research

Scientific inquiry can be undertaken for two different purposes: (1) to solve an existing problem that a particular organization faces or (2) to examine problems that organizations generally encounter and to generate solutions, thereby expanding the knowledge base. Research undertaken to solve an existing problem in a specific setting is *applied research*. In this type of research, the findings are immediately applied to solve the problem. Many professors acting as consultants to organizations do applied research.

Research undertaken to add information to our existing base of knowledge is *basic research*. A large number of issues are of common interest to many organizations—for example, how to increase the productivity of a diverse workforce or how to eradicate sexual harassment in the workplace. The knowledge gained from research on such general issues can become useful later for application in organizational settings, but that is not the primary goal of basic research. The goal is to generate knowledge with which to build better theories that can be tested later. Basic research is often published in academic journals.

The Two Faces of Science: Theory and Empirical Research

Theory and empirical research are the two faces of science. Organizations benefit when good theories are developed and then substantiated through scientific research, because the results can then be confidently used for problem solving.

Theory A *theory* is a postulated network of associations among various factors that a researcher is interested in investigating. For example, given what has been published thus far, you might theorize that self-confident employees perceive their work environment positively, which fosters their productivity, which in turn generates more profits for the company. In constructing this theory, you have postulated a positive relationship among (1) the self-confidence of employees and their positive attitude toward their work environment, (2) their attitude toward the work environment and their productivity, and (3) their productivity and the company's profits.

No doubt, this theory appeals to common sense. But in order to establish whether or not it holds true, we need to actually test it in organizations. Thus, theories offer the basis for doing scientific, data-based research; the theories and research together add to our knowledge. Conducting empirical research without the basis of sound theories does not steer us in the right direction, and building theories without empirically testing them limits their value.

The usefulness of good theories cannot be overstated. A good theory is formulated only after a careful examination of all the previous research and writings on the topic of interest, so that no factor already established as important is inadvertently omitted. Theory building offers unique opportunities to look at phenomena from different perspectives or to add new dimensions to existing ways of examining a phenomenon. New insights and creative ideas for theory building can come through personal observation, intuition, or even informal discussions with employees.

Testable theories are theories whose hypothesized relationships among measurable variables can be empirically tested and verified. When tested and substantiated repeatedly, such theories become the foundation on which subsequent theory building progresses. The next issue of interest is how theories are affirmed through empirical research.

Empirical Research As we have just seen, theories are of no practical use unless we have confidence that they work and can be applied to problem solving in organizational settings. Empirical research allows us to test the value of theories.

Empirical research is research that involves identifying the factors to be studied, gathering the relevant data, analyzing them, and drawing conclusions from the results of data analysis. It could involve simple qualitative analysis of the data, or it could be more complex, using a hypothetico-deductive approach. In *qualitative analysis*, responses to open-ended questions are obtained and meaningfully classified, and certain conclusions are drawn. In the *hypothetico-deductive approach*, a problem is identified, defined, and studied in depth. Then, a theory is formulated. From that theory, testable hypotheses are generated. Next, a research design is developed, relevant data are gathered and analyzed, results are interpreted, and conclusions (or deductions) are drawn from the results. Figure B.1 illustrates this approach.

To be called "scientific," research should conform to certain basic principles. It should be conducted objectively (without subjective biases). It should have a good and rigorous design (which we will examine shortly). It should be testable; that is, the conjectured relationships among factors in a setting should be capable of being tested. It should be replicable; that is, the results must be similar each time similar research is conducted. Finally, the findings should be generalizable (applicable to similar settings). It goes without saying, then, that scientific research offers precision (a good degree of exactitude) and a high degree of confidence in the results of the research (e.g. the researcher can say that 95 percent of the time, the results generated by the research will hold true, with only a 5 percent chance of its not being so).

THE RESEARCH PROCESS

The research process starts with a definition of the problem. To help define the problem, the researcher may interview people and study published materials in the area of interest in order to better understand what is happening in the environment. After defining the problem in clear and precise terms, the researcher develops a

FIGURE B.1 Steps in the Hypothetico-Deductive Approach to Research

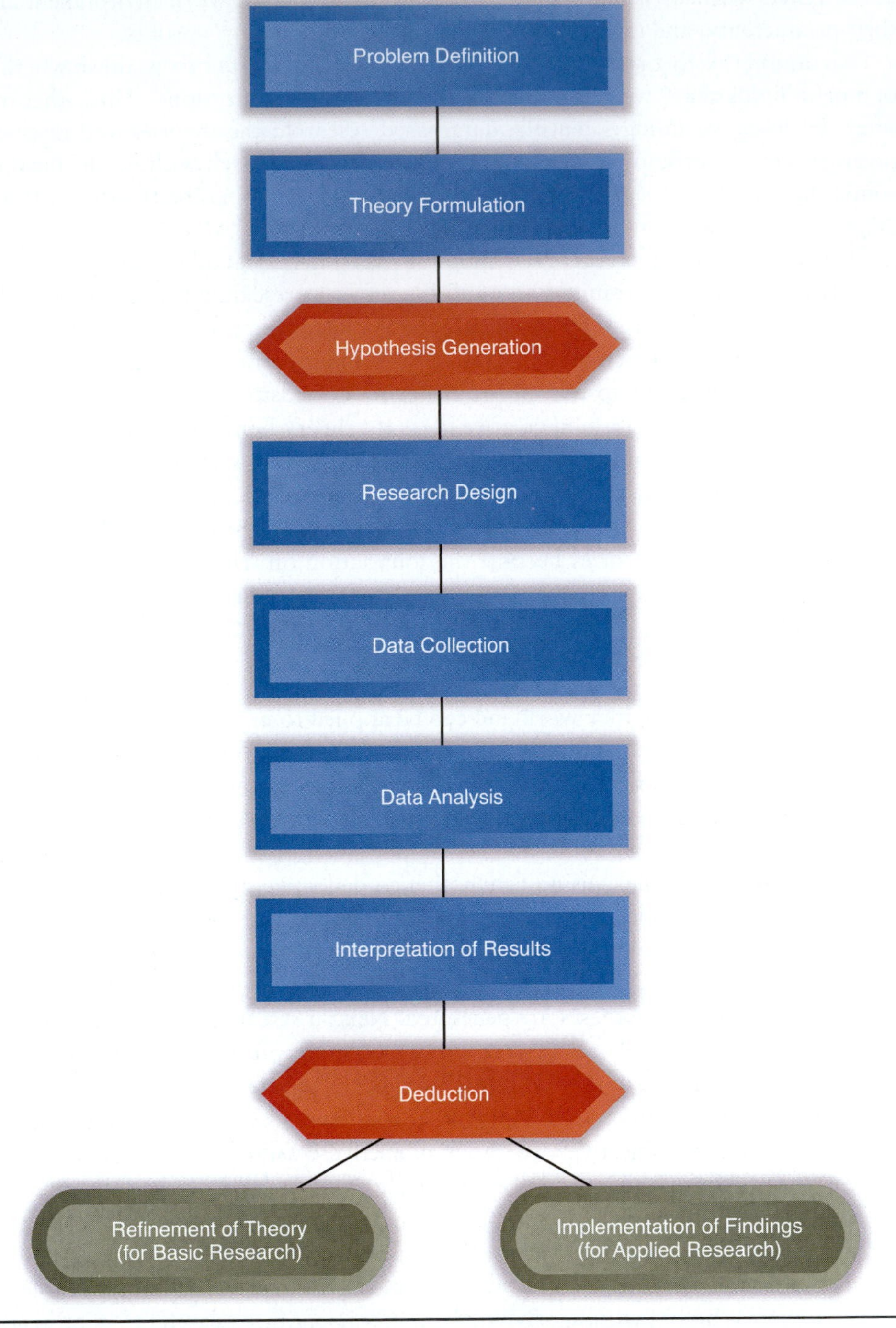

theoretical framework, generates hypotheses, creates the research design, collects data, analyzes data, interprets results, and draws conclusions.

Problem Definition

The first job for the researcher is to define the problem. It is often difficult to state precisely the specific research question to be investigated. The researcher might simply know the broad area of interest—for instance, discrimination—without being clear about which aspect of discrimination to study. In order to focus on the issue to be investigated, the researcher might need to collect some preliminary information that will help to narrow down the issue.

Such information can be obtained by interviewing people in organizations and by doing a literature survey. For example, employees of different gender, race, age, physical ability, and the like may be interviewed to determine the specific aspect of discrimination on which to focus. These interviews also provide insight into what the employees (rather than the researchers) consider important. The literature survey ensures that no pertinent variable is inadvertently omitted and that there is a credible and defensible basis for the research to be done. The researcher conducts an exhaustive search of all the published work in the area of interest to determine what research has been done thus far in the particular area and with what results. The search consumes a lot of time, as one must wade through several psychological, sociological, anthropological, and other relevant journals.

With all this information in hand, the researcher is now ready to define the problem. A well-defined, precise problem statement is a must for any study. The problem definition for the broad topic of discrimination could be this: *What are the important factors that contribute to employees' beliefs that they are being discriminated against by their immediate supervisor in cross-gender or cross-racial supervisor–employee relationships?*

Theoretical Framework

The next step is to develop a theoretical framework for the study. It involves focusing on the pertinent variables for the study and discussing the anticipated or theorized network of connections among the variables. For the discrimination problem, the framework might identify three factors related to employees' beliefs that they were discriminated against by the supervisor: (1) the level of mutual trust that is perceived by the employee to exist between the supervisor and employee (high to low), (2) the manner in which the supervisor offers performance feedback to the employee (in a forthright and helpful manner rather than in a derogatory and hurtful way), and (3) the extent to which the supervisor plays the role of mentor to the employee (training the subordinate and promoting the person's interests in career advancement to being indifferent toward the employee's career progress).

A network of logical connections among these four variables of interest to the study—discrimination (the dependent variable) and trust, performance feedback, and mentoring (the three independent variables)—can then be formulated. These connections with the anticipated nature and direction of the relationships among the variables are postulated in the theoretical framework.

Hypotheses

On the basis of the theoretical framework, the researcher next generates hypotheses. A *hypothesis* is a testable statement of the conjectured relationship between two or more variables. It is derived from the connections postulated in the theoretical framework. An example of a hypothesis is this: The more the employee perceives the supervisor as performing the mentoring role, the less the employee will feel discriminated against by the supervisor. The statement can be tested through data gathering and correlational analysis to see if it is supported.

Research Design

The next step in the research process is research design. Because this step is complex, it is covered in a separate section of the appendix, after the research process.

Data Collection

After creating the research design, the researcher must gather the relevant data. In our example of the discrimination problem, we would collect data on the four variables of interest from employees in one or more organizations, obtain information about their race and gender and that of their supervisors, and seek such demographic data as age, educational level, and position in the organization. This information helps us describe the sample and enables us to see later if demographic characteristics make a difference in the results. For example, we might discover during data analysis that older employees sense less discrimination than their younger counterparts. Such information could even provide a basis for further theory development.

Data Analysis

Having collected the data, the researcher must next analyze it, using statistical procedures to test whether the hypotheses have been substantiated. In the case of the discrimination hypothesis, if a correlational analysis between the variables of mentoring and discrimination indicates a significant negative correlation, the hypothesis will have been supported. In other words, we have been correct in conjecturing that the more the supervisor is perceived as a mentor, the less the employee feels discriminated against. Each of the hypotheses formulated from the theoretical framework is tested, and the results are examined.

Interpreting Results and Drawing Conclusions

The final step is to interpret the results of the data analysis and draw conclusions about them. In our example, if a significant negative relationship is indeed found between mentoring and discrimination, then one of our conclusions might be that mentoring helps fight feelings of discrimination. We might therefore recommend that if the organization wants to create a climate where employees do not feel discriminated against, supervisors should actively engage in mentoring. If the organization accepts this recommendation, it might conduct training programs to make supervisors better mentors. By testing and substantiating each of the hypotheses, we might find a multitude of solutions to overcome the perception of discrimination by employees.

Summary

We can see that every step in the research process is important. Unless the problem is well defined, the research endeavor will be fruitless. If a thorough literature survey is not done, a defensible theoretical framework cannot be developed and useful hypotheses cannot be generated—which compromises effective problem solving. Using the correct methods in data gathering and analysis and drawing relevant conclusions are all indispensable methodological steps for conducting empirical research. We next examine some of the research design issues that are integral to conducting good research.

RESEARCH DESIGN

Issues regarding research design relate particularly to how the variables are measured, how the data are collected, what sampling design is used, and how the data are analyzed. Before decisions in these areas are made, some details about the nature and purpose of the study have to be determined so there is a good match between the purpose of the study and the design choices. If the research design does not mesh with the research goals, the right solutions will not be found.

Important Concepts in Research Design

Five important concepts in research design must be understood before an adequate design can be created: nature of study, study setting, types of study, researcher interference, and time horizon. The *nature of study* is the purpose of the study—whether it is to establish correlations among variables or causation. The *study setting* could be either the environment in which the phenomena studied normally and naturally occur—the *field*—or it could be in a contrived, artificial setting, such as a laboratory. The *type of study* is either experimental (to establish causal connections) or correlational (to establish correlations). An experiment could be conducted in an artificial setting—a *lab experiment*, or it could be conducted in the organization itself where events naturally occur—*field experiment*. *Researcher interference* is the extent to which the researcher manipulates the independent variable and controls other contaminating factors in the study setting that are likely to affect the cause–effect relationship. The *time horizon* is the number of data collection points in the study; the study could be either one-shot (various types of data are collected only once during the investigation) or longitudinal (same or similar data are collected more than once from the same system during the course of the study).

Purpose of Study and Design Choices

One of the primary issues to consider before making any research design decision is the purpose of the study. Is the research to establish a causal relationship (that variable *X* causes variable *Y*), or is it to detect any correlations that might exist between two or more variables? A study to establish a cause–effect relationship differs in many areas (for example, the setting, type of study, extent of researcher interference with the ongoing processes, and time frame of the study) from a study to examine correlations among factors. Figure B.2 depicts the fit between the goal of the study and the characteristics of the study.

Causal Studies

Studies conducted to detect causal relationships call for an experimental design, considerable researcher interference, and a longitudinal time span. The design could consist of laboratory experiments, field experiments, or simulations.

Laboratory Experiments A rigorous causal study may call for a *laboratory experiment*, where participants are exposed to an artificial environment and an artificial stimulus in order to establish a cause–effect relationship. The experiment is set up with maximum researcher interference; both manipulation and controls (described later) are used, and data are collected from the subjects more than once during the experiment (longitudinally). Following is an example of how a lab experiment is conducted.

Suppose a manager wants to know which of two incentives—offering stock options or giving a bonus—would better improve employee productivity. To determine this, the manager has to experiment with each of the two types of incentives to see which offers better results. Not knowing how to proceed, the manager might hire a researcher who is likely to recommend conducting a lab experiment first and then a field experiment. The lab experiment firmly establishes the causal relationship,

FIGURE B.2 Fit between Goal of Study and Study Characteristics

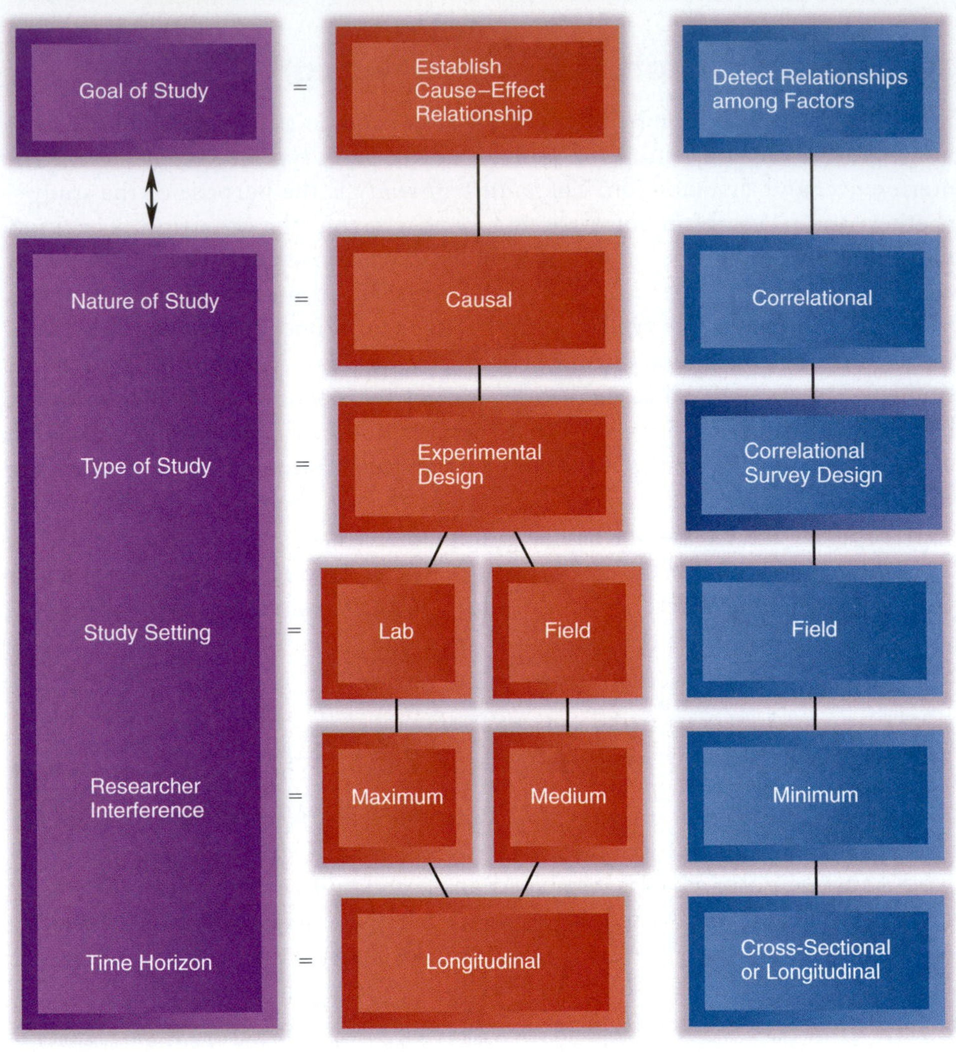

and the field experiment confirms whether or not the causal relationship established during the lab experiment holds good in the organizational setting.

To set up a lab experiment in which thirty subjects participate, the following is done:

1. An artificial setting is created. It will consist of three conference rooms in which the experiment is conducted after regular work hours.
2. A simple task—assembling cardboard houses—is given to the subjects, who take part in the experiment for two hours.
3. The subjects receive an imaginary bonus in the form of cardboard chips and stock options in the form of fake certificates.
4. Each subject is randomly assigned to one of three conference rooms, thus forming three ten-member groups.

For the first hour, all three groups will be assigned the task of assembling the cardboard houses. Thereafter, the researcher manipulates the incentives—giving one group stock options, another a bonus, and a third, called the control group, no incentives at all. The researcher has already exercised tight control to ensure that all three groups have more or less the same types of members in terms of ability, experience, and the like by randomly assigning members to each of the groups. In random assignment, every member has an equal chance of being assigned to any of the groups. This control helps avoid contamination of the cause–effect relationship, since all factors that might affect the causal relationship (age, ability, and so on) are randomly distributed among the groups.

The data are collected at two different times in the following manner. At the end of the first hour, when all three groups have worked without any incentives, the number of cardboard houses built by each group will be recorded by the researcher. The numbers are again counted and recorded at the end of the second hour, after the introduction of the incentives. Determining the difference between the number of houses assembled during the second hour and the number assembled during the first hour for the three groups clarifies the following two issues:

- Do the incentives make any difference at all to performance? Obviously, if the performance has increased during the second hour for either or both of the two groups provided with incentives, while there is no difference for the control group, then it is safe to surmise that either or both of the incentives have caused performance to rise. If there is no difference in the production between the second and first hour for all three groups, then, of course, the incentives have not caused an increase in performance.
- If the incentives do make a difference, which of the two incentives has worked better? By examining which group—the group that received the stock options or the group that received the bonus—performed better during the second hour, we know which of the two incentives worked better. The incentive that increases performance more will obviously be preferred by the company.

Because all possible contaminating factors have been controlled by the random assignment of members to the three groups, the cause–effect relationships found can be accepted with a high degree of confidence.

Field Experiments What occurred in the tightly controlled artificial lab setting may or may not happen in an organizational setting, where many of the factors (such as employees' ages and experience) cannot be controlled and the jobs to be done might be quite complex. But having established a strong causal relationship in the lab setting, the researcher is eager to see if that relationship is generalizable to the organization, or field setting.

For the field experiment, three experimental cells (three branches or departments of the company, or whatever other units are appropriate for the organization) can be chosen. Real bonus and stock options can be offered to two groups, while the third group is treated as a control group and given no incentives. Work performance data can be collected for the three cells before the incentives are introduced and again six months after the incentives are introduced.

While it is possible to manipulate the incentive in a field experiment, it is not possible to control the contaminating factors (ability, experience, and so on). Because employees are already placed, members cannot be randomly assigned to the three units. Under these circumstances, researcher interference can be only partial, since the independent variable can be manipulated but other factors cannot be controlled. Even manipulating the independent variable is not easy, because people in organizations get suspicious and anxious as the word spreads that some strange changes are being made at some sites. Not only does this cause apprehension among employees, but it may also produce invalid results. Because of these difficulties, very few field experiments are conducted in organizational behavior research. However, if the manipulation is successful and the results of the field experiment are similar to those of the lab experiment, the manager can confidently introduce the changes needed to obtain the desired results.

If you read journal articles describing experimental designs, you will want to see how well the manipulations were done and how tightly the contaminating variables were controlled. Were the independent variables successfully manipulated, or did the subjects see through the manipulations? If the subjects in the various groups differed in some characteristics that are relevant to the cause–effect relationship, then it cannot be said with confidence that only the manipulated independent variable caused the dependent variable. Other factors in the setting might also have influenced the dependent variable, and they might be impossible to trace.[1]

Simulations Somewhere between lab and field experiments are *simulations*—experiments that are conducted in settings that closely resemble field settings. The specially created settings look much like actual environments in which events normally occur—for example, offices with desks, computers, and phones. Members of the experimental group are randomly selected and exposed to real-world experiences over a period of time, during which their behavior is studied. A free simulation for studying leadership styles, called "Looking Glass," has been used in management classes. This simulation enables students to study different kinds of behavior as the researcher manipulates some of the stimuli while allowing the flow of events to be governed by the reactions of the participants.[2]

Correlational Studies

Researchers and managers may not be interested in establishing causal connections. Instead, they may want to understand, describe, or predict occurrences in the workplace. In general, they want to know which factors are related to desirable outcomes (such as employee loyalty to the organization) and which to undesirable outcomes (such as high turnover rates). *Correlational studies* are studies that are not specifically geared toward establishing cause–effect relationships. Such studies may be *exploratory*—trying to understand certain relationships; *descriptive*—trying to describe certain phenomena at the workplace; or *analytical*—focusing on testing hypotheses. Correlational studies are always conducted in the field setting with minimum researcher interference, and they can be either one-shot or longitudinal. The vast majority of the research articles published in organizational behavior journals are field studies examining correlations among factors.

To conduct a scientific study, whether causal or correlational, certain research design decisions must be made. As Figure B.3 shows, these decisions involve measurement, issues, data collection methods, sampling design, and data analysis procedures.

FIGURE B.3 Research Design Decisions

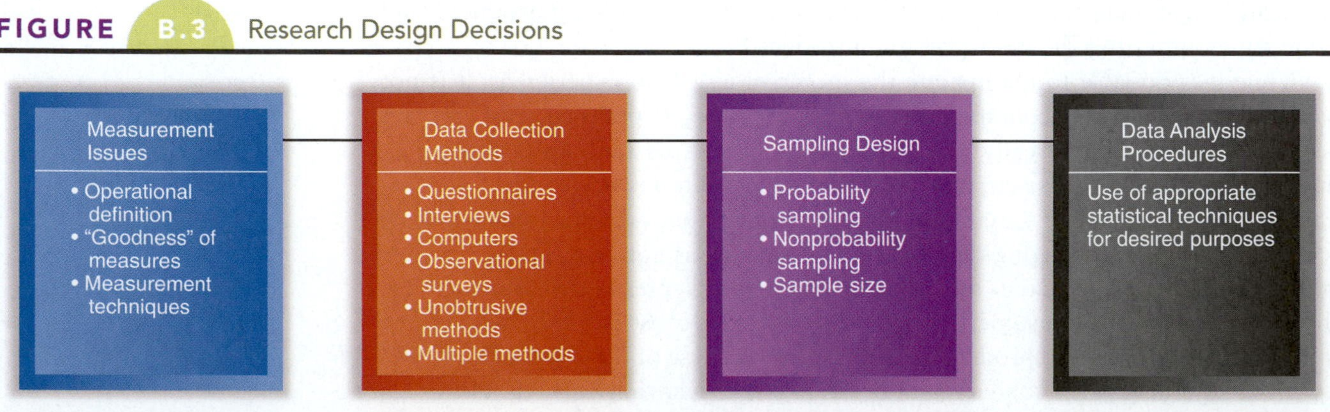

Measurement Issues

We saw earlier that it is difficult to measure attitudes, feelings, and other abstract concepts. Since the measurement of variables in the organizational sciences is not as exact as in the physical sciences, management research cannot be completely scientific. It is possible, however, to minimize biases in measurement by carefully developing valid and reliable measures for even abstract concepts. The primary aspects in measurement are operational definition, the "goodness" of measures, and the measurement techniques to be used.

Operational Definition Attitudes such as job satisfaction and organizational commitment do not easily lend themselves to measurement. To measure them, we first need to translate them into observable behaviors. *Operational definition* is the reduction of the level of abstraction of concepts so as to identify the observable behaviors and measure them.

For example, how can we measure the motivational level of individuals? We know that highly motivated people engage in the following types of behaviors, among others. They are driven by work, and they keep persevering even if they initially fail to accomplish what they want. We can measure the abstract concept of motivation by developing an instrument that asks subjects to respond to several suitably worded questions tapping these behaviors.[3] Most of the abstract concepts that are important to the study of organizational behavior have been operationally defined by scholars, who have developed "good" instruments for measuring them.[4]

"Goodness" of Measures "Good" measurement instruments offer researchers the confidence that they do indeed measure what is desired to be measured and do so in a thorough and accurate manner. The goodness of instruments is established through their validity and reliability.

Validity is our confidence that the instrument used does indeed measure the concept it is supposed to measure. For instance, if a twenty-item instrument is developed to measure job satisfaction, we need to know that it does indeed measure job satisfaction, not employees' general happiness.

Researchers usually establish various types of validity for the measures they use. Among them are content validity, criterion-related validity, predictive validity, construct validity, and convergent and discriminant validity. Journal articles often explain the types of validity established for the instrument used, especially if it is newly developed. In general, only such measures as are both valid and reliable are frequently used by researchers.[5]

Reliability is the ability of an instrument to accurately and stably measure a concept over time and across situations. For example, it is not enough for an instrument to measure job satisfaction; it must do so consistently and accurately time and again in all settings. Most researchers discuss the reliability of their instruments in terms of stability and consistency. Test–retest reliability is one indicator of the stability of a measure over time. Cronbach's alpha and split-half reliability are two indicators of the internal consistency of instruments. These are the terms you are likely to come across in published empirical research.

Authors of studies usually provide details of the measures they use and, at a minimum, cite their source. Journal editors and reviewers try to ensure that studies to be published have used valid and reliable measures. Discriminating readers of journals reporting empirical studies pay attention to the "goodness" of the measures. If variables are not validly and reliably measured, how can we place any confidence in the results of the study?

Measurement Techniques Concepts are not measured solely through questionnaires or interviews. Sometimes, in order to tap certain ideas, feelings, and thoughts that are not easily verbalized, researchers use *projective tests*—word association, sentence completion, thematic apperception tests, and ink-blot tests are some familiar projective tests. In word association (e.g., work could be associated with excitement or drudgery) and sentence completion ("I like") tests, it is expected that the respondent will draw on deeply embedded feelings, attitudes, and orientations when answering. Marketing researchers use these techniques to assess consumer preferences. Thematic apperception tests and ink-blot tests ask the subject to offer a story or interpret an ink blot. They can be interpreted only by trained psychologists.

Data Collection Methods

Data can be collected through questionnaires, interviews, computers, observation, unobtrusive methods, or a combination of these. The most frequently used method in organizational behavior research is questionnaires.

Questionnaires A *questionnaire* is a written set of questions to which respondents record their answers, usually within a close range of alternatives given to them. Questionnaires can be mailed to respondents or administered personally.

Mail questionnaires are commonly used because of the large number of people who can be reached economically even when they are geographically dispersed. As a rule, however, they do not elicit a good response rate, even when stamped, self-addressed envelopes are enclosed for their return. (Researchers sometimes even include, as a small token of their appreciation, a one-dollar bill.) A 30 percent response rate for mail questionnaires is considered good. Mail responses generally fall far short of even this low percentage. Because of the low response rate, certain types of nonresponse biases can creep into research. For example, we cannot know if those who responded to the survey differ from those who did not. Thus, we cannot be sure that the data are representative of the population we are trying to study.

Personally administered questionnaires are questionnaires given to groups of subjects by the researcher, who collects the responses immediately after completion. This method ensures practically a 100 percent response rate. However, many organizations are reluctant to spare company time for the research effort unless the study is of vital importance to them.

Interviews *Interviews* have the potential to elicit a good deal of information. In *structured interviews*, specific questions are asked of all respondents, and the responses are noted by the interviewer. In *unstructured interviews*, there is no predetermined format; questions are framed according to responses given to the previous question. Structured interviews are conducted when the interviewer knows precisely what sort of information is needed. They are efficient in terms of the amount of time involved in both obtaining the required information and categorizing the data obtained. Unstructured interviews are conducted when the researcher wants to explore a problem or become more knowledgeable about particular situations.

Face-to-face interviews offer the researcher the advantage of being able to observe the interviewees as they respond to questions. Nonverbal messages transmitted by the interviewees can be observed and explored further. *Telephone interviews*, on the other hand, help the researcher reach a vast number of geographically dispersed individuals. In both face-to-face and telephone interviews, certain types of biases can enter. The way a question is worded and asked, the inflection of a voice, the frame of mind of the interviewee at the time the interview is conducted, and other factors can all contribute to biases in the data.

Computers *Computer-assisted interviewing* and *computer-aided surveys* will become more popular in the future as more and more people become comfortable using their computers at home and responding to questions contained on diskettes or displayed on Web sites. Interview and questionnaire methods of data collection are greatly facilitated through computers. However, computer literacy of respondents is a prerequisite for using computer-assisted data collection techniques effectively.

Observational Surveys *Observational surveys* are another data collection method whereby information is obtained without asking questions of subjects. In this method, the researcher observes firsthand what is going on and how people are behaving in the work setting. The data are collected by either nonparticipant observers (researchers who observe behavior as outsiders) or participant observers (integral members of the work team). An example of a nonparticipant study is one done by Henry Mintzberg, who observed the nature of managerial work over a period of time.

Like interviews, observational surveys can be either structured or unstructured. In a structured observational survey, the observer identifies the factors that are to be observed. For example, the observer might want to note the number of times a manager gives instructions to staff members and how much time this takes. In an unstructured observational survey, the observer might simply want to know how the manager spends the day at the workplace and might jot down all the activities the manager engages in and the time periods and frequencies involved.

Observational studies help prevent respondent bias, since information is not given by the subjects directly. Any bias that might creep in through the self-consciousness of subjects usually lasts only a few days. Then, subjects begin to function and behave normally, oblivious to the presence of the observer.

However, observer fatigue and observer bias cannot be totally avoided in observational studies. Moreover, when several observers are involved in a large research project, interobserver reliability could become an issue for concern; different observers might interpret and categorize the same behavior differently. This problem can be minimized by training the observers before the start of the project.

Unobtrusive Methods Data collection by *unobtrusive methods* offers valid and reliable information; bias is minimized because the source of the data is tangible elements rather than people. For example, the usage of library books can be determined by the wear and tear on them, a source of information more reliable than surveys of users of the library. The number of empty cans or bottles of pop in the recycling bins outside houses on garbage collection days would offer a good idea of the beverage consumption patterns in households. The personnel records of a company would indicate the absenteeism patterns of employees. Unobtrusive methods thus have the potential to offer the most reliable and unbiased data. They are, however, time consuming and labor intensive; also, the researcher must obtain the company's permission to gain access to such data.

Multiple Methods Each data collection method has advantages and disadvantages. The best approach is using multiple methods of collecting data, since it offers researchers a chance to cross-check the information obtained through the various methods. This approach, however, is expensive and thus is used infrequently in organizational behavior research.

When you read journal articles, you should assess the data collection methods used by the researchers to determine if they are adequate. Authors of published studies often discuss the limitations of their research and the biases they have attempted to minimize. The biases could relate to the types of measures used, the data collection methods adopted, the sampling design, and other research process and design issues. Sophisticated managers pay attention to all research design details in order to evaluate the quality of the research.

Sampling Design

Sampling is the process of drawing a limited number of subjects from a larger population or universe. Since researchers cannot possibly survey the entire universe of people they are interested in studying, they usually draw a sample of subjects from the population for investigation. The sampling design used makes a difference in the generalizability of the findings and determines the usefulness and scientific nature of the study. Sample size is another important issue. There are two broad categories of sampling—probability sampling and nonprobability sampling.

Probability Sampling *Probability sampling* is sampling that ensures that the elements in the population have some known chance, or probability, of being selected for the sample. Because of this, probability sampling designs offer more generalizability than nonprobability designs. There are many probability designs. The *simple random sampling* design, wherein every element in the population has a known and equal chance of being chosen, lends itself to the greatest generalizability. However, other probability designs can be more efficient and offer good generalizability as well. Among them are systematic sampling, stratified random sampling, cluster sampling, and area sampling.

In *systematic sampling*, every *n*th element in the population is chosen as a subject. In *stratified random sampling*, the population is first divided into meaningful strata (for example, blue-collar and white-collar employees); a sample is then drawn from each stratum using either simple random sampling or systematic sampling. *Cluster sampling* is the random selection of chunks (clusters or groups) of elements from the population; every chunk has an equal chance of being selected, and all the members in each chosen chunk participate in the research. For example, in an attitude survey, three departments in an organization can be randomly chosen; all the members of the three departments are the subjects. *Area sampling* is cluster sampling confined to particular geographical areas, such as counties or city blocks. Marketing researchers use cluster and area sampling extensively for surveys.

Nonprobability Sampling For some research projects, probability sampling may be impossible or inappropriate. In such cases, *nonprobability sampling* may be used, even if generalizability is impaired or lost. In nonprobability sampling, the subjects do not have a known probability of being chosen for the study. For instance, the sample of subjects in a study of sexual harassment must come from those who have experienced such harassment; there is nothing to be gained by researching all the employees of the organization. When the choice of subjects for a study involves a limited number of people who are in a position to provide the required information, a probability sampling design is infeasible. The results of such a study are not generalizable; nevertheless, this type of sampling is the best way to learn about certain problems, such as sexual harassment.

Nonprobability sampling includes convenience sampling, judgment sampling, and quota sampling. In *convenience sampling*, information is collected from whoever is conveniently available. In *judgment sampling*, subjects who are in the best position to provide the required information are chosen. In *quota sampling*, people from different groups—some of which are underrepresented—are sampled for comparison purposes. One example might be a study of middle-class African-Americans and whites.

As noted earlier, nonprobability sampling does not lend itself to generalizability. In reading research articles, you should determine the type of sampling design being used and how much generalizability the author claims for the research.

Sample Size Another critical issue in sampling is *sample size*. Too small or too large a sample could distort the results of the research. Tables providing ideal sample sizes for desired levels of precision and confidence are available to researchers. In examining any business report or journal article, you should note the sampling design and the sample size used by the researcher to assess the generalizability of the findings.

Data Analysis Procedures

Beyond good measures, appropriate data collection methods, and an acceptable sampling design, a good research project should also have suitable *data analysis procedures*. Some data cannot be subjected to sophisticated statistical tests. One example is data collected on a *nominal scale*, which divides subjects into mutually exclusive groups, such as men and women or the poor and the rich. Another example is data collected on an *ordinal scale*, which rank-orders the subjects and indicates a preference (X is better than Y). Various simple ways are available to analyze such data that are qualitative or nonparametric in nature. For instance, if we have categorized under distinct headings the verbal responses of organizational members to an open-ended question on how they perceive their work environment, a frequency count of the responses in each category would be adequate to describe how the work environment is perceived. Likewise, to detect if the gender of the worker (male versus female) is independent of members' commitment to the organization (less committed versus more committed), a simple x2 (chi-square) test would suffice.

Sophisticated statistical tests are possible when data have been gathered on interval or ratio scales. Data collected on interval scales—through individuals' responses to questions on equal-appearing multipoint scales—allow for the computation of the arithmetic mean and standard deviation. Data collected on ratio scales also allow us to compute proportions and ratios. For example, an individual who weighs 250 pounds is twice as heavy as one who weighs 125 pounds. Pearson correlations can be calculated, and multiple regression and many multivariate analyses can be made with data obtained on interval and ratio scales. These sorts of analyses cannot be made with data obtained on nominal and ratio scales. Illustrations of the four scales appear in Figure B.4.

One decision that needs to be made before collecting the data is what kinds of analyses are needed to find answers to the research question. This decision will determine which scales should be used in data collection. Sometimes researchers are tempted to apply more sophisticated statistical analyses to data that do not lend themselves to such analyses (this includes sample sizes below thirty). Using inappropriate methods can negatively affect the interpretation of the results and can compromise the problem solution.

Biases in Interpretation of Results

Thus far, we have examined the biases that would result from poor research process and design decisions. Another source of bias is in the interpretation of results. Objectivity plays a large part in the validity of interpretations from the results of data analysis. Objectivity may be difficult, however, if the results of the study do not substantiate the theories painstakingly developed by the researcher.

FIGURE B.4 Illustrations of Four Data Analysis Scales

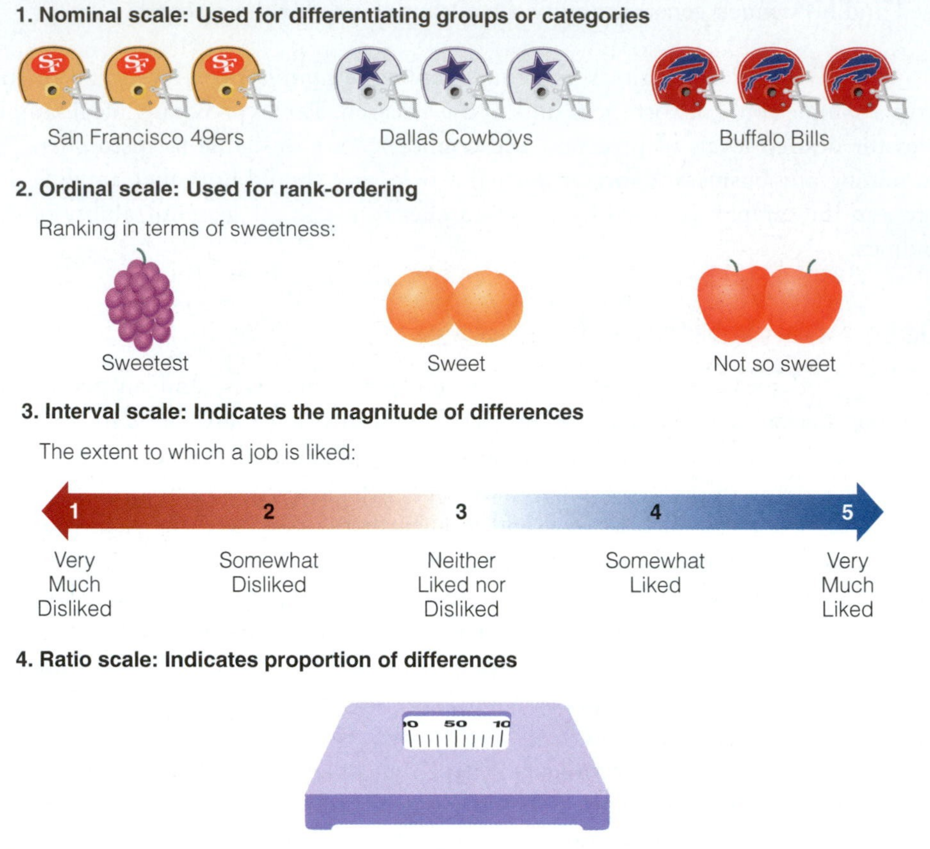

When data analysis does not substantiate one or more of the hypotheses generated, the researcher may be tempted to downplay the results or try to explain them away. For example, a researcher may say that the results were actually in the expected direction even though they were not statistically significant. If a hypothesis has not passed the appropriate statistical test, the hypothesis is just not substantiated, regardless of whether the results were in the theorized direction. When authors try to explain their results, you have to decide for yourself whether the explanations offered are valid.

ORGANIZATIONAL BEHAVIOR RESEARCH AND YOU

It is seldom possible to do completely scientific research in the field of organizational behavior. First, adherence to good research design principles may not always be possible, since certain choices (such as obtaining the most representative sample for better generalizability or utilizing the best data collection methods) may be beyond the researcher's control. Second, attitudes and feelings cannot be measured accurately. Hence, there are likely to be several types of biases in research in this field. However, by paying careful attention to the research process and rigorously making good research design choices, we are able to minimize the biases and enhance the objectivity, testability, replicability, precision and confidence, and generalizability of our research.

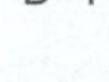

Bias can enter at every stage of the process, from problem definition to problem solution. Errors can creep into experimental designs by way of poor or inadequate manipulations and controls. They can enter into measurement, data collection, sampling, data analysis, interpretation of results, and the drawing of conclusions therefrom.

Unless managers are knowledgeable about some of the methodological flaws that can adversely affect research results, they may inappropriately apply the conclusions drawn in published research to their own settings. Having been exposed to the rudiments of scientific research, *you* can critically examine and evaluate all published works before you assess their usefulness for your organization. For instance, you would not consider applying the results of good research done in a service organization to a manufacturing firm. Good research results in the hands of knowledgeable managers are highly useful tools. That is where research knowledge becomes invaluable. By grasping the essentials of good research, you will become a discriminating consumer of business reports and published articles and can become an effective manager. Research knowledge can often make the difference between managerial excellence and mediocrity.

References

Chapter 1

1. M. Kempner, "Caribou Strives to Become 'No 1 in Experience'," *The Atlanta Journal-Constitution* (June 3, 2007): C1.
2. H. Schwartz, "The Clockwork or the Snakepit: An Essay on the Meaning of Teaching Organizational Behavior," *Organizational Behavior Teaching Review* 11, No. 2 (1987): 19–26.
3. M. Matcho, "Idea Fest," *Fast Company* 66 (January 2003): 95–105, http://www.fastcompany.com/online/66/ideafest.html.
4. H. G. Barkem, J. A. C. Baum, and E. A. Mannix, "Management Challenges in a New Time," *Academy of Management Journal* 45 (2002): 916–930.
5. K. Lewin, "Field Theory in Social Science," selected theoretical papers (edited by Dorin Cartwright) (New York: Harper, 1951).
6. N. Schmitt, ed., Industrial/Organizational Section in *Encyclopedia of Psychology* (Washington, D.C.: American Psychological Association, and New York: Oxford University Press, 2000).
7. R. M. Yerkes, "The Relation of Psychology to Military Activities," *Mental Hygiene* 1 (1917): 371–376.
8. N. Gross, W. Mason, and A. McEachen, *Explorations in Role Analysis: Studies of the School Superintendency Role* (New York: Wiley, 1958).
9. J. S. Adams, A. Tashchian, and T. H. Stone. "Codes of Ethics as Signals for Ethical Behavior," *Journal of Business Ethics 29* (2001): 199–211.
10. F. W. Taylor, *The Principles of Scientific Management* (New York: Norton, 1911).
11. E. A. Locke and G. P. Latham, *A Theory of Goal Setting and Task Performance* (Englewood Cliffs, N.J.: Prentice-Hall, 1990).
12. A. L. Wilkins and W. G. Ouchi, "Efficient Cultures: Exploring the Relationship between Culture and Organizational Performance," *Administrative Science Quarterly 28* (1983): 468–481.
13. M. F. R. Kets de Vries and D. Miller, "Personality, Culture, and Organization," *Academy of Management Review 11* (1986): 266–279.
14. H. Schwartz, *Narcissistic Process and Corporate Decay: The Theory of the Organizational Ideal* (New York: NYU Press, 1990).
15. J. G. March and H. A. Simon, *Organizations* (New York: Wiley, 1958).
16. H. B. Elkind, *Preventive Management: Mental Hygiene in Industry* (New York: B. C. Forbes, 1931).
17. J. C. Quick, "Occupational Health Psychology: Historical Roots and Future Directions," *Health Psychology 18* (1999).
18. K. R. Pelletier, *Mind as Healer, Mind as Slayer: A Holistic Approach to Preventing Stress Disorders* (New York: Delacorte, 1977).
19. D. R. Ilgen, "Health Issues at Work," *American Psychologist* 45 (1990): 273–283.
20. B. M. Staw, L. E. Sandelands, and J. E. Dutton, "Threat-Rigidity Effects in Organizational Behavior: A Multilevel Analysis," *Administrative Science Quarterly* 26 (1981): 501–524.
21. D. Kirkpatrick, "The Net Makes It All Easier—Including Exporting U.S. Jobs," *Fortune* (May 26, 2003): 146.
22. E. V. Brown, President of Proline International, Inc., "Commencement Address—College of Business Administration, the University of Texas at Arlington" (December 2003).
23. T. Reay, K. Golden-Biddle, and K. Germann, "Legitimizing a New Role: Small Wins and Microprocesses of Change," *Academy of Management Journal* 49 (2006): 977–998.
24. R. L. A. Sterba, "The Organization and Management of the Temple Corporations in Ancient Mesopotamia," *Academy of Management Review* 1 (1976): 16–26; S. P. Dorsey, *Early English Churches in America* (New York: Oxford University Press, 1952).
25. Sir I. Moncreiffe of That Ilk, *The Highland Clans: The Dynastic Origins, Chiefs, and Background of the Clans and of Some Other Families Connected to Highland History*, rev. ed. (New York: C. N. Potter, 1982).
26. D. Shambaugh, "The Soldier and the State in China: The Political Work System in the People's Liberation Army," *Chinese Quarterly* 127 (1991): 527–568.
27. L. L'Abate, ed., *Handbook of Developmental Family Psychology and Psychopathology* (New York: Wiley, 1993).
28. J. A. Hostetler, *Communitarian Societies* (New York: Holt, Rinehart & Winston, 1974).
29. J. M. Lewis, "The Family System and Physical Illness," in *No Single Thread: Psychological Health in Family Systems* (New York: Brunner/Mazel, 1976).
30. D. Katz and R. L. Kahn, *The Social Psychology of Organizations*, 2nd ed. (New York: John Wiley & Sons, 1978; H. J. Leavitt, "Applied Organizational Change in Industry: Structural, Technological, and Humanistic Approaches," in J. G. March, ed., *Handbook of Organizations* (Chicago: Rand McNally, 1965), 1144–1170.
31. J. D. Thompson, *Organizations in Action* (New York: McGraw-Hill, 1967).
32. F. J. Roethlisberger and W. J. Dickson, *Management and the Worker* (Cambridge, Mass.: Harvard University Press, 1939).
33. W. L. French and C. H. Bell, *Organization Development*, 4th ed. (Englewood Cliffs, N.J.: Prentice-Hall, 1990).
34. S. G. Barsade and D. E. Gibson, "Why Does Affect Matter in Organizations?," *Academy of Management Perspectives* 21 (2007): 36–59.
35. J. P. Kotter, "Managing External Dependence," *Academy of Management Review* 4 (1979): 87–92.
36. H. K. Steensma and D. G. Corley, "Organizational Context as a Moderator of Theories on Firm Boundaries for Technology Sourcing," *Academy of Management Journal* 44 (2001): 271–291.
37. Caribou corporate information. http://www.cariboucoffee.com/aboutus/http://www.cariboucoffee.com/aboutus/corporateprofile.asp; http://www.cariboucoffee.com/aboutus/pressrelease/05222007.pdf Accessed 7/01/07.
38. Genentech fact sheet. http://www.gene.com/gene/news/kits/biooncology/pdf/oncologypipeline.pdf. Accessed 6/19/07.
39. Google corporate information. http://www.google.com/corporate/. Accessed 5/21/07; K. H. Hammonds, "How Google Grows . . . and Grows . . . and Grows," *FastCompany* 69 (March 2003): 74. http://www.fastcompany.com/magazine/69/google.html
40. The Timberland Company corporate website. http://www.timberland.com/corp/index.jsp?page=corpTimeline; http://www.timberland.com/corp/index.jsp?page=pressreleaseandeid=7500021721 *Fortune* 100 Best

Companies to work for list. http://money.cnn.com/magazines/fortune/bestcompanies/2007/snapshots/78.html Accessed 7/01/07.

41. American Express corporate website. http://home3.americanexpress.com/corp/os/history.asp; http://home3.americanexpress.com/corp/our_story.asp; http://home3.americanexpress.com/corp/gb/themes.asp Accessed 7/01/07.
42. Toyota Company History, Profile, Vision, and Philosophy. http://www.toyota.co.jp/en/index.html.; Toyota Investor fact sheet. http://www.toyota.com/about/shareholder/images/2005factsheet.pdf. Accessed 6/19/07.
43. T. B. Lawrence and V. Corwin, "Being There: The Acceptance and Marginalization of Part-Time Professional Employees," *Journal of Organizational Behavior* 24 (2003): 923–943.
44. M. K. Gowing, J. D. Kraft, and J. C. Quick, *The New Organizational Reality: Downsizing, Restructuring and Revitalization* (Washington, D.C.: American Psychological Association, 1998); T. Tang and R. M. Fuller, "Corporate Downsizing: What Managers Can Do to Lessen the Negative Effects of Layoffs," *SAM Advanced Management Journal 60* (1995): 12–15, 31.
45. L. R. Offermann and M. K. Gowing, "Organizations of the Future," *American Psychologist* 45 (1990): 95–108.
46. J. Chatman, J. Polzer, S. Barsade, and M. Neale, "Being Different Yet Feeling Similar: The Influence of Demographic Composition and Organizational Culture on Work Processes and Outcomes," *Administrative Science Quarterly* 43 (1998): 749–780.
47. L. E. Thurow, *Head to Head: The Coming Economic Battle among Japan, Europe, and America* (New York: William Morrow, 1992).
48. J. E. Patterson, *Acquiring the Future: America's Survival and Success in the Global Economy* (Homewood, Ill.: Dow Jones-Irwin, 1990); H. B. Stewart, *Recollecting the Future: A View of Business, Technology, and Innovation in the Next 30 Years* (Homewood, Ill.: Dow Jones-Irwin, 1989).
49. D. Ciampa, *Total Quality* (Reading, Mass.: Addison-Wesley, 1992).
50. T. J. Douglas and W. Q. Judge, Jr., "Total Quality Management Implementation and Competitive Advantage: The Role of Structural Control and Exploration," *Academy of Management Journal* 44 (2001): 158–169.
51. American Management Association, *Blueprints for Service Quality: The Federal Express Approach* (New York: American Management Association, 1991); P. R. Thomas, L. J. Gallace, and K. R. Martin, *Quality Alone Is Not Enough* (New York: American Management Association, 1992).
52. J. de Mast, "A Methodological Comparison of Three Strategies for Quality Improvement," *International Journal of Quality & Reliability Management* 21 (2004): 198–213.
53. M. Barney, "Motorola's Second Generation," *Six Sigma Forum Magazine* 1 (3) (May 2002): 13.
54. J. A. Edosomwan, "Six Commandments to Empower Employees for Quality Improvement," *Industrial Engineering* 24 (1992): 14–15.
55. M. Baer and M. Frese, "Innovation Is Not Enough: Climates for Initiative and Psychological Safety Advantage: The Role of Structural Control and Exploration," *Journal of Organizational Behavior* 24 (2003): 45–68.
56. See also the five articles in the Special Research Forum on Teaching Effectiveness in the Organizational Sciences, *The Academy of Management Journal* 40 (1997): 1265–1398.
57. L. Proserpio and D. A. Gioia. "Teaching the Virtual Generation," *Academy of Management Learning and Education* 6 (2007): 69–80.
58. R. M. Steers, L. W. Porter, and G. A. Bigley, *Motivation and Leadership at Work* (New York: McGraw-Hill, 1996).
59. H. Levinson, *Executive Stress* (New York: New American Library, 1975).
60. D. L. Whetzel, "The Department of Labor Identifies Workplace Skills," *Industrial/Organizational Psychologist* 29 (1991): 89–90.
61. D. A. Whetton and K. S. Cameron, *Developing Management Skills*, 3rd ed. (New York: HarperCollins, 1995).
62. C. Argyris and D. A. Schon, *Organizational Learning: A Theory of Action Perspective* (Reading, Mass.: Addison-Wesley, 1978).
63. A. Y. Kolb and D. A. Kolb. "Learning Styles and Learning Spaces: Enhancing Experiential Learning in Higher Education, *Academy of Management Learning and Education* 4 (2005): 193–212.
64. R. Ramanjuam and D. M. Rousseau. "The Challenges Are Organizational not Just Clinical," *Journal of Organizational Behavior* 27 (2006): 811–827.
65. M. Kempner, "Caribou Strives to Become 'No 1 in Experience'," *The Atlanta Journal-Constitution* (June 3, 2007): C1.

Chapter 1 Case

1. "Our Company," Johnson & Johnson, http://www.jnj.com/our_company/index.htm (accessed August 15, 2007).
2. "Product Categories," Johnson & Johnson, http://www.jnj.com/product/categories//index.htm (accessed August 15, 2007).
3. *2006 Annual Report,* Johnson & Johnson, http://www.jnj.v1.papiervirtuel.com/report/2007030901/ (accessed August 15, 2007): 5.
4. "Awards & Recognition," Johnson & Johnson, http://www.jnj.com/our_company/awards/index.htm (accessed August 15, 2007).
5. "Our Credo History," Johnson & Johnson, http://www.jnj.com/our_company/our_credo_history/index.htm (accessed August 15, 2007).
6. Author unknown, Johnson & Johnson. *Fortune Small Business* 13(3) (April 2003): 90–93.
7. "Our Credo," Johnson & Johnson, http://www.jnj.com/our_company/our_credo/index.htm (accessed August 15, 2007).
8. Author unknown, *Fortune Small Business.*
9. "Our Credo History."
10. "Our Company."
11. T. Kinni, "Words to Work By: Crafting Meaningful Corporate Ethics Statements." *Harvard Management Communication Letter* (January 2003): 3–4.
12. "Revisions." Johnson & Johnson, http://www.jnj.com/our_company/our_credo_history/revisions/index.htm (accessed August 15, 2007).
13. "Our Credo History."

Chapter 2

1. M. Chase, "Boss Talk: How Genentech Wins at Blockbuster Drugs—CEO to Critics of Prices: 'Give Me a Break'," *The Wall Street Journal* (June 5, 2007): B1.
2. M. A. Hitt, R. E. Hoskisson, and J. S. Harrison, "Strategic Competitiveness in the 1990s: Challenges and Opportunities for U.S. Executives," *Academy of Management Executive* 5 (1991): 7–22.
3. H. G. Barkem, J. A. C. Baum, and E. A. Mannix, "Management Challenges in a New Time," *Academy of Management Journal* 45 (2002): 916–930.
4. S. C. Harper, "The Challenges Facing CEOs: Past, Present, and Future," *Academy of Management Executive* 6 (1992): 7–25.
5. T. R. Mitchell and W. G. Scott, "America's Problems and Needed Reforms: Confronting the Ethic of Personal Advantage," *Academy of Management Executive* 4 (1990): 23–25.
6. B. Spindle, "Sinking in Sync—The Global Slowdown Surprises Economists and Many Companies," *The Wall Street Journal* (December 21, 2000): A1–A10.
7. D. A. Harrison, J. H. Gavin, and A. T. Florey, "Time, Teams, and Task Performance: Changing Effects of Surface- and Deep-Level Diversity on Group Functioning," *Academy of Management Journal* 45 (2003): 1029–1045.
8. J. H. Gavin, J. C. Quick, C. L. Cooper, and J. D. Quick, "A Spirit of Personal Integrity: The Role of Character in Executive Health," *Organizational Dynamics* 32 (2003): 165–179.
9. K. Sera, "Corporate Globalization: A New Trend," *Academy of Management Executive* 6 (1992): 89–96.
10. K. Ohmae, *Borderless World: Power and Strategies in the Interlinked Economy* (New York: Harper & Row, 1990).
11. C. A. Bartlett and S. Ghoshal, *Managing across Borders: The Transnational Solution* (Boston: Harvard Business School Press, 1989).
12. F. Warner, "Learning How to Speak to Gen Y," *Fast Company* 72 (July 2003): 36–37.

13. K. R. Xin and J. L. Pearce, "Guanxi: Connections as Substitutes for Formal Institutional Support," *Academy of Management Journal* 39 (1996): 1641–1658.
14. P. S. Chan, "Franchise Management in East Asia," *Academy of Management Executive* 4 (1990): 75–85.
15. H. Weihrich, "Europe 1992: What the Future May Hold," *Academy of Management Executive* 4 (1990): 7–18.
16. E. H. Schein, "Coming to a New Awareness of Organizational Culture," *MIT Sloan Management Review* 25 (1984): 3–16.
17. S. S. Sarwano and R. M. Armstrong, "Microcultural Differences and Perceived Ethical Problems: An International Business Perspective," *Journal of Business Ethics* 30 (2001): 41–56.
18. R. Sharpe, "Hi-Tech Taboos," *The Wall Street Journal* (October 31, 1995): A1.
19. G. Hofstede, *Culture's Consequences: International Differences in Work-Related Values* (Beverly Hills, Calif.: Sage Publications, 1980).
20. G. Hofstede, "Motivation, Leadership, and Organization: Do American Theories Apply Abroad?" *Organizational Dynamics* (Summer 1980): 42–63.
21. R. Buda and S. M. Elsayed-Elkhouly, "Cultural Differences between Arabs and Americans," *Journal of Cross-Cultural Psychology* 29 (1998): 487–492.
22. G. Hofstede, "Gender Stereotypes and Partner Preferences of Asian Women in Masculine and Feminine Countries," *Journal of Cross Cultural Psychology* 27 (1996): 533–546.
23. G. Hofstede, "Cultural Constraints in Management Theories," *Academy of Management Executive* 7 (1993): 81–94.
24. G. M. Spreitzer, M. W. McCall, Jr., and J. D. Mahoney, "Early Identification of International Executive Potential," *Journal of Applied Psychology* 82 (1997): 6–29.
25. M. A. Hitt, L. Bierman, K. Uhlenbruck, and K. Shimizu, "The Importance of Resources in the Internationalization of Professional Service Firms: The Good, the Bad, and the Ugly," *Academy of Management Journal* 49 (2006): 1137–1157.
26. A. J. Michel, "Goodbyes Can Cost Plenty in Europe," *Fortune* (April 6, 1992): 16.
27. M. Adams, "Building a Rainbow One Stripe at a Time," *HR Magazine* 9 (August 1999): 72–79. Intel, "Diversity at Intel: Our Commitment," 2003, http://www.intel.com/jobs/Diversity/commitment.htm.
28. E. Brandt, "Global HR," *Personnel Journal* 70 (1991): 38–44.
29. P. Chattopadhyay, "Can Dissimilarity Lead to Positive Outcomes: The Influence of Open versus Closed Minds," *Journal of Organizational Behavior* 24 (2003): 295–312.
30. J. C. Quick, J. H. Gavin, C. L. Cooper, and J. D. Quick, "Working Together: Balancing Head and Heart," in R. H. Rozensky, N. G. Johnson, C. D. Goodheart, and W. R. Hammond, eds., *Psychology Builds a Healthy World: Opportunities for Research and Practice*: (Washington, D.C.: American Psychological Association, 2004) 219–232.
31. J. A. Gilbert and J. M. Ivancevich, "Valuing Diversity: A Tale of Two Organizations," *Academy of Management Executive* 4 (2000): 93–105.
32. R. W. Judy and C. D'Amico, *Workforce 2020* (Indianapolis, Ind.: Hudson Institute, 1997). U.S. Department of Labor, "Usual Weekly Earnings Summary," *Labor Force Statistics from the Current Population Survey* (Washington D.C.: U.S. Government, 2002).
33. S. Caudron, "Task Force Report Reveals Coke's Progress on Diversity," *Workforce* 82 (2003): 40, http://www.workforceonline.com/section/03/feature/23/42/44/234246.html.
34. L. S. Gottfredson, "Dilemmas in Developing Diversity Programs," in S. E. Jackson, ed., *Diversity in the Workplace: Human Resources Initiatives* (New York: Guilford Press, 1992), 279–305.
35. U.S. Department of Labor, "Employment Status of the Civilian Population by Sex and Age," (July 2004). Accessed on-line at http://stats.bls.gov/news.release/empsit.t01.htm.
36. "Catalyst Releases 2005 Censuses of Women Board Directors and Corporate Officers," Perspective. Catalyst.org, http://www.catalyst.org/bookstore/perspective/06August.pdf. Accessed 7/2/07.
37. Ibid.
38. Ibid.
39. U.S. Department of Labor, "Highlights of Women's Earnings in 2005," Report 995 (September 2006).
40. A. M. Morrison, R. P. White, E. Van Velsor, and the Center for Creative Leadership, *Breaking the Glass Ceiling: Can Women Reach the Top of America's Largest Corporations?* (Reading, Mass.: Addison-Wesley, 1987).
41. D. E. Arfken, S. L. Bellar, and M. M. Helms, "The Ultimate Glass Ceiling Revisited: The Presence of Women on Corporate Boards," *Journal of Business Ethics* 50 (March 2004): 177–186.
42. "Top Facts about Women-Owned Businesses," Center for Women's Business Research, http://www.womensbusinessresearch.org/facts/index.php. Accessed 7/2/07.
43. L. L. Martins and C. K. Parsons. "Effects of Gender Diversity Management on Perceptions of Organizational Attractiveness: The Role of Individual Differences in Attitudes and Beliefs," *Journal of Applied Psychology* 92 (2007): 865–875.
44. A. Eyring and B. A. Stead, "Shattering the Glass Ceiling: Some Successful Corporate Practices," *Journal of Business Ethics* 17 (1998): 245–251.
45. Catalyst, *Advancing Women in Business: The Catalyst Guide* (San Francisco: Jossey-Bass, 1998).
46. D. L. Nelson and M. A. Hitt, "Employed Women and Stress: Implications for Enhancing Women's Mental Health in the Workplace," in J. C. Quick, L. R. Murphy, and J. J. Hurrell, Jr., eds., *Stress and Well-Being at Work* (Washington, D.C.: American Psychological Association, 1992), 164–177.
47. L. E. Atwater and D. D. Van Fleet, "Another Ceiling: Can Males Compete for Traditionally Female Jobs?" *Journal of Management 23* (1997): 603–626.
48. U.S. Department of Health and Human Services, *Profile of Older Americans* (Washington, D.C.: U.S. Government, 1997).
49. W. B. Johnston, "Global Workforce 2000: The New World Labor Market," *Harvard Business Review* 69 (1991): 115–127.
50. S. E. Jackson and E. B. Alvarez, "Working through Diversity as a Strategic Imperative," in S. E. Jackson, ed., *Diversity in the Workplace: Human Resources Initiatives* (New York: Guilford Press, 1992), 13–36.
51. "Managing Generational Diversity," *HR Magazine* 36 (1991): 91–92.
52. K. Tyler, "The Tethered Generation," *HR* magazine (May 2007): 41–46.
53. C. M. Solomon, "Managing the Baby Busters," *Personnel Journal* (March 1992): 52–59.
54. S. R. Rhodes, "Age-Related Differences in Work Attitudes and Behavior: A Review and Conceptual Analysis," *Psychological Bulletin* 93 (1983): 338–367.
55. B. L. Hassell and P. L. Perrewe, "An Examination of Beliefs about Older Workers: Do Stereotypes Still Exist?" *Journal of Organizational Behavior* 16 (1995): 457–468.
56. U.S. Bureau of the Census, *Population Profile of the United States, 1997* (Washington, D.C.: U.S. Government Printing Office, 1997).
57. W. J. Rothwell, "HRD and the Americans with Disabilities Act," *Training and Development Journal* (August 1991): 45–47.
58. J. Waldrop, "The Cost of Hiring the Disabled," *American Demographics* (March 1991): 12.
59. J. J. Laabs, "The Golden Arches Provide Golden Opportunities," *Personnel Journal* (July 1991): 52–57.
60. L. Winfield and S. Spielman, "Making Sexual Orientation Part of Diversity," *Training and Development* (April 1995): 50–51.
61. N. E. Day and P. Schoenrade, "Staying in the Closet versus Coming Out: Relationships between Communication about Sexual Orientation and Work Attitudes," *Personnel Psychology* 50 (1997): 147–163.
62. J. Landau, "The Relationship of Race and Gender to Managers' Ratings of Promotion Potential," *Journal of Organizational Behavior* 16 (1995): 391–400.
63. P. Barnum, "Double Jeopardy for Women and Minorities: Pay Differences with Age," *Academy of Management Journal* 38 (1995): 863–880.
64. J. E. Rigdon, "PepsiCo's KFC Scouts for Blacks and Women for Its Top Echelons," *The Wall Street Journal* (November 13, 1991): A1.
65. P. A. Galagan, "Tapping the Power of a Diverse Workforce," *Training and Development Journal* 26 (1991): 38–44.

66. C. L. Holladay, J. L. Knight, D. L. Paige, and M. A. Quinones, "The Influence of Framing on Attitudes Toward Diversity Training," *Human Resource Development Quarterly* 14 (2003): 245–263.
67. R. Thomas, "From Affirmative Action to Affirming Diversity," *Harvard Business Review* 68 (1990): 107–117.
68. T. H. Cox, Jr., *Cultural Diversity in Organizations: Theory, Research and Practice* (San Francisco: Berrett-Koehler, 1994).
69. J. Gordon, "Different from What?" *Training* (May 1995): 25–33.
70. M. R. Fusilier, C. D. Aby, Jr., J. K. Worley, and S. Elliott, "Perceived Seriousness of Business Ethics Issues," *Business and Professional Ethics Journal* 15 (1996): 67–78.
71. J. S. Mill, *Utilitarianism, Liberty, and Representative Government* (London: Dent, 1910).
72. K. H. Blanchard and N. V. Peale, *The Power of Ethical Management* (New York: Morrow, 1988).
73. C. Fried, *Right and Wrong* (Cambridge, Mass.: Harvard University Press, 1978).
74. I. Kant, *Groundwork of the Metaphysics of Morals*, trans. H. J. Paton (New York: Harper & Row, 1964).
75. A. Smith, *An Inquiry into the Nature and Causes of the Wealth of Nations*, vol. 10 of The Harvard Classics, ed. C. J. Bullock (New York: P. F. Collier & Son, 1909).
76. R. C. Solomon, "Corporate Roles, Personal Virtues: Aristotelean Approach to Business Ethics," *Business Ethics Quarterly* 2 (1992): 317–339; R. C. Solomon, *A Better Way to Think about Business: How Personal Integrity Leads to Corporate Success* (New York: Oxford University Press, 1999).
77. D. Kemp, "Employers and AIDS: Dealing with the Psychological and Emotional Issues of AIDS in the Workplace," *American Review of Public Administration* 25 (1995): 263–278.
78. J. J. Koch, "Wells Fargo's and IBM's HIV Policies Help Protect Employees' Rights," *Personnel Journal* (April 1990): 40–48.
79. A. Arkin, "Positive HIV and AIDS Policies at Work," *Personnel Management* (December 1994): 34–37.
80. U.S. EEOC. 1980. Discrimination because of Sex under Title VII of the 1964 Civil Rights Act as amended: Adoption of interim guidelines—sexual harassment. *Federal Register* 45: 25024–25025; S. J. Adler, "Lawyers Advise Concerns to Provide Precise Written Policy to Employees," *The Wall Street Journal* (October 9, 1991): B1.
81. L. F. Fitzgerald, F. Drasgow, C. L. Hulin, M. J. Gelfand, and V. J. Magley, "Antecedents and Consequences of Sexual Harassment in Organizations: A Test of an Integrated Model," *Journal of Applied Psychology* 82 (1997): 578–589.
82. E. Felsenthal, "Rulings Open Way for Sex-Harass Cases," *The Wall Street Journal* (June 29, 1998): A10.
83. K. T. Schneider, S. Swan, and L. F. Fitzgerald, "Job-Related and Psychological Effects of Sexual Harassment in the Workplace: Empirical Evidence from Two Organizations," *Journal of Applied Psychology* 82 (1997): 401–415.
84. A. M. O'Leary-Kelly, R. L. Paetzold, and R. W. Griffin, "Sexual Harassment as Aggressive Behavior: An Actor-Based Perspective," *Academy of Management Review* 25 (2000): 372–388.
85. L. M. Goldenhar, N. G. Swanson, J. J. Hurrell, Jr., A. Ruder, and J. Deddens, "Stressors and Adverse Outcomes for Female Construction Workers," *Journal of Occupational Health Psychology* 3 (1998): 19–32; C. S. Piotrkowski, "Gender Harassment, Job Satisfaction and Distress Among Employed White and Minority Women," *Journal of Occupational Health Psychology* 3 (1998): 33–42.
86. G. N. Powell and S. Foley, "Something to Talk About: Romantic Relationships in Organizational Settings," *Journal of Management* 24 (1998): 421–448.
87. R. A. Posthuma, C. P. Maertz, Jr., and J. B. Dworkin. "Procedural Justice's Relationship with Turnover: Explaining Past Inconsistent Findings," *Journal of Organizational Behavior* 28 (2007): 381–398.
88. D. Fields, M. Pang, and C. Chio, "Distributive and Procedural Justice as Predictors of Employee Outcomes in Hong Kong," *Journal of Organizational Behavior* 21 (2000): 547–562.
89. H. L. Laframboise, "Vile Wretches and Public Heroes: The Ethics of Whistleblowing in Government," *Canadian Public Administration* (Spring 1991): 73–78.
90. A. Nyberg, "Whistle-Blower Woes," *CFO Magazine* 19 (October 2003): 50, http://www.cfo.com/article/1,5309,10790,00.html.
91. D. B. Turban and D. W. Greening, "Corporate Social Performance and Organizational Attractiveness to Prospective Employees," *Academy of Management Journal* 40 (1996): 658–672.
92. Task Force on Management of Innovation, *Technology and Employment: Innovation and Growth in the U.S. Economy* (Washington, D.C.: U.S. Government Research Council, 1987).
93. C. H. Ferguson, "Computers and the Coming of the U.S. Keiretsu," *Harvard Business Review* 68 (1990): 55–70.
94. J. Collins, *Good to Great: Why Some Companies Make the Leap . . . and Others Don't* (New York: HarperCollins, 2001).
95. C. Arnst, "The Networked Corporation," *Business Week* (June 26, 1995): 86–89.
96. J. A. Senn, *Information Systems in Management*, 4th ed. (Belmont, Calif.: Wadsworth, 1990).
97. D. K. Sorenson, O. Bouhaddou, and H. R. Warner, *Knowledge Engineering in Health Informatics* (New York: Springer, 1999).
98. M. T. Damore, "A Presentation and Examination of the Integration of Unlawful Discrimination Practices in the Private Business Sector with Artificial Intelligence" (Thesis, Oklahoma State University, 1992).
99. A. Tanzer and R. Simon, "Why Japan Loves Robots and We Don't," *Forbes* (April 16, 1990): 148–153.
100. E. Fingleton, "Jobs for Life: Why Japan Won't Give Them Up," *Fortune* (March 20, 1995): 119–125.
101. M. Iansitu, "How the Incumbent Can Win: Managing Technological Transitions in the Semiconductor Industry," *Management Science* 46 (2000): 169–185.
102. M. B. W. Fritz, S. Narasimhan, and H. Rhee, "Communication and Coordination in the Virtual Office," *Journal of Management Information Systems* 14 (1998): 7–28.
103. M. Apgar, IV, "The Alternative Workplace: Changing Where and How People Work," *Harvard Business Review* (May–June 1998): 121–136.
104. D. L. Nelson, "Individual Adjustment to Information-Driven Technologies: A Critical Review," *MIS Quarterly* 14 (1990): 79–98.
105. S. Armour, "Hi, I'm Joan and I'm a Workaholic," *USA Today* (May 23, 2007).
106. M. Allen, "Legislation Could Restrict Bosses from Snooping on Their Workers," *The Wall Street Journal* (September 24, 1991): B1–B8.
107. K. D. Hill and S. Kerr, "The Impact of Computer-Integrated Manufacturing Systems on the First Line Supervisor," *Journal of Organizational Behavior Management* 6 (1984): 81–87.
108. M. Reitzig, "Strategic Management of Intellectual Property," *MIT Sloan Management Review* 45 (Spring 2004): 35–40.
109. J. Anderson, "How Technology Brings Blind People into the Workplace," *Harvard Business Review* 67 (1989): 36–39.
110. D. L. Nelson and M. G. Kletke, "Individual Adjustment during Technological Innovation: A Research Framework," *Behaviour and Information Technology* 9 (1990): 257–271.
111. D. Mankin, T. Bikson, B. Gutek, and C. Stasz, "Managing Technological Change: The Process Is the Key," *Datamation* 34 (1988): 69–80.
112. T. Simons, R. Friedman, L. A. Liu, and J. M. Parks. "Racial Differences in Sensitivity to Behavioral Integrity: Attitudinal Consequences, In-Group Effects and 'Trickle Down' among Black and Non-Black Employees," *Journal of Applied Psychology* 92 (2007): 650–665.
113. J. McGregor, A. McConnon, and A. Weintraub, "The 25 Most Innovative Companies: The Leaders in Nurturing Cultures of Creativity, *BusinessWeek* 4034 (May 14, 2007): 52.

Chapter 2 Case

1. BellwetherReport.com, Current Research on Timberland Co., *M2PressWire* (February 13, 2007), from Newspaper Source database (accessed August 21, 2007).
2. Datamonitor, The Timberland Company: Company Profile. *Datamonitor.com* (August 2006): 1–8, reference code 4905.
3. *Timberland 2006 Annual Report*: 3.
4. Ibid.
5. D. Power, "Timberland Kicks Up Customization," *Women's Wear Daily* 190(78) (October 12, 2005): 10.

6. Ibid.
7. J. Leand, "Timberland Launches PreciseFit," *SGB* 39(2) (February 2006): 9.
8. J. Reingold, "Walking the Walk," *Fast Company* 100 (November 2005): 80.
9. Ibid.
10. M. Frazier, "Timberland 'Walks the Walk'," *Advertising Age* 78(24) (June 11, 2007): S8.
11. "Global Human Rights Standards," The Timberland Company (2007), http://www.timberland.com/timberlandseve/content.jsp?pageName=timberlanserve_inform (accessed August 21, 2007).
12. J. Reingold, 80–85.
13. Ibid.

Chapter 2 Cohesion Case: Part 1

1. "BP Global—About BP—Who We Are" (2007), BP PLC, http://www.bp.com/subsection.do?categoryId=4 &contentId=2006741 (accessed, August 19, 2007); "BP Global—About BP—BP" (2007), BP PLC, http://www.bp.com/genericarticle.do?categoryId=9 &contentId=2002350 (accessed, August 19, 2007).
2. "Early History—About BP," BP.com (2007), BP PLC, http://www.bp.com/sectiongenericarticle.do? categoryId=901444 &contentId=7027521 (accessed, August 19, 2007).
3. "History of BP—Late Century—About BP," BP.com (2007), BP PLC, http://www.bp.com/sectiongenericarticle. do?categoryId=901444 &contentId=7027525 (accessed, August 19, 2007).
4. Ibid.
5. S. Patton, "In Sync with His CEO; For Five years, BP CIO John Leggate Has Managed People and IT Systems in Concert with His CEO's Acquisition-Hungry Strategy," *CIO* 17(13) (April 15, 2004): 1.
6. J. Elkington, "John Browne," *Time* 163(17) (April 26, 2004): 73.
7. Ibid.
8. E. Armstrong, "A Decade of Sustainability," *The Engineer* (November 27–December 10, 2006): 16.
9. R. Crain, "BP Should Have Concentrated on Being a Better Oil Company," *Advertising Age* 77(34) (September 21, 2006): 14.
10. "Supersize Me. *Petroleum Economist* (December 2006): 1; M. B. Powers, "'Deficiencies' Cited at BP Site in Final Report on Fatal Blast," *ENR: Engineering News-Record* 258(12) (March 26, 2007): 13.
11. "Business: Paying the Price; BP," *The Economist* 382(8512) (January 20, 2007): 76.
12. S. Reed, "BP Feels the Heat; 2006 Was a Horror, and Problems Remain. Will John Browne Leave Early?" *Business Week* (January 22, 2007): 52.
13. "Business: Paying the Price; BP."
14. J. Birger, "What Pipeline Problem?" *Fortune* 154(5) (2006): 23–26.
15. "Mind the Gap," *Petroleum Economist* (September 2006): 1.
16. J. Birger, "What Pipeline Problem?" 24.
17. "Business: Beyond Propriety; BP," *The Economist* 380(8484) (July 1, 2006): 70.
18. "BP Facing Big Fine," *Daily Mail* (November 30, 2006): 16.
19. S. Fleming, "BP Mired in Fresh Problems as Refinery Blaze Hits Profits," *Daily Mail* (April 25, 2007), from Newspaper Source database (accessed August 17, 2007).
20. M. Hawthorne, "BP Gets Break on Dumping in Lake: Refinery Expansion Entices Indiana," *Chicago Tribune* (July 15, 2007), from Newspaper Source database (accessed August 17, 2007); J. Tankersley and M. Hawthorne, "Illinois Lawmakers Bash BP Plan to Dump Waste in Lake Michigan," *Chicago Tribune* (July 24, 2007), from Newspaper Source database (accessed August 17, 2007).
21. S. Reed, "BP Takes It Slow and Steady," *Business Week Online* (February 7, 2007): 2 (accessed August 17, 2007).
22. J. Bush and S. Reed, "The Kremlin's Big Squeeze," *Business Week* (April 30, 2007): 42–43.
23. "El Jef del Petroleo," *Wall Street Journal* (Eastern edition) (June 27, 2007): A12.
24. S. Reed, "Refilling BP's Tank: New CEO Hayward Has Major Safety and Expansion Issues to Resolve," *Business Week* (July 23, 2007): 35.

Chapter 3

1. M. Malseed, "The Story of Sergey Brin." February 2007. http://www.momentmag.com/Exclusive/2007/2007-02/200702-BrinFeature.html.
2. K. Lewin, "Formalization and Progress in Psychology," in D. Cartwright, ed., *Field Theory in Social Science* (New York: Harper, 1951).
3. N. S. Endler and D. Magnusson, "Toward an Interactional Psychology of Personality," *Psychological Bulletin* 83 (1976): 956–974.
4. J. R. Terborg, "Interactional Psychology and Research on Human Behavior in Organizations," *Academy of Management Review* 6 (1981): 561–576.
5. C. Spearman, "General Intelligence: Objectively Determined and Measured," *American Journal of Psychology* 15 (1904), 201–293.
6. F. L. Schmidt and J. Hunter, "General Mental Ability in the World of Work: Occupational Attainment and Job Performance," *Journal of Personality and Social Psychology,* 86(1) (2004): 162–173.
7. C. Bertua, N. Anderson, and J. F. Salgado, "The Predictive Validity of Cognitive Ability Tests: A UK Meta-Analysis," *Journal of Occupational and Organizational Psychology* 78 (2004), 387–409.
8. T. J. Bouchard, Jr., "Twins Reared Together and Apart: What They Tell Us about Human Diversity," in S. W. Fox, ed., *Individuality and Determinism* (New York: Plenum Press, 1984).
9. R. D. Arvey, T. J. Bouchard, Jr., N. L. Segal, and L. M. Abraham, "Job Satisfaction: Environmental and Genetic Components," *Journal of Applied Psychology* 74 (1989): 235–248.
10. G. Allport, *Pattern and Growth in Personality* (New York: Holt, 1961).
11. R. B. Cattell, *Personality and Mood by Questionnaire* (San Francisco: Jossey-Bass, 1973).
12. J. M. Digman, "Personality Structure: Emergence of a Five-Factor Model," *Annual Review of Psychology* 41 (1990): 417–440.
13. T. A. Judge, J. J. Martocchio, and C. J. Thoresen, "Five-Factor Model of Personality and Employee Absence," *Journal of Applied Psychology* 82 (1997): 745–755.
14. H. J. Bernardin, D. K. Cooke, and P. Villanova, "Conscientiousness and Agreeableness as Predictors of Rating Leniency," *Journal of Applied Psychology* 85 (2000): 232–234.
15. S. E. Seibert and M. L. Kraimer, "The Five-Factor Model of Personality and Career Success," *Journal of Vocational Behavior* 58 (2001): 1–21.
16. T. A. Judge and R. Ilies, "Relationships of Personality to Performance Motivation: A Meta-Analytic Review," *Journal of Applied Psychology* 87 (2002): 797–807.
17. G. M. Hurtz and J. J. Donovan, "Personality and Job Performance: The Big Five Revisited," *Journal of Applied Psychology* 85 (2000): 869–879.
18. S. T. Bell. "Deep-Level Composition Variables as Predictors of Team Performance: A Meta-Analysis," *Journal of Applied Psychology* 92(3) (2007): 595–615.
19. J. F. Salgado, S. Moscoso, and M. Lado, "Evidence of Cross-Cultural Invariance of the Big Five Personality Dimensions in Work Settings," *European Journal of Personality* 17 (2003): S67–S76; C. Rodriguez and T. H. Church, "The Structure and Personality Correlates of Affect in Mexico: Evidence of Cross-Cultural Comparability Using the Spanish Language," *Journal of Cross-Cultural Psychology* 34 (2003): 211–230.
20. H. C. Triandis, "Cultural Influences on Personality," *Annual Review of Psychology* 53 (2002): 133–160.
21. M. R. Barrick and M. K. Mount, "The Big Five Personality Dimensions and Job Performance: A Meta-Analysis," *Personnel Psychology* 44 (1991): 1–26.
22. D. D. Clark and R. Hoyle, "A Theoretical Solution to the Problem of Personality-Situational Interaction," *Personality and Individual Differences* 9 (1988): 133–138.
23. D. Byrne and L. J. Schulte, "Personality Dimensions as Predictors of Sexual Behavior," in J. Bancroft, ed., *Annual Review of Sexual Research,* vol. 1 (Philadelphia: Society for the Scientific Study of Sex, 1990).

24. T. A. Judge, E.A. Locke, and C. C. Durham, "The Dispositional Causes of Job Satisfaction: A Core Self-Evaluation Approach," *Research in Organizational Behavior* 19 (1997): 151–88.
25. M. Erez and T.A., Judge, "Relationship of Core Self-Evaluations to Goal Setting, Motivation and Performance," *Journal of Applied Psychology* 86 (2001):1270–79.
26. R. F. Piccolo, T. A Judge, K. Takahashi, N. Watanabe, and E. A Locke, "Core Self-Evaluations in Japan: Relative Effects on Job Satisfaction, Life Satisfaction, and Happiness," *Journal of Organizational Behavior* 26(8) (2005): 965–984.
27. J. B. Rotter, "Generalized Expectancies for Internal vs. External Control of Reinforcement," *Psychological Monographs* 80, whole No. 609 (1966).
28. T. A. Judge and J. E. Bono, "Relationship of Core Self-Evaluations Traits—Self-Esteem, Generalized Self-Efficacy, Locus of Control, and Emotional Stability—with Job Satisfaction and Job Performance: A Meta-Analysis," *Journal of Applied Psychology* 86 (2001): 80–92.
29. S. S. K. Lam and J. Shaubroeck, "The Role of Locus of Control in Reactions to Being Promoted and to Being Passed Over: A Quasi Experiment," *Academy of Management Journal* 43 (2000): 66–78.
30. G. Chen, S. M. Gully, J. Whiteman, and R. N. Kilcullen, "Examination of Relationships Among Trait-Like Individual Differences, State-Like Individual Differences, and Learning Performance," *Journal of Applied Psychology* 85 (2000): 835–847; G. Chen, S. M. Gully, and D. Eden, "Validation of a New General Self-Efficacy Scale," *Organizational Research Methods* 4 (2001): 62–83.
31. A. Bandura, *Self-Efficacy: The Exercise of Control* (San Francisco: Freeman, 1997).
32. D. R. Avery, "Personality as a Predictor of the Value of Voice," *The Journal of Psychology* 137 (2003): 435–447.
33. B. W. Pelham and W. B. Swann, Jr., "From Self-Conceptions to Self-Worth: On the Sources and Structure of Global Self-Esteem," *Journal of Personality and Social Psychology* 57 (1989): 672–680.
34. A. H. Baumgardner, C. M. Kaufman, and P. E. Levy, "Regulating Affect Interpersonally: When Low Esteem Leads to Greater Enhancement," *Journal of Personality and Social Psychology* 56 (1989): 907–921.
35. J. Schimel, T. Pyszczynski, J. Arndt, and J. Greenberg, "Being Accepted for Who We Are: Evidence That Social Validation of the Intrinsic Self Reduces General Defensiveness," *Journal of Personality and Social Psychology* 80 (2001): 35–52.
36. P. Tharenou and P. Harker, "Moderating Influences of Self-Esteem on Relationships between Job Complexity, Performance, and Satisfaction," *Journal of Applied Psychology* 69 (1984): 623–632.
37. R. T. Keller. "Predicting Job Performance from Individual Characteristics among R&D Engineers," *The Business Review*, Cambridge 8(1) (2007): 12–18.
38. R. A. Ellis and M. S. Taylor, "Role of Self-Esteem within the Job Search Process," *Journal of Applied Psychology* 68 (1983): 632–640.
39. J. Brockner and T. Hess, "Self-Esteem and Task Performance in Quality Circles," *Academy of Management Journal* 29 (1986): 617–623.
40. B. R. Schlenker, M. F. Weingold, and J. R. Hallam, "Self-Serving Attributions in Social Context: Effects of Self-Esteem and Social Pressure," *Journal of Personality and Social Psychology* 57 (1990): 855–863.
41. M. K. Duffy, J. D. Shaw, and E. M. Stark, "Performance and Satisfaction in Conflicted Interdependent Groups: When and How Does Self-Esteem Make a Difference?" *Academy of Management Journal* 43 (2000): 772–782.
42. T. Mussweiler, S. Gabriel, and G. V. Bodenhausen, "Shifting Social Identities as a Strategy for Deflecting Threatening Social Comparisons," *Journal of Personality and Social Psychology* 79 (2000): 398–409.
43. Erez and Judge, "Relationship of Core Self-Evaluations to Goal Setting." Same REF as 25.
44. M. Snyder and S. Gangestad, "On the Nature of Self-Monitoring: Matters of Assessment, Matters of Validity," *Journal of Personality and Social Psychology* 51 (1986): 123–139.
44a. G. Toegel, N Anand, M. Kilduff. " Emotion Helpers: The Role of High Positive Affectivity and High Self monitoring Monitoring Managers," *Personnel Psychology* 60(2) (2007): 337–365.
45. A. Mehra, M. Kilduff, and D. J. Brass, "The Social Networks of High and Low Self-Monitors: Implications for Workplace Performance," *Administrative Science Quarterly* 46 (2001): 121–146.
46. W. H. Turnley and M. C. Bolino, "Achieving Desired Images While Avoiding Undesired Images: Exploring the Role of Self-Monitoring in Impression Management," *Journal of Applied Psychology* 86 (2001): 351–360.
47. M. Kilduff and D. V. Day, "Do Chameleons Get Ahead? The Effects of Self-Monitoring on Managerial Careers," *Academy of Management Journal* 37 (1994): 1047–1060.
48. A. H. Church, "Managerial Self-Awareness in High-Performing Individuals in Organizations," *Journal of Applied Psychology* 82 (1997): 281–292.
49. C. Douglas and W. L. Gardner, "Transition to Self-Directed Work Teams: Implications of Transition Time and Self-Monitoring for Managers' Use of Influence Tactics," *Journal of Organizational Behavior* 25 (2004): 45–67.
50. A. M. Isen and R. A. Baron, "Positive Affect and Organizational Behavior," in B. M. Staw and L. L. Cummings, eds., *Research in Organizational Behavior* 12 (Greenwich, Conn.: JAI Press, 1990).
51. D. Watson and L. A. Clark, "Negative Affectivity: The Disposition to Experience Aversive Emotional States," *Psychological Bulletin* 96 (1984): 465–490.
52. R. Ilies and T. Judge, "On the Heritability of Job Satisfaction: The Mediating Role of Personality," *Journal of Applied Psychology* 88 (2003): 750–759.
53. J. M. George, "State or Trait," *Journal of Applied Psychology* 76 (1991): 299–307.
54. J. M. George, "Mood and Absence," *Journal of Applied Psychology* 74 (1989): 287–324.
55. S. Lyubormirsky, L. King, and E. Diener, "The Benefits of Frequent Positive Affect: Does Happiness Lead to Success?" *Psychological Bulletin* 131(6) (2005): 803–855.
56. M. J. Burke, A. P. Brief, and J. M. George, "The Role of Negative Affectivity in Understanding Relations between Self-Reports of Stressors and Strains: A Comment on the Applied Psychology Literature," *Journal of Applied Psychology* 78 (1993): 402–412.
57. S. Barsade, A. Ward, J. Turner, and J. Sonnenfeld, "To Your Heart's Content: A Model of Affective Diversity in Top Management Teams," *Administrative Science Quarterly* 45 (2000): 802–836.
58. J. Schaubroeck, F. O. Walumbwa, D. C. Ganster, and S. Kepes, "Destructive Leader Traits and the Neutralizing Influence of an 'Enriched' Job," *Leadership Quarterly* 18(3) (2007): 236–251.
59. W. Mischel, "The Interaction of Person and Situation," in D. Magnusson and N. S. Endler, eds., *Personality at the Crossroads: Current Issues in Interactional Psychology* (Hillsdale, N.J.: Erlbaum, 1977).
60. H. Rorschach, *Psychodiagnostics* (Bern: Hans Huber, 1921).
61. C. G. Jung, *Psychological Types* (New York: Harcourt & Brace, 1923).
62. Consulting Psychologists Press.
63. R. Benfari and J. Knox, *Understanding Your Management Style* (Lexington, Mass.: Lexington Books, 1991).
64. O. Kroeger and J. M. Thuesen, *Type Talk* (New York: Delacorte Press, 1988).
65. S. Hirsch and J. Kummerow, *Life Types* (New York: Warner Books, 1989).
66. I. B. Myers and M. H. McCaulley, *Manual: A Guide to the Development and Use of the Myers-Briggs Type Indicator* (Palo Alto, Calif.: Consulting Psychologists Press, 1990).
67. G. P. Macdaid, M. H. McCaulley, and R. I. Kainz, *Myers-Briggs Type Indicator: Atlas of Type Tables* (Gainesville, Fla.: Center for Application of Psychological Type, 1987).
68. J. B. Murray, "Review of Research on the Myers-Briggs Type Indicator," *Perceptual and Motor Skills* 70 (1990): 1187–1202.
69. J. G. Carlson, "Recent Assessment of the Myers-Briggs Type Indicator," *Journal of Personality Assessment* 49 (1985): 356–365.
70. A. Thomas, M. Benne, M. Marr, E. Thomas, and R. Hume, "The Evidence Remains Stable: The MBTI Predicts Attraction and Attrition in an Engineering Program," *Journal of Psychological Type* 55 (2000): 35–42.

71. C. Walck, "Training for Participative Management: Implications for Psychological Type," *Journal of Psychological Type* 21 (1991): 3–12.
72. J. Michael, "Using the Myers-Briggs Indicator as a Tool for Leadership Development: Apply with Caution," *Journal of Leadership & Organizational Studies* 10 (2003): 68–78.
73. E. C. Webster, *The Employment Interview: A Social Judgment Process* (Schomberg, Canada: SIP, 1982).
73a. J. Ward, M. J. Lankau, A. C. Amason, J. A. Sonnenfeld, and B. R. Agle, "Improving the Performance of Top Management Teams," *MIT Sloan Management Review* 48(3) (2007): 85–90.
74. N. Adler, *International Dimensions of Organizational Behavior*, 2nd ed. (Boston: PWS-Kent, 1991).
75. L. R. Offerman and M. K. Gowing, "Personnel Selection in the Future: The Impact of Changing Demographics and the Nature of Work," in Schmitt, Borman & Associates, eds., *Personnel Selection in Organizations* (San Francisco: Jossey-Bass, 1993).
76. J. Park and M. R. Banaji, "Mood and Heuristics: The Influence of Happy and Sad States on Sensitivity and Bias in Stereotyping," *Journal of Personality and Social Psychology* 78 (2000): 1005–1023.
77. M. W. Levine and J. M. Shefner, *Fundamentals of Sensation and Perception* (Reading, Mass.: Addison-Wesley, 1981).
78. R. L. Dipboye, H. L. Fromkin, and K. Willback, "Relative Importance of Applicant Sex, Attractiveness, and Scholastic Standing in Evaluations of Job Applicant Resumes," *Journal of Applied Psychology* 60 (1975): 39–43.
79. I. H. Frieze, J. E. Olson, and J. Russell, "Attractiveness and Income for Men and Women in Management," *Journal of Applied Social Psychology* 21 (1991): 1039–1057.
80. P. Ekman and W. Friesen, *Unmasking the Face* (Englewood Cliffs, N.J.: Prentice-Hall, 1975).
81. J. E. Rehfeld, "What Working for a Japanese Company Taught Me," *Harvard Business Review*, (November–December 1990): 167–176.
82. M. W. Morris and R. P. Larrick, "When One Cause Casts Doubt on Another: A Normative Analysis of Discounting in Causal Attribution," *Psychological Review* 102 (1995): 331–355.
83. G. B. Sechrist and C. Stangor, "Perceived Consensus Influences Intergroup Behavior and Stereotype Accessibility," *Journal of Personality and Psychology* 80 (2001): 645–654; A. Lyons and Y. Kashima, "How Are Stereotypes Maintained Through Communication? The Influence of Stereotype Sharedness," *Journal of Personality and Social Psychology* 85 (2003): 989–1005.
84. L. Copeland, "Learning to Manage a Multicultural Workforce," *Training* (May 1988): 48–56.
85. S. Ferrari, "Human Behavior in International Groups," *Management International Review* 7 (1972): 31–35.
86. A. Feingold, "Gender Differences in Effects of Physical Attractiveness on Romantic Attraction: A Comparison across Five Research Paradigms," *Journal of Personality and Social Psychology* 59 (1990): 981–993.
87. M. Snyder, "When Belief Creates Reality," *Advances in Experimental Social Psychology* 18 (1984): 247–305.
88. M. Biernat, "Toward a Broader View of Social Stereotyping," *American Psychologist* 58 (2003): 1019–1027.
89. E. Burnstein and Y. Schul, "The Informational Basis of Social Judgments: Operations in Forming an Impression of Another Person," *Journal of Experimental Social Psychology* 18 (1982): 217–234.
90. T. DeGroot and S. Motowidlo, "Why Visual and Vocal Cues Can Affect Interviewers' Judgments and Predict Job Performance," *Journal of Applied Psychology* 84. (1999): 986–993; M. C. L. Greene and L. Mathieson, *The Voice and Its Disorders* (London: Whurr, 1989).
91. R. L. Gross and S. E. Brodt, "How Assumptions of Consensus Undermine Decision Making," *MIT Sloan Management Review* 42 (Winter 2001): 86–94.
92. R. Rosenthal and L. Jacobson, *Pygmalion in the Classroom: Teacher Expectations and Pupils' Intellectual Development* (New York: Holt, Rinehart & Winston, 1968).
93. D. Eden and Y. Zuk, "Seasickness as a Self-Fulfilling Prophecy: Raising Self-Efficacy to Boost Performance at Sea," *Journal of Applied Psychology* 80 (1995): 628–635.
94. N. M. Kierein and M. A. Gold, "Pygmalion in Work Organizations: A Meta-Analysis," *Journal of Organizational Behavior* 21 (2000): 913–928.
95. D. Eden, "Pygmalion without Interpersonal Contrast Effects: Whole Groups Gain from Raising Manager Expectations," *Journal of Applied Psychology* 75 (1990): 394–398.
96. R. A. Giacolone and P. Rosenfeld, eds., *Impression Management in Organizations* (Hillsdale, N.J.: Erlbaum, 1990); J. Tedeschi and V. Melburg, "Impression Management and Influence in the Organization," in S. Bacharach and E. Lawler, eds., *Research in the Sociology of Organizations* (Greenwich, Conn.: JAI Press, 1984), 31–58.
97. A. Colella and A. Varma, "The Impact of Subordinate Disability on Leader–Member Exchange Relationships," *Academy of Management Journal* 44 (2001): 304–315.
98. D. C. Gilmore and G. R. Ferris, "The Effects of Applicant Impression Management Tactics on Interviewer Judgments," *Journal of Management* (December 1989): 557–564.
99. C. K. Stevens and A. L. Kristof, "Making the Right Impression: A Field Study of Applicant Impressions Management during Job Interviews," *Journal of Applied Psychology* 80 (1995): 587–606.
100. S. J. Wayne and R. C. Liden, "Effects of Impression Management on Performance Ratings: A Longitudinal Study," *Academy of Management Journal* 38 (1995): 232–260.
101. R. A. Baron, "Impression Management by Applicants during Employment Interviews: The 'Too Much of a Good Thing' Effect," in R. W. Eder and G. R. Ferris, eds., *The Employment Interview: Theory, Research, and Practice* (Newbury Park, Calif.: Sage Publications, 1989).
102. F. Heider, *The Psychology of Interpersonal Relations* (New York: Wiley, 1958).
103. B. Weiner, "An Attributional Theory of Achievement Motivation and Emotion," *Psychological Review* (October 1985): 548–573.
104. P. D. Sweeney, K. Anderson, and S. Bailey, "Attributional Style in Depression: A Meta-Analytic Review," *Journal of Personality and Social Psychology* 51 (1986): 974–991.
105. P. Rosenthal, D. Guest, and R. Peccei, "Gender Differences in Managers' Causal Explanations for Their Work Performance," *Journal of Occupational and Organizational Psychology* 69 (1996): 145–151.
106. J. Silvester, "Spoken Attributions and Candidate Success in Graduate Recruitment Interviews," *Journal of Occupational and Organizational Psychology* 70 (1997): 61–71.
107. L. Ross, "The Intuitive Psychologist and His Shortcomings: Distortions in the Attribution Process," in L. Berkowitz, ed., *Advances in Experimental Social Psychology* (New York: Academic Press, 1977); M. O'Sullivan, "The Fundamental Attribution Error in Detecting Deception: The Boy-Who-Cried Wolf Effect," *Personality & Social Psychology Bulletin* 29 (2003): 1316–1327.
108. D. T. Miller and M. Ross, "Self-Serving Biases in the Attribution of Causality: Fact or Fiction?" *Psychological Bulletin* 82 (1975): 313–325.
109. J. R. Schermerhorn, Jr., "Team Development for High-Performance Management," *Training and Development Journal* 40 (1986): 38–41.
110. J. G. Miller, "Culture and the Development of Everyday Causal Explanation," *Journal of Personality and Social Psychology* 46 (1984): 961–978.
111. G. Si, S. Rethorst, and K. Willimczik, "Causal Attribution Perception in Sports Achievement: A Cross-Cultural Study on Attributional Concepts in Germany and China," *Journal of Cross-Cultural Psychology* 26 (1995): 537–553.
112. http://www.google.com/corporate/execs.html#sergey
113. http://www.google.com/intl/en/corporate/tenthings.html

Chapter 3 Case

1. J. Hopkins, "Entrepreneurs Are Born, But Can They Be Taught?" *USA Today* (April 7, 2004), from MasterFILE Premier database (accessed July 7, 2004).
2. Virgin Companies, http://www.virgin.com/Companies.aspx?Region=6 (accessed September 11, 2007).
3. "Virgin.com—Richard's Autobiography," http://www.virgin.com/AboutVirgin/RichardBranson/RichardsAutobiography.aspx (accessed September 11, 2007).

4. Ibid.
5. Ibid.
6. B. Morris, "Richard Branson: What a Life: 'I Don't Think of Work as Work and Play as Play. It's All Living'," *Fortune* (October 6, 2003), http://www.fortune.com/fortune/subs/article/0,15114,488581-2,00.html, part 2, page 1 of 4 (accessed July 7, 2004).
7. J. Shepler, "Richard Branson's Virgin Success: The Incredible Triumph of an Enigmatic Entrepreneur," JohnShepler.com, http://www.johnshepler.com, page 1 of 6 (accessed July 7, 2004).
8. B. Morris, "Richard Branson: What a Life." http://www.fortune.com/fortune/subs/article/0,15114,488581,00.html, part 1, pages 2 and 3 of 4 (accessed July 7, 2004).
9. J. Shepler, "Richard Branson's Virgin Success," page 2 of 6 (accessed July 7, 2004).
10. B. Morris, "Richard Branson: What a Life." http://www.fortune.com/fortune/subs/article/0,15114,488581-2,00.html, part 2, page 1 of 4 (accessed July 7, 2004).
11. "Virgin.com—What We're About," http://www.virgin.com/AboutVirgin/WhatWeAreAbout/WhaWeAreAbout.aspx (accessed September 11, 2007).
12. B. Morris, "Richard Branson: What a Life." http://www.fortune.com/fortune/subs/article/0,15114,488581-2,00.html, part 2, page 1 of 4 (accessed July 7, 2004).
13. Ibid, page 2 of 4.
14. B. Morris, "Richard Branson: What a Life." http://www.fortune.com/fortune/subs/article/0,15114,488581-3,00.html, part 3, page 2 of 5 (accessed July 7, 2004).
15. Ibid, pages 2 and 3 of 5.

Chapter 4

1. http://www.timberland.com/investorRelations/index.jsp.
2. http://www.greenbiz.com/news/news_third.cfm?NewsID=30215.
3. http://www.timberland.com/corp/index.jsp?page=pressrelease&eid=7500016561.
4. A. H. Eagly and S. Chaiken, *The Psychology of Attitudes* (Orlando, Fla.: Harcourt Brace Jovanovich, 1993).
5. M. J. Rosenberg, C. I. Hovland, W. J. McGuire, R. P. Abelson, and J. H. Brehm, *Attitude Organization and Change* (New Haven, Conn.: Yale University Press, 1960).
6. L. Festinger, *A Theory of Cognitive Dissonance* (Evanston, Ill.: Row, Peterson, 1957).
7. R. H. Fazio and M. P. Zanna, "On the Predictive Validity of Attitudes: The Roles of Direct Experience and Confidence," *Journal of Personality* 46 (1978): 228–243.
8. A. Tversky and D. Kahneman, "Judgment under Uncertainty: Heuristics and Biases," in D. Kahneman, P. Slovic, and A. Tversky, eds., *Judgment under Uncertainty* (New York: Cambridge University Press, 1982): 3–20.
9. D. Rajecki, *Attitudes*, 2nd ed. (Sunderland, Mass.: Sinauer Associates, 1989).
10. I. Ajzen and M. Fishbein, "Attitude–Behavior Relations: A Theoretical Analysis and Review of Empirical Research," *Psychological Bulletin* 84 (1977): 888–918.
11. B. T. Johnson and A. H. Eagly, "Effects of Involvement on Persuasion: A Meta-Analysis," *Psychological Bulletin* 106 (1989): 290–314.
12. K. G. DeBono and M. Snyder, "Acting on One's Attitudes: The Role of History of Choosing Situations," *Personality and Social Psychology Bulletin* 21 (1995): 629–636.
13. I. Ajzen and M. Fishbein, *Understanding Attitudes and Predicting Social Behavior* (Englewood Cliffs, N.J.: Prentice-Hall, 1980).
14. I. Ajzen, "From Intentions to Action: A Theory of Planned Behavior," in J. Kuhl and J. Beckmann, eds., *Action-Control: From Cognition to Behavior* (Heidelberg: Springer, 1985).
15. I. Ajzen, "The Theory of Planned Behavior," *Organizational Behavior and Human Decision Processes* 50 (1991): 1–33.
16. A. Sagie and M. Krausz, "What Aspects of the Job Have Most Effect on Nurses?" *Human Resource Management Journal* 13 (2003): 46–62.
17. C. P. Parker, B. B. Baltes, S. A. Young, J. W. Huff, R. A. Altman, H. A. LaCost, and J. E. Roberts, "Relationships between Psychological Climate Perceptions and Work Outcomes: A Meta-Analytic Review," *Journal of Organizational Behavior* 24 (2003): 389–416.
18. J. Lemmick and J. Mattsson, "Employee Behavior, Feelings of Warmth and Customer Perception in Service Encounters," *International Journal of Retail & Distribution Management* 30 (2002): 18–44.
19. E. A. Locke, "The Nature and Causes of Job Satisfaction," in M. Dunnette, ed., *Handbook of Industrial and Organizational Psychology* (Chicago: Rand McNally, 1976).
20. P. C. Smith, L. M. Kendall, and C. L. Hulin, *The Measurement of Satisfaction in Work and Retirement* (Skokie, Ill.: Rand McNally, 1969).
21. R. Ilies and T. A. Judge, "On the Heritability of Job Satisfaction: The Mediating Role of Personality," *Journal of Applied Psychology* 88 (2003): 750–759.
22. D. J. Weiss, R. V. Davis, G. W. England, and L. H. Lofquist, *Manual for the Minnesota Satisfaction Questionnaire* (Minneapolis: Industrial Relations Center, University of Minnesota, 1967).
23. C. D. Fisher, "Why Do Lay People Believe That Satisfaction and Performance Are Correlated? Possible Sources of a Commonsense Theory," *Journal of Organizational Behavior* 24 (2003): 753–777.
24. M. T. Iaffaldano and P. M. Muchinsky, "Job Satisfaction and Job Performance: A Meta-Analysis," *Psychological Bulletin* 97 (1985): 251–273.
25. L. A. Bettencourt, K. P. Gwinner, and M. L. Meuter, "A Comparison of Attitude, Personality, and Knowledge Predictors of Service-Oriented Organizational Citizenship Behaviors," *Journal of Applied Psychology* 86 (2001): 29–41.
26. Aplus.Net, "Aplus.Net Is Put to the Test with Firestorm 2003 and Passes with Flying Colors," http://www.aplus.net/comp_info_20031105.html, November 6, 2003.
27. D. W. Organ, *Organizational Citizenship Behavior: The Good Soldier Syndrome* (Lexington, Mass.: Lexington Books, 1988).
28. P. M. Podsakoff, S. B. Mackenzie, and C. Hui, "Organizational Citizenship Behaviors and Managerial Evaluations of Employee Performance: A Review and Suggestions for Future Research," G. Ferris, ed., in *Research in Personnel and Human Resources Management* (Greenwich, Conn.: JAI Press, 1993): 1–40.
29. K. Lee., and N. J. Allen, "Organizational Citizenship Behavior and Workplace Deviance: The Role of Affect and Cognitions," *Journal of Applied Psychology* 87(1), (2002): 131–142.
30. O. Christ, R. Van Dick, and U. Wagner, "When Teachers Go the Extra Mile: Foci of Organizational Identification as Determinants of Different Forms of Organizational Citizenship Behavior Among Schoolteachers," *British Journal of Educational Psychology* 73 (2003): 329–341.
31. G. L. Blakely, M. C. Andrews, and J. Fuller, "Are Chameleons Good Citizens: A Longitudinal Study of the Relationship between Self-Monitoring and Organizational Citizenship Behavior," *Journal of Business & Psychology* 18 (2003): 131–144.
32. W. H. Bommer, E. W. Miles, and S. L. Grover, "Does One Good Turn Deserve Another? Coworker Influences on Employee Citizenship," *Journal of Organizational Behavior* 24 (2003): 181–196.
33. C. Ostroff, "The Relationship between Satisfaction, Attitudes and Performance: An Organizational Level Analysis," *Journal of Applied Psychology* 77 (1992): 963–974.
34. R. Griffin and T. Bateman, "Job Satisfaction and Organizational Commitment," in C. Cooper and I. Robertson, eds., *International Review of Industrial and Organizational Psychology* (New York: Wiley, 1986).
35. A. R. Wheeler, V. C. Gallagher, R. L. Brouer, and C. J. Sablynski, "When Person-Organization (Mis)fit and (Dis)satisfaction Lead to Turnover: The Moderating Role of Perceived Job Mobility," *Journal of Managerial Psychology* 22(2): 203–219.
36. H. Y. Choi and H. Choi, "An Exploratory Study and Design of Cross-Cultural Impact of Information Systems Managers' Performance, Job Satisfaction, and Managerial Values," *Journal of Global Information Management* 11 (2003): 1–30.

37. X. Huang and E. Van De Vliert, "Where Intrinsic Job Satisfaction Fails to Work: National Moderators of Intrinsic Motivation," *Journal of Organizational Behavior* 24 (2003): 133–250.

38. L. Sun, S. Aryee, and K. S. Law, "High-Performance Human Resource Practices, Citizenship Behavior, and Organizational Performance: A Relational Perspective," *Academy of Management Journal* 50(3): 558 –577.

39. S. L. Robinson and R. J. Bennett, "A Typology of Deviant Workplace Behaviors: A Multidimensional Scaling Study," *Academy of Management Journal* 38(2) (1995): 555–572.

40. M. E. Heilman and V. B. Alcott, "What I Think You Think of Me: Women's Reactions to Being Viewed as Beneficiaries of Preferential Selection," *Journal of Applied Psychology* 86 (2001): 574–582.

41. M. E. Heilman, C. J. Block, and P. Stathatos, "The Affirmative Action Stigma of Incompetence: Effects of Performance Information Ambiguity," *Academy of Management Journal* 40 (1997): 603–625.

42. R. T. Mowday, L. W. Porter, and R. M. Steers, *Employee–Organization Linkages: The Psychology of Commitment* (New York: Academic Press, 1982).

43. H. S. Becker, "Notes on the Concept of Commitment," *American Journal of Sociology* 66 (1960): 32–40.

44. J. P. Meyer, N. J. Allen, and C. A. Smith, "Commitment to Organizations and Occupations: Extension and Test of a Three-Component Model," *Journal of Applied Psychology* 78 (1993): 538–551.

45. J. P. Curry, D. S. Wakefield, J. L. Price, and C. W. Mueller, "On the Causal Ordering of Job Satisfaction and Organizational Commitment," *Academy of Management Journal* 29 (1986): 847–858.

46. T. N. Bauer, T. Bodner, B. Erdogan, D. M. Truxillo, and J. S. Tucker, "Newcomer Adjustment during Organizational Socialization: A Meta-Analytic Review of Antecedents, Outcomes, and Methods," *Journal of Applied Psychology* 92(3) (2007): 707–721.

47. B. Benkhoff, "Ignoring Commitment Is Costly: New Approaches Establish the Missing Link between Commitment and Performance," *Human Relations* 50 (1997): 701–726; N. J. Allen and J. P. Meyer, "Affective, Continuance, and Normative Commitment to the Organization: An Examination of Construct Validity," *Journal of Vocational Behavior* 49 (1996): 252–276.

48. M. J. Somers, "Organizational Commitment, Turnover, and Absenteeism: An Examination of Direct and Interaction Effects," *Journal of Organizational Behavior* 16 (1995): 49–58; L. Lum, J. Kervin, K. Clark, F. Reid, and W. Sirola, "Explaining Nursing Turnover Intent: Job Satisfaction, Pay Satisfaction, or Organizational Commitment?" *Journal of Organizational Behavior* 19 (1998): 305–320.

49. F. Stinglhamber and C. Vandenberghe, "Organizations and Supervisors as Sources of Support and Targets of Commitment," *Journal of Organizational Behavior* 24 (2003): 251–270.

50. R. Eisenberger *et al.,* "Reciprocation of Perceived Organizational Support," *Journal of Applied Psychology* 86 (2001): 42–51; J. E. Finegan, "The Impact of Person and Organizational Values on Organizational Commitment," *Journal of Occupational and Organizational Psychology* 73 (2000): 149–169.

51. E. Snape and T. Redman, "Too Old or Too Young? The Impact of Perceived Age Discrimination," *Human Resource Management Journal* 13 (2003): 78–89.

52. F. Luthans, H. S. McCaul, and N. C. Dodd, "Organizational Commitment: A Comparison of American, Japanese, and Korean Employees," *Academy of Management Journal* 28 (1985): 213–219.

53. C. Wong and I. Wong, "The Role of Perceived Quality of Social Relationships within Organizations in Chinese Societies," *International Journal of Management* 20 (2003): 216–223.

54. D. J. Koys, "The Effects of Employee Satisfaction, Organizational Citizenship Behavior, and Turnover on Organizational Effectiveness: A Unit-Level, Longitudinal Study," *Personnel Psychology* 54 (2001): 101–114.

55. J. A. Conger, "The Necessary Art of Persuasion," *Harvard Business Review* 76 (1998): 84–96.

56. J. Cooper and R. T. Croyle, "Attitudes and Attitude Change," *Annual Review of Psychology* 35 (1984): 395–426.

57. P. Sellers, "The Trials of John Mack," *Fortune* (August 11, 2003): 98–102.

58. D. M. Mackie and L. T. Worth, "Processing Deficits and the Mediation of Positive Affect in Persuasion," *Journal of Personality and Social Psychology* 57 (1989): 27–40.

59. J. W. Brehm, *Responses to Loss of Freedom: A Theory of Psychological Reactance* (New York: General Learning Press, 1972).

60. D. DeSteno, R. E. Petty, and D. D. Rucker, "Discrete Emotions and Persuasion: The Role of Emotion-Induced Expectancies," *Journal of Personality & Social Psychology* 86 (2004): 43–56.

61. R. Petty, D. T. Wegener, and L. R. Fabrigar, "Attitudes and Attitude Change," *Annual Review of Psychology* 48 (1997): 609–647.

62. P. Brinol and R. E. Petty, "Overt Head Movements and Persuasion: A Self-Validation Analysis," *Journal of Personality & Social Psychology* 84 (2003): 1123–1139.

63. W. Wood, "Attitude Change: Persuasion and Social Influence," *Annual Review of Psychology* 51 (2000): 539–570.

64. N. H. Frijda, "Moods, Emotion Episodes, and Emotions," in M. Lewis and J. M. Haviland, eds., *Handbook of Emotions* (New York: Guilford Press, 1993): 381–403.

65. A. Ortony, G. L. Clore, and A. Collins, *The Cognitive Structure of Emotions* (Cambridge, England: Cambridge University Press, 1988).

66. R. S. Lazarus, *Emotion and Adaptation* (New York: Oxford University Press, 1991).

67. H. M. Weiss, K. Suckow, and R. Cropanzano, "Effects of Justice Conditions on Discrete Emotions," *Journal of Applied Psychology* 84 (1999): 786–794.

68. T. B. Lawrence and S. L. Robinson, "Ain't Misbehavin: Workplace Deviance as Organizational Resistance," *Journal of Management* 33(3) (2007): 378–394.

69. B. L. Fredrickson and C. Brannigan, "Positive Emotions," in. G. Bonnano and T. Mayne, eds., *Emotions: Current Issues and Future Directions* (New York: Guilford Press, 2001): 123–152.

70. A. M. Isen and R. A. Baron, "Positive Affect as a Factor in Organizational Behavior," *Research in Organizational Behavior* 13 (1991): 1–53.

71. S. G. Barsade and D. E. Gibson, "Why Does Affect Matter in Organizations?" *The Academy of Management Perspectives* 21 (1) (2007): 36–59.

72. S. G. Barsade, "The Ripple Effect: Emotional Contagion and Its Influence on Group Behavior," *Administrative Science Quarterly* 47 (2002): 644–675.

73. J. E. Dutton, P. J. Frost, M. C. Worline, J. M. Lilius, and J. M., Kanov, "Leading in Times of Trauma," *Harvard Business Review* 80(1) (2002): 54–61.

74. T. A. Stewart, "The Highway of the Mind," *Harvard Business Review* 82 (2004): 116–116.

75. F. Navran, "Your Role in Shaping Ethics," *Executive Excellence* 9 (1992): 11–12.

76. K. Labich, "The New Crisis in Business Ethics," *Fortune* (April 20, 1992): 167–176.

77. L. S. Paine, *Value Shift: Why Companies Must Merge Social and Financial Imperatives to Achieve Superior Performance* (New York: McGraw-Hill, 2003).

78. D. B. Turban and D. M. Cable, "Firm Reputation and Applicant Pool Characteristics," *Journal of Organizational Behavior* 24 (2003): 733–751.

79. E. A. Lind, J. Greenberg, K. S. Scott, and T. D. Welchans, "The Winding Road from Employee to Complainant: Situational and Psychological Determinants of Wrongful-Termination Claims," *Administrative Science Quarterly* 45 (2000): 557–590.

80. Miriam Schulman, "LittleBrother Is Watching You," http://www.scu.edu/ethics/publications/iie/v9n2/brother.html.

81. G. Flynn, "Make Employee Ethics Your Business," *Personnel Journal* (June 1995): 30–40.

82. M. S. Baucus and D. A. Baucus, "Paying the Piper: An Empirical Examination of Longer-Term Financial Consequences of Illegal Corporate Behavior," *Academy of Management Journal* 40 (1997): 129–151.

83. J. O. Cherrington and D. J. Cherrington, "A Menu of Moral Issues: One Week in the Life of *The Wall Street Journal*," *Journal of Business Ethics* 11 (1992): 255–265.

84. B. L. Flannery and D. R. May, "Environmental Ethical Decision Making in the U.S. Metal-Finishing Industry," *Academy of Management Journal* 43 (2000): 642–662.
85. K. R. Andrews, "Ethics in Practice," *Harvard Business Review* 89 (1989): 99–104.
86. M. Rokeach, *The Nature of Human Values* (New York: Free Press, 1973).
87. M. Rokeach and S. J. Ball-Rokeach, "Stability and Change in American Value Priorities, 1968–1981," *American Psychologist* 44 (1989): 775–784.
88. S. P Eisner, "Managing Generation Y," *S.A.M. Advanced Management Journal* 70(4) (2005): 4–15.
89. G. W. England, "Organizational Goals and Expected Behavior of American Managers," *Academy of Management Journal* 10 (1967): 107–117.
90. E. C. Ravlin and B. M. Meglino, "Effects of Values on Perception and Decision Making: A Study of Alternative Work Values Measures," *Journal of Applied Psychology* 72 (1987): 666–673.
91. E. C. Ravlin and B. M. Meglino, "The Transitivity of Work Values: Hierarchical Preference Ordering of Socially Desirable Stimuli," *Organizational Behavior and Human Decision Processes* 44 (1989): 494–508.
92. B. M. Meglino, E. C. Ravlin, and C. L. Adkins, "A Work Values Approach to Corporate Culture: A Field Test of the Value Congruence Process and Its Relationship to Individual Outcomes," *Journal of Applied Psychology* 74 (1989): 424–432.
93. T. A. Judge and R. D. Bretz, Jr., "Effects of Work Values on Job Choice Decisions," *Journal of Applied Psychology* 77 (1992): 261–271.
94. Tony Jones, "Survey Finds Big Business Lacking in Social Responsibility," Australian Broadcasting Corporation (October 13, 2003), http://www.abc.net.au/lateline/content/2003/s966137.htm; RepuTex, http://www.reputex.com.au.
95. R. H. Doktor, "Asian and American CEOs: A Comparative Study," *Organizational Dynamics* 18 (1990): 46–56.
96. R. L. Tung, "Handshakes across the Sea: Cross-Cultural Negotiating for Business Success," *Organizational Dynamics* (Winter 1991): 30–40.
97. C. Gomez, B. L. Kirkman, and D. L. Shapiro, "The Impact of Collectivism and In-Group/Out-Group Membership on the Evaluation Generosity of Team Members," *Academy of Management Journal* 43 (2000): 1097–1106; J. Zhou and J. J. Martocchio, "Chinese and American Managers' Compensation Award Decisions: A Comparative Policy-Capturing Study," *Personnel Psychology* 54 (2001): 115–145.
98. A. J. Ali and M. Amirshahi, "The Iranian Manager: Work Values and Orientations," *Journal of Business Ethics* 40 (2002): 133–143.
99. R. Neale and R. Mindel, "Rigging Up Multicultural Teamworking," *Personnel Management* (January 1992): 27–30.
100. K. Hodgson, "Adapting Ethical Decisions to a Global Marketplace," *Management Review* 81 (1992): 53–57.
101. J. B. Rotter, "Generalized Expectancies for Internal versus External Control of Reinforcement," *Psychological Monographs* 80 (1966): 1–28.
102. L. K. Trevino and S. A. Youngblood, "Bad Apples in Bad Barrels: A Causal Analysis of Ethical Decision-Making Behavior," *Journal of Applied Psychology* 75 (1990): 378–385.
103. H. M. Lefcourt, *Locus of Control: Current Trends in Theory and Research*, 2nd ed. (Hillsdale, N.J.: Erlbaum, 1982).
104. N. Machiavelli, *The Prince*, trans. George Bull (Middlesex, England: Penguin Books, 1961).
105. R. Christie and F. L. Geis, *Studies in Machiavellianism* (New York: Academic Press, 1970).
106. R. A. Giacalone and S. B. Knouse, "Justifying Wrongful Employee Behavior: The Role of Personality in Organizational Sabotage," *Journal of Business Ethics* 9 (1990): 55–61.
107. S. B. Knouse and R. A. Giacalone, "Ethical Decision Making in Business: Behavioral Issues and Concerns," *Journal of Business Ethics* 11 (1992): 369–377.
108. L. Kohlberg, "Stage and Sequence: The Cognitive Developmental Approach to Socialization," in D. A. Goslin, ed., *Handbook of Socialization Theory and Research* (Chicago: Rand McNally, 1969): 347–480.
109. C. I. Malinowski and C. P. Smith, "Moral Reasoning and Moral Conduct: An Investigation Prompted by Kohlberg's Theory," *Journal of Personality and Social Psychology* 49 (1985): 1016–1027.
110. M. Brabeck, "Ethical Characteristics of Whistleblowers," *Journal of Research in Personality* 18 (1984): 41–53.
111. W. Y. Penn and B. D. Collier, "Current Research in Moral Development as a Decision Support System," *Journal of Business Ethics* 4 (1985): 131–136.
112. Trevino and Youngblood, "Bad Apples in Bad Barrels."
113. C. Gilligan, *In a Different Voice: Psychological Theory and Women's Development* (Cambridge, Mass.: Harvard University Press, 1982).
114. S. Jaffee and J. S. Hyde, "Gender Differences in Moral Orientation: A Meta-Analysis," *Psychological Bulletin* 126 (2000): 703–726.
115. G. R. Franke, D. F. Crown, and D. F. Spake, "Gender Differences in Ethical Perceptions of Business Practices: A Social Role Theory Perspective," *Journal of Applied Psychology* 82 (1997): 920–934.
116. S. A. Goldman and J. Arbuthnot, "Teaching Medical Ethics: The Cognitive-Developmental Approach," *Journal of Medical Ethics* 5 (1979): 171–181.
117. http://www.kld.com/research/socrates/businessethics100/2007/company_spotlight.html.
118. http://www.timberland.com/corp/index.jsp?page=pressrelease&eid=8500007642.

Chapter 4 Case

1. "About CCI," http://www.caninecompanions.org/national/about_cci.html (accessed August 23, 2007); "CCI / Facts and FAQs," http://www.caninecompanions.org/national/facts_faqs.html (accessed August 23, 2007).
2. "CCI / Facts and FAQs."
3. Ibid.
4. "CCI/Our Services," http://www.caninecompanions.org/national/our_services.html (accessed August 23, 2007); "CCI / Service Dogs and Skilled Companions," http://www.caninecompanions.org/national/service_dogs.html (accessed August 23, 2007).
5. "CCI/Facility Dogs," http://www.caninecompanions.org/national/facility_dogs.html (accessed August 23, 2007).
6. "CCI/Hearing Dogs," http://www.caninecompanions.org/national/hearing_dogs.html (accessed August 23, 2007).
7. "CCI / Facts and FAQs."
8. Ibid.
9. Author unknown, "Basketball Hall of Famer Bill Walton Raises and Trains Assistance Dog, Presents to Man With Quadriplegia," *Ascribe Health & Fitness News Services* (August 20, 2003): 3–4, from Newspaper Source database (accessed June 23, 2004).
10. L. S. Ball, "Pups Waggle into Texas Workplace as Future Helpers in Training," *The Dallas Morning News* (January 25, 2003), from Newspaper Source (accessed June 23, 2004).
11. A. Nelson, "Dogs of Destiny: For Families Who Raise Pups Training to Become Service Animals, the Work Is Rewarding but Sometimes Sad," *Columbia Daily Tribune* (November 24, 2006), from Newspaper Source database (accessed August 23, 2007).
12. D. S. Morris, "Given Lemons, Boy Makes Aid: 8-Year-old Uses Gift of Lemonade Stand to Raise More than $20,000 for Canine Training Group," *Newsday* (January 14, 2007), from Newspaper Source database (accessed August 23, 2007).

Chapter 5

1. S. Gerstenzang, "CEO think tank," *Working Mother* 29 (9) (November 2006): 49–54.
2. L. W. Porter, G. Bigley, and R. M. Steers, *Motivation and Leadership at Work*, 7th ed. (New York: McGraw-Hill, 2002).
3. J. P. Campbell and R. D. Pritchard, "Motivation Theory in Industrial and Organizational Psychology," in M. D. Dunnette, ed., *Handbook of Industrial and Organizational Psychology* (Chicago: Rand McNally, 1976), 63–130.
4. M. Weber, *The Protestant Ethic and the Spirit of Capitalism* (London: Talcott Parson, tr., 1930).
5. S. Freud, *Civilization and Its Discontents*, trans. and ed. J. Strachey (New York: Norton, 1961).

6. P. D. Dunlop and K. Lee, "Workplace Deviance, Organizational Citizenship Behavior, and Business Unit Performance: The Bad Apples Do Spoil the Whole Barrel," *Journal of Organizational Behavior* 25 (2004): 67–80.
7. K. J. Sweetman, "Employee Loyalty around the Globe," *Sloan Management Review* 42 (2001): 16.
8. B. S. Frey, *Not Just for the Money: An Economic Theory of Personal Motivation* (Brookfield, Vt.: Edgar Elger, 1997).
9. J. L. Matjasko and A. F. Feldman, "Bringing Work Home: The Emotional Experiences of Mothers and Fathers," *Journal of Family Psychology* 20 (2006): 47–55.
10. F. J. Roethlisberger, *Management and Morale* (Cambridge, Mass.: Harvard University Press, 1941).
11. A. Smith, *An Inquiry into the Nature and Causes of the Wealth of Nations*, Vol. 10 of *The Harvard Classics*, C. J. Bullock, ed. (New York: Collier, 1909).
12. J. Jennings, *Less Is More: How Great Companies Use Productivity as a Competitive Tool in Business* (New York: Portfolio, 2002).
13. F. W. Taylor, *The Principles of Scientific Management* (New York: Norton, 1911).
14. Hearings before Special Committee of the House of Representatives to Investigate the Taylor and Other Systems of Shop Management under Authority of House Resolution 90, Vol. 3, 1377–1508 contains Taylor's testimony before the committee from Thursday, January 25, through Tuesday, January 30, 1912.
15. J. Breal, "Secret sauce," *Fast Company* 115 (May 2007): 61–63.
16. L. Van Dyne and J. L. Pierce, "Psychological Ownership and Feelings of Possession: Three Field Studies Predicting Employee Attitudes and Organizational Citizenship Behavior," *Journal of Organizational Behavior* 25 (2004): 439–459.
17. A. H. Maslow, "A Theory of Human Motivation," *Psychological Review* 50 (1943): 370–396.
18. W. James, *The Principles of Psychology* (New York: H. Holt & Co., 1890; Cambridge, Mass.: Harvard University Press, 1983).
19. J. Dewey, *Human Nature and Conduct: An Introduction to Social Psychology* (New York: Holt, 1922).
20. S. Freud, *A General Introduction to Psycho-Analysis: A Course of Twenty-Eight Lectures Delivered at the University of Vienna* (New York: Liveright, 1963); A. Adler, *Understanding Human Nature* (Greenwich, Conn.: Fawcett, 1927).
21. L. W. Porter, "A Study of Perceived Need Satisfactions in Bottom and Middle Management Jobs," *Journal of Applied Psychology* 45 (1961): 1–10.
22. E. E. Lawler, III and J. L. Suttle, "A Causal Correlational Test of the Need Hierarchy Concept," *Organizational Behavior and Human Performance* 7 (1973): 265–287.
23. D. M. McGregor, *The Human Side of Enterprise* (New York: McGraw-Hill, 1960).
24. D. M. McGregor, "The Human Side of Enterprise," *Management Review* (November 1957): 22–28, 88–92.
25. E. E. Lawler, G. E. Lawford, S. A. Mohrman, and G. E. Ledford, Jr., *Strategies for High Performance Organizations—The CEO Report: Employee Involvement, TQM, and Reengineering Programs in Fortune 1000 Corporations* (San Francisco: Jossey-Bass, Inc., 1998).
26. J. Boorstin, "No Preservatives. No Unions. Lots of Dough," *Fortune* 148 (September 15, 2003): 127–129.
27. G. E. Forward, D. E. Beach, D. A. Gray, and J. C. Quick, "Mentofacturing: A Vision for American Industrial Excellence," *Academy of Management Executive* 5 (1991): 32–44.
28. C. P. Alderfer, *Human Needs in Organizational Settings* (New York: Free Press, 1972).
29. B. Schneider and C. P. Alderfer, "Three Studies of Need Satisfactions in Organizations," *Administrative Science Quarterly* 18 (1973): 489–505.
30. H. A. Murray, *Explorations in Personality: A Clinical and Experimental Study of Fifty Men of College Age* (New York: Oxford University Press, 1938).
31. D. C. McClelland, *Motivational Trends in Society* (Morristown, N.J.: General Learning Press, 1971).
32. J. P. Chaplin and T. S. Krawiec, *Systems and Theories of Psychology* (New York: Holt, Rinehart & Winston, 1960).
33. D. C. McClelland, "Achievement Motivation Can Be Learned," *Harvard Business Review* 43 (1965): 6–24.
34. E. A. Ward, "Multidimensionality of Achievement Motivation among Employed Adults," *Journal of Social Psychology* 134 (1997): 542–544.
35. A. Sagie, D. Elizur, and H. Yamauchi, "The Structure and Strength of Achievement Motivation: A Cross-Cultural Comparison," *Journal of Organizational Behavior* 17 (1996): 431–444.
36. D. C. McClelland and D. Burnham, "Power Is the Great Motivator," *Harvard Business Review* 54 (1976): 100–111; J. Hall and J. Hawker, *Power Management Inventory* (The Woodlands, Tex.: Teleometrics International, 1988).
37. F. Luthans, "Successful versus Effective Real Managers," *Academy of Management Executive* 2 (1988): 127–131.
38. S. Schachter, *The Psychology of Affiliation* (Stanford, Calif.: Stanford University Press, 1959).
39. N. W. van Yperen and M. Hagedoorn, "Do High Job Demands Increase Intrinsic Motivation or Fatigue or Both? The Role of Job Control and Job Social Support," *Academy of Management Journal* 46 (2003): 339–348.
40. F. Herzberg, B. Mausner, and B. Snyderman, *The Motivation to Work* (New York: Wiley, 1959).
41. F. Herzberg, *Work and the Nature of Man* (Cleveland: World, 1966).
42. D. S. Hamermesh, "The Changing Distribution of Job Satisfaction," *Journal of Human Resources* 36 (2001): 1–30.
43. J. Marquez, "Winning Women Back," *Workforce Management* 86(7) (April 9, 2007): 20–21.
44. F. J. Leach and J. D. Westbrook, "Motivation and Job Satisfaction in One Government Research and Development Environment," *Engineering Management Journal* 12 (2000): 3–8.
45. D. L. Nelson and B. L. Simmons, "Health Psychology and Work Stress: A More Positive Approach," in J. C. Quick and L. E. Tetrick, eds., *Handbook of Occupational Health Psychology* (Washington D. C.: American Psychological Association, 2003), 97–119.
46. K. S. Cameron, J. E. Dutton, and R. E. Quinn, eds., *Positive Organizational Scholarship: Foundations of a New Discipline* (San Francisco: Berrett-Keohler, 2003).
47. J. Loehr and T. Schwartz, "The Making of a Corporate Athlete," *Harvard Business Review* 79 (2001): 120–129.
48. J. Loehr and T. Schwartz, *The Power of Full Engagement: Managing Energy, Not Time, Is the Key to High Performance and Personal Renewal* (New York: Free Press, 2003).
49. P. M. Blau, *Exchange and Power in Social Life* (New York: Wiley, 1964).
50. A. Etzioni, "A Basis for Comparative Analysis of Complex Organizations," in A. Etzioni, ed., *A Sociological Reader on Complex Organizations*, 2nd ed., (New York: Holt, Rinehart & Winston, 1969), 59–76.
51. O. Janssen, "Job Demands, Perceptions of Effort–Reward Fairness and Innovative Work Behavior," *Journal of Occupational & Organizational Psychology* 73 (2000): 287–302.
52. R. Cropanzano, B. Goldman, and R. Folger, "Deontic Justice: The Role of Moral Principles in Workplace Fairness," *Journal of Organizational Behavior* 24 (2003): 1019–1024.
53. J. P. Campbell, M. D. Dunnette, E. E. Lawler, III, and K. E. Weick, Jr., *Managerial Behavior, Performance and Effectiveness* (New York: McGraw-Hill, 1970).
54. S. S. Masterson and C. L. Stamper, "Perceived Organizational Membership: An Aggregate Framework Representing the Employee—Organization Relationship," *Journal of Organizational Behavior* 24 (2003): 473–490.
55. J. S. Adams, "Inequity in Social Exchange," in L. Berkowitz, ed., *Advances in Experimental Social Psychology*, Vol. 2 (New York: Academic Press, 1965), 267–299; J. S. Adams, "Toward an Understanding of Inequity," *Journal of Abnormal and Social Psychology* 67 (1963): 422–436.
56. J. Nelson-Horchler, "The Best Man for the Job Is a Man," *Industry Week* (January 7, 1991): 50–52.
57. P. D. Sweeney, D. B. McFarlin, and E. J. Inderrieden, "Using Relative Deprivation Theory to Explain Satisfaction with Income and Pay Level: A Multistudy Examination," *Academy of Management Journal* 33 (1990): 423–436.

58. R. C. Huseman, J. D. Hatfield, and E. A. Miles, "A New Perspective on Equity Theory: The Equity Sensitivity Construct," *Academy of Management Review* 12 (1987): 222–234.
59. D. McLoughlin and S. C. Carr, "Equity and Sensitivity and Double Demotivation," *Journal of Social Psychology* 137 (1997): 668–670.
60. K. E. Weick, M. G. Bougon, and G. Maruyama, "The Equity Context," *Organizational Behavior and Human Performance* 15 (1976): 32–65.
61. R. Coles, *Privileged Ones* (Boston: Little, Brown, 1977).
62. J. A. Colquitt and J. Greenberg, "Organizational Justice: A Fair Assessment of the State of the Literature," in J. Greenberg, ed., *Organizational Behavior: The State of the Science,* 2nd ed. (Mahwah, N.J.: Erlbaum Associates, 2003).
63. J. Greenberg, "Equity and Workplace Status: A Field Experiment," *Journal of Applied Psychology* 73 (1988): 606–613.
64. J. Greenberg. "Losing Sleep over Organizational Justice: Attenuating Insomniac Reactions to Underpayment Inequity with Supervisory Training in Interactional Justice," *Journal of Applied Psychology* 91 (2006): 58–69.
65. J. Greenberg and B. Alge, "Aggressive Reactions to Workplace Injustice," in R. W. Griffin, A. O'Leary-Kelly, and J. Collins, eds., *Dysfunctional Behavior in Organizations, Vol. 1: Violent Behaviors in Organizations* (Greenwich, CT: JAI, 1998), 119–145.
66. R. A. Cosier and D. R. Dalton, "Equity Theory and Time: A Reformulation," *Academy of Management Review* 8 (1983): 311–319.
67. J. E. Martin and M. W. Peterson, "Two-Tier Wage Structures: Implications for Equity Theory," *Academy of Management Journal* 30 (1987): 297–315.
68. V. H. Vroom, *Work and Motivation* (New York: Wiley, 1964/1970).
69. U. R. Larson, "Supervisor's Performance Feedback to Subordinates: The Effect of Performance Valence and Outcome Dependence," *Organizational Behavior and Human Decision Processes* 37 (1986): 391–409.
70. M. C. Kernan and R. G. Lord, "Effects of Valence, Expectancies, and Goal-Performance Discrepancies in Single and Multiple Goal Environments," *Journal of Applied Psychology* 75 (1990): 194–203.
71. R. J. Sanchez, D. M. Truxillo, and T. N. Bauer, "Development and Examination of an Expectancy-Based Measure of Test-Taking Motivation," *Journal of Applied Psychology* 85 (2000): 739–750.
72. W. VanEerde and H. Thierry, "Vroom's Expectancy Models and Work-Related Criteria: A Meta-Analysis," *Journal of Applied Psychology* 81 (1996): 575–586.
73. E. D. Pulakos and N. Schmitt, "A Longitudinal Study of a Valence Model Approach for the Prediction of Job Satisfaction of New Employees," *Journal of Applied Psychology* 68 (1983): 307–312.
74. F. J. Landy and W. S. Becker, "Motivation Theory Reconsidered," in L. L. Cummings and B. M. Staw, eds., *Research in Organizational Behavior* 9 (Greenwich, Conn.: JAI Press, 1987), 1–38.
75. L. Kohlberg, "The Cognitive-Developmental Approach to Socialization," in D. A. Goslin, ed., *Handbook of Socialization Theory and Research* (Chicago: Rand McNally, 1969).
76. N. J. Adler, *International Dimensions of Organizational Behavior,* 4th ed. (Mason, OH: South-Western, 2001).
77. G. Hofstede, "Motivation, Leadership, and Organization: Do American Theories Apply Abroad?" *Organizational Dynamics* 9 (1980): 42–63.
78. G. H. Hines, "Cross-Cultural Differences in Two-Factor Theory," *Journal of Applied Psychology* 58 (1981): 313–317.
79. M. C. Bolino and W. H. Turnley. "Old Faces, New Places: Equity Theory in Cross-Cultural Contexts," *Journal of Organizational Behavior* (in press).
80. B. Mannino, "Top 5," *Working Mother* 30(6) (July 2007): 74–76.

Chapter 5 Case

1. "Pixar Company FAQs," http://www.pixar.com/companyinfo/faq/faq.htm (accessed August 23, 2007).
2. "Pixar Corporate Overview," http://www.pixar.com/companyinfo/about_us/overview.htm (accessed August 23, 2007); R. Grover, "A Pixar Exec's Fairy-Tale Story," *Business Week Online* (January 26, 2006), from Academic Search Premier database (accessed August 23, 2007).
3. P. Burrows, R. Grover, and H. Green, "Steve Jobs' Magic Kingdom," *Business Week* (February 6. 2006), from Academic Search Premier database (accessed August 23, 2007).
4. Burrows, Grover, and Green, page 2 of 9.
5. Ibid, page 3 of 9.
6. Ibid.
7. "Pixar Corporate Overview," http://www.pixar.com/companyinfo/about_us/overview.htm (accessed August 23, 2007).
8. C. Gant, "Gone Fishin'—Pixar Studios and the Fish That Ate Disney," *The Australian* (December 20, 2003), page 5 of 6, from Newspaper Source database (accessed June 26, 2004).
9. "Pixar Corporate Overview"; P. Burrows, "Pixar's Unsung Hero," *Business Week* (June 30, 2003), from Business Source Premier database (accessed June 26, 2004).
10. "Pixar Corporate Overview"; "Meet the Execs," http://www.pixar.com/companyinfo/about_us/execs.htm (accessed August 23, 2007).
11. "Pixar Awards," http://www.pixar.com/companyinfo/press_box/awards.htm (accessed August 23, 2007).
12. C. Gant, page 4 of 6.
13. C. Gant, page 2 of 6.

Chapter 6

1. B. Bremner, "Toyota: A Carmaker Wired to Win," *Business Week Online* (April 25, 2007): 21.
2. I. P. Pavlov, *Conditioned Reflexes* (New York: Oxford University Press, 1927).
3. B. Cannon, "Walter B. Cannon: Reflections on the Man and His Contributions," *Centennial Session,* American Psychological Association Centennial Convention, Washington, D.C., 1992.
4. B. F. Skinner, *The Behavior of Organisms: An Experimental Analysis* (New York: Appleton-Century-Crofts, 1938).
5. B. F. Skinner, *Science and Human Behavior* (New York: Free Press, 1953).
6. F. Luthans and R. Kreitner, *Organizational Behavior Modification and Beyond* (Glenview, Ill.: Scott, Foresman, 1985).
7. A. D. Stajkovic and F. Luthans, "A Meta-Analysis of the Effects of Organizational Behavior Modification on Task Performance, 1975–95," *Academy of Management Journal* 40 (1997): 1122–1149.
8. C. B. Cadsby, F. Song, and F. Tapon. "Sorting and Incentive Effects of Pay for Performance: An Experimental Investigation," *Academy of Management Journal* 50 (2007): 387–405.
9. J. Hale, "Strategic Rewards: Keeping Your Best Talent from Walking Out the Door," *Compensation & Benefits Management* 14 (1998): 39–50.
10. B. F. Skinner, *Contingencies of Reinforcement: A Theoretical Analysis* (New York: Appleton-Century-Crofts, 1969).
11. J. P. Chaplin and T. S. Krawiec, *Systems and Theories of Psychology* (New York: Holt, Rinehart & Winston, 1960).
12. M. Maccoby, J. Hoffer Gittell, and M. Ledeen, "Leadership and the Fear Factor," *Sloan Management Review* 148 (Winter 2004): 14–18.
13. A. Bandura, *Social Learning Theory* (Englewood Cliffs, N.J.: Prentice-Hall, 1977); A. Bandura, "Self-Efficacy: Toward a Unifying Theory of Behavioral Change," *Psychological Review* 84 (1977): 191–215.
14. J. J. Martocchio and E. J. Hertenstein, "Learning Orientation and Goal Orientation Context: Relationships with Cognitive and Affective Learning Outcomes," *Human Resource Development Quarterly* 14 (2003): 413–434.
15. A. Bandura, "Regulation of Cognitive Processes through Perceived Self-Efficacy," *Developmental Psychology* (September 1989): 729–735.
16. J. M. Phillips and S. M. Gully, "Role of Goal Orientation, Ability, Need for Achievement, and Locus of Control in the Self-Efficacy and Goal-Setting Process," *Journal of Applied Psychology* 82 (1997): 792–802.
17. J. C. Weitlauf, R. E. Smith, and D. Cervone, "Generalization Effects of Coping-Skills Training: Influence of Self-Defense Training on Women's

Efficacy Beliefs, Assertiveness, and Aggression," *Journal of Applied Psychology* 85 (2000): 625–633.

18. A. D. Stajkovic and F. Luthans, "Social Cognitive Theory and Self-Efficacy: Going Beyond Traditional Motivational and Behavioral Approaches," *Organizational Dynamics* (Spring 1998): 62–74.
19. A. D. Stajkovic and F. Luthans, "Self-Efficacy and Work-Related Performance: A Meta-Analysis," *Psychological Bulletin* 124 (1998): 240–261.
20. V. Gecas, "The Social Psychology of Self-Efficacy," *Annual Review of Sociology* 15 (1989): 291–316.
21. J. B. Vancouver and L. N. Kendall. "When Self-Efficacy Negatively Relates to Motivation and Performance in a Learning Context," *Journal of Applied Psychology* 91 (2006): 1146–1153.
22. O. Isachsen and L. V. Berens, *Working Together: A Personality Centered Approach to Management* (Coronado, Calif.: Neworld Management Press, 1988); O. Krueger and J. M. Thuesen, *Type Talk* (New York: Tilden Press, 1988).
23. E. A. Locke and G. P. Latham, *A Theory of Goal Setting and Task Performance* (Englewood Cliffs, N.J.: Prentice-Hall, 1990).
24. A. D. Stajkovic, E. A. Locke, and E. S. Blair. "A First Examination of the Relationships between Primed Subconscious Goals, Assigned Conscious Goals, and Task Performance," *Journal of Applied Psychology* 91 (2006): 1172–1180.
25. T. O. Murray, *Management by Objectives: A Systems Approach to Management* (Fort Worth, Tex.: Western Company, n.d.).
26. W. T. Brooks and T. W. Mullins, *High Impact Time Management* (Englewood Cliffs, N.J.: Prentice-Hall, 1989).
27. G. H. Seijts, G. P. Latham, K. Tasa, and B. W. Latham, "Goal Setting and Goal Orientation: An Integration of Two Different Yet Related Literatures," *Academy of Management Journal* 47 (2004): 227–239.
28. E. A. Locke, "Toward a Theory of Task Motivation and Incentives," *Organizational Behavior and Human Performance* 3 (1968): 157–189.
29. J. C. Quick, "Dyadic Goal Setting within Organizations: Role Making and Motivational Considerations," *Academy of Management Review* 4 (1979): 369–380.
30. D. McGregor, "An Uneasy Look at Performance Appraisal," *Harvard Business Review* 35 (1957): 89–94.
31. J. R. Hollenbeck, C. R. Williams, and H. J. Klein, "An Empirical Examination of the Antecedents of Commitment to Difficult Goals," *Journal of Applied Psychology* 74 (1989): 18–23.
32. R. C. Rodgers and J. E. Hunter, "The Impact of Management by Objectives on Organizational Productivity," unpublished paper (Lexington: University of Kentucky, 1989).
33. E. A. Locke, K. N. Shaw, L. M. Saari, and G. P. Latham, "Goal Setting and Task Performance: 1969–1980," *Psychological Bulletin* 90 (1981): 125–152.
34. D. B. Fedora, W. D. Davis, J. M. Maslync, and K. Mathiesond, "Performance Improvement Efforts in Response to Negative Feedback: The Roles of Source Power and Recipient Self-Esteem," *Journal of Management* 27 (2001): 79–98.
35. J. C. Quick, "Dyadic Goal Setting and Role Stress," *Academy of Management Journal* 22 (1979): 241–252.
36. G. S. Odiorne, *Management by Objectives: A System of Managerial Leadership* (New York: Pitman, 1965).
37. American Management Association, *Blueprints for Service Quality: The Federal Express Approach* (New York: American Management Association, 1991).
38. G. P. Latham and G. A. Yukl, "A Review of Research on the Application of Goal Setting in Organizations," *Academy of Management Journal* 18 (1975): 824–845.
39. P. F. Drucker, *The Practice of Management* (New York: Harper & Bros., 1954).
40. R. D. Prichard, P. L. Roth, S. D. Jones, P. J. Galgay, and M. D. Watson, "Designing a Goal-Setting System to Enhance Performance: A Practical Guide," *Organizational Dynamics* 17 (1988): 69–78.
41. C. L. Hughes, *Goal Setting: Key to Individual and Organizational Effectiveness* (New York: American Management Association, 1965).
42. M. E. Tubbs and S. E. Ekeberg, "The Role of Intentions in Work Motivation: Implications for Goal-Setting Theory and Research," *Academy of Management Review* 16 (1991): 180–199.
43. S. Vatave, "Managing Risk," *Supervision* 65 (2004): 6–9.
44. J. R. Hollenbeck and A. P. Brief, "The Effects of Individual Differences and Goal Origin on Goal Setting and Performance," *Organizational Behavior and Human Decision Processes* 40 (1987): 392–414.
45. R. A. Katzell and D. E. Thompson, "Work Motivation: Theory and Practice," *American Psychologist* 45 (1990): 144–153; M. W. McPherson, "Is Psychology the Science of Behavior?" *American Psychologist* 47 (1992): 329–335.
46. E. A. Locke, "The Ideas of Frederick W. Taylor: An Evaluation," *Academy of Management Review* 7 (1982): 15–16; R. M. Yerkes and J. D. Dodson, "The Relation of Strength of Stimulus to Rapidity of Habit-Formation," *Journal of Comparative Neurology and Psychology* 18 (1908): 459–482.
47. F. L. Schmidt and J. Hunter, "General Mental Ability in the World of Work: Occupational Attainment and Job Performance," *Journal of Personality and Social Psychology* 86 (2004): 162–173.
48. R. L. Cardy, *Performance Management: Concepts, Skills, and Exercises* (Armonk, New York and London, England: M.E. Sharpe, 2004).
49. P. Cappelli and N. Rogovsky, "Employee Involvement and Organizational Citizenship: Implications for Labor Law Reform and 'Lean Production,'" *Industrial & Labor Relations Review* 51 (1998): 633–653.
50. B. Erdogan, M. L. Kraimer, and R. C. Liden, "Procedural Justice as a Two-Dimensional Construct: An Examination in the Performance Appraisal Account," *Journal of Applied Behavioral Science* 37 (2001): 205–222.
51. S. E. DeVoe and S. S. Iyengar, "Managers' Theories of Subordinates: A Cross-Cultural Examination of Manager Perceptions of Motivation and Appraisal of Performance," *Organizational Behavior and Human Decision Processes* 93 (2004): 47–61.
52. I. M. Jawahar and C. R. Williams, "Where All the Children Are Above Average: The Performance Appraisal Purpose Effect," *Personnel Psychology* 50 (1997): 905–925.
53. M. E. Tubbs and M. L. Trusty, "Direct Reports of Motivation for Task Performance Levels: Some Construct-Related Evidence," *Journal of Psychology* 135 (2001): 185–205.
54. R. R. Kilburg, *Executive Coaching: Developing Managerial Wisdom in a World of Chaos* (Washington, D.C.: American Psychological Association, 2000).
55. H. H. Meyer, E. Kay, and J. R. P. French, "Split Roles in Performance Appraisal," *Harvard Business Review* 43 (1965): 123–129.
56. W. Lam, X. Huang, and E. Snape. "Feedback-Seeking Behavior and Leader-Member Exchange: Do Supervisor-Attributed Motives Matter?" *Academy of Management Journal* 50 (2007): 348–363.
57. W. A. Fisher, J. C. Quick, L. L. Schkade, and G. W. Ayers, "Developing Administrative Personnel through the Assessment Center Technique," *Personnel Administrator* 25 (1980): 44–46, 62.
58. J. S. Goodman, R. E. Wood, and M. Hendrickx, "Feedback Specificity, Exploration, and Learning," *Journal of Applied Psychology* 89 (2004): 248–262.
59. M. B. DeGregorio and C. D. Fisher, "Providing Performance Feedback: Reactions to Alternative Methods," *Journal of Management* 14 (1988): 605–616.
60. G. C. Thornton, "The Relationship between Supervisory and Self-Appraisals of Executive Performance," *Personnel Psychology* 21 (1968): 441–455.
61. A. S. DeNisi and A. N. Kluger, "Feedback Effectiveness: Can 360-Degree Appraisals Be Improved?" *Academy of Management Executive* 14 (2000): 129–140.
62. F. Luthans and S. J. Peterson, "360-Degree Feedback with Systematic Coaching: Empirical Analysis Suggests a Winning Combination," *Human Resource Management* 42 (2003): 243–256.
63. G. Toegel and J. A. Conger, "360-Degree Assessment: Time for Reinvention," *Academy of Management Learning and Education* 2 (2003): 297–311.
64. L. Hirschhorn, "Leaders and Followers in a Postindustrial Age: A Psychodynamic View," *Journal of Applied Behavioral Science* 26 (1990): 529–542.
65. F. M Jablin, "Superior-Subordinate Communication: The State of the Art," *Psychological Bulletin* 86 (1979): 1201–1222.
66. J. Pfeffer, "Six Dangerous Myths about Pay," *Harvard Business Review* 76 (1998): 108–119.

67. "Six Employee Types Prefer Different Rewards," *HRFocus* 84(4) (April 2007): 12.
68. M. Erez, "Work Motivation from a Cross-Cultural Perspective," in A. M. Bouvy, F. J. R. Van de Vijver, P. Boski, and P. G. Schmitz, eds., *Journeys into Cross-Cultural Psychology* (Amsterdam, Netherlands: Swets & Zeitlinger, 1994), 386–403.
69. George T. Milkovich and Jerry M. Newman, *Compensation*, 4th ed. (Homewood, Ill.: Irwin, 1993).
70. S. Kerr, "On the Folly of Rewarding A, While Hoping for B," *Academy of Management Journal* 18 (1975): 769–783.
71. J. M. Bardwick, *Danger in the Comfort Zone* (New York: American Management Association, 1991).
72. M. J. Martinko and W. L. Gardner, "The Leader/Member Attributional Process," *Academy of Management Review* 12 (1987): 235–249.
73. K. N. Wexley, R. A. Alexander, J. P. Greenawalt, and M. A. Couch, "Attitudinal Congruence and Similarity as Related to Interpersonal Evaluations in Manager-Subordinate Dyads," *Academy of Management Journal* 23 (1980): 320–330.
74. H. H. Kelley, *Attribution in Social Interaction* (New York: General Learning Press, 1971).
75. H. H. Kelley, "The Processes of Causal Attribution," *American Psychologist* 28 (1973): 107–128.
76. B. Raabe and T. A. Beehr, "Formal Mentoring versus Supervisor and Coworker Relationships: Differences in Perceptions and Impact," *Journal of Organizational Behavior* 24 (2003): 271–293.
77. A. M. Young and P. L. Perrewe, "What Did You Expect? An Examination of Career-Related Support and Social Support among Mentors and Protégés," *Journal of Management* 26 (2000): 611–633.
78. K. Doherty, "The Good News about Depression," *Business and Health* 3 (1989): 1–4.
79. K. E. Kram, "Phases of the Mentor Relationship," *Academy of Management Journal* 26 (1983): 608–625.
80. T. D. Allen, L. T. Eby, M. L. Poteet, E. Lentz, and L. Lima, "Career Benefits Associated with Mentoring for Protégés: A Meta-Analysis," *Journal of Applied Psychology* 89 (2004): 127–136.
81. T. N. Bauer and S. G. Green, "Development of Leader–Member Exchange: A Longitudinal Test," *Academy of Management Journal* 39 (1996): 1538–1567.
82. K. E. Kram and L. A. Isabella, "Mentoring Alternatives: The Role of Peer Relationships in Career Development," *Academy of Management Journal* 28 (1985): 110–132.
83. J. Greco, "Hey, Coach!" *Journal of Business Strategy* 22 (2001): 28–32.
84. M. Spector and G. Chon, "Toyota University Opens Admissions to Outsiders," *The Wall Street Journal* (March 5, 2007): Section B1.

Chapter 6 Case

1. "Our Story—About American Express," http://www.americanexpress.com/corp/os/history.asp (accessed September 8, 2007).
2. S. Dunford, "Heal Tyself: Learning Network Concentrates on Its Own Learning and Development," *TD* (October 2006): 33–34.
3. Ibid, 33.
4. Ibid, 33–34.
5. Simba Information, "AMEX Finds Manager Support Trumps Delivery in Sustaining Performance Improvement," *Corporate Training & Development Advisor* 11(19) (September 29, 2006): 2.
6. Ibid, 3.
7. Ibid.

Chapter 7

1. "New Research on Timberland Co." M2PressWIRE (February 13, 2007).
2. J. Barling, E. K. Kelloway, and M. R. Frone, eds., *Handbook of Work Stress* (Thousand Oaks, CA: Sage Publications, 2005).
3. J. C. Quick, J. D. Quick, D. L. Nelson, and J. J. Hurrell, Jr., *Preventive Stress Management in Organizations* (Washington, D.C.: American Psychological Association, 1997).
4. S. Benison, A. C. Barger, and E. L. Wolfe, *Walter B. Cannon: The Life and Times of a Young Scientist* (Cambridge, Mass.: Harvard University Press, 1987).
5. W. B. Cannon, "Stresses and Strains of Homeostasis," *American Journal of the Medical Sciences* 189 (1935): 1–14.
6. W. B. Cannon, *The Wisdom of the Body* (New York: Norton, 1932).
7. R. S. Lazarus, *Psychological Stress and the Coping Process* (New York: McGraw-Hill, 1966).
8. C. Liu, P. E. Spector, and L. Shi, "Cross-National Job Stress: A Quantitative and Qualitative Study," *Journal of Organizational Behavior* 28 (2007): 209–239.
9. D. Katz and R. L. Kahn, *The Social Psychology of Organizations*, 2nd ed. (New York: Wiley, 1978), 185–221.
10. H. Levinson, "A Psychoanalytic View of Occupational Stress," *Occupational Mental Health* 3 (1978): 2–13.
11. P. L. Perrewé, K. L. Zellars, G. R. Ferris, A. M. Rossi, C. J. Kacmar, and D. A. Ralston, "Neutralizing Job Stressors: Political Skill as an Antidote to the Dysfunctional Consequences of Role Conflict," *Academy of Management Journal* 47 (2004): 141–152.
12. T. L. Friedman, *The Lexus and the Olive Tree* (New York: Vintage Anchor, 2000).
13. T. Theorell and R. A. Karasek, "Current Issues Relating to Psychosocial Job Strain and Cardiovascular Disease," *Journal of Occupational Health Psychology* 1 (1996): 9–26.
14. D. T. Hall and J. Richter, "Career Gridlock: Baby Boomers Hit the Wall," *Academy of Management Executive* 4 (1990): 7–22.
15. N. P. Podsakoff, J. A. LePine, and M. A. LePine, "Differential Challenge Stressor-Hindrance Stressor Relationships with Job Attitudes, Turnover Intentions, Turnover, and Withdrawal Behavior: A Meta-Analysis," *Journal of Applied Psychology* 92 (2007): 438–454.
16. S. Zuboff, *In the Age of the Smart Machine: The Future of Work and Power* (New York: Basic Books, 1988).
17. R. L. Kahn, D. M. Wolfe, R. P. Quinn, J. D. Snoek, and R. A. Rosenthal, *Organizational Stress: Studies in Role Conflict and Ambiguity* (New York: Wiley, 1964).
18. L. B. Hammer, T. N. Bauer, and A. A. Grandey, "Work-Family Conflict and Work-Related Withdrawal Behaviors," *Journal of Business and Psychology* 17 (2003): 419–436.
19. M. F. Peterson, et al., "Role Conflict, Ambiguity, and Overload: A 21-Nation Study," *Academy of Management Journal* 38 (1995): 429–452.
20. P. D. Bliese and C. A. Castro, "Role Clarity, Work Overload and Organizational Support: Multilevel Evidence of the Importance of Support," *Work & Stress* 14 (2000): 65–74.
21. A. Skogstad, S. Einarsen, T. Torsheim, M. S. Aasland, and H. Hetland, "The Destructiveness of Laissez-Faire Leadership Behavior," *Journal of Occupational Health Psychology* 12 (2007): 80–92.
22. P. J. Frost, *Toxic Emotions at Work: How Compassionate Managers Handle Pain and Conflict* (Boston, MA: Harvard Business School Press, 2003).
23. S. Grebner, N. K. Semmer, L. L. Faso, S. Gut, W. Kalin, and A. Elfering, "Working Conditions, Well-Being, and Job-Related Attitudes Among Call Centre Agents," *European Journal of Work and Organizational Psychology* 12 (2003): 341–365.
24. M. P. Bell, J. C. Quick, and C. Cycota, "Assessment and Prevention of Sexual Harassment: An Applied Guide to Creating Healthy Organizations," *International Journal of Selection and Assessment* 10 (2002): 160–167.
25. L. T. Hosmer, "Trust: The Connecting Link between Organizational Theory and Philosophical Ethics," *Academy of Management Review* 20 (1995): 379–403; V. J. Doby and R. D. Caplan, "Organizational Stress as Threat to Reputation: Effects on Anxiety at Work and at Home," *Academy of Management Journal* 38 (1995): 1105–1123.
26. R. T. Keller, "Cross-Functional Project Groups in Research and New Product Development: Diversity, Communications, Job Stress, and Outcomes," *Academy of Management Journal* 33 (2001): 547–555.

27. M. F. Peterson and P. B. Smith, "Does National Culture or Ambient Temperature Explain Cross-National Differences in Role Stress? No Sweat!" *Academy of Management Journal* 40 (1997): 930–946.

28. K. K. Gillingham, "High-G Stress and Orientational Stress: Physiologic Effects of Aerial Maneuvering," *Aviation, Space, and Environmental Medicine* 59 (1988): A10–A20.

29. R. S. DeFrank, "Executive Travel Stress: Perils of the Road Warrior," *Academy of Management Executive* 14 (2000): 58–72.

30. M. Westman, "Strategies for Coping with Business Trips: A Qualitative Exploratory Study," *International Journal of Stress Management* 11 (2004): 167–176.

31. R. S. Bhagat, S. J. McQuaid, S. Lindholm, and J. Segovis, "Total Life Stress: A Multimethod Validation of the Construct and Its Effect on Organizationally Valued Outcomes and Withdrawal Behaviors," *Journal of Applied Psychology* 70 (1985): 202–214.

32. J. C. Quick, J. R. Joplin, D. A. Gray, and E. C. Cooley, "The Occupational Life Cycle and the Family," in L. L'Abate, ed., *Handbook of Developmental Family Psychology and Psychopathology* (New York: John Wiley, 1993).

33. S. Shellenbarger, "Work & Family," *The Wall Street Journal* (January 31, 1996): B1.

34. S. A. Lobel, "Allocation of Investment in Work and Family Roles: Alternative Theories and Implications for Research," *Academy of Management Review* 16 (1991): 507–521.

35. G. Porter, "Organizational Impact of Workaholism: Suggestions for Researching the Negative Outcomes of Excessive Work," *Journal of Occupational Health Psychology* 1 (1996): 70–84.

36. J. W. Pennebaker, C. F. Hughes, and R. C. O'Heeron, "The Psychophysiology of Confession: Linking Inhibitory and Psychosomatic Processes," *Journal of Personality and Social Psychology* 52 (1987): 781–793.

37. J. Loehr and T. Schwartz, "The Making of a Corporate Athlete," *Harvard Business Review* 79 (2001): 120–129.

38. J. D. Quick, R. S. Horn, and J. C. Quick, "Health Consequences of Stress," *Journal of Organizational Behavior Management* 8 (1986): 19–36.

39. R. M. Yerkes and J. D. Dodson, "The Relation of Strength of Stimulus to Rapidity of Habit-Formation," *Journal of Comparative Neurology and Psychology* 18 (1908): 459–482.

40. J. E. McGrath, "Stress and Behavior in Organizations," in M. D. Dunnette, ed., *Handbook of Industrial and Organizational Psychology* (Chicago: Rand McNally, 1976), 1351–1395.

41. T. A. Wright, R. Cropanzano, and D. G. Meyer, "State and Trait Correlates of Job Performance: A Tale of Two Perspectives," *Journal of Business and Psychology* 18 (2004): 365–383.

42. W. B. Cannon, *Bodily Changes in Pain, Hunger, Fear, and Rage* (New York: Appleton, 1915).

43. P. A. Herbig and F. A. Palumbo, "Karoshi: Salaryman Sudden Death Syndrome," *Journal of Managerial Psychology* 9 (1994): 11–16.

44. S. Sauter, L. R. Murphy, and J. J. Hurrell, Jr., "Prevention of Work-Related Psychological Distress: A National Strategy Proposed by the National Institute for Occupational Safety and Health," *American Psychologist* 45 (1990): 1146–1158.

45. R. Cropanzano, D. E. Rupp, and Z. S. Byrne, "The Relationship of Emotional Exhaustion to Work Attitudes, Job Performance, and Organizational Citizenship Behaviors," *Journal of Applied Psychology* 88 (2003): 160–169.

46. A. A. Grandey, "When 'The Show Must Go On': Surface Acting and Deep Acting as Determinants of Emotional Exhaustion and Peer-Rated Service Delivery," *Academy of Management Journal* 46 (2003): 86–96.

47. I. Wylie, "Routing Rust-Out," © 2004 Gruner & Jahr USA Publishing. First published in *Fast Company* Magazine (January 2004): 40. Reprinted with permission, http://www.fastcompany.com/magazinee/78/5things.html.

48. H. Selye, *Stress in Health and Disease* (Boston: Butterworth, 1976).

49. B. G. Ware and D. L. Block, "Cardiovascular Risk Intervention at a Work Site: The Ford Motor Company Program," *International Journal of Mental Health* 11 (1982): 68–75.

50. B. S. Siegel, *Love, Medicine, and Miracles* (New York: Harper & Row, 1986).

51. D. B. Kennedy, R. J. Homant, and M. R. Homant, "Perceptions of Injustice as a Predictor of Support for Workplace Aggression," *Journal of Business and Psychology* 18 (2004): 323–336.

52. N. Bolger, A. DeLongis, R. C. Kessler, and E. A. Schilling, "Effects of Daily Stress on Negative Mood," *Journal of Personality and Social Psychology* 57 (1989): 808–818.

53. B. A. Macy and P. H. Mirvis, "A Methodology for Assessment of Quality of Work Life and Organizational Effectiveness in Behavioral-Economic Terms," *Administrative Science Quarterly* 21 (1976): 212–226.

54. F. K. Cocchiara and J. C. Quick, "The Negative Effects of Positive Stereotypes: Ethnicity-Related Stressors and Implications on Organizational Health," *Journal of Organizational Behavior,* 25 (2004): 781–785.

55. J. M. Ivancevich, M. T. Matteson, and E. Richards, "Who's Liable for Stress on the Job?" *Harvard Business Review* 64 (1985): 60–72.

56. Frank S. Deus v. Allstate Insurance Company, civil action no. 88-2099, U.S. District Court, Western District of Louisiana.

57. R. S. DeFrank and J. M. Ivancevich, "Stress on the Job: An Executive Update," *Academy of Management Executive* 12 (1998): 55–66.

58. P. Wilson and M. Bronstein, "Employers: Don't Panic about Workplace Stress," *Personnel Today* (November 4, 2003): 10.

59. J. E. Bono and M. A. Vey, "Personality and Emotional Performance: Extraversion, Neuroticism, and Self-Monitoring," *Journal of Occupational Health Psychology* 12 (2007): 177–192.

60. C. S. Troutman, K. G. Burke, and J. D. Beeler, "The Effects of Self-Efficacy, Assertiveness, Stress, and Gender on Intention," *Journal of Applied Business Research* 16 (2000): 63–75.

61. S. E. Taylor, L. C. Klein, G. P. Lewis, T. L. Gruenewald, R. A. R. Burung, and J. A. Updegraff, "Biobehavioral Responses to Stress in Females: Tend-and-Befriend, Not Fight-or-Flight," *Psychological Review* 107 (2000): 411–429.

62. D. L. Nelson and J. C. Quick, "Professional Women: Are Distress and Disease Inevitable?" *Academy of Management Review* 10 (1985): 206–218; T. D. Jick and L. F. Mitz, "Sex Differences in Work Stress," *Academy of Management Review* 10 (1985): 408–420.

63. L. Verbrugge, "Recent, Present, and Future Health of American Adults," *Annual Review of Public Health* 10 (1989): 333–361.

64. M. D. Friedman and R. H. Rosenman, *Type A Behavior and Your Heart* (New York: Knopf, 1974).

65. L. Wright, "The Type A Behavior Pattern and Coronary Artery Disease," *American Psychologist* 43 (1988): 2–14.

66. J. M. Ivancevich and M. T. Matteson, "A Type A–B Person–Work Environment Interaction Model for Examining Occupational Stress and Consequences," *Human Relations* 37 (1984): 491–513.

67. S. O. C. Kobasa, "Conceptualization and Measurement of Personality in Job Stress Research," in J. J. Hurrell, Jr., L. R. Murphy, S. L. Sauter, and C. L. Cooper, eds., *Occupational Stress: Issues and Developments in Research* (New York: Taylor & Francis, 1988), 100–109.

68. J. Borysenko, "Personality Hardiness," *Lectures in Behavioral Medicine* (Boston: Harvard Medical School, 1985).

69. J. S. House, K. R. Landis, and D. Umberson, "Social Relationships and Health," *Science* 241 (1988): 540–545.

70. J. Bowlby, *A Secure Base* (New York: Basic Books, 1988).

71. C. Hazan and P. Shaver, "Love and Work: An Attachment-Theoretical Perspective," *Journal of Personality and Social Psychology* 59 (1990): 270–280.

72. J. C. Quick, D. L. Nelson, and J. D. Quick, *Stress and Challenge at the Top: The Paradox of the Successful Executive* (Chichester, England: Wiley, 1990).

73. J. C. Quick, J. R. Joplin, D. L. Nelson, and J. D. Quick, "Self-Reliance for Stress and Combat" (*Proceedings of the 8th Combat Stress Conference,* U.S. Army Health Services Command, Fort Sam Houston, Texas, September 23–27, 1991): 1–5.

74. J. C. Dvorak, "Baffling," *PC Magazine* 3 (November 4, 2003): 61, http://www.pcmag.com/article2/0,4149,1369270,00.asp.

75. O. Janssen, "How Fairness Perceptions Make Innovative Behavior More or Less Stressful," *Journal of Organizational Behavior* 25 (2004): 201–215; T. A. Judge and J. A. Colquitt, "Organizational Justice and Stress: The Mediating Role of Work–Family Conflict," *Journal of Applied Psychology* 89 (2004): 395–404.

76. K. Hickox, "Content and Competitive," *Airman* (January 1994): 31–33.
77. A. Drach-Zahavy and A. Freund, "Team Effectiveness under Stress: A Structural Contingency Approach," *Journal of Organizational Behavior* 28 (2007): 423–450.
78. R. W. Griffin, A. O'Leary-Kelly, and J. M. Collins, eds., *Dysfunctional Behavior in Organizations: Violent and Deviant Behavior* (Stamford, Conn.: JAI Press, 1998).
79. W. L. French and C. H. Bell, Jr., *Organizational Development: Behavioral Science Interventions for Organization Improvement*, 4th ed. (Englewood Cliffs, N.J.: Prentice-Hall, 1990).
80. M. Macik-Frey, J. C. Quick, and J. D. Quick, "Interpersonal Communication: The Key to Unlocking Social Support for Preventive Stress Management," in C. L. Cooper, ed., *Handbook of Stress, Medicine, and Health, Revised Edition* (Boca Raton, FL: CRC Press): in press.
81. J. C. Quick and C. L. Cooper, *FAST FACTS: Stress and Strain, Second Edtion* (Oxford, England: Health Press, 2003).
82. M. E. P. Seligman, *Learned Optimism* (New York: Knopf, 1990).
83. F. Luthans, "Positive Organizational Behavior: Developing and Managing Psychological Strengths for Performance Improvement," *Academy of Management Executive* 16 (2002): 57–75.
84. W. T. Brooks and T. W. Mullins, *High-Impact Time Management* (Englewood Cliffs, N.J.: Prentice-Hall, 1989).
85. M. Westman and D. Eden, "Effects of a Respite from Work on Burnout: Vacation Relief and Fade-Out," *Journal of Applied Psychology* 82 (1997): 516–527.
86. C. P. Neck and K. H. Cooper, "The Fit Executive: Exercise and Diet Guidelines for Enhancing Performance," *Academy of Management Executive* 14 (2000): 72–84.
87. M. Davis, E. R. Eshelman, and M. McKay, *The Relaxation and Stress Reduction Workbook*, 3rd ed. (Oakland, Calif.: New Harbinger, 1988).
88. H. Benson, "Your Innate Asset for Combating Stress," *Harvard Business Review* 52 (1974): 49–60.
89. D. Ornish, *Dr. Dean Ornish's Program for Reversing Cardiovascular Disease* (New York: Random House, 1995).
90. J. W. Pennebaker, *Opening Up: The Healing Power of Expressing Emotions* (New York: Guilford, 1997).
91. M. E. Francis and J. W. Pennebaker, "Putting Stress into Words: The Impact of Writing on Physiological, Absentee, and Self-Reported Emotional Well-Being Measures," *American Journal of Health Promotion* 6 (1992): 280–287.
92. Z. Solomon, B. Oppenheimer, and S. Noy, "Subsequent Military Adjustment of Combat Stress Reaction Casualties: A Nine-Year Follow-Up Study," in N. A. Milgram, ed., *Stress and Coping in Time of War: Generalizations from the Israeli Experience* (New York: Brunner/Mazel, 1986), 84–90.
93. D. Wegman and L. Fine, "Occupational Health in the 1990s," *Annual Review of Public Health* 11 (1990): 89–103; J. C. Quick, "Occupational Health Psychology: Historical Roots and Future Directions," *Health Psychology* 17 (1999): 82–88.
94. D. Gebhardt and C. Crump, "Employee Fitness and Wellness Programs in the Workplace," *American Psychologist* 45 (1990): 262–272.
95. T. Wolf, H. Randall, and J. Faucett, "A Survey of Health Promotion Programs in U.S. and Canadian Medical Schools," *American Journal of Health Promotion* 3 (1988): 33–36.
96. S. Weiss, J. Fielding, and A. Baum, *Health at Work* (Hillsdale, N.J.: Erlbaum, 1990).
97. J. B. Bennett, R. F. Cook, and K. R. Pelletier, "Toward an Integrated Framework for Comprehensive Organizational Wellness: Concepts, Practices, and Research in Workplace Health Promotion," in J. C. Quick and L. E. Tetrick, eds., *Handbook of Occupational Health Psychology*: (Washington, D.C.: American Psychological Association, 2003): 69–95.
98. K. King, "Timberland Among Top Ten '100 Best Corporate Citizens'" (May 1, 2006), http://www.timberland.com/corp; C. Vanderbeck, "The Timberland Company Named a 2006 Working Mother 100 Best Company by Working Mother Magazine" (September 26, 2006), http://www.timberland.com/corp.; "2001 Excellence in Corporate Philanthropy Awards Honor IBM and Timberland," *Business Wire* (December 3, 2001).

Chapter 7 Case

1. "Our Mission and History," *Where Science Meets Life: Genentech 2007 Corporate Overview*, 2; "Genentech Fast Facts," Genentech, http://www.gene.com/gene/about/news/kits/corporate/fastFacts.jsp (accessed September 14, 2007).
2. "Our Marketed Products," *Where Science Meets Life*, 1.
3. "Our People and Workplace," *Where Science Meets Life*, 5.
4. Ibid.
5. Ibid.
6. "Culture," Genentech, http://www.gene.com/gene/careers/culture//index.jsp (accessed September 14, 2007).
7. "Employee Health, Safety and Wellness," Genentech, http://www.gene.com/gene/about/environmental/involvement/index.jsp (accessed September 14, 2007).
8. "Employee Wellness," Genentech, http://www.gene.com/gene/about/environmental/involvement/wellness.jsp (accessed September 14, 2007).
9. Ibid.
10. Ibid
11. Ibid.

Chapter 7 Cohesion Case: Part 2

1. M. B. Powers, "'Deficiencies' Cited at BP Site in Final Report on Fatal Blast," *ENR: Engineering News-Record* 258(12) (March 26, 2007): 13.
2. J. Birger, "What Pipeline Problem?" *Fortune* 154(5) (2006): 23–26.
3. "BP Facing Big Fine," *Daily Mail* (November 30, 2006): 16.
4. S. Fleming, "BP Mired in Fresh Problems as Refinery Blaze Hits Profits," *Daily Mail* (April 25, 2007), from Newspaper Source database (accessed August 17, 2007).
5. M. Hawthorne, "BP Gets Break on Dumping in Lake: Refinery Expansion Entices Indiana," *Chicago Tribune* (July 15, 2007), from Newspaper Source database (accessed August 17, 2007); J. Tankersley and M. Hawthorne, "Illinois Lawmakers Bash BP Plan to Dump Waste in Lake Michigan," *Chicago Tribune* (July 24, 2007), from Newspaper Source database (accessed August 17, 2007).
6. R. Crain, "BP Should Have Concentrated on Being a Better Oil Company," *Advertising Age* 77(34) (September 21, 2006): 14.
7. J. Hovanec, "BP Ahead of the Curve," *The Times* (Munster, IN) (May 26, 2006), from Newspaper Source database (accessed August 17, 2007).
8. "Business: Beyond Propriety; BP," *The Economist* 380(8484) (July 1, 2006): 70.
9. R. Crain, "BP Should Have Concentrated."
10. Ibid.
11. M. Hawthorne, "Federal Officials to Ask BP to Help Clean Up Lake Michigan," *Chicago Tribune* (August 14, 2007), from Newspaper Source database (accessed August 17, 2007).
12. J. Tankersley and M. Hawthorne, "Illinois Lawmakers Bash BP Plan to Dump Waste in Lake Michigan," *Chicago Tribune* (July 24, 2007), from Newspaper Source database (accessed August 17, 2007).
13. Ibid.
14. Ibid.
15. T. Coyne, "BP Scuttles Lake Discharge Plan: Public Opposition to More Pollutants in Lake Michigan Not Behind Decision, Officials Say," Associated Press article appearing in *South Bend Tribune* (August 24, 2007): A1, A6.
16. "Mind the Gap," *Petroleum Economist* (September 2006): 1
17. S. Patton, "In Sync with His CEO; For Five years, BP CIO John Leggate Has Managed People and IT Systems in Concert with His CEO's Acquisition-Hungry Strategy," *CIO* 17(13) (April 15, 2004): 1.
18. "Mind the Gap.".
19. Ibid.
20. "BP Blames Managers for Texas City," *Occupational Hazards* (June 2007): 22.
21. S. Patton, "In Sync with His CEO."
22. M. M. Plunkett, L. E. Homer, and P. Bellinger, "Enhancing Executive Accountability for Behaviours," *Organization Development Journal* 25(1) (Spring 2007):. P81–P84.

Chapter 8

1. "Caribou Coffee Brews up Innovative Customer Service Using IBM Retail Systems," IBM Press Room (March 3, 2006), http://www.ibm.com/press/us/en/pressrelease/19487.wss?re=caribou.
2. D. L. Whetzel, "The Department of Labor Identifies Workplace Skills," *The Industrial/Organizational Psychologist* (July 1991): 89–90.
3. M. Macik-Frey, J. C. Quick, and J. D. Quick, "Interpersonal Communication: The Key to Unlocking Social Support for Preventive Stress Management," in C. L. Cooper, ed., *Handbook of Stress, Medicine, and Health, Revised Edition* (Boca Raton, FL: CRC Press), in press.
4. J. M. Brett, M. Olekalns, R. Friedman, N. Goats, C. Anderson, and C. C. Lisco, "Sticks And Stones: Language, Face, and Online Dispute Resolution," *Academy of Management Journal* 50 (2007): 85–99.
5. *Richness* is a term originally coined by W. D. Bodensteiner, "Information Channel Utilization under Varying Research and Development Project Conditions" (Ph.D. diss., University of Texas at Austin, 1970).
6. B. Barry and I. S. Fulmer, "The Medium and the Message: The Adaptive Use of Communication Media in Dyadic Influence," *Academy of Management Review* 29 (2004): 272–292.
7. R. Reik, *Listen with the Third Ear* (New York: Pyramid, 1972).
8. E. Rautalinko and H. O. Lisper, "Effects of Training Reflective Listening in a Corporate Setting," *Journal of Business and Psychology* 18 (2004): 281–299.
9. A. G. Athos and J. J. Gabarro, *Interpersonal Behavior: Communication and Understanding in Relationships* (Englewood Cliffs, N.J.: Prentice-Hall, 1978).
10. A. D. Mangelsdorff, "Lessons Learned from the Military: Implications for Management" (Distinguished Visiting Lecture, University of Texas at Arlington, 29 January 1993).
11. D. A. Morand, "Language and Power: An Empirical Analysis of Linguistic Strategies Used in Superior–Subordinate Communication," *Journal of Organizational Behavior* 21 (2000): 235–249.
12. S. Bates, "How Leaders Communicate Big Ideas to Drive Business Results," *Employment Relations Today* 33 (Fall 2006): 13–19.
13. F. Luthans, "Successful versus Effective Real Managers," *Academy of Management Executive* 2 (1988): 127–132.
14. L. E. Penley, E. R. Alexander, I. E. Jernigan, and C. I. Henwood, "Communication Abilities of Managers: The Relationship of Performance," *Journal of Management* 17 (1991): 57–76.
15. J. A. LePine and L. Van Dyne, "Voice and Cooperative Behavior as Contrasting Forms of Contextual Performance: Evidence of Differential Relationships with Big Five Personality Characteristics and Cognitive Ability," *Journal of Applied Psychology* 86 (2001): 326–336.
16. F. M. Jablin, "Superior-Subordinate Communication: The State of the Art," *Psychological Bulletin* 86 (1979): 1201–1222; W. C. Reddin, *Communication within the Organization: An Interpretive Review of Theory and Research* (New York: Industrial Communication Council, 1972).
17. B. Barry and J. M. Crant, "Dyadic Communication Relationships in Organizations: An Attribution Expectancy Approach," *Organization Science* 11 (2000): 648–665.
18. J. C. Quick, D. L. Nelson, and J. D. Quick, *Stress and Challenge at the Top: The Paradox of the Successful Executive* (Chichester, England: Wiley, 1990).
19. J. Silvester, F. Patterson, A. Koczwara, and E. Ferguson, "'Trust Me . . .': Psychological and Behavioral Predictors of Perceived Physician Empathy," *Journal of Applied Psychology* 92 (2007): 519–527.
20. S. E. Moss and J. I. Sanchez, "Are Your Employees Avoiding You? Managerial Strategies for Closing the Feedback Gap," *Academy of Management Executive* 18 (2004): 32–44.
21. G. T. Kumkale and D. Albarracin, "The Sleeper Effect in Persuasion: A Meta-Analytic Review," *Psychological Bulletin* 130 (2004): 143–172.
22. A. Furhham and P. Stringfield, "Congruence in Job-Performance Ratings: A Study of 360 Degree Feedback Examining Self, Manager, Peers, and Consultant Ratings," *Human Relations* 51 (1998): 517–530.
23. J. W. Gilsdorf, "Organizational Rules on Communicating: How Employees Are—and Are Not—Learning the Ropes," *Journal of Business Communication* 35 (1998): 173–201.
24. E. A. Gerloff and J. C. Quick, "Task Role Ambiguity and Conflict in Supervision–Subordinate Relationships," *Journal of Applied Communication Research* 12 (1984): 90–102.
25. E. H. Schein, "Reassessing the 'Divine Rights' of Managers," *Sloan Management Review* 30 (1989): 63–68.
26. D. Tannen, *That's Not What I Mean! How Conversational Style Makes or Breaks Your Relations with Others* (New York: Morrow, 1986); D. Tannen, *You Just Don't Understand* (New York: Ballentine, 1990).
27. D. G. Allen and R. W. Griffeth, "A Vertical and Lateral Information Processing: The Effects of Gender, Employee Classification Level, and Media Richness on Communication and Work Outcomes," *Human Relations* 50 (1997): 1239–1260.
28. K. L. Ashcraft, "Empowering 'Professional' Relationships," *Management Communication Quarterly* 13 (2000): 347–393.
29. G. Hofstede, *Culture's Consequences: International Differences in Work-Related Values* (Beverly Hills, Calif.: Sage Publications, 1980).
30. G. Hofstede, "Motivation, Leadership, and Organization: Do American Theories Apply Abroad?" *Organizational Dynamics* 9 (1980): 42–63.
31. H. Levinson, *Executive* (Cambridge, Mass.: Harvard University Press, 1981).
32. P. Benimadhu, "Adding Value through Diversity: An Interview with Bernard F. Isautier," *Canadian Business Review* 22 (1995): 6–11.
33. M. J. Gannon and Associates, *Understanding Global Cultures: Metaphorical Journeys through 17 Countries* (Thousand Oaks, Calif.: Sage Publications, 1994).
34. T. M. Karelitz and D. V. Budescu, "You Say 'Probable' and I Say 'Likely': Improving Interpersonal Communication with Verbal Probability Phrases," *Journal of Experimental Psychology: Applied* 10 (2004): 25–41.
35. T. Wells, *Keeping Your Cool under Fire: Communicating Nondefensively* (New York: McGraw-Hill, 1980).
36. R. D. Laing, *The Politics of the Family and Other Essays* (New York: Pantheon, 1971).
37. H. S. Schwartz, *Narcissistic Process and Corporate Decay: The Theory of the Organizational Ideal* (New York: New York University Press, 1990).
38. W. R. Forrester and M. F. Maute, "The Impact of Relationship Satisfaction on Attribution, Emotions, and Behaviors Following Service Failure," *Journal of Applied Business Research* (2000): 1–45.
39. M. L. Knapp, *Nonverbal Communication in Human Interaction* (New York: Holt, Rinehart & Winston, 1978); J. McCroskey and L. Wheeless, *Introduction to Human Communication* (New York: Allyn & Bacon, 1976).
40. A. M. Katz and V. T. Katz, eds., *Foundations of Nonverbal Communication* (Carbondale, Ill.: Southern Illinois University Press, 1983).
41. M. D. Lieberman, "Intuition: A Social Cognitive Neuroscience Approach," *Psychological Bulletin* (2000): 109–138.
42. E. T. Hall, *The Hidden Dimension* (Garden City, N.Y.: Doubleday Anchor, 1966).
43. E. T. Hall, "Proxemics," in A. M. Katz and V. T. Katz, eds., *Foundations of Nonverbal Communication* (Carbondale, Ill.: Southern Illinois University Press, 1983).
44. R. T. Barker and C. G. Pearce, "The Importance of Proxemics at Work," *Supervisory Management* 35 (1990): 10–11.
45. R. L. Birdwhistell, *Kinesics and Context* (Philadelphia: University of Pennsylvania Press, 1970).
46. M. G. Frank and P. Ekman, "Appearing Truthful Generalizes Across Different Deception Situations," *Journal of Personality and Social Psychology* 86 (2004): 486–495.
47. S. L. Sporer and B. Schwandt, "Moderators of Nonverbal Indicators of Deception," *Psychology, Public Policy, and Law* 13 (2007): 1–34.

48. P. Ekman and W. V. Friesen, "Research on Facial Expressions of Emotion," in A. M. Katz and V. T. Katz, eds., *Foundations of Nonverbal Communication* (Carbondale, Ill.: Southern Illinois University Press, 1983).
49. H. H. Tan, M. D. Foo, C. L. Chong, and R. Ng, "Situational and Dispositional Predictors of Displays of Positive Emotions," *Journal of Organizational Behavior* 24 (2003): 961–978.
50. C. Barnum and N. Wolniansky, "Taking Cues from Body Language," *Management Review* 78 (1989): 59.
51. Katz and Katz, *Foundations of Nonverbal Communication,* 181.
52. R. Gifford, C. F. Ng, and M. Wilkinson, "Nonverbal Cues in the Employment Interview: Links between Applicant Qualities and Interviewer Judgments," *Journal of Applied Psychology* 70 (1985): 729–736.
53. P. J. DePaulo and B. M. DePaulo, "Can Deception by Salespersons and Customers Be Detected through Nonverbal Behavioral Cues?" *Journal of Applied Social Psychology* 19 (1989): 1552–1577.
54. P. Ekman, *Telling Lies* (New York: Norton, 1985); D. Goleman, "Nonverbal Cues Are Easy to Misinterpret," *New York Times* (September 17, 1991): B5.
55. J. J. Lynch, *A Cry Unheard: New Insights into the Medical Consequences of Loneliness* (Baltimore, MD: Bancroft Press, 2000).
56. J. C. Quick, J. H. Gavin, C. L. Cooper, and J. D. Quick, "Working Together: Balancing Head and Heart," in N. G. Johnson, R. H. Rozensky, C. D. Goodheart, and R. Hammond, eds., *Psychology Builds a Healthy World*: (Washington, D.C.: American Psychological Association, 2004), 219–232.
57. J. C. Quick, C. L. Cooper, J. D. Quick, and J. H. Gavin, *The Financial Times Guide to Executive Health* (London, UK: Financial Times–Prentice Hall, 2003).
58. K. M. Wasylyshyn, "Coaching the Superkeepers," in L. A. Berger and D. R. Berger, eds., *The Talent Management Handbook: Creating Organizational Excellence by Identifying, Developing, and Positioning Your Best People*: (New York, NY: McGraw-Hill, 2003), 320–336.
59. J. C. Quick and M. Macik-Frey, "Behind the Mask: Coaching through Deep Interpersonal Communication," *Consulting Psychology Journal: Practice and Research* 56 (2004): 67–74.
60. B. Drake and K. Yuthas, "It's Only Words—Impacts of Information Technology on Moral Dialogue," *Journal of Business Ethics* 23 (2000): 41–60.
61. N. Frohlich and J. Oppenheimer, "Some Consequences of E-Mail vs. Face-to-Face Communication in Experiment," *Journal of Economic Behavior & Organization* 35 (1998): 389–403.
62. J. Kruger, N. Epley, J. Parker, and Z. Ng, "Egocentrism over E-mail: Can We Communicate as Well as We Think?", *Journal of Personality and Social Psychology* 89 (2005): 925–936.
63. C. Brod, *Technostress: The Human Cost of the Computer Revolution* (Reading, Mass.: Addison-Wesley, 1984).
64. S. Kiesler, "Technology and the Development of Creative Environments," in Y. Ijiri and R. L. Kuhn, eds., *New Directions in Creative and Innovative Management* (Cambridge, Mass.: Ballinger Press, 1988).
65. S. Kiesler, J. Siegel, and T. W. McGuire, "Social Psychological Aspects of Computer-Mediated Communication," *American Psychologist* 39 (1984): 1123–1134.
66. G. Hayes, "Caribou Coffee Offers Free Wi-Fi Service for Customers," *Caribou Coffee Press Room* (August 28, 2006), http://www.cariboucoffee.com/aboutus/pressrelease/08282006.pdf

Chapter 8 Case

1. "About Us," Whole Foods Market, http://www.wholefoodsmarket.com/company/facts.html (accessed September 26, 2007); "Welcome to Whole Foods Market," Whole Foods Market, http://www.wholefoodsmarket.com/company/index.html (accessed September 26, 2007).
2. "Our History," Whole Foods Market, http://www.wholefoodsmarket.com/company/history.html (accessed October 10, 2007).
3. D. Kesmodel and J. Eig, "Unraveling Rahodeb: A Grocer's Brash Style," *The Wall Street Journal*, Eastern edition (July 20, 2007): A1+.
4. D. Kesmodel, "Court Clears Whole Foods Deal; FTC Loses Appeal to Delay Acquisition of Wild Oats, but Other Options Remain," *The Wall Street Journal*, Eastern edition (August 24. 2007): A2.
5. D. Kesmodel, "Whole Foods Wins Ruling on Wild Oats," *The Wall Street Journal*, Eastern edition (August 17, 2007): A3.
6. Kesmodel and Eig, "Unraveling Rahodeb."
7. Ibid.
8. D. Kesmodel, "SEC Opens Informal Inquiry of Whole Foods CEO Postings." *The Wall Street Journal*, Eastern edition (July 14, 2007),: A2.
9. D. Kesmodel and J. R. Wilke, "Whole Foods Is Hot, Wild Oats a Dud—So Said 'Rahodeb'," *The Wall Street Journal*, Eastern edition (July 12, 2007): A1+.
10. Ibid.
11. Kesmodel and Eig, "Unraveling Rahodeb."
12. Ibid.
13. Ibid.
14. Ibid.
15. Kesmodel, "Whole Foods Wins Ruling on Wild Oats,"
16. Kesmodel and Wilke, "Whole Foods Is Hot." —
17. "Declaration of Interdependence," Whole Foods Market, http://www.wholefoodsmarket.com/cgi-bin/print10pt.cgi?url=/company/declaration.html (accessed September 26, 2007).

Chapter 9

1. D. Kiley, "The Toyota Way to No. 1," *Business Week Online* (April 26, 2007): 10, http://www.businessweek.com/autos/content/apr2007/bw20070425_861247.htm?chan=search; M. Fackler, "A Global Toyota Faces Dilution of Its Culture: A Critical Mission Is Spreading 'The Way'," *International Herald Tribune* (February 15, 2007): 3.
2. G. Garcia, "Measuring Performance at Northrop Grumman," *Knowledge Management Review* 3 (2001): 22–25.
3. A. M. Towsend, S. M. DeMarie, and A. R. Hendrickson, "Virtual Teams: Technology and the Workplace of the Future," *Academy of Management Executive* 12 (1998): 17–29.
4. D. M. McGregor, *The Human Side of Enterprise* (New York: McGraw-Hill, 1960).
5. J. R. Katzenbach and D. K. Smith, "The Discipline of Teams," *Harvard Business Review* 71 (1993): 111–120.
6. K. L. Bettenhausen and J. K. Murnighan, "The Development and Stability of Norms in Groups Facing Interpersonal and Structural Challenge," *Administrative Science Quarterly* 36 (1991): 20–35.
7. I. Adarves-Yorno, T. Postmes, and S. A. Haslam, "Creative Innovation or Crazy Irrelevance? The Contribution of Group Norms and Social Identity to Creative Behavior," *Journal of Experimental Social Psychology* 43 (2007): 410–416.
8. D. Tjosvold and Z. Yu, "Goal Interdependence and Applying Abilities for Team In-Role and Extra-Role Performance in China," *Group Dynamics: Theory, Research, and Practice* 8 (2004): 98–111.
9. V. U. Druskat and S. B. Wolff, "Building the Emotional Intelligence of Groups," *Harvard Business Review* 79 (2001): 80–90.
10. I. Summers, T. Coffelt, and R. E. Horton, "Work-Group Cohesion," *Psychological Reports* 63 (1988): 627–636.
11. D. C. Man and S. S. K. Lam, "The Effects of Job Complexity and Autonomy on Cohesiveness in Collectivistic and Individualistic Work Groups: A Cross-Cultural Analysis," *Journal of Organizational Behavior* 24 (2003): 979–1001.
12. K. H. Price, "Working Hard to Get People to Loaf," *Basic and Applied Social Psychology* 14 (1993): 329–344.
13. R. Albanese and D. D. Van Fleet, "Rational Behavior in Groups: The Free-Riding Tendency," *Academy of Management Review* 10 (1985): 244–255.
14. E. Diener, "Deindividuation, Self-Awareness, and Disinhibition," *Journal of Personality and Social Psychology* 37 (1979): 1160–1171.
15. S. Prentice-Dunn and R. W. Rogers, "Deindividuation and the Self-Regulation of Behavior," in P. Paulus, ed., *Psychology of Group Influence* (Hillsdale, N.J.: Erlbaum, 1989), 87–109.
16. B. M. Bass and E. C. Ryterband, *Organizational Psychology*, 2nd ed. (Boston: Allyn & Bacon, 1979).

17. W. G. Bennis and H. A. Shepard, "A Theory of Group Development," *Human Relations* 9 (1956): 415–438.
18. S. Caudron, "Monsanto Responds to Diversity," *Personnel Journal* (November 1990): 72–80.
19. D. L. Fields and T. C. Bloom, "Employee Satisfaction in Work Groups with Different Gender Composition," *Journal of Organizational Behavior* 18 (1997): 181–196.
20. D. C. Lau and J. K. Murnighan, "Demographic Diversity and Faultlines: The Compositional Dynamics of Organizational Groups," *Academy of Management Review* 23 (1998): 325–340.
21. B. Tuckman, "Developmental Sequence in Small Groups," *Psychological Bulletin* 63 (1965): 384–399; B. Tuckman and M. Jensen, "Stages of Small-Group Development," *Group and Organizational Studies* 2 (1977): 419–427.
22. D. Nichols, "Quality Program Sparked Company Turnaround," *Personnel* (October 1991): 24. For a commentary on Wallace's hard times and subsequent emergence from Chapter 11 bankruptcy, see R. C. Hill, "When the Going Gets Tough: A Baldrige Award Winner on the Line," *Academy of Management Executive* 7 (1993): 75–79.
23. S. Weisband and L. Atwater, "Evaluating Self and Others in Electronic and Face-to-Face Groups," *Journal of Applied Psychology* 84 (1999): 632–639.
24. C. J. G. Gersick, "Time and Transition in Work Teams: Toward a New Model of Group Development," *The Academy of Management Journal* 31 (1988): 9–41.
25. M. Hardaker and B. K. Ward, "How to Make a Team Work," *Harvard Business Review* 65 (1987): 112–120.
26. C. R. Gowen, "Managing Work Group Performance by Individual Goals and Group Goals for an Interdependent Group Task," *Journal of Organizational Behavior Management* 7 (1986): 5–27.
27. K. L. Bettenhausen and J. K. Murnighan, "The Emergence of Norms in Competitive Decision-Making Groups," *Administrative Science Quarterly* 30 (1985): 350–372; K. L. Bettenhausen, "Five Years of Groups Research: What We Have Learned and What Needs to Be Addressed," *Journal of Management* 17 (1991): 345–381.
28. J. E. McGrath, *Groups: Interaction and Performance* (Englewood Cliffs, N.J.: Prentice-Hall, 1984).
29. K. L. Gammage, A. V. Carron, and P. A. Estabrooks, "Team Cohesion and Individual Productivity," *Small Group Research* 32 (2001): 3–18.
30. S. E. Seashore, *Group Cohesiveness in the Industrial Work Group* (Ann Arbor, Mich.: University of Michigan, 1954).
31. S. M. Klein, "A Longitudinal Study of the Impact of Work Pressure on Group Cohesive Behaviors," *International Journal of Management* 12 (1996): 68–75.
32. N. Steckler and N. Fondas, "Building Team Leader Effectiveness: A Diagnostic Tool," *Organizational Dynamics* 23 (1995): 20–35.
33. A. Carter and S. Holmes, "Curiously Strong Teamwork," *Business Week* 4023 (February 26, 2007): 90–92.
34. G. Parker, *Team Players and Teamwork* (San Francisco: Jossey-Bass, 1990).
35. N. R. F. Maier, "Assets and Liabilities in Group Problem Solving: The Need for an Integrative Function," *Psychological Review* 74 (1967): 239–249.
36. T. A. Stewart, "The Search for the Organization of Tomorrow," *Fortune* (May 18, 1992): 92–98.
37. J. R. Goktepe and C. E. Schneier, "Role of Sex, Gender Roles, and Attraction in Predicting Emergent Leaders," *Journal of Applied Psychology* 74 (1989): 165–167.
38. W. R. Lassey, "Dimensions of Leadership," in W. R. Lassey and R. R. Fernandez, eds., *Leadership and Social Change* (La Jolla, Calif.: University Associates, 1976), 10–15.
39. J. D. Quick, G. Moorhead, J. C. Quick, E. A. Gerloff, K. L. Mattox, and C. Mullins, "Decision Making among Emergency Room Residents: Preliminary Observations and a Decision Model," *Journal of Medical Education* 58 (1983): 117–125.
40. W. J. Duncan and J. P. Feisal, "No Laughing Matter: Patterns of Humor in the Workplace," *Organizational Dynamics* 17 (1989): 18–30.
41. A. Hunter, "Best Practice Club," *Personnel Today* (April 15, 2003): 8.
42. S. S. Webber and R. J. Klimoski, "Crews: A Distinct Type of Work Team," *Journal of Business and Psychology* 18 (2004): 261–279.
43. P. F. Drucker, "There's More than One Kind of Team," *The Wall Street Journal* (February 11, 1992): A16.
44. B. L. Kirkman, C. B. Gibson, and D. L. Shapiro, "'Exporting' Teams: Enhancing the Implementation and Effectiveness of Work Teams in Global Affiliates," *Organizational Dynamics* 30 (2001): 12–29.
45. A. Taylor and H. R. Greve, "Superman or the Fantastic Four? Knowledge Combination and Experience in Innovative Teams," *Academy of Management Journal* 49 (2006): 723–740.
46. P. M. Podsakoff, M. Ahearne, and S. B. MacKenzie, "Organizational Citizenship Behavior and the Quantity and Quality of Work Group Performance," *Journal of Applied Psychology* 82 (1997): 262–270.
47. L. Hirschhorn, *Managing in the New Team Environment*, (Upper Saddle River, N.J.: Prentice-Hall), 521A.
48. G. Chen and R. J. Klimoski, "The Impact of Expectations on Newcomer Performance in Teams as Mediated by Work Characteristics, Social Exchanges, and Empowerment," *Academy of Management Journal* 46 (2003): 591–607.
49. B. Beersma, J. R. Hollenbeck, S. E. Humphrey, H. Moon, D. E. Conlon, and D. R. Ilgen, "Cooperation, Competition, and Team Performance: Toward a Contingency Approach," *Academy of Management Journal* 46 (2003): 572–590.
50. W. L. Mohr and H. Mohr, *Quality Circles: Changing Images of People at Work* (Reading, Mass.: Addison-Wesley, 1983).
51. R. W. Griffin, "A Longitudinal Assessment of the Consequences of Quality Circles in an Industrial Setting," *Academy of Management Journal* 31 (1988): 338–358.
52. P. Shaver and D. Buhrmester, "Loneliness, Sex-Role Orientation, and Group Life: A Social Needs Perspective," in P. Paulus, ed., *Basic Group Processes* (New York: Springer-Verlag, 1985), 259–288.
53. P. Chattopadhyay, M. Tluchowska, and E. George, "Identifying the Ingroup: A Closer Look at the Influence of Demographic Dissimilarity on Employee Social Identity," *Academy of Management Review* 29 (2004): 180–202.
54. E. V. Hobman, P. Bordia, and C. Gallois, "Consequences of Feeling Dissimilar from Others in a Work Team," *Journal of Business and Psychology* 17 (2003): 301–325.
55. A. E. Randel and K. S. Jaussi, "Functional Background Identity, Diversity, and Individual Performance in Cross-Functional Teams," *Academy of Management Journal* 46 (2003): 763–774.
56. J. S. Bunderson, "Team Member Functional Background and Involvement in Management Teams: Direct Effects and the Moderating Role of Power Centralization," *Academy of Management Journal* 46 (2003): 458–474.
57. G. S. Van Der Vegt, E. Van De Vliert, and A. Oosterhof, "Informational Dissimilarity and Organizational Citizenship Behavior: The Role of Intrateam Interdependence and Team Identification," *Academy of Management Journal* 46 (2003): 715–727.
58. A. Pirola-Merlo and L. Mann, "The Relationship between Individual Creativity and Team Creativity: Aggregating Across People and Time," *Journal of Organizational Behavior* 25 (2004): 235–257.
59. L. Thompson, "Improving the Creativity of Organizational Work Groups," *Academy of Management Executive* 17 (2003): 96–111.
60. C. Ford and D. M. Sullivan, "A Time for Everything: How the Timing of Novel Contributions Influences Project Team Outcomes," *Journal of Organizational Behavior* 25 (2004): 279–292.
61. B. L. Kirman and D. L. Shapiro, "The Impact of Cultural Values on Job Satisfaction and Organizational Commitment in Self-Managing Work Teams: The Mediating Role of Employee Resistance," *Academy of Management Journal* 44 (2001): 557–569.
62. K. W. Thomas and B. A. Velthouse, "Cognitive Elements of Empowerment: An 'Interpretive' Model of Intrinsic Task Motivation," *Academy of Management Review* 15 (1990): 666–681.
63. R. R. Blake, J. S. Mouton, and R. L. Allen, *Spectacular Teamwork: How to Develop the Leadership Skills for Team Success* (New York: Wiley, 1987).
64. American Management Association, *Blueprints for Service Quality: The Federal Express Approach*, AMA Management Briefing (New York: AMA, 1991).
65. W. C. Byham, *ZAPP! The Human Lightning of Empowerment* (Pittsburgh, Pa.: Developmental Dimensions, 1989).

66. F. Shipper and C. C. Manz, "Employee Self-Management without Formally Designated Teams: An Alternative Road to Empowerment," *Organizational Dynamics* (Winter 1992): 48–62.
67. P. Block, *The Empowered Manager: Positive Political Skills at Work* (San Francisco: Jossey-Bass, 1987).
68. V. J. Derlega and J. Grzelak, eds., *Cooperation and Helping Behavior: Theories and Research* (New York: Academic Press, 1982).
69. G. S. Van der vegt, J. S. Bunderson, and A. Oosterhof, "Expertness Diversity and Interpersonal Helping in Teams: Why Those Who Need the Most Help End up Getting the Least," *Academy of Management Journal* 49 (2006): 877–893.
70. A. G. Athos and J. J. Gabarro, *Interpersonal Behavior: Communication and Understanding in Relationships* (Englewood Cliffs, N.J.: Prentice-Hall, 1978).
71. C. Douglas and W. L. Gardner, "Transition to Self-Directed Work Teams: Implications of Transition Time and Self-Monitoring for Managers' Use of Influence Tactics," *Journal of Organizational Behavior* 25 (2004): 47–65.
72. C. Douglas, J. S. Martin, and R. H. Krapels, "Communication in the Transition to Self-Directed Work Teams," *Journal of Business Communication*" 43 (2006): 295–321.
73. J. L. Cordery, W. S. Mueller, and L. M. Smith, "Attitudinal and Behavioral Effects of Autonomous Group Working: A Longitudinal Field Study," *Academy of Management Journal* 34 (1991): 464–476.
74. M. Workman and W. Bommer, "Redesigning Computer Call Center Work: A Longitudinal Field Experiment," *Journal of Organizational Behavior* 25 (2004): 317–337.
75. G. Moorhead, C. P. Neck, and M. S. West, "The Tendency Toward Defective Decision Making within Self-Managing Teams: The Relevance of Groupthink for the 21st Century," *Organizational Behavior & Human Decision Processes* 73 (1998): 327–351.
76. B. M. Staw and L. D. Epstein, "What Bandwagons Bring: Effects of Popular Management Techniques on Corporate Performance, Reputation, and CEO Pay," *Administrative Science Quarterly* 45 (2000): 523–556.
77. R. M. Robinson, S. L. Oswald, K. S. Swinehart, and J. Thomas, "Southwest Industries: Creating High-Performance Teams for High-Technology Production," *Planning Review* 19, published by the Planning Forum (November–December 1991): 10–47.
78. A. Lienert, "Forging a New Partnership," *Management Review* 83 (1994): 39–43.
79. S. Thiagaraian, "A Game for Cooperative Learning," *Training and Development* (May 1992): 35–41.
80. D. C. Hambrick and P. Mason, "Upper Echelons: The Organization as a Reflection of Its Top Managers," *Academy of Management Review* 9 (1984): 193–206.
81. D. C. Hambrick, "The Top Management Team: Key to Strategic Success," *California Management Review* 30 (1987): 88–108.
82. A. D. Henderson and J. W. Fredrickson, "Top Management Team Coordination Needs and the CEO Pay Gap: A Competitive Test of Economic and Behavioral Views," *Academy of Management Journal* 44 (2001): 96–117.
83. D. C. Hambrick and G. D. S. Fukutomi, "The Seasons of a CEO's Tenure," *Academy of Management Review* 16 (1991): 719–742.
84. J. C. Quick, D. L. Nelson, and J. D. Quick, "Successful Executives: How Independent?" *Academy of Management Executive* 1 (1987): 139–145.
85. I. Adizes, "Communication Strategies for Leading Teams," *Leader to Leader* (Winter 2004): 10–15.
86. L. G. Love, "The Evolving Pinnacle of the Corporation: An Explanatory Study of the Antecedents, Processes, and Consequences of Co-CEOs," 2003 (The University of Texas at Arlington).
87. N. J. Adler, *International Dimensions of Organizational Behavior* (Mason, Ohio: South-Western, 2001).
88. I. D. Steiner, *Group Process and Productivity* (New York: Academic Press, 1972).
89. U. Glunk, M. G. Heijltjes, and R. Olie, "Design Characteristics and Functioning of Top Management Teams in Europe," *European Management Journal* 19 (2001): 291–300.
90. J. W. Pfeiffer and C. Nolde, eds., *The Encyclopedia of Team-Development Activities* (San Diego: University Associates, 1991).
91. A. Chozick, "Toyota Appoints First Foreigner to Firm's Board," *The Wall Street Journal* (April 13, 2007): 6.

Chapter 9 Case

1. "Stryker History," The Stryker Corporation, http://www.stryker.com/myhsp/corporate/AboutUs/History/index.htm (accessed September 29, 2007).
2. K. Yung, "Kalamazoo Firm Finds Success in Innovation," *Detroit Free Press* (August 12, 2007), from Newspaper Source database (accessed September 26, 2007).
3. K. Norris, "Kalamazoo, Mich., Firm Makes Instruments and Body Parts for an Aging Nation," *Detroit Free Press* (January 3, 2005), from Newspaper Source database (accessed September 26, 2007).
4. "About Stryker," The Stryker Corporation, http://www.stryker.com/myhsp/corporate/AboutUs/index.htm (accessed September 29, 2007); "Stryker: Company Profile," *Datamonitor.com* (August 2006), reference code 3629: 4–5; A. Weintraub, "Stryker," *Business Week* (March 26, 2007): 66–67; Yung, "Kalamazoo Firm Finds Success in Innovation,"
5. R. Wagner and J. K. Harter, "Assembling the Right Talents at Stryker," *Gallup Management Journal* (September 14, 2006), available at http://gmj.gallup.com (accessed September 26, 2007): 1–2.
6. Ibid, 2.
7. Ibid, 3.
8. Ibid, 4.
9. Ibid.
10. Ibid, 5.

Chapter 10

1. M. Herper, "Genentech's Next Act," *Forbes.com* (January 26, 2007), http://www.forbes.com/business/2007/01/25/genentech-new-direction-biz-cz_mh_0126genentech.html
2. http://www.gene.com/gene/about/corporate/growthstrategy/index.jsp?q=genentech%2C+decision+making&sourceid=navclient-ff&ie=UTF-8&rlz=1B2GGFB_enUS210US210&aq=t
3. H. A. Simon, *The New Science of Management Decision* (New York: Harper & Row, 1960).
4. R. Walker, "Brand Blue," *Fortune* (April 28, 2003): 118B–118H, http://www.fortune.com/fortune/smallbusiness/articles/0,15114,426909,00.html.
5. G. Huber, *Managerial Decision Making* (Glenview, Ill.: Scott, Foresman, 1980).
6. H. A. Simon, *Administrative Behavior* (New York: Macmillan, 1957).
7. E. F. Harrison, *The Managerial Decision-Making Process* (Boston: Houghton Mifflin, 1981).
8. R. L. Ackoff, "The Art and Science of Mess Management," *Interfaces* (February 1981): 20–26.
9. R. M. Cyert and J. G. March, eds., *A Behavioral Theory of the Firm* (Englewood Cliffs, N.J.: Prentice-Hall, 1963).
10. M. D. Cohen, J. G. March, and J. P. Olsen, "A Garbage Can Model of Organizational Choice," *Administrative Science Quarterly* 17 (1972): 1–25.
11. J. G. March and J. P. Olsen, "Garbage Can Models of Decision Making in Organizations," in J. G. March and R. Weissinger-Baylon, eds., *Ambiguity and Command* (Marshfield, Mass.: Pitman, 1986), 11–53.
12. D. van Knippenberg, B. van Knippenberg, and E. van Dijk, "Who Takes the Lead in Risky Decision Making? Effects of Group Members'

Risk Preferences and Prototypicality," *Organizational Behavior and Human Decision Processes* 83 (2000): 213–234.

13. K. R. MacCrimmon and D. Wehrung, *Taking Risks* (New York: Free Press, 1986).
14. T. S. Perry, "How Small Firms Innovate: Designing a Culture for Creativity," *Research Technology Management* 28 (1995): 14–17.
15. B. M. Staw, "Knee-Deep in the Big Muddy: A Study of Escalating Commitment to a Chosen Course of Action," *Organizational Behavior and Human Performance* 16 (1976): 27–44; B. M. Staw, "The Escalation of Commitment to a Course of Action," *Academy of Management Review* 6 (1981): 577–587.
16. B. M. Staw and J. Ross, "Understanding Behavior in Escalation Situations," *Science* 246 (1989): 216–220.
17. T. Freemantle and M. Tolson, "Space Station Had Political Ties in Tow," *Houston Chronicle* (August 4, 2003), http://www.chron.com/cs/CDA/ssistory.mpl/space/2004947.
18. L. Festinger, *A Theory of Cognitive Dissonance* (Evanston, Ill.: Row, Peterson, 1957).
19. B. M. Staw, "The Escalation of Commitment: An Update and Appraisal," in Z. Shapira, ed., *Organizational Decision Making* (Cambridge, England: Cambridge University Press, 1997).
20. D. M. Boehne and P. W. Paese, "Deciding Whether to Complete or Terminate an Unfinished Project: A Strong Test of the Project Completion Hypothesis," *Organizational Behavior and Human Decision Processes* 81 (2000): 178–194; H. Moon, "Looking Forward and Looking Back: Integrating Completion and Sunk Cost Effects within an Escalation-of-Commitment Progress Decision," *Journal of Applied Psychology* 86 (2000): 104–113.
21. D. M. Rowell, "Concorde: An Untimely and Unnecessary Demise," (April 11, 2003), http://www.thetravelinsider.info/2003/0411.htm.
22. G. McNamara, H. Moon, and P. Bromiley, "Banking on Commitment: Intended and Unintended Consequences of an Organization's Attempt to Attenuate Escalation of Commitment," *Academy of Management Journal* 45 (2002): 443–452.
23. G. Whyte, "Diffusion of Responsibility: Effects on the Escalation Tendency," *Journal of Applied Psychology* 76 (1991): 408–415.
24. C. G. Jung, *Psychological Types* (London: Routledge & Kegan Paul, 1923).
25. W. Taggart and D. Robey, "Minds and Managers: On the Dual Nature of Human Information Processing and Management," *Academy of Management Review* 6 (1981): 187–195; D. Hellreigel and J. W. Slocum, Jr., "Managerial Problem-Solving Styles," *Business Horizons* 18 (1975): 29–37.
26. G. A. Stevens and J. Burley, "Piloting the Rocket of Radical Innovation," *Research Technology Management* 46 (2003): 16–26.
27. J. C. White, P. R. Varadarajan, and P. A. Dacin, "Market Situation Interpretation and Response: The Role of Cognitive Style, Organizational Culture, and Information Use," *Journal of Marketing* 67 (2003): 63–73.
28. I. I. Mitroff and R. H. Kilmann, "On Organization Stories: An Approach to the Design and Analysis of Organization through Myths and Stories," in R. H. Killman, L. R. Pondy, and D. P. Slevin, eds., *The Management of Organization Design* (New York: Elsevier–North Holland, 1976).
29. I. B. Myers, *Gifts Differing* (Palo Alto, Calif.: Consulting Psychologists Press, 1980).
30. A. Saleh, "Brain Hemisphericity and Academic Majors: A Correlation Study," *College Student Journal* 35 (2001): 193–200.
31. N. Khatri, "The Role of Intuition in Strategic Decision Making," *Human Relations* 53 (2000): 57–86.
32. H. Mintzberg, "Planning on the Left Side and Managing on the Right," *Harvard Business Review* 54 (1976): 51–63.
33. D. J. Isenberg, "How Senior Managers Think," *Harvard Business Review* 62 (1984): 81–90.
34. R. N. Beck, "Visions, Values, and Strategies: Changing Attitudes and Culture," *Academy of Managment Executive* 1 (1987): 33–41.
35. K. G. Ross, G. A. Klein, P. Thunholm, J. F. Schmitt, and H. C Baxter, "The Recognition-Primed Decision Model," *Military Review, Fort Leavenworth* 84 (2004): 6–10.
36. C. I. Barnard, *The Functions of the Executive* (Cambridge, Mass.: Harvard University Press, 1938).
37. R. Rowan, *The Intuitive Manager* (New York: Little, Brown, 1986).
38. W. H. Agor, *Intuition in Organizations* (Newbury Park, Calif.: Sage, 1989).
39. Isenberg, "How Senior Managers Think."
40. H. A. Simon, "Making Management Decisions: The Role of Intuition and Emotion," *Academy of Management Executive* 1 (1987): 57–64.
41. J. L. Redford, R. H. McPhierson, R. G. Frankiewicz, and J. Gaa, "Intuition and Moral Development," *Journal of Psychology* 129 (1994): 91–101.
42. R. Wild, "Naked Hunch; Gut Instinct Is Vital to Your Business," *Success* (June 1998), http://www.findarticles.com/cf_dls/m3514/n6_v45/20746158/p1/article.jhtml.
43. W. H. Agor, "How Top Executives Use Their Intuition to Make Important Decisions," *Business Horizons* 29 (1986): 49–53.
44. O. Behling and N. L. Eckel, "Making Sense Out of Intuition," *Academy of Management Executive* 5 (1991): 46–54.
45. L. R. Beach, *Image Theory: Decision Making in Personal and Organizational Contexts* (Chichester, England: Wiley, 1990).
46. E. Bonabeau, "Don't Trust Your Gut," *Harvard Business Review* 81 (2003): 116–126.
47. L. Livingstone, "Person-Environment Fit on the Dimension of Creativity: Relationships with Strain, Job Satisfaction, and Performance" (Ph.D. diss., Oklahoma State University, 1992).
48. M. A. West and J. L. Farr, "Innovation at Work," in M. A. West and J. L. Farr, eds., *Innovation and Creativity at Work: Psychological and Organizational Strategies* (New York: Wiley, 1990), 3–13.
49. G. Morgan, *Riding the Waves of Change* (San Francisco: Jossey-Bass, 1988).
50. G. Wallas, *The Art of Thought* (New York: Harcourt Brace, 1926).
51. H. Benson and W. Proctor, *The Break-Out Principle* (Scribner: New York, 2003).
52. G. L. Fricchione, B. T. Slingsby, and H. Benson, "The Placebo Effect and the Relaxation Response: Neural Processes and Their Coupling to Constitutive Nitric Oxide," *Brain Research Reviews* 35 (2001): 1–19.
53. M. D. Mumford and S. B. Gustafson, "Creativity Syndrome: Integration, Application, and Innovation," *Psychological Bulletin* 103 (1988): 27–43.
54. T. Poze, "Analogical Connections—The Essence of Creativity," *Journal of Creative Behavior* 17 (1983): 240–241.
55. I. Sladeczek and G. Domino, "Creativity, Sleep, and Primary Process Thinking in Dreams," *Journal of Creative Behavior* 19 (1985): 38–46.
56. F. Barron and D. M. Harrington, "Creativity, Intelligence, and Personality," *Annual Review of Psychology* 32 (1981): 439–476.
57. R. J. Sternberg, "A Three-Faced Model of Creativity," in R. J. Sternberg, ed., *The Nature of Creativity* (Cambridge, England: Cambridge University Press, 1988), 125–147.
58. A. M. Isen, "Positive Affect and Decision Making," in W. M. Goldstein and R. M. Hogarth, eds., *Research on Judgment and Decision Making* (Cambridge, England: Cambridge University Press, 1997).
59. G. L. Clore, N. Schwartz, and M. Conway, "Cognitive Causes and Consequences of Emotion," in R. S. Wyer and T. K. Srull (eds.), *Handbook of Social Cognition* (Hillsdale, N.J.: Erlbaum, 1994): 323–417.
60. B. L. Frederickson, "What Good Are Positive Emotions?" *Review of General Psychology* 2 (1998): 300–319.
61. B. L. Frederickson, "The Role of Positive Emotions in Positive Psychology," *American Psychologist* 56 (2001): 218–226.
62. T. M. Amabile, S. G. Barsade, J. S. Mueller, and B. M. Staw, "Affect and Creativity at Work," *Administrative Science Quarterly* 50(3) (2005): 367–403.
63. E. R. Hirt, G. M. Levine, H. E. McDonald, R. J. Melton, and L. L. Martin, "The Role of Mood in Quantitative and Qualitative Aspects of Performance: Single or Multiple Mechanisms?" *Journal of Experimental Social Psychology* 33 (1997): 602–629.
64. J. M.George and Z. Zhou, "Understanding When Bad Moods Foster Creativity and Good Ones Don't: The Role of Context and Clarity of Feelings," *Journal of Applied Psychology* 87 (2002): 687–697.
65. J. Zhou, "When the Presence of Creative Coworkers Is Related to Creativity: Role of Supervisor Close Monitoring, Developmental Feedback, and Creative Personality," *Journal of Applied Psychology* 88 (2003): 413–422.

66. C. Axtell, D. Holman, K. Unsworth, T. Wall, and P. Waterson, "Shopfloor Innovation: Facilitating the Suggestion and Implementation of Ideas," *Journal of Occupational Psychology* 73 (2000): 265–285.
67. B. Kijkuit and J. van den Ende, "The Organizational Life of an Idea: Integrating Social Network, Creativity, and Decision-Making Perspectives," *Journal of Management Studies* 44(6) (2007): 863–882.
68. T. M. Amabile, R. Conti, H. Coon, J. Lazenby, and M. Herron, "Assessing the Work Environment for Creativity," *Academy of Management Journal* 39 (1996): 1154–1184.
69. T. Tetenbaum and H. Tetenbaum, "Office 2000: Tear Down the Wall," *Training* (February 2000): 58–64.
70. D. M. Harrington, "Creativity, Analogical Thinking, and Muscular Metaphors," *Journal of Mental Imagery* 6 (1981): 121–126; R. M. Kanter, *The Change Masters* (New York: Simon & Schuster, 1983).
71. T. M. Amabile, B. A. Hennessey, and B. S. Grossman, "Social Influences on Creativity: The Effects of Contracted-for Reward," *Journal of Personality and Social Psychology* 50 (1986): 14–23.
72. Livingstone, "Person-Environment Fit."
73. R. L. Firestein, "Effects of Creative Problem-Solving Training on Communication Behaviors in Small Groups," *Small Group Research* (November 1989): 507–521.
74. R. Von Oech, *A Whack on the Side of the Head* (New York: Warner, 1983).
75. A. G. Robinson and S. Stern, *How Innovation and Improvement Actually Happen* (San Francisco: Berrett-Koehler, 1997).
76. K. Unsworth, "Unpacking Creativity," *Academy of Management Review* 26 (2001): 289–297.
77. M. F. R. Kets de Vries, R. Branson, and P. Barnevik, "Charisma in Action: The Transformational Abilities of Virgin's Richard Branson and ABBS's Percy Barnevik," *Organizational Dynamics* 26 (1998): 7–21.
78. M. Kostera, M. Proppe, and M. Szatkowski, "Staging the New Romantic Hero in the Old Cynical Theatre: On Managers, Roles, and Change in Poland," *Journal of Organizational Behavior* 16 (1995): 631–646.
79. J. Pfeffer, "Seven Practices of Successful Organizations," *California Management Review* 40 (1998): 96–124.
80. L. A. Witt, M. C. Andrews, and K. M. Kacmar, "The Role of Participation in Decision Making in the Organizational Politics—Job Satisfaction Relationship," *Human Relations* 53 (2000): 341–358.
81. C. R. Leana, E. A. Locke, and D. M. Schweiger, "Fact and Fiction in Analyzing Research on Participative Decision Making: A Critique of Cotton, Vollrath, Froggatt, Lengnick-Hall, and Jennings," *Academy of Management Review* 15 (1990): 137–146; J. L. Cotton, D. A. Vollrath, M. L. Lengnick-Hall, and K. L. Froggatt, "Fact: The Form of Participation Does Matter—A Rebuttal to Leana, Locke, and Schweiger," *Academy of Management Review* 15 (1990): 147–153.
82. G. Hamel, "Reinvent Your Company," *Fortune* 141 (June 12, 2000): 98–118.
83. T. W. Malone, "Is Empowerment Just a Fad? Control, Decision Making, and Information Technology," *Sloan Management Review* 38 (1997): 23–35.
84. IBM Customer Success Stories, "City and County of San Francisco Lower Total Cost of Ownership and Build on Demand Foundation" (February 3, 2004), http://www-306.ibm.com/software/success/cssdb.nsf/cs/LWRT-5VTLM2?OpenDocument&Site=lotusmandc.
85. T. L. Brown, "Fearful of 'Empowerment': Should Managers Be Terrified?" *Industry Week* (June 18, 1990): 12.
86. L. Hirschhorn, "Stresses and Patterns of Adjustment in the Postindustrial Factory," in G. M. Green and F. Baker, eds., *Work, Health, and Productivity* (New York: Oxford University Press, 1991), 115–126.
87. P. G. Gyllenhammar, *People at Work* (Reading, Mass.: Addison- Wesley, 1977).
88. R. Tannenbaum and F. Massarik, "Participation by Subordinates in the Managerial Decision-Making Process," *Canadian Journal of Economics and Political Science* 16 (1950): 408–418.
89. H. Levinson, *Executive* (Cambridge, Mass.: Harvard University Press, 1981).
90. J. S. Black and H. B. Gregersen, "Participative Decision Making: An Integration of Multiple Dimensions," *Human Relations* 50 (1997): 859–878.
91. G. Stasser, L. A. Taylor, and C. Hanna, "Information Sampling in Structured and Unstructured Discussion of Three- and Six-Person Groups," *Journal of Personality and Social Psychology* 57 (1989): 67–78.
92. E. Kirchler and J. H. Davis, "The Influence of Member Status Differences and Task Type on Group Consensus and Member Position Change," *Journal of Personality and Social Psychology* 51 (1986): 83–91.
93. R. F. Maier, "Assets and Liabilities in Group Problem Solving," *Psychological Review* 74 (1967): 239–249.
94. M. E. Shaw, *Group Dynamics: The Psychology of Small Group Behavior*, 3rd ed. (New York: McGraw-Hill, 1981).
95. P. W. Yetton and P. C. Bottger, "Individual versus Group Problem Solving: An Empirical Test of a Best Member Strategy," *Organizational Behavior and Human Performance* 29 (1982): 307–321.
96 W. Watson, L. Michaelson, and W. Sharp, "Member Competence, Group Interaction, and Group Decision Making: A Longitudinal Study," *Journal of Applied Psychology* 76 (1991): 803–809.
97. M. A. Serva, M. A. Fuller, and R. C. Mayer, "The Reciprocal Nature of Trust: A Longitudinal Study of Interacting Teams," *Journal of Organizational Behavior* 26 (2005): 625–649.
98. I. Janis, *Victims of Groupthink* (Boston: Houghton Mifflin, 1972).
99. M. A. Hogg and S. C. Hains, "Friendship and Group Identification: A New Look at the Role of Cohesiveness in Groupthink," *European Journal of Social Psychology* 28 (1998): 323–341.
100. P. E. Jones and H. M. P. Roelofsma, "The Potential for Social Contextual and Group Biases in Team Decision Making: Biases, Conditions, and Psychological Mechanisms," *Ergonomics* 43 (2000): 1129–1152; J. M. Levine, E. T. Higgins, and H. Choi, "Development of Strategic Norms in Groups," *Organizational Behavior and Human Decision Processes* 82 (2000): 88–101.
101. A. L. Brownstein, "Biased Predecision Processing," *Psychological Bulletin* 129 (2003): 545–568.
102. C. P. Neck and G. Moorhead, "Groupthink Remodeled: The Importance of Leadership, Time Pressure, and Methodical Decision-Making Procedures," *Human Relations* 48 (1995): 537–557.
103. J. Schwartz and M. L. Ward, "Final Shuttle Report Cites 'Broken Safety Culture' at NASA," *New York Times* (August 26, 2003), http://www.nytimes.com/2003/08/26/national/26CND-SHUT.html?ex=1077253200&en=882575f2c17ed8ff&ei=5070.
104. C. Ferraris and R. Carveth, "NASA and the Columbia Disaster: Decision Making by Groupthink?" in Proceedings of the 2003 Convention of the Association for Business Communication Annual Convention, http://www.businesscommunication.org/conventions/Proceedings/2003/PDF/03ABC03.pdf.
105. A. C. Homan, D. van Knippenberg, G. A. Van Kleef, and K. W. C. De Dreu, "Bridging Faultlines by Valuing Diversity: Diversity Beliefs, Information Elaboration, and Performance in Diverse Work Groups," *Journal of Applied Psychology* 92(5) (2007):1189–1199.
106. G. Moorhead, R. Ference, and C. P. Neck, "Group Decision Fiascoes Continue: Space Shuttle *Challenger* and a Revised Groupthink Framework," *Human Relations* 44 (1991): 539–550.
107. J. R. Montanari and G. Moorhead, "Development of the Groupthink Assessment Inventory," *Educational and Psychological Measurement* 49 (1989): 209–219.
108. P. t'Hart, "Irving L. Janis' Victims of Groupthink," *Political Psychology* 12 (1991): 247–278.
109. A. C. Mooney, P. J. Holahan, and A. C. Amason, "Don't Take it Personally: Exploring Cognitive Conflict as a Mediator of Affective Conflict," *Journal of Management Studies* 44(5) (2007): 733–758.
110. J. A. F. Stoner, "Risky and Cautious Shifts in Group Decisions: The Influence of Widely Held Values," *Journal of Experimental Social Psychology* 4 (1968): 442–459.
111. S. Moscovici and M. Zavalloni, "The Group as a Polarizer of Attitudes," *Journal of Personality and Social Psychology* 12 (1969): 125–135.
112. G. R. Goethals and M. P. Zanna, "The Role of Social Comparison in Choice of Shifts," *Journal of Personality and Social Psychology* 37 (1979): 1469–1476.
113. A. Vinokur and E. Burnstein, "Effects of Partially Shared Persuasive Arguments on Group-Induced Shifts: A Problem-Solving Approach," *Journal of Personality and Social Psychology* 29 (1974): 305–315.

114. L. Armstrong, "Toyota's Scion: A Siren to Young Buyers?" *Business Week* (March 4, 2002), http://www.businessweek.com/bwdaily/dnflash/mar2002/nf2002034_8826.htm.

115. Edmunds.com, Inc., "Toyota Courts NetGen Youth with Echo Subcompact" (January 1, 1999), http://www.edmunds.com/news/autoshows/articles/44460/page020.html.

116. B. Young, "Mixing It Up: Crossover Vehicles Borrow Best of Cars, SUVs, Trucks," *Los Angeles Times*, http://www.latimes.com/extras/autoleasing/mixing.html.

117. K. Dugosh, P. Paulus, E. Roland, and H. Yang, "Cognitive Stimulation in Brainstorming," *Journal of Personality and Social Psychology* 79 (2000): 722–735.

118. B. A. Nijstad, W. Stroebe, and H. F. M. Lodewijkx, "Production Blocking and Idea Generation: Does Blocking Interfere with Cognitive Processes?" *Journal of Experimental Social Psychology* 39 (2003): 531–549.

119. W. H. Cooper, R. B. Gallupe, S. Pollard, and J. Cadsby, "Some Liberating Effects of Anonymous Electronic Brainstorming," *Small Group Research* 29 (1998): 147–178.

120. A. Van de Ven and A. Delbecq, "The Effectiveness of Nominal, Delphi and Interacting Group Decision-Making Processes," *Academy of Management Journal* 17 (1974): 605–621.

121. A. L. Delbecq, A. H. Van de Ven, and D. H. Gustafson, *Group Techniques for Program Planning: A Guide to Nominal, Group, and Delphi Processes* (Glenview, Ill.: Scott, Foresman, 1975).

122. R. A. Cosier and C. R. Schwenk, "Agreement and Thinking Alike: Ingredients for Poor Decisions," *Academy of Management Executive* 4 (1990): 69–74.

123. D. M. Schweiger, W. R. Sandburg, and J. W. Ragan, "Group Approaches for Improving Strategic Decision Making: A Comparative Analysis of Dialectical Inquiry, Devil's Advocacy, and Consensus," *Academy of Management Journal* 29 (1986): 149–159.

124. G. Whyte, "Decision Failures: Why They Occur and How to Prevent Them," *Academy of Management Executive* 5 (1991): 23–31.

125. E. E. Lawler III and S. A. Mohrman, "Quality Circles: After the Honeymoon," *Organizational Dynamics* (Spring 1987): 42–54.

126. T. L. Tang and E. A. Butler, "Attributions of Quality Circles' Problem-Solving Failure: Differences among Management, Supporting Staff, and Quality Circle Members," *Public Personnel Management* 26 (1997): 203–225.

127. S. R. Olberding, "Toyota on Competition and Quality Circles," *The Journal for Quality and Participation* 21 (1998): 52–54.

128. J. Schilder, "Work Teams Boost Productivity," *Personnel Journal* 71 (1992): 67–72.

129. L. I. Glassop, "The Organizational Benefits of Teams," *Human Relations* 55 (2002): 225–249.

130. C. J. Nemeth, "Managing Innovation: When Less Is More," *California Management Review* 40 (1997): 59–68.

131. L. Scholten, D. van Knippenberg, B. A. Nijstad, and K. W. C. De Dreu, "Motivated Information Processing and Group Decision-Making: Effects of Process Accountability on Information Processing and Decision Quality," *Journal of Experimental Social Psychology* 43(4) (2007): 539–552.

132. N. Adler, *International Dimensions of Organizational Behavior*, 3rd ed. (Cincinnati, Ohio: South-Western, 1997).

133. S. C. Peppas, "Attitudes of Hispanics and Non-Hispanics in the US: A Comparative Study of Business Ethics," *Management Research News* 29(3) (2006): 92–105.

134. G. K. Stephens and C. R. Greer, "Doing Business in Mexico: Understanding Cultural Differences," *Organization Dynamics* 24 (1995): 39–55.

135. C. R. Greer and G. K. Stephens, "Escalation of Commitment: A Comparison of Differences between Mexican and U. S. Decision Makers," *Journal of Management* 27 (2001): 51–78.

136. K. W. Phillips and D. L. Lloyd, "When Surface and Deep-Level Diversity Collide: The Effects on Dissenting Group Members," *Organizational Behavior and Human Decision Processes* 99(2) (2006): 143–160.

137. T. Simons, L. H. Pelled, and K. A Smith, "Making Use of Difference: Diversity, Debate, and Decision Comprehensiveness in Top Management Teams," *Academy of Management Journal* 42(6) (1999): 662–673.

138. S. Elbanna and J. Child, "The Influence of Decision, Environmental and Firm Characteristics on the Rationality of Strategic Decision-Making," *Journal of Management Studies* 44(4) (2007): 561–591.

139. J. Khan, "It's Alive!" *Wired Magazine* 10.03 (March 2002), http://www.wired.com/wired/archive/10.03/everywhere_pr.html.

140. J. Wybo, "FMIS: A Decision Support System for Forest Fire Prevention and Fighting," *IEEE Transactions on Engineering Management* 45 (1998): 127–131.

141. M. S. Poole, M. Holmes, and G. DeSanctis, "Conflict Management in a Computer-Supported Meeting Environment," *Management Science* 37 (1991): 926–953.

142. S. S. K. Lam and J. Schaubroeck, "Improving Group Decisions by Better Pooling Information: A Comparative Advantage of Groups Decision Support Systems," *Journal of Applied Psychology* 85 (2000): 565–573.

143. O. Thomas, "At Shell, Everyone's the Answer Man," *Business 2.0* (February 2004): 55, http://www.business2.com/b2/web/articles/0,17863,582181,00.html.

144. P. Kaihla, "The Matchmaker in the Machine," *Business 2.0* (February 2004): 52, http://www.business2.com/b2/web/articles/0,17863,582487,00.html.

145. A. T. McCartt and J. Rohrbaugh, "Managerial Openness to Change and the Introduction of GDSS: Explaining Initial Success and Failure in Decision Conferencing," *Organization Science* 6 (1995): 569–584.

146. P. L. McLeod, R. S. Baron, M. W. Marti, and K. Yoon, "The Eyes Have It: Minority Influence in Face-to-Face and Computer-Mediated Group Discussion," *Journal of Applied Psychology* 82 (1997): 706–718.

147. A. M. Townsend, S. M. DeMarie, and A. R. Hendrickson, "Virtual Teams: Technology and the Workplace of the Future," *Academy of Management Executive* 12 (1998): 17–29.

148. M. S. Poole, M. Holmes, and G. DeSanctis, "Conflict Management in a Computer-Supported Meeting Environment," *Management Science* 37 (1991): 926–953.

149. S. S. K. Lam and J. Schaubroeck, "Improving Group Decisions by Better Pooling Information: A Comparative Advantage of Groups Decision Support Systems," *Journal of Applied Psychology* 85 (2000): 565–573.

150. L. M. Jessup and J. F. George, "Theoretical and Methodological Issues in Group Support Systems," *Small Group Research* 28 (1997): 394–413.

151. E. Bonabeau, "Predicting the Unpredictable," *Harvard Business Review* 80 (2002): 109–117.

152. K. Blanchard and N. V. Peale, *The Power of Ethical Management* (New York: Fawcett Crest, 1988).

153. C. Schneider, "War Dance: Will SEC Go Light on DOD Contractors?" *CFO Magazine* April 7, 2003, http://www.cfo.com/article/1,5309,9121,00.htmlz?f=related.

154. M. McGraw, "Another Whistleblower Down the Tubes," *Bulletin of the Atomic Scientists* 46 (June 1990), http://www.thebulletin.org/issues/1990/j90/j90mcgraw.html.

155. http://www.businessweek.com/investor/content/jan2007/pi20070111_061787.htm?chan=search

156. A. Weintraub, "Can Avastin Cure Genentech's Slide?" *Business Week Online* (July 6, 2004), http://www.businessweek.com/technology/content/jul2004/tc2004076_9274_tc055.htm?chan=search

Chapter 10 Case

1. B. Leavy, "A Leader's Guide to Creating an Innovation Culture," *Strategy & Leadership* 33(4): 38, from ABI/Inform Research database (accessed October 11, 2007).
2. Ibid.
3. Ibid.
4. B. Hindo, "At 3M: A Struggle between Efficiency and Creativity," *Business Week*, IN: Inside Innovation Supplement 4038 (June 11, 2007): 8.
5. Ibid.
6. Ibid.
7. "Scrutinizing Six Sigma: The Story on 3M's Evaluation of the Program Triggered a Vigorous Debate among Readers," *Business Week* 4041 (July 2, 2007): 90.
8. Hindo, "At 3M: A Struggle between Efficiency and Creativity."
9. Ibid. .
10. "Scrutinizing Six Sigma."

11. S. Sanders, "The Quality/Creativity Paradox," *Quality Progress* 40(8) (August 2007): 1.
12. "Scrutinizing Six Sigma."
13. P. Georgescu, "Creativity to the Rescue," *Fortune* 156(8) (October 15, 2007): 74.
14. Leavy, "A Leader's Guide to Creating an Innovation Culture."
15. Ibid.
16. B. Hindo and B. Grow, "Six Sigma: So Yesterday? In an Innovation Economy, It's No Longer a Cure-All," *Business Week*, IN: Inside Innovation Supplement 4038 (June 11, 2007): 11.
17. "Scrutinizing Six Sigma."
18. Ibid.

Chapter 11

1. R. Verkaik, "Google Is Watching You," *The Independent* (May 24, 2007), http://news.independent.co.uk/sci_tech/article2578479.ece.
2. M. J. Miller, "Google's Schmidt Clears the Air" *PC Magazine* (March 17, 2006), http://www.pcmag.com/article2/0,1895,1939258,00.asp.
3. G. C. Homans, "Social Behavior as Exchange," *American Journal of Sociology* 63 (1958): 597–606.
4. R. D. Middlemist and M. A. Hitt, *Organizational Behavior: Managerial Strategies for Performance* (St. Paul, Minn.: West Publishing, 1988).
5. C. Barnard, *The Functions of the Executive* (Cambridge, Mass.: Harvard University Press, 1938).
6. Reuters Limited, "Canadian Carty Had Rough Ride at American Airlines," *USA Today* (April 25, 2003), http://www.usatoday.com/travel/news/2003/2003-04-25-aa-carty-profile.htm.
7. J. R. P. French and B. Raven, "The Bases of Social Power," in D. Cartwright, ed., *Group Dynamics: Research and Theory* (Evanston, Ill.: Row, Peterson, 1962); T. R. Hinkin and C. A. Schriesheim, "Development and Application of New Scales to Measure the French and Raven (1959) Bases of Social Power," *Journal of Applied Psychology* 74 (1989): 561–567.
8. K. D. Elsbach and G. Elofson, "How the Packaging of Decision Explanations Affects Perceptions of Trustworthiness," *Academy of Management Journal* 43 (1) (2000): 80–89.
9. P. M. Podsakoff and C. A. Schriesheim, "Field Studies of French and Raven's Bases of Power: Critique, Reanalysis, and Suggestions for Future Research," *Psychological Bulletin* 97 (1985): 387–411.
10. M. A. Rahim, "Relationships of Leader Power to Compliance and Satisfaction with Supervision: Evidence from a National Sample of Managers," *Journal of Management* 15 (1989): 545–556.
11. C. Argyris, "Management Information Systems: The Challenge to Rationality and Emotionality," *Management Science* 17 (1971): 275–292; J. Naisbitt and P. Aburdene, *Megatrends 2000* (New York: Morrow, 1990).
12. P. P. Carson, K. D. Carson, E. L. Knight, and C. W. Roe, "Power in Organizations: A Look through the TQM Lens," *Quality Progress* (November 1995): 73–78.
13. Inside Innovation, "Marissa Mayer: The Talent Scout," *Business Week online* (June19, 2006), http://www.businessweek.com/magazine/content/06_25/b3989422.htm.
14. M. Velasquez, D. J. Moberg, and G. F. Cavanaugh, "Organizational Statesmanship and Dirty Politics: Ethical Guidelines for the Organizational Politician," *Organizational Dynamics* 11 (1982): 65–79.
15. D. E. McClelland, *Power: The Inner Experience* (New York: Irvington, 1975).
16. S. Finkelstein, *Why Smart Executives Fail: And What You Can Learn from Their Mistakes* (New York: Portfolio, 2003).
17. N. Shahinpoor and B. F Matt, "The Power of One: Dissent and Organizational Life," *Journal of Business Ethics* 74(1) (2007): 37–49.
18. N. Machiavelli, *The Prince,* trans. by G. Bull (Middlesex, England: Penguin Books, 1961).
19. S. Chen, A. Y. Lee-Chai, and J. A. Bargh, "Relationship Orientation as a Moderator of the Effects of Social Power," *Journal of Personality and Social Psychology* 80, No. 2 (2001): 173–187.
20. J. Pfeffer and G. Salancik, *The External Control of Organizations* (New York: Harper & Row, 1978).
21. T. M. Welbourne and C. O. Trevor, "The Roles of Departmental and Position Power in Job Evaluation," *Academy of Management Journal* 43 (4) (2000): 761–771.
22. R. H. Miles, *Macro Organizational Behavior* (Glenview, Ill.: Scott, Foresman, 1980).
23. D. Hickson, C. Hinings, C. Lee, R. E. Schneck, and J. M. Pennings, "A Strategic Contingencies Theory of Intraorganizational Power," *Administrative Science Quarterly* 14 (1971): 219–220.
24. C. R. Hinings, D. J. Hickson, J. M. Pennings, and R. E. Schneck, "Structural Conditions of Intraorganizational Power," *Administrative Science Quarterly* 19 (1974): 22–44.
25. A. Etzioni, *Modern Organizations* (Upper Saddle River, N.J.: Prentice-Hall, 1964).
26. R. Kanter, "Power Failure in Management Circuits," *Harvard Business Review* (July–August 1979): 31–54.
27. F. Lee and L. Z. Tiedens, "Who's Being Served? 'Self-Serving' Attributions in Social Hierarchies," *Organizational Behavior and Human Decision Processes* 84 (2) (March 2001): 254–287.
28. M. Korda, *Power: How to Get It, How to Use It* (New York: Random House, 1975).
29. S. R. Thye, "A Status Value Theory of Power in Exchange Relations," *American Sociological Review* (2000): 407–432.
30. B. T. Mayes and R. T. Allen, "Toward a Definition of Organizational Politics," *Academy of Management Review* 2 (1977): 672–678.
31. M. Valle and P. L. Perrewe, "Do Politics Perceptions Relate to Political Behaviors? Tests of an Implicit Assumption and Expanded Model," *Human Relations* 53 (2000): 359–386.
32. W. A. Hochwarter, "The Interactive Effects of Pro-Political Behavior and Politics Perceptions on Job Satisfaction and Affective Commitment," *Journal of Applied Social Psychology* 33 (2003): 1360–1378.
33. W. A. Hochwarter, K. M. Kacmar, D. C. Treadway, and T. S. Watson, "It's All Relative: The Distinction and Prediction of Political Perceptions Across Levels," *Journal of Applied Social Psychology* 33 (2003): 1955–2016.
34. D. A. Ralston, "Employee Ingratiation: The Role of Management," *Academy of Management Review* 10 (1985): 477–487; D. R. Beeman and T. W. Sharkey, "The Use and Abuse of Corporate Politics," *Business Horizons* (March–April 1987): 25–35.
35. C. O. Longnecker, H. P. Sims, and D. A. Gioia, "Behind the Mask: The Politics of Employee Appraisal," *Academy of Management Executive* 1 (1987): 183–193.
36. Inside Innovation, "Marissa Mayer: The Talent Scout."
37. M. Valle and P. L. Perrewe, "Do Politics Perceptions Relate to Political Behaviors? Tests of an Implicit Assumption and Expanded Model," *Human Relations* 53, No. 3 (2000): 359–386.
38. D. Butcher and M. Clarke, "Organizational Politics: The Cornerstone for Organizational Democracy," *Organizational Dynamics* 31 (2002): 35–46.
39. D. Kipnis, S. M. Schmidt, and I. Wilkinson, "Intraorganizational Influence Tactics: Explorations in Getting One's Way," *Journal of Applied Psychology* 65 (1980): 440–452; D. Kipnis, S. Schmidt, C. Swaffin-Smith, and I. Wilkinson, "Patterns of Managerial Influence: Shotgun Managers, Tacticians, and Bystanders," *Organizational Dynamics* (Winter 1984): 60–67; G. Yukl and C. M. Falbe, "Influence Tactics and Objectives in Upward, Downward, and Lateral Influence Attempts," *Journal of Applied Psychology* 75 (1990): 132–140.
40. G. R. Ferris and T. A. Judge, "Personnel/Human Resources Management: A Political Influence Perspective," *Journal of Management* 17 (1991): 447–488.
41. G. Yukl, P. J. Guinan, and D. Sottolano, "Influence Tactics Used for Different Objectives with Subordinates, Peers, and Superiors," *Groups & Organization Management* 20 (1995): 272–296.
42. C. A. Higgins, T. A. Judge, and G. R. Ferris, "Influence Tactics and Work Outcomes: A Meta-Analysis," *Journal of Organizational Behavior* 24 (2003): 89–106.

43. K. K. Eastman, "In the Eyes of the Beholder: An Attributional Approach to Ingratiation and Organizational Citizenship Behavior," *Academy of Management Journal* 37 (1994): 1379–1391.
44. K. J. Harris, K. M. Kacmar, S. Zivnuska, and J. D. Shaw, "The Impact of Political Skill on Impression Management Effectiveness," *Journal of Applied Psychology* 92(1) (2007): 278–285.
45. D. C. Treadway, G. R. Ferris, A. B. Duke, G. L. Adams, and J. B. Thatcher, "The Moderating Role of Subordinate Political Skill on Supervisors' Impressions of Subordinate Ingratiation and Ratings of Subordinate Interpersonal Facilitation," *Journal of Applied Psychology* 92(3) (2007): 848–855.
46. R. A. Gordon, "Impact of Ingratiation on Judgments and Evaluations: A Meta-Analytic Investigation," *Journal of Personality and Social Psychology* 71 (1996): 54–70.
47. A. Drory and D. Beaty, "Gender Differences in the Perception of Organizational Influence Tactics," *Journal of Organizational Behavior* 12 (1991): 249–258.
48. S. Wellington, M. B. Kropf, and P. R. Gerkovich, "What's Holding Women Back?" *Harvard Business Review* (June 2003): 2–4.
49. P. Perrewe and D. Nelson, "Gender and Career Success: The Facilitative Role of Political Skill," *Organizational Dynamics* 33 (2004): 366–378.
50. R. Y. Hirokawa and A. Miyahara, "A Comparison of Influence Strategies Utilized by Managers in American and Japanese Organizations," *Communication Quarterly* 34 (1986): 250–265.
51. P. David, M. A. Hitt, and J. Gimeno, "The Influence of Activism by Institutional Investors on R&D," *Academy of Management Journal* 44 (1) (2001): 144–157.
52. G. R. Ferris, P. L. Perrewe, W. P. Anthony, and D. C. Gilmore, "Political Skill at Work," *Organizational Dynamics* 28 (2000): 25–37.
53. D. C. Treadway, W. A. Hochwarter, G. R. Ferris, C. J. Kacmar, C. Douglas, A. P. Ammeter, and M. R. Buckley, "Leader Political Skill and Employee Reactions," *Leadership Quarterly* 15 (2004): 493–513.
54. K. K. Ahearn, G. R. Ferris, W. A. Hochwarter, C. Douglas, A. P. Ammeter, "Leader Political Skill and Team Performance," *Journal of Management* 30(3) (2004): 309–327.
55. P. L. Perrewé, K. L. Zellars, G. R. Ferris, A. M. Rossi, C. J. Kacmar, C. J., and D. A. Ralston, "Neutralizing Job Stressors: Political Skill as an Antidote to the Dysfunctional Consequences of Role Conflict Stressors," *Academy of Management Journal* 47 (2004): 141–152.
56. Ferris, G.R., Treadway, D.C., Kolodinsky, R.W., Hochwarter, W.A., Kacmar, C.J., Douglas, C., & Frink, D.D. "Development and Validation of the Political Skill Inventory." *Journal of Management,* 31(2005):126–152.
57. G. Ferris, S. Davidson, P. Perrewé. "Developing Political Skill at Work." *Training.* 42(2005) : 40–45.
58. F. R. Blass and G. R. Ferris, "Leader Reputation: The Role of Mentoring, Political Skill, Contextual Learning, and Adaptation," *Human Resource Management,* 46(1)(2007): 5–19.
59. K. Kumar and M. S. Thibodeaux, "Organizational Politics and Planned Organizational Change," *Group and Organization Studies* 15 (1990): 354–365.
60. McClelland, *Power.*
61. Beeman and Sharkey, "Use and Abuse of Corporate Politics," 37.
62. C. P. Parker, R. L. Dipboye, and S. L. Jackson, "Perceptions of Organizational Politics: An Investigation of Antecedents and Consequences," *Journal of Management* 21 (1995): 891–912.
63. S. J. Ashford, N. P. Rothbard, S. K. Piderit, and J. E. Dutton, "Out on a Limb: The Role of Context and Impression Management in Selling Gender-Equity Issues," *Administrative Science Quarterly* 43 (1998): 23–57.
64. J. Zhou and G. R. Ferris, "The Dimensions and Consequences of Organizational Politics Perceptions: A Confirmatory Analysis," *Journal of Applied Social Psychology* 25 (1995): 1747–1764.
65. M. L. Seidal, J. T. Polzer, and K. J. Stewart, "Friends in High Places: The Effects of Social Networks on Discrimination in Salary Negotiations," *Administrative Science Quarterly* 45 (2000): 1–24.
66. J. J. Gabarro and J. P. Kotter, "Managing Your Boss," *Harvard Business Review* (January–February 1980): 92–100.
67. P. Newman, "How to Manage Your Boss," Peat, Marwick, Mitchell & Company's *Management Focus* (May–June 1980): 36–37.
68. F. Bertolome, "When You Think the Boss Is Wrong," *Personnel Journal* 69 (1990): 66–73.
69. J. Conger and R. Kanungo, *Charismatic Leadership: The Elusive Factor in Organizational Effectiveness* (New York: Jossey-Bass, 1988).
70. G. M. Spreitzer, M. A. Kizilos, and S. W. Nason, "A Dimensional Analysis of the Relationship between Psychological Empowerment and Effectiveness, Satisfaction, and Strain," *Journal of Management* 23 (1997): 679–704.
71. R. C. Ford and M. D. Fottler, "Empowerment: A Matter of Degree," *Academy of Management Executive* 9 (1995): 21–31.
72. M. Holbrook, "Employee Commitment Is Crucial," *Human Resources* (May 2007): 66.
73. J. Simons, "Merck's Man in the Hot Seat," *Fortune* (February 23, 2004): 111–114.
74. S. Finkelstein, *Why Smart Executives Fail: And What You Can Learn from Their Mistakes* (New York: Portfolio, 2003).
75. J. P. Kotter, "Power, Dependence, and Effective Management," *Harvard Business Review* 55 (1977): 125–136; J. P. Kotter, *Power and Influence* (New York: Free Press, 1985).
76. R. Hof, "Is Google Too Powerful?" *Business Week online* (April 9, 2007), http://www.businessweek.com/magazine/content/07_15/b4029001.htm.

Chapter 11 Case

1. B. Schlender and C. Tkaczyk, "Pixar's Magic Man." *Fortune* (May 29, 2006), page 3 of 7, from Academic Search Premier database (accessed August 23, 2007).
2. Ibid, page 4 of 7.
3. Ibid.
4. Ibid.
5. Ibid.
6. Ibid, page 5 of 7.
7. P. Burrows, R. Grover, and H. Green, "Steve Jobs' Magic Kingdom," *Business Week* (February 6, 2006), page 3 of 9, from Academic Search Premier database (accessed August 23, 2007).
8. "Pixar Corporate Overview," http://www.pixar.com/companyinfo/about_us/overview.htm (accessed August 23, 2007).
9. R. Grover, "How Bob Iger Unchained Disney," *Business Week* (February 5, 2007), from ABI / INFORM Research database (accessed August 23, 2007).
10. R. Grover, "Pixar Exec's Fairy-Tale Story," *Business Week Online* (January 26, 2006), page 1 of 2, from Academic Search Premier database (accessed August 23, 2007).
11. Ibid, page 2 of 2.
12. Ibid.
13. Burrows, Grover, and Green, " Steve Jobs' Magic Kingdom.".
14. Schlender and Tkaczyk, "Pixar's Magic Man," page 6 of 7.

Chapter 12

1. G. Farrell, "A CEO and a Gentleman," *USA Today* (April 24, 2005), http://www.usatoday.com/money/companies/management/2005-04-24-chenault-usat_x.htm.
2. J. P. Kotter, "What Leaders Really Do," *Harvard Business Review* 68 (1990): 103–111.
3. E. Florian, "2004 America's Most Admired Companies: Fred Smith of FedEx," *Fortune* (March 8, 2004): 88a, http://www.fortune.com/fortune/subs/article/0,15114,592448,00.html.
4. D. A. Plowman, S. Solansky, T. E. Beck, L. Baker, M. Kulkarni, and D. V. Travis, "The Role of Leadership in Emergent, Self-Organization," *Leadership Quarterly* 18(4) (2007): 341–356.
5. A. Zaleznik, "HBR Classic—Managers and Leaders: Are They Different?" *Harvard Business Review* 70 (1992): 126–135.
6. W. G. Rowe, "Creating Wealth in Organizations: The Role of Strategic Leadership," *Academy of Management Executive* 15 (2001): 81–94.

7. R. M. Stogdill, "Personal Factors Associated with Leadership: A Survey of the Literature," *Journal of Psychology* 25 (1948): 35–71.
8. R. D. Arvey, Z. Zhang, B. J. Avolio, and R. F. Krueger, "Developmental and Genetic Determinants of Leadership Role Occupancy among Women," *Journal of Applied Psychology* 92(3) (2007): 693–706.
9. K. Lewin, R. Lippitt, and R. K. White, "Patterns of Aggressive Behavior in Experimentally Created 'Social Climates,'" *Journal of Social Psychology* 10 (1939): 271–299.
10. S. D. Sidle, "The Danger of Do Nothing Leaders," *The Academy of Management Perspectives* 21(2) (2007): 75–77.
11. R. M. Stodgill and A. E. Coons, eds., *Leader Behavior: Its Description and Measurement*, research monograph no. 88 (Columbus, Ohio: Bureau of Business Research, The Ohio State University, 1957).
12. A. W. Halpin and J. Winer, "A Factorial Study of the Leader Behavior Description Questionnaire," in R. M. Stogdill and A. E. Coons, eds., *Leader Behavior: Its Description and Measurement*, research monograph no. 88 (Columbus, Ohio: Bureau of Business Research, The Ohio State University, 1957), 39–51.
13. E. A. Fleishman, "Leadership Climate, Human Relations Training, and Supervisory Behavior," *Personnel Psychology* 6 (1953): 205–222.
14. R. Kahn and D. Katz, "Leadership Practices in Relation to Productivity and Morale," in D. Cartwright and A. Zander, eds., *Group Dynamics, Research and Theory* (Elmsford, NY: Row, Paterson, 1960).
15. R. R. Blake and J. S. Mouton, *The Managerial Grid III: The Key to Leadership Excellence* (Houston: Gulf, 1985).
16. W. Vandekerckhove and R. Commers, "Downward Workplace Mobbing: A Sign of the Times?" *Journal of Business Ethics* 45 (2003): 41–50.
17. F. E. Fiedler, *A Theory of Leader Effectiveness* (New York: McGraw-Hill, 1964).
18. F. E. Fiedler, *Personality, Motivational Systems, and Behavior of High and Low LPC Persons*, tech. rep. no. 70-12 (Seattle: University of Washington, 1970).
19. J. T. McMahon, "The Contingency Theory: Logic and Method Revisited," *Personnel Psychology* 25 (1972): 697–710; L. H. Peters, D. D. Hartke, and J. T. Pohlman, "Fiedler's Contingency Theory of Leadership: An Application of the Meta-Analysis Procedures of Schmidt and Hunter," *Psychological Bulletin* 97 (1985): 224–285.
20. F. E. Fiedler, "The Contingency Model and the Dynamics of the Leadership Process," in L. Berkowitz, ed., *Advances in Experimental and Social Psychology*, vol. 11 (New York: Academic Press, 1978).
21. S. Arin and C. McDermott, "The Effect of Team Leader Characteristics on Learning, Knowledge Application, and Performance of Cross-Functional New Product Development Teams," *Decision Sciences* 34 (2003): 707–739.
22. F. E. Fiedler, "Engineering the Job to Fit the Manager," *Harvard Business Review* 43 (1965): 115–122.
23. R. J. House, "A Path–Goal Theory of Leader Effectiveness," *Administrative Science Quarterly* 16 (1971): 321–338; R. J. House and T. R. Mitchell, "Path–Goal Theory of Leadership," *Journal of Contemporary Business* 3 (1974): 81–97.
24. C. A. Schriescheim and V. M. Von Glinow, "The Path–Goal Theory of Leadership: A Theoretical and Empirical Analysis," *Academy of Management Journal* 20 (1977): 398–405; E. Valenzi and G. Dessler, "Relationships of Leader Behavior, Subordinate Role Ambiguity, and Subordinate Job Satisfaction," *Academy of Management Journal* 21 (1978): 671–678; N. R. F. Maier, *Leadership Methods and Skills* (New York: McGraw-Hill, 1963).
25. J. P. Grinnell, "An Empirical Investigation of CEO Leadership in Two Types of Small Firms," *S.A.M. Advanced Management Journal* 68 (2003): 36–41.
26. V. H. Vroom and P. W. Yetton, *Leadership and Decision Making* (Pittsburgh: University of Pittsburgh, 1973).
27. V. H. Vroom, "Leadership and the Decision-Making Process," *Organizational Dynamics* 28 (2000): 82–94.
28. W. J. Duncan, K. G. LaFrance, and P. M. Ginter, "Leadership and Decision Making: A Retrospective Application and Assessment," *Journal of Leadership & Organizational Studies* 9 (2003): 1–20.
29. P. Hersey and K. H. Blanchard, "Life Cycle Theory of Leadership," *Training and Development* 23 (1969): 26–34; P. Hersey, K. H. Blanchard, and D. E. Johnson, *Management of Organizational Behavior: Leading Human Resources*, 8th ed. (Upper Saddle River, N.J.: Prentice-Hall, 2001).
30. B. M. Bass, *Bass and Stogdill's Handbook of Leadership: Theory, Research, and Managerial Applications*, 3rd ed. (New York: Free Press, 1990).
31. G. B. Graen and M. Uhl-Bien, "Relationship-Based Approach to Leadership: Development of Leader–Member Exchange (LMX) Theory of Leadership over 25 Years," *Leadership Quarterly* 6 (1995): 219–247; C. R. Gerstner and D. V. Day, "Meta-Analytic Review of Leader–Member Exchange Theory: Correlates and Construct Issues," *Journal of Applied Psychology* 82 (1997): 827–844; R. C. Liden, S. J. Wayne, and R. T. Sparrowe, "An Examination of the Mediating Role of Psychological Empowerment on the Relations between the Job, Interpersonal Relationships, and Work Outcomes," *Journal of Applied Psychology* 85 (2001): 407–416.
32. J. Townsend, J. S. Phillips, and T. J. Elkins, "Employee Retaliation: The Neglected Consequence of Poor Leader–Member Exchange Relations," *Journal of Occupational Health Psychology* 5 (2000): 457–463.
33. D. Nelson, R. Basu, and R. Purdie, "An Examination of Exchange Quality and Work Stressors in Leader–Follower Dyads," *International Journal of Stress Management* 5 (1998): 103–112.
34. K. M. Kacmar, L. A. Witt, S. Zivnuska, and S. M. Gully, "The Interactive Effect of Leader–Member Exchange and Communication Frequency on Performance Ratings," *Journal of Applied Psychology* 88 (2003): 764–772.
35. A. G. Tekleab and M. S. Taylor, "Aren't There Two Parties in an Employment Relationship? Antecedents and Consequences of Organization–Employee Agreement on Contract Obligations and Violations," *Journal of Organizational Behavior* 24 (2003): 585–608.
36. D. A. Hoffman, S. J. Gerras, and F. P. Morgeson, "Climate as a Moderator of the Relationship Between Leader–Member Exchange and Content Specific Citizenship: Safety Climate as an Exemplar," *Journal of Applied Psychology* 88 (2003): 170–178.
37. S. Kerr and J. M. Jermier, "Substitutes for Leadership: Their Meaning and Measurement," *Organizational Behavior and Human Performance* 22 (1978): 375–403.
38. P. M. Podsakoff, S. B. MacKenzie, and W. H. Bommer, "Meta-Analysis of the Relationships between Kerr and Jermier's Substitutes for Leadership and Employee Job Attitudes, Role Perceptions, and Performance," *Journal of Applied Psychology* 81 (1996): 380–399.
39. B. C. Skaggs and M. Youndt, "Strategic Positioning, Human Capital, and Performance in Service Organizations: A Customer Interaction Approach," *Strategic Management Journal* 25 (2004): 85–99.
40. J. M. Burns, *Leadership* (New York: Harper & Row, 1978); T. O. Jacobs, *Leadership and Exchange in Formal Organizations* (Alexandria, Va.: Human Resources Research Organization, 1971).
41. B. M. Bass, "From Transactional to Transformational Leadership: Learning to Share the Vision," *Organizational Dynamics* 19 (1990): 19–31; B. M. Bass, *Leadership and Performance beyond Expectations* (New York: Free Press, 1985).
42. P. M. Podsakoff, S. B. MacKenzie, and W.H. Bommer, "Transformational Leader Behaviors and Substitutes for Leadership as Determinants of Employee Satisfaction, Commitment, Trust, and Organizational Citizenship Behaviors," *Journal of Management* 22 (1996): 259–298.
43. T. A. Judge and R. F. Piccolo, "Transformational and Transactional Leadership: A Meta-Analytic Test of their Relative Validity," *Journal of Applied Psychology* 89 (2004): 755–768.
44. P. Wang, and F. O. Walumbwa. "Family-Friendly Programs, Organizational Commitment, and Work Withdrawal: The Moderating Role of Transformational Leadership," *Personnel Psychology* 60(2) (2007): 397–427.
45. W. Bennis, "Managing the Dream: Leadership in the 21st Century," *Training* 27 (1990): 43–48.
46. P. M. Podsakoff, S. B. MacKenzie, R. H. Moorman, and R. Fetter, "Transformational Leader Behaviors and Their Effects on Followers' Trust in Leader, Satisfaction, and Organizational Citizenship Behaviors," *Leadership Quarterly* 1 (1990): 107–142.
47. MyPrimeTime, Inc., "Great Entrepreneurs—Biography: Howard Schultz, Starbucks," http://www.myprimetime.com/work/ge/schultzbio/index.shtml.

48. C. P. Egri and S. Herman, "Leadership in the North American Environmental Sector: Values, Leadership Styles, and Contexts of Environmental Leaders and Their Organizations," *Academy of Management Journal* 43 (2000): 571–604.
49. T. A. Judge and J. E. Bono, "Five-Factor Model of Personality and Transformational Leadership," *Journal of Applied Psychology* 85 (2001): 751–765.
50. J. E. Bono and T. A. Judge, "Self-Concordance at Work: Toward Understanding the Motivational Effects of Transformational Leaders," *Academy of Management Journal* 46 (2003): 554–571.
51. T. Dvir, D. Eden, B. J. Avolio, and B. Shamir, "Impact of Transformational Leadership on Follower Development and Performance: A Field Experiment," *Academy of Management Journal* 45 (2002): 735–744.
52. The Jargon Dictionary, "The **R** Terms: Reality-Distortion Field," http://info.astrian.net/jargon/terms/r/reality-distortion_field.html.
53. R. J. House and M. L. Baetz, "Leadership: Some Empirical Generalizations and New Research Directions," in B. M. Staw, ed., *Research in Organizational Behavior*, vol. 1 (Greenwood, Conn.: JAI Press, 1979), 399–401.
54. J. A. Conger and R. N. Kanungo, "Toward a Behavioral Theory of Charismatic Leadership in Organizational Settings," *Academy of Management Review* 12 (1987): 637–647.
55. A. R. Willner, *The Spellbinders: Charismatic Political Leadership* (New Haven, Conn.: Yale University Press, 1984).
56. D. Waldman, G. G. Ramirez, R. J. House, and P. Puranam, "Does Leadership Matter? CEO Leadership Attributes and Profitability under Conditions of Perceived Environmental Uncertainty," *Academy of Management Journal* 44 (2001): 134–143.
57. J. M. Howell, "Two Faces of Charisma: Socialized and Personalized Leadership in Organizations," in J. A. Conger, ed., *Charismatic Leadership: Behind the Mystique of Exceptional Leadership* (San Francisco: Jossey-Bass, 1988).
58. F. Luthans and B. J. Avolio, "Authentic Leadership: A Positive Development Approach," In K. S. Cameron, J. E. Dutton, and R. E. Quinn, eds., *Positive Organizational Scholarship: Foundations of a New Discipline* (San Francisco, Calif.: Berrett-Koehler, 2004): 241–261.
59. W. L. Gardner, B. J. Avolio, F. Luthans, D. R. May, and F. O. Walumbwa, "Can You See the Real Me? A Self-based Model of Authentic Leader and Follower Development," *The Leadership Quarterly* 16 (2005): 343–372.
60. B. J. Avolio, W. L. Gardner, F. O. Walumbwa, F. Luthans, and D. R. May, "Unlocking the Mask: A Look at the Process by Which Authentic Leaders Impact Follower Attitudes and Behaviors," *The Leadership Quarterly* 15 (2004): 801–823.
61. S. Michie and J. Gooty, "Values, Emotions, and Authentic Leadership Behaviors: Will the Real Leader Please Stand Up?" *The Leadership Quarterly* 16 (2005): 441–457.
62. S. Michie and D. L. Nelson, "The Effects of Leader Compassion Display on Follower Attributions: Building a Socialized Leadership Image," Paper presented at the *Academy of Management Conference* in Honolulu, Hawaii (2005).
63. M. Maccoby, "Narcissistic Leaders: The Incredible Pros, the Inevitable Cons," *Harvard Business Review* 78 (2000): 68–77.
64. D. Sankowsky, "The Charismatic Leader as Narcissist: Understanding the Abuse of Power," *Organizational Dynamics* 23 (1995): 57–71.
65. F. J. Flynn and B. M. Staw, "Lend Me Your Wallets: The Effect of Charismatic Leadership on External Support for an Organization," *Strategic Management Journal* 25 (2004): 309–330.
66. D. Goleman, "What Makes a Leader?" *Harvard Business Review* 82 (2004): 82–91.
67. D. Goleman, "Never Stop Learning," *Harvard Business Review* 82 (2004): 28–30.
68. C. L. Gohm, "Mood Regulation and Emotional Intelligence: Individual Differences," *Journal of Personality and Social Psychology* 84 (2003): 594–607.
69. J. Useem, "A Manager for All Seasons," *Fortune* (April 30, 2001): 66–72.
70. R. C. Mayer, J. H. Davis, and F. D. Schoorman, "An Integrative Model of Organizational Trust," *Academy of Management Review* 20 (1995): 709–734.
71. R. S. Dooley and G. E. Fryxell, "Attaining Decision Quality and Commitment from Dissent: The Moderating Effects of Loyalty and Competence in Strategic Decision-Making Teams," *Academy of Management Journal* 42 (1999): 389–402.
72. A. Malhotra, A. Majchrzak, R. Carman, and V. Lott, "Radical Innovation without Collocation: A Case Study at Boeing-Rocketdyne," *MIS Quarterly* 25 (2001): 229–249.
73. P. Dixon, "Virtual Teams—Global Leadership," *Financial Times* 17 (February 2003), http://www.globalchange.com/vteams.htm.
74. S. W. Lester and H. H. Brower, "In the Eyes of the Beholder: The Relationship between Subordinates' Felt Trustworthiness and Their Work Attitudes and Behaviors," *Journal of Leadership & Organizational Studies* 10 (2003): 17–33.
75. Saj-nicole A. Joni, "The Geography of Trust," *Harvard Business Review* 82 (2003): 82–88.
76. M. E. Heilman, C. J. Block, R. F. Martell, and M. C. Simon, "Has Anything Changed? Current Characteristics of Men, Women, and Managers," *Journal of Applied Psychology* 74 (1989): 935–942.
77. A. H. Eagly, S. J. Darau, and M. Makhijani, "Gender and the Effectiveness of Leaders: A Meta-Analysis," *Psychological Bulletin* 117 (1995): 125–145.
78. M. K. Ryan, S. A. Haslam, and T. Postmes, "Reactions to the Glass Cliff: Gender Differences in the Explanations for the Precariousness of Women's Leadership Positions," *Journal of Organizational Change Management* 20(2) (2007): 182–197.
79. R. K. Greenleaf, L. C. Spears, and D. T. Frick, eds., *On Becoming a Servant-Leader* (San Francisco: Jossey-Bass, 1996).
80. E. P. Hollander and L. R. Offerman, "Power and Leadership in Organizations: Relationships in Transition," *American Psychologist* 45 (1990): 179–189.
81. H. P. Sims, Jr., and C. C. Manz, *Company of Heros: Unleashing the Power of Self-Leadership* (New York: John Wiley & Sons, 1996).
82. C. C. Manz and H. P. Sims, "Leading Workers to Lead Themselves: The External Leadership of Self-Managing Work Teams," *Administrative Science Quarterly* 32 (1987): 106–128.
83. L. Hirschhorn, "Leaders and Followers in a Postindustrial Age: A Psychodynamic View," *Journal of Applied Behavioral Science* 26 (1990): 529–542.
84. R. E. Kelley, "In Praise of Followers," *Harvard Business Review* 66 (1988): 142–148.
85. C. C. Manz and H. P. Sims, "SuperLeadership: Beyond the Myth of Heroic Leadership," *Organizational Dynamics* 20 (1991): 18–35.
86. W. J. Crockett, "Dynamic Subordinancy," *Training and Development Journal* (May 1981): 155–164.
87. N. J. Adler, *International Dimensions in Organizational Behavior* (Boston: PWS-Kent, 1991).
88. F. C. Brodback *et al.*, "Cultural Variation of Leadership Prototypes across 22 European Countries," *Journal of Occupational and Organizational Psychology* 73 (2000): 1–29.
89. B. Alimo-Metcalfe and R. J. Alban-Metcalfe, "The Development of a New Transformational Leadership Questionnaire," *Journal of Occupational and Organizational Psychology* 74 (2001): 1–27.
90. *Fortune Magazine,* "50 Best Companies for Minorities 2003," *Fortune* (July 7, 2003): 103.
91. J. Adamson, *The Denny's Story: How a Company in Crisis Resurrected Its Good Name and Reputation* (John Wiley & Sons, Inc., 2000).
92. T. Lenartowicz and J. P. Johnson, "A Cross-National Assessment of the Values of Latin American Managers: Contrasting Hues or Shades of Gray?" *Journal of International Business Studies* 34 (2003): 266–281.
93. Y. Hui-Chun and P. Miller, "The Generation Gap and Cultural Influence: A Taiwan Empirical Investigation," *Cross Cultural Management* 10 (2003): 23–42.
94. M. Javidan, "Forward-Thinking Cultures," *Harvard Business Review* 85(7, 8) (2007): 20.
95. G. A. Yukl, *Leadership in Organizations*, 2nd ed. (Upper Saddle River, N.J.: Prentice-Hall, 1989).
96. Harvard Business School, "James E. Burke," *Working Knowledge* (October 27, 2003), http://hbswk.hbs.edu/pubitem.jhtml?id=3755&t=leadership.

97. "AmEx's Ken Chenault Talks about Leadership, Integrity, and the Credit Card Business," Published in Knowledge@Wharton (April, 10, 2005), http://knowledge.wharton.upenn.edu/articlepdf/1179.pdf?CFID=19898527&CFTOKEN=39534433&jsessionid=a830dfb2436748503819.

Chapter 12 Case

1. "Company Overview," Google, http://www.google.com/intl/en/corporate/index.html (accessed October 11, 2007); "Google Management," Google, http://www.google.com/intl/en/corporate/execs.html (accessed October 11, 2007).
2. D. A. Nadler, "The CEO's 2nd Act," *Harvard Business Review* 85(1) (January 2007):. 66–72.
3. S. Berfield, ed. "The Best of 2006: Leaders," *Business Week* 4014 (December 18, 2006): 58+.
4. Ibid.
5. A. Lashinsky, "Who's the Boss?" *Fortune* 154(7) (October 2, 2006): 93.
6. Ibid.
7. Nadler, "The CEO's 2nd Act."
8. K. J. Delaney, "Google Displays Core Strength; As Product Line Expands, Search Business Drives Surges in Profit, Revenue," *The Wall Street Journal*, Eastern edition (April 20, 2007): A3.
9. Nadler, "The CEO's 2nd Act."
10. P. Hosking, "For Those Searching for Value, You Must Look Beyond Google," *The Times* (United Kingdom) (February 18, 2006), from Newspaper Source database (accessed October 6, 2007).
11. G. Hamel, "Management a la Google," *The Wall Street Journal*, Eastern edition (April 26, 2006): A16.
12. A. Ignatius, "In Search of the Real Google," *Time* 167(8) (February 20, 2006): 36.
13. Hamel, "Management a la Google."
14. Ibid.
15. Ibid.
16. Berfield, "The Best of 2006."
17. A. Ignatius, "Meet the Google Guys," *Time* 167(2) (February 20, 2006): 40.
18. Ignatius, "In Search of the Real Google"; Ignatius, "Meet the Google Guys.".
19. Ignatius, "In Search of the Real Google."
20. Ibid.
21. Hosking, "For Those Searching for Value."
22. Ibid.

Chapter 13

1. A. Weintraub, "Another Pain for Genentech," *Business Week* (June 12, 2002), http://www.businessweek.com/technology/content/jun2002/tc20020612_8985.htm?chan=search.
2. Definition adapted from D. Hellriegel, J. W. Slocum, Jr., and R. W. Woodman, *Organizational Behavior* (St. Paul: West, 1992) and from R. D. Middlemist and M. A. Hitt, *Organizational Behavior* (St. Paul: West, 1988).
3. D. Tjosvold, *The Conflict-Positive Organization* (Reading, Mass.: Addison-Wesley, 1991).
4. K. Thomas and W. Schmidt, "A Survey of Managerial Interests with Respect to Conflict," *Academy of Management Journal* 19 (1976): 315–318; G. L. Lippitt, "Managing Conflict in Today's Organizations," *Training and Development Journal* 36 (1982): 66–74.
5. M. Rajim, "A Measure of Styles of Handling Interpersonal Conflict," *Academy of Management Journal* 26 (1983): 368–376.
6. D. Goleman, *Emotional Intelligence* (New York: Bantam Books, 1995); J. Stuller, "Unconventional Smarts," *Across the Board* 35 (1998): 22–23.
7. Tjosvold, *The Conflict-Positive Organization*, 4.
8. R. A. Cosier and D. R. Dalton, "Positive Effects of Conflict: A Field Experiment," *International Journal of Conflict Management* 1 (1990): 81–92.
9. D. Tjosvold, "Making Conflict Productive," *Personnel Administrator* 29 (1984): 121–130.
10. A. C. Amason, W. A. Hochwarter, K. R. Thompson, and A. W. Harrison, "Conflict: An Important Dimension in Successful Management Teams," *Organizational Dynamics* 24 (1995): 25–35.
11. T. L. Simons and R. S. Peterson, "Task Conflict and Relationship Conflict in Top Management Teams: The Pivotal Role of Intergroup Trust," *Journal of Applied Psychology* 85 (2000): 102–111.
12. R. Nibler and K. L. Harris, "The Effects of Culture and Cohesiveness on Intragroup Conflict and Effectiveness," *The Journal of Social Psychology* 143 (2003): 613–631.
13. I. Janis, *Groupthink*, 2nd ed. (Boston: Houghton Mifflin, 1982).
14. J. D. Thompson, *Organizations in Action* (New York: McGraw-Hill, 1967).
15. G. Walker and L. Poppo, "Profit Centers, Single-Source Suppliers, and Transaction Costs," *Administrative Science Quarterly* 36 (1991): 66–87.
16. R. Miles, *Macro Organizational Behavior* (Glenview, Ill.: Scott, Foresman, 1980).
17. H. Levinson, "The Abrasive Personality," *Harvard Business Review* 56 (1978): 86–94.
18. J. C. Quick and J. D. Quick, *Organizational Stress and Preventive Management* (New York: McGraw-Hill, 1984).
19. F. N. Brady, "Aesthetic Components of Management Ethics," *Academy of Management Review* 11 (1986): 337–344.
20. J. R. Ogilvie and M. L. Carsky, "Building Emotional Intelligence in Negotiations," *The International Journal of Conflict Management* 13 (2002): 381–400.
21. A. M. Bodtker and R. L. Oliver, "Emotion in Conflict Formation and Its Transformation: Application to Organizational Conflict Management," *International Journal of Conflict Management* 12 (2001): 259–275.
22. D. E. Conlon and S. H. Hunt, "Dealing with Feeling: The Influence of Outcome Representations on Negotiation," *International Journal of Conflict Management* 13 (2002): 35–58.
23. V. K. Raizada, "Multi-Ethnic Corporations and Inter-Ethnic Conflict," *Human Resource Management* 20 (1981): 24–27; T. Cox, Jr., "The Multicultural Organization," *Academy of Management Executive* 5 (1991): 34–47.
24. G. Hofstede, *Culture's Consequences: International Differences in Work-related Values* (Beverly Hills, Calif.: Sage, 1980); G. Hofstede and M. H. Bond, "The Confucius Connection: From Cultural Roots to Economic Growth," *Organizational Dynamics* (Spring 1988): 4–21; G. Hofstede, "Cultural Constraints in Management Theories," *Academy of Management Executive* 7 (1993): 81–94.
25. T. H. Cox, S. A. Lobel, and P. L. McLead, "Effects of Ethnic Group Cultural Differences on Cooperative and Competitive Behavior in a Group Task," *Academy of Management Journal* 34 (1991): 827–847.
26. J. Schopler, C. A. Insko, J. Wieselquist, *et al.*, "When Groups Are More Competitive than Individuals: The Domain of the Discontinuity Effect," *Journal of Personality and Social Psychology* 80 (2001): 632–644.
27. M. Sherif and C. W. Sherif, *Social Psychology* (New York: Harper & Row, 1969).
28. C. Song, S. M. Sommer, and A. E. Hartman, "The Impact of Adding an External Rater on Interdepartmental Cooperative Behaviors of Workers," *International Journal of Conflict Management* 9 (1998): 117–138.
29. W. Tsai and S. Ghoshal, "Social Capital and Value Creation: The Role of Intrafirm Networks," *Academy of Management Journal* 41 (1998): 464–476.
30. M. A. Zarate, B. Garcia, A. A. Garza, and R. T. Hitlan, "Cultural Threat and Perceived Realistic Group Conflict as Dual Predictors of Prejudice," *Journal of Experimental Social Psychology* 40 (2004): 99–105.
31. J. C. Dencker, A. Joshi, and J. J. Martocchio, "Employee Benefits as Context for Intergenerational Conflict," *Human Resource Management Review* 17(2) (2007): 208–220.
32. M. L. Maznevski and K. M. Chudoba, "Bridging Space over Time: Global Virtual-Team Dynamics and Effectiveness," *Organization Science* 11 (2000): 473–492.
33. D. Katz and R. Kahn, *The Social Psychology of Organizations*, 2nd ed. (New York: Wiley, 1978).

34. D. L. Nelson and J. C. Quick, "Professional Women: Are Distress and Disease Inevitable?" *Academy of Management Review* 10 (1985): 206–218; D. L. Nelson and M. A. Hitt, "Employed Women and Stress: Implications for Enhancing Women's Mental Health in the Workplace," in J. C. Quick, J. Hurrell, and L. A. Murphy, eds., *Stress and Well-Being at Work: Assessments and Interventions for Occupational Mental Health* (Washington, D.C.: American Psychological Association, 1992).
35. M. G. Pratt and J. A. Rosa, "Transforming Work-Family Conflict into Commitment in Network Marketing Organizations," *Academy of Management Journal* 46 (2003): 395–418.
36. W. R. Boswell and J. B. Olson-Buchanan, "The Use of Communication Technologies After Hours: The Role of Work Attitudes and Work-Life Conflict," *Journal of Management* 33(4) (2007): 592–610.
37. R. L. Kahn, et al., *Organizational Stress: Studies in Role Conflict and Ambiguity* (New York: Wiley, 1964).
38. J. L. Badaracco, Jr., "The Discipline of Building Character," *Harvard Business Review* (March–April 1998): 115–124.
39. B. Schneider, "The People Make the Place," *Personnel Psychology* 40 (1987): 437–453.
40. C. A. O'Reilly, J. Chatman, and D. F. Caldwell, "People and Organizational Culture: A Profile Comparison Approach to Assessing Person-Organization Fit," *Academy of Management Journal* 34 (1991): 487–516.
41. I. Dayal and J. M. Thomas, "Operation KPE: Developing a New Organization," *Journal of Applied Behavioral Science* 4 (1968): 473–506.
42. R. H. Miles, "Role Requirements as Sources of Organizational Stress," *Journal of Applied Psychology* 61 (1976): 172–179.
43. W. F. G. Mastenbroek, *Conflict Management and Organization Development* (Chichester, England: Wiley, 1987).
44. M. R. Frone, "Interpersonal Conflict at Work and Psychological Outcomes: Testing a Model among Young Workers," *Journal of Occupational Health Psychology* 5 (2000): 246–255.
45. K. Thomas, "Conflict and Conflict Management," in M. D. Dunnette, ed., *Handbook of Industrial and Organizational Psychology* (New York: Wiley, 1976).
46. H. H. Meyer, E. Kay, and J. R. P. French, "Split Roles in Performance Appraisal," *Harvard Business Review* 43 (1965): 123–129.
47. T. W. Costello and S. S. Zalkind, *Psychology in Administration: A Research Orientation* (Englewood Cliffs, N.J.: Prentice-Hall, 1963).
48. Snapshot Spy, "Employee Computer & Internet Abuse Statistics," http://www.snapshotspy.com/employee-computer-abuse-statistics.htm; Data sources include U.S. Department of Commerce—Economics and Statistics Administration and the National Telecommunications and Information Administration—Greenfield and Rivet, "Employee Computer Abuse Statistics."
49. P. F. Hewlin, "And the Award for Best Actor Goes to . . . : Facades of Conformity in Organizational Settings," *Academy of Management Review* 28 (2003): 633–642.
50. C. A. Insko, J. Scholper, L. Gaertner, *et al.*, "Interindividual–Intergroup Discontinuity Reduction through the Anticipation of Future Interaction," *Journal of Personality and Social Psychology* 80 (2001): 95–111.
51. D. Tjosvold and M. Poon, "Dealing with Scarce Resources: Open-Minded Interaction for Resolving Budget Conflicts," *Group and Organization Management* 23 (1998): 237–255.
52. R. Miles, *Macro Organizational Behavior;* R. Steers, *Introduction to Organizational Behavior*, 4th ed. (Glenview, Ill.: Harper-Collins, 1991).
53. C. Morrill, M. N. Zold, and H. Rao, "Covert Political Conflict in Organizations: Challenges from Below," *Annual Review of Sociology* 29 (2003): 391–415.
54. A. Tyerman and C. Spencer, "A Critical Text of the Sherrif's Robber's Cave Experiments: Intergroup Competition and Cooperation between Groups of Well-Acquainted Individuals," *Small Group Behavior* 14 (1983): 515–531; R. M. Kramer, "Intergroup Relations and Organizational Dilemmas: The Role of Categorization Processes," in B. Staw and L. Cummings, eds., *Research in Organizational Behavior* 13 (Greenwich, Conn.: JAI Press, 1991), 191–228.
55. A. Carmeli, "The Relationship between Emotional Intelligence and Work Attitudes, Behavior and Outcomes: An Examination among Senior Managers," *Journal of Managerial Psychology* 18 (2003): 788–813.
56. R. Blake and J. Mouton, "Overcoming Group Warfare," *Harvard Business Review* 64 (1984): 98–108.
57. D. G. Ancona and D. Caldwell, "Improving the Performance of New Product Teams," *Research Technology Management* 33 (1990): 25–29.
58. M. A. Cronin and L. R. Weingart, "Representational Gaps, Information Processing, and Conflict in Functionally Diverse Teams," *Academy of Management Review* 32(3) (2007): 761–773.
59. C. K. W. DeDreu and L. R. Weingart, "Task versus Relationship Conflict, Team Performance, and Team Member Satisfaction: A Meta-Analysis," *Journal of Applied Psychology* 88 (2003): 741–749.
60. R. J. Lewicki, J. A. Litterer, J. W. Minton, and D. M. Saunders, *Negotiation*, 2nd ed. (Burr Ridge, Ill.: Irwin, 1994).
61. C. K. W. De Dreu, S. L. Koole, and W. Steinel, "Unfixing the Fixed Pie: A Motivated Information-Processing Approach to Integrative Negotiation," *Journal of Personality and Social Psychology* 79 (2000): 975–987.
62. M. H. Bazerman, J. R. Curhan, D. A. Moore, and K. L. Valley, "Negotiation," *Annual Review of Psychology* 51 (2000): 279–314.
63. I. Ayers and P. Siegelman, "Race and Gender Discrimination in Bargaining for a New Car," *American Economic Review* 85 (1995): 304–321.
64. L. J. Kray, L. Thompson, and A. Galinsky, "Battle of the Sexes: Gender Stereotype Confirmation and Reactance in Organizations," *Journal of Personality and Social Psychology* 80 (2001): 942–958.
65. K. W. Thomas, "Conflict and Conflict Management," in M. D. Dunnette, ed., *Handbook of Industrial and Organizational Psychology* (Chicago: Rand McNally, 1976), 900.
66. S. Steinberg, "Airbus Workers in France, Germany Strike against Massive Job Cuts" (March 1, 2007), http://www.wsws.org/articles/2007/mar2007/airb-m01.shtml.
67. C. K. W. De Dreu and A. E. M. Van Vianen, "Managing Relationship Conflict and the Effectiveness of Organizational Teams," *Journal of Organizational Behavior* 22 (2001): 309–328.
68. R. A. Baron, S. P. Fortin, R. L. Frei, L. A. Hauver, and M. L. Shack, "Reducing Organizational Conflict: The Role of Socially Induced Positive Affect," *International Journal of Conflict Management* 1 (1990): 133–152.
69. S. L. Phillips and R. L. Elledge, *The Team Building Source Book* (San Diego: University Associates, 1989).
70. Gladwin and Walter, "How Multinationals Can Manage," 228.
71. L. A. Dechurch, K. L. Hamilton, and C. Haas, "Effects of Conflict Management Strategies on Perceptions of Intragroup Conflict," *Group Dynamics: Theory, Research, and Practice* 11(1) (2007): 66–78.
72. K. W. Thomas, "Toward Multidimensional Values in Teaching: The Example of Conflict Behaviors," *Academy of Management Review* 2 (1977): 484–490.
73. S. Alper, D. Tjosvold, and K. S. Law, "Conflict Management, Efficacy, and Performance in Organizational Teams," *Personnel Psychology* 53 (2000): 625–642.
74. W. King and E. Miles, "What We Know and Don't Know about Measuring Conflict," *Management Communication Quarterly* 4 (1990): 222–243.
75. J. Barker, D. Tjosvold, and I. R. Andrews, "Conflict Approaches of Effective and Ineffective Project Managers: A Field Study in a Matrix Organization," *Journal of Management Studies* 25 (1988): 167–178.
76. M. Chan, "Intergroup Conflict and Conflict Management in the R&D Divisions of Four Aerospace Companies," *IEEE Transactions on Engineering Management* 36 (1989): 95–104.
77. M. K. Kozan, "Cultural Influences on Styles of Handling Interpersonal Conflicts: Comparisons among Jordanian, Turkish, and U.S. Managers," *Human Relations* 42 (1989): 787–799.
78. S. McKenna, "The Business Impact of Management Attitudes towards Dealing with Conflict: A Cross-Cultural Assessment," *Journal of Managerial Psychology* 10 (1995): 22–27.
79. Z. Ma, "Chinese Conflict Management Styles and Negotiation Behaviours: An Empirical Test," *International Journal of Cross Cultural Management* 7(1) (2007): 101–119.
80. Tjosvold, *The Conflict-Positive Organization.*
81. P. J. Frost, *Toxic Emotions at Work: How Compassionate Managers Handle Pain and Conflict* (Harvard Business School Press, 2003).

82. J. R. Ogilvie and M. L. Carsky, "Building Emotional Intelligence in Negotiations," *The International Journal of Conflict Management* 13 (2002): 381–400.
83. "Genentech's Medicine Man" *Business Week Online* (October 6, 2003), http://www.businessweek.com/magazine/content/03_40/b3852085.htm?chan=search.

Chapter 13 Case

1. R. Frank and E. Cheney, "Canadian Club: A Brewing Family Feud Poses Risks for Molson Beer Empire," *The Wall Street Journal*, Eastern edition (June 29, 2004): A1.
2. E. Cheney and R. Frank, "Molson Chairman Resists Calls for Ouster Amid a Family Feud," *The Wall Street Journal*, Eastern edition (June 23, 2004): B46; R. Frank and D. K. Berman, "Molson, Coors Talks Heat Up, but a Deal Faces Several Hurdles," *The Wall Street Journal*, Eastern edition (July 19, 2004): B2.
3. Frank and Berman, "Molson, Coors Talks Heat Up."
4. Frank and Cheney, "Canadian Club: A Brewing Family Feud Poses Risks"; Frank and Berman, "Molson, Coors Talks Heat Up."
5. Molson Press Release (2004) "Molson and Coors Announce Merger of Equals to Create World's Fifth Largest Brewer," http://micro.newswire.ca/release.cgi?rkey=1207225107&view=53454-0&Start=0 (accessed July 22, 2004).
6. D. Kesmodel, "Boss Talk: How 'Chief Beer Taster" Blended Molson, Coors," *The Wall Street Journal*, Eastern edition (October 1, 2007): B1; H. Landi, "Go Global, Think Local: With a Strong Foundation in North America, the World's Fifth Largest Brewer Is on the Move," *Beverage World* (July 2007): 46.
7. A. Holloway, "The Molson Way," *Canadian Business* 80(8) (April 9, 2007): 36.
8. Ibid.
9. Landi, "Go Global, Think Local."
10. Kesmodel, "Boss Talk: How 'Chief Beer Taster" Blended Molson, Coors."
11. Landi, "Go Global, Think Local."
12. Holloway, "The Molson Way," 46.
13. Landi, "Go Global, Think Local," 48.
14. Holloway, "The Molson Way," 36.
15. Landi, "Go Global, Think Local," 46.
16. A. Holloway, "Eric Molson," *Canadian Business* 80(11) (May 21, 2007): 94.
17. Landi, "Go Global, Think Local," 48.
18. D. Kesmodel and D. Ball, "Miller, Coors to Shake Up U.S. Beer Market," *The Wall Street Journal*, Online edition (October 10, 2007)" A1+.

Chapter 13 Cohesion Case: Part 3

1. "BP Global—About BP—Who We Are" (2007), BP PLC, http://www.bp.com/subsection.do?categoryId=4 &contentId=2006741 (accessed, August 19, 2007); "BP Global—About BP—BP" (2007), BP PLC, http://www.bp.com/genericarticle.do?categoryId=9 &contentId=2002350 (accessed, August 19, 2007).
2. J. Elkington, "John Browne," *Time* 163(17) (April 26, 2004): 73.
3. C. Cummins, C. Mollenkamp, A. O. Patrick, and G. Charzan, "Scandal, Crises Hasten Exit for British Icon; BP Chief's Tenure Was Increasingly Rocky; Then He Lied to Court; Hiding an Escort Service," *The Wall Street Journal* (Eastern Edition) (May 2, 2007): A1+, from ABI/Inform database (accessed August 17, 2007); S. Patton, "In Sync with His CEO; For Five Years, BP CIO John Leggate Has Managed People and IT Systems in Concert with His CEO's Acquisition-Hungry Strategy," *CIO* 17(1) (April 15, 2004): 1+, from ABI/Inform database (accessed August 17, 2007).
4. Patton, "In Sync with His CEO."
5. Cummins, Mollenkamp, et al., "Scandal, Crises Hasten Exit for British Icon."
6. Patton, "In Sync with His CEO."
7. Elkington, "John Browne."
8. S. Reed, "BP Takes It Slow and Steady," *Business Week Online* (February 7, 2007): 2 (accessed August 17, 2007).
9. Elkington, "John Browne."
10. Cummins, Mollenkamp, et al., "Scandal, Crises Hasten Exit for British Icon."
11. Elkington, "John Browne."
12. E. Armstrong, "A Decade of Sustainability," *The Engineer* (November 27–December 10, 2006): 16.
13. R. Crain, "BP Should Have Concentrated on Being a Better Oil Company," *Advertising Age* 77(34) (September 21, 2006): 14.
14. "Business: Paying the Price; BP," *The Economist* 382(8512) (January 20, 2007): 76, from ABI/Inform database (accessed August 17, 2007).
15. J. Lohan, "BP Blast Panel Blasts CEO," *ICIS Chemical Business* (January 22–28, 2007): 4.
16. N. Davis and S. Baumgarten, "BP: Waiting for the Shoe to Drop," *ICIS Chemical Business* (January 22–28, 2007): 4.
17. "Business: Paying the Price; BP."
18. Ibid.
19. Ibid.
20. S. Reed, "Refilling BP's Tank: New CEO Hayward Has Major Safety and Expansion Issues to Resolve," *Business Week* (July 23, 2007): 34–35.
21. N. Davis, "BP's New Chief Has a Tough Act to Follow," *ICIS Chemical Business* (May 14, 2007): 19.
22. Reed, "BP Takes It Slow and Steady."
23. Cummins, Mollenkamp, et al., "Scandal, Crises Hasten Exit for British Icon."
24. "Business: Paying the Price; BP."
25. Ibid.
26. Reed, "Refilling BP's Tank."

Chapter 14

1. L. Chappell, "Toyota to Send 30,000 Workers Back to Boot Camp," *Automotive News* (81)(6254) (May 7, 2007): 4.
2. G. W. England and I. Harpaz, "How Working Is Defined: National Contexts and Demographic and Organizational Role Influences," *Journal of Organizational Behavior* 11 (1990): 253–266.
3. L. R. Gomez-Mejia, "The Cross-Cultural Structure of Task-Related and Contextual Constructs," *Journal of Psychology* 120 (1986): 5–19.
4. A. Wrzesniewski and J. E. Dutton, "Crafting a Job: Revisioning Employees as Active Crafters of Their Work," *Academy of Management Review* 26 (2001): 179–201.
5. F. W. Taylor, *The Principles of Scientific Management* (New York: Norton, 1911).
6. T. Bell, *Out of This Furnace* (Pittsburgh: University of Pittsburgh Press, 1941).
7. P. Cappelli, "A Market-Driven Approach to Retaining Talent," *Harvard Business Review* 78 (2000): 103–111.
8. N. D. Warren, "Job Simplification versus Job Enlargement," *Journal of Industrial Engineering* 9 (1958): 435–439.
9. C. R. Walker, "The Problem of the Repetitive Job," *Harvard Business Review* 28 (1950): 54–58.
10. T. Moller, S. E. Mathiassen, H. Franzon, and S. Kihlberg, "Job Enlargement and Mechanical Exposure Variability in Cyclic Assembly Work," *Ergonomics* 47 (2004): 19–40.
11. C. R. Walker and R. H. Guest, *The Man on the Assembly Line* (Cambridge, Mass.: Harvard University Press, 1952).
12. M. A. Campion, L. Cheraskin, and M. J. Stevens, "Career-Related Antecedents and Outcomes of Job Rotation," *Academy of Management Journal* 37 (1994): 1518–1542.
13. E. Santora, "Keep Up Production Through Cross-Training," *Personnel Journal* (June 1992): 162–166.
14. R. P. Steel and J. R. Rentsch, "The Dispositional Model of Job Attitudes Revisited: Findings of a 10-Year Study," *Journal of Applied Psychology* 82 (1997): 873–879; C.-S. Wong, C. Hui, and K. S. Law, "A Longitudinal Study of the Job Perception–Job Satisfaction Relationship: A Text of the Three Alternative Specifications," *Journal of Occupational & Organizational Psychology* 71 (Part 2, 1998): 127–146.

15. F. Herzberg, "One More Time: How Do You Motivate Employees?" *Harvard Business Review* 46 (1968): 53–62.
16. R. N. Ford, "Job Enrichment Lessons from AT&T," *Harvard Business Review* 51 (1973): 96–106.
17. R. J. House and L. A. Wigdor, "Herzberg's Dual-Factor Theory of Job Satisfaction and Motivation: A Review of the Evidence and a Criticism," *Personnel Psychology* 20 (1967): 369–389.
18. A. N. Turner and P. R. Lawrence, *Industrial Jobs and the Worker* (Cambridge, Mass.: Harvard University Press, 1965).
19. J. R. Hackman and G. R. Oldham, "The Job Diagnostic Survey: An Instrument for the Diagnosis of Jobs and the Evaluation of Job Redesign Projects," *Technical Report No. 4* (New Haven, Conn.: Department of Administrative Sciences, Yale University, 1974).
20. J. R. Hackman and G. R. Oldham, "Development of the Job Diagnostic Survey," *Journal of Applied Psychology* 60 (1975): 159–170.
21. E. Sadler-Smith, G. El-Kot, and M. Leat, "Differentiating Work Autonomy Facets in a Non-Western Context," *Journal of Organizational Behavior* 24 (2003): 709–731.
22. P. H. Birnbaum, J. L. Farh, and G. Y. Y. Wong, "The Job Characteristics Model in Hong Kong," *Journal of Applied Psychology* 71 (1986): 598–605.
23. J. R. Hackman and G. R. Oldham, *Work Design* (Reading, Mass.: Addison-Wesley, 1980).
24. H. P. Sims, A. D. Szilagyi, and R. T. Keller, "The Measurement of Job Characteristics," *Academy of Management Journal* 19 (1976): 195–212.
25. H. P. Sims and A. D. Szilagyi, "Job Characteristic Relationships: Individual and Structural Moderators," *Organizational Behavior and Human Performance* 17 (1976): 211–230.
26. Y. Fried, "Meta-Analytic Comparison of the Job Diagnostic Survey and Job Characteristic Inventory as Correlates of Work Satisfaction and Performance," *Journal of Applied Psychology* 76 (1991): 690–698.
27. D. R. May, R. L. Gilson, and L. M. Harter, "The Psychological Conditions of Meaningfulness, Safety, and Availability and the Engagement of the Human Spirit at Work," *Journal of Occupational and Organizational Psychology* 77 (2004): 11–37.
28. R. Wagner, "Nourishing Employee Engagement," *Gallup Management Journal* (February 12, 2004): 1–7, http://gmj.gallup.com/content/default.asp?ci=10504.
29. J. Loehr and T. Schwartz, *The Power of Full Engagement: Managing Energy, Not Time, Is the Key to High Performance and Personal Renewal* (New York: Free Press, 2003).
30. M. F. R. Kets de Vries, "Creating Authentizotic Organizations: Well-Functioning Individuals in Vibrant Companies," *Human Relations* 54 (2001): 101–111.
31. G. R. Salancik and J. Pfeffer, "A Social Information Processing Approach to Job Attitudes and Task Design," *Administrative Science Quarterly* 23 (1978): 224–253.
32. J. Pfeffer, "Management as Symbolic Action: The Creation and Maintenance of Organizational Paradigms," in L. L. Cummings and B. M. Staw, eds., *Research in Organizational Behavior*, vol. 3 (Greenwich, Conn.: JAI Press, 1981), 1–52.
33. C. Clegg and C. Spencer, "A Circular and Dynamic Model of the Process of Job Design," *Journal of Occupational & Organizational Psychology* 80 (2007): 321–S339.
34. J. Thomas and R. Griffin, "The Social Information Processing Model of Task Design: A Review of the Literature," *Academy of Management Review* 8 (1983): 672–682.
35. D. J. Campbell, "Task Complexity: A Review and Analysis," *Academy of Management Review* 13 (1988): 40–52.
36. A. M. Grant, "Relational Job Design and the Motivation to Make a Prosocial Difference," *Academy of Management Review* 32 (2007): 393–417.
37. D. R. May, K. Reed, C. E. Schwoerer, and P. Potter, "Ergonomic Office Design and Aging: A Quasi-Experimental Field Study of Employee Reactions to an Ergonomics Intervention Program," *Journal of Occupational Health Psychology* 9 (2004): 123–135.
38. M. A. Campion and P. W. Thayer, "Job Design: Approaches, Outcomes, and Trade-Offs," *Organizational Dynamics* 16 (1987): 66–79.
39. J. Teresko, "Emerging Technologies," *Industry Week* (February 27, 1995): 1–2.
40. M. A. Campion and C. L. McClelland, "Interdisciplinary Examination of the Costs and Benefits of Enlarged Jobs: A Job Design Quasi-Experiment," *Journal of Applied Psychology* 76 (1991): 186–199.
41. B. Kohut, *Country Competitiveness: Organizing of Work* (New York: Oxford University Press, 1993).
42. J. C. Quick and L. E. Tetrick, eds., *Handbook of Occupational Health Psychology* (Washington, D.C.: American Psychological Association, 2002).
43. W. E. Deming, *Out of the Crisis* (Cambridge, Mass.: MIT Press, 1986).
44. L. Thurow, *Head to Head: The Coming Economic Battle among Japan, Europe, and America* (New York: Morrow, 1992).
45. M. A. Fruin, *The Japanese Enterprise System—Competitive Strategies and Cooperative Structures* (New York: Oxford University Press, 1992).
46. W. Niepce and E. Molleman, "Work Design Issue in Lean Production from a Sociotechnical System Perspective: Neo-Taylorism or the Next Step in Sociotechnical Design?" *Human Relations* 51 (1998): 259–287.
47. S. K. Parker, "Longitudinal Effects of Lean Production on Employee Outcomes and the Mediating Role of Work Characteristics," *Journal of Applied Psychology* 88 (2003): 620–634.
48. E. Furubotn, "Codetermination and the Modern Theory of the Firm: A Property-Rights Analysis," *Journal of Business* 61 (1988): 165–181.
49. H. Levinson, *Executive: The Guide to Responsive Management* (Cambridge, Mass.: Harvard University Press, 1981).
50. B. Gardell, "Scandinavian Research on Stress in Working Life" (Paper presented at the IRRA Symposium on Stress in Working Life, Denver, September 1980).
51. L. Levi, "Psychosocial, Occupational, Environmental, and Health Concepts; Research Results and Applications," in G. P. Keita and S. L. Sauter, eds., *Work and Well-Being: An Agenda for the 1990s* (Washington, D.C.: American Psychological Association, 1992), 199–211.
52. L. R. Murphy and C. L. Cooper, eds., *Healthy and Productive Work: An International Perspective* (London and New York: Taylor & Francis, 2000).
53. R. L. Kahn, *Work and Health* (New York: Wiley, 1981); M. Gowing, J. Kraft, and J. C. Quick, *The New Organizational Reality: Downsizing, Restructuring, and Revitalization* (Washington, D.C.: American Psychological Association, 1998).
54. F. J. Landy, "Work Design and Stress," in G. P. Keita and S. L. Sauter, eds., *Work and Well-Being: An Agenda for the 1990s* (Washington, D.C.: American Psychological Association, 1992), 119–158.
55. C. Gresov, R. Drazin, and A. H. Van de Ven, "Work-Unit Task Uncertainty, Design, and Morale," *Organizational Studies* 10 (1989): 45–62.
56. A. M. Grant, E. M. Campbell, G. Chen, K. Cottone, D. Lapedis, and K. Lee, "Impact and the Art of Motivation Maintenance: The Effects of Contact with Beneficiaries on Persistence Behavior," *Organizational Behavior and Human Decision Processes* 103 (2007): 53–67.
57. Y. Baruch, "The Status of Research on Teleworking and an Agenda for Future Research," *International Journal of Management Review* 3 (2000): 113–129.
58. K. E. Pearlson and C. S. Saunders, "There's No Place Like Home: Managing Telecommuting Paradoxes," *Academy of Management Executive* 15 (2001): 117–128.
59. S. Caudron, "Working at Home Pays Off," *Personnel Journal* (November 1992): 40–47.
60. D. S. Bailey and J. Foley, "Pacific Bell Works Long Distance," *HRMagazine* (August 1990): 50–52.
61. S. M. Pollan and M. Levine, "Asking for Flextime," *Working Women* (February 1994): 48.
62. S. A. Rogier and M. Y. Padgett, "The Impact of Utilizing a Flexible Work Schedule on the Perceived Career Advancement Potential of Women," *Human Resource Development Quarterly* 15 (2004): 89–106.
63. S. Zuboff, *In the Age of the Smart Machine: The Future of Work and Power* (New York: Basic Books, 1988).
64. B. A. Gutek and S. J. Winter, "Computer Use, Control over Computers, and Job Satisfaction," in S. Oskamp and S. Spacapan, eds., *People's Reactions to Technology in Factories, Offices, and Aerospace: The Claremont Symposium on Applied Social Psychology* (Newbury Park, Calif.: Sage, 1990), 121–144.
65. L. M. Schleifer and B. C. Amick III, "System Response Time and Method of Pay: Stress Effects in Computer-Based Tasks," *International Journal of Human-Computer Interaction* 1 (1989): 23–39.

66. K. Voight, "Virtual Work: Some Telecommuters Take Remote Work to the Extreme," *The Wall Street Journal Europe* (February 1, 2001): 1.
67. B. M. Staw and R. D. Boettger, "Task Revision: A Neglected Form of Work Performance," *Academy of Management Journal* 33 (1990): 534–559.
68. H. S. Schwartz, "Job Involvement as Obsession Compulsion," *Academy of Management Review* 7 (1982): 429–432.
69. C. J. Nemeth and B. M. Staw, "The Tradeoffs of Social Control and Innovation in Groups and Organizations," in L. Berkowitz, ed., *Advances in Experimental Social Psychology*, vol. 22 (New York: Academic Press, 1989), 175–210.
70. G. Salvendy, *Handbook of Industrial Engineering: Technology and Operations Management* (New York: John Wiley & Sons, 2001).
71. D. M. Herold, "Using Technology to Improve Our Management of Labor Market Trends," in M. Greller, ed., "Managing Careers with a Changing Workforce," *Journal of Organizational Change Management* 3 (1990): 44–57.
72. D. A. Whetten and K. S. Cameron, *Developing Management Skills*, 6th Edition (Upper Saddle River, N.J.: Prentice Hall, 2004).
73. "Toyota to Adopt Production Line Capable of Assembling 8 Models,: *Nikkei Report* (March 5, 2007).

Chapter 14 Case

1. "Careers—Who We Are," The Coca-Cola Company, http://www.thecoca-colacompany/careers/careers_who_we_are.html (accessed November 1, 2007).
2. "Our Company—Beliefs," The Coca-Cola Company, http://www.thecoca-colacompany/ourcompany/ourbeliefs.html (accessed November 1, 2007).
3. "Careers—Our Company, Your Career," The Coca-Cola Company, http://www.thecoca-colacompany/careers/index.html (accessed November 1, 2007).
4. "Careers—Meet Our People," The Coca-Cola Company, http://www.thecoca-colacompany/careers/meet_our_people.html (accessed November 1, 2007).
5. "Careers—Our Company, Your Career."
6. "Careers—Meet Our People," The Coca-Cola Company, "Hector, Supply Chain General Management," http://www.thecoca-colacompany/careers/meet_our_people_hector.html (accessed November 1, 2007).
7. "Careers—Meet Our People," The Coca-Cola Company, "Joycelyn, Brand Management," http://www.thecoca-colacompany/careers/meet_our_people_ joycelyn.html (accessed November 1, 2007).
8. "Careers—Meet Our People," The Coca-Cola Company, "Mary Page, Strategic Planning," http://www.thecoca-colacompany/careers/meet_our_people_mary.html (accessed November 1, 2007).
9. "Careers—Meet Our People," The Coca-Cola Company, "Rebecca, Global Marketing," http://www.thecoca-colacompany/careers/meet_our_people_rebecca_gm.html (accessed November 1, 2007).
10. Careers—Meet Our People," The Coca-Cola Company, "Tor, Sales Director," http://www.thecoca-colacompany/careers/meet_our_people_ tor.html (accessed November 1, 2007).
11. "Careers—Meet Our People," The Coca-Cola Company, "Tania, Information Technology General Management," http://www.thecoca-colacompany/careers/meet_our_people_ tania.html (accessed November 1, 2007).
12. "Careers—Meet Our People," The Coca-Cola Company, "Vikram, Strategic Growth," http://www.thecoca-colacompany/careers/meet_our_people_ vikram.html (accessed November 1, 2007).

Chapter 15

1. Timberland Company, *2006 Annual Report* (August 3, 2007), http://thomson.mobular.net/thomson/7/2467/2741.
2. J. Child, *Organization* (New York: Harper & Row, 1984).
3. P. Lawrence and J. Lorsch, "Differentiation and Integration in Complex Organizations," *Administrative Science Quarterly* 12 (1967): 1–47.
4. P. Lawrence and J. Lorsch, *Organization and Environment: Managing Differentiation and Integration*, rev. ed. (Cambridge, Mass.: Harvard University Press, 1986).
5. J. Hage, "An Axiomatic Theory of Organizations," *Administrative Science Quarterly* 10 (1965): 289–320.
6. W. Ouchi and J. Dowling, "Defining the Span of Control," *Administrative Science Quarterly* 19 (1974): 357–365.
7. L. Porter and E. Lawler, III, "Properties of Organization Structure in Relation to Job Attitudes and Job Behavior," *Psychological Bulletin* 65 (1965): 23–51.
8. J. Ivancevich and J. Donnelly, Jr., "Relation of Organization and Structure to Job Satisfaction, Anxiety-Stress, and Performance," *Administrative Science Quarterly* 20 (1975): 272–280.
9. R. Dewar and J. Hage, "Size, Technology, Complexity, and Structural Differentiation: Toward a Theoretical Synthesis," *Administrative Science Quarterly* 23 (1978): 111–136.
10. Lawrence and Lorsch, "Differentiation and Integration," 1–47.
11. J. R. R. Galbraith, *Designing Complex Organizations* (Reading, Mass.: Addison-Wesley-Longman, 1973).
12. W. Altier, "Task Forces: An Effective Management Tool," *Management Review* 76 (1987): 26–32.
13. P. Lawrence and J. Lorsch, "New Managerial Job: The Integrator," *Harvard Business Review* 45 (1967): 142–151.
14. J. Lorsch and P. Lawrence, "Organizing for Product Innovation," *Harvard Business Review* 43 (1965): 110–111.
15. D. Pugh, D. Hickson, C. Hinnings, and C. Turner, "Dimensions of Organization Structure," *Administrative Science Quarterly* 13 (1968): 65–91; B. Reimann, "Dimensions of Structure in Effective Organizations: Some Empirical Evidence," *Academy of Management Journal* 17 (1974): 693–708; S. Robbins, *Organization Theory: The Structure and Design of Organizations*, 3rd ed. (Englewood Cliffs, N.J.: Prentice-Hall, 1990).
16. H. Mintzberg, *The Structuring of Organizations* (Englewood Cliffs, N.J.: Prentice-Hall, 1979).
17. J. A. Kuprenas, "Implementation and Performance of a Matrix Organization Structure," *International Journal of Project Management* 21 (2003): 51–62.
18. Mintzberg, *Structuring of Organizations*.
19. K. Weick, "Educational Institutions as Loosely Coupled Systems," *Administrative Science Quarterly* (1976): 1–19.
20. D. Miller and C. Droge, "Psychological and Traditional Determinants of Structure," *Administrative Science Quarterly* 31 (1986): 540; H. Tosi, Jr., and J. Slocum, Jr., "Contingency Theory: Some Suggested Directions," *Journal of Management* 10 (1984): 9–26.
21. C. B. Clott, "Perspectives on Global Outsourcing and the Changing Nature of Work," *Business and Society Review* 109 (2004): 153–170.
22. P. Puranam, H. Singh, and M. Zollo, "Organizing for Innovation: Managing the Coordination-Automomy Dilemma in Technology Acquisitions," *Academy of Management Journal* 49 (2006): 263–280.
23. D. Mack and J. C. Quick, "EDS: An Inside View of a Corporate Life Cycle Transition," *Organizational Dynamics* 30 (2002): 282–293.
24. M. Meyer, "Size and the Structure of Organizations: A Causal Analysis," *American Sociological Review* 37 (1972): 434–441; J. Beyer and H. Trice, "A Reexamination of the Relations between Size and Various Components of Organizational Complexity," *Administrative Science Quarterly* 24 (1979): 48–64; B. Mayhew, R. Levinger, J. McPherson, and T. James, "Systems Size and Structural Differentiation in Formal Organizations: A Baseline Generator for Two Major Theoretical Propositions," *American Sociological Review* 37 (1972): 26–43.
25. M. Gowing, J. Kraft, and J. C. Quick, *The New Organizational Reality: Downsizing, Restructuring, and Revitalization* (Washington, D.C.: American Psychological Association, 1998).
26. Amy J. Hillman and Albert A. Cannella Jr., "Organizational Predictors of Women on Corporate Boards," *Academy of Management Journal* 50 (2007): 941–952.
27. B. A. Pasternack and A. J. Viscio, *The Centerless Corporation: A New Model for Transforming Your Organization for Growth and Prosperity* (New York: Simon & Schuster, 1999).

28. J. Woodward, *Industrial Organization: Theory and Practices* (London: Oxford University Press, 1965).
29. C. Perrow, "A Framework for the Comparative Analysis of Organizations," *American Sociological Review* 32 (1967): 194–208; D. Rosseau, "Assessment of Technology in Organizations: Closed versus Open Systems Approaches," *Academy of Management Review* 4 (1979): 531–542.
30. Perrow, "A Framework for the Comparative Analysis of Organizations," 194–208.
31. J. D. Thompson, *Organizations in Action* (New York: McGraw-Hill, 1967).
32. P. Nemetz and L. Fry, "Flexible Manufacturing Organizations: Implication for Strategy Formulation and Organization Design," *Academy of Management Review* 13 (1988): 627–638; G. Huber, "The Nature and Design of Post-Industrial Organizations," *Management Science* 30 (1984): 934.
33. E. Feitzinger and H. L. Lee, "Mass Customization at Hewlett-Packard: The Power of Postponement," *Harvard Business Review* 75 (1997): 116–121.
34. S. M. Davis, *Future Perfect* (Reading, Mass.: Addison-Wesley, 1987).
35. J. R. Baum and S. Wally, "Strategic Decision Speed and Firm Performance," *Strategic Management Journal* 24 (2003): 1107–1129.
36. Thompson, *Organizations in Action*.
37. H. Downey, D. Hellriegel, and J. Slocum, Jr., "Environmental Uncertainty: The Construct and Its Application," *Administrative Science Quarterly* 20 (1975): 613–629.
38. G. Vroom, "Organizational Design and the Intensity of Rivalry," *Management Science* 52 (2006): 1689–1702.
39. S. Faraj and Y. Xiao, "Coordination in Fast-Response Organizations," *Management Science* 52 (2006): 1155–1169.
40. T. Burns and G. Stalker, *The Management of Innovation* (London: Tavistock, 1961); Mintzberg, *Structuring of Organizations*.
41. M. Chandler and L. Sayles, *Managing Large Systems* (New York: Harper & Row, 1971).
42. G. Dess and D. Beard, "Dimensions of Organizational Task Environments," *Administrative Science Quarterly* 29 (1984): 52–73.
43. J. Courtright, G. Fairhurst, and L. Rogers, "Interaction Patterns in Organic and Mechanistic Systems," *Academy of Management Journal* 32 (1989): 773–802.
44. R. Daft, *Organization Theory and Design*, 7th ed. (Mason, OH: South-Western/Thomson Learning, 2000).
45. D. Miller, "The Structural and Environmental Correlates of Business Strategy," *Strategic Management Journal* 8 (1987): 55–76.
46. R. S. Kaplan and D. P. Norton, "How to Implement a New Strategy without Disrupting Your Organization," *Harvard Business Review* (March 2006): 100–109.
47. W. R. Scott, *Organizations: Rational, Natural, and Open Systems*, 4th ed. (Upper Saddle River, N.J.: Prentice-Hall, 1997).
48. D. Miller and P. Friesen, "A Longitudinal Study of the Corporate Life Cycle," *Management Science* 30 (1984): 1161–1183.
49. M. H. Overholt, "Flexible Organizations: Using Organizational Design as a Competitive Advantage," *Human Resource Planning* 20 (1997): 22–32; P. W. Roberts and R. Greenwood, "Integrating Transaction Cost and Institutional Theories: Toward a Constrained-Efficiency Framework for Understanding Organizational Design Adoption," *Academy of Management Review* 22 (1997): 346–373.
50. C. W. L. Hill and G. R. Jones, *Strategic Management Theory*, 5th ed. (Boston: Houghton Mifflin, 2000).
51. Daft, *Organization Theory and Design*.
52. C. M. Savage, *5th Generation Management, Revised Edition: Co-creating through Virtual Enterprising, Dynamic Teaming, and Knowledge Networking* (Boston: Butterworth-Heinemann, 1996).
53. S. M. Davis, *Future Perfect* (Perseus Publishing, 1997).
54. A. Boynton and B. Victor, "Beyond Flexibility: Building and Managing a Dynamically Stable Organization," *California Management Review* 8 (Fall 1991): 53–66.
55. P. J. Brews and C. L. Tucci, "Exploring the Structural Effects of Internetworking," *Strategic Management Journal* 25 (2004): 429–451.
56. J. Fulk, "Global Network Organizations: Emergence and Future Prospects," *Human Relations* 54 (2001): 91–100.
57. The use of the theatrical troupe as an analogy for virtual organizations was first used by David Mack, circa 1995.
58. E. C. Kasper-Fuehrer and N. M. Ashkanasy, "Communicating Trustworthiness and Building Trust in Interorganizational Virtual Organizations," *Journal of Management* 27 (2001): 235–254.
59. R. Teerlink and L. Ozley, *More than a Motorcycle: The Leadership Journey at Harley-Davidson* (Boston: Harvard Business School Press, 2000).
60. W. A. Cohen and N. Cohen, *The Paranoid Organization and 8 Other Ways Your Company Can Be Crazy: Advice from an Organizational Shrink* (New York: American Management Association, 1993).
61. P. E. Tetlock, "Cognitive Biases and Organizational Correctives: Do Both Disease and Cure Depend on the Politics of the Beholder?" *Administrative Science Quarterly* 45 (2000): 293–326.
62. M. F. R. Kets de Vries and D. Miller, "Personality, Culture, and Organization," *Academy of Management Review* 11 (1986): 266–279.
63. "Timberland Announces the Appointment of Four Category Presidents," About Us, http://www.timberland.com/corp.

Chapter 15 Case

1. G. B. Friesen, "Organization Design for the 21st Century," *Consulting to Management* 16(3) (September 2005): 32+, from ABI/INFORM Research database (accessed November 1, 2007).
2. Ibid.
3. "Administrator Unveils Next Steps of NASA Transformation," *Goddard News* 1(7) (July 2005): 1.
4. Ibid.
5. Ibid.
6. T. N. Carroll, T. J. Gormley, V. J. Bilardo, R. M. Burton, and K. L. Woodman, "Designing a New Organization at NASA: An Organization Design Process Using Simulation," *Organization Science* 17(2): 202, from ABI/INFORM Research database (accessed November 1, 2007).
7. Ibid
8. Ibid.
9. Ibid.
10. Ibid.
11. Ibid.

Chapter 16

1. Caribou Corporate Web site. http://www.cariboucoffee.com/aboutus/.
2. G. Flight, "Grinding out Success Next to Starbucks," *Business 2.0* (March 15, 2007), http://money.cnn.com/magazines/business2/business2_archive/2006/10/01/8387114/index.htm
3. T. E. Deal and A. A. Kennedy, *Corporate Cultures* (Reading, Mass.: Addison-Wesley, 1982).
4. W. Ouchi, *Theory Z* (Reading, Mass.: Addison-Wesley, 1981).
5. T. J. Peters and R. H. Waterman, *In Search of Excellence* (New York: Harper & Row, 1982).
6. M. Gardner, "Creating a Corporate Culture for the Eighties," *Business Horizons* (January–February 1985): 59–63.
7. Definition adapted from E. H. Schein, *Organizational Culture and Leadership* (San Francisco: Jossey-Bass, 1985), 9.
8. C. D. Sutton and D. L. Nelson, "Elements of the Cultural Network: The Communicators of Corporate Values," *Leadership and Organization Development* 11 (1990): 3–10.
9. http://www.google.com/corporate/culture.html.
10. J. Pagel, "Eskimo Joe's Getting Older, But Still Fun at 21," *Amarillo Business Journal* (November 20, 1996), http://www.businessjournal.net/entrepreneur1196.html.
11. A. Bandura, *Social Learning Theory* (Englewood Cliffs, N.J.: Prentice-Hall, 1977).

12. J. A. Chatman, "Leading by Leveraging Culture," *California Management Review* 45 (2003): 20–34.
13. J. M. Beyer and H. M. Trice, "How an Organization's Rites Reveal Its Culture," *Organizational Dynamics* 16 (1987): 5–24.
14. H. M. Trice and J. M. Beyer, "Studying Organizational Cultures through Rites and Ceremonials," *Academy of Management Review* 9 (1984): 653–669.
15. "Voices from Berkshire's Annual Meeting," *Business Week* (May 8, 2007), http://www.businessweek.com/bwdaily/dnflash/content/may2007/db20070507_344372.htm?chan=search.
16. H. Levinson and S. Rosenthal, *CEO: Corporate Leadership in Action* (New York: Basic Books, 1984).
17. V. Sathe, "Implications of Corporate Culture: A Manager's Guide to Action," *Organizational Dynamics* 12 (1987): 5–23.
18. "Wal-Mart Culture Stories—The Sundown Rule," http://www.walmartchina.com/english/walmart/rule/sun.htm.
19. J. Martin, M. S. Feldman, M. J. Hatch, and S. B. Sitkin, "The Uniqueness Paradox in Organizational Stories," *Administrative Science Quarterly* 28 (1983): 438–453.
20. http://news-service.stanford.edu/news/2005/june15/jobs-061505.html.
21. B. Durrance, "Stories at Work," *Training and Development* (February 1997): 25–29.
22. B. Siuru, "2003 Saturn L Series," http://www.autowire.net/2002-40.html.
23. R. Goffee and G. Jones, "What Holds the Modern Company Together?" *Harvard Business Review* (November–December 1996): 133–143.
24. C. Argyris and D. A. Schon, *Organizational Learning* (Reading, Mass.: Addison-Wesley, 1978).
25. L. Hoeber, "Exploring the Gaps between Meanings and Practices of Gender Equity in a Sport Organization," *Gender Work and Organization* 14(3) (2007): 259–280.
26. D. J. McAllister and G. A. Bigley, "Work Context and the Definition of Self: How Organizational Care Influences Organization-Based Self-Esteem," *Academy of Management Journal* 45 (2002): 894–905.
27. "Sounds Like a New Woman," *New Woman* (February 1993): 144.
28. M. Peterson, "Work, Corporate Culture, and Stress: Implications for Worksite Health Promotion," *American Journal of Health Behavior* 21 (1997): 243–252.
29. R. Targos, "Big Bad Hog—Harley-Davidson Customer Service," *Child Care Business*, http://www.childcarebusiness.com/articles/161cover.html.
30. J. Rosenthal and M. A. Masarech, "High-Performance Cultures: How Values Can Drive Business Results," *Journal of Organizational Excellence* (Spring 2003): 3–18.
31. "Earthlink—Core Values and Beliefs," http://www.earthlink.net/about/cvb.
32. L. Smircich, "Concepts of Culture and Organizational Analysis," *Administrative Science Quarterly* (1983): 339–358.
33. Y. Weiner and Y. Vardi, "Relationships between Organizational Culture and Individual Motivation: A Conceptual Integration," *Psychological Reports* 67 (1990): 295–306.
34. M. R. Louis, "Surprise and Sense Making: What Newcomers Experience in Entering Unfamiliar Organizational Settings," *Administrative Science Quarterly* 25 (1980): 209–264.
35. D. Ravasi and M. Schultz, "Responding to Organizational Identity Threats: Exploring the Role of Organizational Culture," *Academy of Management Journal*,49(3) (2006): 433–458.
36. http://www.mcdonalds.com/corp/about/mcd_history_pg1.html.
37. T. L. Doolen, M. E. Hacker, and E. M. van Aken, "The Impact of Organizational Context on Work Team Effectiveness: A Study of Production Teams," *IEEE Transactions on Engineering Management* 50 (2003): 285–296.
38. D. D. Van Fleet and R. W. Griffin, "Dysfunctional Organization Culture: The Role of Leadership in Motivating Dysfunctional Work Behaviors," *Journal of Managerial Psychology* 21(8) (2006): 698–708.
39. P. Bamberger and M. Biron, "Group Norms and Excessive Absenteeism: The Role of Peer Referent Others," *Organizational Behavior and Human Decision Processes* 103(2) (2007): 179–196.
40. J. P. Kotter and J. L. Heskett, *Corporate Culture and Performance* (New York: Free Press, 1992).
41. Deal and Kennedy, *Corporate Cultures*.
42. D. R. Katz, *The Big Store* (New York: Viking, 1987).
43. G. G. Gordon, "Industry Determinants of Organizational Culture," *Academy of Management Review* 16 (1991): 396–415.
44. G. Donaldson and J. Lorsch, *Decision Making at the Top* (New York: Basic Books, 1983).
45. R. H. Kilman, M. J. Saxton, and R. Serpa, eds., *Gaining Control of the Corporate Culture* (San Francisco: Jossey-Bass, 1986).
46. J. P. Kotter, *A Force for Change: How Leadership Differs from Management* (New York: Free Press, 1990); R. M. Kanter, *The Change Masters* (New York: Simon & Schuster, 1983).
47. T. Peters and N. Austin, *A Passion for Excellence: The Leadership Difference* (New York: Random House, 1985).
48. Schein, *Organizational Culture and Leadership*.
49. R. R. Sims and J. Brinkmann, "Enron Ethics (or Culture Matters More than Codes)," *Journal of Business Ethics* 45 (2003): 243–256.
50. M. H. Kavanagh and N. M. Ashkanasy, "The Impact of Leadership and Change Management Strategy on Organizational Culture and Individual Acceptance of Change during a Merger," *British Journal of Management Supplement* 17(1) (2006): S81–S103.
51. J. A. Pearce II, T. R. Kramer, and D. K. Robbins, "Effects of Managers' Entrepreneurial Behavior on Subordinates," *Journal of Business Venturing* 12 (1997): 147–160.
52. P. W. Braddy, A. W. Meade, and C. M. Kroustalis, "Organizational Recruitment Website Effects on Viewers' Perceptions of Organizational Culture," *Journal of Business and Psychology* 20(4) (2006): 525–543.
53. http://money.cnn.com/magazines/fortune/fortune_archive/2006/01/23/8366992/index.htm.
54. A. Xenikou and M. Simosi, "Organizational Culture and Transformational Leadership as Predictors of Business Unit Performance," *Journal of Managerial Psychology* 21(6) (2006): 566–579.
55. D. C. Feldman, "The Multiple Socialization of Organization Members," *Academy of Management Review* 6 (1981): 309–318.
56. R. Pascale, "The Paradox of Corporate Culture: Reconciling Ourselves to Socialization," *California Management Review* 27 (1985): 26–41.
57. D. L. Nelson, "Organizational Socialization: A Stress Perspective," *Journal of Occupational Behavior* 8 (1987): 311–324.
58. D. M. Cable, L. Aiman-Smith, P. W. Mulvey, and J. R. Edwards, "The Sources and Accuracy of Job Applicants' Beliefs about Organizational Culture," *Academy of Management Journal* 43 (2000): 1076–1085.
59. J. Chatman, "Matching People and Organizations: Selection and Socialization in Public Accounting Firms," *Administrative Science Quarterly* 36 (1991): 459–484.
60. D. L. Nelson, J. C. Quick, and M. E. Eakin, "A Longitudinal Study of Newcomer Role Adjustment in U.S. Organizations," *Work and Stress* 2 (1988): 239–253.
61. N. J. Allen and J. P. Meyer, "Organizational Socialization Tactics: A Longitudinal Analysis of Links to Newcomers' Commitment and Role Orientation," *Academy of Management Journal* 33 (1990): 847–858.
62. T. N. Bauer, E. W. Morrison, and R. R. Callister, "Organizational Socialization: A Review and Directions for Future Research," *Research in Personnel and Human Resources Management* 16 (1998): 149–214.
63. D. M. Cable and C. K. Parsons, "Socialization Tactics and Person–Organization Fit," *Personnel Psychology* 54 (2001): 1–23.
64. M. R. Louis, "Acculturation in the Workplace: Newcomers as Lay Ethnographers," in B. Schneider, ed., *Organizational Climate and Culture* (San Francisco: Jossey-Bass, 1990), 85–129.
65. D. M. Rousseau, "Assessing Organizational Culture: The Case for Multiple Methods," in B. Schneider, ed., *Organizational Climate and Culture* (San Francisco: Jossey-Bass, 1990).
66. R. A. Cooke and D. M. Rousseau, "Behavioral Norms and Expectations: A Quantitative Approach to the Assessment of Organizational Culture," *Group and Organizational Studies* 12 (1988): 245–273.
67. R. H. Kilmann and M. J. Saxton, *Kilmann-Saxton Culture-Gap Survey* (Pittsburgh: Organizational Design Consultants, 1983).
68. W. J. Duncan, "Organizational Culture: 'Getting a Fix' on an Elusive Concept," *Academy of Management Executive* 3 (1989): 229–236.

69. C. Yang, "Merger of Titans, Clash of Cultures," *BusinessWeek Online* (July 14, 2003), http://www.businessweek.com/magazine/content/03_8/b3841042_mz005.htm.
70. R. A. Weber and C. F. Camerer, "Cultural Conflict and Merger Failure: An Experimental Approach," *Management Science* 49 (2003): 400–415.
71. S. Buchheit, W. R. Pasewark, and J. R. Strawser, "No Need to Compromise: Evidence of Public Accounting's Changing Culture Regarding Budgetary Performance," *Journal of Business Ethics* 42 (2003): 151–163.
72. N. J. Adler, *International Dimensions of Organizational Behavior*, 2nd ed. (Boston: PWS Kent, 1991).
73. A. Laurent, "The Cultural Diversity of Western Conceptions of Management," *International Studies of Management and Organization* 13 (1983): 75–96.
74. P. C. Earley and E. Mosakowski, "Creating Hybrid Team Cultures: An Empirical Test of Transnational Team Functioning," *Academy of Management Journal* 43 (2000): 26–49.
75. P. Bate, "Using the Culture Concept in an Organization Development Setting," *Journal of Applied Behavior Science* 26 (1990): 83–106.
76. K. R. Thompson and F. Luthans, "Organizational Culture: A Behavioral Perspective," in B. Schneider, ed., *Organizational Climate and Culture* (San Francisco: Jossey-Bass, 1990).
77. S. Seren and U. Baykal, "Relationships between Change and Organizational Culture in Hospitals," *Journal of Nursing Scholarship* 39(2) (2007): 191–197.
78. V. Sathe, "How to Decipher and Change Corporate Culture," in R. H. Kilman et al., *Managing Corporate Cultures* (San Francisco: Jossey-Bass, 1985).
79. M. E. Johnson-Cramer, S. Parise, and R. L. Cross, "Managing Change through Networks and Values," *California Management Review* 49(3) (2007): 85–109.
80. J. B. Shaw, C. D. Fisher, and W. A. Randolph, "From Maternalism to Accountability: The Changing Cultures of Ma Bell and Mother Russia," *Academy of Management Executive* 5 (1991): 7–20.
81. D. Lei, J. W. Slocum, Jr., and R. W. Slater, "Global Strategy and Reward Systems: The Key Roles of Management Development and Corporate Culture," *Organizational Dynamics* 19 (1990): 27–41.
82. S. H. Rhinesmith, "Going Global from the Inside Out," *Training and Development Journal* 45 (1991): 42–47.
83. A. Pater and A. van Gils, "Stimulating Ethical Decision Making in a Business Context: Ethics of Ethical and Professional Codes," *European Management Journal* 21 (December 2003): 762–772.
84. L. K. Trevino and K. A. Nelson, *Managing Business Ethics: Straight Talk about How to Do It Right* (New York: John Wiley & Sons, 1995).
85. A. Bhide and H. H. Stevenson, "Why Be Honest if Honesty Doesn't Pay?" *Harvard Business Review* (September–October 1990): 121–129.
86. C. Driscoll and M. McKee, "Restoring a Culture of Ethical and Spiritual Values: A Role for Leader Storytelling," *Journal of Business Ethics* 73(2) (2007): 205–217.
87. C. Gallo, "How Cisco's CEO Works the Crowd," *Business Week* (October, 11, 2006), http://www.businessweek.com/smallbiz/content/oct2006/sb20061011_917113.htm?campaign_id=nws_insdr_oct13&link_position=link15.
88. "Business Ethics Names 100 Best Corporate Citizens," *Business Ethics* (Spring 2004), http://www.business-ethics.com/100best.htm.
89. S. W. Gellerman, "Why Good Managers Make Bad Ethical Choices," *Harvard Business Review* 64 (1986): 85–90.
90. J. R. Detert, R. G. Schroeder, and J. J. Mauriel, "A Framework for Linking Culture and Improvement Initiatives in Organizations," *Academy of Management Review* 25 (2000): 850–863.
91. P. Panchak, "Executive Word—Manufacturing in the U.S. Pays Off," *Industry Week* (December 1, 2002), http://www.industryweek.com / CurrentArticles/Asp/articles.asp?ArticleId=1365.
92. A. Bernstein, "Low-Skilled Jobs: Do They Have to Move?" *Business Week* (February 26, 2001): 92.
93. R. Bruce, "A Case Study of Harley-Davidson's Business Practices," http://stroked.virtualave.net/casestudy.shtml.
94. T. A. Williams, "Do You Believe in Baldrige?" *Quality Magazine* 43 (2004): 6.
95. Caribou Corporate Web site, "Rainforest Alliance Bestows Corporate Green Globe Award to Caribou Coffee," http://www.cariboucoffee.com/aboutus/pressroom.asp.
96. http://www.cariboucoffee.com/aboutus/socialresponsibility.asp.

Chapter 16 Case

1. "Special Report: The Car Company in Front—Toyota," *The Economist* 374(8411) (January 29, 2005): 73, from ABI/INFORM Research database (accessed October 22 2007).
2. Ibid.
3. "Toyota Up Close," Toyota, http://www.toyota.co.jp/en/about_toyota/outline/index.html (accessed October 26, 2007).
4. "Survey: Inculcating Culture," *The Economist* 378(8461) (January 21, 2006): 13, from ABI/INFORM Research database (accessed October, 22 2007).
5. "Special Report: The Car Company in Front—Toyota."
6. Ibid.
7. "Survey: Inculcating Culture,"
8. "Special Report: The Car Company in Front—Toyota."
9. S. Cook, S. Macaulay, and Coldicott, "Facing the Devil in the Detail," *Training Journal* (October 2005): 32, from ABI/INFORM Research database (accessed October 11, 2007).
10. N. Shirouzu, "Paranoid Tendency: As Rivals Catch Up, Toyota CEO Spurs Big Efficiency Drive; Culture of Institutional Worry Drives Mr. Watanabe; How Paint Is Like 'Fondue'; Finding Limits to Improvement," *The Wall Street Journal*, Eastern edition (December 9, 2006): A1+, from ABI/INFORM Research database (accessed October 22, 2007).
11. Ibid.
12. Ibid.
13. "Special Report: The Car Company in Front—Toyota."
14. "Paranoid Tendency: As Rivals Catch Up."

Chapter 17

1. A. Lashinsky, "Life Inside Google," *Fortune*, http://money.cnn.com/galleries/2007/fortune/0701/gallery.Google_life/index.html.
2. "Google's Gourmet Food," *Fortune*, http://money.cnn.com/galleries/2007/fortune/0701/gallery.Google_food/index.html.
3. http://money.cnn.com/magazines/fortune/bestcompanies/2007/pay/.
4. J. H. Greenhaus, *Career Management* (Hinsdale, Ill.: CBS College Press, 1987).
5. D. T. Hall, *Careers in Organizations* (Pacific Palisades, Calif.: Goodyear, 1976).
6. J. H. Greenhaus, *Career Management;* T. G. Gutteridge and F. L. Otte, "Organizational Career Development: What's Going On Out There?" *Training and Development Journal* 37 (1983): 22–26.
7. M. B. Arthur, P. H. Claman, and R. J. DeFillippi, "Intelligent Enterprise, Intelligent Careers," *Academy of Management Executive* (November 1995): 7–22.
8. M. Lips-Wiersma and D. T. Hall, "Organizational Career Development Is Not Dead: A Case Study on Managing the New Career During Organizational Change," *Journal of Organizational Behavior* 28(6) (2007): 771–792.
9. D. Jemielniak, "Managers as Lazy, Stupid Careerists?" *Journal of Organizational Change Management* 20(4) (2007): 491–508.
10. T. Lee, "Should You Stay Energized by Changing Jobs Frequently?" *CareerJournal* (January 11, 1998), http://www.careerjournal.com/jobhunting/strategies/19980111-reisberg.html.

11. P. Buhler, "Managing in the '90s," *Supervision* (July 1995): 24–26.
12. D. T. Hall and J. E. Moss, "The New Protean Career Contract: Helping Organizations and Employees Adapt," *Organizational Dynamics* (Winter 1998): 22–37.
13. S. A. Zahra, R. L. Priem, and A. A. Rasheed, "Understanding the Causes and Effects of Top Management Fraud," *Organizational Dynamics* 36(2) (2007): 122–139.
14. A. Fisher, "Don't Blow Your New Job," *Fortune* (June 22, 1998): 159–162.
15. D. Goleman, *Working with Emotional Intelligence* (New York: Bantam, 1998).
16. A. Fisher, "Success Secret: A High Emotional IQ," *Fortune* (October 26, 1998): 293–298.
17. M. L. Maynard, "Emotional Intelligence and Perceived Employability for Internship Curriculum," *Psychological Reports* 93 (December 2003): 791–792.
18. K. V. Petrides, A. Furnham, and G. N. Martin, "Estimates of Emotional and Psychometric Intelligence," *Journal of Social Psychology* 144 (April 2004): 149–162.
19. C. Stough and D. de Guara, "Examining the Relationship between Emotional Intelligence and Job Performance," *Australian Journal of Psychology* 55 (2003): 145.
20. C. Chermiss, "The Business Case for Emotional Intelligence," *The Consortium for Research on Emotional Intelligence in Organizations* (2003), http://www.eiconsortium.org/research/business_case_for_ei.htm; L. M. Spencer, Jr. and S. Spencer, *Competence at Work: Models for Superior Performance* (New York: John Wiley & Sons, 1993); L. M. Spencer, Jr., D. C. McClelland, and S. Kelner, *Competency Assessment Methods: History and State of the Art* (Boston: Hay/McBer, 1997).
21. Chermiss, "The Business Case for Emotional Intelligence."
22. D. E. Super, *The Psychology of Careers* (New York: Harper & Row, 1957); D. E. Super and M. J. Bohn, Jr., *Occupational Psychology* (Belmont, Calif.: Wadsworth, 1970).
23. J. L. Holland, *The Psychology of Vocational Choice* (Waltham, Mass.: Blaisdell, 1966); J. L. Holland, *Making Vocational Choices: A Theory of Careers* (Englewood Cliffs, N.J.: Prentice-Hall, 1973).
24. F. T. L. Leong and J. T. Austin, "An Evaluation of the Cross-Cultural Validity of Holland's Theory: Career Choices by Workers in India," *Journal of Vocational Behavior* 52 (1998): 441–455.
25. C. Morgan, J. D. Isaac, and C. Sansone, "The Role of Interest in Understanding the Career Choices of Female and Male College Students," *Sex Roles* 44 (2001): 295–320.
26. S. H. Osipow, *Theories of Career Development* (Englewood Cliffs, N.J.: Prentice-Hall, 1973).
27. J. P. Wanous, T. L. Keon, and J. C. Latack, "Expectancy Theory and Occupational/Organizational Choices: A Review and Test," *Organizational Behavior and Human Performance* 32 (1983): 66–86.
28. P. O. Soelberg, "Unprogrammed Decision Making," *Industrial Management Review* 8 (1967): 19–29.
29. J. P. Wanous, *Organizational Entry: Recruitment, Selection, and Socialization of Newcomers* (Reading, Mass.: Addison-Wesley, 1980).
30. S. L. Premack and J. P. Wanous, "A Meta-Analysis of Realistic Job Preview Experiments," *Journal of Applied Psychology* 70 (1985): 706–719.
31. Idaho State Police, "Realistic Job Preview," http://www.isp.state.id.us/hr/trooper_info/realistic_job.html.
32. P. W. Hom, R. W. Griffeth, L. E. Palich, and J. S. Bracker, "An Exploratory Investigation into Theoretical Mechanisms Underlying Realistic Job Previews," *Personnel Psychology* 41 (1998): 421–451.
33. J. A. Breaugh, "Realistic Job Previews: A Critical Appraisal and Future Research Directions," *Academy of Management Review* 8 (1983): 612–619.
34. G. R. Jones, "Socialization Tactics, Self-Efficacy, and Newcomers' Adjustment to Organizations," *Academy of Management Journal* 29 (1986): 262–279.
35. M. R. Buckley, D. B. Fedor, J. G. Veres, D. S. Wiese, and S. M. Carraher, "Investigating Newcomer Expectations and Job-Related Outcomes," *Journal of Applied Psychology* 83 (1998): 452–461.
36. M. R. Buckley, D. B. Fedor, S. M. Carraher, D. D. Frink, and D. Marvin, "The Ethical Imperative to Provide Recruits Realistic Job Previews," *Journal of Managerial Issues* 9 (1997): 468–484.
37. J. O. Crites, "A Comprehensive Model of Career Adjustment in Early Adulthood," *Journal of Vocational Behavior* 9 (1976): 105–118; S. Cytrynbaum and J. O. Crites, "The Utility of Adult Development in Understanding Career Adjustment Process," in M. B. Arthur, D. T. Hall, and B. S. Lawrence, eds., *Handbook of Career Theory* (Cambridge: Cambridge University Press, 1989), 66–88.
38. D. E. Super, "A Life-Span, Life-Space Approach to Career Development," *Journal of Vocational Behavior* 16 (1980): 282–298; L. Baird and K. Kram, "Career Dynamics: Managing the Superior/Subordinate Relationship," *Organizational Dynamics* 11 (1983): 46–64.
39. D. J. Levinson, *The Seasons of a Man's Life* (New York: Knopf, 1978); D. J. Levinson, *The Seasons of a Woman's Life,* 1997.
40. D. J. Levinson, "A Conception of Adult Development," *American Psychologist* 41 (1986): 3–13.
41. D. L. Nelson, "Adjusting to a New Organization: Easing the Transition from Outsider to Insider," in J. C. Quick, R. E. Hess, J. Hermalin, and J. D. Quick, eds., *Career Stress in Changing Times* (New York: Haworth Press, 1990), 61–86.
42. J. P. Kotter, "The Psychological Contract: Managing the Joining Up Process," *California Management Review* 15 (1973): 91–99.
43. D. M. Rousseau, "New Hire Perceptions of Their Own and Their Employers' Obligations: A Study of Psychological Contracts," *Journal of Organizational Behavior* 11 (1990): 389–400; D. L. Nelson, J. C. Quick, and J. R. Joplin, "Psychological Contracting and Newcomer Socialization: An Attachment Theory Foundation," *Journal of Social Behavior and Personality* 6 (1991): 55–72.
44. S. D. Pugh, D. P. Skarlicki, and B. S. Passell, "After the Fall: Layoff Victims' Trust and Cynicism in Reemployment," *Journal of Occupational and Organizational Psychology* 76 (June 2003): 201–212.
45. D. L. Nelson, "Organizational Socialization: A Stress Perspective," *Journal of Occupational Behavior* 8 (1987): 311–324.
46. R. A. Dean, K. R. Ferris, and C. Konstans, "Reality Shock: Reducing the Organizational Commitment of Professionals," *Personnel Administrator* 30 (1985): 139–148.
47. Nelson, "Adjusting to a New Organization," 61–86.
48. G. Chen and R. J. Kilmoski, "The Impact of Expectations on Newcomer Performance in Teams as Mediated by Work Characteristics, Social Exchanges, and Empowerment," *Academy of Management Journal* 46 (October 2003): 591–607.
49. D. L. Nelson and C. D. Sutton, "The Relationship between Newcomer Expectations of Job Stressors and Adjustment to the New Job," *Work and Stress* 5 (1991): 241–254.
50. A. M. Saks, "Longitudinal Field Investigation of the Moderating and Mediating Effects of Self-Efficacy on the Relationship between Training and Newcomer Adjustment," *Journal of Applied Psychology* 80 (1995): 211–225.
51. G. F. Dreher and R. D. Bretz, Jr., "Cognitive Ability and Career Attainment: Moderating Effects of Early Career Success," *Journal of Applied Psychology* 76 (1991): 392–397.
52. D. L. Nelson and J. C. Quick, "Social Support and Newcomer Adjustment in Organizations: Attachment Theory at Work?" *Journal of Organizational Behavior* 12 (1991): 543–554.
53. Author conversation with Mark Phillips, Assistant Professor of Management, Abilene Christian University (July 2004).
54. TechRepublic Staff, "Most Organizations Wing It with New Employees," *TechRepublic* (April 5, 2002), http://techrepublic.com.com/5100-6317_111051414.html.
55. R. Pascale, "The Paradox of Corporate Culture: Reconciling Ourselves to Socialization," *California Management Review* 27 (1985): 27–41.
56. K. M. Davey and J. Arnold, "A Multi-Method Study of Accounts of Personal Change by Graduates Starting Work: Self-Ratings, Categories, and Women's Discourses," *Journal of Occupational and Organizational Psychology* 73 (2000): 461–486.
57. Levinson, "A Conception of Adult Development," 3–13.
58. J. W. Walker, "Let's Get Realistic about Career Paths," *Human Resource Management* 15 (1976): 2–7.
59. E. H. Buttner and D. P. Moore, "Women's Organizational Exodus to Entrepreneurship: Self-Reported Motivations and Correlates," *Journal*

of Small Business Management 35 (1997): 34–46; Center for Women's Business Research Press Release, "Privately Held, 50% or More Women-Owned Businesses in the United States" (2004), http://www.nfwbo.org/pressreleases/nationalstatetrends/total.htm.

60. D. G. Collings, H. Scullion, and M. J. Morley, "Changing Patterns of Global Staffing in the Multinational Enterprise: Challenges to the Conventional Expatriate Assignment and Emerging Alternatives," *Journal of World Business* 42(2) (2007): 198–213.
61. B. Filipczak, "You're on Your Own," *Training* (January 1995): 29–36.
62. K. E. Kram, *Mentoring at Work: Developmental Relationships in Organizational Life* (Glenview, Ill.: Scott, Foresman, 1985).
63. C. Orpen, "The Effects of Monitoring on Employees' Career Success," *Journal of Social Psychology* 135 (1995): 667–668.
64. J. Arnold and K. Johnson, "Mentoring in Early Career," *Human Resource Management Journal* 7 (1997): 61–70.
65. B. P. Madia and C. J. Lutz, "Perceived Similarity, Expectation–Reality Discrepancies, and Mentors' Expressed Intention to Remain in the Big Brothers/Big Sisters Programs," *Journal of Applied Social Psychology* 34 (March 2004): 598–622.
66. "A Guide to the Mentor Program Listings," *Mentors Peer Resources*, http://www.mentors.ca/mentorprograms.html.
67. B. R. Ragins, "Diversified Mentoring Relationships in Organizations: A Power Perspective," *Academy of Management Review* 22 (1997): 482–521.
68. R. Friedman, M. Kan, and D. B. Cornfield, "Social Support and Career Optimism: Examining the Effectiveness of Network Groups among Black Managers," *Human Relations* 51 (1998): 1155–1177.
69. S. E. Seibert, M. L. Kraimer, and R. C. Liden, "A Social Capital Theory of Career Success," *Academy of Management Journal* 44 (2001): 219–237.
70. PricewaterhouseCoopers Czech Republic, "Graduate Recruitment—FAQs," http://www.pwcglobal.com/cz/eng/car-inexp/main/faq.html.
71. M. A. Covaleski, M. W. Dirsmuth, J. B. Heian, and S. Samuel, "The Calculated and the Avowed: Techniques of Discipline and Struggles over Identity in Big Six Public Accounting Firms," *Administrative Science Quarterly* 43 (1998): 293–327.
72. B. R. Ragins and J. L. Cotton, "Easier Said Than Done: Gender Differences in Perceived Barriers to Gaining a Mentor," *Academy of Management Journal* 34 (1991): 939–951; S. D. Phillips and A. R. Imhoff, "Women and Career Development: A Decade of Research," *Annual Review of Psychology* 48 (1997): 31–43.
73. W. Whiteley, T. W. Dougherty, and G. F. Dreher, "Relationship of Career Mentoring and Socioeconomic Origin to Managers' and Professionals' Early Career Progress," *Academy of Management Journal* 34 (1991): 331–351; G. F. Dreher and R. A. Ash, "A Comparative Study of Mentoring among Men and Women in Managerial, Professional, and Technical Positions," *Journal of Applied Psychology* 75 (1990): 539–546; T. A. Scandura, "Mentorship and Career Mobility: An Empirical Investigation," *Journal of Organizational Behavior* 13 (1992): 169–174.
74. G. F. Dreher and T. H. Cox, Jr., "Race, Gender, and Opportunity: A Study of Compensation Attainment and Establishment of Mentoring Relationships," *Journal of Applied Psychology* 81 (1996): 297–309.
75. D. D. Horgan and R. J. Simeon, "Mentoring and Participation: An Application of the Vroom–Yetton Model," *Journal of Business and Psychology* 5 (1990): 63–84.
76. B. R. Ragins, J. L. Cotton, and J. S. Miller, "Marginal Mentoring: The Effects of Type of Mentor, Quality of Relationship, and Program Design on Work and Career Attitudes," *Academy of Management Journal* 43 (2000): 1177–1194.
77. R. T. Brennan, R. C. Barnett, and K. C. Gareis, "When She Earns More Than He Does: A Longitudinal Study of Dual-Earner Couples," *Journal of Marriage and Family* 63 (2001): 168–182.
78. F. S. Hall and D. T. Hall, *The Two-Career Couple* (Reading, Mass.: Addison-Wesley, 1979).
79. J. S. Boles, M. W. Johnston, and J. F. Hair, Jr., "Role Stress, Work–Family Conflict, and Emotional Exhaustion: Inter-Relationships and Effects on Some Work-Related Consequences" *Journal of Personal Selling and Sales Management* 17 (1998): 17–28.
80. B. Morris, "Is Your Family Wrecking Your Career? (and Vice Versa)," *Fortune* (March 17, 1997): 70–80.
81. D. L. Nelson, J. C. Quick, M. A. Hitt, and D. Moesel, "Politics, Lack of Career Progress, and Work/Home Conflict: Stress and Strain for Working Women," *Sex Roles* 23 (1990): 169–185.
82. L. E. Duxbury and C. A. Higgins, "Gender Differences in Work–Family Conflict," *Journal of Applied Psychology* 76 (1991): 60–74.
83. R. G. Netemeyer, J. S. Boles, and R. McMurrian, "Development and Validation of Work–Family Conflict and Family–Work Conflict Scales," *Journal of Applied Psychology* 81 (1996): 400–410.
84. N. Yang, C. C. Chen, J. Choi, and Y. Zou, "Sources of Work–Family Conflict: A Sino–U.S. Comparison of the Effects of Work and Family Demands," *Academy of Management Journal* 43 (2000): 113–123.
85. A. Iiris Aaltio, and H. Jiehua Huang, "Women Managers' Careers in Information Technology in China: High Flyers with Emotional Costs?"*Journal of Organizational Change Management* 20(2) (2007): 227–244.
86. D. L. Nelson and M. A. Hitt, "Employed Women and Stress: Implications for Enhancing Women's Mental Health in the Workplace," in J. C. Quick, L. R. Murphy, and J. J. Hurrell, eds., *Stress and Well-Being at Work: Assessments and Interventions for Occupational Mental Health* (Washington, D.C.: American Psychological Association, 1992), 164–177.
87. Mitchell Gold Co., "Day Care," http://www.mitchellgold.com/daycare.asp.
88. D. Machan, "The Mommy and Daddy Track," *Forbes* (April 6, 1990): 162.
89. E. M. Brody, M. H. Kleban, P. T. Johnsen, C. Hoffman, and C. B. Schoonover, "Work Status and Parental Care: A Comparison of Four Groups of Women," *Gerontological Society of America* 27 (1987): 201–208; J. W. Anastas, J. L. Gibson, and P. J. Larson, "Working Families and Eldercare: A National Perspective in an Aging America," *Social Work* 35 (1990): 405–411.
90. Cincinnati Area Senior Services, "Corporate Elder Care Program," http://www.senserv.org/elder.htm.
91. E. E. Kossek, J. A. Colquitt, and R. A. Noe, "Caregiving, Well-Being, and Performance: The Effects of Place and Provider as a Function of Dependent Type and Work–Family Climates," *Academy of Management Journal* 44 (2001): 29–44.
92. Harvard University Office of Human Resources, "Work/Life Support Services—Elder Care Resources," http://atwork.harvard.edu/worklife/eldercare/.
93. M. Richards, "'Daddy Track' Is Road Taken More Often," *The Morning Call* (July 28, 2004), http://www.mcall.com/business/local/all-daddyjul28,0,1869593.story?coll=all-businesslocal-hed.
94. L. J. Barham, "Variables Affecting Managers' Willingness to Grant Alternative Work Arrangements," *Journal of Social Psychology* 138 (1998): 291–302.
95. J. Kaplan, "Hitting the Wall at Forty," *Business Month* 136 (1990): 52–58.
96. M. B. Arthur and K. E. Kram, "Reciprocity at Work: The Separate Yet Inseparable Possibilities for Individual and Organizational Development," in M. B. Arthur, D. T. Hall, and B. S. Lawrence, eds., *Handbook of Career Theory* (Cambridge: Cambridge University Press, 1989).
97. K. E. Kram, "Phases of the Mentoring Relationship," *Academy of Management Review* 26 (1983): 608–625.
98. B. Rosen and T. Jerdee, *Older Employees: New Roles for Valued Resources* (Homewood, Ill.: Irwin, 1985).
99. J. W. Gilsdorf, "The New Generation: Older Workers," *Training and Development Journal* (March 1992): 77–79.
100. J. F. Quick, "Time to Move On?" in J. C. Quick, R. E. Hess, J. Hermalin, and J. D. Quick, eds., *Career Stress in Changing Times* (New York: Haworth Press, 1990), 239–250.
101. D. Machan, "Rent-an-Exec," *Forbes* (January 22, 1990): 132–133.
102. E. McGoldrick and C. L. Cooper, "Why Retire Early?" in J. C. Quick, R. E. Hess, J. Hermalin, and J. D. Quick, eds., *Career Stress in Changing Times* (New York: Haworth Press, 1990), 219–238.
103. E. Daspin, "The Second Midlife Crisis," *The Baltimore Sun* (originally published in *The Wall Street Journal*) (May 10, 2004), http://www.baltimoresun.com/business/bal-crisis051004,0,614944.story?coll=bal-business-headlines.
104. S. Kim and D. C. Feldman, "Working in Retirement: The Antecedents of Bridge Employment and Its Consequences for Quality of Life in Retirement," *Academy of Management Journal* 43 (2000): 1195–1210.

105. Lawrence Livermore Retiree Program, "Tasks Requested by Lab Programs," http://www.llnl.gov/aadp/retiree/tasks.html.
106. E. Schein, *Career Anchors* (San Diego: University Associates, 1985).
107. G. W. Dalton, "Developmental Views of Careers in Organizations," in M. B. Arthur, D. T. Hall, and B. S. Lawrence, eds., *Handbook of Career Theory* (Cambridge: Cambridge University Press, 1989), 89–109.
108. D. C. Feldman, "Careers in Organizations: Recent Trends and Future Directions," *Journal of Management* 15 (1989): 135–156.
109. B. O'Reilly, "The Job Drought," *Fortune* (August 24, 1992): 62–74.
110. A. S. Grove, "A High-Tech CEO Updates His Views on Managing and Careers," *Fortune* (September 18, 1995): 229–230.
111. M. Kaplan, "Want a Job at Google? Try These Brainteasers First," *Business 2.0* (August 30, 2007), http://money.cnn.com/2007/08/29/technology/brain_teasers.biz2/index.htm.

Chapter 17 Case

1. "Corporate Profile," Caribou Coffee, http://www.cariboucoffee.com/aboutus/corporate profile.asp (accessed October 22, 2007).
2. M. Frazier, "Starbucks It Isn't—And Purposely So," *Advertising Age*, Midwest region edition 76(11) (March 14, 2005): 12.
3. Ibid.
4. "Careers," Caribou Coffee, http://www.cariboucoffee.com/careers/ (accessed October 22, 2007).
5. "Store Managers—Pay and Benefits," Caribou Coffee, http://www.cariboucoffee.com/careers/storemanagers_paybenefits.asp (accessed October 22, 2007).
6. "Careers," Caribou Coffee.
7. "Careers—Store Managers," Caribou Coffee, http://www.cariboucoffee.com/careers/storemanagers.asp (accessed October 22, 2007).
8. "Store Managers—Training Paths," Caribou Coffee.
9. Ibid.
10. Ibid.
11. Ibid.
12. "Store Managers—Support Center," Caribou Coffee, http://www.cariboucoffee.com/careers/supportcenter.asp (accessed October 22, 2007).
13. Ibid.
14. "Store Managers—Pay and Benefits," Caribou Coffee.
15. "Store Managers—Training Paths," Caribou Coffee.

Chapter 18

1. American Express Corporate Web site press room, "American Express Business Travel Attracts More Than $1 Billion In New Business Globally within First 100 Days of 2007," http://home3.americanexpress.com/corp/pc/2007/aebt100.asp.
2. http://home3.americanexpress.com/corp/pc/2007/axiom.asp.
3. http://home3.americanexpress.com/corp/pc/2007/regus.asp.
4. http://corp.americanexpress.com/gcs/travel/us/land/accenturestudy.aspx.
5. M. A. Verespej, "When Change Becomes the Norm," *Industry Week* (March 16, 1992): 35–38.
6. P. Mornell, "Nothing Endures but Change," *Inc.* 22 (July 2000): 131–132, http://www.inc.com/magazine/20000701/19555.html.
7. H. J. Van Buren III, "The Bindingness of Social and Psychological Contracts: Toward a Theory of Social Responsibility in Downsizing," *Journal of Business Ethics* 25 (2000): 205–219.
8. United States Embassy in Mexico press release, "Response to Criticism of U.S. Agricultural Policy and NAFTA" (December 5, 2002), http://www.usembassy-mexico.gov/releases/ep021205realitiesNAFTA.htm.
9. M. Stevenson, "Mexican Farmers Renew NAFTA Protests," *Yahoo! News* (January 20, 2003).
10. M. McCarthy, "PR Disaster as Coke Withdraws 'Purest' Bottled Water in Britain," *The New Zealand Herald* (March 20, 2004), http://www.nzherald.co.nz/business/businessstorydisplay.cfm?storyID=3555911&thesection=business&thesubsection=world&thesecondsubsection=europe.
11. L. Hirschhorn and T. Gilmore, "The New Boundaries of the 'Boundaryless' Company," *Harvard Business Review* (May–June 1992): 104–115.
12. http://www.microsoft.com/presspass/Press/2002/Jul02/07-11NavisionAcquisitionPR.mspx.
13. http://www.microsoft.com/msft/acquisitions/history.mspx.
14. L. R. Offerman and M. Gowing, "Organizations of the Future: Changes and Challenges," *American Psychologist* (February 1990): 95–108.
15. W. B. Johnston, "Global Work Force 2000: The New World Labor Market," *Harvard Business Review* (March–April 1991): 115–127.
16. "50 Best Companies for Minorities: Full List," *Fortune* (June 28, 2004), http://www.fortune.com/fortune/diversity/subs/fulllist/0,20548,,00.html.
17. http://www.dennys.com/en/cms/Diversity/36.html.
18. G. Bylinsky, "Hot New Technologies for American Factories," *Fortune* (June 26, 2000): 288A–288K.
19. http://home3.americanexpress.com/corp/pc/2007/axiom.asp.
20. R. M. Kanter, "Improving the Development, Acceptance, and Use of New Technology: Organizational and Interorganizational Challenges," in *People and Technology in the Workplace* (Washington, D.C.: National Academy Press, 1991), 15–56.
21. Gap Inc. press release, "Gap Inc. Joins the Ethical Trading Initiative," *CSRwire* (April 28, 2004), http://www.csrwire.com/article.cgi/2683.html.
22. "Gap Inc. 2003 Social Responsibility Report," *Gap Inc.* (September 17, 2004), http://ccbn.mobular.net/ccbn/7/645/696/index.html.
23. S. A. Mohrman and A. M. Mohrman, Jr., "The Environment as an Agent of Change," in A. M. Mohrman, Jr., et al., eds., *Large-Scale Organizational Change* (San Francisco: Jossey-Bass, 1989), 35–47.
24. T. D'Aunno, M. Succi, and J. A. Alexander, "The Role of Institutional and Market Forces in Divergent Organizational Change," *Administrative Science Quarterly* 45 (2000): 679–703.
25. Intel press release, Santa Clara, Calif. (April 21, 2004), http://www.manufacturing.net/Intel-Opening-Arizona-Chip-Plant.aspx?menuid=278
26. Q. N. Huy, "Emotional Balancing of Organizational Continuity and Radical Change: The Contribution of Middle Managers," *Administrative Science Quarterly* 47 (March 1, 2002): 31–69.
27. D. Nadler, "Organizational Frame-Bending: Types of Change in the Complex Organization," in R. Kilmann and T. Covin, eds., *Corporate Transformation* (San Francisco: Jossey-Bass, 1988), 66–83.
28. K. Belson, "AT&T Plans to Raise Its Rates for Residential Calling Plans," *The New York Times* (August 4, 2004), http://www.businessweek.com/technology/content/nov2007/tc20071128_603655.htm
29. L. Ackerman, "Development, Transition, or Transformation: The Question of Change in Organizations," *OD Practitioner* (December 1986): 1–8.
30. T. D. Jick, *Managing Change* (Homewood, Ill.: Irwin, 1993), 3.
31. J. M. Bloodgood and J. L. Morrow, "Strategic Organizational Change: Exploring the Roles of Environmental Structure, Internal Conscious Awareness, and Knowledge," *Journal of Management Studies* 40 (2003): 1761–1782.
32. D. Miller and M. J. Chen, "Sources and Consequences of Competitive Inertia. A Study of the U.S. Airline Industry," *Administrative Science Quarterly* 39 (1994): 1–23.
33. S. L. Brown and K. M. Eisenhardt, "The Art of Continuous Change: Linking Complexity Theory and Time-Paced Evolution in Relentlessly Shifting Organizations," *Administrative Science Quarterly* 42 (1997): 1–34.
34. J. Child and C. Smith, "The Context and Process of Organizational Transformation: Cadbury Ltd. in Its Sector," *Journal of Management Studies* 12 (1987): 12–27.
35. J. Amis, T. Slack, and C. R. Hinings, "The Pace, Sequence, and Linearity of Radical Change," *Academy of Management Journal* 47 (2004): 15–39.
36. R. M. Kanter, *The Change Masters* (New York: Simon & Schuster, 1983).
37. J. R. Katzenbach, *Real Change Leaders* (New York: Times Business, 1995).
38. J. L. Denis, L. Lamothe, and A. Langley, "The Dynamics of Collective Leadership and Strategic Change in Pluralistic Organizations," *Academy of Management Journal* 44 (2001): 809–837.

39. M. Beer, *Organization Change and Development: A Systems View* (Santa Monica, Calif.: Goodyear, 1980): 78.
40. K. Whalen-Berry and C. R. Hinings, "The Relative Effect of Change Drivers in Large-Scale Organizational Change: An Empirical Study," in W. Passmore and R. Goodman, eds., *Research in Organizational Change and Development* 14 (New York: JAI Press, 2003): 99–146.
41. J. L. Denis, L. Lamothe, and A. Langley, "The Dynamics of Collective Leadership and Strategic Change in Pluralistic Organizations," *Academy of Management Journal* 44 (2001): 809–837.
42. F. Cheyunski and J. Millard, "Accelerated Business Transformation and the Role of the Organizational Architect," *Journal of Applied Behavioral Science* 34 (1998): 268–285.
43. N. A. M. Worren, K. Ruddle, and K. Moore, "From Organizational Development to Change Management: The Emergence of a New Profession," *Journal of Applied Behavioral Science* 35 (1999): 273–286.
44. P. G. Audia, E. A. Locke, and K. G. Smith, "The Paradox of Success: An Archival and a Laboratory Study of Strategic Persistence Following Radical Environmental Change," *Academy of Management Journal* 43 (2000): 837–853.
45. V. Bellou, "Psychological Contract Assessment after a Major Organizational Change: The Case of Mergers and Acquisitions," *Employee Relations* 29(1) (2007): 68–88.
46. J. W. Brehm, *A Theory of Psychological Reactance* (New York: Academic Press, 1966).
47. J. A. Klein, "Why Supervisors Resist Employee Involvement," *Harvard Business Review* 62 (1984): 87–95.
48. B. L. Kirkman, R. G. Jones, and D. L. Shapiro, "Why Do Employees Resist Teams? Examining the 'Resistance Barrier' to Work Team Effectiveness," *International Journal of Conflict Management* 11 (2000): 74–92.
49. D. L. Nelson and M. A. White, "Management of Technological Innovation: Individual Attitudes, Stress, and Work Group Attributes," *Journal of High Technology Management Research* 1 (1990): 137–148.
50. T. Diefenbach, "The Managerialistic Ideology of Organisational Change Management," *Journal of Organizational Change Management* 20(1) (2007): 126–144.
51. D. Klein, "Some Notes on the Dynamics of Resistance to Change: The Defender Role," in W. G. Bennis, K. D. Benne, R. Chin, and K. E. Corey, eds., *The Planning of Change*, 3rd ed. (New York: Holt, Rinehart & Winston, 1969), 117–124.
52. T. G. Cummings and E. F. Huse, *Organizational Development and Change* (St. Paul, Minn.: West, 1989).
53. N. L. Jimmieson, D. J. Terry, and V. J. Callan, "A Longitudinal Study of Employee Adaptation to Organizational Change: The Role of Change-Related Information and Change-Related Self Efficacy," *Journal of Occupational Health Psychology* 9 (2004): 11–27.
54. N. DiFonzo and P. Bordia, "A Tale of Two Corporations: Managing Uncertainty during Organizational Change," *Human Resource Management* 37 (1998): 295–303.
55. J. de Vries, C. Webb, and J. Eveline, "Mentoring for Gender Equality and Organisational Change," *Employee Relations* 28(6) (2006): 573–587.
56. M. Johnson-Cramer, S. Parise, and R. Cross, "Managing Change through Networks and Values," *California Management Review* 49(3) (2007): 85–109.
57. L. P. Livingstone, M. A. White, D. L. Nelson, and F. Tabak, "Delays in Technological Innovation Implementations: Some Preliminary Results on a Common but Understudied Occurrence," working paper, Oklahoma State University.
58. P. Neves and A. Caetano, "Social Exchange Processes in Organizational Change: The Roles of Trust and Control," *Journal of Change Management* 6(4) (2006): 351–364.
59. G. Lindsay, "Prada's High-Tech Misstep," *Business 2.0* (February 25, 2004): 72–75, http://www.business2.com/b2/web/articles/0,17863,594365,00.html.
60. M. Hickins, "Reconcilable Differences," *Management Review* 87 (1998): 54–58.
61. J. P. Kotter and L. A. Schlesinger, "Choosing Strategies for Change," *Harvard Business Review* 57 (1979): 109–112; W. Bridges, *Transitions: Making Sense of Life's Changes* (Reading, Mass.: Addison-Wesley, 1980); H. Woodward and S. Buchholz, *Aftershock: Helping People through Corporate Change* (New York: Wiley, 1987).
62. S. Michailova, "Contrasts in Culture: Russian and Western Perspectives on Organizational Change," *Academy of Management Executive* 14 (2000): 99–112.
63. S. E. Herzig and N. L. Jimmieson, "Middle Managers' Uncertainty Management during Organizational Change," *Leadership & Organization Development Journal* 27(8) (2006): 628–645.
64. K. Lewin, "Frontiers in Group Dynamics," *Human Relations* 1 (1947): 5–41.
65. C. Bareil, A. Savoie, and S. Meunier, "Patterns of Discomfort with Organizational Change," *Journal of Change Management* 7(1) (2007): 13–24.
66. W. McWhinney, "Meta-Praxis: A Framework for Making Complex Changes," in A. M. Mohrman, Jr., et al., eds., *Large-Scale Organizational Change* (San Francisco: Jossey-Bass, 1989), 154–199.
67. M. Beer and E. Walton, "Developing the Competitive Organization: Interventions and Strategies," *American Psychologist* 45 (1990): 154–161.
68. B. Bertsch and R. Williams, "How Multinational CEOs Make Change Programs Stick," *Long Range Planning* 27 (1994): 12–24.
69. J. Amis, T. Slack, and C. R. Hinings, "Values and Organizational Change," *Journal of Applied Behavioral Science* 38 (2002): 356–385.
70. W. L. French and C. H. Bell, *Organization Development: Behavioral Science Interventions for Organization Improvement*, 4th ed. (Englewood Cliffs, N.J.: Prentice-Hall, 1990); W. W. Burke, *Organization Development: A Normative View* (Reading, Mass.: Addison-Wesley, 1987).
71. A. Huczynski, *Encyclopedia of Organizational Change Methods* (Brookfield, Vt.: Gower, 1987).
72. A. O. Manzini, *Organizational Diagnosis* (New York: AMACOM, 1988).
73. M. R. Weisbord, "Organizational Diagnosis: Six Places to Look for Trouble with or without a Theory," *Group and Organization Studies* (December 1976): 430–444.
74. H. Levinson, *Organizational Diagnosis* (Cambridge, Mass.: Harvard University Press, 1972).
75. J. Nicholas, "The Comparative Impact of Organization Development Interventions," *Academy of Management Review* 7 (1982): 531–542.
76. D. M. Herold, D. B. Fedor, and S. D. Caldwell, "Beyond Change Management: A Multilevel Investigation of Contextual and Personal Influences on Employees' Commitment to Change," *Journal of Applied Psychology* 92(4) (2007): 942–951.
77. G. Odiorne, *Management by Objectives* (Marshfield, Mass.: Pitman, 1965).
78. E. Huse, "Putting in a Management Development Program That Works," *California Management Review* 9 (1966): 73–80.
79. J. P. Muczyk and B. C. Reimann, "MBO as a Complement to Effective Leadership," *Academy of Management Executive* (May 1989): 131–138.
80. L. L. Berry and A. Parasuraman, "Prescriptions for a Service Quality Revolution in America," *Organizational Dynamics* 20 (1992): 5–15.
81. "Five Companies Win 1992 Baldrige Quality Awards," *Business America* (November 2, 1992): 7–16.
82. D. M. Anderson, "Hidden Forces," *Success* (April 1995): 12.
83. T. A. Stewart and A. P. Raman, "Lessons from Toyota's Long Drive," *Harvard Business Review* 85(7/8) (2007): 74–83.
84. W. G. Dyer, *Team Building: Issues and Alternatives*, 2nd ed. (Reading, Mass.: Addison-Wesley, 1987).
85. E. Stephan, G. Mills, R. W. Pace, and L. Ralphs, "HRD in the Fortune 500: A Survey," *Training and Development Journal* (January 1988): 26–32.
86. A. Edmondson, "Psychological Safety and Learning Behavior in Work Teams," *Administrative Science Quarterly* 44 (1999): 350–383.
87. M. Whitmire and P. R. Nienstedt, "Lead Leaders into the '90s," *Personnel Journal* (May 1991): 80–85.
88. http://www.teambuildinginc.com/services4_teamconcepts.htm.
89. http://www.teambuildinginc.com/services5.htm.
90. E. Salas, T. L. Dickinson, S. I. Tannenbaum, and S. A. Converse, *A Meta-Analysis of Team Performance and Training, Naval Training System Center Technical Reports* (Orlando, Fla.: U.S. Government, 1991).
91. E. Schein, *Its Role in Organization Development*, vol. 1 of *Process Consultation* (Reading, Mass.: Addison-Wesley, 1988).

92. H. Hornstein, "Organizational Development and Change Management: Don't Throw the Baby Out with the Bath Water," *Journal of Applied Behavioral Science* 37 (2001): 223–226.
93. D. Filipowski, "How Federal Express Makes Your Package Its Most Important," *Personnel Journal* (February 1992): 40–46; P. Galagan, "Training Delivers Results to Federal Express," *Training and Development* (December 1991): 27–33.
94. R. W. Revans, *Action Learning* (London: Blonde & Briggs, 1980).
95. I. L. Goldstein, *Training in Organizations*, 3rd ed. (Pacific Grove, Calif.: Brooks/Cole, 1993).
96. J. A. Conger and R. M. Fulmer, "Developing Your Leadership Pipeline," *Harvard Business Review* 81 (2003): 76–84.
97. D. A. Ready and J. A. Conger, "Why Leadership Development Efforts Fail," *MIT Sloan Management Review* 44 (2003): 83–89.
98. M. Jay, "Understanding How to Leverage Executive Coaching," *Organization Development Journal* 21 (2003): 6–13.
99. D. Goleman, R. Boyaysis, and A. McKee, *Primal Leadership: Learning to Lead with Emotional Intelligence* (Harvard Business School Press, 2004).
100. K. M. Wasylyshyn, "Executive Coaching: An Outcome Study," *Consulting Psychology Journal* 55 (2003): 94–106.
101. J. W. Smither, M. London, R. Flautt, Y. Vargas, and I. Kucine, "Can Working with an Executive Coach Improve Multisource Feedback Ratings over Time? A Quasi-Experimental Field Study," *Personnel Psychology* 56 (2003): 23–44.
102. "Occupational Stress and Employee Stress," *American Psychological Association* (June 6, 2004), http://www.psychologymatters.org/karasek.html.
103. American Psychological Association, "Psychologically Healthy Workplace Awards," http://apahelpcenter.mediaroom.com/file.php/mr_apahelpcenter/spinsite_docfiles/134/phwa_magazine_2007.pdf.
104. D. A. Nadler, "Concepts for the Management of Organizational Change," in J. R. Hackman, E. E. Lawler III, and L. W. Porter, eds., *Perspectives on Organizational Behavior* (New York: McGraw-Hill, 1983).
105. Cummings and Huse, *Organizational Development*; P. E. Connor and L. K. Lake, *Managing Organizational Change* (New York: Praeger, 1988).
106. R. L. Lowman, "Ethical Human Resource Practice in Organizational Settings," in D. W. Bray, ed., *Working with Organizations* (New York: Guilford Press, 1991).
107. H. Kelman, "Manipulation of Human Behavior: An Ethical Dilemma for the Social Scientist," in W. Bennis, K. Benne, and R. Chin, eds., *The Planning of Change* (New York: Holt, Rinehart, & Winston, 1969).
108. A. M. Pettigrew, R. W. Woodman, and K. S. Cameron, "Studying Organizational Change and Development: Challenges for Future Research," *Academy of Management Journal* 44 (2001): 697–713.
109. R. A. Katzell and R. A. Guzzo, "Psychological Approaches to Worker Productivity," *American Psychologist* 38 (1983): 468–472.
110. R. A. Guzzo, R. D. Jette, and R. A. Katzell, "The Effects of Psychologically Based Intervention Programs on Worker Productivity," *Personnel Psychology* 38 (1985): 275–291.
111. Goldstein, *Training in Organizations*.
112. T. Covin and R. H. Kilmann, "Participant Perceptions of Positive and Negative Influences on Large-Scale Change," *Group and Organization Studies* 15 (1990): 233–248.
113. C. M. Brotheridge, "The Role of Fairness in Mediating the Effects of Voice and Justification on Stress and Other Outcomes in a Climate of Organizational Change," *International Journal of Stress Management* 10 (2003): 253–268.
114. http://home3.americanexpress.com/corp/gb/themes.asp.

Chapter 18 Case

1. "Corporate Time Line," Cisco Systems, http://newsroom.cisco.com/dlls/corporate_timeline.pdf (accessed October 24, 2007).
2. "Cisco Today—Executive Thought Leadership," Cisco Systems, http://tools.cisco.com/dlls/tln/page/executives/chambers/today (accessed October 24, 2007); "Office Locations—Cisco.com," Cisco Systems, http://www.cisco.com/web/siteassets/contacts/offices (accessed October 24, 2007).
3. Cisco Today—Executive Thought Leadership."
4. Ibid.
5. "Executive Leadership: John Chambers, President and Chief Executive Officer," Cisco Systems, http://newsroom.cisco.com/dlls/tln/exec_team/chambers/index.html (accessed September 29, 2004).
6. "The Economist Intelligence Unit" (2006), *Summary: Foresight 2020: Economic, Industry and Corporate Trends; Report from The Economist Intelligence Unit Sponsored by Cisco Systems*, http://tools.cisco.com/dlls/tln/media/research/2006/2020foresight/Foersight-2020-executive-summary.pdf (accessed October 24, 2007).
7. Ibid.
8. Ibid.
9. Ibid.
10. Ibid.
11. Ibid.
12. B. White, "Boss Talk: No Longer Just 'Plumbers'; Aiming to Rival Sony, Apple, John Chambers Takes Cisco Beyond Routers and Switches," *The Wall Street Journal*, Eastern edition (August 7, 2007), from ABI/INFORM Research database (accessed October 24, 2007).
13. J. Carless "The Network Is the Platform: The Network Is the Most Cost-Effective Platform Companies Can Use to Integrate Complex Interactions for Increased Value and Growth," *News@Cisco* (January 24, 2006), http://newsroom.cisco.com/dlls/2006/ts_012406.html, (accessed October 24, 2007).
14. "Corporate Overview," Cisco Systems, http://newsroom.cisco.com/dlls/corpinfo/corporate_overview.html, (accessed October 24, 2007).
15. Ibid.
16. "Linksys.com—Company/About Linksys/Company Profile," http://www.linksys.com/serlet/satellite?c=L_Content_C1&childpagename=... (accessed October 24, 2007).
17. B. White, "Business Technology: Cisco's Consumer Push Plods Along; CEO Chambers to Outline Vision for Seamless In-Home Network," *The Wall Street Journal*, Eastern edition (January 9, 2007), from ABI/INFORM Research database (accessed October 24, 2007).
18. "Corporate Overview," Cisco Systems.
19. Ibid.
20. "John Chambers, Chairman and Chief Executive Officer—Executive Thought Leadership," Cisco Systems, http://tools.cisco.com/dlls/tln/page/executives/chambers (accessed October 27, 2007).

Chapter 18 Cohesion Case: Part 4

1. S. Reed, "BP Feels the Heat; 2006 Was a Horror, and Problems Remain. Will John Browne Leave Early?" *Business Week* (January 22, 2007): 52+, from ABI/Inform database (accessed August 17, 2007).
2. S. Patton, "In Sync with His CEO; For Five Years, BP CIO John Leggate Has Managed People and IT Systems in Concert with His CEO's Acquisition-Hungry Strategy," *CIO* 17(1) (April 15, 2004): 1+, from ABI/Inform database (accessed August 17, 2007).
3. J. Birger, "What Pipeline Problem?" *Fortune* 154(5) (2006): 23–26.
4. Reed, "BP Feels the Heat."
5. Ibid.
6. J. Laws, "It's the Culture, Stupid," *Occupational Health & Safety* 75(10) (October 2006): 4.
7. M. B. Powers, "'Deficiencies' Cited at BP Site in Final Report on Fatal Blast," *Engineering News-Record* 258(12) (March 26, 2007): 13.
8. E. Armstrong, "A Decade of Sustainability," *The Engineer* (November 27–December 10, 2006): 16; J. Elkington, "John Browne," *Time* 163(17) (April 26, 2004): 73.
9. C. Cummins, C. Mollenkamp, A. O. Patrick, and G. Charzan, "Scandal, Crises Hasten Exit for British Icon; BP Chief's Tenure Was Increasingly Rocky; Then He Lied to Court; Hiding an Escort Service," *The Wall Street Journal* (Eastern Edition) (May 2, 2007): A1+, from ABI/Inform database (accessed August 17, 2007).
10. Ibid.
11. Ibid.
12. Birger, "What Pipeline Problem?"
13. J. Sonnenfeld, "The Real Scandal at BP," *Business Week* (May 14, 2007): 98.
14. Cummins, Mollenkamp, et al., "Scandal, Crises Hasten Exit for British Icon."
15. Ibid.

16. Sonnenfeld, "The Real Scandal at BP."
17. S. Reed, "Refilling BP's Tank: New CEO Hayward Has Major Safety and Expansion Issues to Resolve," *Business Week* (July 23, 2007): 34–35.
18. Reed, "BP Feels the Heat."
19. S. Reed, "BP Takes It Slow and Steady," *Business Week Online* (February 7, 2007): 2 (accessed August 17, 2007).
20. Ibid.
21. Reed, "Refilling BP's Tank."

Appendix A

1. F. W. Taylor, *The Principles of Scientific Management* (New York: Norton, 1911).
2. M. Weber, *The Protestant Ethic and the Spirit of Capitalism* (London: Talcott Parson, tr., 1930).
3. W. B. Cannon, *Bodily Changes in Pain, Hunger, Fear, and Rage* (New York: Appleton, 1915).
4. F. J. Roethlisberger and W. J. Dickson, *Management and the Worker* (Cambridge, Mass.: Harvard University Press, 1939).
5. K. Lewin, R. Lippitt, and R. K. White, "Patterns of Aggressive Behavior in Experimentally Created 'Social Climates,'" *Journal of Social Psychology* 10 (1939): 271–299; A. H. Maslow, *Motivation and Personality* (New York: Harper & Row, 1954); F. Herzberg, B. Mausner, and B. Snyderman, *The Motivation to Work*, 2nd ed. (New York: Wiley, 1959); E. A. Locke, "Toward a Theory of Task Motivation and Incentives," *Organizational Behavior and Human Performance* 3 (1968): 157–189; R. M. Stogdill, *Handbook of Leadership: A Survey of Theory and Research* (New York: Free Press, 1974); G. A. Yukl, *Leadership in Organizations*, 3rd ed. (Englewood Cliffs, N.J.: Prentice-Hall, 1995).
6. G. C. Homans, *The Human Group* (New York: Harcourt Brace Jovanovich, 1950).
7. J. R. Hackman and G. Oldham, *Work Redesign* (Reading, Mass.: Addison-Wesley, 1980); P. C. Smith, L. M. Kendall, and C. L. Hulin, *The Measurement of Satisfaction in Work and Retirement* (Chicago: Rand McNally, 1969).
8. N. R. F. Maier, *Psychology in Industry: A Psychological Approach to Industrial Problems*, 2nd ed. (Boston: Houghton Mifflin, 1955).
9. R. C. Solomon, "Corporate Roles, Personal Virtues: An Aristotelian Approach to Business Ethics," *Business Ethics Quarterly*, 2 (1992): 317–339.
10. R. C. Solomon, *A Better Way to Think about Business: How Personal Integrity Leads to Corporate Success* (New York: Oxford University Press, 1999).
11. M. E. P. Seligman, *Learned Optimism* (New York: Knopf, 1990) and M. E. P. Seligman and M. Csikszentmihalyi, "Positive Psychology," *American Psychologist*, 55 (2000): 5–14.
12. B. L. Simmons, *Eustress at Work: Accentuating the Positive* (unpublished doctoral dissertation, Oklahoma State University, 2000).
13. F. Luthans, "Positive Organizational Behavior: Developing and Managing Psychological Strengths," *Academy of Management Executive*, 16 (2002): 57–72; "The Need for and Meaning of Positive Organizational Behaviors," *Journal of Organizational Behavior*, 23 (2002): 695–706.
14. B. J. Avolio, *Full Leadership Development: Building the Vital Forces in Organizations* (Thousand Oaks, CA: Sage Publications, 1999).
15. F. J. Roethlisberger, *Management and Morale* (Cambridge, Mass: Harvard University Press, 1941).
16. J. G. Adair, "The Hawthorne Effect: A Reconsideration of Methodological Artifact," *Journal of Applied Psychology* 69 (1984): 334–345.
17. F. J. Roethlisberger, W. J. Dickson, and H. A. Wright, *Management and the Worker: An Account of a Research Program Conducted by the Western Electric Company, Hawthorne Works, Chicago* (Cambridge, Mass.: Harvard University Press, 1950); A. G. Athos and J. J. Gabarro, *Interpersonal Behavior: Communication and Understanding in Relationships* (Englewood Cliffs, N.J.: Prentice-Hall, 1978).

Appendix B

1. Two sources for further reference on experimental design are D. T. Campbell and J. C. Stanley, *Experimental and Quasi-Experimental Designs for Research* (Chicago: Rand McNally, 1966); and T. D. Cook and D. T. Campbell, *Quasi-Experimentation: Design and Analysis Issues for Field Settings* (Boston: Houghton Mifflin, 1979).
2. M. L. Lombardo, M. McCall, and D. L. DeVries, *Looking Glass* (Glenview, Ill.: Scott, Foresman, 1983).
3. Elaboration of how such measures are developed is beyond the scope of this appendix but can be found in U. Sekaran, *Research Methods for Business: A Skill Building Approach*, 2nd ed. (New York: Wiley, 1992).
4. Several measures are available in *Psychological Measurement Yearbooks*; J. L. Price, *Handbook of Organizational Measurement* (Lexington, Mass.: D. C. Heath, 1972); and *Michigan Organizational Assessment Packages* (Ann Arbor, Mich.: Institute of Survey Research).
5. One such instrument is the Job Descriptive Index, which is used to measure job satisfaction. It was developed by P. C. Smith, L. Kendall, and C. Hulin. See their book *The Measurement of Satisfaction in Work and Retirement* (Chicago: Rand McNally, 1969), pp. 79–84.

Glossary

A

adaptive culture An organizational culture that encourages confidence and risk taking among employees, has leadership that produces change, and focuses on the changing needs of customers.

adhocracy A selectively decentralized form of organization that emphasizes the support staff and mutual adjustment among people.

administrative orbiting Delaying action on a conflict by buying time.

advancement The second, high-achievement-oriented career stage in which the individual focuses on increasing competence.

affect The emotional component of an attitude.

affective commitment A type of organizational commitment based on an individual's desire to remain in an organization.

anthropocentric Placing human considerations at the center of job design decisions.

anthropology The science of the learned behavior of human beings.

anticipatory socialization The first socialization stage, which encompasses all of the learning that takes place prior to the newcomer's first day on the job.

artifacts Symbols of culture in the physical and social work environment.

assumptions Deeply held beliefs that guide behavior and tell members of an organization how to perceive and think about things.

attitude A psychological tendency expressed by evaluating an entity with some degree of favor or disfavor.

attribution theory A theory that explains how individuals pinpoint the causes of their own behavior and that of others.

authentic leadership A style of leadership that includes transformational, charismatic, or transactional approaches as the situation demands.

authority The right to influence another person.

authority-compliance manager (9,1) A leader who emphasizes efficient production.

autocratic style A style of leadership in which the leader uses strong, directive, controlling actions to enforce the rules, regulations, activities, and relationships in the work environment.

B

barriers to communication Aspects of the communication content and context that can impair effective communication in a workplace.

behavioral measures Personality assessments that involve observing an individual's behavior in a controlled situation.

benevolent An individual who is comfortable with an equity ratio less than that of his or her comparison other.

bounded rationality A theory that suggests there are limits to how rational a decision maker can actually be.

brainstorming A technique for generating as many ideas as possible on a given subject, while suspending evaluation until all the ideas have been suggested.

bridge employment Employment that takes place after retiring from a full-time position but before permanent withdrawal from the workforce.

C

career The pattern of work-related experiences that span the course of a person's life.

career anchors A network of self-perceived talents, motives, and values that guide an individual's career decisions.

career ladder A structured series of job positions through which an individual progresses in an organization.

career management A lifelong process of learning about self, jobs, and organizations; setting personal career goals; developing strategies for achieving the goals, and revising the goals based on work and life experiences.

career path A sequence of job experiences that an employee moves along during his or her career.

career plateau A point in an individual's career in which the probability of moving further up the hierarchy is low.

centralization The degree to which decisions are made at the top of the organization.

challenge The call to competition, contest, or battle.

change The transformation or modification of an organization and/or its stakeholders.

change agent The individual or group that undertakes the task of introducing and managing a change in an organization.

change and acquisition The third socialization stage, in which the newcomer begins to master the demands of the job.

character assassination An attempt to label or discredit an opponent.

character theory An ethical theory that emphasizes the character, personal virtues, and integrity of the individual.

charismatic leadership A leader's use of personal abilities and talents in order to have profound and extraordinary effects on followers.

classical conditioning Modifying behavior so that a conditioned stimulus is paired with an unconditioned stimulus and elicits an unconditioned response.

coercive power Power that is based on an agent's ability to cause an unpleasant experience for a target.

cognitive dissonance A state of tension that is produced when an individual experiences conflict between attitudes and behavior.

cognitive moral development The process of moving through stages of maturity in terms of making ethical decisions.

cognitive style An individual's preference for gathering information and evaluating alternatives.

collectivism A cultural orientation in which individuals belong to tightly knit social frameworks, and they depend strongly on large extended families or clans.

communication The evoking of a shared or common meaning in another person.

communicative disease The absence of heartfelt communication in human relationships leading to loneliness and social isolation.

communicator The person originating a message.

compensation A compromise mechanism in which an individual attempts to make up for a negative situation by devoting himself or herself to another pursuit with increased vigor.

compensation award An organizational cost resulting from court awards for job distress.

complexity The degree to which many different types of activities occur in the organization.

conflict Any situation in which incompatible goals, attitudes, emotions, or behaviors lead to disagreement or opposition for two or more parties.

consensus An informational cue indicating the extent to which peers in the same situation behave in a similar fashion.

consequential theory An ethical theory that emphasizes the consequences or results of behavior.

consideration Leader behavior aimed at nurturing friendly, warm working relationships, as well as encouraging mutual trust and interpersonal respect within the work unit.

consistency An informational cue indicating the frequency of behavior over time.

contextual variables A set of characteristics that influence the organization's design processes.

continuance commitment A type of organizational commitment based on the fact that an individual cannot afford to leave.

conversion A withdrawal mechanism in which emotional conflicts are expressed in physical symptoms.

counterdependence An unhealthy, insecure pattern of behavior that leads to separation in relationships with other people.

counter-role behavior Deviant behavior in either a correctly or incorrectly defined job or role.

country club manager (1,9) A leader who creates a happy, comfortable work environment.

creativity A process influenced by individual and organizational factors that results in the production of novel and useful ideas, products, or both.

cross-training A variation of job enlargement in which workers are trained in different specialized tasks or activities.

D

data Uninterpreted and unanalyzed facts.

defensive communication Communication that can be aggressive, attacking, and angry, or passive and withdrawing.

Delphi technique Gathering the judgments of experts for use in decision making.

democratic style A style of leadership in which the leader takes collaborative, responsive, interactive actions with followers concerning the work and work environment.

devil's advocacy A technique for preventing groupthink in which a group or individual is given the role of critic during decision making.

dialectical inquiry A debate between two opposing sets of recommendations.

differentiation The process of deciding how to divide the work in an organization.

discounting principle The assumption that an individual's behavior is accounted for by the situation.

disenchantment Feeling negativity or anger toward a change.

disengagement Psychological withdrawal from change.

disidentification Feeling that one's identity is being threatened by a change.

disorientation Feelings of loss and confusion due to a change.

displacement An aggressive mechanism in which an individual directs his or her anger toward someone who is not the source of the conflict.

distinctiveness An informational cue indicating the degree to which an individual behaves the same way in other situations.

distress The adverse psychological, physical, behavioral, and organizational consequences that may arise as a result of stressful events.

distributive bargaining A negotiation approach in which the goals of the parties are in conflict, and each party seeks to maximize its resources.

distributive justice The fairness of the outcomes that individuals receive in an organization.

diversity All forms of individual differences, including culture, gender, age, ability, religion, personality, social status, and sexual orientation.

divisionalized form A moderately decentralized form of organization that emphasizes the middle level and standardization of outputs.

dual-career partnership A relationship in which both people have important career roles.

due process nonaction A procedure set up to address conflicts that is so costly, time-consuming, or personally risky that no one will use it.

dynamic follower A follower who is a responsible steward of his or her job, is effective in managing the relationship with the boss, and practices self-management.

dysfunctional conflict An unhealthy, destructive disagreement between two or more people.

E

effective decision A timely decision that meets a desired objective and is acceptable to those individuals affected by it.

ego-ideal The embodiment of a person's perfect self.

eldercare Assistance in caring for elderly parents and/or other elderly relatives.

emotional contagion A dynamic process through which the emotions of one person are transferred to another either consciously or unconsciously through nonverbal channels.

emotions Mental states that typically include feelings, physiological changes, and the inclination to act.

empowerment Sharing power within an organization.

enacted values Values reflected in the way individuals actually behave.

encounter The second socialization stage in which the newcomer learns the tasks associated with the job, clarifies roles, and establishes new relationships at work.

engagement The expression of oneself as one performs in work or other roles.

engineering The applied science of energy and matter.

entitled An individual who is comfortable with an equity ratio greater than that of his or her comparison other.

environment Anything outside the boundaries of an organization.

environmental uncertainty The amount and rate of change in the organization's environment.

equity sensitive An individual who prefers an equity ratio equal to that of his or her comparison other.

ergonomics The science of adapting work and working conditions to the employee or worker.

escalation of commitment The tendency to continue to support a failing course of action.

espoused values What members of an organization say they value.

establishment The first career stage in which the person learns the job and begins to fit into the organization and occupation.

ethical behavior Acting in ways consistent with one's personal values and the commonly held values of the organization and society.

eustress Healthy, normal stress.

executive coaching A technique in which managers or executives are paired with a coach in a partnership to help the executive perform more efficiently.

expatriate manager A manager who works in a country other than his or her home country.

expectancy The belief that effort leads to performance.

expert power The power that exists when an agent has specialized knowledge or skills that the target needs.

expert system A computer-based application that uses a representation of human expertise in a specialized field of knowledge to solve problems.

extinction The attempt to weaken a behavior by attaching no consequences to it.

extraversion A preference indicating that an individual is energized by interaction with other people.

F

fantasy A withdrawal mechanism that provides an escape from a conflict through daydreaming.

feedback Information fed back that completes two-way communication.

feeling Making decisions in a personal, value-oriented way.

femininity The cultural orientation in which relationships and concern for others are valued.

first-impression error The tendency to form lasting opinions about an individual based on initial perceptions.

fixation An aggressive mechanism in which an individual keeps up a dysfunctional behavior that obviously will not solve the conflict.

flexible work schedule A work schedule that allows employees discretion in order to accommodate personal concerns.

flextime An alternative work pattern that enables employees to set their own daily work schedules.

flight/withdrawal A withdrawal mechanism that entails physically escaping a conflict (flight) or psychologically escaping (withdrawal).

followership The process of being guided and directed by a leader in the work environment.

formal leadership Officially sanctioned leadership based on the authority of a formal position.

formal organization The official, legitimate, and most visible part of the system.

formalization The degree to which the organization has official rules, regulations, and procedures.

functional conflict A healthy, constructive disagreement between two or more people.

fundamental attribution error The tendency to make attributions to internal causes when focusing on someone else's behavior.

G

garbage can model A theory that contends that decisions in organizations are random and unsystematic.

gateways to communication Pathways through barriers to communication and antidotes to communication problems.

general self-efficacy An individual's general belief that he or she is capable of meeting job demands in a wide variety of situations.

glass ceiling An intangible barrier that keeps women and minorities from rising above a certain level in organizations.

goal setting The process of establishing desired results that guide and direct behavior.

group Two or more people with common interests, objectives, and continuing interaction.

group cohesion The "interpersonal glue" that makes members of a group stick together.

group polarization The tendency for group discussion to produce shifts toward more extreme attitudes among members.

groupthink A deterioration of mental efficiency, reality testing, and moral judgment resulting from pressures within the group.

guanxi The Chinese practice of building networks for social exchange.

H

Hawthorne studies Studies conducted during the 1920s and 1930s that discovered the existence of the informal organization.

heuristics Shortcuts in decision making that save mental activity.

hierarchy of authority The degree of vertical differentiation across levels of management.

homeostasis A steady state of bodily functioning and equilibrium.

hygiene factor A work condition related to dissatisfaction caused by discomfort or pain.

I

identification A compromise mechanism whereby an individual patterns his or her behavior after another's.

impoverished manager (1,1) A leader who exerts just enough effort to get by.

impression management The process by which individuals try to control the impressions others have of them.

incremental change Change of a relatively small scope, such as making small improvements.

individual differences The way in which factors such as skills, abilities, personalities, perceptions, attitudes, values, and ethics differ from one individual to another.

individualism A cultural orientation in which people belong to loose social frameworks, and their primary concern is for themselves and their families.

inequity The situation in which a person perceives he or she is receiving less than he or she is giving, or is giving less than he or she is receiving.

influence The process of affecting the thoughts, behavior, and feelings of another person.

informal leadership Unofficial leadership accorded to a person by other members of the organization.

informal organization The unofficial and less visible part of the system.

information Data that have been interpreted, analyzed, and have meaning to some user.

Information Communication Technology (ICT) The various new technologies, such as e-mail, voice mail, teleconferencing, and wireless access, which are used for interpersonal communication.

information power Access to and control over important information.

initiating structure Leader behavior aimed at defining and organizing work relationships and roles, as well as establishing clear patterns of organization, communication, and ways of getting things done.

instrumental values Values that represent the acceptable behaviors to be used in achieving some end state.

instrumentality The belief that performance is related to rewards.

integrated involvement Closeness achieved through tasks and activities.

integration The process of coordinating the different parts of an organization.

integrative approach The broad theory that describes personality as a composite of an individual's psychological processes.

integrative negotiation A negotiation approach that focuses on the merits of the issues and seeks a win–win solution.

interactional psychology The psychological approach that says in order to understand human behavior, we must know something about the person and about the situation.

intergroup conflict Conflict that occurs between groups or teams in an organization.

interorganizational conflict Conflict that occurs between two or more organizations.

interpersonal communication Communication between two or more people in an organization.

interpersonal conflict Conflict that occurs between two or more individuals.

interrole conflict A person's experience of conflict among the multiple roles in his or her life.

intragroup conflict Conflict that occurs within groups or teams.

intrapersonal conflict Conflict that occurs within an individual.

intrarole conflict Conflict that occurs within a single role, such as when a person receives conflicting messages from role senders about how to perform a certain role.

introversion A preference indicating that an individual is energized by time alone.

intuition A fast, positive force in decision making that is utilized at a level below consciousness and involves learned patterns of information.

intuition Gathering information through "sixth sense" and focusing on what could be rather than what actually exists.

J

job A set of specified work and task activities that engage an individual in an organization.

Job Characteristics Model A framework for understanding person–job fit through the interaction of core job dimensions with critical psychological states within a person.

Job Diagnostic Survey (JDS) The survey instrument designed to measure the elements in the Job Characteristics Model.

job enlargement A method of job design that increases the number of activities in a job to overcome the boredom of overspecialized work.

job enrichment Designing or redesigning jobs by incorporating motivational factors into them.

job redesign An OD intervention method that alters jobs to improve the fit between individual skills and the demands of the job.

job rotation A variation of job enlargement in which workers are exposed to a variety of specialized jobs over time.

job satisfaction A pleasurable or positive emotional state resulting from the appraisal of one's job or job experiences.

job sharing An alternative work pattern in which more than one person occupies a single job.

Judging Preference Preferring closure and completion in making decisions.

jurisdictional ambiguity The presence of unclear lines of responsibility within an organization.

L

laissez-faire style A style of leadership in which the leader fails to accept the responsibilities of the position.

language The words, their pronunciation, and the methods of combining them used and understood by a group of people.

leader An advocate for change and new approaches to problems.

leader–member relations The quality of interpersonal relationships among a leader and the group members.

leadership The process of guiding and directing the behavior of people in the work environment.

Leadership Grid An approach to understanding a leader's or manager's concern for results (production) and concern for people.

leadership training and development A variety of techniques that are designed to enhance individuals' leadership skills.

lean production Using committed employees with ever-expanding responsibilities to achieve zero waste, 100 percent good product, delivered on time, every time.

learning A change in behavior acquired through experience.

least preferred coworker (LPC) The person a leader has least preferred to work with over his or her career.

legitimate power Power that is based on position and mutual agreement; agent and target agree that the agent has the right to influence the target.

locus of control An individual's generalized belief about internal control (self-control) versus external control (control by the situation or by others).

loss of individuality A social process in which individual group members lose self-awareness and its accompanying sense of accountability, inhibition, and responsibility for individual behavior.

M

Machiavellianism A personality characteristic indicating one's willingness to do whatever it takes to get one's own way.

machine bureaucracy A moderately decentralized form of organization that emphasizes the technical staff and standardization of work processes.

maintenance The third career stage in which the individual tries to maintain productivity while evaluating progress toward career goals.

maintenance function An activity essential to effective, satisfying interpersonal relationships within a team or group.

management The study of overseeing activities and supervising people in organizations.

management by objectives (MBO) A goal-setting program based on interaction and negotiation between employees and managers.

management by objectives (MBO) An organization-wide intervention technique that involves joint goal setting between employees and managers.

manager An advocate for stability and the status quo.

masculinity The cultural orientation in which assertiveness and materialism are valued.

meaning of work The way a person interprets and understands the value of work as part of life.

mechanistic structure An organizational design that emphasizes structured activities, specialized tasks, and centralized decision making.

medicine The applied science of healing or treatment of diseases to enhance an individual's health and well-being.

mentor An individual who provides guidance, coaching, counseling, and friendship to a protégé.

mentoring A work relationship that encourages development and career enhancement for people moving through the career cycle.

message The thoughts and feelings that the communicator is attempting to elicit in the receiver.

moral maturity The measure of a person's cognitive moral development.

motivation The process of arousing and sustaining goal-directed behavior.

motivation factor A work condition related to satisfaction of the need for psychological growth.

moving The second step in Lewin's change model, in which new attitudes, values, and behaviors are substituted for old ones.

Myers-Briggs Type Indicator (MBTI) instrument An instrument developed to measure Carl Jung's theory of individual differences.

N

need for achievement A manifest (easily perceived) need that concerns individuals' issues of excellence, competition, challenging goals, persistence, and overcoming difficulties.

need for affiliation A manifest (easily perceived) need that concerns an individual's need to establish and maintain warm, close, intimate relationships with other people.

need for power A manifest (easily perceived) need that concerns an individual's need to make an impact on others, influence others, change people or events, and make a difference in life.

need hierarchy The theory that behavior is determined by a progression of physical, social, and psychological needs, including lower-order needs and higher-order needs.

negative affect An individual's tendency to accentuate the negative aspects of himself or herself, other people, and the world in general.

negative consequences Results of a behavior that a person finds unattractive or aversive.

negativism An aggressive mechanism in which a person responds with pessimism to any attempt at solving a problem.

nominal group technique (NGT) A structured approach to group decision making that focuses on generating alternatives and choosing one.

nonaction Doing nothing in hopes that a conflict will disappear.

nondefensive communication Communication that is assertive, direct, and powerful.

nonprogrammed decision A new, complex decision that requires a creative solution.

nonverbal communication All elements of communication that do not involve words.

normative commitment A type of organizational commitment based on an individual's perceived obligation to remain with an organization.

norms of behavior The standards that a work group uses to evaluate the behavior of its members.

O

objective knowledge Knowledge that results from research and scientific activities.

one-way communication Communication in which a person sends a message to another person and no feedback, questions, or interaction follow.

operant conditioning Modifying behavior through the use of positive or negative consequences following specific behaviors.

opportunistic "what's in it for me" manager (Opp) A leader whose style aims to maximize self-benefit.

opportunities Favorable times or chances for progress and advancement.

organic structure An organizational design that emphasizes teamwork, open communication, and decentralized decision making.

organization development (OD) A systematic approach to organizational improvement that applies behavioral science theory and research in order to increase individual and organizational well-being and effectiveness.

organization man manager (5,5) A middle-of-the-road leader.

organizational behavior The study of individual behavior and group dynamics in organizations.

organizational citizenship behavior Behavior that is above and beyond the call of duty.

organizational commitment The strength of an individual's identification with an organization.

organizational (corporate) culture A pattern of basic assumptions that are considered valid and that are taught to new members as the way to perceive, think, and feel in the organization.

organizational design The process of constructing and adjusting an organization's structure to achieve its goals.

organizational life cycle The differing stages of an organization's life from birth to death.

organizational politics The use of power and influence in organizations.

organizational socialization The process by which newcomers are transformed from outsiders to participating, effective members of the organization.

organizational structure The linking of departments and jobs within an organization.

overdependence An unhealthy, insecure pattern of behavior that leads to preoccupied attempts to achieve security through relationships.

P

participation problem A cost associated with absenteeism, tardiness, strikes and work stoppages, and turnover.

participative decision making Decision making in which individuals who are affected by decisions influence the making of those decisions.

paternalistic "father knows best" manager (9+9) A leader who promises reward and threatens punishment.

people The human resources of the organization.

Perceiving Preference Preferring to explore many alternatives and flexibility.

perceptual screen A window through which we interact with people that influences the quality, accuracy, and clarity of the communication.

performance appraisal The evaluation of a person's performance.

performance decrement A cost resulting from poor quality or low quantity of production, grievances, and unscheduled machine downtime and repair.

performance management A process of defining, measuring, appraising, providing feedback on, and improving performance.

personal power Power used for personal gain.

personality A relatively stable set of characteristics that influence an individual's behavior.

personality hardiness A personality resistant to distress and characterized by commitment, control, and challenge.

person–role conflict Conflict that occurs when an individual is expected to perform behaviors in a certain role that conflict with his or her personal values.

phased retirement An arrangement that allows employees to reduce their hours and/or responsibilities in order to ease into retirement.

planned change Change resulting from a deliberate decision to alter the organization.

political behavior Actions not officially sanctioned by an organization that are taken to influence others in order to meet one's personal goals.

political skill The ability to get things done through favorable interpersonal relationships outside of formally prescribed organizational mechanisms.

position power The authority associated with the leader's formal position in the organization.

positive affect An individual's tendency to accentuate the positive aspects of himself or herself, other people, and the world in general.

positive consequences Results of a behavior that a person finds attractive or pleasurable.

power The ability to influence another person.

power distance The degree to which a culture accepts unequal distribution of power.

powerlessness A lack of power.

preventive stress management An organizational philosophy that holds that people and organizations should take joint responsibility for promoting health and preventing distress and strain.

primary prevention The stage in preventive stress management designed to reduce, modify, or eliminate the demand or stressor causing stress.

procedural justice The fairness of the process by which outcomes are allocated in an organization.

process consultation An OD method that helps managers and employees improve the processes that are used in organizations.

professional bureaucracy A decentralized form of organization that emphasizes the operating core and standardization of skills.

programmed decision A simple, routine matter for which a manager has an established decision rule.

projection Overestimating the number of people who share our own beliefs, values, and behaviors.

projective test A personality test that elicits an individual's response to abstract stimuli.

psychoanalysis Sigmund Freud's method for delving into the unconscious mind to better understand a person's motives and needs.

psychological contract An implicit agreement between an individual and an organization that specifies what each is expected to give and receive in the relationship.

psychological intimacy Emotional and psychological closeness to other team or group members.

psychology The science of human behavior.

punishment The attempt to eliminate or weaken undesirable behavior by either bestowing negative consequences or withholding positive consequences.

Q

quality circle (QC) A small group of employees who work voluntarily on company time, typically one hour per week, to address work-related problems such as quality control, cost reduction, production planning and techniques, and even product design.

quality program A program that embeds product and service quality excellence in the organizational culture.

quality team A team that is part of an organization's structure and is empowered to act on its decisions regarding product and service quality.

R

rationality A logical, step-by-step approach to decision making, with a thorough analysis of alternatives and their consequences.

rationalization A compromise mechanism characterized by trying to justify one's behavior by constructing bogus reasons for it.

realistic job preview (RJP) Both positive and negative information given to potential employees about the job they are applying for, thereby giving them a realistic picture of the job.

receiver The person receiving a message.

referent power An elusive power that is based on interpersonal attraction.

reflective listening A skill intended to help the receiver and communicator clearly and fully understand the message sent.

refreezing The final step in Lewin's change model, in which new attitudes, values, and behaviors are established as the new status quo.

reinforcement The attempt to develop or strengthen desirable behavior by either bestowing positive consequences or withholding negative consequences.

reinvention The creative application of new technology.

reward power Power based on an agent's ability to control rewards that a target wants.

richness The ability of a medium or channel to elicit or evoke meaning in the receiver.

risk aversion The tendency to choose options that entail fewer risks and less uncertainty.

robotics The use of robots in organizations.

role negotiation A technique whereby individuals meet and clarify their psychological contract.

rule-based theory An ethical theory that emphasizes the character of the act itself rather than its effects.

S

satisfice To select the first alternative that is "good enough," because the costs in time and effort are too great to optimize.

secondary prevention The stage in preventive stress management designed to alter or modify the individual's or the organization's response to a demand or stressor.

secrecy Attempting to hide a conflict or an issue that has the potential to create conflict.

selective perception The process of selecting information that supports our individual viewpoints while discounting information that threatens our viewpoints.

self-esteem An individual's general feeling of self-worth.

self-fulfilling prophecy The situation in which our expectations about people affect our interaction with them in such a way that our expectations are confirmed.

self-image How a person sees himself or herself, both positively and negatively.

self-interest What is in the best interest and benefit to an individual.

self-managed team A team that makes decisions that were once reserved for managers.

self-monitoring The extent to which people base their behavior on cues from other people and situations.

self-reliance A healthy, secure, *interdependent* pattern of behavior related to how people form and maintain supportive attachments with others.

self-report questionnaire A common personality assessment that involves an individual's responses to a series of questions.

self-serving bias The tendency to attribute one's own successes to internal causes and one's failures to external causes.

sensing Gathering information through the five senses.

simple structure A centralized form of organization that emphasizes the upper echelon and direct supervision.

Six Sigma A high-performance system to execute business strategy that is customer driven, emphasizes quantitative decision making, and places a priority on saving money.

skill development The mastery of abilities essential to successful functioning in organizations.

skills training Increasing the job knowledge, skills, and abilities that are necessary to do a job effectively.

social decision schemes Simple rules used to determine final group decisions.

social information-processing (SIP) model A model that suggests that the important job factors depend in part on what others tell a person about the job.

social learning The process of deriving attitudes from family, peer groups, religious organizations, and culture.

social loafing The failure of a group member to contribute personal time, effort, thoughts, or other resources to the group.

social perception The process of interpreting information about another person.

social power Power used to create motivation or to accomplish group goals.

social responsibility The obligation of an organization to behave in ethical ways.

sociology The science of society.

sociotechnical systems (STS) Giving equal attention to technical and social considerations in job design.

specialization The degree to which jobs are narrowly defined and depend on unique expertise.

standardization The degree to which work activities are accomplished in a routine fashion.

status structure The set of authority and task relations among a group's members.

stereotype A generalization about a group of people.

strain Distress.

strategic change Change of a larger scale, such as organizational restructuring.

strategic contingencies Activities that other groups depend on in order to complete their tasks.

stress The unconscious preparation to fight or flee that a person experiences when faced with any demand.

stressor The person or event that triggers the stress response.

strong culture An organizational culture with a consensus on the values that drive the company and with an intensity that is recognizable even to outsiders.

strong situation A situation that overwhelms the effects of individual personalities by providing strong cues for appropriate behavior.

structure The systems of communication, authority and roles, and workflow.

superordinate goal An organizational goal that is more important to both parties in a conflict than their individual or group goals.

survey feedback A widely used method of intervention whereby employee attitudes are solicited using a questionnaire.

synergy A positive force that occurs in groups when group members stimulate new solutions to problems through the process of mutual influence and encouragement within the group.

T

task An organization's mission, purpose, or goal for existing.

task environment The elements of an organization's environment that are related to its goal attainment.

task function An activity directly related to the effective completion of a team's work.

task revision The modification of incorrectly specified roles or jobs.

task structure The degree of clarity, or ambiguity, in the work activities assigned to the group.

task-specific self-efficacy An individual's beliefs and expectancies about his or her ability to perform a specific task effectively.

team building An intervention designed to improve the effectiveness of a work group.

team manager (9,9) A leader who builds a highly productive team of committed people.

teamwork Joint action by a team of people in which individual interests are subordinated to team unity.

technocentric Placing technology and engineering at the center of job design decisions.

technological interdependence The degree of interrelatedness of the organization's various technological elements.

technology The intellectual and mechanical processes used by an organization to transform inputs into products or services that meet organizational goals.

technology The tools, knowledge, and/or techniques used to transform inputs into outputs.

technostress The stress caused by new and advancing technologies in the workplace.

telecommuting Transmitting work from a home computer to the office using a modem.

terminal values Values that represent the goals to be achieved or the end states of existence.

tertiary prevention The stage in preventive stress management designed to heal individual or organizational symptoms of distress and strain.

Theory X A set of assumptions of how to manage individuals who are motivated by lower-order needs.

Theory Y A set of assumptions of how to manage individuals who are motivated by higher-order needs.

thinking Making decisions in a logical, objective fashion.

360-degree feedback A process of self-evaluation and evaluations by a manager, peers, direct reports, and possibly customers.

time orientation Whether a culture's values are oriented toward the future (long-term orientation) or toward the past and present (short-term orientation).

trait theory The personality theory that states that in order to understand individuals, we must break down behavior patterns into a series of observable traits.

transformational change Change in which the organization moves to a radically different, and sometimes unknown, future state.

transformational coping A way of managing stressful events by changing them into less subjectively stressful events.

transnational organization An organization in which the global viewpoint supersedes national issues.

triangulation The use of multiple methods to measure organizational culture.

two-way communication A form of communication in which the communicator and receiver interact.

Type A behavior pattern A complex of personality and behavioral characteristics, including competitiveness, time urgency, social status insecurity, aggression, hostility, and a quest for achievements.

U

uncertainty avoidance The degree to which a culture tolerates ambiguity and uncertainty.

unfreezing The first step in Lewin's change model, in which individuals are encouraged to discard old behaviors by shaking up the equilibrium state that maintains the status quo.

unplanned change Change that is imposed on the organization and is often unforeseen.

upper echelon A top-level executive team in an organization.

V

valence The value or importance one places on a particular reward.

values Enduring beliefs that a specific mode of conduct or end state of existence is personally or socially preferable to an opposite or converse mode of conduct or end state of existence.

virtual office A mobile platform of computer, telecommunication, and information technology and services.

W

whistle-blower An employee who informs authorities of the wrongdoings of his or her company or coworkers.

withdrawal The final career stage in which the individual contemplates retirement or possible career changes.

work Mental or physical activity that has productive results.

work simplification Standardization and the narrow, explicit specification of task activities for workers.

work team A group of people with complementary skills who are committed to a common mission, performance goals, and approach for which they hold themselves mutually accountable.

workaholism An imbalanced preoccupation with work at the expense of home and personal life satisfaction.

workplace deviance behavior Any voluntary counterproductive behavior that violates organizational norms and causes some degree of harm to organizational functioning.

Z

zone of indifference The range in which attempts to influence a person will be perceived as legitimate and will be acted on without a great deal of thought.

Company Index

Q

R

S

T

U

V

W

X

Y

Z

Name Index

Subject Index

A

B

C

D

E

F

G

H

I

J

K

L

M

N

O

P

Q

R

S

T

U

V

W

Y

Z